Business
Plans
Handbook

Business Plans Handbook

A COMPILATION OF ACTUAL BUSINESS PLANS DEVELOPED BY BUSINESSES THROUGHOUT NORTH AMERICA

VOLUME

9

Jacqueline K. Mueckenheim,
Project Editor

GALE®

THOMSON
™
GALE

Detroit • New York • San Diego • San Francisco • Cleveland • New Haven, Conn. • Waterville, Maine • London • Munich

Business Plans Handbook, 9th Volume

Project Editor
Jacqueline K. Mueckenheim

Editorial
Eric Hoss, Paul Lewon

Imaging and Multimedia
Jeffrey Lee Matlock

Product Design
Mike Logusz, Tracey Rowens

Composition and Electronic Capture
Keith Helmling, Mary Beth Trimper

Typesetter
Shelly Andrews

ISBN 0-7876-5309-8
ISSN 1084-4473

Printed in the United States of America
10 9 8 7 6 5 4 3 2 1

Contents

Business Plans

Appendixes

Highlights

Business Plans Handbook, Volume 9 (BPH-9) is a collection of actual business plans compiled by entrepreneurs seeking funding for small businesses throughout North America. For those looking for examples of how to approach, structure, and compose their own business plans, *BPH-9* presents 24 sample plans, including plans for the following businesses:

- Caviar Company
- Commercial Airline
- Computer Training Service Business
- Dollar Store
- Electronic Document Security Company
- Golf Driving Range

- Internet Communications Service Provider
- Internet Travel Agency Business
- Marble Quarry
- Online Publishing System Company
- Science Information Website Company
- Wireless Systems Provider

FEATURES AND BENEFITS

BPH-9 offers many features not provided by other business planning references including:

○ Twenty-four business plans, each of which represent an owner's successful attempt at clarifying (for themselves and others) the reasons that the business should exist or expand and why a lender should fund the enterprise.

○ Two fictional plans that are used by business counselors at a prominent small business development organization as examples for their clients. (You will find these in the Business Plan Template Appendix.)

○ An expanded directory section that includes: listings for venture capital and finance companies, which specialize in funding start-up and second-stage small business ventures, and a comprehensive listing of Service Corps of Retired Executives (SCORE) offices. In addition, the Appendix also contains updated listings of all Small Business Development Centers (SBDCs); associations of interest to entrepreneurs; Small Business Administration (SBA) Regional Offices; and consultants specializing in small business planning and advice. It is strongly advised that you consult supporting organizations while planning your business, as they can provide a wealth of useful information.

○ A Small Business Term Glossary to help you decipher the sometimes confusing terminology used by lenders and others in the financial and small business communities.

○ A cumulative index, outlining each plan profiled in the complete *Business Plans Handbook* series.

○ A Business Plan Template which serves as a model to help you construct your own business plan. This generic outline lists all the essential elements of a complete business plan and their components, including the Summary, Business History and Industry Outlook, Market Examination, Competition, Marketing, Administration and Management, Financial Information, and other key sections. Use this guide as a starting point for compiling your plan.

○ Extensive financial documentation required to solicit funding from small business lenders. *BPH-9* contains the most comprehensive financial data within the series to date. You will find examples of: Cash Flows, Balance Sheets, Income Projections, and other financial information included with the textual portions of the plan.

Introduction

Perhaps the most important aspect of business planning is simply *doing* it. More and more business owners are beginning to compile business plans even if they don't need a bank loan. Others discover the value of planning when they *must* provide a business plan for the bank. The sheer act of putting thoughts on paper seems to clarify priorities and provide focus. Sometimes business owners completely change strategies when compiling their plan, deciding on a different product mix or advertising scheme after finding that their assumptions were incorrect. This kind of healthy thinking and re-thinking via business planning is becoming the norm. The editors of *Business Plans Handbook, Volume 9 (BPH-9)* sincerely hope that this latest addition to the series is a helpful tool in the successful completion of your business plan, no matter what the reason for creating it.

This ninth volume, like each volume in the series, offers genuine business plans used by real people. *BPH-9* provides 24 business plans used by actual entrepreneurs to gain funding support for their new businesses. The business and personal names and addresses and general locations have been changed to protect the privacy of the plan authors.

NEW BUSINESS OPPORTUNITIES

As in other volumes in the series, *BPH-9* finds entrepreneurs engaged in a wide variety of creative endeavors. Examples include a proposal for a concert promotions company; a company who offers gourmet caviar for sale; and a retail store where each item costs just $1—those popular "dollar stores." In addition, several e-commerce based plans are provided, including an Internet-based travel agency, an Internet business development consulting firm, and a company that offers an online publishing service. Social entrepreneurship is also profiled in this volume with a plan for a non-profit youth outreach ministry.

Comprehensive financial documentation has become increasingly important as today's entrepreneurs compete for the finite resources of business lenders. Our plans illustrate the financial data generally required of loan applicants, including Income Statements, Financial Projections, Cash Flows, and Balance Sheets.

ENHANCED APPENDIXES

In an effort to provide the most relevant and valuable information for our readers, we have updated the coverage of small business resources. For instance, you will find: a directory section, which includes listings of all of the Service Corps of Retired Executives (SCORE) offices; an informative glossary, which includes small business terms; and a cumulative index, outlining each plan profiled in the complete *Business Plans Handbook* series. In addition we have updated the list of Small Business Development Centers (SBDCs); Small Business Administration Regional Offices; venture capital and finance companies, which specialize in funding start-up and second-stage small business enterprises; associations of interest to entrepreneurs; and consultants, specializing in small business advice and planning. For your reference, we have also reprinted the business plan template, which provides a comprehensive overview of the essential components of a business plan and two fictional plans used by small business counselors.

SERIES INFORMATION

If you already have the first eight volumes of *BPH*, with this ninth volume, you will now have a collection of over 220 real business plans (not including the one updated plan in the second volume, whose original appeared in the first, or the two fictional plans in the Business Plan Template Appendix section of the second, third, fourth, fifth, sixth, and seventh volumes); contact information for hundreds of organizations and agencies offering business expertise; a helpful business plan template; a foreword providing advice and instruction to entrepreneurs on how to begin their research; more than 1,500 citations to valuable small business development material; and a comprehensive glossary of terms to help the business planner navigate the sometimes confusing language of entrepreneurship.

ACKNOWLEDGMENTS

The Editors wish to sincerely thank the many contributors to *BPH-9*, including:

- Leslie A. Colston, Set Free Publications
- Julian Cook, Newlines Airlines LLC
- L. Joshua Eikov, Virtual Technologies LLC
- Charles Epstein, BackBone Inc.
- Seth Goldhammer, Chris Gray, Kaj Gronholm, Derek Kumm, and Kate Tallman, Leeds School of Business, Deming Center of Entrepreneurship (University of Colorado, Boulder)
- Michael Goldstein, Professional Planning Associates
- Adam Greengrass, BizPlanSource Inc.
- Scott Lockett, Tindell Associates LLC
- David Satterthwaite, Prisma Microfinance
- Lee Toh, Mangabay Business Plans & Development—Subsidiary of Innis Asset Allocation

The Editors would also like to express their gratitude to Shelly Andrews, Contributing Editor & Typesetter, for her talent, dedication, and hard work on behalf of this publication.

COMMENTS WELCOME

Your comments on *Business Plans Handbook* are appreciated. Please direct all correspondence, suggestions for future volumes of *BPH*, and other recommendations to the following:

Managing Editor, Business Product
Business Plans Handbook
The Gale Group
27500 Drake Rd.
Farmington Hills, MI 48331-3535
Phone: (248)699-4253
Fax: (248)699-8052
Toll-Free: 800-347-GALE
E-mail: BusinessProducts@gale.com

Airline Company

BUSINESS PLAN

SKYTRAILS AIRLINE, LTD.

London Stansted Airport
London, United Kingdom

SkyTrails Airline plans to establish itself as a niche player in the long-haul market of business travel. By continuously focusing on the needs of the premium-class business traveller, SkyTrails will provide the best value proposition in the markets it serves. It will offer customers a compelling value proposition: a high level of service and comfort at 50 percent of the current published business-class fare.

- EXECUTIVE SUMMARY

- THE COMPANY

- REGULATORY ENVIRONMENT

- MARKET ANALYSIS

- FINANCIALS

- APPENDIX

AIRLINE COMPANY
BUSINESS PLAN

EXECUTIVE SUMMARY

Purpose

Having successfully raised £1.3 million from angel investors, SkyTrails is now looking to raise £25 million from investors who are interested in the opportunity presented by SkyTrails and believe in its growth potential. This is a unique opportunity to invest in a new concept in the aviation industry which offers attractive returns and a clear exit strategy in the public markets within 3 to 5 years.

Vision

SkyTrails' aim is to establish itself as a niche player in the long-haul market of business travel.

By continuously focusing on the needs of the premium-class business traveller, SkyTrails will provide the best value proposition in the markets it serves.

Overview

SkyTrails is the project name for a new airline company that will focus on single class long-haul scheduled flights. SkyTrails will capitalise on the widening gap in long-haul travel between business and economy class. Based at London Stansted Airport (STN), SkyTrails will initially focus on the busiest transatlantic route, London to New York, by offering a STN-JFK service. SkyTrails will operate Boeing 757-200 aircraft configured with 80 seats which will provide a very spacious and pleasant environment. The aircraft will be equipped with the latest technology in order to enable the business traveller to use his time efficiently while travelling. The company will start by leasing two aircraft and expand its fleet to 6 aircraft by the second year of operation.

SkyTrails will be a "business to business" airline and will focus exclusively on the premium/business segment of the market. It will offer customers a compelling value proposition: a high level of service and comfort at 50 percent of the current published business-class fare. SkyTrails will charge £1,800 for a roundtrip ticket as opposed to £3,580 (for companies with high volume demand, SkyTrails will offer further discounts down to £1,400 for bulk purchase). In addition to an attractive price, SkyTrails will offer passengers considerable time savings, convenience, and will focus on creating a lifestyle appeal.

The business model contemplated enables the company to reach a break-even point with 40 passengers per flight (50 percent load factor) which significantly reduces the risks associated with typical airlines that need a greater number of passengers to break-even. In many ways, the SkyTrails model replicates the benefits of the very successful regional jet model on a long-haul basis.

By the end of the fourth year SkyTrails will achieve sales of £218 million, EBITDAR of £72 million and net income after taxes of £32 million.

Market Potential

- The London-New York route is the busiest transatlantic route with over 3.8 million passengers carried in 1999. The Civil Aviation Authority (CAA) estimates that approximately 30 percent of passengers were business travellers (1.14 million passengers).
- In 1999, over 2.65 million passengers in Stansted's catchment area travelled to the USA. Given that no airline currently serves the North Atlantic route from Stansted, SkyTrails will be uniquely positioned to take advantage of the unserved demand that exists.
- Stansted is the fastest growing airport in Europe with 9.9 million passengers for 1999.

It is the hub of low cost airlines Go Fly, Ryanair, and Buzz, all of which are experiencing tremendous growth and an increase in business travellers. They claim that as many as 40 percent of their passengers are travelling on business.

- Stansted benefits from an Open Skies Agreement with the USA. This enables SkyTrails to operate flights to any city in the USA without having to obtain special rights under the Bermuda II Bilateral Agreement which apply to Heathrow and Gatwick.
- SkyTrails has already obtained landing and takeoff slots at Stansted and JFK airports for its initial flights.
- Total traffic from U.K. airports to the USA amounted to 16.2 million passengers in 1999. After launching the JFK route, SkyTrails will then be able to expand by targeting other attractive markets in the USA (Boston, Chicago, Washington, D.C., etc.) as well as other continents depending on the regulatory environment. With a break-even point of 40 passengers per flight, SkyTrails will also be able to target medium and low density routes offering an enormous potential for growth and an important competitive advantage.

Management

It is important to note that during the first 12 months the operations will be handled by TravelAir which has ETOPS certification, thus taking away much of the operational burden from SkyTrails' management and ensuring a timely launch.

Markus Friedman, Chairman
CEO of EBEL Watches (1991-1999)
CEO of CWS (1964-1991)

William Scott, Founder and Managing Director
Assistant to CEO, Southern Winds (airline in Argentina) (1999)
Associate, Global Transportation, Chase Manhattan Bank (1995-1998)
M.B.A., Columbia Business School (2000)/ B.Sc. Economics, London School of Economics (1995)

Frederick Rodmann, Finance Director
Assistant General Manager, Pegasus Airline (1992-2000)
Audit Senior, Price Waterhouse (1986-1992)

Joseph Orr, Corporate Sales Manager
Airline Manager, Lastminute.com (2000)
National Account Manager, Virgin Atlantic Airways (1994-2000)

Oleg Schweitz, Marketing Director
Director of Marketing, Paramount Comedy Chanel (1997-2000)
Brand Manager, AT&T Communications (1996-1997)
Marketing Manager, Warner Bros. (1993-1996)

Ken Loman, Technical Director
Technical General Manager, Accountable Manager, Qatar Airways (1997-98)
Technical General Manager, Accountable Manager, CityFlyer Express (1991-97)
Project/Development Engineer, Air Europe (1988-91)

John MacDonald (Founder/Chairman CityFlyer Express 1992-1998)

Ryan Roland (Professor, Columbia Business School)

Non-Executive Directors

Competition

The London-New York route is currently served by British Airways (11x/day), American Airlines (7x/day), Virgin Atlantic Airways (5x/day), United Airlines (4x/day), and Continental Airlines (2x/day). These airlines operate out of Heathrow and Gatwick with wide-body aircraft (B747s, B777s, B767s, A340s, A300s, DC-10s) in a two- or three-class configuration. British Airways has introduced a fourth class of service, World Traveller Plus, which is equivalent to Virgin's Premium Economy.

By targeting such a dense route, SkyTrails initial market share will not be significant enough to be considered as a threat by the major transatlantic carriers. Existing players will only be able to react with price which is only one aspect of the SkyTrails concept and by no means the most important.

Key Success Factors

SkyTrails believes that the following factors will be key to the company's success:

Management and Culture
SkyTrails has hired experienced airline professionals in order to ensure the operations are well managed. Blending experienced airline professionals with a young creative management team will be a successful combination which will continuously look for innovation while maintaining a high level of professionalism. Getting the right combination will be key in executing this venture successfully. The company will also focus on building a strong corporate culture that will help to differentiate itself from the competition and sustain a high level of motivation while maintaining cost control.

More than just an airline, a lifestyle
SkyTrails will differentiate itself as much as possible from the traditional airlines. SkyTrails will be to the airline industry what the boutique hotels (Royalton, W Hotel, Mercer Hotel, etc.) are to the hotel industry. Passengers flying on SkyTrails will identify to a lifestyle. SkyTrails has hired industrial designer Ric Sloan to work on the interior of the aircraft. Ric Sloan is one of the leading contemporary industrial designers and is viewed by many as one of the world's most fashionable.

Superior Product and Service
With an 80-passenger configuration, the cabin of the Boeing 757 will look more like a private jet than like a large mass transportation aircraft. Boarding and disembarking will be much faster given the low number of passengers. SkyTrails will reduce the overall travelling time by at least 1 hour and 30 minutes for passengers flying to and from the city of London, Canary Wharf, and the fast growing Cambridge area. Providing a personalized and comfortable experience is key in retaining customers and getting repeat business. A strong emphasis will be placed on this aspect of the business: particular attention will be paid to the design of the cabin, the technology available, efficiency of processes, and quality of service offered by the cabin crew. SkyTrails will continuously innovate and have the ability to introduce new products to market in a shorter timeframe than its competitors.

Strong Sales team
SkyTrails will market its services to companies directly. Its ability to acquire corporate clients will be extremely important to the success of the venture. SkyTrails will offer discounts for volume travel and will also partner with select hotels in order to offer all-in packages.

Low Cost Operation
As a new airline, SkyTrails will have a significant cost advantage over the existing airlines that have large overhead expenses. By focusing on a single type of aircraft, a

single class of travel, and initially a single route, systems will be simple and costs will be kept to a minimum. SkyTrails will continuously focus on maintaining a low cost base in order to keep this advantage.

Low Break-Even Point
By operating the B757, SkyTrails will have lower operating costs and a low break-even point (40 passengers/50 percent load factor) significantly reducing the risks associated with traditional airlines. With such a low break-even point, SkyTrails will be able to make it through economic downturns with less pain than its competitors. It will also enable SkyTrails to consider medium and low density routes on a long-haul basis offering more point to point services.

The Internet
Maximizing the potential of the Internet will be key in keeping low distribution and administrative costs. SkyTrails will have a strong Internet presence and will use the Internet for customer interaction as well as internal functions.

Operating Strategy: One type of aircraft, one class of service

Strategy

SkyTrails will operate a single type of aircraft: The Boeing 757-200. By operating this aircraft type on the transatlantic route, SkyTrails will have significantly lower operating costs per trip. The trip cost for the B757-200 will be approximately £25,000 one way as opposed to £75,000 for a B747 operated by existing carriers. This demonstrates the lower risk associated with this operation. It will also enable the company to offer direct services where others offer indirect services. Moreover, it will be able to offer greater frequency than competitors operating larger aircraft. Focusing on a single aircraft type enables the company to minimize the costs of training and maintenance. SkyTrails will offer only one class of travel which facilitates processes (marketing, purchasing, training, systems, etc.). In order to provide a high quality service to its customers, SkyTrails will implement productivity and profit-based incentives for personnel.

Pricing Strategy: Simple, £900 One Way
SkyTrails will not need sophisticated yield management systems to determine the price of each ticket. However, SkyTrails will hire an experienced yield analyst in order to maximize revenues. SkyTrails will offer a simple fare structure which will be comprised of a maximum of four different fare types.

This pricing structure will be very attractive for the small and medium enterprises (SME) who do not have access to large volume corporate discounts with the major carriers.

Sales, Marketing, and Distribution Strategy
1. *Corporates:* SkyTrails is a business to business airline. It will focus its efforts on targeting corporate travel managers directly through a strong sales force, partnerships with credit card companies, or other entities that have access to corporate clients. SkyTrails will offer flexible pricing to suit companies' travel requirements.

2. *End-users:* In order to attract the traveller directly, SkyTrails' marketing strategy will focus on the lifestyle and convenience rather than price because in many cases price is not the primary issue for the business traveller. SkyTrails will only use electronic tickets which will be distributed through agents, the Internet, and our call center. SkyTrails will also distribute through travel agents as they still have a significant position in the corporate market.

Growth Strategy

SkyTrails will initially target the high volume routes in which it will only be a small player and not be perceived a real threat to the larger airlines. The following U.S. cities are obvious targets: New York, Boston, Washington, D.C., and Chicago. However, the medium term objective is not to increase capacity on these large routes but rather to focus on medium to low density routes where competitors flying wide-body equipment will not be able to operate profitably. London to Bradley Airport (Hartford, Connecticut) is a perfect example of such a route.

Financial Summary and Funding Requirement

Management currently estimates the total funding requirements at £25 million. This takes into account the start-up costs, the on-going operating costs, the costs of incorporating additional aircraft, and the minimum cash requirements to satisfy the CAA.

Income Statement

£	2002	2003	2004	2005
Number of Aircraft	2	5	7	9
Load Factor	51%	59%	67%	68%
Total Sales	**30,550,315**	**77,046,634**	**164,108,039**	**218,156,052**
EBITDAR	11,804	16,701,194	50,804,281	72,763,402
EBITDAR Margin	0.00%	21.70%	31.00%	33.40%
EBITDA	-4,984,748	5,825,332	30,197,385	45,204,782
EBITDA Margin	-16.30%	7.60%	18.40%	20.70%
Net Income	**-4,323,273**	**5,616,514**	**20,701,527**	**31,719,327**
Net Margin	**-14.20%**	**7.30%**	**12.60%**	**14.50%**

Valuation

EBITDAR	£72MM	£72MM	£72MM
EBITDAR Multiple	5	6	7
Value	**£364MM**	**£437MM**	**£509MM**

The table above outlines the value of the company in 2005. This assumes conservative cash flow multiples and we therefore believe that these valuations are on the low side of the spectrum.

THE COMPANY
Vision

SkyTrails' aim is to establish itself as a niche player in the long-haul market of business travel.

By continuously focusing on the needs of the premium class business traveller, SkyTrails will provide the best value proposition in the markets it serves.

Values

Safety	People and People	Simpler
Technology	Success Is in Details	Professional Service
Change	Innovate	

We exist to provide a valuable service to our customers, a rewarding opportunity for our employees, and profitability to our shareholders. We believe that success in this endeavor depends on our employees. Satisfied employees lead to satisfied customers, which lead to satisfied shareholders. To achieve this, we enable our employees to act with an entrepreneurial spirit, and we value those willing to take responsibility for their actions and the consequences of those actions. We treat employees as family, which fosters intimacy, informality, strong relationships, caring attitudes, and it makes work more fun. We give employees the opportunity to become shareholders and to participate in the financial benefits of ownership. People take better care of things they own. We treat employees with respect, which encourages them to treat each other and every customer with respect. We want our customers to experience legendary service that makes a lasting impression. Providing exceptional value to customers requires hard work and concentration. Hard work is most effective when processes are simple. Simplicity reduces costs and speeds processes. We do not cut corners. We believe in doing things right the first time. We take pride in our efforts as well as the rewards. Throughout this endeavor, safety will be the overriding force behind any decision.

During the start-up phase, the operations side of the business will be outsourced to TravelAir reducing management needs and ensuring a timely launch.

Management

Our aim is to achieve a good balance between senior airline professionals and creative young managers.

Markus Friedman, Chairman (59)
After graduating from the University of Geneva in Law and Political sciences in 1964, Mr. Friedman joined CWS, a Swiss-based company producing industrial hygienic products and soon became CEO. In 1991, after 27 years at CWS, Mr. Friedman left the company and joined EBEL, the Swiss watch manufacturer, as CEO. He brought in Investcorp as a shareholder and restructured the company. In October 1999, Mr. Friedman orchestrated the sale of EBEL to LVMH, the French luxury goods group and left EBEL. Mr. Friedman is a shareholder in Avcon, a Swiss-based company that manages a fleet of private jets.

William Scott, Founder and Managing Director (27)
Mr. Scott has been actively involved in the airline industry since he joined Chase Manhattan Bank's Aerospace Group in 1995. He was involved in aircraft financing, airline privatisation and restructuring, and M&A transactions. More recently, Mr. Scott worked for Southern Winds, a regional airline in Argentina founded in 1996. He worked closely with the CEO in raising equity and on strategic issues. Mr. Scott holds a B.Sc. Economics from the London School of Economics and an M.B.A. from the Columbia Business School.

Frederick Rodmann, Finance Director (35)
Mr. Rodmann has been Assistant General Manager of Pegasus Airlines , a Turkish charter airline, since 1992. As Assistant General Manager he was actively involved in many aspects of Pegasus business and has wide aviation experience. Mr. Rodmann assisted Aer Lingus, the Irish flag carrier, to sell Pegasus Airlines to its current owners, the Cukurova Group in 1994. Under his stewardship Pegasus has made profits in each of the last six years and has grown its fleet from two to sixteen aircraft. Prior to joining Pegasus, Mr. Rodmann worked for Price Waterhouse in Dublin from 1986 to 1992. Mr. Rodmann is a member of the Institute of Chartered Accountants in Ireland. He also holds a Bachelor of Commerce degree from University College Galway, Ireland.

Joseph Orr, Corporate Sales Manager (32)
Mr. Orr has gained over 7 years of sales experience within the airline industry. The majority of this was at Virgin Atlantic where he worked within the Corporate Sales Department. His last role of National Account Manager gave him sole responsibility for a number of Virgin's largest volume clients—a portfolio that was valued at £35m. Prior to this, Mr. Orr was Area Sales Manager covering the city of London. Though the smallest geographical territory within this team, it was the highest revenue generating area and had the highest proportion of clients contracted to Virgin. Mr. Orr left Virgin Atlantic earlier in 2000 and was appointed head of Airline Supply at lastminute.com prior to joining SkyTrails. He holds a Bachelor of Arts in Business Studies with travel modules.

Oleg Schweitz, Marketing Director (31)

Mr. Schweitz brings over 10 years of marketing and branding experience to SkyTrails. Having spent 3 years in International media planning at the CIA Group, he then moved to Warner Bros as Marketing Manager, overseeing all Interactive Entertainment products published across Europe. Mr. Schweitz joined AT&T as Brand Manager in 1996 with responsibility for brand marketing and advertising strategy during its key consolidation period in the U.K. Most recently Mr. Schweitz has been the Marketing Director with Paramount Television responsible for marketing and airtime sales revenue for the Digital, Cable, and Satellite broadcaster and a marketing department of eight. Mr. Schweitz is a qualified Chartered Marketer with the Chartered Institute of Marketing.

Ken Loman, Technical Director (39)

Mr. Loman has accumulated over 20 years of experience in the industry. On leaving the Royal Air Force in 1985, Mr. Loman worked with Jersey European in the Maintenance Control Department. In 1988 he moved to work with Air Europe as a Project/Development Engineer within the Technical Services Department. In 1991, he became involved in the start-up of CityFlyer Express as Technical General Manager. The airline achieved the First JAR 145 Approval for which he was the Accountable Manager. Late 1997 Mr. Loman worked on a short-term contract involved in the re-launch of Qatar Airways until late 1998. Since this time Mr. Loman has been working on a consultancy basis for a number of aviation related entities.

Non-Executive Directors

John MacDonald, Director (subject to clearance from non-compete with British Airways)

Mr. MacDonald is an active entrepreneur and general manager with skills in the identification and analysis of business opportunities, and their subsequent implementation and management. John MacDonald has a proven track record in founding, developing, and selling airline companies. In 1982, he founded and was the Managing Director of Connectair Limited, a commuter airline for British Caledonian. Connectair was successfully sold to ILG, Air Europe in 1988. From 1991 to 1999, John MacDonald was the Executive Chairman of CityFlyer Express, the premier British Airways Express Franchise. CityFlyer Express was sold to British Airways in 1999.

John MacDonald is a Non-Executive Director of Cannons Group plc and Positek Limited. Mr. MacDonald holds a B.A. from Southampton University and an M.B.A. from Cranfield University.

Ryan Roland, Director

Educated primarily in the Great Britain, Professor Roland earned B.Sc. and Ph.D. degrees in Chemistry from University College, London University. He also received degrees in Business Administration from Manchester (Dip. B.A.), Harvard (M.B.A.) and Columbia Business Schools (Ph.D.).

Professor Roland served on the faculties of the UCLA Graduate School of Management and Harvard Business School before joining the Columbia Business School faculty in 1979. He has also served as a Visiting Professor at INSEAD, Fontainebleau, France, Hong Kong University of Science and Technology, and the China Europe International Business School.

He has undertaken both educational and consulting activities for major corporations in the United States and overseas. Included are: AT&T; Aetna; American Cyanamid; Bankers Trust; Bell Canada, Bell Laboratories; Bell Communications Research; BOC; Ceverceria Cuahtemoc (Mexico); Chase Manhattan Bank; Chemical Bank; CIGNA; Ciba-Geigy; Cluett Peabody; Corning; Digital Equipment; Equifax; The Equitable Life Assurance Society of the United States; Essilor of America; FMC; General Foods; General Electric; Goodyear; GTE.; Hoescht-Celanese; IBM; Johnson & Johnson; L'Air Liquide; MacDonalds; McGraw-Hill;

Merck; PaineWebber; Pfizer; Singer; Sony; Stone Container; Thompson; and Unilever. Professor Roland is widely published. His articles have appeared in numerous journals and reviews. Professor Roland has also published five books.

In order to remain competitive, corporations have become more cost conscious and have taken steps to tighten their travel and entertainment budgets, often by requiring their employees to travel on a specific airline or in economy class. SkyTrails believes there is a fantastic opportunity to create a single class long-haul airline that will bridge the growing gap between business and economy class travel. London Stansted Airport offers attractive opportunities for long-haul travel and JFK is the most popular airport in the New York area. We believe that targeting the London-New York route makes sense because it is the busiest transatlantic route with 3.8 million passengers in 1999.

Tighter Travel and Entertainment Budgets

Travel and entertainment budgets of large and small companies represent on average 7 percent of operating costs and are the third largest category of controllable corporate expense behind salaries and data processing. These costs are coming under increasing scrutiny as companies try to maintain their profitability levels. As a result of this trend, more and more companies are implementing strict travel policies and are forcing employees to travel economy class. While this is still predominantly a phenomenon occurring for short-haul flights, some companies have already implemented these rules on long-haul flights as well. Only large companies with enough bargaining power obtain discounts from airlines for business class travel. These discounts range from 15 percent to 50 percent, depending on the size of the company travel budget. Large corporations therefore continue to allow their passengers to fly business class on long-haul travel because they benefit from these discounts. For smaller companies, the choice is more difficult: either pay full fare business class and travel in comfort or pay full fare economy class and travel in a cramped environment resulting in employee fatigue and inefficiency. Many companies do not have any other choice but to force employees to travel economy as business class is too expensive.

Bridging the Business-Economy Gap

The opportunity has been created by a widening gap in long-haul travel between economy class and business class, both in terms of price and service offered. Prompted by the introduction in the early 1990s of Virgin's Upper-Class, a business-first product, competitors have had to either improve the quality of their business class (British Airways) or follow suit by eliminating first class services and offering a business-first product (Continental Airlines). As a result of these changes, business class on long-haul flights has improved significantly but prices have also increased accordingly. Conversely economy class has seen very little improvement and overall economy class prices have decreased as a result of over capacity.

The following table gives us an overview of this trend:

Round-trip fare LON-NYC £	1994	2001	% Change
Business Class	1,959	3,580	82%
Full-Fare Economy	817	884	8%
Deep Discount Economy	254	208	-18%

There is a segment of the business travel market that cannot or will not continue to pay business class fares for long-haul travel. These business travellers are getting the worst deal since they are paying full-fare economy as they need the flexibility to change their ticket but are getting the same service as a leisure traveller paying a deeply discounted economy fare.

- SkyTrails will provide an attractive alternative: A "Business Class type" service for £1,800

LONDON-NEW YORK /STANSTED-JFK

While the overall transatlantic market is very competitive and many airlines have recently complained of over capacity in the market, fares have only been reduced in the economy class cabin where we tend to see a larger portion of deeply discounted fares. SkyTrails believes that it is the best strategy to start competing on the busiest transatlantic route where we only need a small share of the market to achieve profitability. In 1999, over 3.8 million passengers flew between London and New York (source: CAA). SkyTrails' initial share of the market will be approximately 2 percent. It will be difficult for established airlines to react in such a dense market. With higher fixed costs and larger market shares, established players will be reluctant to do so. The cost of competing on price would by far outweigh the cost of accepting a small erosion in their market share.

STANSTED AIRPORT

Stansted is London's third international gateway and one of the fastest growing airports in Europe. Growing at over 30 percent per annum, it served 9.9 million passengers in 1999. Stansted has a catchment area of 11.5 million people representing 20 percent of the U.K. population. Stansted is operated by the British Airport Authority (BAA), a publicly traded company. The BAA has a keen interest to see Stansted grow and has invested over $750 million since 1986.

Existing Unserved Market for Transatlantic Services

Currently, no airline is offering a service to New York from Stansted Airport which means that SkyTrails will have no direct competition within the Stansted catchment area. In 1999, 2.65 million passengers in Stansted's catchment area travelled to the USA (source: CAA). These passengers will naturally prefer flights from Stansted. The low cost airlines operating out of Stansted—Ryanair, Go Fly, and Buzz—are all recording an increase in business travellers. These cost conscious business travellers are natural customers for SkyTrails.

Stansted's Catchment Area

Excluding Central London, total population of Stansted's catchment area is 11.5 million. The catchment area includes Essex, Suffolk, Norfolk, Cambridgeshire, Northamptonshire, Leicestershire, Lincolnshire, Bedfordshire, and Hertfordshire.

The most interesting region of Stansted's catchment area is Cambridge. Over the past three years, Cambridge has transformed itself into the home of fast-growing high technology companies. Over 1,200 companies employing over 35,000 people are based in the Cambridge area. Also, 12 major global corporations have established research centres in the area including Microsoft, Nokia, and Xerox.

Easy Access

The Stansted Express rail link runs every 15 minutes to/from Liverpool Street Station (heart of the city of London) right into the terminal building at Stansted airport. Travelling time is 41 minutes. Passengers working in London will be able to leave their offices 70 minutes before takeoff time, a convenience no other airline can offer.

Stansted is located just 30 miles from the North East of London and only 15 miles away from London's orbital motorway (M25). Stansted is adjacent to Junction 8 on the M11 which makes access easy for people working in Canary Wharf.

London Stansted Airport also offers easy onward travel facilities to Cambridge, Ipswich, and Norwich either by road, train, bus, or coach.

	Stansted	**Heathrow**	**Gatwick**
London (Financial District)	41 min	60 min	50 min
Canary Wharf	90 min	90 min	120 min
Cambridge	25 min	1h 20 min	1h 30 min

Market Acceptance

More and more business travellers use Stansted as an alternative to Heathrow and Gatwick, both of which have become very hectic. In 1998, 32 percent of passengers travelling through Stansted were business travellers. A survey conducted by the *Financial Times* in November 1999 on 800 business travellers working in the city of London revealed that business travellers rated Stansted higher than both Heathrow and Gatwick.

Friendly Regulatory Environment

Slots are available at Stansted and new airlines have the priority when applying for these. Slots are distributed for each season and airlines need to apply approximately three months in advance (June deadline for winter schedule). SkyTrails has already secured slots at Stansted for its desired schedule.

Airlines flying out of Stansted are not governed by the Bermuda II Bilateral Agreement between the U.K. and USA. Stansted falls under the regional airports category which enjoy open skies with the USA. This means that airlines will automatically be granted traffic rights for flights from Stansted to the USA.

For further information on the regulatory environment please see the Appendix.

Lower Costs

Charges at Stansted are at least 20 percent below those of Heathrow and Gatwick. In addition, SkyTrails has negotiated attractive deals with suppliers who are eager to see transatlantic services from Stansted.

JFK AIRPORT

JFK is the largest and best known airport in the New York area. The new start-up JetBlue is based at JFK and will potentially be beneficial for SkyTrails in terms of connecting traffic.

Regulatory Environment

JFK has a slot restriction from 2 P.M. to 8 P.M. but under the new entrant rule, SkyTrails has been able to obtain the slots required for the initial two daily flights.

For further information on the regulatory environment please see the Appendix.

Lifestyle

Service/Product

SkyTrails will introduce a single class concept to long-haul air travel. The newly designed class will provide a "high tech," spacious, and comfortable environment. In many ways, SkyTrails aims to create a "boutique" airline which replicates the concept of boutique hotels and targets the same type of customers.

In order to achieve this goal, SkyTrails will hire and partner with well known designers and suppliers for various aspects of the business. The seats and aircraft cabin will be designed by Ric Sloan, one of the most fashionable industrial designers of the moment. He was featured in *Forbes* magazine (12 May 2001) as "one designer to watch." SkyTrails will partner with a fashion designer for the uniforms and with well known restaurants for the catering.

SkyTrails' primary target will be young executives (25-45) that are lifestyle driven.

Comfort

In addition to a standard airline four abreast seating configuration, SkyTrails will also offer a unique meeting room environment enabling passengers to conduct business in an office setting while travelling.

Seats will have a 52-inch pitch and will recline at least 150 degrees, very similar to the current business class of traditional carriers. SkyTrails will make a special effort to offer good lighting for passengers, something which is lacking in today's airlines. Given the number of proposed seats, each passenger will enjoy considerable improvement in air quality over the established operators, an issue that is attracting increasing attention in the media.

Technology

SkyTrails will ensure that the aircraft is equipped with the amenities business travellers need in order to continue working while travelling. Again, SkyTrails will aim to provide these services at a fair price in order to stimulate their use rather than high prices which are prohibitive. SkyTrails aims to create a business centre in the aircraft where passengers will be able to use telephone, fax, and printer. Each seat will be equipped with a laptop power supply. SkyTrails will also provide e-mail access and use of a personal mobile phone for each passenger.

Convenience

SkyTrails will focus on offering a high quality service from the time of booking right to the time at which the passenger arrives at hotel/home in the destination city. Passengers will have the choice of booking a seat through the Internet, a call centre, or a travel agency.

e-tickets: Tickets will be 100 percent electronic and the passenger will only need their passport and confirmation number in order to access the aircraft. They will be able to print a copy of their itinerary from the website or will get confirmation numbers from the call centre.

Free transfers to/from airports: A free shared limousine service will be offered between JFK and Manhattan on arrival and departure. On the Stansted side, free rail ticket to/from Liverpool Street station will be offered or a free car service to/from Cambridge.

Valet Parking Service: SkyTrails will offer a complimentary valet parking service at Stansted which will save time for passengers wishing to drive to the airport.

Larger carry-on luggage: The increased space on board will also accommodate larger carry-on luggage which is a sensitive issue for business travellers who do not wish to check in their luggage.

No more check-in: Allowing larger carry-on luggage enables us to abolish the concept of check-in and simply close the gate 15 minutes prior to takeoff. For those passengers with lots of luggage, SkyTrails will offer a door-to-door service for an extra fee. By abolishing check-in, SkyTrails will not only avoid many delays but it will also save money that other airlines spend on lost and damaged luggage.

Reduced overall transfer time: Passengers working in the city of London and Canary Wharf will save at least 1 hour from the moment they leave their office to the time of takeoff. On arriving in New York, they will save at least 30 minutes as they will not have to wait for their luggage and for a taxi. Boarding and disembarking the aircraft will be much faster due to the smaller number of passengers on each flight. Passengers travelling in the opposite direction can expect similar advantages over the competition.

Personalized service: SkyTrails will have individual DVD players for passengers to view the movie of their choice. On the catering side, SkyTrails intends to offer a choice of cuisine by partnering with well known brands. On the night flight from New York, passengers will have the option to order their breakfast on the train into Liverpool Street station, therefore giving them more time to sleep on the aircraft.

SkyTrails will accommodate passengers in departure and arrival lounge. The arrival lounge in Stansted will have shower facilities to accommodate business travellers going straight to work.

Finally, SkyTrails will offer enhanced shopping on-board through extensive product offerings. SkyTrails will sell exclusive products not widely available in traditional stores.

SkyTrails will take special care in hiring and training the cabin crew as the level of on-board service is highly dependent on the quality of these people.

Frequent Flyer Program
Major airlines have been successful at retaining customers by giving them frequent flyer miles each time they travel. As customers get more miles, they gain privileges which include access to airport lounges, upgrades, free flights, and other benefits. In addition, major airlines, through global partnerships are able to offer these programs on many different airlines.

SkyTrails will introduce a frequent flyer program of its own which will be very simple and easy to understand. Most airlines have very complicated programs which often make it difficult for customers to redeem their miles. SkyTrails will offer frequent flyer Internet cash/points that customers will be able to spend on specific websites. SkyTrails will partner with selected e-commerce sites in order to provide this service. SkyTrails believes that its value proposition combined with good service and a simple and innovative frequent flyer program will be sufficient to retain customers.

SkyTrails' primary objective is to establish itself as a niche player in the long-haul market of business travel by providing a high level of service and comfort at an attractive price. The use of a simplified organizational structure, a common aircraft type, and a policy of system wide commonality will significantly reduce operating costs over the more traditional airlines. This, coupled with our focus on premium long-haul passengers, will enable us to achieve much higher margins than our competitors.

Operating Strategy

Focus on a single type of aircraft and a single class of travel
SkyTrails opted for the B757-200 based upon its capacity, range, operating costs, reliability, and availability. By operating a narrow body aircraft on long-haul flights, SkyTrails is able to reduce significantly the operating costs and offer more frequencies. By operating a single aircraft type, SkyTrails will minimize costs associated with training and maintenance programs. Pilot commonality, aircraft interchangeability, technician interchangeability, great economies of scale in spares holdings are some of the benefits associated with single aircraft type operation. Also by offering a single class of service, SkyTrails reduces significantly the complexity of serving three different classes (i.e., catering, marketing, purchasing, systems, etc.).

Ensure service-oriented personnel through productivity and profit-based incentives
SkyTrails wishes to maintain labour cost flexibility by providing a portion of total compensation in the form of profit sharing. Maintaining high productivity of the work force is also an important aspect that management will focus on. SkyTrails believes that employee ownership is fundamental to its success and will provide schemes to promote this.

Focus on long-haul, point-to-point, nonstop services
SkyTrails will initially focus on the London-New York route where it can operate profitably with a small share of the market. SkyTrails will maintain this focus in the future by choosing routes where a large market already exists. Following New York, SkyTrails will start services to Boston, Chicago, and Washington, D.C.

Outsource non-passenger related activities
SkyTrails will outsource many services to quality companies in areas where there is no direct contact with the passengers. SkyTrails aims to offer a quality service to its passengers and will therefore ensure that only its staff interact directly with the customers.

Pricing Strategy

Simple and Transparent Fare Structure
SkyTrails will use a simple yield management system to determine the best price for each single seat in the aircraft. SkyTrails will have a simple fare structure with three different fares. SkyTrails will monitor the purchasing patterns and will be able to restrict the amount of discounted fares on certain flights.

Fare Type	Restrictions	One way Fare	Round-trip Fare
Flexible	Changeable and Refundable No Fee	£900	£1,800
Advance	2 weeks advance booking Nonrefundable Changeable with Fee	£700	£1,400
One month advance	For travel booked 1 month in advance Nonrefundable Nonchangeable	£500	£1,000

Flexible	This fare is designed for business travellers who make travel plans at the last minute and who often have to change their travelling plans. It is fully changeable and refundable without any fees nor restrictions. This fare is 50 percent cheaper than current published business class fares.
Advance	This fare is designed for the business traveller who has fixed engagements and is price conscious. This ticket is equivalent to a premium economy fare on Virgin.
One month advance	This fare will be used to stimulate leisure travellers to travel on Saturdays or to book one month in advance. It will be very difficult for business travellers to get access to these fares because of their booking and flying patterns.

In order to attract large corporations, SkyTrails will offer one way fully flexible tickets between £1,400 and £1,700 depending on the volumes involved. While large corporations already get deals at around £1,000 one way, small and medium enterprises (SME) have no means to achieve any significant discount from the full fare business class (£3,580 rtn) SkyTrails will offer very attractive alternatives for the SME market.

SkyTrails will use special promotions in the first months of operations in order to attract as many customers as possible and get them to experience the service. The initial objective is to focus on load factors rather than yields in order to penetrate the market and stimulate product trial.

In order to be successful in the market of business travel, SkyTrails needs to convince two decision makers: 1.) the travel manager or person who makes the travel policy for a company and 2.) the traveller himself. The travel manager and the traveller make decisions based on different criteria and it is important to satisfy both decision makers in order to ensure success.

The travel manager is mainly driven by price and his objective is to negotiate the best deal for his company. On the other hand, the traveller is driven by frequent flyer programs, comfort, convenience, and lifestyle. SkyTrails will have a sales team that will focus on travel managers of large and small companies and will have a conceptual and lifestyle driven communication strategy that will appeal to the traveller.

Marketing and Sales Strategy

Large Volume Companies (1000+ sectors per annum)
SkyTrails will target the large financial institutions and other companies with a major presence in both London and New York. In the city of London and in Canary Wharf there is great concentration of London-New York premium class traffic. The Top 20 London-New York spending companies account for close to 100,000 premium sectors per annum (sectors: one-way ticket). These companies are able to negotiate discounts of up to 50 percent off published fares and are often tied in to global deals with the major airlines. While SkyTrails can still offer more attractive deals to these large corporates, it does not anticipate obtaining primary carrier status. SkyTrails will most certainly get secondary or tertiary status therefore capturing up to 20 percent of these companies' volumes. It will sign commercial agreements with these companies.

Sales and Distribution

	Name	**Estimated Sectors/Year***
1	Credit Suisse First Boston	10,000
2	JP Morgan	10,000
3	Goldman Sachs	9,200
4	Morgan Stanley	7,400
5	Deutsche Bank	7,400
6	Merrill Lynch	5,500
7	Chase Manhattan	5,500
8	UBS	5,500
9	Lehman Brothers	4,500
10	IBM	4,500
11	PricewaterhouseCoopers	4,500
10	Warburg Dillon Read	3,600
11	Seagram	3,500
12	Citibank	2,900
13	Reuters	2,800
14	Marsh	2,600
15	GE	2,200
16	Diageo	2,000
17	Barclays	1,500
19	Natwest	1,400
20	Cable and Wireless	1,400
	Total	**97,900**

London originating only

Medium Volume Companies (50-1000 sectors)
SkyTrails has already identified over 200 companies in this category. These companies are the most attractive for SkyTrails because they have a weaker purchasing power than the large volume companies and therefore do not get discounts in excess of 30 percent off published fares.

Small and Medium Enterprises (up to 50 sectors)

SkyTrails will also target the small and medium enterprises (SMEs) market. The Stansted catchment area of London, North London, Essex, Cambridgeshire, Hertfordshire, Essex, East Anglia, and the Southern Midlands has a proliferation of SMEs, many of which are subsidiaries of U.S. based companies. SkyTrails will offer a compelling value proposition to these SMEs based on corporate discounts from an already competitive pricing structure. British Airways and other major transatlantic airlines do not offer corporate discounts in the SME market.

SkyTrails will hire a strong sales team that will target companies directly. SkyTrails will also team up with a major credit card company and large business travel agencies that will give SkyTrails access to a large number of SMEs. SkyTrails believes that getting companies enrolled will be a critical success factor and will ensure that its value proposition is well communicated to the businesses likely to use the service.

Electronic Ticketing

SkyTrails will offer customers quicker, easier, more convenient ways to arrange travel through the use of e-ticketing or "ticketless travel." An e-ticket entitles a passenger to all the same conditions of a conventional paper ticket, however instead of being printed, the e-ticket is stored in the SkyTrails e-ticket database. The customer simply receives a paper itinerary/receipt for Customs and Immigration.

Distribution and Revenue Management

SkyTrails will use an integrated ticketless software (Open Skies by HP) which offers an online booking engine as an alternative to traditional airline distribution through Computer Reservation System (CRS). Open Skies also offers streamlined revenue accounting, airport functionality, and a customer database function. The Open Skies system is currently used by Go, Easyjet, JetBlue, Buzz, CityBird, and many others.

Travel Agency

SkyTrails will form relationships with the key U.K. business travel agents giving them an opportunity to increase their commission by taking some of the risk. Travel agents will be able to buy in bulk in advance and get higher commissions than if they simply book tickets on an ad hoc basis.

Travel agents' commissions in the U.K. have declined from 9 percent to 7 percent in recent years and are set to reduce further in 2001. SkyTrails will offer attractive returns for agency partners—well above U.K. industry standards.

Call Centres

SkyTrails will operate an efficient, customer oriented call centre open 24 hours a day in order to serve individuals, corporate clients, or travel agents. Fully trained staff will also be able to handle website enquiries.

Direct Sales through the Internet

Harnessing the power of the Internet will be key to the success of SkyTrails. It is the most cost effective distribution method and SkyTrails will heavily promote its website to attract direct passengers. A user friendly website will be set up to sell tickets, select seats, choose meals, check punctuality, etc. In addition, the website will enable passengers to choose connecting flights with European low cost airlines (Ryanair, Go Fly, Virgin Express, Easyjet, Buzz) and also with U.S. low cost airlines. This will enable SkyTrails to expand its target market by capturing connecting passengers as well as point-to-point passengers.

An extranet corporate booking tool will be developed for use by corporate clients.

SkyTrails will form strategic partnerships with leading travel, luxury goods, and financial websites targeting similar audiences with hyperlinks between websites.

Advertising and Communication

SkyTrails' customer base is well defined which will enable SkyTrails to focus its advertising efforts to specific locations and specific newspapers and magazines.

Phase I: Market Penetration in high density routes

Growth Strategy

SkyTrails will initially target the most dense transatlantic market starting with New York. We will then expand to Boston, Washington, D.C., Dulles, and Chicago.

By targeting very dense markets, SkyTrails will only need a small portion of the overall market in order to be profitable.

Phase II: Extend service to medium/low density long haul routes

We see much larger potential in medium to low density long haul routes where the traditional airlines are not present today. These destinations include Stewart Airport or Whiteplains Airport which are located in New York state but within easy reach of Greenwich and Stamford (Connecticut) which are key business centres. Passengers will be able to bypass the large hubs for long haul flights in the same way the regional jet is able to bypass hubs on short haul flights.

	JFK	JFK	BOS	IAD	ORD	SWF	FLL	BDL
Launch Date	Feb 02	Mar 04	Mar 03	Jun 03	Sep 03	Mar 04	Mar 05	Mar 05
Daily Frequency	2x	1x	1x	1x	1x	1x	1x	1x

JFK: New York   **BOS:** Boston   **IAD:** Washington Dulles
ORD: Chicago O'Hare   **SWF:** Stewart airport (New York)   **FLL:** Fort Lauderdale (Florida)
BDL: Hartford (Connecticut)

Other Opportunities

While scheduled long haul flights will clearly be our focus, SkyTrails will take advantage of opportunities in the high-end segment of the leisure market where we are seeing strong growth. Such opportunities could fit in nicely with the business travel which tends to be low at weekends and during the summer season.

SkyTrails will also consider ad hoc charters and corporate charters on a case by case basis.

Air Operator's Certificate and Operating License

Operations

In order to conduct commercial flights, SkyTrails will need an Air Operator's Certificate (AOC) and an Operating Licence which are granted by the U.K. Civil Aviation Authority. In order to get an AOC and an Operating Licence, the company has to comply with safety, financial, and other requirements laid down by the CAA/JAA. The application process can take over 12 months to complete. In order to avoid relying on this process to start operations, SkyTrails will use the AOC and operating license of TravelAir in the first year of operations. By using an existing airline, SkyTrails significantly reduces the risk of delays in the start-up phase. SkyTrails will in effect outsource the operations to this existing airline for the first 12 months which will enable SkyTrails to focus on the commercial aspects of the business. From the passenger's perspective, TravelAir will be invisible. The crew will have SkyTrails uniforms and the aircraft will have SkyTrails livery. TravelAir has tremendous experience with B757 ETOPS (Extended Twin Operations) operations and is viewed by many as the best quality charter airline in the U.K.

Slots

Through TravelAir, SkyTrails has obtained landing and takeoff slots at both Stansted and JFK for the following times:

	Flight 01	**Flight 02**
London Stansted	15:00	19:00
New York JFK	18:00	22:00

	Flight 03	**Flight 04**
New York JFK	19:15	23:15
London Stansted	07:00	11:00

TravelAir will transfer all the slots obtained to SkyTrails once it obtains its own AOC.

Airports

In order to maintain a high level of customer service, SkyTrails will either employ its own staff or ensure the ground handling agent has dedicated staff for all aspects of airport handling involving contact with customers. For other aspects of ground handling, SkyTrails will initially outsource its needs until critical mass has been established. SkyTrails will lease space in each airport for lounges and offices.

Maintenance and Training

Heavy maintenance and training will be outsourced, initially to TravelAir.

Aircraft

The Boeing 757-200 is one of the most popular commercial aircraft ever built. Over 800 B757s are currently in service. Boeing is starting to deliver a stretched version, the B757-300 and is presently evaluating the possibility of building an extra long range B757. The B757-200 is usually configured to accommodate 180 passengers in a two-class configuration. The B757-200 has a high level of dispatch reliability (in excess of 99 percent).

The other possibilities for SkyTrails could have been the B767 which is a wide body aircraft. SkyTrails believes that the risk involved with operating a B767 are 30 percent higher and also limit the ability to expand in smaller markets. SkyTrails could have considered the BBJ which is equivalent to a B737 long range. Unfortunately, the BBJ is still in its early days and the lack of availability in the market is what has driven our decision towards the B757. The BBJ could be ideally suited for smaller markets.

B757-200 Specifications

Design range, miles (km)	4,550 miles (7,315km)
Maximum gross weight—Takeoff	255,000 lb (115,660 kg)
Typical operating empty weight	128,730 lb (58,390 kg)
Engines	Pratt & Whitney PW2040/PW2037
	Rolls Royce RB211-535
Maximum fuel capacity, U.S. gal (L)	11,526 gal (43,625L)
Lower-hold cargo volume	1,670 ft3 (47.3 m3)

REGULATORY ENVIRONMENT

Bilateral Agreement between U.S. and U.K.

Flights from major international airports in the U.K. to the U.S. are regulated by a Bilateral Agreement between the two countries. The government negotiates routes for its country and then distributes these to the airline of its choice. Usually airlines have to submit an application detailing why its proposed service is in the best national interest. This creates a barrier to entry which is difficult to overcome. In addition, landing and takeoff slots at London Heathrow and

London Gatwick are difficult to obtain creating another barrier to entry. These barriers to entry give a strong advantage to existing airlines. However, U.S. and U.K. government have been negotiating possible liberalization of skies. If this happens, we expect to see additional capacity out of Heathrow to the USA which may have an impact on yields.

Open Skies for Regional Airports (Bermuda II Agreement)
International flights from all the regional airports in the U.K. (Stansted, Birmingham, Manchester, etc.) are regulated by this Agreement with the U.S. which enables all national airlines of each country to operate an unlimited number of flights between these airports and any U.S. international airport. SkyTrails will therefore be able to benefit from this Agreement by operating out of Stansted. SkyTrails will still have to apply for the routes but these will be automatically granted. The application was filed on 12 September 2000.

A more detailed overview of the regulatory environment written by Eugene Stokes, Aviation Partner at Smyth Adair Benson, is provided in the Appendix.

Major Airlines Characteristics:

Focus on hubs
In order to increase load factors, major airlines have adopted a hub and spoke strategy which consists of centralising flights at an airport therefore benefiting from connecting passengers in addition to origination and destination passengers. As a result of this strategy, many passengers are forced to make stopovers, increasing their travelling time.

SkyTrails will offer point to point services which offer significant time savings for premium passengers.

High fixed costs
Major airlines have large overhead costs and many are tied in to labour contracts which prevent them from reducing these costs significantly.

SkyTrails will maintain a lower cost base and therefore maintain a competitive advantage.

Lack of customer focus
Overall, airlines tend to lack customer focus. By focusing on hubs and alliances, airlines gain efficiencies but these strategies are of limited benefit to the customers.

SkyTrails will offer an individual service and its success will be built on customer focus.

Consolidation with major alliances: Star Alliance, One World
While most industries have consolidated in the past few years through mergers and acquisitions, the airline industry's consolidation is based predominantly on alliances and minority equity stakes. Starting with code-share agreements and extending these to full alliances have been the common pattern followed by airlines around the world. These alliances enable airlines to benefit from each others network and distribution capability. While very beneficial to the airlines, it is arguable whether the consumer really benefits from these alliances as they tend to reduce competition. Customer satisfaction usually suffers as a result of this consolidation, creating an opportunity for SkyTrails.

The most successful alliance to date is the Star Alliance which is comprised of Lufthansa, United, SAS, Thai, Varig, Air New Zealand, Ansett Australia, All Nippon Airways, and recently Singapore Airlines. Its main competitor, One World, is comprised of British Airways, American Airlines, Cathay Pacific Airways, Qantas, Finnair, and Iberia. Another important combination is Virgin-Singapore Airlines. Singapore now owns 49

MARKET ANALYSIS

Global Airline Industry

percent of Virgin Atlantic and the two airlines will be a strong competitor on the transatlantic market.

Following Swissair's acquisition of 85 percent of Sabena, other European airlines have started to talk about possible mergers and acquisition. On the U.S. side, United and U.S. Airways have announced a merger which has prompted other talks within the major airlines. This consolidation will be closely monitored by the regulatory bodies and it is uncertain how many will be approved.

SkyTrails will not take part in any alliance and will remain committed to its niche strategy. The larger the alliances become, the more opportunities there are for niche airlines to prosper.

Low Cost Airlines are gaining market share

Following the continued success of Southwest Airlines, many start-up airlines have emerged in the past ten years, both in Europe and in the U.S. The low cost airlines focus on short-haul traffic and have been key in stimulating demand by offering extremely low fares. These airlines initially targeted the leisure traveller but in recent years they have attracted a growing amount of business travellers who were not satisfied with the high prices charged by the major airlines. The main challenge faced by these young companies is that of safety. After the ValueJet accident in Florida, customers were concerned that low cost airlines did not maintain their aircraft correctly and were more dangerous to fly than the majors.

While low cost airlines continue to thrive in the U.S., the more recent European additions such as Easyjet, Virgin Express, Go Fly, Ryanair, and others are experiencing tremendous growth and are presenting a serious challenge to the major airlines short-haul strategies.

SkyTrails will benefit from this trend as passengers are now used to flying with newer airlines which do not have the history of State-Owned carriers.

Regional Airlines are increasing point-to-point travel

The Regional Airlines are by far the most profitable segment of the market with net margins as high as 15 percent. They benefit from very fuel efficient modern aircraft (Regional Jets) and are able to focus on high yield passengers by providing point-to-point services and more frequencies. By using smaller jets, boarding and disembarking times are reduced which enables fast turnaround of the aircraft. Companies such as Comair and Atlantic Coast in the U.S. and Crossair, Air Littoral, and British Regional Airlines in Europe have grown tremendously in the past five years.

SkyTrails is in effect an extension of the Regional Airlines by offering point to point services on a long-haul basis.

The Market

Breakdown of Passengers on London to New York route April 1999-March 2000

	JFK	Newark	Total New York
Heathrow	2,499,983	709,104	3,209,087
Gatwick	134,226	492,547	626,773
Total London	2,634,209	1,201,651	**3,835,860**

N.B. In the above table, connecting traffic through London is included and accounts for 1.2 million passengers.

Top 10 U.S. Destinations from Heathrow October 1998- September 1999

City	Airport	Business	Leisure	Total
New York	JFK	861,179	1,738,393	2,599,572
Los Angeles	LAX	313,806	1,073,360	1,387,167
Chicago	ORD	421,807	736,109	1,157,916
San Francisco	SFO	286,101	749,969	1,036,070
Washington, D.C.	IAD	358,403	654,786	1,013,189
Boston	BOS	286,406	525,556	811,961
Miami	MIA	158,855	459,399	618,255
Newark	EWR	171,880	492,303	664,183
Seattle	SEA	102,157	188,329	290,486
Philadelphia	PHL	107,265	181,572	288,837
Total		**3,067,859**	**6,799,776**	**9,867,636**

Stansted Catchment Area Originating Traffic to New York

	Inner Catchment*	Inner and Outer Catchment**
Total Traffic	406,338	744,839
Origin/Destination Passengers	357,508	647,437
	88.00%	*86.90%*
Business Passengers	125,585	232,392
	30.90%	*31.20%*

N.B. In the above table, connecting traffic through London is excluded.

*Inner Catchment: *Essex, Suffolk, Norfolk, Cambridgeshire*
**Inner & Outer Catchment: *Inner and Hertfordshire, Bedfordshire, Northamptonshire,*
               Leicestershire, Nottinghamshire, Lincolnshire.

Both catchment areas exclude the city of London which is a key market for SkyTrails.

SkyTrails Share of New York market from inner and outer catchment area

SkyTrails Load Factor	Share of Total	Share of O&D Traffic*	Share of Business Travellers
80%	23.00%	26.10%	74.40%
70%	20.10%	22.90%	65.10%
60%	17.20%	19.60%	55.80%
50%	14.40%	16.30%	46.50%

*Origin and Destination

Inner and Outer Catchment

SkyTrails Load Factor	Share of Total	Share of O&D Traffic	Share of Business Travellers
80%	12.50%	14.40%	40.20%
70%	11.00%	12.60%	35.20%
60%	9.40%	10.80%	30.20%
50%	7.80%	9.00%	25.10%

Focus on Point to Point Traffic

The majority of the business traffic between London and New York is point to point as business travellers from other European capitals tend to fly direct.

Connecting Traffic

While SkyTrails will focus primarily on point to point, it will benefit from connecting traffic originating in secondary cities in the U.K., Europe, and the U.S. Premium travellers in those cities have to connect in a hub in order to travel to the U.S. and they could easily combine a low-cost European flight into Stansted with a SkyTrails flight to the U.S. The following table highlights the various secondary cities that are served by a low-cost airline operating at Stansted and with arrival and departure times within 2 hours of a SkyTrails flight:

Airline	Secondary European City
Go Fly	Bologna, Copenhagen, Edinburgh, Faro, Malaga, Palma
Ryanair	Cork, Kerry, Knock, Nimes, Biarritz, Carcassone (Toulouse), Perpignan, St. Etienne (Lyon), Venice, Pisa, Glasgow, Anconna, Malmo, Brescia, Dinard
Buzz	Dusseldorf, Bordeaux, Berlin, Marseilles

Airline	Secondary American City
American	Albany, Baltimore, Boston, Buffalo, Cleveland, Hartford, Los Angeles, Philadelphia, Pittsburgh, Raleigh/Durham, Rochester, San Juan (P.R.), Syracuse, Washington
American West	Las Vegas
Delta	Albany, Atlanta, Baltimore, Boston, Los Angeles, Philadelphia, Pittsburgh, Richmond, Rochester, Washington
National Airlines	Los Angeles, Las Vegas
Northwest	Detroit
TWA	Las Vegas, Los Angeles, San Francisco, St. Louis
United	Boston, Los Angeles, Washington, D.C.

Competition

Premium Capacity on the London-New York Route (Sept.-Dec. 2000)

Airline	Daily Frequencies	Premium Seats one-way/day*	% Total Capacity
British Airways	11x	936	42.40%
American Airlines	7x	403	18.20%
Virgin Atlantic	5x	275	12.50%
United Airlines	4x	273	12.30%
Continental Airlines	2x	139	6.30%
Other**	n/a	103	4.70%
SkyTrails***	2x	80	3.60%
Total		**2,209**	**100%**

Premium Seats: 80 percent LF on First Class, Business Class, BA World Traveller Plus, VS Premium economy, plus 10 percent of economy passengers where no Premium Economy equivalent exists

**Other includes 10 percent of premium seats on KLM/AF/EI*

***Assumes 50 percent LF*

Market Shares on Planned Routes for SkyTrails:

Carrier	NYC	BOS	WAS	ORD	MIA
British Airways	42.40%	37.60%	41.70%	20.00%	57.70%
American Airlines	18.20%	34.80%	0.00%	37.60%	18.80%
United Airlines	12.50%	9.40%	37.80%	27.40%	0.00%
Virgin Atlantic	12.30%	7.60%	8.90%	5.60%	8.00%
Continental Airlines	6.30%	0.00%	0.00%	0.00%	0.00%
Nondirect OA	4.70%	2.30%	2.50%	3.20%	3.30%
SkyTrails Airways	3.60%	8.30%	9.10%	6.20%	12.20%
Total	**100%**	**100%**	**100%**	**100%**	**100%**

Product on the London-New York Route

Business Class	AA	BA	UA	CO	VS
Equipment	A300/767	747	763	777	747
Pitch (inches)	50	72	135	153	150
Recline (degrees)	127	180	135	153	150

British Airways (BA)

BA is the market leader with over 40 percent of premium capacity. BA has run into a number of difficulties in the past year and reported disappointing results in 1999. The airline has clearly stated its strategy to focus on the business and premium traveller. BA has introduced a full-sleeper Business Class. We believe that BA is right to focus on the business segment but by offering a full-sleeper Business Class, they are taking the risk that First Class passengers downgrade to Business Class. In addition, by providing this higher quality product, BA is betting that it will be able to continue increasing the price of its business class product. It is simply widening the gap between business class and economy. BA recently introduced World Traveller Plus, which corresponds to Virgin's Premium Economy. The pricing will be similar to SkyTrails but the product is simply an economy class with more legroom. Although BA does offer a good product, it has been harmed by bad press, disappointing results, and unmotivated staff. BA's global strategy with American Airlines has been delayed by the regulatory bodies but BA is still trying to make it work under a weaker form. While BA and AA combined will be a powerful team, the culture and product do not seem to be aligned today.

American Airlines (AA)

AA has 7 daily frequencies with B767 and A300 offering 18.1 percent of the market capacity. AA's service and product standards are below that of the competition. As mentioned earlier, AA's alliance with BA, if it goes through, will be a powerful combination in terms of size and resources.

Virgin Atlantic Airways (Virgin)

Virgin's share of the premium segment is 12.3 percent. Virgin is by far the most innovative player in today's market. Virgin was the first airline to introduce a business-first service in the early 1990s and is the only airline to offer a premium economy section on long-haul flights. Virgin has a code-share agreement with Continental which enables both airlines to sell tickets on each others' flights. The recent sale of 49 percent of Virgin to Singapore Airlines will also provide Virgin with an increase in connecting passengers from Asia. Virgin is also rumoured to be considering a first-class only concept operating BBJs, ACJs, or Bombardier's Global Connector. This does not represent a threat to SkyTrails as Virgin is targeting the First Class passenger.

United Airlines (United)

United has the same share of the premium market as Virgin with 12.3 percent. United is one of the leading airlines in the Star Alliance which provides much connecting traffic. United's product is industry standard and is viewed as a follower rather than a market leader.

Continental Airlines (CO)

CO is more of a niche player in this market with only two flights a day. It operates out of Gatwick to Newark. However, its code-share with Virgin gives it access to Heathrow and JFK. Continental is a strong player at Newark where it controls over 50 percent of the landing and takeoff slots. It is planning to increase its presence at Newark by building a new terminal for additional wide body aircraft. In May 2001, Continental started a service from Stansted to Newark with a B757. This certainly helps to raise the profile of Stansted as a gateway to the U.S. Continental's B757 only has 16 business class seats and its early morning departure from Stansted does not suit the London or Canary Wharf based traveller.

British Midland (BM)

BM has been attempting to obtain traffic rights from Heathrow to the USA, so far unsuccessfully. It is determined to keep trying to get into the market. BM has ordered Airbus A330s which will be delivered in summer 2001 and which it intends to use on routes to the USA. British Midland has obtained rights to fly from Manchester to the USA but not from Heathrow.

FINANCIALS

Funding Needs

SkyTrails' total funding needs amount to £25 million. The following table summarises the uses of funds to August 2003 which is the point when accumulated net uses of funds reaches its highest point:

GBP £	Sources and Uses until Aug 03
Total Funds Raised	26,359,750
Aircraft Reconfiguration	-10,150,000
Aircraft Leasing	-11,127,588
Aircraft Deposits	-3,558,620
Advertising Expense	-5,558,690
Operating Profit	13,732,027
Cash Balance Aug 2003	9,696,879

SkyTrails has to set aside a Bond which is required by the CAA in order to protect consumers during the period that SkyTrails is operating under TravelAir's AOC. SkyTrails also needs to have sufficient funds to satisfy the CAA that it can survive with no revenues for 3 months at the time it applies for its own AOC.

Valuation

In order to value airline companies on the same basis, we use the Enterprise Value (EV) to EBITDAR multiple. EBITDAR is cash flow before rentals (operating leases) which, for SkyTrails amounts to £72.6 million at the end of the fourth fiscal year. The following table shows the multiples for European publicly traded airlines:

	BA	Lufthansa	KLM	SAirGroup	Alitalia	Air France	Ryanair	Average
1998/1999	9.5	4.5	6.5	6	5.6	5.9	14	**7.4**
1999/2000	15.3	5.9	8.5	9.3	10	4.4	12.2	**9.3**
2000/2001	12.9	5.6	6.4	7.5	8.2	4.4	11.2	**8.0**
2001/2002	10.1	4.9	5.5	6.8	7.6	3.1	10.1	**6.9**

EBITDAR: Airlines are valued based on EBITDAR multiples (as opposed to EBITDA) because airlines have different mixes of operating leases and on-balance sheet financing for aircraft which therefore would distort valuations based on EBITDA multiples.

If we take a very high discount rate of 50 percent to account for the risk involved and assume that we are four years away from the end of the fourth fiscal year, we get the following present values:

EBITDAR Multiple	**5**	**6**	**7**
PV with 50% annual discount	£72MM	£86MM	£100MM

Operating Margins

The financial model produces an operating margin at the end of year 4 of 21.3 percent. Margins well in excess of this are currently being attained by regional carriers, even though the more traditional airlines do not reach these heights. We believe this margin is on the low side because we have made conservative assumptions. We will attain margins similar to the better regional carriers as our strategy is similar to theirs. The table below shows the operating margins obtained by a selection of regional and non-regional airlines and was sourced from *Airline Business* magazine.

Operating Margin	**1999**	**1998**
Regional		
Atlas Air	28.90%	32.20%
Ryanair	22.70%	24.10%
Southwest Airlines	21.80%	21.80%
GB Airways	19.20%	14.50%
Westjet Airlines	19.00%	11.20%
Skywest Airlines	18.30%	16.50%
Majors		
Delta	9.00%	12.50%
Northwest Airlines	6.90%	-2.10%
Lufthansa	5.70%	9.00%
Air France	3.50%	2.90%
British Airways	0.90%	5.00%

Assumptions

Revenues

Aircraft

SkyTrails will start operations with two B757-200 with an 80-seat configuration. The following table shows aircraft addition through the period of the plan:

	Feb 2	Mar 3	Jun 3	Sep 3	Mar 4	Mar 5
Additions	2	1	1	1	2	2
Total B757	**2**	**3**	**4**	**5**	**7**	**9**

Load Factors

We have assumed that the first two flights reach their break-even load factor after 12 months.

Fares

Fare type	Fare	Definition	Distribution method
Full fare	1,800	A fully refundable, fully changeable, flexible fare	Sold through SkyTrails call centre or website
Full fare TA	1,600	A fully refundable, fully changeable, flexible fare	Sold through travel agents
Corporate	1,400	A fully refundable, fully changeable, flexible fare with a corporate discount for volume purchase	Sold through travel agents or through SkyTrails call centre or website
Restricted	1,400	A 14-day advance purchase fare with fees for changes and cancellation	Sold through SkyTrails call centre or website
Restricted TA	1,260	A 14-day advance purchase fare with fees for changes and cancellation	Sold through travel agents
Full Restricted	1,000	A nonchangeable, nonrefundable fare	Sold through SkyTrails call centre or website
Full Restricted TA	900	A nonchangeable, nonrefundable fare	Sold through travel agents

Other Revenue: £1,000 per sector is assumed for Cargo and Duty Free revenue.

The following table breaks down the mix of fares assumed in each year:

Fare	2001-2002 % of seats	2002-2003 % of seats	2003-2004 % of seats	2004-2005 % of seats
£1,800	2.40%	6.14%	7.25%	7.37%
£1,600	4.80%	5.29%	5.48%	5.58%
£1,400	38.40%	44.07%	53.53%	56.22%
£1,260	14.40%	12.78%	8.05%	7.29%
£1,000	16.00%	13.21%	14.10%	13.94%
£900	24.00%	18.51%	11.59%	9.61%
Weighted average price	£1,215	£1,272	£1,314	£1,327
Total round-trip passengers	**7,578**	**62,136**	**124,431**	**164,575**

Variable Costs

	STN	JFK	BOS	IAD	ORD	SFW	FLL	BDL
Fuel (US$ per U.S. Gallon)	1	1	1	1	1	1	1	1
Consumption (Gal/hr)	1,110	1,110	1,110	1,110	1,110	1,110	1,110	1,110
Maintenance (Round Trip) £		6,533	6,409	7,150	7,582	6,519	8,207	6,519
Landing Fees £	208	437	280	246	326	142	182	142
Navigation Fees £		2,410	2,384	2,431	2,998	2,410	3,117	2,410
Pax Services* (per pax) £	120	120	120	120	120	120	120	120
Ground Handling £	850	2,223	1,834	1,882	1,544	1,434	1,334	1,434

Pax Services include: catering(£30), frequent flyer contribution(£25), in-flight products(£10), ground transfers (£20), distribution cost (£5), Lounge U.S. (£5), airport passenger handling (£9), credit card commission (£16)

N.B. These figures are based on current prices obtained from suppliers

Fixed Costs

Direct Costs

Flight-Deck Crew

11 flight crews are assumed for the first two aircraft. Each flight crew is composed of a captain and a first officer. Captain cost is assumed at £6,850 per month and first officer at £4,760. These figures include social charges, accommodation, and transport.

Cabin Crew

11 cabin crews are assumed for the first two aircraft. Each cabin crew comprises 1 purser, 2 senior cabin crew, and 3 junior cabin crew at a cost of £2,367, £1,878, and £1,670 respectively.

Insurance

$25,000 per month per aircraft.

Leasing

- $315,000 per month per aircraft for the first two aircraft which is based on current market conditions.
- $335,000 per month per aircraft for the next two aircraft as we assume used aircraft will be leased.
- $420,000 per month per aircraft for aircraft 5-9 as we assume new aircraft will be leased.

Security Deposits

The standard 3-month rental is assumed.

Reconfiguration Costs

We assumed £2,000,000 per aircraft for the first two aircraft of which 25 percent is paid 6 months prior to delivery and 75 percent is paid thirty days net. All other reconfiguration costs are assumed thirty days net.

TravelAir Management Fee

$42,000 per month for the first two aircraft and $15,000 per month for additional aircraft. This is consistent with the contract signed with TravelAir. We assume SkyTrails will get its own AOC in the thirteenth month of operation at which point SkyTrails will no longer pay a fee to TravelAir but incurs higher payroll cost as it takes all the operations in-house.

Salaries

These include salaries and benefits for the Ground Operations/Customer Service, Sales, Marketing, Finance and Administration, and Technical departments. These are projected according to a manpower plan.

Indirect Costs

£	Pre-Ops	Year 1	Year 2	Year 3	Year 4
Advertising Expense	858,690	2,200,000	4,500,000	5,150,000	5,400,000
Internet and Technology	60,000	180,000	240,000	240,000	240,000
Legal	183,000	120,000	120,000	120,000	120,000
Rent (offices/lounge, etc.)	397,000	228,000	312,000	384,000	384,000
Other	216,500	1,096,000	1,211,000	1,886,000	1,671,000
Total	**1,715,190**	**3,824,000**	**6,383,000**	**7,780,000**	**7,815,000**

Exchange Rate: £1=$1.45

SkyTrails will using hedging techniques for both fuel and currency in order to minimize its exposure.

Interest Income: Interest rate is assumed at 3.5 percent per annum.

Annual Income Statement (£)

FYE DECEMBER	2001	2002	2003	2004	2005
Revenue					
Total Passenger Revenue	-	29,320,595	74,422,654	158,860,079	212,059,412
Charter Revenue	-	-	-	-	-
Other Revenue	-	1,229,720	2,623,980	5,247,960	6,096,640
Total Revenue	**-**	**30,550,315**	**77,046,634**	**164,108,039**	**218,156,052**
Operating Expenses					
Salaries and Benefits	927,000	5,235,170	8,536,105	1,907,550	23,441,555
Fuel	-	6,556,655	14,070,125	25,600,793	34,235,586
Maintenance	-	4,016,690	8,619,536	15,683,369	20,973,152
Landing Fees	-	396,585	789,766	1,250,127	1,528,248
Navigation Fees	-	1,481,813	3,158,926	5,780,160	7,805,474
Pax Services	-	5,848,188	14,401,162	29,749,429	39,761,225
Ground Handling	-	1,858,722	3,842,269	6,351,984	8,108,271
Air 2000 Management Fee	137,931	626,897	57,931	-	0
Insurance	-	413,793	758,621	1,310,345	1,724,138
Other Expenses	1,097,190	4,104,000	6,111,000	7,670,000	7,815,000
Total Operating Expenses	**2,162,121**	**30,538,511**	**60,345,440**	**113,303,758**	**145,392,650**
EBITDAR	**2,162,121**	**11,804**	**16,701,194**	**50,804,281**	**72,763,402**
EBITDAR MARGIN	N/A	0.0%	21.7%	31.0%	33.4%
Aircraft Rental	-	4,996,552	10,875,862	20,606,897	27,558,621
EBITDA	**(2,162,121)**	**4,984,748**	**5,825,332**	**30,197,385**	**45,204,782**
EBITDA MARGIN	N/A	-16.3%	7.6%	18.4%	20.7%
Depreciation	-	-	1,200,000	2,000,000	2,800,000
EBIT	**(2,162,121)**	**(4,984,748)**	**4,625,332**	**28,197,385**	**42,404,782**
EBIT MARGIN	N/A	-16.3%	6.0%	17.2%	19.4%
Interest Expense					
Interest Income	241,902	661,475	722,477	1,376,225	2,908,543
Income Before Taxes	**(1,920,219)**	**4,323,273**	**5,347,809**	**29,573,610**	**45,313,324**
MARGIN	N/A	-14.2%	6.9%	18.0%	20.8%
Taxes 30%	-	-	268,705	8,872,083	13,593,997
Net Income	**(1,920,219)**	**(4,323,273)**	**5,616,514**	**20,701,527**	**31,719,327**
MARGIN	N/A	-14.2%	7.3%	12.6%	14.5%

APPENDIX A

Regulatory Environment and Licensing Issues

Eugene Stokes
Partner
Head of Aviation Regulatory and Commercial
Smyth Adair Benson

For the past 15 years Eugene Stokes has been a recognised specialist with an international reputation in regulatory, commercial, EC, and competition law affecting air transport and the travel industry: he advises airlines, airports, banks, governments, and regulatory authorities on a wide range of regulatory, legal, and aeropolitical issues, has been involved in all aspects of the liberalisation of aviation in the European Community and advises on both contentious and noncontentious commercial and competition issues in the aviation sector.

During this period, his airline clients have been numerous but have included United Airlines, Delta Airlines, ANA, Cathay Pacific, Philippine Airlines, Swissair, CityFlyer Express, British Caledonian, Dan-Air, and Avianca, and he has advised the new low cost U.K. scheduled carrier EasyJet since its start-up.

SkyTrails—Licensing Requirements
SkyTrails is an English registered company and its principal place of business will be in England. Under European Community Law, every air transport undertaking with its registered office and principal place of business in a Member State of the European Union must hold an operating licence granted by that Member State in accordance with the EC Licensing Regulation (Council Regulation EEC No: 2407/92). In the United Kingdom the grant of operating licences is delegated to the Civil Aviation Authority. While the EC Market Access Regulation (Council Regulation EEC No: 2408/92) provides that all holders of EC operating licences have the right (virtually unrestricted) to operate any services between any two points in the European Community ("community carriers") it leaves the rights of Community carriers to operate to points outside the FU unaffected. Community carriers require to be separately licensed by their states to perform such services according to the requirements of bilateral air services agreements between the Member States which licences them and the relevant states outside the European Union.

The bilateral air service agreement between the U.K. and the U.S. is quite restrictive, but the proposed route London Stansted/New York JFK is available under it. An application will need to be made to the CAA for a route licence following the grant of which the U.K. government (the Department of the Environment Transport and the Regions or "DETR") will be asked to designate the applicant (i.e. by diplomatic note inform the U.S. government [Department of Transportation or "DOT"] that the applicant has been designated for service under the bilateral by the U.K. government).

The requirements of an EC operating licence are quite onerous and include the issue by the CAA of an Air Operators Certificate (AOC) and demonstration to the CAA's satisfaction of stringent financial fitness requirements (which require it to be demonstrated that the applicant can discharge its financial obligations in its business for the first two years and this without any revenue for the first three months). For a new airline, these requirements (particularly the AOC requirements which relate to safety and technical competence) can take many months to process. Because SkyTrails wishes to commence service early in 2001 it has decided to contract with an existing U.K. operating licence holder to operate the services on its behalf until such time as its own operating licence is granted.

While it is permitted to enter into such an operating agreement, it is a requirement of U.K. law that an undertaking which makes seats available on an aircraft (or holds itself out as being able to make seats on an aircraft available) while not the operator of the aircraft, must (except in certain circumstances which will not apply to SkyTrails) be licensed. The applicable licence is an Air Travel Organiser's Licence (ATOL) the primary purpose of which is to protect the consumer who has advanced moneys to a seat provider in advance of receiving evidence of his contract with the actual operator.

Because of the hybrid nature of the operation, the CAA can apply the financial fitness standards of the EC licensing regulation to SkyTrails even during the period when it holds an ATOL (the financial fitness standards for which are somewhat different).

This "hybrid" arrangement whereby a new airline operation commences through the combination of an ATOL (held by the new airline pending grant of its own operating licence) and an operating agreement between the new airline and an existing U.K. operator is somewhat frowned upon by the European Commission (although it is not technically contrary to relevant EC legislation). While a number of U.K. airlines have commenced service in this way, the U.K. CAA now looks for a commitment to work towards the grant of an operating licence as soon as possible.

Route Licence

The Process

SkyTrails has selected TravelAir as the operator of the initial services. TravelAir will be required to apply for the route licence for the Stansted/JFK route and seek designation by the U.K. government. Once application has been made to the CAA it will be published in the CAA's Official Record after which there will be a 21-day period for objections to be lodged. Only other U.K. operators have the right to object but, given the CAA's pro-competitive licensing policy and the availability of this route under the U.K./U.S. bilateral, it is not anticipated that any such objector would have reasonable grounds. The possibility of an objection cannot, however, be entirely dismissed. An objection does delay the process which to some competitors might be regarded as a reason for objecting in itself even though the objection might need to be withdrawn later when grounds for the objection would need to be filed. Generally, we would not expect any other U.K. carrier to behave in such a manner.

Assuming there is no objection, TravelAir will be able to proceed after a 21-day period to grant of the licence by the CAA (who will wish to ensure that TravelAir is financially fit to operate the route—this depending to a large extent on the financial arrangements between SkyTrails and TravelAir). Following grant of the route licence to TravelAir, the process of designation by the U.K. government can be completed in a matter of days and it is not anticipated that the process of grant of an operating permit by the U.S. DOT would occupy any substantial passage of time.

If there is an objection to the application to the CAA, the CAA will fix a date for a hearing and require written submissions from the applicant and the objectors. The entire hearing process can take between three and six months and there are provisions for appeal to the Secretary of State which is a written process. It is, however, considered extremely unlikely that even if there were objections they would proceed to a hearing because there are no obvious good grounds for an objection to be made out.

On the grant of its own operating licence, SkyTrails would apply for its own route licence, having agreed with TravelAir that TravelAir would apply for its own route licence to be revoked at the appropriate point.

ATOL

SkyTrails will apply for an ATOL in time to be ready to sell with the appropriate lead time. On grant to it of its operating licence the ATOL will be revoked.

Other Considerations

The U.K./U.S. bilateral requires fare to be filed and approved by the governments. SkyTrails' fares will be substantially below those of their competitors at the outset. While this will obviously be of concern to those competitors, it is not expected that they will succeed in persuading their governments to disallow them. Nevertheless they may try to squeeze a new carrier like SkyTrails out of the market by lowering their own fares. Whether such price pressure is lawful will depend on the application of general principles of anti-trust/competition law, but these principles are well known to the competitors concerned who will be well aware of the consequences of proceeding unlawfully.

Business Development Firm

NKR CONSULTING

8444 Temas Park Road
Raleigh, North Carolina 27601

This plan raised over $500,000 in "seed money" for NKR Consulting. The firm operates as a vertically integrated branding, marketing, and business development solutions provider. Its primary services include media planning, media buying, creative services, and web design. NKR focuses on serving early-stage Internet and technology companies, traditional economy businesses seeking to expand their presence onto the Internet, and Internet "orphans"—Internet companies that have been abandoned by investors.

- BUSINESS OVERVIEW

- OBJECTIVES & STRATEGY

- COMPANY & SERVICE OVERVIEW

- CURRENT CLIENTS

- BUSINESS STRATEGY

- MANAGEMENT

- PROJECTED PROFIT & LOSS

BUSINESS
OVERVIEW

NKR Consulting, Inc., is a privately held North Carolina corporation, which was formed in April of 2000 as an LLC and subsequently converted to a C Corporation. We have offices at 8444 Temas Park Road, Raleigh, North Carolina. We are considering opening offices in Orlando, Florida, and in Austin, Texas, to attract and service clients.

NKR Consulting (NKR) currently operates as a vertically integrated branding, marketing, and business development solutions provider. We provide business planning, strategy, and branding execution for our clients, including media planning, media buying, creative services, and web design. Clients may benefit from the complete suite of services or choose the offerings that best fit their needs. The business concentrates on providing these services to early-stage Internet and technology companies, traditional economy businesses seeking to expand their presence onto the Internet, and Internet "orphans"—those Internet companies that have been abandoned by investors.

The company's services are becoming increasingly valuable, and it continues to attract clients with its ability to provide innovative outsource solutions through its unique combination of business disciplines and strength of vendor/alliance relationships.

Early on, management identified a significant opportunity to provide innovative branding solutions. To achieve this goal, we have dedicated resources toward the identification of highly complementary technologies and vendors that will constitute the basis for our migration from our current "analog" branding services practice to a knowledge-powered, web-enabled "digital" solution for marketing-related services. Through these efforts we have identified these targets, focused our efforts, and gained very favorable agreements that we believe will deliver the technology mechanism for the business to evolve into a global provider of web-enabled marketing solutions.

Upon funding, the company will initiate the integration of Internet-enabled marketing solutions that will power our current "analog" services with an innovative "digital" format that utilizes knowledge management technology in a new way. Although knowledge management has been used in the IT industry and within the management consulting world, it has never been deployed in a marketing or branding arena. Within our current business, applications of the system are limitless. We will use the system for the re-purposing of market research, industry analysis, audio and video presentations, and text, financial data, legal documentation—anything related to the storage, retrieval, and archiving of intellectual and creative assets.

The time, cost, and risk of integrating these systems is significantly mitigated by a plan that incorporates OEM license agreements from complementary technology providers. These superior technologies, currently in existence, would significantly benefit from OEM relationships aggregated under an NKR-branded, web-enabled, open technology platform. The branded platform will operate globally utilizing a revolutionary Palladium Info Management (PIM) system.

The PIM system technology was originally developed by a Japanese technology firm and later readied for market by a major international computer firm. The company has a unique opportunity to leverage a valuable and extensive menu of MJ Computers technologies through a very favorable license entered into by the PIM developer, IdeaDigit Inc. (IDI) of San Francisco. The basis of the license provides global, unlimited use of the MJ technology to IDI—a unique agreement by MJ regarding its product licenses. The PIM system will provide a web-enabled technology overlay to all of the marketing and branding related technologies combined under the OEM license program.

Over the first several months of operations, management has analyzed current market conditions and forecast trends in its core segment. The company now requires further investment to fund both its current analog business model of providing end-to-end branding solutions in addition to development of the proposed digital platform. To accomplish our goals, we have outlined a three-phase plan for growth:

- In our current Phase I business, we will increase human and technical resources to increase capacity for client service, expand the current "analog" business offerings, and continue to explore complementary alliances, technologies, and financial partners.

- In Phase II, we will "digitize" our analog practice to enable the management of tacit knowledge within the creative services (advertising, branding, marketing, and design) market. Unprecedented in our industry, the implementation of knowledge management technology in the creative services should make NKR unique in appeal. We will expand our capacity for services on a global basis through technology provided by our OEM partners. Our agreement with IDI should enable us to effectively deploy our digital services strategy and provide the systems, personnel, and capacity for successful implementation of the Phase III plan.

- Our Phase III initiatives involve expanding this digital offering to build branded, sophisticated marketing solutions required to promote an Internet Virtual Incubation Network (IVIN) to incubators on a global basis. IVIN would be formed as a joint venture among existing incubators seeking knowledge management solutions and which understand the powerful benefits of forming a global knowledge exchange alliance. IVIN will leverage the core knowledge base of incubators to accelerate the development and increase value of their early-stage investments. Phase III of this plan presents the IVIN project as a new business model that more appropriately addresses the needs for business acceleration and delivers an exchange mechanism to enable the monetization of tacit knowledge.

OBJECTIVES & STRATEGY

COMPANY & SERVICE OVERVIEW

Current Strategic Relationships

Management has identified a compelling opportunity to facilitate the construction and administration of the Internet-enabled technology solution discussed in this plan. IDI (developer of an Internet-enabled advanced "Knowledge Management" system) has agreed in principal with NKR to enter into a global, exclusive (to certain defined vertical markets) technology license with NKR to provide its technology as the overlay system to facilitate the formation of OEM relationships with marketing and business development technology providers.

We have also elevated our traditional client/provider relationship with Copper Knowledge (Copper), now a subsidiary of FITQ Corporation, to that of a strategic alliance. As a result, NKR provides clients superior graphic and website design in addition to programming and maintenance at a lower cost. In exchange, NKR benefits from client referrals and engagements from Copper. We consider the fostering of additional strategic relationships to be a significant step toward the fulfillment of our digital platform and advancement toward providing a total end-to-end branding solution to the marketplace with greater profitability.

In addition to the two formal alliances discussed above, we have strategic relationships with the following companies. These relationships will enable us to expand our analog services and to expand internationally.

Buxite:	A Toronto-based consulting firm that provides web development and architecture. Focuses on U.S. and Canada and provides entry into Canada. (Formerly Mindz.)
eSleuth:	A Massachusetts-based consulting firm that provides competitive intelligence, industry research, and market analysis for Internet companies.
Hired Guns, Inc.:	A Chicago-based consulting firm that provides outsourced sales and business development solutions for companies in the telecommunications industry.
HireUps!:	An Ohio-based consulting firm that provides executive recruiting services.
Dennis Financial:	A Virginia-based consulting firm that provides financial modeling and strategy for start-ups.

Analog Branding Services

Our plan identifies a new opportunity—moving the current "analog" branding business to a "digital" version through the licensing of complementary web-enabled marketing technologies under favorable OEM license agreements. NKR currently provides the analog model of its services through its core business competencies, which include planning, marketing, advertising, media buying, etc., as described below. We are in the process of growing our team of specialists to expand our core competencies.

NKR plans to become a premier provider of vertically integrated marketing and business development services for Internet and technology-related businesses. As we acknowledge the continuing demand for these analog services, we are assembling the technology structure to transition to the digital, knowledge-powered practice.

Current "Analog" Services Offered

- **Brand strategy:** brand positioning, brand migration, brand revitalization, alliance architecture
- **Communications:** sales collateral, promotional items, public relations, advertising, point-of-sale systems, direct mail, training material
- **Brand development:** brand assessment, competitive analysis
- **Identity:** logo development, brand naming
- **Electronic:** web applications, presentations
- **Business plans:** review, writing

New Offering: Rich Media

We have developed an innovative rich media streaming ad concept that presents a unique opportunity to offer spot commercial advertising as is normally associated with the television and billboard industries. Our Rich Media concept envisions two eight-second spots that run on each page of our client's site as three vignette stills, or "webboards."

The Rich Media concept combines the best aspects of a web-based advertising banner campaign, a billboard campaign, and a television/cable spot media buy. The spots run when a user clicks on one of the webboards representing the advertised product. The client's name, product, and/or message are viewed on a webboard that remains on the web page in six-minute increments. These lifestyle ads, coupons for discounts on products, and often loyalty points that may be redeemed for cash or prizes encourage the user/viewer to take action to acquire the products used in the spots, building consumer loyalty.

Our research shows that our ad concept is unique, and that while being a strong differentiator for our client, it affords both revenue opportunities and a point of differentiation. Producing these rich media segments affords us exceptionally high margins.

UniversityDigs.com (UD)

UD is a portal that provides solutions to off-campus collegiate housing needs. The portal will offer turnkey housing solutions that appeal to its target market. NKR has provided the initial planning, financial modeling, marketing strategy, media strategy, and a new method of rich media advertising.

ElderStats product

ElderStats is an Internet-delivered application that facilitates the tracing and sharing of personal and healthcare-related information combined with a valuable tacit knowledge base and "life buoys"—instant access to relevant and contextual information about eldercare management. RETT, the developer of ElderStats, specializes in the eldercare market, and plans to market this knowledge management tool in 10 specific vertical markets with little existing competition. NKR structured the business plan, financial modeling, and competitive analysis, in addition to marketing strategy.

Obsidian Portal International

Obsidian Portal International (OPI) is an early-stage developer of worldwide logistics systems for business-to-business applications. OPI's principals constituted a part of the core management team for a Fortune 50 firm's enterprise. NKR was selected as the exclusive brand strategy and marketing alliance architect, and will direct the commercial launch of OPI's worldwide logistics application.

L-5 Productions

L-5 Productions is a global Internet entertainment software publisher for the personal computer, video game consoles and next-generation interactive entertainment platforms, personal digital assistants (PDAs), and cell phones. L-5's principals are the original developers and producers of one of the video game industry's most successful franchises, Blast Cuts. NKR, in addition to a new corporate identity, has provided a market entry and branding strategy for the company's innovative episodic game format that delivers games in segments via the Internet in "game capsules."

EarthMeldFinancial.com (EMF)

EMF is a rapidly expanding international financial portal providing online financial news, investment tools, and transaction services. Based in Australia, EMF is leveraging its highly trafficked websites and Internet portals, direct access share trading companies, and other brokerage and clearing firms to create an international network of online transaction businesses dealing in worldwide stocks, foreign currency exchange, and other financial services such as insurance.

NKR has been retained to drive the development and strategic branding initiative of a unique web-investment site that leverages EMF's distribution assets in the United States and Australia. NKR has directed the branding strategy, including corporate identity, site design and technology implementation.

Integral to our business strategy are three key components:

1. Superior client service

As a part of our goal to provide our clients with superior services, we will continually develop additional support services when requested to ensure our position as their provider of choice. By delivering high-quality service, the company should benefit from long-term client engagements and repeat business. We believe we will continue to gain new clients with greater ease as our reputation for quality service becomes widely known.

CURRENT CLIENTS

BUSINESS STRATEGY

2. Geographic Reach

While headquartered in North Carolina, management is considering opening an executive suite satellite office in Las Vegas, Nevada, to procure and service existing clients in the Western United States and, ultimately, to oversee the construction of the Global Incubator Network, as described. Additional office presence in Nevada and California for the company will be considered as the client base grows. Website and graphic design services, programming, and illustration services for all of its clients will be provided in Nevada, unless another web development firm is identified in another part of the country.

3. Technology/Internet Infrastructure

The NKR website has been developed and serves well as an account administration tool and sales development resource. Prospective clients have researched and contacted the company through the website, and the site has provided a common platform for client contact, account management, and file sharing. Management believes that a continued collaboration with Copper will greatly enhance the operability and economy of further WNKR site development and promotion. Copper will make available to us two tools they have developed: a wireless enabled management resource system named Copper Blue; and a proprietary e-mail promotion system, Copper News. Copper News will allow us to disperse our lists in a "forward-able" format, enabling us to track the forwarded distribution and build our audience and client base. This technology combination will add a significant dimension to the NKR platform and dramatically increase the efficiencies and economies of using the Internet to manage growth, coordinate internal staff activity, and provide a common platform as we begin moving toward the digital practice.

Phase II: Shift to "Digital" Creative Services

As discussed above, while providing innovative, albeit analog, solutions for emerging brands, we have identified a marketing-related technology that should enable us to build an NKR-branded, knowledge-powered and web-enabled platform for creative services.

Our proposed solution provides the framework for an Internet-enabled marketing community that delivers superior marketing solutions to a global market through "digital" management of creative services. A knowledge management system created by our OEM partner, IDI, provides the foundation for a worldwide networked branding and marketing resource that is central to the NKR business model. The NKR-branded system will deliver an exchange mechanism that will enable the re-purposing of prior work within the creative services (advertising, branding, marketing, and design) market. Knowledge-based services and content can be contributed, accessed, lawfully re-purposed and paid for through the system. The system and exchange that we are building also allows for the monetization of tacit knowledge, providing significantly greater revenue opportunities than in a purely "analog" branding model.

Knowledge Management: Revolutionizing Creative Services

IdeaDigit Inc. (IDI) is a technology company that has developed a powerful software application, LodorPIM™. LodorPIM™ is a revolutionary content capturing and classification tool that allows users to capture, catalog, and retrieve relevant information by operating within the users' context. LodorPIM™ revolutionizes the way intellectual capital is captured and how knowledge is managed and exchanged.

Built upon Coyote V, an object-oriented intelligent infrastructure produced by MJ Computers, this PIM system is an information classification and cataloging tool. The system allows users to index information wherever it resides (intranet, extranet, Internet, or local hard drive) and in whatever format it may exist (text, graphics, audio, video, or multiple media). Once indexed with the Lodor PIM™ tool, users can recall stored assets by using multiple dynamic search methodologies and locate materials of high relevance from multiple disciplines, languages, and knowledge storage systems.

Although Knowledge Management has been used in the IT industry and within the Management Consulting world to capture best practices, it has never, to our knowledge, been deployed in a marketing or branding arena. Within our current business, applications of the system are limitless: we will use the system for the re-purposing of market research, industry analysis, audio and video presentations, and text, financial data, legal documentation—anything related to the storage, retrieval, and archiving of intellectual and creative assets.

The IDI Knowledge Management and Business Processes System, combined with worldwide marketing, branding, and advertising support relationships, partnerships and alliances, will provide the basis from which NKR Consulting will position itself as an end-to-end solutions provider, entering the market with digital creative services.

Examples of Use: Digital Creative Services

We believe that most vertical markets are inefficient in their creative processes because they rely on tacit knowledge for both business management and for growth. This is certainly the case in the creative industries such as advertising and marketing/branding, where creative processes aren't shared. Other businesses within the community are viewed as competition, and productive collaboration is rarely encouraged. We propose to initiate and drive the shift towards the digitizing, and the subsequent monetizing of ideas within many vertical markets.

Through the delivery of our analog creative services, we will support a strategy involving the powering of our business offerings by IDI's system described above. The knowledge management system should enable us to provide creative services that will reduce our time to market and will add value (by saving time, money, and energy, etc.) to both our clients and to their offerings.

As a virtual creative incubator, rather than providing desks, phone systems, and a water cooler, we will become the vertically integrated supplier of:

- Vertically integrated web-based technology for marketing solutions
- Common platform to access knowledge and creative input, both in-house and in-network
- A branded community for creative services commerce
- Branding services that include planning, creative media buying, and ad serving

By deploying our digital strategy, we will be able to create a core set of strategic alliances in each of our markets. Our clients will be able to use the system internally and will also have the option to join our community, having access to all other client knowledge. We then plan to create a subscriber-only global exchange specifically serving the branding, marketing, advertising, and design industries. By developing the operating systems upon a global knowledge exchange platform, we hope to become the de facto global resource for branding solutions.

To demonstrate the expanded service offering Phase II will provide, we have provided a table that offers a quick view of the current analog practice combined with the digital solutions described below. As NKR migrates from the analog practice to that of digital, we will continue to offer analog services to those clients seeking traditional solutions in combination with digitally enhanced capability.

KNOWLEDGE MANAGEMENT SOLUTIONS
Business Processes
Enterprise Portals
Nugents

RICH MEDIA ADVERTISING
Production
Ad Scheduling and Traffic

E-MAIL SOLUTIONS
List Brokerage
Opt-in e-mail marketing
Opt-in List Management

DIRECT MARKETING SOLUTIONS
Electronic File Cards
Automated List Manager
Turn-key Reporting
Instant Financial Analysis

MEDIA PURCHASING SOLUTIONS
Electronic File Cards
Schedule Manager
Inventory Management
Traffic Management
Turn-key Reporting and Instant Financial Analysis

ELECTRONIC DOCUMENT MANAGEMENT
Electronic
Paper, Video, Audio
Storage/Retrieval

PATENT and TRADEMARK SEARCH
Web-enabled
Federal PTO Direct
Automated Form Completion

URL/DOMAIN SOLUTIONS
Brokerage Appraisals
Auto-negotiated and Auctions
Registration Management and Bulk Registration
Automated Form Completion

BRAND STRATEGY
Brand Positioning
Brand Migration
Brand Revitalization
Alliance Architecture

BRAND DEVELOPMENT
Brand Assessment

IDENTITY
Logo Development
Brand Naming

ELECTRONIC
Web Applications
Presentations

BUSINESS PLANS
Review
Writing

COMMUNICATIONS
Sales Collateral
Promotional Items
Public Relations
Advertising
Point-of-Sale Systems
Direct Mail
Training Material

Kurt F. Xavier   **MANAGEMENT**
Chairman, President & Chief Executive Officer

Throughout his 16-year career as a marketing, branding, and business development professional, Kurt has consulted Fortune 1000 companies, government agencies, and nascent companies alike, compiling a significant track record of success in the process.

Most recently he has completed strategic initiatives for LOPA International, HUT Learning, and FITQ. As a director and the president of NKR Consulting, Kurt led numerous teams to deliver successful business strategies for both public and private enterprises in broad vertical markets including: transportation and logistics, healthcare, real estate, wireless networking, software development, and bottled beverages.

Kurt distinguished his career as an innovator and change agent when charged with concept, branding, and business development responsibilities for strategic initiatives within Mount Richmont Inc., an international owner and franchiser of gasoline and convenience stores. Prior to joining Mount Richmont, he served as vice president of creative strategies and a member of the executive committee for Tuscany Partners (TP), Florida's then second-largest marketing and communications firm. Prior to joining TP, he served as director of new business at JET Management. Notable clients during his career have included some of the largest players in the above-mentioned industries.

Kurt has served as a featured speaker and honored panelist for many of the most prestigious marketing and research institutes in the world. Moreover, he has been profiled in numerous business and industry publications including the *Wall Street Journal,* the *New York Times, Nation's Restaurant News, Progressive Grocer,* and *Convenience Store News.* Kurt received his marketing and creative education (B.S.) degrees from Notre Dame University as well as from the University of Virginia. He has served on over a dozen nationally based charitable boards serving the healthcare and social needs of underprivileged children and their families.

Jeremy Irons
Vice President Sales

Jeremy Irons has more than 10 years of sales and sales management experience in the high-tech industry. Most recently, he served as the head of the Canadian operations of Notts

Communications. While at Notts he created valuable partnerships and strategic distribution channels for all of Notts' products and services throughout Canada. Jeremy secured relationships with Microsoft, Hewlett Packard, IBM, Unisys, KPMG and many other high-profile industry giants. Prior to Notts, he managed the Canadian group at ePinnacleDot, selling to mostly the top 250 Canadian industrial companies. Prior to that he was sales manager at IBM where he introduced state-of-the-art computer systems used by the Canadian government, and developed and managed the entire check-processing solution targeting the financial community in Brazil.

In addition to his sales background, Jeremy possesses valuable technical experience having developed engineering software for CAD/CAM applications and AI analysis. He received his Computer Science B.S. degree from the top educational institution in Quebec, the Technology Institute of Quebec. Over the years Jeremy has developed a multicultural background with a comprehensive knowledge of the business cultures in the U.S., Canada, and Brazil.

Kim Fritz
Vice President Operations

Kim Fritz is an accomplished executive officer with expertise in implementing Information Technology infrastructures that improve business with positive impacts on the bottom line. She has extensive experience developing successful IT strategies and business plans and a demonstrated ability to analyze business requirements and create effective technical solutions.

Kim was the founder and CEO of Hercules Communications Networks, a manufacturer and designer of wireless broadband products. Prior to Hercules, she was the chief technologist for Logic Maneuvers. Kim served as president and chief executive officer of Borne Technologies, Inc., a CTI (computer telephony integration) based systems integration company that was sold to a publicly traded company. Borne created and developed a global systems architecture that allowed users to access their e-mail text-to-speech via any touch-tone or cellular telephone. The company also developed an international data network that had an emphasis in telemedicine, which was accessible via telephone. Prior to founding Hercules she founded Diamond Information Systems. The company provided consulting services in information technology and financial information systems including, LAN/WAN systems design, and the design and construction of Mammoth Computers. The company was sold in 1994.

Kim attended Ohio State University and is a graduate of the Advanced Management Program at Harvard University. She is a member of a half dozen prestigious communications and engineering groups, including the International Telecommunications Union (ITU) and the Institute of Electrical and Electronics Engineers (IEEE).

Nick Masters
Chief Technical Officer

Nick Masters is an experienced and accomplished Internet and network architect possessing more than 12 years of experience in Internet protocols, internetworking infrastructure, business development cycles, and marketing program implementation. As the managing partner for a successful web hosting organization, he has been instrumental in building a core business from the ground up. Nick has demonstrated an outstanding proficiency in managing large project teams and creating incremental revenue sources to build an infrastructure for sustained growth within an organization.

As a manager of multiple projects with compressed timelines and large budgets to facilitate company growth in accordance with its strategic business plan, Nick had previously served KoreView Systems after leaving Copper Networks, Inc., as a key network manager. He has also successfully served other networking technology and business efficiency developers such as NetLook System, eBunk Corporation, Inc., and Raton Research, Inc.

Nick has detailed knowledge of all systems and issues that impact network operations including security, Internet routing infrastructure (backbone), virtual private networking, e-commerce, and integration of multiple vendor relationships to provide seamless data continuity and maximize customer uptime.

Nick is an active member of the web hosting community and continues to provide counsel and support to nonprofit organizations and entrepreneurs wishing to build a presence on the World Wide Web.

Brian Forbes
Interactive Media Strategist

Brian Forbes can be seen every weeknight demonstrating innovative products on a local Chicago TV station and is the new technology writer for the *Chicago Tribune*. He also writes regularly for national magazines about home design, construction, and trends. He has also reported/produced for various other television entities, both publicly and privately financed.

This past year Brian hosted/produced/wrote award-winning children's videos. In addition, he is an instructor and speaker for media training workshops, does voiceover work, and produces video news releases and corporate videos.

For 10 years Brian was a full-time television news reporter. Brian has been honored with numerous Emmy Awards for his news series work and has received national awards from various other national news, healthcare, and family organizations

Brian began his undergraduate education at the University of Kentucky and received his Doctorate in Dentistry from Northwestern University in Chicago. He holds a master's in Public Health from Washington University.

Projected Profit and Loss

For Years ending 30 June

Revenue:	Year 1	Year 2	Year 3
Branding			
Marketing	$620,000	$620,000	$620,000
Advertising	$93,569	$117,386	$142,905
Strategy	$325,000	$643,500	$721,500
e-Commerce	$258,000	$315,000	$342,000
e-tailing	$258,000	$324,000	$360,000
Data Mining	$100,500	$500,205	$900,825
Total Revenue	**$1,565,069**	**$2,025,661**	**$2,193,230**
Operating Expenses			
General and Administration	$167,500	$708,000	$399,500
IT Services	$143,975	$349,350	$199,200
Marketing	$845,000	$1,534,800	$803,100
Sales	$122,693	$331,789	$166,732
Total Operating Expenses	**$1,279,168**	**$2,923,939**	**$1,568,532**
EBITDA	$285,901	$(898,278)	$624,698
Depreciation	$1,139	$633	$633
Amortization of Start-up Costs	$34,286	$34,286	$34,286
EBIT	$250,476	$(933,196)	$589,779
Interest			
Taxes	$100,191	$(373,278)	$235,912
Net Income	**$150,286**	**$(559,918)**	**$353,868**

Caviar Company

BUSINESS PLAN

CAVIAR DELIGHTS

19331 Madison Avenue
New York, New York 10016

When Caviar Delights was bought by its present owner from a bankruptcy court, the company had been out of business for more than two years and had only a handful of sales in the year prior to its demise. By closely following this informal business plan—and using his own cash and credit—the new owner took Caviar Delights from $0 to $2 million in sales in the firm's first year of operation. Contributor: Scott Lockett of Tindell Associates.

- ASSUMPTIONS

- INITIAL CONSIDERATIONS

- PROJECTIONS

- PRODUCTS

- MARKET

- ADVERTISING

- INITIAL FIRST STEPS

- ORGANIZATION

- COMPLICATIONS

- CONCLUSION

ASSUMPTIONS

- We've got caviar.
- We've got credit.
- The old customers return.
- Ed (me, the owner) stays alive until Jan 1.
- Washington Avenue location remains headquarters location.
- Inventory moved to Washington Avenue site.

**INITIAL
CONSIDERATIONS**

The gourmet market will be hard to crack initially. We should restart the existing caviar business with caviar—plus a few new products—and focus on them. The resulting cash flow will allow us to re-evaluate and enter the gourmet market without a drain on the company's limited resources. Based on the 1999 sales figures, the retail market is miniscule (less than 1 percent of total sales). The company should focus on its wholesale customers and increase margins, prices, and volume, then re-evaluate the retail (mail order) gourmet market in January 2001.

The objective is to position Caviar Delights as the pre-eminent caviar and gourmet provider in the country. In order to achieve this, the strategy will be to:

1. Rebuild the caviar distribution and packing of Caviar Delights
2. Acquire private-label gourmet items and integrate them into the caviar markets
3. Continue to add new products to the private-label offerings
4. Expand sales into new geographic markets
5. Strengthen sales in the company's existing markets

PROJECTIONS

Here are our sales projections for the next three years:

- Sales for fiscal year 2000: $2,300,000
- Sales for fiscal year 2001: $4,600,000
- Sales for fiscal year 2002: $9,000,000

These numbers are ambitious, but with increased marketing and a sales force, they are easily achievable. The numbers for 2000 are based on sales from 1999 (exclusive of old accounts receivable). Sales from May to December 1999 were $1,094,559 ($136,820 per month). Projections for fiscal years 2001 and 2002 include assumptions of a nationwide sales force.

PRODUCTS

Historical sales show that Caviar Delights derived nearly 100 percent of its revenue from caviar sales. Foie gras and smoked salmon accounted for less than 1 percent of these sales.

In order to achieve our short-term goals, the product line must be increased. The establishment of complementary products within the current lines will make the company less dependent on the whims of the caviar market. It will also increase profit margins.

With the proper selection of items, all of the existing markets can be penetrated. Each of the items must meet rigid standards of quality and low cost. The standard markup for new and private label items is a minimum of 50 percent.

The current list of products to offer includes: caviar (Beluga, Osetra, Sevruga, Salmon, Paddle), smoked salmon, foie gras, coffee, spices, hot sauce, pies, cakes, sausage, and pasta.

All of this is Caviar Delight's private label. Possible other products are Ehmer Meats and Edwards Hams. These new products will contribute a 25 percent increase in revenue over 1999.

In 1999 Caviar Delights had 233 clients. These customers are spread across the country. While the market penetration in greater New York City is small, there is certainly ample room for growth in this same region. With the addition of two salespeople, the company can concentrate on new business in New York City while managers Ed and Charlie concentrate on the previous clients.

MARKET

The two new salespeople will easily contribute an increase of 10 percent in revenue over 1999. They will be supported by a new nationwide sales force in place by 2001, along with a new retail mail order and Internet division.

The sales force will be a "straight commission"-based system. In 2001, the addition of representative firms may help speed the transition to nationwide sales. A sales system utilizing the software packages Act! and Access will be implemented, and the sales force will be trained to use it. This new software will allow all interactions with clients to be easily logged and accessed, and will create targeted profiles of customers, which can be manipulated for specific marketing initiatives.

It's unknown if any consistent advertising was conducted for the company in 1999 before it went bankrupt. But that's all in the past.

ADVERTISING

We know the most effective method of advertising Caviar Delights is targeted advertising. To achieve our goals, we will send customers on the old company's mailing list a letter notifying them of our purchase of Caviar Delights. These mailings will be followed by phone calls from Ed or Charlie.

New efforts will target each customer based on his/her profile. New markets will be targeted based on the specifics of the market (i.e., caterers will receive marketing showing offerings specific to caterers).

Monthly specials will increase sales and flatten the cyclical nature of the past caviar business.

Attendance at the Fancy Food Shows as an exhibitor should continue.

1. Create brochure with old and new products by October 1.
2. Send letter to previous Caviar Delights customers and alert them of the purchase by September 23.
3. Put up informational web page by October 1 with a fully functional web page (online ordering) by December 1.
4. No catalog yet. Will re-evaluate whether one should be produced when we consider retail expansion in January.
5. Ed helps bring back old customers while the two new salespeople will concentrate on new business. Charlie will handle most of the old customers after Ed hands them off.
6. Salespeople will be paid strictly on commission. Initial thought is 8 percent of collected gross sales.
7. Increase efforts to understand our customers, tailor the product offerings for the particular customers, and up sell.

INITIAL FIRST STEPS

ORGANIZATION

In order to maximize profits for Ed and Charlie, the number of employees on the payroll should be kept to a minimum. Here is an overview of the company's key employees and/or positions to be filled in the near future:

Ed: President. Helps make transition smooth while old customers get used to the idea that the previous caviar company now has a new vision and a new name. Assists in the recovery of old clients. Transitions out of operations and to the head office by January 1, 2001.

Charlie: Operations Manager. Oversees company. Maintains financial controls, records, and accountability. Manages caviar processing. Directs salespeople. Purchases products. Sustains old clients. Assists with new business.

Administrative Assistant: Assists Charlie, answers phones, performs data entry, general and administrative tasks. Makes coffee, buys Diet Coke.

Two Salespeople: Focus on new business. Some interface with old clients once Ed and Charlie have recovered them.

Caviar Processors: Pack caviar. Seasonally adjusted numbers depending on how many are contracted for this function.

Possible additions: Contract legal consultation and an annual audit by a certified public account.

COMPLICATIONS

In order for this to work, we must have credit or more cash. Why?

Old customers may not return. Caviar may be too scarce or expensive to get. We must be able to maintain the current markup and reduce costs. The key to introducing a private label is price and service. If the company cannot maintain competitive prices then the private label won't sell.

The sales force must be motivated to sell. And a straight commission sales force may not work. If using representative firms, there may be pressure from other companies they represent which could undermine our success.

CONCLUSION

The short-term future looks a little scary.

However, once the caviar sales are restored, the cash flow from this company is bound to be huge.

The first few months will be lean, so credit is absolutely necessary. An infusion of cash from some source can replace the credit, but repayment may dilute earnings and delay build up of cash necessary for expansion. It will also violate the principle of limiting the number of people involved.

As a final thought, it's entirely possible that Caviar Delights could be structured so that it becomes a public offering within five years. Then the money will really flow.

Computer Training Service Business

BUSINESS PLAN

ENHANCED OCCUPATIONS CENTER

1211 Bailey Drive
Seattle, Washington 98121

Computer training services have an excellent profitability level and growth rate. Our competitive edge along with new training techniques puts EOC at the forefront of training services. We are living in an age where computer knowledge is a must and the market for computer training services is booming.

- EXECUTIVE SUMMARY

- COMPANY HISTORY

- SERVICES

- MARKET ANALYSIS SUMMARY

- BUSINESS STRATEGY & IMPLEMENTATION

- MANAGEMENT SUMMARY

- FINANCIAL PLAN

- APPENDIX

COMPUTER TRAINING SERVICE BUSINESS
BUSINESS PLAN

EXECUTIVE SUMMARY

Enhanced Occupations Center is a computer training service business located at 1505 N. Fifth Street, Seattle, Washington. This business plan was developed for the purpose of a business loan in the amount of $71,500. Our projected sales for 2000 alone are $122,448 and our projected profits are over $30,000.

Computer training services, as shown in our plan, have an excellent profitability level and growth rate. Our competitive edge along with new training techniques puts EOC at the forefront of training services. We are living in an age where computer knowledge is a must and the market for computer training services is booming. Our training center will differ from the traditional computer training services (usually offered by colleges and universities) because of our added personal touch.

Objectives

The Enhanced Occupations Center (EOC) knows firsthand that computer training has to meet all of its customers' needs in order to have a tangible lasting impact. When you measure across multiple customer segments—each of which has its own priorities—you see how much more training must do to consistently and simultaneously satisfy participants, managers, and executives. Training then can move to close those gaps and deliver more real value. Closing those gaps between employer skill needs and employee skills development is the main objective of EOC.

EOC's other objectives are:

- To meet the computer training needs of computer users and area businesses by the way of Skill Assessment and Goal-Based Training.
- Retain new and current students through Step-Level Based computer training.
- Re-assess students upon completion of computer training to record skill level improvements.
- Monitor outcomes of student completions after a 30-day period to track new employment or computer-related improvements.
- Adjust the computer training program as needed and according to outcomes.
- Continue to assess our own staff's computer training skill level and effectiveness.
- Sales of $122,448 in 2000 and $200,192 by 2002.

Mission

EOC's mission is to understand what our students and businesses hope to achieve and dedicate our computer training and development to the fulfillment of those goals. The computer training we provide is contributing visibly and substantially to the fulfillment of our area business's strategies.

EOC will maintain financial balance, charge a high value for our services, and deliver an even higher value to our clients. EOC will make computer user techniques accessible to hundreds of computer users who would otherwise not have the updated knowledge to use them. EOC will make a profit and generate cash. We will provide a rewarding work environment and fair compensation to our employees, ultimately provide excellent value to our customers and a fair return to our owners.

EOC's keys to success include: implementing an effective cash flow plan, achieving efficiency, running our training like a business, and maintaining a serious business discipline to everything in our training.

EOC's cash flow plan is to:

- Maintain enough money on hand each month to pay the cash obligations the following month.
- Identify and eliminate deficiencies or surpluses in cash.
- Alter business financial plans to provide more cash if deficiencies are found.
- Invest any revealed excess cash in an accessible, interest bearing, low-risk account, such as a savings account or short-term CD or T-bill.
- Eliminate credit and terms to customers.
- Clearly understand the computer training market, distributions costs and competition, and continually adjusting accordingly.
- Keep enough cash, as an added cushion for security, on hand to cover expenses.
- Reduce accountant expenses by producing our own summary statistics and projections.

To achieve effectiveness EOC will:

- Link our training and development to business strategy by understanding what our customers hope to achieve and dedicating training and development to the fulfillment of those goals.
- Focus on business issues rather than training content by working tirelessly to offer training that matches new and emerging demands.
- Let our customer demand shape our training and development offerings by providing a core curriculum designed to train individuals in basic skills and core competencies. We will also conduct ongoing needs assessments across the organization aimed at making training more strategic and providing training that has more business impact.
- Clarify our training and development business mission by avoiding trying to be all things to all people. EOC will offer more than training to develop employee skills. The training EOC will provide will also contribute—visible and substantially—to fulfillment of our customers' business strategies.
- See training and development as an enterprise, not as a function by:

    1. Maintaining intense focus on our customers, their issues, and their needs.
    2. Being systematic in our efforts to meet those needs efficiently, consistently, and reliably.
    3. Daring to pursue missions that are linked to the business strategy and focused on business issues; willingly tackling big challenges, even those that are difficult and risky; being ambitious, alert, confident, and pragmatic.

To achieve cost efficiency EOC will:

- Expose hidden costs for businesses by allowing them to see their "true" training costs such as lost productivity, wasted training investments, or lost opportunity. Teaching these businesses how to measure training costs, and what they are getting back from their training.
- Aggressively reduce costs by eliminating duplication.
- Build and maintain reliable systems and processes by putting reliable training and development systems and processes in place.
- Operate as a variable cost, not a fixed expense, by understanding that customers spend only at their own initiative. Making training a variable cost makes especially good sense now that the pace of change in business—and the resulting demands for

learning—are accelerating so dramatically. We found that there's no better stimulus to innovate, improve, and become more efficient than having to earn the right to serve customers, each and every day.

- Be flexible and opportunistic in sourcing by strategically linking and focusing on business issues, allowing customers to consistently define the value derived from the training. Clarify precisely what our customers expect from the training; negotiate a results contract; guarantee customer satisfaction.

To maintain a serious business discipline EOC will:

- Continually adapt to ongoing change in the business environment.
- Promote learning not as an ideal but as a way to fulfill specific business-driven objectives.
- Be entrepreneurial—live with risk.
- Structure training to provide exactly what is needed.
- Divide customers into segments and provide each segment appropriate forms of value.
- Document customers' expectations.
- Write results contracts specifying value to be delivered, at what price, customers' role in achieving targeted results.
- Offer service guarantees.

COMPANY HISTORY

The Enhanced Occupations Center (EOC) is a product of a similar computer training program developed and implemented by Serena Bolton, for the University of Washington Office of Community and Business Partnerships. The program was developed for the University of Washington to provide basic computer training to the North Seattle Community area residents and Peters school's Leadership Academy.

The training was provided for four parents per session, two sessions per week for 15-20 sessions. Upon completion of the program the students will received a certificate. The sessions were made up of four core areas of Microsoft Office® training and those core areas were:

1. Word Processing
2. Access Database
3. Publisher 98
4. Internet

Serena learned from the project and the community that there is a growing need for computer training that is based on the student or employer's goals and skills assessment needs. After the four-month project ended, and for a year after the program, Serena analyzed, researched, and redeveloped the program based on those needs.

The Enhanced Occupations Center differs from the University of Washington project to the following:

1. Training is based on skill assessment and goals
2. Outcome of the training is monitored
3. Microsoft Office User Specialist (MOUS) Testing is offered
4. Students are retained through Step-Level program
5. Training is re-evaluated continuously
6. Other occupational programs will be implemented in conjunction with the computer training, such as the Secretarial Program

During her year of research and studies, Serena developed her knowledge base of curriculum development and delivery, return on investment for Technology-Based Training (TBT), training management systems, development teams for creating TBTs, ensuring transfer of learning to the job, leveraging technology for human performance improvement and computer training statistics.

Now Serena was ready to bring all of the above components together, along with the communities' needs, and package them into a plan for the birth of her vision. Basing the program on the same centralized idea, Microsoft Office® Training, Serena created the Enhanced Occupations Center.

The computer training project developed for the Leadership Academy and AECC21, by Serena Bolton, has been maintained by the University of Washington Office of Community and Business Partnerships, and is taking place at the Maple Business Center in Seattle. After speaking with Martin Rawlins, Director of the Office, there is still a growing need for basic and advanced computer training. Martin has offered technical assistance and support to EOC and the assistance has been welcomed and accepted.

EOC has also been approved by the Microsoft Office User Specialist Program to operate as an Authorized Test Center. This approval gives EOC full authorization to use the Microsoft Office® logo on our printed and televised materials. Microsoft will also provide the security of having MicroShare, a technical support team, available to EOC 24-hours a day.

EOC is a sole proprietorship and operated by Serena Bolton, a Certified Microsoft Office User Specialist. Serena has eleven years of hands-on computer use and training experience, and is also a Microsoft Certified Testing Administrator.

Company Ownership

Total start-up expense (including professional fees, website, and related expenses) come to $79,454. Required start-up assets include $22,880 in short-term assets (office furniture, etc.) and $15,000 in initial cash to handle the first three months of training operations as sales play through the cash flow. The details are included in the following chart.

Start-up Summary

Start-up Plan
Start-up Expenses

Temporary Help	$1,120
Stationery, etc.	$250
Building Improvements	$500
Telephone	$250
Utilities	$410
Insurance	$475
Rent	$1,400
Professional Development	$7,500
9 Computer Packages	$10,000
6 Printers	$1,074
1 Training Projector	$4,700
8 Transcription Machines	$2,000
1 Fax/Copier	$500
8 Computer Tables	$600
11 Computer Chairs	$1,000
4 File Cabinets	$360
2 Work Centers	$800
1 Desk	$150
Advertisements	$16,420
Books/Materials	$7,500

Start-up Summary

Continued

Assessment Software	$7,445
Other	$0
Total Start-up Expense	**$56,954**
Start-up Assets Needed	
Cash Requirements	$15,000
Start-up inventory	$0
Other Short-term Assets	$0
Total Short-term Assets	**$15,000**
Long-term Assets	$0
Total Assets	**$15,000**
Total Start-up Requirements:	**$79,454**
Left to finance:	$71,509
Start-up Funding Plan	
Investment	
Investor 1	$0
Investor 2	$0
Other	$7,945
Total Investment	**$7,945**
Short-term Liabilities	
Unpaid Expenses	$0
Short-term Loans	$0
Interest-free Short-term Loans	$0
Subtotal Short-term Liabilities	$0
Long-term Liabilities	$0
Total Liabilities	**$0**
Loss at Start-up	**$7,055**
Total Capital	**$15,000**
Total Capital and Liabilities	**$15,000**
Checkline	**$0**

Company Location and Facilities

The Enhanced Occupations Center will be located at 1505 N. Fifth Street, Seattle, Washington. The suite is approximately 850 square feet and encompasses two offices, a receptionist area, and a 700-foot open training area. The suite is housed inside a secure building. There are restroom facilities and a drinking fountain located in the foyer area. The doors on the building automatically lock at 4:55 P.M. Anyone entering after that time must use a personal code.

The building is located between Marshall and Stanton roads and is near one of the state's largest employers, General Hospital. Other businesses located in the building are: Private Management, Temporary Placement Services, Pager Company, and a Credit Counselor business. The building is surrounded by restaurants, stores, etc.

SERVICES

EOC will offer the following training and assessment services. Each element of service will be implemented in overlapping phases.

PHASE 1

Microsoft Office®-based computer training including the following:

a) Word Processing Software
b) PowerPoint Presentation Software
c) Access Database/Customer Records Software
d) Excel Spreadsheet/Invoicing Software
e) Publisher Desktop Publishing/Graphics Software
f) Outlook E-Mail/Calendar/Scheduling Software
g) FrontPage Web Page Development (coming soon)
h) Internet Online Technology

PHASE 2

The Occupational Skills Assessments are for the following areas:

Office Skills Testing
- Receptionist
- Secretarial
- Telephone
- Customer Service

Call Center Testing
- Telemarketing
- Data Entry
- Data Analysis

Office Management Testing
Computer Literacy Testing

PHASE 3

Microsoft Office User Specialist (MOUS) Certification Testing

Payment Methods

Class tuition payments must be paid to EOC in full, before the student can take a class. EOC will offer several payment options to the student such as: Visa, MasterCard, money orders, and personal checks.

Service Description

We will provide core curriculum designed to train individuals from basic computer skills to certification competencies. Students will be retained through Step-Level Based Training indicated below:

- **Basic/Level 1**—consists of students who have had little or no computer training.
- **Advanced/Level 2**—consists of students who have had at-home or on-the-job experience with the majority of software packages.
- **Intermediate/Level 3**—consists of certification training of students in preparation for the Microsoft Office User Specialist Certification Test.
- Microsoft Office User Specialist Program—EOC is part of the MicroShare family of Authorized Test Centers (ATCs) that administer and offer assessment tests for the Microsoft Office® User Specialist (MOUS) program. About 90 percent of the Fortune 500 companies use Microsoft Office products. An ever-increasing number of individuals in these companies are looking for ways to give themselves a competitive edge to move up the career ladder.

- As an ATC, we have the opportunity to give our customers this competitive edge by helping them prove their expertise and skill in using Microsoft Office products. When passing or failing the test the student will receive a printout stating the results of the exam to take with them. If the student has passed the test, they will receive a Certification certificate in the mail 2-4 weeks later.

Microsoft Office User Specialist Certification Test

The test consists of actually taking the exam to be come a Microsoft Office User Specialist. This certification will give the student the credentials needed to prove that the student knows how to use Microsoft Office Applications efficiently and productively.

EOC believes that assessing a customer before and after a class will give us the real value of our training. EOC also will follow up 30 days after the training to see if the student actually retained what was learned and if the student was able to apply the skills in their current environment.

EOC also believes in assessing our own staff. We will conduct ongoing Skill Level Needs Assessments of our own employees across the Center, aimed at making computer training more strategic and providing computer training that has more of a business impact. We will continually seek to be effective for future student and business needs. Our key focus is to utilize our program outcomes to improve and increase our computer training effectiveness in the workplace.

EOC Company Assessment Program

EOC will provide an assessment service to local businesses as their pre-interviewing process. There will be a fee attached to this service. The assessment appointment will be by the company and they will give instructions as to our location, etc. EOC will only do business transactions with the company.

Training Schedule

The typical computer training class will run 2 hours, twice a week, for four weeks or a total of 16 hours of training. Our capacity for weekly classes, for one month, would be a total of 72 students.

Our workshops are one day, eight-hour classes. These classes are geared towards the individual wanting to brush up or learn a skill quickly without the long-term commitment.

The computer training classes will be scheduled as listed below. The specific subject of the class won't be established until we receive customer response to advertising and promotions.

Tentative Class Schedule

Monday-Thursday	**$125/Book $20**
8:30-10:00	Class preparation/marketing—Trainer
10:00-12:00	Class
12:00-12:30	Lunch—Trainer
12:30-2:30	Class
2:30-3:00	Return Phone Calls/Miscellaneous—Trainer
3:00-5:00	Class
5:00-5:30	Day's Review—Trainer

Friday Workshops	**$49-$179**
8:30-10:00	Workshop preparation/marketing—Trainer
10:00-12:00	Workshop 1#
12:00-12:30	Lunch—Trainer
12:30-2:30	Workshop 2#
2:30-3:00	Return Phone Calls/Miscellaneous—Trainer
3:00-5:00	Workshop 3#
5:00-5:30	Day's Review—Trainer

Saturdays-Workshops	**$49-$179**
9:00-12:00	Class/Includes Break—All
12:00-12:30	Lunch—All
12:30-4:30	Class/Includes Break—All

EOC differs from the traditional learning environments where the classes are large and sometimes overwhelming to new students. EOC believes that by having smaller classes (no more than 8 students) the trainer can be more attentive to the majority of the students' needs. We focus on quality training, not quantity. Our fees are justified by the specialization of our personalized services.

Competitive Comparison

Once we learn the immediate needs of our typical customer, we can create our marketing literature to address these problems and our solutions to them, such as:

Sales Literature

Are you being turned down for jobs because you don't know Windows, Microsoft Word, or PowerPoint? If so, call the Enhanced Occupations Center at 643-1000 for personalized hands-on training in the most popular software packages.

EOC will capitalize on the 80-20 rule and target low-maintenance customers that bring us the most revenues for the least effort. According to W.E.B. Business Consultants, 80 percent of computer training revenues come from 20 percent of our customers. We will use a program for tracking customers, sales, and our time. And then we will focus our efforts on the best 20 percent of our customers. We will target these people first and give them preferred status. EOC will then market our services to everyone else. We will "weed out" the customers that want to nickel and dime EOC, and make us rework a project over and over while they keep changing their minds about what they want.

EOC's sales literature includes:

- Brochure
- Business Cards
- Flyers
- Newsletters
- Introductory Letters
- Promotional tote bags, etc.
- CompuFax Sheet
- Web Presence

Technology

Enhanced Occupations Center will maintain the latest Windows® capabilities including:

1. Complete e-mail facilities on the Internet, for working with students directly through e-mail delivery of schedules and information.
2. Complete presentation facilities for preparation and delivery of multimedia presentations on Windows machines, in formats that include on-disk presentation, live presentation, or video presentation.
3. Complete desktop publishing facilities for delivery of regular advertising and promotional materials.

Future Services

We will be adding these products and services in the near future:

Secretarial Training Classes —The student will learn about daily routines, telephone usage, mail services and shipping, travel arrangements, keeping accurate records, office machines, telecommunications equipment, computer systems, database management systems, computer communications, computerized spreadsheets software, data security, keyboarding skills, word processing, computer terms, writing business letters, and other written communications, forms of address, legal documents and terms, correct English usage, spelling, pronunciation, punctuation, numerals, bookkeeping and accounting, business and personal taxes, banking, special business and financial information for the small business secretary, and career advancement.

Retail Self-paced Learning manuals—The student will be able to order or purchase outright, computer workbooks to use as added supplements.

Senior Citizens Classes—Seniors will be picked up at their location and brought to the center for two hours to learn the basics of using a computer. These students will not be able to keep materials. This service will be at a senior discounted rate.

Web Page Design Classes—The student will learn the basics of how to design a web page. This class will be a 2-8 hour class and will have a fee of $135 tuition and $20 for the book.

Computer Question/Help desk—This service will only be available to current students who have computer questions related or not related to the subject they are currently studying.

MARKET ANALYSIS SUMMARY

The U.S. Census Bureau County Population report from 1998 states that the 14 most common purposes of the computer being used at home are word processing, calendar/scheduling, e-mail, bookkeeping, customer records, inventory control, invoicing, sales/marketing, desktop publishing, graphics and design, analysis, programming, spreadsheets and databases. The number one main purpose for computer use is word processing. The number one software used for these applications is Microsoft Word.

EOC will be focusing on new computer users and employed computer users that need to gain skills or update current skills. Our most important group of potential customers are those employed with high-technology businesses. These are entry-level employees or managers. We realize businesses do not want to waste their time or risk their money with training organizations that are fast paced with low skills retention outcomes.

The U.S. Census Bureau County Population report from 1998 states that there are approximately 436,084 people living in King County. As of the fall of 1989, nearly 1 in 3 persons age 3 and above will have used a computer. Overall about 1 in 6 adults has a home computer. More than 1 in 3 adults uses a computer at work. Women use computers 43 percent more than men. Persons in managerial and professional positions (56 percent) and technical and administrative positions (55 percent) were most likely to use computers.

Market Segmentation

Market Analysis

Potential Customers	Growth	2000	2001	2002	2003	2004	CAGR
Managerial or Professional	56%	244,207	380,963	594,302	927,111	1,446,293	56.00%
Women	43%	187,516	268,148	383,452	548,336	784,120	43.00%
Technical and Administrative	55%	239,846	371,761	576,230	893,157	1,384,393	55.00%
Other	46%	200,598	292,873	427,595	624,289	911,462	46.00%
Total	**50.93%**	**872,167**	**1,313,745**	**1,981,579**	**2,992,893**	**4,526,268**	**50.93%**

EOC will focus on the following segments. These segments are more interesting than other groups because they have the specific computer training needs EOC intends to meet.

Target Market Strategy

- Microsoft Training for Fortune 500 company employees.
- Training real estate agents on realty software and basic Windows and Microsoft Office software.
- Training real estate agents on basic desktop publishing skills—scanning color photos, creating flyers for property, etc.
- Training physicians in specific specialties to use their patient management software.
- Training people on how to get the most from the Internet.
- Training business people on how to keep up with their websites, from e-mail management to web page creation.
- Training office personnel on how to use Microsoft Office or other office packages.
- Training the first-time computer owner on how to use their home PC.
- Setting up newsletter templates and teaching businesses how to keep up with the in-house or company newsletter.
- Training sales managers on how to use database software to track their sales and marketing functions.
- Training individuals who are looking for better employment on how to use the latest software packages.

These strategies are most effective when put into a formula in the following order:

1. Identifying the symptoms
2. Diagnosis of the problem
3. Prognosis
4. Treatment
5. Follow-up/Outcome Management

Additional Target Marketing Strategies

Our slogan "Training with a personal touch" emphasizes one of our major benefits and we will use this slogan throughout our literature, advertising, and graphics.

The following functions will be assigned to our marketing tools:

- Get name recognition
- Obtain leads
- Turn qualified prospect into a customer
- Ensure customer loyalty
- Stimulate training Center traffic
- Sell service directly
- Introduce new service
- Sell a special service package

The following are low cost/no cost marketing methods:

- Form relationships with noncompeting businesses.
- Get to know other computer professionals.
- Combine services in virtual corporations to provide turnkey solutions to clients.
- Do cooperative mailings with other noncompeting professionals.
- Volunteer to speak in clubs, associations, workshops, or seminars on our specialty.
- Periodically ask customers for referrals.
- Join a barter exchange.
- Produce a periodic newsletter.
- Write articles for local newspapers or upload them to Internet bulletin boards.
- Join Internet newsgroups and mail lists.
- Submit press releases.

The following are for fee marketing methods:

- Join associations
- Conduct seminars
- Conduct contests
- Offer freebees

EOC has two marketing formulas in place and they are:

Formula #1
1. Get a list of companies together that we think may need our services (such as new businesses from the County Clerk's office or the *Seattle Journal*).
2. Call these people and find out the contact person and if they need our services.
3. Mail a letter, brochure, and card to the interested companies.
4. Follow-up with another call to the contact person.
5. Continue to call these people periodically.
6. Keep good records of companies and contact logs.

Formula #2
1. Get a list of companies together that we think may need our services (such as new businesses from the County Clerk's office or the *Seattle Journal*).
2. Call these people and find out the contact person and if they need our services.
3. Ask them if they would like a FREE subscription to our computer newsletter that we will fax them periodically.
4. Fax the newsletter to those who are interested, and include mail enrollment information as well. Mail information to those people who don't want newsletters but are still interested in our services.

5. Follow-up in a week to see what they thought and if we can help them with anything.
6. Continue to send our fax newsletter regularly.
7. Keep good records of contacts and logs.

Other Strategies:

- Join America's Learning Exchange resource database that will promote our training to employers, workers, and life-long learners via the Internet.
- Create alliances with grassroots organizations and staffing organizations.
- Assist in job placement upon completion of Certification testing.
- Create website for schedule information, applications, and book purchasing.
- Register with government programs for SBA certification and other government procurement opportunities.
- Network amongst family and friends for "word of mouth" opportunities to gather referrals.
- Contact students from previous classes.

Market Needs

Our target market is very dependent on reliable information technology. They use the computers for a complete range of functions, beginning with core administration information such as accounting, shipping, and inventory. They also use computers for communications within the business and outside the business, and for personal productivity. The businesses are not, however, large enough to have dedicated computer training personnel such as the MIS departments in large businesses. Ideally, they come to us for a long-term alliance, looking for reliable training service and support to substitute for the lack of their in-house trainer. These are not businesses that want to shop for rock-bottom prices. They want to have reliable providers of training expertise.

Market Trends

One important trend is that we live in an age where one-stop shopping is the preferred purchasing method. All you need to do is head down to your local Wal-Mart Supercenter for a 31-inch television, diapers, and a gallon of milk, while you simultaneously let them rotate your tires and have your hair done.

Now the technical professional has a similar resource. With the growing popularity of the Microsoft Office User Specialist Certification and use of Microsoft Office products, EOC is offering students the "one-stop-shop computer training and certification" approach. A student will no longer have to go from one seminar to another, or from one instructor's methods to another. At EOC students can begin at the basic level of instruction and follow through all the way to certification, without going through the added stress of familiarizing themselves all over again.

Market Growth and Industry

According to the America's Career Infonet Report, the top three fastest growing occupations in Washington are:

- Computer Engineers—102 percent increase forecast between 1994 and 2005.
- Systems analysts, electronic data processing—98 percent increase between 1994 and 2005.
- Electronic pagination system operators—80 percent increase between 1994 and 2005.

Listed below are the occupations with the largest number of projected openings in Washington during the 1994-2005 time period.

1. General Office Clerks
2. Teachers

3. Clerical and administrative support workers
4. Receptionists and information clerks
5. Systems analysts, electronic data processing

All of the above occupations will require computer knowledge or computer training from their candidates.

By the year 2002, almost every household will have a computer and almost all businesses will be utilizing a computer for one reason or another. Computer training will no longer be a choice—it will be a requirement. EOC will be in place and established, already serving the training needs of employment candidates and businesses.

Among industries, computer use was most common in finance, insurance, and real estate, where 2 in 3 workers used them. According to *Training Magazine*'s 1999 Industry Report in 1999, training budgets crept up to $62.5 billion. Of that sum, $15 billion will go to outside providers of training products and services. Of all formal training 33 percent will be devoted to teaching computer skills. Of all computer-skills training, 74 percent of the training will be delivered in a classroom by a live instructor.

Competition and Buying Patterns

EOC's main competitors could be considered local colleges, universities, and continuing education providers, but in reality they are not.

In a sense, these "competitors" actually welcome computer training companies who cater to the smaller class sizes and novice computer users. It gives them the opportunity to cut back on waiting lists and also expedite their schedules, increasing the quantity and decreasing the quality. Computer Training companies rank second in selected training sources organizations choose to utilize.

EOC has heard time and time again, from students who have withdrawn from educational institutions because the classes are "too large and move too quickly through the materials." These students want and need computer training classes that are small and Skill Level Based oriented. The students also want improved teaching methods outside the traditional lecture learning style. They seek retention of skills learned. They want hands-on learning and they want to be able to go home or to work and begin using their new skills right away. Here are some other reasons that people will want to come to EOC for training:

1. They have specific projects they want to create and their training will be learning-specific.
2. They only need to learn a few things about a program and do not need a full course.
3. Their schedule varies and they need a flexible training schedule.
4. They are in a hurry. They do not have time to fit in a class at the local university or college. They want to be trained now!
5. They are nervous in large groups or formal education facilities and want a more relaxed learning environment such as our Center.
6. They feel like they are slow learners and would be more comfortable in a Center environment.

According to the American Society for Training and Development (ASTD), "leading edge companies are responding to the need of skilled employees by providing more training (usually outsourced) because it makes sense from both a business standpoint and from a recruitment standpoint," said Laurie Bassi, ASTD Vice President of Research.

The huge need for skilled employees is being driven by technology and companies are scrambling to meet the technological requirements of their business.

The 1999 State of Industry report found that most firms increased the amount of money they spent on employees by about $150 per employee from 1996 to 1997, but that the leading edge firms surveyed doubled that with an average increase of $300 per employee. Typical total expenditures for training grew from $1.4 million in 1996 to $2 million in 1997 for average firms, and leading edge firms increased spending from $3.4 million to $4.1 million in the same period. Projected expenditures for 1998 show that the gap between the average firm and leading edge firms will continue to widen, with industry average increasing to $2.1 million while leading edge firms are projected to spend $4.7 million on training.

ASTD has found that companies that invest the most in workplace learning find higher net sales per employee, higher gross profits per employee, and a higher ratio in market-to-book values, compared with companies who invest less in workplace learning.

The information technology and transportation/public utility sectors spent the most on training ($3.9 million and $3.8 million respectively) and these sectors also led in terms of money spent per employee on training ($1,004 per employee and $943 per employee respectively).

Outsourcing of training grew by 20 percent, from $461,000 per firm in 1996 to $513,000 in 1997, and was predicted to grow to $522,000 in 1998.

In 1998 job-specific technical skills (including the use of technology) were the most frequent kinds of training delivered (17%), followed by management and supervisor training (12%), computer literacy and applications training (12%). Bringing up the rear was executive development (4%) and basic skills (2%), all which were up from 1996.

The use of learning technologies in training was on the rise—with an increase of 50 percent— but was still relatively low overall.

After carefully researching the computer training market, it has been discovered that some students are more concerned with how you train than with what you are training, even though the two concepts are equally important. EOC focuses on customer care.

The nearest Microsoft Office User Specialist testing center is in Redmond. EOC will be the first in MOUS Training Center to make its presence in Seattle. This groundbreaking opportunity gives EOC time to establish and maintain ongoing relationships with area businesses and students to gain their loyalty should another center open in Seattle. The key element in purchase decisions made at the EOC client level is trust in the professional reputation and reliability of the training center.

BUSINESS STRATEGY & IMPLEMENTATION

We develop marketing materials based on the symptoms of our customers and then we coordinate those materials to focus on solving the typical customer's symptoms. We will then obtain lists of people that fit our typical customer's characteristics.

Our business strategy is to develop a list of people that would most likely exhibit the "symptoms" we have determined our typical customer would have. Once we have our list we will consistently approach them about our services.

One way of approaching our prospects would be the Letter-Series Method. The Letter-Series Method consists of sending our prospects a series of four different professionally written letters (1 per week) before we ever call them. The letters would be personal, meaning the letter would state "Dear Mr. Smith" instead of "Dear Prospective Customer." By sending customers four letters we will establish EOC in their minds as a professional, persistent business entity.

The letters will be written in advance. They will cover a different topic each time. They will contain computer hints or a copy of our newsletter. We won't try to push or sell in these letters.

By the fourth letter, they will know that we intend to call them. We will make sure we do call them when we say we will.

Here is the possible structure for our four letters:

Letter one

> Introduce ourselves and our philosophy. Build trust. Don't try to sell in this letter. Go over our attitudes, specialty, history, qualifications, and philosophy. It will be like a resume to introduce EOC.

Letter two

> Introduce our company.

Letter three

> Cover a topic we feel may interest the prospect based on our knowledge of their "symptoms" and characteristics.

Letter four

> Cover another topic we feel may interest them and let them know we will be calling on a specific day/time.

> We will then create reminder and follow-up letters as well. These letters will include:

- Appointment reminder
- Thank you for the appointment
- Broken appointment/no show—will call back later
- Thank you for your business
- Thank you for your referral

EOC will make it a point to sign and hand-address our envelopes. We believe this will significantly increase the probability of our letters being opened. And an individually signed letter is much more personal.

On the fifth week, we will call to make an appointment to come in and talk with the prospect. We will have a written telephone script before we start calling.

A Harvard Business School study indicates that it "takes five contacts from an unknown company to an individual before he or she will feel comfortable enough to do business with the company." We will start with 350 or more prospects. We won't mail them all at once. We will stagger the mailing so that we will be able to contact them personally after they have received their fourth letter. This will be our initial implementation of the business, along with our current waiting list of students.

That list includes:

Myrna Armstrong	Susan Gregory	Sheila Noble
Jennifer Armstrong	Irene Bailey	Deborah Steel
John Armstrong	Missy Williams	Bella McCormick
Barnard Ashton	James Allen	Tina Thompson
Cherry Ashton	Donald Ray	Rolanda Jenkins
Mary Evory	Willa Chatman	Daniel Fisher
Samual Harmon	Cecelia Barnes	Melissa McCray
Lori Dickie	Wilonda Black	Lisa Jarrett
Cyndi Donaldson	Rev. Stephanie Smith	

Once our students respond to our advertisements or referrals, they will enter into our pre-registration process. Once they have submitted their registration form/agreement letter and payment, they will be invited to the orientation and skill assessment. After they have been assessed they will be placed in a basic beginner's, advanced, or intermediate class—whichever meets their training needs.

After students complete their level they will be assessed and an outcome report will be written. Each student will be evaluated after each level they pass. The student will then again be placed. Once the student has completed all of the levels, or does not want to go any further, they will have a closing assessment. Each student will receive technical support for 30 days after which they will be contacted and a follow-up report will be done on the skills they have learned and the skills they use.

We will start with a critical competitive edge: there is no local competitor we know of that offers the MOUS Certification testing, small retention based classes, or individual student attention. Most of the local training facilities are not flexible to students' needs. Our positioning on this point is very hard to match, but only if we maintain this focus in our strategy, marketing, business development, and fulfillment. We should be aware that the tendency to dilute this personal touch, with larger classes that require longer student commitment, could weaken the importance of our competitive edge.

Competitive Edge

Marketing in a high-end computer training business depends on recognition for expertise. It starts with our known contacts in positions to recommend us, and continues with long-term efforts to develop recognition in professional forums.

We will develop and maintain a database of people in the right positions. It starts with contacts we bring in as we start the business. From there we add enquiries and participants in forums and seminars, and newsletter subscribers. We use the database to make regular contact with mailings for additional forums and seminars.

Marketing Strategy

Seattle Community College's Continuing Education offers similar courses to EOC. Seattle prices its computer classes at $119 for 5-8 hours of training and $20 for the book. We will follow suit but market our classes at $125 for the class and $20 for the book. We can ask for more because our classes are smaller and we are able to give more individualized attention to our students. We also are able to give discounts on some of our manuals because we manufacture them ourselves.

Pricing Strategy

The going rate for private training is between $25-$60 per hour depending on what is being taught. For businesses the rate is between $40-45 per hour for on-site training of 1-2 students, with a minimum of a two-hour visit. If people are going to have a large group trained at their location, we would charge a per person rate instead of an hourly one. For an 8-hour course, we would charge $300 for the first two students, and $110 for each additional student. Our fees will be set to cover a reference book, training, and 60 days of follow-up phone support.

For the periodic Computer Upgrading workshops, a two-hour class, the fee will be $49 per person, and includes a copy of "How to buy the right computer."

For the periodic Basic Four workshops, a one-day or eight-hour class, the fee will be $179 per person, and includes a workbook, copies of "How to buy the right computer" and "The Beginner's Inspirational Guide to Computer Tips and Shortcuts," and a light lunch.

Promotion Strategy

The biggest mistake that computer-based business owners make is using a shotgun versus a laser beam approach to their business. Most of us in the computer industry have a tendency to be good at many different computer tasks. We might be good at desktop publishing, recommending software, customizing software, and doing basic PC repair. We might think that because we are good at all of these things we should do them all. We will have a broader customer base. We can service more people and thus should make more money.

This seems like the logical conclusion, but in reality it does not work. We spread ourselves to thin. At EOC we believe the more specific you get about what you do and who you do it for, the easier our service is to sell. We are working with a laser beam approach when we focus in this way. A laser beam is concentrated and works in a powerful way. We believe in focusing on one aspect of the computer industry for a specific type of client. In doing this we become three things: 1) a specialist, 2) known as an expert in our field, 3) all our marketing efforts fall into place, 4) we minimize, if not eliminate, much of our competition.

Because we do not want to grow too fast, our main form of promotional strategy in the beginning will be word of mouth and referrals.

Distribution Strategy

EOC's delivery method will have a large bearing on how we develop our program, so we have given this process up-front consideration. We have chosen to use the learning center method to deliver our training.

The training distribution will begin with first completing a needs assessment on the customer. Once the customer has been assessed they will be placed in a class that meets their assessment needs. Once the customer completes the class, they will again be assessed and go through an outcome procedure. The customer then has the choice of going up to the next level. If a customer chooses to dropout, they can return and be tested and placed again.

The following distribution tools will be used to aid in our classroom delivery:

- Printed material
- Instructor-led classroom presentation
- CD-ROM
- Internet
- Professional Speakers
- Tours/Field Trips

Our goal, in the near future, is to implement a Distributed Learning Framework (DLF). A web-enabled DLF can be accessed by users in a consistent and convenient manner from any location on the Internet. The DLF would manage other application data such as:

- Registration
- Users
- Learners Profiles
- Schedules
- Progress and Performance data
- Discussion Forums
- E-mail
- Surveys

The benefits of this approach would be:

- Accessibility
- Flexibility

- Extensibility
- Reusability
- Interoperability
- Durability

In the future, learning frameworks will evolve to embrace new technologies such as electronic commerce and knowledge management best practices to solve business issues such as skill gaps, corporate virtual campuses, career development, and help desks. Distributed learning frameworks also will link to enterprise resource planning, human resources, and financial systems.

EOC will use the accelerated-learning theory called the multiple intelligences theory. This theory was developed by the Harvard psychologist Howard Gardner and his team of researchers at the Graduate School of Education. What Gardner and his team put forth is the fact that there is no single way in which everyone thinks and learns. Instead, there are many forms of intelligence, many ways by which people learn, understand, think, problem-solve, and relate to the world. Gardner proposed a system of eight distinct intelligences. EOC will incorporate activities into our computer training program that exercises all eight of these intelligences.

Training Strategy

In brief, here are Gardner's eight multiple intelligences:

1. Verbal-linguistic—(speaking, reading, writing). This intelligence shows up in writers, storytellers, lawyers, politicians, and television talk-show hosts. **EOC training incorporation will include: group discussions.**
2. Logical-mathematical—(scientific reasoning). Obvious possessors are scientists, statisticians, and computer programmers. **EOC training incorporation will include: calculations and other math operations.**
3. Visual-spatial—(visualizing through lines, shape, volume, etc.). Think of architects, graphic designers, painters, decorators, film directors, chess players, engineers, and sculptors are examples of this type of brilliance. **EOC training incorporation will include: charts, graphs, and PowerPoint presentations.**
4. Bodily-kinesthetic—(control and interpretation of muscular or physical sensations). Geniuses here may be actors, athletes, dancers, physical therapists, mechanics, carpenters, jewelers, and craftspeople. **EOC training incorporation will include: Hands-on learning and stretching breaks.**
5. Musical-rhythmic—(recognize and use rhythmic and tonal patterns). Musicians, disc jockeys, and studio engineers and those who learn best when music is playing. **EOC training incorporation will include: Using soft music in the background.**
6. Interpersonal—(ability to work cooperatively with others). This form of intelligence is highly developed in teachers, therapists, managers, salespeople, public relations, and religious leaders. **EOC training incorporation will include: paired sharing, interactive games and exercises, group and peer teaching.**
7. Intrapersonal—(self-smart). This intelligence shows up in theologians, entrepreneurs, philosophers, and therapists. **EOC training incorporation will include: self-esteem activities, self-paced learning, and individualized instruction.**
8. Naturalistic—(nature-smart). This intelligence likes animals and organic systems better than people. **EOC training incorporation will include: Field trips and time outdoors.**

Instruction Method

All training programs have four major ingredients: information, performance outcomes, instructional methods, and instructional media. EOC will carefully account for and include each of these ingredients in our instructional methods.

All courses will include information to be trained. Course information can be classified as one of five types: facts, concepts, processes, procedures, and principles. The information will be decided by both looking at the knowledge and skill requirements of the job and the knowledge and skill level of the intended audience. Subtracting the knowledge and skills of the intended audience from those of the job, EOC will be able to derive final course content.

EOC's performance outcome will be a clearly defined statement of what the learners will be doing when they have achieved the purpose of the course or lesson. The performance outcomes will be mirrored with what must be done on the job. They are then written in the form of learning objectives. For each of our lessons we have at least one major learning objective and many will include supporting objectives as well.

Instructional methods are two types: informational displays and practice exercises with feedback. EOC will mainly use the practice exercise with feedback method.

Our instructional methods will be delivered through a mix of media that include: instructor, computer, workbook, overhead transparencies, flipchart, and perhaps a video.

EOC is obliged to offer training that works in today's society. While the modern employees are the best-educated in history, they are still required to absorb tremendous amounts of information and apply vast amounts of knowledge. EOC will use every theory, tool, and technique that will help employees learn while unleashing every available type of intelligence, gift, and aspect of humanity at their disposal.

Marketing Programs

The letters, brochures, business cards, flyers, and other literature will act as our representative. Here are some of our marketing programs and strategies:

Using sales letter strategies such as:

- Knowing our target audience—Know our objective or specific purpose of our letter.
- Being objective—Thinking like the reader.
- Using catchy salutation—Like "Here's some timely information for Ms. Wilson."
- Get to the point—Try and keep the letter short. One or two paragraphs.
- Vary the length of our paragraphs—A couple of 3-4 line paragraphs followed by a one-liner ads impact.
- Tell the reader what we want them to do next—Such as "I will call you on Thursday morning to iron out the details."
- Provide the facts—Give enough facts to our customer for them to make a decision.
- Address the reader's primary concern—"What is in it for me?"
- Add a P.S.—This is the second most read part of the letter. The first is the first paragraph or headline.
- Keep it short—No longer than one page.
- Talk to them friendly one-on-one—Use the word "you."
- Avoid jargon—Be clear and concise.
- Hand sign all of our letters.

Designing good ad copy to reach our customers:

- Choose the proper publication
- Have a goal for our advertisement
- Involve the audience
- Inform the buyer
- Headline and illustrations grab attention
- Give them something
- Always be specific
- Make our offer a good one
- Be creative in our media choices such as unusual avenues like fax newsletters, mall kiosks, fax-on-demand, publicity stunts, online marketing, anything unusual to reach our target market
- Small, classified ads
- Track our results
- Keep all our customers/prospects in a database and stay in touch with them regularly
- Gradually increase the size of our ad and track the results
- Advertise regularly and consistently
- Evaluate our efforts

Customer loyalty is much more important to EOC than customer satisfaction. We will serve our customers so well they will brag about EOC to others. This will keep them loyal and also provides a continual flow of customers.

Self-Evaluation Program

We will maintain our customers' happiness by utilizing our Self-Evaluation Program in which we will continually ask ourselves these following questions:

1. Is EOC's service the best it can be?
2. Is the appearance of our trainers, business surroundings, and product packaging professional?
3. Can we clearly describe our business in 25 words or less? Can our customers describe our business in 25 words or less?
4. Do our customers know about all of our products and services?
5. Do we have a well-developed marketing plan that we follow on a consistent basis?
6. What if our marketing plans work? Will we be able to handle the increased volume of sales without harming our customers or the quality of our work product?
7. Do we treat others with honesty and respect at all times?

EOC will continue to listen to ours customers and stay in regular contact with our customers by offering:

- Workshops and seminars.
- Private sales or classes.
- Giving them informative newsletters, articles, or tip sheets that can help them in their businesses, such as a computer tips and tricks newsletter.

EOC also will have a program in place for dropping customers who meet the following criteria:

- They complain about our prices and are always trying to get us to cut our rates.
- They complain about our competitors.
- Clients who miss appointments.
- Clients who can't make up their mind.
- Clients who hover over us while we work.

- Clients who owe us money or keep saying they'll pay us "when their funding comes in."

Sales Strategy

EOC's sales strategy is to get people to talk about themselves—their wants, desires, needs, and fears. Then use the information to help make a sale. Our sales goal is to remember why people buy.

The majority of people buy on emotion and justify their decision with facts and reason. They may buy for power, prestige, security, happiness, or freedom. EOC's service will appeal to these basic emotional needs first. After the prospect decides to buy our service for an emotional reason, they will be given facts by EOC to back up their decision.

EOC will establish trust and rapport with all of our prospective customers. We also will be prepared or anticipate objections. With those objections, we will make a list, learn from them and then come up with the answers to them. EOC will review the list of objections and possible solutions frequently.

EOC will have quantitative, reasonable sales goals by asking ourselves the following questions:

- What is our net profits per sale?
- What was our business activity over the last 12 months?
- How did last year's activity compare to the year before? Did you show an increase or decrease in sales? By what percent?
- What is the lifetime value of a customer? How much will our average customer buy over the months or years that they stay with us?
- How much of this is profit? What is the net profit/customer over the life of the customer?

We will also research our past and decide what is working and what is not. Based on our past performance we will decide on a goal that is attainable. We will then work backwards from our goal to decide what we will have to do to reach it.

EOC sales concentration will also be focused on reversing the risk from our customers to our Center by offering guaranteed learning. If at the end of a course students don't feel like they have learned what was covered in class, we will work with them at no additional charge until they are comfortable with the material.

EOC believes that being in the right place at the right time is 50 percent of obtaining a successful sale. Product knowledge is 25 percent and the last 25 percent is our human relations skills. Being very knowledgeable and extremely helpful are the ingredients to a successful sale.

Listed are some valuable secrets we have learned:

- Be out there—Be in as many places as possible. Look as big as we possibly can.
- Be free with our knowledge—Give prospects a "taste" of what we know without expectations of reimbursement.
- Look for long-term alliances in every situation—Don't be satisfied with just one sale. Learn from experiences and successes of others. Continually look for ways we can ride the coattails of others' successes.
- Be helpful and friendly—Being free with our knowledge, without an invoice, gets people "hooked" on our organization.
- People do business with people, not with companies.

- Ask customers why they choose EOC—Learn what we did right and repeat it.

Sometimes having too many customers can be bad for business. Raising rates through a letter can serve three purposes:

- It helps to get rid of deadwood customers. They don't call anymore because they can't afford the rates.
- The trainer can work less and earn more.
- It is a great opportunity to reiterate all of our services.

Finally, it is our goal to deliver more than what we promise and never build up hopes.

Sales Forecast

The peaks and valleys for this business in the U.S. are from about September 6 through November 22. For some reason people think "school" in the fall, and they take more classes. Two of our worst times are from November 22 through January 7 and the month of March. Obviously, the holidays are getting in the way from November 22 through January 7. People are too busy with taxes in March, but it will pick up in April and May as people file their tax returns.

It's during our "valley" periods that we will concentrate on a saturation of workshops and seminars, where no long-term commitment is required of the customer. We will also do holiday specials. For everyone who has inquired about our classes during the year, we will do a mailing around November 5 and offer them a really good deal on training during our "valley" period.

Sales Forecast	FY2001	FY2002	FY2003
Sales	$122,448	$200,192	$200,192
Other	$0	$0	$0
Total Sales	$122,448	$200,192	$200,192
Direct Cost of Sales			
Sales	$0	$0	$0
Other	$0	$0	$0
Subtotal Cost of Sales	**$0**	**$0**	**$0**

Strategic Alliances

Living and volunteering in the Seattle community for the past 34 years has given computer trainer Serena Bolton an opportunity to build many business alliances within the King County area. Those alliances include:

University of Washington—Office of Business and Community Partnerships
Stephens Capital Development
Seattle Board of Education
Seattle Police Department
Employment Opportunities Unlimited
Jason's Staffing
General Hospital
Generation Learning Solutions
TechTool Publishers
Microsoft /MicroShare Testing
Senior Citizens Centers
Webber Real Estate
Dr. Waylon Nestle, D.S.S.
UAW 451

Ballinger Center
Career Pathways

Other alliances will be created through public relations programs.

Turning Points

Seattle, Washington is at a business industry turning point. With Boeing being phased out as the number one employer, people are scrambling to adjust their skills. Those employees that have been laid off or bought out are finding the world outside is not what it used to be before they entered Boeing. Those employees are now finding their skills to be outdated or unusable in the workforce today.

They lack the computer skills needed to become employable once again. They are also finding that more and more certifications are now being required criteria for employment.

EOC is strategically positioning itself to be in place for these workers and others that are in need of basic computer training. EOC is also positioning itself to meet the needs of employers who are requesting advanced training and certifications. EOC will be the gap filler between the employer and the employee.

EOC knows that no business is without frustrations and disappointments. Yet, we strive to know what to expect in advance, so we are better prepared to deal with the built-in frustrations of this business. We expect a certain amount of "no shows." This is why we require payment up front as a guarantee of attendance. We know that about 1 out of every 5 people who sign up could possibly back out due to sickness, emergencies, and sometimes people just change their mind. In this case we make sure we do not spend our money before it has cleared.

MANAGEMENT SUMMARY

Personnel Plan

EOC will consist of three employees. Serena Bolton will participate full-time in the business as Director and Computer Instructor. The other three positions are currently vacant and will be filled as needed. Listed below are the job descriptions.

- **Director and Computer Instructor,** Serena Bolton, will maintain credentials needed to provide the most efficient and thorough computer training statewide. She will also be in charge of upgrading the skills of her staff.
- **Receptionist/Secretary,** Vacant, will handle all incoming calls and walk-ins, mail, correspondence, data entry, filing, ordering of supplies, scheduling, and play a supportive role to the Director. Candidate will also be required to take EOC classes and become certified.
- **Assistant Trainer,** Vacant, will be in charge of helping in the computer lab during class sessions, assist with development of computer training manuals, provide training in absence of Director, maintain maintenance of computer equipment, and play a supportive role to the Director. Candidate will be required to become MOUS certified within 60 days.
- **Van Driver,** Vacant, will be in charge of picking up seniors and dropping them off in a safe and courteous manner. Will be required to take EOC classes.

The projected salaries for each of these positions is hourly at $8.00 with no benefits at this time.

Personnel Plan	FY2001	FY2002	FY2003
Receptionist/Secretary	$9,920	$16,640	$16,640
Trainer's Assistant	$9,920	$16,640	$16,640
Van Driver	$9,920	$16,640	$16,640
Other	$17,360	$29,120	$29,120
Total Payroll	**$47,120**	**$79,040**	**$79,040**
Total Headcount	**0**	**3**	**3**
Payroll Burden	**$7,068**	**$11,856**	**$11,856**
Total Payroll Expenditures	**$54,188**	**$90,896**	**$90,896**

We want to finance growth mainly through cash flow. We recognize that this means we will have to grow more slowly.

FINANCIAL PLAN

The most important factor in our case is sales. We will develop a permanent system with ongoing marketing and sales development.

We are also assuming an initial short-term loan of $71,500 which includes start-up capital of $15,000.

Our financial plan depends on important assumptions, most of which are shown in the following table as annual assumptions.

Important Assumptions

Some of the more important underlying assumptions are:

- We assume a strong economy, without major recession.
- We assume, of course, that there are no unforseen changes in technology to make the use of computers and the need of computer training obsolete.

General Assumptions	FY2001	FY2002	FY2003
Short-term Interest Rate %	10.00%	10.00%	10.00%
Long-term Interest Rate %	10.00%	10.00%	10.00%
Payment Days Estimator	30	30	30
Collection Days Estimator	45	45	45
Inventory Turnover Estimator	6.00	6.00	6.00
Tax Rate %	25.00%	25.00%	25.00%
Expenses in Cash %	10.00%	10.00%	10.00%
Sales on Credit %	0.00%	0.00%	0.00%
Personnel Burden %	15.00%	15.00%	15.00%

Our monthly units break-even is 72 students. The monthly sales break-even is $10,403. Our average per-unit revenue is $145 per class and our estimated average fixed cost is $10,396 per month.

Break-even Analysis

Break-even Analysis:	
Monthly Units Break-even	72
Monthly Sales Break-even	$10,403

Assumptions:	
Average Per-Unit Revenue	$145.00
Average Per-Unit Variable Cost	$0.10
Estimated Monthly Fixed Cost	$10,396

Projected Profit and Loss

Our projected profit and loss is shown on the following table, with sales increasing more than 30 percent. We show a break-even profit the first year. We prefer to project conservatively so that we make sure we have enough cash.

The detailed monthly projections are included in appendices.

Profit and Loss (Income Statement)	FY2001	FY2002	FY2003
Sales	$122,448	$200,192	$200,192
Direct Cost of Sales	$0	$0	$0
Production Payroll	$0	$0	$0
Other	$0	$0	$0
Total Cost of Sales	**$0**	**$0**	**$0**
Gross Margin	$122,448	$200,192	$200,192
Gross Margin %	100.00%	100.00%	100.00%
Operating Expenses			
Sales and Marketing Expenses			
Sales and Marketing Payroll	$0	$0	$0
Advertising/Promotion	$7,130	$11,960	$11,960
Travel	$0	$0	$0
Miscellaneous	$0	$0	$0
Total Sales and Marketing Expenses	**$0**	**$0**	**$0**
Sales and Marketing %	0.00%	0.00%	0.00%
General and Administrative Expenses			
General and Administrative Payroll	$0	$0	$0
Payroll Expense	$47,120	$79,040	$79,040
Payroll Burden	$7,068	$11,856	$11,856
Depreciation	$1,696	$0	$0
Leased Van	$2,625	$4,500	$4,500
Telephone	$350	$600	$600
Utilities	$1,435	$2,140	$2,140
Insurance	$950	$1,900	$1,900
Rent	$4,200	$8,400	$8,400
Total General and Administrative Expenses	**$0**	**$0**	**$0**
General and Administrative %	0.00%	0.00%	0.00%
Other Expenses			
Other Payroll	$0	$0	$0
Accounting Services	$1,400	$2,400	$2,400
Total Other Expenses	**$0**	**$0**	**$0**
Other %	0.00%	0.00%	0.00%
Total Operating Expenses	**$73,974**	**$122,796**	**$122,796**
Profit Before Interest and Taxes	$48,474	$77,396	$77,396
Interest Expense Short-term	($590)	($1,461)	($2,810)
Interest Expense Long-term	$0	$0	$0
Taxes Incurred	$12,266	$19,714	$20,052
Extraordinary Items	$0	$0	$0
Net Profit	$36,798	$59,143	$60,155
Net Profit/Sales	30.05%	29.54%	30.05%

The following cash flow projections show the annual amounts only. Cash flow projections are critical to our success. Reflected in this chart are the only remaining months of 2000. The annual cash flow figures are included here and the more important detailed monthly numbers are included in the appendices.

Projected Cash Flow

Projected Cash Flow	FY2001	FY2002	FY2003
Net Profit	$36,798	$59,143	$60,155
Plus:			
Depreciation	$1,696	$0	$0
Change in Accounts Payable	$128	$4,103	($310)
Current Borrowing (repayment)	($7,868)	($13,488)	($13,488)
Increase (decrease) Other Liabilities	$0	$0	$0
Long-term Borrowing (repayment)	$0	$0	$0
Capital Input	$0	$0	$0
Subtotal	**$30,754**	**$49,758**	**$46,357**
Less:			
Change in Accounts Receivable	$0	$0	$0
Change in Inventory	$0	$0	$0
Change in Other Short-term Assets	$0	$0	$0
Capital Expenditure	$0	$0	$0
Dividends	$0	$0	$0
Subtotal	**$0**	**$0**	**$0**
Net Cash Flow	**$30,754**	**$49,758**	**$46,357**
Cash Balance	**$45,754**	**$95,513**	**$141,870**

The balance sheet in the following table shows sufficient growth of net worth, and a sufficiently healthy financial position. The monthly estimates are included in the appendices.

Projected Balance Sheet

Assets			
Short-term Assets	FY2001	FY2002	FY2003
Cash	$45,754	$95,513	$141,870
Accounts Receivable	$0	$0	$0
Inventory	$0	$0	$0
Other Short-term Assets	$0	$0	$0
Total Short-term Assets	**$45,754**	**$95,513**	**$141,870**
Long-term Assets			
Capital Assets	$0	$0	$0
Accumulated Depreciation	$1,696	$1,696	$1,696
Total Long-term Assets	**($1,696)**	**($1,696)**	**($1,696)**
Total Assets	**$44,058**	**$93,817**	**$140,174**
Liabilities and Capital			
Accounts Payable	$128	$4,232	$3,922
Short-term Notes	($7,868)	($21,356)	($34,844)
Other Short-term Liabilities	$0	$0	$0
Subtotal Short-term Liabilities	**($7,740)**	**($17,124)**	**($30,922)**
Long-term Liabilities	$0	$0	$0
Total Liabilities	**($7,740)**	**($17,124)**	**($30,922)**

Projected Cash Flow

Projected Balance Sheet

Projected Balance Sheet

Continued

	FY2001	FY2002	FY2003
Paid in Capital	$7,945	$7,945	$7,945
Retained Earnings	$7,055	$43,853	$102,996
Earnings	$36,798	$59,143	$60,155
Total Capital	$51,798	$110,941	$171,095
Total Liabilities and Capital	$44,058	$93,817	$140,174
Net Worth	$51,798	$110,941	$171,095

Business Ratios

The following table shows the projected ratios. We expect to maintain healthy ratios for profitability, risk, and return.

Ratio Analysis

Profitability Ratios:	FY2001	FY2002	FY2003
Gross Margin	100.00%	100.00%	100.00%
Net Profit Margin	30.05%	29.54%	30.05%
Return on Assets	83.52%	63.04%	42.91%
Return on Equity	71.04%	53.31%	35.16%
Activity Ratios			
AR Turnover	0.00	0.00	0.00
Collection Days	0	0	0
Inventory Turnover	0.00	0.00	0.00
Accts Payable Turnover	208.73	12.17	12.17
Total Asset Turnover	**2.78**	**2.13**	**1.43**
Debt Ratios			
Debt to Net Worth	-0.15	-0.15	-0.18
Short-term Liability to Liability	0.00	0.00	0.00
Liquidity Ratios			
Current Ratio	0.00	0.00	0.00
Quick Ratio	0.00	0.00	0.00
Net Working Capital	$53,494	$112,637	$172,791
Interest Coverage	0.00	0.00	0.00
Additional Ratios			
Assets to Sales	0.36	0.47	0.70
Debt/Assets	-18%	-18%	-22%
Current Debt/Total Assets	-18%	-18%	-22%
Acid Test	0.00	0.00	0.00
Asset Turnover	2.78	2.13	1.43
Sales/Net Worth	2.36	1.80	1.17
Dividend Payout	$0	$0	$0

This page left intentionally blank to accommodate tabular matter following.

APPENDIX

Sales Forecast

Sales	Jun	Jul	Aug	Sep	Oct	Nov	Dec
Sales	$20,016	$14,896	$14,896	$24,352	$33,920	$8,488	$5,880
Other	$0	$0	$0	$0	$0	$0	$0
Total Sales	**$20,016**	**$14,896**	**$14,896**	**$24,352**	**$33,920**	**$8,488**	**$5,880**
Direct Cost of Sales							
Sales	$0	$0	$0	$0	$0	$0	$0
Other	$0	$0	$0	$0	$0	$0	$0
Subtotal Cost of Sales	**$0**	**$0**	**$0**	**$0**	**$0**	**$0**	**$0**

Personnel Plan

Personnel	Jun	Jul	Aug	Sep	Oct	Nov	Dec
Receptionist/Secretary	$1,280	$1,280	$1,600	$1,280	$1,600	$1,280	$1,600
Trainer's Assistant	$1,280	$1,280	$1,600	$1,280	$1,600	$1,280	$1,600
Van Driver	$1,280	$1,280	$1,600	$1,280	$1,600	$1,280	$1,600
Other	$2,240	$2,240	$2,800	$2,240	$2,800	$2,240	$2,800
Total Payroll	**$6,080**	**$6,080**	**$7,600**	**$6,080**	**$7,600**	**$6,080**	**$7,600**
Total Headcount	**3**	**3**	**3**	**3**	**3**	**3**	**3**
Payroll Burden	**$912**	**$912**	**$1,140**	**$912**	**$1,140**	**$912**	**$1,140**
Total Payroll Expenditures	**$6,992**	**$6,992**	**$8,740**	**$6,992**	**$8,740**	**$6,992**	**$8,740**

General Assumptions

	Jun	Jul	Aug	Sep	Oct	Nov	Dec
Short-term Interest Rate %	10.00%	10.00%	10.00%	10.00%	10.00%	10.00%	10.00%
Long-term Interest Rate %	10.00%	10.00%	10.00%	10.00%	10.00%	10.00%	10.00%
Payment Days Estimator	30	30	30	30	30	30	30
Collection Days Estimator	45	45	45	45	45	45	45
Inventory Turnover Estimator	6.00	6.00	6.00	6.00	6.00	6.00	6.00
Tax Rate %	25.00%	25.00%	25.00%	25.00%	25.00%	25.00%	25.00%
Expenses in Cash %	10.00%	10.00%	10.00%	10.00%	10.00%	10.00%	10.00%
Sales on Credit %	0.00%	0.00%	0.00%	0.00%	0.00%	0.00%	0.00%
Personnel Burden %	15.00%	15.00%	15.00%	15.00%	15.00%	15.00%	15.00%

Jan	Feb	Mar	Apr	May	FY2001	FY2002	FY2003
$0	$0	$0	$0	$0	$122,448	$200,192	$200,192
$0	$0	$0	$0	$0	$0	$0	$0
$0	**$0**	**$0**	**$0**	**$0**	**$122,448**	**$200,192**	**$200,192**
$0	$0	$0	$0	$0	$0	$0	$0
$0	$0	$0	$0	$0	$0	$0	$0
$0	**$0**	**$0**	**$0**	**$0**	**$0**	**$0**	**$0**

Jan	Feb	Mar	Apr	May	FY2001	FY2002	FY2003
$0	$0	$0	$0	$0	$9,920	$16,640	$16,640
$0	$0	$0	$0	$0	$9,920	$16,640	$16,640
$0	$0	$0	$0	$0	$9,920	$16,640	$16,640
$0	$0	$0	$0	$0	$17,360	$29,120	$29,120
$0	**$0**	**$0**	**$0**	**$0**	**$47,120**	**$79,040**	**$79,040**
0	**0**	**0**	**0**	**0**	**0**	**3**	**3**
$0	**$0**	**$0**	**$0**	**$0**	**$7,068**	**$11,856**	**$11,856**
$0	**$0**	**$0**	**$0**	**$0**	**$54,188**	**$90,896**	**$90,896**

Jan	Feb	Mar	Apr	May	FY2001	FY2002	FY2003
10.00%	10.00%	10.00%	10.00%	10.00%	10.00%	10.00%	10.00%
10.00%	10.00%	10.00%	10.00%	10.00%	10.00%	10.00%	10.00%
30	30	30	30	30	30	30	30
45	45	45	45	45	45	45	45
6.00	6.00	6.00	6.00	6.00	6.00	6.00	6.00
25.00%	25.00%	25.00%	25.00%	25.00%	25.00%	25.00%	25.00%
10.00%	10.00%	10.00%	10.00%	10.00%	10.00%	10.00%	10.00%
0.00%	0.00%	0.00%	0.00%	0.00%	0.00%	0.00%	0.00%
15.00%	15.00%	15.00%	15.00%	15.00%	15.00%	15.00%	15.00%

Profit and Loss (Income Statement)

	Jun	Jul	Aug	Sep	Oct	Nov	Dec
Sales	$20,016	$14,896	$14,896	$24,352	$33,920	$8,488	$5,880
Direct Cost of Sales	$0	$0	$0	$0	$0	$0	$0
Production Payroll	$0	$0	$0	$0	$0	$0	$0
Other	$0	$0	$0	$0	$0	$0	$0
Total Cost of Sales	**$0**	**$0**	**$0**	**$0**	**$0**	**$0**	**$0**
Gross Margin	$20,016	$14,896	$14,896	$24,352	$33,920	$8,488	$5,880
Gross Margin %	100.00%	100.00%	100.00%	100.00%	100.00%	100.00%	100.00%

Operating Expenses

Sales and Marketing Expenses

	Jun	Jul	Aug	Sep	Oct	Nov	Dec
Sales and Marketing Payroll	$0	$0	$0	$0	$0	$0	$0
Advertising/Promotion	$920	$920	$1,150	$920	$1,150	$920	$1,150
Travel	$0	$0	$0	$0	$0	$0	$0
Miscellaneous	$0	$0	$0	$0	$0	$0	$0
Total Sales and Marketing Expenses	**$0**	**$0**	**$0**	**$0**	**$0**	**$0**	**$0**
Sales and Marketing %	0.00%	0.00%	0.00%	0.00%	0.00%	0.00%	0.00%

General and Administrative Expenses

	Jun	Jul	Aug	Sep	Oct	Nov	Dec
General and Administrative Payroll	$0	$0	$0	$0	$0	$0	$0
Payroll Expense	$6,080	$6,080	$7,600	$6,080	$7,600	$6,080	$7,600
Payroll Burden	$912	$912	$1,140	$912	$1,140	$912	$1,140
Depreciation	$1,696	$0	$0	$0	$0	$0	$0
Leased Van	$375	$375	$375	$375	$375	$375	$375
Telephone	$50	$50	$50	$50	$50	$50	$50
Utilities	$115	$90	$410	$115	$90	$410	$115
Insurance	$0	$475	$0	$0	$475	$0	$0
Rent	$0	$700	$700	$700	$700	$700	$700
Total General and Administrative Expenses	**$0**	**$0**	**$0**	**$0**	**$0**	**$0**	**$0**
General and Administrative %	0.00%	0.00%	0.00%	0.00%	0.00%	0.00%	0.00%

Other Expenses

	Jun	Jul	Aug	Sep	Oct	Nov	Dec
Other Payroll	$0	$0	$0	$0	$0	$0	$0
Accounting Services	$200	$200	$200	$200	$200	$200	$200
Total Other Expenses	**$0**	**$0**	**$0**	**$0**	**$0**	**$0**	**$0**
Other %	0.00%	0.00%	0.00%	0.00%	0.00%	0.00%	0.00%
Total Operating Expenses	**$10,348**	**$9,802**	**$11,625**	**$9,352**	**$11,780**	**$9,647**	**$11,330**

	Jun	Jul	Aug	Sep	Oct	Nov	Dec
Profit Before Interest and Taxes	$9,668	$5,094	$3,271	$15,000	$22,140	($1,159)	($5,450)
Interest Expense Short-term	($9)	($19)	($28)	($37)	($47)	($56)	($66)
Interest Expense Long-term	$0	$0	$0	$0	$0	$0	$0
Taxes Incurred	$2,419	$1,278	$825	$3,759	$5,547	($276)	($1,346)
Extraordinary Items	$0	$0	$0	$0	$0	$0	$0
Net Profit	$7,258	$3,835	$2,474	$11,278	$16,640	($827)	($4,038)
Net Profit/Sales	36.26%	25.74%	16.61%	46.31%	49.06%	-9.74%	-68.68%

Jan	Feb	Mar	Apr	May	FY2001	FY2002	FY2003
$0	$0	$0	$0	$0	$122,448	$200,192	$200,192
$0	$0	$0	$0	$0	$0	$0	$0
$0	$0	$0	$0	$0	$0	$0	$0
$0	$0	$0	$0	$0	$0	$0	$0
$0	**$0**	**$0**	**$0**	**$0**	**$0**	**$0**	**$0**
$0	$0	$0	$0	$0	$122,448	$200,192	$200,192
0.00%	0.00%	0.00%	0.00%	0.00%	100.00%	100.00%	100.00%
$0	$0	$0	$0	$0	$0	$0	$0
$0	$0	$0	$0	$0	$7,130	$11,960	$11,960
$0	$0	$0	$0	$0	$0	$0	$0
$0	$0	$0	$0	$0	$0	$0	$0
$0	**$0**	**$0**	**$0**	**$0**	**$0**	**$0**	**$0**
0.00%	0.00%	0.00%	0.00%	0.00%	0.00%	0.00%	0.00%
$0	$0	$0	$0	$0	$0	$0	$0
$0	$0	$0	$0	$0	$47,120	$79,040	$79,040
$0	$0	$0	$0	$0	$7,068	$11,856	$11,856
$0	$0	$0	$0	$0	$1,696	$0	$0
$0	$0	$0	$0	$0	$2,625	$4,500	$4,500
$0	$0	$0	$0	$0	$350	$600	$600
$90	$0	$0	$0	$0	$1,435	$2,140	$2,140
$0	$0	$0	$0	$0	$950	$1,900	$1,900
$0	$0	$0	$0	$0	$4,200	$8,400	$8,400
$0	**$0**	**$0**	**$0**	**$0**	**$0**	**$0**	**$0**
0.00%	0.00%	0.00%	0.00%	0.00%	0.00%	0.00%	0.00%
$0	$0	$0	$0	$0	$0	$0	$0
$0	$0	$0	$0	$0	$1,400	$2,400	$2,400
$0	**$0**	**$0**	**$0**	**$0**	**$0**	**$0**	**$0**
0.00%	0.00%	0.00%	0.00%	0.00%	0.00%	0.00%	0.00%
$90	**$0**	**$0**	**$0**	**$0**	**$73,974**	**$122,796**	**$122,796**
($90)	$0	$0	$0	$0	$48,474	$77,396	$77,396
($66)	($66)	($66)	($66)	($66)	($590)	($1,461)	($2,810)
$0	$0	$0	$0	$0	$0	$0	$0
($6)	$16	$16	$16	$16	$12,266	$19,714	$20,052
$0	$0	$0	$0	$0	$0	$0	$0
($18)	$49	$49	$49	$49	$36,798	$59,143	$60,155
0.00%	0.00%	0.00%	0.00%	0.00%	30.05%	29.54%	30.05%

Projected Cash Flow

	Jun	Jul	Aug	Sep	Oct	Nov	Dec
Net Profit	$7,258	$3,835	$2,474	$11,278	$16,640	($827)	($4,038)
Plus:							
Depreciation	$1,696	$0	$0	$0	$0	$0	$0
Change in Accounts Payable	$3,541	($0)	($337)	$2,088	$2,138	($5,409)	($996)
Current Borrowing							
(repayment)	($1,124)	($1,124)	($1,124)	($1,124)	($1,124)	($1,124)	($1,124)
Increase (decrease)							
Other Liabilities	$0	$0	$0	$0	$0	$0	$0
Long-term Borrowing							
(repayment)	$0	$0	$0	$0	$0	$0	$0
Capital Input	$0	$0	$0	$0	$0	$0	$0
Subtotal	**$11,371**	**$2,710**	**$1,013**	**$12,242**	**$17,655**	**($7,360)**	**($6,158)**
Less:							
Change in Accounts Receivable	$0	$0	$0	$0	$0	$0	$0
Change in Inventory	$0	$0	$0	$0	$0	$0	$0
Change in Other							
Short-term Assets	$0	$0	$0	$0	$0	$0	$0
Capital Expenditure	$0	$0	$0	$0	$0	$0	$0
Dividends	$0	$0	$0	$0	$0	$0	$0
Subtotal	**$0**	**$0**	**$0**	**$0**	**$0**	**$0**	**$0**
Net Cash Flow	**$11,371**	**$2,710**	**$1,013**	**$12,242**	**$17,655**	**($7,360)**	**($6,158)**
Cash Balance	**$26,371**	**$29,081**	**$30,094**	**$42,336**	**$59,991**	**$52,631**	**$46,473**

Jan	Feb	Mar	Apr	May	FY2001	FY2002	FY2003
($18)	$49	$49	$49	$49	$36,798	$59,143	$60,155
$0	$0	$0	$0	$0	$1,696	$0	$0
($1,009)	($16)	$43	$43	$43	$128	$4,103	($310)
$0	$0	$0	$0	$0	($7,868)	($13,488)	($13,488)
$0	$0	$0	$0	$0	$0	$0	$0
$0	$0	$0	$0	$0	$0	$0	$0
$0	$0	$0	$0	$0	$0	$0	$0
($1,028)	$33	$92	$92	$92	$30,754	$49,758	$46,357
$0	$0	$0	$0	$0	$0	$0	$0
$0	$0	$0	$0	$0	$0	$0	$0
$0	$0	$0	$0	$0	$0	$0	$0
$0	$0	$0	$0	$0	$0	$0	$0
$0	$0	$0	$0	$0	$0	$0	$0
$0	$0	$0	$0	$0	$0	$0	$0
$0	$0	$0	$0	$0	$0	$0	$0
($1,028)	$33	$92	$92	$92	$30,754	$49,758	$46,357
$45,445	$45,479	$45,571	$45,662	$45,754	$45,754	$95,513	$141,870

Projected Balance Sheet

Assets

Short-term Assets	Jun	Jul	Aug	Sep	Oct	Nov	Dec
Cash	$26,371	$29,081	$30,094	$42,336	$59,991	$52,631	$46,473
Accounts Receivable	$0	$0	$0	$0	$0	$0	$0
Inventory	$0	$0	$0	$0	$0	$0	$0
Other Short-term Assets	$0	$0	$0	$0	$0	$0	$0
Total Short-term Assets	**$26,371**	**$29,081**	**$30,094**	**$42,336**	**$59,991**	**$52,631**	**$46,473**
Long-term Assets							
Capital Assets	$0	$0	$0	$0	$0	$0	$0
Accumulated Depreciation	$1,696	$1,696	$1,696	$1,696	$1,696	$1,696	$1,696
Total Long-term Assets	**($1,696)**	**($1,696)**	**($1,696)**	**($1,696)**	**($1,696)**	**($1,696)**	**($1,696)**
Total Assets	**$24,675**	**$27,385**	**$28,398**	**$40,640**	**$58,295**	**$50,935**	**$44,777**
Liabilities and Capital							
Accounts Payable	$3,541	$3,540	$3,203	$5,291	$7,430	$2,021	$1,025
Short-term Notes	($1,124)	($2,248)	($3,372)	($4,496)	($5,620)	($6,744)	($7,868)
Other Short-term Liabilities	$0	$0	$0	$0	$0	$0	$0
Subtotal Short-term Liabilities	**$2,417**	**$1,292**	**($169)**	**$795**	**$1,810**	**($4,723)**	**($6,843)**
Long-term Liabilities	$0	$0	$0	$0	$0	$0	$0
Total Liabilities	**$2,417**	**$1,292**	**($169)**	**$795**	**$1,810**	**($4,723)**	**($6,843)**
Paid in Capital	$7,945	$7,945	$7,945	$7,945	$7,945	$7,945	$7,945
Retained Earnings	$7,055	$7,055	$7,055	$7,055	$7,055	$7,055	$7,055
Earnings	$7,258	$11,093	$13,567	$24,845	$41,485	$40,658	$36,620
Total Capital	**$22,258**	**$26,093**	**$28,567**	**$39,845**	**$56,485**	**$55,658**	**$51,620**
Total Liabilities and Capital	**$24,675**	**$27,385**	**$28,398**	**$40,640**	**$58,295**	**$50,935**	**$44,777**
Net Worth	**$22,258**	**$26,093**	**$28,567**	**$39,845**	**$56,485**	**$55,658**	**$51,620**

	Jan	Feb	Mar	Apr	May	FY2001	FY2002	FY2003
	$45,445	$45,479	$45,571	$45,662	$45,754	$45,754	$95,513	$141,870
	$0	$0	$0	$0	$0	$0	$0	$0
	$0	$0	$0	$0	$0	$0	$0	$0
	$0	$0	$0	$0	$0	$0	$0	$0
	$45,445	**$45,479**	**$45,571**	**$45,662**	**$45,754**	**$45,754**	**$95,513**	**$141,870**
	$0	$0	$0	$0	$0	$0	$0	$0
	$1,696	$1,696	$1,696	$1,696	$1,696	$1,696	$1,696	$1,696
	($1,696)	**($1,696)**	**($1,696)**	**($1,696)**	**($1,696)**	**($1,696)**	**($1,696)**	**($1,696)**
	$43,749	**$43,783**	**$43,875**	**$43,966**	**$44,058**	**$44,058**	**$93,817**	**$140,174**
	$16	$0	$43	$86	$128	$128	$4,232	$3,922
	($7,868)	($7,868)	($7,868)	($7,868)	($7,868)	($7,868)	($21,356)	($34,844)
	$0	$0	$0	$0	$0	$0	$0	$0
	($7,852)	**($7,868)**	**($7,825)**	**($7,782)**	**($7,740)**	**($7,740)**	**($17,124)**	**($30,922)**
	$0	$0	$0	$0	$0	$0	$0	$0
	($7,852)	**($7,868)**	**($7,825)**	**($7,782)**	**($7,740)**	**($7,740)**	**($17,124)**	**($30,922)**
	$7,945	$7,945	$7,945	$7,945	$7,945	$7,945	$7,945	$7,945
	$7,055	$7,055	$7,055	$7,055	$7,055	$7,055	$43,853	$102,996
	$36,601	$36,651	$36,700	$36,749	$36,798	$36,798	$59,143	$60,155
	$51,601	**$51,651**	**$51,700**	**$51,749**	**$51,798**	**$51,798**	**$110,941**	**$171,095**
	$43,749	**$43,783**	**$43,875**	**$43,966**	**$44,058**	**$44,058**	**$93,817**	**$140,174**
	$51,601	**$51,651**	**$51,700**	**$51,749**	**$51,798**	**$51,798**	**$110,941**	**$171,095**

Concert Promotions Company

BUSINESS PLAN

GOOD VIBRATIONS, INC.

145 Mueller Avenue, Suite 13
Lansing, Michigan 48901

Good Vibrations, Inc. (GVI), is a home-based concert promoting corporation. GVI's keys to success include: implementing an effective cash flow plan, communicating with our customers and clients regularly, and targeting our most ready-to-buy customers or clients first.

- EXECUTIVE SUMMARY

- COMPANY SUMMARY

- PROMOTIONAL SERVICES

- MARKET ANALYSIS SUMMARY

- STRATEGY

- MANAGEMENT SUMMARY

- FINANCIAL PLAN

- APPENDIX

EXECUTIVE SUMMARY

Good Vibrations, Inc. (GVI), is a home-based concert promoting corporation, located at 145 Mueller Avenue, Suite 13, Lansing, Michigan. This business plan was developed for the purpose of applying for a business loan in the amount of $19,550. The start-up costs for this business are $29,550. The owner's equity is $10,000. Projected sales for 2002 alone are $377,250 and our projected profits are over $147,000.

GVI's keys to success include: implementing an effective cash flow plan, communicating with our customers and clients regularly, and targeting our most ready-to-buy customers or clients first.

The business of concert promotions, as shown in our plan, has an excellent profitability level and growth rate. Our competitive edge along with new promotion techniques puts GVI in the forefront of promotional services. We are living in an age where more and more new talent is being introduced into the concert mainstream. Our concert promotion services will differ from the traditional concert promoters because of our added personal touch. The highlights of our business plan are shown below.

Objectives

Our objectives for the business are to:

- Sell 80 percent to 90 percent of an arena's capacity per concert
- Host at least 10-20 concerts a year
- Create an ongoing relationship between GVI, the artist, and the concert attendees that will continue throughout each year

Mission

Our mission is to provide the best and most unique quality of entertainment that the music industry has to offer to our concert attendees. Also, to meet the artists' performance needs with professionalism and expertise. We will establish an excellent business relationship with each arena facility owner so that the event is profitable to all parties involved.

Effective Facets of Promotions

RESEARCH:
Always ask questions, gather information, meet people, and learn more about our market.

QUANTITY:
We must do everything we can to let all potential attendees know of an event. Many avenues must be pursued to make sure no stone is left unturned in terms of promotion.

FREQUENCY & DISTRIBUTION:
If we wait until the last six days before an event to bombard the market, it is too late. People plan their "free time" weeks and months ahead. We must give our audience plenty of advance notice.

12 Keys to Outstanding Success

Below are 12 key marketing ingredients that we will apply to make significant growth almost straight away. They are as follows:

1. Understand that marketing our business provides the ultimate return on our money. Work "on" our business, not "in" it.
2. Only use direct-response marketing, not "institutional."

3. Communicate with our customers and clients regularly.
4. Run simple low-cost, or no-cost tests on every aspect of marketing to find our biggest sales appeal.
5. Target our most ready-to-buy customers or clients first.
6. Create a systematic, high profit back end.
7. Always reverse the risk our customers feel before they buy.
8. Give our reasons why our sponsoring of events will benefit, add value, and solve problems for the client.
9. Always include testimonials or endorsements in all our marketing.
10. Always think in terms of the customer or client's "What's in it for me?" question.
11. Implementing an effective cash flow plan.
12. Achieving efficiency.

Good Vibrations, Inc., is a home-based corporation located at 145 Mueller Avenue, Suite 13, Lansing, Michigan. Our present office is small but is in a room of its own to keep our home and work lives separate. Our office will contain bookshelves, file cabinet, desk with computer, sitting chairs, a fax, a copier, and space for a small waiting area.

COMPANY SUMMARY

Good Vibrations, Inc., is a corporation, owned by its principal investor and operator, Roland Wilson.

Company Ownership

Roland's plan is to be home-based for the period of three years after which he will seek the use of an office/hall building for his offices. GVI's regular business hours will run from 12:00 noon until 9:00 P.M., Monday through Friday. On Saturdays or concert days the hours will vary. Most of the business will be handled at our home office. As other business warrants, we will use hotel facilities and clients' offices for the larger more in-depth meetings.

Operations

The process of promoting a concert will begin with:

1. Choosing a date, artists, and location
2. Project expenses
3. Project sponsorships needed
4. Project ticket sales
5. If concert selection is feasible, begin concert promotion schedule

Total start-up expenses (including legal costs, advertising and promotions, stationery, and related expenses) come to $29,550. Start-up assets required include $2,000 in short-term assets (office furniture, etc.) and $10,000 in initial cash to handle the first few months of operations as sales play through the cash flow. The details are included in the following chart.

Start-up Summary

Start-up Plan
Start-up Expenses

Legal and Accounting Expenses	$500
Stationery, etc.	$300
Brochures and Promotional Items	$3,150
Consultants	$1,000
Insurance	$500
Office Furniture	$2,000
Research and Development	$1,000

Start-up Summary

Continued

Computer and Printer	$1,200
Travel	$3,000
Meals	$400
Security	$6,000
Accommodations	$500
Other	$0
Total Start-up Expense	**$19,550**
Start-up Assets Needed	
Cash Requirements	$10,000
Start-up inventory	$0
Other Short-term Assets	$0
Total Short-term Assets	**$10,000**
Long-term Assets	$0
Total Assets	**$10,000**
Total Start-up Requirements:	**$29,550**
Left to finance:	$0
Start-up Funding Plan	
Investment	
Owner	$10,000
Investor 2	$0
Other	$0
Total Investment	**$10,000**
Short-term Liabilities	
Unpaid Expenses	$0
Short-term Loans	$19,550
Interest-free Short-term Loans	$0
Subtotal Short-term Liabilities	$19,550
Long-term Liabilities	$0
Total Liabilities	**$19,550**
Loss at Start-up	($19,550)
Total Capital	**($9,550)**
Total Capital and Liabilities	**$10,000**
Checkline	$0

PROMOTIONAL SERVICES

GVI will offer the following promotional services to our clients:

- Distribute Public Service Announcements
- Purchase Radio Ads
- Purchase Newspaper Ads
- Offer Bulletin Announcements, Newsletters, and Personal Letters
- Print Bulletin Inserts/Flyers
- Submit Concert Information to the Press
- Display Posters
- Provide Press Kits
- Setup Telephone Interviews with Local Radio Stations
- Handle Merchandising of T-shirts, Posters, CDs, etc.

- Provide Lodging and Transportation
- Setup Facility and Site Selection
- Provide Food and Beverages for Artist
- Handle Technical Specifications, including Sound, System Needs, Lighting Needs, etc.

We will use several types of promotional strategies for our events, but the majority of our market will be reached by radio. **Promotional Strategies**

Media Profile/Demographics

1. **WWCK 105.5 FM**—265,000 listeners per day and, through the use of repeater facilities, are a major presence in the radio market throughout south central Michigan. Market: Lansing is the 16th ranked radio metro in the U.S. 42.9 percent of the adult 25+ population has at least some college education. Lansing metro retail sales total $5.4 billion per year. 95 percent of metro residents drive to work.

2. **WDZZ 92.7 FM**—100,000+ listeners per day. Target audience 92.7 3,000 watts 18-54 age group. #1 Urban Adult Contemporary alternative work station reaching adults of all ages. Is #1 in reaching our core audience of 18-34 urban listeners.

We will also use Print Media, Television, Online Information Services, Posters, Banners, and Event Programs.

Print Media (advertisements placed):

- Major Newspapers: *Oakland Press, Saginaw News, Detroit News, Detroit Free Press, Grand Rapids Press, Lansing State Journal, Ann Arbor News, Bay City Times, Kalamazoo Gazette, Chicago Tribune, Saturday Star (Ontario Edition).*

- Music Magazines: *Current Magazine, Jam Rag, Metro Times, Orbit, Between the Lines, Music Review Magazine, The Buzz! News, Real Detroit, Repeat the Beat, Mirror, BPM Culture, DJ, Revolution, DJ Times.*

In addition to advertisements placed, five waves of press releases with follow-up issued to 250 local newspapers and other periodicals in Michigan, Ohio, Illinois, Indiana, Wisconsin, and Windsor, Canada, listing supporting company as a major sponsor of the event.

Television

- Five waves of press releases with follow-up issued to 60 television stations in Michigan, Ohio, Illinois, Indiana, Wisconsin, and Windsor, Canada, listing supporting company as a major sponsor of the event.

Online Information Services

- Five waves of press releases with follow-up issued to over 2000 international magazines, newspapers, and major music/information sites. Third-party sponsoring will be made available to supporting company where suitable in posting company's banners on major websites.

Posters

- Logo inclusion on 2000 11' x 17' three-color posters regionally distributed.

Banners

- Sponsor's banners prominently displayed at major traffic flow points. Banners will be prominently displayed at the entrance to the event, Major sponsors will have their banners on stage either across the front or as a backdrop behind the entertainers.

Event Program

- Prominent logo inclusion in 10,000 copies of the official program for the Good Vibes Explosion 2002 and listing of supporting company as a categorized sponsor.

Dealing with Local Media

We will use the following methods in dealing with the media.

Create our own cover letter on our organization. Thank them for their time and commitment to working for the community to keep them informed of special programs. Make it personal and warm. Build an ongoing relationship.

Deliver the Press Kit in person if possible. Both the fact sheet and release should be in the hands of media representatives two to three weeks before the concert date, to accommodate deadlines and schedules, and facilitate coverage. But even if we don't make the deadlines for the concert, we will submit the information and make contact with editors and assignment desks to keep them aware that our ongoing events for the community through concerts and programs will enrich the community.

The Press Kit includes the following:

1. A Black and White Publicity Photo of the Artists (make sure we know how many to send).

2. Artist Fact Sheet. This has generic information about the artist.

3. News Release for Concert Night. The release is only intended to supply generic information for local communicators to build on. All details that the public needs to know in order to be aware of the event and consider attending should be in the local release. Always doublecheck to be sure that the information on how media people can reach us for questions or interview requests is clearly displayed.

   An important thing: Our office has clearly identified on the news release who media representatives should contact for information about our concert. If this information is not accurate please correct the contact persons name and daytime phone number before sending it to the media.

4. Sample Community Bulletin Board Announcement and/or PSA. Since formats of these vary widely, adapt the sample to suit requirements.

Media Contact Tips

Media Contacts: If we have not contacted local editors and news directors for previous events in our community, now is the time! Call for an appointment. If an in-person meeting is not possible, ask to speak on the phone or ask if they want to suggest a more convenient time to call back. Personal contact is extremely helpful in getting coverage.

Accompany your release by a call before or after it is received, or arrange an appointment so we can present it in person. In our contacts with local media, make it clear that concerts such as this one held at our local arenas are planned as an enrichment event to the community at large and that the community is invited, without a charge. Some news people assume events are for paying attendees only, so your casual mentions about the fact that the whole county is invited may be helpful in getting coverage.

Invite the editor or news director to attend the concert, underscoring its community-wide aspect, and the fact that you believe it will be a very special event.

Good Vibrations is focusing on four target audience groups that are of all racial backgrounds. The men's and women's age groups are:

1. 18-24
2. 25-34
3. 35-44
4. 45-54

Our marketing survey has revealed that, on average, approximately two thirds of concert attendees are female and one third are male. According to the U.S. Census Bureau, Census 2000, these people are between the ages of 18-54 who possess disposable incomes of $10,000-$40,000. According to Arbitron, most are employed with high school diplomas and 57.8 percent have some college education.

According to the Lansing Area Chamber of Commerce the year round population for Ingham County is 436,000 and 125,000 for the city of Lansing. According to Arbitron the median annual household income is $42,784 and median home value is $50,500.

Lansing Area Access/Restaurant/Tours/Traffic Flows

- Immediately adjacent to the Lansing IMA Arena is I-69 which sees over 25,000 cars pass by each day according to the Lansing Area Chamber of Commerce.
- The IMA has the convenience of being within 100 minutes of at least four major state universities, threee major concert arenas, and the State Capitol.
- With the intersection of I-496 and I-69 in Lansing, it is favorably positioned near the corridor, which is one of the county's major north-south interstate highway systems.
- A major shopping complex, The Westinghouse Center, is within walking distance as well as a number of dining and fast food establishments.

Currently Good Vibrations, Inc., is conducting a feasibility study in hopes of bringing at least four concerts to the lower Michigan area in 2002. These concerts will also feature food and novelties booths.

We expect a modest 5 percent growth in our target market over the next four years. The growth will increase our Ingham County target market from 236,683 to 287,691 by 2005.

Market Analysis

Potential Customers	Growth	2001	2002	2003	2004	2005	CAGR
Age Group 18-24	5%	41,869	43,962	46,160	48,468	50,891	5.00%
Age Group 25-34	5%	61,054	64,107	67,312	70,678	74,212	5.00%
Age Group 35-44	5%	70,052	73,555	77,233	81,095	85,150	5.00%
Age Group 45-54	5%	63,708	66,893	70,238	73,750	77,438	5.00%
Other	0%	0	0	0	0	0	0.00%
Total	**5.00%**	**236,683**	**248,517**	**260,943**	**273,991**	**287,691**	**5.00%**

Target Market Segment Strategy

Our strategy is to target individuals aged 18-54 because they are the largest population of music buyers and concert attendees. We will reach the 18-34 group by marketing some of the newest and heart-throbbing talents. For our 35-54 group we will market our older and more overlooked artists that this age group will recognized from the 1960s to the 1980s, from their school/college days along with the other R&B artists and music that appeals to them.

We cannot survive just waiting for the customer to come to us. Instead, we must get better at focusing on the specific market segments whose needs match our offerings. Focusing on targeted segments is the key to our future.

Therefore, we need to focus our marketing message and our product offerings. We need to develop our message, communicate it, and make good on it.

Our target market covers 15 lower Michigan counties, and people aged 18-54 which totals over 2.9 million individuals. This market is the largest segment of people that generally purchase tickets to music concerts. We expect 18 percent of this market to be urban males, 30 percent to be urban females, 15 percent to be suburban males and 37 percent to be suburban females.

Market Growth/ Industry

Attendance for top tours fell in 1999 while concert grosses jumped.

Analysis: The good news for the concert industry is that music fans in North America forked over a record $1.5 billion to buy concert tickets in 1999, according to industry trade magazine StarRate. The bad news for fans is that this feat was accomplished by increasing ticket prices rather than by increasing attendance.

StarRate's annual analysis of the concert business found that the average consumer paid $43.63 to see one of the top 50 tours in 1999, up more than $10 per ticket from 1998. But only 27.4 million tickets to the top 50 tours were sold in 1999, a decrease of 1.1 million from the previous year.

Aging rockers the Rolling Stones—who haven't been shy about asking a premium for tickets in recent years—were 1999's top grossing act, ringing up $66.7 million in ticket sales in North America, according to StarRate. The Stones' "No Security" tour, for which fans paid an average of nearly $110 per ticket, topped 1999's gross charts despite drawing nearly a half million fewer fans in North America than did the No. 2 Bruce Springsteen tour, for which tickets cost an average of about $60.

Trade magazine *Entertainment Business*, whose statistics include shows outside North America (and which has a slightly different reporting period), pegged the Stones' 1999 take at $89.2 million and named the band as the top touring act of the 1990s, with more than $750 million in ticket sales for the decade. Their closest competitors were the Grateful Dead ($285 million) and U2 ($282.5 million).

The Rolling Stones sold out 42 of 45 shows reported *Entertainment Business* for 1999, but there are signs that high ticket prices kept fans away from some events. Sting's "Brand New Day" tour, for example, attracted a disappointing average of 4,600 fans per city, perhaps because the typical ticket sold for nearly $80.

Neil Young, with an average ticket price near $70, averaged attendance of less than 5,000 per city. Meanwhile, Tom Petty and the Heartbreakers and John Mellencamp, acts with fan bases similar to Young's, both charged about half as much for tickets as Young did and both drew an average of well over 10,000 fans per city.

Premium prices weren't charged by every act in the top 10. The average NSync ticket went for $28.62; the Dave Matthews Band, $34.44; Shania Twain, $37.65; Backstreet Boys,

$37.24; the George Strait Country Music Festival, $40.80; and Neil Diamond, $36.86. All had prices comfortably below the average. Among StarRate's top 50 tours, the lowest ticket prices were charged by the Goo Goo Dolls, $19.37.

The spike in 1999's average ticket prices can be attributed in large part to the Rolling Stones, who charged a much higher ticket price for their "No Security" arena tour than for their "Bridges to Babylon" stadium tour of 1998, which commanded prices in the $65 range. But also feeding the trend is the increasingly common practice of charging significantly higher prices for venues' best seats.

Also contributing to rising ticket prices is the rapid consolidation of the concert promotions business, which had traditionally been controlled by independent promoters who generally booked concerts in one region. That changed in 1997, when a new company called BEST Entertainment snapped up many of the top independents. BEST's big catch of 1999 was The Next Adventure, which, rather than controlling a region, specializes in promoting major stadium tours like "Bridges to Babylon."

BEST is particularly powerful in the amphitheater market because, during its buying spree, the company purchased promoters who also owned venues. BEST now owns venues in about 30 of top 50 markets, and it self-produced about 20 amphitheater tours in the summer of 1999.

These efforts have made BEST the dominant player in the industry. According to StarRate, BEST had a hand in more than 60 percent of the 200 top-grossing concert dates of 1999. BEST-promoted shows grossed $310 million in 1999, according to *Entertainment Business,* well ahead of the $118 million take of the number two player, House of Blues Concerts.

BEST's strategy for recouping its approximately $1.5 billion investment in the concert business has been to increase sales of sponsorships—which includes the placement of a business' name on a venue—and to sell more advertising. BEST also has increased the marketing muscle behind the subscription series at its amphitheaters.

Demographics are also working to increase ticket prices. As the spending power of baby boomers grows, so does the amount of money they will spend to see their favorite acts. That fact isn't lost on the acts and their management, who demand more money from promoters. Thus tours like those of the Rolling Stones, Bette Midler (with an average ticket price of $81.23, according to StarRate), and Andrea Bocelli ($101.34) can command higher ticket prices than ever.

One of the more encouraging signs to those in the concert industry was the emergence of acts that appeal to young audiences. While surveys of the top-grossing tours are often dominated by long-established acts, 1999's top tours included teen favorites NSync and Backstreet Boys.

Also of note is Shania Twain, who began her first headlining tour in 1997 and quickly emerged as the hottest country act since Garth Brooks.

Indicators weren't as positive for country music as a whole, however, as the genre didn't have the benefit of a Garth Brooks tour in 1999. The George Strait Festival continued to roll, and Brooks & Dunn grossed an estimated $10 million, according to *Entertainment Business.* But overall, gross country concert dollars were down 16 percent from 1998.

Despite the festival's calamitous end, Woodstock '99 was the single highest-grossing concert event of the year, according to *Entertainment Business.* Nearly 187,000 people attended the July 22-25 event, and its total ticket gross was nearly $29 million.

The year-end charts issued by both StarRate and *Entertainment Business* are compiled from unaudited box office reports voluntarily filed by concert promoters, and promoters are told that the numbers they report should reflect the face price of tickets. The numbers don't include taxes, ticketing company convenience fees, parking, and other charges.

Top 10 Tours (StarRate)
Act/Gross (in millions)

1. Rolling Stones/$66.7
2. Bruce Springsteen and the E Street Band/$61.4
3. NSync/$51.5
4. Dave Matthews Band/$48.5
5. Shania Twain/$40.8
6. Cher/$37.7
7. Backstreet Boys/$37.1
8. Elton John/$32.5
9. George Strait Country Music Festival/$32.4
10. Bette Midler/$31.7

Top 10 Tours *(Entertainment Business)*
Act/Gross (in millions)

1. Rolling Stones/$89.2
2. Bruce Springsteen and the E Street Band/$53
3. Dave Matthews Band/$44.6
4. NSync/$44.3
5. Shania Twain/$36.6
6. George Strait Country Music Festival/$32.4
7. Cher/$31.5
8. Neil Diamond/$31.3
9. Celine Dion/$26.8
10. Backstreet Boys/$24.5

As you can see Good Vibrations, Inc., has chosen a prime time to start a concert promotions business.

STRATEGY

As stated above our strategy is a combination of promotions and target marketing. We will focus on concert attendees ages 18-54 and utilize our detailed promotional strategies to reach these individuals. The target customer will also consist of baby boomers and R&B music lovers.

Implementation Steps

Before we begin our marketing and promotions, we will confirm all of the following items:

- Check with other area concert arenas, churches, radio stations, and promoters for conflicting events
- Confirm our concert location in writing
- Confirm the date and artist in writing with the agent
- Confirm that the radio station will support us
- Thoroughly read artist's rider and contract to be sure we can fulfill it

14 Weeks Prior to Concert

Our tour posters, mailers, tickets, and flyers are ordered from the printer. The cost of our promotional pieces and tickets are to be absorbed by getting a local business to use the backs of tickets as a coupon, or by placing logos on our promotional pieces. Also, we are seeking to partner with our local radio station. We can do this by placing their logo on our promotional items in exchange for substantial discounts for on-air advertising and underwriting. The most important thing we will do is to start a "word of mouth" campaign immediately. We will make calls to local clubs, etc., and get the word out about our event. This is very effective and helps get the "buzz" going. This will begin immediately!

Determining what type of concert we are promoting we then acquire our mailing labels for a regional mailing for that particular industry. At least two to three times the venue capacity are mailed out. If the venue holds 500, between 1000-1500 mailers are sent out. All local barber shops and beauty salons are then contacted.

Next ticket sales at ticket outlets and music stores are set up. They are then listed on our promotional materials. All outlets are informed that the receipts and excess tickets are to be picked up no later than the day before the concert. Our music stores are then informed that even if they sell all of their allotted tickets UNDER NO CIRCUMSTANCES should they tell their customers the concert is sold out unless we personally tell them so.

13 Weeks Prior to Concert

Our mailing is sent out. We will use volunteers to help with our bulk mailing and as a back up we will contact our printer; they offer mailing services to promoters for a very reasonable fee.

12 Weeks Prior to Concert

Our flyers advertising the concert will be distributed throughout our city. Distribute flyers advertising the concert to all major clubs in the area. Also, flyers will be posted in local businesses and restaurants. Flyers are also distributed to our ticket outlets, and posters are being displayed in a prominent location in the selling outlets.

Our tour publicist is provided the following information:

1. Venue name
2. Venue street address, including city and state
3. Show time
4. Ticket prices (specify ticket breakdown... $9 groups/$12 advanced, etc.)
5. Local phone number for ticket information
6. The name of the radio station(s) we are doing our primary promotions with, including the call letters, phone numbers, and the name of our contact at the station

If any stations or newspapers contact us directly, they will be supplied with all the details of our concert.

11 Weeks Prior to Concert

Tickets will be distributed to our outlets. They are adequately supplied with tickets, flyers, and a poster. The poster is hung in a prominent location.

8 Weeks Prior to Concert

Our partnering with a local radio station is arranged and they have started running spots/ underwriting announcements—approximately 20 per week . We have inquired with the radio station about contests and giveaways, such as tickets, CDs, cassettes, and "prize packages." Most stations jump at the chance to center a huge promotion surrounding a concert. We are working mainly with our local station. The amount of "free" promotion they give us each time they giveaway tickets on the air will offset our expense of supplying them with a reasonable amount of free tickets. We will target our ticket giveaway at 20 pair of tickets. The product giveaway is available through management or the station can contact the radio promotions department at the artist's record company. We will always begin our radio campaign at least eight weeks before our concert. We are airing between 3-6 spots or more each day. Our radio promotion is always started early on. We can always reduce spots when we sell out our concert.

Also, the stations in our area are provided with all the information regarding our concert. We understand that waiting too late to begin our radio promotion will adversely affect our ticket sales. Although radio advertising does cost, it is an incredible means to effectively communicate with the concertgoers that will attend our concert.

6 Weeks Prior to Concert

We are following up to see that our local radio station received promotional giveaway products, including ticket giveaways. We are also contacting the artist's management about a radio interview. This is scheduled by week four.

4 Weeks Prior to Concert

We are now running the second "flight" of spots/underwriting announcements with our local radio station. Approximately 20 per week up to our show date or until the tickets have sold out. Radio spots will remain airing until the day of the show unless we sell out our tickets. We also are sending out a second mailing to "concertgoers" in our area at this time. Lists are available from Dunhams Direct.

Concert posters are placed in prominent locations throughout our community such as: local grocery stores, arcades, malls, restaurants, and any industry-owned businesses. We are also making sure all posters are still up at our area barber shops and beauty salons.

3 Weeks Prior to Concert

Arrange for a volunteer to call all major clubs to remind them about the concert. This is a very important part of the last-minute promotion of our concert. Even though we may have already contacted our local clubs, we are going ahead and giving them another "reminder" call. It is also being mentioned that we have group rate tickets available to groups of ten or more. Connecting with our local clubs is a vital link to the success of our concert.

Week of Concert

All ticket monies and/or tickets are picked up from the outlets no later than the day prior to the concert. This will give us time to make an accounting of all tickets sold at advance and group rates. Group rates will not be applicable at the door nor should any tickets not already paid for be held at the door. It is common for people to call, ask us to hold 30 tickets, and then not show up or appear with just a few people.

If we have not already discussed arrival times and last-minute details with the artist's road manager, he/she will be called to confirm appropriate arrangements.

Hotels are reserved and prepaid in the artist's name. There is often confusion at the desk so we will be sure that the artist's name is correctly spelled and, if possible, a confirmation number is assigned and given to the road manager.

Day of Concert

We are making sure that our crew will be present at the pre-determined time. The hall manager should have the building open and ready for set-up.

We will brief ushers and staff on their duties at least two hours before concert time. We are making sure they are aware of the fact that due to recording contracts, no tape recorders or video cameras are permitted in the hall without written approval of the record company or management. Photographs are not permitted.

We are meeting with our road manager to cover details on set-up and load-out as well as sound check, etc.

We have tables set up at the rear of the concert arena and have several people available to help with sales of records and T-shirts, etc.

We have an expense record sheet completed (door sales can be added following the concert) and receipts on hand so we can settle up quickly if percentages are involved.

Meal(s) for artists and crew are provided.

Preparation time with artists and crew usually takes place an hour or so prior to the concert. Doors usually open to the public 30-45 minutes before concert time.

Mailing list cards are passed out (if appropriate) to get the name and address of all who attended so we can send flyers to them in the future. More concertgoers will fill out cards if a drawing is attached. Drop boxes are placed by entrances for cards.

After the Concert

We are making sure that enough crew members are present to help artists with load-out.

- We will then send thank-you notes to all volunteers.
- We pay all our bills.

Sound Check

Sound check should be scheduled at least two hours before the concert start time. A set time should be agreed upon before the event date. Plan to keep people out of the arena during sound check. The sound system and stage should be set when artists arrive. They usually like to take their time during sound check to make sure things go as smooth as possible during the concert. We will have our most qualified sound engineer on hand to run the sound. If additional equipment is rented or brought in, we will be certain that the sound engineer is experienced in operating it or has someone with him who is. Also, we must be sure that the sound engineer is at the site the whole time (sound check, concert time, and tear down). Concert order, track queues, and equipment instructions should be completed prior to sound checks.

Product Sales

GVI will have at least two trustworthy, responsible individuals available to handle the sale of merchandise. We may need more sales personnel depending on the size of the building. The vendor should provide a starting bank for the sales personnel for transactions. Sales personnel will be expected at the product table one hour prior to the concert, during the concert, and one hour after the concert.

It is necessary for the promoter to provide at least one to two eight-foot tables (depending on the size of the building) to display the products. We will place the tables in areas most heavily traveled by the concert attendees—near entrances and exits closest to parking areas.

The artist may have the right, but not the obligation, to sell products at the concert. The artist pays no charges or fees on merchandise sold at the event if stated in their contracts.

Logistical Specifications

Lodging /Transportation

When necessary, we will provide one double room at a national chain hotel (Holiday Inn or like quality). The hotel should be as close as possible to the concert site. Confirmation of reservation should be returned with the Concert Confirmation Form.

When the artist is flying to the event, we will provide transportation to and from the airport, concert site and hotel. We will be notified of the cost of the air fare. We plan to pay this at the time the airplane ticket is booked. The artist arrival time, flight number, airline, etc., will be communicated with us as soon as possible prior to the event.

Possible Competition

The following are possible competitors:

1. XYZ Music Presents
2. WHYZ Presents
3. Mega Explosion Concert
4. River Run Casino
5. MTV ABX
6. Chandler Park Music Festival
7. Industry & Stoned Productions
8. Molehill Productions

These companies are listed as "possible" competition because we know with our unique marketing strategies and professionalism we can gain an edge over them.

Competitive Edge

Good Vibrations, Inc., currently has artists waiting to be promoted year round, instead of just during the summer. Our competitive edge will be that we will continuously market the artist and be more than a seasonal promoter. We operate with the utmost professionalism and offer quality service to all of our clients, not just the most famous ones.

Pricing

Our ticket pricing will average about $35 for floor tickets and $27.50 for general admissions. Our average arena capacity will be about 2,500 to 4,500 seating capacity. Each concert will be budgeted out in regards to individual charges such as but not limited to:

- Arena rental
- Ticketmaster fees
- Stage use
- Forklift
- Spotlights
- Novelty Sales
- Parking
- Insurance Bond
- Switchboard
- House sound
- Risk Management
- Technical Director
- Security
- Stage hands
- Follow spots
- Set-up/Clean-up
- Utilities

- Marquee set-up
- First Aid
- Lighting Design Fee

AIDCA, or attention, interest, desire, conviction and action are the five stages of the sales call are how we'll approach our prospective clients. If this approach fails, we will politely thank them for their time and discontinue the call.

**Sales Strategy/
AIDCA**

Possible Leads

Possible leads will derive from advertising firms, martial arts, travel agencies, automotive dealers, airlines, apparel, electronic stores, art supplies, youth organizations and centers, athletic organizations, ball clubs and organization, bartending schools, band instruments, beauty salons and schools, banks, cellular services and pagers, bible schools, colleges, pool parlors, bookstores, beverage manufacturers, sporting goods, apartments, pet supplies, car alarms, churches, basketball clubs, hockey clubs, soccer clubs, credit card companies, fast-food restaurants, employment agencies, fitness clubs, vitamin and health stores, travel agencies, furniture stores, manufacturers, grocers, hotels and motels, ice cream manufacturers, music stores, mobile home manufacturers, and brokers, and many more.

Key points of interest for sales calls:

- Strive to set-up an appointment as opposed to a sale.
- Target your sales drives.
- Keep features in reserve as aids to tip the balance in your favor.
- Elaborate on product or service features, benefits, and company knowledge.
- Never criticize the competition, but always aim to outperform it.
- Above all, SMILE!

Sales of sponsorships will be based on the collective expenses of each individual concert. Our goal is to know the total expenses of each concert before we promote it. Once we know the expense total, we will know how many sponsorships we need to sell.

Sponsorship/Advertising will play a vital role in the success and growth of Good Vibrations. Before the first ticket is sold, sponsorship and program advertising is our primary resource to ensure a successful event for Lansing and Ingham County. Without such support, Good Vibrations would simply cease to get off the launching pad. This year is our inaugural year and we anticipate it to be a watershed for the four-concert event called the "Good Vibes Explosion 2002."

Sponsorships

Good Vibrations's use of Internet, television, radio, and print advertising, as well as commissioned art posters, official programs, brochures, flyers, T-shirts, banners, direct e-mail, and extensive signage will blanket south central Michigan and deliver sponsor/advertiser's and the Good Vibrations's messages. We estimate that the event marketing campaign will generate 2.9 million impressions within 90 minutes of Lansing, effectively tapping into a market with an Effective Buying Income (EBI) of $38 billion.

The different sponsorship/advertising packages and their corresponding benefits and features are described within the following pages. Each package delivers incredible value, allowing your company to fulfill its marketing missions in a cost effective, culturally beneficial manner. All sponsors receive an entertainment package consisting of tickets and backstage and hospitality passes to all indoor and outdoor events. If our sponsors do not see an "exact fit," we are open and willing to create a special program for their company.

Sponsorship Title Endowment

Marquee Sponsor	$25,000.00
Corporate Sponsor	$15,000.00
Principal Sponsor	$10,000.00
Patron Sponsor	$5,000.00
Associate Sponsor	$2,500.00
Affiliate Sponsor	$1,000.00
Booster	$500.00

Marquee Sponsor

The Marquee Sponsor will achieve unparalleled exposure at an unsurpassed value for their company through title sponsorship of the Good Vibes Explosion 2002. Grab the attention of a desirable target with millions of favorable impressions. Demonstrate their company's commitment to community service and preservation of America's unique musical heritage. Receive top billing across all the board in all media in all mentions.

The benefits afforded to the sole Marquee Sponsor of the Good Vibes Explosion 2002 will include:

- Their company's name will become the lead part of the Festival's name, i.e.: "The (corporate identity or product brand)" Good Vibes Explosion 2002.
- Full inclusion in primary position of all paid and trade television, radio and print advertising and promotional pieces, press releases, indoor event signage, and public service announcements.
- Continuous listings and press coverage in print, radio, and television during said event.
- Top billing mentions during emcee breaks and intros at indoor and outdoor events.
- License to use event name and trademarks in your company's promotional activities, subject to GVI review.
- First choice vendor booth placement (booth at GVI's expense) with product exclusivity at event with right to sell, use, or display products (within GVI's guidelines).
- Paramount banner placement at all indoor and outdoor events (subject to venue rules).
- Marquee sponsor title appearing on Good Vibes Explosion 2002 T-shirts.
- Largest size sponsor advertisement in the official Good Vibes Explosion 2002 program guide, published by Small Business Designs and Graphics and distributed at the event and in south central Michigan.
- Lead appearances in all event program, brochures, posters and flyers, and event website for one year, with linking.
- First option to be involved in video and audio recording and broadcast projects.
- Additional banner placements (up to four total) at indoor and outdoor events.
- Additional signage at concession and souvenir areas.
- Custom entertainment package to reward employees, customers, and others. Consists of eight VIP passes which feature a "Meet and Greet" session with headlining artists (subject to artist contractual riders) in addition to total access to all events and 20 sponsorship passes which allow for seats in both indoor events.

Corporate Sponsor

For the Corporate Sponsor we will tailor their contribution to a slightly more modest level than the Marquee Sponsorship, but they will receive incredible exposure nonetheless. Each opportunity to announce and credit the event will be followed immediately by a phrase such as "Presented by (their company or product brand)". Show the target audience their company's strong commitment to new American music and community service.

The Benefits afforded to Corporate Sponsors of the Good Vibes Explosion 2002 will include:

- Full inclusion in secondary position of all paid and trade television, radio and print advertising and promotional pieces, press releases, indoor event signage, and public service announcements.
- Continuous listings and press coverage in print, radio, and television during said event.
- Prominent mentions during emcee breaks and intros at indoor and outdoor events.
- License to use event name and trademarks in your company's promotional activities, subject to GVI review.
- Preferred vendor booth placement (booth at GVI's expense) with product exclusivity at event with right to sell, use, or display products (within GVI's guidelines).
- Preferred stage wings banner placement at all indoor and outdoor events (subject to venue rules).
- Second largest size sponsor advertisement in the official Good Vibes Explosion's program guide, published by Small Business Designs and Graphics and distributed at the event and south central Michigan.
- Corporate sponsor title appearing on Good Vibes Explosion 2002 T-shirts.
- Second largest appearances in all event program, brochures, posters and flyers and event website for one year, with linking.
- Additional signage at concession and souvenir areas.
- Custom entertainment package to reward employees, customers, and others. Consists of six VIP passes which feature a "Meet and Greet" session with headlining artists (subject to artist contractual riders) in addition to total access to all events and 12 sponsorship passes which allow for seats in all events.

We're adding this sponsorship level for sponsors who are trying to reach a new, expanded market (from local to regional or national).

Principal Sponsor

The benefits afforded to Principal Sponsors of the Good Vibes Explosion 2002 will include:

- Full inclusion in third position of all paid and trade television, radio and print advertising and promotional pieces, press releases, indoor event signage, and public service announcements.
- Continuous listings and press coverage in print, radio, and television during said event.
- Mentions during emcee breaks and intros at indoor and outdoor events.
- Vendor booth placement (booth at GVI's expense) with product exclusivity at event with right to sell, use, or display products (within GVI's guidelines).
- Stage wings banner placement at all indoor and outdoor events (subject to venue rules).
- Third largest size sponsor advertisement in the official Good Vibes Explosion 2002 program guide, published by Small Business Designs and Graphics and distributed at the event and south central Michigan.
- Principal sponsor title appearing on Good Vibes Explosion 2002 T-shirts.
- Third largest appearances in all event program, brochures, posters and flyers, and event website for one year, with linking.
- Custom entertainment package to reward employees, customers, and others. Consists of four VIP passes which feature a "Meet and Greet" session with headlining artists (subject to artist contractual riders) in addition to total access to all events and eight sponsorship passes which allow for seats in all events.

Patron Sponsor

No sponsorship can do so much for so little money. Gain millions of favorable impressions at an incredible value. This is the minimum level of sponsorship necessary to receive television-advertising benefits. Help one of the first and best American music festivals to grow and touch people with the uplifting power of Rap and Dance music.

The benefits afforded to Patron Sponsors of the Good Vibes Explosion 2002 will include:

- Inclusions in all paid and trade radio and print advertising and promotional pieces, press releases, and indoor event signage and public service announcements.
- Mentions during emceed breaks and intros at indoor and outdoor events.
- Vendor booth placement (booth at GVI's expense) with product exclusivity at event with right to sell, use, or display products (within GVI's guidelines).
- Stage wings banner placement at all indoor and outdoor events (subject to venue rules).
- One-fourth size sponsor advertisement in the official Good Vibes Explosion 2002 program guide published by Small Business Designs and Graphics and distributed at the event and south central Michigan.
- Patron sponsor title appearing on Good Vibes Explosion T-shirts.
- Appearances in all event program, brochures, posters and flyers, and event website for one year, with linking.
- Custom entertainment package to reward employees, customers, and others. Consists of two VIP passes which feature a "Meet and Greet" session with headlining artists (subject to artist contractual riders) in addition to total access to all events and six sponsorship passes which allow for seats in all events.

Associate Sponsor

The Associate Sponsor will be able to promote their company to thousands of potential local customers who are proven spenders! This is the minimum level of sponsorship necessary to qualify for booth space at the event.

The benefits afforded to Associate Sponsors of the Good Vibes Explosion 2002 will include:

- Inclusions in all paid and trade radio and print advertising and promotional pieces, press releases, and indoor event signage and public service announcements.
- Mentions during emceed breaks and intros at indoor and outdoor events.
- Stage wings banner placement at all indoor and outdoor events (subject to venue rules).
- One-fourth size black and white sponsor advertisement in the official Good Vibes Explosion 2002 program guide, published by Small Business Designs and Graphics and distributed at the event and south central Michigan.
- Associate sponsor title appearing on Good Vibes Explosion 2002 T-shirts.
- Appearances in all event posters and flyers, and event website for one year.
- Custom entertainment package to reward employees, customers, and others. Consists of two VIP passes which feature a "Meet and Greet" session with headlining artists (subject to artist contractual riders) in addition to total access to all events and four sponsorship passes which allow for seats in all events.

Affiliate Sponsor

The Affiliate Sponsor will be able to promote their company to thousands of potential local customers who are proven spenders!

The benefits afforded to Affiliate Sponsors of the Good Vibes Explosion 2002 will include:

- Inclusions in print advertising, press releases, and indoor event signage and public service announcements.

- Mentions during emceed breaks and intros at indoor and outdoor events.
- Business card-size black and white sponsor advertisement in the official Good Vibes Explosion 2002 program guide, published by Small Business Designs and Graphics and distributed at the event and south central Michigan.
- Affiliate sponsor title appearing on Good Vibes Explosion 2002 T-shirts.
- Appearances in all event posters and flyers, and event website.
- Custom entertainment package consisting of two VIP passes which feature a "Meet and Greet" session with headlining artists (subject to artist contractual riders) in addition to total access to all events and two sponsorship passes which allow for seats in all events.

Booster Sponsor

The Booster Sponsor will be able to promote their company to thousands of potential local customers who are proven spenders!

The benefits afforded to Booster Sponsors of the Good Vibes Explosion 2002 will include:

- Mentions during emceed breaks.
- Mention in the official Good Vibes Explosion 2002 program guide, published by Small Business Designs and Graphics and distributed at the event and south central Michigan.
- Booster sponsor title appearing on Good Vibes Explosion 2002 T-shirts.
- Appearances in all event posters and event website.
- Custom entertainment package consisting of two VIP passes which feature a "Meet and Greet" session with headlining artists (subject to artist contractual riders).

Sales Forecast

We plan to host four concerts a year over the next three years. In 2002 we will host concerts on the following dates:

- Valentine's Day, February 14
- Easter, March 30
- Mother's Day, May 19
- Michigan State University Smash Month Concert, September 21

The following table gives a rundown on forecasted sales. We anticipate selling at least half of the available seats or 2,500 tickets for each of the first three concerts at our lowest price of $27.50. This would average approximate sales of $68,750 each for the first three concerts. For the Michigan State University concert we anticipate a sellout crowd of 4,500 seats at our maximum price of $37 or at least $166,500 in projected sales as recent similar concerts have shown. Then in 2003 we plan to increase our $27.50 tickets to $37, and our $37 tickets to $47. In 2004 we plan to increase our $37 tickets to $42 and our $47 tickets to $52. Those increases will help to promote growth in our cash flow. We also plan to have teen parties every month starting in January 2002. The ticket costs to the parties will be $10 a ticket for the first year and $15 a ticket for the second year. The parties will be for 50 to 100 teens. Our conservative sales forecast reflects the lower number of teens attending or purchasing tickets.

We expect our expenses to decrease about 10 percent as our events become annual events and not much advertising and marketing is required.

Sales Forecast

Continued

Sales Forecast

Sales	FY2002	FY2003	FY2004
Valentine's Day Concert	$68,750	$92,500	$105,000
Easter Concert	$68,750	$92,500	$105,000
Mother's Day Concert	$68,750	$92,500	$105,000
Michigan State University			
Smash Month Concert	$165,600	$211,500	$234,000
Teen Parties	$4,500	$6,000	$9,000
Total Sales	**$377,250**	**$495,000**	**$558,000**
Direct Cost of Sales			
Valentine's Day Concert	$28,050	$25,245	$22,721
Easter Concert	$28,050	$25,245	$22,721
Mother's Day Concert	$28,050	$25,245	$22,721
Michigan State University			
Smash Month Concert	$39,550	$35,595	$32,036
Teen Parties	$1,800	$2,400	$2,400
Subtotal Cost of Sales	**$125,500**	**$113,730**	**$102,599**

Milestones

The accompanying table lists important program milestones, with dates and managers in charge, and budgets for each. The budgets are set for the cost of everything except the cost of the artist and will be adjusted depending on which artist we choose to use. The milestone schedule indicates our emphasis on planning for implementation. Our pre-paid sponsorships will help to offset any additional costs needed outside our budget.

What the table doesn't show is the commitment behind it. We will hold monthly follow-up meetings every month to discuss the variance and course corrections.

Milestone	Start Date	End Date	Budget	Manager	Department
Valentines Day Concert	9/6/2001	2/14/2002	$30,000	Roland Wilson	Promotions
Easter Day Concert	12/22/2001	3/30/2002	$30,000	Roland Wilson	Promotions
Mother's Day Concert	2/10/2002	5/19/2002	$30,000	Roland Wilson	Promotions
Michigan State University					
Smash Month Concert	6/15/2002	9/21/2002	$45,000	Roland Wilson	Promotions
Totals			**$135,000**		

MANAGEMENT SUMMARY

The initial management team depends on the founder himself, and additional back-up if needed. As we grow, we will take on additional office help and sales people.

Personnel Plan

Roland Wilson will arrange the concerts, make sure everything goes according to schedule, that and the bills are paid in full and on time. For the first year he will not receive any pay. All the profits will be put back into the business. Within the second year Roland will seek to hire a staff that includes a Secretary and Sponsorship Sales Rep, each being paid $25,000 a year without benefits. Roland will begin receiving an Owner's Draw in the amount of $1000 per week the third year. He will initially cut costs in the start-up phase by offering college student's working internships with his company.

Personnel Plan	FY2002	FY2003	FY2004
Secretary/Receptionist	$0	$25,000	$27,000
Sponsorship Sales Rep	$0	$25,000	$27,000
Owner's Draw	$0	$0	$52,000
Total Payroll	**$0**	**$50,000**	**$106,000**
Total Headcount	1	3	3
Payroll Burden	$0	$7,500	$15,900
Total Payroll Expenditures	**$0**	**$57,500**	**$121,900**

FINANCIAL PLAN

- We want to finance growth mainly through cash flow. We recognize that this means we will have to grow more slowly than we might like.
- The most important factor in our case is sponsorship sales. The sales will offset any expenses we incur with promoting our concerts.
- We are also assuming start-up capital of $10,000.

Important Assumptions

The financial plan depends on important assumptions, most of which are shown in the following table as annual assumptions. At least we are planning on the problem and dealing with it. Interest rates, tax rates, and personnel burden are based on conservative assumptions.

Some of the more important underlying assumptions are:

- We assume a strong economy, without major recession.
- We assume, of course, that there are no unforeseen changes in concert promotions to make our musical artists immediately obsolete.

General Assumptions	FY2002	FY2003	FY2004
Short-term Interest Rate %	10.00%	10.00%	10.00%
Long-term Interest Rate %	10.00%	10.00%	10.00%
Payment Days Estimator	30	30	30
Collection Days Estimator	45	45	45
Inventory Turnover Estimator	6.00	6.00	6.00
Tax Rate %	25.00%	25.00%	25.00%
Expenses in Cash %	10.00%	10.00%	10.00%
Sales on Credit %	0.00%	0.00%	0.00%
Personnel Burden %	15.00%	15.00%	15.00%

Break-even Analysis

Our break-even analysis will be based on each concert and the following facts:

- Cost of promoting the event
- Cost of talent and talents expenses
- Cost of location and amenities
- How much in sponsorships do we need to sell and by what timeframe

All of the costs for these items are yet to be determined.

Projected Profit and Loss

Our projected profit and loss is shown on the following table, with sales modestly increasing over the next three years.

Projected Profit and Loss (Income Statement)	FY2002	FY2003	FY2004
Sales	$377,250	$495,000	$558,000
Direct Cost of Sales	$125,500	$113,730	$102,599
Production Payroll	$0	$0	$0
Other	$0	$0	$0
Total Cost of Sales	**$125,500**	**$113,730**	**$102,599**
Gross Margin	$251,750	$381,270	$455,401
Gross Margin %	66.73%	77.02%	81.61%
Operating Expenses			
Sales and Marketing Expenses			
Sales and Marketing Payroll	$0	$0	$0
Advertising/Promotion	$8,600	$7,740	$6,966
Travel	$12,000	$12,000	$12,000
Sound	$4,000	$4,000	$4,000
Accommodations	$2,000	$2,000	$2,000
Security	$24,000	$24,000	$24,000
Miscellaneous	$0	$0	$0
Total Sales and Marketing Expenses	**$0**	**$0**	**$0**
Sales and Marketing %	0.00%	0.00%	0.00%
General and Administrative Expenses			
General and Administrative Payroll	$0	$0	$0
Payroll Expense	$0	$50,000	$106,000
Payroll Burden	$0	$7,500	$15,900
Depreciation	$0	$0	$0
Telephone	$600	$600	$600
Business Insurance	$500	$500	$500
Concert Facility Insurance	$500	$500	$500
Total General & Administrative Expenses	**$0**	**$0**	**$0**
General and Administrative %	0.00%	0.00%	0.00%
Other Expenses			
Other Payroll	$0	$0	$0
Accountant	$935	$1,020	$1,020
Total Other Expenses	**$0**	**$0**	**$0**
Other %	0.00%	0.00%	0.00%
Total Operating Expenses	**$53,135**	**$109,860**	**$173,486**
Profit Before Interest and Taxes	$198,615	$271,410	$281,915
Interest Expense Short-term	$1,955	$1,955	$1,955
Interest Expense Long-term	$0	$0	$0
Taxes Incurred	$49,165	$67,364	$69,990
Extraordinary Items	$0	$0	$0
Net Profit	**$147,495**	**$202,091**	**$209,970**
Net Profit/Sales	**39.10%**	**40.83%**	**37.63%**

The following cash flow projections show the annual amounts only. Cash flow projections are critical to our success. The monthly cash flow is shown in the illustration, with one bar representing the cash flow per month, and the other the monthly balance. The annual cash flow figures are included here and the more important detailed monthly numbers are included in the appendices.

Projected Cash Flow

Projected Cash Flow	FY2002	FY2003	FY2004
Net Profit	$147,495	$202,091	$209,970
Plus:			
Depreciation	$0	$0	$0
Change in Accounts Payable	$69,305	($55,813)	$3,825
Current Borrowing (repayment)	$0	$0	$0
Increase (decrease) Other Liabilities	$0	$0	$0
Long-term Borrowing (repayment)	$0	$0	$0
Capital Input	$0	$0	$0
Subtotal	**$216,800**	**$146,278**	**$213,795**
Less:			
Change in Accounts Receivable	$0	$0	$0
Change in Inventory	$0	$0	$0
Change in Other Short-term Assets	$0	$0	$0
Capital Expenditure	$0	$0	$0
Dividends	$0	$0	$0
Subtotal	**$0**	**$0**	**$0**
Net Cash Flow	**$216,800**	**$146,278**	**$213,795**
Cash Balance	**$266,800**	**$272,078**	**$586,873**

The balance sheet in the following table shows managed but sufficient growth of net worth, and a sufficiently healthy financial position. The monthly estimates are included in the appendices.

Projected Balance Sheet

Projected Balance Sheet	FY2002	FY2003	FY2004
Assets			
Short-term Assets			
Cash	$226,800	$373,078	$586,873
Accounts Receivable	$0	$0	$0
Inventory	$0	$0	$0
Other Short-term Assets	$0	$0	$0
Total Short-term Assets	**$226,800**	**$373,078**	**$586,873**
Long-term Assets			
Capital Assets	$0	$0	$0
Accumulated Depreciation	$0	$0	$0
Total Long-term Assets	**$0**	**$0**	**$0**
Total Assets	**$226,800**	**$373,078**	**$586,873**
Liabilities and Capital			
Accounts Payable	$69,305	$13,492	$17,316
Short-term Notes	$19,550	$19,550	$19,550
Other Short-term Liabilities	$0	$0	$0
Subtotal Short-term Liabilities	**$88,855**	**$33,042**	**$36,866**
Long-term Liabilities	$0	$0	$0
Total Liabilities	**$88,855**	**$33,042**	**$36,866**

Projected Cash Flow

Projected Balance Sheet

Projected Balance Sheet	Paid in Capital	$10,000	$10,000	$10,000
	Retained Earnings	($19,550)	$127,945	$330,036
Continued	Earnings	$147,495	$202,091	$209,970
	Total Capital	**$137,945**	**$340,036**	**$550,006**
	Total Liabilities and Capital	**$226,800**	**$373,078**	**$586,873**
	Net Worth	**$137,945**	**$340,036**	**$550,006**

Risks

Our risks for concert promotions are minimal. Our sponsorships will cover the out-of-pocket expenses up front. Any ticket sales will be mostly profit. In case of a concert cancellation, it will be stated in our contracts with the artists that they will be responsible for any fees or expenses we incur because of their cancellation.

Exit Strategy

We will consider using one of the forms of exit listed below, should our business come short of meeting our objectives over the next five years.

- Selling all or a portion of the business
- Passing the business on to a family member
- Selling to an Employee Stock Ownership Plan (ESOP)
- Taking the company public
- Liquidation

Each of the above forms of exit involves a variety of considerations. These considerations will be worked out between the owner, legal counsel, an accountant, and GVI's staff.

This page left intentionally blank to accommodate tabular matter following.

APPENDIX

Sales Forecast

Sales	Oct	Nov	Dec	Jan	Feb	Mar	Apr
Valentine's Day Concert	$0	$0	$0	$0	$68,750	$0	$0
Easter Concert	$0	$0	$0	$0	$0	$68,750	$0
Mother's Day Concert	$0	$0	$0	$0	$0	$0	$0
Michigan State University Smash Month Concert	$0	$0	$0	$0	$0	$0	$0
Teen Parties	$0	$0	$0	$500	$500	$500	$500
Total Sales	**$0**	**$0**	**$0**	**$500**	**$69,250**	**$69,250**	**$500**

Direct Cost of Sales							
Valentine's Day Concert	$0	$0	$0	$0	$28,050	$0	$0
Easter Concert	$0	$0	$0	$0	$0	$28,050	$0
Mother's Day Concert	$0	$0	$0	$0	$0	$0	$0
Michigan State University Smash Month Concert	$0	$0	$0	$0	$0	$0	$0
Teen Parties	$0	$0	$0	$200	$200	$200	$200
Subtotal Cost of Sales	**$0**	**$0**	**$0**	**$200**	**$28,250**	**$28,250**	**$200**

Personnel Plan

Personnel	Oct	Nov	Dec	Jan	Feb	Mar	Apr
Secretary/Receptionist	$0	$0	$0	$0	$0	$0	$0
Sponsorship Sales Rep	$0	$0	$0	$0	$0	$0	$0
Owner's Draw	$0	$0	$0	$0	$0	$0	$0
Total Payroll	**$0**	**$0**	**$0**	**$0**	**$0**	**$0**	**$0**
Total Headcount	1	1	1	1	1	1	1
Payroll Burden	$0	$0	$0	$0	$0	$0	$0
Total Payroll Expenditures	**$0**	**$0**	**$0**	**$0**	**$0**	**$0**	**$0**

General Assumptions

	Oct	Nov	Dec	Jan	Feb	Mar	Apr
Short-term Interest Rate %	10.00%	10.00%	10.00%	10.00%	10.00%	10.00%	10.00%
Long-term Interest Rate %	10.00%	10.00%	10.00%	10.00%	10.00%	10.00%	10.00%
Payment Days Estimator	30	30	30	30	30	30	30
Collection Days Estimator	45	45	45	45	45	45	45
Inventory Turnover Estimator	6.00	6.00	6.00	6.00	6.00	6.00	6.00
Tax Rate %	25.00%	25.00%	25.00%	25.00%	25.00%	25.00%	25.00%
Expenses in Cash %	10.00%	10.00%	10.00%	10.00%	10.00%	10.00%	10.00%
Sales on Credit %	0.00%	0.00%	0.00%	0.00%	0.00%	0.00%	0.00%
Personnel Burden %	15.00%	15.00%	15.00%	15.00%	15.00%	15.00%	15.00%

May	Jun	Jul	Aug	Sep	FY2002	FY2003	FY2004
$0	$0	$0	$0	$0	$68,750	$92,500	$105,000
$0	$0	$0	$0	$0	$68,750	$92,500	$105,000
$68,750	$0	$0	$0	$0	$68,750	$92,500	$105,000
$0	$0	$0	$0	$166,500	$166,500	$211,500	$234,000
$500	$500	$500	$500	$500	$4,500	$6,000	$9,000
$69,250	**$500**	**$500**	**$500**	**$167,000**	**$377,250**	**$495,000**	**$558,000**
$0	$0	$0	$0	$0	$28,050	$25,245	$22,721
$0	$0	$0	$0	$0	$28,050	$25,245	$22,721
$28,050	$0	$0	$0	$0	$28,050	$25,245	$22,721
$0	$0	$0	$0	$39,550	$39,550	$35,595	$32,036
$200	$200	$200	$200	$200	$1,800	$2,400	$2,400
$28,250	**$200**	**$200**	**$200**	**$39,750**	**$125,500**	**$113,730**	**$102,599**

May	Jun	Jul	Aug	Sep	FY2002	FY2003	FY2004
$0	$0	$0	$0	$0	$0	$25,000	$27,000
$0	$0	$0	$0	$0	$0	$25,000	$27,000
$0	$0	$0	$0	$0	$0	$0	$52,000
$0	**$0**	**$0**	**$0**	**$0**	**$0**	**$50,000**	**$108,000**
1	1	1	1	1	1	3	3
$0	$0	$0	$0	$0	$0	$7,500	$15,900
$0	**$0**	**$0**	**$0**	**$0**	**$0**	**$57,500**	**$121,900**

May	Jun	Jul	Aug	Sep	FY2002	FY2003	FY2004
10.00%	10.00%	10.00%	10.00%	10.00%	10.00%	10.00%	10.00%
10.00%	10.00%	10.00%	10.00%	10.00%	10.00%	10.00%	10.00%
30	30	30	30	30	30	30	30
45	45	45	45	45	45	45	45
6.00	6.00	6.00	6.00	6.00	6.00	6.00	6.00
25.00%	25.00%	25.00%	25.00%	25.00%	25.00%	25.00%	25.00%
10.00%	10.00%	10.00%	10.00%	10.00%	10.00%	10.00%	10.00%
0.00%	0.00%	0.00%	0.00%	0.00%	0.00%	0.00%	0.00%
15.00%	15.00%	15.00%	15.00%	15.00%	15.00%	15.00%	15.00%

Profit and Loss (Income Statement)

	Oct	Nov	Dec	Jan	Feb	Mar	Apr
Sales	$0	$0	$0	$500	$69,250	$69,250	$500
Direct Cost of Sales	$0	$0	$0	$200	$28,250	$28,250	$200
Production Payroll	$0	$0	$0	$0	$0	$0	$0
Other	$0	$0	$0	$0	$0	$0	$0
Total Cost of Sales	**$0**	**$0**	**$0**	**$200**	**$28,250**	**$28,250**	**$200**
Gross Margin	$0	$0	$0	$300	$41,000	$41,000	$300
Gross Margin %	0.00%	0.00%	0.00%	60.00%	59.21%	59.21%	60.00%
Operating Expenses							
Sales and Marketing Expenses							
Sales and Marketing Payroll	$0	$0	$0	$0	$0	$0	$0
Advertising/Promotion	$0	$0	$0	$2,150	$2,150	$0	$2,150
Travel	$0	$0	$0	$0	$3,000	$3,000	$0
Sound	$0	$0	$0	$0	$1,000	$1,000	$0
Accommodations	$0	$0	$0	$0	$500	$500	$0
Security	$0	$0	$0	$0	$6,000	$6,000	$0
Miscellaneous	$0	$0	$0	$0	$0	$0	$0
Total Sales and							
Marketing Expenses	**$0**	**$0**	**$0**	**$0**	**$0**	**$0**	**$0**
Sales and Marketing %	0.00%	0.00%	0.00%	0.00%	0.00%	0.00%	0.00%
General and Administrative Expenses							
General and Administrative							
Payroll	$0	$0	$0	$0	$0	$0	$0
Payroll Expense	$0	$0	$0	$0	$0	$0	$0
Payroll Burden	$0	$0	$0	$0	$0	$0	$0
Depreciation	$0	$0	$0	$0	$0	$0	$0
Telephone	$50	$50	$50	$50	$50	$50	$50
Business Insurance	$500	$0	$0	$0	$0	$0	$0
Concert Facility Insurance	$0	$0	$0	$500	$0	$0	$0
Total General and							
Administrative Expenses	**$0**	**$0**	**$0**	**$0**	**$0**	**$0**	**$0**
General and Administrative %	0.00%	0.00%	0.00%	0.00%	0.00%	0.00%	0.00%
Other Expenses							
Other Payroll	$0	$0	$0	$0	$0	$0	$0
Accountant	$0	$85	$85	$85	$85	$85	$85
Total Other Expenses	$0	$0	$0	$0	$0	$0	$0
Other %	0.00%	0.00%	0.00%	0.00%	0.00%	0.00%	0.00%
Total Operating Expenses	**$550**	**$135**	**$135**	**$2,785**	**$12,785**	**$10,635**	**$2,285**
Profit Before Interest							
and Taxes	($550)	($135)	($135)	($2,485)	$28,215	$30,365	($1,985)
Interest Expense Short-term	$163	$163	$163	$163	$163	$163	$163
Interest Expense Long-term	$0	$0	$0	$0	$0	$0	$0
Taxes Incurred	($178)	($74)	($74)	($662)	$7,013	$7,551	($537)
Extraordinary Items	$0	$0	$0	$0	$0	$0	$0
Net Profit	($535)	($223)	($223)	($1,986)	$21,039	$22,652	($1,611)
Net Profit/Sales	0.00%	0.00%	0.00%	-397.19%	30.38%	32.71%	-322.19%

May	Jun	Jul	Aug	Sep	FY2002	FY2003	FY2004
$69,250	$500	$500	$500	$167,000	$377,250	$495,000	$558,000
$28,250	$200	$200	$200	$39,750	$125,500	$113,730	$102,599
$0	$0	$0	$0	$0	$0	$0	$0
$0	$0	$0	$0	$0	$0	$0	$0
$28,250	**$200**	**$200**	**$200**	**$39,750**	**$125,500**	**$113,730**	**$102,599**
$41,000	$300	$300	$300	$127,250	$251,750	$381,270	$455,401
59.21%	60.00%	60.00%	60.00%	76.20%	66.73%	77.02%	81.61%
$0	$0	$0	$0	$0	$0	$0	$0
$0	$0	$0	$2,150	$0	$8,600	$7,740	$6,966
$3,000	$0	$0	$0	$3,000	$12,000	$12,000	$12,000
$1,000	$0	$0	$0	$1,000	$4,000	$4,000	$4,000
$500	$0	$0	$0	$500	$2,000	$2,000	$2,000
$6,000	$0	$0	$0	$6,000	$24,000	$24,000	$24,000
$0	$0	$0	$0	$0	$0	$0	$0
$0	**$0**	**$0**	**$0**	**$0**	**$0**	**$0**	**$0**
0.00%	0.00%	0.00%	0.00%	0.00%	0.00%	0.00%	0.00%
$0	$0	$0	$0	$0	$0	$0	$0
$0	$0	$0	$0	$0	$0	$50,000	$106,000
$0	$0	$0	$0	$0	$0	$7,500	$15,900
$0	$0	$0	$0	$0	$0	$0	$0
$50	$50	$50	$50	$50	$600	$600	$600
$0	$0	$0	$0	$0	$500	$500	$500
$0	$0	$0	$0	$0	$500	$500	$500
$0	**$0**	**$0**	**$0**	**$0**	**$0**	**$0**	**$0**
0.00%	0.00%	0.00%	0.00%	0.00%	0.00%	0.00%	0.00%
$0	$0	$0	$0	$0	$0	$0	$0
$85	$85	$85	$85	$85	$935	$1,020	$1,020
$0	$0	$0	$0	$0	$0	$0	$0
0.00%	0.00%	0.00%	0.00%	0.00%	0.00%	0.00%	0.00%
$10,635	**$135**	**$135**	**$2,285**	**$10,635**	**$53,135**	**$109,860**	**$173,486**
$30,365	$165	$165	($1,985)	$116,615	$198,615	$271,410	$281,915
$163	$163	$163	$163	$163	$1,955	$1,955	$1,955
$0	$0	$0	$0	$0	$0	$0	$0
$7,551	$1	$1	($537)	$29,113	$49,165	$67,364	$69,990
$0	$0	$0	$0	$0	$0	$0	$0
$22,652	$2	$2	($1,611)	$87,339	$147,495	$202,091	$209,970
32.71%	0.31%	0.31%	-322.19%	52.30%	39.10%	40.83%	37.63%

Projected Cash Flow

	Oct	Nov	Dec	Jan	Feb	Mar	Apr
Net Profit	($535)	($223)	($223)	($1,986)	$21,039	$22,652	($1,611)
Plus:							
Depreciation	$0	$0	$0	$0	$0	$0	$0
Change in Accounts Payable	$465	($271)	$0	$1,968	$39,781	($1,403)	($38,704)
Current Borrowing (repayment)	$0	$0	$0	$0	$0	$0	$0
Increase (decrease) Other Liabilities	$0	$0	$0	$0	$0	$0	$0
Long-term Borrowing (repayment)	$0	$0	$0	$0	$0	$0	$0
Capital Input	$0	$0	$0	$0	$0	$0	$0
Subtotal	**($70)**	**($494)**	**($223)**	**($18)**	**$60,820**	**$21,249**	**($40,315)**
Less:							
Change in Accounts Receivable	$0	$0	$0	$0	$0	$0	$0
Change in Inventory	$0	$0	$0	$0	$0	$0	$0
Change in Other Short-term Assets	$0	$0	$0	$0	$0	$0	$0
Capital Expenditure	$0	$0	$0	$0	$0	$0	$0
Dividends	$0	$0	$0	$0	$0	$0	$0
Subtotal	**$0**	**$0**	**$0**	**$0**	**$0**	**$0**	**$0**
Net Cash Flow	**($70)**	**($494)**	**($223)**	**($18)**	**$60,820**	**$21,249**	**($40,315)**
Cash Balance	**$9,930**	**$9,436**	**$9,213**	**$9,195**	**$70,015**	**$91,264**	**$50,949**

May	Jun	Jul	Aug	Sep	FY2002	FY2003	FY2004
$22,652	$2	$2	($1,611)	$87,339	$147,495	$202,091	$209,970
$0	$0	$0	$0	$0	$0	$0	$0
$38,704	($40,107)	$0	$1,403	$67,469	$69,305	($55,813)	$3,825
$0	$0	$0	$0	$0	$0	$0	$0
$0	$0	$0	$0	$0	$0	$0	$0
$0	$0	$0	$0	$0	$0	$0	$0
$0	$0	$0	$0	$0	$0	$0	$0
$61,356	**($40,105)**	**$2**	**($208)**	**$154,808**	**$216,800**	**$146,278**	**$213,795**
$0	$0	$0	$0	$0	$0	$0	$0
$0	$0	$0	$0	$0	$0	$0	$0
$0	$0	$0	$0	$0	$0	$0	$0
$0	$0	$0	$0	$0	$0	$0	$0
$0	$0	$0	$0	$0	$0	$0	$0
$0	**$0**	**$0**	**$0**	**$0**	**$0**	**$0**	**$0**
$61,356	**($40,105)**	**$2**	**($208)**	**$154,808**	**$216,800**	**$146,278**	**$213,795**
$112,304	**$72,199**	**$72,201**	**$71,992**	**$226,800**	**$226,800**	**$373,078**	**$586,873**

Projected Balance Sheet

Assets

Short-term Assets	Oct	Nov	Dec	Jan	Feb	Mar	Apr
Cash	$9,930	$9,436	$9,213	$9,195	$70,015	$91,264	$50,949
Accounts Receivable	$0	$0	$0	$0	$0	$0	$0
Inventory	$0	$0	$0	$0	$0	$0	$0
Other Short-term Assets	$0	$0	$0	$0	$0	$0	$0
Total Short-term Assets	**$9,930**	**$9,436**	**$9,213**	**$9,195**	**$70,015**	**$91,264**	**$50,949**
Long-term Assets							
Capital Assets	$0	$0	$0	$0	$0	$0	$0
Accumulated Depreciation	$0	$0	$0	$0	$0	$0	$0
Total Long-term Assets	**$0**	**$0**	**$0**	**$0**	**$0**	**$0**	**$0**
Total Assets	**$9,930**	**$9,436**	**$9,213**	**$9,195**	**$70,015**	**$91,264**	**$50,949**
Liabilities and Capital							
Accounts Payable	$465	$194	$194	$2,163	$41,944	$40,541	$1,837
Short-term Notes	$19,550	$19,550	$19,550	$19,550	$19,550	$19,550	$19,550
Other Short-term Liabilities	$0	$0	$0	$0	$0	$0	$0
Subtotal Short-term Liabilities	**$20,015**	**$19,744**	**$19,744**	**$21,713**	**$61,494**	**$60,091**	**$21,387**
Long-term Liabilities	$0	$0	$0	$0	$0	$0	$0
Total Liabilities	**$20,015**	**$19,744**	**$19,744**	**$21,713**	**$61,494**	**$60,091**	**$21,387**
Paid in Capital	$10,000	$10,000	$10,000	$10,000	$10,000	$10,000	$10,000
Retained Earnings	($19,550)	($19,550)	($19,550)	($19,550)	($19,550)	($19,550)	($19,550)
Earnings	($535)	($758)	($982)	($2,968)	$18,072	$40,723	$39,112
Total Capital	**($10,085)**	**($10,308)**	**($10,532)**	**($12,518)**	**$8,522**	**$31,173**	**$29,562**
Total Liabilities and Capital	**$9,930**	**$9,436**	**$9,213**	**$9,195**	**$70,015**	**$91,264**	**$50,949**
Net Worth	**($10,085)**	**($10,308)**	**($10,532)**	**($12,518)**	**$8,522**	**$31,173**	**$29,562**

May	Jun	Jul	Aug	Sep	FY2002	FY2003	FY2004
$112,304	$72,199	$72,201	$71,992	$226,800	$226,800	$373,078	$586,873
$0	$0	$0	$0	$0	$0	$0	$0
$0	$0	$0	$0	$0	$0	$0	$0
$0	$0	$0	$0	$0	$0	$0	$0
$112,304	**$72,199**	**$72,201**	**$71,992**	**$226,800**	**$226,800**	**$373,078**	**$586,873**
$0	$0	$0	$0	$0	$0	$0	$0
$0	$0	$0	$0	$0	$0	$0	$0
$0	**$0**	**$0**	**$0**	**$0**	**$0**	**$0**	**$0**
$112,304	**$72,199**	**$72,201**	**$71,992**	**$226,800**	**$226,800**	**$373,078**	**$586,873**
$40,541	$434	$434	$1,837	$69,305	$69,305	$13,492	$17,316
$19,550	$19,550	$19,550	$19,550	$19,550	$19,550	$19,550	$19,550
$0	$0	$0	$0	$0	$0	$0	$0
$60,091	**$19,984**	**$19,984**	**$21,387**	**$88,855**	**$88,855**	**$33,042**	**$36,866**
$0	$0	$0	$0	$0	$0	$0	$0
$60,091	**$19,984**	**$19,984**	**$21,387**	**$88,855**	**$88,855**	**$33,042**	**$36,866**
$10,000	$10,000	$10,000	$10,000	$10,000	$10,000	$10,000	$10,000
($19,550)	($19,550)	($19,550)	($19,550)	($19,550)	($19,550)	$127,945	$330,036
$61,764	$61,765	$61,767	$60,156	$147,495	$147,495	$202,091	$209.970
$52,214	**$52,215**	**$52,217**	**$50,606**	**$137,945**	**$137,945**	**$340,036**	**$550,006**
$112,304	**$72,199**	**$72,201**	**$71,992**	**$226,800**	**$226,800**	**$373,078**	**$586,873**
$52,214	**$52,215**	**$52,217**	**$50,606**	**$137,945**	**$137,945**	**$340,036**	**$550,006**

Counseling Center

BUSINESS PLAN

1600 West Main Street
Ann Arbor, Michigan 48106

The Juniper Counseling Center (JCC) is a mental and health counseling/education center focusing on teen mothers, troubled children/youth, and senior citizens with mental/health issues. The business plan was developed for the purpose of a start-up business loan in the amount of $20,935.

- EXECUTIVE SUMMARY

- COMPANY SUMMARY

- SERVICES

- MARKET ANALYSIS SUMMARY

- STRATEGY & IMPLEMENTATION SUMMARY

- MANAGEMENT SUMMARY

- FINANCIAL PLAN

- APPENDIX

COUNSELING CENTER
BUSINESS PLAN

EXECUTIVE SUMMARY

The Juniper Counseling Center (JCC) is a mental and health counseling/education center focusing on teen mothers, troubled children/youth, and senior citizens with mental/health issues. JCC is located at 1600 West Main Street in Ann Arbor, Michigan. The business plan was developed for the purpose of a start-up business loan in the amount of $20,935. The total amount needed to open JCC is $26,935. The owner's investment is $6,000.

Our projected sales for 2002 is over $290,000 and our first year projected net profits are well over $40,000.

Juniper's keys to success include: marketing, service quality, growth potential, implementing an effective cash flow plan, achieving efficiency, running our counseling center professionally, and maintaining a serious business discipline in everything we do.

Mental and health counseling and educational training services, as shown in our plan, have an excellent profitability level and growth rate. Our competitive edge along with new counseling techniques put JCC in the forefront of counseling and educational services. We are living in an age where new techniques for mental and health counseling are in great demand. Our center will differ from the traditional counseling services because of our added personal touch.

Objectives

Our objectives are to:

- Provide counseling to individuals, couples, and families.
- Provide various therapeutic group sessions (i.e., bereavement, divorce, teen parenting, senior citizens' health issues, troubled children/youth).
- Provide health prevention and maintenance groups.
- Provide various disease-focused therapeutic groups.

Mission

JCC's mission is to empower disadvantaged and disenfranchised individuals, families, and youths to take control of their destiny and function productively by providing them with the necessary skills to realize their dreams, through counseling, education, social skills training, motivation, and participating in the treatment of abnormal behaviors to become successful.

Keys to Success

Juniper's keys to success include: marketing, service quality, growth potential, implementing an effective cash flow plan, achieving efficiency, running our counseling center professionally, and maintaining a serious business discipline in everything we do.

JCC's cash flow plan is to:

- Maintain enough money on hand each month to pay the cash obligations the following month.
- Identify and eliminate deficiencies or surpluses in cash.
- Alter business financial plans to provide more cash if deficiencies are found.
- Invest any revealed excess cash in an accessible, interest-bearing, low-risk account such as a savings account or short-term CD or T-bill.
- Clearly understand the mental health education market and competition while continually adjusting accordingly.

- Keep enough cash, as needed cushion for security, on hand to cover expenses.
- Reduce accountant expenses by producing our own summary statistics and projections via accounting software Therapist Helper.

Our vision is to move Washtenaw County's disenfranchised population to a condition of empowerment and self-determination, by enabling them to employ innovative strategies to produce desirable actions that lead to healthy results. JCC is dedicated to the community it serves. Through seminars, therapeutic groups, individual, couples, and family counseling, the center strives to raise public awareness to the needs of at-risk residents within our community. Services are designed to strengthen and increase self-esteem, self-respect, and respect for others in society, promote health, and to address issues relating to improving the quality of their lives.

COMPANY SUMMARY

The founder and owner is Rolanda K. Walker, R.N., MSW, Ph.D. It is a privately owned corporation.

Company Ownership

JCC will be located at 1600 West Main Street, Ann Arbor, Michigan.

Company Location and Facilities

The process of the JCC business operations is as follows:

Business Operations

- Counseling hours will be 9:00 A.M. until 5:00 P.M., Monday through Friday with flexible weekend and evening hours.
- Clients will come for services via physicians and school referrals, court orders, and by word-of-mouth. Per request, some clients with special needs will receive home visits.
- A client's first visit will be called in to the client's insurance company for approval of services.
- The client must have prior permission from the insurance company before they can receive services.
- On the day of the initial in-take, the client is assessed and a treatment plan is sent to the insurance company.
- The insurance will return payment for services in about 14 days.

Our total start-up costs are $26,935, which is mostly for furniture, equipment, working capital, and expenses associated with opening our first office. Direct owner investment will be $6,000. JCC will seek a commercial loan for the remaining $20,935 needed to start up the business. The assumptions are shown in the following table.

Start-up Summary

Start-up Expenses

2-Surge Protectors	$60
4-Computers	$4,000
Copy Machine	$600
Laser Printer	$2,000
Adding Machine	$30
Electric Typewriter	$120
Fax Machine	$300
12-Clip Boards	$12
4-Waste Baskets	$12

Start-up Summary

Continued

File Folders	$75
4-Desk Organizers	$200
4-Floor Mates	$184
Hole Punchers	$12
Paper	$60
4-Wall Clock	$80
Pens/Pencils/Markers/Paper Clips/Tacks	$60
3-Large Bulletin Boards	$90
2-Paper Shredder	$50
2-Paper Stand	$30
4-File Cabinets	$240
1-Supply Cabinet	$200
Wall Pictures	$350
1-Oval Table	$400
12-Chairs	$312
4-Desk Lamps	$60
1-Standing Lamp	$30
2-TV/VCR	$500
Entrance Rug	$90
Computer Disks	$16
Envelopes	$50
Labels	$25
File Guides	$60
Organizer Compartment	$30
Laminator	$200
Paper/Plastic Cutter	$60
Electric Stapler	$70
Tape	$8
3-Desk Calendars	$18
Pencil Sharpeners	$35
3-Office Chairs	$130
1-Executive Chair	$500
3-Desks	$900
3-Love Seats	$600
3-Guest Chairs	$390
3-Book Shelves	$300
Childrens' Table & Chairs	$100
Childrens' Games	$150
Teaching Aids	$200
Childrens' Toys	$150
Carpeting	$2,000
Group Room Furniture	$752
Therapist Software Programs	$930
Kitchen Furniture	$450
3-Staplers	$24
Tablets/Rolodex	$30
Legal	$1,500
Stationery, etc.	$300
Brochures	$300
Professional Development	$500
Other	$0
Total Start-up Expense	**$20,935**

Start-up Assets Needed

Cash Requirements	$6,000
Start-up inventory	$0
Other Short-term Assets	$0
Total Short-term Assets	**$6,000**
Long-term Assets	$0
Total Assets	**$6,000**
Total Start-up Requirements:	**$26,935**
Left to finance:	$0

Start-up Funding Plan
Investment

Investor 1	$0
Investor 2	$0
Owner's Equity	$6,000
Total investment	**$6,000**

Short-term Liabilities

Unpaid Expenses	$0
Short-term Loans	$20,935
Interest-free Short-term Loans	$0
Subtotal Short-term Liabilities	$20,935
Long-term Liabilities	$0
Total Liabilities	**$20,935**
Loss at Start-up	**($20,935)**
Total Capital	**($14,935)**
Total Capital and Liabilities	**$6,000**
Checkline	**$0**

SERVICES

Services offered include education, training, and counseling to empower and implement a change in a person's behavior and thinking.

JCC will also provide the following services to individuals, families, couples, and youth:

- Violence/Conflict Resolutions
- Positive growth
- Bereavement
- Families in Crisis
- Grandparents Parenting
- Teen Parenting
- Relationship Problems
- Out-of-Control children and teen youths
- Health Services Utilization
- Alcohol/Substance Abuse
- Employment Difficulties
- Home Visits Available

MARKET ANALYSIS SUMMARY

JCC will be focusing on providing education and counseling services to teen mothers, out-of-control children/youth, individuals with mental health disorders, and senior citizens with mental and health issues.

- According to the National Campaign to Prevent Teen Pregnancy 1996 Michigan Report, a total of 29,840 15 to 19-year-olds gave birth.
- About 20 percent of U.S. children and adolescents (15 million), ages 9 to 17, have diagnosable psychiatric disorders (MECA, 1996, the Surgeon General, 1999)
- Chronic disease, memory impairment, and depressive symptoms affect large numbers of older people, and the risk of such problems often increases with age. In 1995, almost 60 percent of people age 70 and older report having arthritis, up slightly from the proportion reporting arthritis in 1984. The prevalence of arthritis and other chronic diseases, such as hypertension, heart disease, cancer, diabetes, and stroke are also reported, and vary by race and ethnicity. Increases in memory impairment and depressive symptoms occur with advancing age: one third or more of men and women age 85 and older have moderate or severe memory impairment and 23 percent of this group experience severe depressive symptoms.

Target Market Segment Strategy

The U.S Census Bureau County Population report of 1998 states that there are approximately 436,084 people living in Washtenaw County. Any of these individuals is a possible client for JCC.

JCC knows we cannot survive just waiting for the customer to come to us. Instead, we must get better at focusing on the specific market segments whose needs match our offering. Focusing on targeted segments is the key to our future. Therefore, we will focus our marketing message and our service offerings. We will develop our message, communicate it to our referral partners, and make good on it.

Teen Mothers

Nearly one million teen girls get pregnant each year. More than four out of 10 young women get pregnant at least once before they turn 20. Each year the federal government alone spends about $40 billion to help families that began with a teenage birth.

In Michigan, 11,350 15 to 17-year-olds gave birth, and 18,490 18 to 19-year-olds gave birth. Michigan ranks 24 (Rank of 1=largest decrease) for teen pregnancy rate with 87 pregnancies per 1,000 girls. Teen pregnancies were down in all age groups ranging from girls aged 14 and younger to girls aged 15 to 19-year-olds. Twenty-two percent of births in Michigan are to teens who have already had a birth.

Hispanic/Latina girls were the highest in birth rates among different racial/ethnic groups with African Americans being the second highest and White (non-Hispanic) being the third highest. From 1991-1998 African American girls has had the highest decrease in births with a 35% decrease. White (non-Hispanic) came in second with a 22% decrease and Hispanic/Latina with a 3% decrease in births. Asian/Pacific Islanders had an increase of 7% in teen births. JCC will continue this fight against teen pregnancy through our educational and counseling programs for teens.

Troubled Children/ Youth

On January 17, 2001 David Satcher, M.D., Surgeon General of the United States of America unveiled a compelling report on youth violence to the frontline caregivers of our nation. The report was commissioned after the now infamous 1999 Columbine event that focused America's attention on children's behavior and their sometimes inability to cope with stress. In the report, Dr. Satcher invites families, school personnel, and public health communities to take a proactive role in the prevention of youth violence. "This is no time to let down our guard on youth violence," said Dr. Satcher.

Dr. Satcher's public health perspective identifies behavioral, environmental, and biological factors associated with youth violence. The report goes on to encourage our nation to take steps in educating individuals, communities, and primary care physicians to protect themselves from these risks. Dr. Satcher's public health approach offers a practical, goal-oriented, and community-based strategy for promoting and maintaining health. "The most urgent need now is a national resolve to confront the problem of youth violence systematically using research-based approaches and to correct damaging myths and stereotypes that interfere with the risk at hand," said Satcher.

According to the American Academy of Child and Adolescent Psychiatry (AACAP) the needs and voice of child and adolescent psychiatry have been buried under the sweeping forces of federal mandates and national medical organizations' consensus on the oversupply of specialists. They have failed to recognize the continuing critical shortage of child and adolescent psychiatrists. There is a danger of becoming marginalized when the profession cannot provide needed services and contribute to society. The serious undersupply of practitioners has resulted in children receiving inadequate care from mental health profession-als who lack the necessary training.

Report of the Surgeon General's Conference on Children's Mental Health: A National Action Agenda released the following information on January 3, 2001. From this information a report was developed and is the culmination of nearly a year of significant activities that were launched with the March 22, 2000, White House Meeting on Children's Mental Health. The report emphasizes the magnitude of the problem facing us in the United States. One in 10 children and adolescents suffers from a mental illness severe enough to cause some level of impairment. The report also emphasizes that it is estimated that fewer than 1 in 5 of these children receive needed treatment in any given year.

As stated in the foreword to the report, "The burden of suffering experienced by children with mental health needs and their families has created a health crisis in this country. Growing numbers of children are suffering needlessly because their emotional, behavioral, and developmental needs are not being met.... It is time that we as a Nation took seriously the task of preventing mental health problems and treating mental illnesses in youth."

Prevalence and Magnitude of Child and Adolescent Psychiatric Problems

- The Center for Mental Health Services (1998) estimated that 9 to 13 percent of U.S. children and adolescents, ages 9 to 17, meet the definition of "serious emotional disturbance" and 5 to 9 percent of U.S. children and adolescents, "extreme functional impairment."
- Only about 20 percent of emotionally disturbed children and adolescents receive some kind of mental health services (the Surgeon General, 1999), and only a small fraction of them receive evaluation and treatment by child and adolescent psychiatrists.
- The demand for the services of child and adolescent psychiatry is projected to increase by 100 percent by 2020. (U.S. Bureau of Health Professions, DHHS, 2000).
- The population of children and adolescents under age 18 is projected to grow by more than 40 percent in the next 50 years from the current 70 million to more than 100 million by 2050 (U.S. Bureau of the Census, 1999).

**Senior Citizens
Health Status**

Older Americans are living longer and living better than ever before. But many of those age 65 and older face disability, chronic health conditions, or economic stress according to a new federal indicators report that describes the status of the nation's older population.

Population:

The number and proportion of older people in the U.S. population has grown and generally will continue to grow at a very rapid pace. Aging in the twenty-first century will be characterized by a steep rise in the population age 85 and older and increased racial and ethnic diversity.

- The number of older people in the U.S. has increased tenfold since 1900. Today, an estimated 35 million people, 13 percent of the population, are age 65 and older. By 2030, 20 percent of Americans, about 70 million, will have passed their sixty-fifth birthday. The population age 85 and above is currently the fastest-growing segment of the older population; its growth is particularly important for anticipating health care and assistance needs, because these individuals tend to be in poorer health and require more services than people below age 85.
- The racial and ethnic makeup of the U.S. is changing, and the older population is no exception. In 2000, an estimated 84 percent of the population age 65 and older is non-Hispanic white, 8 percent non-Hispanic black, 6 percent Hispanic, 2 percent non-Hispanic Asian and Pacific Islander, and less than 1 percent non-Hispanic American Indian and Alaska Native. By 2050, those proportions are projected to be substantially different: 64 percent of the older population is expected to be non-Hispanic white, 16 percent Hispanic, 12 percent non-Hispanic black, and 7 percent non-Hispanic Asian and Pacific Islander, with the non-Hispanic American Indian and Alaska Native populations remaining at less than 1 percent.
- Today's older Americans are better educated than their counterparts 50 years ago, a factor that can positively influence socioeconomic status and health. In 1998, a high school diploma was held by some 67 percent of older Americans, compared with just 18 percent in 1950. About 15 percent of older Americans had earned at least a bachelor's degree in 1998, increasing from 4 percent in 1950.

Health Status:

Older Americans are living longer and feeling better. An overwhelming majority rate their health as good or excellent. Men and women report comparable levels of well-being. Disability rates are declining as well. But large numbers of older people find their health threatened by memory impairments, depression, chronic conditions, and disability, especially at very advanced ages, which can substantially diminish quality of life.

- Americans born at the beginning of the twenty-first century are expected to live almost 30 years longer than those born at the turn of the twentieth century. In 1997, a newborn baby girl could expect to live 79 years and a boy 74 years, compared to 51 years for a girl and 48 years for a boy born in 1900. Life expectancy varies by race, however. The average life expectancy for a white baby born in 1997 was 6 years higher than for a black baby born in the same year.
- Despite the prevalence of illness or chronic conditions, the proportion of Medicare beneficiaries age 65 and older with a chronic disability was 21 percent in 1994, down from 24 percent in 1982. During this time period, the older population grew significantly, and the number of older people estimated to have functional limitations increased by 600,000. This was considerably fewer, however, than the 1.5 million increase projected had disability rates not declined.

Overall teen pregnancies have decreased but they are still too high. The overall U.S. teenage pregnancy rate declined 17 percent between 1990 and 1996 (the most recent year available), from 117 pregnancies per 1,000 women aged 15-19 to 97 per 1,000. The national teen birth rate declined 3 percent between 1998 and 1999, reaching a rate of 49.6 births per 1,000 women ages 15-19—the lowest rate ever recorded. Since 1991, the teen birth rate has declined 20 percent. Nearly one million teen girls get pregnant each year. More than four out of 10 young women get pregnant at least once before they turn 20. Each year the federal government alone spends about $40 billion to help families that began with a teenage birth. Yet, much work is needed to be done in order to keep teen pregnancy down, such as more educational and counseling programs.

About 20 percent of U.S. children and adolescents (15 million), ages 9 to 17, have diagnosable psychiatric disorders (MECA, 1996, the Surgeon General, 1999). "There is a dearth of child psychiatrists.... Furthermore, many barriers remain that prevent children, teenagers, and their parents from seeking help from the small number of specially trained professionals.... This places a burden on pediatricians, family physicians, and other gatekeepers to identify children for referral and treatment decisions." (Mental Health: A Report of the Surgeon General, 1999). The population of children and adolescents under age 18 is projected to grow by more than 40 percent in the next 50 years from the current 70 million to more than 100 million by 2050 (U.S. Bureau of the Census, 1999).

The number of older people in the U.S. has increased tenfold since 1900. Today, an estimated 35 million people, 13 percent of the population, are age 65 and older. By 2030, 20 percent of Americans, about 70 million, will have passed their sixty-fifth birthday. The population age 85 and above is currently the fastest growing segment of the older population; its growth is particularly important for anticipating health care and assistance needs, because these individuals tend to be in poorer health and require more services than people below age 85.

The global population is aging at a rate unprecedented in history. In the U.S., the population age 65 and older is expected to double by 2030. The Forum developed the report "Older Americans 2000: Key Indicators of Well-Being" to regularly track trends as society and individuals look for ways to address the aging boom. Today's report, which brings together information from more than a dozen national data sources for the first time, will serve as a baseline for future updates.

> *Americans age 65 and older are an important and growing segment of our population. While many federal agencies provide data on this diverse population, it is sometimes difficult to understand how this group is faring. For the first time, the federal statistical system has come together to provide a unified picture of the overall health and well-being of older Americans.*
>
> —Katherine K. Wallman, Chief Statistician, U.S. Office of Management and Budget

As a Registered Nurse and Health Psychologist, Rolanda K. Walker is equipped with advanced training and information about the interaction of psychological and medical conditions (or psychomedical disorders). This includes information about psychological difficulties that can be caused by medical conditions, as well as psychological factors which can complicate or delay recovery from medical conditions. This is the kind of expertise that will stimulate further thought about the assessment and treatment of patients with psychomedical disorders. This is the expertise that will give Juniper Counseling Center a cutting edge over their competition.

Industry Analysis and Trends

Competition

| **STRATEGY &** **IMPLEMENTATION** **SUMMARY** | JCC will focus on servicing Washtenaw County and the surrounding areas. The three population segments will be individuals, families, and couples. The target customer is usually a person or persons with some type of behavioral dysfunction. |

Competitive Edge

We start with a critical competitive edge: there is no competitor we know of that can claim anywhere near as much specific expertise on the problems and opportunities of psychological treatment as JCC. Our positioning on this point is very hard to match, so we must maintain our focus in our strategy, marketing and business development, and fulfillment. We should be aware that the tendency to dilute this expertise with more generalized counseling work could weaken the importance of our competitive edge.

Also, our potential competitor does not make home visits. Our staff is prepared to take our services to our clients. Older citizens many times are unable to leave their home for reasons such as lack of transportation, limited mobility, fear of driving, and issues of personal safety, to name a few. We will provide a holistic approach to total wellness by including intensive medical education pertaining to all medical diagnosis and treatments.

Price of Service

Prices will vary according to a person's insurance coverage and their ability to pay. Generally the cost of service averages about $75.00 per one-hour session. There will be one group session with 10 clients at $30 per client for the length of 52 weeks.

Sales Strategy

Sales in our business is client service. It is repeat business. One doesn't sell a session, one develops a treatment plan that works for the client.

We expect to see at least 15 clients per day. Dr. Walker will consult with 5 clients at an average of $75 per session, and each of her therapists will consult with 5 clients at an average of $75 per session. There will be at least one ongoing group session per week, averaging 10 clients at $30 per client, running for 52 weeks.

We expect to make enough money to expand the programs that Dr. Walker will implement in order to reach all disenfranchised individuals in the surrounding area.

Sales Forecast

We expect sales to increase as our staff and referral base increase. The following table gives a run-down on forecasted sales.

Sales	FY2002	FY2003	FY2004
Therapist/Counseling Sessions	$292,500	$292,500	$292,500
Medical/Mental Health Group Sessions	$15,600	$15,600	$15,600
Total Sales	**$308,100**	**$308,100**	**$308,100**
Direct Cost of Sales			
Therapist/Counseling Sessions	$0	$0	$0
Medical/Mental Health Group Sessions	$0	$0	$0
Subtotal Cost of Sales	**$0**	**$0**	**$0**

MANAGEMENT SUMMARY

JCC's staff has an accumulated 75 years plus in the Health Care industry related to experience. All are well versed in the evolution of the Health Care industry and share a vision for the successful positioning of Juniper Counseling Center within the Health Care Industry.

Our professional staff come to you with many years of experience, compassion, sensitivity to cultural values which affect the treatment outcome, and a strong desire to make life the best that it can be for all of its citizens.

Our management team consists of founder Rolanda K. Walker (RN, MSW, ACSW, Ph.D.), who has worked in the Health Care arena for over 20 years as a Registered Nurse/Health Educator and Social Worker for the last 5 years. Dr. Walker is a graduate from Wayne State University as a Health Educator and is also graduate from University of Detroit Mercy's MSW program. She is currently finishing up her Ph.D in Health Psychology from the University of Michigan-Ann Arbor.

Our professional support team will consist of of three registered nurses who will provide health education through medical seminars, groups, and individual counseling.

The following table summarizes our personnel expenditures for the first three years. We believe this plan is a compromise between fairness and expedience and meets the commitment of our mission statement. A professional staff of three RNs, 3-4 Therapists, Office Manager, Billing Clerk, Payroll Manager, Accountant, and Cleaning Crew will be assembled. These individuals will provide health education through seminars, groups, and individual counseling.

Personnel Plan

All the therapists will be paid 50-50. This means that for all counseling services provided, the therapist will be paid one-half of the amount the insurance company pays. For example, if a insurance company pays $75.00 per session, the therapist will be paid $37.50 per session.

Personnel Plan	FY2002	FY2003	FY2004
3 Therapists	$146,252	$146,252	$146,252
3 Nurses	$5,200	$5,200	$5,200
Office Manager	$21,840	$21,840	$21,840
Billing Clerk	$3,744	$3,744	$3,744
Payroll Manager	$4,160	$4,160	$4,160
Accountant	$2,500	$2,500	$2,500
Cleaning Person	$1,952	$1,952	$1,952
Other	$0	$0	$0
Total Payroll	**$185,648**	**$185,648**	**$185,648**
Total Headcount	**11**	**11**	**11**
Payroll Burden	**$27,847**	**$27,847**	**$27,847**
Total Payroll Expenditures	**$213,494**	**$213,494**	**$213,494**

FINANCIAL PLAN

The financial plan is for rapid, but controlled growth. Initial capitalization is pegged at 150K with cash streaming in from referrals over a period of six months. We plan to increase our clientele and cashflow through networking.

Important Assumptions

General Assumptions	FY2002	FY2003	FY2004
Short-term Interest Rate %	10.00%	10.00%	10.00%
Long-term Interest Rate %	10.00%	10.00%	10.00%
Payment Days Estimator	30	30	30
Collection Days Estimator	14	14	14
Inventory Turnover Estimator	6.00	6.00	6.00
Tax Rate %	25.00%	25.00%	25.00%
Expenses in Cash %	10.00%	10.00%	10.00%
Sales on Credit %	75.00%	75.00%	75.00%
Personnel Burden %	15.00%	15.00%	15.00%

Break-even Analysis

The following table summarizes our break-even analysis. With approximate fixed cost of $2000 per month at the outset (a bare minimum), we need to bill $4000 to cover our costs. We really don't expect to reach break-even until a few months into the business operation.

Break-even Analysis:

Monthly Units Break-even	53
Monthly Sales Break-even	$4,000

Assumptions:

Average Per-Unit Revenue	$75.00
Average Per-Unit Variable Cost	$37.50
Estimated Monthly Fixed Cost	$2,000

Projected Profit and Loss

Our projected profit and loss is shown in the following table, with a net sales of more than $40,000 the first year to more than $60,000 through the third, and profits almost negligible for the start-up phase of this business.

Detailed monthly projections are included in the appendices.

Profit and Loss (Income Statement)	FY2002	FY2003	FY2004
Sales	$308,100	$308,100	$308,100
Direct Cost of Sales	$0	$0	$0
Production Payroll	$0	$0	$0
Other	$0	$0	$0
Total Cost of Sales	**$0**	**$0**	**$0**
Gross Margin	$308,100	$308,100	$308,100
Gross Margin %	100.00%	100.00%	100.00%
Operating expenses:			
Sales and Marketing Expenses			
Sales and Marketing Payroll	$0	$0	$0
Advertising/Promotion	$900	$450	$450
Miscellaneous	$0	$0	$0
Total Sales and Marketing Expenses	**$0**	**$0**	**$0**
Sales and Marketing %	0.00%	0.00%	0.00%

General and Administrative Expenses	FY2002	FY2003	FY2004
General and Administrative Payroll	$0	$0	$0
Payroll Expense	$185,648	$185,648	$185,648
Payroll Burden	$27,847	$27,847	$27,847
Depreciation	$0	$0	$0
Utilities	$1,500	$1,500	$1,500
Insurance	$600	$600	$600
Rent	$12,000	$12,000	$12,000
Total General &			
Administrative Expenses	**$0**	**$0**	**$0**
General and Administrative %	0.00%	0.00%	0.00%
Other Expenses			
Other Payroll	$0	$0	$0
Telephone	$1,380	$1,380	$1,380
Total Other Expenses	**$0**	**$0**	**$0**
Other %	0.00%	0.00%	0.00%
Total Operating Expenses	**$229,874**	**$229,425**	**$229,425**
Profit Before Interest and Taxes	$78,226	$78,675	$78,675
Interest Expense Short-term	$2,094	$2,094	$2,094
Interest Expense Long-term	$0	$0	$0
Taxes Incurred	$19,033	$19,145	$19,145
Extraordinary Items	$0	$0	$0
Net Profit	$57,099	$57,436	$57,436
Net Profit/Sales	18.53%	18.64%	18.64%

Cash flow projections are the most critical indicator of our business's success. Attainment of the targeted population participation will ensure the accumulation of required cash to execute the running of the organization. The annual cash flow figures are included here and the more important detailed monthly numbers are included in the appendices.

Projected Cash Flow

Projected Cash Flow	FY2002	FY2003	FY2004
Net Profit	$57,099	$57,436	$57,436
Plus:			
Depreciation	$0	$0	$0
Change in Accounts Payable	$2,618	$50	($4)
Current Borrowing (repayment)	$0	$0	$0
Increase (decrease) Other Liabilities	$0	$0	$0
Long-term Borrowing (repayment)	$0	$0	$0
Capital Input	$0	$0	$0
Subtotal	$59,717	$57,486	$57,432
Less:			
Change in Accounts Receivable	$8,295	$0	$0
Change in Inventory	$0	$0	$0
Change in Other Short-term Assets	$0	$0	$0
Capital Expenditure	$0	$0	$0
Dividends	$0	$0	$0
Subtotal	$8,295	$0	$0
Net Cash Flow	**$51,422**	**$57,486**	**$57,432**
Cash Balance	**$57,422**	**$114,908**	**$172,340**

Projected Balance Sheet

The balance sheet in the following chart shows managed but sufficient growth of net worth and a sufficiently healthy financial position. The monthly estimates are included in the appendices.

Assets

Short-term Assets	FY2002	FY2003	FY2004
Cash	$57,422	$114,908	$172,340
Accounts Receivable	$8,295	$8,295	$8,295
Inventory	$0	$0	$0
Other Short-term Assets	$0	$0	$0
Total Short-term Assets	**$65,717**	**$123,203**	**$180,635**
Long-term Assets			
Capital Assets	$0	$0	$0
Accumulated Depreciation	$0	$0	$0
Total Long-term Assets	**$0**	**$0**	**$0**
Total Assets	**$65,717**	**$123,203**	**$180,635**
Liabilities and Capital			
Accounts Payable	$2,618	$2,668	$2,664
Short-term Notes	$20,935	$20,935	$20,935
Other Short-term Liabilities	$0	$0	$0
Subtotal Short-term Liabilities	**$23,553**	**$23,603**	**$23,599**
Long-term Liabilities	$0	$0	$0
Total Liabilities	**$23,553**	**$23,603**	**$23,599**
Paid in Capital	$6,000	$6,000	$6,000
Retained Earnings	($20,935)	$36,164	$93,600
Earnings	$57,099	$57,436	$57,436
Total Capital	**$42,164**	**$99,600**	**$157,036**
Total Liabilities and Capital	**$65,717**	**$123,203**	**$180,635**
Net Worth	**$42,164**	**$99,600**	**$157,036**

This page left intentionally blank to accommodate tabular matter following.

APPENDIX

Sales Forecast

Sales	Apr	May	Jun	Jul	Aug	Sep
Therapist/Counseling Sessions	$22,500	$28,125	$22,500	$22,500	$22,500	$22,500
Medical/Mental Health Group Sessions	$1,200	$1,500	$1,200	$1,200	$1,200	$1,200
Total Sales	**$23,700**	**$29,625**	**$23,700**	**$23,700**	**$23,700**	**$23,700**

Direct Cost of Sales						
Therapist/Counseling Sessions	$0	$0	$0	$0	$0	$0
Medical/Mental Health Group Sessions	$0	$0	$0	$0	$0	$0
Subtotal Cost of Sales	**$0**	**$0**	**$0**	**$0**	**$0**	**$0**

Personnel Plan

Personnel	Apr	May	Jun	Jul	Aug	Sep
3 Therapists	$11,250	$14,063	$11,250	$11,250	$11,250	$11,250
3 Nurses	$400	$500	$400	$400	$400	$400
Office Manager	$1,680	$2,100	$1,680	$1,680	$1,680	$1,680
Billing Clerk	$288	$360	$288	$288	$288	$288
Payroll Manager	$320	$400	$320	$320	$320	$320
Accountant	$200	$225	$200	$200	$200	$200
Cleaning Person	$150	$188	$150	$150	$150	$150
Other	$0	$0	$0	$0	$0	$0
Total Payroll	**$14,288**	**$17,835**	**$14,288**	**$14,288**	**$14,288**	**$14,288**
Total Headcount	**11**	**11**	**11**	**11**	**11**	**11**
Payroll Burden	**$2,143**	**$2,675**	**$2,143**	**$2,143**	**$2,143**	**$2,143**
Total Payroll Expenditures	**$16,431**	**$20,510**	**$16,431**	**$16,431**	**$16,431**	**$16,431**

General Assumptions

	Apr	May	Jun	Jul	Aug	Sep
Short-term Interest Rate %	10.00%	10.00%	10.00%	10.00%	10.00%	10.00%
Long-term Interest Rate %	10.00%	10.00%	10.00%	10.00%	10.00%	10.00%
Payment Days Estimator	30	30	30	30	30	30
Collection Days Estimator	14	14	14	14	14	14
Inventory Turnover Estimator	6.00	6.00	6.00	6.00	6.00	6.00
Tax Rate %	25.00%	25.00%	25.00%	25.00%	25.00%	25.00%
Expenses in Cash %	10.00%	10.00%	10.00%	10.00%	10.00%	10.00%
Sales on Credit %	75.00%	75.00%	75.00%	75.00%	75.00%	75.00%
Personnel Burden %	15.00%	15.00%	15.00%	15.00%	15.00%	15.00%

Oct	Nov	Dec	Jan	Feb	Mar	FY2002	FY2003	FY2004
$28,125	$22,500	$28,125	$28,125	$22,500	$22,500	$292,500	$292,500	$292,500
$1,500	$1,200	$1,500	$1,500	$1,200	$1,200	$15,600	$15,600	$15,600
$29,625	**$23,700**	**$29,625**	**$29,625**	**$23,700**	**$23,700**	**$308,100**	**$308,100**	**$308,100**
$0	$0	$0	$0	$0	$0	$0	$0	$0
$0	$0	$0	$0	$0	$0	$0	$0	$0
$0	**$0**	**$0**	**$0**	**$0**	**$0**	**$0**	**$0**	**$0**

Oct	Nov	Dec	Jan	Feb	Mar	FY2002	FY2003	FY2004
$14,063	$11,250	$14,063	$14,063	$11,250	$11,250	$146,252	$146,252	$146,252
$500	$400	$500	$500	$400	$400	$5,200	$5,200	$5,200
$2,100	$1,680	$2,100	$2,100	$1,680	$1,680	$21,840	$21,840	$21,840
$360	$288	$360	$360	$288	$288	$3,744	$3,744	$3,744
$400	$320	$400	$400	$320	$320	$4,160	$4,160	$4,160
$225	$200	$225	$225	$200	$200	$2,500	$2,500	$2,500
$188	$150	$188	$188	$150	$150	$1,952	$1,952	$1,952
$0	$0	$0	$0	$0	$0	$0	$0	$0
$17,836	**$14,288**	**$17,836**	**$17,836**	**$14,288**	**$14,288**	**$185,648**	**$185,648**	**$185,648**
11	**11**	**11**	**11**	**11**	**11**	**11**	**11**	**11**
$2,675	**$2,143**	**$2,675**	**$2,675**	**$2,143**	**$2,143**	**$27,847**	**$27,847**	**$27,847**
$20,511	**$16,431**	**$20,511**	**$20,511**	**$16,431**	**$16,431**	**$213,495**	**$213,495**	**$213,495**

Oct	Nov	Dec	Jan	Feb	Mar	FY2002	FY2003	FY2004
10.00%	10.00%	10.00%	10.00%	10.00%	10.00%	10.00%	10.00%	10.00%
10.00%	10.00%	10.00%	10.00%	10.00%	10.00%	10.00%	10.00%	10.00%
30	30	30	30	30	30	30	30	30
14	14	14	14	14	14	14	14	14
6.00	6.00	6.00	6.00	6.00	6.00	6.00	6.00	6.00
25.00%	25.00%	25.00%	25.00%	25.00%	25.00%	25.00%	25.00%	25.00%
10.00%	10.00%	10.00%	10.00%	10.00%	10.00%	10.00%	10.00%	10.00%
75.00%	75.00%	75.00%	75.00%	75.00%	75.00%	75.00%	75.00%	75.00%
15.00%	15.00%	15.00%	15.00%	15.00%	15.00%	15.00%	15.00%	15.00%

Profit and Loss (Income Statement)

	Apr	May	Jun	Jul	Aug	Sep
Sales	$23,700	$29,625	$23,700	$23,700	$23,700	$23,700
Direct Cost of Sales	$0	$0	$0	$0	$0	$0
Production Payroll	$0	$0	$0	$0	$0	$0
Other	$0	$0	$0	$0	$0	$0
Total Cost of Sales	**$0**	**$0**	**$0**	**$0**	**$0**	**$0**
Gross Margin	$23,700	$29,625	$23,700	$23,700	$23,700	$23,700
Gross Margin %	100.00%	100.00%	100.00%	100.00%	100.00%	100.00%
Operating Expenses:						
Sales and Marketing Expenses						
Sales and Marketing Payroll	$0	$0	$0	$0	$0	$0
Advertising/Promotion	$75	$75	$75	$75	$75	$75
Miscellaneous	$0	$0	$0	$0	$0	$0
Total Sales and Marketing Expenses	**$0**	**$0**	**$0**	**$0**	**$0**	**$0**
Sales and Marketing %	0.00%	0.00%	0.00%	0.00%	0.00%	0.00%
General and Administrative Expenses						
General and Administrative Payroll	$0	$0	$0	$0	$0	$0
Payroll Expense	$14,288	$17,835	$14,288	$14,288	$14,288	$14,288
Payroll Burden	$2,143	$2,675	$2,143	$2,143	$2,143	$2,143
Depreciation	$0	$0	$0	$0	$0	$0
Utilities	$125	$125	$125	$125	$125	$125
Insurance	$0	$100	$0	$100	$0	$100
Rent	$1,000	$1,000	$1,000	$1,000	$1,000	$1,000
Total General and Administrative Expenses	**$0**	**$0**	**$0**	**$0**	**$0**	**$0**
General and Administrative %	0.00%	0.00%	0.00%	0.00%	0.00%	0.00%
Other Expenses						
Other Payroll	$0	$0	$0	$0	$0	$0
Telephone	$115	$115	$115	$115	$115	$115
Total Other Expenses	**$0**	**$0**	**$0**	**$0**	**$0**	**$0**
Other %	0.00%	0.00%	0.00%	0.00%	0.00%	0.00%
Total Operating Expenses	**$17,746**	**$21,925**	**$17,746**	**$17,846**	**$17,746**	**$17,846**
Profit Before Interest and Taxes	$5,954	$7,700	$5,954	$5,854	$5,954	$5,854
Interest Expense Short-term	$174	$174	$174	$174	$174	$174
Interest Expense Long-term	$0	$0	$0	$0	$0	$0
Taxes Incurred	$1,445	$1,881	$1,445	$1,420	$1,445	$1,420
Extraordinary Items	$0	$0	$0	$0	$0	$0
Net Profit	$4,335	$5,644	$4,335	$4,260	$4,335	$4,260
Net Profit/Sales	18.29%	19.05%	18.29%	17.97%	18.29%	17.97%

	Oct	Nov	Dec	Jan	Feb	Mar	FY2002	FY2003	FY2004
	$29,625	$23,700	$29,625	$29,625	$23,700	$23,700	$308,100	$308,100	$308,100
	$0	$0	$0	$0	$0	$0	$0	$0	$0
	$0	$0	$0	$0	$0	$0	$0	$0	$0
	$0	$0	$0	$0	$0	$0	$0	$0	$0
	$0	**$0**	**$0**	**$0**	**$0**	**$0**	**$0**	**$0**	**$0**
	$29,625	$23,700	$29,625	$29,625	$23,700	$23,700	$308,100	$308,100	$308,100
	100.00%	100.00%	100.00%	100.00%	100.00%	100.00%	100.00%	100.00%	100.00%
	$0	$0	$0	$0	$0	$0	$0	$0	$0
	$75	$75	$75	$75	$75	$75	$900	$450	$450
	$0	$0	$0	$0	$0	$0	$0	$0	$0
	$0	**$0**	**$0**	**$0**	**$0**	**$0**	**$0**	**$0**	**$0**
	0.00%	0.00%	0.00%	0.00%	0.00%	0.00%	0.00%	0.00%	0.00%
	$0	$0	$0	$0	$0	$0	$0	$0	$0
	$17,836	$14,288	$17,836	$17,836	$14,288	$14,288	$185,648	$185,648	$185,648
	$2,675	$2,143	$2,675	$2,675	$2,143	$2,143	$27,847	$27,847	$27,847
	$0	$0	$0	$0	$0	$0	$0	$0	$0
	$125	$125	$125	$125	$125	$125	$1,500	$1,500	$1,500
	$0	$100	$0	$100	$0	$100	$600	$600	$600
	$1,000	$1,000	$1,000	$1,000	$1,000	$1,000	$12,000	$12,000	$12,000
	$0	**$0**	**$0**	**$0**	**$0**	**$0**	**$0**	**$0**	**$0**
	0.00%	0.00%	0.00%	0.00%	0.00%	0.00%	0.00%	0.00%	0.00%
	$0	$0	$0	$0	$0	$0	$0	$0	$0
	$115	$115	$115	$115	$115	$115	$1,380	$1,380	$1,380
	$0	**$0**	**$0**	**$0**	**$0**	**$0**	**$0**	**$0**	**$0**
	0.00%	0.00%	0.00%	0.00%	0.00%	0.00%	0.00%	0.00%	0.00%
	$21,826	**$17,846**	**$21,826**	**$21,926**	**$17,746**	**$17,846**	**$229,874**	**$229,425**	**$229,425**
	$7,799	$5,854	$7,799	$7,699	$5,954	$5,854	$78,226	$78,675	$78,675
	$174	$174	$174	$174	$174	$174	$2,094	$2,094	$2,094
	$0	$0	$0	$0	$0	$0	$0	$0	$0
	$1,906	$1,420	$1,906	$1,881	$1,445	$1,420	$19,033	$19,145	$19,145
	$0	$0	$0	$0	$0	$0	$0	$0	$0
	$5,718	$4,260	$5,718	$5,643	$4,335	$4,260	$57,099	$57,436	$57,436
	19.30%	17.97%	19.30%	19.05%	18.29%	17.97%	18.53%	18.64%	18.64%

Projected Cash Flow

	Apr	May	Jun	Jul	Aug	Sep
Net Profit	$4,335	$5,644	$4,335	$4,260	$4,335	$4,260
Plus:						
Depreciation	$0	$0	$0	$0	$0	$0
Change in Accounts Payable	$2,553	$467	($467)	$65	($65)	$65
Current Borrowing (repayment)	$0	$0	$0	$0	$0	$0
Increase (decrease) Other Liabilities	$0	$0	$0	$0	$0	$0
Long-term Borrowing (repayment)	$0	$0	$0	$0	$0	$0
Capital Input	$0	$0	$0	$0	$0	$0
Subtotal	**$6,887**	**$6,111**	**$3,868**	**$4,325**	**$4,269**	**$4,325**
Less:						
Change in Accounts Receivable	$8,181	$2,045	($2,045)	$114	$0	$0
Change in Inventory	$0	$0	$0	$0	$0	$0
Change in Other Short-term Assets	$0	$0	$0	$0	$0	$0
Capital Expenditure	$0	$0	$0	$0	$0	$0
Dividends	$0	$0	$0	$0	$0	$0
Subtotal	**$8,181**	**$2,045**	**($2,045)**	**$114**	**$0**	**$0**
Net Cash Flow	**($1,294)**	**$4,065**	**$5,913**	**$4,211**	**$4,269**	**$4,325**
Cash Balance	**$4,706**	**$8,771**	**$14,684**	**$18,896**	**$23,165**	**$27,490**

Projected Balance Sheet

Assets						
Short-term Assets	**Apr**	**May**	**Jun**	**Jul**	**Aug**	**Sep**
Cash	$4,706	$8,771	$14,684	$18,896	$23,165	$27,490
Accounts Receivable	$8,181	$10,227	$8,181	$8,295	$8,295	$8,295
Inventory	$0	$0	$0	$0	$0	$0
Other Short-term Assets	$0	$0	$0	$0	$0	$0
Total Short-term Assets	**$12,887**	**$18,998**	**$22,866**	**$27,191**	**$31,460**	**$35,785**
Long-term Assets						
Capital Assets	$0	$0	$0	$0	$0	$0
Accumulated Depreciation	$0	$0	$0	$0	$0	$0
Total Long-term Assets	$0	$0	$0	$0	$0	$0
Total Assets	**$12,887**	**$18,998**	**$22,866**	**$27,191**	**$31,460**	**$35,785**
Liabilities and Capital						
Accounts Payable	$2,553	$3,020	$2,553	$2,618	$2,553	$2,618
Short-term Notes	$20,935	$20,935	$20,935	$20,935	$20,935	$20,935
Other Short-term Liabilities	$0	$0	$0	$0	$0	$0
Subtotal Short-term Liabilities	**$23,488**	**$23,955**	**$23,488**	**$23,553**	**$23,488**	**$23,553**
Long-term Liabilities	$0	$0	$0	$0	$0	$0
Total Liabilities	**$23,488**	**$23,955**	**$23,488**	**$23,553**	**$23,488**	**$23,553**
Paid in Capital	$6,000	$6,000	$6,000	$6,000	$6,000	$6,000
Retained Earnings	($20,935)	($20,935)	($20,935)	($20,935)	($20,935)	($20,935)
Earnings	$4,335	$9,978	$14,313	$18,572	$22,907	$27,167
Total Capital	**($10,600)**	**($4,957)**	**($622)**	**$3,637**	**$7,972**	**$12,232**
Total Liabilities and Capital	**$12,887**	**$18,998**	**$22,866**	**$27,191**	**$31,460**	**$35,785**
Net Worth	**($10,600)**	**($4,957)**	**($622)**	**$3,637**	**$7,972**	**$12,232**

Oct	Nov	Dec	Jan	Feb	Mar	FY2002	FY2003	FY2004
$5,718	$4,260	$5,718	$5,643	$4,335	$4,260	$57,099	$57,436	$57,436
$0	$0	$0	$0	$0	$0	$0	$0	$0
$336	($336)	$336	$65	($466)	$65	$2,618	$50	($4)
$0	$0	$0	$0	$0	$0	$0	$0	$0
$0	$0	$0	$0	$0	$0	$0	$0	$0
$0	$0	$0	$0	$0	$0	$0	$0	$0
$0	$0	$0	$0	$0	$0	$0	$0	$0
$6,054	**$3,924**	**$6,054**	**$5,708**	**$3,868**	**$4,325**	**$59,717**	**$57,486**	**$57,432**
$2,074	($2,074)	$2,074	$0	($2,074)	$0	$8,295	$0	$0
$0	$0	$0	$0	$0	$0	$0	$0	$0
$0	$0	$0	$0	$0	$0	$0	$0	$0
$0	$0	$0	$0	$0	$0	$0	$0	$0
$0	$0	$0	$0	$0	$0	$0	$0	$0
$2,074	**($2,074)**	**$2,074**	**$0**	**($2,074)**	**$0**	**$8,295**	**$0**	**$0**
$3,980	**$5,997**	**$3,980**	**$5,708**	**$5,942**	**$4,325**	**$51,422**	**$57,486**	**$57,432**
$31,470	**$37,467**	**$41,448**	**$47,156**	**$53,098**	**$57,422**	**$57,422**	**$114,908**	**$172,340**

Oct	Nov	Dec	Jan	Feb	Mar	FY2002	FY2003	FY2004
$31,470	$37,467	$41,448	$47,156	$53,098	$57,422	$57,422	$114,908	$172,340
$10,369	$8,295	$10,369	$10,369	$8,295	$8,295	$8,295	$8,295	$8,295
$0	$0	$0	$0	$0	$0	$0	$0	$0
$0	$0	$0	$0	$0	$0	$0	$0	$0
$41,839	**$45,762**	**$51,816**	**$57,525**	**$61,393**	**$65,717**	**$65,717**	**$123,203**	**$180,635**
$0	$0	$0	$0	$0	$0	$0	$0	$0
$0	$0	$0	$0	$0	$0	$0	$0	$0
$0	$0	$0	$0	$0	$0	$0	$0	$0
$41,839	**$45,762**	**$51,816**	**$57,525**	**$61,393**	**$65,717**	**$65,717**	**$123,203**	**$180,635**
$2,954	$2,618	$2,954	$3,019	$2,553	$2,618	$2,618	$2,668	$2,664
$20,935	$20,935	$20,935	$20,935	$20,935	$20,935	$20,935	$20,935	$20,935
$0	$0	$0	$0	$0	$0	$0	$0	$0
$23,889	**$23,553**	**$23,889**	**$23,954**	**$23,488**	**$23,553**	**$23,553**	**$23,603**	**$23,599**
$0	$0	$0	$0	$0	$0	$0	$0	$0
$23,889	**$23,553**	**$23,889**	**$23,954**	**$23,488**	**$23,553**	**$23,553**	**$23,603**	**$23,599**
$6,000	$6,000	$6,000	$6,000	$6,000	$6,000	$6,000	$6,000	$6,000
($20,935)	($20,935)	($20,935)	($20,935)	($20,935)	($20,935)	($20,935)	$36,164	$93,600
$32,885	$37,144	$42,862	$48,505	$52,840	$57,099	$57,099	$57,436	$57,436
$17,950	**$22,209**	**$27,927**	**$33,570**	**$37,905**	**$42,164**	**$42,164**	**$99,600**	**$157,036**
$41,839	**$45,762**	**$51,816**	**$57,525**	**$61,393**	**$65,717**	**$65,717**	**$123,203**	**$180,635**
$17,950	**$22,209**	**$27,927**	**$33,570**	**$37,905**	**$42,164**	**$42,164**	**$99,600**	**$157,036**

Dollar Store

BUSINESS PLAN

DOLLAR DAZE

3535 Lincoln Plaza Drive
Dayton, Ohio 45402

Dollar Daze is a business specializing in general merchandise. The store has access to the purchasing power of buying centers offering merchandise at prices 10 to 30 percent below wholesale with immediate delivery and low to no minimum orders. These centers are well stocked and prepared to meet the increased demands of the peak selling seasons. Our mission is to provide the Dayton area with a wide variety of quality general merchandise generally priced at one dollar, in a clean and friendly atmosphere.

- EXECUTIVE SUMMARY

- COMPANY SUMMARY

- PRODUCTS

- MARKET ANALYSIS SUMMARY

- STRATEGY & IMPLEMENTATION SUMMARY

- MANAGEMENT SUMMARY

- FINANCIAL PLAN

- APPENDIX

EXECUTIVE SUMMARY

Dollar Daze is a business specializing in general merchandise. It will be located in the brand-new Town Square Plaza, which is in a high traffic area. The space will be next to Nicky's, a café and bakery. The space is easily accessible and provides ample parking for its customers. The space is visible from all points within the center itself as well as the traffic from Martin and Washington Streets. The business is a retail establishment selling current dollar variety merchandise at retail. The majority of the merchandise is priced within a one-dollar price range, thus attracting the widest possible range of customers.

Dollar Daze has access to the purchasing power of buying centers offering merchandise at prices 10 to 30 percent below wholesale with immediate delivery and low to no minimum orders. These centers are well stocked and prepared to meet the increased demands of the peak selling seasons such as Seasonal Changes, Back-to-School, Holiday Needs, etc. Since delivery from these centers to the business takes only five to ten days, Dollar Daze is assured of a well-stocked store regardless of seasonal demands. Also, since these buying centers are able to deliver in such a short time, there is not a necessity to carry an extremely large inventory in advance of peak selling periods.

Dollar Daze attracts its customers through the use of specialized advertisements, handbills, news releases in newspapers, as well as the traffic flow of which the area itself generates.

A Grand Opening will commence after Dollar Daze has been in business for six to eight weeks. This event will be held on a Saturday. Dollar Daze's owner Melinda Parker will coordinate the Grand Opening. It will include a local political official, ribbon-cutting ceremonies, pictures, speaking, etc. Professional news releases will be submitted to the local and market area newspapers, and possibly radio and television.

The storeowner of Dollar Daze has access to over 250 of the best buying centers in the country. The buying centers provide inventory and fixtures. Melinda Parker will take a buying trip for initial inventory with her close friend and professional buyer Jill Smythson. All staff will be provided with in-store training.

According to the information contained in this business plan, we feel that Dollar Daze is a sound business investment for the financial institution to consider for a loan in the amount of $35,000.

Key to Success

The key to our successful retail business is our flexibility. The buying habits of customers change and vary. The availability of equally varied merchandise gives us the freedom to change with our customers.

Mission

Our mission is to provide the Dayton area with a wide variety of quality general merchandise generally priced at one dollar, in a clean and friendly atmosphere.

COMPANY SUMMARY

Dollar Daze will rent a 1,300-square-foot space, having 1,000 square feet of selling space from Noel Sparks. Located in the brand-new Town Square Plaza, it is a high traffic area. The space will be next to Nicky's, a café and bakery. The space is easily accessible and provides ample parking for its customers. The space is visible from all points within the center itself as well as the traffic from Martin and Washington Streets.

Proposed hours of operation are from 9:00 A.M. to 7:00 P.M., Monday through Saturday and 12:00 P.M. to 6:00 P.M. on Sunday. Dollar Daze will also maintain extended holiday hours. The business will be closed Christmas Day as well as three other national holidays yet to be decided.

Since the selected location is in the heart of one of the busiest retail corridors in the area, we feel that this space is the best possible location in Dayton and surrounding areas.

Dollar Daze is a sole-proprietorship and is registered to the owner, Melinda Parker.

Company Ownership

Start-up costs will be financed through a combination of owner investment and a short-term loan. The start-up chart shows the distribution of financing.

Start-up Summary

Those expenses include:

- Inventory, fixtures, and supply fees of $24,400
- Marketing/advertising fees of $600 for our grand opening
- Build-out fees of $3,000 for our location including our sign
- Deposits on location, utilities, telephone, and insurance

Start-up Plan
Start-up Expenses

Deposit on Location	$2,500
Rent (2 months)	$2,000
Build-out of location (including sign)	$3,000
Telephone Deposits/2 months' payments	$750
Credit Card Machine	$150
License and Permits	$100
Insurance (6 months)	$300
Advertising (2 months)	$600
Miscellaneous	$200
Total Start-up Expense	**$9,600**

Start-up Assets Needed

Cash Requirements	$6,000
Start-up Inventory	$24,400
Other Short-term Assets	$0
Total Short-term Assets	**$30,400**

Long-term Assets	$0
Total Assets	**$30,400**

Total Start-up Requirements:	**$40,000**
Left to Finance:	$0

Start-up Funding Plan
Investment

Melinda Parker	$5,000
Investor 2	$0
Other	$0
Total Investment	**$5,000**

Start-up Summary

Continued

Short-term Liabilities	
Unpaid Expenses	$0
Short-term Loans	$35,000
Interest-free Short-term Loans	$0
Subtotal Short-term Liabilities	$35,000
Long-term Liabilities	$0
Total Liabilities	**$35,000**
Loss at Start-up	**($9,600)**
Total Capital	**($4,600)**
Total Capital and Liabilities	**$30,400**
Checkline	**$0**

Equipment and Supplies

Listed below is our equipment and supplies list:

Inventory at cost
Gondolas
Shelving
Pegboard & Slatwall
Pegboard & Slatwall Hooks
Cash Register (Multi-Department)
2 Rolls Register Tape
2,000 Plastic Bags
12 Shopping Baskets
1 2-Line Labeler
6 Rolls for Labeler
Tissue Paper
Weekly Bookkeeping & Record System
Inventory Control System
Supplier/Order System
Advertising Manual
Training Manual
Promotional Idea Manual
Custom Designed Handbills
Customer Register Cards
Pre-opening Guide
Store Merchandise Guide
Store Manual
Buyers Guide
Newsletter Service

PRODUCTS

Our product line will include items from the following categories:

- Hardware
- Toys
- Gift Items
- Office Supplies
- Schools Supplies
- Baby Products
- Bath Products
- Cleaning Products

- Pet Supplies
- Safety & Security Items
- Kitchen Items

We will always have an abundant selection of items available from which to choose.

The Dayton market faces the economic challenges of poverty, single parenthood, and public assistance, plus the generational squeeze of caring for the young and elderly at the same time. The majority of their budget goes to basics, such as rent and groceries. They are top-ranked for buying major household appliances and baby products and they tend to purchase fast food and takeout food.

MARKET ANALYSIS SUMMARY

General Statistics for 1999 in the 45402 zip code area are as follows:

Total Population - 39,889

Number of Households - 14,344

Population by Race
White - 11.8%
Black - 86.5%
Asian Pacific Islander - 0.1%
Other - 1.6%

Population by Gender
Male - 46.2%
Female - 53.8%

Income Figures
Median Household Income - $21,729
   Household Income Under $50K - 75.3%
   Household Income $50K-$100K - 20.8%
   Household Income Over $100K - 4.0%

1990 Housing Figures
Average Home Value - $38,152
Average Rent - $272

Dollar Daze will provide high quality merchandise at a discount price range to its customers. Since the majority of its items offered will be in the one-dollar price range, Dollar Daze will be able to maintain its competitiveness.

Market Segmentation

The target female market is in a growing community that has a population in excess of 39,889 people, well over 14,344 households, of which approximately 53.8 percent are female. The median family income for Dayton is $21,729.

The approaches to be used to attract these customers will be a website, radio and print advertising, signs in the store windows, and word of mouth advertising from our satisfied customers.

Target Market Segment Strategy

Industry Analysis

In 1999, retail sales grew 9 percent to almost $3 trillion dollars. General merchandise and apparel grew to $784.5 billion, a 7.6 percent rise over 1998. According to the Department of Commerce, Internet shopping reached $5.3 billion or .64 percent of U.S. retail sales in 1999. The growth of traditional U.S. retailing should not be robust due to a dearth of economically favorable store locations. Many companies have responded by using their capital for other purposes such as reducing long-term debt and repurchasing their common stock.

Some companies can continue to grow their store count where they have a very specific demographic group to serve and locations can be developed in sparse locations at minimal costs. General Washington and Family Cents Savings for instance, continue to expand their store counts. Keys to their success are convenient locations, relatively small stores, and the ability to provide most nonfood merchandise to their lower-income customer bases.

The retailing industry is mature and slow growing. These factors mean companies will have to do a better job of managing their operations. Specifically, retailers must close unprofitable stores, locate in regions with faster growth, and manage their inventory better. Retailers must also invest in automated processes to keep their costs down. Some companies have taken steps to reduce their exposure to economic cycles and consumer trends.

Traditional retailers may have finally recognized the potential of Internet commerce and its impact on their business. Initially, retailers had just a website that was more for informational purposes than e-commerce transactional purposes. However, beginning in the year 2000, several retailers will devote more time to developing full blown e-commerce sites. Most notably, Target Stores plans to launch a major e-commerce program in the year 2000. Savings Marts' purchase of Billings in March 1999 is significant. It allows Savings Marts to use Billings's expertise and technology in direct marketing to further promote and enhance Savings Marts's Yonkers.com Internet site. Picway also launched a comprehensive Internet site focused on their shoe retailing concept.

Industry Trends

Consumers are more value conscious than they've been in the past. Their shopping habits have shifted from department stores to discounters and mass merchandisers. Many consumers can find the same items at a mass merchandiser that they can find at a department store at a substantially lower price.

Competition and Buying Patterns

There is currently no other store of this kind in the area, which ensures its success!

Dollar Daze will offer a wide selection of general merchandise priced at only one dollar. Having over 25,000 different items to choose from for its inventory selection insures that Dollar Daze will be able to maintain a full and diverse inventory for its customers. It will have suppliers that can deliver these items within 5-10 working days, so the shelves and walls will remain full and well-stocked.

The Christmas season has traditionally been important to retailers but there has been lackluster growth in the past few years despite the booming economy. Part of the problem is shifting demographics. Older people tend to buy fewer items as they age. Since the baby boom generation is approaching their fifties, they will have less need for more items. So the target market of these stores lean towards men and women ages 18-49.

Some retailers have responded by offering theme promotions during other parts of the year, such as Valentine's Day, Independence Day, and Easter. Retailers are also requiring their suppliers to develop unique and exclusive merchandise and product assortments for their stores to avoid competition with another store for the same product.

Consumers are much more value-oriented which has contributed to the growth of mass merchandise stores. Another indication is the growth of the wholesale club and dollar store concept over the past two decades. These stores allow consumers to buy products in bulk and get more products for their money. These stores mostly carry fast-moving merchandise brands which are number one or two in their respective product categories.

The Dayton area continues to expand, offering the retail establishments an ever-growing opportunity for success.

Melinda Parker has chosen three strategies for implementation of Dollar Daze and they are:

1. to build sales volume
2. to create a customer database
3. to develop an effective product line and pricing strategy

STRATEGY & IMPLEMENTATION SUMMARY

During the first few years, the store's sales, she hopes, will grow through the use of promotional campaigns, magazine advertisements, and website sales. Trisha will develop the customer database through careful selection and screening of mailing lists. She plans to select an inventory she feels is affordable and unique when compared to the other dollar store products. For her pricing strategy, she will establish an ongoing campaign to purchase products at pennies less than her competitors, whereas sometimes she can sell items at $.99 instead of $1.00.

Dollar Daze will be locally owned and operated, insuring that the needs and desires of the local community are met. It will also be able to provide special ordering of items for its customers and offer a personal and friendly atmosphere that you cannot find in larger chain variety stores.

Competitive Edge

Our sales strategy is to:

Sales Strategy

- develop a website for e-commerce sales within the next year
- provide quality customer service
- have a "no cash refund/exchanges only" policy
- accept all major credit cards
- survey our customers regarding products they would like to see added to our store
- sponsor school and other community events
- automate our sales process, such as using bar codes and a Point-of-Purchase cash register to track inventory and sales

Revenues of stores of this nature, using the available demographics, average between $176 to $177 in sales per square foot of selling space during their first year of business. This business projected its first year at 90 percent of low average.

Sales Forecast

Each year reflects an increase of 5 percent per year in fixed expenses to more than keep up with the current consumer price index (CPI).

Year 2 reflects a conservative growth rate of 15 percent. Year 3 reflects a growth rate of 10 percent. The information in the chart below is based on a 1,300-square-foot unit with 1,000 square feet of actual selling space.

Sales Forecast

Continued

Sales	FY2002	FY2003	FY2004
Row 1	$158,400	$182,160	$200,376
Other	$0	$0	$0
Total Sales	**$158,400**	**$182,160**	**$200,376**
Direct Cost of Sales			
Row 1	$91,080	$104,742	$115,216
Other	$0	$0	$0
Subtotal Cost of Sales	**$91,080**	**$104,742**	**$115,216**

MANAGEMENT SUMMARY

Melinda Parker, owner of Dollar Daze, has a B.A. degree in Marketing. For two years she has managed a dollar store similar to Dollar Daze. She has a full understanding of how to operate and manage a dollar store and its employees.

Personnel Plan

The personnel plan is included in the following table. It shows the owner's salary (Other) and two full-time salaries for cashiers. There will be no benefits offered at this time. Cashiers will have other duties as assigned.

Personnel Plan	FY2002	FY2003	FY2004
Cashier (1)	$6,000	$6,000	$6,000
Cashier (2)	$6,000	$6,000	$6,000
Other	$18,000	$18,000	$18,000
Total Payroll	**$30,000**	**$30,000**	**$30,000**
Total Headcount	3	3	3
Payroll Burden	$4,500	$4,500	$4,500
Total Payroll Expenditures	**$34,500**	**$34,500**	**$34,500**

FINANCIAL PLAN

Our financial plan includes:

- moderate growth with a steady cash flow
- investing residual profits into company expansion
- repayment of our loan calculated at a high A.P.R. of 10 percent and at a 10-year-payback on our $35,000 loan

Important Assumptions

We do not sell anything on credit. The personnel burden is low because benefits are not paid to our staff. We will continue to work on a short-term interest rate that is lower. We are also assuming the economy will continue to grow and there will continue to be a need for stores such as Dollar Daze.

General Assumptions	FY2002	FY2003	FY2004
Short-term Interest Rate %	10.00%	10.00%	10.00%
Long-term Interest Rate %	10.00%	10.00%	10.00%
Payment Days Estimator	30	30	30
Collection Days Estimator	45	45	45
Inventory Turnover Estimator	6.00	6.00	6.00
Tax Rate %	25.00%	25.00%	25.00%
Expenses in Cash %	10.00%	10.00%	10.00%
Sales on Credit %	0.00%	0.00%	0.00%
Personnel Burden %	15.00%	15.00%	15.00%

A break-even analysis label has been completed on the basis of average costs/prices. With fixed costs averaging $5,979 and $176 to $177 in sales per square foot, we need $7,972 in sales per month to break-even.

Break-even Analysis:

Monthly Units Break-even	7,972
Monthly Sales Break-even	$7,972

Assumptions:

Average Per-Unit Revenue	$1.00
Average Per-Unit Variable Cost	$0.25
Estimated Monthly Fixed Cost	$5,979

We predict advertising costs will go down in the next three years as word of our store gets out to the public. Our net profit/sales ratio will be low the first year. We expect this ratio to rise at least 12 percent the second year and at least 3 percent in our third year. Normally, a start-up concern will operate with negative profits through the first two years. We will avoid that kind of operating loss on our second year by knowing our competitors and having a full understanding of our target markets.

Profit and Loss (Income Statement)	FY2002	FY2003	FY2004
Sales	$158,400	$182,160	$200,376
Direct Cost of Sales	$91,080	$104,742	$115,216
Production Payroll	$0	$0	$0
Other	$6,000	$0	$0
Total Cost of Sales	**$97,080**	**$104,742**	**$115,216**
Gross Margin	$61,320	$77,418	$85,160
Gross Margin %	38.71%	42.50%	42.50%
Operating Expenses:			
Sales and Marketing Expenses			
Sales and Marketing Payroll	$0	$0	$0
Rent	$10,000	$12,000	$12,000
Repairs and Maintenance	$550	$600	$600
Insurance	$300	$600	$600
Professional Fees	$600	$600	$600
Interest and Bank Charges	$300	$300	$300
Advertising	$3,000	$2,000	$1,000
Telephone	$750	$900	$900
Utilities	$3,000	$3,000	$3,000
Operating Supplies	$1,200	$1,200	$1,200
Loan Payment	$6,391	$6,972	$6,972
Capital Purchases	$2,000	$2,000	$2,000
Travel	$0	$0	$0
Miscellaneous	$14,400	$1,200	$1,200
Total Sales and Marketing Expenses	**$0**	**$0**	**$0**
Sales and Marketing %	0.00%	0.00%	0.00%

Projected Profit and Loss

Continued

General and Administrative Expenses	FY2002	FY2003	FY2004
General and Administrative Payroll	$0	$0	$0
Payroll Expense	$30,000	$30,000	$30,000
Payroll Burden	$4,500	$4,500	$4,500
Depreciation	$0	$0	$0
Other	$0	$0	$0
Total General and Administrative Expenses	**$0**	**$0**	**$0**
General and Administrative %	0.00%	0.00%	0.00%
Other Expenses			
Other Payroll	$0	$0	$0
Other	$0	$0	$0
Total Other Expenses	**$0**	**$0**	**$0**
Other %	0.00%	0.00%	0.00%
Total Operating Expenses	**$76,991**	**$65,872**	**$64,872**
Profit Before Interest and Taxes	($15,671)	$11,546	$20,288
Interest Expense Short-term	$3,500	$3,500	$3,500
Interest Expense Long-term	$0	$0	$0
Taxes Incurred	($4,793)	$2,012	$4,197
Extraordinary Items	$0	$0	$0
Net Profit	($14,378)	$6,035	$12,591
Net Profit/Sales	-9.08%	3.31%	6.28%

Projected Cash Flow

We are positioning ourselves in the market as a medium risk concern with steady cash flows.

	FY2002	FY2003	FY2004
Net Profit	($14,378)	$6,035	$12,591
Plus:			
Depreciation	$0	$0	$0
Change in Accounts Payable	$2,992	$8,210	$318
Current Borrowing (repayment)	$0	$0	$0
Increase (decrease) Other Liabilities	$0	$0	$0
Long-term Borrowing (repayment)	$0	$0	$0
Capital Input	$0	$0	$0
Subtotal	($11,387)	$14,244	$12,909
Less:			
Change in Accounts Receivable	$0	$0	$0
Change in Inventory	($9,825)	$1,150	$1,573
Change in Other Short-term Assets	$0	$0	$0
Capital Expenditure	$0	$0	$0
Dividends	$0	$0	$0
Subtotal	($9,825)	$1,150	$1,573
Net Cash Flow	**($1,562)**	**$13,094**	**$11,337**
Cash Balance	**$4,438**	**$17,532**	**$28,869**

All of our tables will be updated monthly to reflect past performance and future assumptions. Future assumptions will not be based on past performance but rather on economic cycle activity, regional industry strength, and future cash flow possibilities. We expect a solid growth in net worth by the year 2005.

Projected Balance Sheet

Assets	FY2002	FY2003	FY2004
Short-term Assets			
Cash	$4,438	$17,532	$28,869
Accounts Receivable	$0	$0	$0
Inventory	$14,575	$15,725	$17,298
Other Short-term Assets	$0	$0	$0
Total Short-term Assets	**$19,013**	**$33,258**	**$46,167**
Long-term Assets			
Capital Assets	$0	$0	$0
Accumulated Depreciation	$0	$0	$0
Total Long-term Assets	**$0**	**$0**	**$0**
Total Assets	**$19,013**	**$33,258**	**$46,167**
Liabilities and Capital			
Accounts Payable	$2,992	$11,201	$11,520
Short-term Notes	$35,000	$35,000	$35,000
Other Short-term Liabilities	$0	$0	$0
Subtotal Short-term Liabilities	**$37,992**	**$46,201**	**$46,520**
Long-term Liabilities	$0	$0	$0
Total Liabilities	**$37,992**	**$46,201**	**$46,520**
Paid in Capital	$5,000	$5,000	$5,000
Retained Earnings	($9,600)	($23,978)	($17,944)
Earnings	($14,378)	$6,035	$12,591
Total Capital	**($18,978)**	**($12,944)**	**($353)**
Total Liabilities and Capital	**$19,013**	**$33,258**	**$46,167**
Net Worth	**($18,978)**	**($12,944)**	**($353)**

APPENDIX

Sales Forecast

Sales	Mar	Apr	May	Jun	Jul	Aug	Sep
Row 1	$12,672	$14,256	$11,880	$11,088	$11,088	$9,500	$14,256
Other	$0	$0	$0	$0	$0	$0	$0
Total Sales	**$12,672**	**$14,256**	**$11,880**	**$11,088**	**$11,088**	**$9,500**	**$14,256**
Direct Cost of Sales							
Row 1	$7,286	$8,197	$6,831	$6,376	$6,376	$5,463	$8,197
Other	$0	$0	$0	$0	$0	$0	$0
Subtotal Cost of Sales	**$7,286**	**$8,197**	**$6,831**	**$6,376**	**$6,376**	**$5,463**	**$8,197**

Personnel Plan

Personnel	Mar	Apr	May	Jun	Jul	Aug	Sep
Cashier (1)	$500	$500	$500	$500	$500	$500	$500
Cashier (2)	$500	$500	$500	$500	$500	$500	$500
Other	$1,500	$1,500	$1,500	$1,500	$1,500	$1,500	$1,500
Total Payroll	**$2,500**	**$2,500**	**$2,500**	**$2,500**	**$2,500**	**$2,500**	**$2,500**
Total Headcount	3	3	3	3	3	3	3
Payroll Burden	$375	$375	$375	$375	$375	$375	$375
Total Payroll Expenditures	**$2,875**	**$2,875**	**$2,875**	**$2,875**	**$2,875**	**$2,875**	**$2,875**

General Assumptions

	Mar	Apr	May	Jun	Jul	Aug	Sep
Short-term Interest Rate %	10.00%	10.00%	10.00%	10.00%	10.00%	10.00%	10.00%
Long-term Interest Rate %	10.00%	10.00%	10.00%	10.00%	10.00%	10.00%	10.00%
Payment Days Estimator	30	30	30	30	30	30	30
Collection Days Estimator	45	45	45	45	45	45	45
Inventory Turnover Estimator	6.00	6.00	6.00	6.00	6.00	6.00	6.00
Tax Rate %	25.00%	25.00%	25.00%	25.00%	25.00%	25.00%	25.00%
Expenses in Cash %	10.00%	10.00%	10.00%	10.00%	10.00%	10.00%	10.00%
Sales on Credit %	0.00%	0.00%	0.00%	0.00%	0.00%	0.00%	0.00%
Personnel Burden %	15.00%	15.00%	15.00%	15.00%	15.00%	15.00%	15.00%

Oct	Nov	Dec	Jan	Feb	FY2002	FY2003	FY2004
$14,256	$15,840	$22,972	$9,504	$11,088	$158,400	$182,160	$200,376
$0	$0	$0	$0	$0	$0	$0	$0
$14,256	**$15,840**	**$22,972**	**$9,504**	**$11,088**	**$158,400**	**$182,160**	**$200,376**
$8,197	$9,108	$13,208	$5,465	$6,376	$91,080	$104,742	$115,216
$0	$0	$0	$0	$0	$0	$0	$0
$8,197	**$9,108**	**$13,208**	**$5,465**	**$6,376**	**$91,080**	**$104,742**	**$115,216**

Oct	Nov	Dec	Jan	Feb	FY2002	FY2003	FY2004
$500	$500	$500	$500	$500	$6,000	$6,000	$6,000
$500	$500	$500	$500	$500	$6,000	$6,000	$6,000
$1,500	$1,500	$1,500	$1,500	$1,500	$18,000	$18,000	$18,000
$2,500	**$2,500**	**$2,500**	**$2,500**	**$2,500**	**$30,000**	**$30,000**	**$30,000**
3	3	3	3	3	3	3	3
$375	$375	$375	$375	$375	$4,500	$4,500	$4,500
$2,875	**$2,875**	**$2,875**	**$2,875**	**$2,875**	**$34,500**	**$34,500**	**$34,500**

Oct	Nov	Dec	Jan	Feb	FY2002	FY2003	FY2004
10.00%	10.00%	10.00%	10.00%	10.00%	10.00%	10.00%	10.00%
10.00%	10.00%	10.00%	10.00%	10.00%	10.00%	10.00%	10.00%
30	30	30	30	30	30	30	30
45	45	45	45	45	45	45	45
6.00	6.00	6.00	6.00	6.00	6.00	6.00	6.00
25.00%	25.00%	25.00%	25.00%	25.00%	25.00%	25.00%	25.00%
10.00%	10.00%	10.00%	10.00%	10.00%	10.00%	10.00%	10.00%
0.00%	0.00%	0.00%	0.00%	0.00%	0.00%	0.00%	0.00%
15.00%	15.00%	15.00%	15.00%	15.00%	15.00%	15.00%	15.00%

Profit and Loss (Income Statement)

	Mar	Apr	May	Jun	Jul	Aug
Sales	$12,672	$14,256	$11,880	$11,088	$11,088	$9,500
Direct Cost of Sales	$7,286	$8,197	$6,831	$6,376	$6,376	$5,463
Production Payroll	$0	$0	$0	$0	$0	$0
Other	$6,000	$0	$0	$0	$0	$0
Total Cost of Sales	**$13,286**	**$8,197**	**$6,831**	**$6,376**	**$6,376**	**$5,463**
Gross Margin	($614)	$6,059	$5,049	$4,712	$4,712	$4,037
Gross Margin %	-4.85%	42.50%	42.50%	42.50%	42.50%	42.49%
Operating expenses:						
Sales and Marketing Expenses						
Sales and Marketing Payroll	$0	$0	$0	$0	$0	$0
Rent	$0	$0	$1,000	$1,000	$1,000	$1,000
Repairs and Maintenance	$0	$50	$50	$50	$50	$50
Insurance	$0	$0	$0	$0	$0	$0
Professional Fees	$50	$50	$50	$50	$50	$50
Interest and Bank Charges	$25	$25	$25	$25	$25	$25
Advertising	$0	$0	$300	$300	$300	$300
Telephone	$0	$0	$75	$75	$75	$75
Utilities	$250	$250	$250	$250	$250	$250
Operating Supplies	$100	$100	$100	$100	$100	$100
Loan Payment	$0	$581	$581	$581	$581	$581
Capital Purchases	$0	$0	$0	$0	$0	$0
Travel	$0	$0	$0	$0	$0	$0
Miscellaneous	$1,200	$1,200	$1,200	$1,200	$1,200	$1,200
Total Sales and Marketing Expenses	**$0**	**$0**	**$0**	**$0**	**$0**	**$0**
Sales and Marketing %	0.00%	0.00%	0.00%	0.00%	0.00%	0.00%
General and Administrative Expenses						
General and Administrative Payroll	$0	$0	$0	$0	$0	$0
Payroll Expense	$2,500	$2,500	$2,500	$2,500	$2,500	$2,500
Payroll Burden	$375	$375	$375	$375	$375	$375
Depreciation	$0	$0	$0	$0	$0	$0
Other	$0	$0	$0	$0	$0	$0
Total General and Administrative Expenses	**$0**	**$0**	**$0**	**$0**	**$0**	**$0**
General and Administrative %	0.00%	0.00%	0.00%	0.00%	0.00%	0.00%
Other Expenses						
Other Payroll	$0	$0	$0	$0	$0	$0
Other	$0	$0	$0	$0	$0	$0
Total Other Expenses	**$0**	**$0**	**$0**	**$0**	**$0**	**$0**
Other %	0.00%	0.00%	0.00%	0.00%	0.00%	0.00%
Total Operating Expenses	**$4,500**	**$5,131**	**$6,506**	**$6,506**	**$6,506**	**$6,506**
Profit Before Interest and Taxes	($5,114)	$928	($1,457)	($1,794)	($1,794)	($2,469)
Interest Expense Short-term	$292	$292	$292	$292	$292	$292
Interest Expense Long-term	$0	$0	$0	$0	$0	$0
Taxes Incurred	($1,351)	$159	($437)	($521)	($521)	($690)
Extraordinary Items	$0	$0	$0	$0	$0	$0
Net Profit	($4,054)	$477	($1,312)	($1,564)	($1,564)	($2,071)
Net Profit/Sales	-31.99%	3.35%	-11.04%	-14.11%	-14.11%	-21.79%

	Sep	Oct	Nov	Dec	Jan	Feb	FY2002	FY2003	FY2004
	$14,256	$14,256	$15,840	$22,972	$9,504	$11,088	$158,400	$182,160	$200,376
	$8,197	$8,197	$9,108	$13,208	$5,465	$6,376	$91,080	$104,742	$115,216
	$0	$0	$0	$0	$0	$0	$0	$0	$0
	$0	$0	$0	$0	$0	$0	$6,000	$0	$0
	$8,197	**$8,197**	**$9,108**	**$13,208**	**$5,465**	**$6,376**	**$97,080**	$104,742	$115,216
	$6,059	$6,059	$6,732	$9,764	$4,039	$4,712	$61,320	$77,418	$85,160
	42.50%	42.50%	42.50%	42.50%	42.50%	42.50%	38.71%	42.50%	42.50%
	$0	$0	$0	$0	$0	$0	$0	$0	$0
	$1,000	$1,000	$1,000	$1,000	$1,000	$1,000	$10,000	$12,000	$12,000
	$50	$50	$50	$50	$50	$50	$550	$600	$600
	$50	$50	$50	$50	$50	$50	$300	$600	$600
	$50	$50	$50	$50	$50	$50	$600	$600	$600
	$25	$25	$25	$25	$25	$25	$300	$300	$300
	$300	$300	$300	$300	$300	$300	$3,000	$2,000	$1,000
	$75	$75	$75	$75	$75	$75	$750	$900	$900
	$250	$250	$250	$250	$250	$250	$3,000	$3,000	$3,000
	$100	$100	$100	$100	$100	$100	$1,200	$1,200	$1,200
	$581	$581	$581	$581	$581	$581	$6,391	$6,972	$6,972
	$0	$0	$1,000	$1,000	$0	$0	$2,000	$2,000	$2,000
	$0	$0	$0	$0	$0	$0	$0	$0	$0
	$1,200	$1,200	$1,200	$1,200	$1,200	$1,200	$14,400	$1,200	$1,200
	$0	**$0**	**$0**	**$0**	**$0**	**$0**	**$0**	**$0**	**$0**
	0.00%	0.00%	0.00%	0.00%	0.00%	0.00%	0.00%	0.00%	0.00%
	$0	$0	$0	$0	$0	$0	$0	$0	$0
	$2,500	$2,500	$2,500	$2,500	$2,500	$2,500	$30,000	$30,000	$30,000
	$375	$375	$375	$375	$375	$375	$4,500	$4,500	$4,500
	$0	$0	$0	$0	$0	$0	$0	$0	$0
	$0	$0	$0	$0	$0	$0	$0	$0	$0
	$0	**$0**	**$0**	**$0**	**$0**	**$0**	**$0**	**$0**	**$0**
	0.00%	0.00%	0.00%	0.00%	0.00%	0.00%	0.00%	0.00%	0.00%
	$0	$0	$0	$0	$0	$0	$0	$0	$0
	$0	$0	$0	$0	$0	$0	$0	$0	$0
	$0	**$0**	**$0**	**$0**	**$0**	**$0**	**$0**	**$0**	**$0**
	0.00%	0.00%	0.00%	0.00%	0.00%	0.00%	0.00%	0.00%	0.00%
	$6,556	**$6,556**	**$7,556**	**$7,556**	**$6,556**	**$6,556**	**$76,991**	**$65,872**	**$64,872**
	($497)	($497)	($824)	$2,208	($2,517)	($1,844)	($15,671)	$11,546	$20,288
	$292	$292	$292	$292	$292	$292	$3,500	$3,500	$3,500
	$0	$0	$0	$0	$0	$0	$0	$0	$0
	($197)	($197)	($279)	$479	($702)	($534)	($4,793)	$2,012	$4,197
	$0	$0	$0	$0	$0	$0	$0	$0	$0
	($592)	($592)	($837)	$1,437	($2,107)	($1,602)	($14,378)	$6,035	$12,591
	-4.15%	-4.15%	-5.28%	6.26%	-22.16%	-14.45%	-9.08%	3.31%	6.28%

Projected Cash Flow

	Mar	Apr	May	Jun	Jul	Aug
Net Profit	($4,054)	$477	($1,312)	($1,564)	($1,564)	($2,071)
Plus:						
Depreciation	$0	$0	$0	$0	$0	$0
Change in Accounts Payable	$5,712	$3,148	($2,261)	$1,116	$792	($2,530)
Current Borrowing (repayment)	$0	$0	$0	$0	$0	$0
Increase (decrease) Other Liabilities	$0	$0	$0	$0	$0	$0
Long-term Borrowing (repayment)	$0	$0	$0	$0	$0	$0
Capital Input	$0	$0	$0	$0	$0	$0
Subtotal	**$1,658**	**$3,625**	**($3,573)**	**($448)**	**($773)**	**($4,600)**
Less:						
Change in Accounts Receivable	$0	$0	$0	$0	$0	$0
Change in Inventory	($7,286)	($720)	($2,732)	($910)	$0	($1,826)
Change in Other Short-term Assets	$0	$0	$0	$0	$0	$0
Capital Expenditure	$0	$0	$0	$0	$0	$0
Dividends	$0	$0	$0	$0	$0	$0
Subtotal	**($7,286)**	**($720)**	**($2,732)**	**($910)**	**$0**	**($1,826)**
Net Cash Flow	**$8,944**	**$4,345**	**($841)**	**$462**	**($773)**	**($2,774)**
Cash Balance	**$14,944**	**$19,289**	**$18,448**	**$18,910**	**$18,137**	**$15,363**

Projected Balance Sheet

Assets						
Short-term Assets	**Mar**	**Apr**	**May**	**Jun**	**Jul**	**Aug**
Cash	$14,944	$19,289	$18,448	$18,910	$18,137	$15,363
Accounts Receivable	$0	$0	$0	$0	$0	$0
Inventory	$17,114	$16,394	$13,662	$12,752	$12,752	$10,926
Other Short-term Assets	$0	$0	$0	$0	$0	$0
Total Short-term Assets	**$32,058**	**$35,683**	**$32,110**	**$31,662**	**$30,889**	**$26,289**
Long-term Assets						
Capital Assets	$0	$0	$0	$0	$0	$0
Accumulated Depreciation	$0	$0	$0	$0	$0	$0
Total Long-term Assets	**$0**	**$0**	**$0**	**$0**	**$0**	**$0**
Total Assets	**$32,058**	**$35,683**	**$32,110**	**$31,662**	**$30,889**	**$26,289**
Liabilities and Capital						
Accounts Payable	$5,712	$8,860	$6,599	$7,715	$8,506	$5,976
Short-term Notes	$35,000	$35,000	$35,000	$35,000	$35,000	$35,000
Other Short-term Liabilities	$0	$0	$0	$0	$0	$0
Subtotal Short-term Liabilities	**$40,712**	**$43,860**	**$41,599**	**$42,715**	**$43,506**	**$40,976**
Long-term Liabilities	$0	$0	$0	$0	$0	$0
Total Liabilities	**$40,712**	**$43,860**	**$41,599**	**$42,715**	**$43,506**	**$40,976**
Paid in Capital	$5,000	$5,000	$5,000	$5,000	$5,000	$5,000
Retained Earnings	($9,600)	($9,600)	($9,600)	($9,600)	($9,600)	($9,600)
Earnings	($4,054)	($3,577)	($4,889)	($6,453)	($8,017)	($10,088)
Total Capital	**($8,654)**	**($8,177)**	**($9,489)**	**($11,053)**	**($12,617)**	**($14,688)**
Total Liabilities and Capital	**$32,058**	**$35,683**	**$32,110**	**$31,662**	**$30,889**	**$26,289**
Net Worth	**($8,654)**	**($8,177)**	**($9,489)**	**($11,053)**	**($12,617)**	**($14,688)**

Sep	Oct	Nov	Dec	Jan	Feb	FY2002	FY2003	FY2004
($592)	($592)	($837)	$1,437	($2,107)	($1,602)	($14,378)	$6,035	$12,591
$0	$0	$0	$0	$0	$0	$0	$0	$0
$9,197	($4,757)	$3,177	$9,775	($20,523)	$146	$2,992	$8,210	$318
$0	$0	$0	$0	$0	$0	$0	$0	$0
$0	$0	$0	$0	$0	$0	$0	$0	$0
$0	$0	$0	$0	$0	$0	$0	$0	$0
$0	$0	$0	$0	$0	$0	$0	$0	$0
$8,605	**($5,349)**	**$2,340**	**$11,213**	**($22,629)**	**($1,455)**	**($11,387)**	**$14,244**	**$12,909**
$0	$0	$0	$0	$0	$0	$0	$0	$0
$5,468	$0	$1,822	$8,200	($5,465)	($6,376)	($9,825)	$1,150	$1,573
$0	$0	$0	$0	$0	$0	$0	$0	$0
$0	$0	$0	$0	$0	$0	$0	$0	$0
$0	$0	$0	$0	$0	$0	$0	$0	$0
$5,468	**$0**	**$1,822**	**$8,200**	**($5,465)**	**($6,376)**	**($9,825)**	**$1,150**	**$1,573**
$3,137	**($5,349)**	**$518**	**$3,013**	**($17,164)**	**$4,921**	**($1,562)**	**$13,094**	**$11,337**
$18,500	**$13,152**	**$13,669**	**$16,682**	**($482)**	**$4,438**	**$4,438**	**$17,532**	**$28,869**

Sep	Oct	Nov	Dec	Jan	Feb	FY2002	FY2003	FY2004
$18,500	$13,152	$13,669	$16,682	($482)	$4,438	$4,438	$17,532	$28,869
$0	$0	$0	$0	$0	$0	$0	$0	$0
$16,394	$16,394	$18,216	$26,416	$20,951	$14,575	$14,575	$15,725	$17,298
$0	$0	$0	$0	$0	$0	$0	$0	$0
$34,894	**$29,546**	**$31,885**	**$43,098**	**$20,469**	**$19,013**	**$19,013**	**$33,258**	**$46,167**
$0	$0	$0	$0	$0	$0	$0	$0	$0
$0	$0	$0	$0	$0	$0	$0	$0	$0
$0	**$0**	**$0**	**$0**	**$0**	**$0**	**$0**	**$0**	**$0**
$34,894	**$29,546**	**$31,885**	**$43,098**	**$20,469**	**$19,013**	**$19,013**	**$33,258**	**$46,167**
$15,173	$10,416	$13,593	$23,368	$2,845	$2,992	$2,992	$11,201	$11,520
$35,000	$35,000	$35,000	$35,000	$35,000	$35,000	$35,000	$35,000	$35,000
$0	$0	$0	$0	$0	$0	$0	$0	$0
$50,173	**$45,416**	**$48,593**	**$58,368**	**$37,845**	**$37,992**	**$37,992**	**$46,201**	**$46,520**
$0	$0	$0	$0	$0	$0	$0	$0	$0
$50,173	**$45,416**	**$48,593**	**$58,368**	**$37,845**	**$37,992**	**$37,992**	**$46,201**	**$46,520**
$5,000	$5,000	$5,000	$5,000	$5,000	$5,000	$5,000	$5,000	$5,000
($9,600)	($9,600)	($9,600)	($9,600)	($9,600)	($9,600)	($9,600)	($23,978)	($17,944)
($10,679)	($11,271)	($12,107)	($10,670)	($12,777)	($14,378)	($14,378)	$6,035	$12,591
($15,279)	**($15,871)**	**($16,707)**	**($15,270)**	**($17,377)**	**($18,978)**	**($18,978)**	**($12,944)**	**($353)**
$34,894	**$29,546**	**$31,885**	**$43,098**	**$20,469**	**$19,013**	**$19,013**	**$33,258**	**$46,167**
($15,279)	**($15,871)**	**($16,707)**	**($15,270)**	**($17,377)**	**($18,978)**	**($18,978)**	**($12,944)**	**($353)**

Electronic Document Security Company

BUSINESS PLAN   GOLDTRUSTMARK.COM

445 Lockheed Avenue
Overland Park, Kansas 66213

GoldTrustMark.com provides Internet-enabled electronic document security. By providing an integrated bundle of technological tools, GoldTrustMark.com aims to position itself as the market leader in providing electronic document watermarking security solutions to the financial services industry and other knowledge-intensive industries.

- COMPANY SNAPSHOT

- THE OPPORTUNITY

- THE SOLUTION

- MARKET ANALYSIS

- COMPETITIVE ANALYSIS

- MARKETING STRATEGY

- MANAGEMENT TEAM

- FINANCIAL OVERVIEW

- APPENDIX A: MARKET RESEARCH FINDINGS

- APPENDIX B: FINANCIAL PROJECTIONS

**COMPANY
SNAPSHOT**

Management:
Bill Piller, Founder
Edward Reins, CTO
Jonathan Kosow, Director, Sales/Marketing
Maxine Stein, Esq, Director, Sales

Board of Advisors:
Frank Letterman, Co-Chairman—Letterman Capital
Jimmy Douglas, CIO—Manhattan Solutions, Inc.
Robert Timperton, Director, Kingston Mist Fund—Rising Sun Fruits
Henry Gonzalez, President—Gonzalez Enterprises
Mark Rubin, Managing Director—Whitehall & Rubin Co.
Edward Gargant, President—Gargant Technologies, Inc.

Industry: Electronic Document Security

Web Design: Luminary Studios

Database Management: InforPen

Nonprofit Partner: Habitat for Humanity

PR Agency: Bowdent Communications

Bank: Imperial Bank

Law Firms: Davis, Smith & Flounder; White & Trent

Use of Funds: Product development, technology development, marketing/sales, and distribution

Current Investors: ($150,000)

**Business
Description**

GoldTrustMark.com provides Internet-enabled electronic document security. The company's mission is to enable any document or contract intensive industries to take full advantage of the opportunities presented by the Electronic Signatures Act and Global and National Commerce Act, and Revised Article 9 of the Uniform Commercial Code. The GoldTrustMark.com solution contains processes for document watermarking and security, and aims to move these industries from the traditional paper-based system into the realm of electronic content management and security. GoldTrustMark.com's solution is a proprietary watermarking technology that, unlike any technologies on the market today, ensures the integrity of text and image documents in both digital and analog formats.

The company will deliver its solution using a software-based product, meaning that clients will not have to make significant investments in information technology hardware or infrastructure in order to take advantage of it. Instead, GoldTrustMark.com functionality will be accessible via a standard software package, accessible by any permissioned user. State-of-the-art security and encryption technology will guarantee the safety of all information transferred across the network, and advanced watermarking functionality will secure the documents prior to transmission and upon receipt.

Finally, the solution's wireless accessibility will ensure that users can watermark their documents from their laptop or personal digital assistant (PDA). By providing this integrated bundle of technological tools, GoldTrustMark.com aims to position itself as the market leader in providing electronic document watermarking security solutions to the financial services and other knowledge-intensive industries.

Market Needs

Businesses currently have several document security needs, which are not being met:

- Improved document security
- Technology that doesn't allow for the manipulation of text
- Improved document integrity verification
- Document authenticity

Service Features

GoldTrustMark.com will directly address the needs of clients by delivering a comprehensive, software-based, document watermarking and security solution for the financial services profession. Service features will include:

- Document watermarking functionality
- Comprehensive document security package
- Secure online transactions
- Wireless access

Security Features

The company has developed a proprietary watermarking technology that, unlike most digital watermarking programs, protects both text and images before, during, and after their electronic transmission. Furthermore this technology is unique in that it enables a document to be watermarked in both digital and analog formats.

Market Opportunity

On October 1, 2000, the United States took a substantial step toward bringing the business world up to speed with the rapidly evolving landscape of e-commerce when the "Electronic Signatures in Global and National Commerce Act" (E-Sign) came into effect. This legislation is designed to bridge the gap between business transactions and online technology. Its fundamental purpose is to remove the existing legal impediments to the use of electronic contracts in order to facilitate the growth of e-commerce. The goal of E-Sign is to permit contracting parties to take advantage of the efficiencies that only the digital world can offer. Instantaneous exchange of documents between contracting parties eliminates the time loss to traditional carriers such as mail or the quality degradation that results from repeated faxing.

Such increased efficiencies are also the goal of Revised Article 9 of the Uniform Commercial Code—a regulation that requires all transactions related to the creation of a security interest in "goods, documents, instruments, general intangibles, chattel paper or accounts" as well as the sale of the latter two items, to be registered with the Secretary of State in the state(s) where these transactions take place. Given the wide scope of transactions covered (the definition above covers security sales of nearly every type), to date, this has been a paper- and time-intensive process. But with the passing of a Revised Article 9 (effective July 1, 2001), all of these filings will be handled electronically—a move that will result in increased efficiencies, as well as an anticipated elimination of "dual filing" which still exists in approximately 20 percent of states.

As required by law for E-Sign and Revised Article 9 to work, there must be protocols in place to ensure that issues such as authenticity, integrity, and security are adequately addressed. It is critical when facilitating an electronic transaction to maintain the integrity of the data being transmitted. The document being sent must be the same as the one received, with no unauthorized or accidental alterations during or after delivery. The need to establish authenticity and maintain data integrity naturally leads to the enforceability of an electronic transaction. If neither authenticity nor data integrity can be preserved during the course of a transaction, then the underlying deal may be subject to repudiation.

One of the pitfalls of E-Sign is the lack of guidance in prescribing the type of technology that must be used for an electronic record to meet the functional equivalence standard. E-Sign has left it to the contracting parties to determine for themselves the best method to ensure authentication and data integrity.

GoldTrustMark.com has developed a proprietary document watermarking system that safeguards the integrity of both electronic and hard-copy documents. The company's watermarking method is unique in that it functions in—and is automatically transferred between—digital and analog versions of the same document. This unique technological facet positions GoldTrustMark.com to be able to take advantage of the increased demand for electronic document security. It is anticipated that the passing of this Act will cause contract-intensive industries to rely increasingly on electronic documents, and the resultant increased need for security and authentication technologies by these firms signifies a considerable market opportunity for the company's watermarking technology.

COMPETITIVE ADVANTAGE

While there are providers of digital document security solutions, GoldTrustMark.com's proprietary technology is the only one that functions in both digital and analog environments. GoldTrustMark.com technology will reduce costs for clients, for it will not require them to invest in IT hardware. Furthermore, the company's value-added wireless interface—a feature that is not offered by any competitors—will allow client firms to watermark their records regardless of their location. These facts will enable the company to deliver a highly flexible solution that is specifically tailored to the document security needs of the financial services profession, and which allows firms to take advantage of the Electronic Signatures in Global and National Commerce Act. As a result, the company will enjoy a number of sustainable competitive advantages: proprietary technology, incumbent advantages, and learning curve advantages.

Market Entry

In entering the market and positioning itself in front of potential clients, GoldTrustMark.com will utilize a dual-track approach. First off, the company will forge a series of strategic alliances with world-class products and service providers, whose offerings complement its own: manufacturers and distributors of computer hardware, such as scanners and PCs, as well as with document storage providers. These alliances will not only provide GoldTrustMark.com with strong client referral channels, but will also provide it with increased visibility and credibility. In addition, the company will employ a more traditional marketing approach by engaging in selective target marketing and direct advertising to target financial services firms.

As an initial step in its marketing efforts, GoldTrustMark.com will launch an operational website, focused on the needs of financial services professionals in its first tier target markets. This version of the site will be accessible only to a select number of users, most notably some of the local attorneys who have signed letters of intent to subscribe to the company's service. The site's functionality will be limited, but will include links to alliance partners and a working demo of GoldTrustMark.com functionality.

GoldTrustMark.com will derive its revenues from two primary revenue streams:

- Software licensing fees
- Partnership fees

As information technology has taken an increasingly pivotal role in organizations and enterprises from all industries and economic sectors, the exchange of data and conclusion of agreements in the electronic medium has taken on crucial importance as a means of increasing operational efficiency and effectiveness. Organizations in both the private and public sectors recognize that switching from paper-based to electronically based transactional and archival systems will result in both speedier transactions, as well as substantial cost savings in the areas of transactional processing, approval, communications, and archiving. Federal and state governments have also recognized the important role of electronically enabling transactions—a situation, which has recently resulted in two key pieces of legislation and regulation in this area.

The Electronic Signatures in Global and National Commerce Act, known as E-Sign, was signed by President Clinton last summer and went into effect on October 1, 2000. In short, it gives electronic signatures the same standing as their paper and pen counterparts. While many have viewed the effects of this piece of legislation to be solely upon electronic signatures, they are indeed much wider. More broadly, E-Sign directly addresses the legitimacy and legality of all electronic records and notices, establishing them as satisfying the same requirements as their hard-copy counterparts. Furthermore, it makes the use of electronic records in place of hard-copy records acceptable in a broad range of instances where record retention is required. Thus, overall, the purpose of the Act is to establish that electronic records and signatures can replace paper in most transactions.

However, one thing the Act does not do is specify how these records and signatures will be secured and verified. In fact, the Act does not even outline what an electronic signature specifically is, other than to describe it as an "electronic sound, symbol, or process, attached to or logically associated with a contract or other record and executed or adopted by a person with the intent to sign the record."

In this regard, E-Sign may in fact at first appear more confusing than it is helpful. While many have touted it as a piece of legislation that is designed to revolutionize the manner in which transactions are conducted, its direct effects are nowhere near as far reaching. Instead of mandating a change in the way that business is transacted, the Act merely gives rise to the possibility of a new way of conducting business by recognizing the legitimacy of the electronic medium. It leaves the decision as to what shape these new types of legally valid electronic transactions will take up to the market.

Article 9 of the Uniform Commercial Code requires that all transactions related to the creation of a security interest in "goods, documents, instruments, general intangibles, chattel paper, or accounts" as well as the sale of the latter two items, must be registered with the Secretary of State in the state(s) where these transactions take place. Given the wide scope of transactions covered (the definition above covers security sales of nearly every type), to date, this has been a paper- and time-intensive process. But with the passing of Revised Article 9 (effective July 1, 2001), all of these filings will be handled electronically—a move that will result in increased efficiencies, as well as an anticipated elimination of "dual filing," which still exists in approximately 20 percent of states.

Revised Article 9, therefore, essentially applies the principles set forth in E-Sign and applies them specifically to the realm of securities sales and trades. Naturally, it sets forth concrete guidelines for the length of time for which these electronic records must be maintained, when they must be filed, etc. However, much like E-Sign, it is technologically neutral, meaning that it does not prescribe any particular technologies for use in these new electronic transactions.

Putting These New Regulations into Practice

Whatever shape they do take, in order to be truly viable for business purposes, electronic records and signatures will have to satisfy the same two key criteria as their analog counterparts:

Authentication
It must be known that the record or signature was indeed generated by the person(s) who claim to have generated it. In short, it must be established that it is not a forgery. Off-line, this is most often done by signing documents in person, but the more impersonal nature of electronic communication renders this impossible in the vast majority of cases.

Integrity
Once generated or signed by the author(s), it must be known that the record or signature is not altered in transit or during storage. In the analog realm, this fact is most often ensured by signing multiple copies of an identical document, for each of the transacting parties to retain in their records. Once again, however, this is not easily replicated in the digital realm.

In order to reap the full benefits of these new government regulations, document integrity and authentication must not only be established at the time of the electronic transaction (i.e., when the "electronic signing" takes place), but must be maintained for the life of the electronic record (for archival purposes and future reference). Furthermore, in the case of some government regulations, uniqueness of a given electronic file will need to be proven. In other words, in cases where possession of an electronic document signifies ownership or control of the particular agreement it contains, the uniqueness of the original version of an electronic file will need to be proven, as opposed to any copies that may have been made of it.

The Market Response

The key nature of these criteria for the success of electronic records and signatures as a transactional medium signals a clear opportunity for providers of electronic signatures and certificates, as well as companies that provide digital security (to ensure integrity). This situation has the potential to open a Pandora's box of incompatible, ineffective, or outright insecure document security technology development and several years of struggle before second-generation systems emerge, which will provide ease of use with effective multi-tier security mechanisms.

Currently, companies like Wappa Technologies, Bet-Net, NetLine Certification, PenLore, NNQ, and others are offering technologies ranging from RSA encryption to digital signatures and digital certificates.

Each of the above technologies relies on some form of encryption, and as such exhibits the associated vulnerability to hacking. Encryption-based security mechanisms in general are designed to provide security during document transmission, but not before and after. Digital signatures do provide a document authentication capability before and after receipt but have a number of shortcomings aside from hackability. One is that currently, they are designed to work on text only. Graphics, pictures, or images are unprotected. Another is the technique's inherent design for use in the digital domain only, limiting the naturally occurring nondigital transmission of documents by hand, mail, Xerox™ or fax.

Thus, while these technologies will enable businesses to take advantage of the electronic exchange of records and signatures, they will not ensure their integrity if they are transferred to hard copy—a conversion that will doubtless be necessary in any number of industries and situations.

President Clinton's signing of the Digital Signature Act opened a new category of document management possibilities for broad range of companies in information industries. The law recognizes all electronic documents as legal and binding, rendering the distinction between hard-copy documents and their digital versions obsolete in legal terms. Instead of relying on hard-copy document management, businesses are now able to store their archives in electronic form. However, there are currently no document security companies which specifically address these needs in this new electronically enabled context. As a result, businesses currently have numerous document security needs which are not being met:

Identifying Market Needs

- Improved document security
- Improved document integrity verification
- Document authentication

THE SOLUTION

GoldTrustMark.com recognizes that high levels of security are crucial for companies who produce, share, transmit, and store extremely confidential documents. These documents and information are one of the foundations of any business's competitive advantage. Consequently, the company is taking great steps to ensure that its clients have access to the most rigorous, state-of-the-art security features. User confidence is of the paramount concern to GoldTrustMark.com, and that's why the company has developed one of the most sophisticated and advanced maximum security systems available online.

GoldTrustMark.com Security

Watermarking Functionality
GoldTrustMark.com is developing a one-of-a-kind, proprietary watermarking technology which will securely watermark either hard copy and/or electronic documents, and render those documents tamperproof. This technology will allow GoldTrustMark.com users to add an extra layer of protection to their business-critical documents, and enable them to keep track of any time their documents have been changed.

Secure GoldTrustMark.com IDs
All users will be required to register a password and user identification number with GoldTrustMark.com. Users will individually create and control these access numbers, allowing them to change their log-in details to ensure maximum sustained security. Subscribing firms will, of course, have the ability to cut off the accessibility of terminated employees. Finally, as an added security feature, GoldTrustMark.com will maintain a user log for client firms to review.

Wireless Access
GoldTrustMark.com will provide its subscribers with wireless access to all of their archived documents. By doing so, users will be able to access any of their documents using a wireless modem or personal digital assistant (PDA).

In designing its technology, GoldTrustMark.com has been careful to ensure that it affords its clients maximum flexibility in applying its watermarking and security solution. As a result, GoldTrustMark.com's watermarking technology is equally applicable to both analog (hard copy) and digital documents and, within the digital realm, with all leading programming languages and applications. The company's intent is to ensure that its solution evolves to

GoldTrustMark.com Technology Compatibility

support technological advances, ensuring that its clients have continued access to the most flexible and effective watermarking and security solution.

For example, given the increasing profile of Extensible Markup Language (XML) as a web formatting specification, GoldTrustMark.com has ensured that its solution is fully XML compatible and complies with all XML specifications. Moving forward, the company will ensure such compatibility and compliance for all major technology standards.

In short, GoldTrustMark.com's technology will render documents completely tamperproof—not only at the time of their creation, but throughout their life span. Therefore, the company's technology will be critical both in transactional and archival environments. This fact, alongside the solution's flexibility and technological compatibility, will ensure that it is applicable to a wide range of document and transaction types:

Application Example 1: Financial Services Industry

Through the application of GoldTrustMark.com's technology, financial services firms will be able to realize increased efficiencies through converting their existing paper records into electronic format. Given the relative flexibility of E-Sign, financial services firms will be able to scan their existing hard-copy records into the digital realm and watermark them with GoldTrustMark.com's technology, thereby authenticating them and ensuring their integrity for the life of the document. Similarly, financial services firms will be able to conclude any new legal documents or agreements solely in the electronic realm. In both cases, the authenticity and integrity of documents will be ensured in both electronic and hard-copy formats, given the attributes of GoldTrustMark.com's technology.

Application Example 2: Major Retail Service Providers

Firms in the retail industry will benefit from GoldTrustMark.com's technology by applying it to any and all online agreements concluded with partners and customers. For example, numerous credit card issuers currently afford new customers the ability to sign up for a new credit card online. However, current security and encryption technology does not allow authenticated, unalterable copies of these new cardmember agreements to be distributed to both contracting parties at the time the agreement is concluded. GoldTrustMark.com's technology will do just that, providing each contracting party with an authenticated legal copy of the cardmember agreement, which cannot be altered in either digital or hardcopy format.

Application Example 3: Online Transactions

Parties to online transactions—whether they be purchases at such leading consumer sites as Amazon.com or Priceline.com, or auction agreements between individuals on sites such as eBay—will enjoy benefits similar to those described in the example above. Both parties to a transaction will be provided with an authenticated copy of their agreement, which will preserve its integrity in both digital and analog formats.

Application Example 4: Academic Records

Academic institutions will benefit from GoldTrustMark.com's solution by utilizing it to authenticate and ensure the integrity of students' transcript records. Application of GoldTrustMark.com technology will ensure that student records cannot be tampered with once entered, and will facilitate the electronic transmission of transcripts between academic institutions and other interested parties—a process, which is currently limited to the hard-copy realm, given the need for thorough watermarking.

The previous examples illustrate just a few of the myriad potential applications for GoldTrustMark.com's watermarking technology. As they illustrate, the company's technology is applicable to any number of functional and industry contexts and, in each case, provides a thorough solution to the unique watermarking and security needs of each situation.

In other words, GoldTrustMark.com delivers value to the client by rendering a more efficient and effective solution to existing document security—one which not only bolsters security in existing transactions and archives, but which enables new types of transactions that are not currently possible because of the inadequacy of existing security and watermarking solutions.

Specifically, GoldTrustMark.com's technology solution delivers value to its clients by addressing their three most pressing current market needs:

- Improved document security
- Improved document integrity verification
- Document authentication

While GoldTrustMark.com recognizes the vast opportunity for document security and management in all knowledge industries, given the management team's experience and the need for a focused market entry approach, the company will initially beta test in one of the most document-intensive industries in the U.S.—the financial services profession. A large number of the millions of documents produced for this industry are being transmitted across the Internet, with no level of security, either pre- or post-transmission.

As the second largest revenue-generating service in the U.S., the financial industry is inundated with documents, both hard copy and electronic. And perhaps, no other industry wastes as many resources creating, filing, searching, and retrieving documents. Upon successful completion of testing in this industry, GoldTrustMark.com will quickly expand into other vertical markets.

In order to add depth to the understanding of the target market, GoldTrustMark.com conducted extensive market research with financial services professionals across the United States. The primary research initiative was intended to probe financial services professionals' need for the increased security effectiveness in document transmission and management, as well as the increased online visibility, which the company's services afford. The results indicate a market fertile for the development of the GoldTrustMark.com concept, and are included in Appendix A of this document.

There are only a handful of companies that compete in the watermarking arena. There are two that have emerged as the market leaders. These two companies are Javelin and Globe Marking. Both companies have a digital watermarking process and engage in various forms of watermark protection:

Javelin
Javelin is a developer of patented digital watermarking technologies for multimedia content distribution. Their technology can only survive in electronic format.

Globe Marking
Globe Marking is the leading developer of digital watermarking technologies. Their technologies can allow digital data to be imperceptibly embedded in digital visual content, including movies, photographic, or artistic images. These technologies are used

Value Proposition

MARKET ANALYSIS

Target Market Segmentation

Primary Market Research Findings

COMPETITIVE ANALYSIS

Overview of Competition

in a wide variety of applications, including solutions that deter counterfeiting, piracy, and other unauthorized uses. Their system enables communications capabilities within electronic content only.

GoldTrustMark.com's Competitive Advantage

GoldTrustMark.com differentiates itself from all of the above competitors by being the only industry player to focus specifically upon the electronic security of documents. The GoldTrustMark.com solution will reduce costs for clients, for it will not require them to invest in IT hardware or infrastructure. Furthermore, the company's value-added wireless inter-face—a feature that is not offered by any of the competitors—will allow client firms and financial services professionals to watermark and transmit their records regardless of their location.

These facts will enable the company to deliver a highly flexible solution that is specifically tailored to document security needs of the financial services profession. GoldTrustMark.com's sustainable competitive advantages will be a result of its product/service offerings and market entry position.

Proprietary Technology

The GoldTrustMark.com record management solution will be based upon the company's proprietary watermarking technology, which significantly improves on existing technologies in the market. The GoldTrustMark.com watermark is the only one that will survive in both digital and analog environments. This will pose an obstacle to other market players who wish to develop similarly rich functionality in their technology solutions.

Incumbent Advantages

By being the first player in its market niche, GoldTrustMark.com will be offering a unique value proposition to financial professionals, and will therefore be able to garner a substantial share of the legal document security market. For these clients, the cost of switching to an alternate solution will exceed the cost of retaining GoldTrustMark.com as their record management provider, providing the company with significant incumbent advantages.

Learning-Curve Advantages

By working longer and more extensively with clients in the legal profession than any other company, GoldTrustMark.com will be able to evolve its product and service offerings to meet the changing needs of its clients. This will afford the company significant learning-curve advantages.

MARKETING STRATEGY

Overall Strategy

In entering the market and positioning itself in front of potential clients, GoldTrustMark.com will utilize a dual-track approach. First off, the company will forge a series of strategic alliances with world-class product and service providers, whose offerings complement its own. These alliances will not only provide GoldTrustMark.com with strong client referral channels, but will also provide it with increased visibility and credibility. In addition, the company will employ a more traditional marketing approach by engaging in selective target marketing and direct advertising to target financial services firms.

Strategic Alliances

GoldTrustMark.com aims to forge a series of strategic alliance partnerships with leading providers of web and technology products and services. The company's web partners will play a crucial role in the development and launch of the GoldTrustMark.com online service, and will be retained as service providers following the launch. Affiliated partners, on the other hand, will serve as a referral channel, spreading brand knowledge of the GoldTrustMark.com solution to their existing clients in the legal profession. In return, GoldTrustMark.com will refer its clients to affiliated partners for services that are complementary to the company's solution.

Affiliated Partners

GoldTrustMark.com intends to conclude agreements with key strategic alliance partners, whose product and service offerings complement its own. These types of partners will help provide the company with a steady stream of client referrals and will enable it to offer its subscribers a complete document security solution. Keeping these goals in mind, the following types of partners are currently being given priority by GoldTrustMark.com:

Computer Hardware

The company recognizes that certain clients will wish to invest in technology hardware, which will enhance their ability to internally manage their documents and knowledge in tandem with the GoldTrustMark.com service. Consequently, GoldTrustMark.com will form alliance partnerships with world-class manufacturers of hardware such as PCs, scanners, and document shredders. The company has already approached and is in negotiation with several leading hardware manufacturers and distributors.

Document Management Services

GoldTrustMark.com realizes that there are a number of service providers, whose offerings will complement its own. For example, client companies may wish to archive selected documents in both electronic and hard-copy form. Similarly, some client companies may wish to outsource the destruction of hard-copy documents, which have been stored electronically. Consequently, GoldTrustMark.com aims to form alliance partnerships with leading providers of services in areas such as traditional hard-copy document storage and document destruction, among others. The company is currently in discussion with a number of leading traditional document management service providers.

Internet Security Companies

There are numerous companies that are offering technologies ranging from RSA encryption to digital signatures and digital certificates. Through partnerships with companies such as Atlanta Bright Solutions, Kippers, LPW, and a host of other companies, we will leverage off their existing sales and marketing platforms.

Direct Marketing Channels

In addition to approaching potential clients through affiliate partner referrals, GoldTrustMark.com will also employ more traditional direct marketing mechanisms to target prospective client financial services firms:

Selective target marketing

GoldTrustMark.com will initially concentrate its services on financial services firms located in its primary target markets: New York, Miami, and Atlanta. The company selected these targets as a result of focus groups and a broad primary research study to identify financial services firms most interested in the service.

Direct advertising

The company will focus its advertising campaign on trade journals and newspapers, taking out full-page ads in trade journals for the legal community. GoldTrustMark.com is also negotiating with many different annual legal conferences to be the electronic document and knowledge management speaker for the legal profession. GoldTrustMark.com will also obtain trade booths at many trade shows and legal seminars.

Branding

With the aid of Luminary Studios, GoldTrustMark.com has developed an eye-catching logo which embodies the company's intended image. In developing this logo, GoldTrustMark.com conducted an extensive branding exercise and identified some core values that it felt will be critical to the success of its service. The color blue was chosen as a symbol of the stability and reliability of the company's service. Gold was chosen to reference the speed of the GoldTrustMark.com document watermarking functionality. Finally, the box around the word "gold" symbolizes the safety and security, which the company's solution affords its clients.

Site Launch

As an initial step in its marketing efforts, GoldTrustMark.com will launch an operational site, focused on the needs of financial services professionals in its first-tier target markets. This version of the site will be accessible only to a select number of users, most notably some of the local attorneys who have signed letters of intent to subscribe to the company's service. Although the site's functionality will be limited, it will include a working demo of the document watermarking functionality

GoldTrustMark.com believes that this will serve as a constructive first step, as it will allow the company to fine-tune the features and content of the site prior to its full, nationwide launch, which will follow in a few months' time.

THE MANAGEMENT TEAM

GoldTrustMark.com is currently conducting a nationwide search for a Chief Executive Officer to add to its management team. The company's existing management team is in the process of interviewing numerous executive search firms, with the aim of retaining one to assist in filling this vacant position.

Bill Piller, President and Founder

Mr. Piller founded GoldTrustMark.com in February 2000 and is currently responsible for all aspects of the company's management and administration. Prior to founding GoldTrustMark.com, he was a Senior Consultant with Zocari Strategies, a boutique management-consulting firm located in downtown New York. Mr. Piller worked in the emerging technology practice at Zocari, specializing in business plan development, strategy, and market research. He has also been an angel investor and board member for several start-up businesses over the past five years. Mr. Piller holds a B.A. from Yale, and is presently pursuing a master's degree in New Media and Technology.

Edward Reins, Chief Technology Officer

Mr. Reins founded Monumental M Technologies, a Miami-based audio and multimedia copyright protection company which developed a watermarking and copyright protection system recognized by the worldwide media protection industry. During the development phase, Mr. Reins was granted several patents in media copyright protection technologies. Monumental M has since merged with NuKoppe Research to become WKO Corp. Mr. Reins holds a BSEE from Texas A&M and is a Ph.D. candidate at the Massachusetts Institute of Technology.

Jonathan Kosow, Director of Marketing

Mr. Kosow is in charge of developing, managing, and coordinating the initial sales and marketing efforts for GoldTrustMark.com. He is currently Vice President of Sales and Marketing at Second Century Group of Minneapolis. Mr. Kosow has specialized in building national sales forces in financial services industries for the past five years. Prior to joining Second Century, he opened the retail division of a national subprime mortgage lender and was directly responsible for the marketing efforts of its 10 offices in five states. Mr. Kosow holds a B.A. in English from Christendom College.

Maxine Stein, Director of Sales

Ms. Stein is the president and founder of Advanced Career Strategies, an agency providing consulting to professionals in career and networking services. Prior to founding Advanced Career Strategies, she worked as a legal recruiter for both Fortune 500 companies and niche financial services firms. Ms. Stein has spent her entire professional career selling services to the financial services community. She has a B.S. in Human Resources from the University of Dallas and an M.B.A. from the University of South Carolina.

GoldTrustMark.com will derive its revenues from two primary revenue streams:

FINANCIAL OVERVIEW

Revenue Streams

Software Licensing Fees

GoldTrustMark.com subscribers will be charged a monthly software licensing fee for the use of the company's knowledge management software functionality. The company will implement a tiered pricing model, charging client companies a licensing fee based on the number of potential end users they employ.

Partnership Fees

GoldTrustMark.com will receive a partnership or referral fee from partners, to which the company has referred its customers for service or product purchase. These fees will apply to partners who provide hardware, scanning, and document destruction services, among others.

For a summary of management's financial projections, please refer to Appendix B.

Phase I—Strategic Positioning

GoldTrustMark.com Roll-Out Timeline

January-March 2001
- Complete phase one-product development
- File patent application
- Forge alliances with strategic partners
- Begin key staff hiring
- Fund additional operating expenses
- Security Audit

Phase I Benchmarks:
- Successful initial product launch
- Completion of senior management team by hiring highly experienced CEO
- Completion of core product development for initial site software

Phase II—Soft Launch

April-August 2001
- Launch full product version with initial subscribers in pilot program
- Hire staff for key company functions
- Enhance product features beyond initial version
- Develop marketing strategies, messages, and sales team
- Complete Board of Directors and Advisors; fund additional operating expenses

Phase II Benchmarks:
- Complete partnerships necessary to launch fully functional site
- Complete initial success tests with trial companies
- Develop marketing material and tactics
- Complete hiring of "launch" staff

Phase III—Full Launch

September-December 2001
- Hire full team for product launch
- Launch national business-to-business marketing campaign
- Fund additional operating expenses
- Obtain additional venture financing

Phase III Benchmarks:
- Achieve profitability

APPENDIX A: MARKET RESEARCH FINDINGS

In order to add depth to the understanding of the target market, GoldTrustMark.com conducted extensive market research with financial services firms across the United States. The primary research initiative was intended to probe financial service professionals' need for the increased efficiency and effectiveness in document and knowledge management, as well as the increased online visibility, which the company's services afford. The results indicate a market fertile for the development of the GoldTrustMark.com concept.

Profile of Survey Participants

Sample Groups:	Leading financial services firms
Location:	Greater New York, Miami, Atlanta, and Houston
Response Rate:	19 percent of 270 organizations contacted
Individual Contacts at Firms:	Associate financial services professionals and partners

Survey Findings and Analysis

Survey participants were asked to respond to three fundamental questions regarding their firms' current and intended use of the Internet, which gave a broad indication of the market acceptance of the GoldTrustMark.com concept.

1. Does your firm currently utilize the Internet as a business tool?

- 62 percent of total respondents said their firm maintained a website and significantly utilized the Internet as a business tool.
- Results varied widely by geographic dispersion. 56 percent of respondents in Atlanta do not have a website or significantly utilize the Internet as a business tool. In contrast, only 20 percent of Miami respondents did not have a website or significantly utilize the Internet.

	Yes	No
New York	68%	32%
Miami	80%	20%
Atlanta	22%	56%
Houston	67%	33%

2. Does your firm see the Internet as a viable tool to support your regional or statewide expansion?

- Most respondents believed that the Internet is a viable tool for supporting the regional or statewide expansion of their financial services firm. This finding remained consistent across regions.

	Yes	No
New York	71%	29%
Miami	90%	10%
Atlanta	100%	0%
Houston	78%	22%

3. Would your firm be interested in participating in a service like GoldTrustMark.com?

- 54 percent of respondents stated they would be interested or might be interested in participating in a service like GoldTrustMark.com, while 41 percent stated they would not be interested in participating at this time.
- Respondents in Atlanta and New York were most interested in GoldTrustMark.com, while those in Miami were the least interested.

	Yes	No	Maybe
New York	26%	43%	30%
Miami	20%	40%	40%
Atlanta	44%	44%	11%
Houston	22%	67%	11%

Given the survey findings, GoldTrustMark.com has narrowed its first-tier target market to include those cities, in which a substantial number of financial services firms have already embraced Internet technologies as a business tool. The company's second-tier target market will include cities whose strategic Internet adoption among financial services firms is not currently as high, but where financial services firms realize the value of the Internet as a strategic business tool and are highly-interested in adopting new, web-based ways of working.

Software Revenue

The Software Revenue is based on the assumption of the following income source:

a. Yearly software charge that will average $7,500/firm per year. This fee is based on conversations with other software companies who charge fees on a per seat basis.

The company is projecting to sign-up the following number of new clients to use its service.

Year 1:	112
Year 2:	515
Year 3:	640
Total:	**1,267**

The software and general maintenance fees are the same for every client.

APPENDIX B: FINANCIAL PROJECTIONS

Assumptions

Salary Expenses

The company anticipates the following salaries:

	Y1	Y2	Y3
CEO (1)	94,500	94,500	94,500
President (1)	63,000	63,000	63,000
CTO (1)	63,000	63,000	63,000
COO (1)		70,000	70,000
Directors (3 @ 45.5K)	136,500	136,500	136,500
Office manager	28,000	28,000	28,000
Administrative (2 @ 25K)	50,000	50,000	50,000
Salespeople Y1=3 @ 35K	105,000		
Y2=6 @ 42K; 3 @ 35K		357,000	
Y3=10@42K			420,000
Total salaries per full year	**540,000**	**862,000**	**925,000**

Payroll Taxes	**Y1**	**Y2**	**Y3**
CEO	6,330	6,330	6,330
President	4,820	4,820	4,820
CTO	4,820	4,820	4,820
COO	–	5,355	5,355
Directors	10,442	10,442	10,442
Office manager	2,142	2,142	2,142
Admin	3,825	3,825	3,825
Salespeople	8,033	27,311	32,130
Unemployment	3,000	4,000	4,000
Total payroll taxes (full year)	**43,411**	**69,044**	**73,864**

Employee Benefits

Projected to be 10 percent of total salaries:

Y1	Y2	Y3
54,000	86,200	92,500

Other Expenses

Other expense were estimates per client.

This page left intentionally blank to accommodate tabular matter following.

Projected Income Statement for the Year Ended December 31, 2001

Revenue	Month 1	Month 2	Month 3	Month 4	Month 5	Month 6
Software Revenue						
Software Fees	$-	$-	$-	$-	$-	$75,000
Other	$-	$-	$-	$-	$-	$-
Total Revenue	**$-**	**$-**	**$-**	**$-**	**$-**	**$75,000**
Expenses						
Hardware Acquisition	$-	$-	$-	$-	$-	$100,000
Salaries	$-	$-	$-	$-	$-	$45,000
Payroll Taxes	$-	$-	$-	$-	$-	$3,618
Employee Benefits	$-	$-	$-	$-	$-	$4,500
Marketing and Travel	$-	$-	$-	$-	$-	$8,570
Rent	$-	$-	$-	$-	$-	$2,200
Public Relations and Advertising	$-	$-	$-	$-	$-	$8,570
Office Expense	$-	$-	$-	$-	$-	$1,000
Legal and Professional	$-	$-	$1,000	$1,000	$1,000	$1,000
Equipment Leasing Expense	$-	$-	$-	$-	$-	$3,000
Web Hosting Expense	$-	$-	$-	$-	$-	$1,430
Utilities and Telephone	$-	$-	$-	$-	$-	$2,000
Insurance Expense	$-	$-	$-	$-	$-	$5,000
Other	$-	$-	$-	$-	$-	$5,000
Total Expenses	**$-**	**$-**	**$1,000**	**$1,000**	**$1,000**	**$190,888**
Net Income	**$-**	**$-**	**$(1,000)**	**$(1,000)**	**$(1,000)**	**$(115,888)**
Number of clients signed this month	-	-	-	-	-	10
Total Client Base	-	-	-	-	-	**10**

Month 7	Month 8	Month 9	Month 10	Month 11	Month 12
$90,000	$105,000	$120,000	$135,000	$150,000	$165,000
$-	$-	$-	$-	$-	$-
$90,000	**$105,000**	**$120,000**	**$135,000**	**$150,000**	**$165,000**
$-	$-	$-	$-	$-	$-
$45,000	$45,000	$45,000	$45,000	$45,000	$45,000
$3,618	$3,618	$3,618	$3,618	$3,618	$3,618
$4,500	$4,500	$4,500	$4,500	$4,500	$4,500
$8,570	$8,570	$8,570	$8,570	$8,570	$8,570
$2,200	$2,200	$2,200	$2,200	$2,200	$2,200
$8,570	$8,570	$8,570	$8,570	$8,570	$8,570
$1,000	$1,000	$1,000	$1,000	$1,000	$1,000
$1,000	$1,000	$1,000	$1,000	$1,000	$1,000
$3,000	$3,000	$3,000	$3,000	$3,000	$3,000
$1,430	$1,430	$1,430	$1,430	$1,430	$1,430
$2,000	$2,000	$2,000	$2,000	$2,000	$2,000
$5,000	$5,000	$5,000	$5,000	$5,000	$5,000
$5,000	$5,000	$5,000	$5,000	$5,000	$5,000
$90,888	**$90,888**	**$90,888**	**$90,888**	**$90,888**	**$90,888**
$(888)	**$14,112**	**$29,112**	**$44,112**	**$59,112**	**$74,112**
12	14	16	18	20	22
22	**36**	**52**	**70**	**90**	**112**

Projected Income Statement for the Year Ended December 31, 2002

Revenue	Quarter 1	Quarter 2	Quarter 3	Quarter 4	Total
Software Revenue					
Software Fees	$825,000	$900,000	$1,012,500	$1,125,000	$3,862,500
Other	$-	$-	$-	$-	$-
Total Revenue	**$825,000**	**$900,000**	**$1,012,500**	**$1,125,000**	**$3,862,500**
Expenses					
Technology Maintenance	$20,000	$20,000	$-	$-	$40,000
Hardware Acquisition	$100,000	$-	$-	$-	$100,000
Salaries	$215,500	$215,500	$215,500	$215,500	$862,000
Payroll Taxes	$17,261	$17,261	$17,261	$17,261	$69,044
Employee Benefits	$21,550	$21,550	$21,550	$21,550	$86,200
Marketing and Travel	$50,000	$50,000	$50,000	$50,000	$200,000
Rent	$10,000	$10,000	$10,000	$10,000	$40,000
Public Relations and Advertising	$50,000	$50,000	$50,000	$50,000	$200,000
Office Expense	$3,000	$3,000	$3,000	$3,000	$12,000
Legal and Professional	$10,000	$10,000	$10,000	$10,000	$21,000
Equipment Leasing Expense	$15,000	$15,000	$15,000	$15,000	$60,000
Web Hosting Expense	$7,500	$7,500	$7,500	$7,500	$30,000
Utilities and Telephone	$8,000	$8,000	$8,000	$8,000	$32,000
Insurance Expense	$6,250	$6,250	$6,250	$6,250	$25,000
Other	$15,000	$15,000	$15,000	$15,000	$60,000
Total Expenses	**$549,061**	**$444,061**	**$422,061**	**$422,061**	**$1,837,244**
Net Income	**$275,939**	**$455,939**	**$590,439**	**$702,939**	**$2,025,256**
Number of clients signed this month	110	120	135	150	515
Total Client Base	**222**	**342**	**477**	**627**	**627**

Projected Income Statement
for the Year Ended December 31, 2003

Revenue	Quarter 1	Quarter 2	Quarter 3	Quarter 4	Total
Software Revenue					
Software Fees	$1,200,000	$1,200,000	$1,200,000	$1,200,000	$4,800,000
Other	$-	$-	$-	$-	$-
Total Revenue	**$1,200,000**	**$1,200,000**	**$1,200,000**	**$1,200,000**	**$4,800,000**
Expenses					
Technology Maintenance	$20,000	$-	$20,000	$-	$40,000
Hardware Acquisition	$-	$-	$-	$-	$-
Salaries	$231,250	$231,250	$231,250	$231,250	$925,000
Payroll Taxes	$18,460	$18,460	$18,460	$18,460	$73,864
Employee Benefits	$23,125	$23,125	$23,125	$23,125	$92,500
Marketing and Travel	$50,000	$50,000	$50,000	$50,000	$200,000
Rent	$12,000	$12,000	$12,000	$12,000	$48,000
Public Relations and Advertising	$50,000	$50,000	$50,000	$50,000	$200,000
Office Expense	$3,000	$3,000	$3,000	$3,000	$12,000
Legal and Professional	$3,000	$3,000	$3,000	$3,000	$12,000
Equipment Leasing Expense	$15,000	$15,000	$15,000	$15,000	$60,000
Web Hosting Expense	$7,500	$7,500	$7,500	$7,500	$30,000
Utilities and Telephone	$10,000	$10,000	$10,000	$10,000	$40,000
Insurance Expense	$6,250	$6,250	$6,250	$6,250	$25,000
Other	$20,000	$20,000	$20,000	$20,000	$80,000
Total Expenses	**$469,591**	**$449,591**	**$469,591**	**$449,591**	**$1,838,364**
Net Income	**$730,409**	**$750,409**	**$730,409**	**$750,409**	**$2,961,636**
Number of clients signed this month	160	160	160	160	640
Total Client Base	**787**	**947**	**1,107**	**1,267**	**1,267**

Financial Services Company

BUSINESS PLAN   PRISMA MICROFINANCE, INC.

2 Claremont Street
Boston, Massachusetts 02118

Prisma MicroFinance, Inc., is a private, mission-driven company with operating subsidiaries in Central America that provide "microcredit" to entrepreneurs. Since 1995, Prisma has provided lending and savings services to people in the developing world considered "unbankable" by formal financial institutions. By operating a profitable private-equity funded business in the Nicaraguan microfinance market—where most competitors are nonprofits—the company seeks to revolutionize and to grow the world's microfinance industry.

- EXECUTIVE SUMMARY

- COMPANY OVERVIEW

- TARGET MARKET

- OPERATIONS & MANAGEMENT

- GROWTH STRATEGY & MILESTONES

- MARKETING & SALES STRATEGY

- FINANCIAL ANALYSIS

- IMPACT ANALYSIS & SOCIAL RETURN ON INVESTMENT

- APPENDIX

EXECUTIVE SUMMARY
Who We Are

Prisma MicroFinance, Inc., is a private, mission-driven company with operating subsidiaries in Central America that provide "microcredit" to entrepreneurs. Since 1995, Prisma has provided lending and savings services to people in the developing world considered "unbankable" by formal financial institutions. By operating a profitable private-equity funded business in the Nicaraguan microfinance market—where most competitors are nonprofits—the company seeks to revolutionize and to grow the world's microfinance industry. The company upholds a dual mission of providing affordable capital to "unbankable" individuals while operating an efficient, profitable business.

Why We Do It

At Prisma MicroFinance, access to affordable credit is considered a right, not a privilege. Providing affordable capital is a business model that will allow the company to offer reliable financial returns and significant social returns to its investors, while providing a valuable service to its borrowers. "We believe in doing well by doing good."

The Management

Prisma's management team has a total of over 25 years of experience in the microfinance industry. They have worked together for five years and their track record proves that they have the necessary skills to guide the company as it expands throughout Nicaragua and Central America.

The Market

The worldwide microfinance market is large, underserved, and growing at a rate of 30 percent annually. The worldwide market is estimated to be $270 billion, with current annual cash turnover of $2.5 billion. The Nicaraguan market is $300 million, with $50 million being lent at rates averaging 60 percent APR. There are more than 20 significant entities in Nicaragua providing microfinance services, with no single one holding more than 13 percent of market share.

The Customers

Prisma's customers are individuals who are not in an economic position to secure funding from traditional financial institutions. The majority are small-business owners, operating in the Nicaraguan capitol of Managua. Prisma has a strong lending history with taxicab owner-operators, and it plans to solidify its reputation within this market. By FY2004, its customer base will be an equal split of micro, small, and medium-size business owners.

Competitive Advantage and Profitability

Prisma embodies a profitable business model with four major components: local and inexpensive labor, market penetration in cooperative taxi financing, externalization of costs by partnering with third parties, and the use of effective technology. Unlike its competition, Prisma has operated without subsidies or grants since day one for over five years while also providing healthy returns to its financial backers. Moreover, Prisma lends at rates of 31-34 percent APR, two thirds of the average competitor's rate.

Marketing and Sales

Prisma's marketing and sales strategy has been extremely successful, yet extremely cheap. As word of mouth has been Prisma's biggest source of sales, marketing activities have been focused on keeping clients happy and recognizing their accomplishments. The social structure and business culture that has made this approach a success in Nicaragua exists throughout Central America.

	FY2001	FY2002	FY2003	FY2004	**Financials**
Total Revenue	**252,843**	**711,608**	**1,187,556**	**2,065,688**	
Net Income	23,888	53,781	417,534	931,289	
% Growth in Net Income by Year	-19%	125%	676%	123%	
ROA (Industry Standard = 3.08%)	1.00%	0.60%	3.50%	4.10%	

FY2001

Key Milestones

- Raise Series "B" $1.5 million Investment Round
- Grow loan portfolio to $1 million
- Make 2,000th loan
- Diversify portfolio to 60/40 taxi/non-taxi loans
- Expand board to 7 members
- Establish Advisory Board
- Report on new location for central office

FY2002

- Close Series "B" $1.5 million Investment Round
- Grow loan portfolio to $4 million with debt
- Make 4,000th loan
- Diversify portfolio to 50/50 taxi/non-taxi loans
- Expand Central Managua office
- Complete Central American expansion report

FY2003

- Raise Series "C" $4 million Investment Round
- Grow loan portfolio to $5 million
- Make 6,000th loan
- Diversify portfolio to 40/60 taxi/non-taxi
- Open second Nicaraguan office
- Lay groundwork for operations in second country

FY2004

- Close Series "C" $4 million Investment Round
- Grow loan portfolio to $10 million
- Make 10,000th loan
- Achieve balanced "Prisma Portfolio," even split of Micro, Small, Medium loans
- Open third and fourth Nicaraguan Offices
- Begin operations in second Central American country

Funding Goals

Prisma is raising $1.5 million in its Series "B" round to grow and expand business, both the total number of customers it serves and the region in which it offers service. The company has planned an aggressive, but realistic, expansion strategy. By the end of FY2004, Prisma will be lending 4,800 loans profitably in four Nicaraguan cities and a second Central American country with a total lending portfolio of $10.56 million.

Use of Funds

Prisma seeks to expand its current successful model. The funds from the sale of stock will be used to leverage debt in order to expand the loan portfolio.

COMPANY OVERVIEW

Prisma MicroFinance, Inc.'s, Mission Statement:

To provide our customers superior financial services, fostering opportunities for wealth and employment creation, while maximizing social and economic returns for our investors.

The Company

Prisma MicroFinance, Inc. (Prisma) is a United States corporation registered in the state of Massachusetts. The company was founded to be a development bank—making loans in small amounts widely available to people in the developing world. This growing industry is known as "microfinance."

The necessary capital to operate Prisma is raised through private equity and debt from individual and institutional investors in the developed world. With $1.5 million in new equity, the company will be able to support expansion efforts and leverage at least this amount in debt financing. This capital will accelerate growth, exponentially increasing the number of customers and amount lent. Prisma's customers are primarily business owners who do not have access to affordable capital to finance their operations because they are considered unbankable by traditional financial institutions. Although these poor business owners may operate on a very small scale, their operations are profitable. They remain locked in the poverty cycle because of the premium they pay for being perceived as a risky investment. Prisma's experience, and that of the microfinance industry in general, has proven just the opposite. Lending to poor individuals poses risks because of the precarious nature of their cash flows, but providing them access to affordable capital allows them to even out cash flows and break out of the poverty cycle.

Prisma does not conduct its operations for charity. It is at the forefront of the B2-4B revolution—meaning it is finding business solutions for the four million poor people of the world. Companies such as Hewlett-Packard are investing significant capital into this area not only because of the social upshot, but because it is good business. Prisma has operated profitably for five years by targeting a market opportunity that is large, underserved, and in which the competition is fragmented by industry standards. Prisma offers less expensive products to consumers with better service than its competitors.

Company Name

"Prisma" means "prism" in Spanish. Prisma MicroFinance, Inc. "refracts" private capital investment from the developed world, funneling it to small business owners in Central America who traditionally have lacked access to capital but who are entrepreneurial and commercially savvy operators.

Prisma's spectrum covers providing access to credit and financial services for people living in the developing world. The diversity in loan size creates a balanced portfolio serving a range of people. A single loan officer can easily and profitably manage a cost-effective portfolio that includes loans of different sizes. In this way, Prisma embraces its dual business focus of:

- Providing capital to "unbankable" clients
- Ensuring market rate returns for investors

Company History

Prisma was begun in 1995 as a savings and loan cooperative called SINAI, R. L. (Support and Incentives for Autonomous Initiatives) founded by a Nicaraguan, Roger Aburto, and an American, David J. Satterthwaite. They shared a common interest in assisting poor business owners overcome barriers to success. The two founders started operations completely through grassroots efforts with $1,000 in personal start-up capital and a $4,000 loan from American businessman George Kraus, who is now a Board Member. For its first two years, the company conducted its activities out of a single room in Roger's house with a home computer.

Prisma has grown steadily from the beginning, averaging 387 percent annual growth rate as measured by total loan portfolio under management.

Prisma Growth: 1996-2000

Year	1996	1997	1998	1999	2000
Number of Loans, Year End	99	310	530	395	236
Portfolio Balance	$39,400	$396,557	$698,381	$649,066	$855,177
Total Number of					
Loans Made	**257**	**607**	**1,099**	**1,419**	**1,519**

The organization's growth has been funded completely with private investment. In December of 2000, the Nicaraguan loan portfolio was at just over $850,000 distributed to 236 loans. The average loan is $3,000 and is repaid within 22 months. Phenomenally, in 1,500 loans, Prisma's default rate is less than 1 percent. The single most limiting factor throughout Prisma's history has been lack of capital. At present, the organization has nearly 200 approved loans waiting for sufficient funds to grant them.

Prisma's first client in 1995, Arroya Rios Vallejos, borrowed $500 for inventory for her corner store. She has since received and repaid four loans, and now owns her own home.

Unlike the overwhelming majority of microfinance institutions that depend on donations, Prisma's entire loan portfolio has instead been financed by debt from individuals and commercial institutions. Prisma has consistently offered interest rates at 31-36 percent APR, significantly lower than the competition's rates of 60-80 percent APR. The company has continually sought to maintain efficient and modern operations, thus creating a vibrant business culture prepared to confront a demanding marketplace.

Products Offered

Prisma is a financial institution. Its principal operations are as a lender to customers typically viewed by the industry as "unbankable." Prisma makes loans, at risk-adjusted market rates, from $50 to $15,000 dollars. This range is often referred to in the lending profession as "microfinance" because of the size of the loans.

All customers require a co-signer and character references for loan approval, creating a circle of trust for lenders. All loans over $500 require guarantees and/or collateral. Interest rates start at 24 percent a year, plus fees. Loan interest rates vary depending on loan size, customers' credit, and other risk factors. Loan terms have ranged from 3 months to 3 years. For the Nicaraguan operations, the median loan term to date from the last 300 loans was 2.4 years.

Prisma has ongoing relationships with customers over the life of the loan. By maintaining contact with customers, early interventions save troubled loans. For example, the company offers customers in good standing (taxi owners in particular) additional working capital lines of credit. This ensures that their business is not disrupted due to cash flow crunches or unexpected occurrences including a car accident, a sick family member, or "inclement weather." Prisma also encourages evening out cash flows by requiring that customers put 5 percent of every loan into a savings account. For first-time borrowers, this amount is folded into the loan amount.

Borrowers in good standing, called class "A" customers, gain more latitude in available credit, which they use to restructure existing loans or get new ones. Customers increase their standard of living as a direct result of these loans.

Loan Products

- Micro Loans ($50-250)—primarily made to low-income individuals for consumer purchases and micro-entrepreneurs for business-related expenses. Micro loans are most often made to women. Business owners buy inventory and consumers purchase domestic appliances, such as refrigerators or stoves.
- Small Loans ($251-1,000)—primarily made to business owners. They purchase inventory and/or capital investments like machinery—freezers, sewing machines, or power tools.
- Medium Loans ($1,001-15,000)—primarily made to taxi owners to purchase new vehicles. These loans assist business owners graduating from small loans and growing owner-operated businesses seeking to expand. Extensive due diligence and more rigorous guarantees are required.

Sources of Revenue

LOAN REVENUE: The revenue stream from a loan is derived from three sources.

1. **Interest:** A 24 percent annual rate is carried over the term of the loan. This rate is considerably lower than competitors' rates, which average at least 60 percent in the Nicaraguan microfinance industry. This revenue source accounts for 51 percent of Prisma's historical income.
2. **Legal Fee:** A flat legal fee is charged for the origination of every loan, usually $30, which is carried over the life of the loan.
3. **Origination Fee:** A 6 percent origination fee is charged that is carried over the life of the loan. This fee accounts for 7 percent of Prisma's historical income.

Additional revenue is derived from:

- **Loan Late Payment Charges:** Delinquent clients pay an extra 0.5 percent on the late balance. Almost 20 percent of the outstanding loans are assessed a late fee at some point during the life of the loan. But, at any one time, only 5 percent are in arrears. This revenue source accounts for 8 percent of Prisma's historical income.
- **Savings Accounts:** All clients are required to maintain a savings deposit with a balance of at least 5 percent of the amount borrowed. Prisma provides customers the initial 5 percent required in the loan itself. Savings accounts earn 8 percent annual interest. As this rate is on the high end of the market, the majority of customers carry at least a portion of their savings with Prisma. Savings account volume in Nicaraguan has been 5-10 percent of the total loan portfolio.
- **Currency Exchange:** Prisma conducts all operations in U.S. dollars because the local economies in which Prisma operates currently, and plans to operate in the future, are less stable. Operations in dollars minimize the currency risk and economic influences on the value of the portfolio. Loans are made and collected in dollars; however, the accounts for subsidiary operations must, by law, be carried on the books of the subsidiary companies in the local currency. On average, currency exchanges accounts for 15 percent of Prisma's historical net income.
- **Automobile Insurance:** This is a new product offering for Prisma; 50 policies have been sold since March 2000. Although it is a lucrative new offering, income is not realized for a policy sale until the end of the fiscal year. In fact, it is carried on the books as a liability. Offering insurance is a value added for several reasons. One, the company ensures that all cars it finances are insured. Two, competitive advantage lending to taxi drivers provides a captive market for the product. Last, profitably expanding services beyond just lending is a positive entry to offering additional products and services to customers that trust the company.

Smart people are not confined to the developed world.... Any company that doesn't figure out a way to get connected with the poor [of the Third World] will not tap huge potential.

—Carly Fiorina, CEO, Hewlett-Packard

The Global Microfinance Market

Prisma MicroFinance, Inc., operates in the large, growing, yet underserved market of microfinance lending. The MicroCredit Virtual Library estimates that there are currently 7,000 microfinance institutions worldwide, serving approximately 16 million poor people. The total cash turnover for these institutions is $2.5 billion.

Of the estimated 500 million people who operate micro or small businesses around the world, only 10 million have access to financial support for their businesses (Source: Micro-credit Summit).

Worldwide demand for credit by this population is almost limitless. Based on an average loan size worldwide of $550, demand for microloans is approximately $270 billion. The annual growth rate of the world microloan portfolio is 30 percent, with some estimates as high as 70 percent (Source: Micro-credit Summit).

The spectacular growth rate of the microfinance industry is in large part due to the difficulty that the vast majority of people in the developing world face in gaining access to credit. The strict demands and cronyism of commercial banks makes it nearly impossible for an average citizen to get a loan.

Demand in Nicaragua

Prisma focuses its activities in the markets with which it is most familiar—Central America. With five years of profitable operations in Nicaragua, the company knows how to conduct successful business in these markets. Currently, the company operates in Managua, the capitol city of Nicaragua, and has made approximately 1,500 loans to date. Lending is limited only by the amount of capital available to lend.

Nicaragua is an attractive market for microfinance. Despite the American image of the country as economically volatile and politically unstable, Nicaragua has had open markets since 1990. In 1990, Nicaraguans elected as president Violetta Barrios de Chamorro who enacted market economy reforms in 1991, privatizing 351 state industries. The 1996 election of Arnoldo Alleman marked the continuation of government policies favoring a market economy. These policies remain in place today.

The economy largely consists of coffee, cereal grains, sesame, cotton, and bananas. Agriculture provides 34 percent of Nicaragua's GDP, the highest in Central America; however, over the past decade, there has been a shift in the workforce away from the agricultural sector toward urban, service sector jobs. Approximately 46 percent of the labor force is now employed in the service industry, compared to 28 percent in agriculture and 26 percent in manufacturing, construction, and mining. Nicaragua's major trading partner is the United States and its major exports are cotton, sugar, seafood, meat, and gold. Economic highlights about the country include:

- GDP of $2. 01 billion in 1998
- GDP per capita of $420
- Population of just over 4, 800,000
- Inflation rate consistently under 10 percent since 1994

The Nicaraguan Small Business Bureau estimates that the number of micro and small, nonagricultural businesses in Nicaragua is 152,607, excluding informal businesses, such as street hawkers and market vendors. Micro and small businesses are defined as having less than 5 employees. They employ 267,000 individuals, and are largely family-run enterprises. Informal businesses, typically a one-person operation, are estimated to be up to double those numbers. The government estimates that 60 percent of urban economic activity is conducted at the small, micro, or informal sector—a major driver of the local economy. With the average micro or small loan in Nicaragua estimated to be $585, based on industry data, this indicates an almost $300 million market in Nicaragua alone. The microfinance market, as a segment, is currently underserved. The total outstanding loan portfolio for Nicaraguan microfinance institutions is $47.9 million. Based on Prisma's experience, approximately 50 percent of all businesses in the country have access to some form of credit, either from formal institutions, family/friends, nonprofit microfinance lenders, or moneylenders. This number skews disproportionately to the larger companies, namely those with at least 20 employees or who are involved in export. Lending available to this population is at rates or terms less attractive than Prisma offers. Nonprofit lenders typically charge 60-80 percent APR, moneylenders are as high as 40 percent a month, and capital from family/friends is highly limited.

Within the large number of businesses operating in Nicaragua, there are numerous segments that are especially attractive for microfinance lending. Some unifying characteristics include:

- a high asset turnover rate
- the ability to provide collateral like property or equipment
- a network of co-signers

Specific businesses that have been excellent customers to date include:

- taxi drivers: make daily or weekly payments and provide excellent collateral
- employee associations: act as an intermediary, thus improving the security of consumer loans
- community banks: increase the efficiency of servicing microloans

The Prisma target customer is a self-employed businessperson, either female or male, who lives in an urban area with his or her family. One of the most lucrative market segments Prisma loans to is taxi owners.

The Nicaraguan Microfinance Market

Although the countries in Central America are diverse, all have one thing in common: taxi cooperatives. There are more than 8,000 taxis operating in Nicaragua and the market is expanding. The Transportation Department estimates the number of new licenses granted will increase the total at least 10 percent a year for the next three years.

In Nicaragua, taxis are owner-operated and are considered medium-sized businesses. The owners are called "taxistas." They are organized nationally into 240 cooperatives. The cooperative structure gives the members bargaining power, purchasing power, and a strong social network.

In 2000, Prisma held about 2 percent of the taxi finance market within a fragmented market where no single competitor dominates. Taxi financing is a patchwork of banks, finance companies, car dealers, and other sources of informal financing. No financial institution has captured this market.

Expansion Strategy: Prisma will specialize in financing "taxistas" as a spearhead to establishing operations nationwide in Nicaragua and in other countries in Central America.

Prisma has made 250 loans to date to this population. Because the market is regulated through licenses, business is lucrative for the "taxistas" and loan repayment has been impeccable.

Furthermore, in a recent Prisma survey of 80 drivers, 80 percent said they had or needed financing, whereas only half have existing access to financing.

Of the 3,200 "taxistas" who currently want financing, Prisma is positioned to capture the best of these clients, assuming the following:

- Prisma's 4-year track record of successfully working with taxi owner-operators will continue
- The average "taxista" loan to date of $5,993 for a term of 2.4 years is indicative of this market
- Any potential "taxistas" who are bad credit risks can be replaced because Prisma offers better credit terms
- A taxi is replaced every five years

This market segment is worth $11.52 million. For Prisma, further penetration into this market is currently limited only by capital. The Nicaraguan operations currently have 200 pending loans that have been approved, but there is not sufficient capital to lend.

Prisma will specialize in financing "taxistas" as a spearhead to establishing operations nationwide in Nicaragua and in other countries in Central America. Small, low overhead offices will be established in other urban centers. Strategic partnerships with a national bank and car dealers will enable Prisma to centralize lending and collections processes while still maintaining national coverage. This strategy coincides with market trends: new licenses are currently overwhelmingly granted outside the capitol.

Taxi owners are low-risk customers with excellent sources for collateral. They have the insured vehicle itself and an operating license that has value within the cooperative with which Prisma has outstanding relations. Moreover, the cooperatives must co-sign on a Prisma loan. This provides an important set of organizational incentives to re-pay loans. Finally, all taxi loans must be guaranteed by a lien on real-estate.

Serving this market segment is an excellent example of Prisma's double bottom line. Loans made by Prisma to "taxistas" serve independent business people while also placing large amounts of capital quickly and securely. A loan to this population enables a customer to have an annual income of approximately $1,000, almost twice the national average. Given that the average "taxista" has 6 dependents, Prisma's lending helps a huge number of people achieve a decent, although still precarious, standard of living. In this way, the Prisma social return, like the Prisma loan portfolio, is balanced: the emerging middle-class is encouraged while also supporting those on the economic margins.

Nicaraguan Competition

The total outstanding loan portfolio for Nicaraguan microfinance institutions is $47.9 million and Prisma currently has 1.2 percent of the market. Prisma's major competitors, in order of threat to the company, are:

- Other microfinance institutions
- Other formal lending institutions
- Money lenders
- Family/friends
- Potential customers not borrowing

Prisma is confident that its customer network is established enough to overcome the first three threats through word of mouth. In reverse order, here is an overview of each.

Potential Customers Not Borrowing: The most common action by potential customers at this time is not to access capital or credit, due to fear, lack of understanding, or no market opportunity. This dynamic clearly drags the economy in a number of ways, creating a significant dis-incentive for individuals to participate in the market economy.

Borrowing from Family and Friends: When individuals cannot turn to institutions, they turn to family and friends. On the practical level, this typically results in under-capitalization of potential successful businesses because family and friends are confronting the same dearth of capital.

Money Lenders: These are usually local individuals that lend money to people at interest rates that reflect their ability to provide capital quickly for their customers with limited focus on due diligence. Interest rates for this immediate access to capital are frequently as high as 480 percent APR. Prisma's significantly lower interest rates make it an attractive alternative to money lenders even if the turn-around on loan issuance is not immediate.

Other Formal Lending Institutions: There are a wide variety of formal lending institutions in Nicaragua who serve business owners. For the most part, these institutions would only be interested in Prisma's clients who take out the largest loans, namely the taxi cooperatives, because the others would be viewed as too risky. Prisma has a competitive advantage over formal lending institutions because it has been directly serving this target market for five years, knows the customers, and wants to serve them where the formal banks do not.

Other Microfinance Institutions: These institutions are Prisma's biggest threat. Many have as much experience as Prisma; however, their interest rates are much higher, hovering anywhere between 60-100 percent APR. Prisma's competitive advantage over these institutions is that its interest rates are considerably lower. Prisma is also a nimble company, with the ability to adapt its loans to the needs of the customer. Prisma is among the top twenty players in the Nicaraguan microfinance landscape, which controls at least 80 percent of the total market, the remainder of the market being served by money lenders. Even with this relatively small number of players in the market, it is still fragmented, with the largest organization controlling approximately 13 percent and the smallest less than 1 percent. The following table gives a breakdown of competitors' loan portfolios and growth.

Nicaraguan Microfinance Institutions: Portfolio and Client Data in Thousands of Dollars (Source: ASOMIF)

Institution	1997 Portfolio	1999 Portfolio	Clients	Average Loan Amount	Portfolio Growth
FAMA	2,688.10	6,230.90	15,218	409.4	132%
FDL	1,935.60	5,858.90	6,609	886.5	203%
ACODEP	1,180.60	4,563.90	14,769	309	287%
FINDE	1,128.00	3,505.20	2,862	1,224.70	211%
CEPRODEL	1,103.60	2,930.00	4,125	710.3	165%
CHISPA	1,646.00	2,524.60	6,557	385	53%
PRESTANIC	3,247.00	2,480.50	5,502	450.8	-24%
CARUNA	1,227.90	2,302.90	6,213	370.7	88%
ASODERI	976.5	2,238.20	3,500	639.5	129%
FIDESA	988.4	2,092.70	1,542	1,357.10	112%
F.J.N.	893.9	2,010.00	2,435	825.5	125%
FINCA	650	1,680.00	14,351	117.1	158%
FUNDENUSE	441.6	1,062.00	2,370	448.1	140%

Institution	1997 Portfolio	Portfolio	1999 Clients	Average Loan Amount	Portfolio Growth
FUDESI	453.6	1,000.00	955	1,047.10	120%
F/LEON 2000	379	979.2	2,367	413.7	158%
F/4i 2000	210	789.4	2,213	356.7	276%
CESADE	200	430.5	850	506.5	115%
CARMA	160	250.7	300	835.7	57%
FONDEFER	190	198.6	1,309	151.7	5%
OTRAS	3,500.00	4,135.10	16,319	253.4	18%
PRISMA	**396.5**	**649.06**	**863**	**752.1**	**63.67%**

Potential future competition: In this growing market, there are potential future competitors. Banks may move "down the line" to capture a portion of this market share, and direct competitors within Nicaragua may expand their operations. Prisma will draw on the relationships it has established throughout the Nicaraguan microfinance industry, its knowledge of government regulations, and its understanding of industry dynamics to preempt this competition.

Barriers to Entry

In-House Knowledge: Running a microfinance company requires extensive knowledge of banking, financial management, sales, and community outreach. A successful MFI needs a staff with a unique blend of skills. Prisma MicroFinance has attracted employees that bring these skills and has also spent time and energy on professional development. Organizations interested in starting a microfinance company will have to be dedicated to developing the requisite internal capacity as Prisma has done, and this can be costly and time consuming.

Staffing: Microfinance has been driven by nongovernmental agencies. As such, management and individuals working in the field usually come from a social service delivery background rather than a business background. However, microfinance is based on business fundamentals. Attracting individuals from the business sector has historically proven challenging because of the pay differential and lack of compensation incentives such as employment stock option plans. Prisma has already been able to attract staff from the business sector by offering competitive salaries; by converting to a for-profit stock company Prisma is now in a position to offer ESOPs, thus narrowing the differential between for-profit and nonprofit compensation packages. New ventures not in a position to do this will be hard pressed to attract employees with the skills necessary to run a successfully microfinance company.

OPERATIONS & MANAGEMENT

Management

The managers and directors have worked together since the beginning of operations in Nicaragua in 1995, boasting over 25 years of combined experience in the microfinance industry.

President, CEO, & Co-Founder: David J. Satterthwaite has six years of microfinance experience in Nicaragua and Latin America. David has also worked as a business consultant, researcher, and teaching assistant. He graduated with honors from Haverford College in Pennsylvania and is currently completing graduate work in Social Economy at Boston College.

General Manager (COO): Carlos Alberto Aburto Villalta has been responsible for Nicaraguan operations since 1998 and held previous management positions within the company prior to becoming COO. He holds a five-year undergraduate business degree from the Universidad

Centro Americano (UCA) in Managua, Nicaragua, and is currently a candidate for a master's degree in business from the UCA.

Portfolio Manager: Honey Maria Aburto Villalta has been the loan portfolio manager since 1998. She holds a five-year undergraduate law degree from the Universidad Centro Americano (UCA) in Managua, Nicaragua, and is currently a candidate for her master's degree in labor law from the UCA.

Board of Directors

Roger Aburto: Co-founder of Prisma. Roger currently runs Xilonem, a cooperative spin-off from Prisma, which manages the insurance fund and past-due collections. Roger's experience includes: manager for a regional micro-credit fund for 8 years, a small-business owner, and a veteran. His education includes graduate work on the Nicaraguan informal economy.

Richard Burnes: Co-founder and Principle of Charles River Ventures (CRV is not associated with Prisma). Rick has been an investor in Prisma since its beginning in 1995.

George Kraus: As a retired entrepreneur, George supports a variety of humanitarian and business projects in Nicaragua. He has been an investor in Prisma since its beginning in 1995.

Staff

No.	Name	Position	Monthly Wage
1	Róger Aburto García	Director	$500
2	David Satterthwaite (in the U.S.)	President	$2,400
3	Carlos Aburto Villalta	General Manager	$500
4	Ivette López Blanco (PT)	Assistant Manager	$270
5	Honey Aburto Villalta (PT)	Portfolio Manager	$270
6	Carlos García Palma	Accountant	$295
7	Rafael Gutiérrez Román	Information Technology	$295
8	Rafael Gutiérrez Tellez	Collections	$200
9	Ramón Román Gutiérrez	Legal Council	$275
10	Ernestina Olivares Vallejos	Teller	$200
11	Armando López Torrez	Security	$75
12	Pablo D. Johanes López	Market Investigation and Development	$175
Total Monthly Payroll			**$5,056**

Board of Advisors

Erica Mills, Master of Public Administration, marketing and communications consultant
Drew Tulchin, Master of Business Administration, business consultant
Brady Miller, former Director of Finance for Ex-Officio, finance consultant

Professional Staff

Nicaraguan Professionals:
Marco Morales, CPA
Oscar Silva, Legal Counsel, Delaney y Asociados

United States Professionals:
Tom Herman, Legal Counsel, Smith & Duggan, LLP
Howard Brady, CPA, MFI Consulting, Inc.
Daniel MacLeod, Graphic Designer, Visual Braille, Inc.

1. Clients visit a Prisma office to request an application.
2. Clients with strong references receive an application; careful track is kept of who receives them.
3. If, upon review of the application by the Credit Committee, the customer is deemed to be an acceptable credit risk, preliminary approval is granted.
4. A site visit is made to interview the customer, verify application details, and review collateral.
5. Clients provide all necessary paperwork—including signatures and guarantees. The complexity of this process depends on loan size.
6. Larger loans, including taxi loans, can take months because of the due diligence involved. It includes a police record review.
7. The process is uniform and straightforward to ensure all customers receive the same treatment.

The Prisma Sales Experience

Prisma's operations and management has five years of successful, profitable lending experience in the Nicaraguan market. The company has developed successful activities for ensuring it is providing excellent service and developing strong relationships with solid customers, ensuring that the loans will be repaid.

Operations

Key Management Philosophy: Prisma conducts business in a highly professional and open manner. The company's philosophy is centered on knowing customers, working with them to be successful, making sure they understand how their loans work, and rewarding good behavior.

Streamlined Processing: Customers are classified from A-D based factors including: payment timeliness, credit history, savings, referring new business, and peer performance (those they referred or referred them). The taxi co-ops are classified according to the same criteria by each co-op as a group. There are rewards and tangible benefits for "A" customers, knowledge of which is spread among customers through word of mouth.

Balanced and Cost-effective Loan Portfolio: The existing relationship with Taxi Cooperatives provides an inroad for nationwide market penetration. A single loan officer covers the costs of his/her position with only 20 taxi loans (approximately $5,000 each). Microfinance industry data indicates loan officers can manage 150-300 loans at one time. Therefore, because the breakeven point for an additional lender is low, Prisma can financially afford to have a balanced portfolio with an equal number of micro and small loans. Although smaller loans are less lucrative, they are financially viable for the business and promote the social mission of ensuring there is access to credit for all. In addition, they provide the benefits of being repaid faster, requiring less due diligence, and producing a high number of referrals.

Hand-held Technology and Centralized Due Diligence: In order to minimize infrastructure costs, back-office support for loan officers will be centralized. Loan officers will utilize advanced technology to conduct their business. Hand-held devices will be used in the field to mechanize the application and monitoring process. The loan portfolio data is stored electronically to minimize onerous paperwork. This equipment investment pays for itself in the reduced paperwork, time savings (especially in approving applications and transferring data). Electronic loan processing and bi-weekly visits to the main office will allow the due-diligence of loan guarantees to be performed with adequate legal review, in a timely manner.

In addition to this technology, Prisma will also take advantage of technology being designed by groups like Hewlett Packard's World e-Inclusion team that is developing networked tools with the express purpose of making microlending more efficient. With a commitment of selling, leasing, or donating $1 billion in products and services to this initiative, it could prove a valuable source of technology enhancement.

Strategic Banking Partnership: To minimize expansion costs and accelerate the amount of lending possible, Prisma plans to partner with a bank with national presence. By utilizing their existing infrastructure and brokering the deals, remote offices avoid the complications of handling cash. This provides benefits in efficiency and also safety/security. Prisma has a developed a relationship with Banco de Finanza, a national leader in web-based delivery of banking services.

Vested Managers: A generous Employee Stock Option Plan creates a vested management team. Vested managers are important to providing motivation for the growth strategy. With these economic incentives for employees, Prisma has a competitive advantage compared to other microfinance lenders, including:

- nonprofits—unable to offer their managers a portion of the potential upside
- newly established stock companies controlled by directors from the nonprofit sector—unlikely to implement market-based incentives due to employee culture bias

GROWTH STRATEGY & MILESTONES

Growth Strategy

Prisma's market niche in taxi financing allows management to plan significant portfolio growth while minimizing overhead. Prisma will specialize in taxi financing as a spearhead to establishing operations nationwide in Nicaragua and in other countries in Central America. Using Prisma's specialization in taxi finance in this way drives penetration of the micro-credit market while still maintaining healthy profit margins.

In fiscal year 2002, Prisma will relocate its Managua office to prepare for national and international expansion. The new office space will accommodate the additional staff needed for expansion, while remaining in a geographically strategic location that will be convenient for Prisma's borrowers. In FY2003, the first satellite office in Nicaragua will be established, with two more additional national offices in FY2004. Also, in FY2004 Prisma will begin operating in a second country in Central America, to be determined depending on market opportunity.

Loan Officers: Prisma can realistically project rapid portfolio growth because of the proven demand for taxi financing and Prisma's track record financing taxis. Assuming that a single loan officer will manage 200 loans (a conservative estimate by industry standards), management estimates needing 25 loan officers by FY2004 when the total loan portfolio will be worth almost $11 million, distributed among 4,800 clients.

Scalability: Management forecasts steady profits for FY2001, although net income is projected to be slightly lower than FY2000 due to the integration of the U.S. operations. FY2002 will see a 100 percent growth in net income over FY2001, although management will advise reinvesting the profit into the company to support the growth strategy. Investment toward scalability during these two years will begin to pay off in FY2003, when management forecasts a 10.9 percent return on shareholder equity. Between FY2002 and FY2004, the portfolio balance per loan officer in order to break-even drops from an aggressive (but tenable) $470,000 down to $225,000 (total portfolio/total expenses). Securing the taxi financing niche and introducing operational improvements such as the use of hand-held technology makes the Prisma business model scalable.

Taxi Financing Market Share: Assuming that three-fourths of all medium-sized loans will be taxi loans and a 10 percent annual growth in the taxi sector, Prisma will claim a 22 percent market share by FY2004.

Central American Expansion: Nicaragua serves as a launch pad for entering the Central American market. In FY2004, Prisma plans to open operations in a second Central American country. This is a large and important market. (A Central American target market analysis can be found in the appendices.) The central challenge in expansion will be hiring effective management; for this reason, we are adopting a conservative expansion schedule. The taxi finance market will serve as a spearhead regardless of which country is deemed most appropriate.

Scalability Goal: Equity in Prisma is a long-term, non-liquid investment. The objective of achieving scale in the microfinance industry requires patient capital. "Scale" signifies at least the $50 million portfolio necessary to credibly solicit commercial capital investment. This will take 5-10 years. Scale is Prisma's mandate in order to be a leader in establishing new private equity capital markets for the microfinance industry.

The founders' choice in 1995 not to accept donations or subsidies to run this business was unheard of in the microfinance field at the time. However, since day one, Prisma has been dedicated to utilizing the essential potential of microfinance to eradicate poverty: making it economically attractive for capitalists to invest in "unbankable" business people. This choice has resulted in two truisms: private capital seeks scale to maximize profits and in order to achieve scale, equity is required. Therefore, consideration of the liquid event on this investment is imperative.

Financial Return & Exit Strategy

Because there are currently no secondary markets for Prisma stock and no one has yet to systematically "securitize" microloans, the most viable exit strategy for investors is acquisition.

Prisma has had discussions with major U.S. banks and has a clear understanding of what characteristics would be needed in order for an acquisition to occur. A national or international loan portfolio in taxi finance and a total loan portfolio of at least $50 million will make Prisma an attractive acquisition to larger banking institutions. These are the principal reasons that Prisma seeks to capture a niche market and grow its loan portfolio—to bring value to investors supporting micro-loans, which at present are unproven in secondary markets.

First and foremost, Prisma is committed to providing its investors with dividends, even in the early stages of growth. Prisma has been profitable for five years, since its first day of operation. This proven viability legitimizes the plan of paying dividends. Management thinks it imprudent to forecast the value of dividends at this time. The financial projections indicate healthy profits in FY2003 and FY2004 of 10.9 percent and 11.5 percent respectively, once scale is achieved.

Financial Returns to Investors

Moreover, Prisma seeks capital appreciation for its investors. Prisma anticipates that capital appreciation will be augmented in the future by the creation of business spin-offs and offering of additional products. Business spin-offs could include auto repair, auto parts, car insurance and collections. Additional products might be credit cards, mortgage financing, or home-improvement loans.

Like a bank, Prisma is a profitable lending business. But Prisma stands apart from its commercial counterparts for two reasons:

Social Returns to Investors

- it targets people without access to traditional, financial resources
- it is a business that realizes social as well as economic returns

Social returns constitute positive impact beyond the immediate benefits offered by a product —in this case small loans. Micro-lending is a business and development strategy widely acknowledged to bring extensive and diverse social returns to local communities. Well-managed, sustainable programs have been proven to successfully empower borrowers, strengthen families, catalyze communities, and expand local markets.

When an individual generates income from a small loan, the benefits extend a great distance and in many directions. Borrowers become more responsive to the needs of their families, and more active in their communities. Breadwinners are able to provide improved healthcare and education to their families, so children grow up healthier and with greater opportunities to realize their own potential. Families become stronger through access to working capital and the resulting opportunities. The fabric of communities becomes more tightly woven when it has a greater stake in its own development and can realize the benefits of its own efforts.

Prisma's clients and investors are able to realize tremendous social returns precisely because the company is profitable. Based on our estimates, every dollar lent generates $21 of social benefit for the borrower. For Prisma, profitability and sustainability are indicators that customers are using and repaying their loans successfully. This, in turn, means resources are more readily available for loans, and the social returns mentioned above go hand in hand with the unfettered availability and successful use of working capital.

Finally, as a market-driven social initiative, Prisma provides social returns at a larger scale with accelerated impact because it attracts investment.

MARKETING & SALES STRATEGY
Marketing Strategy

Because Prisma is mindful of the fiscal operations and expenses necessary to run a profitable enterprise, the marketing budget is, by design, small and highly focused on very basic, interpersonal efforts. Only those activities that provide proven return and bring in new loans to achieve the intended growth and projection figures are undertaken.

Grassroots marketing and establishing trust with customers has been the hallmark of the Nicaraguan operations to date. These efforts led to a 207 percent growth in Prisma's loan portfolio between 1996-2000. Ensuring positive customer experience has led to word of mouth as the leading source for new client acquisition. In a country like Nicaragua, where relationships and community are the mainstays of business activity, the "word on the street" is the best marketing channel and a strong indicator of a company's reputation. It is also inexpensive.

Other channels for publicity, especially formal channels including print media, television, and radio, will not yield sufficient response for their cost. The target customers are typically distrustful and skeptical of formal institutions, if not outright intimidated. Therefore, relationship marketing like face-to-face communication and rewarding referrals has a much larger impact, not to mention lower acquisition cost.

Marketing activities follow the same standards as operations, described earlier. This includes knowing customers, working with them to be successful, making sure they understand how their loans work, and rewarding good behavior. Customers are classified from A-D based factors including: payment timeliness, credit history, savings, referring new business, and peer performance (those they referred or referred them). The taxi co-ops are classified according to the same criteria by each co-op as a group. There are known rewards and tangible benefits for "A" customers—including better interest rates.

New loans are most easily made through the "chain of trust," whereby existing or old clients vouch (co-sign) for new customers. The practice of allowing "A" clients to co-sign, helping friends and family secure loans, provides Prisma with essentially a free sales force, minimizes default rates, and provides a support network to support struggling customers. Customers are highly loyal; they support the lending institution because they are supporting each other and helping themselves.

Promotional activities include simple and basic activities for existing customers and important members of the community including receptions, small gifts, and a newsletter. An annual reception is held to thank customers and share what the organization is doing. Customers feel valued and that they are contributing to economic development in their country. "A" clients receive little gifts on holidays. These gifts are inexpensive but customers appreciate them.

Marketing in New Markets

When entering a new market—first in other cities in Nicaragua and later in other Central American countries—the same tactics will be used. A major key to success is in effective new hires with strong professional and social networks that can share what Prisma does. Word of mouth is effective among family, friends, and the taxi co-operatives—all of which have connections in locations targeted for expansion and are just waiting for Prisma to establish operations there.

Indicators for measuring the success of marketing efforts is in how little money is spent to achieve Prisma's growth milestones. Customer satisfaction will remain the lynchpin of Prisma's marketing strategy.

Sales Strategy

As noted in previous sections, this enterprise is not starting from scratch. Prisma has five years of profitable operations upon which to base its sales activities. Most of the efforts will be on maintaining the current methods and practices that have made the company successful to date—lending to individuals in groups that know each other, providing excellent service, building trust with customers, and working with customers to ensure a successful loan.

The Nicaraguan operation has worked well with the taxi cooperatives. Since 80 percent of taxi drivers report requiring external funding to ensure they can operate successfully, this is a target market with very likely customers. Furthermore, most cannot or choose not to be served by more formal banks. Even better, the taxi cooperatives are close-knit business and social circles. Therefore, taxi drivers easily see what a loan from Prisma does for their business because a co-worker and friend has directly benefited from it. Drivers ensure their colleagues do not default on their loans because they are co-signers and do not want to lose this resource for affordable capital (and an "A" rating). In the event of a default, the entire cooperative could lose the lending service and the co-signers will be stuck with the bill.

FINANCIAL ANALYSIS

Capital Structure

Prisma's business model makes two assumptions:

1. Equity capital is the only source of capital that will enable the company to achieve its expansion goals while maintaining a solid balance sheet.
2. U.S. investors are looking to invest in companies that value social responsibility.

Prisma's five years of profitable operations confirms the first assumption. From its inception, Prisma has been financed through debt. Prisma has serviced these debts and remained profitable, but relying solely on debt capital has limited the company's growth as evidenced by the fact that Prisma has 200 approved loans waiting to be financed.

The *New York Times'* front-page article "On Wall Street, More Investors Push Social Goals," from February 11, 2001, bolsters the second assumption. Increasingly, investors are realizing that there "is a correlation between good practices and good investment results" and are placing their money accordingly. An analysis of "Socially Responsible Investing" proves that investors are increasingly adopting an investment approach that integrates social and environmental concerns into investment decisions. Prisma provides a viable option for investors interested in making money and making a difference.

**Financial
Projections**

Prisma's fiscal year runs July 1 through June 30. The $1.5 million currently being raised in Series "B" round is scheduled to close in July 2001. Therefore, the equity appears in FY2002, beginning July 2001. During fiscal year 2001, the management established a U.S. office to raise funds and promote the company's activities. A central strategy is leveraging equity with additional debt to grow operations. In FY2002, a conservative leverage ratio of less than 1 to 1 is assumed; a similar ratio is also assumed in FY2003.

The $1.5 million of sought equity will fully impact revenue in FY2002. By FY2003, management projects a 10.9 percent return on $2.7 million in equity. By comparison, ROE for other financially self-sufficient microfinance institutions is 6.05 percent according to the *MicroBanking Bulletin*. Return on assets for these institutions hovers at 3.08 percent; by FY2004 management projects ROA of 4.1 percent. Throughout FY2002 and FY2003, investment in scaling operations is assumed. The goal is to achieve appropriate scale to secure another round of equity investment of $4 million in July of 2003 (beginning of FY2004).

Additional assumptions in the financials include:

- Interest Earned: As of FY2002, 17 percent net interest margin is assumed matching historical performance.
- Cost of Capital: 13 percent annual rate, based on current relationships with creditors and management's knowledge of the capital market for socially responsible investment instruments.
- Loan Officer Capacity: Each loan officer will manage 200 clients, which is low by industry standards.
- Taxes: Both U.S. and Nicaragua tax liabilities and expenses are included in the projections, assuming a combined rate of 35 percent.

**IMPACT ANALYSIS
& SOCIAL RETURN
ON INVESTMENT**

To claim that tangible assets should be measured and valued, while intangibles should not—or could not—is like stating that "things" are valuable, while "ideas" are not.

—Barach Lev, Professor Stern School of Business, New York University

Social Impact

Receiving a Prisma loan generates significant social impact in the following areas:

- Human Capital Development: Relates to improved economic standing, heightened self-esteem and sense of empowerment, and creation of a stable financial situation for borrowers
- Community Development: Resulting from borrowers' improved economic standing and ability to give back to the community
- Corporate Governance: Refers to the equity incentives that Prisma will offer to its employees and its ethic of empowering its staff through inclusive decision-making roles
- Socially Responsible Market Creation: Speaks to the industry-wide desired outcome of Prisma's activities, which is to be at the forefront of developing viable products to improve the situation of the world's four billion poor people, or the B2-4B revolution

Human Capital Development

Prisma's impact on human capital development results from the positive externalities generated by each dollar lent. The positive externalities start a ripple effect, which leads to improved diet as a result of having a stable cash flow and increased education level for borrowers' children who can stay in school rather than be forced to drop out to increase family income. Improvements to borrowers' lives can be seen in all areas of basic need as a result of having a higher standing of living.

Community Development

In addition to improving individual borrower's economic situation, Prisma's loans also fuel community development, which in essence is the aggregated effect of the individual loans. The loans improve the standing of individual borrowers, thus stabilizing economies at the community level.

The sense of empowerment that comes from economic stability also leads to greater community involvement. This involvement can take many forms, including being involved with public health projects such as latrine building, providing for community members who are sick or in a time of crisis, and skills transfer to other local business owners. These activities and interactions build healthy, sustainable communities.

Corporate Governance

Prisma is offering a balanced, inclusive equity structure that extends to every employee. Senior management is indigenous, except for David Satterthwaite, the CEO and President, who worked in Nicaragua for five years. There is local representation on the board, currently one third of the membership. Equity incentives in Latin America, including ESOPs, are far from the norm, especially for a small company. However, by doing so Prisma is promoting a new business culture of equitable private property ownership in an American company—this is globalization at its most positive.

Creating a commercial market that benefits poor people

According to Jeffrey Ashe, founder of Boston's Working Capital and former Vice-President of Accion International, there are approximately four billion people throughout the developing world without access to affordable credit. Entrepreneurs with excellent skills and incredible ideas are restricted in their opportunity due to lack of financial resources. Even the small amount of money needed as investment capital to start micro-enterprises like weaving baskets and selling them at the local market is beyond the grasp of the majority of the world's poor.

The world's "unbankable" populations have three options:

1. gather limited resources from family and friends
2. borrow from a moneylender at exorbitant rates
3. turn to a microfinance institution like Prisma

Frequently, family and friends cannot generate the necessary capital and the moneylender's rates are too high to be able to pay them back. This being the case, only a loan from an institution like Prisma can result in the successful growth of a new business that may break the cycle of poverty.

According to industry sources, less than $10 billion currently is invested in the worldwide microfinance industry. This does not even scratch the surface towards serving this market.

Microcredit is not a panacea solution for social problems. But, it is a useful tool for many to bridge the gap out of poverty and improve their lives. In addition to this activity providing a social return, there are equally compelling market driven motivations to undertake these operations using private capital—providing this service produces financial return.

As with any industry sector, once an example of a successful model is provided, others will enter the field. Following Prisma's lead, microfinance will become a viable commercial market, serving billions of the world's poor.

SROI Methodology and Analysis

While some of Prisma's Social Impact Areas are easily quantifiable, others are best evaluated in terms of qualitative impact analysis. Human Capital Development and Community Economic Development are included in the quantitative analysis using number of dollars lent as the unit of measurement. The qualitative methods analyze aspects of all four impact areas. The following sections outline Prisma's quantitative and qualitative methodology for measuring SROI.

Quantitative Analysis

Current SROI Analysis: In developing its quantitative methodology, Prisma has drawn from models developed by Roberts Endowed Development Fund (REDF), one of the leaders in social enterprise. The use of a social benefit/cost ratio, adjusted for present value, gives a clear sign as to whether the social benefits outweigh the social costs and by what degree. Based on traditional cost/benefit analysis benchmarks, if the ratio is greater than or equal to one, the project should be pursued.

SROI Ratio = Present Value of Social Benefits/Present Value of Social Costs

Social Benefits

Social benefits accounted for in the quantitative analysis of SROI include ripple effects from improving one's financial situations through receiving a loan. These include:

- Improved health for all family members, leading to higher productivity on a long-term basis
- Increased education for borrowers' children as they are not required to drop out of school in order to supplement the family's income
- Increased civic participation as a result of a heightened level of confidence and overall sense of self-worth

These benefits are cited extensively in microfinance literature, including by industry leaders such as FINCA and Accion International. The dollar amounts in the table below are taken from the financial projections for Prisma's loan portfolio. They represent the total number of dollars Prisma expects to lend in each year. (Social benefit and social cost are calculated on a per year basis and then aggregated.) As social benefits are directly correlated to loans, the social benefits are captured in terms of dollars lent to borrowers.

Social Costs

Prisma has always borrowed capital at market rates therefore eliminating the social cost of subsidies or grants often included as social costs in SROI analysis. We have included a small social cost that reflects loan loss due to Prisma's choice to make loans to extremely high-risk individuals. As the company's loan loss has historically been under 1 percent, the estimated social cost per dollar lent of $. 05 used in the model reflects our acknowledgment that in undertaking an expansion strategy into new geographic markets, we run the risk of an increase in the loan loss rate.

Prisma's SROI Ratio:

2000-2004	2000	2001	2002	2003	2004	Total
Benefits	$906,272	$1,309,380	$4,427,150	$5,449,600	$10,648,000	$22,740,402
PV of Benefits	$906,272	$1,138,591	$3,347,561	$3,583,200	$6,088,029	$15,063,654
Costs	$45,336	$65,469	$221,358	$272,480	$532,400	$1,137,043
Present Value of Costs	$45,336	$56,930	$167,378	$179,160	$304,401	$753,205

Present Value of Social Benefits/Present Value of Social Costs = $15,063, 654/753, 205 = $21

A benefit/cost ratio of 21 means that for every unit of cost, 21 units of social benefit are derived. As the unit of measurement in this model is dollars, the social return is interpreted as $21 of social benefit for every $1 of social cost incurred. The fact that Prisma's SROI ratio is as high as 21 indicates that in terms of benefit/cost analysis, it is an attractive project, with an extremely high social return on investment.

Future SROI Analysis: Ideally, Prisma would quantify its SROI in terms of the increase in income derived directly from the loan. Measuring income generated specifically from a Prisma loan is complicated in that it would involve measuring a portion of each borrower's increase in income, rather than their total income. This approach would require an in-depth understanding of loan usage and the borrower's expenditures. Prisma proposes to develop this understanding through the qualitative methods described below.

A SROI analysis based on incremental increases in income would enable Prisma to project the increase per month in income over time. The company would then calculate the social net present value of that increase and calculate the appropriate social internal rate of return.

Qualitative Analysis

Prisma has historically collected some of the information described below, such as customer finances, professional activities, age, and gender. Based on its experience, Prisma believes the most effective way to gather information on a going forward basis is to administer question-naires at the loan's beginning, closing, and annually thereafter (on a voluntary basis), in conjunction with qualitative interviews. These new methods will standardize the process of information gathering and enable Prisma to do more rigorous quantitative analysis, in addition to maintaining a clear sense of its customer base—even as it rapidly expands. Information gathered from customers will include both economic and social indicators.

Economic Indicators

As a bank, Prisma must make loans that are fiscally responsible and will be paid back. Therefore, it needs to determine a borrower's financial status before, during, and at the end of the loan. During the loan application process, loan officers will collect information about customers and their finances, including their professional activities, income, historical income, family financial resources, and projected future income. This builds on the information Prisma currently collects and believes is reasonable to collect in the future.

Social Indicators

Because of the level of trust Prisma staff establishes with customers, they have been consistently helpful in providing information enabling us to track their status. At the time of the loan, social indicators including age, gender, economic condition of borrower, number of family members, and current income are provided. Throughout the term of the loan, it is easy to track the number of employees, business income, and changes in standard of living. This is done implicitly by following the timeliness of loan payments and seeing if loan payments are made on time or late. Receipt of late payments usually indicates a change for the worse in the borrower's status. Prisma will also begin using a standardized method for tracking the ongoing conversations Prisma staff has with customers, through which much information about social indicators is gathered. At the end of the loan, the same information will be formally gathered with an exit questionnaire. Plus, because of its active involvement in the communities it serves and the fact that many customers renew loans for additional working capital, Prisma will be able to track social indicators longitudinally.

Information gathered through loan review, questionnaires, and interviews will be included in Prisma's Annual Report. This will enable our investors to track the SROI and ensure that Prisma stays true to its mandate of doing well by doing good.

If we are looking for one single action which will enable the poor to overcome their poverty, I would focus on credit.

—Dr. Muhammad Yunus
Founder, The Grameen Bank

APPENDIX

Target Market—Microfinance in Central America

Market Description

Prisma MicroFinance, Inc., is a U.S. microfinance company with Nicaraguan operations where loans are made to residents in the urban area of capitol, Managua. The loans range in size from U.S. $50-$15,000, and are used for both personal and business purposes. Loans to taxi cab cooperatives account for the larger loans and act as a subsidy for the smaller loans to individuals, primarily women.

Market Size and Trends

Managua is Nicaragua's economic center and has a population of more than 1,000,000. Although Nicaragua's economy is still driven by agriculture, service jobs in the urban areas represent an increasing number of jobs.

This trend holds true throughout Central America. The table below demonstrates the size of the market for international microfinance in Central America's urban areas—the geographic areas that Prisma will target as it expands—expressed in terms of population and GDP. The countries are ranked by size of capital city, beginning with the largest, Guatemala City.

Country/ Capital City	Population–Country/ Population–Capital City	GDP (in US$)/ GDP per capita
Guatemala	12,700,000	$18.9 million
Guatemala City	2,000,000	$1,750
El Salvador	5,900,000	$11.9 billion
San Salvador	1,300,000	$1,960
Nicaragua	4,275,000	$2.3 billion
Managua	1,000,000	$430
Honduras	5,800,000	$4.49 billion
Tegucigalpa	800,000	$774
Panama	2,800,000	$9.14 billion
Panama City	700,000	$3,310

Costa Rica	3,700,000	$5 billion
San Jose	330,000	$1,351
Belize	250,000	$700 million
Belize City	55,000	$3,000

Many Central American countries are rebuilding after years of political, social, and economic unrest. Microentrepreneurs play an integral role as economic drivers in this rebuilding and will need access to affordable capital.

Prisma's target customers include:

Target Customers

- Taxi cab drivers
- Microentrepreneurs
- Women

These target customers look for microfinance institutions (MFIs) that are professional, while still understanding the specific needs of poorer borrowers. They would not have access to banks or traditional financial institutions, so if they decide to take out a loan their options are limited to friends/family, moneylenders, or MFIs. The resources of friends and family are extremely limited, and the exorbitant rates charged by moneylenders (ranging from 360-480 percent APR) make them unattractive in terms of repayment possibilities. (Moneylenders are attractive because there are no conditions to qualify for a loan.) Prisma is in competition with other MFIs.

Prisma has been in operation for six years. In each of these six years, it has expanded its outreach and refined its operations. With a strong management team in place, Prisma is now ready to significantly expand its operations. It is already the market leader for lending to taxi cab cooperatives and plans to make this its market niche over the next year. This will position Prisma to expand its outreach to other microentrepreneurs and individuals, particularly women.

Market Readiness

Through its experience in the Managua area, Prisma has learned that there is a significant demand for microloans. With its economy continuing to grow, this demand will only increase.

Strategic Opportunities

Other capitol cities throughout Central America are experiencing a similar shift toward an expansion of economic activity in the urban centers. The need for microentrepreneurs to access affordable capital will expand along with the urban-based economies. Clearly, there is a demand for reputable MFIs to meet this need and Prisma has established a way to reach this market.

Golf Driving Range

BUSINESS PLAN

MOUNTAIN CEDAR GOLF CLUB

1175 Mountain Cedar Drive
Kerrville, Texas 78028

Mountain Cedar Golf Club is a driving range located in the suburbs of San Antonio, Texas. This plan raised $1.5 million in capital for the company's owners.

- EXECUTIVE SUMMARY

- BUSINESS DESCRIPTION

- PRODUCTS

- MARKETING

- COMPETITION

- OPERATIONS

- FINANCIALS

- RISK FACTORS

EXECUTIVE SUMMARY

Mountain Cedar Golf Club (MCGC) is a state-of-the-art golf driving range to be located on the southeast side of Kerrville, Texas. This metropolitan San Antonio area has no golf driving ranges to compare to this one. Most of the ranges are located in out-of-the-way areas and are operating on a short-term basis until the land is developed for some other use. Our intent is to build a golf driving range that will become the premier range in the United States.

Locating the range in San Antonio's northern development corridor provides many opportunities for revenue growth as it is close to many of the various tourist attractions that make this city one of the most popular vacation and convention cities in Texas as well as the Southwestern U.S.

A typical driving range operates on a "Mom and Pop" basis with much manual labor and very little revenue other than that produced by the buckets of balls sold. MCGC will operate with a multi-tiered 50-station deck, debit card ball dispensing, integrated POS computer, a pro shop, batting cages, restaurant, professional PGA and LPGA instruction, corporate memberships, plus targeted e-mail and Internet marketing.

MCGC is pioneering a concept in corporate sponsorship of the range. By soliciting corporate sponsorship from noncompeting companies, the additional revenue is expected to be $500,000 the first year with significant increases the following years.

Another aspect, only practiced by a handful of ranges, is that of selling memberships to the range. This is very similar to traditional golf club memberships. The membership will include perks and special advantages for the golfer. The benefit to MCGC will be a steady stream of revenue as well as a target audience for marketing.

The bottom line for this company is as follows: First year revenue $4,102,287 with expenses of $1,170,614 and a net profit before taxes of $2,931,623. We are seeking start-up financing of $1.5 million dollars in return for a 30 percent equity position in the company.

As a benefit to MCGC and the community, MCGC will offer low-cost/free lessons to children in the greater San Antonio area. We want to promote the advantages of golf to all in the community, which will create long-term value and enhanced quality of life.

MCGC's home page is located at www.mountaincedargolf.com. Its phone number is (210) 730-1839. E-mail: info@mountaincedargolf.com.

BUSINESS DESCRIPTION

In the United States there are more golf courses than there are McDonald's restaurants. There are over 26 million golfers in the U.S., and of these more than six million are avid golfers and play an average of 25 or more rounds per year. Since 1996 the number of golfers has increased by two million (8.2%), yet the number of practice facilities has grown by only 3 percent. These numbers show an incredible opportunity upon which to capitalize.

The golf range industry has gone through major changes over the last 10 years. What used to be a "mom and pop" dominated industry has given way to large, automated ranges owned by publicly traded companies. From 1994 to 1999 the number of large ranges (51 or more tee stations) has grown from 336 to 495 (8.1%). The number of customers has increased 9.3 percent, yet the number of tee stations has grown by only 3 percent. The company believes that these numbers combined with the limited availability of practice facilities in metropolitan San Antonio has created a market that is "primed" for a state-of-the-art, centrally located facility.

MCGC is to be located on a 15-acre tract in a southeastern region of Kerrville called Jalapeno Junction, situated just north of San Antonio. It's part of a 300-acre mixed-use development that includes retail, office, hotel, and residential units. Specifically, the plan is highlighted by a new Town Center, as well as 1.9 million square feet of office space, a 625-room hotel, 135,000 square feet of neighborhood retail space, and approximately 1,900 residential units. Six thousand residential units already have been built on a site across the street from Jalapeno Junction. There are approximately 50,000 people within walking distance of the proposed site of MCGC.

MCGC will be located north of I-604, one of the busiest highways in the state, and will serve a market of nearly 1.5 million people with a golf range that is state of the art, featuring the following:

- Multi-tiered tee stations served by automatic ball and debit card systems
- PGA and LPGA professional golf instruction for all ages
- Heated grass and turf tees
- Water and sand hazards
- Putting green
- Corporate and individual memberships
- Pro shop and club repair
- Family-oriented environment

MCGC will provide the surrounding neighborhoods with wholesome activities and create long-term value and enhanced quality of life. The design will complement the surrounding hill country park land and fit within the city of San Antonio's historic tradition.

PRODUCTS

Traditionally, golf ranges have relied solely on revenue generated by ball sales. While MCGC will derive a major portion of its revenue from buckets of range balls, it will use new and innovative ways to increase revenues.

With the usual golf range very little thought goes into other ways to capitalize on the captive market. There are thousands of ways to increase revenue with a little extra planning and thought. At MCGC, we are planning to increase the revenue substantially by adding additional services. These services include corporate sponsorship advertising on the grounds of MCGC, PGA and LPGA professional instructors, a pro shop, food service, leagues, and corporate and individual memberships.

The largest increase in revenue will come from advertising sales at MCGC. Advertising at MCGC will serve two purposes: 1) to increase revenues, and 2) reduce costs through innovative, new programs, and media.

Advertising revenue will come from several innovative sources.

- The range balls will have sponsorship directly on the balls. This will reduce and perhaps eliminate the cost of range balls.
- With so many corporations headquartered or operating within 25 miles of MCGC we will have plenty of "official sponsors" of MCGC. Potential sponsors include airlines, phone companies, Internet providers, hotels, car dealers, well-known restaurants, credit cards, delivery companies (i.e., FedEx), etc.
- Between each tee is a tee divider. These dividers provide excellent opportunity for smaller companies to advertise. Potential advertisers include local restaurants, florists, newspapers, etc.

- Our website will be state of the art, also. Golfers will be able to sign up for tee times and purchase memberships and gifts online. Targeting advertising from golf companies and MCGC will increase revenues.

Ninety-three percent of golf ranges in the U.S. have some sort of golf instruction program. At MCGC we will offer only the best in PGA and LPGA trained professionals. Programs will include group, individual, team lessons, and a golf school. Golf has become a way of life for many, and a great way to reduce stress and have fun. We do not think this should be limited to people in the mid- to upper-income brackets. As a benefit to the community, we will offer free or reduced cost lessons to children in the city of San Antonio.

MCGC's facilities will include a pro shop that caters to all levels of golf. In addition to traditional golf items, gift certificates will be available. Approximately 1,000 square feet of the facility will be used for the pro shop. The pro shop's merchandise will available for sale on our website, giving an additional avenue for increased revenue.

Food Service is often overlooked when developing a golf range. At MCGC, food service will be tied directly to our golf services. The close proximity of MCGC to many of the major tourist attractions will afford it many lunchtime customers. Daily specials that include lunch and golf will be offered as well as "a la carte" items.

An additional source of revenue to supplement buckets of balls and increase attendance at the facility is league play. At MCGC we will offer lunch-time and weekend leagues for all levels. While increasing revenue for MCGC, it will also foster a sense of community for the players.

Membership Packages

One of the newest concepts in golf ranges is to offer memberships in a manner similar to golf clubs. This is an exciting concept not only because it initially increases revenues, but also because it ensures a steady income flow throughout the year. Golfers who are members are more likely to come to practice when they have a financial tie to MCGC.

We see memberships growing exponentially in years two through five as MCGC becomes more popular, and at the same time tee times become more difficult to secure.

Although membership will not be required, we will offer comprehensive membership packages, each with a variety of privileges. Below is a sample of our membership packages.

Masters Member ($1,000 per year; initiation fee of $150)

- 60-day advance booking for tee-time
- 50 percent discount on pre-paid ball cards
- 10 percent discount at the Golf Pro Shop
- 10 percent discount on lessons at the Mountain Cedar Golf Club
- Complimentary locker and bag storage

Tour Member ($500 per year; initiation fee of $75)

- 7-day advance booking for tee-time
- 20 percent discount on pre-paid ball cards
- 5 percent discount at the Golf Pro Shop
- 5 percent discount on lessons at the Mountain Cedar Golf Club

Standard Member ($200 per year; initiation fee of $50)

- 48-hour advance booking for tee-time

Corporate Member ($3,000 per year; initiation fee of $500)

The corporate membership program will enable companies to entertain clients, host business meetings and special events, and allow their employees to practice their games year-round. Corporate privileges include:

- 25 hours free tee-time with unlimited balls (10 percent off after first 25 hours)
- 60-day advance booking for tee-time
- No minimum on number of stalls reserved
- 20 percent discount on pre-paid ball cards (limit $2,500)
- Access to locker rooms
- One free Ryder Cup Room rental (9 A.M. to 5 P.M.)
- 50 percent discount on one Ryder Cup Room rental (9 A.M. to 11 P.M.)

Off-Peak Member ($1,295 per year; initiation fee of $150)

- Unlimited balls year-round
- Monday through Friday, 9 a.m. to 11 A.M., and 2 P.M. to 5 P.M.

Marketing is divided into two categories: start-up and ongoing.

MARKETING

Start-Up Marketing

Start-up marketing will include print and radio advertising, PR, direct market mailing, and a "killer" website.

Beginning one month before the opening we will begin running ads in San Antonio's major newspapers, culminating in full-page ads three days before opening. Also one month before opening, we will run strategically placed radio ads. The most likely stations are the top four FM stations (including the classical station) in the market; while the best time slots for us are during National Public Radio broadcasts. A flood of press releases should garner plenty of free coverage in local press.

Direct marketing will produce the largest immediate return. Every corporation and office within a 25-mile radius will be targeted. The mailing will announce our opening, encourage purchase of corporate memberships, and include discounts for the grand opening.

The website will be used to build the MCGC brand. By offering grand opening specials available only online, the site will generate traffic that will be used later for targeted advertising from golf companies and MCGC. The site will be visually appealing, database driven, and dynamically produced. Content (instructional and coupons) will encourage users to return again and again.

Ongoing Marketing

As the MCGC brand develops, we want to emphasize that golf is a way of life and a family sport. Marketing will concentrate on targeted direct marketing to current MCGC golfers and corporate memberships. Targeted advertising to businesses within 25 miles of MCGC will increase. Local print and radio advertising will become a small percentage of total advertising. The location in Jalapeno Junction allows what we call incidental advertising. The total traffic passing by on I-604 will provide tremendous "free" advertising to entice new customers to practice at MCGC. Once we have a customer, we do not plan to let go. The customer base will be monetized as much as possible.

COMPETITION

On the surface, competition with MCGC appears to be significant. There are five golf ranges within 15 miles of the planned site of MCGC. The ranges are West Bitters Golf Course and Driving Range, Top Hills Golf Club, Ruling 10 Golf Center, Red Peppers Golf Course, and Clemray Golf Center. On closer inspection, the competition from these existing ranges is small. These ranges serve some of the projected customers of MCGC; however, the location and accessibility of each is not ideal. MCGC will have one of the best locations of any golf range in Texas or the Southwest.

Key Discriminators for MCGC

- Location: Situated in or near Jalapeno Junction are one million people within a 50-mile radius. Over 50,000 people are within walking distance to the facility. MCGC is located on I-604, one of the highest traveled roads in the area. It is in close proximity to the major theme parks, park lands, riding ranches, shooting ranges, large public cave systems, a plethora of shopping malls and restaurants, and many other unique tourist attractions which make San Antonio a prime vacation and convention city.
- Multi-tiered heated tee stations
- Grass and turf tees
- Debit card payment and disbursement systems
- Corporate and individual memberships
- Reduced fee/free lessons for students and disadvantaged players
- PGA and LPGA class A professionals

Weaknesses

- Start-up cost; location is very expensive
- New concept in revenue production; few driving ranges sell advertising space. No models to follow
- High salaries required for top talent
- State-of-the-art driving ranges are new and reliability unproven

OPERATIONS

MCGC realizes that human resources are vital to the start-up and growth of MCGC. Our employees will drive the success of the company. MCGC management structure will require several key people to oversee operations.

With the diverse operations of MCGC, the General Manager will oversee a facilities manager, head golf professional, and sales manager. Each of these managers will have several employees to oversee. Recruitment for these managerial positions is a challenge. We expect to hire above-average people to fill each position and significant recruitment costs will occur. Also, compensation will be above the norm for these positions. Our philosophy is that hiring the best will only produce the best for the company and we are willing to pay higher salaries for higher performance.

Expenditures for professional support services are expected to be significant at start-up with a major reduction in these expenses once the business is operational. The only continuing professional expenditure is predicted to be accounting services with minor expenditures for legal advice.

The facilities to be built and maintained will house a pro shop, dining area, kitchen, locker rooms, meeting rooms, multi-tiered tees stations, storage sheds, and offices. Finished interior space is to be approximately 3,000 square feet. The final facilities design requires review and approval by several city agencies.

Following are tables with details of the projected financial performance of MCGC. The numbers for revenue are extremely conservative. The table showing performance comparisons illustrates the performance of driving ranges from average and top 5 percent of all ranges in the U.S. We are projecting MCGC to perform above the 5 percent range. Because of the location and love for golf in the San Antonio area we are projecting MCGC to be one of the top performing ranges in the U.S. There are no numbers for rent or mortgage expense because MCGC expects to operate with no long-term debt.

The Mountain Cedar Golf Club versus Other Driving Ranges
Industry Comparison

Year 1	Top 25%	Top 5%	MCGC
Revenue	$803,845	$2,011,904	$4,102,237
Expenses			
Payroll	150,384	267,989	466,686
General Administration	4,429	106,973	106,973
Range Ball Replacement	18,649	44,999	65,000
Fertilizers and Chemical	3,513	10,714	10,714
Irrigation and Water	7,237	39,476	30,000
Equipment Lease—Maintenance	17,622	53,741	53,741
Cost of Pro Shop Merchandise	88,664	223,280	225,000
Cost of Food and Beverage	10,220	51,586	50,000
Advertising and Marketing	12,308	37,797	50,000
Facility Insurance	13,290	37,500	37,500
Property Tax	19,572	57,738	25,000
Utilities	20,409	49,999	50,000
Total Expenses	**366,297**	**981,792**	**1,170,614**
Net Income BTD	**$437,548**	**$1,030,112**	**$2,941,466**

The Mountain Cedar Golf Club
Revenue by Quarter
2002

	1st quarter	2nd quarter	3rd quarter	4th quarter	Average/qtr	Annual
Ball Sales (50 stations)						
Estimated Station use	30%	35%	40%	35%	35%	
Stations occupied per hour	15	17.5	20	18	17.5	
Buckets Sold per Customer	2	2	3	2	2.25	
Hours of Operation (per day)	8	17	17	17	14.75	
Daily Customers	120	297.5	340	298	263.75	
Buckets Sold per Day	240	595	1,020	595	612.5	
Buckets Sold per quarter	21,600	53,550	91,800	53,550	55,125	220,500
Average Fee per Bucket	12.00	12.00	12.00	12.00	12.00	12.00
Seasonal Ball Revenue	**$259,200**	**$642,600**	**$1,101,600**	**$642,600**	**$661,500**	**$2,646,000**
Pro Shop						
TOTAL	**45,355.10**	**112,442.86**	**192,759.18**	**112,442.86**	**115,750.00**	**463,000.00**
Membership Sales						
TOTAL	**2,448.98**	**6,071.43**	**10,408.16**	**6,071.43**	**6,250.00**	**25,000.00**
Instruction						
TOTAL	**13,518.37**	**33,514.29**	**57,453.06**	**33,514.29**	**34,500.00**	**138,000.00**
Food and Beverage						
TOTAL	**30,000.00**	**37,500.00**	**45,000.00**	**37,500.00**	**37,500.00**	**150,000.00**
Interest						
TOTAL	**0**	**8,063.00**	**8,063.00**	**8,063.00**	**6,047.00**	**30,237.00**
Batting Cage						
TOTAL	**7,500.00**	**75,000.00**	**45,000.00**	**22,500.00**	**37,500.00**	**150,000.00**
Advertising						
TOTAL	**125,000.00**	**125,000.00**	**125,000.00**	**125,000.00**	**125,000.00**	**500,000.00**
TOTAL REVENUES						**$4,102,237.00**

The Mountain Cedar Golf Club
5-Year Revenue and Expense Projection

Revenue	2002	2003	2004	2005	2006
Ball Revenue	2,646,000	3,572,100	4,822,335	6,510,152	8,788,706
Pro Shop	463,000	625,050	718,808	826,629	950,623
Membership	25,000	75,000	93,750	117,188	146,484
Instruction	138,000	276,000	345,000	431,250	539,063
Food and Beverage	150,000	300,000	375,000	468,750	585,938
Interest	30,237	41,727	57,583	79,464	109,661
Batting Cage	150,000	187,500	234,375	292,969	366,211
Advertising	500,000	625,000	781,250	976,563	1,220,703
Total Revenue	**$4,102,237**	**$5,702,377**	**$7,428,100**	**$9,702,964**	**$12,707,388**
Growth	-	39%	30%	31%	31%
Expense					
Payroll	466,686	583,358	641,693	705,863	776,449
General Administration	106,973	117,670	129,437	142,381	156,619
Range Ball Replacement	65,000	81,250	101,563	126,953	158,691
Fertilizers and Chemical	10,714	11,785	12,964	14,260	15,686
Irrigation and Water	30,000	33,000	36,300	39,930	43,923
Equipment Lease—Maintenance	53,741	59,115	65,027	71,529	78,682
Cost of Pro Shop Merchandise	225,000	303,750	349,313	401,709	461,966
Cost of Food and Beverage	50,000	100,000	125,000	156,250	195,313
Advertising and Marketing	50,000	62,500	78,125	97,656	122,070
Facility Insurance	37,500	41,250	45,375	49,913	54,904
Property Tax	25,000	27,500	30,250	33,275	36,603
Utilities	50,000	57,500	66,125	76,044	87,450
Total Expense	**$1,170,614**	**$1,478,678**	**$1,681,171**	**$1,915,763**	**$2,188,356**
Net Profit (EBTDA)	**$2,931,623**	**$4,223,698**	**$5,746,929**	**$7,787,200**	**$10,519,031**
Growth	-	44%	36%	36%	35%

RISK FACTORS

An investment in MCGC involves a high degree of risk. Prospective investors should carefully consider the following risk factors before making any investment:

Limited Operating History

MCGC is not yet operating as a golf practice facility. MCGC is currently in negotiations with the city for surplus park land in the Jalapeno Junction area. There are no guarantees that these negotiations will be successful. Failure to obtain land in Jalapeno Junction will significantly hinder the ability of MCGC to go forward with its plans. Further, there can be no assurance that MCGC will be able to achieve significant revenues or any net income in the future. Accordingly, any investment in MCGC involves a high degree of risk, and purchasers should be prepared to lose their entire investment.

Technological and Market Uncertainty

The development of MCGC's products and services may be impeded by problems relating to the development, production, distribution, or marketing of its products and services, which problems may be beyond the financial and technical abilities of MCGC to solve. Further, there can be no assurance that services and products developed by competitors of MCGC will not significantly limit the potential market for MCGC. Finally, there can be no assurance that laws, rules, or regulations will be adopted in such a manner as will materially adversely affect MCGC.

Competition

MCGC is attempting to entire a highly competitive business which is dominated by two already established golf ranges (Clemray and West Bitters). Additionally, there are three other ranges farther away that may influence the business performance of MCGC. The golf range in Top Hills is operated by the National Park Service and as such has limitless resources. The Red Peppers Golf Course has significant resources at its disposal. There is no assurance that MCGC will be able to compete against the other golf ranges.

Dependence on Location

MCGC's success is based on being able to successfully negotiate with the city for surplus park land. If the land is acquired, there are no assurances that MCGC will be successful. There are a number of factors which are beyond the control of MCGC. With its proximity to many tourist hot spots and employment centers, the business plan is based on the assumption that there will be many mid-day golfers. There are no assurances that mid-day golf will become a reality. Finally, MCGC will be located near three neighborhoods. There is a possibility that the neighborhood associations could attempt to limit the lighting at night or shorten the business hours of operation.

Grocery Store

BUSINESS PLAN

VIKING GROCERY STORES

3816 South Johnson Street
Springfield, Missouri 65802

This business plan is prepared to obtain joint financing in the amount of $2,746,000, to begin work on site preparation and modifications, purchase equipment, and to cover expenses in the first year of operations. We are seeking joint financing from our local Economic Development Fund.

- EXECUTIVE SUMMARY

- COMPANY SUMMARY

- PRODUCTS

- MARKET ANALYSIS SUMMARY

- STRATEGY & IMPLEMENTATION SUMMARY

- MANAGEMENT SUMMARY

- FINANCIAL PLAN

- APPENDIX

EXECUTIVE SUMMARY

Viking Grocery Stores–Springfield, will be located in the old Lloyd building, located at 3816 South Johnson Street, in the heart of Springfield, Missouri. This business plan is prepared to obtain joint financing in the amount of $2,746,000, to begin work on site preparation and modifications, purchase equipment, and to cover expenses in the first year of operations. We are seeking joint financing from our local Economic Development Fund.

Viking Stores–Springfield, will be incorporated initially as a corporation. This will shield the owners and all other investors from issues of personal liability. The investors will be treated as shareholders and therefore will not be liable for more than their personal investment. Owner Jones Stewart will contribute $70,000 ($20,000 in sweat equity and $50,000 in cash) towards this business venture.

The financing, in addition to the capital contributions from the owner and shareholders, will allow our store to successfully open and maintain operations through the year. A large initial capital investment will allow our store to provide its customers with a fully featured grocery store. A unique, upscale, and innovative environment is required to provide the customer with an atmosphere that will inspire continued use. The successful operation of year one will provide our store with customers that will allow it to be self-sufficient in year two.

The Viking Store concept, as shown in our plan, has an excellent profitability level and growth rate. Our competitive edge, along with new retail techniques and technology, puts our store in the forefront of the retailing of perishable and nonperishable consumer goods. We are living in an age where unique grocery store environments are in great demand. Our store will differ from the traditional grocery store because of our added personal touch.

Objectives

As a leading wholesale distributor, our commitment is to provide quality products and services in a cost-effective manner, enabling Viking retailers to excel in serving their customers. If you're interested in being supplied by Viking Stores, Inc., the initial, minimum objectives are:

- A clean environment in which to shop
- A safe place to shop
- Value
- Great, friendly service
- Our shop will be good neighbors and will be involved in the community
- Our store will be at least 25,000 square feet
- Store will have minimum weekly retail sales of $75,000 which is equivalent to approximately $35,000 of purchases weekly at the wholesale level
- Generate capital by leasing remaining space to two other business tenants

Mission

Our most fundamental philosophy is the concern for people. This strong belief in people is the determining factor that motivates our operations in developing our relationship with our employees and customers.

We believe that our responsibility for customer satisfaction is not focused solely on the sale of a product, but rather is the total relationship a customer experiences when interacting with our organization. We believe in honesty and truth in all transactions and in providing products of the highest quality and at fair prices. We should do everything possible to provide outstanding service in marketing the products we sell.

Our philosophy of concern for people gives our Viking Store the drive to be a good corporate citizen. We believe we have a responsibility to be a good neighbor in maintaining our property in first-class condition and by making the appearance of our plant, facilities, equipment, and grounds as attractive as possible, making them an asset to the communities that support our company.

We at Viking Store of Springfield, are committed to bringing you the best all-around shopping experience. Our nice pledge campaign includes an intense training session for all of our employees, and a firm understanding and commitment to deliver these pledge points at the Viking Store in Springfield, Missouri.

Advantage of Selling Viking Brands

- Viking Stores' commitment to quality over the years has strengthened the integrity of the Viking brand. Most private labels can't hold a candle to the quality of Viking products.
- Viking Stores, Inc., regularly evaluates and audits the Viking product mix to keep variety consistent with consumer wants and needs.
- An extensive line of over 2,000 Viking products can be sold throughout your store—from the produce department to the health and beauty care aisle.
- An overwhelming acceptance of products bearing the Viking name has made this brand one of the top sellers in the Midwest. An established loyalty among customers keeps them buying Viking brands.
- Offers customers a double-your-money-back guarantee which encourages them to buy with confidence.
- Allows the retail store to be part of a community contribution program. This program also promotes loyalty for Viking brand products.

COMPANY SUMMARY

Viking Grocery Stores–Springfield will be part of Viking Stores, Inc., a premier regional grocery/drugstore retailer and wholesale distributor based in Kansas City, Missouri. As a result of five acquisitions since 1999, Viking Stores, Inc., now owns and operates 113 supermarkets and 21 drugstores throughout Missouri and Illinois.

Viking Stores, Inc., also distributes more than 40,000 private label and national brand products to more than 325 independently owned grocery stores in Missouri, Illinois, and Arkansas and serves as wholesale distributor to 8,700 convenience stores in nine states throughout the Midwest.

Company History

At the end of 1917, a group of independent grocers discussed forming a cooperative to create buying power for group members. In early 1918, 27 members incorporated the Kansas City Grocery Company, a name it kept until 1954 when the company became Viking Stores, Inc., In 1959, the company produced its first private-label Viking brand product—coffee.

Although the company changed its cooperative status to "for profit status" in the early 1970s, the publicly held company did not become publicly traded on the NASDAQ until August 2000 following Viking Stores' merger with Morgan Food Town in St. Louis, Missouri. For the fiscal year ending March 25, 2000, Viking Stores and Morgan Food Town had combined revenues of $3.8 billion, $1.2 billion of which was retail grocery sales.

Company Ownership

The Viking Store–Springfield will be a corporation. Currently it will be owned and operated by Jones Stewart and his investors.

Location

We have located the ideal location for our operation. Our store will be located at 3816 South Johnson Street, Springfield, Missouri.

This site will contribute to our success due to being formally used as a grocery store.

Also a real estate company, Viking Stores' Market Space Corporation is in business to offer buildings and properties for sale or lease. Their buildings can be converted to meet various business needs and offer prime locations and ample parking. Throughout Missouri, Arkansas, and Illinois, they have existing improved properties as well as outparcels and land for sale. Market Space Corporation can provide demographic information on their locations to expedite any purchase transactions. Leasing is also an option. Both stand-alone buildings and tenant space within buildings where others businesses operate can be leased. Examples would include strip malls housing such operations as dry cleaners, video stores, hair salons, pizza shops, etc.

Hours of Operation

Store hours will be 7 days a week from 10:00 A.M. until 10:00 P.M. Checks and all major credit cards will be accepted. A food stamp policy along with other policies will be in place.

Start-up Summary

Start-up costs will be financed through a combination of owner investment, short-term loans, and long-term borrowing. The start-up chart shows the distribution of financing.

Start-up Plan
Start-up Expenses

Working Capital	$100,000
Accounting	$10,000
Legal (contingency)	$15,000
Office Supplies	$15,000
Administrative Consultants	$75,000
Building Repair Equipment	$1,250,000
Insurance	$55,000
Roof Repairs	$150,000
HVAC Installation	$100,000
Build Out	$100,000
Electrical Repairs	$75,000
Masonry/concrete	$65,000
Expensed equipment	$10,000
Flooring	$42,000
Plumbing	$79,000
Doors and Hardware	$33,000
Glazing	$12,000
Security System	$25,000
Sprinkler System	$65,000
Specialties: Tap fees, etc.	$45,000
Asphalt	$43,000
Architect	$22,000
Engineer, Attorney	$20,000
Project Management Fee	$50,000
Miscellaneous	$0
Total Start-up Expense	**$2,456,000**

Start-up Assets Needed

Cash Requirements	$0
Start-up inventory	$400,000
Other Short-term Assets	$0
Total Short-term Assets	**$400,000**
Long-term Assets	$0
Total Assets	**$400,000**
Total Start-up Requirements:	**$2,856,000**
Left to finance:	$2,786,000

Start-up Funding Plan
Investment

Investor 1	$0
Investor 2	$0
Owner's Investment	$70,000
Total Investment	**$70,000**

Short-term Liabilities

Unpaid Expenses	$0
Short-term Loans	$0
Interest-free Short-term Loans	$0
Subtotal Short-term Liabilities	$0
Long-term Liabilities	$0
Total Liabilities	**$0**
Loss at Start-up	**$330,000**
Total Capital	**$400,000**
Total Capital and Liabilities	**$400,000**
Checkline	**$0**

PRODUCTS

The store will sell over 40,000 private label and national brand products to the community.

MARKET ANALYSIS SUMMARY

By household size, grocery spending ranges from an average of $51 per week in one-person households to $130 per week in households of five or more. Per-person spending is inversely correlated with household size: per-person weekly expenditures are only $23 in households with five or more members but $35 in one-person homes, according to the the Food Marketing Institute.

To make our advertising and printing dollars work their smartest, we need a team that will work its hardest. The Viking Creative Services Department is ready to meet those needs by providing everything from concepts and design to printing and signage. They are experts in the process of creating and printing advertising, brochures, newsletters, business forms, stationery/business cards, P.O.S. materials, screen-printed clothing/merchandise, and weekly 4-color grocery insert mailers/circulars. Whether we need a bag stuffer, a new logo, billboard advertising, radio spots, TV commercials, or a video, their creative and professional team of associates and state-of-the-art printing equipment offer customers high-quality products in a timely and efficient manner.

Market Segmentation

Seventy-three percent of our shoppers are female head of the households, 11 percent are male head of the households, 15 percent are both and 1 percent are other. Household Income: Average weekly household spending ranges from $68 for shoppers earning under $15,000 to $118 for those earning more than $75,000 per year. Spending on groceries at the consumer's primary store also increases with income from $57 per week for those families earning $15,000 or less per year to $95 per week for those earning over $75,000.

Target Market Segment Strategy

Our store will meet the grocery needs of the surrounding neighborhood of female or male head of households earning $15,000 per year or more.

We will reach our consumers by taking full advantage of Viking Stores' single clearinghouse for manufacturers' coupons, Viking and manufacturers' in-ad coupons, and warehouse damage coupons. Our redemption programs will include Viking gift certificates, selling-show vouchers, and mail-in rebates. Other services include the Viking Gift Certificate program, in-ad coupon redemption, and scan-down service to manufacturers and brokers.

Technology: Electronic Marketing

Viking is committed to keeping up with technology changes, thereby gaining a competitive edge in the marketplace. Computers and other information systems are integrated to provide management information and time-saving tools.

These include:

- E-mail systems
- Standard accounting software
- Computer-based training

Support is always available to answer system and software development questions, or provide programming solutions as new industry developments appear.

To support our retail store(s), electronic marketing allows us to access complete data analysis and marketing services. These services include data storage, strategic planning/consultation, sourcing for card/key tag manufacturing, custom marketing program development, promotions and campaigns, electronic marketing training and education, retailer-specific data analysis, and support of third-party programs.

Promotions

Building store traffic, generating consumer excitement, accelerating sales and profits, and positioning our store competitively in the market will be relatively simplified by the use of the Sales Promotions Department at Vikings. By combining their purchasing programs with trendsetting insight, Viking has created over 100 profit-generating retail promotions each year. Viking retailers select those promotions that best meet their unique marketing needs. Backed by TV spots, circulars, P.O.S. materials, sweepstakes and more, this promotional activity is key to our retail success.

We will also promote our store using information gathered from our Mystery Shopper Program. This program was developed to provide monthly feedback to owners and managers on the status and condition of the stores. The program focuses on these major areas:

- Internal and external store appearance
- Product availability
- Point-of-purchase materials
- Food service

- Uniforms
- Most importantly, the quality of service received at the register

Each store is visited by a mystery shopper once a month, making sure that all shifts are experienced at least twice a year. Employees are eligible to earn cash incentives and top stores are honored with awards quarterly.

In order to portray the professional image that Viking Stores' customers have come to expect, a selection of uniforms are available. Uniform requirements are facilitated with the use of a contracted distribution and laundry service.

According to FMI United States regional average weekly household spending in 1999 was fairly equal across regions, with shoppers in the Midwest spending $83; the South, $83; the East, $98; and the West, $92 per week.

Industry Analysis

As a progressive leader in the food distribution industry, Viking Stores, Inc., based in Kansas City, Missouri, owns and operates 113 supermarkets and drugstores in Missouri and Illinois under the Ames' Markets, Family Supermarkets, Food Fair, Gordon's Markets, Sunshine Markets, and The Bond banners. Under the direction of corporate leadership and a Board of Directors, Viking Stores, Inc., will continue to foster innovation and support and promote growth of the company to ensure its success.

Sales for Viking Stores' retail grocery segment increased 59.1 percent to $148 million during the first quarter of fiscal 2001, reflecting additional sales from the acquisition of 23 Gordon's Markets and three Sunshine Markets in fiscal 2000. Comparable store sales increased approximately 4.4 percent in the first quarter, primarily because of the company's promotional programs and continued emphasis on product-line expansion.

Grocery distribution segment sales for the quarter declined 2.5 percent to $360 million from $369.3 million for fiscal 2000. Convenience store distribution sales also declined 1.8 percent to $211.5 from $215.4 million. Sales declines in both distribution segments were associated principally with the elimination of intercompany sales for Gordon's Markets and Sunshine Markets.

Gross margin for the quarter widened to 13.1 percent from 12.2 percent, reflecting the higher margins associated with the retail grocery operations acquired in fiscal 2000.

"We are very pleased to begin fiscal 2001 with solid profitability," said William Miller, Viking Stores' President and Chief Executive Officer. "Excluding non-recurring items, this represents the second consecutive quarter of earnings improvement. We are very committed to our retail strategy and believe the approach is beginning to show meaningful results. As we continue integrating our retail acquisitions and bring their performance to optimal levels through enriched promotional programs and expanding product lines, we expect financial profitability to accelerate."

Mr. Miller stated, "Earlier this week, St. Louis, Missouri-based Morgan Food Town shareholders approved the previously announced merger with Viking Stores. Our shareholders also approved certain changes to Viking Stores' charter which were necessary to complete the merger. We are very pleased to welcome Morgan Food Town into Viking Stores rapidly growing retail operations. Adding Morgan's 73 supermarkets and deep-discount drugstores more than doubles our retail store base to 113, gives us a well respected regional name, and significant presence in the greater St. Louis market. The merger represents a significant step forward in our strategic plan to become a major regional retail grocery operator."

Competition

Marketed at a lower shelf price than national brands, Viking brand products give Viking retailers a competitive advantage. Viking Stores backs Viking brands with year-round promotional support including a big fall and early spring sale.

The store will be in walking distance of area shoppers, whereas the next nearest grocery store is two to three miles from our store location.

**STRATEGY &
IMPLEMENTATION
SUMMARY**

Viking will help us grow and develop our store. Building a new store or undergoing expansion can be a tremendous challenge for retailers, especially when trying to run a business at the same time. Viking store development services include everything from securing real estate and financing to construction and decor. It's another area in which Viking helps retailers solidify strong market positions.

In addition to our store will be space available for two other retail establishments.

Competitive Edge

Viking provides a service which helps us manage the information related to our retail business more effectively. Viking Stores, Inc., offers us the complete integration of pricing, promotions, scanning, receiving, and electronic payment systems, including EBT and human resource functions at store and corporate levels. Their commitment to putting retailers in the fast lane with state-of-the-art, point-of-sale technology keeps us on the leading edge.

Sales Strategy

Our store will sell mostly the Viking store brand instead of the national brands. We feel this is a growing trend amongst shoppers.

Purchases of store or lower-priced brands, instead of national brands, decreased with slightly more than one in ten consumers (15 percent) doing so "pretty much every time" they shop—down three percentage points from 1991. Over half of consumers (52 percent) are doing so "every time" or "fairly often" when they shop. Almost one in four (22 percent) of larger households (five or more members) report purchasing store brands "every time" they shop and almost as many (18 percent) with annual incomes under $15,000 said they buy store brands "every time" they shop according to FMI.

**Sales Forecast and
Additional Income**

The following table gives a run-down on forecasted sales and income. Our sales are based on the industry standard of $11.17 per square foot (store size: 25,000 square feet) for our weekly sales estimate. We expect our sales to grow at least 1 percent per new store brand item added to our product line for a total of 10 percent per year. We also expect to cut cost approximately 10 percent a year through bartering and other means of relationship building.

The remaining 25,000 net square footage not being used for the grocery store will be leased to the public at $4 a square foot.

Sales Forecast	FY2002	FY2003	FY2004
Sales 25,000 square feet @			
$11.17 per square foot per week	$14,521,000	$15,973,100	$17,570,410
Other	$0	$0	$0
Total Sales	**$14,521,000**	**$15,973,100**	**$17,570,410**

Direct Cost of Sales	FY2002	FY2003	FY2004
Sales 25,000 square feet @			
$11.17 per square foot per week	$6,066,660	$5,459,994	$4,913,994
Other	$0	$0	$0
Subtotal Cost of Sales	**$6,066,660**	**$5,459,994**	**$4,913,994**

Purchasing from suppliers throughout the world, Viking Stores warehouses over 40,000 products in St. Louis, Illinois, Kansas City, and Tulsa, Oklahoma. Supplying nearly 500 stores with these quality products at the lowest cost can only be achieved through a proficient distribution system. Viking Stores' state-of-the-art facilities combine manual labor with mechanical technology for optimum efficiency. Viking Stores' streamlined warehouse operations and sophisticated systems expedite product flow and reduce costs in procurement, inventory control and labor.

Warehousing and Transportation

Today, Viking Stores, Inc., Transportation has two locations, one based in Kansas City, the other in Tulsa. Its combined fleet of 245 full-time drivers travel over 12.5 million miles per year. They utilize 116 tractors, 193 dry van trailers, and 176 refrigerated trailers. In a typical week, they average 2,397 delivery stops, delivering between 28 and 33 million pounds of product. Viking Stores' routing department builds 1,234 truckloads of product per week with an average load size of 25,000-28,000 pounds. Viking Stores Transportation utilizes the latest computer technology including the TRUCKS Routing System, CADEC on-board computers, and the Maintenance Control and Management System.

Much has changed over the years in the transportation system at Viking Stores including the fleet design, safety, and performance of the vehicles used in transporting product. Associated Markets' trucks of the 1940s, not much more than delivery vans, used to service the company's customers. For years, Viking used Delivery Line to carry its groceries, while it had its own drivers (about 20 in 1965) to haul perishables. The truck used was an early 1950s model with a 30-foot trailer.

Viking started its own transportation department in 1967, the same year that many Delivery drivers lost their jobs during a labor dispute. Viking hired many of these drivers. Four people in routing, two in dispatch, and 75 drivers hit the road. The Viking tractor/trailer (40-footer) was one of the first owned outright by Viking Stores.

The trailer of the 1980s and 1990s was the 50-footer, more than twice the size of the Associated Market's trucks of the 1940s. It was nationally recognized for its safety-conscious design. Viking Stores, Inc., has been praised for having one of the most cost-effective fleets anywhere. In 1989, a complex computer program called TRUCKS was used to organize each and every trailer load of product. It could route 100 loads in less than 5 minutes. Viking Stores' transportation fleet also became involved in backhauling activities.

People are our most valuable asset and Viking Stores' ProActive Consulting Services provides a complete line of human resource services designed to help us develop the greatest potential from our associates. The people we employ are also a major investment in our company. It is their goal to help us fully capitalize on this investment. Viking Stores' staff is highly experienced in the retail supermarket industry and familiar with its unique problems and opportunities.

MANAGEMENT SUMMARY

Our store will hire one Manager, one Assistant Manager, four Cashiers, four Laborers/Stockers, and four Administrative Workers. Our Store Manager will have a college degree and several years of experience with managing a retail store.

Personnel Plan

The personnel plan is included in the following table. It shows the Manager's hourly pay, followed by that of the rest of the staff. Each of these positions will overlap to make sure the customers are receiving excellent customer service and that adequate help is on hand.

Personnel Plan	FY2002	FY2003	FY2004
Other	$0	$0	$0
1 Manager@ $22/hour	$45,760	$45,760	$45,760
1 Assistant Manager @$18/hour	$37,440	$37,440	$37,440
4 Cashiers@ $9/hour	$74,880	$74,880	$74,880
4 Administrative Workers@ $9/hour	$74,880	$74,880	$74,880
4 Laborers/Stockers@ $7.50/hour	$62,400	$62,400	$62,400
Total Payroll	**$295,360**	**$295,360**	**$295,360**
Total Headcount	**15**	**15**	**15**
Payroll Burden	**$44,304**	**$44,304**	**$44,304**
Total Payroll Expenditures	**$339,664**	**$339,664**	**$339,664**

FINANCIAL PLAN

Viking stores prides itself on being in touch with the financial side of the business at all times. This starts with our budgeting program that sets sales goals, establishes payroll budgets, and creates criteria for gross margin, shrink, expenses, and profit. Exception reporting directs operations in the right direction, saving time, and measuring results.

We will manage and grow our store with a full range of financial services that include five-year financial planning, business valuations, estate planning, buying/selling a store, and financing assistance. Viking will save us valuable time and money plus the headaches and worry often associated with complex money matters.

From Viking, we will receive a complete portfolio of financial, accounting, and payroll services, including comparative operating statements, bank reconciliations, sales tax returns, payroll tax returns, periodic and operational review, cash flows, break-even analyses, financial projections, wages, taxes, deductions, check printing, and deposit advice. It is these kinds of thorough information and accurate recordkeeping that allow Viking retailers to make sound business decisions for the future.

Important Assumptions

We do not sell anything on credit.

General Assumptions	FY2002	FY2003	FY2004
Short-term Interest Rate %	10.00%	10.00%	10.00%
Long-term Interest Rate %	10.00%	10.00%	10.00%
Payment Days Estimator	30	30	30
Collection Days Estimator	45	45	45
Inventory Turnover Estimator	15.70	15.70	15.70
Tax Rate %	25.00%	25.00%	25.00%
Expenses in Cash %	10.00%	10.00%	10.00%
Sales on Credit %	0.00%	0.00%	0.00%
Personnel Burden %	15.00%	15.00%	15.00%

Break-even Analysis

By using a conservative markup of 50 percent, we will have to sell $120,000 worth of goods to break even. A break-even analysis table has been completed on the basis of average costs/prices.

Break-even Analysis:

Monthly Units Break-even	80,000
Monthly Sales Break-even	$80,000

Assumptions:

Average Per-Unit Revenue	$1.00
Average Per-Unit Variable Cost	$0.25
Estimated Monthly Fixed Cost	$60,000

We predict consulting and accounting costs will go down in the next three years. Normally, a start-up concern will operate with negative profits through the first two years. We will avoid that kind of operating loss by knowing our competitiors and our target markets.

Projected Profit and Loss

Profit and Loss (Income Statement)	FY2002	FY2003	FY2004
Sales	$14,521,000	$15,973,100	$17,570,410
Direct Cost of Sales	$6,066,660	$5,459,994	$4,913,994
Production Payroll	$0	$0	$0
Other	$0	$0	$0
Total Cost of Sales	**$6,066,660**	**$5,459,994**	**$4,913,994**
Gross Margin	$8,454,340	$10,513,106	$12,656,416
Gross Margin %	58.22%	65.82%	72.03%
Operating Expenses			
Sales and Marketing Expenses			
Sales and Marketing Payroll	$0	$0	$0
Advertising/Promotion	$13,000	$0	$0
Travel	$0	$0	$0
Miscellaneous	$0	$0	$0
Total Sales and Marketing Expenses	**$0**	**$0**	**$0**
Sales and Marketing %	0.00%	0.00%	0.00%
General and Administrative Expenses			
General and Administrative Payroll	$0	$0	$0
Payroll Expense	$295,360	$295,360	$295,360
Payroll Burden	$44,304	$44,304	$44,304
Depreciation	$0	$0	$0
Leased Equipment	$0	$0	$0
Utilities	$0	$0	$0
Insurance	$0	$0	$0
Rent	$0	$0	$0
Total General and Administrative Expenses	**$0**	**$0**	**$0**
General and Administrative %	0.00%	0.00%	0.00%
Other Expenses			
Other Payroll	$0	$0	$0
Contract/Consultants	$0	$0	$0
Total Other Expenses	**$0**	**$0**	**$0**
Other %	0.00%	0.00%	0.00%
Total Operating Expenses	**$352,664**	**$339,664**	**$339,664**

Projected Profit and Loss

Continued

	FY2002	FY2003	FY2004
Profit Before Interest and Taxes	$8,101,676	$10,173,442	$12,316,752
Interest Expense Short-term	$0	$0	$0
Interest Expense Long-term	$0	$0	$0
Taxes Incurred	$2,025,419	$2,543,361	$3,079,188
Extraordinary Items	$0	$0	$0
Net Profit	$6,076,257	$7,630,082	$9,237,564
Net Profit/Sales	41.84%	47.77%	52.57%

Projected Cash Flow

We are positioning ourselves in the market as a medium risk concern with steady cash flows. Accounts payable is paid at the end of each month while sales are in cash, giving the Viking Store–Springfield an excellent cash structure.

Projected Cash Flow	FY2002	FY2003	FY2004
Net Profit	**$6,076,257**	**$7,630,082**	**$9,237,564**
Plus:			
Depreciation	$0	$0	$0
Change in Accounts Payable	$581,567	$25,135	($2,571)
Current Borrowing (repayment)	$0	$0	$0
Increase (decrease) Other Liabilities	$0	$0	$0
Long-term Borrowing (repayment)	$0	$0	$0
Capital Input	$0	$0	$0
Subtotal	**$6,657,824**	**$7,655,216**	**$9,234,993**
Less:			
Change in Accounts Receivable	$0	$0	$0
Change in Inventory	$2,547	($40,255)	($36,229)
Change in Other Short-term Assets	$0	$0	$0
Capital Expenditure	$0	$0	$0
Dividends	$0	$0	$0
Subtotal	**$2,547**	**($40,255)**	**($36,229)**
Net Cash Flow	**$6,655,276**	**$7,695,471**	**$9,271,222**
Cash Balance	**$6,655,276**	**$14,350,747**	**$23,621,970**

Projected Balance Sheet

All of our tables will be updated monthly to reflect past performance and future assumptions. Future assumptions will not be based on past performance but rather on economic cycle activity, regional industry strength, and future cash flow possibilities. We expect solid growth in net worth beyond the year 2002.

Projected Balance Sheet			
Assets			
Short-term Assets	FY2002	FY2003	FY2004
Cash	$6,655,276	$14,350,747	$23,621,970
Accounts Receivable	$0	$0	$0
Inventory	$402,547	$362,293	$326,063
Other Short-term Assets	$0	$0	$0
Total Short-term Assets	**$7,057,824**	**$14,713,040**	**$23,948,033**
Long-term Assets			
Capital Assets	$0	$0	$0
Accumulated Depreciation	$0	$0	$0
Total Long-term Assets	**$0**	**$0**	**$0**
Total Assets	**$7,057,824**	**$14,713,040**	**$23,948,033**

Liabilities and Capital	FY2002	FY2003	FY2004
Accounts Payable	$581,567	$606,701	$604,130
Short-term Notes	$0	$0	$0
Other Short-term Liabilities	$0	$0	$0
Subtotal Short-term Liabilities	**$581,567**	**$606,701**	**$604,130**
Long-term Liabilities	$0	$0	$0
Total Liabilities	**$581,567**	**$606,701**	**$604,130**
Paid in Capital	$70,000	$70,000	$70,000
Retained Earnings	$330,000	$6,406,257	$14,036,338
Earnings	$6,076,257	$7,630,082	$9,237,564
Total Capital	**$6,476,257**	**$14,106,338**	**$23,343,903**
Total Liabilities and Capital	**$7,057,824**	**$14,713,040**	**$23,948,033**
Net Worth	**$6,476,257**	**$14,106,338**	**$23,343,902**

APPENDIX

Sales Forecast

Sales	May	Jun	Jul	Aug	Sep	Oct	Nov
Sales 25,000 square feet							
@ $11.17/square foot/week	$1,396,250	$1,117,000	$1,117,000	$1,117,000	$1,117,000	$1,396,250	$1,117,000
Other	$0	$0	$0	$0	$0	$0	$0
Total Sales	**$1,396,250**	**$1,117,000**	**$1,117,000**	**$1,117,000**	**$1,117,000**	**$1,396,250**	**$1,117,000**
Direct Cost of Sales							
Sales 25,000 square feet							
@ $11.17/square foot/week	$400,000	$400,000	$526,666	$526,666	$526,666	$526,666	$526,666
Other	$0	$0	$0	$0	$0	$0	$0
Subtotal Cost of Sales	**$400,000**	**$400,000**	**$526,666**	**$526,666**	**$526,666**	**$526,666**	**$526,666**

Personnel Plan

	May	Jun	Jul	Aug	Sep	Oct	Nov
1 Manager@ $22/hour	$4,400	$3,520	$3,520	$3,520	$3,520	$4,400	$3,520
1 Assistant Manager							
@$18/hour	$3,600	$2,880	$2,880	$2,880	$2,880	$3,600	$2,880
4 Cashiers@ $9/hour	$7,200	$5,760	$5,760	$5,760	$5,760	$7,200	$5,760
4 Administrative Workers							
@ $9/hour	$7,200	$5,760	$5,760	$5,760	$5,760	$7,200	$5,760
4 Laborers/Stockers							
@ $7.50/hour	$6,000	$4,800	$4,800	$4,800	$4,800	$6,000	$4,800
Total Payroll	**$28,400**	**$22,720**	**$22,720**	**$22,720**	**$22,720**	**$28,400**	**$22,720**
Total Headcount	**15**	**15**	**15**	**15**	**15**	**15**	**15**
Payroll Burden	**$4,260**	**$3,408**	**$3,408**	**$3,408**	**$3,408**	**$4,260**	**$3,408**
Total Payroll Expenditures	**$32,660**	**$26,128**	**$26,128**	**$26,128**	**$26,128**	**$32,660**	**$26,128**

General Assumptions

	May	Jun	Jul	Aug	Sep	Oct	Nov
Short-term Interest Rate %	10.00%	10.00%	10.00%	10.00%	10.00%	10.00%	10.00%
Long-term Interest Rate %	10.00%	10.00%	10.00%	10.00%	10.00%	10.00%	10.00%
Payment Days Estimator	30	30	30	30	30	30	30
Collection Days Estimator	45	45	45	45	45	45	45
Inventory Turnover Estimator	15.70	15.70	15.70	15.70	15.70	15.70	15.70
Tax Rate %	25.00%	25.00%	25.00%	25.00%	25.00%	25.00%	25.00%
Expenses in Cash %	10.00%	10.00%	10.00%	10.00%	10.00%	10.00%	10.00%
Sales on Credit %	0.00%	0.00%	0.00%	0.00%	0.00%	0.00%	0.00%
Personnel Burden %	15.00%	15.00%	15.00%	15.00%	15.00%	15.00%	15.00%

	Dec	Jan	Feb	Mar	Apr	FY2002	FY2003	FY2004
	$1,396,250	$1,396,250	$1,117,000	$1,117,000	$1,117,000	$14,521,000	$15,973,100	$17,570,410
	$0	$0	$0	$0	$0	$0	$0	$0
	$1,396,250	**$1,396,250**	**$1,117,000**	**$1,117,000**	**$1,117,000**	**$14,521,000**	**$15,973,100**	**$17,570,410**
	$526,666	$526,666	$526,666	$526,666	$526,666	$6,066,660	$5,459,994	$4,913,994
	$0	$0	$0	$0	$0	$0	$0	$0
	$526,666	**$526,666**	**$526,666**	**$526,666**	**$526,666**	**$6,066,660**	**$5,459,994**	**$4,913,994**

	Dec	Jan	Feb	Mar	Apr	FY2002	FY2003	FY2004
	$4,400	$4,400	$3,520	$3,520	$3,520	$45,760	$45,760	$45,760
	$3,600	$3,600	$2,880	$2,880	$2,880	$37,440	$37,440	$37,440
	$7,200	$7,200	$5,760	$5,760	$5,760	$74,880	$74,880	$74,880
	$7,200	$7,200	$5,760	$5,760	$5,760	$74,880	$74,880	$74,880
	$6,000	$6,000	$4,800	$4,800	$4,800	$62,400	$62,400	$62,400
	$28,400	**$28,400**	**$22,720**	**$22,720**	**$22,720**	**$295,360**	**$295,360**	**$295,360**
	15	**15**	**15**	**15**	**15**	**15**	**15**	**15**
	$4,260	**$4,260**	**$3,408**	**$3,408**	**$3,408**	**$44,304**	**$44,304**	**$44,304**
	$32,660	**$32,660**	**$26,128**	**$26,128**	**$26,128**	**$339,664**	**$339,664**	**$339,664**

	Dec	Jan	Feb	Mar	Apr	FY2002	FY2003	FY2004
	10.00%	10.00%	10.00%	10.00%	10.00%	10.00%	10.00%	10.00%
	10.00%	10.00%	10.00%	10.00%	10.00%	10.00%	10.00%	10.00%
	30	30	30	30	30	30	30	30
	45	45	45	45	45	45	45	45
	15.70	15.70	15.70	15.70	15.70	15.70	15.70	15.70
	25.00%	25.00%	25.00%	25.00%	25.00%	25.00%	25.00%	25.00%
	10.00%	10.00%	10.00%	10.00%	10.00%	10.00%	10.00%	10.00%
	0.00%	0.00%	0.00%	0.00%	0.00%	0.00%	0.00%	0.00%
	15.00%	15.00%	15.00%	15.00%	15.00%	15.00%	15.00%	15.00%

Profit and Loss (Income Statement)

	May	Jun	Jul	Aug	Sep	Oct	Nov
Sales	$1,396,250	$1,117,000	$1,117,000	$1,117,000	$1,117,000	$1,396,250	$1,117,000
Direct Cost of Sales	$400,000	$400,000	$526,666	$526,666	$526,666	$526,666	$526,666
Production Payroll	$0	$0	$0	$0	$0	$0	$0
Other	$0	$0	$0	$0	$0	$0	$0
Total Cost of Sales	**$400,000**	**$400,000**	**$526,666**	**$526,666**	**$526,666**	**$526,666**	**$526,666**
Gross Margin	$996,250	$717,000	$590,334	$590,334	$590,334	$869,584	$590,334
Gross Margin %	71.35%	64.19%	52.85%	52.85%	52.85%	62.28%	52.85%
Operating Expenses							
Sales and Marketing Expenses							
Sales and Marketing Payroll	$0	$0	$0	$0	$0	$0	$0
Advertising/Promotion	$1,250	$1,000	$1,000	$1,000	$1,000	$1,250	$1,000
Travel	$0	$0	$0	$0	$0	$0	$0
Miscellaneous	$0	$0	$0	$0	$0	$0	$0
Total Sales and Marketing Expenses	**$0**	**$0**	**$0**	**$0**	**$0**	**$0**	**$0**
Sales and Marketing %	0.00%	0.00%	0.00%	0.00%	0.00%	0.00%	0.00%
General and Administrative Expenses							
General and Administrative Payroll	$0	$0	$0	$0	$0	$0	$0
Payroll Expense	$28,400	$22,720	$22,720	$22,720	$22,720	$28,400	$22,720
Payroll Burden	$4,260	$3,408	$3,408	$3,408	$3,408	$4,260	$3,408
Depreciation	$0	$0	$0	$0	$0	$0	$0
Leased Equipment	$0	$0	$0	$0	$0	$0	$0
Utilities	$0	$0	$0	$0	$0	$0	$0
Insurance	$0	$0	$0	$0	$0	$0	$0
Rent	$0	$0	$0	$0	$0	$0	$0
Total General and Administrative Expenses	**$0**	**$0**	**$0**	**$0**	**$0**	**$0**	**$0**
General and Administrative %	0.00%	0.00%	0.00%	0.00%	0.00%	0.00%	0.00%
Other Expenses							
Other Payroll	$0	$0	$0	$0	$0	$0	$0
Contract/Consultants	$0	$0	$0	$0	$0	$0	$0
Total Other Expenses	**$0**	**$0**	**$0**	**$0**	**$0**	**$0**	**$0**
Other %	0.00%	0.00%	0.00%	0.00%	0.00%	0.00%	0.00%
Total Operating Expenses	**$33,910**	**$27,128**	**$27,128**	**$27,128**	**$27,128**	**$33,910**	**$27,128**
Profit Before Interest and Taxes	$962,340	$689,872	$563,206	$563,206	$563,206	$835,674	$563,206
Interest Expense Short-term	$0	$0	$0	$0	$0	$0	$0
Interest Expense Long-term	$0	$0	$0	$0	$0	$0	$0
Taxes Incurred	$240,585	$172,468	$140,802	$140,802	$140,802	$208,919	$140,802
Extraordinary Items	$0	$0	$0	$0	$0	$0	$0
Net Profit	$721,755	$517,404	$422,405	$422,405	$422,405	$626,756	$422,405
Net Profit/Sales	51.69%	46.32%	37.82%	37.82%	37.82%	44.89%	37.82%

Dec	Jan	Feb	Mar	Apr	FY2002	FY2003	FY2004
$1,396,250	$1,396,250	$1,117,000	$1,117,000	$1,117,000	$14,521,000	$15,973,100	$17,570,410
$526,666	$526,666	$526,666	$526,666	$526,666	$6,066,660	$5,459,994	$4,913,994
$0	$0	$0	$0	$0	$0	$0	$0
$0	$0	$0	$0	$0	$0	$0	$0
$526,666	**$526,666**	**$526,666**	**$526,666**	**$526,666**	**$6,066,660**	**$5,459,994**	**$4,913,994**
$869,584	$869,584	$590,334	$590,334	$590,334	$8,454,340	$10,513,106	$12,656,416
62.28%	62.28%	52.85%	52.85%	52.85%	58.22%	65.82%	72.03%
$0	$0	$0	$0	$0	$0	$0	$0
$1,250	$1,250	$1,000	$1,000	$1,000	$13,000	$0	$0
$0	$0	$0	$0	$0	$0	$0	$0
$0	$0	$0	$0	$0	$0	$0	$0
$0	**$0**	**$0**	**$0**	**$0**	**$0**	**$0**	**$0**
0.00%	0.00%	0.00%	0.00%	0.00%	0.00%	0.00%	0.00%
$0	$0	$0	$0	$0	$0	$0	$0
$28,400	$28,400	$22,720	$22,720	$22,720	$295,360	$295,360	$295,360
$4,260	$4,260	$3,408	$3,408	$3,408	$44,304	$44,304	$44,304
$0	$0	$0	$0	$0	$0	$0	$0
$0	$0	$0	$0	$0	$0	$0	$0
$0	$0	$0	$0	$0	$0	$0	$0
$0	$0	$0	$0	$0	$0	$0	$0
$0	$0	$0	$0	$0	$0	$0	$0
$0	**$0**	**$0**	**$0**	**$0**	**$0**	**$0**	**$0**
0.00%	0.00%	0.00%	0.00%	0.00%	0.00%	0.00%	0.00%
$0	$0	$0	$0	$0	$0	$0	$0
$0	$0	$0	$0	$0	$0	$0	$0
$0	**$0**	**$0**	**$0**	**$0**	**$0**	**$0**	**$0**
0.00%	0.00%	0.00%	0.00%	0.00%	0.00%	0.00%	0.00%
$33,910	**$33,910**	**$27,128**	**$27,128**	**$27,128**	**$352,664**	**$339,664**	**$339,664**
$835,674	$835,674	$563,206	$563,206	$563,206	$8,101,676	$10,173,442	$12,316,752
$0	$0	$0	$0	$0	$0	$0	$0
$0	$0	$0	$0	$0	$0	$0	$0
$208,919	$208,919	$140,802	$140,802	$140,802	$2,025,419	$2,543,361	$3,079,188
$0	$0	$0	$0	$0	$0	$0	$0
$626,756	$626,756	$422,405	$422,405	$422,405	$6,076,257	$7,630,082	$9,237,564
44.89%	44.89%	37.82%	37.82%	37.82%	41.84%	47.77%	52.57%

Projected Cash Flow

	May	Jun	Jul	Aug	Sep	Oct	Nov
Net Profit	$721,755	$517,404	$422,405	$422,405	$422,405	$626,756	$422,405
Plus:							
Depreciation	$0	$0	$0	$0	$0	$0	$0
Change in Accounts Payable	$476,384	$22,533	$166,878	($84,229)	$0	$59,479	($59,479)
Current Borrowing (repayment)	$0	$0	$0	$0	$0	$0	$0
Increase (decrease) Other Liabilities	$0	$0	$0	$0	$0	$0	$0
Long-term Borrowing (repayment)	$0	$0	$0	$0	$0	$0	$0
Capital Input	$0	$0	$0	$0	$0	$0	$0
Subtotal	**$1,198,139**	**$539,937**	**$589,283**	**$338,176**	**$422,405**	**$686,235**	**$362,925**
Less:							
Change in Accounts Receivable	$0	$0	$0	$0	$0	$0	$0
Change in Inventory	($94,268)	$0	$96,815	$0	$0	$0	$0
Change in Other Short-term Assets	$0	$0	$0	$0	$0	$0	$0
Capital Expenditure	$0	$0	$0	$0	$0	$0	$0
Dividends	$0	$0	$0	$0	$0	$0	$0
Subtotal	**($94,268)**	**$0**	**$96,815**	**$0**	**$0**	**$0**	**$0**
Net Cash Flow	**$1,292,406**	**$539,937**	**$492,468**	**$338,176**	**$422,405**	**$686,235**	**$362,925**
Cash Balance	**$1,292,406**	**$1,832,344**	**$2,324,812**	**$2,662,987**	**$3,085,392**	**$3,771,627**	**$4,134,552**

Dec	Jan	Feb	Mar	Apr	FY2002	FY2003	FY2004
$626,756	$626,756	$422,405	$422,405	$422,405	$6,076,257	$7,630,082	$9,237,564
$0	$0	$0	$0	$0	$0	$0	$0
$59,479	$0	($59,479)	$0	$0	$581,567	$25,135	($2,571)
$0	$0	$0	$0	$0	$0	$0	$0
$0	$0	$0	$0	$0	$0	$0	$0
$0	$0	$0	$0	$0	$0	$0	$0
$0	$0	$0	$0	$0	$0	$0	$0
$686,235	**$626,756**	**$362,925**	**$422,405**	**$422,405**	**$6,657,824**	**$7,655,216**	**$9,234,993**
$0	$0	$0	$0	$0	$0	$0	$0
$0	$0	$0	$0	$0	$2,547	($40,255)	($36,229)
$0	$0	$0	$0	$0	$0	$0	$0
$0	$0	$0	$0	$0	$0	$0	$0
$0	$0	$0	$0	$0	$0	$0	$0
$0	**$0**	**$0**	**$0**	**$0**	**$2,547**	**($40,255)**	**($36,229)**
$686,235	**$626,756**	**$362,925**	**$422,405**	**$422,405**	**$6,655,276**	**$7,695,471**	**$9,271,222**
$4,820,787	**$5,447,542**	**$5,810,467**	**$6,232,872**	**$6,655,276**	**$6,655,276**	**$14,350,747**	**$23,621,970**

Projected Balance Sheet

Assets

Short-term Assets	May	Jun	Jul	Aug	Sep	Oct	Nov
Cash	$1,292,406	$1,832,344	$2,324,812	$2,662,987	$3,085,392	$3,771,627	$4,134,552
Accounts Receivable	$0	$0	$0	$0	$0	$0	$0
Inventory	$305,732	$305,732	$402,547	$402,547	$402,547	$402,547	$402,547
Other Short-term Assets	$0	$0	$0	$0	$0	$0	$0
Total Short-term Assets	$1,598,139	$2,138,076	$2,727,359	$3,065,535	$3,487,939	$4,174,174	$4,537,099
Long-term Assets							
Capital Assets	$0	$0	$0	$0	$0	$0	$0
Accumulated Depreciation	$0	$0	$0	$0	$0	$0	$0
Total Long-term Assets	$0	$0	$0	$0	$0	$0	$0
Total Assets	**$1,598,139**	**$2,138,076**	**$2,727,359**	**$3,065,535**	**$3,487,939**	**$4,174,174**	**$4,537,099**
Liabilities and Capital							
Accounts Payable	$476,384	$498,917	$665,796	$581,567	$581,567	$641,046	$581,567
Short-term Notes	$0	$0	$0	$0	$0	$0	$0
Other Short-term Liabilities	$0	$0	$0	$0	$0	$0	$0
Subtotal Short-term Liabilities	**$476,384**	**$498,917**	**$665,796**	**$581,567**	**$581,567**	**$641,046**	**$581,567**
Long-term Liabilities	$0	$0	$0	$0	$0	$0	$0
Total Liabilities	**$476,384**	**$498,917**	**$665,796**	**$581,567**	**$581,567**	**$641,046**	**$581,567**
Paid in Capital	$70,000	$70,000	$70,000	$70,000	$70,000	$70,000	$70,000
Retained Earnings	$330,000	$330,000	$330,000	$330,000	$330,000	$330,000	$330,000
Earnings	$721,755	$1,239,159	$1,661,564	$2,083,968	$2,506,373	$3,133,128	$3,555,533
Total Capital	**$1,121,755**	**$1,639,159**	**$2,061,564**	**$2,483,968**	**$2,906,373**	**$3,533,128**	**$3,955,533**
Total Liabilities and Capital	**$1,598,139**	**$2,138,076**	**$2,727,359**	**$3,065,535**	**$3,487,939**	**$4,174,174**	**$4,537,099**
Net Worth	**$1,121,755**	**$1,639,159**	**$2,061,564**	**$2,483,968**	**$2,906,373**	**$3,533,128**	**$3,955,533**

	Dec	Jan	Feb	Mar	Apr	FY2002	FY2003	FY2004
	$4,820,787	$5,447,542	$5,810,467	$6,232,872	$6,655,276	$6,655,276	$14,350,747	$23,621,970
	$0	$0	$0	$0	$0	$0	$0	$0
	$402,547	$402,547	$402,547	$402,547	$402,547	$402,547	$362,293	$326,063
	$0	$0	$0	$0	$0	$0	$0	$0
	$5,223,334	$5,850,090	$6,213,015	$6,635,419	$7,057,824	$7,057,824	$14,713,040	$23,948,033
	$0	$0	$0	$0	$0	$0	$0	$0
	$0	$0	$0	$0	$0	$0	$0	$0
	$0	$0	$0	$0	$0	$0	$0	$0
	$5,223,334	**$5,850,090**	**$6,213,015**	**$6,635,419**	**$7,057,824**	**$7,057,824**	**$14,713,040**	**$23,948,033**
	$641,046	$641,046	$581,567	$581,567	$581,567	$581,567	$606,701	$604,130
	$0	$0	$0	$0	$0	$0	$0	$0
	$0	$0	$0	$0	$0	$0	$0	$0
	$641,046	**$641,046**	**$581,567**	**$581,567**	**$581,567**	**$581,567**	**$606,701**	**$604,130**
	$0	$0	$0	$0	$0	$0	$0	$0
	$641,046	**$641,046**	**$581,567**	**$581,567**	**$581,567**	**$581,567**	**$606,701**	**$604,130**
	$70,000	$70,000	$70,000	$70,000	$70,000	$70,000	$70,000	$70,000
	$330,000	$330,000	$330,000	$330,000	$330,000	$330,000	$6,406,257	$14,036,338
	$4,182,288	$4,809,044	$5,231,448	$5,653,853	$6,076,257	$6,076,257	$7,630,082	$9,237,564
	$4,582,288	**$5,209,044**	**$5,631,448**	**$6,053,853**	**$6,476,257**	**$6,476,257**	**$14,106,338**	**$23,343,903**
	$5,223,334	**$5,850,090**	**$6,213,015**	**$6,635,419**	**$7,057,824**	**$7,057,824**	**$14,713,040**	**$23,948,033**
	$4,582,288	**$5,209,044**	**$5,631,448**	**$6,053,852**	**$6,476,257**	**$6,476,257**	**$14,106,338**	**$23,343,902**

Import/Export Store

BUSINESS PLAN   CENTRAL IMPORT/EXPORT

67110 Middlebelt Road
Livonia, Michigan 48154

Central Import/Export will be a start-up wholesale distribution/retail store. This import/export business will be run by owner Ramon Juarez as a Limited Liability Company. Central sells quality products and provides excellent customer service for Mexican food and product lovers. Central will offer these products, imported directly from Mexico, to the state of Michigan.

- EXECUTIVE SUMMARY

- COMPANY SUMMARY

- PRODUCTS AND SIC CODES

- MARKET ANALYSIS SUMMARY

- STRATEGY & IMPLEMENTATION SUMMARY

- MANAGEMENT SUMMARY

- FINANCIAL PLAN

- APPENDIX

EXECUTIVE SUMMARY

Central Import/Export will be a start-up wholesale distribution/retail store. This import/export business will be run by owner Ramon Juarez as a Limited Liability Company. Central sells quality products and provides excellent customer service for Mexican food and product lovers. Central will offer these products, imported directly from Mexico, to the state of Michigan. The business will be located at 67110 Middlebelt Road, Livonia, Michigan, and will also have an export market in Mexico that serves youth and adults. Our intent is to provide the community and state with unique Mexican food products and merchandise.

The business will be financed with $17,195 of the owner's money and $17,805 from a business loan. Starting costs are $35,000. Sales are estimated at $73,000 per year by the first year. A positive cash flow will be produced at the end of the first year.

The closest import/export business of Mexican products is in Detroit, Michigan, some 20 miles away. Livonia is an urban city of approximately 104,000 people, which is also located in Michigan containing approximately 9,295,297 people.

Objectives

Central's objectives are to:

- achieve a profit in the first year
- establish an import/export business in the city of Livonia, Michigan
- create jobs
- provide quality products and customer service at a reasonable price
- achieve the largest market share in the city for imported products
- increase average length of customer relationships and decrease customer turnover

Export Policy Commitment Statement

The mission of Central Import/Export is to provide quality products to the United States and Mexico's retail market. Our company is willing to utilize necessary resources to ensure the success of our import/export venture. Central is also committed to providing in-depth service to this market in terms of assistance in distribution, advertising, and promotion.

The overall goals are to:

- develop long-term relationships with the Mexican wholesalers and resellers
- successfully compete in the Mexican and U.S. markets

The short-term goals are to:

- secure contracts with major wholesalers in the Mexican market
- develop prosperous business relationships with these wholesalers

The long-term goal is to, within eight years:

- establish a strong market presence
- obtain a market share of 3 percent
- provide custom brokering services

The goal of Central Import/Export is to supply restaurants, gift shops, landscaping companies, and party stores with imported frozen foods and interior/exterior decorations imported from Mexico, and to sell to walk-in customers out of our retail store. We will also provide an export service from Livonia, Michigan, to Mexico, which includes packaging, delivery service, and transportation of local business goods.

Central Import/Export will play a significant role in improving the U.S. balance of trade while protecting our competitiveness and improving our profits. Entering the Mexican marketplace offers many benefits for our business, including:

- increased growth
- increased profits
- extended product/service life cycles
- increased numbers of customers
- tax advantages
- added product/service lines
- improved competitiveness
- favorable publicity and recognition
- enhance domestic competitiveness
- gain global market share
- reduce dependence on existing markets
- exploit corporate technology and know-how
- extend the sales potential of existing products
- stabilize seasonal market fluctuations
- enhance potential for corporate expansion
- sell excess production capacity
- gain information about foreign competition

Key Advantages of Exporting

The name of the business is Central Import/Export. This name was chosen to identify the company with the products and methods in which they will be sold. The name has also been registered in Wayne County. The business will be a wholesale distribution and retail store of Mexican products, frozen foods, decorations, furniture, and leather goods.

COMPANY SUMMARY

Central Import/Export will be registered as a Limited Liability Company with the owner being Ramon Juarez.

Company Ownership

Forty-five percent of start-up costs will go to assets. Total start-up expenses (transportation costs and deposits) total $35,000. Start-up assets required include $6,000 in inventory and $9,153 in working capital. The owner's investment includes purchasing truck, equipment, and fixtures totaling $17,195. The remaining amount needed for start-up is $17,805, which Central will finance with a commercial loan.

Start-up Summary

Start-up Plan
Start-up Expenses

Cooler	$2,553
Freezer	$450
Supplies (bags, office)	$250
Price Tag Gun	$105
Cash Register	$213
Fax Machine	$157
Truck	$6,200
Truck License Tags	$370

Start-up Summary

Continued

Truck Repairs and Maintenance	$3,010
Travel	$700
Hauling Fees	$1,200
Shelves	$550
Display Cases	$200
Counter	$200
Rent	$2,100
Permits/Registrations	$25
Grand Opening	$544
Consultants	$270
Import Bond	$750
Other	$0
Total Start-up Expenses	**$19,847**
Start-up Assets Needed	
Cash Requirements	$9,153
Start-up inventory	$6,000
Other Short-term Assets	$0
Total Short-term Assets	**$15,153**
Long-term Assets	$0
Total Assets	**$15,153**
Total Start-up Requirements:	**$35,000**
Left to finance:	$0
Start-up Funding Plan	
Investment	
Owner's Equity	$17,195
Other	$0
Total Investment	**$17,195**
Short-term Liabilities	
Unpaid Expenses	$0
Short-term Loans	$17,805
Interest-free Short-term Loans	$0
Subtotal Short-term Liabilities	$17,805
Long-term Liabilities	$0
Total Liabilities	**$17,805**
Loss at Start-up	**($19,847)**
Total Capital	**($2,652)**
Total Capital and Liabilities	**$15,153**
Checkline	**$0**

Location and Facilities

We currently lease a building/warehouse located at the corner of Schoolcraft Road and Middlebelt Road, Livonia, Michigan. Nearby is I-96, with eastbound and westbound exits. Also located in the vicinity is a medium size congregational church. The building is located in the center of Livonia's Hispanic population.

The building is approximately 640 square feet and contains an employee restroom, shelving and store fixtures, coolers, and counters. The parking is limited, but arrangements are being made to utilize adjacent parking for customer overflow.

This wholesale distribution and retail import/export business will have unique items imported directly from Mexico and exported directly into Mexico. The majority of these items will be hand-picked. Customers can buy food products, decorations, landscaping products, and more. The store will be open from 9:30 A.M. to 8:00 P.M. Monday thru Saturday, and 9:30 A.M. to 5:00 P.M. Sundays.

Business Operations

We will have one full-time employee and one part-time employee. The owner's draw will be a salary of $16,632 and the part-time employee will be paid approximately $6.83 an hour. We will not be offering benefits for the first few years. Employees will maintain the building's cleanliness.

Inventory will be purchased through several vendors that include: Flores del Rio, Milagro X Guago, Chili Pepper Produce, San Juan, A.Q. MER. V., and Zentavo. We estimate our inventory to turnover 6 times a year. Starting inventory will be $6,000 with a markup of 100 percent or more.

The following are our operation policies and will be posted throughout the store:

- No cash refunds
- $25 fee for check returns
- Accepting credit cards: Visa, Mastercharge, Discover, and American Express

The owner has basic knowledge of bookkeeping and is familiar with accounting software. An accountant will be hired in the future to examine records and make recommendations.

An attorney will be retained in the future to handle legal aspects of the business.

Ramon Juarez has over 14 years of import/export experience and will be attending Schoolcraft Community College, majoring in International Trade. He is therefore technically qualified to handle the products the business will offer. Central will be aided in development by a licensed U.S. Customs Broker, Manuel Rodriguez. Central will also utilize the services of International Trade Administration of the U.S. Department of Commerce (ITA/DOC), World Trade Center Institutes, Small Business Development Centers, Global Trade Point Network, Fedworld, International Trade Law, U.S. Customs, Trade Show Central, MCB Publications, American Chamber of Commerce of Mexico, and SBA Export Small Business Development Center.

We will open our store in the month of January. We hope to capitalize on the buyers of Mexican products who normally travel to Detroit, by giving them a closer location. Opening during this time will give us the opportunity to establish new customer relationships before the peak in our spring season.

Central is aware of the many international laws that can affect our export activities. Five of the most prominent laws and agreements that have influenced our decisions and actions in business with Mexico are:

Import/Export Laws and Licensing

- Antitrust Laws
- Antiboycott Regulations
- Foreign Corrupt Practices
- World Trade Organization
- NAFTA

Central understands that all goods and services leaving the United States require some form of export licensing. By obtaining a general export license from the Export Administration Regulations (EAR), Central is essentially receiving authorization from the U.S. government to export our products.

According to exporting rules, Central will verify that our customer is not:

- on the Table of Denial Orders (TDO)
- on the list of Specially Designated Nationals (SDN)
- located in an embargoed country
- involved with the production of nuclear, chemical, or biological weapons

Central has acquired the assistance of a customs broker to manage any additional import/export issues.

PRODUCTS & SIC CODES

Listed below is the Mexican food product line and its Standard Industry Codes:

• candy, chewing gum, other confections	SIC 2064-2067
• fats and oils	SIC 207
• beverages	SIC 208
• miscellaneous food and kindred products	SIC 209
• snack foods	SIC Snack Food Concordance
• candy confectionery and chocolate products	SIC 2064-68
• canned frozen and preserved fruits, veggies	SIC 203
• cookies and crackers	SIC 2032
• frozen food	SIC 2037, 2038
• pasta	SIC 2099
• snack food	SIC 2096
• processed food and beverages	SIC 20
• meat products	SIC 201
• dairy products	SIC 202
• preserved fruits and veggies	SIC 203
• grain mill products	SIC 204
• sugar and confectionery products	SIC 206

Inventory

Inventory will be controlled by indexing the products as they are brought in and as they are sold. Central's tracking system will tell the management what merchandise is in stock, what is on order, when it will arrive, and what was sold. With such a system, Central can plan purchases more intelligently and quickly recognize the fast moving items we need to reorder and the slow moving items we should mark down or specially promote.

Inventory will turn approximately 6 times a year. We will keep 25 percent of our initial inventory or $1500 worth of goods on hand at all times. For inventory valuation we will use the Last In, First Out (LIFO) method. We will sell the recently purchased inventory first. This method will help us pay less in taxes.

Suppliers will be independent craftspeople, import sources, distributors, and manufacturers. We have established a list of possible suppliers and requested quotes, prices, and available discounts. We also will ask for customer references. We will establish accounts with these suppliers prior to opening our store.

The goods to be imported into the U.S. and sold from the retail location include processed food and beverages, meat products, dairy products, preserved fruits and vegetables, sugar and confectionery products, candy, chewing gum and other confections, fats and oils, beverages, Miscellaneous food and kindred products, snack foods, decorations, furniture, and leather goods.

The goods to be export into Mexico and sold to retailers include toys, rebuilt auto parts, tennis shoes, and tools.

Central will use the cost-plus method of international pricing. Cost-plus method is based on our domestic price plus exporting costs (documentation expenses, freight charges, customs duties, and international sales and promotional costs). Any costs not applicable, such as domestic marketing costs, are subtracted. The cost-plus method allows us to maintain our domestic profit margin percentage, and thus to set a suitable price. This method does not, however, take into account local market conditions. So we continually research the local foreign market in order to maintain our competitiveness.

Pricing Methods

Consumer goods marketers who wonder where their growth will come from in the future should explore multicultural markets. While sizable population increases among nonwhites are a given, many marketers haven't awoken to ethnic buying-power growth.

MARKET ANALYSIS SUMMARY

The New America Marketbasket Index points out that household expenditures among multicultural families will grow faster than white households. The study, developed by New America Strategies Group and DemoGraph Corporation, looked at 13 different key areas of consumer spending—such as entertainment, clothing, vehicle, and home purchases—by race. It offers projections from 1995 to 1998 based on purchase behavior trends from 1992 to 1995.

The Index documents the accelerating purchasing power, financial strength, and upward mobility of African, Asian, and Hispanic American consumers by analyzing household spending, and tracks their per-household spending growth based on a weighted average of multicultural household expenditures compared to that of white households.

In 10 of the 13 categories, minorities posted stronger growth than white households. Only in restaurant expenditures, public transportation, and rent did white growth exceed that of minorities. Expenditures from multicultural households exceeded white households in five categories—groceries, entertainment, personal care products, clothing, and education.

Why the greater increases from minorities? Laura Teller, chief executive officer of Miami-based DemoGraph, attributes it to a strong economy, near full employment, and minorities having more money to spend. "A rising tide lifts all the ships," she said. "The economic expansion has more money flowing into those communities."

The study forecasts healthcare outlays and entertainment spending growing nearly three to three-and-a-half times faster in minority households compared to white families. Electric utility expenditures grew twice as fast in minority households.

"Grocery and clothing expenditures are higher due to the size of the households," Teller said, citing the fact that minorities have more family members in average households. Multicultural households also have more people contributing to the family income, especially in Hispanic homes, she added.

The study projected Asian Americans to increase average spending 17.7 percent from 1995 to 1998. African Americans were close behind at 17.6 percent, while Hispanic expenditure growth was 15.5 percent. Whites, meanwhile, spent only 13.7 percent more over the three-year period.

DemoGraph projected expenditure increases through extrapolating data from the 1995 U.S. Consumer Expenditure Survey, U.S. Center for Educational Statistics, the National Auto Dealers Association, and the Harvard Joint Center for Housing Studies. The company didn't factor out inflation since it believed that it affects all groups equally.

While some of the gains occur in smaller-ticket items, such as groceries and clothing, multicultural families tend to outspend whites in more expensive goods, such as cars and homes. Minorities plan to increase spending on vehicles by 37.2 percent, while growth for whites is about 13.4 percent between 1995 and 1998. Minorities will boost their spending on home ownership by 16.9 percent, compared to 12.4 percent for whites. The study said 40 percent of all first-time home buyers between 1995 and 1998 are multicultural consumers.

"Multicultural families are becoming part of the burgeoning middle class," Teller said. "Their first purchase is a car, and they also have a high desire to own their home."

Most of the expenditure increase from African Americans can be attributed to increased spending on clothing, entertainment, and healthcare. Hispanics are expected to have large increases in vehicle purchases, clothing, and entertainment, while gains in Asian expenditures are in restaurants, vehicles, and education. Whites spent more of their dollars in restaurants, clothes, and public transportation.

For several demographic categories, expenditures on rent are expected to decline, due to those families moving into their first homes. Spending by African Americans on rent is projected to decline 13 percent, and 20.2 percent for Hispanics. Both whites and Asian Americans plan to increase average spending for rent by 6.3 percent. African Americans are expected to decrease spending on public transportation.

"Multicultural consumers are purchasing the good life," Teller says. However, an economic recession could definitely curb spending. Teller said that while Asian Americans save more than other minorities, African Americans and Hispanics have a smaller savings and income cushion if the economy falters. "Losing jobs would be a big shock to their systems," Teller says.

The Hispanic population has grown at a steady pace for the last 20 years and is continuing to grow. The number of people buying and renovating homes and landscapes is increasing according to the Home Builders Association. Hispanics, ages 0 to 64 with an income of $15,000 and up will be targeted for Mexican food, African Americans and Anglo Americans, ages 35 to 64 with an income of $15,000 and up will be targeted for the home and garden decorations.

Market Segmentation

Our customers are multicultural, male and female, ages 0 to 64, employed and unemployed and live in Michigan. According to the U.S. Census Bureau, Michigan's total population is 9,295,297: 4,512,781 are male and 4,782,516 are female. 7,786,237 or 84% of Michigan residents are between the ages of 0 to 64. 18% of the Michigan residents are multicultural with 1,291,706 being African American; 55,638 being American Indian, Eskimo, or Aleut; 104,983 being Asian or Pacific Islander; 86,884 being "other"; and 201,596 being Hispanic. Wayne County, where Central will be located, has a population of 437,349 as of July 1, 1999, which was an increase of 6,890 over the 1990 census.

According to Tradeport.org, Mexico is the most Spanish-speaking country in the world. Its population is approximately 98,552,776 (July 1998 est.): 70% of the people live in urban areas; 36% of the population is 0-14 years of age (male 17,883,007, female 17,193,082); 60% of the population is 15-64 (male 28,932,074, female 30,511,443); and 4% are 65 years and over (male 1,808,581, female 2,224,589). Population growth is approximately 1.77%.

Central has products for the entire age group, both male and female mestizos (Amerindian-Spanish) individuals. We will market our products to those individuals that make up 96 percent of Mexico's population.

Market Analysis

Potential Customers	Growth	2001	2002	2003	2004	2005	CAGR
Caucasian	1%	7,554,490	7,630,035	7,760,335	7,783,398	7,861,232	1.00%
African Americans	1%	1,291,706	1,304,623	1,317,669	1,330,846	1,344,154	1.00%
American Indian, Eskimo, or Aleut	1%	55,638	56,194	56,756	57,324	57,897	1.00%
Hispanic	2%	201,596	205,023	208,508	212,053	215,658	1.70%
Asian or Pacific Islander	1%	104,983	106,033	107,093	108,164	109,246	1.00%
Other	1%	86,884	87,753	88,631	89,517	90,412	1.00%
Total	**1.02%**	**9,295,297**	**9,389,661**	**9,484,992**	**9,581,302**	**9,678,599**	**1.02%**

Target Market/ Export Program Strategy

To keep track of our target market growth, we have implemented the following market research program in which we will:

- Keep abreast of world events that influence the international marketplace, watch for announcements of specific projects, or simply visit likely markets. For example, a thawing of political hostilities often leads to the opening of economic channels between countries.
- Analyze trade and economic statistics. Trade statistics are generally compiled by product category and by country. These statistics provide the U.S. firm with information concerning shipments of products over specified periods of time. Demographic and general economic statistics, such as population size and makeup, per capita income, and production levels by industry can be important indicators of the market potential for a company's products.
- Obtain advice from experts. There are several ways of obtaining this advice:
    - –Contact experts at the U.S. Department of Commerce and other government agencies.
    - –Attend seminars, workshops, and international trade shows.
    - –Hire an international trade and marketing consultant.
    - –Talk with successful exporters of similar products.
    - –Contact trade and industry association staff.

Gathering and evaluating secondary market research can be complex and tedious. However, several publications are available that can help us simplify the process.

Our Export Program Strategy is simply that Central will treat our export sales no differently than its domestic sales, using existing personnel and organizational structures. As international sales and inquiries increase, then we may separate the management of our exports from that of our domestic sales.

The advantages of separating our international from domestic business include the centralization of specialized skills needed to deal with international markets and the benefits of a focused marketing effort that is more likely to increase export sales. A possible disadvantage is that segmentation might be a less efficient use of corporate resources.

When we separate international from domestic business, we may do so at different levels in the organization. For example, when Central first begins to export, we may create an export department with a full- or part-time manager who reports to the head of domestic sales and marketing. At later stages, we may choose to increase the autonomy of the export department to the point of creating an international division that reports directly to the president.

Larger companies at advanced stages of exporting may choose to retain the international division or to organize along product or geographic lines. Since Central has distinct product lines we may create an international department in each product division. A company with products that have common end users may organize geographically. For example, it may form a division for Europe and another for the Pacific Rim.

Because we are a small company, our initial needs may be satisfied by a single export manager who has responsibility for the full range of international activities. Regardless of how we organize our exporting efforts, the key is to facilitate the marketer's job. Good marketing skills will help Central operate in unfamiliar markets. Experience has shown that a company's success in foreign markets depends less on the unique attributes of its products than on its marketing methods.

Once Central is organized to handle exporting markets other than Mexico, a proper channel of distribution will be carefully chosen for each market. These channels include sales representatives, agents, distributors, retailers, and end users.

Advertising and Promotion Strategies

Advertising will be accomplished by mailing flyers to potential buyers. A newspaper ad will run announcing our Grand Opening. We will have our logo and business information printed on our delivery truck, which will be visible throughout the city. We believe flyers and word-of-mouth networking should be sufficient advertising for our product. This promotional strategy is also very inexpensive.

To build our export trade leads we will utilize the following resources:

- National Export Offer Service
- Commercial news USA
- Export Yellow Pages
- ComFind—Global Business Directory
- Network of Americas—Export Directory

To develop leads for service matchmaking we will utilize the following resources:

- Import-Export Bulletin Boards—Post buy/sell offers
- IBEX—International Business Exchange
- Free Web Trader
- Global Trade Point Network
- Global Traders Forum
- The Netsource Trade Center
- GoldSite Europe
- The Trading Floor
- Trade Compass
- Barter Worldwide, Inc.
- ITEX Barter Industry
- alt.business.import-export
- International Business Newsgroup
- Inter-American Development Bank
- African Development Bank
- Asia Development Bank
- Bidworld.com

Future forms of promotion may include trade press ads, trade shows, catalog shows, cross border buying trips, trade missions, and a website.

World trade is increasingly important to the strength of our economy and to the growth of U.S. companies. Exporting and importing creates jobs and provides small firms with growth, new markets, and additional profits.

Every billion earned in U.S. export dollars generates about 20,000 jobs. There has never been a better time for American businesses to begin exporting. As the world economy becomes more interdependent, the opportunities for small businesses become more attractive.

Exporting is booming in the United States, and small businesses are beginning to realize that the world is their market. A business does not have to be big to sell in the global marketplace. Experience shows that small businesses do export successfully. Finding your niche in the world market is similar to finding it in the U.S. market. Many of the same qualities that make small business owners successful in the United States apply to success in global markets.

- Based on 1992 data from the U.S. Department of Commerce, small firms (fewer than 500 employees) represented 95.7 percent of exporters of goods in 1992. Of the 112,854 goods exporters, 108,026 were small firms.
- By major industry, in 1992, 9.3 percent of manufacturing firms exported goods or services. Comparable figures for other industries include 8.0 percent of wholesale trade firms, 1.5 percent of retail and service firms, 1.0 percent of finance, insurance, and real estate firms, and only 0.3 percent of construction firms.
- By race or origin in 1992 the percent that exported goods or services was 2.7 percent for Hispanic-owned firms, 2.3 percent for Asian, Pacific, American Indian, or Aleut Eskimo owned firms, 1.8 percent for white-owned firms, and 0.8 percent for black-owned firms.

In 1992 Michigan had a total of 6,338 exporters and from those 1,838 had 1 to 19 employees, similar to Central.

Industry Analysis and Trends

Central will save its customers hundreds of dollars by cutting our shipping costs. We will pick up our inventory and drop off our inventory. While Central will not be the only store selling Mexican products, it will have the advantage of selling products at a lower price with a larger variety. Livonia customers no longer will have to drive to Detroit, Michigan, to purchase similar goods.

Competition and Buying Patterns

Thousands of small firms already compete in the global market. They account for 97 percent of companies involved in direct merchandise exporting, yet generate only about 30 percent of the dollar value of the nation's export sales. Small firms, then, represent the largest pool for potential growth in export sales.

Entering the Mexican market will not be difficult. The same import strategies applied in the U.S. market can be used to develop export markets. Central understands selling abroad demands hard work, perseverance, and a commitment of resources. It requires planning, market research, and attention to detail. It may also involve changes, like new packaging and metric conversion.

Central has taken the mystery out of exporting by using these fundamental elements of the exporting process:

- Analyzing the capabilities of our small business
- Knowing the export potential of our product/service
- Identifying foreign markets that are right for us

STRATEGY & IMPLEMENTATION SUMMARY

- Studying market-entry strategies and export procedures
- Learning how to process exports

We will implement our import segment of our business by e-mailing a list of goods we are interested in purchasing to our Mexican contact, Rosa Marie Juarez, located in Nuevo Laredo, Mexico. She will then purchase merchandise and our U.S. customs broker will prepare the documentation. The merchandise is then brought into the U.S. to be housed in a warehouse in Laredo, Texas. The goods will then be picked up by Ramon Juarez (who will be bringing with him items to be exported) and brought back to Michigan for distribution.

Our implementation of our export segment consists of receiving e-mail from our Mexican contact, Rosa Marie Juarez, requesting U.S. merchandise to be exported. We will then purchase the merchandise and e-mail a list of products to our customs broker for documentation. The merchandise will be transported to Laredo, Texas. We will then deliver the items to be exported and pick up items to be imported.

Competitive Edge

Our location is a very important competitive edge. The nearest import/exporter of Mexican goods is in Detroit, Michigan. There are a few local stores selling the goods such as Target, Kmart, Jason's Music Shop, and a few party stores. These stores are selling the product at a higher retail cost than Central. Central will take these stores and distribute our goods to them, saving them transportation and shipping costs.

Sales Strategy

Central will initially open as a wholesale distribution and retail store with a variety of Mexican food, and interior and exterior decorations made of brass ceramic, wrought iron, clay, and wood. After establishing ourselves as a retail import/export store, we will then begin to distribute our products to gift shops, restaurants, landscaping companies, and other retail shops selling similar products.

Sales Forecast

The following chart gives a rundown on forecasted sales.

Sales Forecast

Sales	2001	2002	2003
Row 1	$73,000	$73,000	$73,000
Other	$0	$0	$0
Total Sales	**$73,000**	**$73,000**	**$73,000**
Direct Cost of Sales			
Row 1	$15,000	$18,000	$18,000
Other	$0	$0	$0
Subtotal Cost of Sales	**$15,000**	**$18,000**	**$18,000**

Strategic Alliances

Central has taken the time to form alliances both here, in the United States, and across the border of Mexico. Those alliances are as follows:

The United States

- Chili Pepper Produce—Distributor
- Manuel Rodriguez—Customs Broker
- U.S. Department of Commerce, International Trade Administration—Support
- World Trade Organization—Support
- National Trade Data Bank—Research

Mexico

- Rosa Marie Juarez—Buyer
- Milagro X Guago—Vendor
- Flores del Rio—Vendor
- Fontino Ltd.
- Goodrich ltda.
- Hong Kong Knitting Co. Ltd

The risks of this business are low. Items that will be imported or exported vary according to demand and there will be a pre-arrangement for purchasing and selling goods beforehand.   **Risks**

The difficulties the business foresees are:

- small size of the parking lot
- constant changes in import/export regulations
- cost of transporting increases with fuel increases
- transportation breakdowns

The solutions for these difficulties are to:

- work out an agreement with adjacent businesses for use of their parking area for overflow traffic
- stay informed on changes of regulations through personal research and assistance from our Customs Agent
- increase the volume of merchandise purchased and decrease number of trips made to Mexico
- keep truck on a consistent maintenance program until new truck can be purchased

The owner has injected $17,195 of the $35,000 capital needed to start the business. Therefore, 49 percent of the risk is with the owner's money. In the event of business failure it is estimated that the owner's assets and current income would produce the $17,805 needed to repay the loan.

Ramon Juarez has been transporting merchandise and personal belongings to and from Michigan to Texas and Mexico as a nonprofit group for the past 14 years. He regularly visits family and friends in Mexico and has gained a good knowledge of driving time, cost, and requirements for transportation of goods. Ramon is a full-time employee as an engineer for Ford Motor Company. It is the intent of the owner to be the key manpower in starting this business. Ramon Juarez will be assisted by one part-time employee.   **MANAGEMENT SUMMARY**

The complexities and dynamics of international trade are such that Ramon has found it extremely advantageous to obtain the services of a customs broker in order to facilitate the importation of goods. Ramon will also be assisted by Manuel Rodriguez, a U.S. Customs Broker. Mr. Rodriguez's operation transcends Customs, calling for contact with over 40 other government agencies such as the U.S. Department of Agriculture (USDA) on meat importation, the Environmental Protection Agency (EPA) on vehicle emission standards, or the Food and Drug Administration (FDA) on product safety. For these reasons, the services of a Customs Broker are highly recommended for Central.

Mr. Rodriguez will act as an agent for Ramon in conducting customs business on his behalf. Mr. Rodriguez will also prepare and file the necessary customs entries, arrange for the payment of duties found due, take steps to the effective release of the goods in customs custody, and represent Ramon in custody matters. Mr. Rodriguez has an excellent understanding of trade requirements and procedures and customs tariff regulations. Furthermore, Mr. Rodriguez will assist Ramon with advice on other transportation options, types of carriers, and shipping routes. Mr. Rodriguez will assist with exchange rates, appraisals, and proper classifications and duties. Mr. Rodriguez is aware of potential problems involving every entry item represented, including cargo handling. This includes all factors affecting appraisement, exchange rates, and many regulations concerning calculation of duties.

Central believes very strongly that relationships should be forthright, work should be structured with enough room for creativity, and pay should commensurate with the amount and quality work completed. No person is better than another except in ability, knowledge, and experience.

Personnel Plan

It is the intent of the owners to operate the business with one full-time employee and one part-time employee. The employees will be proficient in English and Spanish to communicate with Hispanics as well as other ethnic groups. As the business grows, a third employee will be added to conduct sales outside the Livonia area. The personnel plan is included in the following table. It shows the one part-time employee salary for driver/customer service representative and a total of two employees, one being the owner.

Personnel Plan	2001	2002	2003
Personnel			
Driver/Customer Service Representative	$6,552	$6,552	$6,552
Other	$0	$0	$0
Total Payroll	**$6,552**	**$6,552**	**$6,552**
Total Headcount	**2**	**2**	**2**
Payroll Burden	**$983**	**$983**	**$983**
Total Payroll Expenditures	**$7,535**	**$7,535**	**$7,535**

FINANCIAL PLAN

Our financial plan anticipates the following:

- Growth will be moderate, cash flows steady
- Marketing will remain below 15 percent of sales
- The company will invest residual profits into financial markets and company expansion

Important Assumptions

Our financial plan depends on important assumptions, most of which are shown in the following table as annual assumptions:

Some of the more important underlying assumptions are:

- We assume strong economy, both in the U.S. and Mexico
- We assume, of course, that there are no unforseen changes in the use of the product which make the need for the product obsolete.

General Assumptions	2001	2002	2003
Short-term Interest Rate %	10.00%	10.00%	10.00%
Long-term Interest Rate %	10.00%	10.00%	10.00%
Payment Days Estimator	30	30	30
Collection Days Estimator	45	45	45
Inventory Turnover Estimator	6.00	6.00	6.00
Tax Rate %	25.00%	25.00%	25.00%
Expenses in Cash %	10.00%	10.00%	10.00%
Sales on Credit %	0.00%	0.00%	0.00%
Personnel Burden %	15.00%	15.00%	15.00%

A break-even analysis table has been completed on the basis of average per-unit revenue. With fixed costs of $3,720, we need to generate sales of at least $1,333 per month or sell approximately $50 worth of goods per day.

Break-even Analysis (margin heading)

Break-even Analysis:

Monthly Units Break-even	1,333
Monthly Sales Break-even	$1,333

Assumptions:

Average Per-Unit Revenue	$1.00
Average Per-Unit Variable Cost	$0.25
Estimated Monthly Fixed Cost	$1,000

Central will have a profit to sales ratio of just over 11 percent. Normally, a start-up concern will operate with negative profits through the first two years. We will avoid this kind of operating loss by knowing our competitors and our target market.

Projected Profit and Loss (margin heading)

Profit and Loss (Income Statement)	2001	2002	2003
Sales	$73,000	$73,000	$73,000
Direct Cost of Sales	$15,000	$18,000	$18,000
Production Payroll	$0	$0	$0
Working Capital	$0	$0	$0
Total Cost of Sales	**$15,000**	**$18,000**	**$18,000**
Gross Margin	$58,000	$55,000	$55,000
Gross Margin %	79.45%	75.34%	75.34%
Operating Expenses			
Sales and Marketing Expenses			
Sales and Marketing Payroll	$0	$0	$0
Truck Maintenance	$2,640	$2,640	$2,640
Travel	$2,400	$2,400	$2,400
Telephone	$456	$456	$456
Total Sales and Marketing Expenses	**$0**	**$0**	**$0**
Sales and Marketing %	0.00%	0.00%	0.00%

Projected Profit and Loss

Continued

General and Administrative Expenses			
General and Administrative Payroll	$0	$0	$0
Payroll Expense	$6,552	$6,552	$6,552
Payroll Burden	$983	$983	$983
Depreciation	$0	$0	$0
Truck	$4,200	$4,200	$4,200
Utilities	$1,200	$1,200	$1,200
Insurance	$1,332	$1,332	$1,332
Rent	$3,600	$3,600	$3,600
Total General and Administrative Expenses	**$0**	**$0**	**$0**
General and Administrative %	0.00%	0.00%	0.00%
Other Expenses			
Other Payroll	$0	$0	$0
Bank Loan Repayment	$3,744	$3,744	$3,744
Owner's Withdrawals	$16,632	$16,632	$16,632
Customs Broker	$900	$900	$900
Total Other Expenses	**$0**	**$0**	**$0**
Other %	0.00%	0.00%	0.00%
Total Operating Expenses	**$44,639**	**$44,639**	**$44,639**
Profit Before Interest and Taxes	$13,361	$10,361	$10,361
Interest Expense Short-term	$1,781	$1,781	$1,781
Interest Expense Long-term	$0	$0	$0
Taxes Incurred	$2,895	$2,145	$2,145
Extraordinary Items	$0	$0	$0
Net Profit	$8,686	$6,436	$6,436
Net Profit/Sales	11.90%	8.82%	8.82%

Projected Cash Flow

We are positioning ourselves in the market as a low-risk concern with steady cash flows. Accounts payable are paid at the end of each month, while sales are in cash and credit cards, giving Central excellent cash structure. Intelligent marketing will secure a cash balance of $32,072 by 2001.

Projected Cash Flow	2001	2002	2003
Net Profit	$8,686	$6,436	$6,436
Plus:			
Depreciation	$0	$0	$0
Change in Accounts Payable	$5,046	($657)	($45)
Current Borrowing (repayment)	$0	$0	$0
Increase (decrease) Other Liabilities	$0	$0	$0
Long-term Borrowing (repayment)	$0	$0	$0
Capital Input	$9,153	$0	$0
Subtotal	**$22,884**	**$5,779**	**$6,391**
Less:			
Change in Accounts Receivable	$0	$0	$0
Change in Inventory	$0	$1,200	$0
Change in Other Short-term Assets	$0	$0	$0
Capital Expenditure	$0	$0	$0
Dividends	$0	$0	$0
Subtotal	**$0**	**$1,200**	**$0**
Net Cash Flow	**$22,884**	**$4,579**	**$6,391**
Cash Balance	**$32,037**	**$36,616**	**$43,007**

All of our tables will be updated monthly to reflect past performance and future assumptions. Future assumptions will not be based on past performance, but rather on economic cycle activity, regional and international industry, strength, and future cash flow possibilities. We expect a solid growth in net worth beyond the year 2002.

Projected Balance Sheet
Assets

Short-term Assets	2001	2002	2003
Cash	$32,037	$36,616	$43,007
Accounts Receivable	$0	$0	$0
Inventory	$6,000	$7,200	$7,200
Other Short-term Assets	$0	$0	$0
Total Short-term Assets	**$38,037**	**$43,816**	**$50,207**
Long-term Assets			
Capital Assets	$0	$0	$0
Accumulated Depreciation	$0	$0	$0
Total Long-term Assets	$0	$0	$0
Total Assets	**$38,037**	**$43,816**	**$50,207**
Liabilities and Capital			
Accounts Payable	$5,046	$4,389	$4,345
Short-term Notes	$17,805	$17,805	$17,805
Other Short-term Liabilities	$0	$0	$0
Subtotal Short-term Liabilities	**$22,851**	**$22,194**	**$22,150**
Long-term Liabilities	$0	$0	$0
Total Liabilities	**$22,851**	**$22,194**	**$22,150**
Paid in Capital	$26,348	$26,348	$26,348
Retained Earnings	($19,847)	($11,161)	($4,726)
Earnings	$8,686	$6,436	$6,436
Total Capital	**$15,187**	**$21,622**	**$28,058**
Total Liabilities and Capital	**$38,037**	**$43,816**	**$50,207**
Net Worth	**$15,187**	**$21,622**	**$28,058**

Projected Balance Sheet

The following table shows the projected ratios. We expect to maintain healthy ratios for profitability, risk, and return.

Business Ratios

Ratio Analysis

Profitability Ratios:	2001	2002	2003	RMA
Gross Margin	79.45%	75.34%	75.34%	0
Net Profit Margin	11.90%	8.82%	8.82%	0
Return on Assets	22.83%	14.69%	12.82%	0
Return on Equity	57.19%	29.76%	22.94%	0
Activity Ratios				
AR Turnover	0.00	0.00	0.00	0
Collection Days	0	0	0	0
Inventory Turnover	2.50	2.73	2.50	0
Accounts Payable Turnover	10.13	12.17	12.17	0
Total Asset Turnover	**1.92**	**1.67**	**1.45**	**0**

Business Ratios

Continued

Debt Ratios				
Debt to Net Worth	1.50	1.03	0.79	0
Short-term Liability to Liability	1.00	1.00	1.00	0
Liquidity Ratios				
Current Ratio	1.66	1.97	2.27	0
Quick Ratio	1.40	1.65	1.94	0
Net Working Capital	$15,187	$21,622	$28,058	0
Interest Coverage	7.50	5.82	5.82	0
Additional Ratios				
Assets to Sales	0.52	0.60	0.69	0
Debt/Assets	60%	51%	44%	0
Current Debt/Total Assets	60%	51%	44%	0
Acid Test	1.40	1.65	1.94	0
Asset Turnover	1.92	1.67	1.45	0
Sales/Net Worth	4.81	3.38	2.60	0
Dividend Payout	$0	$0	$0	$0

This page left intentionally blank to accommodate tabular matter following.

APPENDIX

Sales Forecast

Sales	Jan	Feb	Mar	Apr	May	Jun	Jul
Row 1	$3,162	$4,704	$5,270	$4,740	$5,146	$3,360	$3,360
Other	$0	$0	$0	$0	$0	$0	$0
Total Sales	**$3,162**	**$4,704**	**$5,270**	**$4,740**	**$5,146**	**$3,360**	**$3,360**
Direct Cost of Sales							
Row 1	$0	$0	$3,000	$0	$3,000	$0	$3,000
Other	$0	$0	$0	$0	$0	$0	$0
Subtotal Cost of Sales	**$0**	**$0**	**$3,000**	**$0**	**$3,000**	**$0**	**$3,000**

Personnel Plan

Personnel	Jan	Feb	Mar	Apr	May	Jun	Jul
Driver/Customer Service Representative	$546	$546	$546	$546	$546	$546	$546
Other	$0	$0	$0	$0	$0	$0	$0
Total Payroll	**$546**	**$546**	**$546**	**$546**	**$546**	**$546**	**$546**
Total Headcount	2	2	2	2	2	2	2
Payroll Burden	$82	$82	$82	$82	$82	$82	$82
Total Payroll Expenditures	**$628**	**$628**	**$628**	**$628**	**$628**	**$628**	**$628**

General Assumptions

	Jan	Feb	Mar	Apr	May	Jun	Jul
Short-term Interest Rate %	10.00%	10.00%	10.00%	10.00%	10.00%	10.00%	10.00%
Long-term Interest Rate %	10.00%	10.00%	10.00%	10.00%	10.00%	10.00%	10.00%
Payment Days Estimator	30	30	30	30	30	30	30
Collection Days Estimator	45	45	45	45	45	45	45
Inventory Turnover Estimator	6.00	6.00	6.00	6.00	6.00	6.00	6.00
Tax Rate %	25.00%	25.00%	25.00%	25.00%	25.00%	25.00%	25.00%
Expenses in Cash %	10.00%	10.00%	10.00%	10.00%	10.00%	10.00%	10.00%
Sales on Credit %	0.00%	0.00%	0.00%	0.00%	0.00%	0.00%	0.00%
Personnel Burden %	15.00%	15.00%	15.00%	15.00%	15.00%	15.00%	15.00%

	Aug	Sep	Oct	Nov	Dec	2001	2002	2003
	$6,572	$5,580	$6,200	$10,800	$14,106	$73,000	$73,000	$73,000
	$0	$0	$0	$0	$0	$0	$0	$0
	$6,572	**$5,580**	**$6,200**	**$10,800**	**$14,106**	**$73,000**	**$73,000**	**$73,000**
	$0	$3,000	$0	$3,000	$0	$15,000	$18,000	$18,000
	$0	$0	$0	$0	$0	$0	$0	$0
	$0	**$3,000**	**$0**	**$3,000**	**$0**	**$15,000**	**$18,000**	**$18,000**

	Aug	Sep	Oct	Nov	Dec	2001	2002	2003
	$546	$546	$546	$546	$546	$6,552	$6,552	$6,552
	$0	$0	$0	$0	$0	$0	$0	$0
	$546	**$546**	**$546**	**$546**	**$546**	**$6,552**	**$6,552**	**$6,552**
	2	2	2	2	2	2	2	2
	$82	$82	$82	$82	$82	$983	$983	$983
	$628	**$628**	**$628**	**$628**	**$628**	**$7,535**	**$7,535**	**$7,535**

	Aug	Sep	Oct	Nov	Dec	2001	2002	2003
	10.00%	10.00%	10.00%	10.00%	10.00%	10.00%	10.00%	10.00%
	10.00%	10.00%	10.00%	10.00%	10.00%	10.00%	10.00%	10.00%
	30	30	30	30	30	30	30	30
	45	45	45	45	45	45	45	45
	6.00	6.00	6.00	6.00	6.00	6.00	6.00	6.00
	25.00%	25.00%	25.00%	25.00%	25.00%	25.00%	25.00%	25.00%
	10.00%	10.00%	10.00%	10.00%	10.00%	10.00%	10.00%	10.00%
	0.00%	0.00%	0.00%	0.00%	0.00%	0.00%	0.00%	0.00%
	15.00%	15.00%	15.00%	15.00%	15.00%	15.00%	15.00%	15.00%

Profit and Loss (Income Statement)

	Jan	Feb	Mar	Apr	May	Jun	Jul
Sales	$3,162	$4,704	$5,270	$4,740	$5,146	$3,360	$3,360
Direct Cost of Sales	$0	$0	$3,000	$0	$3,000	$0	$3,000
Production Payroll	$0	$0	$0	$0	$0	$0	$0
Working Capital	$0	$0	$0	$0	$0	$0	$0
Total Cost of Sales	**$0**	**$0**	**$3,000**	**$0**	**$3,000**	**$0**	**$3,000**
Gross Margin	$3,162	$4,704	$2,270	$4,740	$2,146	$3,360	$360
Gross Margin %	100.00%	100.00%	43.07%	100.00%	41.70%	100.00%	10.71%

Operating Expenses
Sales and Marketing Expenses

	Jan	Feb	Mar	Apr	May	Jun	Jul
Sales and Marketing Payroll	$0	$0	$0	$0	$0	$0	$0
Truck Maintenance	$220	$220	$220	$220	$220	$220	$220
Travel	$200	$200	$200	$200	$200	$200	$200
Telephone	$38	$38	$38	$38	$38	$38	$38
Total Sales and Marketing Expenses	**$0**	**$0**	**$0**	**$0**	**$0**	**$0**	**$0**
Sales and Marketing %	0.00%	0.00%	0.00%	0.00%	0.00%	0.00%	0.00%

General and Administrative Expenses

	Jan	Feb	Mar	Apr	May	Jun	Jul
General and Administrative Payroll	$0	$0	$0	$0	$0	$0	$0
Payroll Expense	$546	$546	$546	$546	$546	$546	$546
Payroll Burden	$82	$82	$82	$82	$82	$82	$82
Depreciation	$0	$0	$0	$0	$0	$0	$0
Truck	$350	$350	$350	$350	$350	$350	$350
Utilities	$100	$100	$100	$100	$100	$100	$100
Insurance	$111	$111	$111	$111	$111	$111	$111
Rent	$300	$300	$300	$300	$300	$300	$300
Total General and Administrative Expenses	**$0**	**$0**	**$0**	**$0**	**$0**	**$0**	**$0**
General and Administrative %	0.00%	0.00%	0.00%	0.00%	0.00%	0.00%	0.00%

Other Expenses

	Jan	Feb	Mar	Apr	May	Jun	Jul
Other Payroll	$0	$0	$0	$0	$0	$0	$0
Bank Loan Repayment	$312	$312	$312	$312	$312	$312	$312
Owner's Withdrawals	$1,386	$1,386	$1,386	$1,386	$1,386	$1,386	$1,386
Customs Broker	$75	$75	$75	$75	$75	$75	$75
Total Other Expenses	**$0**	**$0**	**$0**	**$0**	**$0**	**$0**	**$0**
Other %	0.00%	0.00%	0.00%	0.00%	0.00%	0.00%	0.00%
Total Operating Expenses	**$3,720**	**$3,720**	**$3,720**	**$3,720**	**$3,720**	**$3,720**	**$3,720**

	Jan	Feb	Mar	Apr	May	Jun	Jul
Profit Before Interest and Taxes	($558)	$984	($1,450)	$1,020	($1,574)	($360)	($3,360)
Interest Expense Short-term	$148	$148	$148	$148	$148	$148	$148
Interest Expense Long-term	$0	$0	$0	$0	$0	$0	$0
Taxes Incurred	($177)	$209	($400)	$218	($431)	($127)	($877)
Extraordinary Items	$0	$0	$0	$0	$0	$0	$0
Net Profit	**($530)**	**$627**	**($1,199)**	**$654**	**($1,292)**	**($381)**	**($2,631)**
Net Profit/Sales	**-16.75%**	**13.32%**	**-22.75%**	**13.79%**	**-25.10%**	**-11.35%**	**-78.31%**

Aug	Sep	Oct	Nov	Dec	2001	2002	2003
$6,572	$5,580	$6,200	$10,800	$14,106	$73,000	$73,000	$73,000
$0	$3,000	$0	$3,000	$0	$15,000	$18,000	$18,000
$0	$0	$0	$0	$0	$0	$0	$0
$0	$0	$0	$0	$0	$0	$0	$0
$0	**$3,000**	**$0**	**$3,000**	**$0**	**$15,000**	**$18,000**	**$18,000**
$6,572	$2,580	$6,200	$7,800	$14,106	$58,000	$55,000	$55,000
100.00%	46.24%	100.00%	72.22%	100.00%	79.45%	75.34%	75.34%
$0	$0	$0	$0	$0	$0	$0	$0
$220	$220	$220	$220	$220	$2,640	$2,640	$2,640
$200	$200	$200	$200	$200	$2,400	$2,400	$2,400
$38	$38	$38	$38	$38	$456	$456	$456
$0	**$0**	**$0**	**$0**	**$0**	**$0**	**$0**	**$0**
0.00%	0.00%	0.00%	0.00%	0.00%	0.00%	0.00%	0.00%
$0	$0	$0	$0	$0	$0	$0	$0
$546	$546	$546	$546	$546	$6,552	$6,552	$6,552
$82	$82	$82	$82	$82	$983	$983	$983
$0	$0	$0	$0	$0	$0	$0	$0
$350	$350	$350	$350	$350	$4,200	$4,200	$4,200
$100	$100	$100	$100	$100	$1,200	$1,200	$1,200
$111	$111	$111	$111	$111	$1,332	$1,332	$1,332
$300	$300	$300	$300	$300	$3,600	$3,600	$3,600
$0	**$0**	**$0**	**$0**	**$0**	**$0**	**$0**	**$0**
0.00%	0.00%	0.00%	0.00%	0.00%	0.00%	0.00%	0.00%
$0	$0	$0	$0	$0	$0	$0	$0
$312	$312	$312	$312	$312	$3,744	$3,744	$3,744
$1,386	$1,386	$1,386	$1,386	$1,386	$16,632	$16,632	$16,632
$75	$75	$75	$75	$75	$900	$900	$900
$0	**$0**	**$0**	**$0**	**$0**	**$0**	**$0**	**$0**
0.00%	0.00%	0.00%	0.00%	0.00%	0.00%	0.00%	0.00%
$3,720	**$3,720**	**$3,720**	**$3,720**	**$3,720**	**$44,639**	**$44,639**	**$44,639**
$2,852	($1,140)	$2,480	$4,080	$10,386	$13,361	$10,361	$10,361
$148	$148	$148	$148	$148	$1,781	$1,781	$1,781
$0	$0	$0	$0	$0	$0	$0	$0
$676	($322)	$583	$983	$2,559	$2,895	$2,145	$2,145
$0	$0	$0	$0	$0	$0	$0	$0
$2,028	**($966)**	**$1,749**	**$2,949**	**$7,678**	**$8,686**	**$6,436**	**$6,436**
30.86%	**-17.32%**	**28.21%**	**27.30%**	**54.43%**	**11.90%**	**8.82%**	**8.82%**

Projected Cash Flow

	Jan	Feb	Mar	Apr	May	Jun	Jul
Net Profit	($530)	$627	($1,199)	$654	($1,292)	($381)	($2,631)
Plus:							
Depreciation	$0	$0	$0	$0	$0	$0	$0
Change in Accounts Payable	$2,666	$335	$2,081	($2,073)	$2,046	($2,346)	$1,958
Current Borrowing (repayment)	$0	$0	$0	$0	$0	$0	$0
Increase (decrease) Other Liabilities	$0	$0	$0	$0	$0	$0	$0
Long-term Borrowing (repayment)	$0	$0	$0	$0	$0	$0	$0
Capital Input	$3,051	$3,051	$3,051	$0	$0	$0	$0
Subtotal	**$5,187**	**$4,013**	**$3,933**	**($1,419)**	**$754**	**($2,727)**	**($674)**
Less:							
Change in Accounts Receivable	$0	$0	$0	$0	$0	$0	$0
Change in Inventory	$0	$0	$0	$0	$0	$0	$0
Change in Other Short-term Assets	$0	$0	$0	$0	$0	$0	$0
Capital Expenditure	$0	$0	$0	$0	$0	$0	$0
Dividends	$0	$0	$0	$0	$0	$0	$0
Subtotal	**$0**	**$0**	**$0**	**$0**	**$0**	**$0**	**$0**
Net Cash Flow	**$5,187**	**$4,013**	**$3,933**	**($1,419)**	**$754**	**($2,727)**	**($674)**
Cash Balance	**$14,340**	**$18,353**	**$22,286**	**$20,867**	**$21,621**	**$18,894**	**$18,220**

Aug	Sep	Oct	Nov	Dec	2001	2002	2003
$2,028	($966)	$1,749	$2,949	$7,678	$8,686	$6,436	$6,436
$0	$0	$0	$0	$0	$0	$0	$0
($1,259)	$1,742	($1,823)	$2,958	($1,238)	$5,046	($657)	($45)
$0	$0	$0	$0	$0	$0	$0	$0
$0	$0	$0	$0	$0	$0	$0	$0
$0	$0	$0	$0	$0	$0	$0	$0
$0	$0	$0	$0	$0	$9,153	$0	$0
$769	**$776**	**($74)**	**$5,907**	**$6,440**	**$22,884**	**$5,779**	**$6,391**
$0	$0	$0	$0	$0	$0	$0	$0
$0	$0	$0	$0	$0	$0	$1,200	$0
$0	$0	$0	$0	$0	$0	$0	$0
$0	$0	$0	$0	$0	$0	$0	$0
$0	$0	$0	$0	$0	$0	$0	$0
$0	**$0**	**$0**	**$0**	**$0**	**$0**	**$1,200**	**$0**
$769	**$776**	**($74)**	**$5,907**	**$6,440**	**$22,884**	**$4,579**	**$6,391**
$18,989	**$19,765**	**$19,691**	**$25,598**	**$32,037**	**$32,037**	**$36,616**	**$43,007**

Projected Balance Sheet

Assets

Short-term Assets	Jan	Feb	Mar	Apr	May	Jun	Jul
Cash	$14,340	$18,353	$22,286	$20,867	$21,621	$18,894	$18,220
Accounts Receivable	$0	$0	$0	$0	$0	$0	$0
Inventory	$6,000	$6,000	$6,000	$6,000	$6,000	$6,000	$6,000
Other Short-term Assets	$0	$0	$0	$0	$0	$0	$0
Total Short-term Assets	**$20,340**	**$24,353**	**$28,286**	**$26,867**	**$27,621**	**$24,894**	**$24,220**
Long-term Assets							
Capital Assets	$0	$0	$0	$0	$0	$0	$0
Accumulated Depreciation	$0	$0	$0	$0	$0	$0	$0
Total Long-term Assets	$0	$0	$0	$0	$0	$0	$0
Total Assets	**$20,340**	**$24,353**	**$28,286**	**$26,867**	**$27,621**	**$24,894**	**$24,220**
Liabilities and Capital							
Accounts Payable	$2,666	$3,001	$5,082	$3,009	$5,055	$2,709	$4,666
Short-term Notes	$17,805	$17,805	$17,805	$17,805	$17,805	$17,805	$17,805
Other Short-term Liabilities	$0	$0	$0	$0	$0	$0	$0
Subtotal Short-term Liabilities	**$20,471**	**$20,806**	**$22,887**	**$20,814**	**$22,860**	**$20,514**	**$22,471**
Long-term Liabilities	$0	$0	$0	$0	$0	$0	$0
Total Liabilities	**$20,471**	**$20,806**	**$22,887**	**$20,814**	**$22,860**	**$20,514**	**$22,471**
Paid in Capital	$20,246	$23,297	$26,348	$26,348	$26,348	$26,348	$26,348
Retained Earnings	($19,847)	($19,847)	($19,847)	($19,847)	($19,847)	($19,847)	($19,847)
Earnings	($530)	$97	($1,102)	($448)	($1,740)	($2,121)	($4,752)
Total Capital	**($131)**	**$3,547**	**$5,399**	**$6,053**	**$4,761**	**$4,380**	**$1,749**
Total Liabilities and Capital	**$20,340**	**$24,353**	**$28,286**	**$26,867**	**$27,621**	**$24,894**	**$24,220**
Net Worth	**($131)**	**$3,547**	**$5,399**	**$6,053**	**$4,761**	**$4,380**	**$1,749**

	Aug	Sep	Oct	Nov	Dec	2001	2002	2003
	$18,989	$19,765	$19,691	$25,598	$32,037	$32,037	$36,616	$43,007
	$0	$0	$0	$0	$0	$0	$0	$0
	$6,000	$6,000	$6,000	$6,000	$6,000	$6,000	$7,200	$7,200
	$0	$0	$0	$0	$0	$0	$0	$0
	$24,989	**$25,765**	**$25,691**	**$31,598**	**$38,037**	**$38,037**	**$43,816**	**$50,207**
	$0	$0	$0	$0	$0	$0	$0	$0
	$0	$0	$0	$0	$0	$0	$0	$0
	$0	$0	$0	$0	$0	$0	$0	$0
	$24,989	**$25,765**	**$25,691**	**$31,598**	**$38,037**	**$38,037**	**$43,816**	**$50,207**
	$3,407	$5,149	$3,326	$6,284	$5,046	$5,046	$4,389	$4,345
	$17,805	$17,805	$17,805	$17,805	$17,805	$17,805	$17,805	$17,805
	$0	$0	$0	$0	$0	$0	$0	$0
	$21,212	**$22,954**	**$21,131**	**$24,089**	**$22,851**	**$22,851**	**$22,194**	**$22,150**
	$0	$0	$0	$0	$0	$0	$0	$0
	$21,212	**$22,954**	**$21,131**	**$24,089**	**$22,851**	**$22,851**	**$22,194**	**$22,150**
	$26,348	$26,348	$26,348	$26,348	$26,348	$26,348	$26,348	$26,348
	($19,847)	($19,847)	($19,847)	($19,847)	($19,847)	($19,847)	($11,161)	($4,726)
	($2,724)	($3,690)	($1,942)	$1,007	$8,686	$8,686	$6,436	$6,436
	$3,777	**$2,811**	**$4,559**	**$7,508**	**$15,187**	**$15,187**	**$21,622**	**$28,058**
	$24,989	**$25,765**	**$25,691**	**$31,598**	**$38,037**	**$38,037**	**$43,816**	**$50,207**
	$3,777	**$2,811**	**$4,559**	**$7,508**	**$15,187**	**$15,187**	**$21,622**	**$28,058**

Internet Communications Service Provider

BUSINESS PLAN   APPIAN WAY COMMUNICATIONS NETWORK, LTD.

119 Melton Boulevard
Houston, Texas 77032

Appian Way Communications Network is a rapidly growing ISP and systems integrator which intends to become a leader in providing businesses, educational institutions, and governmental organizations with high-quality, cost-effective business solutions. Specifically, it helps customers take full advantage of the Internet without having to develop and maintain their own Internet technology, or hire and retain an extensive Internet staff. This business plan raised over $2 million for the company, and was successful for getting its sales up to $16 million in less than 2 years.

- INTRODUCTION

- INDUSTRY BACKGROUND & OPPORTUNITY

- THE APPIAN WAY COMMUNICATIONS NETWORK STRATEGY

- GROWTH STRATEGIES

- SERVICES

- CUSTOMERS

- SALES & MARKETING

- COMPETITION

- BUSINESS PRINCIPALS

- FINANCIAL PROJECTIONS

INTRODUCTION

Appian Way Communications Network is a rapidly growing ISP and systems integrator that targets middle-market businesses, educational institutions, the hospitality industry, and government organizations.

Our primary services include:

- dedicated Internet access through our highly reliable network, which provides our customers with Internet access that is "always on"
- wireless data services up to 5MB
- co-location services, in which we provide secure space to house customer-owned Internet equipment
- managed application hosting, in which we provide a server for the customer's exclusive use to install any software application the customer chooses
- custom Internet appliance solutions
- data center services include, among others, our co-location services and our managed application hosting services. These are similar to the services offered by computer service providers—or CSPs—which house, maintain, and supply power to their customers' Internet equipment.

We believe our growth and success in serving our target customer base is the direct result of our competitive strengths, including:

- a network that permits our customers to bypass congested Internet exchanges and access points and avoid Internet exchange breakdowns, increasing the speed and reliability of our customers' Internet connection
- Internet access that we can tailor to meet each customer's needs
- knowledgeable and responsive customer support by our network experts
- business Internet solutions that allow our customers to outsource a significant portion of their Internet technology and staff
- a senior management team with more than 20 years of combined experience in designing, implementing and managing teleCommunications Network.

INDUSTRY BACKGROUND & OPPORTUNITY

The Internet was originally conceived as a communications tool to be used by a limited number of researchers and academics. Today, it has escalated into a web of approximately 70 million interconnected users. The Internet has evolved from a static, text-based medium to a graphically rich communications infrastructure. The creation and rapid development of the desktop computer simplified access to the Internet, encouraging consumers to seek information through this new medium.

As the breadth of the information expanded, the Internet's applications and users grew as well. Businesses began investigating the potential of the Internet to reach the growing volume of customers on the Internet. To capture this emerging customer base, businesses needed a presence on the Internet and applications to facilitate electronic commerce.

The Internet Infrastructure

The Internet has emerged as a significant global business communications medium, enabling millions of people to communicate, publish and retrieve information, and conduct business electronically. A multi-tiered system of local, regional, and national ISPs has evolved to provide access to the Internet, transport data and, more recently, to provide value-added

Internet services. ISPs exchange data in packets generated by their customers through direct or indirect connections with other ISPs. To meet the needs of ISPs to exchange data at centralized points, large ISPs have established a series of central Internet exchanges, which facilitate the transmission of data.

Despite the relatively centralized nature of these exchange points, data traveling across the Internet often makes multiple connections or "hops" through a variety of local, regional, and national ISPs, as it moves from the originating site, through a central exchange point, and to its final destination. While these centralized points have the advantage of having dozens of ISPs interconnected and exchanging Internet data, they increasingly face congestion problems that cause significantly longer response times for a user.

In addition, because data traveling across the Internet must often make connections through multiple ISPs, the failure of a single ISP's Internet connection can interrupt a user's Internet transmission. Many ISPs have sought to improve data transmission reliability and speed by establishing private "peering connections" and network access points. This permits the ISPs to directly exchange Internet traffic while reducing the number of hops in their Internet connection and avoiding the often congested major Internet exchanges.

The Growth of the Internet

The Internet has experienced tremendous growth and has become a global medium for communications and commerce. According to International Data Corporation (or IDC) the ISP market in the United States reached $10.7 billion in 1998, representing a 43 percent increase over 1997 revenues. Business-related Internet operations generated approximately $2.9 billion of the $10.7 billion aggregate 1998 ISP revenue. Moreover, IDC predicts revenues generated by business-related ISPs will increase by 75.9 percent to $5.1 billion in 1999 and reach $12 billion by 2003, growing at a compound annual growth rate of 32.5 percent from 1998 to 2003. In addition, IDC estimates that the total value of goods and services purchased over the Internet will increase from $50.5 billion in 1998 to approximately $734 billion by the end of 2002.

Trends contributing to the growth of the business-related Internet market include:

- the increasing availability of high bandwidth capacity
- the proliferation of Internet access and ancillary Internet services
- the competitive need of small and mid-sized businesses to automate key business processes
- the convenience and speed of conducting business over the Internet
- the availability of Internet-enabled packaged software applications
- an increase in the amount and diversity of business and educational information available on the Internet and the web
- recent enhancements in the Internet's security and reliability

The demand generated by these new dynamics, combined with business customers' high quality service requirements, has fueled the growth of dedicated access connections and other Internet-related products and services for businesses.

Web Hosting and Co-Location

To realize the opportunities of the Internet, companies must develop an attractive Internet presence using a website that is easily accessible to potential customers. However, rapid Internet and technology growth have outpaced the ability of many businesses to develop the necessary internal information technology knowledge and tools.

A variety of companies, including web hosting companies and ISPs, have begun to focus on providing Internet co-location and other web-related services to their customers. Typically, companies offering these services build networks of numerous geographically dispersed data centers to be physically close to their customers. This reduces the cost of the services and the risk of transmission delay and data loss as data travels through multiple network connections. According to IDC, corporate Internet access and value-added services, such as web hosting and co-location, are the fastest-growing services offered by ISPs. Corporate access revenue and value-added services revenue were $5.9 billion in 1998 and are expected to grow to approximately $25 billion by 2003.

The Trend Toward Outsourcing of Internet Operations

Many businesses lack the resources and expertise to cost-effectively develop, maintain, and continually upgrade their network facilities and systems. Also, individuals with the expertise to establish and maintain sophisticated Internet technology are in great demand and their services are costly. Furthermore, businesses often find it difficult to keep up with new technologies and to integrate them into their infrastructure. Even if enterprises possess the necessary resources to accomplish these tasks, we believe that they often determine that this ongoing and significant investment in their own Internet technology and personnel is an inefficient use of their overall resources. Consequently, many enterprises are seeking outsourcing arrangements for their Internet needs. These arrangements allow enterprises to focus on their core operations, enhance the reliability and performance of their websites and reduce their Internet-related operating expenses.

The Convergence of Services in the Communications Industry

The traditional divisions within the communications industry are disappearing due to new regulations, customer demand, and technology evolution. Regulatory changes in the United States and around the world have opened the communications industry to increased competition. In particular, the Telecommunications Act of 1996 provides for comprehensive reform of telecommunications laws in the United States and is designed to foster competition in the local telecommunications marketplace.

With greater competition in the communications industry, customers have increasingly demanded that communications providers offer multiple services at lower prices. These services may include local and long-distance calling, wireless, Internet access, and high-speed dedicated lines. Also included are ancillary services such as single bill presentment, call forwarding, caller identification, voicemail, and similar services.

We believe that these integrated providers will increase efficiency in the deployment of communications services by selling multiple services in bundles over a single connection.

Enhancements in switching technologies are beginning to permit the delivery of numerous services over a single network, offering cost savings over traditional networks which were designed to deliver a limited number of services. We believe that as competition increases, providers who offer a range of services in a cost-effective manner will be best positioned to capitalize on the convergence of services within the communications industry. These providers will offer a well-designed package of services they can tailor to satisfy each customer's needs.

THE APPIAN WAY COMMUNICATIONS NETWORK STRATEGY

We intend to become a leader in providing businesses, educational institutions, and governmental organizations with high quality, cost-effective business solutions that will allow our customers to take advantage of the Internet without having to develop and maintain their own Internet technology and hire and retain an extensive Internet staff. To achieve this objective, we intend to continue to rely on the following core elements of our business strategy:

Providing Highly Reliable Internet Access

We intend to continue increasing the capacity, fault-tolerance, and geographic reach of our network to support customer growth. Our network is designed to respond quickly, be secure, and provide continuous availability to our clients. We can deliver our services to customers throughout the world from our Chicago data center. We connect our customers' Internet traffic to four very large ISPs who provide access to the central Internet exchanges. Our innovative network architecture often permits our customers' Internet traffic to bypass congested points on the Internet and avoid breakdowns at the Internet exchanges, which increases the speed and reliability of their Internet connection. We proactively manage and monitor traffic on the Internet and reroute traffic to provide high quality access.

Increasing the Percentage of Our Revenues from Value-Added Data Center Services

We intend to generate a higher percentage of our revenues from our value-added data center services, which typically provide higher margins than our Internet access services. We believe that value-added services are among the fastest-growing segments of the Internet marketplace. Our data center services provide a variety of options to our customers, and we work with their management and information technology teams to analyze their varied Internet service needs and choose the option that best addresses those needs.

We have offered our co-location services since September 1996, and as of December 1, 1999, we had 36 co-location customers. We have offered our managed application hosting services since September 1999, and, as of December 1, 1999, had six managed application hosting customers. We intend to emphasize our managed application hosting business in our marketing, and we have allocated greater resources to developing these services.

Targeting Middle Market Business, Educational, and Governmental Customers

The Internet service needs of middle market businesses, educational institutions, and governmental organizations differ significantly from those of the typical individual consumer because Internet access and related services are often critical to enterprise customers' businesses. They demand dedicated, high-speed Internet access and knowledgeable, prompt and responsive customer support. When marketing our services, we focus on creating the best solution to meet our customers' needs and not simply promoting our technology. Compared to individual consumers, enterprise customers are usually less price sensitive and more willing to pay a premium for custom solutions that meet their needs. As a result, we believe that providing services to enterprise customers generates greater revenues and higher margins per customer than servicing individual consumers.

Providing Superior Customer Support by Network Experts

Enterprise customers seeking broader access to the Internet increasingly face significant technological challenges, in part because the Internet is an evolving and rapidly growing medium. In addition, as new and more complex applications for the Internet are developed, we believe that even sophisticated users will increasingly encounter problems. Unlike many other ISPs who outsource their technical support to independent call centers, the Appian Way Communications Network, Ltd., professionals who implemented our network are among those who respond to and resolve customer inquiries and problems. We intend to continue providing superior customer support by hiring only customer support personnel who can demonstrate the ability to understand and manage our network. We believe that our strong emphasis on the superior customer support provided by our network experts has resulted in a high level of customer satisfaction and significant subscriber growth from customer referrals.

We intend to further develop our business by focusing on the core elements of our business strategy discussed above and pursuing the following key growth strategies:

GROWTH STRATEGIES

Expanding Our Network Nationally and Internationally

We intend to build more data centers and POPs in the United States and pursue international opportunities. We believe that having a number of widely distributed and networked data centers and POPs improves network performance and reliability. We intend to add data centers in the following metropolitan areas by the end of 2000: Washington, D.C., Houston, San Francisco, Cincinnati, New York, Seattle and Miami. We intend to establish data centers in Las Vegas and Paris by the end of the first quarter of 2001.

Before purchasing or leasing a new data center, we will evaluate the market opportunity in the proposed location by analyzing Internet usage statistics and specific economic criteria as well as pre-selling our services in that market. For any given location we expect to require at least six months to select the appropriate site, construct or acquire the necessary facilities, install equipment, and hire the operations and sales personnel needed to conduct business at the site. We have already identified suitable sites for some of our proposed data center locations. We also intend to supplement the data center expansion by establishing POPs throughout the United States and at various international sites to aggregate and transport traffic to and from our planned data centers.

Broadening Our Marketing Activities

We intend to expand our marketing efforts to increase our customer base. We also intend to increase market awareness of our name and our commitment to reliable service and superior customer support. Therefore, while continuing to encourage referrals from existing customers, we are increasing print publication, radio, outdoor, and direct mail advertising and telemarketing in targeted metropolitan areas.

Pursuing Strategic Sales and Distribution Alliances

We are pursuing strategic sales and distribution alliances in markets where there are substantial opportunities to attract new customers. We believe that establishing relationships with businesses that provide products and services which complement our service offerings will permit us to use their expertise and market access, while lowering our costs of entering new markets. These relationships will also give us additional customer referrals and new solutions to offer existing customers.

For example, we currently obtain customer referrals through our Valued Internet Partner, or VIP program, in which we pay our partners a fee for referring new customers who ultimately purchase our services. We will also pursue strategic alliances with value-added resellers or other authorized partners through our Appian Way Affiliate Partner (or AWAP) program, which permits others to resell our services directly to customers in specified markets. We intend to further expand our customer base by establishing additional distribution relationships with network integrators, value-added resellers, system vendors, consulting companies, and other ISPs.

Engaging in Strategic Acquisitions

We will continue to consider acquisitions of strategically located operations and customer lists and associated customer accounts. In addition, we may consider acquisitions of businesses, including other ISPs, with complementary products, services, or technologies. We may also consider acquisitions that can provide personnel who augment our team of network experts.

Eventually Becoming an Integrated Communications Provider, Offering Both Voice and Data Services

We plan to pursue a long-term strategy of providing a complete portfolio of voice and data communications services. To achieve our goal, we plan to become a competitive local exchange carrier, or CLEC, which would permit us to provide voice and other data services to complement our current services. We believe that technology advancements and customer preferences are driving the convergence of communications services toward service providers who can offer multiple communication services through a single network. We also believe that to remain competitive in the face of these changes, we must eventually become a single-source provider of voice and data communications services.

We create tailored solutions for our customers based on their business and technical requirements, modifying these solutions as our customers' needs evolve. Unlike many other ISPs that outsource their technical support to independent call centers, our highly reliable services are supported by our knowledgeable and responsive network experts, some of whom are the same professionals that implemented our network.

SERVICES

Our primary services include dedicated Internet access, co-location services, and managed application hosting. We also offer web hosting, e-mail services, and domain name services.

Our customer contracts require us to provide our services for a one-year, two-year, or three-year term and contain, among other things, a limited service level warranty related to the continuous availability of service on a 24-hours-per-day, seven-days-per-week basis, except for scheduled maintenance periods. This warranty provides a credit for free service for disruptions in our Internet access services. At the end of the term of a contract, a customer may elect to extend the contract's term on a month-to-month basis. Any change or upgrade in service, however, typically requires a new contract for a new term.

Our Internet access services are designed to deliver the ease of expansion, high availability, and performance required by moderate to high volume Internet operations that are central to a customer's business.

Internet Access

Through our co-location services, we provide secure space to house customer-owned Internet equipment. Based upon their business and technical requirements, customers may select from shared cabinet facilities, exclusive cabinets, or custom-built rooms with additional security features. All co-location facilities include dedicated electrical power circuits to ensure that we meet each customer's power requirements. Because the Internet operations of our co-location customers frequently require hardware and software upgrades, we give customers unlimited but secure access to their leased co-location space. Additional space, electrical power, and Internet services can be tailored to meet our customers' needs.

Co-location

Our Trenton, New Jersey, data center houses the computers that operate the core functions of our business, including communications equipment, data storage and retrieval systems, security software and hardware, and related customer support. Our data center provides customers with a secure, climate-controlled facility that they cannot readily or inexpensively create at their own place of business. The data center contains:

- a power supply with a back-up generator
- fire suppression and containment capabilities
- raised floors
- fully redundant HVAC
- high levels of physical security

We offer the following co-location services:

- **Switch Hotel**—A dedicated, enclosed custom-built room with separate dedicated power circuits, providing additional security via key-card entry, access barriers, motion camera and tiles bolted to the floor.

- **Cabinet Co-Location**—Mid-level service providing an exclusive cabinet for the customer. This is an economical solution for customers co-locating multiple servers.
- **Server Co-Location**—Entry-level service providing an economical solution for customers co-locating a single server. The customer's server shares space in a cabinet with the servers of other customers.

We intend to open new data centers in Washington, D.C., Houston, San Francisco, Cincinnati, New York, Seattle and Miami before the end of 2000. We believe our data centers will be an important factor in attracting customers and marketing our data center services.

Managed Application Hosting

Our managed application hosting service, which we first introduced in September 1999, provides a server for the customer's exclusive use to install any software application the customer chooses. In addition, we will provide all required maintenance on the server hardware. This service, which is similar to the services being offered by computer service providers (CSPs) is targeted to businesses with high volumes of Internet traffic and with Internet-based applications and web services that are extremely important to their daily operations.

Unlike typical web hosting operations that host multiple customers' websites on a single server, we provide our managed application hosting services with only one customer per server. As a result, a customer need not be concerned about how its actions or applications might impact other customers' applications housed on the same server, or how its server might be affected by other customers' actions or applications.

Our managed application hosting services offer a suite of applications from leading software vendors that is designed to meet the Internet operations needs of middle market companies. We also offer proprietary e-commerce and web development software as additional options for our managed application customers. We presently offer these software products only in conjunction with our managed application hosting services. We implement the applications selected by the customer in our data center, configure them to meet the needs of the customer, and package them with a server, security, Internet access, back-up, and operational support. A customer may also use software applications it obtains from others on the server we provide to the customer in our data center.

Our managed application hosting services are compatible with the products of many leading hardware and software system vendors, including Cobalt Networks, VA Linux Systems, Hewlett-Packard Company, Sun Microsystems, Silicon Graphics, Microsoft Corporation, and Macromedia Corporation. This multi-vendor flexibility enables our customers to select their own technical solutions and to integrate their Internet operations with their existing information technology. We offer our customers four different levels of managed application hosting service that range from simple to comprehensive solutions, each of which can be tailored to meet the specific needs of a given customer. In addition, our customers can augment their services with hardware or software that we provide or software that they purchase directly from others.

The Portable, Instant Internet

Ever think about using the Internet "on the fly" to look up information or send a quick e-mail? How many times have you not gone online because of the inconvenience of sitting down at your PC, turning it on, waiting for it to boot, clicking on an ISP icon, and waiting again for your modem to dial in and connect?

But imagine simply picking up a device the size of a clipboard, switching it on, and being instantly online from the comfort of your couch, kitchen table, or backyard lounge chair. What if you could access the Internet when you wanted, where you wanted, without using a PC or an appliance that competes with your TV program?

Using the National Semiconductor GEODE™, Appian Way Communications Network has developed AXCESS-NOW™, a working prototype for a powerful, convenient Internet access device that can make web browsing as easy as using the telephone. AXCESS-NOW™ will allow you to tap into the vast universe of information available on the Internet, wherever you are in and around the house.

A Powerful Concept for Portable Access

For example, if you're in the kitchen, use AXCESS-NOW™ to find a great dinner recipe online in minutes. If you're working on your car and need to know the answer to a diagnostic problem, get online with AXCESS-NOW™ right in your garage. If you're watching baseball and want to compare stats or find out more about the team, AXCESS-NOW™ can connect you to the Internet quickly and conveniently.

AXCESS-NOW™ isn't designed to replace conventional PCs as a productivity tool. Rather, it complements the PC as a single-application device, making it more convenient for Internet users to send or receive e-mail, chat, or browse websites instantly. Its portability and ease of use delivers the ultimate Internet experience.

Appian Way Communications Network is providing AXCESS-NOW™ to its customers by designing specific applications and developing their own Internet access devices with a variety of features and connection options.

Design Features for Single Application Use

AXCESS-NOW™ employs sophisticated wireless (radio frequency) data transmission technology to make it a truly mobile device, providing convenience similar to that of a cordless telephone. As an example an AXCESS-NOW™ could be 1.3 pounds, 6" x 9" featuring an LCD touchscreen supporting high-resolution graphics. Additionally, it comes with a stylus, enabling users to navigate the web using AXCESS-NOW's touchscreen technology.

AXCESS-NOW™ is completely integrated and sealed: There are no internal parts that can be upgraded, added, or removed, and there is no software to load. It's designed with dual Universal System Bus (USB) ports to add peripheral options such as a keyboard, mouse, printer, or gaming input device. While there are no disk or floppy drives, and no PC Card slots, the design would support these items if a customer application needed to feature them.

The AXCESS-NOW™ design includes three components: The AXCESS-NOW™ mobile display tablet, the charging unit, and a base station transceiver that can be plugged into any power outlet near an RJ-11 telephone jack. Depending upon how clients choose a solution, it could use a coaxial cable Internet connection as well. The design can support DSL and ISDN as well as cable and legacy 56K interconnect protocols, and it is Ethernet network ready. Eventually, pending availability of such services, "persistent" or instant-on service similar to cable television will be available, enabling users to pick up AXCESS-NOW™ and turn it on with instant, no dial-up access.

The transceiver base station, which delivers the Internet data via RF signals to the hand-held AXCESS-NOW™ unit, can be tucked out of sight or placed among other home entertainment system components. The charging unit is an inconspicuous desktop cradle similar to those that come with cordless telephones.

AXCESS-NOW™ is designed to carry a charge for up to six hours, with 20 hours of standby (out of cradle) power. It has a range of up to 500 feet from the base station, allowing freedom of mobility throughout a house, office, or even the immediate neighborhood. It will provide the Internet access of a PC in a product as portable and easy to use as a cordless phone.

Making Information Access Available

There are still variables that will determine when such a device will find favor in a vast numbers of homes and offices around the U.S. For example, one factor in mass-market acceptance of AXCESS-NOW™ devices is the maturation of the telecom and datacom industry infrastructures to support persistent Internet connections.

But with the acceptance of devices such as the VCR, the cellular telephone, and compact disc/DVD players, the industry won't be far behind in providing the technology infrastructure necessary to make AXCESS-NOW™ a reality. And in time, these and other technological improvements will likely bring the cost of AXCESS-NOW™ devices into a comfortable price range for consumers. Similarly, Internet services are very likely to evolve into either cable- or telephone-based access standards that will make persistent Internet connections possible.

CUSTOMERS

Most of our customers are middle-market businesses, educational institutions, independent hotels or chains, and governmental organizations, but our customer base also includes other ISPs and several larger companies. The Internet service needs of our target customers differ significantly from those of typical individual consumers. Enterprises often view their Internet access and related services as critical to their business. They demand dedicated, high-speed Internet access and knowledgeable, prompt and often highly technical customer support.

When marketing our services, we focus on creating the best solutions to meet our customers' needs and not simply promoting our technology. We work with our customers' management and information technology teams to analyze their Internet needs and create solutions to specifically address those needs. Compared to individual consumers, enterprise customers are usually less price sensitive and more willing to pay a premium for creative solutions crafted to meet their needs. As a result, we believe that providing Internet services to enterprise customers generates greater revenues and higher margins per customer than servicing individual consumers.

As of September 1, 1999, we had 250 customers. We provide service to a number of enterprises, including:

- Houston Convention and Visitors' Bureau
- National League Baseball Player's Association
- Las Vegas Chamber of Commerce
- St. Louis Chamber of Commerce
- Adam's Mark Hotel
- Smith, Black, and Davis, CPAs

SALES AND MARKETING

We sell our services through a consultative approach developed by our management team based on their cumulative business experience. We use local technology-oriented sales personnel to understand individual customer needs and make the proper recommendations regarding tailored Internet-based solutions. The local field sales staff is supported by our in-house tele-sales staff based at our corporate headquarters in Chicago.

We refer to our employees who use the telephone to directly market and sell our services as our tele-sales staff. We use our tele-sales staff or our CAP partners, discussed below, to complete sales to smaller customers and to target customers in markets where we do not have field sales staff. In addition, we hire independent telemarketing firms to generate business leads. To support our sales efforts, we have also begun a new advertising and media campaign to build awareness of our name and quality of service. We intend to expand our field sales force, further develop our indirect distribution channels, and use telemarketing firms to increase sales leads and grow our customer base.

Field Sales

Our field sales force consists of technically competent, locally based, and experienced Internet sales representatives. These individuals have strong Internet technical backgrounds and understand the local telecommunications tariffs as well as the needs of their local business communities. In general, members of our field sales staff pursue leads generated by our telemarketing campaign and our outdoor advertising efforts. Our field sales personnel also make "cold calls" on potential customers. Most larger sales are closed by a field salesperson who visits the customer. We believe that this localized approach allows us to provide better solutions for our customers' needs.

Tele-sales

We are looking to staff a phone room to contact smaller potential customers in the geographic areas we serve as well as potential customers in new markets. We expect our tele-sales staff to develop the interest of large customers and close sales to small customers without requiring a face-to-face meeting between the customer and a member of our field sales force.

Indirect Sales

We are developing relationships with partners, including value-added resellers, network integrators, and web design companies, to use the expertise of their established sales organizations to help increase our sales. As an example, our Valued Internet Partner (or VIP program) is an agency relationship that offers referral fees to VIP partners who bring us sales opportunities that ultimately result in sales of our services. We intend to expand the VIP program into each new market area we enter.

Also, our Appian Way Affiliate Partner program (AWAP program) allows authorized partners to resell our services and maintain a direct relationship with customers in their local markets. In markets we have not identified as a high priority for our network expansion, we forward leads directly to our AWAP partners so they can arrange a visit to the customer. We provide service and technical support 24 hours a day, every day of the year and invoice the partners at a reduced rate, allowing them to profit from the resale of our services.

Internet Sales

We use the Internet as another source to generate sales. Our tele-sales staff handles many inquiries regarding our services received via e-mail, either closing the sale or passing the leads to our field sales force. We are internally developing systems and applications that will allow us to receive, accept, and implement sales electronically via the Internet.

Telemarketing

We will begin a telemarketing campaign in March 2000 using an outside telemarketing firm that we pay on an hourly basis. We also compensate the firm with performance-based bonuses. We create a sales script used by the telemarketers and train all telemarketing personnel. Our telemarketing program seeks to generate leads from small to medium-sized businesses that are pre-qualified for our services in our market areas. We may establish an internal telemarketing department to ensure the quality of our sales efforts.

Strategic Marketing and Reseller Alliances

We enter into strategic marketing and reseller alliances with partners to bundle and sell our services with those of the partners. For example, our agreement allows us to resell Potter's unique national dial-up service—MIA—bundled with our Internet access service. In addition, MIA jointly funds our marketing efforts for national dial-up services in geographic areas where this service can be offered. MIA also promotes our services as one of a dedicated number of its Internet access referral partners.

Branding

As a component of our marketing efforts, we plan to invest aggressively in building the Appian Way Communications Network brand. We will begin an outdoor and radio advertising campaign in the markets we currently serve. We intend to increase customer awareness of us and our services through an integrated marketing plan, which combines online and traditional advertising in business and trade publications, trade show participation, direct mail, and public relations campaigns.

COMPETITION

In addition to other national, regional, and local ISPs, our current and prospective competitors include long distance and local exchange telecommunications carriers, cable television operators and their affiliates, satellite, and wireless communications companies and providers of co-location and other data center services. We also anticipate that if we offer services as a CLEC, we will face new competitors that already have established a market presence for local telecommunications access.

The principal competitive factors in our market include:

- Internet system engineering expertise and advanced technical functions
- price of services
- availability and quality of customer service and support
- timing of introductions of new services
- network capability
- network security
- reliability of services
- financial resources
- variety and quality of services
- ease of expansion
- ability to maintain, expand, and add new distribution channels
- broad geographic presence
- brand name
- conformity with industry standards

ISPs

Our primary competitors include other ISPs with a significant national presence that focus on business customers, such as GTE Internetworking, PSINet, Concentric Network, MindSpring Enterprises, Verio and Intermedia Internet. We also compete with smaller regional and local ISPs in our targeted geographic regions such as Knit-Wit and Glendale. Our customer base includes smaller ISPs, which may also compete with us for customers in their markets.

Value-Added Services Providers

As we increasingly generate revenues from our value-added data center services, competition from other value-added service providers will become more intense. Our competitors in this market include co-location providers like Oasis Communications, Western EarthCenter, Digit 7, and ITJump. They also include application service providers such as I-Fleet and Market Networks.

All of the major long distance companies—including AT&T, MCI Worldcom, and Sprint—offer Internet access services and compete with us. The relatively recent sweeping reforms in the federal regulation of the telecommunications industry brought about by the Telecommunications Act of 1996 have created greater opportunities for local exchange carriers, including the regional Bell operating companies, to enter the Internet access market.

We believe that many long-distance and local telecommunications carriers will seek to acquire ISPs, enter into joint ventures with them, and purchase Internet access wholesale from ISPs to address the Internet access requirements of those carriers' current enterprise customers. Worldcom's acquisition of UUNET, GTE's acquisition of BBN, and Cable & Wireless's acquisition of InternetMCI are indicative of this trend. Accordingly, we expect to experience increased competition from the traditional large telecommunications carriers.

Telecommunications Carriers

Many of the major cable television operators, such as MediaOne, have begun to offer or have announced an intention to offer Internet access through their existing cable infrastructure. Seeking to take advantage of this installed cable infrastructure and the Internet access opportunities it affords, many telecommunications providers have acquired cable companies, such as AT&T's acquisition of TCI and @Home.

While many cable companies are faced with large-scale upgrades of their existing plant equipment and infrastructure to support connections to the Internet and become competitive, we believe that some smaller enterprise customers may be attracted by the combined services already being offered by cable operators. Other alternative service communications companies have also announced plans to enter the Internet access market with various wireless and satellite services and technologies.

Cable Operators, Direct Broadcast Satellite, and Wireless Communications Companies

Appian Way Communications Network is the result of a joint marketing effort of two independent companies: Majestic Digital and GVC Communications, Inc.

BUSINESS PRINCIPALS

Majestic Digital (MD) is an Internet management and services company which provides Internet strategy consulting and comprehensive technology solutions to Fortune companies and other corporate users of information technology. MD helps businesses identify how the Internet can be used to their competitive advantage and use our expertise in creative design and systems engineering to design, develop, and deploy advanced Internet applications and solutions.

Majestic Digital

Through its KOOR™ program, MD acts in the capacity for many high-tech and Internet based start-up and established businesses. In this capacity MD carries out the following mission:

- To provide technology vision and leadership for developing and implementing IT initiatives that create and maintain leadership for the enterprise in a constantly changing and intensely competitive marketplace.
- To report to a senior functional executive (EVP, COO, CFO) or CEO.
- To help the organization shape and develop IT policies and IT strategy with the idea of coordination of its business strategies.

Majestic Digital Project Responsibilities

- Business technology planning process—sponsor collaborative planning processes
- Applications development—new and existing for enterprise initiatives and overall coordination for SBU/divisional initiatives

- Partnerships—establishing strategic relationships with key IT suppliers and consultants
- Technology transfer—provide enabling technologies that make it easier for customers and suppliers to do business with our enterprise as well as increase revenue and profitability

MD's principal architect is David Stryker. From 1996 to March 1999, Mr. Stryker served as President and Chief Executive Officer of DigitJive Technologies, Inc., a computer telephony integration (CTI) based systems integration company that was sold to a publicly traded company named TKN. DigitJive created and developed a global systems architecture that allowed a user to access their e-mail text-to-speech via any touch-tone or cellular telephone. The company also developed an international data network that had an emphasis in telemedicine, which was accessible via telephone.

Prior to founding DigitJive, Mr. Stryker served as chief technology officer at LuftMark Corporation where he developed customer service plans following TQM protocols, and created and implemented the systems architecture for online systems. He was responsible for negotiating and developing strategic alliances and software site-licenses. He founded Diamond D Information Systems in 1991. This company provided consulting services in information technology and financial information systems, including LAN/WAN design online systems and the design and construction of Waterloo Computers. Diamond D was sold in early 1995.

Mr. Stryker brings significant experience in the areas of strategic planning, project management, systems architecture, and sales and marketing. Additionally, Mr. Stryker has written and published several white papers in the areas of e-commerce, knowledge management, and executive information management. Mr. Stryker received his Bachelor of Science degree in International Business from Texas A&M University.

GVC Communications

Products and Services Offered by the Company

- website development
- website hosting
- mail hosting
- nationwide dial-up access
- computer sales
- computer service depot
- dedicated access
- co-location of servers

GVC Communications Certifications

- Solomon Accounting Software
- MicroBiz Point-of-sale Software
- MetaInfo Server Software
- IBM Business Partner
- Hewlett Packard Business Partner and Warranty Service Center
- Data General Business Partner
- Microsoft Product Specialist

Hernando Browning—Hernando Browning has over 12 years sales, operations, and information management experience. From 1989 to 1991 Hernando held several different management positions with Berwett Computers, finishing his time there as Repair Depot Sales Director. After leaving Berwett Hernando started his own consulting group, and serviced the business community with a specialty in Point of Sales systems and LAN installations. GVC was founded by Hernando in 1997.

Hernando also has an outstanding record for public and military service. He served as a police officer for Hamilton County in Cincinnati, Ohio, and enjoyed a 13-year career in the United States Air Force. He is a decorated veteran of the Desert Storm conflict and is currently on active duty with the Ohio National Guard. Hernando's specialties include strategic planning, network design and installation, procurement, and network operations.

Ken Gillette—Ken Gillette has over 12 years of operations and information management experience. As a solutions integrator he designed and implemented a system for a major Fortune 100 firm that helped them settle over 35,000 bankruptcy claims between 1991 and 1993. Ken then developed and implemented various systems for the federal court system between 1993 and 1995.

In 1995 Ken went to work for the accounting firm of Slinger, Bastian & Klip, LLP where he managed the information systems for the Chicago office of this prestigious firm. Ken continued here until 1999 when he formed his own consulting group and joined GVC as its Chief Operating Officer.

Ken has a strong background in systems development, network planning, and installation of both hardware and cabling.

Tim Sullivan—Tim Sullivan has been an attorney in Wyoming since 1979, first practicing under the shingle of Yemen Hottsfer III. Since 1984 Tim has practiced law under his own name, specializing in real estate and corporate and commercial law (both transactional and litigation).

Tim graduated from Ohio State University with a B.A. in Marketing, and then obtained his J.D. in 1979 from the University of Cincinnati Law School.

- IT infrastructure and architecture (e.g., computers and networks)
- Training—provide training for all IT users to ensure productive use of existing and new systems
- Customer satisfaction—interact with internal and external clients to ensure continuous customer satisfaction

GVC Communications Principals

GVC Communications Responsibilities

**FINANCIAL
PROJECTIONS**

	2000	2001	2002
Income			
Small business	$6,856,000	$32,280,000	$65,560,000
Consumer	$2,224,000	$14,120,000	$28,240,000
Total Retail	**$9,080,000**	**$46,400,000**	**$93,800,000**
Hospitality	$2,101,680	$6,104,880	$10,008,000
Equipment Sales	$3,600,000	$16,000,000	$33,000,000
Total Income	**$14,781,680**	**$68,504,880**	**$136,808,000**
Expenses			
Research and Development	$1,978,168	$6,450,488	$12,680,800
Infrastructure	$1,016,421	$6,606,527	$13,975,264
Sales and Marketing	$3,445,420	$16,126,220	$32,702,000
Overhead	$5,912,672	$25,801,952	$51,723,200
Total Expenses	**$12,352,681**	**$48,985,187**	**$111,081,264**
Pre-tax Income	$2,428,999	$19,519,693	$25,726,736
Subscriber Base	224,000	1,120,000	2,240,000
Wireless Installations	28	35	44

Internet Software Company

BUSINESS PLAN   POGGLE, INC.

14001 Harmony Street
San Diego, California 92101

Poggle's vision is to develop software to improve information retrieval and in so doing to provide total freedom and access to stored information, regardless of the language used to create or search for the information. It is the company's vision to extend this capability beyond normal computing boundaries to include text as well as voice recognition information usage.

- EXECUTIVE SUMMARY

- MARKETING PLAN

- SALES PLAN

- ORGANIZATION & OPERATIONS

- FINANCIAL PROJECTIONS

**EXECUTIVE
SUMMARY
Overview**

E-business today has embodied an electronic transformation of our culture. This transformation has emerged in the use of technology, which has become pervasive throughout our daily life. One of the problems that this use of technology has brought to us is the user unfriendliness that is often its byproduct. One of the latest trends has been to enable users to utilize technology more effectively, with less hassle and to make technology transparent in its use.

Intrigued by the communication and language barriers that would prevent e-business from flourishing, Poggle decided to invent a software technology to overcome the situation. There are over 6,000 languages spoken today in 288 countries. Poggle set out to build a software engine that could easily and quickly facilitate the use of these languages in e-business environments. Poggle subsequently introduced a product at an October 2000 international exhibition to enthusiastic crowds that waited in long lines to see live demonstrations of their technology.

The result has been an overwhelming success. Poggle's new technology has resulted in several new products that are destined to transform the degree to which international users utilize e-business. Poggle's focus is to extend this technology beyond language and geographical boundaries, allowing anyone to participate, be connected to, and effectively utilize the global e-business community.

Poggle has subsequently positioned itself as a dynamic, exciting, growth-oriented software company that designs and develops software focused on making user environments easier and friendlier to use. Today, Poggle's suite of products support the same functionality in multiple languages. Poggle's focus is to make cross-language communication the defacto standard for the future of e-business.

**Poggle's Vision—To
Improve Information
Retrieval**

Poggle's vision is to develop software to improve information retrieval and in so doing to provide total freedom and access to stored information, regardless of the language used to create or search for the information. It is the company's vision to extend this capability beyond normal computing boundaries to include text as well as voice recognition information usage.

Furthermore, the company's vision includes becoming an e-industry leader in designing communication enhancement' products and services that facilitate e-business, Internet usage, and electronic communication transactions.

Accurate and timely access to information has always been essential for companies and individuals to make sound business decisions. One of the problems on the Internet today is that companies in general have neglected to address the impediments users face when accessing required information in a multilingual global economy. Additionally, Internet users are easily disconnected if they make a simple typographical error or misspell the website names they want to connect with. Poggle's vision is to address this information discontinuity with a solution designed specifically to enhance capability and functionality while improving user friendliness.

In this rapidly changing information age, businesses have been hindered by the "dead-ends" prohibiting the flow of accurate and timely information. As the Internet continues to grow, so does the demand for a more streamlined and time efficient use of the web. Without using the exact website address format or if the search entry contains foreign characters or errors, Internet users are not able to search and retrieve the precise information they are seeking. This is where Poggle comes in.

Poggle's mission is to enhance e-business communication by developing premium products and services utilizing Poggle's technology. Initially, major goals are to provide products that enhance the Internet experience. The Internet itself does not drive the entire world of e-business, but it is a substantial place to start. Ultimately, the company intends to develop products that enhance non-Internet related e-business transactions, and through these to set the standard for the next generation of e-business software technologies.

Specifically in relation to the Internet, Poggle plans to address the difficulties that international e-business customers currently face. Poggle's mission includes:

- Making Access to Information Easier (Enterprise Business)
- Improve Communication and Data Exchange (Business to Business)
- Connect People Worldwide (Business to Consumer)
- Help businesses reach worldwide audiences (Business to Consumer, Business to Business)
- Enhance Internet communication by developing premium products and services

Poggle's Mission

In e-business today, a loyal customer is one that has had a satisfying experience. Poggle defines satisfaction in this area as having four components: Accuracy, Availability, Advisory, and Partnership.

- Accuracy—The focus of Poggle's products is to deliver accurate information in a timely manner.
- Availability—Poggle's products are designed to facilitate availability of information to market sectors that previously would have had difficulty in accessing that information.
- Advisory—The company's products deliver content that is advisory in nature. In so doing, the customer is assured of a quality response to the information they are seeking.
- Partnership—Poggle remains focused on collaborating with its customers in order to assure that those customers receive the highest level of service available.

Poggle's Focus—Customer Satisfaction

Poggle's strategic growth plan is comprised of three components that will enable the company to obtain its goal as a leading designer, developer, and marketer of low cost, high quality intelligent software.

- The first component is internal new product development. Poggle will develop software for its competitive market edge.
- The second component is external integration of Poggle products into potential strategic business partners' browsers, e-mail systems, websites, wireless devices and applications, global telephone systems and directories, home entertainment devices and database packages.
- The third component is aggressive sales and marketing. Poggle intends to develop a sales and marketing campaign focused primarily on the U.S. Fortune 1000, as well as the top 1,000 international companies, end users of those companies, and their affiliates.

Marketing & Growth Strategies

Poggle's products are unique in the capabilities they bring to market. There is no direct competition for the company's products. Poggle's products are focused on the globalization of information distribution and access, while competitor's products are more niche focused.

Competitive Summary

Business Model

Poggle's business model is comprised of three components, Participate, Connect, and Utilize.

- Participate—Poggle's products allow users from any geographic location or verbal language to participate fully in the global e-business community.
- Connect—Poggle's products facilitate international users' connection to e-business, for these users will no longer face a language or spelling barrier.
- Utilize—Poggle's products allow any user to effectively utilize e-business by making it user-friendlier. Being able to communicate in your natural language without worrying about misspelling will greatly enhance users' experience of e-business.

Operations

An in-house staff of individuals with extensive experience in all related industries will comprise the operational team. These individuals will have, at a minimum, the following expertise:

- Product Development—focused on the ability to develop and package software products and bring those products to market.
- Marketing—extensive knowledge of merchandising, promotions, advertising, sales, operations, and planning.
- Sales—strong administration and order processing capabilities coupled with day-to-day sales management expertise.
- Accounting—extensive capabilities in cash flow management, budgeting, and managing receivables in addition to forecasting.

Each of these operational divisions will share a focus on success, achievement, and the creation and maintenance of value and customer satisfaction.

Management Team

The company's management team consists of three highly skilled individuals who together founded the company in September 2000. These individuals have extensive knowledge and expertise in the technology behind Poggle's applications. Furthermore, they share a vision for Poggle's future and they excel at keeping the company on track to achieving that vision.

As the company grows, the three founders intend to bring on an executive team skilled in the daily operations as well as the strategic and tactical management and oversight of the organization. The founders intend to then divide their talents to areas best served by them.

Financial Requirement and Use

The company is seeking pre-IPO equity/debt funding of $1.6 million in order to launch and promote the company's products and services. The company is projecting net profit of $944,000 on $3.4 million gross, or approximately 29% of sales, over the course of the first 12 months of operation.

Summary

Today's e-business landscape is one that is painted with many companies in many geographies worldwide. In this environment, there is no real solution to the language barriers that exist to totally effective use of e-business.

Poggle's vision is to facilitate global e-business by providing applications and tools that will dissolve the barriers created by the multi-lingual global economy. No company ever has taken on this challenge and presented a solution that is both affordable and easy to access and use. This is what differentiates Poggle's approach and is what generates the value that Poggle intends to bring to market.

This business plan represents management's best current estimate of the potential of the business. It must be recognized that no business is free of major risks and few business plans are free of errors of omission or commission.

MARKETING PLAN

Market Overview

In its simplest sense, e-business is the use of technologies to improve and transform key business processes. Most companies understand this and are on their way in the evolution from traditional business practices to e-business. They have begun to technologically enable core processes to strengthen customer service operations, streamline supply chains, and reach existing and new customers. The accessibility and broad reach of technology has forever changed customers' expectations regarding support and response. Customers today expect accurate, round-the-clock service. Hence, the requirement for a massively scalable, reliable, and secure electronic foundation that includes reliable and available servers, industry-leading software and middleware, and worldwide consulting services from experts with industry-specific knowledge—all supported by a scalable and robust infrastructure.

In a few short years, e-business has gone from concept to undeniable reality. The reason behind this is that it works for everyone: consumers, businesses, and governments. The primary values of e-business—cost savings, revenue growth, and customer satisfaction—are proving to be just the tip of the iceberg. Having realized the benefit of technologically enabling individual business processes, many companies are now seeking further return on investment by integrating new and existing e-business applications and technologies. For example, two billion Internet-ready devices like smart phones, PDAs, and other pervasive computing applications are expected to be in consumers' hands in the next two years. These devices and applications are prime candidates to better serve customers and improve efficiency. The key to success is finding a way to give customers what they want without the expense of traditional business operations.

Once a business e-business-enables its operations, it can find itself in new terrain, where all of its competitors and customers are also operating as e-businesses (by 2003, the Net will generate two billion dollars in sales). At that point, "buy, sell, trade online" does not apply just to stocks and financial units, but to many transactions in which an enterprise engages. These e-marketplaces have already proven to be the most fluid and changing aspect of e-business leading the next generation of the technology landscape.

International E-Business and Internet Growth

The growth of e-business will drive much more than just the use of the Internet. In the United States, the growth of the Internet is expected to slow down somewhat due to saturation. At the same time, the outlook for growth internationally is excellent. Once the rest of the world comes online, the Internet will face infrastructure issues. One of the qualities that makes the Internet unique—its unstructured approach—is proving to be one of its greatest challenges.

As the Internet grows to billions of users, its infrastructure will need to be improved dramatically to make it more scalable and secure. Small business Internet access projections show that Internet usage will be 54 percent of the population by the end of 2001. A worldwide Internet population forecast by IDC indicates that there will be half a billion Internet users by 2003. This opens the door to companies like Poggle that have developed products designed to simplify the Internet's infrastructure, or at least how that infrastructure is perceived by individual users. It's not the infrastructure that exists that is the problem, it's the user-friendliness of being able to access and effectively utilize that infrastructure, and that is where Poggle comes into the picture.

Worldwide Internet revenue estimates indicate that the United States and Western Europe will lead the way in Internet commerce. The United States currently has almost 60 percent of Internet traffic. This leaves a tremendous amount of growth for international users.

Market Trends

The number of websites, e-mail users, and size of databases increases daily. Customers want a user-friendly online experience, however, this is becoming more difficult because of the sheer number of users. Certain trends have begun to surface that prove the need for Poggle's products. These include:

1. An American Internet user survey found that about 15.9 million Americans using the Internet during 1997 canceled their Internet service because web surfing and e-mailing were too difficult.
2. Existing Internet search engines do not tolerate typographical errors that users typically make such as adding an extra period or omitting a dot or comma in a website address.
3. Online customers are less than satisfied when they find shopping malls bottlenecked with data and language barriers.
4. Navigating through a complex network of more than 1 billion web pages full of structured content becomes more frustrating for the Internet user. Since more websites and pages appear while others change faster than search engines can index them, Internet users fail to make the right connection as no search engine has indexed more than 33 percent of them.
5. Misspelled product and company names with less than 100 percent accurate web addresses lead users to dead ends. This creates frustration for the end user and means a loss of sales revenue for the company.
6. Current search engines are not everything that they profess to be. They do not address a user's grammar, spelling, frequency of word use, etc. Search engines are important to Internet use, but they are intolerant of human errors.

The Poggle Business Model

The purpose of Poggle's business model is to explain the overall philosophy of how the company intends to develop, market, and sell its products. Poggle's business model is comprised of three essential ingredients that, when combined, create a powerful central theme: Participate, Connect, and Utilize.

- **Participate**—Poggle products are designed to enhance users' participation in the global e-business economy. Prior to Poggle's applications, an international user whose first language was not English started with a disadvantage. Now with Poggle applications, this user will be able to participate more fully, without having to worry about their English spelling capabilities.
- **Connect**—Poggle products enable users in any location worldwide to connect to technology (such as the Internet) and take full advantage of search engine capabilities, without having to worry about spelling, or about the Internet addresses relating to the information they seek.
- **Utilize**—Poggle products allow users to more fully utilize the e-business technologies such as the Internet. Poggle's software enables users to work more effectively, moving into the background many functions that previously took a great deal of time and effort to utilize.

There are technological changes taking place in the development of information retrieval and processing. These changes are quickly altering the way Internet technology is processed. Poggle is faced primarily with indirect competition from the companies that offer the information process capability.

Poggle is primarily an Application Services Provider (ASP). The ASP business model is one where the company hosts their application on their website and offers other applications, or users, access to that software remotely. In addition to the ASP model, Poggle products also fit into the Client-Server model, where a remote application makes calls to a centralized application (in this case the remote application is Poggle's browser plug in, and the centralized application is Poggle's ASP software).

Competitive Analysis

Being successful in the highly competitive e-business marketplace today is not about the creativity of the idea or even the capability and functionality of the technology. What makes one company successful over another is how effective their technology is at enabling users and creating value for them. Too many companies have assumed that just because they have a catchy idea or a useful product in their minds, that the public will also think so.

Poggle's technology is practically assured of success because its focus is communications, which is the core focus of e-business. By facilitating enhanced communications, Poggle products will create more efficiency and productivity and will spark a new level of inter-global e-business operations. This success will also be Poggle's success.

Conclusion

SALES PLAN

Selling Strategies

The sales strategy that Poggle intends to undertake is a multifaceted approach utilizing front-end and back-end revenue streams. Front-end revenue streams are those that are paid directly by the users who will directly utilize Poggle's ASP software from the Poggle website. Back-end revenue streams are those where incremental "value-added" services are utilized by companies and partners and where Poggle makes some kind of commission or referral fee from their use. Additional back-end revenue streams include services that are utilized transparently and visitors to the Poggle website, such as advertising and click-through revenues.

Front-end revenue streams are comprised of the direct sales of Poggle products.

Front-End Revenue

The following revenue streams comprise back-end incremental revenue that are not considered to be the primary sources of income for Poggle, but nonetheless will generate limited income.

Back-End Revenue

- Licensing Programs—Strategic partnerships with leading companies that want to build Poggle's software into their products will create licensing opportunities for the company.
- Products and Services Sold to the Poggle User Community—The company will feature specific products and/or services on the company's website that are relevant to the interests of the Poggle user community. These products will generate additional income for Poggle while providing niche-targeted incremental value to Poggle users.
- Click-Through Incremental Revenue—The company will allow content focused banner advertising on its website that brings incremental value to Poggle users. The company will be remunerated for each "click-through" that a user follows from the Poggle site.

- Sponsorships/Co-Branding—The company will sponsor specific opportunities, products, or services that bring incremental value to the Poggle users. Additionally, Poggle will co-brand other incremental products and/or services.

Strategic Partners

Poggle values strategic partnerships and sees them as a way to leverage brand identity while bringing the company's software to large numbers of existing users with minimal marketing efforts on Poggle's behalf. Additionally, Poggle views its strategic partners as all having value-added technology where Poggle's technology, combined with that owned by the strategic partner, together creates a more powerful value proposition than either could separately.

Strategic partners will be added as the company continues to grow. Strategic partnerships that are currently under development include the following companies: Excite, Lycos, InfoSeek, and Yahoo!

Advertising Plan

Poggle's advertising plan is to take heavy advantage of Internet based advertising campaigns, specifically focused on search engine sites. Additionally, Poggle will take advantage of traditional advertising media's as well, including newspaper, magazine, and possibly radio and television depending on projected growth.

Promotions and Public Relations

The public relations strategy has been to create a brand identity for Poggle with the public and business community.

Launch plans include a Media Tour in the top five "global markets" including China, Japan, Korea, the Middle East, and non-Latin Europe. This will give Poggle an opportunity to personally meet with distinguished members of the trade and consumer press and provide them with one-on-one demonstrations.

Online publicity will increase with the launch announcement, distribution of the free download, and online interviews of Poggle's management team. Press relations will continue with high-tech print trade publications, editors, online e-zines, and press releases, awards programs, high-tech analysts, media events, radio, TV, web casts, editorial reviews/calendars, tradeshows, and promotional opportunities.

ORGANIZATION & OPERATIONS

Organization

MANAGEMENT TEAM

Poggle's management team has a wide degree of experience in different corporate focuses. The current team is comprised of the three founders of the company. Their core strengths are in the engineering and software development areas. Once fully funded, Poggle intends to hire an experience management team to oversee operations of the company and to assure financial projections are met.

Operations

PRODUCT DEVELOPMENT

The product development department is responsible for software development and product packaging. The company's founders will oversee all operations of this department.

CUSTOMER SERVICE/PRODUCT SUPPORT

The company is committed to superior levels of customer satisfaction. To this end Poggle intends to build an internal customer service department. This department will be staffed by knowledgeable people who are also skilled in being effective on the telephone in interpersonal relationship management.

MATERIALS AND PURCHASING

The responsibility of this department will be the establishment of new sources of supply, management of the ordering process, procurement, and stocking.

SALES

The sales department is responsible for the achievement of Poggle revenue targets, management and growth of the distribution channels, and pursuit of corporate strategic relationships.

MARKETING

The marketing department is responsible for implementation of the marketing plan, overseeing the development of pricing and price lists, catalogues, and selling sheets. Additionally, this department handles all research and advertising.

LEGAL & ACCOUNTING

The legal department is responsible for management of Poggle's copyrights, trademarks, and patents, in addition to contract negotiation.

INTELLECTUAL PROPERTY PROTECTION

Poggle has aggressively moved to protect its developed intellectual property rights such as trademarks, product designs, and proprietary concepts. These rights are protected through patent application trademark registrations, the maintenance of trade secrets, the development of trade presentation and, when necessary, appropriate action against those who are, in the company's opinion, unfairly competing. Several trademarks have been issued by the United States Department of Commerce. The current registered trademark and future patent beneficiary is Poggle, Incorporated. Poggle will be filing additional trademark registrations and patents for their other technologies in China, Japan, Korea, the Middle East, and Europe.

FINANCIAL PROJECTIONS

Financial Requirement and Use

The company's products are currently available through its website. Once this business plan is funded, the company intends to hire an executive management team along with several other individuals in compliance with the implementation of the company's organizational plan. Additional funds will be utilized to cover operations, sales, marketing, and product development costs for the remainder of 2001. Funds will be utilized to cover expenses estimated at just over $1.6 million for the first 12 months of operation. See the following financial statements for the background on this figure.

Statement of First-Year Cash Flow (in thousands)

Revenue	Unit Price	Month-1	Month-2	Month-3	Month-4	Month-5	Month-6
Product 1	$25,000.00	-	-	-	50,000	75,000	100,000
Product 2	$54.80	-	5,480	27,400	54,800	82,200	109,600
Product 3	$19.95	-	998	1,995	2,993	3,990	4,988
Product 4	$25,000.00	-	-	-	25,000	25,000	25,000
Product 5	$9.95	-	498	995	1,493	1,990	2,488
Product 6	$2,500.00	-	25,000	50,000	75,000	100,000	125,000
Product 7	$3,500.00	-	35,000	70,000	105,000	140,000	175,000
Total Revenue							
(Gross Profit)		**-**	**66,975**	**150,390**	**314,285**	**428,180**	**542,075**
Expenses							
Advertising		2,500	2,625	2,756	2,894	3,039	3,191
Shipping		250	263	276	289	304	319
Insurance		500	500	500	500	500	500
Professional Services		1,000	10,500	11,025	11,576	12,155	12,763
Rent		5,000	5,000	5,000	5,000	5,000	5,000
Repair & Maintenance		500	500	500	500	500	500
Payroll		40,000	40,000	50,000	60,000	70,000	70,000
Supplies		500	500	500	500	500	500
Travel & Entertainment		5,000	5,250	5,513	5,788	6,078	6,381
Product Development		5,000	5,250	5,513	5,788	6,078	6,381
Administration		1,000	1,050	1,103	1,158	1,216	1,276
Computer Expense		7,500	7,875	8,269	8,682	9,116	9,572
Utilities		1,000	1,050	1,103	1,158	1,216	1,276
Trade Shows		3,500	3,675	3,859	4,052	4,254	4,467
Miscellaneous		500	5,250	5,513	5,788	6,078	6,381
Total Expenses		**87,250**	**89,288**	**101,427**	**113,673**	**126,032**	**128,508**
Net Profit Before Taxes		**(87,250)**	**(22,313)**	**48,963**	**200,612**	**302,148**	**413,567**
Net Profit as % of Sales						70.6%	76.3%

Month-7	Month-8	Month-9	Month-10	Month-11	Month-12	Year One Total	% of Revenue
125,000	150,000	175,000	200,000	225,000	250,000	1,350,000	18.9%
137,000	164,400	191,800	219,200	246,600	274,000	1,512,480	21.2%
5,985	6,983	7,980	8,978	9,975	10,973	65,835	0.9%
25,000	25,000	25,000	25,000	25,000	25,000	225,000	3.1%
2,985	3,483	3,980	4,478	4,975	5,473	32,835	0.5%
150,000	175,000	200,000	225,000	250,000	275,000	1,650,000	23.1%
21,000	245,000	280,000	315,000	350,000	385,000	2,310,000	32.3%
655,970	**769,865**	**883,760**	**997,655**	**1,111,550**	**1,225,445**	**7,146,150**	**100.0%**
3,350	3,518	3,694	3,878	4,072	4,276	39,793	0.6%
335	352	369	388	407	428	3,979	0.1%
500	500	500	500	500	500	6,000	0.1%
13,401	14,071	14,775	15,513	16,289	17,103	159,171	2.2%
5,000	5,000	5,000	5,000	5,000	5,000	60,000	0.8%
500	500	500	500	500	500	6,000	0.1%
85,000	85,000	85,000	110,000	110,000	110,000	915,000	12.8%
500	500	500	500	500	500	6,000	0.1%
6,700	7,036	7,387	7,757	8,144	8,552	79,586	1.1%
6,700	7,036	7,387	7,757	8,144	8,552	79,586	1.1%
1,340	1,407	1,477	1,551	1,551	1,710	15,917	0.2%
10,051	10,553	11,081	11,635	11,635	12,828	119,378	1.7%
1,340	1,407	1,477	1,551	1,551	1,710	15,917	0.2%
4,690	4,925	5,171	5,430	5,430	5,986	55,710	8.0%
6,700	7,036	7,387	7,757	7,757	8,552	79,586	1.1%
146,109	**148,839**	**151,706**	**151,706**	**179,717**	**186,196**	**1,641,623**	**23.0%**
509,861	**621,026**	**732,054**	**817,938**	**928,673**	**1,039,249**	**5,505,524**	
77.7%	80.7%	82.8%	82.0%	83.5%	84.8%	77.0%	

Statement of Three-Year Profit and Loss

Three-Year Projection	Year One	Year Two	Year Three
Revenue		15%	20%
Product 1	$1,350,000	$1,552,500	1,863,000
Product 2	1,512,480	1,739,352	2,087,222
Product 3	65,835	75,710	90,852
Product 4	225,000	258,750	310,500
Product 5	32,835	37,760	45,312
Product 6	1,650,000	1,897,500	2,277,000
Product 7	2,310,000	2,656,500	3,187,800
Total Revenue	**3,992,835**	**4,591,760**	**5,510,112**
Expenses			
Advertising	39,793	43,772	49,025
Shipping	3,979	4,377	4,902
Insurance	6,000	6,600	7,392
Professional Services	159,171	175,088	196,099
Rent	60,000	66,000	73,920
Repair and Maintenance	6,000	6,600	7,392
Payroll	915,000	1,006,500	1,127,280
Supplies	6,000	6,600	7,392
Travel & Entertainment	79,586	87,544	98,049
Product Development	79,586	87,544	98,049
Administration	15,917	17,509	19,610
Computer Expense	119,378	131,316	147,074
Utilities	15,917	17,509	19,610
Trade Shows	55,710	61,281	68,635
Miscellaneous	79,586	87,544	98,049
Total Expenses	**1,641,623**	**1,805,785**	**2,022,479**
Net Profit Before Taxes	**$2,351,212**	**$2,785,975**	**$3,487,633**
Net Profit as % of Revenue	58.90%	60.70%	63.30%

Internet Travel Agency Business

BUSINESS PLAN

MEMORY LANE CRUISES

7616 Wylie Wood Street
Jackson, Mississippi 39204

The Internet travel industry has experienced dramatic growth in recent years, and forecasts call for similar levels of success in the future. Memory Lane Cruises provides superior web-based travel services to its customers via solid business strategies, solid marketing, and cutting-edge Internet technology. This limited plan was used to successfully obtain a Small Business Adminstration loan. Its author employs this shorter format when seeking funding in the $75,000 to $200,000 range; plans for greater sums are more extensive and detailed.

- EXECUTIVE SUMMARY

- THE COMPANY'S HISTORY

- INTERNET TRAVEL SERVICE

- THE INTERNET TRAVEL INDUSTRY

- THE COMPANY'S PLANNED OPERATIONS

- BUDGET & SALES PROJECTIONS

- USE OF PROCEEDS

- MANAGEMENT

- CONCLUSION

EXECUTIVE SUMMARY

Memory Lane Cruises, Inc., a Mississippi corporation, has developed the infrastructure to become an extremely profitable enterprise in the burgeoning Internet travel agency business. MLC will carve a niche in the cruise sector of this $1.875 billion industry, utilizing leads generated by the website of an affiliated company. The company will combine Internet technology with solid marketing and business strategies, resulting in a virtual travel agency providing efficient cost-effective service to its customers nationwide.

The Internet has expanded the horizons of the travel industry. Previously an agency's marketing area was limited to its local area, its customers restricted to those within driving distance to the agencies office. The Internet has dramatically changed permitting business to be conducted nationally and internationally. Most current travel agency Internet usage is by existing agencies attempting to expand their business. They continue to have the fixed office expenses attendant with a retail business. MLC will take the concept one step further by eliminating the retail aspects and operating the business through its computer system.

MLC's sister company, TripBlaster, operates a successful website for travel agencies specializing in booking cruises. This site allows agents to advertise cruises and to receive inquiries via e-mail, faxes, or telephone. Furthermore, the site operates so that consumers can request specific parameters for their cruise and be referred to cruises meeting their criteria. The inquiries exceed the available cruise choices at the site. MLC plans to make these inquiries their initial customer base. MLC will use their cruise affiliations to meet the needs of these consumers.

The management of MLC is uniquely qualified to operate the Internet travel agency. Its principals combine experience in Internet travel agent technology with sales and marketing experience.

The company is seeking debt financing in the sum of $100,000 to complete the launch of the business. To assist potential lenders this plan will describe the company's history, the Memory Lane Cruises website, overview of the Internet travel agency, the company's planned operations, the operating budget and revenue potential, business plan timetable, use of proceeds, management and financial information including projected balance sheets, income statements, cash flow projections, and break-even analysis.

THE COMPANY'S HISTORY

The company is a logical business extension of affiliated company TripBlaster's Internet cruise travel business. The business (described in greater detail in this plan) provides an advertising vehicle for travel agents specializing in cruise travel. The website matches customers with cruises. Management observed two phenomenas:

1. A significant number of consumer requests could not be satisfied by existing advertisers.
2. These requests represented a significant amount of potential travel agency commissions.

Based on these observations MLC was created.

Developmental work is near completion. A staff has been retained and training sessions have been tentatively scheduled. In addition marketing campaigns have been developed. The company is prepared to be fully operational within 30 days of funding.

Based on management's experience with the cruise travel website and after conferring with industry consultants, MLC projects the following revenues for the first three years of operations.

Year	Projected Revenues ($)
1	518,906
2	648,632
3	810,790

General

INTERNET TRAVEL SERVICE

The principals of Memory Lane Cruises, Inc., also operate the Memory Lane Cruises Internet travel service. Combined with the company's own web page, this service will be a primary source of potential customers.

Operations of the website

The Memory Lane Cruises site matches consumers with appropriate cruises offered by advertising travel agents. Upon opening the attractive page with color graphics and an easy-to-use interactive format, the consumer sees a listing of three categories:

- Cruise Lines
- Cruise Destinations
- Other Destinations

The potential customer clicks on their choice and a screen appears describing the available cruises meeting their requirements. If they want to receive a quote or receive further information, they click the quote button.

The screen that appears contains a questionnaire with general information which must be completed for the process to continue. Questions include:

- Name
- Telephone number
- E-mail address
- A contact time
- The number of cabins required

After the general information is completed, specific reservation information is requested. This questionnaire queries on details of the cruise requested. This includes the customer's available sailing dates, price categories, type and location of room, previous cruising background, and availability for cruises on short notice. After completing the questionnaires, the consumer submits the information by activating the submit button.

The information is e-mailed to the Memory Lane Cruises databank and the advertising travel agent which posted the cruise listing. Many times the listed cruises are no longer available or the location requested is not among the listings, or the pricing requested is not available. In those instances TripBlaster will refer these potential customers to MLC. Other advertisers on the website have agreed to this arrangement. MLC will not compete with these agencies at this site. The company believes that this will be a steady source of potential customers.

THE INTERNET TRAVEL INDUSTRY

The Internet travel industry has experienced dramatic growth. The ability to purchase airline tickets, make hotel reservations, and book cruises via the Internet has evolved from a novelty to a tool utilized by millions of consumers. The strength of this market is illustrated by sales projections that predict $8.8 billion in travel bookings by the year 2002. Below are the actual figures for 1996-1997 and projections for 1998-2002.

Year	Revenues ($billions)
1996	0.275
1997	0.827
1998	1.875
1999	3.2
2000	4.736
2001	6.57
2002	8.88

The percentage of nonairline revenues is projected to increase substantially. In 1997 nonairline bookings were approximately 10 percent of total bookings ($82 million). Projections for the year 2002 are for an estimated 25 percent of the market ($2.2 billion). These projections indicate the potential strength of Internet travel businesses.

Presently no company dominates the market. Jupiter Communications reports that 81 percent of revenues are generated by 44 percent of the sites. There is definitely room for an innovative Internet cruise travel organization in this rapidly expanding market.

THE COMPANY'S PLANNED OPERATIONS

General

The company will be strictly an Internet operation. There will be no walk-in customers, nor will there be a marketing area limited by geography. Operations will take advantage of modern electronic and telephonic communications. The company's office will be minimal, functioning as a communications center housing the company's agent and computer systems.

Operations

Initially operations will consist of two agents dealing with the public and travel industry professionals and one management member specializing in marketing and Internet technology. A typical transaction would take place as follows:

1. The agent will contact a potential customer obtained through the TripBlaster site or from the company's site. The agent will have all relevant information needed to assist the customer derived from Internet site questionnaires.

2. Consulting the company's data base of available cruises containing relevant data such as departure data, prices, availabilities, and port visits, the agent can match the customer with an appropriate cruise.

3. The booking information is e-mailed to the cruise line or cruise agent.

4. Confirmations are sent to the customer.

Preliminary Procedures

Training

The company has retained a travel industry professional to train the initial agents. The trainer will be at the company's facilities for approximately five days. During this period the consultant will:

- Train agents on basic cruise industry procedures and regulations
- Train agents on sales techniques
- Review office systems

The company believes that this training period and the company's computer systems will assure efficient operations as soon as possible. (Additionally, the industry professional has agreed to work with the agency on a consulting basis.)

Industry Licensing and Registration
Cruise Line International Association

Membership in the CLIA is essential for the operation of any cruise line business. Cruise lines and agents require membership before dealing with travel agents. The company will apply as soon as possible. The requirements for membership are:

- Application
- $300 fee
- Two-day training program for agents

Cruise Line Registration

Registration with cruise lines is required in order to be able to book cruises and receive commissions. Cruise lines require:

- CLIA certificates
- Business references
- Business cards
- Business license
- Taxpayer identification number
- W-9 form

This process generally takes at least two weeks. The company plans to register with as many cruise lines as possible.

The company plans to market their services utilizing a web page, Internet advertising, and public relations activities. Below is a description of each activity. | **Marketing**

The company website

Management's expertise in website design and Internet technology will result in an effective website presentation. It is anticipated that the site will be similar to the TripBlaster web page. In addition to attractive color graphics, the emphasis will be on interactive features. The information gathered by interactive customer questionnaires will assist sales efforts as well as developing a database for future marketing efforts. The site will also list available cruises as well as discussing the company's ability to find a cruise to meet anyone's travel needs. It is estimated that the site will cost $3,500 to implement.

Internet Advertising

Internet banner advertising along with text-based listings on major search engines as well as other noncompeting travel websites will be an ongoing marketing vehicle. These banners or small advertisements appear throughout the World Wide Web usually at the top of various related Internet sites. The company will position their advertisements at travel related areas with links to the company web page. MLC will also retain a banner on the Infoseek search engine. The Infoseek search engine banner will be viewed by 200,000 persons monthly. TripBlaster has agreed to pass its 15 percent agency commission along to Memory Lane Cruises to facilitate growth.

Public Relations

MLC will promote its services using tradition public relations methods, as well as Internet related activities. In the traditional area, public relations activities include:

- Press releases
- Promotional events
- Magazine articles

In the Internet arena, the company may provide online travel news or produce an online newsletter.

The company's operating philosophy is to emphasize marketing while providing efficient service using technology and a limited number of personnel.

BUDGET & SALES PROJECTIONS

The company has analyzed its estimated operating expenses and has designed a projected budget for the first year of operations. Expenses are heavily devoted to marketing, while operating and administrative expenses are limited. Below is the proposed budget.

Budget

Use	Amount ($)
Salary and Taxes (agents)	4,800
Salary and Taxes (officers)	2,400
Rent	400
Utilities and Telephone	500
Internet Advertising	3,750
Public Relations/Promotions	750
Insurance	50
Miscellaneous Expenses	632
Total	**13,832**

Notes:
1. Salaries assume two agents and one officer.
2. Internet advertising includes funds for the Infoseek search engine banner plus other banner and Internet advertising.
3. Miscellaneous is a 5 percent of expenses reserve for unanticipated expenses items.

Sales Projections

MLC's sales projections have been conservatively calculated based upon the following assumptions:

- Commission of 10 percent per booked cruise
- Average cruise price of $3,000
- 100 sales per month for the first quarter
- 25 percent increase per quarter for the first year
- 25 percent yearly increases in the second and third year

Based on these assumptions sales for the first year are calculated to be $518,906. Sales for the second and third year are projected to be $648,632 and $810,790.

USE OF PROCEEDS

The company is seeking $100,000 in debt financing. The initial capitalization will be $30,000 contributed by management. Proceeds will be allocated to operating expenses for the first 6 months, equipment, and other start-up expenses. Below is the estimated allocation of funds.

Use	Amount ($)
Six months' operating expenses	79,695
Computer equipment	7,500
Internet site production	5,000
Deposits	5,000
Reserve	2,805
Total	**100,000**

Below is a brief description of each use.

Six Months' Operating Expenses—Funds for this use are necessitated by the time required to set up operations and to gain the full revenue impact of the marketing program. The funds are also required because of the cruise lines' commission payment policy. Commissions are paid after the cruise is completed, therefore payment time from booking the cruise to receiving payment can be as much as 60 days.

Equipment—The equipment category includes expenditures for an Internet server, computers, and related items.

Website Production—This category encompasses all expenses required to design and produce the company's website.

Deposits—Included in this category are deposits that may be required to secure Internet banner space or as required by cruise lines.

MLC is led by a management team with over 50 years of combined business experience. Areas of expertise include Internet technology, sales, marketing, and training and management. Initially the company will utilize travel consultants to assist in the technical aspects of the travel industry, however, management's operating of the TripBlaster-Memory Lane Cruises website has provided the necessary industry exposure to operate a travel agency business. Below is a brief description of the business background of each officer.

MANAGEMENT

Brad Sterling—Mr. Sterling founded TripBlaster in 1996. TripBlaster has grown from an Internet design shop to become a one-stop resource for Worldwide Web Technology, including design, hosting, and advertising. The company also owns several commercial websites, including Memory Lane Cruises and the online magazine Traveler's Log.

Prior to founding TripBlaster, from 1988 to 1995 Mr. Sterling was an account manager/trainer for Supreme X Health Plan, a Medicaid-based health maintenance organization located in Reno, Nevada. From 1976 to 1988, he served as corporate trainer and general manager for Amope Research. Mr. Sterling will devote approximately 20 hours per week to MLC.

Karen Watkins (Vice-President)—From 1969 to 1986 Ms. Watkins was employed with the consumer products division of the international corporation Kashi & Milliken. From 1986 to 1990 she served as a corporate trainer, training all new hires in all aspects of sales and marketing. From 1990 to 1996 she was an account manager selling the company's products to food and drug retailers and mass merchants at the corporate and retail level. Ms. Watkins will devote 40 or more hours per week to the company's business.

Lois Boiler—Ms. Boiler has been vice-president of TripBlaster since 1992. She is the administrator of the company's operations and accounting systems and is involved in all areas of long-range planning. Since 1979 she has held administrative and consulting positions at financial and educational institutions. Ms. Boiler has earned a Bachelor of

Fine Arts degree from the University of Chicago. She will devote 10 hours per week to MLC.

CONCLUSION

Memory Lane Cruises, Inc., has developed a business strategy that combines Internet technology with the company's experience in operating an Internet travel page. This approach emphasizes limited operating expenses with a ready-made market from the TripBlaster-Memory Lane Cruises web page enhanced by a new web page and Internet advertising. The revenue producing potential is impressive.

Memory Lane Cruises, Inc., represents an excellent opportunity for a financial institution seeking a profitable, long-term relationship.

Marble Quarry

BUSINESS PLAN

VOMARTH MARBLE QUARRY

Via di San Sebastianello 5
I-00184 Rome, Italy

Based near Rome, this Italian-based company quarries, manufactures, and distributes its own world-renowned marble. Recently the firm sought out additional monies to market directly to consumers, architects, and designers living in the United States as it recognized how American Baby Boomers are craving more upscale luxury products (including marble) in their lives. This plan persuaded numerous investors to give the company US$6 million to start a vitally important new distribution operation in the United States.

- VOMARTH SNAPSHOT

- THE COMPANY: HISTORICAL BRIEF

- THE OPPORTUNITY

- THE STRATEGY

- STRATEGY SNAPSHOT

- MARKETING STRATEGY

- MARKET & PRODUCT ANALYSIS

- COMPETITIVE ANALYSIS

- EXECUTIVE MANAGEMENT

- FINANCIAL SUMMARY

**VOMARTH
SNAPSHOT**

Management:
Ed Mastian, CEO
Bonnie Slinger, CFO & COO
Chuck Wilson, Quarry Master
Nicholas Kitt, Production Manager

Board of Directors:
Jeff DiMuzio (Italy)
Brian Davis (England)
Michael Thompson (United States)
Jimmy Duthow (United States)
Frank Steinker (Germany)
John O'Reilly (Ireland)

Industry: Dimensional stone

Web Design: Proactive

Bank: PNC Bank

Accountant: Anderson Accounting

Use of funds: Acquisitions, distribution, marketing/sales, products diversification

Current investors: US$6 million Private Investors, Personal Funds, Operations Proceeds

Current Valuation: US$65+ million

Business Description: Vomarth quarries, manufactures, and distributes its own various colors and grades of marble. Its unique products are used for purpose of construction and renovation. Currently, its natural stone products are manufactured in Ireland and distributed in most major areas of the U.S. and parts of Europe.

The company plans to consolidate the traditionally fragmented industry through developing retail stores. This will allow them to brand a portfolio of marble and natural stone products, which will be recognized and trusted throughout the world for its quality. Vomarth will earn in the stone industry the status that Andersen Windows established among the manufacturers of custom windows.

The company will acquire stone retail/fabrication businesses that have been identified and qualified by the company's acquisition team. The acquisitions will have proven track records of profitable sales and will be the dominant (or have the possibility to be the dominant) stone business in their market area.

Market Needs: The market currently has the following needs:

- Consumers have no well-known brand name to trust when they go to buy stone. We intend to brand the totality of the stone buying experience and exploit this opportunity in the market.
- Localized sales by a nationally trusted name.
- Once the decision is made to have a granite counter top, the consumers want it immediately. We will satisfy this need.

Market Opportunity: Note that every new construction site or existing commercial/ residential building has a need for dimensional stone products. *Floor Covering Weekly* estimates that the retail floor covering market alone, being the most profitable segment of dimensional stone industry, is estimated at US$40.8 billion with the typical residential customer spending between $2,000 to $5,000 for stone work per kitchen and $2,000 to $5,000 per bathroom.

In tandem with this highly profitable market, the company will achieve US$600 million in annual sales of its natural stone products with a short-term goal in this planned retail project of US$80 million in five years. Our plan is to use this retail business to allow us to connect to the end consumers and promote our branded portfolio of luxury stones. In time, as we will be the first to understand and implement this strategy in the stone business, we can be the trusted stone brand in the consumer's mind.

Competitive Advantage: The company controls the supply of the product through its quarrying operations. Managing product distribution from quarry to end consumers will give the company the first of its many edges by competitive prices and providing consistent quality.

More importantly, a proven management team of seasoned industry experts with over 100 years of experience between them runs the company. Since the early days, this team has delivered nearly 12 times its original investments through proving up to 1.6 million tons of marble on just the first five of the 100 acres owned by the company. Furthermore, its management has established a network of distributors with hundreds of dedicated sales personnel. Such methods result in a doubling of sales each year between 1996 and 1999.

In terms of innovation, the company has developed products in the past with special backings and surfacing for use on yachts and elevators. Dynamically innovative, the company already utilizes the most advanced stone engineering techniques in its tile plant to process marble tiles from small blocks of exotic stone.

In terms of fulfillment, quality control, and service, the company has already perfected the complex logistics of fulfillment through its proprietary quality control operations. In its planned retail business, we can achieve a turn-around time of 10 days for our custom counter tops from template to installation. Finally, coating technologies to enhance durability and simplify maintenance are fully integrated into the company's products.

Market Entry: In the United States, the company' dimensional stone products are sold through 20 of the most prestigious regional distributors. They have an average of more than 400 active retail customers, and together they reach a retail segment of 4,100 retail stores. Vomarth has product leverage and an operational familiarity with these distributors. The venerable list includes Big Apple Granite & Marble (New York) and Kipper Johnson (West and East Coast).

The company's product is also sold through a large international Italian distributor, who promotes Vomarth at international trade shows. Being actively promoted with such a distinguished company puts the company's marble in front of a wide and diverse group of regional distributors, major contractors, and prominent architects and interior designers. With a little targeted marketing, the company is achieving its aim in reaching these professionals. It is the intention to use the present distribution channels to sell our portfolio of branded marble and granite.

Finally, because of its retail acquisition strategy in the United States, the economies of purchasing and distribution will allow the company to give their clients better value to the end consumer, which will greatly increase its field of prospects.

Value to Purchaser: The appearance of exotic marble creates a memorable impression of elegance that architects and interior decorators seek for their best clients. Lifestyle choices, fashion trends, and the growing cultural trend of "bringing nature inside" have caught on with Baby Boomers. The kitchen and bathroom are now areas in the home that receive the most attention, and as it happens it is where the use of natural materials like stone can make all the difference. Since 80 percent of the housing stock in the States was built before 1980, this leaves a huge market for our products in the remodeling sector.

Strong and durable, stones in foyers, kitchens, fireplace surrounds, and bathrooms are all strong selling points for any building or home that is on the market. In our increasingly health-conscious world, polished stone surfaces is one of the purest environments for those who suffer from dust and other allergies.

THE COMPANY: HISTORICAL BRIEF

Dating from the Pre-Cambrian period over 750 million years ago, Vomarth marble shows twisted and interlocking bands of serpentine in varying shades of sepia, cream, green, blue, red, brown, and gray interrupted by veins of crystalline calcite and dolomite.

Noted for its wide variety of colorful shades, Vomarth's marble is sometimes used as a semi-precious stone and is preferred by famous sculptors to create national monuments and treasured pieces of art, notable architects and designers have also taken advantage of its rare beauty to add elegance and prestige to their buildings. In fact, many publications around the globe have said our marble may be "the world's most beautiful stone."

Sawn marble—along with granite, limestone, slate, and other semi-precious stones—constitutes the dimensional stone industry. The dimensional stone industry is a US$60 billion-per-year world market with thousands of quarries supplying stone and thousands of commercial fabricators serving the end-user.

Vomarth was founded by Ed Danesi and his daughter Bonnie Slinger. The Danesi family has traditionally been in the marble business and has contributed their quarries as their investment in Vomarth. The quarries include the Kolpart and Loperizo leases and lands of 100 acres, which are in the main marble area in the geological area known as the "Vomarth Marble Formation" north of Rome. Just the first eight of the 100 acres have proven reserved of 3.2 million tons of marble, estimated by independent geologists and verified by accountants Arthur Anderson at a very conservative US$65 million and by some experts to be as high as US$140 million.

Along with a grant aid of US$415,000 from an Italian government agency and US$4.5 million of private equity financing (1996), Vomarth Marble Quarry (Vomarth) was formed with the objective of utilizing new technology to produce and market commercial-grade blocks, slabs, and tiles from the company's own marble reserves of exotic Italian marble.

The first several years were spent developing the quarry, building the tile plant, and selecting and installing state-of-the-art machinery and equipment. Currently, it is the most advanced quarrying and fabrication company in Ireland and has all the necessary equipment to produce marble blocks suitable for the construction industry that as recent as five years earlier, were only suitable for small giftware pieces.

Since the initial foundational stage, the company has experienced steady growth. It is now a regular exhibitor at every major stone trade show in the world where its products easily and consistently sell out. As a result, Vomarth products are delivered to no less than 20 major regional distributors, together reaching over 4,100 retail stores. Sales revenue has doubled each year between 1996 and 1999. This is a result of the company forming strategic alliances with dominant companies in the industry located in Italy and Ireland.

As a result of these successes and a seasoned managerial team with a proven track record in place, the company now feels comfortable to seek financing to implement its retail acquisition strategy.

Vomarth has identified an opportunity in the dimensional stone business that it is uniquely qualified to capitalize on. Since Vomarth has a presence across the supply chain through its primary marble extraction business and its wholesale distribution of that marble, the company now intends to add the final element—retailing. Implementation of this element strengthens opportunities in each of the three areas to create an extremely competitive stone business.

THE OPPORTUNITY

Apart from the large growing market in the existing stone business, we believe that a whole new customer will enter the market as the effects of the increasing volume of business drive down the costs of stone. Like Henry Ford and his low cost motor car which made transport suddenly available for the ordinary man, so too will the reduction in the costs of slab granite coming from South America and China create a whole new market.

The world market for dimensional natural stone at the retail level is valued at US$60 billion a year and is growing at the rate of approximately 20 percent per year, according to Jeffrey Matthews in his report "Marble & Limestone Market Study."

This report estimates the market in the United States for dimensional natural stone at US$5 billion, and 80 percent of this is imported. *Floor Covering Weekly* estimates the retail floor covering market alone at US$40.8 billion per year. End-users of natural stone products are divided between commercial and residential. Large commercial construction consists of jobs in excess of US$100,000, while large residential construction consists of jobs in excess of US$15,000. A typical residential customer spends from US$2,000 to US$5,000 for stonework per kitchen and a similar amount per bathroom.

As this is the fastest growing segment of the market, with natural stone increasingly taking market share from ceramic tiles and other artificial products, this means that **every new construction site or existing commercial building or residence with floors, walls, bathrooms, a staircase, or a kitchen is a potential customer for natural stone products.**

This is a tremendous market opportunity when one considers that residential construction happens to be the most profitable segment of the natural stone industry and favored by demographical factors. Namely, the "Baby Boomer" generation has come of age, and this 35-53 age group, estimated at 80 million, is now the largest spending demographic in the United States. As consumers they have come to expect and demand the most for their money, and an investment in natural stone yields the best possible value.

We see a lot of opportunity for which we are uniquely qualified to exploit, such as:

- Changing an old system of distribution that sometimes has to go through "10 different hands" from the time the stone leaves the ground until it is installed in the kitchen. There is a better way.
- The current traditional closed shop in the stone business is at last opening up because of the ubiquitous Internet and the full information today's consumer now has available to them. In effect, consumers can identify marble from a small village in Ireland and tell their stone shop all about it.
- We believe we can own the space in the consumers mind when it comes to identifying marble and granite, as there is no well-known stone brand today.
- Strategic alliances with powerful complementary businesses is already part of this company, and we intend to continue this in our retail stores.

- Our European ethos can be advantageous to our retail stores that have proven to be a compelling attraction for consumers of other European luxury products.
- Since this is an industry that traditionally spends nothing on advertising, there is an enormous first-mover advantage for any stone company that advertises and more importantly, to initiate a public relations program that creates some excitement.
- The stone industry's highly fragmented entities make it a perfect candidate for consolidation. There is a growing tension between regional distributors and their stone retailers. This has begun to change business relationships. We are seeing that as some retailers get larger, they are bypassing their regional distributor, and in turn distributors are directly bidding on retail jobs.
- The accelerated growth generated by the acquisitions of retail fabricators will provide currency for more acquisitions, creating a snowball effect. In essence, the opportunity here is the creation of a "category-killer," the first of its kind that consolidates the dimensional stone industry. Vomarth is this company.

By owning and controlling the stone at its source and marketing these brands through company-owned retail showrooms, the company retains market initiative to ensure delivering of consistently high-quality products at truly competitive prices from source to finish.

THE STRATEGY

Vomarth Marble Quarry will achieve US$600 million in annual sales of its natural stone products, with a short-term goal of US$80 million in five years. We will accomplish this goal through a two-prong strategy: that of introducing a portfolio of branded marble and granite products including the world-famous Vomarth and secondly, by the acquisition of 18 stone retail/fabrication centers across the United States, and by doing so consolidate a fragmented, and resource-poor industry.

According to the branding part of its strategy, Vomarth will develop its Vomarth brand into a portfolio of stones trusted to be the highest quality in the dimensional stone industry. Besides its own Italian Vomarth Aqua, that is already recognized as the leading luxury marble in the world, Vomarth will brand granite and other exotic and neutral field-type marbles and process them with its proprietary surfacing techniques. The company intends to align with other quarries that are the sources of other stones in order to brand and organize their distribution.

By controlling the stone at its source and marketing these brands through company-owned retail showrooms, the company can establish a well-known brand in the stone industry for the first time. Furthermore, through its investments and experience in technology, the company has also developed new uses for stone such as lightweight stone panels that can be used where heavier format stone would be prohibitive.

The key to implementing our branding strategy is retail; the company's acquisition team will identify and qualify several stone retail/fabricators that will have a proven track record of profitable sales and will be the dominant (or have the possibility to be the dominant) stone business in their market area.

Within the first few years, Vomarth plans to achieve US$30 million in sales by using the established sales organizations of the acquired retail stone fabricators. Much of the sales and projects in these acquired businesses are organized through personal contacts with the end-users. Knowing what these customers expect and value is essential to delivering a product that will please them. Personnel and stonemasons at the acquired businesses will be retrained to communicate the value of Vomarth's products and services to the customers, and to deliver that value by way of quality products and services on a consistent basis.

The company will strive to become recognized as the foremost expert in natural stone fabrication and installation. This will allow Vomarth to promote its own brands and create more business for its portfolio of stone brands through its distribution network.

The stream of Vomarth natural stone products will increase quickly with each profitable acquisition, supported by targeted advertising and promotions of the expanding network of retail centers. The brands will become recognized and trusted for quality and value. Sales figures will further increase.

With increased economies of purchasing, streamlined distribution, and professionally managed retailers, the company seeks to increase net margins in the acquired businesses from the current 12.5 percent to 20 percent within one year of takeover. In addition, as most sales require a deposit, the call on the company's cash resources will be limited.

Over time, the company expects to meet or exceed the following objectives:

Sales	**US$600 Million**
Retail Outlets	110
Vomarth Portfolio	10 stones
Net Margins	25%

In purchasing of retail stores, Vomarth regards the change of ownership to be a traumatic and sensitive issue and so will develop a plan to ensure that the introduction of the acquired retail outlets be achieved with the least possible interruption to these businesses. In addition, Vomarth recognizes that the fair treatment of employees in a dynamic environment is critical to the success of the plan.

Regional distributors in major areas across the United States will stock sufficient quantities of Vomarth stone products so that a full range of product will be within driving distance of 80 percent of the U.S. population. In the meantime, Vomarth will continue with its development of the quarry and manufacturing plant. New advances in technology and equipment will be introduced which will enable the company to offer additional products and increase the uses of its existing products. This emphasis on sales of the company's own branded products at the retail end will have a major effect on the quarry's profitability.

The company intends to use the Internet to educate and generate customers for its stores, and so will provide a localized source for a nationally promoted product.

Within five years the company expects to meet or exceed the following short-term objectives:

Sales	**US$118 Million**
Retail Outlets	27
Vomarth Portfolio	2
Net Margins	20%

This dynamic growth opportunity for Vomarth is within its grasp because the experience and vision of its key people, who have grown up in the stone business, are proven innovators in the business and have kept up with the industry's cutting-edge technology.

The company maintains a clear conception of its market niche and its competitive advantage. Vomarth keeps itself positioned to capitalize on every situation that will create opportunity and value within the area of the company's core competencies. Last but not least, Vomarth is implementing systems to ensure that the company can consistently deliver both products and service as offered by defining what constitutes real value to the customer and by setting a higher standard than the competition in both manufacturing and in over-the-top service.

STRATEGY SNAPSHOT

Action Steps:

- Vomarth acquires retail shops with a proven track record of profitability to generate strong business cash flow.
- The retail shops allow Vomarth to connect to the end consumer and market its Vomarth and other branded products directly to the public.
- The company will then use its raw material extraction alliances to extend and expand its portfolio of stone brands.
- Targeted marketing at this point will enable Vomarth to become the dominant stone brand in the world, potentially having a global market share as high as 40 percent.

Ensuring correct installation and maintenance procedures will provide long-term immunity from competitors that compromise on this element of the process for short-term gain.

MARKETING STRATEGY

The company's promotional strategy relies heavily on communicating the value of its products and services to the customer. The company will market by directly interfacing with the end-users, architects, and designers through consistent advertising in selected publications. Advertisements promoting Vomarth products have already run in upscale magazines such as *Architectural Digest, House Beautiful, Florida Design, Southern Living,* and *Southern Accents.* In addition, the company's showrooms will feature several striking floor designs.

The coverage the company receives in marble trade magazines and in prestigious publications such as *Hibernia Magazine* enhances its public image. Vomarth will utilize both a "push" strategy and a "pull" strategy in promoting its products. It will maximize its considerable channels of distribution to push the offering to the market.

Currently, the company's dimensional stone products are sold through 20 of the most prestigious regional distributors in the United States. Each has an average of 400 active customers, and combined they reach a retail segment of 4,100 shops. Vomarth will continue to maintain and develop these important relationships.

In addition to the United States, distributors in Italy, Ireland, the United Kingdom, France, and Germany are preparing to promote the company's product line. Later this year regional distributors will be set up in Portugal, Spain, Mexico, and Argentina when more products become available.

The company further intends to begin aggressively promoting its brands of natural stone products directly to the end consumer when it has its own retail stores in the United States. Our showrooms and the showrooms of the regional distributors, in addition to the company's displays at trade shows, will likewise increase consumer awareness of the company's products. As consumer demand develops for the company's brands, the "pull" strategy will begin to take effect throughout the supply chain. With the help of a sophisticated website, Vomarth can use the Internet to create awareness and pull in consumers.

MARKET & PRODUCT ANALYSIS

The world market for dimensional natural stone at the retail level is valued at US$60 billion. The overall U.S. floor covering market is estimated at US$40.8 billion per year. There are currently very few domestic producers of marble tile, and the variety of their stone is quite limited.

Critic Charles H. Caffin (1903) enthused, "No description can give an adequate idea of its stateliness, the exquisite mystery of graded greens and grays black, their tempestuous streaking and tender veining and the perfect texture of their polished surface. The most heedless visitor cannot pass them un-admired [for] the connoisseur will be enthusiastic."

The company fills a demand for luxury stones fabricated to exact specifications. Vomarth communicates regularly with regional distributors, local fabricators and architects, designers and end-users to identify their needs and consistently deliver a quality product and service unavailable elsewhere.

The company's marble products offer an attractive value to buyers who desire a high-quality exclusive product. The appearance of exotic marble creates a memorable impression of elegance that architects and interior decorators designers seek for their best clients. Fashion trends, lifestyle choices, and the current economic growth period in the United States all contribute to the increased use of natural stone and today's growing cultural trend of "bringing nature inside"; of creating a more natural, more relaxed (though still sophisticated) space in which to live and grow.

End users of natural stone products are divided between commercial and residential. Large commercial construction consists of jobs in excess of US$100,000; large residential construction consists of jobs in excess of US$15,000.

The major market segments for the company's natural stone products are as follows:

Commercial:

Large new construction	12%
Small new construction	16%
Large renovation	6%
Small renovation	6%
	40%

Residential:

Large new construction	11%
Small new construction	18%
Large renovation	20%
Small renovation	21%
	60%

Total:	**100%**

The company will market its own portfolio of branded stones through the regional distributors, retail home improvement centers, and stone retail/fabrication businesses.

Having our own retail stores will make it possible for prospective buyers to connect with the actual quarry owners, which is unusual in the retail sector of the stone industry. This direct connection between raw material producer and end-user is one of the unique pluses we will bring to our customers.

The use of natural stone is increasing in use in the U.S. with the bulk of the market located in just five geographic areas: New York, Florida, Illinois, California, and Texas. Throughout the United States and Europe marble and other natural stones have traditionally been used on the most prestigious commercial and residential projects. All developed regions of the globe are markets for natural stone tiles and slabs.

Renovators will see an immediate transformation by replacing existing materials with Vomarth natural stone in foyers, kitchens, fireplace surrounds, and baths. In effect, every new construction site or existing commercial building or residence with floors, walls, bathrooms, a staircase, or a kitchen is a potential customer for Vomarth natural stone products. These are also strong selling points for any building or home that is on the market.

Architects and interior decorators/designers will benefit from introducing a client to a special product. A satisfied client often translates to another assignment. Architects need the materials they specify to make a positive aesthetic statement while at the same time offering ease of installation, durability, reliability, uniformity, and ease of maintenance. They will specify a material that has these qualities, and Vomarth consistently meet these demands.

Both residential and commercial building owners are increasingly choosing natural stone over synthetic hard coverings because of its natural beauty and durability. In the United States, since 80 percent of residential housing was built before 1980, the renovations market has created further demand for Vomarth products.

In addition, our increasingly health-conscious world supports bringing nature inside to create a more relaxed and positive living environment. Polished stone flooring is one of the purest environments for those who suffer from dust and other allergies, with a bonus of low maintenance.

Vomarth's branded Vomarth products possess superior strength and durability and can be installed by any trained stonemason. The company uses the most innovative stone engineering to produce its tiles and slabs. Vomarth manufactures exotic marble three-eighths inch and three-quarter inch tiles and slabs. Italian Vomarth Blue is a translucent aqua-green color mixed with variegation of dark and pale shades of blue. This stone makes a striking impression in the following formats:

- Vomarth marble slabs: 8' x 4' slabs used by marble fabricators for counter tops, vanity tops, and worktops
- Vomarth marble tiles: 12" x 12" and larger polished square tiles used in the floor and wall covering business
- Vomarth panels: 7mm panel slabs, thin, lightweight and extremely strong panels for specialty requirements such as elevators or aircraft
- Other: Vanity units, table tops, fireplace surrounds, and columns

The company will develop and expand its portfolio of branded luxury stones to include a selection of both exotic and neutral field-type marbles.

The company's tile plant in Italy has recently begun to make many of its specialty Aqua and Cream tiles directly blocks, and it is the only plant in the world with the equipment capable of processing these difficult-to-work luxury stones into tile.

Vomarth will offer luxury stones and engineered stone products unavailable anywhere else. In addition, Vomarth will continue to develop and sell products with special backings and surfacing for use on unique projects such as yachts and elevators. It will also utilize the most advanced stone engineering techniques to facilitate special effects such as book matching and quarter book matching, that attract high-end prospects to the company's products.

All of these stones will be processed through the company's stone engineering and surface techniques to meet the demands of architects and builders. Vomarth has access to technology including the development of a coating substance that when applied makes the marble scratchproof, graffiti proof, and easier to clean and maintain. A quick buffing by the regular maintenance person restores the finish to its original luster. Such advanced stone engineering is a key element of the Vomarth brand name.

Should there be any need for expert consultation, the company's factory, sales office, and showroom in Recess, Ireland are staffed to provide expert advice on any questions relating to maintenance or repairs. The regional distributors who handle Vomarth stone products are also fully capable of performing installation and repairs if tiles should need replacement. The company stands ready to take back any of its products that are flawed in any way and guarantees customer satisfaction. To date, the quality control in the factory has been effective and the company has never had to take any product back.

Vomarth is presenting the market with two main offerings:

1. The company will offer stone distributors a nationally promoted stone brand that is the recognized standard in the industry and also the best value. With the exclusive Irish Vomarth as the foundation, we will add granite and other marble, both exotic and neutral field-type stones, to broaden the portfolio.
2. Vomarth will offer consumers the ultimate stone-buying experience through our own retail showrooms and provide the most professional selection, fabrication, and installation on the market. We will brand the totality of that purchasing experience and not just our natural stone products alone.

The beauty, strength, and endurance of natural stone make it the covering of choice in both new and renovation construction. It is little wonder that currently, the natural stone industry continues to expand at rates exceeding 20 percent per year.

COMPETITIVE ANALYSIS

The company has already shown its ability to compete in its existing quarrying business. From a standing start just over three years ago, its products are now available throughout the United States. No other company in this industry has achieved such market penetration so fast.

By acquiring their own stone retailers, Vomarth can further increase sales of Vomarth. The Vomarth plan has four major competitive advantages over the existing stone retailers:

1. With seven retail units in one geographic region, Vomarth can purchase slab and tile in container loads, which is economically efficient. Apart from the cost savings this represents, it means that we can always select the best quality stones direct from the quarries for our customers.
2. Seven retail units in one area also facilitate the operation of a central, highly automated fabrication workshop. Apart from providing a consistent level of quality, it will also allow us to deliver customized products such as granite counter tops within 10 days. Such a rate of turnaround is a first in the industry and currently not available in the market.
3. Our retail showrooms will have designers who are also salespeople, and they will work in teams both in the retail showrooms and outside sales. This is novel in an industry that traditionally has not made full use of a professional, dedicated sales force.
4. Installation: We regard this as the critical element in our whole plan. Installation is the point where the customers have the most connection to the product and the retailer and as well where the retailer has the most opportunity to make a positive impact on the customer. We intend to be the best installers in our market area.

Vomarth has identified five well-run companies in the retailing of stone that represents the typical competitors we will have:

1. Renaissance Stones (Miami, Florida)
2. K. Neopolitan (Washington, D.C.)
3. Masterpiece Stones (Dallas, Texas)
4. The Stone House (Orlando, Florida)
5. Hill's Granite & Marble (San Francisco, California)

The following is an analysis of the competitive strengths and weaknesses of each.

Renaissance Stones

Reliability	Renaissance products are of high quality and very reliable
Established Brand	Sells marble, but there is little brand recognition
Customer Loyalty	Very loyal customer base
Profit Margins	Gross margins in excess of 50%
Distribution Process	Purchasing can be improved
Advertising	Very little needed
Market Share	Local only, less than 1% of total U.S. market
Competitive Advantage	No product advantage, but quality service
Retail/Commercial	80% of business is retail
Technology	Slow to react to industry innovations

K. Neopolitan

Reliability	Highly reliable products, but a notch below Renaissance
Established Brands	Sells marble, but there is little brand recognition
Customer Loyalty	Very loyal customer base
Profit Margins	Gross profit is 40%
Distribution	Purchasing needs improvement
Advertising	Local and small scale
Market Share	Under 1% of total U.S. market
Competitive Advantage	No product advantage
Retail/commercial	Most of business is retail
Technology	Slow to react to industry innovations

Masterpiece Stones

Reliability	Produces a high-quality and reliable product equal to Renaissance
Established Brands	Sells marble, but there is little brand recognition
Customer Loyalty	Slightly less customer loyalty than Renaissance
Profit Margin	Gross profit 40%
Distribution	Purchasing needs significant improvement
Advertising	Some advertising is done
Market Share	Under 1% of total U.S. market
Competitive Advantage	Some price advantage; no product advantage
Retail/Commercial	Higher percentage of commercial jobs
Technology	Slow to react to industry innovations

The Stone House

Reliability	Their product is equal to Masterpiece and just below Renaissance
Established Brands	Sells established marble, but there is little brand recognition
Customer Loyalty	Slightly less customer loyalty than Renaissance
Profit Margin	Gross profit slightly less than 40%
Distribution	Purchasing needs improvement
Advertising	Local print advertising only
Market Share	Under 1% of total U.S. market
Competitive Advantage	Great showroom; no other special advantage
Retail/Commercial	Mostly retail; 10% commercial
Technology	Slow to react to industry innovations

Hill's Granite & Marble

Reliability	Equal to Renaissance: highest-quality product
Established Brands	Sells marble, but there is little brand recognition
Customer Loyalty	Very loyal customer base
Profit Margin	Gross profit approximately 50%
Distribution	Purchasing can be improved
Advertising	Very little needed
Market Share	Under 1% of total U.S. market
Competitive Advantage	No product advantage; high-quality workmanship
Retail/Commercial	Even mix
Technology	Slow to react to industry innovations

EXECUTIVE MANAGEMENT

Ed Danesi, age 64, is Chairman of the Board and CEO. Danesi is an Italian national and has been actively involved in marble for the last 42 years from quarrying to production and from fabrication to retail sales. He spends most of his time meeting with potential customers and developing new markets. He began his career in the marble business at age 22 when he began managing a marble processing plant. Ed has quarried Vomarth, processed the stone, and sold finished products from his marble shop near Rome. Recently he set up regional and international distributors for Vomarth in every section of the United States.

Bonnie Slinger, 36, is the CFO and COO. She holds an Honors Bachelor of Commerce degree from University College Rome and worked at the accounting firm of Smallton Douglas in London for two years prior to joining the company in 1994. Since March of that year Bonnie has held the position of Managing Director of Ed Danesi Marble Ltd., a subsidiary of Vomarth and a company she founded and owned. Bonnie directed the development of the quarry and the purchase and commissioning of the tile manufacturing plant. She also set up the company's office systems, including the MIS and accounting systems.

Chuck Wilson, 43, is the Quarrymaster. Chuck has been involved in the Vomarth business all of his life. His family was associated with the Italian White Marble Company and the Quest Black Marble quarries near Rome. He managed both marble quarries and factories at different times in his career. He commissioned a marble manufacturing plant in Texas in the early 1990s and trained the entire staff on the proper working of marble fabrication. Chuck is a master at quarry management and has increased production from 480 tons in 1995 to 6,000 tons in 1999.

Nicholas Kitt, 36, is the Production Manager. Before joining Vomarth, Nicholas managed a large manufacturing company with 10 locations in Europe and Asia. After continuing his education by completing management courses in both England and France, Nicholas was put in charge of production and logistics for all 10 of that company's facilities. He built and established Vomarth's marble manufacturing plant in Rome and has taken the plant from zero production to producing 7,400 square feet per month. He is responsible for delivering the finished product to customers.

FINANCIAL SUMMARY

The company is seeking US$12 million in a second round of outside investment to fund acquisitions, operations, marketing/sales, and personnel growth. Vomarth is expected to generate the majority of its revenue through:

- Sales of natural stone products in its retail showrooms
- Sales of Vomarth-branded marble and granite
- Consultation services to professionals

The company currently has assets worth US$65 million.

The following is a summary of the company's financial projections:

Projections

Financials (millions)	Year 1	Year 2	Year 3	Year 4	Year 5
Sales Revenue	4.22	15.80	30.34	61.82	118.47

Revenue Model

The company will generate the following revenue streams, with a specific focus on transitioning the business from its historical emphasis on fabrication and quarrying operation to retail and consulting revenue incurred through its retail stores.

Revenue Source	Description
Fabrication	Raw material extraction & manufacture of Vomarth
Consultation	Expert industry knowledge with access to specialist suppliers
Retail Sales	The Ed Danesi Collection of Marble & Granite

Exit Strategies

Vomarth is an attractive IPO option given the company's following successes:

- Notable revenue flows
- Leveraged production, distribution, and dedicated sales team
- Selling into a fast-growing market
- Large, versatile, and growing client base

Nonprofit Youth Outreach Ministry

BUSINESS PLAN   LIFE WORKS CINCINNATI

4556 Colerain Avenue
Cincinnati, Ohio 45231

In 1996, a local Midwestern branch of this international Christian organization started "from scratch" with no donors and no revenue. The next year the still-struggling group commissioned this plan. By following its advice, five years later the youth ministry became highly solvent. More importantly, this plan has helped the organization easily meet or exceed its spiritual-based goals positively affecting thousands of young people's lives in the metropolitan region it serves. This plan was provided by Scott Lockett of Tindell Associates.

- OUR MISSION

- OUR GOALS

- STRATEGIC PLAN HIGHLIGHTS

NONPROFIT YOUTH OUTREACH MINISTRY
BUSINESS PLAN

OUR MISSION

We are committed to following Jesus's commandment to go and spread His Gospel.

OUR GOALS

We have identified numerous goals and related action steps to take to help us achieve success in our Father's work.

Spread the Gospel to Youth

As a mission community of believers, Life Works Cincinnati is here to spread the Gospel to every teenager in the area. We can do this by:

1) Reaching all the high schools in the area by 2000.

- Work with Martin Luther King High School to continue tutoring program for students in the fall of 1997.
- Start a club at Martin Luther King High School and Thomas Edison in the fall of 1997.
- Begin contact work and campaigners at Country Day and Episcopal in the spring of 1997.
- Organize contact work at Bishop Ireton in the fall of 1998.
- Initiate work at Catholic High School and Bryant in the fall of 1999.

2) Sending 200 kids to summer camp by 2000.

- 50 high school kids to Adirondacks in 1998.
- 200 high school kids to Colorado in 1999 and 50 junior high kids to North Carolina.
- 300 high school kids to Colorado and North Carolina in 2000.

3) Holding fall outreach camps and spring campaigner camps each year.

- 80 kids in fall 1997 to Shenandoah.
- 20 campaigners skiing and to Summit Lake in spring 1998.
- 150 kids in fall 1998 to Shenandoah.
- 40 campaigners skiing and to Summit Lake in spring 1999.

4) Implementing "Moms in Touch" by fall 1998.

- Gather information during summer 1998.
- Recruit prayer warriors summer 1998.
- Begin fall 1998.

Support Our Ministry's Workers

We are committed to the welfare and spiritual health of those who do this ministry, that they may do it out of a consistent and growing relationship with Christ and His Church. We can do this by:

1) Recruiting and developing leaders.

- Be Biblically based and Christ-centered as an organization and as individuals.
- Contact churches and colleges for recruitment.
- Require all leaders to attend two leadership conferences each year.
- Ask leaders to attend weekly training and fellowship meetings.

2) Recruiting and developing new and old committee members.

- Hold committee meetings once a month.
- Contact churches and parents for interest.
- Have members attend one committee conference.
- Train committee in "Taking Donors Seriously."

3) Pursuing excellence in all we do.

- Be wise stewards of the resources entrusted to us.
- Strive for excellence in all services, programs, and activities.
- Be unwilling to accept mediocrity.
- Seek to improve our skills, techniques, materials, and approaches.

4) Nurturing and developing our human resources.

- Cooperate with each other and become interdependent and mutually supportive.
- Make honesty and integrity non-negotiable for all board, staff, and volunteers.
- Build on our commitment to help our staff and volunteers spread the Gospel.
- Assure that our staff and associates grow continually toward both their professional and spiritual goals.
- Cultivate and respect diversity in attitude, denomination, and action insofar as it supports our vision and values.
- Honoring the dignity of and respecting the value of each individual as an important contributor to the success of the organization.

We are committed to being light for Christ in the greater Cincinnati community. We can do this by: **Be Light for Christ**

1) Forming long-term relationships with local churches.

- Contact two new churches each month and provide them with Life Works information.
- Hold a yearly pastor's lunch and invite all senior and youth pastors.
- Invite churches to partner with Life Works by providing volunteer leaders, committee members, and financial support.
- Attend church mission conferences.

2) Building bonds with parents.

- Begin Caring Adult Fellowship (CAF) for parents of students.
- Use CAF to serve as a core prayer and fellowship group for each school.
- Hold parent nights for each school.
- Invite parents to be adult guests at camp.
- Encourage families to attend Life Works family camps in the area.

We are committed to operating an ongoing and energizing ministry to Cincinnati and the metro area. We can do this by: **An Ongoing Commitment**

1) Ensuring that the area has adequate funds to carry out our mission.

- Provide the fundraising necessary to meet the budget each year: 1997–$100,000; 1998– $150,000; 1999–$200,000.
- Be a liaison between the community and Life Works.
- Increase the number of churches giving each year until 2000 by 100 percent.

- Secure 50 new individual donors each year.
- Give businesses the opportunity to invest in the lives of young people.

2) Partnering with urban areas.

- Raise support for inner city areas.
- Hold joint events with areas in close proximity to Cincinnati.

STRATEGIC PLAN HIGHLIGHTS

The heart of our mission is reaching out to area youth and sharing the Gospel of Jesus Christ. We can accomplish this if we follow a strategic plan which strives to meet the following goals over the next three years:

Year One Goals:

- Life Works in five high schools
- $105,000 budget
- 20 people on committee
- 25 leaders
- two interns
- one staff member

Year Two Goals:

- Life Works in six high schools
- $150,000 budget
- 30 people on committee
- 30 leaders
- two interns
- one staff member

Year Three Goals:

- Life Works in every high school in the area
- $200,000 budget
- 40 people on committee
- 50 leaders
- two interns
- two staff members

Online Publishing System

BUSINESS PLAN

MOONBEAM PUBLISHING

11050 Sterling Road
Newark, New Jersey 07102

Combining the flexibility and interactivity of the web with advanced database driven digital printing, MoonBeam gives organizations the agility to produce on-demand narrowly targeted print documents.

- MISSION STATEMENT

- STRATEGIC OBJECTIVE

- THE COMPANY

- PRODUCTS & SERVICES

- TARGET MARKETS

- MARKETING

- MANAGEMENT

MISSION STATEMENT

To develop a profitable, fast-growing company whose core print products and print delivery systems help clients (Fortune 500 companies, franchises, government agencies, etc.) save time to market and control expenses on print and marketing programs. MoonBeam's proprietary process enables these companies to realize the benefits of "live" print documents which are more focused and printed in smaller quantities to reflect the shorter window of opportunity for sales in today's fast-paced economy.

STRATEGIC OBJECTIVE

To secure the growth capital necessary to:

- Launch an aggressive marketing campaign
- Develop technology and services
- Develop and expand markets and distribution channels
- Increase sales force

THE COMPANY

MoonBeam's proprietary online publishing system provides users with the easiest, fastest, most flexible, and economical means of delivering print communications on the market today. Combining the flexibility and interactivity of the web with advanced database driven digital printing, MoonBeam gives organizations the agility to produce on-demand narrowly targeted print documents. Additionally, the MoonBeam solution centralizes the print process, saving users time finalizing their print order and saving the clients' money by processing orders together.

Companies can now:

- effect cost savings using a "just in time" document assembly and delivery system which eliminates the problem of too many or too few documents
- quickly—and affordably—respond to market demand, maximizing sales opportunities and minimizing sales costs
- realize a higher return on investment in all print communications with a combination of precision-targeting and unrivaled matching of print need to print run

How it Works

MoonBeam provides a web-based order entry system that allows anyone—from corporate to consumer end-users—to select, edit, assemble, and deliver products in any quantity. These print products are customized using our "point and click" design tools. These newly developed documents are orderable through the company's proprietary storefront application, and printed by the company's high-end digital presses. Those corporate customers that require standard lithographic printing and storage will be serviced by partnerships with national fulfillment houses, giving customers a complete "pick, pack, and deliver" solution.

PRODUCTS & SERVICES

MoonBeam's core product and service offerings are as follows:

- **Online Order Entry:** An easy-to-use web-based order entry system that enables organizations to assemble and deliver targeted print runs. MoonBeam's process has the built-in intelligence to determine which printing press or methodology is best suited and most economical for that particular print job and assign print vendors, thereby automatically lowering print costs by printing centrally.

- **Online Editing:** The process enables users to create and recreate "live" documents, with little or no design training, that can be output via the most efficient and cost efficient print option available. Leveraging the flexibility and interactivity of the web, a "live" document is a print product that is easy to create, customize (promoting re-use), and deliver in economic quantities. (Live documents are more effective than static documents because they are based on the most current and relevant information. They are less costly because they are adapted from existing documents and design elements.)

Using the company's online design tools, customers can now prepare documents to be printed in runs of 250-10,000 with an economy that rivals traditional lithographic printing by eliminating waste, and improving response rates through documents that are "on target and on time."

- **Digital Printing:** MoonBeam owns and operates a digital printing press and several large format printers as well as commercial-grade copy machines (both color and black and white). The company's relationships with other strategically deployed digital press operators assures uninterrupted production during peak output times without further capital expense.

- **System Integration:** MoonBeam's software engineers build customized print on demand solutions across all vertical markets. The company's integration services are provided directly to the end user or through an "e-print" authorized web shop. MoonBeam's solutions include mass runs of identification cards, editable documents issued from complaint centers, brochure requests for colleges, editable business cards for local business, aftermarket sales programs, personalized travel brochures, brandable sales kits for channel partners, and more.

- **System Integration for Fulfillment Houses:** Fulfillment houses store and ship printed materials as well as other products for large enterprise clients on an as-needed basis. However, new print technologies that reduce paper overhead are posing significant challenges to fulfillment houses that are premised on "store and retrieve" business models. MoonBeam provides consultation and systems integration enabling fulfillment houses to modify their existing systems to more efficiently execute orders from existing inventories; moreover, MoonBeam will help migrate these companies to a print-on-demand environment that will keep them viable and competitive as the industry moves toward a "virtual" warehousing (or point, click, and fulfill) approach.

- **Database Driven Marketing Programs:** From "affinity" marketing efforts to event-driven initiatives or special one-time offers, the company's storefront technology enables organizations to rapidly and affordably ramp up a print-based campaign. Launched from websites with ties to backend databases, or via a MoonBeam storefront, marketing departments can compose and deliver customized documents in real time, based on the marketing objectives of a particular campaign, and further personalized using specific information gleaned from customer profiles housed in their database.

MoonBeam will generate revenues by:

- Fee Per Transaction
- Programming, Systems Integration, and Consultation
- Printing
- Database Management
- Report Generation

- Specialized Identification Card Programs
- License Fees for Specialized Software Programming (Centralized Print Platform, Restaurant Complaint Center Management, Automotive Sales Program, Self-service print center)

TARGET MARKETS

MoonBeam will target potential solutions partners (printers, fulfillment houses, web design shops) and marketing executives with Fortune 5,000 companies. MoonBeam's e-print solutions support strategic business functions for leading companies in every industry, including:

- Hotel/Hospitality Industry
- Cruise Lines
- Car Rental Companies
- Credit Card Companies
- Insurance Companies
- Financial Services
- Healthcare
- Pharmaceuticals
- Government
- Telecommunications
- Retail
- Insurance

MARKETING

The company's initial marketing campaign will focus on servicing a limited number of companies in select strategic markets (e.g., strategic solutions partners—web shops, fulfillment houses, printers—and Fortune 5,000 organizations). This will enable the company to efficiently and expeditiously prove the value of the technology, accelerate profitability, and carve out niche markets as it expands into other industries and aggregates market share.

MANAGEMENT

MoonBeam's senior management combines digital printing, information technology, fulfillment, and marketing experience. The company's CEO has founded several successful companies, including a print supplies distributor that was sold to a publicly traded company.

Retail Business Incubator

BUSINESS PLAN   ACME INCUBATORS

163 Perkins Street
Jackson, Michigan 49204

Business incubation programs have become essential economic development tools for communities that are trying to improve their economies and keep them healthy over the long run. The programs—which house very-early stage companies and provide them with a full array of business planning, management, and financial services—yield excellent returns. According to research, a high percentage (84%) of the companies that "graduate" from incubation programs remain in their communities, and an average 87 percent of incubator graduates are still in business.

- EXECUTIVE SUMMARY

- APPENDIX

**EXECUTIVE
SUMMARY**

Need

The number of businesses being started in the U.S. has more than doubled during the past decade, with well over 520,000 new business incorporations during the first nine months of 1988 alone. But the percentage of those that survive has remained the same (according to the Massachusetts Institute of Technology) or declined (according to Dun & Bradstreet). Either way, business start-ups are facing tough odds nationwide. According to the Federal Small Business Administration (SBA), 80 percent of all new small firms opened in 1988 will fail by 1993—out of money or energy or both.

Is there any way for entrepreneurs to combat these statistics? One increasingly popular economic support tool is the business incubator which, as the name implies, is a place designed to foster the growth of small companies.

Business incubation programs have become essential economic development tools for communities that are trying to improve their economies and keep them healthy over the long run. The programs—which house very-early stage companies and provide them with a full array of business planning, management, and financial services—yield excellent returns. According to research, a high percentage (84%) of the companies that "graduate" from incubation programs remain in their communities, and an average 87 percent of incubator graduates are still in business.

A retail business incubator located in Jackson is needed and will be the ideal project to stimulate and promote community and organization partnerships, along with economic growth. It can accomplish this by providing the opportunity for job placement, on-the-job training, entrepreneurial training, business development and technical assistance, career counseling, small business financing, space for business start-ups, space for existing business owners, and space for community organizations. This retail incubator could also satisfy the one-stop-shop needs of the community.

Purpose

A retail incubator's main purpose would be to catalyze the process of starting and growing retail business. A proven model, it will provide entrepreneurs with the expertise, networks, and tools they need to make their ventures successful. This retail incubation program will diversify economies, commercialize technologies, create jobs, and build wealth. It will also shield new businesses from the harsh environment they face during the first few years of existence—the most critical period.

While the Jackson retail incubator won't work magic, it can provide an encouraging place for young companies to make their start. Oscar Wright, California's Small Business Advocate, is coordinating with numerous public and private entities to encourage and assist in the creating of incubators in the state. Mr. Wright comments: "Incubators are on the cutting edge of developing new and strategic tools for small business success and local economic diversity. Incubators afford each community an opportunity to address specific concerns germane to their own economic reality." Even though we currently have a business incubator in Jackson, it has been proven that no two incubators will be exactly alike, reflecting differing and divergent needs.

Highly adaptable, incubators have differing goals: to diversify rural economies, to provide employment for and increase the wealth of depressed inner cities, and to transfer technology from universities and major corporations.

For National Business Incubator Association's (NBIA) *1998 State of the Business Incubation Industry*, surveys were mailed to all incubators in North America. Responses represented 67 percent of the 587 business incubation programs identified in NBIA's database as of spring 1998.

Researchers discovered the following:

- North American incubators have created nearly 19,000 companies still in business and more than 245,000 jobs
- Most incubator facilities (75%) are less than 40,000 square feet (the average is 36,657 square feet; median is 16,000 square feet)
- Incubators overall each served an average of 20 entrepreneurial firms in 1997 (the median number reported was 12)
- NBIA member incubators served, on average, twice as many client companies and nearly twice as many graduates as nonmember incubators
- Client companies in member incubators created, on average, one third more jobs than client companies of nonmember incubators

Primary Sponsors of Incubators

Nonprofit, Public, or Private

51 percent of all North American facilities, these incubators are sponsored by government and nonprofit organizations, and are primarily for economic development. This mission includes job creation, economic diversification, and/or expansion of the tax base.

Academic-Related

27 percent of all North American facilities, these incubators are affiliated with universities and colleges and share some of the same objectives of public and private incubators. In addition, they provide faculty with research opportunities, and alumni, faculty, and associated groups with start-up business opportunities. (This percentage includes some of the Hybrid responses that noted universities, community colleges or technical colleges.)

Hybrid

16 percent of all North American facilities, these incubators are joint efforts among government, nonprofit agencies, and/or private developers. These partnerships may offer the incubator access to government funding and resources, and private sector expertise and financing.

Private, for Profit

8 percent of all North American facilities, these incubators are run by investment groups or by real estate development partnerships. Their primary interests are economic reward for investment in tenant firms, new technology applications, and other technological transfers, and added value through development of commercial and industrial real estate.

Other

5 percent of all North American facilities, these incubators are sponsored by a variety of non-conventional sources such as art organizations, Native American, church groups, chambers of commerce, port districts, etc.

Incubator Focus

- 43%—Mixed Use
- 25%—Technology (general)
- 10%—Manufacturing
- 9%—Targeted
- 6%—Service
- 5%—Empowerment
- 2%—Other

The *1998 State of the Business Incubation Industry* contains 67 charts and graphs profiling the industry and highlighting results. Some findings:

- Forty-five (45) percent of today's incubators are urban, 36 percent are rural, and the remaining 19 percent are suburban.
- Most (43 percent) are mixed use and another 25 percent are technology. Ten (10) percent focus on manufacturing companies and 6 percent on service companies. The study revealed growth of the newer, "targeted" incubators—ones that focus on a specific industry such as software, food manufacturing, multimedia, or the arts. They are 9 percent of the total.
- The average incubator was established in 1991.
- The average operating expenses are between $72,320 and $207,500.
- There is no such thing as a standard size for incubators. The average incubator is 36,657 square feet, the mean is 16,000 square feet and the range is from 600 to 500,000 square feet. (These numbers exclude space rented to tenants not receiving incubation services.)
- Eighty-five (85) percent of all senior incubator managers have a college degree or post-graduate education.
- The average incubator offers full incubation services to 20 in-house and affiliate companies; member incubators serve an average of 24.

A relatively new concept in economic development circles, business incubation has grown markedly—from 12 North American programs in 1980 to the 587 identified by this study.

The *1998 State of the Business Incubation Industry* joins "The Impact of Incubator Investments" study (conducted in 1997 by Ohio University, the Southern Technology Council, University of Michigan and NBIA to paint a picture of today's incubators and the effect they're having. There's no question they are viable economic development tools. Through research we now know incubators are better at what they do if their managers remain involved through membership in the association, the industry's best professional development resource.

Economic Impact

The results of the largest study ever conducted on business incubation show that these support programs for entrepreneurial firms have impressive, measurable impacts on the companies they serve. In addition, experts are calling business incubators a "best value" in economic development, based on low program costs and high return on investment to communities.

"Business incubation programs treat entrepreneurial companies as important community and national resources, and they provide assistance that ensures company success. This study should convince communities that if they don't already have a business incubation program, they'll want to start thinking about one," says Dinah Adkins, executive director of the NBIA, Athens, Ohio.

The study, completed in October 1997, was conducted by the University of Michigan, NBIA, Ohio University and the Southern Technology Council under a grant from the U.S. Department of Commerce Economic Development Administration. It examined the impacts of business incubators, which house very-early stage companies and provide on-site management and a full array of business planning, management, and financial services. Entrepreneurial companies stay in an incubator for an average of two to three years, then graduate to become free standing.

Some of the most important results of the study—which enlisted incubator companies, graduates, managers, and stakeholders—show how effective business incubators are:

- Retail incubator companies experience very healthy growth. The average firm's sales increased by more than 400 percent from the time it entered until the time it left the incubator. In addition, the average annual growth in sales per firm in all types of incubators was $239,535.
- Business incubation programs produce graduate firms with high survival rates. A reported 87 percent of incubated companies that fulfilled program graduation requirements are still in business.
- Business incubation programs create new jobs for a low subsidy cost and a good return on investment. The estimated cost per job created in relation to public grants was $1,109. It's not uncommon for the cost per job of other job-generating economic development programs to be three to six times higher.
- Most firms that graduate from business incubators—an average of 84 percent— remain in their communities.
- Business incubation programs assist companies that create many new jobs. In 1996 incubators reported, on average, that their firms had created 468 jobs directly and 234 additional "spin-off" jobs in the community for a total of 702 jobs.
- Despite their early stage, most incubator firms provide employee benefits.
- Retail incubators contribute to their client companies' success and expand community resources, increasing early-stage capital, access to entrepreneurship education, and other sources of help to young companies.
- Retail incubation programs improve local community image.

Earlier studies and surveys had suggested that business incubation was a successful economic development strategy. "The anecdotal information said the same thing, but there had been no large-scale, national study of the industry to confirm that," says research team member Larry Molnar, director, EDA University Center for Economic Diversification, University of Michigan Business School, Ann Arbor.

"Incubation is highly adaptable, which is another reason it's such a good economic development tool," Adkins says.

The research analysis also led investigators to formulate policy recommendations. They urge incubation program sponsors at all levels to, among other things: (1) invest more heavily in incubators as a major tool in economic development, (2) target their investments to the best program type for their community resources and (3) seek evidence that any program they support adheres to the authentic definition of an incubator and strives to institute best practices. They also charged the business incubation industry with developing standard impact measures and distributing to incubators a simple toolkit, developed by the researchers, that will make data collection easy at the local level.

"Adding these measures to incubators' total evaluation process will help them track their growth and effectiveness. It will also allow the industry to create a national database, making it possible to study and improve the business incubation process in years to come," says team member Hugh Sherman, assistant professor of policy and strategy, management systems department, Ohio University in Athens.

Incubator's Delivery

There is no single formula for retail incubators. In general, however, they are defined as physical facilities that provide new firms with the supportive network necessary to increase their probability of survival during the crucial early years when they are most vulnerable. Most start-ups are short of everything but the founder's energy, and a Jackson retail incubator is one way of building on that spirit while cushioning the demands on things formative businesses don't have—particularly working capital.

Industry leaders pinpoint three areas in which a facility should "deliver" in order to rightfully be called an incubator:

1. The facility should provide flexible space for a number of companies at a rent that is either below average for the area, or an exceptional value for the services provided. There should be plenty of room for each business to expand.
2. Shared equipment and services are provided that would otherwise be unavailable or unaffordable to help businesses cut costs. Receptionist, photocopying and conference rooms are most popular, with security, phone answering/message center, computer access, word processing, typing, audiovisual equipment and shipping/receiving also in high demand.
3. The incubator should offer experienced management advice and access to professional expertise, backed by a policy which ensures that each participating business completes a thorough business plan and any other strategic planning necessary.

Most incubators with a success rate of over 80 percent also meet a fourth criteria: access to capital. Facilities with in-house funding are often difficult to get into because they evaluate businesses more strictly, but knowing that funding is available when needed helps both the individual business and the incubator management to prosper.

Incubator Characteristics

Incubators come in different forms. According to NBIA statistics, most (47 percent) are nonprofit, operated by groups ranging from community development organizations to municipal governments seeking to create new jobs and increase local tax bases. Academic related incubators (14 percent) serve as a link between innovations developed by universities or colleges and the businesses that market them to the general public. The so-called "mixed" incubator or "hybrid," which links private companies and public institutions in an effort to create new business, comprises 14 percent.

A growing number (25 percent) are for-profit incubators, which make money by acquiring part ownership in their tenant companies or from rental payments. For-profit operations are expected to grow to at least half the total of all incubators in the next few years. The future is private, for-profit incubators. Of that there is little doubt, the only uncertainty is timing (The NBIA's Adkins, however, contends that nonprofit incubators are still growing at an extremely rapid rate—faster than for-profits—and will continue to be a strong component of the overall mix).

While the major goal of for-profit incubators is to make money—they are in the business of helping young companies because it pays—their motivation is not dissimilar to that of their tenants. Says the owner of one: "Why are we for-profit? Because like the people in the incubator, we're entrepreneurs, too. It sets up the right incentives for us. We survive because we run it like a business."

Just as incubators come in different forms, their size also varies. The largest, measured by land area, is Science Park in New Haven, Connecticut, with 10 buildings on 80 acres. The Charleston Business and Technology Center in South Carolina has the greatest number of tenants—147 in one building. The University City Science Center in Philadelphia consists of

1,100,000 square feet sprawled over 10 square blocks and divided among approximately 100 tenants. Their proudest boast: graduating over 500 businesses. In addition, California is home to the largest incubator in the Western U.S.—the San Pedro Venture Center.

Unlike the traditional incubator in the East, where older buildings were used for facilities, San Pedro boasts of "modern, clean, new surroundings and a 1,000-line Centrex communication system from Pacific Bell," states Manager Frans Verschoor. "We've also just opened a 5,000-square-foot pre-school daycare center, built according to state requirements at a cost of $100,000, that can accommodate 45 children. Operated by the local YWCA, which is paying $1 annually for rent, its central location means parents will never be further than 800 feet, or one minute, from their children," Verschoor comments.

"The pre-school center, the first we know of nationwide in an incubator setting, was constructed in recognition that the requirements of time have changed the traditional roles of women, who are now equally part of the workforce. The growth of single-parent families is also a factor. Having on-site daycare facilities helps the parent, the employer, and the child."

The San Pedro Venture Center, which opened in September 1988, will ultimately house 125 tenants in 11 buildings situated on 10 acres. It currently provides office suites (492 to 785 square feet) or combination office/warehouse spaces (584 to 1,400 square feet), each of which functions as a totally independent unit. Each unit has air conditioning/heating, lights, blinds, restroom, and transformer (to provide a range of power from normal household to industrial strength). All a tenant needs to bring is a desk and chair to set up operations. Each unit is individually alarmed, and connected to a central system complete with camera surveillance.

Not only space, but leases are flexible, unlike typical five-year contracts, it would require a minimum of only six months. While there is no long-term obligation, most tenants signed up for three years.

A host of "pay as you use them" services is available for tenants, including a fax machine, photocopying, and secretarial services, a conference room (with another under construction that will accommodate up to 400 people for seminars and social gatherings), mailroom, and staffed reception area. These services are provided at cost; the developers receive their income solely from rent.

Verschoor has also negotiated with service firms in the Los Angeles area (including accounting, tax, marketing, legal, advertising, and business planning) which have agreed to give sizeable discounts to San Pedro Venture Center tenants. "Not only does this give tenants access to first-rate counsel," Verschoor emphasizes, "but the arrangement makes sense for the consultants. A small company today could be a Fortune 500 in the future."

Additionally, the center can connect tenants with funding sources, both public and private, and has hooked up with NASA's computer database—the largest in the world—which, in Verschoor's words, "is ready to go when tenant needs for information so require."

While Verschoor uses the number of new tenants—now averaging one a week—as one indicator of success, he is most proud of the resultant job creation. "We're located within the San Pedro/Wilmington Enterprise Zone, where the goal is to establish 1,350 new and lasting jobs within the next five years. In its first five months of operation alone, the San Pedro Venture Center created 30 of those jobs."

Model Incubator

Incubator Benefits

Business

It's clear that retail incubators can significantly cut down on a start-up's overhead. They allow entrepreneurs to focus on the development of their ventures, rather than on the more mundane aspects of running a business. As a former incubator tenant in Washington, D.C., comments: "Why should you deal with issues such as what phone system or Xerox to buy? It makes far more sense to rent space in an incubator and concentrate on the success of your business."

Community

In addition to surveying companies, incubation professionals, and community stakeholders, the research team conducted a macroeconomic study in four communities to analyze the expanded impacts of incubators, such as how many direct and community spin-off, or "indirect," jobs they add and what effect they have on the tax base.

The return on investment was clearly healthy. "Looking at the operating subsidies these incubators received and the jobs and local taxes they produced, we estimate the return on public investment at $4.96 for every $1 of public operating subsidies," says Larry Molnar. This calculation did not include state or federal taxes, he notes. "The numbers make it clear that business incubators add considerable resources to—not take resources from—their communities," Molnar adds.

The research team confirmed another important fact about incubators: They are not all alike. Although some impacts were similar regardless of incubator type, other impacts related directly to an incubator's mission and goals.

"For instance, firms in all types of business incubators had similar average increases in their annual gross revenues. But firms from technology incubators created more jobs than other types of incubators," says team member Lou Tornatzky, director of the Southern Technology Council, Research Triangle Park, North Carolina. Incubators that are focused on low-income people and minorities were rated high by their community stakeholders in assisting minorities and women business owners and enhancing the business climate. The study divided incubators into three main categories according to the main types of firms served—mixed use, technology, and empowerment/neighborhood revitalization. There are many other subtypes, though, including manufacturing, arts, software, kitchen, and multimedia incubators.

Phases of Project

For planning purposes it will be beneficial to divide the project into phases and establish the timelines for each distinct phase. The usual divisions are: Feasibility (average time is three months); Development (average nine months); Renovation (average time ranges from three months to one year); and the Early Stage Operations during which the project will experience operational losses (average time is 18 months.) The delineation of each phase's time period is particularly important for those phases that occur after you "sign on the line" as owners or lessees of a facility, thus incurring fixed operational costs.

The availability of funds may necessitate that the renovation work on the facility be divided into phases. Certain sections of the facility may have to remain undeveloped until operating revenues generate enough to support increased mortgage, another tenant is located, or there is an allocation of operating budget revenues for renovation of the next phase.

We will identify portions of the facility we will probably lease first. Create a leasing schedule and, if possible, we will attempt to lease in concentrated areas of the building. Certain portions of the facility may be leased to tenants before renovations while other portions could be used during renovations.

When we formulate the project's classifications and timeline, we will remember that each situation is unique. Though this section sites the most commonly used divisions in the planning process many projects "go their own way" and may require classifications which are exceptions to these rules.

There are four phases in the incubator development process: preliminary planning, initiation and start-up, fine-tuning operations, and growing client firms. The following is a snapshot of the first phase.

- **Preliminary Planning**—Identify potential stakeholders. These will be the movers and shakers in our community: the successful entrepreneurs, politicians, administrators and community activists who are tied to economic development. After identifying stakeholders, we will get a good handle on their goals and objectives.
- **Conduct a Needs Assessment**—Identify local entrepreneurial base and gaps in the existing business and financial services for entrepreneurs in the community and barriers to accessing these services. This information would come directly from the entrepreneurs. This assessment will also let us know if the community's entrepreneurs and stakeholders mesh. This could be accomplished by facilitating a strategic planning session to allow the stakeholders and project developers to step back and take a look at the implications of their goals and objectives. Also a focus group would be developed of both experienced and start-up entrepreneurs in the sessions.
- **Choosing the Right Real Estate**—The following items will be taken into account when choosing a building: zoning, building codes, location factors, traffic, hazards, leasable space, security, insurance, access to facilities, material flow, staging areas, floor loads, ventilation, heating and cooling, electrical service, and plumbing.
- **Evaluate Organizational Issues, Financing Options**—Identify the relationship between the owner, the developer, and management. At this point, the decisions on legal structure of the incubator ownership and evaluation of potential sources of financing for development and operations.
- **Determine Support Services and Operating Pro Forma**—Determine the composition, organization, pricing and legal structure of shared services, management assistance, consulting, and business financing programs. To determine these factors we would do an operating scheme for the incubator—based on acquisition or site costs, construction costs, market analysis, rental rates, and lease-up schedule.
- **Select a Management Team and Finalize Business Plan**—Select a management team that is committed to the community, have sympathy for the need of start-up businesses, flexible, creative, steady under stress, high level of interpersonal skills, and they can mentor, administrate, handle public relations, facilitate and can be a friend. Included in our business plan will be preliminary drawings and a client outreach recruitment plan, fine-tuned construction costs, market and economic information, monthly cash-flow projections for the next five years, description of management team, description of legal and organization structure. We will then nail down our financing—get lenders, grantors, and equity partners to come up with money to start the project.

Service Programs

Our service program will precede the operation of the business incubator. A good business assistance service program will serve as one of our most effective tenant and client recruitment tools. Recruiting will begin well in advance of the availability of space for lease. It would be quite acceptable to begin our service delivery up to a year in advance of available space for lease or facility occupancy.

Our service program will be more concerned with the content and quality of each service provided rather than the number of services provided.

The typical management assistance service programs include office practice services, general management assistance services, and technical services. The following list is a sample of one menu of services provided by a business incubator located in Pennsylvania that has been in operation for more than three years.

Level One—Office Practice Services:

- Clerical services
- Switchboard services
- Voice mailbox/electronic mailbox
- Telephone equipment
- Least cost routing for telephone calls
- FAX service
- Postal service
- Overnight courier service
- Notary services
- Photocopier
- VCR/TV equipment station
- Audiovisual equipment rental
- Conference room
- Canteen and coffee service
- Sports ticket purchasing
- Auto service discounts
- Audiotape/videotape/journal clip services
- Annual exhibit event
- Group purchasing/warehouse membership
- Furniture rental
- Laser printing and clip art graphics
- Printing services
- Exhibit area
- Desktop Publishing Services
- Workshops/Seminars

Level Two—Management Services:

- Capital formation
- Customized job training
- Entrepreneurial classes/training
- Technical and commercial communications
- Technical writing—second draft
- Bookkeeping/accounting
- Facts about starting and operating a business in Michigan
- Legal referral
- One hour legal briefings
- New Venture Developments
- Business Plan preparation
- Employment services
- Maintenance of facilities/equipment
- Micro-loans
- Shipping and receiving services
- Marketing service sampler

- Marketing
  - –Direct mail campaign
  - –Worksheet series
  - –Federal/state procurement
  - –Offense/defense tactics
  - –Panel presentation
  - –Export assistance
  - –Market research
  - –Printed circuit design

A portion of these services will be offered at first for little or no fee in order to introduce and stimulate initial usage per client. This would be equivalent to a special introductory offer.

It is possible that our management assistance program would charge a fee unless our program's third party funding support restricts or prohibits charging a fee.

We will be proactive in order to generate and maintain a sufficient client base for the service program. One strategy to build our client base volume necessary to continue development of the service program is to accept nontenant client companies.

Responding to an informal e-mail survey and phone interviews by the NBIA, business incubator managers said that their programs' successful entrepreneurial firms had the following characteristics:

Program Management

- An effective management team that works cooperatively and consists of members selected to provide a range of knowledge and skills
- Sound financing, the earlier the better. Funding is directly related to a firm's success, and in some cases it can be the deciding factor between a business venture's success or failure
- Principals that are able to focus on a lead product or service, and avoid over-investing in development and diversification
- Principals that make business decisions based on a clear understanding of the market and the competition, rather than their own enchantment with their product or service
- Principals that keep on top of best business practices by surrounding themselves with knowledgeable people, by remaining open to their advice and ideas, and by being willing and ready to make changes based on new information
- A well-researched business plan in place that provides clear direction and focus
- Principals that are good money managers and remain in control of the venture's books
- Entrepreneurs who are passionate about their ventures and communicate that excitement to potential funders, customers, and mentors.

Entrepreneurial failures often lacked some or all of these elements, according to survey respondents.

The incubator manager should be able to explain why business planning is important, both during start-up efforts and afterwards. Some firms may never prepare a business plan, because they aren't eligible for venture capital, for instance, but they are the same companies that tend to make "seat-of-the pants decisions," and to lack a clear vision of their future.

Principles of the Incubator

As listed in the NBIA Regional Training Institute curriculum, these 10 principles state that incubators should:

1. Concentrate on the development or collection of support services that nurture start-up or emerging businesses. Providing below-market rental rates should not be the primary focus of the incubator.
2. Value growth and development of individual companies beyond their ability to pay rent.
3. Be judged on their ability to create new businesses or help nurture emerging companies, not on the number of jobs directly created. Successful, growing businesses will create employment opportunities.
4. Be structured so that the property element takes a secondary position relative to programs since serving businesses is the core of quality incubation programs. However, the facility can offer the following tangible and intangible benefits:
     a. a positive cash flow resulting from successful incubator facilities management
     b. a centralized place for entrepreneurs to meet
     c. a focus for small business support programs in the community
     d. opportunities for valuable interchanges among entrepreneurial firms
5. Be viewed as one possible component of an integrated, overall, regional economic development plan and be designed to reflect the strengths and weaknesses of the region.
6. Be structured so that program outcomes match both the short- and long-term benefits required by sponsors.
7. Work from a clear mission statement with quantifiable goals and objectives tied to an evaluation process which rewards quality performance.
8. Be run by highly skilled, street-smart managers who are willing to wear a large number of hats, e.g., those of: general business counselor, triage nurse, facilities manager, psychologist, investment banker, etc.
9. Recognize the inevitable tension faced by the manager, who functions as both advocate for the companies and landlord of a facility.
10. Set up and run operational policies and systems in a businesslike fashion.

Staffing

Many incubation programs are hard to staff. A number of "pressures" on the incubator program drive up expenses and drive down revenue. Many business incubation programs respond to these income pressures by restructuring their staff in one of the following ways:

1. Balancing the duties and responsibilities of the incubator manager between facility management and the delivery of management assistance services to the tenant companies. If the duties and responsibilities do not emphasize the management assistance side of the equation, most managers will spend the majority of their time on the property and will neglect client services.
2. Carefully considering the need to have a full-time staff member attend to the central switchboard and clerical/word processing services for the tenant companies. This is a key position. The switchboard is the lifeline of communication between the incubator and its marketplace. The impression of the incubator's quality is most influenced by the style and content of the switchboard services. The skill to operate a switchboard is rare. Many secretaries have clerical skills and consider the switchboard a "prison sentence." Someone who enjoys the interaction of a switchboard and has word processing skills as well is invaluable.

3. A full-time switchboard/word processing staff person with a part-time manager is more effective than a full-time manager and a part-time switchboard/word processing staff person. If we can afford to have both positions full-time, that is great. However, many incubation projects are forced to operate with part-time staff support and you cannot have a part-time switchboard service: business communication requirements are not part-time. Management assistance, however, can be scheduled into a part-time manager's work week.

4. Utilizing community organizations' school-to-work and on-the-job training participants, is another way of addressing staffing needs. This concept accomplishes two objectives:

    a. It helps community organizations to place their program completers

    b. It maintains an ongoing pool of incubator staff candidates.

The following steps will be used to reach an acquisition lease price for using a facility as a business incubator.

Targeting a Facility

1. We will examine floor plans and use our best judgment to sketch partitions on the floor plans to accommodate tenant spaces of 140, 400, 1,100, 3,000, and 6,000 square feet. For each large space we will have two spaces of the next smaller size.

2. Measure the linear feet of each designated area.

3. Measure the net rentable square feet of the partitions.

4. Grade and label our leasable spaces A, B, C, or D based on the quality of the space and its location.

5. Seek input from three or four commercial realtors regarding market lease rates for similar property and set our market value at the average.

6. Calculate the potential revenue at full occupancy by listing A space at full market value, B space at 90 percent of market, C space at 80 percent of market, and D space at 70 percent of market. The total is our potential full occupancy revenue.

7. Starting with this potential full occupancy figure, we will subtract 8 percent for vacancy and 6 percent as bad debt expense.

8. Next we will subtract at least $.90 but no more than $1.40 per square foot for contributions toward our service program and staff.

9. We then will subtract fixed costs for taxes, insurance, etc.

10. By calculating $.90 per square foot for maintenance, cleaning, and repairs, we will subtract it from our balance. The rate can be adjusted up or down depending upon the condition of the facility.

11. This final figure is the amount we may spend on a lease or mortgage at "full occupancy," regardless of when this is achieved.

12. We will follow a conservative schedule of what we anticipate will be leased to tenants such as:

    a. 10 percent pre-leased

    b. 40 percent lease-up achieved by end of year one

    c. 50 percent lease-up achieved by end of year two

    d. 80 percent lease-up achieved by end of year three

13. These steps can determine what we will have available for lease or mortgage payments through the first three years.

We will then ask ourselves the following questions: Is there is enough money to support our monthly payment with the anticipated subsidy for the first there years? Is there enough money to support an unsubsidized program at "full occupancy"?

If the answer is yes, we will hire an engineer to corroborate our partitioning plan and construct a rough estimate of our renovation costs. If not, we will go back to the property owner to re-negotiate and acquisition cost or lease rate.

Based on both the engineer's assessment of renovation and the evaluation of our leasing plan, we can weigh the advantages and disadvantages of constructing a new facility versus proceeding with acquisition and renovation.

Industry "Rules of Thumb"

- We should be able to demonstrate that the facility will break even at 67 percent occupancy or less.
- We will need at least 30,000 square fee gross space to have any hope of breaking even.
- The candidate facilities that look the best financially would be our targeted facilities. We will need to focus on what the facility will generate in income as an incubator than on the actual market value of the property. The purchase price will be dictated by our calculations.
- Having collected the operating data and renovation estimates, we would then be ready to negotiate a tough acquisition price and terms payment.

Strategic Planning Issues

As development plans are prepared, there are a number of strategic issues that need to be addressed. The issues listed below represent very important, basic questions that will be answered as we move forward with the program.

1. Who will fund the phases of this program?
2. Will this program be place on a plan to self-sustain?
3. How large should the facility be?
4. How should we structure management assistance services within the program?
5. What comes first?

Most business incubators struggle to attain break-even operating status. Those that generate an operating surplus usually achieve returns on investment that would not excite an investor. Many business incubation programs fall victim to sustaining a difficult facility and having client bases that do not generate user fees sufficient to meet management and office practice costs.

Hopefully, our program will generate regular operating profits or our program's budget and cash flow will never become a concern. The income potential of a building can increase its market value and, hopefully, each audit will show an increase in the physical assets of the corporation so our facility's assessed value will increase our net worth annually.

Most business incubators that achieve self-sustaining operations have more than 30,000 square feet of net rentable space and can generate revenues more than $1.50 per square foot above facility fixed costs. However, with very few exceptions, business incubators cannot support adequate returns on investments to more than one stakeholder organization.

Funding Sources

Retail incubators have received loan and grant funding from literally hundreds of public and private funding sources. The following are a few planning issues to be considered relating to funding:

A. Establishing a nonprofit public or private corporation that will offer access to the widest range of funding sources.

B. If we plan on accessing federal funds from an organization such as EDA we will plan on allowing nine months to one year for a decision.

C. After our investment in facility renovation/acquisition, we will plan on raising funds to cover an average of 18 months of operational losses.

D. Federal and state public funds to support business incubators are growing in number and dollar volume allocated.

E. Most business incubators have not received grant funding support beyond three years.

F. We will research the dozens of ways to structure the acquisition or lease of the facility that involve creative financing techniques with the seller that will produce far greater cost savings benefits than do most third party grants and loans.

G. Unfortunately, there are more funding sources available for facility acquisition and renovation than for service delivery and early stage operational losses.

H. It is difficult to repay money borrowed for delivery of services and the early stage operational losses of our facility unless we have a substantial return on our leasing plan once we achieve a high occupancy rate. We may be able to support these early stage operational losses via debt financing if the money we borrow is a program-related investment from a foundation. The program-related investment usually provides us with a long-term, unsecured, zero-interest loan.

I. It is now easier to raise grant funds for new construction than it has been in the past.

J. We have to beware of agreements accompanying the acceptance of a grant such as:
   - Agreement to have tenant companies sign lease agreements with strict employment clauses.
   - Agreeing to create dramatic job growth in early years.
   - Agreeing to maintain the incubator program for 15 years or longer.

K. Beware of being pressured into undercapitalizing our project.

L. Within our proposal narrative we will discuss the entrepreneurs and prospects we have met, surveyed, and served rather than to speak philosophically about our marketing approach for locating tenant prospects.

M. If training must be offered as a condition to our funding, we will make sure that training includes nontenant business training as well as tenant company training.

N. Establish a for-profit organization and utilize venture capitalists.

Marketing Strategy

Underlying the retail incubator marketing plan is an exploration of the question: Are there prospective customers for a business incubation program in this community? The following questions are suggested to serve as a catalyst to stimulate some creative ways of identifying collection points where our prospective clients may congregate.

1. Are there any clusters of businesses that appear to be significant or emerging in markets that appear to have a positive near-term future?
2. If so, what do these cluster companies purchase in some volume that could be supplied locally?
3. Do the owners of these cluster companies ever meet together?
4. What topics would attract these prospective entrepreneurs to attend a meeting at which the incubation program plan could be introduced and discussed?

In addition to answering these four questions, we would identify a minimum of five or more key contact points in the community whom new entrepreneurs can call or visit to receive information and resources to start their company. These contacts would be educated on the objectives of the incubation program. These contacts would also refer to the incubator those entrepreneurs who show the best promise of business survival and who express an interest in facilities which offer an accompanying access to services.

Identifying these key contact points and answers to the preceding questions will help us to locate potential clients. It will also be important for us to be able to assess the demand for a business incubation program. In addition to conducting a traditional survey and collecting demographic statistics, an alternative approach of assessing client demand will be to offer a demonstration of some components of our management assistance services program. We can then gauge an indication of demand by recording the number and type of participants who access our services.

These services can be demonstrated by a variety of ways: one-day workshops, a series of workshops, one-on-one counseling assistance, etc. These ongoing workshops provided by the incubator will be designed to help the program assess the level of entrepreneurial activity in the area as well as to market the incubator itself.

Once we have gathered this information allowing us to identify sources of potential clients as well as assess market demand for management assistance services, we will be ready to consider other important questions as we prepare our marketing plan.

1. How can we position ourselves, our staff, and board to initiate marketing and sales activities rather than just to react to opportunities for promoting our program?
2. Do we plan to escrow/allocate funds for marketing and sales activities?
3. Do we us the word "incubator" as the primary descriptor to prospective tenants?
4. Do we split our potential customers into vertical segments to help target special features of our program to customers?
5. Do we have plans to develop a "constancy of purpose" among our staff and stakeholders regarding the continuing development and effective implementation of our marketing plan.
6. Do we have plans to establish a "track system" to guide our staff and board through the correct process of presenting the facilities and services of our program to prospective tenants?
7. Do we have a clear statement of how we are distinguished from your competitors?
8. Are we planning to become an active member in our state and national incubation associations?
9. Will our marketing materials focus primarily on what just happened vs. what is planned to happen?
10. Will our incubation program staff and service providers have regular planning sessions to focus on new services for our existing clients and to plan activities that demonstrate our services to prospective clients?
11. Will we actively use our clients' successes to market to target groups?

Creative Funding Strategies

Because financial resources are limited, one solution we will use is to be creative in negotiating acquisition, renovation, lease agreements, and leasehold improvements. We will use the following suggestions to get our creative thought processes flowing.

A. Remember to ignore the asking prices on the property/facility. Do our calculations as detailed and make an offer to purchase or lease based on the income value of the property—not the market value.
B. Request that seller carry a portion of the lease/mortgage, receiving monthly payments based on a graduated scale as defined by a prorated three-year lease plan. This will allow us to pay more only after we have rented a larger percentage of our space.
C. Consider capital equipment needs and seek contributions for the phone system, office equipment, furniture, etc., from companies that manufacture and/or sell these products.
D. Ask area banks to pool funds via a CRA plan for leasehold improvements. Then base our leasehold improvements on tenant loans a few percentage points higher than CRA

terms, amortizing the payments to the length of the leases. This will enable us to have the tenants pay for more of the capital improvements as well as encourage longer lease agreements.

E. Permit the anchor tenant to sublease to others as long as the tenant agrees to commit to a larger square foot area than they currently need, but eventually plan to utilize. Give them a lower rate on the extended space allowing them to gain a margin of income on that space.

F. Include the rental space, leased furniture, and a package of office practice services in one flat rate monthly charge. When using this method, we will calculate the square foot rate of this office at double our normal lease cost. The services fee should be calculated at an hourly rate based on defined usage—assume the maximum number of hours whether or not they use their full allotment. The sum of all three factors equals the monthly charge.

G. Determine whether the seller has the opportunity to obtain a tax deduction for the amount of the difference between the market appraisal and the sales price. Such a tax deduction would create an incentive for the seller to discount the sale price by the net effect of the tax deduction.

H. Attempt to restrict grant funds to a specific portion of the facility in order to increase project flexibility and leverage other sources of debt equity.

I. Identify our net rentable lease units as A, B, C, or D grade space. Attempt to package A space with some B, C, and/or D space per tenant. This will prevent the possibility that we will rent the A space first and experience the increased difficulty of lease the B, C, and D space. Price the lease rates accordingly.

Community Reinvestment Act (CRA)

The CRA, revised in 1989, offers the incubation industry two opportunities: to obtain bank participation in an incubator development project, and to obtain money for revolving loan funds or other lending programs in order to extend credit to incubator tenants and the small- and minority-business community.

Banks can fulfill some of their CRA compliance factors related to their effectiveness in communicating with—and working with—community groups by participating in the development of a business incubator. There are a number of services the incubators can provide to banks with good data about what's happening economically in their neighborhoods and alert banks to the latest neighborhood business trends. Additionally, they can provide banks with a wide range of services including helping to review loan packages and other technical assistance.

Incubation Part of Policy Statement

After a broad-based community task force assesses the credit needs of the community—which is always the first step—it is commonly found that almost every market reports the same needs: financing for small businesses for working capital and for fixed assets. This would be included in the needs statement, the policy statement asks the banks to come with a plan to address these needs. And that's where an incubator can fit in.

The CRA implementation plan can specifically include funding for an incubator project or loans for incubator clients and small businesses.

Raising Awareness

Federal Reserve states that "Support of small business incubator programs affords institutions an opportunity to provide other services which can stimulate small-business development. These activities, in our view, would be included as part of an institution's record of performance under CRA."

Washington added that this communiqué, received in November 1988, placed incubator projects under the category of "other activities" in which financial institutions may engage in order to receive CRA credits. According to Washington, banks can help incubators address two pressing needs: funding for incubator project and loans for start-up businesses.

According to Washington, an incubator looking to secure these kinds of CRA-related funds from banks must first participate in the formation of a community group such as a city-county reinvestment task force. This task force represents all segments of the community, which is responsible for coordinating and assisting with the assessment of needs and eventually developing a plan.

Funding for projects is not a given. An incubator has to be a viable project and be on the alert for opportunities to promote its work.

Banks must be shown that incubators can offer them a good deal that will help them meet the regulators' CRA expectations.

One group meets with a consortium of seven banks. The group meets with top officers once a month to help them meet CRA requirements. This group has adequate information about their real estate transactions, where they might be lagging behind and what they may do to better market their services in terms of meeting CRA requirements.

Blending bank funds with government and foundation sources creates a solid building block and helps the incubator to be viewed as less risky. The incubator can also engineer some other CRA-related deals: seed capital and subordinate loan pools to help meet the needs of minorities and underserved people in the community.

Another way a bank can help is to provide scholarships for low-income entrepreneurs and owners of small businesses or start-ups to take classes.

The retail incubator can also assist with providing a one-on-one service covering the "pre-application" loan process for a possible citywide seed-capital revolving loan fund; this service can be funded by the Small Business Development Center (SBDC).

Utilizing the CRA is an excellent way for our incubator to leverage financial support, both for ourselves and, perhaps more importantly, our tenants.

Empowerment Zone Initiatives

In December of 1994, Detroit, Atlanta, Baltimore, Chicago, New York, and a partnership of Philadelphia and Camden were awarded empowerment zones.

Detroit's winning proposal was the result of many people representing the community and the gamut of public and private organizations throughout Detroit and the metropolitan area. The vision expressed, the projects proposed, and the commitment guaranteed, truly set Detroit's proposal apart from any of the other submissions.

According to a the *Jackson Journal* article dated September 27, 2000, and entitled "Gore envisions cash aid for Jackson," it is possible that Jackson, Michigan, may have another opportunity to apply for an empowerment zone designation. A state-of-the-art business incubator could play a role in the strategic plan to outline programs and strategies aimed at reducing the effects of poverty in the inner city. It could also assist in bringing together unlikely groups of community residents, city and state officials, and representatives of local business and financial institutions to work side by side to determine the best ways to address poverty issues in their communities.

The business incubator will also assist with the framework of the EZ/EC programs' four key principles:

- **Economic Opportunity,** including job creation within the community and throughout the region, entrepreneurial initiatives, small business expansion, and training for jobs that offer upward mobility
- **Sustainable Community Development,** to advance the creation of livable and vibrant communities through comprehensive approaches that coordinate economic, physical, environmental, community, and human development
- **Community-Based Partnerships,** involving participation of all segments of the community, including the political and governmental leadership, community groups, health and social service groups, environmental groups, religious organizations, the private and nonprofit sectors, centers of learning, other community institutions, and individual citizens
- **Strategic Vision for Change,** which identifies what the community will become and a strategic map for revitalization

Since the aim of the EZ/EC Initiative is to serve as a catalyst for locally generated strategies, its accountability can be assured through the development of benchmarks such as a business incubator. The initiative's design reflects the benefit of prior experience and knowledge of successful economic development efforts by combining targeted tax incentives with such things as direct financial assistance, job readiness training and placement services, improvements to physical infrastructure and public safety, and the development of strong community partnerships shown to be essential for long-term success.

Like Detroit, Jackson can also empower itself through the strength of a city committed to a new economic future. Our future can also be built upon:

- New economic foundations blending business into the neighborhood, linking training and jobs to Zone residents, offering real access to new financial resources
- The proposed Zone's new vitality can succeed by citywide and regional cooperation. We can build and maintain a positive flow of employment, capital and innovation. Each section of our Plan can also demonstrate a commitment to build new bridges across all economic and social sectors, while removing barriers between citizens, government, foundations, institutions, and our regional neighbors.

By sponsoring small business incubators in their state, state governments can encourage local economic growth through job creation and job retention, the revitalization of underutilized property and the establishment of public-private partnerships.

Partnering for Economic Development

As a focal point of entrepreneurial activity, our business incubator may provide key leadership to the new business formation component of our community's economic development plan.

The most important planks in our economic development plan are retention and expansion of new businesses. The other area of economic development has to do with all of those areas that affect business development. It includes education, taxation, infrastructure, and availability of financing—whether you are expanding or relocating or creating a new business.

After looking at who's doing what in our community and how we are accomplishing our overall economic development, the city, county, and private sector are becoming more educated to the significance of new business formation and to the role it could play in Jackson's economic development.

By bringing together the Jackson Chamber of Commerce, Small Business Development Center, Community Capital Development Corporation, Jackson Area Investment Fund, colleges and universities, Small Business Administration, Business Information Center, Women's Business Center, City of Jackson, Michigan Minority Business Development Center, Enterprise Community, Career Alliance, Metropolitan Chamber of Commerce, Jackson County Planning Commission, HUD, and our local banks into a partnership, we could create a Council of Small Business Enterprises (COSBE). The retail incubator will be the nucleus of these community partnerships and for a new business council component in our economic development plan. This concept can continue to grow by forming linkages with other organizations interested in economic growth.

National Business Incubator Association (NBIA)

Membership in NBIA

A key alliance and support system for the proposed Jackson business incubator will be our membership with the National Business Incubation Association (NBIA). It is the world's leading organization advancing business incubation and entrepreneurship. It provides thousands of professionals with the information, education, advocacy, and networking resources to bring excellence to the process of assisting early-stage companies. It is also the world's largest membership organization for those involved with business incubation programs, and it is committed to advancing the business incubation industry by providing research, technical assistance, and educational opportunities for business incubation professionals, business service providers, investors, and others involved in helping start-up businesses grow and thrive.

NBIA Activities

NBIA offers professional development activities and specialized training to help business assistance professionals create and administer effective incubation programs. The Association's public awareness activities educate entrepreneurs, public sector leaders, corporations, and investors on the benefits of business incubation. NBIA also conducts research, compiles statistics, produces publications that provide hands-on approaches to developing and managing effective programs, tracks relevant legislative initiatives, and maintains a speakers' bureau and referral service. It creates partnerships with leading private-sector and public-sector entities to further the interests of the industry and its members.

Who belongs to NBIA?

- Incubator executive directors, managers, and staff
- Incubator developers and researchers
- Business assistance professionals
- Economic development professionals
- University-related research park managers
- Corporate joint venture partners
- Industry consultants
- Venture capital investors
- Educational institutions
- People exploring feasibility of business incubation for their communities
- Anyone interested in business incubation

NBIA Objectives

- Provide information, research, and networking resources to help members develop and manage successful incubation programs

- Monitor and disseminate knowledge of industry developments, trends, and best practices
- Inform and educate leaders, potential supporters, and stakeholders of the significant benefits of incubation
- Build public awareness of business incubation as a valuable business development tool
- Expand capacity to create valuable resources for members through partnerships
- Engage and represent all segments of the industry
- Create value for members

Member Benefits

- Subscription to *NBIA Review* and *NBIA Updates*
- NBIA Member Directory
- Access to members-only section of NBIA website
- Eligibility to join NBIA's member-only listserve
- Information research, referral, documentation, and dissemination service
- Legislative and government program updates
- Special money-saving programs for goods and services with leading providers
- Targeted member mailings including industry press releases and media tool kit
- Eligibility to vote in NBIA elections and run for the NBIA board

Members-only Discounts on:

- NBIA bookstore purchases, including important publications for incubator managers, developers, and clients

Incubator Risks and Failures

Incubator developers are always interested in what makes an incubator work. But we found it can be more useful at what makes an incubator fail. We found there to be five main stumbling blocks to success.

1. **Expecting too much too quickly.** The dynamics behind incubators can be very complicated, which means everything does not come together as quickly as a real estate operation might. But people don't understand that. Some developers believe they can acquire a building and put out a sign shortly thereafter. They fully believe that once the incubator opens, the jobs and companies will flow in. This type of expectation leads to frustration and dissatisfaction at best and failure at worst. Developers also must manage expectations of the public. This is always tough. When city councils and economic development administrators get involved in a job creation goal, they want the community to see immediate results. But they must be made to understand that it takes two to five years for most companies to become viable in the marketplace.
2. **Selecting the wrong manager.** Because the incubator manager is the key person running the incubator—and sometimes the only person—he or she must be well-rounded, well-organized, have good business sense, and be a skilled networker. The latter is especially important. The ability to gain resources and cooperation from important institutions, individuals, and organizations often spells the difference between success and failure.
3. **Overestimating the incubator's role.** Economic development planners can make the error of viewing an incubator as a cure-all for economic growth. It can make a significant contribution, but it cannot cure all the economic ills of a region. The existence of an incubator most likely won't influence a large industry to relocate, for instance. Incubators can make a contribution to expansion and retention of industries already in a region by training, expanding and providing additional resources to

companies there. The most important purpose of an incubator is to work with entrepreneurs to accelerate the development of emerging companies. That must be the key focus of management. Thinking that incubators are there to create jobs is a mistake; jobs follow the companies, not vice versa.

4. **Overspending.** Some incubators don't understand the dynamics of their own business—and an incubator is a business after all. The ability to manage cash flow and stay within the boundaries of the operating budget are as critical to incubators as they are for any business.

5. **Failure to leverage resources.** It takes an incubator a few years to get running and become financially stable. Developers must set a realistic timeframe, then leverage resources. As an example, the Austin Technology Incubator in Texas looked for funding for three years out. Its city council committed to $50,000 a year for each three years. The Chamber of Commerce put in $25,000 a year for each of the three years. The incubator raised $50,000 a year from private sources. In addition to that, private companies—such as accounting, law, and marketing firms—made three-year commitments of in-kind support amount to about $100,000 a year. Resources are thus leveraged and, as a bonus, a lot of people gain a stake in the incubator's success. Although Austin did not start out doing so, more incubators are taking equity in client companies as another important leveraging tool.

Funding Needs

Until a building has been located and our calculations completed it is difficult to pinpoint exact funding needs. According to NBIA, the average start-up of a business incubator is between $72,320 to 207,500. The breakdown is as follows:

	Low Estimate	High Estimate	
Leasehold Improvements	$0	$25,000	Note 1
Telephone System	$700	$30,500	Note 2
Furnishings	$29,900	$47,000	Note 2
Office Equipment	$1,650	$18,750	Note 2
Organizational Costs/Other	$3,600	$7,750	Note 3
Additional Funds	$20,000	$50,000	Note 4
Initial Marketing	$3,500	$5,000	Note 5
Prepaid Rent/Utility Deposit	$9,000	$17,500	
Travel and Lodging	$1,500	$2,500	
Supplies	$2,500	$3,500	
Total Investment	**$72,350**	**$207,500**	

Note 1. Real Estate costs include the cost of modifying a leasehold to meet criteria for business incubator standards. The cost of such leasehold improvements may be paid by the landlord as a part of the lease negotiation, or may be paid by the Proprietor. These costs have been estimated to be from $0 to $25,000.

Note 2. Total purchase price for this item is represented by the high estimate figure. The equipment may be purchased through a vendor. The initial investment under an equipment lease is represented by the low estimate figure which includes a deposit and six month's payments. Furnishings include desks, chairs, and file cabinets for clients.

Note 3. Organizational Costs include the cost of attorney fees, financial advisors, and other costs associated with the new company.

Note 4. This figure includes cash reserves for the initial start-up period, including salary for Proprietor or General Manager. This is an estimate, and there is no assurance that additional capital will not be necessary during the start-up period.

Note 5. This figure represents costs of an initial marketing and public relations campaign.

Summary

Retail incubators are proven tools for creating jobs, encouraging technology transfer, and starting new businesses. Set up to assist in the growth and development of new enterprises, incubators are themselves a growth industry. In 13 years, their number has increased thirty-fold, to more than 500 in 1993. A new incubator becomes operational each week, on average. More than 9,000 small firms currently reside in incubators; thousands more are program "graduates," having moved on to occupy commercial space within their communities.

Retail incubators accelerate the development of successful entrepreneurial companies by providing hands-on assistance and a variety of business and technical support services during the vulnerable early years. Typically, incubators provide space for a number of businesses under one roof with such amenities as flexible space and leases; office services and equipment on a pay-as-you-go basis; an on-site incubator manager as a resource for business advice; orchestrated exposure to a network of outside business and technical consultants, often providing accounting, marketing, engineering and design advice; assistance with financing; and opportunities to network and transact business with other firms in the same facility. Incubators reduce the risks involved in business start-ups, and their young tenant companies gain access to facilities and equipment and equipment that might otherwise be unavailable or unaffordable.

Our incubation program's main goal is to produce successful graduate-businesses that are financially viable when they "graduate" from the incubator, usually within two or three years of entering the program. Research shows that more than 80 percent of firms that have ever been incubated are still in operation. And research on graduates by Coopers & Lybrand has found that these graduates are increasing revenues and creating jobs.

Formalization of the industry was accelerated from 1984 through 1987 by the active involvement of the U.S. Small Business Administration's Office of Private Sector Initiatives. Under the direction of John Cox, now SBA's Director of Finance and Investment, the agency held a series of regional conferences and published a newsletter and several incubator handbooks.

The National Business Incubation Association was formed by industry leaders in 1985, and by 1987 was recognized as the main source of information on incubators. NBIA's membership today numbers over 700 and is primarily composed of incubator developers and managers. Its mission is to provide training and a clearinghouse for information on incubator management and development issues and on tools for assisting start-up and fledgling firms. This organization will provide the technical support and research needed, plus ongoing support in the developmental and completion stages of our incubator.

Retail Clothing Store

BUSINESS PLAN

BOSTON RAGS CLOTHING STORE

423 West Oaks Boulevard
Hartford, Connecticut 06103

This plan outlines how Boston Rags, a start-up retail men's, women's, and children's clothing store, will provide the Hartford community with unique clothing they would normally purchase outside of the state.

EXECUTIVE SUMMARY

Boston Rags Clothing Store will be a start-up retail men's, women's, and children's clothing store specializing in unique clothing from other parts of the U.S. This business will be a casual urban wear traditional clothing store which will be run by the owners, Nancy Seymour and Joanne Arbor, as a Partnership. It will be located at 423 West Oaks Boulevard, near downtown Hartford, Connecticut. This store will also have a local market and will serve both youth and adults. Our intent is to provide the community with unique clothing they would normally purchase outside of the state.

The business will be financed with $18,299 of the owners' money plus $35,444 from a business loan. Starting costs are $53,743. Sales are estimated at $187,500 per year by the first year. A positive cash flow will be produced at the end of the first year.

There are no other urban wear stores located within 20 miles of the location selected for this store. Hartford is in an urban city of approximately 104,000 people which is also a part of Hartford County area containing approximately 408,000 people.

Nancy Seymour receives a Veteran's pension (from her late husband) which is adequate for support without drawing from the business. Joanne Arbor is employed full-time by Central Connecticut State University, which is also adequate support without drawing from the business. Joanne has managerial experience and basic knowledge of accounting. She has at least 7 years of retail experience.

Objectives

Boston Rags's main objectives are to:

- Establish a unique clothing retail business in the city of Hartford, Connecticut
- Create jobs
- Provide quality clothing and customer service at a reasonable price
- Achieve the largest market share in the city for urban wear
- Be an active and vocal member of the community, and to provide continual re-investment through participation in community activities and financial contributions
- Achieve a profit within the first year
- Continually and consistantly increase total number of customers per year
- Increase average length of customer relationships and decrease customer turnover

Mission

Boston Rags Clothing Store is a retail clothing store specializing in unique clothing and accessories. We encourage customers to be experimental with new clothing styles. Our mission is to understand what our customers' needs and hopes are after buying urban wear clothing.

Boston Rags will maintain financial balance while delivering a quality product to our customers. We will make our clothing accessible throughout our community by way of establishing a retail location, fashion shows, and events. We will make a profit and generate cash. We will provide a rewarding work environment and fair compensation to our employees, ultimately provide excellent value to our customers, and a fair return to our owners.

Boston Rags's keys to success include: implementing an effective cash flow plan, achieving efficiency, running our retail store professionally, and maintaining a serious business discipline to everything we do.

Boston Rags's cash flow plan is to:

- Maintain enough money on hand each month to pay the cash obligations the following month.
- Identify and eliminate deficiencies or surpluses in cash.
- Alter business financial plans to provide more cash if deficiencies are found.
- Invest any revealed excess cash in an accessible, interest bearing, low-risk account such as a savings account or short-term CD or T-bill.
- Eliminate credit and terms to customers (not credit card sales).
- Clearly understand the urban wear market, distribution costs and competition, and continually adjust accordingly.
- Keep enough cash, as needed cushion for security, on hand to cover expenses.
- Reduce accountant expenses by producing our own summary statistics and projections via accounting software.

Keys to Success

The business will be named "Boston Rags Clothing Store." This is to identify the store with the city of Boston, Massachusetts, where most of the store's inventory will be purchased. The name is registered in Hartford County under an assumed name.

Boston Rags Clothing Store's primary goal is to find customers and keep them coming back.

Boston Rags is designed to help customers change their look without buying an entirely new wardrobe. We will cater to the person wanting to build a new wardrobe by purchasing clothing and accessory pieces to add to clothing they already have.

Customers will rely on the business they purchase pieces from to give them continuous help and personal opinions. Theirs is a business that repeats and it will be easy to establish a strong clientele.

Customers will save money from having to buy a complete outfit by just purchasing pieces. They will also enjoy shopping in stores that are well inventoried and serviced-minded, such as Boston Rags.

Boston Rags will set the pace for urban fashion for all seasons. Last year's outfit will be accessorized to be this year's outfit. People like to buy clothing pieces and accessories to continue wearing clothing that would be out-of-date otherwise.

Boston Rags will also cater to all types of customers and for all occasions other than routine shopping. Examples: Wives buying gifts for their husbands, friends buying gifts for their friends, etc. Boston Rags's store will be a source of wearable gifts.

Retail profits can be as high as 65-85 percent on clothing and accessory pieces. The sales and profit margins in a specialty clothing and accessory store are higher than the average retail store. We have the opportunity to profit successfully.

The urban clothing market is the most exciting, fastest growing market for consumers. They will always look for unique clothing pieces and they will not hesitate to buy them.

COMPANY SUMMARY

The business will be retail sales of urban clothing and associated products. Nancy Seymour will hold 50 percent ownership and Joanne Arbor will also hold 50 percent ownership. It will

Company Ownership

be set up as a partnership at start-up and then phase into a Limited Liability Corporation by the second year.

Start-up Summary

Total start-up expense (including fixtures, equipment, and grand opening) is $53,743. Start-up assets required $19,000 in inventory. With the owners' investment of $18,299, the amount of additional start-up funds needed are $35,444. The details are included in the following chart and table. It is planned to start the business in the month of December because this is the Christmas seasonal month in which retail store are known to have high sales. Once established, business volume may be somewhat cyclical for that reason.

Start-up Plan
Start-up Expenses

Grand Opening	$2,000
Rent Deposit	$2,200
Salaries and Wages	$1,200
Payroll Taxes	$180
Insurance	$219
Telephone Deposit	$300
Utilities Deposit	$840
Office Supplies	$250
Advertising	$600
Accounting/Legal	$400
Fixtures	$3,755
Expensed Equipment	$4,500
Repairs and Maintance	$6,900
Carpet	$1,300
Floor Tile	$800
Sign	$1,000
Counter	$4,000
Travel	$4,200
Burglar Alarm	$99
Other	$0
Total Start-up Expense	**$34,743**

Start-up Assets Needed

Cash Requirements	$0
Start-up Inventory	$19,000
Other Short-term Assets	$0
Total Short-term Assets	**$19,000**
Long-term Assets	$0
Total Assets	**$19,000**
Total Start-up Requirements:	**$53,743**
Left to Finance:	**$0**

Start-up Funding Plan
Investment

Personal Investment	$18,299
Other	$0
Total Investment	**$18,299**

Short-term Liabilities

Unpaid Expenses	$0
Short-term Loans	$35,444
Interest-free Short-term Loans	$0
Subtotal Short-term Liabilities	**$35,444**
Long-term Liabilities	$0
Total Liabilities	**$35,444**
Loss at Start-up	**($34,743)**
Total Capital	**($16,444)**
Total Capital and Liabilities	**$19,000**
Checkline	**$0**

Boston Rags Clothing Store will be located at 423 West Oaks Boulevard, Hartford, Connecticut. The store is approximately 2500 square feet. It contains two dressing rooms and a unisex restroom. Parking space is available in front of the store with additional spaces in the rear for overflow. The are a variety of businesses in the area that include Burger King, White Castle, and a flower shop along with Central Connecticut State University. This variety of businesses creates a constant flow of traffic during most business hours.

Company Location and Facilities

While a clothing retail store is not unique in itself, this business will have one-of-a-kind items and provide personal one-on-one attention to customers after hours when needed. Customers can buy sweaters, dress slacks, dress shirts, coats, jogging suits, jean outfits, childrens' items, catalog items, and more. The store hours will be 7 days a week. Store hours will be from 10A.M. to 10P.M., Monday through Saturday, and 11:00A.M. to 8:00P.M. on Sundays.

Business Operations

We will have two full-time employees. The wages for these employees will be $6.00 hour. We will not be offering benefits for the first couple of years. Employees will do the cleaning of the building.

The inventory will be purchased through several vendors that include: BRG Sportswear, Inc., White Sail, USA 66, Wonder, Inc., ABX, and Mark Zap Clothing, Inc. We estimate our inventory to turn over 8 times a year. Starting inventory will be $19,000 with the markup of up to 100 percent.

The following are our operation policies and will be posted throughout the store:

- 30-day layaway with 50 percent down, nonrefundable
- 30-day exchange policy, no cash refunds (this will be written on our receipts)
- $25 fee for check returns
- 2 items at a time in the dressing room
- Accepting credit cards, Visa, Mastercharge, Discover, and American Express

The owners have enlisted the professional services of Mitchell's Accounting and Investment Services to handle Boston Rags's business functions and needs. The following will be conducted by Mitchell's accounting firm:

- Weekly payroll
- Compliance with all Connecticut Sales Tax requirements
- Generate Profit and Loss Statements as required
- Consultation on an as-needed basis
- Generate all 941 requirements as required by Federal, State, and Local Taxes

- Generate all W-2s as required
- Filing all required personal tax returns will be at the current cost rates for Schedule C's and other business returns

This accounting firm will be phased out as we learn how to use the appropriate accounting software to manage our own books.

Ms. Arbor has combined managerial experience of 12 years and has also taken business management classes at Smith Community College and Hartford Business Institute. She is therefore technically qualified to handle the products the store will offer. Boston Rags will be aided in development by Ventures store out of Boston, Massachusetts, and Wonderkins Store out of New York, New York. Ventures and Wonderkins sell similar products to Boston Rags. The owners of Ventures are also close friends of Ms. Arbor. Boston Rags will also utilize the SBA Business Information Center for additional resources and business training.

The owners have referred to an attorney but will not retain an attorney until a later date. The attorney will be used for recommendations in respect to future incorporation as a Limited Liability Corporation. The attorney will also handle any future permit or certificate needs.

PRODUCTS

Urban wear has increased in popularity as the number of new musical hip-hop artists' popularity has increased over the past several years. Boston Rags will sell products similar to one hip-hop artist, Mark Zap, who has a store in New York. Like Mark's store, Boston Rags's line of clothing of more than 32 pieces, include denim, leather, twill and linen bottoms, linen and silk shirts, silk/cashmere sweater vests, T-shirts, and hats.

Boston Rags, like Mark Zap's, decided to carry a line of clothing that is a "more simple" but still gives off "a chameleon type of feel" in which "it can fit into any type of setting—not too bright or loud." According to Mark Zap this type of urban wear has projected sales in the range of $15 million to $18 million depending on store size. New growth developments in the urban wear industry have made obtaining the clothing much more simple and easy. This clothing can also be sold at festivals and fashion shows.

Inventory

Boston Rags's inventory tracking system will tell Boston Rags's management what merchandise is in stock, what is on order, when it will arrive, and what was sold. With such a system Boston Rags can plan purchases more intelligently and quickly recognize the fast moving items we need to reorder and the slow moving items we should markdown or specially promote.

We will control inventory right at the cash register with our point-of-sale (POS) software and equipment. Our POS software records each sale when it happens, so inventory records are always up-to-date. We will get more information about the sale than we would gather with a manual system. By running reports based on this information, we will be able to make better decisions.

Our POS equipment includes electronic cash drawers, bar-code scanners, credit card readers, and receipt printers. Our POS software package includes integrated accounting modules, including general ledger, accounts receivable, accounts payable, purchasing, and inventory control systems. In essence, our POS system is an all-in-one way to keep track of our business cash flow. The reporting capabilities of our POS programs include sales, costs, and profits by salesperson or by category for the day, month, and year-to-date.

We will count our inventory once every two weeks (the count cycle). Processing paperwork and placing orders with our vendors will take two weeks (the order cycle). The order will take two weeks to get to us (delivery cycle). Therefore, we will need six weeks worth of inventory from the first day of the count cycle to stay in operation until our merchandise arrives. We will have on hand a six-week supply of inventory and turn it over 8 times a year. According to *Retail in Detail* by Ronald L. Bond, "estimating sales for a new retail store is very difficult, and loaded with uncertainties." Bond suggests the retailer start with a range from $75 to $200 per square foot per year. We will use the very conservative figure of $75 per square foot per year, similar to Ventures in Boston, Massachusetts.

For inventory valuation we will use the Last In, First Out (LIFO) method. We will sell the most recently purchased inventory first. This method will also help us pay less in taxes.

Our inventory control system will tell us when to buy replacement inventory, what to buy, what not to buy, and how much to buy.

Suppliers will be independent craftspeople, import sources, distributors, and manufacturers. We have established a list of possible suppliers and requested quotes, prices, available discounts, and delivery terms. We have also asked them for customer references. We will also try and establish accounts with these suppliers prior to opening our store.

MARKET ANALYSIS SUMMARY

Consumer expenditures for retail sales rose to $1,139,457 in Hartford, Connecticut, and to $5,842,488 in Hartford County in 1999.

The continuous formation of new musical groups that wear urban clothing helps fuel our business, as does our free music CD store giveaways.

Market Segmentation

According to the Hartford Chamber of Commerce, there are approximately 150,000 males and 165,000 females in Hartford County, totaling 315,000 people. Of those 315,000 people, 186,000 are between the ages of 18 and 54 years of age. Seventy-six percent of the 315,000 people have a household income of more than $15,000. Boston Rags's target market is men and women between the ages of 18 and 54 with a household income of $15,000 or more.

Market Analysis

Potential Customers	Growth	2000	2001	2002	2003	2004	CAGR
Women and Girls	5%	407,000	427,350	448,718	471,154	494,712	5.00%
Men and Boys	5%	407,000	427,350	448,718	471,154	494,712	5.00%
Other	0%	0	0	0	0	0	0.00%
Total	**5.00%**	**814,000**	**854,700**	**897,436**	**942,308**	**989,424**	**5.00%**

Target Market and Program Strategies

Near the business thoroughfare is a new residential subdivision under development, where houses are priced at $100,000 and above. Also in the area is the campus of Central Connecticut State University, and downtown Hartford, all which serve Boston Rags's potential customers. Boston Rags's customers are employed men and women, between the ages of 18 to 54 years old with a household medium income of $32,000 and above.

We will use flyers and other literature to act as our representative. Here are some of our marketing programs and strategies:

Designing good ad copy to reach our customers.

- Choose the proper publication
- Have a goal for our advertisement
- Involve the audience

- Inform the buyer
- Headline and illustrations grab attention
- Give them something
- Always be specific
- Make our offer a good one
- Be creative in our media choices—such as unusual avenues like—fax newsletters, mall kiosks, fax-on-demand, publicity stunts, online marketing, anything unusual to reach our target market
- Small classified ads
- Track our results
- Keep all our customers/prospects in a database and stay in touch with them regularly
- Gradually increase the size of our ad and tract the results
- Advertise regularly and consistently
- Evaluate our efforts

Customer loyalty is much more important to Boston Rags than customer satisfaction. We will serve our customers so well they will brag about Boston Rags to others. This will keep them loyal, and also provide a continual flow of customers. We will maintain our customers' happiness by using our Self-Evaluation Program.

Self-Evaluation Program asks the following questions:

- Are Boston Rags's products the best they can be?
- Is the appearance of our cashiers, managers, business surroundings, and appearance of our store professional?
- Can we clearly describe our business in 25 words or less? Can our customers describe our business in 25 words or less?
- Do our customers know about all of our products and services?
- Do we have a well-developed marketing plan that we follow on a consistent basis?
- What if our marketing plans work? Will we be able to handle the increased volume of sales without harming our customers or the quality of our work product?
- Do we treat others with honesty and respect at all times?

Advertising and Promotional Strategy

Boston Rags will try out our promotion on a small portion of our target audience before we roll out the promotion to the rest of the target market. Our tests will include variation on our basic offer, on the text or composition of our message, and on our presentation. The benefits from testing will provide to us early feedback on the response rates and margins used in our break-even calculations for that particular promotion. Testing will also help us roll out successful ideas and omit the not-so-successful ones.

With our promotions we will compare results, analyze, track responses, and measure profitability to insure our promotions are profitable.

Our advertising budget will be equal to 2 or 3 percent of our projected gross sales which averages out to be $5,627 or $457 a month after initial start-up. The budget will be based on the cost method which theorizes that an advertiser can't afford to spend more than he or she has. We will increase this amount for our grand opening.

We have taken the following steps to insure our dollars will be wisely spent on advertising.

1. Established our target market by asking ourselves who our customers are and therefore whom we want to reach with our advertising.
2. Setting a rough budget for broadcast advertising.

3. Contacted sales managers at TV and radio stations in our area and arrange to have a salesperson visit us.
4. Talked to other business people in our area about their experiences with broadcast advertising.
5. Asked about the "audience delivery" of the available spots.
6. Inquired about the production of our commercial.

We then compared various proposals and looked at the cost per thousands and negotiated the most attractive deal based on which outlet offers the most cost-effective way of reaching our audience. We will also buy time well in advance to lower the cost.

Our direct mail campaign will begin by getting our name on as many mailing lists as possible. We will then take note of our reaction to each piece of mail we receive and save the ones that communicate most effectively, noticing the colors, key words, and types of inserts that can be adapted to our own mailer. To get the readers involved we will include stickers that say Yes or No to be pasted on the order form. We will continue to build our direct mailing program with the resources from the Direct Marketing Association (DMA).

We plan to target our advertising to focus as narrowly as possible to the media that will reach our customers. Our customers' location, age, income, interests, and other information will be used to guide us to the right media.

Our printed ads will attract attention through a truly arresting headline and visual element. It will appeal to the reader's self-interest or announce news. It will communicate our company's unique advantage and it will prove our advantage over our competitor. Finally, it will motivate readers to take action. Our printed ads will not be a "hard sell" but it will be an all-out attempt to attract, communicate with, and motivate the reader. All of our ads will answer the customer's number one question: "What is in it for me?"

Our radio and television ads will deliver our message to more customers than any other type of ad campaign. We have a clear understanding of our market so the money spent on broadcast advertising isn't wasted.

For television ads, we will stick to 30-second spots which are standard in the industry. We understand that generally rates vary widely during the first quarter of the year, and sometimes during the third quarter or late in the fourth quarter, which are traditionally slow seasons for many businesses. We will try to avoid paying full rates during the rest of the year or during popular shows or prime time. We will also stretch our dollar by bartering our products for air time.

Our other methods of marketing will include direct mail, encompassing a wide variety of marketing materials, including brochures, catalogs, postcards, newsletters, and sales letters.

Point-of-Purchase (POP) advertising appears in various forms inside our retail store. It is designed to influence the buying behavior of our customers. POP advertising may take many forms in our store, each bearing a sales message. Here are a few examples:

- Counter cards and displays
- Window displays
- Floor stands and cutouts
- Animated displays run by electricity
- Pennants, banners, plaques, streamers

Industry Analysis and Trends

According to the 1994 U.S. Industrial Outlook stores selling mostly nondurables accounted for nearly 64 percent total retail sales, with 1993 revenues topping 1.3 trillion, up 5.7 percent over 1992. Sales of durable goods totaled 757 billion in current dollars, up more than seven percent from 1992 and accounted for 36 percent of the total.

According to *The Guide to Retail Business Planning* retail operations in the United States generated $2.34 trillion in sales from more than 1.5 million establishments in 1995. From 1994 to 1995 the sector as a whole grew at a rate of approximately 5 percent and represents the second-largest industry in our economy after the service industry.

Retailing has experienced more changes during the past decade than it did in the preceding generations. Although one can argue that retailing is still a domain of small businesses (that is, approximately 75 percent of all retail stores have annual sales of less than $1 million), in recent years slightly more than 80 percent of all sales were generated by stores with sales above $1 million. In addition, the growth of discount retailers has increased at a rate, some experts claim, three times that of the industry. This is due primarily to companies like Wal-Mart (which has been credited with creating one out of every 16 new jobs in the United States in 1994) and to an increase in wholesale membership clubs, such as Toys "R" Us and Circuit City.

Retail customers of the 1990s are significantly different from retail customers of a decade ago, and retail strategies need to be reassessed in view of the changing demographics and new buying patterns.

Competition and Buying Patterns

Boston Rags is located on a strip that includes a variety of businesses, but none of which create any competition. Traffic is moderate to heavy, especially near the lunch and dinner hours. The closest competing urban wear store is at least 20 miles away, located in the Hartford Valley Mall. There are no other urban wear stores in the direct vicinity of Boston Rags's location.

According to the Arbitron, Spring 2000, U.S. Dept. of Labor, Bureau of Labor Statistics, Consumer Expenditure Survey, 1998, Hartford County and surrounding areas spend in the following patterns:

Women's and Girls' Clothing

- $449.4 Thousand each Month
- $103.7 Thousand each Week
- $14.8 Thousand each Day
- $1,477 each Hour (ten-hour business day)

Men's and Boys' Clothing

- $323.4 Thousand each Month
- $74.6 Thousand each Week
- $10.6 Thousand each Day
- $1063 each Hour (ten-hour business day)

The Consumer Spending Patterns Report states that the average amount spent on clothing per household is:

	Per year	**Per week**
Women's Apparel	$1060	$28.38
Men's Apparel	$636	$12.22
Girls' Apparel	$265	$5.09
Boys' Apparel	$219	$4.21

Boston Rags uses a strategy of total market service. Our promise is in our location and the products we sell, the people we attract, and the atmosphere we create.

We will create an atmosphere that lures the "Hardcore" urban clothing fans.

Ultimately, we aren't selling either clothing or accessories. We are selling the look. We want to be part of the activity, part of the memory, part of the tradition of dressing in the latest fashions.

Strategic Assumptions:

1. Every person is a potential customer and all potential markets experience growth.
2. Marketing to one segment of the population will lead to an expansion in overall market growth.

STRATEGY & IMPLEMENTATION SUMMARY

Our location is a very important competitive edge. We are there, right at the point of entering or exiting downtown Hartford. The nearest competitor is at least 20 miles away.

The other competitive edge we have developed is the atmosphere and reputation. Boston Rags will bring a part of the Boston, Massachusetts, urban clothing experience to Hartford, Connecticut. That is why we are developing our fashion shows, musical guest appearances, etc. This advantage is important to us because our prices are slightly higher than other urban wear store locations in Connecticut. We will also offer more personal attention to our customers than the larger mall retail stores. We have direct connections to one of the top urban wear retailers in Boston, Massachusetts, called Ventures.

Competitive Edge

It is the intent to start the business selling the clothing people need to create a unique image of themselves. This includes various prints, colors, and styles. To increase sales and promote Boston Rags's store, special events will be held that please people, stimulate interest, pursue leisure, involve social participation, and occur within a specific, prescribed time frame. Some of our special events will include:

Sales Strategy

- Anniversaries
- Bazaars
- Celebrations
- Ceremonies
- Concerts
- Conferences
- Contests
- Conventions
- Exhibits
- Fashion Shows
- Festivals
- Grand Openings
- Open Houses
- Premieres
- Sports Shows
- Testimonials
- Trade Shows

Special events give Boston Rags powerful vehicles to promote our image, products, merchandise, services, and to generate goodwill to the public.

Boston Rags will use these special events to attract customers, sell products, earn profits, make markets aware of new developments, and make communities aware of their policies, goals, and purposes.

We will not be offering credit to our customers. We will accept checks with the assistance of a check verification company. This check verification company offers check verification and check guarantees. So, if a check has been approved by this company and it turns out to be bad, the company will reimburse us for the value of the check, eliminating our risk of getting paid.

We will accept all major credit cards. Accepting credit cards will increase the probability, speed, and size of our customers' sales. It will give us the chance to increase sales by enabling customers to make impulse buys. It will improve our cash flow because we will receive the money within a few days. It also guarantees we will be paid. All potential sales will be attended to in a timely fashion and long-term salesperson/customer relationships will be a major goal of Boston Rags.

Sales Forecast

The peaks for this type of retail business are the months of August through December where sales rise as high as $34,472 for the month of December. The valleys for this type of business are January, June, and July where sales are down as far as $7,968 for the month of January. The remaining months have an average sales of about $13,000.

During the valley periods we will concentrate on a saturation of special events and sales. We will also do holiday specials.

Projected sales based on square footage ranges from $75 to $200. We used the more conservative rate of $75. The store is 2,500 square feet, multiplied by $75 to give us a Gross Sales of $187,500 the first year and maintaining that average through the second year. There will be some cycling, but it will take some experience to ascertain it. Summer months will probably be lower than winter. Computations are base on a 100 percent markup.

Sales Forecast

Sales	FY2001	FY2002	FY2003
Sales	$187,500	$286,118	$384,736
Other	$0	$0	$0
Total Sales	**$187,500**	**$286,118**	**$384,736**
Direct Cost of Sales			
Sales	$28,500	$28,500	$28,500
Other	$0	$0	$0
Subtotal Cost of Sales	**$28,500**	**$28,500**	**$28,500**

Strategic Alliances

Ms. Seymour and Ms. Arbor have begun to build strategic alliances to assist them with buisiness and inventory issues. Those alliances are:

- SBA Business Information Center
- Community Capital Development Corporation
- Hartford Area Investment Fund
- BRG Sportswear, Inc.
- White Sail
- USA 66
- Wonder, Inc.

- ABX
- Mark Zap Clothing, Inc.

Retailers of nondurable merchandise face a dual challenge of a slow-growing market and changes in demographics and consumer buying habits that have spawned structural changes within the industry. Boston Rags will adjust our competitive strategies to these new realities and take advantage of new marketing techniques as electronic retailing, catalog marketing, a smaller store, and improved customer service. By completing these tasks we can succeed in improving our market position in the changing retailing era of the 1990s and beyond.

Risks

The owners are injecting $18,299 of the $53,743 capital needed to start the business. Therefore, 34 percent of the risk is with the owners' money. In the event of business failure it is estimated that the owners' assets and current income would produce the $35,444 needed to repay the loan.

Ms. Arbor has over seven years of experience in retail sales and over five years of managerial experience. She has held positions of responsibility which required meeting company objectives. She receives a sufficient salary from her current job to support her during the incubation period of her business. She will oversee the store on a daily basis. She, along with co-owner Ms. Seymour, will hire two staff persons to work full-time in the store. One person will be responsible for operating the cash register and loss prevention. The other person will be responsible for customer service and inventory control. Ms. Seymour will oversee day-to-day operations along with Ms. Arbor.

MANAGEMENT SUMMARY

Both owners believe very strongly that relationships should be forthright, work should be structured with enough room for creativity, and pay should commensurate with the amount and quality of work completed. No person is better than another, except in ability, knowledge, and experience.

Boston Rags understands the impact hiring and managing our store's staff will have on our business success. Therefore, we have taken the time to make sure all those overseeing the store and those working directly in the store have the qualifications needed to help build our professional image.

Personnel Plan

It is the intent for the owners to be the key manpower in starting this business. They will be assisted by two full-time employees during certain hours. Employee resources include the local University and Career Alliance. Employee's age is not a factor unless they are under 18, they then would need a worker's permit.

The following two employees will be hired:

The Sales Clerk/Loss Prevention Manager will be Moira Rye. Moira has seven years of retail management experience in the area of cashier and loss prevention.

The Customer Service/Inventory Control Manager will be Rhonda Small. Rhonda has nine years of experience in the area of customer service and inventory control.

Both of these employees have an exceptionally high level of retail experience and professionalism needed to deliver excellent customer service for our customers and management of our store.

Personnel Plan

Continued

Personnel	FY2001	FY2002	FY2003
Moira Rye	$6,600	$6,600	$6,600
Rhonda Small	$6,600	$6,600	$6,600
Other	$0	$0	$0
Total Payroll	**$13,200**	**$13,200**	**$13,200**
Total Headcount	0	0	0
Payroll Burden	$1,980	$1,980	$1,980
Total Payroll Expenditures	**$15,180**	**$15,180**	**$15,180**

FINANCIAL PLAN

Our financial plan anticipates the following:

- Growth will be moderate, cash flows steady
- Marketing will remain below 15 percent of sales
- The company will invest residual profits into financial markets and not company expansion (unless absolutely necessary)

Important Assumptions

Our financial plan depends on important assumptions, most of which are shown in the following table as annual assumptions.

Some of the more important underlying assumptions are:

- We assume a strong economy, without major recession
- We assume, of course, that there are no unforeseen changes in the use of clothing which will make the need for clothing obsolete

General Assumptions

	FY2001	FY2002	FY2003
Short-term Interest Rate %	10.00%	10.00%	10.00%
Long-term Interest Rate %	10.00%	10.00%	10.00%
Payment Days Estimator	30	30	30
Collection Days Estimator	0	0	0
Inventory Turnover Estimator	8.00	8.00	8.00
Tax Rate %	25.00%	25.00%	25.00%
Expenses in Cash %	10.00%	10.00%	10.00%
Sales on Credit %	0.00%	0.00%	0.00%
Personnel Burden %	15.00%	15.00%	15.00%

Break-even Analysis

A break-even analysis table has been completed on the basis of average costs/prices. With fixed costs of $7,059, $50 in an average sale, and $10 in average variable costs, we need $8,824 per month to break even.

Break-even Analysis:	
Monthly Units Break-even	176
Monthly Sales Break-even	$8,824
Assumptions:	
Average Per-Unit Revenue	$50.00
Average Per-Unit Variable Cost	$10.00
Estimated Monthly Fixed Cost	$7,059

Boston Rags will have a profit-to-sales ratio of just over 27 percent. Normally, a start-up concern will operate with negative profits through the first two years. We will avoid that kind of operating loss by knowing our competitors and our target markets.

Profit and Loss (Income Statement)	FY2001	FY2002	FY2003
Sales	$187,500	$288,118	$384,736
Direct Cost of Sales	$28,500	$28,500	$28,500
Production Payroll	$0	$0	$0
Other	$0	$0	$0
Total Cost of Sales	**$28,500**	**$28,500**	**$28,500**
Gross Margin	$159,000	$257,818	$356,236
Gross Margin %	84.80%	90.04%	92.59%
Operating expenses:			
Sales and Marketing Expenses			
Sales and Marketing Payroll	$0	$0	$0
Rent	$12,100	$13,200	$13,200
Travel	$2,000	$2,000	$2,000
Burglar Alarm	$1,188	$1,188	$1,188
Total Sales and Marketing Expenses	**$0**	**$0**	**$0**
Sales and Marketing %	0.00%	0.00%	0.00%
General and Administrative Expenses			
General and Administrative Payroll	$0	$0	$0
Payroll Expense	$13,200	$13,200	$13,200
Payroll Burden	$1,980	$1,980	$1,980
Depreciation	$0	$0	$0
Office Supplies	$220	$220	$220
Utilities	$10,080	$10,080	$10,080
Insurance	$876	$876	$876
Telephone	$1,080	$1,080	$1,080
Total General & Administrative Expenses	**$0**	**$0**	**$0**
General and Administrative %	0.00%	0.00%	0.00%
Other Expenses			
Other Payroll	$0	$0	$0
Advertising	$5,027	$5,484	$5,784
Loan Repayment	$6,820	$7,440	$7,440
Inventory	$28,500	$28,500	$28,500
Accounting/legal	$4,800	$4,800	$4,800
Total Other Expenses	**$0**	**$0**	**$0**
Other %	0.00%	0.00%	0.00%
Total Operating Expenses	**$87,871**	**$90,048**	**$90,348**
Profit Before Interest and Taxes	$71,129	$167,570	$265,888
Interest Expense Short-term	$3,544	$3,544	$3,544
Interest Expense Long-term	$0	$0	$0
Taxes Incurred	$16,896	$41,006	$65,586
Extraordinary Items	$0	$0	$0
Net Profit	$50,688	$123,019	$196,758
Net Profit/Sales	27.03%	43.00%	51.14%

Projected Cash Flow

We are positioning ourselves in the market as a medium risk concern with steady cash flows. Accounts payable is paid at the end of each month while sales are in cash and credit cards, giving Boston Rags an excellent cash structure. Intelligent marketing will secure a cash balance of $ 77,443 by 2001.

	FY2001	FY2002	FY2003
Net Profit	**$50,688**	**$123,019**	**$196,758**
Plus:			
Depreciation	$0	$0	$0
Change in Accounts Payable	$14,777	($4,126)	$2,384
Current Borrowing (repayment)	$0	$0	$0
Increase (decrease) Other Liabilities	$0	$0	$0
Long-term Borrowing (repayment)	$0	$0	$0
Capital Input	$0	$0	$0
Subtotal	**$65,466**	**$128,193**	**$200,130**
Less:			
Change in Accounts Receivable	$0	$0	$0
Change in Inventory	($11,875)	$0	$0
Change in Other Short-term Assets	$0	$0	$0
Capital Expenditure	$0	$0	$0
Dividends	$0	$0	$0
Subtotal	**($11,875)**	**$0**	**$0**
Net Cash Flow	**$77,341**	**$128,193**	**$200,130**
Cash Balance	**$77,341**	**$205,635**	**$405,766**

Projected Balance Sheet

All of our tables will be updated monthly to reflect past performance and future assumptions. Future assumptions will not be based on past performance but rather on economic cycle activity, regional industry strength, and future cash flow possibilities. We expect solid growth in net worth beyond the year 2002.

Assets			
Short-term Assets	**FY2001**	**FY2002**	**FY2003**
Cash	$77,341	$205,635	$405,766
Accounts Receivable	$0	$0	$0
Inventory	$7,125	$7,125	$7,125
Other Short-term Assets	$0	$0	$0
Total Short-term Assets	**$84,466**	**$212,760**	**$412,891**
Long-term Assets			
Capital Assets	$0	$0	$0
Accumulated Depreciation	$0	$0	$0
Total Long-term Assets	$0	$0	$0
Total Assets	**$84,466**	**$212,760**	**$412,891**
Liabilities and Capital			
Accounts Payable	$14,777	$10,652	$13,036
Short-term Notes	$35,444	$35,444	$35,444
Other Short-term Liabilities	$0	$0	$0
Subtotal Short-term Liabilities	**$50,221**	**$46,096**	**$48,480**
Long-term Liabilities	$0	$0	$0
Total Liabilities	**$50,221**	**$46,096**	**$48,480**
Paid in Capital	$18,299	$18,299	$18,299

Retained Earnings	($34,743)	$15,945	$138,965
Earnings	$50,688	$123,019	$196,758
Total Capital	$34,244	$157,264	$354,021
Total Liabilities and Capital	**$84,466**	**$212,760**	**$412,891**
Net Worth	**$34,244**	**$157,264**	**$354,021**

The following table shows the projected ratios. We expect to maintain healthy ratios for profitability, risk and return.

Business Ratios

Ratio Analysis

Profitability Ratios:	FY2001	FY2002	FY2003	RMA
Gross Margin	84.80%	90.04%	92.59%	0.42
Net Profit Margin	27.03%	43.00%	51.14%	1
Return on Assets	60.01%	60.49%	48.88%	0
Return on Equity	148.02%	78.22%	55.58%	0

Activity Ratios				
AR Turnover	0.00	0.00	0.00	0
Collection Days	0	0	0	0
Inventory Turnover	2.18	4.00	4.00	0
Accounts Payable Turnover	6.68	12.17	12.17	0
Total Asset Turnover	**2.22**	**1.41**	**0.96**	**0**

Debt Ratios				
Debt to Net Worth	1.47	0.29	0.14	1.4
Short-term Liability to Liability	1.00	1.00	1.00	8.3

Liquidity Ratios				
Current Ratio	1.68	4.41	8.30	1.2
Quick Ratio	1.54	4.26	8.16	0.1
Net Working Capital	$34,244	$157,264	$354,021	0
Interest Coverage	20.07	47.28	75.02	0

Additional Ratios				
Assets to Sales	0.45	0.71	1.05	0
Debt/Assets	59%	23%	12%	0
Current Debt/Total Assets	59%	23%	12%	0
Acid Test	1.54	4.26	8.16	0
Asset Turnover	2.22	1.41	0.96	0
Sales/Net Worth	**5.48**	**1.82**	**1.09**	**0**
Dividend Payout	**$0**	**$0**	**$0**	**$0**

APPENDIX

Sales Forecast

Sales	Dec	Jan	Feb	Mar	Apr	May
Sales	$35,472	$7,968	$13,125	$13,281	$12,343	$12,968
Other	$0	$0	$0	$0	$0	$0
Total Sales	**$35,472**	**$7,968**	**$13,125**	**$13,281**	**$12,343**	**$12,968**
Direct Cost of Sales						
Sales	$0	$4,750	$0	$4,750	$0	$4,750
Other	$0	$0	$0	$0	$0	$0
Subtotal Cost of Sales	**$0**	**$4,750**	**$0**	**$4,750**	**$0**	**$4,750**

Personnel Plan

Personnel	Dec	Jan	Feb	Mar	Apr	May
Moira Rye	$600	$600	$480	$600	$600	$600
Rhonda Small	$600	$600	$480	$600	$600	$600
Other	$0	$0	$0	$0	$0	$0
Total Payroll	**$1,200**	**$1,200**	**$960**	**$1,200**	**$1,200**	**$1,200**
Total Headcount	**0**	**0**	**0**	**0**	**0**	**0**
Payroll Burden	**$180**	**$180**	**$144**	**$180**	**$180**	**$180**
Total Payroll Expenditures	**$1,380**	**$1,380**	**$1,104**	**$1,380**	**$1,380**	**$1,380**

General Assumptions

	Dec	Jan	Feb	Mar	Apr	May	Jun
Short-term Interest Rate %	10.00%	10.00%	10.00%	10.00%	10.00%	10.00%	10.00%
Long-term Interest Rate %10.00%	10.00%	10.00%	10.00%	10.00%	10.00%	10.00%	10.00%
Payment Days Estimator	30	30	30	30	30	30	30
Collection Days Estimator0	0	0	0	0	0	0	0
Inventory Turnover Estimator	8.00	8.00	8.00	8.00	8.00	8.00	8.00
Tax Rate %	25.00%	25.00%	25.00%	25.00%	25.00%	25.00%	25.00%
Expenses in Cash %	10.00%	10.00%	10.00%	10.00%	10.00%	10.00%	10.00%
Sales on Credit %	0.00%	0.00%	0.00%	0.00%	0.00%	0.00%	0.00%
Personnel Burden %	15.00%	15.00%	15.00%	15.00%	15.00%	15.00%	15.00%

	Jun	Jul	Aug	Sep	Oct	Nov	FY2001	FY2002	FY2003
	$8,750	$8,750	$16,562	$14,531	$15,625	$28,125	$187,500	$286,118	$384,736
	$0	$0	$0	$0	$0	$0	$0	$0	$0
	$8,750	**$8,750**	**$16,562**	**$14,531**	**$15,625**	**$28,125**	**$187,500**	**$286,118**	**$384,736**
	$0	$4,750	$0	$4,750	$0	$4,750	$28,500	$28,500	$28,500
	$0	$0	$0	$0	$0	$0	$0	$0	$0
	$0	**$4,750**	**$0**	**$4,750**	**$0**	**$4,750**	**$28,500**	**$28,500**	**$28,500**

	Jun	Jul	Aug	Sep	Oct	Nov	FY2001	FY2002	FY2003
	$480	$480	$600	$480	$600	$480	$6,600	$6,600	$6,600
	$480	$480	$600	$480	$600	$480	$6,600	$6,600	$6,600
	$0	$0	$0	$0	$0	$0	$0	$0	$0
	$960	**$960**	**$1,200**	**$960**	**$1,200**	**$960**	**$13,200**	**$13,200**	**$13,200**
	0	**0**	**0**	**0**	**0**	**0**	**0**	**0**	**0**
	$144	**$144**	**$180**	**$144**	**$180**	**$144**	**$1,980**	**$1,980**	**$1,980**
	$1,104	**$1,104**	**$1,380**	**$1,104**	**$1,380**	**$1,104**	**$15,180**	**$15,180**	**$15,180**

Jul	Aug	Sep	Oct	Nov	FY2001	FY2002	FY2003
10.00%	10.00%	10.00%	10.00%	10.00%	10.00%	10.00%	10.00%
10.00%	10.00%	10.00%	10.00%	10.00%	10.00%	10.00%	
30	30	30	30	30	30	30	30
0	0	0	0	0	0	0	
8.00	8.00	8.00	8.00	8.00	8.00	8.00	8.00
25.00%	25.00%	25.00%	25.00%	25.00%	25.00%	25.00%	25.00%
10.00%	10.00%	10.00%	10.00%	10.00%	10.00%	10.00%	10.00%
0.00%	0.00%	0.00%	0.00%	0.00%	0.00%	0.00%	0.00%
15.00%	15.00%	15.00%	15.00%	15.00%	15.00%	15.00%	15.00%

Profit and Loss (Income Statement)

	Dec	Jan	Feb	Mar	Apr	May
Sales	$35,472	$7,968	$13,125	$13,281	$12,343	$12,968
Direct Cost of Sales	$0	$4,750	$0	$4,750	$0	$4,750
Production Payroll	$0	$0	$0	$0	$0	$0
Other	$0	$0	$0	$0	$0	$0
Total Cost of Sales	**$0**	**$4,750**	**$0**	**$4,750**	**$0**	**$4,750**
Gross Margin	$35,472	$3,218	$13,125	$8,531	$12,343	$8,218
Gross Margin %	100.00%	40.39%	100.00%	64.23%	100.00%	63.37%
Operating Expenses:						
Sales and Marketing Expenses						
Sales and Marketing Payroll	$0	$0	$0	$0	$0	$0
Rent	$0	$1,100	$1,100	$1,100	$1,100	$1,100
Travel	$0	$0	$0	$0	$0	$0
Burglar Alarm	$99	$99	$99	$99	$99	$99
Total Sales & Marketing Expenses	**$0**	**$0**	**$0**	**$0**	**$0**	**$0**
Sales and Marketing %	0.00%	0.00%	0.00%	0.00%	0.00%	0.00%
General and Administrative Expenses						
General & Administrative Payroll	$0	$0	$0	$0	$0	$0
Payroll Expense	$1,200	$1,200	$960	$1,200	$1,200	$1,200
Payroll Burden	$180	$180	$144	$180	$180	$180
Depreciation	$0	$0	$0	$0	$0	$0
Office Supplies	$0	$20	$20	$20	$20	$20
Utilities	$840	$840	$840	$840	$840	$840
Insurance	$0	$0	$219	$0	$0	$219
Telephone	$90	$90	$90	$90	$90	$90
Total General & Administrative Expenses	**$0**	**$0**	**$0**	**$0**	**$0**	**$0**
General and Administrative %	0.00%	0.00%	0.00%	0.00%	0.00%	0.00%
Other Expenses						
Other Payroll	$0	$0	$0	$0	$0	$0
Advertising	$0	$457	$457	$457	$457	$457
Loan Repayment	$0	$620	$620	$620	$620	$620
Inventory	$0	$4,750	$0	$4,750	$0	$4,750
Accounting/legal	$400	$400	$400	$400	$400	$400
Total Other Expenses	**$0**	**$0**	**$0**	**$0**	**$0**	**$0**
Other %	0.00%	0.00%	0.00%	0.00%	0.00%	0.00%
Total Operating Expenses	**$2,809**	**$9,756**	**$4,949**	**$9,756**	**$5,006**	**$9,975**
Profit Before Interest and Taxes	$32,663	($6,538)	$8,176	($1,225)	$7,337	($1,757)
Interest Expense Short-term	$295	$295	$295	$295	$295	$295
Interest Expense Long-term	$0	$0	$0	$0	$0	$0
Taxes Incurred	$8,092	($1,708)	$1,970	($380)	$1,760	($513)
Extraordinary Items	$0	$0	$0	$0	$0	$0
Net Profit	**$24,276**	**($5,125)**	**$5,910**	**($1,140)**	**$5,281**	**($1,539)**
Net Profit/Sales	**68.44%**	**-64.32%**	**45.03%**	**-8.59%**	**42.79%**	**-11.87%**

Jun	Jul	Aug	Sep	Oct	Nov	FY2001	FY2002	FY2003
$8,750	$8,750	$16,562	$14,531	$15,625	$28,125	$187,500	$286,118	$384,736
$0	$4,750	$0	$4,750	$0	$4,750	$28,500	$28,500	$28,500
$0	$0	$0	$0	$0	$0	$0	$0	$0
$0	$0	$0	$0	$0	$0	$0	$0	$0
$0	**$4,750**	**$0**	**$4,750**	**$0**	**$4,750**	**$28,500**	**$28,500**	**$28,500**
$8,750	$4,000	$16,562	$9,781	$15,625	$23,375	$159,000	$257,618	$356,236
100.00%	45.71%	100.00%	67.31%	100.00%	83.11%	84.80%	90.04%	92.59%
$0	$0	$0	$0	$0	$0	$0	$0	$0
$1,100	$1,100	$1,100	$1,100	$1,100	$1,100	$12,100	$13,200	$13,200
$2,000	$0	$0	$0	$0	$0	$2,000	$2,000	$2,000
$99	$99	$99	$99	$99	$99	$1,188	$1,188	$1,188
$0	**$0**	**$0**	**$0**	**$0**	**$0**	**$0**	**$0**	**$0**
0.00%	0.00%	0.00%	0.00%	0.00%	0.00%	0.00%	0.00%	0.00%
$0	$0	$0	$0	$0	$0	$0	$0	$0
$960	$960	$1,200	$960	$1,200	$960	$13,200	$13,200	$13,200
$144	$144	$180	$144	$180	$144	$1,980	$1,980	$1,980
$0	$0	$0	$0	$0	$0	$0	$0	$0
$20	$20	$20	$20	$20	$20	$220	$220	$220
$840	$840	$840	$840	$840	$840	$10,080	$10,080	$10,080
$0	$0	$219	$0	$0	$219	$876	$876	$876
$90	$90	$90	$90	$90	$90	$1,080	$1,080	$1,080
$0	**$0**	**$0**	**$0**	**$0**	**$0**	**$0**	**$0**	**$0**
0.00%	0.00%	0.00%	0.00%	0.00%	0.00%	0.00%	0.00%	0.00%
$0	$0	$0	$0	$0	$0	$0	$0	$0
$457	$457	$457	$457	$457	$457	$5,027	$5,484	$5,784
$620	$620	$620	$620	$620	$620	$6,820	$7,440	$7,440
$0	$4,750	$0	$4,750	$0	$4,750	$28,500	$28,500	$28,500
$400	$400	$400	$400	$400	$400	$4,800	$4,800	$4,800
$0	**$0**	**$0**	**$0**	**$0**	**$0**	**$0**	**$0**	**$0**
0.00%	0.00%	0.00%	0.00%	0.00%	0.00%	0.00%	0.00%	0.00%
$6,730	**$9,480**	**$5,225**	**$9,480**	**$5,006**	**$9,699**	**$87,871**	**$90,048**	**$90,348**
$2,020	($5,480)	$11,337	$301	$10,619	$13,676	$71,129	$167,570	$265,888
$295	$295	$295	$295	$295	$295	$3,544	$3,544	$3,544
$0	$0	$0	$0	$0	$0	$0	$0	$0
$431	($1,444)	$2,760	$1	$2,581	$3,345	$16,896	$41,006	$65,586
$0	$0	$0	$0	$0	$0	$0	$0	$0
$1,293	**($4,332)**	**$8,281**	**$4**	**$7,743**	**$10,035**	**$50,688**	**$123,019**	**$196,758**
14.78%	**-49.50%**	**50.00%**	**0.03%**	**49.55%**	**35.68%**	**27.03%**	**43.00%**	**51.14%**

Projected Cash Flow

	Dec	Jan	Feb	Mar	Apr	May
Net Profit	**$24,276**	**($5,125)**	**$5,910**	**($1,140)**	**$5,281**	**($1,539)**
Plus:						
Depreciation	$0	$0	$0	$0	$0	$0
Change in Accounts Payable	$8,540	($2,482)	($742)	$1,897	($2,270)	$4,411
Current Borrowing (repayment)	$0	$0	$0	$0	$0	$0
Increase (decrease) Other Liabilities	$0	$0	$0	$0	$0	$0
Long-term Borrowing (repayment)	$0	$0	$0	$0	$0	$0
Capital Input	$0	$0	$0	$0	$0	$0
Subtotal	**$32,816**	**($7,607)**	**$5,169**	**$757**	**$3,011**	**$2,872**
Less:						
Change in Accounts Receivable	$0	$0	$0	$0	$0	$0
Change in Inventory	$0	($4,750)	$0	($4,750)	$0	($2,375)
Change in Other Short-term Assets	$0	$0	$0	$0	$0	$0
Capital Expenditure	$0	$0	$0	$0	$0	$0
Dividends	$0	$0	$0	$0	$0	$0
Subtotal	**$0**	**($4,750)**	**$0**	**($4,750)**	**$0**	**($2,375)**
Net Cash Flow	**$32,816**	**($2,857)**	**$5,169**	**$5,507**	**$3,011**	**$5,247**
Cash Balance	**$32,816**	**$29,959**	**$35,127**	**$40,634**	**$43,645**	**$48,892**

Jun	Jul	Aug	Sep	Oct	Nov	FY2001	FY2002	FY2003
$1,293	**($4,332)**	**$8,281**	**$4**	**$7,743**	**$10,035**	**$50,688**	**$123,019**	**$196,758**
$0	$0	$0	$0	$0	$0	$0	$0	$0
($3,828)	$4,894	($4,417)	$5,674	($6,021)	$9,120	$14,777	($4,126)	$2,384
$0	$0	$0	$0	$0	$0	$0	$0	$0
$0	$0	$0	$0	$0	$0	$0	$0	$0
$0	$0	$0	$0	$0	$0	$0	$0	$0
$0	$0	$0	$0	$0	$0	$0	$0	$0
($2,534)	**$562**	**$3,864**	**$5,678**	**$1,722**	**$19,156**	**$65,466**	**$118,894**	**$199,142**
$0	$0	$0	$0	$0	$0	$0	$0	$0
$0	$0	$0	$0	$0	$0	($11,875)	$0	$0
$0	$0	$0	$0	$0	$0	$0	$0	$0
$0	$0	$0	$0	$0	$0	$0	$0	$0
$0	$0	$0	$0	$0	$0	$0	$0	$0
$0	**$0**	**$0**	**$0**	**$0**	**$0**	**($11,875)**	**$0**	**$0**
($2,534)	**$562**	**$3,864**	**$5,678**	**$1,722**	**$19,156**	**$77,341**	**$118,894**	**$199,142**
$46,358	**$46,920**	**$50,785**	**$56,463**	**$58,185**	**$77,341**	**$77,341**	**$196,234**	**$395,376**

Projected Balance Sheet

Assets

Short-term Assets	**Dec**	**Jan**	**Feb**	**Mar**	**Apr**	**May**
Cash	$32,816	$29,959	$35,127	$40,634	$43,645	$48,892
Accounts Receivable	$0	$0	$0	$0	$0	$0
Inventory	$19,000	$14,250	$14,250	$9,500	$9,500	$7,125
Other Short-term Assets	$0	$0	$0	$0	$0	$0
Total Short-term Assets	**$51,816**	**$44,209**	**$49,377**	**$50,134**	**$53,145**	**$56,017**
Long-term Assets						
Capital Assets	$0	$0	$0	$0	$0	$0
Accumulated Depreciation	$0	$0	$0	$0	$0	$0
Total Long-term Assets	$0	$0	$0	$0	$0	$0
Total Assets	**$51,816**	**$44,209**	**$49,377**	**$50,134**	**$53,145**	**$56,017**
Liabilities and Capital						
Accounts Payable	$8,540	$6,058	$5,316	$7,213	$4,943	$9,354
Short-term Notes	$35,444	$35,444	$35,444	$35,444	$35,444	$35,444
Other Short-term Liabilities	$0	$0	$0	$0	$0	$0
Subtotal Short-term Liabilities	**$43,984**	**$41,502**	**$40,760**	**$42,657**	**$40,387**	**$44,798**
Long-term Liabilities	$0	$0	$0	$0	$0	$0
Total Liabilities	**$43,984**	**$41,502**	**$40,760**	**$42,657**	**$40,387**	**$44,798**
Paid in Capital	$18,299	$18,299	$18,299	$18,299	$18,299	$18,299
Retained Earnings	($34,743)	($34,743)	($34,743)	($34,743)	($34,743)	($34,743)
Earnings	$24,276	$19,151	$25,061	$23,921	$29,202	$27,663
Total Capital	**$7,832**	**$2,707**	**$8,617**	**$7,477**	**$12,758**	**$11,219**
Total Liabilities and Capital	**$51,816**	**$44,209**	**$49,377**	**$50,134**	**$53,145**	**$56,017**
Net Worth	**$7,832**	**$2,707**	**$8,617**	**$7,477**	**$12,758**	**$11,219**

	Jun	Jul	Aug	Sep	Oct	Nov	FY2001	FY2002	FY2003
	$46,358	$46,920	$50,785	$56,463	$58,185	$77,341	$77,341	$196,234	$395,376
	$0	$0	$0	$0	$0	$0	$0	$0	$0
	$7,125	$7,125	$7,125	$7,125	$7,125	$7,125	$7,125	$7,125	$7,125
	$0	$0	$0	$0	$0	$0	$0	$0	$0
	$53,483	**$54,045**	**$57,910**	**$63,588**	**$65,310**	**$84,466**	**$84,466**	**$203,359**	**$402,501**
	$0	$0	$0	$0	$0	$0	$0	$0	$0
	$0	$0	$0	$0	$0	$0	$0	$0	$0
	$0	$0	$0	$0	$0	$0	$0	$0	$0
	$53,483	**$54,045**	**$57,910**	**$63,588**	**$65,310**	**$84,466**	**$84,466**	**$203,359**	**$402,501**
	$5,527	$10,420	$6,004	$11,678	$5,657	$14,777	$14,777	$10,652	$13,036
	$35,444	$35,444	$35,444	$35,444	$35,444	$35,444	$35,444	$35,444	$35,444
	$0	$0	$0	$0	$0	$0	$0	$0	$0
	$40,971	**$45,864**	**$41,448**	**$47,122**	**$41,101**	**$50,221**	**$50,221**	**$46,096**	**$48,480**
	$0	$0	$0	$0	$0	$0	$0	$0	$0
	$40,971	**$45,864**	**$41,448**	**$47,122**	**$41,101**	**$50,221**	**$50,221**	**$46,096**	**$48,480**
	$18,299	$18,299	$18,299	$18,299	$18,299	$18,299	$18,299	$18,299	$18,299
	($34,743)	($34,743)	($34,743)	($34,743)	($34,743)	($34,743)	($34,743)	$15,945	$138,965
	$28,956	$24,625	$32,906	$32,910	$40,653	$50,688	$50,688	$123,019	$196,758
	$12,512	**$8,181**	**$16,462**	**$16,466**	**$24,209**	**$34,244**	**$34,244**	**$157,264**	**$354,021**
	$53,483	**$54,045**	**$57,910**	**$63,588**	**$65,310**	**$84,466**	**$84,466**	**$203,359**	**$402,501**
	$12,512	**$8,181**	**$16,462**	**$16,466**	**$24,209**	**$34,244**	**$34,244**	**$157,264**	**$354,021**

Science Information Website Company

BUSINESS PLAN

E-SCIENCE TECHNOLOGIES, INC.

5621 Gateway Road
Boston, Massachusetts 02215

e-Science Technologies, Inc., was founded in late 1999 by a unique team of leading scientists and former Wall Street and Internet executives. The company's objective is to establish its e-Science.net website as the most trusted and comprehensive source of scientific information and services on the Internet for the physical and life sciences, and the impact of science on society.

- EXECUTIVE SUMMARY

- INVESTMENT HIGHLIGHTS

- RISK FACTORS

- THE COMPETITIVE ENVIRONMENT

- THE WEBSITE

- OPERATING STRATEGY

- REVENUE OPPORTUNITIES

- ORGANIZATION & MANAGEMENT

- PRESENT OPPORTUNITY

- APPENDIX

SCIENCE INFORMATION WEBSITE COMPANY
BUSINESS PLAN

EXECUTIVE SUMMARY
Introduction and Overview

e-Science Technologies, Inc., was founded in late 1999 by a unique team of leading scientists and former Wall Street and Internet executives. The company's objective is to establish its e-Science.net website as the most trusted and comprehensive source of scientific information and services on the Internet for the physical and life sciences, and the impact of science on society.

The company's Business Plan is to leverage the power and reach of the Internet to allow individuals, educators, and representatives of private, public, and not-for-profit organizations anywhere in the world to have access to:

1. A full range of online scientific information, including news and live webcasts of major scientific events and breakthroughs in Galileo's Tower™
2. An online laboratory for conducting experiments, called Virtual Lab™ 1.0
3. Monthly commentary and articles from highly regarded professors representing the world's greatest educational institutions
4. A monthly scientific competition for high school students, where a full or partial college scholarship will be awarded to each month's winner
5. Real-time chat forums in Newton's World™ with leading scientists in a variety of scientific fields, including physics, biology, and chemistry

The e-Science.net website will offer both free and subscription-based editorial content and related services. The site's home page will offer a gateway to different levels of editorial content and services segmented by user (e.g., elementary and high school students, adult lay people with an interest in science, and professional scientists and academicians).

The company expects the majority of its paid subscribers to be professional scientists and academicians. In addition to having access to free Basic Content provided to general site visitors, subscribers will have access to Premium Content, private discussion forums and exchanges, and other special features. E-Science.net's Basic and Premium Content will include original articles created by staff writers, features contributed under contract by renowned international scholars and scientists affiliated with the company, and licensed features from third parties.

In addition to generating subscription revenues from visitors that are paid subscribers, e-Science.net will generate significant advertising revenues from companies that want to reach its targeted and specialized community of amateur and professional scientists. Such firms include manufacturers and distributors of science-related products and scientific organizations, as well as traditional consumer products and durable goods manufacturers, retailers, and other online firms. Additional revenues will be earned by facilitating e-commerce transactions with producers and distributors of scientific products and services, offering online tutoring services, and selling e-Science™ branded software.

In August 2000, e-Science Technologies, Inc., was spun off from NetWide Holdings, Inc. ("NHI"), a Delaware corporation which is an incubator of Internet companies. Besides e-Science.net, NHI has also developed a comprehensive business plan for quote-right.com, a website dedicated to providing financial and investment content to online investors.

Business Strategy

The e-Science.net business strategy incorporates in the short term the objectives highlighted below. The company believes that meeting these principal objectives will enable e-Science.net to establish itself as the preeminent online destination for amateur and professional scientists, as well as those with a casual interest in science.

Principal Short-Term Objectives

- Offer users a unique and broad range of scientific features and tools in a single integrated, easy-to-access website.
- Expand the set of existing online scientific communities by allowing site visitors with similar science-related experience to exchange information and gather news and knowledge in a compelling new environment.
- Establish and promote the e-Science.net brand name so that online consumers equate the company with top editorial content, knowledgeable scientists, and a broad range of intellectually rich and fun online experiments.
- Compile and provide to advertisers meaningful demographic data on website visitors.
- Structure alliances with a broad range of science-related vendors to facilitate e-commerce transactions.
- Promote the world's first online laboratory, Virtual Lab™ 1.0, for users of all ages and levels of scientific knowledge.

Corporate Development

In order to achieve its objectives, e-Science.net has undertaken several key development initiatives. Specifically, the company has completed significant market research leading to the creation of this Business Plan: recruited a diversified group of top scientists as advisors, identified key prospective strategic partners, and begun to interview candidates for senior management. Moreover, the company has developed the design for the first generation of its website, including the online laboratory Virtual Lab™ 1.0, and is planning for a "soft" launch of e-Science.net in October 2001.

During the autumn of 2000, the company will seek its first round of outside financing to fund its next growth stage, with a full-scale launch of the e-Science.net website planned for January 2001.

Present Opportunity

e-Science.net is ideally positioned to establish itself as the leader in a valuable online market niche. The company believes that there are no direct competitors, and that other participants in the online market oriented toward people with an interest in science tend to be limited in terms of scope, and focused on a more a narrow audience.

In contrast, e-Science.net offers compelling editorial content and interactive features to a wide array of science-minded individuals, including both amateurs and professionals, from children to adults. The centerpiece of the e-Science.net website is its innovative online laboratory. This multimedia learning application, known as Virtual Lab™ 1.0, offers visitors to e-Science.net the opportunity to perform interesting online experiments as if they were in an actual laboratory, mixing ingredients, changing temperatures, and witnessing the outcome in real time.

In addition to its editorial content and Virtual Lab™ 1.0, e-Science.net offers many other rewarding features, including special discussion forums, science clubs, and scientific competitions for high school students, all intended to create a profound sense of community among its visitors. The company is confident that the community feeling inspired by e-Science.net will attract repeat visitors and enhance its ability to establish itself as the premier online destination for general science.

INVESTMENT HIGHLIGHTS

Opportunity to Establish Leading Position in Major Market Segment

The company believes that it is poised to establish a leading position in the market for general online science information and products. e-Science.net does not believe that there are directly comparable websites currently in operation today that provide the breadth of information and innovation that it will provide to online amateur and professional scientists, as well as those with a casual interest in science.

Innovative Operating Strategy

The company's innovative business model will serve to differentiate it from the competition and achieve its desired market share and revenue targets. Key features of e-Science.net business model include the following three elements:

1. *Broad Target Audience*

In contrast to other more narrowly focused science-related sites, e-Science.net will offer content and features appealing to a broad spectrum of consumers, from those with a casual interest in science to industry professionals. The company estimates that the size of its target online audience is roughly 32 million people in the U.S. alone.

2. *Virtual Lab™ 1.0*

The centerpiece of the e-Science.net website is its innovative online laboratory. This multimedia learning application, known as Virtual Lab™ 1.0, offers visitors to e-Science.net the opportunity to perform interesting online experiments as if they were in an actual laboratory, mixing ingredients, changing temperatures, and witnessing the outcome in real time.

3. *Strategic Approach to Editorial Content*

The company's approach to editorial content is based on providing an enriching breadth of information on science to online visitors. Key content features include: 1. Galileo's Tower™, which will feature scientific news and live webcasts of major scientific events and breakthroughs, and 2. a college- and university-led monthly commentary section with contributions from highly regarded professors at the world's greatest educational institutions. The company expects that featured content will be debated in a lively fashion in real-time chat forums in its Newton's World™.

Leading International Scientific Team

The company's team of scientific advisors, led by Dr. William Newton, Chief Scientist, is composed of a handful of scientists that are world leaders in their field of specialization. This team includes specialists in robotics, biomechanics, engineering mechanics, medicine, psychiatry, environmental studies, and scientific education.

RISK FACTORS

Development of e-Science.net Organization and Website

The company's growth is dependent upon the successful development of its organization and website. e-Science.net has been formed to execute the concept outlined within its Business Plan and as yet has no significant operating history. While the company's first generation website has already been created, further development of editorial content, features, and technology will be required to achieve the company's long-term objectives.

Management of Growth

Subject to the completion of the company's private placement in the autumn of 2000, e-Science.net expects its business to grow rapidly during the remainder of 2000 and in future years. This growth will require a commitment to a substantial marketing plan and an ongoing hiring program, among other things. Rapid growth may place a strain on the company's management, resources and operations. Accordingly, failure to properly manage this growth could have a material adverse effect on the company's business.

Capital Requirements

The company will rely heavily upon its planned autumn 2000 private placement to fund its post-launch period. While the company believes that the amount of capital it plans to raise during this period will be sufficient for the following twelve months of operation, it is possible that additional outside funding will be required to continue operations. If such financing is not available on commercially acceptable terms, e-Science.net may be unable to take advantage of planned business opportunities, which could have a material adverse effect on its business.

Competition with Established Off-line Publications and New Market Entrants

Although the company is confident in its business model, e-Science.net could face intense competition from newly introduced websites in the future and from science-oriented publications with whom consumers may be more immediately familiar. The company's failure to establish a strong market presence early in its development could adversely affect its ability to consummate its planned growth objectives.

Government Regulation

e-Science.net is subject to government regulation applicable to businesses generally, and to businesses that offer information or services online. Although there are currently few laws and regulations governing Internet-based commerce, it is possible that such laws or regulations may be implemented in the future. These laws and regulations may include issues such as copyright, privacy, piracy, and taxation of goods and services distributed via the Internet. The company cannot anticipate the effect that future laws or regulations may have on e-Science.net.

Liability for Content

As a publisher of licensed and original editorial content, the company is not immune from claims relating to defamation, negligence, copyright, and patent or trademark infringement. Such claims, if lodged against e-Science.net and prosecuted successfully, could have a material adverse effect on its business.

THE COMPETITIVE ENVIRONMENT

Overview of Internet Usage Trends

During the last five years, the Internet has become a formidable alternative to traditional media. Never before have consumers been able to seek information, communicate with one another, and execute commercial transactions so quickly and easily. According to a recent study, the number of worldwide web users is expected to grow from approximately 100 million in 1998 to approximately 320 million by 2002. The proliferation of the Internet as a research and commercial tool will make traditional methods of communication almost obsolete, and will further break down national boundaries in the communication and research domain. The accessibility and expanse of the Internet provides a true "marketplace of ideas."

It is not an overstatement to say that the growth of Internet usage across the world was the single most important technological change of the late twentieth century, resulting in business models with vastly lower costs for products and services and significant benefits to all participants. In November 1998, Forrester Research, a Cambridge, Massachusetts-based technology-oriented consultancy, estimated that there was $43.1 billion in commerce conducted over the Internet in 1998, that there would be $109.3 billion in commerce in 1999, and $1.3 trillion in Internet commerce in 2003.

In this setting, not only is the number of new users increasingly rapidly, as well as the sale of goods and services, but the amount of time spent by users of the Internet online has increased significantly as well. In June 1999, Media Metrix estimated that the average hours spent per person per month on the Internet increased by 43.8 percent from May 1998 to May 1999, growing from 5.3 to 7.6 hours per month. More recently, Neilsen/NetRatings estimated that the average time spent online by Internet users was 8.3 hours in December 1999.

As the number of online users has grown dramatically, along with average time spent online, the Internet has become an increasingly attractive medium for niche advertising. Among other attributes, online advertising offers targetability, interactivity, and measurability with precision and timeliness not available in traditional media. For this reason, U.S. advertising via the Internet is forecast by Forrester Research to increase from an estimated $1.3 billion in 1998 to $10.5 billion in 2003.

Moreover, as the Internet continues to evolve, and consumers become aware of websites with compelling new ideas, the market remains extremely receptive to innovative concepts. According to Media Metrix, iwon.net, a sweepstakes website launched in late 1999, had 6.9 million unique visitors in March 2000, a site that didn't exist in March of the previous year, but quickly became a leading website.

The e-Science.net Target Audience

The company believes that its website will appeal to a wide audience, including professional scientists and academicians, science students and "armchair scientists" alike. In assessing the size of its target audience, the company has made certain assumptions profiled below about Internet penetration rates for its various constituencies. In summary, the company believes that e-Science.net's target market in the U.S. alone currently consists of roughly 32 million online users. As Internet usage rates continue to grow, the company expects its total target audience size to grow as well, particularly among students and adult hobbyists. The size of each of the various market segments identified by the company is profiled below:

Projected Market Size for e-Science.net (U.S.)

Category	Total Universe	% Online (Est.)	Total Target Audience
Scientists			
Physicists and Astronomers	18,000	85%	15,300
Chemists	96,000	85%	81,600
Chemical Engineering Technicians (Est.)	109,000	85%	92,650
Science Technicians	227,000	85%	192,950
Agricultural and Food Scientists	21,000	85%	17,850
Biological and Medical Scientists	112,000	85%	95,200
Atmospheric Scientists	8,400	85%	7,140
Science Teachers and Professors			
Primary and Secondary School (Est.)	337,230	85%	286,650
University (including professors, researchers, and assistants)	183,000	85%	155,550
Science Students			
Primary and Secondary (Est.)	40,154,000	45%	18,069,300
University (Est.)	2,400,000	85%	2,040,000
Science Hobbyists			
Adult hobbyists not included in categories above (Est.)	24,402,050	45%	10,980,922
Total	**68,067,680**	**47%**	**32,035,112**

According to a recent poll conducted by *Popular Science*, 60 percent of individuals who use the Internet have searched for science-related information online. Furthermore, the poll shows that 70 percent of people searching for science information online believe the Internet empowers them by providing them with information they are seeking in a timely, efficient, and convenient manner.

e-Science.net intends to establish itself as the dominant participant in the field of science and discovery over the Internet. The current competition in this industry is largely unnoticed by consumers, with very few if any standout websites able to be cited by consumers by name without prompting. The company believes that most science-related websites are restricted to one discrete topic or field and tend to be comprised mostly of static, mundane articles, with little chance for interactivity. Many sites are also geared towards a specific target audience, often not lay people, and tend to be affiliated with a sponsoring organization, such as a science association or think tank.

In terms of sales of educational products, the Software and Information Industry Association recently estimated that educational software for curricular uses approximated $800 million in total U.S. sales, and that other educational software not specifically tied to school curricula accounted for roughly another $1.0 billion in total U.S. sales.

The wide range of fields and topics covered by e-Science.net offers vivid evidence of its scope and diversity. e-Science.net will provide core research and comprehensive information pertaining to the physical and life sciences, as well as the effect of science on society, in a well-organized, logical website.

An overview of how the website will be organized is as follows:

Tier	Consumer	Student	Scientist/Academic
Level	Basic	Intermediate	Complex
Description	Content and features adult science aficionados.	Multi-level content and features for high school, college, and graduate-level science students.	Content and features geared towards the science professional.
Features	*Kids' Corner* (up to eighth grade) • Access to age-appropriate experiments in Virtual Lab™ 1.0. • Access to special science news and features geared towards kids. • Membership in the e-Science™ Future Scientist Club.	• Access to all basic areas of the website, including *Science News* in Galileo's Tower™ and Virtual Lab™ 1.0. • Membership in the e-Science™ Science Student Club. • Access to monthly scientific challenge which rewards high school students with college scholarships.	• Access to all basic areas of the website, including *Science News* in Galileo's Tower™ and Virtual Lab™ 1.0. • Access to Newton's World™. • Eligibility to apply to be an Expert Scientist on the site on selected topics, and to submit original research and articles for publication.

Tier	Consumer	Student	Scientist/Academic
	Adults' Section • Access to *Science News* in Galileo's Tower™. • Access to Virtual Lab™ 1.0. • Membership in the e-Science™ Science Club.		• Eligibility to participate in online forums and private encrypted discussions.
Fees	Access is free, with the exception of Virtual Lab™ 1.0.	Subscription fee of $15.00 per month.	Subscription fee of $19.95 per month.

The e-Science.net website will be segmented in such a manner that it appeals to a broad spectrum of individuals and organizations who are interested in science. The multidimensional design enables the company to perform the following functions for users of its site:

- Guide visitors to specific areas of interest
- Educate visitors about particular scientific issues
- Help visitors assess their individual science information needs
- Initiate action through interactive messaging
- Provide ongoing support through a personalized action plan

Website Features

Science News

The e-Science.net *Science News* center will offer a wide variety of scientific information designed to appeal to all scientists, from the novice to the most expert. Galileo's Tower™ will provide the latest information ranging from cutting edge scientific papers to live webcasts of significant scientific events, such as space shuttle launches and landings.

Virtual Lab™ 1.0

The company believes that its multimedia learning laboratory, Virtual Lab™ 1.0, will be unrivaled in the industry for the foreseeable future. In order to develop Virtual Lab™ 1.0, the company has dedicated considerable resources to employ a team of programmers and technicians over the past six months dedicated to this project alone.

Virtual Lab™ 1.0, which will be available initially in five different languages, has been designed to simulate real life laboratory testing conditions in an online environment. For example, a visitor to the website will be able to "mix" different compounds and molecules into a beaker or other container, apply heat, light, or electricity, and see the results in real time.

Virtual Lab™ 1.0 has been designed to appeal to many different categories of users, from novices to experts, providing an extremely useful and enjoyable online experience. Experiments will be grouped according to scientific category and level of difficulty. Some examples of possible experiments using Virtual Lab™ 1.0 include the following:

Chemistry: "What do you get when Argon and Nitrogen mix?"

Biology: "Genetic Outcomes"

Physics: "The Behavior of Light Rays: Everett's 'Many Worlds' Interpretation of Quantum Mechanics"

Psychology: "How Facial Expressions Affect Mood"

In addition to its online applications, the company has designed Virtual Lab™ 1.0 software for conducting experiments off-line as well. The company will charge individual consumers a $39.00 fee to download Virtual Lab™ 1.0 from e-Science.net. In addition, the company intends to license Virtual Lab™ 1.0 for worldwide distribution to schools and other appropriate end-users. This feature promises to provide tremendous traffic to the company's website, along with substantial interest from commercial sponsors. At present, the company plans to offer new releases of Virtual Lab™ once or twice per year for the foreseeable future.

Newton's World™

The company plans to schedule a live chat every evening on different topics of interest, with e-Science.net's paid subscribers interacting directly with the company's affiliated scientists. Weekly chat schedules and topics will be determined and announced in advance, allowing for maximum participation and ensuring quality in dialogue.

This website feature will create an interactive and personal element that is expected to stimulate recurring traffic. Initially, this feature will follow a "question and answer" format. In addition, as mentioned earlier, the company intends to facilitate private or restricted online conferences and consultations among qualified members. (A sample schedule of topics appears in the appendix.) The company will also allow subscribers to apply for "Expert Scientist" status, which will enable them to host conferences and submit papers, research, and otherwise participate at a higher level on the website when appropriate. Finally, e-Science.net will also organize an Interactive Collegiate Forum with several national universities under the aegis of Newton's World™ to discuss science-related matters.

Specialized Science Clubs

To foster a community feeling and to encourage active and consistent online participation, e-Science.net will form several virtual clubs for its visitors. The clubs will be organized according to the category of visitors (e.g., younger kids, science students, and adults). Clubs that will be introduced include the following:

e-Science™ Future Scientist Club—This club's objective is to encourage a life-long love of science among elementary school children. It will include online science competitions, information on science camps, specialized subgroups (e.g., Future Chemist Club), online science quizzes and other special features geared towards the young scientist.

e-Science™ Science Student Club—This club will focus on secondary school and university science students and will include online competitions, specialized subgroups (e.g., Physics Students Club), chat rooms, information on leading science universities and science programs, information on careers in science, forums to submit ideas to Newton's World™, science quizzes, and other special features geared toward the serious science student.

E-Commerce Links

The company will create links to a variety of manufacturers and distributors of science-related materials, including books, equipment, and supplies.

OPERATING STRATEGY

Emphasis on Innovative, Comprehensive Scientific Content

e-Science.net offers users a unique and broad range of scientific features and tools in a single integrated, easy-to-access website. Editorial content will cover key areas of science, including physics, chemistry, astronomy, the biological sciences, and the impact of science on society. The company is dedicated to updating its content, product, and service offerings continuously in order to meet the ever-changing and growing demand for online science information.

One of the key features offered at e-Science.net will be the company's online laboratory Virtual Lab™ 1.0, which will allow users to mix ingredients, add heat, light, and electricity, and conduct online experiments in real time. The company is also committed to offering other interactive features which will enhance and personalize the visitor's online science experience.

By emphasizing its comprehensive, innovative content, the company believes that it can establish a reputation as the preeminent online destination for amateur and professional scientists, as well as those with a casual interest in science.

Broad Scientific Community Approach

As discussed above, unlike other websites which emphasize only one specialty or topic, e-Science.net will offer content covering a wide range of scientific topics. This will attract the science community at large to the website, greatly enhancing its community appeal. This will also serve to expand the set of existing online scientific communities by allowing site visitors with similar science-related experience to exchange information and gather news and knowledge in a compelling new environment.

Compelling Adjunct Services

e-Science.net's website traffic will be largely driven by its exceptional scientific content. However, the company will offer many adjunct services to its visitors and subscribers which will not only enhance the user's experience on the e-Science.net website, but which will also provide additional revenue streams to the company. For example, the company will structure alliances with a range of science-related vendors to facilitate e-commerce transactions and will offer online tutoring services in selected scientific fields as well.

Aggressive Marketing

Key to the company's operating strategy is its emphasis on establishing e-Science.net as the most trusted and respected name in scientific consultation and services on the Internet. The company believes that the e-Science.net concept will have broad domestic and international appeal, enhanced by the ubiquitous nature of the Internet. Accordingly, the company has adopted a marketing and public relations strategy with the objective of establishing rapid market penetration and a dominant brand identity.

Advertising
Advertising will be the cornerstone of e-Science.net's marketing program and will include online and off-line initiatives. The company believes that "click-through" banner advertising will constitute a key means of driving traffic to its website. In order to attract first-time users to e-Science.net, the company plans to engage in extensive banner advertising on strategic websites that appeal to its target audience. Depending on the source, the company can use banner advertisements to direct users to the e-Science.net home page or to a specific page containing topical information. The company also intends to utilize general off-line advertising through more conventional media. Some off-line outlets under consideration include print advertising (such as *Popular Science* and *Scientific American*), and radio and television advertisements which would air in conjunction with science-oriented programming.

Affiliate Relations
Co-marketing campaigns are a significant part of the company's plan to drive traffic to the e-Science.net website. e-Science.net has identified selected colleges and universities that have moderate to large-scale science programs as well as governmental and non-governmental (NGO) science organizations that the company believes would make strong strategic partners. In some cases, the company expects to have access to these organization's mailing lists and the ability to distribute brochures at the point-of-presence about e-Science.net. (Where

appropriate, the company may participate in fundraising or other forms of support for not-for-profit or educational programs for the advancement of science and scientific causes.)

Public Relations

Because the "Newton" name is one of the most respected and recognized names in the scientific world, the company believes that Dr. William Newton is in a unique position to raise consumer knowledge of scientific issues and increase awareness of the company. e-Science.net intends to leverage Dr. Newton's reputation to spread the company's message of empowering consumers and science professionals alike with information and services of significant interest. Moreover, Dr. Newton and other company scientists will conduct presentations at relevant scientific conferences and publish articles in topical trade journals, supported by an effective public relations firm responsible for promoting e-Science.net.

REVENUE OPPORTUNITIES

Introduction

The company's revenues will be derived primarily through advertising sales, subscription revenues, e-commerce transactions, including sales of e-Science™ branded software, and online tutoring services.

Advertising Revenues

As e-Science.net launches its innovative scientific information and experimentation website, the company believes that advertisers and merchants will have a strong interest in gaining access to its visitors. The company believes that its website will be visited by users receptive to the products being advertised by scientific magazines, educational sites, and medical suppliers, as well as traditional consumer products and durable goods manufacturers, and selected retailers.

Because e-Science.net is a unique concept, there is no comparable website to provide direct comparisons for advertising rates. Taking into account the average rates for Internet advertising, the company plans to charge approximately $40.00 per CPM (cost per thousand impressions) for banner ads in the Basic Content area, and a higher rate for banner ads in the Premium Content area accessible only to paid subscribers.

The company believes it will be able to generate two million visitors per month within (fill in number) months of full launch. (By comparison, according to Media Matrix, a leading Internet traffic monitoring company, Ivillage.net, a website geared toward women, generated 6.7 million unique visitors in May 2000, while OnHealth.net generated 5.2 million unique visitors. Other leading portal sites such as America Online routinely generate over 30 million unique visitors per month, including non-subscribers.)

Subscription Revenues

The company believes that it will successfully convert roughly 10 percent of visitors to its website to paid subscribers. At a monthly subscription fee of $19.95, when the company obtains 2 million unique visitors per month, with 200,000 as paying subscribers, monthly subscription revenues will be $4 million.

E-Commerce Revenues

e-Science.net will establish e-commerce relationships with educational and scientific product manufacturers and retailers. Through these arrangements, visitors to e-Science.net will be afforded access, via direct links, to a large assortment of consumable and durable products, including chemical compounds, beakers, science kits, and measuring devices, among others. For all sales originating via the e-Science.net website, the company will collect a transaction fee from affiliated vendors that is equivalent to a fixed percentage of the product value.

Software Sales

The company will offer proprietary, branded e-Science™ software for sale on its website. Although the company's online laboratory Virtual Lab™ 1.0 will be available to most visitors for free online, selected experiments may be conducted by visitors and subscribers off-line by downloading e-Science™ software for these experiments and associated "virtual ingredients." The company intends to commence development and licensing of e-Science™ software associated with Virtual Lab™ 1.0 before beginning development of other kinds of science-related software. In addition to marketing this software online, it will also be marketed directly to elementary and secondary schools.

Online Tutoring

The company will offer online tutoring services geared towards the estimated 18.1 million online elementary and secondary school science students in the U.S. Tutoring fees will be charged on an hourly basis, at an approximate rate of $45.00 per hour.

ORGANIZATION & MANAGEMENT
Introduction

e-Science.net will be led by Dr. Willaim P. Newton. In addition to Dr. Newton, the company has a distinguished group of scientific advisors, and has begun to recruit members of its senior management team. Profiles of these key individuals are provided below.

> **Jason Lin, Ph.D., PE, Senior Scientific Advisor.** Dr. Jason Lin received his Master's of Science degree from the University of California at Berkeley in 1961 and worked closely with Dr. A. H. Einstein, the son of legendary scientist Albert Einstein. He received his Bachelor of Science degree from Cheng-Kung University and his Ph.D. from Colorado State University in 1966. Dr. Lin performed post doctoral work in Classical Physiology and Medical Instructions at Baylor College of Medicine from 1966 to 1969.
>
> Dr. Lin has taught Biomechanics, CV Flow Dynamics, Biofluid Mechanics, and has researched CV Dynamics, Hemorheology, Cardiovascular Prostheses, and Circulatory Assists. Lin has had scientific papers published in many major scholarly journals. Dr. Lin currently is associated with the University of Miami as a James L. Knight Professor, the University of Nanyang Technological, Singapore as Eminent Professor of Biomedical Engineering, and has been the Herff Chair of Excellence Professor of Biomedical Engineering at Memphis State University. Dr. Lin was granted Visiting Professor status at the Julius Silver Institute of Biomedical Sciences, Department of Biomedical Engineering, Israel Institute of Technology, Haifa, Israel, and has an association with the following educational institutions: the University of Houston, Baylor College of Medicine, King's College Medical School, and the University of London.
>
> Taking a very active role in the medical and scientific communities, Dr. Lin is currently a Director with the National Science Foundation Industry, a member of the Surgery and Bioengineering Study Section, National Institute of Heart, Lung, and Blood, and is on the Scientific Review Board for the Medical Research Council of Canada. In addition, Dr. Lin is currently on the Editorial Board of Transaction American Society of Internal Artificial Organs and Asian Cardiovascular and Thoracic Surgery Annals, and has served as Chairperson of the following causes: Ad Hoc Committee, Surgery and Bioengineering, Omnicath Corporation, Board of Scientific Advisors, AV Healing, and Board of Scientific Advisors, Cardiotech International.
>
> Throughout his career, Dr. Lin has consulted for many organizations and companies, such as the U.S. Food and Drug Administration, the National Institutes of Health, St. Jude Medical Center, Baxter Edwards Laboratories, the World Heart Corporation, Autogenics Europe Ltd, and Beckman-Coulter, among others. Dr. Lin is involved with

the following professional societies: Founding Fellow of American Institute for Medical and Biological Engineers, Fellow of ASME, Senior Member of American Society of Biomedical Engineer, and a Member of the American Society of Artificial Internal, International Society of Biorheology, and Sigma Xi.

Having received numerous awards and honors throughout his career Dr. Lin is the owner of several patents such as the Prosthetic Heart Valve, the Low Turbulence Heart Valve, and the Helicofoil Pump.

William Knaught, Ph.D., Senior Scientific Advisor. Professor Knaught currently teaches Engineering Mechanics at the University of Wisconsin-Milwaukee. He has taught and performed research at various schools in the United States, including the California Institute of Technology and Northwestern University. Dr. Knaught has also worked abroad in England, Poland, Germany, Russia, Italy, Yugoslavia, and China. In 1970 he worked as a Distinguished Visiting Scholar in the Department of Applied Mathematics and Theoretical Physics at the University of Cambridge, United Kingdom. His research has been sponsored by the British Science Council, NATO, NASA, the National Science Foundation, the Office of Naval Research, the National Academy of Sciences, and the National Institute of Standards and Technology.

In 1991, Dr. Knaught was appointed a Fulbright Scholar, and in 1992, he received the Lady Davies Scholarship from the government of Israel. He is a member of the Sigma Xi Research Society and the American Academy of Mechanics, an Associate Member of the Cambridge Philosophical Society in the United Kingdom, and a life member of the New York Academy of Sciences.

Dr. Knaught is one of the co-founders and a co-chairman of the International Conference and Research Workshops on Mesomechanics, which convenes every two years in order to merge interdisciplinary research of a high technology nature involving Physics, Mechanics, and Materials Science. He has been selected an ASEE/NASA Summer Faculty member twice, once in 1996 at the Johnson Space Center-NASA White Sands Test Facility in New Mexico, and again in 1998 at the California Institute of Technology/ Jet Propulsion Laboratory in Pasadena, California.

Since 1987, Dr. Knaught has served as President of Panslavia-International Research Institute, Inc., which assists multinational partners in trade, science, and technology transfer with particular emphasis on global problems of ecology and medical research and development.

Disorado M. Rhadi, M.D., Senior Medical Advisor. Since 1995, Dr. Rhadi has been a Board Certified Pediatrician, following his education which began in 1985 at the Aga Khan University in Pakistan. His duties as a practicing physician have taken him all over the world, where he has gained medical privileges at Rio Grande Regional Medical Center, Edinburg Regional Medical Center, and McAllen Medical Center. His practicing experience in the United States has taken him to Cook County Children's Hospital in Chicago, the University of Illinois Hospital, and Brookdale Hospital Medical Center in Brooklyn, New York.

Kenneth Y. Fraffel, M.A.T., Senior Scientific Advisor. Dedicating his life to teaching, with highlights in Chemistry, Physics, and Earth Science, Mr. Fraffel earned a Bachelor of Science degree in Chemistry from the University of Massachusetts. He went on to earn his Master of Arts in Teaching in Chemistry from Bridgewater College. Having recently retired after teaching for 28 years, Mr. Fraffel is a private investor.

Rey S. Luttin, M.D., Senior Medical Advisor. With his education starting in 1978, Dr. Luttin's specialty is Child and Adolescent Psychiatry. Dr. Luttin completed his Internship and Residency at the University of Missouri, Columbia, in 1987, and a post-residency Fellowship in 1989. His association with several hospitals include Madison Center Hospital, Charter Hospital, and Memorial of South Bend. In his private practice he treats adults, adolescents, and children, networking with local mental health agencies. Having been a leader in his area for more than 10 years, he works closely with social workers, teachers, mental health workers, psychologists, and community organizations.

Namir C. Wassan, Ph.D., Senior Scientific Advisor. Dr. Wassan is associated with the Ministry of Higher Education, King Fahd University of Petroleum and Minerals. In this capacity, he is very much involved in environmental related research, particularly, the engineering aspects. Dr. Wassan will share his works with the company on the many research projects in which he has participated.

The company is currently recruiting key executives for the following positions to round out its management team:

- **President and CEO:** Responsible for implementing the company's comprehensive business strategy on a day-to-day basis, establishing key objectives in connection with this Business Plan, and overseeing key department heads.
- **Vice President, Business Development:** Responsible for creating and implementing the company's worldwide strategic partnerships.
- **Chief Financial Officer:** Responsible for financial planning, financial reporting, financial forecasting, treasury functions and tax planning, and compliance.
- **Chief Technology Officer:** Responsible for website planning and development, continued functionality, feature enhancements, and maintenance.
- **Vice President of Marketing:** Responsible for the external promotion of the company, the creation and implementation of the company's marketing strategy, the development of affiliate relations programs, and the development and implementation of the company's publicity efforts.
- **Editor-in-Chief:** Oversee responsibilities for website content, including both original and licensed content, quality control, and related activities.
- **Director of Research:** Responsible for managing and monitoring research activities, particularly relating to content.
- **Director of Advertising Sales:** Responsible for generating advertising revenues.

Other key positions to be filled include Research Assistants (specializing in various scientific fields), Science Reporters (to cover science news and produce news-based content for the website), Features Managers (to manage specific website features, such as the science clubs and Virtual Lab™ 1.0), Software Developers (to develop and license e-Science™ software), Advertising Salespeople (to assist in sales of banner, button, and sponsorship advertising), technology support staff such as Programmers and Website Support Managers, and other administrative support personnel.

e-Science.net is poised to become a leading destination for online science information and experimentation. The innovative e-Science.net format creates a multi-tiered, multi-subject forum for the exchange of ideas and information pertaining to the physical and life sciences, and the impact of science on society. Access to content on e-Science.net will be stratified in such a way that the site is expected to appeal to amateur and professional scientists alike, from children to adults.

The company's business model will enable it to generate revenues from several diverse sources, including advertising sales, subscriptions, e-commerce, and other special online services. e-Science.net's operating strategy encompasses building brand awareness, attracting strong visitor traffic, creating incentives for casual visitors to become repeat visitors and to subscribe to the company's special services, and creating a community of end-users which is not only self-supporting but also attractive to prospective advertisers and marketing partners. The company believes that there are no science-oriented websites with a similar format and that the competitive field is extremely limited. Furthermore, e-Science.net is being developed by a strong team of Internet entrepreneurs and world-renowned scientists.

In addition to developing its business strategy and assembling its advisory team, the company is presently completing its first generation website and has laid the foundation for its planned growth. In order to achieve its objectives, e-Science.net will seek to raise $X.0 million in equity financing during the autumn of 2000. Proceeds of this financing will be used to develop the second generation of the e-Science.net website, to hire key management and other support personnel, and to commence implementation of the company's sales and marketing initiatives. Subject to financing, the company is preparing for a full launch of the e-Science.net website in January 2001.

In summary, the company is confident in its ability to establish a leading general science website, supported by renowned company scientists in touch with consumer desires and knowledgeable about the Internet. With the energy and commitment of its founding development team, e-Science.net intends to press its competitive advantage in order to redefine the standards by which science-related websites are evaluated.

PRESENT OPPORTUNITY

APPENDIX

Sample Schedule of Website Discussion Topics

Dr. Newton's Weekly Live Chat Symposium Plan

Week 1

M	"Newton's Ideas and Opinion" with Dr. Newton
T	Biology
W	Astronomy, Universe, and Astrology
TR	Space Mission
F	Young Scientists - High School Morning - with Dr. Newton

Week 2

M	Physics & Chemistry
T	Math
W	Culture, Education, World Peace
TR	Electronic, Mechanical, Bioengineering, Robotics
F	Young Scientists - High School Morning - with Staff Professor

Week 3

M	Medicine
T	Computer Age
W	Philosophy and Science
TR	All High Tech and Society

| F | Young Scientist - High School Morning - with Staff Professor |

Week 4

M	Human Bioenergy, Nutrition, Sexuality
T	Science and Religion
W	Politics
TR	Biophysics
F	All Science - Morning with Professor chosen by chatroom students

Skin Cream Formulator

BUSINESS PLAN

LABELLE INDUSTRIES, INC.

4515 Mapletree Boulevard
Grand Rapids, Michigan 49503

LaBelle is a niche player in the specialty skincare business, focusing on value-added products which are not widely or readily available in the United States. We have perfected unique distribution processes resulting in lower distributing costs and high profitability. We have established a network of strategic alliances with a manufacturer who has the capability to ascend from laboratory to commercial scale and manufacture products in accordance with quality specifications.

- EXECUTIVE SUMMARY

- COMPANY SUMMARY

- PRODUCTS/INGREDIENTS

- MARKET ANALYSIS SUMMARY

- STRATEGY & IMPLEMENTATION SUMMARY

- MANAGEMENT SUMMARY

- FINANCIAL PLAN

- APPENDIX

EXECUTIVE SUMMARY

LaBelle Industries, Inc. (LaBelle) is a home-based specialty skin cream formulator, wholesaler and distributor. We sell products to companies ranging from drugstores to consumers. This business is owned and operated by principal investor Roman Miller. He is a strong knowledge-based manager, with a combined 25 years of experience in this industry. LaBelle was created in 2001 and is currently located in Roman's home in Grand Rapids, Michigan. The purpose of the business being home-based is to lower the costs of overhead.

Through Reuben Retro Skincare, we manufacture and distribute an approved skin cream used to improve arthritis in muscle mass. LaBelle also produces one other specialty formula that will be detailed later in this document.

In theory, a wholesale distributor behaves no differently from a retailer: it purchases goods it intends to sell at a profit. The fundamental difference between the two is that retailers sell to the buying public or "the consumer" and distributors sell to retail businesses and fellow wholesale firms. In the strict sense of the term, distributors never sell to the public consumer, although the advent of wholesale membership clubs and other "power retailers" has begun to call that definition into question.

A new, natural product called Nopeinne, conceived by Roman Miller, will soon be available to relieve physical pain and suffering of mankind. An investment into Nopeinne is an adventure into the near future. Nopeinne is a manifestation of remedies used for treatment of wounds and physical disorder that caused pain and suffering among a nomadic people, namely the American Indian, before the settling of the pilgrims in 1620.

LaBelle is a niche player in the specialty skincare business, focusing on value-added products which are not widely or readily available in the United States. We have perfected unique distribution processes resulting in lower distributing costs and high profitability. We have established a network of strategic alliances with a manufacturer who has the capability to ascend from laboratory to commercial scale and manufacture products in accordance with quality specifications.

Our retailers and our customers have given us an opportunity to provide products beyond our present capability. We need to increase our inventory, purchase advertising, and establish marketing and support activities.

Funding Requirements

The total amount needed for this start-up business is $38,178. Roman Miller has invested $7,636 into this business and is seeking a commercial loan of $30,542 to enable us to expand our operation and become a major factor in the production and distribution of skincare products. The funds will be distributed in the following way: $10,000 for research and development of the products, $25,000 for actual production of the product, $2,178 for radio promotions, and $1,000 for television promotions.

Our signature product Nopeinne is manufactured in cream form. We are the only company in the world capable of manufacturing this product using our patented cream formula. Our market research shows that the demand for this product alone justifies the future expansion of our facilities from being home-based to brick and mortar in 2005.

Our objectives are to have:

1. a gross margin of 65 percent or more
2. a net profit above 10 percent of sale
3. sales passing the projected sales of $252,000 by the year 2004

Objectives

We see our mission as not only that of wholesale-distributor, but a trade supplier where we can reach the end-user market with products we consider to be proprietary. We seek a fair and responsible profit, enough to keep the company financially healthy for the long term and to satisfactorily compensate owners and investors for their money and risk.

Mission

The keys to success in this business are:

Keys to Success

- Marketing: either dealing with channel problems and barriers to entry, or solving problems with major advertising and promotion budgets.
- Management: products delivered on time, cost controlled, marketing budgets managed.
- Uncompromising commitment to the quality of the end product: multiple skin cream products.
- Successful niche marketing: we need to find the quality-conscious customer in the right channels, and we need to make sure that customer can find us.
- Almost-automatic development and distribution of our product to maintain high demand needs.

LaBelle Industries Inc., is a privately owned specialty formulator of skin creams and ointments. Our end-users are in all levels of skincare needs ranging from acne to razor bumps to arthritis.

COMPANY SUMMARY

LaBelle is a corporation established in 2001. The company is owned by Roman Miller.

Company Ownership

The hours of business will be from 8:00 A.M. until 5:00 P.M., Monday through Saturday, and closed on all major holidays. Because our business is home-based, it is possible we may work overtime by answering the telephone after 5:00 P.M. or before 8:00 A.M. Any person-to-person contact will be done at the customer's establishment.

Daily Operations

We will perform most of these functions on a daily basis:

- Checking invoices against payments.
- Purchasing inventory.
- Visiting customers for promotion and service evaluation.
- Scheduling deliveries (including immediate deliveries when shortages occur) and monitoring their progress.
- Fielding calls from our manufacturer and retailers.
- Order processing.
- Inventory control.

We will perform these activities on a weekly/monthly basis:

- Maintain our bookkeeping and recordkeeping to ensure our distribution business's cash flow in the short run and avoid confusion at the end of the fiscal year.

We will keep a tight reign on these daily/weekly/monthly duties to improve our business's efficiency and reduce operating problems during the week.

Start-up Summary

The total amount needed for this start-up business is $38,178. Roman Miller has invested $7,636 into this business and is seeking a commercial loan of $30,542 to enable us to expand our operation and become a major factor in the production and distribution of skincare products. The funds will be distributed in the following way: $10,000 for research and development of the products, $25,000 for actual production of the product, $2,178 for radio promotions, and $1,000 for television promotions.

Start-up Plan

Start-up Expenses

Legal	$0
Radio Promotions (3 weeks @ $726)	$2,178
Television (100 spots @ $10)	$1,000
Research and development	$10,000
Other	$0
Total Start-up Expenses	**$13,178**

Start-up Assets Needed

Cash Requirements	$0
Start-up inventory	$25,000
Other Short-term Assets	$0
Total Short-term Assets	**$25,000**
Long-term Assets	$0
Total Assets	**$25,000**
Total Start-up Requirements:	**$38,178**
Left to finance:	$0

Start-up Funding Plan

Investment

Owner's Equity	$7,636
Investor 2	$0
Other	$0
Total Investment	**$7,636**

Short-term Liabilities

Unpaid Expenses	$0
Short-term Loans	$30,542
Interest-free Short-term Loans	$0
Subtotal Short-term Liabilities	$30,542
Long-term Liabilities	$0
Total Liabilities	**$30,542**
Loss at Start-up	**($13,178)**
Total Capital	**($5,542)**
Total Capital and Liabilities	**$25,000**
Checkline	**$0**

LaBelle Industries, Inc. is a home-based business located at 4515 Mapletree Boulevard, Grand Rapids, Michigan 49503. Our present office is small but is in a room of its own to keep our home and work lives separate. Our office contains bookshelves, file cabinet, desk with computer, sitting chairs, a fax, a copier, and space for inventory storage area for additional small products.

We will use restaurants, hotel lobbies, and conference rooms if our home won't accommodate clients comfortably. Also, as we add employees, we will look at taking on additional space or finding a new location. All products will be formulated, packaged, and shipped to the distributors through the Reuben Retro Skincare Company or hand-delivered by the LaBelle manager. This way we cut down on storage space, overstocked inventory, and any other cost surrounding the manufacturing aspect of our business.

Company Locations and Facilities

Our products are skincare creams for acne and razor bumps and medicated therapy in the form of an arthritis cream. The products are all natural with no chemicals. The products also include herbs.

PRODUCTS/ INGREDIENTS

Herbs were used extensively by ancient Romans and Egyptians and are frequently found in the tombs of Pharoahs by archaeologists. Native Americans made use of herbs and their medicineman shared their herbal remedies with less fortunate African Americans who did not have access to a physician or modern medical treatment for physical disorder, pain, and/or injury.

African Americans, during that era, depended exclusively on treatment by midwives among them when incapacitated or physically disabled on a temporary basis. They harvested assorted herbs during the growing season which were then dried by the sun and the wind and even in the shelters of Indians and slaves. Many such wild plants have been used successfully for decades by chefs and cooks at public eating establishments for the purpose of enhancing the flavor of food.

Modern supermarkets stock a complete assortment of familiar herbs, attributed to popular domestic demand. Nopeinne is the creation of an aware male amateur cook who began experimenting with herbs and fruits, based on his knowledge of natural medicinal properties contained in them. Among them are sassafras, sena, and the aloe vera plant, found among plants in many homes and used to treat minor burns. Herb tea is a popular beverage consumed by millions of people around the world. Peppermint, eucalyptus, lemon balm, lavender, compry, Queen Anne's Lace, capsicum, feverfew, ginseng, echinacea, and hot pepper are a few herbs that contain healing properties. Other valuable foods used for medicinal purposes are citrus fruits, bananas, and oranges and are included in fabricating this formula. The extensive use of herbs has been well established by man, including the source of many drugs, although Nopeinne does not contain harmful foreign properties.

Our current and future products consist of the following:

Product Description

    Skincare—facial treatments
    Body and Bath—bath and shower products that are not extensions of a fine fragrance
    Men's Products—men's hair bump treatment
    Other products—medicated therapy cream for arthritis
    Other—new products that don't fit the above categories

A new, natural product called Nopeinne, conceived by a man of vision, will soon be available to relieve physical pain and suffering of mankind. An investment into Nopeinne is an adventure into the near future. Nopeinne is a manifestation of remedies used for treatment of wounds and physical disorder that caused pain and suffering among a nomadic people, namely the American Indian, before the settling of the pilgrims in 1620.

Nopeinne is not expected to accomplish what Viagra did for men, but its purpose is to improve people's physical ability to function. This new product may be the key that will unlock stiff joints and tight muscles while raising the investors' monetary value.

Competitive Comparison

Within our niche we have several significant competitors: Tigerbalm, Flexall, Bengay, Heat, and Asper Cream. In general, however, our competition is not in our niche. We compete against skin cream companies that use chemicals instead of natural herb formulas. It isn't that people choose our competitors instead of our product. Instead they choose lesser quality, chemical-formed creams instead of natural herbs formulas we offer. This will change as we begin letting the public know they now have a choice of getting the same relief and better results without the chemical components. We will continue to examine our rivals' weaknesses and strengths, and continue to strategically promote our strengths and their weaknesses.

Marketing Plan

Our marketing plan consists of providing a direct line of communication regarding our product to current and prospective customers. Our advertising campaign will accomplish the following:

1. Convince customers that our company's products are the best available
2. Enhance our company's image
3. Point out the need and create a desire for our products
4. Announce new products or programs
5. Draw customers to our business

Our advertisements will be simple and easily understood, truthful, informative, sincere, and customer-oriented. We will use the following advertising media for our home-based business:

- Personal contact
- Newspapers
- Magazines
- Newsletters
- Telephone directories
- Radio
- Online/Internet
- Flyers—Direct Mail
- Specialty Items (pencils, calendars, matchbooks, telephone pads, etc.)
- Sales Letters
- Brochures and Catalogs
- Postcards
- Coupon Mailers
- Radio Give-a-Ways

All of our correspondence will be professional, printed on good paper and with clean typing free of any spelling errors.

Our main sourcing contact will be Reuben Retro Skincare, located at 42005 West 45th Street, New York, New York.

Sourcing

Reuben Retro was founded in 1975 by Master Chemist Jean Fream, a graduate of the prestigious Sorbonne in Paris, France. Monsieur Fream's celebrated formulas are manufactured for industry giants such as Loreal and Maybelline.

His insight and genius forms the very core of Reuben Retro's Research and Development Team, combining the master disciplines of European craftsmanship with the latest in scientific technologies and the finest natural ingredients.

For more than two decades, Reuben Retro has developed and manufactured products that make a difference in people's lives. Thousands have discovered our products and have rediscovered beauty once compromised by problematic skin. And more have found our products to be a healthy alternative to harsh medical and pharmaceutical treatments.

For more than 20 years they have used nature as their guide and maintained a natural approach to skincare. Their mission is simple.

LaBelle intends to demystify skincare, improve the way you look, and most importantly, help you feel better about yourself.

We are a highly technical niche player with a specialized product line that is in great demand. We have developed new technology and processes that are in demand by other cosmetic manufacturers as well as by major distributors who do not have the ability to produce our specialty products. We have the management team and the skin cream formulations to become a major player in the specialized niche we serve. We also hope to develop a website in the near future.

Technology

Our future products include:

Future Products

- Bath oils
- Moisturizer
- Additional acne creams
- Shaving bump cream

Our target markets are the retailers who have established relationships with consumers and the consumers themselves via word-of-mouth. We are essentially the distributing arm for these retailers and can provide development services as well as products for them.

MARKET ANALYSIS SUMMARY

The retail businesses are in the business of selling goods, and there are more than 1.5 million of them across the country. The greater the difference between the selling price and the price they pay for the product, the greater their profit. It follows that retailers have (or should have) a keen interest in the way products move from the manufacturer to them because that's where the markup occurs. If they can find a wholesale distributor like LaBelle, who can deliver a product on their shelves at a lower price and still provide exemplary service, few will refuse the chance.

Random test results of Nopeinne exceed anticipated performance at the laboratory level while clinical analysis is pending. This new product netted an impressive percent approval from Michigan and Indiana consumers ranging in age from 13 to 50 and older over a two-year period with no report of side effects.

Market Segmentation

Retailers: our market research indicates about 46 potential retailers within a 1-25 mile radius of our location, who currently sell our competitors products. Our target retailers are drugstores/pharmacies.

Consumers: There are 437,700 individuals in Kent County. Of those 315,008 are adults 18 and older, which are our target consumer market.

Market Analysis

Potential Customers	Growth	2001	2002	2003	2004	2005	CAGR
Target Retailers	10%	46	51	56	62	68	10.27%
Consumers	5%	437,700	459,585	482,564	506,692	532,027	5.00%
Other	0%	0	0	0	0	0	0.00%
Total	**5.00%**	**437,746**	**459,636**	**482,620**	**506,754**	**532,095**	**5.00%**

Target Market Segment Strategy

Retail Business: Retailers are in the business of selling goods, and there are more than 1.5 million of them across the country. The greater the difference between the selling price and the price they pay for the product, the greater their profit. It follows that retailers have (or should have) a keen interest in the way products move from the manufacturer to them because that's where the markup occurs. If they can find a wholesale distributor like LaBelle, who can deliver a product on their shelves at a lower price and still provide exemplary service, few will refuse the chance. We have retailers who will be begging for our products and we anticipate having backorders, so it is only logical that we will devote most of our time meeting this demand.

Consumer Market: This is potentially our biggest market for Nopeinne; it is limited only by our ability to produce. We look at the potential in this market as the basis for our growth. We will market to this group by giving them a clear comparison between the chemical-based products they are now using and our natural products. This marketing strategy will begin by letting the public know they now have a choice of getting the same relief and better results without the chemical components followed by their conversion over to our products.

Market Needs

Many thousands of individuals are immobilized by osteoarthritis or from temporary muscle strain and do not have access to soothing hot baths or physical therapy that relieve suffering, but Nopeinne is instantly available to a victim in pain. Hundreds of thousands of mature persons agonize about debilitating aches and pain while spending as many dollars annually for various health remedies to find relief.

Repulsive blotches on the skin, ugly pimples, sore joints, and muscles unquestionably diminish individual aesthetic qualities, progress, and success, but our Nopeinne formula is the knight in shining armor, prepared to challenge and change that undesirable status. Nopeinne is not expected to accomplish what Viagra did for men, but its purpose is to improve people's physical ability to function. This new product may be the key that will unlock stiff joints and tight muscles while raising the investors' monetary value.

Among them are staggering numbers of high profile men, women, and youths, troubled by ugly, detracting, facial blemishes that beg for attention. Thousands of individuals cannot hold a cup of coffee or a pencil or a pen and vital physical activity is severely restricted by excruciating pain. Medical clinics are filled to capacity each day with victims, untimely inhibited by rheumatism, sore muscles, and joints. Simple fun and games no longer need be curtailed because of inflamed body joints. Nopeinne offers divine redemption to innocent victims of these ailments.

The consumers are seeking more natural products versus products containing artificial or chemical ingredients and to say wholesale trade is immense would be an understatement. The Department of Commerce's most recent Census of Wholesale Trade (1992) reports that merchant wholesalers handled nearly $1.9 trillion (58 percent) of the more than $3.3 trillion total wholesale trade sales. The industry's annual payroll in 1994 topped $127 billion, according to the National Association of Wholesaler-Distributors (NAW), and supplied salaries to more than 4.6 million individuals. All told, the inventories moved by wholesale distribution establishments were valued at more than $177 billion.

Market Trends

One of the more lucrative fields of proven endeavor is that of pharmaceuticals and related medical aids purchased by persons suffering from pain. A plethora of related complaints are documented each year by thousands of doctors and pharmacists. Recent government statistics disclose the fact that 43 million individuals suffer from arthritis while 20 to 40 percent of adults in this country are plagued by acne. Thirteen to fourteen million allergy sufferers were listed between 1990-1998 and 18 million are projected for 1999. Prescription drug sales gross up to $120 billion annually in America and that number is projected to double by 2004.

Market Growth

Caution, reluctance, or procrastination could be costly in this instance because statistically, the American consumer has proven to be reliable in terms of buying health products as rapidly as they are exposed to the marketplace. Consumer confidence in health products has never been higher.

The U.S. cosmetics market, measured in manufacturers' shipments, grew by more than $1 billion in 1998, at a rate of 6.6 percent. Growth was driven by color cosmetics with its focus on teens and 'tweens, and skincare with its dermal patches and pore strips, as well as the impact of niche lines with spa positioning. As for body and bath, there were a few cellulite or slimming body products and the bath market seemed close to saturation. Fragrance exhibited modest growth, fueled by classic scents and limited editions.

Industry Analysis

The skincare industry is characterized by a wide variety of companies ranging in size, from large companies such as St. Ives to smaller specialty firms such as ours. The companies are generally organized by either end-user markets or product technology. In the past decade there has been a general trend in the industry to change emphasis from using chemicals to all natural products. The cost of product development and the need to operate factories at high levels of capacity have caused skincare companies of every size to outsource parts of the skincare cream manufacturing processes. This has created opportunities for smaller companies to create and occupy niches in development and contract manufacturing.

An investment into health-related products has always been a wise and advantageous decision, simply because most Americans are prone to abusing and neglecting their bodies which frequently require costly adjustments to restore a reasonable degree of physical comfort. The American consumer spends $439 billion, $1.5 million annually for healthcare and health products ranging from dieting to exercise to painkillers, marketed for the purpose of securing relief, comfort, and improving physical appearance.

The longevity of the stock market is dependent on the continued desire and need of persons with surplus money to improve their financial status. LaBelle Industries, producer of Nopeinne, is a bonafide, newly organized and registered Michigan business with great potential by its very nature.

Industry Participants

LaBelle and Nopeinne are reaching out to special persons, seriously interested in a high-yielding financial investment. Opportunity is frequently unrecognized by persons preoccupied with other unrelated initiatives of lessor importance. Success, in many instances, is dependent on the willingness of one to take calculated risks of investing in reasonably assured fields of endeavor.

Physical Distribution

Once a sale is made, the product is shipped to the distribution point—our facility. We will be looking at setting up a drop-shipment so goods travel directly from the manufacturer to the customer. Our whole physical distribution process will be fueled by sales.

The following activities will be coordinated in order to physically move our product:

1. Communication between order processing and physical distribution.
2. Warehousing of finished product for distribution.
3. Selection of transportation method to move the finished goods from warehouse.
4. Handling the finished product at the distribution point.

We will also provide necessary delivery service to customers in a timely manner and keep costs under control.

Competition and Buying Patterns

Currently Celebrex and Vioxx cost more than $2 a pill, suggesting that the cost of a new pharmaceutical product is not an issue to persons seeking relief from pain. This inspired an impassioned Michigan vegetarian to create Nopeinne to relieve pain and suffering. Thus now poised to take its place in the marketplace is a new people-pleasing formula for relief.

Main Competitors

Our main skin cream competitors are: Tigerbalm, Flexall, Bengay, Heat, and Asper Cream.

Their shortcoming is that they contain more chemicals than the natural herbs and ingredients of Nopeinne.

Our main wholesale competitors will be power retailers who merge the specialty store concept with the discount store's emphasis on price. These retail warehouses are large stores with products displayed on metal racks in a warehouse setting. There are two distinct types of retail warehouses, the first being a membership and the second a consumer store which is open to the general public.

Their shortcoming, as with other competitors, is service; buyers must travel to them to pick up their goods. Some of the power retailers have just begun to offer delivery services, which is helping retailers to appreciate the value of using a distributor like LaBelle.

STRATEGY & IMPLEMENTATION SUMMARY

We address the market through one business segment: specialty skincare formulas. We are a niche player who has developed strong alliances with retailers who have powerful channel relationships.

Our marketing strategy assumes that we will serve our distributor by being a trade supplier, where we develop and sell our own lines of products based on industry and customer needs.

Our main strategy at LaBelle is to position ourselves at the top of the quality scale, featuring our combination of superb technology and rich, healthy herbs for the buyer who wants the best quality and best price. Tactics underneath that strategy include research and development related to new formulas and new products, choosing the right channels of distribution, and communicating our quality position to the market. Products are mainly those listed under the product description heading. We will continually develop new packaging, channel development, channel marketing programs, our direct sales, and our continued presence in high-end catalog channels and new presence on the web.

LaBelle gives the skincare cream user, who cares about their skin features, a combination of the highest quality all-natural creams and the latest formulations at a relatively good price.	**Value Proposition**

Our competitive edge is in the formulations and distributing processes we have developed for the production of the one product in which we specialize. As detailed above, we are in an excellent position to capture a significant part of the $123 billion-dollar skin cream market. We simply need to establish a marketing program and begin to promote our products.	**Competitive Edge**

Marketing Strategy

Our marketing strategy is to create effective advertisements made simple and which are easily understood, customer-oriented, truthful, informative, sincere, and will explain the who, what, when, where, why, and how of our business. Our advertising plan will instill a desire in people to consider our products and the value of our customer service and an inclination to do business with our company because of the positive messages they receive. Our good advertising will cause action and persuade the prospective customer to go with LaBelle instead of the competition.

We will use advertising to educate consumers who are buying from us. We expect our advertising, especially personal selling, has a cumulative effect. We are expecting the initial response to be slow, but to increase over time. We plan to advertise regularly and continuously on a small scale and then place large advertisements infrequently. By the same token, visiting and calling customers frequently helps to solidify relationships.

Word of mouth is essential to the growth of any business. We know the traditional forms of advertising play only a supporting role, and we will thrive or suffer from our reputation in the marketplace. We believe each satisfied customer has the potential to steer dozens of new ones to us, and each dissatisfied customer is equally capable of wreaking havoc on our business by planting doubt in the minds of existing customers and scaring off potential business.

For individuals who have suffered from facial scars, bumps, acne, or arthritis pain, LaBelle offers exquisite skin cream solutions. Unlike most skin cream manufacturers who use chemicals, LaBelle's all-natural products make no development compromises for standardization.	**Positioning Statements**

We will maintain our pricing positions as a premier provider. We are the best product available from the most discriminating consumer. We intend to maintain our separation from the price competition at the lower end of the business. Our plan calls for no significant changes in pricing. Price increases will be due mostly to the fluctuation of our ingredient prices.	**Pricing Strategy**

Our promotion strategy is to first listen and observe our customers so we know what they consider paramount. We will then tell them how our products and services will supply solutions. We have kept in mind that retail businesses don't buy products and services; they buy the benefits that are derived from them, such as profit and support. As we continue to	**Promotion Strategy**

develop our planned strategy, we will clearly express and promote the features and functions of our products and services that satisfy the prospect's demands.

Our primary contact is the company's national or regional sales manager, or whoever is in charge of making inventory decisions. In entrepreneurial businesses like LaBelle, the owner is usually the sole decisionmaker.

We will also promote our products through seminars and home showings.

Distribution Strategy

Our distribution strategy is guided by security and control. LaBelle will personally deliver the products we buy and sell. We will deliver for security, to ensure the product's safe and timely delivery, and control, to be responsible for as much of the product's movement from the supplier to end user as possible, in order to provide a more comprehensive service and thereby increase revenues. Frankly, we don't want our customers knowing the identity of our manufacturer supplying our product.

Our distribution strategy is also guided by volume. The more the retailer buys, the lower our price. Our first opportunity to increase our margin by increasing our volume arises when we purchase our inventory from our manufacturer. If we can purchase inventory for ten retailers at a time instead of two, we will be devoting less of our money to our cost of goods sold and more to our business bank account. Buying in volume will also improve our relationship with our suppliers, it makes us a more valuable element of our customer base. The more we purchase, the more cost-saving opportunities will be offered to us.

Marketing Programs

Some of our marketing programs will include but will not be limited to:

- Free samples
- Coupons
- Referral Discounts
- Mailers

Sales Strategy

LaBelle's sales strategy includes using the following selling techniques:

1. Telephone Sales
2. Person-to-Person Sales

Our sales strategy is outlined below in three phases.

Phase One is to accommodate our existing customers and to make sure that current orders and subsequent orders are maintained.

Phase Two will commence when our facilities are expanded. We will then be able to develop new products, accept new clients, and contact companies who have shown interest in our products and be able to accommodate their orders. We plan to hire a high-quality salesperson to assist in defining our marketing program.

Phase Three will begin with the hiring of two additional sales representatives who will develop our consumer program wherein we will begin to sell our product directly to an individual via the web.

Savings will be our first transaction between the manufacturer and LaBelle. This is the arena in which price and profit do battle. Our ideal series of events is for LaBelle to pay as little as possible for the merchandise, control its distribution from the manufacturer to the customer/ end user, and incur as few costs as possible in the process.

We will accept credit card, cash, and check sales. Later as we build cash-flow we will consider credit terms with 30-day invoices.

Sales Forecast

Our sales forecast is based on the selling of 5,000 units of the skin cream product. Four thousand units will be sold to retailers at an introductory wholesale price of $7.50 per unit, and 1,000 units will be sold directly to the consumers at $15 per unit. We expect our inventory to turn 4 times a year or every three months, forecasting revenue from sales to average approximately $45,000 per quarter. It costs $5.00 per unit to manufacture this product.

We are expecting to increase sales from $180,000 to $225,000 in the next year, which is slightly more than 24 percent growth. Growth forecast is relatively high for our industry because we are developing new patent formulas. In 2003 and 2004 we expect growth to increase 10 percent per year, to a projected total of $252,000 in 2004. We will spend approximately 30 percent of our original inventory investment to maintain or purchase additional inventory.

We are not projecting significant change in the products, or in the proportion between different products. Our seasonality, as shown in the chart, is still a factor in the business. Overall, sales tend to be steady.

Sales Forecast

Sales	FY2002	FY2003	FY2004
Sales	$180,000	$225,000	$252,000
Other	$0	$0	$0
Total Sales	**$180,000**	**$225,000**	**$252,000**
Direct Cost of Sales			
Sales	$22,500	$36,000	$39,600
Other	$0	$0	$0
Subtotal Cost of Sales	**$22,500**	**$36,000**	**$39,600**

Sales Programs

Specific sales programs:

- Distributor sales
- Web sales
- Retail sales
- Direct sales
- Telephone sales

Strategic Alliances

We depend on our alliance with Reuben Retro to generate continuous leads for our add-on products. We are also developing relationships with other manufacturers to further cut cost and continue sales growth.

MANAGEMENT SUMMARY

As the owner and manager of the business, Roman Miller will have complete control over every aspect of its structure and activity. He will handle daily operations himself. These operations include purchasing and order processing, controlling inventory, setting delivery schedules, defining return policies, and devising pricing methods.

We have a strong manager that can boast of years of experience in skin cream development. Roman has spent four years working and researching the skin cream industry. He has a proven background of expertise and is more than capable of transforming LaBelle into a leading specialty skin cream distributor.

Organizational Structure

Roman Miller, owner, is responsible for overall business management. We will utilize outside support resources as needed.

Management Team

We are currently developing the management team and more skin cream formulations to become a major player in the specialized niche we serve.

Management Team Gaps

We depend on our consultants that include our CPA and our attorney for some key management help. As we grow, we will develop more formulas and more mass production of those new products.

Personnel

Our present plan is to have one manager, Roman Miller. His job is to keep the office running efficiently, everything from scheduling future employees to monitoring deliveries and shipments to hiring and record keeping. He will not receive an owner's draw for the start-up phase of the business.

We are also looking to hire a Distribution Sales Representative (DSR) who will be a capable marketing professional with a background in skincare sales. Our DSR's duties include visiting prospects, discussing ideas for the prospects' purchases, taking notes regarding special product or service requests, providing customers with pricing information and estimates, and arranging for the signing of a contract, if necessary. We would like to bring that person on board late 2002.

Future personnel include one administrative support personnel, a bookkeeper. This bookkeeper will pay bills for inventory, equipment and supplies, as well as handle payroll and general bookkeeping. We will look for someone with basic computer and bookkeeping skills. Until we can hire a bookkeeper, we will utilize a good accounting software package.

We will not be offering any employee benefits for at least two years.

FINANCIAL PLAN

The financial picture is quite encouraging. We will be slow to take on debt over the next three years, but with our increase in sales we do expect to apply for a credit line with the bank in 2005 for expansion on our products and facilities.

Important Assumptions

The assumptions that support our projections are:

The move to larger facilities at some point and the purchase of additional equipment will result in increased production. We have excellent agreements with our primary sources of supply and assume there will be no change in these relationships. We also assume that the demand for Nopeinne and our other products will continue to increase as evidenced in our market research.

On the flip side, another company could develop some of the formulas we have, in which case we would lose some of the technical and market advantage we now have. This will also decrease our valuation. If we cannot find a capable marketing person, who is both sales and technically savvy, in time to get into this market, we would be at a disadvantage. Technology changes, as do buying habits and social structure. But a degree of risk is synonymous to everything one does, so taking a chance is essential for success and perhaps survival. Even with a stagnated economy, we believe there will be little, if any, impact on individual desire to feel good and be free from physical pain and suffering, caused by neglect and/or deficient health care, thus continuing to purchase our products.

General Assumptions	FY2002	FY2003	FY2004
Short-term Interest Rate %	10.00%	10.00%	10.00%
Long-term Interest Rate %	10.00%	10.00%	10.00%
Payment Days Estimator	30	30	30
Collection Days Estimator	45	45	45
Inventory Turnover Estimator	4.00	4.00	4.00
Tax Rate %	25.00%	25.00%	25.00%
Expenses in Cash %	10.00%	10.00%	10.00%
Sales on Credit %	0.00%	0.00%	0.00%
Personnel Burden %	15.00%	15.00%	15.00%

Risks

Developing a strong base of retailers and distributors, paying close attention to customer suggestions and requests, finding a small niche and sticking to what we know best, and coping with a changing economy are all proven ways to keep a wholesale distribution business successful and out of bankruptcy.

As in any business there are risks. Our goal is to recognize crucial warning signs and head off disasters by continually asking ourselves these questions:

1. Are we carrying too many different kinds of products or stocking too much merchandise?
2. Are we blinded by "pride of parenthood," failing to cut back on money-losing operations?
3. Have we carefully analyzed demand for our products, monitored the marketplace, and adjusted quickly to changing conditions?
4. Are some employees making little or no contribution to our bottom line?
5. Are our profits declining despite increased sales, or is our inventory growing due to sliding sales figures?
6. Have we prepared an accurate and realistic cash-flow projection?
7. Are we maintaining unneeded warehouse or office space?
8. Have we diversified away from our main strengths or overexpanded during good times, only to find ourself less liquid than we would like to be?
9. Are we taking stopgap measures like injecting additional cash to meet accounts payable, payroll, and other expenses, rather than facing the real problems and taking the neccessary corrective steps?

Recognizing problems is a step in the right direction. The next step is to take action once we've diagnosed the problem so we can get our wholesale distribution business back on track. When deciding on our course of action, we will create and update an accurate and realistic cash-flow projection that takes into account changing economic realities, look at our operations on an overall basis instead of attacking cost-cutting piecemeal, and analyze both the short- and long-term effects of each cost-cutting activity.

We can avoid or overcome bankruptcy and failure by maintaining assiduous financial and operation control of our wholesale-distribution business, especially during the turbulent start-up period, and we'll set ourselves on a path toward greater productivity and profitability. As we gain experience in the realms of wholesaling, merchandising, distributions and sales, and earn a reputation for providing top-quality customer service, good prices, and good products, we will develop specialized business skills which represent a comparative advantage over competitors in our area and beyond. Diligence and perseverance are as essential for success for a wholesaler or distributor as they are for any other line of work, and sound financial position is the necessary cornerstone for anyone interested in building a winning venture. That doesn't mean we will need millions of dollars; it means we must effectively manage the money we have, whatever the amount.

Break-even Analysis

The break-even analysis shows that LaBelle has a good balance of fixed costs and sufficient sales strength to remain healthy. Our goal is to sell at least 341 products per month or generate at lease $3,406 a month in sales.

Break-even Analysis:

Monthly Units Break-even	341
Monthly Sales Break-even	$3,406

Assumptions:

Average Per-Unit Revenue	$10.00
Average Per-Unit Variable Cost	$5.00
Estimated Monthly Fixed Cost	$1,703

Projected Profit and Loss

This table shows we project a net profit of $108,552 by the end of 2002 and a gross margin of $212,400 by 2004. We hope to gain enough skills by 2004 to release our support consultant completely. The table also includes part of a repayment schedule of our $30,542 loan at 11 percent over a period of 7 years at approximately $523 per month including interest.

Profit and Loss (Income Statement)	FY2002	FY2003	FY2004
Sales	$180,000	$225,000	$252,000
Direct Cost of Sales	$22,500	$36,000	$39,600
Production Payroll	$0	$0	$0
Other	$0	$0	$0
Total Cost of Sales	**$22,500**	**$36,000**	**$39,600**
Gross Margin	$157,500	$189,000	$212,400
Gross Margin %	87.50%	84.00%	84.29%
Operating Expenses			
Sales and Marketing Expenses			
Sales and Marketing Payroll	$0	$0	$0
Advertising/Promotion	$2,000	$15,000	$20,000
Travel	$770	$1,155	$1,733
Miscellaneous	$0	$0	$0
Total Sales and Marketing Expenses	**$0**	**$0**	**$0**
Sales and Marketing %	0.00%	0.00%	0.00%
General and Administrative Expenses			
General and Administrative Payroll	$0	$0	$0
Payroll Expense	$0	$0	$0
Payroll Burden	$0	$0	$0
Depreciation	$0	$0	$0
Leased Equipment	$0	$0	$0
Telephone	$660	$726	$799

	FY2002	FY2003	FY2004
Insurance	$450	$600	$600
Rent	$0	$0	$0
Total General and Administrative Expenses	**$0**	**$0**	**$0**
General and Administrative %	0.00%	0.00%	0.00%
Other Expenses			
Other Payroll	$0	$0	$0
Loan Repayment	$5,230	$6,276	$6,276
Contract/Consultants	$600	$300	$0
Total Other Expenses	**$0**	**$0**	**$0**
Other %	0.00%	0.00%	0.00%
Total Operating Expenses	**$9,710**	**$24,057**	**$29,408**
Profit Before Interest and Taxes	$147,790	$164,943	$182,992
Interest Expense Short-term	$3,054	$3,054	$3,054
Interest Expense Long-term	$0	$0	$0
Taxes Incurred	$36,184	$40,472	$44,984
Extraordinary Items	$0	$0	$0
Net Profit	**$108,552**	**$121,417**	**$134,953**
Net Profit/Sales	**60.31%**	**53.96%**	**53.55%**

Projected Cash Flow

We expect to have a projected cash balance of $356,538 by 2004. In February of 2002 we anticipate a slight decrease in cash flow. Therefore we will heighten our telephone and person-to-person sales efforts beginning in December 2001 to strengthen January 2002 and February 2002 sales and cash flow.

Projected Cash Flow	FY2002	FY2003	FY2004
Net Profit	$108,552	$121,417	$134,953
Plus:			
Depreciation	$0	$0	$0
Change in Accounts Payable	$3,528	$5,554	($164)
Current Borrowing (repayment)	$0	$0	$0
Increase (decrease) Other Liabilities	$0	$0	$0
Long-term Borrowing (repayment)	$0	$0	$0
Capital Input	$0	$0	$0
Subtotal	**$112,104**	**$123,897**	**$135,137**
Less:			
Change in Accounts Receivable	$0	$0	$0
Change in Inventory	($2,500)	$13,500	$3,600
Change in Other Short-term Assets	$0	$0	$0
Capital Expenditure	$0	$0	$0
Dividends	$0	$0	$0
Subtotal	**($2,500)**	**$13,500**	**$3,600**
Net Cash Flow	$114,604	$110,397	$131,537
Cash Balance	**$114,604**	**$225,001**	**$356,538**

As shown in the balance sheet in the following table, we expect a projected healthy growth in net worth, from approximately $103,010 from 2002 to more than $359,380 by the end of 2004. The monthly projections are in the appendices.

Projected Balance Sheet

Projected Balance Sheet

Continued

Projected Balance Sheet	FY2002	FY2003	FY2004
Assets			
Short-term Assets			
Cash	$114,604	$225,001	$356,538
Accounts Receivable	$0	$0	$0
Inventory	$22,500	$36,000	$39,600
Other Short-term Assets	$0	$0	$0
Total Short-term Assets	**$137,104**	**$261,001**	**$396,138**
Long-term Assets			
Capital Assets	$0	$0	$0
Accumulated Depreciation	$0	$0	$0
Total Long-term Assets	**$0**	**$0**	**$0**
Total Assets	**$137,104**	**$261,001**	**$396,138**
Liabilities and Capital			
Accounts Payable	$3,528	$9,082	$8,919
Short-term Notes	$30,542	$30,542	$30,542
Other Short-term Liabilities	$0	$0	$0
Subtotal Short-term Liabilities	**$34,070**	**$39,624**	**$39,461**
Long-term Liabilities	$0	$0	$0
Total Liabilities	**$34,070**	**$39,624**	**$39,461**
Paid in Capital	$7,636	$7,636	$7,636
Retained Earnings	($13,178)	$95,374	$216,790
Earnings	$108,552	$121,417	$134,953
Total Capital	**$103,010**	**$224,426**	**$359,380**
Total Liabilities and Capital	**$137,104**	**$261,001**	**$396,138**
Net Worth	**$103,010**	**$224,426**	**$359,380**

This page left intentionally blank to accommodate tabular matter following.

APPENDIX

Sales Forecast

Sales	Oct	Nov	Dec	Jan	Feb	Mar	Apr
Sales	$17,169	$15,203	$27,658	$11,546	$10,044	$13,195	$13,680
Other	$0	$0	$0	$0	$0	$0	$0
Total Sales	**$17,169**	**$15,203**	**$27,658**	**$11,546**	**$10,044**	**$13,195**	**$13,680**
Direct Cost of Sales							
Sales	$0	$0	$0	$7,500	$0	$0	$7,500
Other	$0	$0	$0	$0	$0	$0	$0

General Assumptions

General Assumptions	Oct	Nov	Dec	Jan	Feb	Mar	Apr
Short-term Interest Rate %	10.00%	10.00%	10.00%	10.00%	10.00%	10.00%	10.00%
Long-term Interest Rate %	10.00%	10.00%	10.00%	10.00%	10.00%	10.00%	10.00%
Payment Days Estimator	30	30	30	30	30	30	30
Collection Days Estimator	45	45	45	45	45	45	45
Inventory Turnover Estimator	4.00	4.00	4.00	4.00	4.00	4.00	4.00
Tax Rate %	25.00%	25.00%	25.00%	25.00%	25.00%	25.00%	25.00%
Expenses in Cash %	10.00%	10.00%	10.00%	10.00%	10.00%	10.00%	10.00%
Sales on Credit %	0.00%	0.00%	0.00%	0.00%	0.00%	0.00%	0.00%
Personnel Burden %	15.00%	15.00%	15.00%	15.00%	15.00%	15.00%	15.00%

May	Jun	Jul	Aug	Sep	FY2002	FY2003	FY2004
$17,048	$13,320	$12,822	$14,968	$13,348	$180,000	$225,000	$252,000
$0	$0	$0	$0	$0	$0	$0	$0
$17,048	**$13,320**	**$12,822**	**$14,968**	**$13,348**	**$180,000**	**$225,000**	**$252,000**
$0	$0	$7,500	$0	$0	$22,500	$36,000	$39,600
$0	$0	$0	$0	$0	$0	$0	$0

May	Jun	Jul	Aug	Sep	FY2002	FY2003	FY2004
10.00%	10.00%	10.00%	10.00%	10.00%	10.00%	10.00%	10.00%
10.00%	10.00%	10.00%	10.00%	10.00%	10.00%	10.00%	10.00%
30	30	30	30	30	30	30	30
45	45	45	45	45	45	45	45
4.00	4.00	4.00	4.00	4.00	4.00	4.00	4.00
25.00%	25.00%	25.00%	25.00%	25.00%	25.00%	25.00%	25.00%
10.00%	10.00%	10.00%	10.00%	10.00%	10.00%	10.00%	10.00%
0.00%	0.00%	0.00%	0.00%	0.00%	0.00%	0.00%	0.00%
15.00%	15.00%	15.00%	15.00%	15.00%	15.00%	15.00%	15.00%

Profit and Loss (Income Statement)

	Oct	Nov	Dec	Jan	Feb	Mar	Apr
Sales	$17,169	$15,203	$27,658	$11,546	$10,044	$13,195	$13,680
Direct Cost of Sales	$0	$0	$0	$7,500	$0	$0	$7,500
Production Payroll	$0	$0	$0	$0	$0	$0	$0
Other	$0	$0	$0	$0	$0	$0	$0
Total Cost of Sales	**$0**	**$0**	**$0**	**$7,500**	**$0**	**$0**	**$7,500**
Gross Margin	$17,169	$15,203	$27,658	$4,046	$10,044	$13,195	$6,180
Gross Margin %	100.00%	100.00%	100.00%	35.04%	100.00%	100.00%	45.18%
Operating Expenses							
Sales and Marketing Expenses							
Sales and Marketing Payroll	$0	$0	$0	$0	$0	$0	$0
Advertising/Promotion	$0	$0	$1,000	$0	$0	$0	$0
Travel	$0	$70	$70	$70	$70	$70	$70
Miscellaneous	$0	$0	$0	$0	$0	$0	$0
Total Sales and							
Marketing Expenses	**$0**	**$0**	**$0**	**$0**	**$0**	**$0**	**$0**
Sales and Marketing %	0.00%	0.00%	0.00%	0.00%	0.00%	0.00%	0.00%
General and							
Administrative Expenses							
General and							
Administrative Payroll	$0	$0	$0	$0	$0	$0	$0
Payroll Expense	$0	$0	$0	$0	$0	$0	$0
Payroll Burden	$0	$0	$0	$0	$0	$0	$0
Depreciation	$0	$0	$0	$0	$0	$0	$0
Leased Equipment	$0	$0	$0	$0	$0	$0	$0
Telephone	$0	$60	$60	$60	$60	$60	$60
Insurance	$0	$0	$0	$150	$0	$0	$150
Rent	$0	$0	$0	$0	$0	$0	$0
Total General and							
Administrative Expenses	**$0**	**$0**	**$0**	**$0**	**$0**	**$0**	**$0**
General and Administrative %	0.00%	0.00%	0.00%	0.00%	0.00%	0.00%	0.00%
Other Expenses							
Other Payroll	$0	$0	$0	$0	$0	$0	$0
Loan Repayment	$0	$0	$523	$523	$523	$523	$523
Contract/Consultants	$50	$50	$50	$50	$50	$50	$50
Total Other Expenses	**$0**	**$0**	**$0**	**$0**	**$0**	**$0**	**$0**
Other %	0.00%	0.00%	0.00%	0.00%	0.00%	0.00%	0.00%
Total Operating Expenses	**$50**	**$180**	**$1,703**	**$853**	**$703**	**$703**	**$853**
Profit Before Interest							
and Taxes	$17,119	$15,023	$25,955	$3,193	$9,341	$12,492	$5,327
Interest Expense Short-term	$255	$255	$255	$255	$255	$255	$255
Interest Expense Long-term	$0	$0	$0	$0	$0	$0	$0
Taxes Incurred	$4,216	$3,692	$6,425	$735	$2,272	$3,059	$1,268
Extraordinary Items	$0	$0	$0	$0	$0	$0	$0
Net Profit	**$12,649**	**$11,076**	**$19,275**	**$2,204**	**$6,815**	**$9,178**	**$3,804**
Net Profit/Sales	**73.67%**	**72.86%**	**69.69%**	**19.09%**	**67.85%**	**69.56%**	**27.81%**

	May	Jun	Jul	Aug	Sep	FY2002	FY2003	FY2004
	$17,048	$13,320	$12,822	$14,968	$13,348	$180,000	$225,000	$252,000
	$0	$0	$7,500	$0	$0	$22,500	$36,000	$39,600
	$0	$0	$0	$0	$0	$0	$0	$0
	$0	$0	$0	$0	$0	$0	$0	$0
	$0	**$0**	**$7,500**	**$0**	**$0**	**$22,500**	**$36,000**	**$39,600**
	$17,048	$13,320	$5,322	$14,968	$13,348	$157,500	$189,000	$212,400
	100.00%	100.00%	41.50%	100.00%	100.00%	87.50%	84.00%	84.29%
	$0	$0	$0	$0	$0	$0	$0	$0
	$0	$0	$0	$1,000	$0	$2,000	$15,000	$20,000
	$70	$70	$70	$70	$70	$770	$1,155	$1,733
	$0	$0	$0	$0	$0	$0	$0	$0
	$0	**$0**	**$0**	**$0**	**$0**	**$0**	**$0**	**$0**
	0.00%	0.00%	0.00%	0.00%	0.00%	0.00%	0.00%	0.00%
	$0	$0	$0	$0	$0	$0	$0	$0
	$0	$0	$0	$0	$0	$0	$0	$0
	$0	$0	$0	$0	$0	$0	$0	$0
	$0	$0	$0	$0	$0	$0	$0	$0
	$0	$0	$0	$0	$0	$0	$0	$0
	$60	$60	$60	$60	$60	$660	$726	$799
	$0	$0	$150	$0	$0	$450	$600	$600
	$0	$0	$0	$0	$0	$0	$0	$0
	$0	**$0**	**$0**	**$0**	**$0**	**$0**	**$0**	**$0**
	0.00%	0.00%	0.00%	0.00%	0.00%	0.00%	0.00%	0.00%
	$0	$0	$0	$0	$0	$0	$0	$0
	$523	$523	$523	$523	$523	$5,230	$6,276	$6,276
	$50	$50	$50	$50	$50	$600	$300	$0
	$0	**$0**	**$0**	**$0**	**$0**	**$0**	**$0**	**$0**
	0.00%	0.00%	0.00%	0.00%	0.00%	0.00%	0.00%	0.00%
	$703	**$703**	**$853**	**$1,703**	**$703**	**$9,710**	**$24,057**	**$29,408**
	$16,345	$12,617	$4,469	$13,265	$12,645	$147,790	$164,943	$182,992
	$255	$255	$255	$255	$255	$3,054	$3,054	$3,054
	$0	$0	$0	$0	$0	$0	$0	$0
	$4,023	$3,091	$1,054	$3,253	$3,098	$36,184	$40,472	$44,984
	$0	$0	$0	$0	$0	$0	$0	$0
	$12,068	**$9,272**	**$3,161**	**$9,758**	**$9,293**	**$108,552**	**$121,417**	**$134,953**
	70.79%	**69.61%**	**24.65%**	**65.19%**	**69.62%**	**60.31%**	**53.96%**	**53.55%**

Projected Cash Flow

Projected Cash Flow	Oct	Nov	Dec	Jan	Feb	Mar	Apr
Net Profit	$12,649	$11,076	$19,275	$2,204	$6,815	$9,178	$3,804
Plus:							
Depreciation	$0	$0	$0	$0	$0	$0	$0
Change in Accounts Payable	$3,933	($343)	$3,703	($1,340)	($3,143)	$686	$5,097
Current Borrowing (repayment)	$0	$0	$0	$0	$0	$0	$0
Increase (decrease) Other Liabilities	$0	$0	$0	$0	$0	$0	$0
Long-term Borrowing (repayment)	$0	$0	$0	$0	$0	$0	$0
Capital Input	$0	$0	$0	$0	$0	$0	$0
Subtotal	**$16,582**	**$10,734**	**$22,978**	**$864**	**$3,671**	**$9,864**	**$8,901**
Less:							
Change in Accounts Receivable	$0	$0	$0	$0	$0	$0	$0
Change in Inventory	$0	$0	$0	($2,500)	$0	$0	$0
Change in Other Short-term Assets	$0	$0	$0	$0	$0	$0	$0
Capital Expenditure	$0	$0	$0	$0	$0	$0	$0
Dividends	$0	$0	$0	$0	$0	$0	$0
Subtotal	**$0**	**$0**	**$0**	**($2,500)**	**$0**	**$0**	**$0**
Net Cash Flow	**$16,582**	**$10,734**	**$22,978**	**$3,364**	**$3,671**	**$9,864**	**$8,901**
Cash Balance	**$16,582**	**$27,315**	**$50,293**	**$53,657**	**$57,328**	**$67,192**	**$76,093**

May	Jun	Jul	Aug	Sep	FY2002	FY2003	FY2004
$12,068	$9,272	$3,161	$9,758	$9,293	$108,552	$121,417	$134,953
$0	$0	$0	$0	$0	$0	$0	$0
($4,259)	($811)	$4,883	($3,872)	($1,005)	$3,528	$5,554	($164)
$0	$0	$0	$0	$0	$0	$0	$0
$0	$0	$0	$0	$0	$0	$0	$0
$0	$0	$0	$0	$0	$0	$0	$0
$0	$0	$0	$0	$0	$0	$0	$0
$7,809	**$8,461**	**$8,044**	**$5,885**	**$8,288**	**$112,080**	**$126,971**	**$134,790**
$0	$0	$0	$0	$0	$0	$0	$0
$0	$0	$0	$0	$0	($2,500)	$13,500	$3,600
$0	$0	$0	$0	$0	$0	$0	$0
$0	$0	$0	$0	$0	$0	$0	$0
$0	$0	$0	$0	$0	$0	$0	$0
$0	**$0**	**$0**	**$0**	**$0**	**($2,500)**	**$13,500**	**$3,600**
$7,809	**$8,461**	**$8,044**	**$5,885**	**$8,288**	**$114,580**	**$113,471**	**$131,190**
$83,902	**$92,363**	**$100,407**	**$106,292**	**$114,580**	**$114,580**	**$228,051**	**$359,240**

Projected Balance Sheet

Assets

Short-term Assets	Oct	Nov	Dec	Jan	Feb	Mar	Apr
Cash	$16,582	$27,315	$50,293	$53,657	$57,328	$67,192	$76,093
Accounts Receivable	$0	$0	$0	$0	$0	$0	$0
Inventory	$25,000	$25,000	$25,000	$22,500	$22,500	$22,500	$22,500
Other Short-term Assets	$0	$0	$0	$0	$0	$0	$0
Total Short-term Assets	**$41,582**	**$52,315**	**$75,293**	**$76,157**	**$79,828**	**$89,692**	**$98,593**

Long-term Assets

	Oct	Nov	Dec	Jan	Feb	Mar	Apr
Capital Assets	$0	$0	$0	$0	$0	$0	$0
Accumulated Depreciation	$0	$0	$0	$0	$0	$0	$0
Total Long-term Assets	**$0**	**$0**	**$0**	**$0**	**$0**	**$0**	**$0**
Total Assets	**$41,582**	**$52,315**	**$75,293**	**$76,157**	**$79,828**	**$89,692**	**$98,593**

Liabilities and Capital

	Oct	Nov	Dec	Jan	Feb	Mar	Apr
Accounts Payable	$3,933	$3,590	$7,293	$5,953	$2,809	$3,495	$8,592
Short-term Notes	$30,542	$30,542	$30,542	$30,542	$30,542	$30,542	$30,542
Other Short-term Liabilities	$0	$0	$0	$0	$0	$0	$0
Subtotal Short-term Liabilities	**$34,475**	**$34,132**	**$37,835**	**$36,495**	**$33,351**	**$34,037**	**$39,134**
Long-term Liabilities	$0	$0	$0	$0	$0	$0	$0
Total Liabilities	**$34,475**	**$34,132**	**$37,835**	**$36,495**	**$33,351**	**$34,037**	**$39,134**
Paid in Capital	$7,636	$7,636	$7,636	$7,636	$7,636	$7,636	$7,636
Retained Earnings	($13,178)	($13,178)	($13,178)	($13,178)	($13,178)	($13,178)	($13,178)
Earnings	$12,649	$23,725	$43,000	$45,204	$52,019	$61,197	$65,001
Total Capital	**$7,107**	**$18,183**	**$37,458**	**$39,662**	**$46,477**	**$55,655**	**$59,459**
Total Liabilities and Capital	**$41,582**	**$52,315**	**$75,293**	**$76,157**	**$79,828**	**$89,692**	**$98,593**
Net Worth	**$7,107**	**$18,183**	**$37,458**	**$39,662**	**$46,477**	**$55,655**	**$59,459**

May	Jun	Jul	Aug	Sep	FY2002	FY2003	FY2004
$83,902	$92,363	$100,407	$106,292	$114,580	$114,580	$228,051	$359,240
$0	$0	$0	$0	$0	$0	$0	$0
$22,500	$22,500	$22,500	$22,500	$22,500	$22,500	$36,000	$39,600
$0	$0	$0	$0	$0	$0	$0	$0
$106,402	**$114,863**	**$122,907**	**$128,792**	**$137,080**	**$137,080**	**$264,051**	**$398,840**
$0	$0	$0	$0	$0	$0	$0	$0
$0	$0	$0	$0	$0	$0	$0	$0
$0	**$0**	**$0**	**$0**	**$0**	**$0**	**$0**	**$0**
$106,402	$114,863	$122,907	$128,792	$137,080	$137,080	$264,051	$398,840
$4,333	$3,522	$8,405	$4,533	$3,528	$3,528	$9,082	$8,919
$30,542	$30,542	$30,542	$30,542	$30,542	$30,542	$30,542	$30,542
$0	$0	$0	$0	$0	$0	$0	$0
$34,875	**$34,064**	**$38,947**	**$35,075**	**$34,070**	**$34,070**	**$39,624**	**$39,461**
$0	$0	$0	$0	$0	$0	$0	$0
$34,875	**$34,064**	**$38,947**	**$35,075**	**$34,070**	**$34,070**	**$39,624**	**$39,461**
$7,636	$7,636	$7,636	$7,636	$7,636	$7,636	$7,636	$7,636
($13,178)	($13,178)	($13,178)	($13,178)	($13,178)	($13,178)	$95,374	$216,790
$77,069	$86,341	$89,502	$99,259	$108,552	$108,552	$121,417	$134,953
$71,527	**$80,799**	**$83,960**	**$93,717**	**$103,010**	**$103,010**	**$224,426**	**$359,380**
$106,402	**$114,863**	**$122,907**	**$128,792**	**$137,080**	**$137,080**	**$264,051**	**$398,840**
$71,527	**$80,799**	**$83,960**	**$93,717**	**$103,010**	**$103,010**	**$224,426**	**$359,380**

Video Production & Distribution Company

BUSINESS PLAN

KITAMON PRODUCTIONS

3550 Alta Vista Drive
San Diego, California 92101

Kitamon is a "next generation" video production and distribution company. Its programming allows viewers to live vicariously through the everyday experiences of their favorite movie, music, sports and fashion celebrities at their most compellingly human moments.

- THE COMPANY

- THE OPPORTUNITY

- TARGET MARKET

- MARKETING

- FINANCIAL SUMMARY

- MANAGEMENT

VIDEO PRODUCTION & DISTRIBUTION COMPANY
BUSINESS PLAN

THE COMPANY

Kitamon is a "next generation" video production and distribution company that meets the exploding demand among increasingly competitive traditional and "new" media channels seeking uniquely compelling, hard-to-access celebrity-focused content. By using both new (Internet, wireless) and traditional (television, radio) media, Kitamon is changing the way celebrities communicate with their fans. Providing access without intrusion, Kitamon's programming allows viewers to live vicariously through the everyday experiences of their favorite movie, music, sports and fashion icons at their most compellingly human moments: in their world with their friends, doing whatever they want to do.

Kitamon has emerged and aggressively consolidated its position as a leading entertainment-based, content producer, distributor, and syndicator, utilizing its access to the most highly prized sources of compelling content as well as its extensive experience with traditional and emergent media. Kitamon's syndication arrangements with a number of major Internet portals, entertainment companies, and online magazines and others will result in ongoing licensing, sponsorship, advertising, and subscription-based revenue and will assure a worldwide audience of millions for Kitamon productions.

A secondary source of revenue will be derived from Kitamon's third-party production. Kitamon's sophisticated production capacity will be provided as a service to entities requiring digital video production, including video content for other websites as well as standard broadcast media outlets.

THE OPPORTUNITY

While there are a few leaders in content syndication for both new and traditional media, Kitamon is the only syndicator based within the entertainment/celebrity genre. Kitamon is more lean, flexible, and focused than traditional entertainment enterprises and better positioned than new media companies without experience in the industry. Upon receipt of funding, the strength of Kitamon's portal, content, and production offerings will present barriers to entry for new and existing competitors:

1. **First to Market:** As the first entity of its kind, Kitamon enjoys a significant and difficult-to-overcome headstart for even the best-funded ventures attempting to compete in this space.
2. **Access:** Kitamon's unfettered access to celebrities, based in part on pre-existing relationships with some of the entertainment industry's leading publicists, assures the company of a steady stream of celebrity subjects.
3. **Unique Content:** Kitamon is the only company focused on distributing real-world, behind-the-scenes celebrity-driven video content via the web. Others, such as MTV, generate celebrity content, but does not syndicate it to other websites.

TARGET MARKET

While Kitamon will market its programming and production services through B-to-B (business to business) channels, its appeal is to the interests of Gen I+. Generation I+ is an emergent term used to define today's 13- to 34-year-olds, the combination of Generation X and Generation Y. Generation I+ is a highly desirable target, one which includes the largest generation since the baby boomers. The U.S. Census Bureau cited an approximately 50 percent section of Generation I—the 15- to 24-year-olds—as having disposable income of over $300 billion in 1998. A respected research analyst has estimated the 16- to 24-year-old subsection of Generation I to make online purchases of approximately $4.5 billion in 2000.

Kitamon will leverage relationships with its distribution partners to generate "brand" recognition. The Kitamon logo will prominently appear on all partner sites; the logo will also discreetly appear on all Kitamon productions the company either syndicates or broadcasts. The logo will be accompanied by the tagline, "Want to see more? Go to www.Kitamon.tv..." Kitamon's distribution partners all have sites that attract high volume, targeted traffic, which will provide the company with immediate and ongoing exposure. Additionally, Kitamon's partners have all agreed to make their newsletter and registration lists available to the company for special direct mailings and offers, providing yet another channel for relationship and brand building.

MARKETING

Kitamon is currently seeking $1.5 million to fund its marketing initiatives, expand its production capabilities, and sustain general operations. The company expects to be profitable from year one and projects a profit of $27.4 by year three.

FINANCIAL SUMMARY

The company was formed in June 1999 by founders bringing a wealth of complementary experiences, skills, and relationships in the fields of entertainment, business, production, syndication, and high-end web design. Kitamon's President and CEO was formerly with NBC and KPMG and is a founding member of one of the world's most exclusive nightclubs. Kitamon's Director brings over 10 years of marketing, advertising, and public relations experience, having founded several prominent and highly successful entertainment-related businesses.

MANAGEMENT

Wireless Systems Integrator

BUSINESS PLAN   SPONGESHARK, LLC.

7100 Montcalm Avenue
Boulder, Colorado 80301

SpongeShark uses the new wireless Bluetooth tech-
nology to provide a superior self check-in solution
to airlines. The SpongeShark solution will elimi-
nate lines so that airline customer service person-
nel will be freed up to handle real problems for the
customer, rather than just checking in passengers.

- EXECUTIVE SUMMARY

- COMPANY OVERVIEW

- PRODUCT & SERVICE

- INDUSTRY & MARKETPLACE ANALYSIS

- MARKETING PLAN

- OPERATIONS PLAN

- DEVELOPMENT PLAN

- MANAGEMENT

- FINANCIAL PLAN

- OFFERING

- APPENDIX

EXECUTIVE SUMMARY

Opportunity

SpongeShark is a systems integrator that provides wireless solutions for the airline industry. Airports are nearing capacity and air travel is expected to increase by 60 percent by 2010. In order to keep their most profitable frequent-flyer customers, airlines must develop new services to handle this traffic increase. Self check-in will be among the most important services airlines will offer their customers. SpongeShark's team, with its combination of airline industry contacts and technical and business expertise, is poised to provide these services to airlines.

Solution

"The passenger agent's role will be completely transformed from one of doing check-ins and transactions to one of solving problems for our customers."

—Senior Director of Customer Service and Development, Air Canada

SpongeShark uses the new wireless Bluetooth technology to provide a superior self check-in solution to airlines. Our solution will include:

- Self check-in (with FAA approved security features)
- Access to flight information/status
- Access to first class upgrades and other offers
- Entertainment and other web-based information

The SpongeShark solution will eliminate lines so that airline customer service personnel will be freed up to handle real problems for the customer, not the mundane task of checking in passengers. Airlines are currently testing self check-in technologies, such as kiosks, but these do not have the capabilities of SpongeShark's Bluetooth-enabled solution.

Bluetooth is a short range, high bandwidth wireless technology that Nokia, Motorola, Ericsson, and personal digital assistant (PDA) manufacturers will be integrating into their devices beginning in 2001. Bluetooth's diffusion rate is expected to be high, reaching 600 million handheld devices by 2004. Due to the exploding growth of the number of Bluetooth-enabled devices, airline passengers will be ready for and expecting the type of service that SpongeShark delivers. Customers will be able to use their own mobile phone or PDA, such as the Palm Pilot, to communicate with the airline information systems via the SpongeShark solution.

Financial Summary

We expect revenues of $60 million and net income of $10 million by 2005. Our software licenses and hardware support generate 30 percent of this revenue on a recurring basis. We are seeking an initial equity investment of $2.5 million to launch the business. This investment will have an ROI of 20 times at our exit event in 2005.

	2001	2002	2003	2004	2005
Airline Customers (cumulative)	1	3	7	12	18
Net Revenues	**261,667**	**4,390,000**	**17,580,000**	**46,600,000**	**59,520,000**
Net Earnings	**-2,085,411**	**-730,382**	**2,282,970**	**7,870,612**	**10,052,394**

SpongeShark was created to provide wireless solutions for the airline industry. We are leveraging the new Bluetooth technology to enhance the customer service for users of Bluetooth-enabled handheld devices. The company was formed as an LLC in Colorado in 2000.

COMPANY OVERVIEW

SpongeShark delivers wireless solutions to the travel industry, enabling our customers to create and deliver innovative marketing programs to their best customers.

Mission Statement

SpongeShark is recruiting engineers and an international business development and sales team. We are beginning negotiations with several major international airlines that have expressed interest in our solution. The SpongeShark team has strong connections throughout the airline industry, and we will leverage these contacts to help refine our solution and provide a foundation for future sales. We are also in discussions with both hardware and software vendors that are developing their Bluetooth products.

Current Status

The SpongeShark solution uses Bluetooth technology to allow airlines to interact with their passengers in a way never before possible. Bluetooth will enable next-generation wireless devices (including cellular phones, personal digital assistants or PDAs and laptops) to communicate (both data and voice) with other Bluetooth-enabled devices within a range of 30-330 feet (approximately 10-100 meters). Bluetooth technology will be part of more than 100 million devices in the U.S. and almost 572 million devices worldwide by 2004, according to predictions of IDC and Dataquest. Bluetooth technology is currently at 721 kbps transfer rate, faster than wireless web, with a second version due with 10 Mbps transfer rate. This Ethernet-quality speed enables high-resolution graphics, audio, and video.

Bluetooth

SpongeShark aims to contract with major international airlines and become their systems integrator for wireless check-in and other enhanced services. Airlines are racing to implement self check-in services, however, none of the current solutions have the advantage of SpongeShark's proximity-based Bluetooth-enabled solution. Only SpongeShark's solution will use the devices that travelers already own, and allow for the airlines to use proximity-based marketing tools. Self check-in solutions are just beginning to come to market, and we intend to seize this window of opportunity and be the first company to offer a Bluetooth solution.

Objectives

Our future vision is to expand our services to other areas of the travel ribbon. As travelers begin to expect Bluetooth wireless services at airports, they will also expect similar services at hotels, resorts, and other modes of transportation. By expanding further into the travel ribbon, SpongeShark will be able to continue its rapid growth beyond the first five years of operation. SpongeShark will be able to leverage the expertise it has gained from our airline integration and offer solutions to these new markets.

SpongeShark will be responsible for installing and maintaining the hardware an airline will need in order to become "Bluetooth-enabled." In addition, SpongeShark will include proprietary software to enable airline content to be displayed on the airline passenger's mobile devices. SpongeShark will be able to provide these services by placing proximity-based Bluetooth servers in key areas of the airport, such as check-in areas, gates owned by the airline, and public areas designated by the airline. A typical airport setup will contain one main SpongeShark server along with several wireless access points in public areas.

PRODUCT & SERVICE

SpongeShark will develop the software to interact with the handheld devices, handle the software integration with the airline databases, arrange the placement of the wireless access points in the airport, enable Internet access to the access points, and perform maintenance and repairs.

SpongeShark will deliver a complete wireless solution, including user interface and database software, integration with legacy systems, network engineering, installation, maintenance, and help desk support.

Airline Passenger's Experience

"The check-in, once again, took forever; even though [the] check-in desks were fully staffed, only one passenger seemed to get through the line every 15 minutes."

—E-pinions.com User

SpongeShark will offer amazing convenience and entertainment to the airline's passengers through their own mobile devices. Mobile devices have seen great improvements to the screen size and clarity in the last few years, and due to the expected convergence of mobile phones with PDAs, the technology will only continue to get better.

Airline passenger's will be able to:

- **Check-in:** At either check-in areas or the gate, customers can register their arrival for a specific flight.
- **Check flight info/status:** The user can check the intended flight's departure time.
- **Check seat arrangements:** Using a graphical layout appropriate for the specific aircraft, a user can check and change if needed his/her seat arrangement.
- **Be alerted to cancellations/delays:** An audible sound and splash screen can alert users to changes in their flight status.
- **Be alerted to time of boarding:** Not only can the users mobile device alert to the correct time of boarding according to the user's status and seat arrangement, the device may also work as a boarding pass.
- **Receive promotions and offers from the airline.**
- **Listen to streaming audio (news, music):** As Bluetooth uses radio frequency, the technology is apt for streaming audio broadcasts.
- **View news, city information, city maps, airport maps:** Users will want assistance finding a connecting gate or determining where the rental agencies are located within the airport. Additionally, users will wish to have city specific information for their arriving city.
- **Watch streaming video:** With 721 kbps, Bluetooth can allow for streaming video.
- **Play networked games:** Users will have the ability to play games either against a computer opponent or against other passengers.
- **Use instant chat:** Passengers can instant message with other passengers, or airline personnel can instant message a passenger if necessary.
- **Access the Internet:** Users will also be able to check e-mail and browse web pages at a faster rate than WAP allows, and free of charge. (Some mobile providers charge air time for WAP use.)

SpongeShark gives airlines a unique competitive edge and therefore increased loyalty by providing these services to passengers.

Industry Analysis

SpongeShark falls within two industries: wireless communications and computer related services.

Wireless Communications: SpongeShark is part of the wireless communications industry (NAICS 51332). This is a very broad industry which includes wireless handset manufacturers to wireless service providers. The wireless communications industry grew 20.8 percent in 1999. By 2002, mobile devices will make up one half of all devices accessing the Internet worldwide. Currently, telecom companies such as Nokia and Ericsson are developing the next generation of mobile devices that will have greater functionality due to increased local processing power and larger, color displays. This will allow for the fusion of the cell phone, PDA, and electronic wallet into a single device.

Computer Related Services: SpongeShark can also be classified as a company which provides "computer related services" (SIC 7379) because we are involved with integrating a Bluetooth communications system with an airline's website or ticketing database.

Marketplace Analysis

SpongeShark will provide wireless technology to the airline industry. Our entry market will be major European airlines and major U.S. airlines that operate in Europe.

Air travelers in European and North American airports will be the first end-users of the SpongeShark service. More than two billion passengers pass through the world's airports each year. This number is projected to increase by 60 percent by 2010. Business travelers are likely to be the first to use the SpongeShark service, since they will be the early adopters of Bluetooth enabled phones.

Customer Analysis

"Airlines are in a race to provide technology-based check-in."

—CIO, ATA

Airlines are in a highly competitive market, and they are always looking for innovative services that will give them an edge over their competitors. The competition is particularly intense for business travelers, who are the most lucrative segment of air travelers. There is an opportunity to improve the experience for business travelers through wireless technology because so many business travelers use wireless handheld devices.

Routine Transactions: Airlines we have spoken with recognize that improvement in customers' air travel experiences can be a competitive advantage. Time spent waiting in line is one of the biggest obstacles that travelers experience. Since SpongeShark allows passengers to complete routine transactions with their mobile devices, there will be fewer people waiting in line for simple transactions with the agent. The shorter line benefits all of the passengers, not just those with a Bluetooth-enabled devices. One major U.S. carrier said that their goal is to automate all of the transactions that would make people wait in line: check-in, rebooking, upgrades, and frequent flyer account transactions.

Entertainment: SpongeShark also offers high-speed Internet access and entertainment to passengers while they wait in the gate area. Airlines can offer this benefit exclusively to customers in its frequent-flyer program, or to those who have membership in their executive service. Once mobile devices have adequate displays, airlines could show previews to all passengers of the pay-per-view entertainment options that will be on the flight. In-flight entertainment is becoming an important new revenue source for airlines.

SpongeShark offers airlines a great opportunity to integrate wireless service with their customer relationship management (CRM) software. The m-Commerce Manager of a major U.S. airline told us that he expects wireless to transform customer relationship management. For example, a business traveler could receive an automatic notification of an upgrade after his flight had been cancelled during his previous trip. Integration with the airline's CRM system will give the airline more touch points with its best customers thereby creating more upselling and crosselling opportunities.

Airlines are using technology as a competitive weapon, and they are in a rush to implement new technology before it has been widely adopted. Icelandair implemented WAP services a year and a half before WAP-enabled phones were available on the market. Similarly, airlines will be in a race to implement Bluetooth services.

As an open standard with many applications, it is widely expected that almost all wireless devices being manufactured by mid to late 2004 will be Bluetooth-enabled. See the chart below for worldwide Bluetooth adoption estimates. Europe is destined to see the earliest growth, considering their dependency on mobile phones currently.

	2000	2001	2002	2003	2004
Mobile handsets with Bluetooth (millions of units)	1.2	28.8	123.7	318	572
Percent of total handsets with Bluetooth	0.30%	5.30%	18.50%	40.80%	65.40%
Growth rates		2329%	330%	157%	80%

(Source: Dataquest, Inc., April 2000)

We also know that airlines readily copy each other's successful technological initiatives. The CIO of ATA told us that airlines have a herd mentality. If one airline announces a new service, others will be sure to follow. SpongeShark needs to be successfully implemented with one key airline, and then our service will be attractive to many other airlines.

"If you wait another two years to start planning your wireless strategy and initiatives, you may have lost your opportunity."

—e-Commerce Specialist, Delta Airlines

Competitor Analysis

There are several alternative check-in technologies that are being tested and implemented in the airline industry.

Barcode Readers. Customers print out barcoded airline tickets when they purchase online using their home PC. In tests the technology didn't work very well and it caused longer lines than the standard system where a flight attendant takes boarding passes.

Handheld Wireless Computers. Northwest Airlines now has handheld computers and printers for its gate agents to take into a long line to check passengers in and print out their boarding passes. Unlike SpongeShark, this does not allow for self-service. Even if these handheld computers reduce waiting time, agents will still be busy dealing with all of the same routine transactions.

Smart Cards. Some airlines are considering embedding frequent flyer cards with a chip or a small antenna which will contain all of the information that they need to check-in for their flight. The cards with the antennas are able to automatically detect a customer's presence and check them in as soon as they walk into the airport. A major U.S. airline rejected this idea because they felt that U.S. travelers would consider the smart card an invasion of their privacy.

In contrast, SpongeShark gives the traveler control of the check-in process: they know when the transaction is complete because the boarding pass is visible on the screen of their handheld device. SpongeShark also offers travelers a wider range of transactions. The SpongeShark system can be implemented to offer simple services at the beginning but can be expanded as the airlines' needs expand. The three technologies above cannot expand beyond the functionality that they currently provide.

Kiosks. Kiosk solutions are being tested by several U.S. and international airlines for self-serve check-in. Unlike SpongeShark, kiosks do not significantly reduce lines at the gate because only one customer can use the kiosk at a time. Where there used to be a line for the desk, there is now a line for the kiosk. Also, kiosks are more expensive to install and maintain than SpongeShark servers and they do not offer Internet access and entertainment options to passengers who are waiting at the gate. Finally, kiosk users have to deal with an unfamiliar user interface whereas SpongeShark users are working with their own mobile device.

Wireless Internet. Those who have subscriptions to wireless Internet services can access the Internet through their WAP-enabled cell phone or PDA. Swissair began testing self-service check-in through the wireless Internet in October 1999. This technology is seriously flawed, however, because passengers can check in while they are still miles away from the airport.

SpongeShark avoids this security problem because our Bluetooth network is a "proximity-based" solution that operates at a maximum range of 330 feet. SpongeShark is superior to the wireless Internet because of the much higher bandwidth. Anybody who has tried to surf the Internet on a mobile phone can tell you that it is very frustrating to wait for the very slow connection. SpongeShark's 721 kbps transfer rate provides a much better experience. Airlines can offer their best customers access to free news and entertainment to encourage participation in their loyalty programs.

Wireless LAN/Internet Kiosks. SpongeShark also competes with companies that are focused on providing Internet access in airports. Travelers can log on at numerous kiosks, plug their laptops into data ports on many pay phones, or visit Internet cafes or business centers which provide access. Wireless LAN's are a new and growing trend in airports. Users can rent or buy an 802.11 card and connect to a wireless network that is accessible through the entire airport.

SpongeShark is a superior service because our service is designed for handheld devices, which are much more convenient to bring on a trip than a laptop computer. In the next few years handheld devices will outsell PCs by a factor of three-to-one.

MARKETING PLAN

SpongeShark's goal is to facilitate wireless check-in and provide entertainment to passengers of all of the major airlines in the world. We will start by signing a contract with one major airline. We will give our first airline customer a tremendous competitive advantage because their gate agents will be freed from routine transactions and will be able to offer more complete customer service to their passengers. Our target market is the 111 major international airlines in Europe, North America, and Asia. Our entry market will be those airlines who are part of an international alliance with other airlines. We will raise our profile in airline technology circles with our presence at major trade shows and advertisements in key trade publications. We will use personal relationships and highly skilled personal sales staff to develop relationships with airlines and acquire the contracts. Our niche is major airlines which are competing on the basis of customer service and the latest technology. Airline executives we have spoken with have indicated that now is the time to begin implementing the technology that SpongeShark offers. Our identity is as wireless experts who can implement the most cutting edge technology for the travel industry.

Target Market Strategy

Our target market is major airlines that fly in Europe, North America, and Asia. There are 111 airlines with over 30 planes which fly in these regions. Our sales assumptions project that we will capture 18 percent of the 86 airlines in the European and North American markets in five years. Representative airlines in this group have the following characteristics:

- 32 major European destinations
- 21 major U.S. destinations
- 400 total gates needing SpongeShark access points
- 56 million passengers per year

Our entry market will be airlines which fly in Europe as part of an international alliance. Passengers who fly with alliance partners often change from one airline to another in major European hubs, which is where SpongeShark's check-in technology would be most useful in the near term based on the fact that Bluetooth adoption will be much faster in Europe. Currently, mobile device penetration is up to 70 percent in some European countries versus under 30 percent in the United States. Many Europeans will be comfortable using their Bluetooth enabled phones to make purchases and access information, and they will expect airlines to provide similar services. One alliance partner who implements the SpongeShark system will encourage their alliance partners to do so as well so that air travelers can enjoy a seamless travel experience. There are currently five major airline alliances with 26 airlines which fly in Europe and North America.

Product and Service Strategy

SpongeShark will be positioned as a tool for airlines to stay in communication with their best customers while they wait in the gate area. Ours is the best solution for airlines because:

SpongeShark frees airline gate agents. Passengers with Bluetooth-enabled devices will be able to perform a wide range of transactions on their own, from simple check in, to rebooking, to changing their seat, to upgrading to first class, to making sure their miles have been credited towards their frequent flyer account. Instead of dealing with lines of customers who need these simple transactions, airline gate agents will spend their time solving real problems for passengers. Airlines will be able to provide a much higher level of service to their passengers as a result.

SpongeShark allows for push marketing. SpongeShark uses Bluetooth, which only works when passengers are near the access point and allows for information to be "pushed" to mobile devices even if the information was not requested by the end user. Airlines have a captive audience with their passengers who are waiting in the gate area. Passengers have the option of "pulling" information from an airline's wireless Internet site, but they may not choose to do so. With SpongeShark, airlines can push promotions and offers to the passengers through their mobile devices. This can build the customer relationship and encourage purchases of additional services.

SpongeShark allows airlines constant contact with passengers at critical moments. Airlines decide at the last minute which passengers will get upgrades to first class based on variables in their CRM system such as number of miles traveled or amount paid for the ticket. Once this is decided, passengers then have to get back in line to claim their upgrade. When flights are rebooked, passengers also have to get back in line to find out that the flight has been cancelled, and again to check in for another flight. SpongeShark allows airlines to push messages directly to the passengers, such as "To thank you for flying with United, we have upgraded you to first class for this flight. Your new seat is 3A." Other self check-in technologies such as kiosks do not offer the constant contact with passengers.

SpongeShark provides the infrastructure to support a wide range of entertainment options. The high bandwidth transmission of Bluetooth gives waiting passengers much faster access to the Internet as well as music and video entertainment. The airlines can control the content that is offered to their passengers, so passengers will know that all of the entertainment they are enjoying has been brought to them by the airline. In the future, when mobile device screens are able to support video, the airline can present previews of pay-per-view options that will be available on the flight. None of the other self check-in technologies can offer this range of entertainment options.

Our pricing assumptions are as follows:

Pricing Strategy

Product or Service	Price
SpongeShark access points	$560 per access point
SpongeShark main airport servers	$4,200 per airport
Annual hardware support fee	$1,000 per access point
Annual software license fee	$1,500 per access point
Typical system integration fee	$120,000 per airline
Typical installation fee	$2,000 per access point

Airlines spend an average of 2.5 percent of their revenues on Information Technology. Twenty-nine percent of airlines spend over 3 percent of their revenues on information technology. Together, the 26 airlines in our entry market had 1999 revenue of $132 billion, which translates to an information technology investment of $3.3 billion in our entry market alone. This year, IT budgets allocated to e-business will increase by 40 percent as airlines shift the focus of their spending from Y2K problems. Ten percent of their e-business investment will be in self-service ticketing and check-in systems such as ours.

A SpongeShark access point can provide service for eight passengers at a time, whereas a customer service agent or a kiosk can only provide service for one passenger at a time. These alternatives are also much more expensive than SpongeShark. This is what airlines are willing to spend on alternatives to SpongeShark technology:

Gate agent:	$46,000 per year, salary, and benefits.
Self-serve kiosks:	$10,000-20,000 per kiosk.
SpongeShark:	$2,000 per access point, hardware cost, and one-year software license.

SpongeShark not only minimizes airlines' expenses, but it also boosts revenue by encouraging more passengers to become loyal customers. Loyal airline passengers outspend other air travelers by a factor of twelve to one.

Distribution Strategy

Our discussions with airline executives have indicated that major airlines do not buy their technology through resellers and consultants, but buy directly from providers after they have figured out what it is that they need through internal processes. Therefore, SpongeShark will be distributed primarily through in-house personal sales. In order to get an introduction to the important decision-makers in the airlines, we will also work through companies that have established strong relationships with them. Our connection with major systems integrators and tour package companies will enhance our credibility in the eyes of airlines.

Major systems integrators like Sabre, Amadeus, and Galileo work closely with Information Technology Directors at many airlines. These are the types of companies who have won contracts to modernize airlines' legacy systems, build websites, and set up online transactions.

Information Technology Directors will turn to them for suggestions for self-service check-in. SpongeShark will work to build relationships with these companies, so that they will recommend our solution.

Tour package companies like the Mark Travel Corporation develop tours for airlines to sell under their own brand name such as American Airlines Vacations. These companies have relationships with several airlines as well as resorts, hotels, and car rental companies. It is important for tour package customers to have a seamless travel experience, checking in with no hassles at their flight, car rental, and resort. SpongeShark will make this a reality once all of the companies implement our solution. Therefore, tour package companies have an interest in introducing SpongeShark to all of the companies it works with, starting with the airlines.

Advertising and Promotion Strategy

The goal of SpongeShark's communications efforts is to position ourselves as the company with the most cutting-edge technology, which is strong enough to be the dominant player in this niche for many decades. We will use a mix of trade shows, advertising, and public relations to spread this message.

SpongeShark will attend all of the major trade shows on the subject of technology in the travel industry. These include IATA Passenger Services 2001, Travel Technology Odyssey, and E-commerce for Travel 2001. Executives who purchase technology for their airlines attend these trade shows to learn about the latest technological trends. Wireless technology is becoming a hot topic at these conferences. Presence at trade shows will establish us as a strong and enduring company.

Print advertising and public relations will also be very important for getting our name out and positioning ourself as a technological leader. We will also devote substantial resources towards getting our product reviewed by influential trade publications such as *Airline InfoTech*. Finally, SpongeShark will publicize any new partnerships with system integrators and our first contract with an airline so that the industry is aware of us and so that the public knows that they can use the service.

SpongeShark will promote our brand within the travel industry so that we are well known as a wireless solutions company. We will not be branded for the airline passengers. The look and feel of our service will be tailored to the specifications of the airlines so that passengers know that the services have been brought to them by their airline.

Sales Strategy

Our product and service will be sold by an internal direct sales force that works with the executives at the headquarter offices of airlines who are responsible for airport technology. Some titles of these executives are Manager of Airport Automation Development, General Manager-Wireless Programs, Director Systems Integration, VP Network Strategy and Profitability, and Director Technical Services. We will make the initial contact through personal relationships that we have within the airline industry.

During our surveys of airline industry executives, we have found that airlines do not buy their technology through consultants or resellers. Instead, they decide internally what they need and who could provide it to them. They generally work through an RFP (request for proposal) system, whereby they solicit multiple bids for a given project. Our sales efforts will focus on convincing these decision makers that our Bluetooth-enabled check-in will be their best solution even before they write the RFP.

After the RFP process is finished, the sale will be closed with a contract between SpongeShark and the airline. At that point, we will begin installing the access points in airports. Integration happens at this time too. We are planning to waive the installation fee for our first airline customer to encourage them to implement the SpongeShark system.

Airlines are constantly struggling to stay competitive. Customer service and entertainment are critical to attract new passengers and to maintain their loyalty. SpongeShark will deliver a complete wireless solution that enhances customer service, improves customer retention, and lowers operating costs to boost airline profits.

SpongeShark will focus on the design and installation of wireless networks that leverages Bluetooth's proximity-based features to drive customer loyalty programs. Our key strengths are:

- Design of Bluetooth-based networks that enable 1-to-1 marketing
- Integration of our networks with legacy information systems

We are not a manufacturing company. Numerous companies are better positioned to build and sell Bluetooth hardware. We will partner with these companies, purchase their components, and build networks to deliver our service.

We are not a content aggregator. Our airline customers will select the news, entertainment, and travel information that they want to deliver to their passengers. The airlines will use our network to deliver this value-added service to their best customers.

We are a wireless solution provider. SpongeShark customers will benefit from our expertise in installation and maintenance of wireless access points.

SpongeShark has a competitive advantage because our Bluetooth network is low cost, flexible, and scalable. These features allow our clients to install and modify the network quickly and easily. Our specific focus on the travel industry gives us an expertise to provide wireless solutions that address the needs of this sector.

Very high reliability and hardware support are key to achieving high transaction usage and positive passenger feedback, especially since our service will be deployed in volume across a wide geography.

In-house staff will perform the majority of our operations. Our internal focus will be on the design and delivery of value-added services on behalf of our customers. Functions that do not directly focus on this task will be outsourced to vendors or strategic partners as follows:

Core functions	Outsourced functions
Business development/Sales	Hardware manufacturing
Marketing	Content aggregation (news, entertainment, etc.)
Software development	Physical repairs
System integration	
Network installation/maintenance	
Account management	

We will round out our current management team with marketers and sales people who possess international experience in the IT and/or travel sectors. In addition, we will seek out software developers and network engineers to perform the system integration functions.

OPERATIONS PLAN

Operations Strategy

Scope of Operations

Ongoing Operations

The SpongeShark solution offers four services to our airline customers: integration, hardware support, software licensing, and security.

Integration

From our interviews, we know the majority of airlines use a Sabre database for flight information and an Oracle database for customer service. This allows SpongeShark to pre-develop most of the software that will be used in communicating information from the airline's databases to our equipment. The SpongeShark main server will do all of the data translation from the airline databases and build an interface layer to communicate to the wireless access points. Most airlines have already experienced integration due to their development of their e-commerce websites. We can leverage off of the airlines' past experience, combined with our own experience, to create a smooth and quick integration for our customers.

Our goal is to achieve consistency and accuracy of information. System integration costs will be bundled with the costs for the servers that are sold to each airline.

Hardware Support & Software Licensing

A per-seat licensing agreement with SpongeShark will ensure the airlines for:

- server diagnostics
- network diagnostics
- hardware repairs
- software bug fixes/patches
- software upgrades
- software updates

The SpongeShark main server for each airport will use a software solution to operate as a router/firewall. Not only does this provide security for wireless access points against hack attempts, but it can facilitate in diagnostics and software upgrades. Main servers can report network and server information in a variety of secure manners to both SpongeShark and to the client. Additionally, software patches, bug fixes, and updates can be sent through the main servers. As mobile devices' displays and memory upgrade, users will expect more dynamic content. SpongeShark can continually update our software, so that the airlines can quickly benefit. Pre-tested firmware upgrades sent over the network will eliminate the need for SpongeShark to send support staff in the field, allow clients to receive updates quicker and more efficiently, and eliminate the need for clients to install any software themselves. While most on-site repair will be outsourced, SpongeShark will bind quality-service agreements with our support/service partners to ensure a positive experience for our clients if repairs are necessary.

Network Security

Since SpongeShark uses a wireless radio frequency, passengers may be apprehensive that their personal data could be "heard" by a third-party device. Embedded in the Bluetooth protocol are authentication and encryption schemes. Bluetooth authentication ensures that information can only be read by the intended device. Additionally, encryption disallows any promiscuous or malicious devices from reading information.

SpongeShark main servers will also act as firewalls, to prevent any intrusions from the Internet interfering with the SpongeShark internal networks created by the wireless access points and the passenger's mobile devices.

Check-in Security

The Federal Aviation Association (FAA) has recently approved self-serve technology for both passenger and baggage check-in. In fact, asking security questions through a digital form allows for better record keeping of the transaction. A description of the check-in process is presented in Appendix A.

We will target European airports as our first marketplace to take advantage of the high adoption rates for handheld devices. In many European countries the adoption rate exceeds 70 percent. We will deploy our service in Asia and North America when the perceived demand is at a sufficient level.

Numerous elements are required to launch this company successfully. Our primary need is for people and partnerships that can drive the company forward. We will seek out strategic partnerships that will accelerate the design, testing, implementation, and expansion of our service such as:

- **System integrators (e.g., Sabre):** To aid in the development of relationships with airline IT management.
- **Handheld device manufacturers (e.g., Ericsson):** To accelerate the adoption of Bluetooth devices with promotion and education.
- **Wireless access server manufacturers (e.g., Red-M):** To facilitate disbursement and price point of our solution.

The first year of operations will focus on two distinct functions: business development and engineering. The key steps in our initial development plan are as follows:

- *Milestone 1:* Obtain Series A funding

- Hire key staff with specific expertise
    - o Senior level management with experience in an international technology rollout
    - o International sales and marketing
    - o Engineering (network design, database programming, interface design, system integration)

- *Milestone 2:* Build a demonstration prototype
    - o Database server (back-end hardware and software)
    - o Network (from airline to Bluetooth server)
    - o Bluetooth server (hardware and application)
    - o End-user interface (front-end application)

- Expand on our current relationships with airlines and airports

- Build the service through engineering while building the market through business development

- Obtain letters of intent from potential customers

- Seek out investors for Series B funding

- Set up agreements with service and equipment vendors

- Negotiate outsourced manufacturing agreements

- Identify European partners for network maintenance

- *Milestone 3:* Sign first sales contract

- Complete first network installation and system integration

- *Milestone 4:* Obtain Series B funding

DEVELOPMENT PLAN

Development Strategy

The development timeline for the first 13 months of operation is shown in below.

Activities & Milestones	1	2	3	4	5	6	7	8	9	10	11	12	13
Hiring select management team	O	O	O										
Close Series A funding				E									
Hire key engineering/ developers for prototype					H								
Develop Bluetooth Server Back End					E	E							
Develop Front End						E	E						
Prototype complete								H					
Sign letter of intent with first customer								M	M	M			
Negotiate outsourced manufacturing agreement									E				
Demo prototype at conferences									M	M			
Begin outsourced manufacturing of servers										E			
First sale										E			
Contract with European technicians (maintenance)										H			
Integration of SpongeShark with Airline network											E	E	E
First airport complete													E

KEY

E = Engineering   H = Hiring   O = Milestone   M = Marketing

MANAGEMENT

Company Organization

SpongeShark is a licensed LLC in the state of Colorado, headed by a dynamic team of five University of Colorado M.B.A.s. Specializing in management, finance, business development, technology, and operations, each member brings a unique set of business skills that construct an energetic driven team. Ownership will be equally divided among the five members.

As SpongeShark expands we will bring on several experienced members. The key requirements to round out the team are business development and sales professionals. SpongeShark's clear vision and growth prospects will allow it to attract top people. Additionally all members of the management team have developed many key relationships and networks that will enable rapid growth.

Management Team

Kaj Gronholm—CEO

Kaj Gronholm has an extensive background in leadership and management. As president of the UC M.B.A. class of 2001, he has helped lead and develop UC's relationship with the business community, M.B.A. class culture, and program direction. Prior to coming to UC, Kaj grew a retail store at an annual growth rate of 50 percent and boosted net profit by over 200 percent. As an entrepreneur, SpongeShark is Kaj's second start-up. The first is a still growing company in the pet industry. Kaj's undergraduate degree is in Physics, awarded by the University of Texas at Austin. While at UT, Kaj developed an extensive knowledge of computers and technology.

Derek Kumm—COO

Derek Kumm bring 5 years of technical project management to SpongeShark. As a project manager for Carnot Technical Services, Derek managed a staff of five technicians and one analyst while being responsible for sales, marketing, planning, budgeting, staffing, and control of field projects. Derek has shown strong leadership at the UC as President of the Graduate Entrepreneurs Association. Additionally, Derek was a managing member of Entrepreneurial Solutions, LLC, an M.B.A. consulting firm.

Seth Goldhammer—CTO

Seth Goldhammer has been building and deploying computer networks and solutions since 1995. Combining management and technical skills, Seth is a key component of SpongeShark's team. Most recently Seth was CEO of Entrepreneurial Solutions, LLC, an M.B.A. consulting firm. Seth is proficient with SQL, Perl, Javascript, VBScript, and HTML, as well as Win2K, NT 4.0 Server, FreeBSD, Linux, Solaris 2.6, MacOS 9.0, and network administration. Seth will be able to leverage these skills to build the SpongeShark technology.

Chris Gray—CFO

Chris Gray, a UC M.B.A., will take on the duties of Chief Financial Officer. Before SpongeShark, Chris managed inside sales and engineering responsibilities for Microminiature Technology, Inc., a manufacturing company in the microelectronics industry. After Microminiature, Chris worked at CDM Optics, Inc., as a Product Development Manager. At CDM Optics, Chris was responsible for marketing of medical products as intern for a start-up company that designs and manufactures digital imaging systems. Chris's experience and training as a UC M.B.A. will enable him to build the network of partnerships needed to build SpongeShark into a leader in the wireless world.

Kate Tallman—CMO

Kate Tallman brings a wealth of experience to SpongeShark. Kate spent time as a research analyst from 1996-1999 analyzing marketing positions and business strategies of healthcare companies. After this, Kate worked in the marketing department of Ecrix Corporation, a data storage company, evaluating e-commerce strategies. Kate is near the top of the UC M.B.A. class, and is specializing in marketing and entrepreneurship.

Advisory Board

Juan Rodriguez

A cofounder of StorageTek, Juan brings tremendous experience in both technology and management to the SpongeShark team. Juan has founded 3 companies since StorageTek, including Exabyte and Ecrix. Juan serves on the board of directors of several start-up companies.

Urs von Euw

Urs is the CIO of Swiss Air Group, the technology arm of Swiss Air. Swiss Air is the leader in wireless check-in services for the airline industry, however, they do not have a Bluetooth solution. Urs is advising SpongeShark on airline needs and current solutions.

Lex Aludeman

Lex was the system administrator for ITN.net, a web development company for the airline industry. Lex brings industry contacts and experience to SpongeShark's team. His knowledge of airline databases and e-commerce systems are being leveraged in building the SpongeShark solution.

FINANCIAL PLAN

Summary

A summary of the financial outlook for SpongeShark is outlined below. Please see Appendix B for a complete set of financial projections, including annual income statements, balance sheets and cash flow statements for 2001 through 2005, as well as monthly income statements and cash flow statements for 2001. An analysis of key financial, profitability, and return ratios is also included in Appendix B.

Sources of Revenue

SpongeShark will generate revenue from five elements of each airline contract. These revenue streams include the sale of access point hardware, fees for system integration with the airline databases and reservation system, installation of the main server and access points, annual hardware support contracts, and annual software license contracts. The breakdown of the revenue streams can be seen in the chart below representing our total revenues of $60 million in our fifth year of operation.

Sources of Revenue

Access points	1%
Hardware support	12%
System integration	8%
Software license	18%
Installation	61%

The hardware support and software license contracts will be sold on a per access point basis and will generate monthly cash flows for SpongeShark. Therefore, 30 percent of our revenues will be recurring on a monthly basis throughout the entire duration of our relationship with an airline.

Financial Projections

SpongeShark expects to acquire our first airline client in Q4 2001. This initial customer will test our system in a major European hub airport and several smaller airports with approximately 50 total access points. We are anticipating break-even to occur in 2002 after acquiring our fourth airline client. Roughly at this same time we expect a substantial increase in revenues due to an increase in customer acquisition, larger contracts with additional access points, and the reoccurring revenues generated from the hardware support and software license contracts. In our fifth year of operations we are anticipating revenues of $60 million while generating net income of $10 million.

A summary of our financial projections can be seen below:

Income Statement	2001	2002	2003	2004	2005
Revenue	262	4,390	17,580	46,600	59,520
Gross Profit	-400	1,668	6,848	18,880	24,740
Operating Expenses	1,685	2,398	4,565	6,117	7,986
EBIT	-2,085	-730	2,283	12,762	16,754
Net Earnings	-2,085	-730	2,283	7,871	10,052
% of Revenue	13%	17%	17%		

Cash Flow					
Cash Flow from Operations	-2,142	-1,845	-1,325	-104	6,678
CAPEX	-114	-172	-312	-456	-648

Balance Sheet					
Cash	244	3,226	1,589	1,029	7,059
Net Fixed Assets	98	229	455	761	1,166
Retained Earnings	-2,085	-2,816	-533	7,338	17,390

Growth

Revenue Annual Growth	1,578%	300%	165%	28%
Net Earnings Annual Growth			245%	28%

The number of clients acquired annually after the initial test market can be seen below:

	2001	2002	2003	2004	2005
New airline clients	1	2	4	5	6
Cumulative clients	1	3	7	12	18

In our fifth year of operation we will have a total of 18 airline clients representing approximately 400 access points per airline. The number of access points increases from the initial number of 50 due to the fact that at this time our clients will be using our service in both European and North American airports.

SpongeShark will be purchasing the servers and access points from outside vendors and will not be designing or assembling these products in-house. In addition, the company will be outsourcing the installation and maintenance of the access points in the airports. Working capital requirements have been estimated using an analysis of comparable firms in the communication services and information technology industries. Please see Appendix B for additional financial assumptions used in constructing these projections.

An initial equity investment of $2,500,000 is required to launch the business and provide funds for research and development, marketing expenses, working capital requirements, and to finance our first installation. We will require an additional round of funding in twelve months of $5,000,000 to fund the rapid growth of the company expected at this time.

SpongeShark is seeking these funds from a variety of sources. Specifically, the company is seeking venture capital or angel investors who are familiar with the wireless communication or airline industries. In addition, other nontraditional sources of funding are being considered. Airlines are currently in a technological race to see who can offer the best customer service using a variety of technologies and they are not interested in developing these services in-house. Therefore, customer advances or customer participation in the development of the company are seen as additional sources of financing.

Technology
Currently it is still unknown whether Bluetooth will be the wireless technology of choice in the future. However, the SpongeShark concept is not technology specific and can be delivered using other wireless technologies. In addition, the adoption rate of Bluetooth-enabled handheld devices could potentially delay the introduction of the SpongeShark wireless service. However, airlines are interested in rolling out these services before widespread adoption of these devices has taken place.

Operations
SpongeShark is currently in the development stage of operations. Therefore, it is possible for the service to take longer to launch than anticipated, delaying the timeline for acquiring our first customer. In addition, an inability to control the costs involved with supplying the service could potentially decrease our net income projections. Since the hardware that we will be utilizing to deliver our service already exists, we hope to minimize any technological hurdles that could potentially delay the introduction of our service.

Competition

There are companies in the marketplace interested in delivering a variety of wireless services to the airline traveler. However, SpongeShark is uniquely focused on delivering services to the airlines to further enhance their customer service. Information technology companies, systems integrators, or communication service companies could move in on the wireless space that SpongeShark will be operating in. However, we expect to develop a niche expertise in delivering customer service solutions via a Bluetooth network. Currently, the focus of many of the companies interested in developing Bluetooth technology are working on building hardware and not services around the technology.

OFFERING

In return for an investment of $2.5 million, SpongeShark is offering a 24 percent share of the company to the investor. We expect that this investment will grow by 80 percent annually over our five-year planning horizon. Details of the valuation and returns to the investor calculations can be found in Appendix B.

Funding Required

SpongeShark is seeking an initial equity investment of $2.5 million to fund research and development, marketing expenses, working capital requirements, and to finance our first installation. A second round investment of $5 million will be required 12 months after the initial round to support additional customer acquisitions and subsequent rapid growth of the company.

Valuation and Offering

SpongeShark's valuation at the time of the anticipated exit event in 2005 is approximately $200 million. The initial $2.5 million investment will acquire 24 percent of the company in preferred Series "A" stock. The investor is expected to gain an internal rate of return of 80 percent and a 20X return on investment at the exit event in five years.

The second round investment of $5 million will acquire an additional 21 percent of the company in preferred Series "B" stock. The second round investor is expected to achieve an internal rate of return of 70 percent and a 8X return on investment at the exit event in four years.

Exit Strategies

The preferred exit strategy in 2005 for SpongeShark investors will be acquisition after the company has proved the business model and has begun to stabilize operations and revenue growth. By the fifth year of operation, SpongeShark will have substantial revenues and a valuable knowledge base regarding delivering wireless technologies to the travel industry. Larger information technology, systems integrators, or wireless communications companies that have not developed a Bluetooth expertise in-house will find SpongeShark to be an attractive acquisition target. An additional liquidity event for our investors will be an initial public offering in 2005. This strategy will depend largely on the market for initial public offerings at the time of exit.

APPENDIX

Appendix A: Check-In Procedures

Premise 1: End user purchases e-ticket prior to departure. The airline reservation system records the transaction.

Premise 2: Handheld device is used as an e-wallet for many other transactions.

    1. Enter check-in "zones" for Bluetooth handheld device users

2. Connect to check-in system using handheld device
   - User is identified via e-wallet technology.
   - User confirms ID with log-in and password.

3. Accept or change ticketing information
   - To accept your seat or review any special requests you may have made when booking, touch the relevant buttons on your handheld device.

4. Change your seat with ease
   - If you want to amend your seat allocation, you will be linked to this screen. To change your seat, just touch an available seat and it's yours.

5. Check-in your baggage
   - If you have baggage to check in, just hand it to the airline customer service officer at the adjacent baggage drop-off counter.

6. Collect your boarding pass instantly
   - Once you finish check-in, your boarding pass is activated on your handheld device.
   - Proceed to the gate to board the plane.

Appendix B: Financial Statements and Assumptions

Income Statement

Income Statement ($)	2001	2002	2003	2004	2005
Net Revenues	261,667	4,390,000	17,580,000	46,600,000	59,520,000
Cost of Goods Sold	661,952	2,722,307	10,731,951	27,720,420	34,780,484
Gross Profit	-400,286	1,667,693	6,848,049	18,879,580	24,739,516
Operating Expenses					
Sales and Marketing	571,500	845,275	1,503,039	2,060,691	2,685,700
Research and Development	459,500	631,975	1,439,574	2,011,152	2,706,185
General and Administration	654,125	920,825	1,622,466	2,045,265	2,593,640
Total Operating Expenses	**1,685,125**	**2,398,075**	**4,565,079**	**6,117,108**	**7,985,526**
Earnings from Operations	**-2,085,411**	**-730,382**	**2,282,970**	**12,762,472**	**16,753,991**
Taxes	**-**		**-**	**4,891,860**	**-6,701,596**
Net Earnings	**-2,085,411**	**-730,382**	**2,282,970**	**7,870,612**	**10,052,394**

Balance Sheet

Balance Sheet ($)	2001	2002	2003	2004	2005
Assets					
Current Assets					
Cash	243,608	3,226,150	1,589,349	1,028,933	7,058,870
Accounts Receivable	65,417	1,097,500	4,395,000	11,650,000	14,880,000
Inventories	26,167	439,000	1,758,000	4,660,000	5,952,000
Other Current Assets	39,250	658,500	2,637,000	6,990,000	8,928,000
Total Current Assets	**374,442**	**5,421,150**	**10,379,349**	**24,328,933**	**36,818,870**
Net Fixed Assets	97,714	228,857	455,429	760,857	1,165,714
Total Assets	**472,156**	**5,650,007**	**10,834,777**	**25,089,790**	**37,984,584**

Balance Sheet

Continued

Liabilities and Shareholders' Equity					
Current Liabilities					
Accounts Payable and					
Accrued Expenses	39,250	658,500	2,637,000	6,990,000	8,928,000
Other Current Liabilities	18,317	307,300	1,230,600	3,262,000	4,166,400
Total Current Liabilities	**57,567**	**965,800**	**3,867,600**	**10,252,000**	**13,094,400**
Stockholders' Equity					
Preferred Stock	2,500,000	7,500,000	7,500,000	7,500,000	7,500,000
Retained Earnings	-2,085,411	-2,815,793	-532,823	7,337,790	17,390,184
Total Equity	**414,589**	**4,684,207**	**6,967,177**	**14,837,790**	**24,890,184**
Total Liabilities					
and Equity	**472,156**	**5,650,007**	**10,834,777**	**25,089,790**	**37,984,584**
Cash Flow Statement ($)	**2001**	**2002**	**2003**	**2004**	**2005**

Cash Flow Statement

Operating Activities					
Net Earnings	-2,085,411	-730,382	2,282,970	7,870,612	10,052,394
Depreciation	16,286	40,857	85,429	150,571	243,143
Working Capital Changes					
(Increase)/Decrease					
Accounts Receivable	-65,417	-1,032,083	-3,297,500	-7,255,000	-3,230,000
(Increase)/Decrease					
Inventories	-26,167	-412,833	-1,319,000	-2,902,000	-1,292,000
(Increase)/Decrease					
Other Current Assets	-39,250	-619,250	-1,978,500	-4,353,000	-1,938,000
Increase/(Decrease)					
Accounts Payable &					
Accrued Expenses	39,250	619,250	1,978,500	4,353,000	1,938,000
Increase/(Decrease)					
Other Current Liabilities	18,317	288,983	923,300	2,031,400	904,400
Net Cash Provided by					
Operating Activities	-2,142,392	-1,845,458	-1,324,801	-104,416	6,677,937
Investing Activities					
Plant and Equipment	-114,000	-172,000	-312,000	-456,000	-648,000
Net Cash Used in					
Investing Activities	-114,000	-172,000	-312,000	-456,000	-648,000
Financing Activities					
Increase/(Decrease)					
Preferred Stock	-	5,000,000	-	-	-
Net Cash Provided/					
(Used) by Financing		- 5,000,000	-	-	-
Increase/(Decrease)					
in Cash	-2,256,392	2,982,542	-1,636,801	-560,416	6,029,937
Cash at Beginning					
of Year	**2,500,000**	**243,608**	**3,226,150**	**1,589,349**	**1,028,933**
Cash at End of Year	**243,608**	**3,226,150**	**1,589,349**	**1,028,933**	**7,058,870**

This page left intentionally blank to accommodate tabular matter following.

Income Statement ($)

	Jan	Feb	Mar	Apr	May
Net Revenues	-	-	-	-	-
Cost of Goods Sold	7,107	7,107	7,107	7,107	7,107
Gross Profit	-7,107	-7,107	-7,107	-7,107	-7,107
Operating Expenses					
Sales and Marketing	95,375	27,042	30,375	77,042	30,375
Research and Development	77,875	23,708	47,875	23,708	47,875
General and Administration	54,510	54,510	54,510	54,510	54,510
Total Operating Expenses	**227,760**	**105,260**	**132,760**	**155,260**	**132,760**
Earnings from Operations	-234,868	-112,368	-139,868	-162,368	-139,868
Taxes	-	-	-	-	-
Net Earnings	**-234,868**	**-112,368**	**-139,868**	**-162,368**	**-139,868**

Cash Flow Statement ($)

Operating Activities	Jan	Feb	Mar	Apr	May	Jun
Net Earnings	-234,868	-112,368	-139,868	-162,368	-139,868	-117,368
Depreciation	1,357	1,357	1,357	1,357	1,357	1,357
Working Capital Changes						
(Increase)/Decrease Accounts Receivable	-	-	-	-	-	-
(Increase)/Decrease Inventories	-	-	-	-	-	-
(Increase)/Decrease Other Current Assets	-3,271	-3,271	-3,271	-3,271	-3,271	-3,271
Increase/(Decrease) Accounts Payable and						
Accrued Expenses	3,271	3,271	3,271	3,271	3,271	3,271
Increase/(Decrease) Other Current Liabilities	1,526	1,526	1,526	1,526	1,526	1,526
Net Cash Provided by Operating Activities	**-231,984**	**-109,484**	**-136,984**	**-159,484**	**-136,984**	**-114,484**
Investing Activities	-	-	-	-	-	-
Plant and Equipment	-82,000	-2,909	-2,909	-2,909	-2,909	-2,909
Net Cash Used in Investing Activities	-82,000	-2,909	-2,909	-2,909	-2,909	-2,909
Financing Activities	-	-	-	-	-	-
Increase/(Decrease) Preferred Stock	-	-	-	-	-	-
Net Cash Provided/(Used) by Financing	-	-	-	-	-	-
Increase/(Decrease) in Cash	-313,984	-112,393	-139,893	-162,393	-139,893	-117,393
Cash at Beginning of Month	**2,500,000**	**2,186,016**	**2,073,623**	**1,933,730**	**1,771,337**	**1,631,443**
Cash at End of Month	**2,186,016**	**2,073,623**	**1,933,730**	**1,771,337**	**1,631,443**	**1,514,050**

Jun	Jul	Aug	Sep	Oct	Nov	Dec
-	-	-	230,417	10,417	10,417	10,417
7,107	7,107	7,107	196,274	136,274	136,274	136,274
-7,107	-7,107	-7,107	34,143	-125,857	-125,857	-125,857
32,042	80,375	27,042	32,375	77,042	35,375	27,042
23,708	47,875	23,708	47,875	23,708	47,875	23,708
54,510	54,510	54,510	54,510	54,510	54,510	54,510
110,260	**182,760**	**105,260**	**134,760**	**155,260**	**137,760**	**105,260**
-117,368	-189,868	-112,368	-100,618	-281,118	-263,618	-231,118
-	-	-	-	-	-	-
-117,368	**-189,868**	**-112,368**	**-100,618**	**-281,118**	**-263,618**	**-231,118**

Jul	Aug	Sep	Oct	Nov	Dec
-189,868	-112,368	-100,618	-281,118	-263,618	-231,118
1,357	1,357	1,357	1,357	1,357	1,357
-	-	-57,604	-2,604	-2,604	-2,604
-4,361	-4,361	-4,361	-4,361	-4,361	-4,361
-3,271	-3,271	-3,271	-3,271	-3,271	-3,271
3,271	3,271	3,271	3,271	3,271	3,271
1,526	1,526	1,526	1,526	1,526	1,526
-191,345	**-113,845**	**-159,699**	**-285,199**	**-267,699**	**-235,199**
-	-	-	-	-	-
-2,909	-2,909	-2,909	-2,909	-2,909	-2,909
-2,909	-2,909	-2,909	-2,909	-2,909	-2,909
-	-	-	-	-	-
-	-	-	-	-	-
-	-	-	-	-	-
-194,254	-116,754	-162,608	-288,108	-270,608	-238,108
1,514,050	**1,319,796**	**1,203,042**	**1,040,434**	**752,325**	**481,717**
1,319,796	**1,203,042**	**1,040,434**	**752,325**	**481,717**	**243,608**

Financial Assumptions

Revenue

Revenue projections assume that the first airline contract will include the sale of 50 access points. This number will increase to 100 access points per airline in 2002, 200 access points per airline in 2003, and 400 access points per airline in 2004 and 2005. The number of access points steadily increases as our clients move from using our service in European airports to both European and North American airports. The number of access points per airline is based on the average number of gates and major airports served by several of our target airline customers. A breakdown of our revenue projections can be seen below:

Revenue	2001	2002	2003	2004	2005
Revenue from sale of access point	100,000	400,000	1,600,000	4,000,000	4,800,000
Revenue from system integration	120,000	240,000	480,000	600,000	720,000
Revenue from installation	0	3,000,000	12,000,000	30,000,000	36,000,000
Revenue from hardware support	16,667	300,000	1,400,000	4,800,000	7,200,000
Revenue from software license	25,000	450,000	2,100,000	7,200,000	10,800,000
Total	**261,667**	**4,390,000**	**17,580,000**	**46,600,000**	**59,520,000**

2001 revenue projections assume that we will not be receiving revenue from the installation of the 50 access points for our first client. SpongeShark will be funding this initial installation to lower the financial barriers for an airline testing our service. In addition, we will only be receiving revenue from the hardware support and software license contracts for four months since we will be acquiring this customer at the beginning of Q4. Our pricing structure can be found in the Marketing Plan.

Cost of Goods Sold

The cost of system integration and the software license contracts is assumed to include the salaries of the software engineers working on these projects. We are assuming that the cost per access point will be $1,200, which includes the cost of one server for every fifty access points. The cost of installation will average $10,000 per access point based on the assumption of approximately $200 per hour labor charge and 50 hours of labor. The cost of hardware support is $1,000 per access point based on a $100 per hour labor charge and 10 hours of labor.

Operating Expenses

Sales and marketing expenses can be seen in the chart below:

Sales and Marketing	2001	2002	2003	2004	2005
Commissions	2,000	8,000	32,000	80,000	96,000
Travel and Entertainment	20,000	40,000	80,000	100,000	120,000
Advertising and Promotion	40,000	80,000	160,000	200,000	240,000
Exhibitions	200,000	250,000	312,500	390,625	488,281
Brochures and Literature	20,000	40,000	80,000	100,000	120,000
Market research	15,000	15,000	15,000	15,000	15,000
Recruiting and Relocation	10,000	0	10,000	0	0
Total	**307,000**	**433,000**	**689,500**	**885,625**	**1,079,281**

Commissions are assumed to be 2 percent of the sale of access points. Travel and entertainment expenses are $20,000 per new airline client. Advertising and promotion expenses are $40,000 per new airline client. Exhibition and trade show expenses are $200,000 in 2001 and grow at 25 percent per year. Brochures and literature are $20,000 per new airline client. Recruiting and relocation includes $10,000 per relocated executive employee.

Sales and marketing salaries, benefits, and headcount for this department can be seen below:

Sales and Marketing

Salaries	2001	2002	2003	2004	2005
Total Salaries	230,000	358,500	707,425	1,021,796	1,396,886
Benefits (15% of salary)	34,500	53,775	106,114	153,269	209,533
Headcount	3	5	10	15	21

Research and development expenses can be seen in the chart below:

Research and Development	2001	2002	2003	2004	2005
Relocation and recruitment	30,000	10,000	20,000	10,000	10,000
Travel and Entertainment	20,000	30,000	45,000	67,500	101,250
Other Expenses	145,000	222,250	503,363	698,031	924,932
Total	**195,000**	**262,250**	**568,363**	**775,531**	**1,036,182**

Relocation and recruitment includes $10,000 per relocated executive employee. Travel and entertainment is assumed to be $20,000 in 2001 with a 50 percent annual growth. Other expenses were assumed to be 50 percent of the research and development salary budget.

Research and Development salaries, benefits, and headcount for this department can be seen below. These totals include the salaries of the software engineers that are figured as cost of goods sold.

Research and

Development Salaries	2001	2002	2003	2004	2005
Total Salaries	290,000	444,500	1,006,725	1,396,061	1,849,864
Benefits (15% of salary)	43,500	66,675	151,009	209,409	277,480
Headcount	4	7	15	22	29

General and administrative expenses can be seen in the chart below:

General and

Administrative	2001	2002	2003	2004	2005
Rent and Utilities	100,000	125,000	500,000	625,000	781,250
Legal and Accounting	50,000	75,000	112,500	168,750	253,125
Telephone, Fax, Networking (total)	15,000	22,500	33,750	50,625	75,938
Travel and Entertainment	50,000	75,000	112,500	168,750	253,125
Insurance	50,000	75,000	112,500	168,750	253,125
Supplies and Postage	1,000	1,500	2,250	3,375	5,063
Total	**266,000**	**374,000**	**873,500**	**1,185,250**	**1,621,625**

The increase in rent and utilities in 2003 is based on the assumption that SpongeShark will move into a larger facility in this year. All other general administrative expenses grow at an annual rate of 50 percent.

General and administrative salaries, benefits, and headcount for this department can be seen below:

General and

Administrative Salaries	2001	2002	2003	2004	2005
Total	337,500	475,500	651,275	747,839	845,231
Benefits (15% of salary)	50,625	71,325	97,691	112,176	126,785
Headcount	6	7	9	10	11

Balance Sheet

Balance sheet assumptions were based on an analysis of comparable companies and industry data from the computer-related services and wireless communication industries. SpongeShark's cash account is inflated in 2005 because we intend to use this cash to fund development and deployment of our service in other areas of the travel ribbon. In addition, our accounts receivables are above average based on the assumption that our installations will take roughly three months to complete at which time we will receive payment from our clients. Also, our inventory requirements are above average as we will require an inventory of access points to satisfy our customer's expansion plans and to realize economies of scale when purchasing the access points from outside vendors. The balance sheet accounts as a percent of revenues can be seen in the chart below:

	SpongeShark	Industry
Accounts Receivable	25.00%	17.90%
Inventory	10.00%	1.00%
Other Current Assets	15.00%	14.00%
Accounts Payable and Accrued Expenses	15.00%	16.30%
Other Current Liabilities	7.00%	6.90%

Property, plant, and equipment assumptions can be seen below:

Plant Assumptions	2001	2002	2003	2004	2005
RedM server	$3,200				
Bluetooth development kit	2,000				
Bluetooth analyzer software	500				
Bluetooth PCMCIA card	500				
Bluetooth phone	200				
Other	3,600				
Development equipment	10,000	20,000	40,000	80,000	160,000
Office equipment, computers, and software	104,000	152,000	272,000	376,000	488,000
Total	**$114,000**	**$172,000**	**$312,000**	**$456,000**	**$648,000**
Depreciation Rate: Years	7	7	7	7	7

Development equipment requirements will grow 100 percent per year from the initial amount of $10,000. Office equipment, computers, and software are assumed to be $8,000 per person.

Ratio Analysis

A summary of the key financial ratios and profitability and return percentages can be seen below. The industry numbers are constructed from a compilation of ratios from comparable companies and industry averages from the computer-related services (SIC 7379) and the communication services (SIC 4899) industries.

Ratios	2001	2002	2003	2004	2005	Industry
Current ratio	6.5	5.61	2.68	2.37	2.81	1.31
Debt to Capital	0	0	0	0	0	0.41
Profitability						
Gross Profit %		37.99%	38.95%	40.51%	41.57%	45.76%
Net Earnings %		12.99%	16.89%	16.89%		14.62%
Returns						
Return on Assets		21.07%	31.37%	26.46%		16.47%
Return on Equity		32.77%	53.04%	40.39%		44.60%

Our current ratio is larger than the industry average because we are anticipating above average accounts receivables. This is a result of the assumption that our installation process will take approximately three months at which time we will receive payment from our airline client. SpongeShark expects to have an all equity capital structure throughout the five-year period.

SpongeShark's return on assets is above the industry average based on the assumption that we will be outsourcing the manufacturing aspects of the business and will not be an asset intensive company. The average gross profit, net earnings, and return on equity for 2003 through 2005 is near the industry average for each figure.

The assumptions and calculations utilized to determine the returns to the investor and capitalization structure can be seen below:

Valuation Calculation

Assumptions

Months until exit	60
Forecast annualized earnings at exit	$10,052,394
P/E ratio at exit	20
Valuation at exit	$201,047,886

Investment Round	First	Second
Month of Investment	0	12
Investor required IRR	80%	70%
Amount of Investment	$2,500,000	$5,000,000
Required Monthly IRR	6.67%	5.83%
Duration of Investment	60	48

Returns	First	Second
Required FV for Investor at exit	$47,239,200	$41,760,500
Individual Investor's Share	23.50%	20.80%
Individual Investor's ROI	1890%	835%
Individual Investor's IRR	80%	70%

Capitalization Table

Investors' Share	44.30%
Founders' Share	55.70%

Handset Technology

Appendix C: Detailed Description of Product and Service

Mobile phones and PDAs do have limitations. Wireless Internet currently receives negative reviews due to the difficulty in typing words. To type, mobile phones force a user to use the number pad, which often means pressing multiple buttons just to type a single letter. Prototype phones have attempted to eliminate this problem by including a keyboard, but the small buttons are often difficult to use. Understanding this limitation, SpongeShark will offer an easy to use menu-like interface to reduce the amount of keystrokes necessary for an end-user.

Menu and icon driven pages will be the most effective on mobile phone displays. The resolution of the screens will allow for creativity similar to current web design, which is also designed for point-and-click navigation. As a result, airlines have the ability to use their pre-existing e-commerce site templates. Not only can this expedite integration, but it can work in tangent with the airline's e-commerce site to build brand recognition for their online services.

Legacy Integration

Converting the travel information into the appropriate format for this new service will require a "transcoding" process which involves filtering and adapting content developed in standard markup languages (which enable browser applications to interpret and display data) to be better suited to end-user devices.

SpongeShark will write a JAVA application to translate the airline's travel-related information into the Wireless Markup Language (WML): a format that can be presented on Wireless Application Protocol (WAP) enabled devices. The resulting WML content will then pass through our wireless access points via Bluetooth to phones and PDA's supporting WAP. The WAP browser has become the standard for mobile Internet use and therefore will not require any pre-installation or purchase by the passenger.

Following is a graphical representation of how SpongeShark's software application translates data into a presentable form for the passenger:

CRS Database	SpongeShark GUI	Bluetooth
(Sabre, Oracle, etc.)	(JAVA, WML, WAP)	PDA, Phone, Notebook

Authentication

To ensure a user's identity, SpongeShark plans to provide a two-level security system. Currently, self-serve kiosks ask for a credit card swipe of the credit card used to make the initial ticket purchase. This is an example of single level security. Every mobile phone and PDA, regardless of manufacturer, carries a unique identification string. SpongeShark will associate this ID with the user for a primary security. Additionally, SpongeShark will ask each user to create a unique username and password for login purposes. An airline using SpongeShark as part of their customer loyalty program could have the username be the frequent flyer membership number of that passenger. Future options in security include biometrics such as voice recognition or digital signatures.

Appendix A - Business Plan Template

Business Plan Template

USING THIS TEMPLATE

A business plan carefully spells out a company's projected course of action over a period of time, usually the first two to three years after the start-up. In addition, banks, lenders, and other investors examine the information and financial documentation before deciding whether or not to finance a new business venture. Therefore, a business plan is an essential tool in obtaining financing and should describe the business itself in detail as well as all important factors influencing the company, including the market, industry, competition, operations and management policies, problem solving strategies, financial resources and needs, and other vital information. The plan enables the business owner to anticipate costs, plan for difficulties, and take advantage of opportunities, as well as design and implement strategies that keep the company running as smoothly as possible.

This template has been provided as a model to help you construct your own business plan. Please keep in mind that there is no single acceptable format for a business plan, and that this template is in no way comprehensive, but serves as an example.

The business plans provided in this section are fictional and have been used by small business agencies as models for clients to use in compiling their own business plans.

GENERIC BUSINESS PLAN

Main headings included below are topics that should be covered in a comprehensive business plan. They include:

Business Summary

Purpose
Provides a brief overview of your business, succinctly highlighting the main ideas of your plan.

Includes
- Name and Type of Business
- Description of Product/Service
- Business History and Development
- Location
- Market
- Competition
- Management
- Financial Information
- Business Strengths and Weaknesses
- Business Growth

Table of Contents

Purpose

Organized in an Outline Format, the Table of Contents illustrates the selection and arrangement of information contained in your plan.

Includes

○ Topic Headings and Subheadings
○ Page Number References

Business History and Industry Outlook

Purpose

Examines the conception and subsequent development of your business within an industry specific context.

Includes

○ Start-up Information
○ Owner/Key Personnel Experience
○ Location
○ Development Problems and Solutions
○ Investment/Funding Information
○ Future Plans and Goals
○ Market Trends and Statistics
○ Major Competitors
○ Product/Service Advantages
○ National, Regional, and Local Economic Impact

Product/Service

Purpose

Introduces, defines, and details the product and/or service that inspired the information of your business.

Includes

○ Unique Features
○ Niche Served
○ Market Comparison
○ Stage of Product/Service Development
○ Production
○ Facilities, Equipment, and Labor
○ Financial Requirements
○ Product/Service Life Cycle
○ Future Growth

Market Examination

Purpose

Assessment of product/service applications in relation to consumer buying cycles.

Includes

- ◯ Target Market
- ◯ Consumer Buying Habits
- ◯ Product/Service Applications
- ◯ Consumer Reactions
- ◯ Market Factors and Trends
- ◯ Penetration of the Market
- ◯ Market Share
- ◯ Research and Studies
- ◯ Cost
- ◯ Sales Volume and Goals

Competition

Purpose

Analysis of Competitors in the Marketplace.

Includes

- ◯ Competitor Information
- ◯ Product/Service Comparison
- ◯ Market Niche
- ◯ Product/Service Strengths and Weaknesses
- ◯ Future Product/Service Development

Marketing

Purpose

Identifies promotion and sales strategies for your product/service.

Includes

- ◯ Product/Service Sales Appeal
- ◯ Special and Unique Features
- ◯ Identification of Customers
- ◯ Sales and Marketing Staff
- ◯ Sales Cycles
- ◯ Type of Advertising/Promotion
- ◯ Pricing
- ◯ Competition
- ◯ Customer Services

Operations

Purpose

Traces product/service development from production/inception to the market environment.

Includes

- Cost Effective Production Methods
- Facility
- Location
- Equipment
- Labor
- Future Expansion

Administration and Management

Purpose

Offers a statement of your management philosophy with an in-depth focus on processes and procedures.

Includes

- Management Philosophy
- Structure of Organization
- Reporting System
- Methods of Communication
- Employee Skills and Training
- Employee Needs and Compensation
- Work Environment
- Management Policies and Procedures
- Roles and Responsibilities

Key Personnel

Purpose

Describes the unique backgrounds of principle employees involved in business.

Includes

- Owner(s)/Employee Education and Experience
- Positions and Roles
- Benefits and Salary
- Duties and Responsibilities
- Objectives and Goals

Potential Problems and Solutions

Purpose

Discussion of problem solving strategies that change issues into opportunities.

Includes

- Risks
- Litigation
- Future Competition
- Economic Impact
- Problem Solving Skills

Financial Information

Purpose

Secures needed funding and assistance through worksheets and projections detailing financial plans, methods of re-payment, and future growth opportunities.

Includes

- Financial Statements
- Bank Loans
- Methods of Repayment
- Tax Returns
- Start-up Costs
- Projected Income (3 years)
- Projected Cash Flow (3 Years)
- Projected Balance Statements (3 years)

Appendices

Purpose

Supporting documents used to enhance your business proposal.

Includes

- Photographs of product, equipment, facilities, etc.
- Copyright/Trademark Documents
- Legal Agreements
- Marketing Materials
- Research and or Studies
- Operation Schedules
- Organizational Charts
- Job Descriptions
- Resumes
- Additional Financial Documentation

Food Distributor

FICTIONAL BUSINESS PLAN

COMMERCIAL FOODS, INC.

3003 Avondale Ave.
Knoxville, TN 37920

October 31, 1992

This plan demonstrates how a partnership can have a positive impact on a new business. It demonstrates how two individuals can carve a niche in the specialty foods market by offering gourmet foods to upscale restaurants and fine hotels. This plan is fictional and has not been used to gain funding from a bank or other lending institution.

- STATEMENT OF PURPOSE

- DESCRIPTION OF THE BUSINESS

- MANAGEMENT

- PERSONNEL

- LOCATION

- PRODUCTS AND SERVICES

- THE MARKET

- COMPETITION

- SUMMARY

- INCOME STATEMENT

- FINANCIAL STATEMENTS

FOOD DISTRIBUTOR
BUSINESS PLAN

STATEMENT OF PURPOSE

Commercial Foods, Inc. seeks a loan of $75,000 to establish a new business. This sum, together with $5,000 equity investment by the principals, will be used as follows:

Merchandise inventory	$25,000
Office fixture/equipment	12,000
Warehouse equipment	14,000
One delivery truck	10,000
Working capital	39,000
Total	**$100,000**

DESCRIPTION OF THE BUSINESS

Commercial Foods, Inc. will be a distributor of specialty food service products to hotels and upscale restaurants in the geographical area of a 50 mile radius of Knoxville. Richard Roberts will direct the sales effort and John Williams will manage the warehouse operation and the office. One delivery truck will be used initially with a second truck added in the third year.

We expect to begin operation of the business within 30 days after securing the requested financing.

MANAGEMENT

A. Richard Roberts is a native of Memphis, Tennessee. He is a graduate of Memphis State University with a Bachelor's degree from the School of Business. After graduation, he worked for a major manufacturer of specialty food service products as a detail sales person for five years, and, for the past three years, he has served as a product sales manager for this firm.

B. John Williams is a native of Nashville, Tennessee. He holds a B.S. Degree in Food Technology from the University of Tennessee. His career includes five years as a product development chemist in gourmet food products and five years as operations manager for a food service distributor.

Both men are healthy and energetic. Their backgrounds complement each other, which will ensure the success of Commercial Foods, Inc. They will set policies together and personnel decisions will be made jointly. Initial salaries for the owners will be $1,000 per month for the first few years. The spouses of both principals are successful in the business world and earn enough to support the families.

They have engaged the services of Foster Jones, CPA, and William Hale, Attorney, to assist them in an advisory capacity.

PERSONNEL

The firm will employ one delivery truck driver at a wage of $8.00 per hour. One office worker will be employed at $7.50 per hour. One part-time employee will be used in the office at $5.00 per hour. The driver will load and unload his own trucks. Mr. Williams will assist in the warehouse operation as needed to assist one stock person at $7.00 per hour. An additional delivery truck and driver will be added the third year.

LOCATION

The firm will lease a 20,000 square foot building at 3003 Avondale Ave., in Knoxville, which contains warehouse and office areas equipped with two-door truck docks. The annual rental is $9,000. The building was previously used as a food service warehouse and very little modification to the building will be required.

		PRODUCTS AND SERVICES

The firm will offer specialty food service products such as soup bases, dessert mixes, sauce bases, pastry mixes, spices, and flavors, normally used by upscale restaurants and nice hotels. We are going after a niche in the market with high quality gourmet products. There is much less competition in this market than in standard run of the mill food service products. Through their work experiences, the principals have contacts with supply sources and with local chefs.

THE MARKET

We know from our market survey that there are over 200 hotels and upscale restaurants in the area we plan to serve. Customers will be attracted by a direct sales approach. We will offer samples of our products and product application data on use of our products in the finished prepared foods. We will cultivate the chefs in these establishments. The technical background of John Williams will be especially useful here.

COMPETITION

We find that we will be only distributor in the area offering a full line of gourmet food service products. Other foodservice distributors offer only a few such items in conjunction with their standard product line. Our survey shows that many of the chefs are ordering products from Atlanta and Memphis because of a lack of adequate local supply.

SUMMARY

Commercial Foods, Inc. will be established as a foodservice distributor of specialty food in Knoxville. The principals, with excellent experience in the industry, are seeking a $75,000 loan to establish the business. The principals are investing $25,000 as equity capital.

The business will be set up as an "S" Corporation with each principal owning 50% of the common stock in the corporation.

Attached is a three year pro forma income statement we believe to be conservative. Also attached are personal financial statements of the principals and a projected cash flow statement for the first year.

PRO FORMA INCOME STATEMENT

	1st Year	2nd Year	3rd Year
Gross Sales	300,000	400,000	500,000
Less Allowances	1,000	1,000	2,000
Net Sales	299,000	399,000	498,000
Cost of Goods Sold	179,400	239,400	298,800
Gross Margin	119,600	159,600	199,200
Operating Expenses			
Utilities	1,200	1,500	1,700
Salaries	76,000	79,000	102,000
Payroll Taxes/Benefits	9,100	9,500	13,200
Advertising	3,000	4,500	5,000
Office Supplies	1,500	2,000	2,500
Insurance	1,200	1,500	1,800
Maintenance	1,000	1,500	2,000
Outside Services	3,000	3,000	3,000
Whse Supplies/Trucks	6,000	7,000	10,000
Telephone	900	1,000	1,200
Rent	9,000	9,500	9,900
Depreciation	2,500	2,000	3,000
Total Expenses	114,400	122,000	155,300
Other Expenses			
Bank Loan Payment	15,000	15,000	15,000
Bank Loan Interest	6,000	5,000	4,000
Total Expenses	**120,400**	**142,000**	**174,300**
Net Profit (Loss)	**(800)**	**17,600**	**24,900**

FINANCIAL STATEMENT I	**Assets**			**Liabilities**	
	Cash	15,000			
	1991 Olds	11,000		Unpaid Balance	8,000
	Residence	140,000		Mortgage	105,000
	Mutual Funds	12,000		Credit Cards	500
	Furniture	5,000		Note Payable	4,000
	Merck Stock	10,000			
		182,200			117,500
	Net Worth				**64,700**
		182,200			**182,200**

FINANCIAL STATEMENT II	**Assets**			**Liabilities**	
	Cash	5,000			
	1992 Buick Auto	15,000		Unpaid Balance	12,000
	Residence	120,000		Mortgage	100,000
	U.S. Treasury Bonds	5,000		Credit Cards	500
	Home Furniture	4,000		Note Payable	2,500
	AT&T Stock	3,000			
		147,000			115,000
	Net Worth				**32,000**
		147,000			**147,000**

Hardware Store

FICTIONAL BUSINESS PLAN

OSHKOSH HARDWARE, INC.

123 Main St.
Oshkosh, WI 54901

June 1994

The following plan outlines how a small hardware store can survive competition from large discount chains by offering products and providing expert advice in the use of any product it sells. This plan is fictional and has not been used to gain funding from a bank or other lending institution.

EXECUTIVE SUMMARY

Oshkosh Hardware, Inc., is a new corporation that is going to establish a retail hardware store in a strip mall in Oshkosh, Wisconsin. The store will sell hardware of all kinds, quality tools, paint, and housewares. The business will make revenue and a profit by servicing its customers not only with needed hardware but also with expert advice in the use of any product it sells.

Oshkosh Hardware, Inc. will be operated by its sole shareholder, James Smith. The company will have a total of four employees. It will sell its products in the local market. Customers will buy our products because we will provide free advice on the use of all of our products and will also furnish a full refund warranty.

Oshkosh Hardware, Inc. will sell its products in the Oshkosh store staffed by three sales representatives. No additional employees will be needed to achieve its short and long range goals. The primary short range goal is to open the store by October 1, 1994. In order to achieve this goal a lease must be signed by July 1, 1994 and the complete inventory ordered by August 1, 1994.

Mr. James Smith will invest $30,000 in the business. In addition, the company will have to borrow $150,000 during the first year to cover the investment in inventory, accounts receivable, and furniture and equipment. The company will be profitable after six months of operation and should be able to start repayment of the loan in the second year.

THE BUSINESS

The business will sell hardware of all kinds, quality tools, paint, and housewares. We will purchase our products from three large wholesale buying groups.

In general our customers are homeowners who do their own repair and maintenance, hobbyists, and housewives. Our business is unique in that we will have a complete line of all hardware items and will be able to get special orders by overnight delivery. The business makes revenue and profits by servicing our customers not only with needed hardware but also with expert advice in the use of any product we sell. Our major costs for bringing our products to market are cost of merchandise of 36%, salaries of $45,000, and occupancy costs of $60,000.

Oshkosh Hardware, Inc.'s retail outlet will be located at 1524 Frontage Road, which is in a newly developed retail center of Oshkosh. Our location helps facilitate accessibility from all parts of town and reduces our delivery costs. The store will occupy 7500 square feet of space. The major equipment involved in our business is counters and shelving, a computer, a paint mixing machine, and a truck.

THE MARKET

Oshkosh Hardware, Inc., will operate in the local market. There are 15,000 potential customers in this market area. We have three competitors who control approximately 98% of the market at present. We feel we can capture 25% of the market within the next four years. Our major reason for believing this is that our staff is technically competent to advise our customers in the correct use of all products we sell.

After a careful market analysis, we have determined that approximately 60% of our customers are men and 40% are women. The percentage of customers that fall into the following age categories are:

Under 16:	0%
17-21:	5%
22-30:	30%
31-40:	30%

41-50:	20%
51-60:	10%
61-70:	5%
Over 70:	0%

The reasons our customers prefer our products is our complete knowledge of their use and our full refund warranty.

We get our information about what products our customers want by talking to existing customers. There seems to be an increasing demand for our product. The demand for our product is increasing in size based on the change in population characteristics.

SALES

At Oshkosh Hardware, Inc. we will employ three sales people and will not need any additional personnel to achieve our sales goals. These salespeople will need several years experience in home repair and power tool usage. We expect to attract 30% of our customers from newspaper ads, 5% of our customers from local directories, 5% of our customers from the yellow pages, 10% of our customers from family and friends, and 50% of our customers from current customers. The most cost effect source will be current customers. In general our industry is growing.

MANAGEMENT

We would evaluate the quality of our management staff as being excellent. Our manager is experienced and very motivated to achieve the various sales and quality assurance objectives we have set. We will use a management information system that produces key inventory, quality assurance, and sales data on a weekly basis. All data is compared to previously established goals for that week, and deviations are the primary focus of the management staff.

GOALS IMPLEMENTATION

The short term goals of our business are:

1. Open the store by October 1, 1994
2. Reach our breakeven point in two months
3. Have sales of $100,000 in the first six months

In order to achieve our first short term goal we must:

1. Sign the lease by July 1, 1994
2. Order a complete inventory by August 1, 1994

In order to achieve our second short term goal we must:

1. Advertise extensively in Sept. and Oct.
2. Keep expenses to a minimum

In order to achieve our third short term goal we must:

1. Promote power tool sales for the Christmas season
2. Keep good customer traffic in Jan. and Feb.

The long term goals for our business are:

1. Obtain sales volume of $600,000 in three years
2. Become the largest hardware dealer in the city
3. Open a second store in Fond du Lac

The most important thing we must do in order to achieve the long term goals for our business is to develop a highly profitable business with excellent cash flow.

FINANCE

Oshkosh Hardware, Inc., faces some potential threats or risks to our business. They are discount house competition. We believe we can avoid or compensate for this by providing quality products complimented by quality advice on the use of every product we sell. The financial projections we have prepared are located at the end of this document.

JOB DESCRIPTION: GENERAL MANAGER

The General Manager of the business of the corporation will be the president of the corporation. He will be responsible for the complete operation of the retail hardware store which is owned by the corporation. A detailed description of his duties and responsibilities is as follows:

Train and supervise the three sales people. Develop programs to motivate and compensate these employees. Coordinate advertising and sales promotion effects to achieve sales totals as outlined in budget. Oversee purchasing function and inventory control procedures to insure adequate merchandise at all times at a reasonable cost.

Sales
Finance

Prepare monthly and annual budgets. Secure adequate line of credit from local banks. Supervise office personnel to insure timely preparation of records, statements, all government reports, control of receivables and payables, and monthly financial statements.

Administration

Perform duties as required in the areas of personnel, building leasing and maintenance, licenses and permits, and public relations.

QUARTERLY FORECASTED BALANCE SHEETS

	Beg. Bal.	1st Qtr	2nd Qtr	3rd Qtr	4th Qtr
Assets					
Cash	30,000	418	(463)	(3,574)	4,781
Accounts Receivable	0	20,000	13,333	33,333	33,333
Inventory	0	48,000	32,000	80,000	80,000
Other Current Assets	0	0	0	0	0
Total Current Assets	30,000	68,418	44,870	109,759	118,114
Land	0	0	0	0	0
Building & Improvements	0	0	0	0	0
Furniture & Equipment	0	75,000	75,000	75,000	75,000
Total Fixed Assets	0	75,000	75,000	75,000	75,000
Less Accum. Depreciation	0	1,875	3,750	5,625	7,500
Net Fixed Assets	0	73,125	71,250	69,375	67,500
Intangible Assets	0	0	0	0	0
Less Amortization	0	0	0	0	0
Net Intangible Assets	0	0	0	0	0
Other Assets	0	0	0	0	0
Total Assets	**30,000**	**141,543**	**116,120**	**179,134**	**185,614**

	Beg. Bal.	1st Qtr	2nd Qtr	3rd Qtr	4th Qtr
Liabilities and Shareholders' Equity					
Short-Term Debt	0	0	0	0	0
Accounts Payable	0	12,721	10,543	17,077	17,077
Dividends Payable	0	0	0	0	0
Income Taxes Payable	0	(1,031)	(2,867)	(2,355)	(1,843)
Accrued Compensation	0	1,867	1,867	1,867	1,867
Other Current Liabilities	0	0	0	0	0
Total Current Liabilities	0	13,557	9,543	16,589	17,101
Long-Term Debt	0	110,000	110,000	160,000	160,000
Other Non-Current Liabilities	0	0	0	0	0
Total Liabilities	0	123,557	119,543	176,589	177,101
Common Stock	30,000	30,000	30,000	30,000	30,000
Retained Earnings	0	(12,014)	(33,423)	(27,455)	(21,487)
Shareholders' Equity	30,000	17,986	(3,423)	2,545	8,513
Total Liabilities & Shareholders' Equity	30,000	141,543	116,120	179,134	185,614

	Beg. Actual	1st Qtr	2nd Qtr	3rd Qtr	4th Qtr	Total
Total Sales	0	60,000	40,000	100,000	100,000	300,000
Goods/Services	0	21,600	14,400	36,000	36,000	108,000
Gross Profit	0	38,400	25,600	64,000	64,000	192,000
Operating Expenses	0	47,645	45,045	52,845	52,845	198,380
Fixed Expenses						
Interest	0	1,925	1,925	2,800	2,800	9,450
Depreciation	0	1,875	1,875	1,875	1,875	7,500
Amortization	0	0	0	0	0	0
Total Fixed Expenses	0	3,800	3,800	4,675	4,675	16,950
Operating Profit (Loss)	0	(13,045)	(23,245)	6,480	6,480	(23,330)

QUARTERLY FORECASTED STATEMENTS OF EARNINGS AND RETAINED EARNINGS

	Beg. Actual	1st Qtr	2nd Qtr	3rd Qtr	4th Qtr	Total
Other Income (Expense)	0	0	0	0	0	0
Interest Income	0	0	0	0	0	0
Earnings (Loss) Before Taxes	0	(13,045)	(23,245)	6,480	6,480	(23,330)
Income Taxes	0	(1,031)	(1,836)	512	512	(1,843)
Net Earnings	0	(12,014)	(21,409)	5,968	5,968	(21,487)
Retained Earnings, Beginning	0	0	(12,014)	(33,423)	(27,455)	0
Less Dividends	0	0	0	0	0	0
Retained Earnings, Ending	0	(12,014)	(33,423)	(27,455)	(21,487)	(21,487)

QUARTERLY FORECASTED STATEMENTS OF CHANGES IN FINANCIAL POSITION

	Beg. Bal.	1st Qtr	2nd Qtr	3rd Qtr	4th Qtr	Total
Sources (Uses) of Cash						
Net Earnings (Loss)	0	(12,014)	(21,409)	5,968	5,968	(21,487)
Depreciation & Amortization	0	1,875	1,875	1,875	1,875	7,500
Cash Provided by Operations	0	(10,139)	(19,534)	7,834	7,834	(13,987)
Dividends	0	0	0	0	0	0
Cash Provided by (Used For) Changes in						
Accounts Receivable	0	(20,000)	6,667	(20,000)	0	(33,333)
Inventory	0	(48,000)	16,000	(48,000)	0	(80,000)
Other Current Assets	0	0	0	0	0	0
Accounts Payable	0	12,	721	(2,178)	6,534 0	17,077
Income Taxes	0	(1,031)	(1,836)	512	512	(1,843)
Accrued Compensation	0	1,867	0	0	0	1,867
Dividends Payable	0	0	0	0	0	0
Other Current Liabilities	0	0	0	0	0	0

	Beg. Bal.	1st Qtr	2nd Qtr	3rd Qtr	4th Qtr	Total
Other Assets	0	0	0	0	0	0
Net Cash Provided by (Used For)						
Operating Activities	0	(54,443)	18,653	(60,954)	512	(96,233)
Investment Transactions						
Furniture & Equipment	0	(75,000)	0	0	0	(75,000)
Land	0	0	0	0	0	0
Building & Improvements	0	0	0	0	0	0
Intangible Assets	0	0	0	0	0	0
Net Cash from Investment Transactions	0	(75,000)	0	0	0	(75,000)
Financing Transactions						
Short-Term Debt	0	0	0	0	0	0
Long-Term Debt	0	110,000	0	50,000	0	160,000
Other Non-Current Liabilities	0	0	0	0	0	0
Sale of Common Stock	30,000	0	0	0	0	0
Net Cash from Financing Transactions	30,000	110,000	0	50,000	0	160,000
Net Increase (Decrease) in Cash	30,000	(29,582)	(881)	(3,111)	8,355	(25,219)
Cash, Beginning of Period	0	30,000	418	(463)	(3,574)	30,000
Cash, End of Period	30,000	418	(463)	(3,574)	4,781	4,781

**FINANCIAL
RATIO ANALYSIS**

	Beg. Actual	1st Qtr	2nd Qtr	3rd Qtr	4th Qtr
Overall Performance					
Return on Equity	0.00	(66.80)	625.45	234.50	70.10
Return on Total Assets	0.00	(8.49)	(18.44)	3.33	3.22
Operating Return	0.00	(9.22)	(20.02)	3.62	3.49
Profitability Measures					
Gross Profit Percent	0.00	64.00	64.00	64.00	64.00
Profit Margin (AIT)	0.00	(20.02)	(53.52)	5.97	5.97
Operating Income per Share	0.00	0.00	0.00	0.00	0.00
Earnings per Share	0.00	0.00	0.00	0.00	0.00
Test of Investment Utilization					
Asset Turnover	0.00	0.42	0.34	0.56	0.54
Equity Turnover	0.00	3.34	(11.69)	39.29	11.75
Fixed Asset Turnover	0.00	0.82	0.56	1.44	1.48
Average Collection Period	0.00	30.00	30.00	30.00	30.00
Days Inventory	0.00	200.00	200.00	200.00	200.00
Inventory Turnover	0.00	0.45	0.45	0.45	0.45
Working Capital Turns	0.00	1.09	1.13	1.07	0.99
Test of Financial Condition					
Current Ratio	0.00	5.05	4.70	6.62	6.91
Quick Ratio	0.00	1.51	1.35	1.79	2.23
Working Capital Ratio	1.00	0.43	0.33	0.57	0.60
Dividend Payout	0.00	0.00	0.00	0.00	0.00
Financial Leverage					
Total Assets	1.00	7.87	(33.92)	70.39	21.80

	Beg. Actual	1st Qtr	2nd Qtr	3rd Qtr	4th Qtr
Debt/Equity	0.00	6.87	(34.92)	69.39	20.80
Debt to Total Assets	0.00	0.87	1.03	0.99	0.95

Year-End Equity History

	Beg. Actual	1st Qtr	2nd Qtr	3rd Qtr	4th Qtr
Shares Outstanding	0	0	0	0	0
Market Price per Share (@20x's earnings)	0.00	0.00	0.00	0.00	0.00
Book Value per Share	0.00	0.00	0.00	0.00	0.00

Altman Analysis Ratio

	Beg. Actual	1st Qtr	2nd Qtr	3rd Qtr	4th Qtr
1.2x (1)	1.20	0.47	0.37	0.62	0.65
1.4x (2)	0.00	(0.12)	(0.40)	(0.21)	(0.16)
3.3x (3)	0.00	(0.35)	(0.72)	0.07	0.07
0.6x (4)	0.00	0.00	0.00	0.00	0.00
1.0x (5)	0.00	0.42	0.34	0.56	0.54
Z Value	1.20	.042	(.041)	1.04	1.10

DETAILS FOR QUARTERLY STATEMENTS OF EARNINGS

Sales

Dollars Sales Forecasted

	Beg. Act.	1st Qtr	2nd Qtr	3rd Qtr	4th Qtr	Total	%Sales	Fixed
Product 1	0	60,000	40,000	100,000	100,000	300,000		
Product 2	0	0	0	0	0	0		
Product 3	0	0	0	0	0	0		
Product 4	0	0	0	0	0	0		
Product 5	0	0	0	0	0	0		
Product 6	0	0	0	0	0	0		
Total Sales	0	60,000	40,000	100,000	100,000	300,000		

**DETAILS FOR
QUARTERLY
STATEMENTS OF
EARNINGS**

...continued

	Beg. Act.	1st Qtr	2nd Qtr	3rd Qtr	4th Qtr	Total	%Sales	Fixed
Cost of Sales								
Dollar Cost Forecasted								
Product 1	0	21,600	14,400	36,000	36,000	108,000	36.00%	0
Product 2	0	0	0	0	0	0	0.00%	0
Product 3	0	0	0	0	0	0	0.00%	0
Product 4	0	0	0	0	0	0	0.00%	0
Product 5	0	0	0	0	0	0	0.00%	0
Product 6	0	0	0	0	0	0	0.00%	0
Total Cost of Sales	0	21,600	14,400	36,000	36,000	108,000		
Operating Expenses								
Payroll	0	12,000	12,000	12,000	12,000	48,000	0.00%	12,000
Paroll Taxes	0	950	950	950	950	3,800	0.00%	950
Advertising	0	4,800	3,200	8,000	8,000	24,000	8.00%	0
Automobile Expenses	0	0	0	0	0		0.00%	0
Bad Debts	0	0	0	0	0	0	0.00%	0
Commissions	0	3,000	2,000	5,000	5,000	15,000	5.00%	0
Computer Rental	0	1,200	1,200	1,200	1,200	4,800	0.00%	1,200
Computer Supplies	0	220	220	220	220	880	0.00%	220
Computer Maintenance	0	100	100	100	100	400	0.00%	100
Dealer Training	0	1,000	1,000	1,000	1,000	4,000	0.00%	1,000
Electricity	0	3,000	3,000	3,000	3,000	12,000	0.00%	3,000
Employment Ads and Fees	0	0	0	0	0	0	0.00%	0
Entertainment: Business	0	1,500	1,500	1,500	1,500	6,000	0.00%	1,500
General Insurance	0	800	800	800	800	32,000	0.00%	800
Health & W/C Insurance	0	0	0	0	0	0	0.00%	0
Interest: LT Debt	0	2,500	2,500	2,500	2,500	10,000	0.00%	2,500
Legal & Accounting	0	1,500	1,500	1,500	1,500	6,000	0.00%	1,500
Maintenance & Repairs	0	460	460	460	460	1,840	0.00%	460

	Beg. Act.	1st Qtr	2nd Qtr	3rd Qtr	4th Qtr	Total	%Sales	Fixed
Office Supplies	0	270	270	270	270	1,080	0.00%	270
Postage	0	85	85	85	85	340	0.00%	85
Prof. Development	0	0	0	0	0	0	0.00%	0
Professional Fees	0	1,000	1,000	1,000	1,000	4,000	0.00%	1,000
Rent	0	8,000	8,000	8,000	8,000	2,000	0.00%	8,000
Shows & Conferences	0	0	0	0	0	0	0.00%	0
Subscriptions & Dues	0	285	285	285	285	1,140	0.00%	285
Telephone	0	1,225	1,225	1,225	1,225	4,900	0.00%	1,225
Temporary Employees	0	0	0	0	0	0	0.00%	0
Travel Expenses	0	750	750	750	750	3,000	0.00%	750
Utilities	0	3,000	3,000	3,000	3,000	12,000	0.00%	3,000
Research & Development	0	0	0	0	0	0	0.00%	0
Royalties	0	0	0	0	0	0	0.00%	0
Other 1	0	0	0	0	0	0	0.00%	0
Other 2	0	0	0	0	0	0	0.00%	0
Other 3	0	0	0	0	0	0	0.00%	0
Total Operating Expenses	0	47,645	45,045	52,845	52,845	198,380		
Percent of Sales	0.00%	79.41	112.61	52.85	52.85	66.13		

DETAILS FOR QUARTERLY STATEMENT OF EARNINGS
...continued

BUSINESS PLAN TEMPLATE

Appendix B -
Organizations, Agencies,
and Consultants

Organizations, Agencies, & Consultants

A listing of Associations and Consultants of interest to entrepreneurs, followed by the 10 Small Business Administration Regional Offices, Small Business Development Centers, Service Corps of Retired Executives offices, and Venture Capital & Finance companies.

ASSOCIATIONS

This section contains a listing of associations and other agencies of interest to the small business owner. Entries are listed alphabetically by organization name.

American Association for Consumer
Benefits
PO Box 100279
Ft. Worth, TX 76185
Free: (800)872-8896
Fax: (817)377-5633
E-mail: AACB_Assoc@yahoo.com
Jerry Clark, Contact

American Association of Family
Businesses
PO Box 547217
Surfside, FL 33154
Phone: (305)864-1184
Fax: (305)864-1187
Craig Gordon, Pres.

American Small Businesses
Association
8773 IL Rte. 75E.
Rock City, IL 61070
Free: (800)942-2722
E-mail: gavazzi.1@osu.edu
Website: http://www.asbaonline.org/
Vernon Castle, Exec. Dir.

American Society of Independent
Business
c/o Keith Wood
777 Main St., Ste. 1600
Fort Worth, TX 76102
Phone: (817)870-1880
Keith Wood, Pres.

American Women's Economic
Development Corporation
216 East 45th St.
New York, NY 10017
Phone: (917)368-6120

Fax: (212)786-7114
E-mail: info@awed.org
Website: http://www.awed.org
Suzanne Israel Tufts, Pres. & CEO

Association for Enterprise
Opportunity
70 E Lake St., Ste. 1120
Chicago, IL 60601
Phone: (312)357-0177
Fax: (312)357-0180
E-mail: aeochicago@ad.com
Christine M. Benuzzi, Exec. Dir.

Association of Small Business
Development Centers
c/o Don Wilson
8990 Burke Lake Rd.
Burke, VA 22015
Phone: (703)764-9850
Fax: (703)764-1234
E-mail: don@asbdc-us.org
Website: http://www.asbdc-us.org
Don Wilson, Pres.

BEST Employers Association
2505 McCabe Way
Irvine, CA 92614
Phone: (714)756-1000
Free: (800)433-0088
Fax: (714)553-0883
Donald R. Lawrenz, Exec. Sec.

Business Market Association
4131 N. Central Expy., Ste. 720
Dallas, TX 75204
R. Mark King, Pres.

Coalition of Americans to Save the
Economy
1100 Connecticut Ave. NW, Ste.
1200
Washington, DC 20036-4101
Phone: (202)293-1414
Fax: (202)293-1702
Barry Maloney, Treas.

Employers of America
520 S Pierce, Ste. 224
Mason City, IA 50401
Phone: (641)424-3187
Free: (800)728-3187
Fax: (641)424-1673
E-mail: employer@employerhelp.org
Website: http://
www.employerhelp.org
Jim Collison, Pres.

Family Firm Institute
221 N. Beacon St.
Boston, MA 02135-1943
Phone: (617)789-4200
Fax: (617)789-4220
E-mail: ffi@ffi.org
Website: http://www.ffi.org
Judy L. Green, Ph.D., Exec. Dir.

Group Purchasing Association
Plaza Tower, 35th Fl.
1001 Howard Ave.
New Orleans, LA 70113-2002
Phone: (504)529-2030
Fax: (504)558-0929
E-mail: lenn@firstgpa.com

Independent Business Alliance
111 John St.
New York, NY 10038
Free: (800)559-2580
Fax: (212)285-1639
Robert J. Levine, CEO

International Association of Business
701 Highlander Blvd., Ste. 500
Arlington, TX 76015-4332
Paula Rainey, Pres.

International Association for Business
Organizations
PO Box 30149
Baltimore, MD 21270
Phone: (410)581-1373
Rudolph Lewis, Exec. Officer

International Council for Small Business
c/o Jefferson Smurfit Center for Entrepreneurial Studies
St. Louis University
3674 Lindell Blvd.
St. Louis, MO 63108
Phone: (314)977-3628
Fax: (314)977-3627
E-mail: icsb@slu.edu
Website: http://www.icsb.org
Sharon Bower, Sec.

National Alliance for Fair Competition
3 Bethesda Metro Center, Ste. 1100
Bethesda, MD 20814
Phone: (410)235-7116
Fax: (410)235-7116
E-mail: ampesq@aol.com
Tony Ponticelli, Exec. Dir.

National Association of Business Leaders
PO Box 766
Bridgeton, MO 63044
Phone: (314)344-1111
Fax: (314)298-9110
E-mail: nabl@nabl.com
Website: http://www.nabl.com/
John Weigel, Contact

National Association for Business Organizations
PO Box 30220
Baltimore, MD 21270
Phone: (410)581-1373
Website: http://www.ameribiz.com/quicklink.htm
Rudolph Lewis, Pres.

National Association of Government Guaranteed Lenders
c/o Tony Wilkinson
PO Box 332
Stillwater, OK 74076
Phone: (405)377-4022
Fax: (405)377-3931
E-mail: twilkinson@naggl.com
Website: http://www.naggl.com/
Tony Wilkinson, Pres./CEO

National Association of Private Enterprise
7819 Shelburne Cir.
Spring, TX 77379-4687
Phone: (281)655-5412
Free: (800)223-6273
Fax: (281)257-3244

E-mail: info@nape.org
Laura Squiers, Exec. Dir.

National Association for the Self-Employed
PO Box 612067
DFW Airport
Dallas, TX 75261-2067
Free: (800)232-NASE
Fax: 800-551-4446
Website: http://www.nase.org
Robert Hughes, Pres.

National Association of Small Business Investment Companies
666 11th St. NW, No. 750
Washington, DC 20001
Phone: (202)628-5055
Fax: (202)628-5080
E-mail: nasbic@nasbic.org
Website: http://www.nasbic.org
Lee W. Mercer, Pres.

National Business Association
PO Box 700728
Dallas, TX 75370
Phone: (972)458-0900
Free: (800)456-0440
Fax: (972)960-9149
E-mail: p.archibald@nationalbusiness.org
Website: http://www.nationalbusiness.org
Pat Archibald, Pres.

National Business Owners Association
820 Gibbon St. Ste. 204
Alexandria, VA 22314
Phone: (202)737-6501
Free: (888)755-NBOA
Fax: (877)626-2329
E-mail: govaffairs@nboa.org
Thomas Rumfelt, Chm.

National Center for Fair Competition
8421 Frost Way
Annandale, VA 22003
Phone: (703)280-4622
Fax: (703)280-0942
E-mail: kentonp1@aol.com
Kenton Pattie, Pres.

National Federation of Independent Business
53 Century Blvd., Ste. 300
Nashville, TN 37214
Phone: (615)872-5800
Free: (800)NFIBNOW

Fax: (615)872-5353
Website: http://www.nfib.org
Jack Faris, Pres. and CEO

National Small Business Benefits Association
2244 N. Grand Ave. E.
Springfield, IL 62702
Phone: (217)753-2558
Fax: (217)753-2558
Les Brewer, Exec.VP

National Small Business United
1156 15th St. NW, Ste. 1100
Washington, DC 20005
Phone: (202)293-8830
Free: (800)345-6728
Fax: (202)872-8543
E-mail: nsbu@nsbu.org
Website: http://www.nsbu.org
Todd McCraken, Pres.

Network of Small Businesses
5420 Mayfield Rd., Ste. 205
Lyndhurst, OH 44124
Phone: (216)442-5600
Fax: (216)449-3227
Irwin Friedman, Chm.

Research Institute for Small and Emerging Business
722 12th St. NW
Washington, DC 20005
Phone: (202)628-8382
Fax: (202)628-8392
E-mail: info@riseb.org
Website: http://www.riseb.org
Mark Schultz, CEO/Pres.

Score Association - Service Corps of Retired Executives
c/o Service Corps of Retired Executives Association
409 3rd St. SW, 6th Fl.
Washington, DC 20024
Phone: (202)205-6762
Free: (800)634-0245
Fax: (202)205-7636
Website: http://www.score.org
W. Kenneth Yancey, Jr., CEO

Small Business Legislative Council
1010 Massachusetts Ave. NW
Washington, DC 20001
Phone: (202)639-8500
Fax: (202)296-5333
Website: http://www.sblc.org
John Satagaj, Pres.

Small Business Network
PO Box 30149
Baltimore, MD 21270
Phone: (410)581-1373
E-mail: natibb@ix.netcom.com
Rudolph Lewis, CEO

Small Business Service Bureau
554 Main St.
PO Box 15014
Worcester, MA 01608-0014
Phone: (508)756-3513
Free: (800)343-0939
Fax: (508)770-0528
E-mail: membership@sbsb.com
Website: http://www.sbsb.com
Francis R. Carroll, Pres.

Small Business Support Center
Association
c/o James S. Ryan
8811 Westheimer Rd., No. 210
Houston, TX 77063-3617
James S. Ryan, Admin.

Small Business Survival Committee
1920 L St., NW, Ste. 200
Washington, DC 20036
Phone: (202)785-0238
Fax: (202)822-8118
E-mail: membership@sbsc.org
Website: http://www.sbsc.org
Christopher Wysocki, Pres.

Support Services Alliance
PO Box 130
Schoharie, NY 12157-0130
Phone: (518)295-7966
Free: (800)836-4772
Fax: (518)295-8556
E-mail: comments@ssainfo.com
Website: http://www.ssainfo.com
Gary Swan, Pres.

CONSULTANTS

*This section contains a listing of consult-
ants specializing in small business
development. It is arranged alphabetically
by country, then by state or province, then
by city, then by firm name.*

CANADA

Alberta

Common Sense Solutions
3405 16A Ave.

Edmonton, AB, Canada
Phone: (403)465-7330
Fax: (403)465-7380
E-mail:
gcoulson@comsensesolutions.com
Website: http://
www.comsensesolutions.com

Varsity Consulting Group
School of Business
University of Alberta
Edmonton, AB, Canada T6G 2R6
Phone: (780)492-2994
Fax: (780)492-5400
Website: http://www.bus.ualberta.ca/
vcg

Viro Hospital Consulting
42 Commonwealth Bldg., 9912 - 106
St. NW
Edmonton, AB, Canada T5K 1C5
Phone: (403)425-3871
Fax: (403)425-3871
E-mail: rpb@freenet.edmonton.ab.ca

British Columbia

SRI Strategic Resources Inc.
4330 Kingsway, Ste. 1600
Burnaby, BC, Canada V5H 4G7
Phone: (604)435-0627
Fax: (604)435-2782
E-mail: inquiry@sri.bc.ca
Website: http://www.sri.com

Andrew R. De Boda Consulting
1523 Milford Ave.
Coquitlam, BC, Canada V3J 2V9
Phone: (604)936-4527
Fax: (604)936-4527
E-mail: deboda@intergate.bc.ca
Website: http://
www.ourworld.compuserve.com/
homepages/deboda

The Sage Group Ltd.
980 - 355 Burrard St.
744 W Haistings, Ste. 410
Vancouver, BC, Canada V6C 1A5
Phone: (604)669-9269
Fax: (604)669-6622

Tikkanen-Bradley
1345 Nelson St., Ste. 202
Vancouver, BC, Canada V6E 1J8
Phone: (604)669-0583
E-mail:
webmaster@tikkanenbradley.com

Website: http://
www.tikkanenbradley.com

Ontario

The Cynton Co.
17 Massey St.
Brampton, ON, Canada L6S 2V6
Phone: (905)792-7769
Fax: (905)792-8116
E-mail: cynton@home.com
Website: http://www.cynton.com

Begley & Associates
RR 6
Cambridge, ON, Canada N1R 5S7
Phone: (519)740-3629
Fax: (519)740-3629
E-mail: begley@in.on.ca
Website: http://www.in.on.ca/
~begley/index.htm

CRO Engineering Ltd.
1895 William Hodgins Ln.
Carp, ON, Canada K0A 1L0
Phone: (613)839-1108
Fax: (613)839-1406
E-mail: J.Grefford@ieee.ca
Website: http://www.geocities.com/
WallStreet/District/7401/

Task Enterprises
Box 69, RR 2 Hamilton
Flamborough, ON, Canada L8N 2Z7
Phone: (905)659-0153
Fax: (905)659-0861

HST Group Ltd.
430 Gilmour St.
Ottawa, ON, Canada K2P 0R8
Phone: (613)236-7303
Fax: (613)236-9893

Harrison Associates
BCE Pl.
181 Bay St., Ste. 3740
PO Box 798
Toronto, ON, Canada M5J 2T3
Phone: (416)364-5441
Fax: (416)364-2875

TCI Convergence Ltd. Management
Consultants
99 Crown's Ln.
Toronto, ON, Canada M5R 3P4
Phone: (416)515-4146
Fax: (416)515-2097
E-mail: tci@inforamp.net
Website: http://tciconverge.com/
index.1.html

Ken Wyman & Associates Inc.
64B Shuter St., Ste. 200
Toronto, ON, Canada M5B 1B1
Phone: (416)362-2926
Fax: (416)362-3039
E-mail:
kenwyman@compuserve.com

JPL Business Consultants
82705 Metter Rd.
Wellandport, ON, Canada L0R 2J0
Phone: (905)386-7450
Fax: (905)386-7450
E-mail:
plamarch@freenet.npiec.on.ca

Quebec

The Zimmar Consulting Partnership
Inc.
Westmount
PO Box 98
Montreal, QC, Canada H3Z 2T1
Phone: (514)484-1459
Fax: (514)484-3063

Saskatchewan

Trimension Group
No. 104-110 Research Dr.
Innovation Place, SK, Canada S7N
3R3
Phone: (306)668-2560
Fax: (306)975-1156
E-mail: trimension@trimension.ca
Website: http://www.trimension.ca

UNITED STATES

Alabama

Business Planning Inc.
300 Office Park Dr.
Birmingham, AL 35223-2474
Phone: (205)870-7090
Fax: (205)870-7103

Tradebank of Eastern Alabama
546 Broad St., Ste. 3
Gadsden, AL 35901
Phone: (205)547-8700
Fax: (205)547-8718
E-mail: mansion@webex.com
Website: http://www.webex.com/~tea

Alaska

AK Business Development Center
3335 Arctic Blvd., Ste. 203
Anchorage, AK 99503
Phone: (907)562-0335
Free: (800)478-3474
Fax: (907)562-6988
E-mail: abdc@gci.net
Website: http://www.abdc.org

Business Matters
PO Box 287
Fairbanks, AK 99707
Phone: (907)452-5650

Arizona

Carefree Direct Marketing Corp.
8001 E Serene St.
PO Box 3737
Carefree, AZ 85377-3737
Phone: (480)488-4227
Fax: (480)488-2841

Trans Energy Corp.
1739 W 7th Ave.
Mesa, AZ 85202
Phone: (480)827-7915
Fax: (480)967-6601
E-mail: aha@clean-air.org
Website: http://www.clean-air.org

CMAS
5125 N 16th St.
Phoenix, AZ 85016
Phone: (602)395-1001
Fax: (602)604-8180

Comgate Telemanagement Ltd.
706 E Bell Rd., Ste. 105
Phoenix, AZ 85022
Phone: (602)485-5708
Fax: (602)485-5709
E-mail: comgate@netzone.com
Website: http://www.comgate.com

Moneysoft Inc.
1 E Camelback Rd. #550
Phoenix, AZ 85012
Free: (800)966-7797
E-mail: mbray@moneysoft.com

Harvey C. Skoog
PO Box 26439
Prescott Valley, AZ 86312
Phone: (520)772-1714
Fax: (520)772-2814

LMC Services
8711 E Pinnacle Peak Rd., No. 340
Scottsdale, AZ 85255-3555
Phone: (602)585-7177
Fax: (602)585-5880
E-mail: louws@earthlink.com

Sauerbrun Technology Group Ltd.
7979 E Princess Dr., Ste. 5
Scottsdale, AZ 85255-5878
Phone: (602)502-4950
Fax: (602)502-4292
E-mail: info@sauerbrun.com
Website: http://www.sauerbrun.com

Gary L. McLeod
PO Box 230
Sonoita, AZ 85637
Fax: (602)455-5661

Van Cleve Associates
6932 E 2nd St.
Tucson, AZ 85710
Phone: (520)296-2587
Fax: (520)296-3358

California

Acumen Group Inc.
Phone: (650)949-9349
Fax: (650)949-4845
E-mail: acumen-g@ix.netcom.com
Website: http://pw2.netcom.com/
~janed/acumen.html

On-line Career and Management
Consulting
420 Central Ave., No. 314
Alameda, CA 94501
Phone: (510)864-0336
Fax: (510)864-0336
E-mail: career@dnai.com
Website: http://www.dnai.com/
~career

Career Paths-Thomas E. Church &
Associates Inc.
PO Box 2439
Aptos, CA 95001
Phone: (408)662-7950
Fax: (408)662-7955
E-mail: church@ix.netcom.com
Website: http://www.careerpaths-
tom.com

Keck & Co. Business Consultants
410 Walsh Rd.
Atherton, CA 94027
Phone: (650)854-9588

Fax: (650)854-7240
E-mail: info@keckco.com
Website: http://www.keckco.com

Ben W. Laverty III, PhD, REA, CEI
4909 Stockdale Hwy., Ste. 132
Bakersfield, CA 93309
Phone: (661)283-8300
Free: (800)833-0373
Fax: (661)283-8313
E-mail: cstc@cstcsafety.com
Website: http://www.cstcsafety.com/
cstc

Lindquist Consultants-Venture
Planning
225 Arlington Ave.
Berkeley, CA 94707
Phone: (510)524-6685
Fax: (510)527-6604

Larson Associates
PO Box 9005
Brea, CA 92822
Phone: (714)529-4121
Fax: (714)572-3606
E-mail: ray@consultlarson.com
Website: http://
www.consultlarson.com

Kremer Management Consulting
PO Box 500
Carmel, CA 93921
Phone: (408)626-8311
Fax: (408)624-2663
E-mail: ddkremer@aol.com

W and J PARTNERSHIP
PO Box 2499
18876 Edwin Markham Dr.
Castro Valley, CA 94546
Phone: (510)583-7751
Fax: (510)583-7645
E-mail:
wamorgan@wjpartnership.com
Website: http://
www.wjpartnership.com

JB Associates
21118 Gardena Dr.
Cupertino, CA 95014
Phone: (408)257-0214
Fax: (408)257-0216
E-mail: semarang@sirius.com

House Agricultural Consultants
PO Box 1615
Davis, CA 95617-1615
Phone: (916)753-3361

Fax: (916)753-0464
E-mail: infoag@houseag.com
Website: http://www.houseag.com/

3C Systems Co.
16161 Ventura Blvd., Ste. 815
Encino, CA 91436
Phone: (818)907-1302
Fax: (818)907-1357
E-mail: mark@3CSysCo.com
Website: http://www.3CSysCo.com

Technical Management Consultants
3624 Westfall Dr.
Encino, CA 91436-4154
Phone: (818)784-0626
Fax: (818)501-5575
E-mail: tmcrs@aol.com

RAINWATER-GISH & Associates,
Business Finance & Development
317 3rd St., Ste. 3
Eureka, CA 95501
Phone: (707)443-0030
Fax: (707)443-5683

Global Tradelinks
451 Pebble Beach Pl.
Fullerton, CA 92835
Phone: (714)441-2280
Fax: (714)441-2281
E-mail: info@globaltradelinks.com
Website: http://
www.globaltradelinks.com

Strategic Business Group
800 Cienaga Dr.
Fullerton, CA 92835-1248
Phone: (714)449-1040
Fax: (714)525-1631

Burnes Consulting
20537 Wolf Creek Rd.
Grass Valley, CA 95949
Phone: (530)346-8188
Free: (800)949-9021
Fax: (530)346-7704
E-mail: kent@burnesconsulting.com
Website: http://
www.burnesconsulting.com

Pioneer Business Consultants
9042 Garfield Ave., Ste. 312
Huntington Beach, CA 92646
Phone: (714)964-7600

Beblie, Brandt & Jacobs Inc.
16 Technology, Ste. 164
Irvine, CA 92618
Phone: (714)450-8790

Fax: (714)450-8799
E-mail: darcy@bbjinc.com
Website: http://198.147.90.26

Fluor Daniel Inc.
3353 Michelson Dr.
Irvine, CA 92612-0650
Phone: (949)975-2000
Fax: (949)975-5271
E-mail:
sales.consulting@fluordaniel.com
Website: http://
www.fluordanielconsulting.com

MCS Associates
18300 Von Karman, Ste. 710
Irvine, CA 92612
Phone: (949)263-8700
Fax: (949)263-0770
E-mail: info@mcsassociates.com
Website: http://
www.mcsassociates.com

Inspired Arts Inc.
4225 Executive Sq., Ste. 1160
La Jolla, CA 92037
Phone: (619)623-3525
Free: (800)851-4394
Fax: (619)623-3534
E-mail: info@inspiredarts.com
Website: http://www.inspiredarts.com

The Laresis Companies
PO Box 3284
La Jolla, CA 92038
Phone: (619)452-2720
Fax: (619)452-8744

RCL & Co.
PO Box 1143
737 Pearl St., Ste. 201
La Jolla, CA 92038
Phone: (619)454-8883
Fax: (619)454-8880

Comprehensive Business Services
3201 Lucas Cir.
Lafayette, CA 94549
Phone: (925)283-8272
Fax: (925)283-8272

The Ribble Group
27601 Forbes Rd., Ste. 52
Laguna Niguel, CA 92677
Phone: (714)582-1085
Fax: (714)582-6420
E-mail: ribble@deltanet.com

Norris Bernstein, CMC
9309 Marina Pacifica Dr. N

Long Beach, CA 90803
Phone: (562)493-5458
Fax: (562)493-5459
E-mail: norris@ctecomputer.com
Website: http://foodconsultants.com/
bernstein/

Horizon Consulting Services
1315 Garthwick Dr.
Los Altos, CA 94024
Phone: (415)967-0906
Fax: (415)967-0906

Brincko Associates Inc.
1801 Avenue of the Stars, Ste. 1054
Los Angeles, CA 90067
Phone: (310)553-4523
Fax: (310)553-6782

Rubenstein/Justman Management
Consultants
2049 Century Park E, 24th Fl.
Los Angeles, CA 90067
Phone: (310)282-0800
Fax: (310)282-0400
E-mail: info@rjmc.net
Website: http://www.rjmc.net

F.J. Schroeder & Associates
1926 Westholme Ave.
Los Angeles, CA 90025
Phone: (310)470-2655
Fax: (310)470-6378
E-mail: fjsacons@aol.com
Website: http://www.mcninet.com/
GlobalLook/Fjschroe.html

Western Management Associates
5959 W Century Blvd., Ste. 565
Los Angeles, CA 90045-6506
Phone: (310)645-1091
Free: (888)788-6534
Fax: (310)645-1092
E-mail: gene@cfoforrent.com
Website: http://www.cfoforrent.com

Darrell Sell and Associates
Los Gatos, CA 95030
Phone: (408)354-7794
E-mail: darrell@netcom.com

Leslie J. Zambo
3355 Michael Dr.
Marina, CA 93933
Phone: (408)384-7086
Fax: (408)647-4199
E-mail:
104776.1552@compuserve.com

Marketing Services Management
PO Box 1377
Martinez, CA 94553
Phone: (510)370-8527
Fax: (510)370-8527
E-mail: markserve@biotechnet.com

William M. Shine Consulting Service
PO Box 127
Moraga, CA 94556-0127
Phone: (510)376-6516

Palo Alto Management Group Inc.
2672 Bayshore Pky., Ste. 701
Mountain View, CA 94043
Phone: (415)968-4374
Fax: (415)968-4245
E-mail: mburwen@pamg.com

BizplanSource
1048 Irvine Ave., Ste. 621
Newport Beach, CA 92660
Free: 888-253-0974
Fax: 800-859-8254
E-mail: info@bizplansource.com
Website: http://
www.bizplansource.com
Adam Greengrass, President

The Market Connection
4020 Birch St., Ste. 203
Newport Beach, CA 92660
Phone: (714)731-6273
Fax: (714)833-0253

Muller Associates
PO Box 7264
Newport Beach, CA 92658
Phone: (714)646-1169
Fax: (714)646-1169

International Health Resources
PO Box 329
North San Juan, CA 95960-0329
Phone: (530)292-1266
Fax: (530)292-1243
Website: http://
www.futureofhealthcare.com

NEXUS - Consultants to
Management
PO Box 1531
Novato, CA 94948
Phone: (415)897-4400
Fax: (415)898-2252
E-mail: jimnexus@aol.com

Aerospace.Org
PO Box 28831
Oakland, CA 94604-8831

Phone: (510)530-9169
Fax: (510)530-3411
Website: http://www.aerospace.org

Intelequest Corp.
722 Gailen Ave.
Palo Alto, CA 94303
Phone: (415)968-3443
Fax: (415)493-6954
E-mail: frits@iqix.com

McLaughlin & Associates
66 San Marino Cir.
Rancho Mirage, CA 92270
Phone: (760)321-2932
Fax: (760)328-2474
E-mail: jackmcla@msn.com

Carrera Consulting Group, a division
of Maximus
2110 21st St., Ste. 400
Sacramento, CA 95818
Phone: (916)456-3300
Fax: (916)456-3306
E-mail:
central@carreraconsulting.com
Website: http://
www.carreraconsulting.com

Bay Area Tax Consultants and
Bayhill Financial Consultants
1150 Bayhill Dr., Ste. 1150
San Bruno, CA 94066-3004
Phone: (415)952-8786
Fax: (415)588-4524
E-mail: baytax@compuserve.com
Website: http://www.baytax.com/

California Business Incubation
Network
101 W Broadway, No. 480
San Diego, CA 92101
Phone: (619)237-0559
Fax: (619)237-0521

G.R. Gordetsky Consultants Inc.
11414 Windy Summit Pl.
San Diego, CA 92127
Phone: (619)487-4939
Fax: (619)487-5587
E-mail: gordet@pacbell.net

Freeman, Sullivan & Co.
131 Steuart St., Ste. 500
San Francisco, CA 94105
Phone: (415)777-0707
Free: (800)777-0737
Fax: (415)777-2420
Website: http://www.fsc-
research.com

Ideas Unlimited
2151 California St., Ste. 7
San Francisco, CA 94115
Phone: (415)931-0641
Fax: (415)931-0880

Russell Miller Inc.
300 Montgomery St., Ste. 900
San Francisco, CA 94104
Phone: (415)956-7474
Fax: (415)398-0620
E-mail: rmi@pacbell.net
Website: http://www.rmisf.com

PKF Consulting
425 California St., Ste. 1650
San Francisco, CA 94104
Phone: (415)421-5378
Fax: (415)956-7708
E-mail: callahan@pkfc.com
Website: http://www.pkfonline.com

Welling & Woodard Inc.
1067 Broadway
San Francisco, CA 94133
Phone: (415)776-4500
Fax: (415)776-5067

Highland Associates
16174 Highland Dr.
San Jose, CA 95127
Phone: (408)272-7008
Fax: (408)272-4040

ORDIS Inc.
6815 Trinidad Dr.
San Jose, CA 95120-2056
Phone: (408)268-3321
Free: (800)446-7347
Fax: (408)268-3582
E-mail: ordis@ordis.com
Website: http://www.ordis.com

Stanford Resources Inc.
20 Great Oaks Blvd., Ste. 200
San Jose, CA 95119
Phone: (408)360-8400
Fax: (408)360-8410
E-mail: sales@stanfordsources.com
Website: http://
www.stanfordresources.com

Technology Properties Ltd. Inc.
PO Box 20250
San Jose, CA 95160
Phone: (408)243-9898
Fax: (408)296-6637
E-mail: sanjose@tplnet.com

Helfert Associates
1777 Borel Pl., Ste. 508
San Mateo, CA 94402-3514
Phone: (650)377-0540
Fax: (650)377-0472

Mykytyn Consulting Group Inc.
185 N Redwood Dr., Ste. 200
San Rafael, CA 94903
Phone: (415)491-1770
Fax: (415)491-1251
E-mail: info@mcgi.com
Website: http://www.mcgi.com

Omega Management Systems Inc.
3 Mount Darwin Ct.
San Rafael, CA 94903-1109
Phone: (415)499-1300
Fax: (415)492-9490
E-mail: omegamgt@ix.netcom.com

The Information Group Inc.
4675 Stevens Creek Blvd., Ste. 100
Santa Clara, CA 95051
Phone: (408)985-7877
Fax: (408)985-2945
E-mail: dvincent@tig-usa.com
Website: http://www.tig-usa.com

Cast Management Consultants
1620 26th St., Ste. 2040N
Santa Monica, CA 90404
Phone: (310)828-7511
Fax: (310)453-6831

Cuma Consulting Management
Box 724
Santa Rosa, CA 95402
Phone: (707)785-2477
Fax: (707)785-2478

The E-Myth Academy
131B Stony Cir., Ste. 2000
Santa Rosa, CA 95401
Phone: (707)569-5600
Free: (800)221-0266
Fax: (707)569-5700
E-mail: info@e-myth.com
Website: http://www.e-myth.com

Reilly, Connors & Ray
1743 Canyon Rd.
Spring Valley, CA 91977
Phone: (619)698-4808
Fax: (619)460-3892
E-mail: davidray@adnc.com

Management Consultants
Sunnyvale, CA 94087-4700
Phone: (408)773-0321

RJR Associates
1639 Lewiston Dr.
Sunnyvale, CA 94087
Phone: (408)737-7720
E-mail: bobroy@rjrassoc.com
Website: http://www.rjrassoc.com

Schwafel Associates
333 Cobalt Way, Ste. 21
Sunnyvale, CA 94085
Phone: (408)720-0649
Fax: (408)720-1796
E-mail: schwafel@ricochet.net
Website: http://www.patca.org

Staubs Business Services
23320 S Vermont Ave.
Torrance, CA 90502-2940
Phone: (310)830-9128
Fax: (310)830-9128
E-mail: Harry_L_Staubs@Lamg.com

Out of Your Mind...and Into the
Marketplace
13381 White Sands Dr.
Tustin, CA 92780-4565
Phone: (714)544-0248
Free: (800)419-1513
Fax: (714)730-1414
E-mail: lpinson@aol.com
Website: http://www.business-
plan.com

Independent Research Services
PO Box 2426
Van Nuys, CA 91404-2426
Phone: (818)993-3622

Ingman Company Inc.
7949 Woodley Ave., Ste. 120
Van Nuys, CA 91406-1232
Phone: (818)375-5027
Fax: (818)894-5001

Innovative Technology Associates
3639 E Harbor Blvd., Ste. 203E
Ventura, CA 93001
Phone: (805)650-9353

Grid Technology Associates
20404 Tufts Cir.
Walnut, CA 91789
Phone: (909)444-0922
Fax: (909)444-0922
E-mail: grid_technology@msn.com

Ridge Consultants Inc.
100 Pringle Ave., Ste. 580
Walnut Creek, CA 94596

Phone: (925)274-1990
Fax: (510)274-1956
E-mail: info@ridgecon.com
Website: http://www.ridgecon.com

Bell Springs Publishing
PO Box 1240
Willits, CA 95490
Phone: (707)459-6372
E-mail: bellsprings@sabernet
Website: http://www.bellsprings.com

Hutchinson Consulting and Appraisal
23245 Sylvan St., Ste. 103
Woodland Hills, CA 91367
Phone: (818)888-8175
Free: (800)977-7548
Fax: (818)888-8220
E-mail: r.f.hutchinson-cpa@worldnet.att.net

Colorado

Sam Boyer & Associates
4255 S Buckley Rd., No. 136
Aurora, CO 80013
Free: (800)785-0485
Fax: (303)766-8740
E-mail: samboyer@samboyer.com
Website: http://www.samboyer.com/

Ameriwest Business Consultants Inc.
PO Box 26266
Colorado Springs, CO 80936
Phone: (719)380-7096
Fax: (719)380-7096
E-mail: email@abchelp.com
Website: http://www.abchelp.com

GVNW Consulting Inc.
2270 La Montana Way
Colorado Springs, CO 80936
Phone: (719)594-5800
Fax: (719)594-5803
Website: http://www.gvnw.com

M-Squared Inc.
755 San Gabriel Pl.
Colorado Springs, CO 80906
Phone: (719)576-2554
Fax: (719)576-2554

Thornton Financial FNIC
1024 Centre Ave., Bldg. E
Fort Collins, CO 80526-1849
Phone: (970)221-2089
Fax: (970)484-5206

TenEyck Associates
1760 Cherryville Rd.

Greenwood Village, CO 80121-1503
Phone: (303)758-6129
Fax: (303)761-8286

Associated Enterprises Ltd.
13050 W Ceder Dr., Unit 11
Lakewood, CO 80228
Phone: (303)988-6695
Fax: (303)988-6739
E-mail: ael1@classic.msn.com

The Vincent Company Inc.
200 Union Blvd., Ste. 210
Lakewood, CO 80228
Phone: (303)989-7271
Free: (800)274-0733
Fax: (303)989-7570
E-mail: vincent@vincentco.com
Website: http://www.vincentco.com

Johnson & West Management
Consultants Inc.
7612 S Logan Dr.
Littleton, CO 80122
Phone: (303)730-2810
Fax: (303)730-3219

Western Capital Holdings Inc.
10050 E Applwood Dr.
Parker, CO 80138
Phone: (303)841-1022
Fax: (303)770-1945

Connecticut

Stratman Group Inc.
40 Tower Ln.
Avon, CT 06001-4222
Phone: (860)677-2898
Free: (800)551-0499
Fax: (860)677-8210

Cowherd Consulting Group Inc.
106 Stephen Mather Rd.
Darien, CT 06820
Phone: (203)655-2150
Fax: (203)655-6427

Greenwich Associates
8 Greenwich Office Park
Greenwich, CT 06831-5149
Phone: (203)629-1200
Fax: (203)629-1229
E-mail: lisa@greenwich.com
Website: http://www.greenwich.com

Follow-up News
185 Pine St., Ste. 818
Manchester, CT 06040
Phone: (860)647-7542

Free: (800)708-0696
Fax: (860)646-6544
E-mail: Followupnews@aol.com

Lovins & Associates Consulting
309 Edwards St.
New Haven, CT 06511
Phone: (203)787-3367
Fax: (203)624-7599
E-mail: Alovinsphd@aol.com
Website: http://www.lovinsgroup.com

JC Ventures Inc.
4 Arnold St.
Old Greenwich, CT 06870-1203
Phone: (203)698-1990
Free: (800)698-1997
Fax: (203)698-2638

Charles L. Hornung Associates
52 Ned's Mountain Rd.
Ridgefield, CT 06877
Phone: (203)431-0297

Manus
100 Prospect St., S Tower
Stamford, CT 06901
Phone: (203)326-3880
Free: (800)445-0942
Fax: (203)326-3890
E-mail: manus1@aol.com
Website: http://www.RightManus.com

Delaware

Focus Marketing
61-7 Habor Dr.
Claymont, DE 19703
Phone: (302)793-3064

Daedalus Ventures Ltd.
PO Box 1474
Hockessin, DE 19707
Phone: (302)239-6758
Fax: (302)239-9991
E-mail: daedalus@mail.del.net

The Formula Group
PO Box 866
Hockessin, DE 19707
Phone: (302)456-0952
Fax: (302)456-1354
E-mail: formula@netaxs.com

Selden Enterprises Inc.
2502 Silverside Rd., Ste. 1
Wilmington, DE 19810-3740
Phone: (302)529-7113

Fax: (302)529-7442
E-mail: selden2@bellatlantic.net
Website: http://
www.seldenenterprises.com

District of Columbia

Bruce W. McGee and Associates
7826 Eastern Ave. NW, Ste. 30
Washington, DC 20012
Phone: (202)726-7272
Fax: (202)726-2946

McManis Associates Inc.
1900 K St. NW, Ste. 700
Washington, DC 20006
Phone: (202)466-7680
Fax: (202)872-1898
Website: http://www.mcmanis-
mmi.com

Smith, Dawson & Andrews Inc.
1000 Connecticut Ave., Ste. 302
Washington, DC 20036
Phone: (202)835-0740
Fax: (202)775-8526
E-mail: webmaster@sda-inc.com
Website: http://www.sda-inc.com

Florida

BackBone, Inc.
20404 Hacienda Court
Boca Raton, FL 33498
Phone: 561-470-0965
Fax: 516-908-4038
E-mail: BPlans@backboneinc.com
Website: http://
www.backboneinc.com
Charles Epstein, President

Whalen & Associates Inc.
4255 Northwest 26 Ct.
Boca Raton, FL 33434
Phone: (561)241-5950
Fax: (561)241-7414
E-mail: drwhalen@ix.netcom.com

E.N. Rysso & Associates
180 Bermuda Petrel Ct.
Daytona Beach, FL 32119
Phone: (386)760-3028
E-mail: erysso@aol.com

Virtual Technocrats LLC
560 Lavers Circle, #146
Delray Beach, FL 33444
Phone: 561-265-3509
Fax: email only

E-mail: josh@virtualtechnocrats.com;
info@virtualtechnocrats.com
Website: http://
www.virtualtechnocrats.com
Josh Eikov, Managing Director

Eric Sands Consulting Services
6193 Rock Island Rd., Ste. 412
Fort Lauderdale, FL 33319
Phone: (954)721-4767
Fax: (954)720-2815
E-mail: easands@aol.com
Website: http://
www.ericsandsconsultig.com

Professional Planning Associates, Inc.
1975 E. Sunrise Blvd. Suite 607
Fort Lauderdale, FL 33304
Phone: 954-764-5204
Fax: 954-463-4172
E-mail: Mgoldstein@proplana.com
Website: http://proplana.com
Michael Goldstein, President

Host Media Corp.
3948 S 3rd St., Ste. 191
Jacksonville Beach, FL 32250
Phone: (904)285-3239
Fax: (904)285-5618
E-mail:
msconsulting@compuserve.com
Website: http://
www.mediaservicesgroup.com

William V. Hall
1925 Brickell, Ste. D-701
Miami, FL 33129
Phone: (305)856-9622
Fax: (305)856-4113
E-mail:
williamvhall@compuserve.com

F.A. McGee Inc.
800 Claughton Island Dr., Ste. 401
Miami, FL 33131
Phone: (305)377-9123

Taxplan Inc.
Mirasol International Ctr.
2699 Collins Ave.
Miami Beach, FL 33140
Phone: (305)538-3303

T.C. Brown & Associates
8415 Excalibur Cir., Apt. B1
Naples, FL 34108
Phone: (941)594-1949
Fax: (941)594-0611
E-mail: tcater@naples.net.com

RLA International Consulting
713 Lagoon Dr.
North Palm Beach, FL 33408
Phone: (407)626-4258
Fax: (407)626-5772

Comprehensive Franchising Inc.
2465 Ridgecrest Ave.
Orange Park, FL 32065
Phone: (904)272-6567
Free: (800)321-6567
Fax: (904)272-6750
E-mail: theimp@cris.com
Website: http://
www.franchise411.com

Hunter G. Jackson Jr. - Consulting
Environmental Physicist
PO Box 618272
Orlando, FL 32861-8272
Phone: (407)295-4188
E-mail: hunterjackson@juno.com

F. Newton Parks
210 El Brillo Way
Palm Beach, FL 33480
Phone: (561)833-1727
Fax: (561)833-4541

Avery Business Development
Services
2506 St. Michel Ct.
Ponte Vedra Beach, FL 32082
Phone: (904)285-6033
Fax: (904)285-6033

Strategic Business Planning Co.
PO Box 821006
South Florida, FL 33082-1006
Phone: (954)704-9100
Fax: (954)438-7333
E-mail: info@bizplan.com
Website: http://www.bizplan.com

Dufresne Consulting Group Inc.
10014 N Dale Mabry, Ste. 101
Tampa, FL 33618-4426
Phone: (813)264-4775
Fax: (813)264-9300
Website: http://www.dcgconsult.com

Agrippa Enterprises Inc.
PO Box 175
Venice, FL 34284-0175
Phone: (941)355-7876
E-mail: webservices@agrippa.com
Website: http://www.agrippa.com

Center for Simplified Strategic
Planning Inc.
PO Box 3324
Vero Beach, FL 32964-3324
Phone: (561)231-3636
Fax: (561)231-1099
Website: http://www.cssp.com

Georgia

Marketing Spectrum Inc.
115 Perimeter Pl., Ste. 440
Atlanta, GA 30346
Phone: (770)395-7244
Fax: (770)393-4071

Business Ventures Corp.
1650 Oakbrook Dr., Ste. 405
Norcross, GA 30093
Phone: (770)729-8000
Fax: (770)729-8028

Informed Decisions Inc.
100 Falling Cheek
Sautee Nacoochee, GA 30571
Phone: (706)878-1905
Fax: (706)878-1802
E-mail: skylake@compuserve.com

Tom C. Davis & Associates, P.C.
3189 Perimeter Rd.
Valdosta, GA 31602
Phone: (912)247-9801
Fax: (912)244-7704
E-mail: mail@tcdcpa.com
Website: http://www.tcdcpa.com/

Illinois

TWD and Associates
431 S Patton
Arlington Heights, IL 60005
Phone: (847)398-6410
Fax: (847)255-5095
E-mail: tdoo@aol.com

Management Planning Associates
Inc.
2275 Half Day Rd., Ste. 350
Bannockburn, IL 60015-1277
Phone: (847)945-2421
Fax: (847)945-2425

Phil Faris Associates
86 Old Mill Ct.
Barrington, IL 60010
Phone: (847)382-4888
Fax: (847)382-4890
E-mail: pfaris@meginsnet.net

Seven Continents Technology
787 Stonebridge
Buffalo Grove, IL 60089
Phone: (708)577-9653
Fax: (708)870-1220

Grubb & Blue Inc.
2404 Windsor Pl.
Champaign, IL 61820
Phone: (217)366-0052
Fax: (217)356-0117

ACE Accounting Service Inc.
3128 N Bernard St.
Chicago, IL 60618
Phone: (773)463-7854
Fax: (773)463-7854

AON Consulting Worldwide
200 E Randolph St., 10th Fl.
Chicago, IL 60601
Phone: (312)381-4800
Free: (800)438-6487
Fax: (312)381-0240
Website: http://www.aon.com

FMS Consultants
5801 N Sheridan Rd., Ste. 3D
Chicago, IL 60660
Phone: (773)561-7362
Fax: (773)561-6274

Grant Thornton
800 1 Prudential Plz.
130 E Randolph St.
Chicago, IL 60601
Phone: (312)856-0001
Fax: (312)861-1340
E-mail: gtinfo@gt.com
Website: http://
www.grantthornton.com

Kingsbury International Ltd.
5341 N Glenwood Ave.
Chicago, IL 60640
Phone: (773)271-3030
Fax: (773)728-7080
E-mail: jetlag@mcs.com
Website: http://www.kingbiz.com

MacDougall & Blake Inc.
1414 N Wells St., Ste. 311
Chicago, IL 60610-1306
Phone: (312)587-3330
Fax: (312)587-3699
E-mail: jblake@compuserve.com

James C. Osburn Ltd.
6445 N. Western Ave., Ste. 304
Chicago, IL 60645

Phone: (773)262-4428
Fax: (773)262-6755
E-mail: osburnltd@aol.com

Tarifero & Tazewell Inc.
211 S Clark
Chicago, IL 60690
Phone: (312)665-9714
Fax: (312)665-9716

Human Energy Design Systems
620 Roosevelt Dr.
Edwardsville, IL 62025
Phone: (618)692-0258
Fax: (618)692-0819

China Business Consultants Group
931 Dakota Cir.
Naperville, IL 60563
Phone: (630)778-7992
Fax: (630)778-7915
E-mail: cbcq@aol.com

Center for Workforce Effectiveness
500 Skokie Blvd., Ste. 222
Northbrook, IL 60062
Phone: (847)559-8777
Fax: (847)559-8778
E-mail: office@cwelink.com
Website: http://www.cwelink.com

Smith Associates
1320 White Mountain Dr.
Northbrook, IL 60062
Phone: (847)480-7200
Fax: (847)480-9828

Francorp Inc.
20200 Governors Dr.
Olympia Fields, IL 60461
Phone: (708)481-2900
Free: (800)372-6244
Fax: (708)481-5885
E-mail: francorp@aol.com
Website: http://www.francorpinc.com

Camber Business Strategy
Consultants
1010 S Plum Tree Ct
Palatine, IL 60078-0986
Phone: (847)202-0101
Fax: (847)705-7510
E-mail: camber@ameritech.net

Partec Enterprise Group
5202 Keith Dr.
Richton Park, IL 60471
Phone: (708)503-4047
Fax: (708)503-9468

Rockford Consulting Group Ltd.
Century Plz., Ste. 206
7210 E State St.
Rockford, IL 61108
Phone: (815)229-2900
Free: (800)667-7495
Fax: (815)229-2612
E-mail:
rligus@RockfordConsulting.com
Website: http://
www.RockfordConsulting.com

RSM McGladrey Inc.
1699 E Woodfield Rd., Ste. 300
Schaumburg, IL 60173-4969
Phone: (847)413-6900
Fax: (847)517-7067
Website: http://
www.rsmmcgladrey.com

A.D. Star Consulting
320 Euclid
Winnetka, IL 60093
Phone: (847)446-7827
Fax: (847)446-7827
E-mail: startwo@worldnet.att.net

Indiana

Modular Consultants Inc.
3109 Crabtree Ln.
Elkhart, IN 46514
Phone: (219)264-5761
Fax: (219)264-5761
E-mail: sasabo5313@aol.com

Midwest Marketing Research
PO Box 1077
Goshen, IN 46527
Phone: (219)533-0548
Fax: (219)533-0540
E-mail: 103365.654@compuserve

Ketchum Consulting Group
8021 Knue Rd., Ste. 112
Indianapolis, IN 46250
Phone: (317)845-5411
Fax: (317)842-9941

MDI Management Consulting
1519 Park Dr.
Munster, IN 46321
Phone: (219)838-7909
Fax: (219)838-7909

Iowa

McCord Consulting Group Inc.
4533 Pine View Dr. NE
PO Box 11024

Cedar Rapids, IA 52410
Phone: (319)378-0077
Fax: (319)378-1577
E-mail: smmccord@hom.com
Website: http://
www.mccordgroup.com

Management Solutions L.C.
3815 Lincoln Pl. Dr.
Des Moines, IA 50312
Phone: (515)277-6408
Fax: (515)277-3506
E-mail: wasunimers@uswest.net

Grandview Marketing
15 Red Bridge Dr.
Sioux City, IA 51104
Phone: (712)239-3122
Fax: (712)258-7578
E-mail: eandrews@pionet.net

Kansas

Assessments in Action
513A N Mur-Len
Olathe, KS 66062
Phone: (913)764-6270
Free: (888)548-1504
Fax: (913)764-6495
E-mail: lowdene@qni.com
Website: http://www.assessments-in-
action.com

Maine

Edgemont Enterprises
PO Box 8354
Portland, ME 04104
Phone: (207)871-8964
Fax: (207)871-8964

Pan Atlantic Consultants
5 Milk St.
Portland, ME 04101
Phone: (207)871-8622
Fax: (207)772-4842
E-mail: pmurphy@maine.rr.com
Website: http://www.panatlantic.net

Maryland

Clemons & Associates Inc.
5024-R Campbell Blvd.
Baltimore, MD 21236
Phone: (410)931-8100
Fax: (410)931-8111
E-mail: info@clemonsmgmt.com
Website: http://
www.clemonsmgmt.com

Imperial Group Ltd.
305 Washington Ave., Ste. 204
Baltimore, MD 21204-6009
Phone: (410)337-8500
Fax: (410)337-7641

Leadership Institute
3831 Yolando Rd.
Baltimore, MD 21218
Phone: (410)366-9111
Fax: (410)243-8478
E-mail: behconsult@aol.com

Burdeshaw Associates Ltd.
4701 Sangamore Rd.
Bethesda, MD 20816-2508
Phone: (301)229-5800
Fax: (301)229-5045
E-mail: jstacy@burdeshaw.com
Website: http://www.burdeshaw.com

Michael E. Cohen
5225 Pooks Hill Rd., Ste. 1119 S
Bethesda, MD 20814
Phone: (301)530-5738
Fax: (301)530-2988
E-mail: mecohen@crosslink.net

World Development Group Inc.
5272 River Rd., Ste. 650
Bethesda, MD 20816-1405
Phone: (301)652-1818
Fax: (301)652-1250
E-mail: wdg@has.com
Website: http://www.worlddg.com

Swartz Consulting
PO Box 4301
Crofton, MD 21114-4301
Phone: (301)262-6728

Software Solutions International Inc.
9633 Duffer Way
Gaithersburg, MD 20886
Phone: (301)330-4136
Fax: (301)330-4136

Strategies Inc.
8 Park Center Ct., Ste. 200
Owings Mills, MD 21117
Phone: (410)363-6669
Fax: (410)363-1231
E-mail: strategies@strat1.com
Website: http://www.strat1.com

Hammer Marketing Resources
179 Inverness Rd.
Severna Park, MD 21146
Phone: (410)544-9191
Fax: (305)675-3277

E-mail: info@gohammer.com
Website: http://www.gohammer.com

Andrew Sussman & Associates
13731 Kretsinger
Smithsburg, MD 21783
Phone: (301)824-2943
Fax: (301)824-2943

Massachusetts

Geibel Marketing and Public
Relations
PO Box 611
Belmont, MA 02478-0005
Phone: (617)484-8285
Fax: (617)489-3567
E-mail: jgeibel@geibelpr.com
Website: http://www.geibelpr.com

Bain & Co.
2 Copley Pl.
Boston, MA 02116
Phone: (617)572-2000
Fax: (617)572-2427
E-mail:
corporate.inquiries@bain.com
Website: http://www.bain.com

Mehr & Co.
62 Kinnaird St.
Cambridge, MA 02139
Phone: (617)876-3311
Fax: (617)876-3023
E-mail: mehrco@aol.com

Monitor Company Inc.
2 Canal Park
Cambridge, MA 02141
Phone: (617)252-2000
Fax: (617)252-2100
Website: http://www.monitor.com

Information & Research Associates
PO Box 3121
Framingham, MA 01701
Phone: (508)788-0784

Walden Consultants Ltd.
252 Pond St.
Hopkinton, MA 01748
Phone: (508)435-4882
Fax: (508)435-3971
Website: http://
www.waldenconsultants.com

Jeffrey D. Marshall
102 Mitchell Rd.
Ipswich, MA 01938-1219

Phone: (508)356-1113
Fax: (508)356-2989

Consulting Resources Corp.
6 Northbrook Park
Lexington, MA 02420
Phone: (781)863-1222
Fax: (781)863-1441
E-mail: res@consultingresources.net
Website: http://
www.consultingresources.net

Planning Technologies Group L.L.C.
92 Hayden Ave.
Lexington, MA 02421
Phone: (781)778-4678
Fax: (781)861-1099
E-mail: ptg@plantech.com
Website: http://www.plantech.com

Kalba International Inc.
23 Sandy Pond Rd.
Lincoln, MA 01773
Phone: (781)259-9589
Fax: (781)259-1460
E-mail: info@kalbainternational.com
Website: http://
www.kalbainternational.com

VMB Associates Inc.
115 Ashland St.
Melrose, MA 02176
Phone: (781)665-0623
Fax: (425)732-7142
E-mail: vmbinc@aol.com

The Company Doctor
14 Pudding Stone Ln.
Mendon, MA 01756
Phone: (508)478-1747
Fax: (508)478-0520

Data and Strategies Group Inc.
190 N Main St.
Natick, MA 01760
Phone: (508)653-9990
Fax: (508)653-7799
E-mail: dsginc@dsggroup.com
Website: http://www.dsggroup.com

The Enterprise Group
73 Parker Rd.
Needham, MA 02494
Phone: (617)444-6631
Fax: (617)433-9991
E-mail: lsacco@world.std.com
Website: http://www.enterprise-
group.com

PSMJ Resources Inc.
10 Midland Ave.
Newton, MA 02458
Phone: (617)965-0055
Free: (800)537-7765
Fax: (617)965-5152
E-mail: psmj@tiac.net
Website: http://www.psmj.com

Scheur Management Group Inc.
255 Washington St., Ste. 100
Newton, MA 02458-1611
Phone: (617)969-7500
Fax: (617)969-7508
E-mail: smgnow@scheur.com
Website: http://www.scheur.com

I.E.E.E., Boston Section
240 Bear Hill Rd., 202B
Waltham, MA 02451-1017
Phone: (781)890-5294
Fax: (781)890-5290

Business Planning and Consulting
Services
20 Beechwood Ter.
Wellesley, MA 02482
Phone: (617)237-9151
Fax: (617)237-9151

Michigan

Walter Frederick Consulting
1719 South Blvd.
Ann Arbor, MI 48104
Phone: (313)662-4336
Fax: (313)769-7505

Set Free Publications
P.O. Box 340
Flint, MI 48501-0340
Phone: (810)523-9167
Fax: (810)564-1744
E-mail:
questions@setfreepublications.com
Website: http://
www.setfreepublications.com
Leslie A. Colston, Business Plan
Writer/Author

Fox Enterprises
6220 W Freeland Rd.
Freeland, MI 48623
Phone: (517)695-9170
Fax: (517)695-9174
E-mail: foxjw@concentric.net
Website: http://www.cris.com/~foxjw

G.G.W. and Associates
1213 Hampton
Jackson, MI 49203
Phone: (517)782-2255
Fax: (517)782-2255

Altamar Group Ltd.
6810 S Cedar, Ste. 2-B
Lansing, MI 48911
Phone: (517)694-0910
Free: (800)443-2627
Fax: (517)694-1377

Sheffieck Consultants Inc.
23610 Greening Dr.
Novi, MI 48375-3130
Phone: (248)347-3545
Fax: (248)347-3530
E-mail: cfsheff@concentric.net

Rehmann, Robson PC
5800 Gratiot
Saginaw, MI 48605
Phone: (517)799-9580
Fax: (517)799-0227
Website: http://www.rrpc.com

Francis & Co.
17200 W 10 Mile Rd., Ste. 207
Southfield, MI 48075
Phone: (248)559-7600
Fax: (248)559-5249

Private Ventures Inc.
16000 W 9 Mile Rd., Ste. 504
Southfield, MI 48075
Phone: (248)569-1977
Free: (800)448-7614
Fax: (248)569-1838
E-mail: pventuresi@aol.com

JGK Associates
14464 Kerner Dr.
Sterling Heights, MI 48313
Phone: (810)247-9055
Fax: (248)822-4977
E-mail: kozlowski@home.com

Minnesota

Health Fitness Corp.
3500 W 80th St., Ste. 130
Bloomington, MN 55431
Phone: (612)831-6830
Fax: (612)831-7264

Consatech Inc.
PO Box 1047
Burnsville, MN 55337

Phone: (612)953-1088
Fax: (612)435-2966

Robert F. Knotek
14960 Ironwood Ct.
Eden Prairie, MN 55346
Phone: (612)949-2875

DRI Consulting
7715 Stonewood Ct.
Edina, MN 55439
Phone: (612)941-9656
Fax: (612)941-2693
E-mail: dric@dric.com
Website: http://www.dric.com

Markin Consulting
12072 87th Pl. N
Maple Grove, MN 55369
Phone: (612)493-3568
Fax: (612)493-5744
E-mail:
markin@markinconsulting.com
Website: http://
www.markinconsulting.com

Minnesota Cooperation Office for
Small Business & Job Creation Inc.
5001 W 80th St., Ste. 825
Minneapolis, MN 55437
Phone: (612)830-1230
Fax: (612)830-1232
E-mail: mncoop@msn.com
Website: http://www.mnco.org

Enterprise Consulting Inc.
PO Box 1111
Minnetonka, MN 55345
Phone: (612)949-5909
Fax: (612)906-3965

Amdahl International
724 1st Ave. SW
Rochester, MN 55902
Phone: (507)252-0402
Fax: (507)252-0402
E-mail: amdahl@best-service.com
Website: http://www.wp.com/
amdahl_int

Power Systems Research
1365 Corporate Center Curve, 2nd Fl.
St. Paul, MN 55121
Phone: (612)905-8400
Free: (888)625-8612
Fax: (612)454-0760
E-mail: Barb@Powersys.com
Website: http://www.powersys.com

Missouri

Business Planning and Development
Corp.
4030 Charlotte St.
Kansas City, MO 64110
Phone: (816)753-0495
E-mail: humph@bpdev.demon.co.uk
Website: http://
www.bpdev.demon.co.uk

CFO Service
10336 Donoho
St. Louis, MO 63131
Phone: (314)750-2940
E-mail: jskae@cfoservice.com
Website: http://www.cfoservice.com

Nebraska

International Management Consulting
Group Inc.
1309 Harlan Dr., Ste. 205
Bellevue, NE 68005
Phone: (402)291-4545
Free: (800)665-IMCG
Fax: (402)291-4343
E-mail: imcg@neonramp.com
Website: http://
www.mgtconsulting.com

Heartland Management Consulting
Group
1904 Barrington Pky.
Papillion, NE 68046
Phone: (402)339-2387
Fax: (402)339-1319

Nevada

The DuBois Group
865 Tahoe Blvd., Ste. 108
Incline Village, NV 89451
Phone: (775)832-0550
Free: (800)375-2935
Fax: (775)832-0556
E-mail: DuBoisGrp@aol.com

New Hampshire

Wolff Consultants
10 Buck Rd.
Hanover, NH 03755
Phone: (603)643-6015

BPT Consulting Associates Ltd.
12 Parmenter Rd., Ste. B-6
Londonderry, NH 03053
Phone: (603)437-8484

Free: (888)278-0030
Fax: (603)434-5388
E-mail: bptcons@tiac.net
Website: http://
www.bptconsulting.com

New Jersey

Bedminster Group Inc.
1170 Rte. 22 E
Bridgewater, NJ 08807
Phone: (908)500-4155
Fax: (908)766-0780
E-mail: info@bedminstergroup.com
Website: http://
www.bedminstergroup.com

Delta Planning Inc.
PO Box 425
Denville, NJ 07834
Phone: (913)625-1742
Free: (800)672-0762
Fax: (973)625-3531
E-mail: DeltaP@worldnet.att.net
Website: http://deltaplanning.com

Kumar Associates Inc.
1004 Cumbermeade Rd.
Fort Lee, NJ 07024
Phone: (201)224-9480
Fax: (201)585-2343
E-mail: mail@kumarassociates.com
Website: http://kumarassociates.com

John Hall & Company Inc.
PO Box 187
Glen Ridge, NJ 07028
Phone: (973)680-4449
Fax: (973)680-4581
E-mail: jhcompany@aol.com

Market Focus
PO Box 402
Maplewood, NJ 07040
Phone: (973)378-2470
Fax: (973)378-2470
E-mail: mcss66@marketfocus.com

Vanguard Communications Corp.
100 American Rd.
Morris Plains, NJ 07950
Phone: (973)605-8000
Fax: (973)605-8329
Website: http://www.vanguard.net/

ConMar International Ltd.
1901 US Hwy. 130
North Brunswick, NJ 08902
Phone: (732)940-8347
Fax: (732)274-1199

KLW New Products
156 Cedar Dr.
Old Tappan, NJ 07675
Phone: (201)358-1300
Fax: (201)664-2594
E-mail: lrlarsen@usa.net
Website: http://
www.klwnewproducts.com

PA Consulting Group
315A Enterprise Dr.
Plainsboro, NJ 08536
Phone: (609)936-8300
Fax: (609)936-8811
E-mail: info@paconsulting.com
Website: http://www.pa-
consulting.com

Aurora Marketing Management Inc.
66 Witherspoon St., Ste. 600
Princeton, NJ 08542
Phone: (908)904-1125
Fax: (908)359-1108
E-mail: aurora2@voicenet.com
Website: http://
www.auroramarketing.net

Smart Business Supersite
88 Orchard Rd., CN-5219
Princeton, NJ 08543
Phone: (908)321-1924
Fax: (908)321-5156
E-mail: irv@smartbiz.com
Website: http://www.smartbiz.com

Tracelin Associates
1171 Main St., Ste. 6K
Rahway, NJ 07065
Phone: (732)381-3288

Schkeeper Inc.
130-6 Bodman Pl.
Red Bank, NJ 07701
Phone: (732)219-1965
Fax: (732)530-3703

Henry Branch Associates
2502 Harmon Cove Twr.
Secaucus, NJ 07094
Phone: (201)866-2008
Fax: (201)601-0101
E-mail: hbranch161@home.com

Robert Gibbons & Company Inc.
46 Knoll Rd.
Tenafly, NJ 07670-1050
Phone: (201)871-3933
Fax: (201)871-2173
E-mail: crisisbob@aol.com

PMC Management Consultants Inc.
6 Thistle Ln.
Three Bridges, NJ 08887-0332
Phone: (908)788-1014
Free: (800)PMC-0250
Fax: (908)806-7287
E-mail: int@pmc-management.com
Website: http://www.pmc-
management.com

R.W. Bankart & Associates
20 Valley Ave., Ste. D-2
Westwood, NJ 07675-3607
Phone: (201)664-7672

New Mexico

Vondle & Associates Inc.
4926 Calle de Tierra, NE
Albuquerque, NM 87111
Phone: (505)292-8961
Fax: (505)296-2790
E-mail: vondle@aol.com

InfoNewMexico
2207 Black Hills Rd., NE
Rio Rancho, NM 87124
Phone: (505)891-2462
Fax: (505)896-8971

New York

Powers Research and Training
Institute
PO Box 78
Bayville, NY 11709
Phone: (516)628-2250
Fax: (516)628-2252
E-mail:
powercocch@compuserve.com
Website: http://
www.nancypowers.com

Consortium House
296 Wittenberg Rd.
Bearsville, NY 12409
Phone: (845)679-8867
Fax: (845)679-9248
E-mail: eugenegs@aol.com
Website: http://www.chpub.com

Progressive Finance Corp.
3549 Tiemann Ave.
Bronx, NY 10469
Phone: (718)405-9029
Free: (800)225-8381
Fax: (718)405-1170

Wave Hill Associates Inc.
2621 Palisade Ave., Ste. 15-C

Bronx, NY 10463
Phone: (718)549-7368
Fax: (718)601-9670
E-mail: pepper@compuserve.com

Management Insight
96 Arlington Rd.
Buffalo, NY 14221
Phone: (716)631-3319
Fax: (716)631-0203
E-mail:
michalski@foodserviceinsight.com
Website: http://
www.foodserviceinsight.com

Samani International Enterprises,
Marions Panyaught Consultancy
2028 Parsons
Flushing, NY 11357-3436
Phone: (917)287-8087
Fax: 800-873-8939
E-mail: vjp2@biostrategist.com
Website: http://
www.biostrategist.com

Marketing Resources Group
71-58 Austin St.
Forest Hills, NY 11375
Phone: (718)261-8882

Mangabay Business Plans &
Development
Subsidiary of Innis Asset Allocation
125-10 Queens Blvd., Ste. 2202
Kew Gardens, NY 11415
Phone: 905-527-1947
Fax: 509-472-1935
E-mail: mangabay@mangabay.com
Website: http://www.mangabay.com
Lee Toh, Managing Partner

ComputerEase Co.
1301 Monmouth Ave.
Lakewood, NY 08701
Phone: (212)406-9464
Fax: (914)277-5317
E-mail: crawfordc@juno.com

Boice Dunham Group
30 W 13th St.
New York, NY 10011
Phone: (212)924-2200
Fax: (212)924-1108

Elizabeth Capen
27 E 95th St.
New York, NY 10128
Phone: (212)427-7654
Fax: (212)876-3190

Haver Analytics
60 E 42nd St., Ste. 2424
New York, NY 10017
Phone: (212)986-9300
Fax: (212)986-5857
E-mail: data@haver.com
Website: http://www.haver.com

The Jordan, Edmiston Group Inc.
150 E 52nd Ave., 18th Fl.
New York, NY 10022
Phone: (212)754-0710
Fax: (212)754-0337

KPMG International
345 Park Ave.
New York, NY 10154-0102
Phone: (212)758-9700
Fax: (212)758-9819
Website: http://www.kpmg.com

Mahoney Cohen Consulting Corp.
111 W 40th St., 12th Fl.
New York, NY 10018
Phone: (212)490-8000
Fax: (212)790-5913

Management Practice Inc.
342 Madison Ave.
New York, NY 10173-1230
Phone: (212)867-7948
Fax: (212)972-5188
Website: http://www.mpiweb.com

Moseley Associates Inc.
342 Madison Ave., Ste. 1414
New York, NY 10016
Phone: (212)213-6673
Fax: (212)687-1520

Practice Development Counsel
60 Sutton Pl. S
New York, NY 10022
Phone: (212)593-1549
Fax: (212)980-7940
E-mail: pwhaserot@pdcounsel.com
Website: http://www.pdcounsel.com

Unique Value International Inc.
575 Madison Ave., 10th Fl.
New York, NY 10022-1304
Phone: (212)605-0590
Fax: (212)605-0589

The Van Tulleken Co.
126 E 56th St.
New York, NY 10022
Phone: (212)355-1390
Fax: (212)755-3061
E-mail: newyork@vantulleken.com

Vencon Management Inc.
301 W 53rd St.
New York, NY 10019
Phone: (212)581-8787
Fax: (212)397-4126
Website: http://www.venconinc.com

Werner International Inc.
55 E 52nd, 29th Fl.
New York, NY 10055
Phone: (212)909-1260
Fax: (212)909-1273
E-mail: richard.downing@rgh.com
Website: http://www.wernertex.com

Zimmerman Business Consulting Inc.
44 E 92nd St., Ste. 5-B
New York, NY 10128
Phone: (212)860-3107
Fax: (212)860-7730
E-mail: ljzzbci@aol.com
Website: http://www.zbcinc.com

Overton Financial
7 Allen Rd.
Peekskill, NY 10566
Phone: (914)737-4649
Fax: (914)737-4696

Stromberg Consulting
2500 Westchester Ave.
Purchase, NY 10577
Phone: (914)251-1515
Fax: (914)251-1562
E-mail:
strategy@stromberg_consulting.com
Website: http://
www.stromberg_consulting.com

Innovation Management Consulting
Inc.
209 Dewitt Rd.
Syracuse, NY 13214-2006
Phone: (315)425-5144
Fax: (315)445-8989
E-mail: missonneb@axess.net

M. Clifford Agress
891 Fulton St.
Valley Stream, NY 11580
Phone: (516)825-8955
Fax: (516)825-8955

Destiny Kinal Marketing Consultancy
105 Chemung St.
Waverly, NY 14892
Phone: (607)565-8317
Fax: (607)565-4083

Valutis Consulting Inc.
5350 Main St., Ste. 7
Williamsville, NY 14221-5338
Phone: (716)634-2553
Fax: (716)634-2554
E-mail: valutis@localnet.com
Website: http://
www.valutisconsulting.com

North Carolina

Best Practices L.L.C.
6320 Quadrangle Dr., Ste. 200
Chapel Hill, NC 27514
Phone: (919)403-0251
Fax: (919)403-0144
E-mail: best@best:in/class
Website: http://www.best-in-
class.com

Norelli & Co.
Bank of America Corporate Ctr.
100 N Tyron St., Ste. 5160
Charlotte, NC 28202-4000
Phone: (704)376-5484
Fax: (704)376-5485
E-mail: consult@norelli.com
Website: http://www.norelli.com

North Dakota

Center for Innovation
4300 Dartmouth Dr.
PO Box 8372
Grand Forks, ND 58202
Phone: (701)777-3132
Fax: (701)777-2339
E-mail: bruce@innovators.net
Website: http://www.innovators.net

Ohio

Transportation Technology Services
208 Harmon Rd.
Aurora, OH 44202
Phone: (330)562-3596

Empro Systems Inc.
4777 Red Bank Expy., Ste. 1
Cincinnati, OH 45227-1542
Phone: (513)271-2042
Fax: (513)271-2042

Alliance Management International
Ltd.
1440 Windrow Ln.
Cleveland, OH 44147-3200
Phone: (440)838-1922
Fax: (440)838-0979

E-mail: bgruss@amiltd.com
Website: http://www.amiltd.com

Bozell Kamstra Public Relations
1301 E 9th St., Ste. 3400
Cleveland, OH 44114
Phone: (216)623-1511
Fax: (216)623-1501
E-mail:
jfeniger@cleveland.bozellkamstra.com
Website: http://
www.bozellkamstra.com

Cory Dillon Associates
111 Schreyer Pl. E
Columbus, OH 43214
Phone: (614)262-8211
Fax: (614)262-3806

Holcomb Gallagher Adams
300 Marconi, Ste. 303
Columbus, OH 43215
Phone: (614)221-3343
Fax: (614)221-3367
E-mail: riadams@acme.freenet.oh.us

Young & Associates
PO Box 711
Kent, OH 44240
Phone: (330)678-0524
Free: (800)525-9775
Fax: (330)678-6219
E-mail: online@younginc.com
Website: http://www.younginc.com

Robert A. Westman & Associates
8981 Inversary Dr. SE
Warren, OH 44484-2551
Phone: (330)856-4149
Fax: (330)856-2564

Oklahoma

Innovative Partners L.L.C.
4900 Richmond Sq., Ste. 100
Oklahoma City, OK 73118
Phone: (405)840-0033
Fax: (405)843-8359
E-mail: ipartners@juno.com

Oregon

INTERCON—The International
Converting Institute
5200 Badger Rd.
Crooked River Ranch, OR 97760
Phone: (541)548-1447
Fax: (541)548-1618
E-mail:
johnbowler@crookedriverranch.com

Talbott ARM
HC 60, Box 5620
Lakeview, OR 97630
Phone: (541)635-8587
Fax: (503)947-3482

Management Technology Associates
Ltd.
2768 SW Sherwood Dr, Ste. 105
Portland, OR 97201-2251
Phone: (503)224-5220
Fax: (503)224-5334
E-mail: lcuster@mta-ltd.com
Website: http://www.mgmt-tech.com

Pennsylvania

Healthscope Inc.
400 Lancaster Ave.
Devon, PA 19333
Phone: (610)687-6199
Fax: (610)687-6376
E-mail: health@voicenet.com
Website: http://www.healthscope.net/

Elayne Howard & Associates Inc.
3501 Masons Mill Rd., Ste. 501
Huntingdon Valley, PA 19006-3509
Phone: (215)657-9550

GRA Inc.
115 West Ave., Ste. 201
Jenkintown, PA 19046
Phone: (215)884-7500
Fax: (215)884-1385
E-mail: gramail@gra-inc.com
Website: http://www.gra-inc.com

Mifflin County Industrial
Development Corp.
Mifflin County Industrial Plz.
6395 SR 103 N
Bldg. 50
Lewistown, PA 17044
Phone: (717)242-0393
Fax: (717)242-1842
E-mail: mcide@acsworld.net

Autech Products
1289 Revere Rd.
Morrisville, PA 19067
Phone: (215)493-3759
Fax: (215)493-9791
E-mail: autech4@yahoo.com

Advantage Associates
434 Avon Dr.
Pittsburgh, PA 15228
Phone: (412)343-1558

Fax: (412)362-1684
E-mail: ecocba1@aol.com

Regis J. Sheehan & Associates
Pittsburgh, PA 15220
Phone: (412)279-1207

James W. Davidson Company Inc.
23 Forest View Rd.
Wallingford, PA 19086
Phone: (610)566-1462

Puerto Rico

Diego Chevere & Co.
Metro Parque 7, Ste. 204
Metro Office
Caparra Heights, PR 00920
Phone: (787)774-9595
Fax: (787)774-9566
E-mail: dcco@coqui.net

Manuel L. Porrata and Associates
898 Munoz Rivera Ave., Ste. 201
San Juan, PR 00927
Phone: (787)765-2140
Fax: (787)754-3285
E-mail:
m_porrata@manuelporrata.com
Website: http://manualporrata.com

South Carolina

Aquafood Business Associates
PO Box 13267
Charleston, SC 29422
Phone: (843)795-9506
Fax: (843)795-9477
E-mail: rraba@aol.com

Profit Associates Inc.
PO Box 38026
Charleston, SC 29414
Phone: (803)763-5718
Fax: (803)763-5719
E-mail: bobrog@awod.com
Website: http://www.awod.com/
gallery/business/proasc

Strategic Innovations International
12 Executive Ct.
Lake Wylie, SC 29710
Phone: (803)831-1225
Fax: (803)831-1177
E-mail: stratinnov@aol.com
Website: http://
www.strategicinnovations.com

Minus Stage
Box 4436
Rock Hill, SC 29731
Phone: (803)328-0705
Fax: (803)329-9948

Tennessee

Daniel Petchers & Associates
8820 Fernwood CV
Germantown, TN 38138
Phone: (901)755-9896

Business Choices
1114 Forest Harbor, Ste. 300
Hendersonville, TN 37075-9646
Phone: (615)822-8692
Free: (800)737-8382
Fax: (615)822-8692
E-mail: bz-ch@juno.com

RCFA Healthcare Management
Services L.L.C.
9648 Kingston Pke., Ste. 8
Knoxville, TN 37922
Phone: (865)531-0176
Free: (800)635-4040
Fax: (865)531-0722
E-mail: info@rcfa.com
Website: http://www.rcfa.com

Growth Consultants of America
3917 Trimble Rd.
Nashville, TN 37215
Phone: (615)383-0550
Fax: (615)269-8940
E-mail: 70244.451@compuserve.com

Texas

Integrated Cost Management Systems
Inc.
2261 Brookhollow Plz. Dr., Ste. 104
Arlington, TX 76006
Phone: (817)633-2873
Fax: (817)633-3781
E-mail: abm@icms.net
Website: http://www.icms.net

Lori Williams
1000 Leslie Ct.
Arlington, TX 76012
Phone: (817)459-3934
Fax: (817)459-3934

Business Resource Software Inc.
2013 Wells Branch Pky., Ste. 305
Austin, TX 78728
Free: (800)423-1228

Fax: (512)251-4401
E-mail: info@brs-inc.com
Website: http://www.brs-inc.com

Erisa Adminstrative Services Inc.
12325 Hymeadow Dr., Bldg. 4
Austin, TX 78750-1847
Phone: (512)250-9020
Fax: (512)250-9487
Website: http://www.cserisa.com

R. Miller Hicks & Co.
1011 W 11th St.
Austin, TX 78703
Phone: (512)477-7000
Fax: (512)477-9697
E-mail: millerhicks@rmhicks.com
Website: http://www.rmhicks.com

Pragmatic Tactics Inc.
3303 Westchester Ave.
College Station, TX 77845
Phone: (409)696-5294
Free: (800)570-5294
Fax: (409)696-4994
E-mail: ptactics@aol.com
Website: http://www.ptatics.com

Perot Systems
12404 Park Central Dr.
Dallas, TX 75251
Phone: (972)340-5000
Free: (800)688-4333
Fax: (972)455-4100
E-mail: corp.comm@ps.net
Website: http://
www.perotsystems.com

ReGENERATION Partners
3838 Oak Lawn Ave.
Dallas, TX 75219
Phone: (214)559-3999
Free: (800)406-1112
E-mail: info@regeneration-
partner.com
Website: http://www.regeneration-
partners.com

High Technology Associates—
Division of Global Technologies Inc.
1775 St. James Pl., Ste. 105
Houston, TX 77056
Phone: (713)963-9300
Fax: (713)963-8341
E-mail: hta@infohwy.com

MasterCOM
103 Thunder Rd.
Kerrville, TX 78028

Phone: (830)895-7990
Fax: (830)443-3428
E-mail:
jmstubblefield@mastertraining.com
Website: http://
www.mastertraining.com

PROTEC
4607 Linden Pl.
Pearland, TX 77584
Phone: (281)997-9872
Fax: (281)997-9895
E-mail: p.oman@ix.netcom.com

Bastian Public Relations
614 San Dizier
San Antonio, TX 78232
Phone: 210-404-1839
E-mail: info@bastianpr.com
Website: http://www.bastianpr.com
Lisa Bastian CBC

Business Strategy Development
Consultants
PO Box 690365
San Antonio, TX 78269
Phone: (210)696-8000
Free: (800)927-BSDC
Fax: (210)696-8000

Tom Welch, CPC
6900 San Pedro Ave., Ste. 147
San Antonio, TX 78216-6207
Phone: (210)737-7022
Fax: (210)737-7022
E-mail: bplan@iamerica.net
Website: http://
www.moneywords.com

Utah

Business Management Resource
PO Box 521125
Salt Lake City, UT 84152-1125
Phone: (801)272-4668
Fax: (801)277-3290
E-mail: pingfong@worldnet.att.net

Virginia

Tindell Associates
209 Oxford Ave.
Alexandria, VA 22301
Phone: 703-683-0109
Fax: 703-783-0219
E-mail: scott@tindell.net
Website: http://www.tindell.net
Scott Lockett, President

Elliott B. Jaffa
2530-B S Walter Reed Dr.
Arlington, VA 22206
Phone: (703)931-0040
E-mail:
thetrainingdoctor@excite.com
Website: http://www.tregistry.com/
jaffa.htm

Koach Enterprises - USA
5529 N 18th St.
Arlington, VA 22205
Phone: (703)241-8361
Fax: (703)241-8623

Federal Market Development
5650 Chapel Run Ct.
Centreville, VA 20120-3601
Phone: (703)502-8930
Free: (800)821-5003
Fax: (703)502-8929

Huff, Stuart & Carlton
2107 Graves Mills Rd., Ste. C
Forest, VA 24551
Phone: (804)316-9356
Free: (888)316-9356
Fax: (804)316-9357
Website: http://www.wealthmgt.net

AMX International Inc.
1420 Spring Hill Rd. , Ste. 600
McLean, VA 22102-3006
Phone: (703)690-4100
Fax: (703)643-1279
E-mail: amxmail@amxi.com
Website: http://www.amxi.com

Charles Scott Pugh (Investor)
4101 Pittaway Dr.
Richmond, VA 23235-1022
Phone: (804)560-0979
Fax: (804)560-4670

John C. Randall and Associates Inc.
PO Box 15127
Richmond, VA 23227
Phone: (804)746-4450
Fax: (804)730-8933
E-mail: randalljcx@aol.com
Website: http://
www.johncrandall.com

McLeod & Co.
410 1st St.
Roanoke, VA 24011
Phone: (540)342-6911
Fax: (540)344-6367
Website: http://www.mcleodco.com/

Salzinger & Company Inc.
8000 Towers Crescent Dr., Ste. 1350
Vienna, VA 22182
Phone: (703)442-5200
Fax: (703)442-5205
E-mail: info@salzinger.com
Website: http://www.salzinger.com

The Small Business Counselor
12423 Hedges Run Dr., Ste. 153
Woodbridge, VA 22192
Phone: (703)490-6755
Fax: (703)490-1356

Washington

Burlington Consultants
10900 NE 8th St., Ste. 900
Bellevue, WA 98004
Phone: (425)688-3060
Fax: (425)454-4383
E-mail:
partners@burlingtonconsultants.com
Website: http://
www.burlingtonconsultants.com

Perry L. Smith Consulting
800 Bellevue Way NE, Ste. 400
Bellevue, WA 98004-4208
Phone: (425)462-2072
Fax: (425)462-5638

St. Charles Consulting Group
1420 NW Gilman Blvd.
Issaquah, WA 98027
Phone: (425)557-8708
Fax: (425)557-8731
E-mail:
info@stcharlesconsulting.com
Website: http://
www.stcharlesconsulting.com

Independent Automotive Training
Services
PO Box 334
Kirkland, WA 98083
Phone: (425)822-5715
E-mail: ltunney@autosvccon.com
Website: http://www.autosvccon.com

Kahle Associate Inc.
6203 204th Dr. NE
Redmond, WA 98053
Phone: (425)836-8763
Fax: (425)868-3770
E-mail:
randykahle@kahleassociates.com
Website: http://
www.kahleassociates.com

Dan Collin
3419 Wallingord Ave N, No. 2
Seattle, WA 98103
Phone: (206)634-9469
E-mail: dc@dancollin.com
Website: http://members.home.net/
dcollin/

ECG Management Consultants Inc.
1111 3rd Ave., Ste. 2700
Seattle, WA 98101-3201
Phone: (206)689-2200
Fax: (206)689-2209
E-mail: ecg@ecgmc.com
Website: http://www.ecgmc.com

Northwest Trade Adjustment
Assistance Center
900 4th Ave., Ste. 2430
Seattle, WA 98164-1001
Phone: (206)622-2730
Free: (800)667-8087
Fax: (206)622-1105
E-mail: matchingfunds@nwtaac.org
Website: http://www.taacenters.org

Business Planning Consultants
S 3510 Ridgeview Dr.
Spokane, WA 99206
Phone: (509)928-0332
Fax: (509)921-0842
E-mail: bpci@nextdim.com

Wisconsin

White & Associates Inc.
5349 Somerset Ln. S
Greenfield, WI 53221
Phone: (414)281-7373
Fax: (414)281-7006
E-mail: wnaconsult@aol.com

SMALL BUSINESS ADMINISTRATION REGIONAL OFFICES

This section contains a listing of Small Business Administration offices arranged numerically by region. Service areas are provided. Contact the appropriate office for a referral to the nearest field office, or visit the Small Business Administration online at www.sba.gov.

Region 1

U.S. Small Business Administration
10 Causeway St.

Boston, MA 02222-1093
Phone: (617)565-8415
Fax: (617)565-8420
Serves Connecticut, Maine, Massachusetts, New Hampshire, Rhode Island, and Vermont.

Region 2

U.S. Small Business Administration
26 Federal Plaza, Ste. 3108
New York, NY 10278
Phone: (212)264-1450
Fax: (212)264-0038
Serves New Jersey, New York, Puerto Rico, and the Virgin Islands.

Region 3

Serves Delaware, the District of Columbia, Maryland, Pennsylvania, Virginia, and West Virginia. For the nearest field office, visit the Small Business Administration online at www.sba.gov.

Region 4

U.S. Small Business Administration
233 Peachtree St. NE
Harris Tower 1800
Atlanta, GA 30303
Phone: (404)331-4999
Fax: (404)331-2354
Serves Alabama, Florida, Georgia, Kentucky, Mississippi, North Carolina, South Carolina, and Tennessee.

Region 5

U.S. Small Business Administration
500 W. Madison St., Ste. 1240
Chicago, IL 60661-2511
Phone: (312)353-5000
Fax: (312)353-3426
Serves Illinois, Indiana, Michigan, Minnesota, Ohio, and Wisconsin.

Region 6

U.S. Small Business Administration
4300 Amon Carter Blvd.
Dallas/Fort Worth, TX 76155
Phone: (817)885-6581
Fax: (817)885-6588
Serves Arkansas, Louisiana, New Mexico, Oklahoma, and Texas.

Region 7

U.S. Small Business Administration
323 W. 8th St., Ste. 307
Kansas City, MO 64105-1500
Phone: (816)374-6380
Fax: (816)374-6339
Serves Iowa, Kansas, Missouri, and Nebraska.

Region 8

U.S. Small Business Administration
721 19th St., Ste. 400
Denver, CO 80202
Phone: (303)844-0500
Fax: (303)844-0506
Serves Colorado, Montana, North Dakota, South Dakota, Utah, and Wyoming.

Region 9

U.S. Small Business Administration
455 Market St., Ste. 2200
San Francisco, CA 94105
Phone: (415)744-2118
Fax: (415)744-2119
Serves American Samoa, Arizona, California, Guam, Hawaii, Nevada, and the Trust Territory of the Pacific Islands.

Region 10

U.S. Small Business Administration
1200 6th Ave., Ste. 1805
Seattle, WA 98101-1128
Phone: (206)553-5676
Fax: (206)553-2872
Serves Alaska, Idaho, Oregon, and Washington.

SMALL BUSINESS DEVELOPMENT CENTERS

This section contains a listing of all Small Business Development Centers organized alphabetically by state/U.S. territory name, then by city, then by agency name.

Alabama

Auburn University
SBDC
108 College of Business

Auburn, AL 36849-5243
Phone: (334)844-4220
Fax: (334)844-4268
Garry Hannem, Dir.

Alabama Small Business
Procurement System
University of Alabama at
Birmingham
SBDC
1717 11th Ave. S., Ste. 419
Birmingham, AL 35294-4410
Phone: (205)934-7260
Fax: (205)934-7645
Charles Hobson, Procurement Dir.

University of Alabama at
Birmingham
Alabama Small Business
Development Consortium
SBDC
1717 11th Ave. S., Ste. 419
Birmingham, AL 35294-4410
Phone: (205)934-7260
Fax: (205)934-7645
John Sandefur, State Dir.

Alabama A & M University
University of Alabama at Huntsville
NE Alabama Regional Small
Business Development Center
PO Box 168
225 Church St., NW
Huntsville, AL 35804-0168
Phone: (205)535-2061
Fax: (205)535-2050
Jeff Thompson, Dir.

Jacksonville State University
Small Business Development Center
114 Merrill Hall
700 Pelham Rd. N.
Jacksonville, AL 36265
Phone: (205)782-5271
Fax: (205)782-5179
Pat Shaddix, Dir.

University of West Alabama
SBDC
Station 35
Livingston, AL 35470
Phone: (205)652-3665
Fax: (205)652-3516
Paul Garner, Dir.

University of South Alabama
Small Business Development Center
College of Business, Rm. 8
Mobile, AL 36688

Phone: (334)460-6004
Fax: (334)460-6246

Alabama State University
SBDC
915 S. Jackson St.
Montgomery, AL 36104-5714
Phone: (334)229-4138
Fax: (334)269-1102
Lorenza G. Patrick, Dir.

Troy State University
Small Business Development Center
Bibb Graves, Rm. 102
Troy, AL 36082-0001
Phone: (205)670-3771
Fax: (205)670-3636
Janet W. Kervin, Dir.

University of Alabama
Alabama International Trade Center
Small Business Development Center
Bidgood Hall, Rm. 250
Box 870397
Tuscaloosa, AL 35487-0396
Phone: (205)348-7011
Fax: (205)348-9644
Paavo Hanninen, Dir.

Alaska

University of Alaska (Fairbanks)
Small Business Development Center
510 Second Ave., Ste. 101
Fairbanks, AK 99701
Phone: (907)474-6700
Fax: (907)474-1139
Billie Ray Allen, Dir.

University of Alaska (Juneau)
Small Business Development Center
612 W. Willoughby Ave., Ste. A
Juneau, AK 99801
Phone: (907)463-1732
Fax: (907)463-3929
Norma Strickland, Acting Dir.

Kenai Peninsula Small Business
Development Center
PO Box 3029
Kenai, AK 99611-3029
Phone: (907)283-3335
Fax: (907)283-3913
Mark Gregory

University of Alaska (Matanuska-
Susitna)
Small Business Development Center
201 N. Lucile St., Ste. 2-A

Wasilla, AK 99654
Phone: (907)373-7232
Fax: (907)373-7234
Timothy Sullivan, Dir.

Arizona

Central Arizona College
Pinal County Small Business
Development Center
8470 N. Overfield Rd.
Coolidge, AZ 85228
Phone: (520)426-4341
Fax: (520)426-4363
Carol Giordano, Dir.

Coconino County Community
College
Small Business Development Center
3000 N. 4th St., Ste. 25
Flagstaff, AZ 86004
Phone: (520)526-5072
Fax: (520)526-8693
Mike Lainoff, Dir.

Northland Pioneer College
Small Business Development Center
PO Box 610
Holbrook, AZ 86025
Phone: (520)537-2976
Fax: (520)524-2227
Mark Engle, Dir.

Mohave Community College
Small Business Development Center
1971 Jagerson Ave.
Kingman, AZ 86401
Phone: (520)757-0894
Fax: (520)757-0836
Kathy McGehee, Dir.

Yavapai College
Small Business Development Center
Elks Building
117 E. Gurley St., Ste. 206
Prescott, AZ 86301
Phone: (520)778-3088
Fax: (520)778-3109
Richard Senopole, Director

Cochise College
Small Business Development Center
901 N. Colombo, Rm. 308
Sierra Vista, AZ 85635
Phone: (520)515-5478
Fax: (520)515-5437
E-mail: sbdc@trom.cochise.cc.az.us
Shelia Devoe Heidman, Dir.

Arizona Small Business Development
Center Network
2411 W. 14th St., Ste. 132
Tempe, AZ 85281
Phone: (602)731-8720
Fax: (602)731-8729
E-mail: york@maricopa.bitnet
Michael York, State Dir.

Maricopa Community Colleges
Arizona Small Business Development
Center Network
2411 W. 14th St., Ste. 132
Tempe, AZ 85281
Phone: (602)731-8720
Fax: (602)731-8729
Michael York, Dir.

Eastern Arizona College
Small Business Development Center
622 College Ave.
Thatcher, AZ 85552-0769
Phone: (520)428-8590
Fax: (520)428-8462
Greg Roers, Dir.

Pima Community College
Small Business Development and
Training Center
4905-A E. Broadway Blvd., Ste. 101
Tucson, AZ 85709-1260
Phone: (520)206-4906
Fax: (520)206-4585
Linda Andrews, Dir.

Arizona Western College
Small Business Development Center
Century Plz., No. 152
281 W. 24th St.
Yuma, AZ 85364
Phone: (520)341-1650
Fax: (520)726-2636
John Lundin, Dir.

Arkansas

Henderson State University
Small Business Development Center
1100 Henderson St.
PO Box 7624
Arkadelphia, AR 71923
Phone: (870)230-5224
Fax: (870)230-5236
Jeff Doose, Dir.

Genesis Technology Incubator
SBDC Satellite Office
University of Arkansas—Engineering
Research Center

Fayetteville, AR 72701-1201
Phone: (501)575-7473
Fax: (501)575-7446
Bob Penquite, Business Consultant

University of Arkansas at Fayetteville
Small Business Development Center
Business Administration Bldg., Ste.
106
Fayetteville, AR 72701
Phone: (501)575-5148
Fax: (501)575-4013
Ms. Jimmie Wilkins, Dir.

Small Business Development Center
1109 S. 16th St.
PO Box 2067
Ft. Smith, AR 72901
Phone: (501)785-1376
Fax: (501)785-1964
Vonelle Vanzant, Business
Consultant

University of Arkansas at Little Rock,
Regional Office (Fort Smith)
Small Business Development Center
1109 S. 16th St.
PO Box 2067
Ft. Smith, AR 72901
Phone: (501)785-1376
Fax: (501)785-1964
Byron Branch, Business Specialist

University of Arkansas at Little Rock,
Regional Office (Harrison)
Small Business Development Center
818 Hwy. 62-65-412 N
PO Box 190
Harrison, AR 72601
Phone: (870)741-8009
Fax: (870)741-1905
Bob Penquite, Business Consultant

University of Arkansas at Little Rock,
Regional Office (Hot Springs)
Small Business Development Center
835 Central Ave., Box 402-D
Hot Springs, AR 71901
Phone: (501)624-5448
Fax: (501)624-6632
Richard Evans, Business Consultant

Arkansas State University
Small Business Development Center
College of Business
Drawer 2650
Jonesboro, AR 72467
Phone: (870)972-3517
Fax: (501)972-3868
Herb Lawrence, Dir.

University of Arkansas at Little Rock
SBDC
Little Rock Technology Center Bldg.
100 S. Main St., Ste. 401
Little Rock, AR 72201
Phone: (501)324-9043
Fax: (501)324-9049
Janet Nye, State Dir.

University of Arkansas at Little Rock,
Regional Office (Magnolia)
Small Business Development Center
600 Bessie
PO Box 767
Magnolia, AR 71753
Phone: (870)234-4030
Fax: (870)234-0135
Mr. Lairie Kincaid, Business
Consultant

University of Arkansas at Little Rock,
Regional Office (Pine Bluff)
Small Business Development Center
The Enterprise Center III
400 Main, Ste. 117
Pine Bluff, AR 71601
Phone: (870)536-0654
Fax: (870)536-7713
Russell Barker, Business Consultant

University of Arkansas at Little Rock,
Regional Office (Stuttgart)
Small Business Development Center
301 S. Grand, Ste. 101
PO Box 289
Stuttgart, AR 72160
Phone: (870)673-8707
Fax: (870)673-8707
Larry Lefler, Business Consultant

Mid-South Community College
SBDC
2000 W. Broadway
PO Box 2067
West Memphis, AR 72303-2067
Phone: (870)733-6767

California

Central Coast Small Business
Development Center
6500 Soquel Dr.
Aptos, CA 95003
Phone: (408)479-6136
Fax: (408)479-6166
Teresa Thomae, Dir.

Sierra College Small Business
Development Center

560 Wall St., Ste. J
Auburn, CA 95603
Phone: (916)885-5488
Fax: (916)823-2831
Mary Wollesen, Dir.

Weill Institute Small Business
Development Center
1706 Chester Ave., Ste. 200
Bakersfield, CA 93301
Phone: (805)322-5881
Fax: (805)322-5663
Jeffrey Johnson, Dir.

Butte College
Small Business Development Center
260 Cohasset Rd., Ste. A
Chico, CA 95926
Phone: (916)895-9017
Fax: (916)895-9099
Kay Zimmerlee, Dir.

Southwestern College
Small Business Development and
International Trade Center
900 Otay Lakes Rd., Bldg. 1600
Chula Vista, CA 91910
Phone: (619)482-6393
Fax: (619)482-6402
Mary Wylie, Dir.

Contra Costa SBDC
2425 Bisso Ln., Ste. 200
Concord, CA 94520
Phone: (510)646-5377
Fax: (510)646-5299
Debra Longwood, Dir.

North Coast Small Business
Development Center
207 Price Mall, Ste. 500
Crescent City, CA 95531
Phone: (707)464-2168
Fax: (707)465-6008
Fran Clark, Dir.

Imperial Valley Satellite SBDC
Town & Country Shopping Center
301 N. Imperial Ave., Ste. B
El Centro, CA 92243
Phone: (619)312-9800
Fax: (619)312-9838
Debbie Trujillo, Satellite Mgr.

Export SBDC/El Monte Outreach
Center
10501 Valley Blvd., Ste. 106
El Monte, CA 91731
Phone: (818)459-4111

Fax: (818)443-0463
Charles Blythe, Manager

North Coast
Small Business Development Center
520 E St.
Eureka, CA 95501
Phone: (707)445-9720
Fax: (707)445-9652
Duff Heuttner, Bus. Counselor

Central California
Small Business Development Center
3419 W. Shaw Ave., Ste. 102
Fresno, CA 93711
Phone: (209)275-1223
Fax: (209)275-1499
Dennis Winans, Dir.

Gavilan College Small Business
Development Center
7436 Monterey St.
Gilroy, CA 95020
Phone: (408)847-0373
Fax: (408)847-0393
Peter Graff, Dir.

Accelerate Technology Assistance
Small Business Development Center
4199 Campus Dr.
University Towers, Ste. 240
Irvine, CA 92612-4688
Phone: (714)509-2990
Fax: (714)509-2997
Tiffany Haugen, Dir.

Amador SBDC
222 N. Hwy. 49
PO Box 1077
Jackson, CA 95642
Phone: (209)223-0351
Fax: (209)223-5237
Ron Mittelbrunn, Mgr.

Greater San Diego Chamber of
Commerce
Small Business Development Center
4275 Executive Sq., Ste. 920
La Jolla, CA 92037
Phone: (619)453-9388
Fax: (619)450-1997
Hal Lefkowitz, Dir.

Yuba College SBDC
PO Box 1566
15145 Lakeshore Dr.
Lakeport, CA 95453
Phone: (707)263-0330
Fax: (707)263-8516
George McQueen, Dir.

East Los Angeles SBDC
5161 East Pomona Blvd., Ste. 212
Los Angeles, CA 90022
Phone: (213)262-9797
Fax: (213)262-2704

Export Small Business Development
Center of Southern California
110 E. 9th, Ste. A669
Los Angeles, CA 90079
Phone: (213)892-1111
Fax: (213)892-8232
Gladys Moreau, Dir.

South Central LA/Satellite
SBDC
3650 Martin Luther King Blvd., Ste.
246
Los Angeles, CA 90008
Phone: (213)290-2832
Fax: (213)290-7191
Cope Norcross, Satellite Mgr.

Alpine SBDC
PO Box 265
3 Webster St.
Markleeville, CA 96120
Phone: (916)694-2475
Fax: (916)694-2478

Yuba/Sutter Satellite
SBDC
10th and E St.
PO Box 262
Marysville, CA 95901
Phone: (916)749-0153
Fax: (916)749-0155
Sandra Brown-Abernathy, Dir.

Valley Sierra SBDC
Merced Satellite
1632 N St.
Merced, CA 95340
Phone: (209)725-3800
Fax: (209)383-4959
Nick Starianoudakis, Satellite Mgr.

Valley Sierra Small Business
Development Center
1012 11th St., Ste. 300
Modesto, CA 95354
Phone: (209)521-6177
Fax: (209)521-9373
Kelly Bearden, Dir.

Napa Valley College Small Business
Development Center
1556 First St., Ste. 103
Napa, CA 94559
Phone: (707)253-3210

Fax: (707)253-3068
Chuck Eason, Dir.

Inland Empire Business Incubator
SBDC
155 S. Memorial Dr.
Norton Air Force Base, CA 92509
Phone: (909)382-0065
Fax: (909)382-8543
Chuck Eason, Incubator Mgr.

East Bay Small Business
Development Center
519 17th. St., Ste. 210
Oakland, CA 94612
Phone: (510)893-4114
Fax: (510)893-5532
Napoleon Britt, Dir.

International Trade Office
SBDC
3282 E. Guasti Rd., Ste. 100
Ontario, CA 91761
Phone: (909)390-8071
Fax: (909)390-8077
John Hernandez, Trade Manager

Coachella Valley SBDC
Palm Springs Satellite Center
501 S. Palm Canyon Dr., Ste. 222
Palm Springs, CA 92264
Phone: (619)864-1311
Fax: (619)864-1319
Brad Mix, Satellite Mgr.

Pasadena Satellite
SBDC
2061 N. Los Robles, Ste. 106
Pasadena, CA 91104
Phone: (818)398-9031
Fax: (818)398-3059
David Ryal, Satellite Mgr.

Pico Rivera SBDC
9058 E. Washington Blvd.
Pico Rivera, CA 90660
Phone: (310)942-9965
Fax: (310)942-9745
Beverly Taylor, Satellite Mgr.

Eastern Los Angeles County Small
Business Development Center
375 S. Main St., Ste. 101
Pomona, CA 91766
Phone: (909)629-2247
Fax: (909)629-8310
Toni Valdez, Dir.

Pomona SBDC
375 S. Main St., Ste. 101

Pomona, CA 91766
Phone: (909)629-2247
Fax: (909)629-8310
Paul Hischar, Satellite Manager

Cascade Small Business
Development Center
737 Auditorium Dr., Ste. A
Redding, CA 96001
Phone: (916)247-8100
Fax: (916)241-1712
Carole Enmark, Dir.

Inland Empire Small Business
Development Center
1157 Spruce St.
Riverside, CA 92507
Phone: (909)781-2345
Free: (800)750-2353
Fax: (909)781-2353
Teri Ooms, Dir.

California Trade and Commerce
Agency
California SBDC
801 K St., Ste. 1700
Sacramento, CA 95814
Phone: (916)324-5068
Fax: (916)322-5084
Kim Neri, State Dir.

Greater Sacramento SBDC
1410 Ethan Way
Sacramento, CA 95825
Phone: (916)563-3210
Fax: (916)563-3266
Cynthia Steimle, Director

Calaveras SBDC
PO Box 431
3 N. Main St.
San Andreas, CA 95249
Phone: (209)754-1834
Fax: (209)754-4107

San Francisco SBDC
711 Van Ness, Ste. 305
San Francisco, CA 94102
Phone: (415)561-1890
Fax: (415)561-1894
Tim Sprinkles, Director

Orange County Small Business
Development Center
901 E. Santa Ana Blvd., Ste. 101
Santa Ana, CA 92701
Phone: (714)647-1172
Fax: (714)835-9008
Gregory Kishel, Dir.

Southwest Los Angeles County
Westside Satellite
SBDC
3233 Donald Douglas Loop S., Ste. C
Santa Monica, CA 90405
Phone: (310)398-8883
Fax: (310)398-3024
Sue Hunter, Admin. Asst.

Redwood Empire Small Business
Development Center
520 Mendocino Ave., Ste. 210
Santa Rosa, CA 95401
Phone: (707)524-1770
Fax: (707)524-1772
Charles Robbins, Dir.

San Joaquin Delta College Small
Business Development Center
445 N. San Joaquin, 2nd Fl.
Stockton, CA 95202
Phone: (209)474-5089
Fax: (209)474-5605
Gillian Murphy, Dir.

Silicon Valley SBDC
298 S. Sunnyvale Ave., Ste. 204
Sunnyvale, CA 94086
Phone: (408)736-0680
Fax: (408)736-0679
Eliza Minor, Director

Southwest Los Angeles County Small
Business Development Center
21221 Western Ave., Ste. 110
Torrance, CA 90501
Phone: (310)787-6466
Fax: (310)782-8607
Susan Hunter, Dir.

West Company SBDC
367 N. State St., Ste. 208
Ukiah, CA 95482
Phone: (707)468-3553
Fax: (707)468-3555
Sheilah Rogers, Director

North Los Angeles Small Business
Development Center
4717 Van Nuys Blvd., Ste. 201
Van Nuys, CA 91403-2100
Phone: (818)907-9922
Fax: (818)907-9890
Wilma Berglund, Dir.

Export SBDC Satellite Center
5700 Ralston St., Ste. 310
Ventura, CA 93003
Phone: (805)658-2688

Fax: (805)658-2252
Heather Wicka, Manager

Gold Coast SBDC
5700 Ralston St., Ste. 310
Ventura, CA 93003
Phone: (805)658-2688
Fax: (805)658-2252
Joe Higgins, Satellite Mgr.

High Desert SBDC
Victorville Satellite Center
15490 Civic Dr., Ste. 102
Victorville, CA 92392
Phone: (619)951-1592
Fax: (619)951-8929
Janice Harbaugh, Business
Consultant

Central California - Visalia Satellite
SBDC
430 W. Caldwell Ave., Ste. D
Visalia, CA 93277
Phone: (209)625-3051
Fax: (209)625-3053
Randy Mason, Satellite Mgr.

Colorado

Adams State College
Small Business Development Center
School of Business, Rm. 105
Alamosa, CO 81102
Phone: (719)587-7372
Fax: (719)587-7603
Mary Hoffman, Dir.

Community College of Aurora
Small Business Development Center
9905 E. Colfax
Aurora, CO 80010-2119
Phone: (303)341-4849
Fax: (303)361-2953
E-mail: asbdc@henge.com
Randy Johnson, Dir.

Boulder Chamber of Commerce
Small Business Development Center
2440 Pearl St.
Boulder, CO 80302
Phone: (303)442-1475
Fax: (303)938-8837
Marilynn Force, Dir.

Pueblo Community College (Canon
City)
Small Business Development Center
3080 Main St.
Canon City, CO 81212
Phone: (719)275-5335

Fax: (719)275-4400
Elwin Boody, Dir.

Pikes Peak Community College
Small Business Development Center
Colorado Springs Chamber of
Commerce
CITTI Bldg.
1420 Austin Bluff Pkwy.
Colorado Springs, CO 80933
Phone: (719)592-1894
Fax: (719)533-0545
E-mail: sbdc@mail.uccs.edu
Iris Clark, Dir.

Colorado Northwestern Community
College
Small Business Development Center
50 College Dr.
Craig, CO 81625
Phone: (970)824-7078
Fax: (970)824-1134
Ken Farmer, Dir.

Delta Montrose Vocational School
Small Business Development Center
1765 US Hwy. 50
Delta, CO 81416
Phone: (970)874-8772
Free: (888)234-7232
Fax: (970)874-8796
Bob Marshall, Dir.

Community College of Denver
Greater Denver Chamber of
Commerce
Small Business Development Center
1445 Market St.
Denver, CO 80202
Phone: (303)620-8076
Fax: (303)534-3200
Tamela Lee, Dir.

Office of Business Development
Colorado SBDC
1625 Broadway, Ste. 1710
Denver, CO 80202
Phone: (303)892-3809
Free: (800)333-7798
Fax: (303)892-3848
Lee Ortiz, State Dir.

Fort Lewis College
Small Business Development Center
136-G Hesperus Hall
Durango, CO 81301-3999
Phone: (970)247-7009
Fax: (970)247-7623
Jim Reser, Dir.

Front Range Community College (Ft.
Collins)
Small Business Development Center
125 S. Howes, Ste. 105
Ft. Collins, CO 80521
Phone: (970)498-9295
Fax: (970)204-0385
Frank Pryor, Dir.

Morgan Community College (Ft.
Morgan)
Small Business Development Center
300 Main St.
Ft. Morgan, CO 80701
Phone: (970)867-3351
Fax: (970)867-3352
Dan Simon, Dir.

Colorado Mountain College
(Glenwood Springs)
Small Business Development Center
831 Grand Ave.
Glenwood Springs, CO 81601
Phone: (970)928-0120
Free: (800)621-1647
Fax: (970)947-9324
Alisa Zimmerman, Dir.

Small Business Development Center
1726 Cole Blvd., Bldg. 22, Ste. 310
Golden, CO 80401
Phone: (303)277-1840
Fax: (303)277-1899
Jayne Reiter, Dir.

Mesa State College
Small Business Development Center
304 W. Main St.
Grand Junction, CO 81505-1606
Phone: (970)243-5242
Fax: (970)241-0771
Julie Morey, Dir.

Aims Community College
Greeley/Weld Chamber of Commerce
Small Business Development Center
902 7th Ave.
Greeley, CO 80631
Phone: (970)352-3661
Fax: (970)352-3572
Ron Anderson, Dir.

Red Rocks Community College
Small Business Development Center
777 S. Wadsworth Blvd., Ste. 254
Bldg. 4
Lakewood, CO 80226
Phone: (303)987-0710

Fax: (303)987-1331
Jayne Reiter, Acting Dir.

Lamar Community College
Small Business Development Center
2400 S. Main
Lamar, CO 81052
Phone: (719)336-8141
Fax: (719)336-2448
Dan Minor, Dir.

Small Business Development Center
Arapahoe Community College
South Metro Chamber of Commerce
7901 S. Park Plz., Ste. 110
Littleton, CO 80120
Phone: (303)795-5855
Fax: (303)795-7520
Selma Kristel, Dir.

Pueblo Community College Small
Business Development Center
900 W. Orman Ave.
Pueblo, CO 81004
Phone: (719)549-3224
Fax: (719)549-3338
Rita Friberg, Dir.

Morgan Community College
(Stratton)
Small Business Development Center
PO Box 28
Stratton, CO 80836
Phone: (719)348-5596
Fax: (719)348-5887
Roni Carr, Dir.

Trinidad State Junior College
Small Business Development Center
136 W. Main St.
Davis Bldg.
Trinidad, CO 81082
Phone: (719)846-5645
Fax: (719)846-4550
Dennis O'Connor, Dir.

Front Range Community College
(Westminster)
Small Business Development Center
3645 W. 112th Ave.
Westminster, CO 80030
Phone: (303)460-1032
Fax: (303)469-7143
Leo Giles, Dir.

Connecticut

Bridgeport Regional Business
Council

Small Business Development Center
10 Middle St., 14th Fl.
Bridgeport, CT 06604-4229
Phone: (203)330-4813
Fax: (203)366-0105
Juan Scott, Dir.

Quinebaug Valley Community
Technical College
Small Business Development Center
742 Upper Maple St.
Danielson, CT 06239-1440
Phone: (860)774-1133
Fax: (860)774-7768
Roger Doty, Dir.

University of Connecticut (Groton)
Small Business Development Center
Administration Bldg., Rm. 300
1084 Shennecossett Rd.
Groton, CT 06340-6097
Phone: (860)405-9009
Fax: (860)405-9041
Louise Kahler, Dir.

Middlesex County Chamber of
Commerce
SBDC
393 Main St.
Middletown, CT 06457
Phone: (860)344-2158
Fax: (860)346-1043
John Serignese

Greater New Haven Chamber of
Commerce
Small Business Development Center
195 Church St.
New Haven, CT 06510-2009
Phone: (203)782-4390
Fax: (203)787-6730
Pete Rivera, Regional Dir.

Southwestern Area Commerce and
Industry Association (SACIA)
Small Business Development Center
1 Landmark Sq., Ste. 230
Stamford, CT 06901
Phone: (203)359-3220
Fax: (203)967-8294
Harvey Blomberg, Dir.

University of Connecticut
School of Business Administration
Connecticut SBDC
2 Bourn Place, U-94
Storrs, CT 06269
Phone: (860)486-4135
Fax: (860)486-1576

E-mail: oconnor@ct.sbdc.uconn.edu
Dennis Gruel, State Dir.

Naugatuck Valley Development
Center
Small Business Development Center
100 Grand St., 3rd Fl.
Waterbury, CT 06702
Phone: (203)757-8937
Fax: (203)757-8937
Ilene Oppenheim, Dir.

University of Connecticut (Greater
Hartford Campus)
Small Business Development Center
1800 Asylum Ave.
West Hartford, CT 06117
Phone: (860)570-9107
Fax: (860)570-9107
Dennis Gruel, Dir.

Eastern Connecticut State University
Small Business Development Center
83 Windham St.
Williamantic, CT 06226-2295
Phone: (860)465-5349
Fax: (860)465-5143
Richard Cheney, Dir.

Delaware

Delaware State University
School of Business Economics
SBDC
1200 N. Dupont Hwy.
Dover, DE 19901
Phone: (302)678-1555
Fax: (302)739-2333
Jim Crisfield, Director

Delaware Technical and Community
College
SBDC
Industrial Training Bldg.
PO Box 610
Georgetown, DE 19947
Phone: (302)856-1555
Fax: (302)856-5779
William F. Pfaff, Dir.

University of Delaware
Delaware SBDC
Purnell Hall, Ste. 005
Newark, DE 19716-2711
Phone: (302)831-1555
Fax: (302)831-1423
Clinton Tymes, State Dir.

Small Business Resource &
Information Center
SBDC
1318 N. Market St.
Wilmington, DE 19801
Phone: (302)571-1555
Fax: (302)571-5222
Barbara Necarsulmer, Mgr.

District of Columbia

Friendship House/Southeastern
University
SBDC
921 Pennsylvania Ave., SE
Washington, DC 20003
Phone: (202)547-7933
Fax: (202)806-1777
Elise Ashby, Dir.

George Washington University
East of the River Community
Development Corp.
SBDC
3101 MLK Jr. Ave., SE, 3rd Fl.
Washington, DC 20032
Phone: (202)561-4975
Howard Johnson, Accounting
Specialist

Howard University
George Washington Small Business
Legal Clinic
SBDC
2000 G St., NW, Ste. 200
Washington, DC 20052
Phone: (202)994-7463
Jose Hernandez, Counselor

Howard University
Office of Latino Affairs
SBDC
2000 14th St., NW, 2nd Fl.
Washington, DC 20009
Phone: (202)939-3018
Fax: (202)994-4946
Jose Hernandez, Gov. Procurement
Specialist

Howard University
SBDC
Satellite Location
2600 6th St., NW, Rm. 125
Washington, DC 20059
Phone: (202)806-1550
Fax: (202)806-1777
Terry Strong, Acting Regional Dir.

Marshall Heights Community
Development Organization
SBDC
3917 Minnesota Ave., NE
Washington, DC 20019
Phone: (202)396-1200
Terry Strong, Financing Specialist

Washington District Office
Business Information Center
SBDC
1110 Vermont Ave., NW, 9th Fl.
Washington, DC 20005
Phone: (202)737-0120
Fax: (202)737-0476
Johnetta Hardy, Marketing Specialist

Florida

Central Florida Development Council
Small Business Development Center
600 N. Broadway, Ste. 300
Bartow, FL 33830
Phone: (941)534-4370
Fax: (941)533-1247
Marcela Stanislaus, Vice President

Florida Atlantic University (Boca
Raton)
Small Business Development Center
777 Glades Rd.
Bldg. T9
Boca Raton, FL 33431
Phone: (561)362-5620
Fax: (561)362-5623
Nancy Young, Dir.

UCF Brevard Campus
Small Business Development Center
1519 Clearlake Rd.
Cocoa, FL 32922
Phone: (407)951-1060

Dania Small Business Development
Center
46 SW 1st Ave.
Dania, FL 33304-3607
Phone: (954)987-0100
Fax: (954)987-0106
William Healy, Regional Mgr.

Daytona Beach Community College
Florida Regional SBDC
1200 W. International Speedway Blvd.
Daytona Beach, FL 32114
Phone: (904)947-5463
Fax: (904)258-3846
Brenda Thomas-Ramos, Dir.

Florida Atlantic University
Commercial Campus
Small Business Development Center
1515 W. Commercial Blvd., Rm. 11
Ft. Lauderdale, FL 33309
Phone: (954)771-6520
Fax: (954)351-4120
Marty Zients, Mgr.

Minority Business Development
Center
SBDC
5950 West Oakland Park Blvd., Ste.
307
Ft. Lauderdale, FL 33313
Phone: (954)485-5333
Fax: (954)485-2514

Edison Community College
Small Business Development Center
8099 College Pkwy. SW
Ft. Myers, FL 33919
Phone: (941)489-9200
Fax: (941)489-9051
Dan Regelski, Management
Consultant

Florida Gulf Coast University
Small Business Development Center
17595 S. Tamiami Trail, Ste. 200
Midway Ctr.
Ft. Myers, FL 33908-4500
Phone: (941)948-1820
Fax: (941)948-1814
Dan Regleski, Management
Consultant

Indian River Community College
Small Business Development Center
3209 Virginia Ave., Rm. 114
Ft. Pierce, FL 34981-5599
Phone: (561)462-4756
Fax: (561)462-4796
Marsha Thompson, Dir.

Okaloosa-Walton Community
College
SBDC
1170 Martin Luther King, Jr. Blvd.
Ft. Walton Beach, FL 32547
Phone: (850)863-6543
Fax: (850)863-6564
Jane Briere, Mgr.

University of North Florida
(Gainesville)
Small Business Development Center
505 NW 2nd Ave., Ste. D

PO Box 2518
Gainesville, FL 32602-2518
Phone: (352)377-5621
Fax: (352)372-0288
Lalla Sheehy, Program Mgr.

University of North Florida
(Jacksonville)
Small Business Development Center
College of Business
Honors Hall, Rm. 2451
4567 St. John's Bluff Rd. S
Jacksonville, FL 32224
Phone: (904)620-2476
Fax: (904)620-2567
E-mail: smallbiz@unf.edu
Lowell Salter, Regional Dir.

Gulf Coast Community College
SBDC
2500 Minnesota Ave.
Lynn Haven, FL 32444
Phone: (850)271-1108
Fax: (850)271-1109
Doug Davis, Dir.

Brevard Community College
(Melbourne)
Small Business Development Center
3865 N. Wickham Rd.
Melbourne, FL 32935
Phone: (407)632-1111
Fax: (407)634-3721
Victoria Peak, Program Coordinator

Florida International University
Small Business Development Center
University Park
CEAS-2620
Miami, FL 33199
Phone: (305)348-2272
Fax: (305)348-2965
Marvin Nesbit, Dir.

Florida International University
(North Miami Campus)
Small Business Development Center
Academic Bldg. No. 1, Rm. 350
NE 151 and Biscayne Blvd.
Miami, FL 33181
Phone: (305)919-5790
Fax: (305)919-5792
Roy Jarrett, Regional Mgr.

Miami Dade Community College
Small Business Development Center
6300 NW 7th Ave.
Miami, FL 33150
Phone: (305)237-1906

Fax: (305)237-1908
Frederic Bonneau, Regional Mgr.

Ocala Small Business Development
Center
110 E. Silver Springs Blvd.
PO Box 1210
Ocala, FL 34470-6613
Phone: (352)622-8763
Fax: (352)651-1031
E-mail: sbdcoca@mercury.net
Philip Geist, Program Dir.

University of Central Florida
Small Business Development Center
College of Business Administration,
Ste. 309
PO Box 161530
Orlando, FL 32816-1530
Phone: (407)823-5554
Fax: (407)823-3073
Al Polfer, Dir.

Palm Beach Gardens
Florida Atlantic University
SBDC
Northrop Center
3970 RCA Blvd., Ste. 7323
Palm Beach Gardens, FL 33410
Phone: (407)691-8550
Fax: (407)692-8502
Steve Windhaus, Regional Mgr.

Procurement Technical Assistance
Program
University of West Florida
Small Business Development Center
19 W. Garden St., Ste. 302
Pensacola, FL 32501
Phone: (850)595-5480
Fax: (850)595-5487
Martha Cobb, Dir.

University of West Florida
Florida SBDC Network
19 West Garden St., Ste. 300
Pensacola, FL 32501
Phone: (850)595-6060
Fax: (850)595-6070
E-mail: fsbdc@uwf.edu
Jerry Cartwright, State Dir.

Seminole Community College
SBDC
100 Weldon Blvd.
Sanford, FL 32773
Phone: (407)328-4722
Fax: (407)330-4489
Wayne Hardy, Regional Mgr.

Florida Agricultural and Mechanical
University
Small Business Development Center
1157 E. Tennessee St.
Tallahassee, FL 32308
Phone: (904)599-3407
Fax: (904)561-2049
Patricia McGowan, Dir.

University of South Florida—CBA
SBDC Special Services
4202 E. Fowler Ave., BSN 3403
Tampa, FL 33620
Phone: (813)974-4371
Fax: (813)974-5020
Dick Hardesty, Procurement Mgr.

University of South Florida (Tampa)
Small Business Development Center
1111 N. Westshore Dr., Annex B,
Ste. 101-B
Tampa, FL 33607
Phone: (813)554-2341
Free: (800)733-7232
Fax: (813)554-2356
Irene Hurst, Dir.

Georgia

University of Georgia
Small Business Development Center
230 S. Jackson St., Ste. 333
Albany, GA 31701-2885
Phone: (912)430-4303
Fax: (912)430-3933
E-mail: sbdcalb@uga.cc.uga.edu
Sue Ford, Asst. District Dir.

NE Georgia District
SBDC
1180 E. Broad St.
Athens, GA 30602-5412
Phone: (706)542-7436
Fax: (706)542-6823
Gayle Rosenthal, Mgr.

University of Georgia
Chicopee Complex
Georgia SBDC
1180 E. Broad St.
Athens, GA 30602-5412
Phone: (706)542-6762
Fax: (706)542-6776
E-mail: sbdcath@uga.cc.uga.edu
Hank Logan, State Dir.

Georgia State University
Small Business Development Center
University Plz.

Box 874
Atlanta, GA 30303-3083
Phone: (404)651-3550
Fax: (404)651-1035
E-mail: sbdcatl@uga.cc.uga.edu
Lee Quarterman, Area Dir.

Morris Brown College
Small Business Development Center
643 Martin Luther King, Jr., Dr. NW
Atlanta, GA 30314
Phone: (404)220-0205
Fax: (404)688-5985
Ray Johnson, Center Mgr.

University of Georgia
Small Business Development Center
1054 Claussen Rd., Ste. 301
Augusta, GA 30907-3215
Phone: (706)737-1790
Fax: (706)731-7937
E-mail: sbdcaug@uga.cc.uga.edu
Jeff Sanford, Area Dir.

University of Georgia (Brunswick)
Small Business Development Center
1107 Fountain Lake Dr.
Brunswick, GA 31525-3039
Phone: (912)264-7343
Fax: (912)262-3095
E-mail: sbdcbrun@uga.cc.uga.edu
David Lewis, Area Dir.

University of Georgia (Columbus)
Small Business Development Center
North Bldg., Rm. 202
928 45th St.
Columbus, GA 31904-6572
Phone: (706)649-7433
Fax: (706)649-1928
E-mail: sbdccolu@uga.cc.uga.edu
Jerry Copeland, Area Dir.

DeKalb Chamber of Commerce
DeKalb Small Business Development
Center
750 Commerce Dr., Ste. 201
Decatur, GA 30030-2622
Phone: (404)373-6930
Fax: (404)687-9684
E-mail: sbdcdec@uga.cc.uga.edu
Eric Bonaparte, Area Dir.

Gainesville Small Business
Development Center
500 Jesse Jewel Pkwy., Ste. 304
Gainesville, GA 30501-3773
Phone: (770)531-5681
Fax: (770)531-5684

E-mail: sbdcgain@uga.cc.uga.edu
Ron Simmons, Area Dir.

Kennesaw State University
Small Business Development Center
1000 Chastain Rd.
Kennesaw, GA 30144-5591
Phone: (770)423-6450
Fax: (770)423-6564
E-mail: sbdcmar@uga.cc.uga.edu
Carlotta Roberts, Area Dir.

Southeast Georgia District (Macon)
Small Business Development Center
401 Cherry St., Ste. 701
PO Box 13212
Macon, GA 31208-3212
Phone: (912)751-6592
Fax: (912)751-6607
E-mail: sbdcmac@uga.cc.uga.edu
Denise Ricketson, Area Dir.

Clayton State College
Small Business Development Center
PO Box 285
Morrow, GA 30260
Phone: (770)961-3440
Fax: (770)961-3428
E-mail: sbdcmorr@uga.cc.uga.edu
Bernie Meincke, Area Dir.

University of Georgia
SBDC
1770 Indian Trail Rd., Ste. 410
Norcross, GA 30093
Phone: (770)806-2124
Fax: (770)806-2129
E-mail: sbdclaw@uga.cc.edu
Robert Andoh, Area Dir.

Floyd College
Small Business Development Center
PO Box 1864
Rome, GA 30162-1864
Phone: (706)295-6326
Fax: (706)295-6732
E-mail: sbdcrome@uga.cc.uga.edu
Drew Tonsmeire, Area Dir.

University of Georgia (Savannah)
Small Business Development Center
450 Mall Blvd., Ste. H
Savannah, GA 31406-4824
Phone: (912)356-2755
Fax: (912)353-3033
E-mail: sbdcsav@uga.cc.uga.edu
Lynn Vos, Area Dir.

Georgia Southern University
Small Business Development Center

325 S. Main St.
PO Box 8156
Statesboro, GA 30460-8156
Phone: (912)681-5194
Fax: (912)681-0648
E-mail: sbdcstat@uga.cc.uga.edu
Mark Davis, Area Dir.

University of Georgia (Valdosta)
Small Business Development Center
Baytree W. Professional Offices
1205 Baytree Rd., Ste. 9
Valdosta, GA 31602-2782
Phone: (912)245-3738
Fax: (912)245-3741
E-mail: sbdcval@uga.cc.uga.edu
Suzanne Barnett, Area Dir.

University of Georgia (Warner
Robins)
Small Business Development Center
151 Osigian Blvd.
Warner Robins, GA 31088
Phone: (912)953-9356
Fax: (912)953-9376
E-mail: sbdccwr@uga.cc.uga.edu
Ronald Reaves, Center Mgr.

Guam

Pacific Islands SBDC Network
UOG Station
303 University Dr.
Mangilao, GU 96923
Phone: (671)735-2590
Fax: (671)734-2002
Dr. Sephen L. Marder, Dir.

Hawaii

Kona Circuit Rider
SBDC
200 West Kawili St.
Hilo, HI 96720-4091
Phone: (808)933-3515
Fax: (808)933-3683
Rebecca Winters, Business
Consultant

University of Hawaii at Hilo
Small Business Development Center
200 W. Kawili St.
Hilo, HI 96720-4091
Phone: (808)974-7515
Fax: (808)974-7683
Website: http://www.maui.com/
~sbdc/hilo.html
Dr. Darryl Mleynek, State Director

University of Hawaii at West Oahu
SBDC
130 Merchant St., Ste. 1030
Honolulu, HI 96813
Phone: (808)522-8131
Fax: (808)522-8135
Laura Noda, Center Dir.

Maui Community College
Small Business Development Center
Maui Research and Technology
Center
590 Lipoa Pkwy., No. 130
Kihei, HI 96779
Phone: (808)875-2402
Fax: (808)875-2452
David B. Fisher, Dir.

University of Hawaii at Hilo
Business Research Library
SBDC
590 Lipoa Pkwy., No. 128
Kihei, HI 96753
Phone: (808)875-2400
Fax: (808)875-2452

Kauai Community College
Small Business Development Center
3-1901 Kaumualii Hwy.
Lihue, HI 96766-9591
Phone: (808)246-1748
Fax: (808)246-5102
Randy Gringas, Center Dir.

Idaho

Boise State University
Small Business Development Center
1910 University Dr.
Boise, ID 83725
Phone: (208)385-3875
Free: (800)225-3815
Fax: (208)385-3877
Robert Shepard, Regional Dir.

Idaho State University (Idaho Falls)
Small Business Development Center
2300 N. Yellowstone
Idaho Falls, ID 83401
Phone: (208)523-1087
Free: (800)658-3829
Fax: (208)523-1049
Betty Capps, Regional Dir.

Lewis-Clark State College
Small Business Development Center
500 8th Ave.
Lewiston, ID 83501
Phone: (208)799-2465

Fax: (208)799-2878
Helen Le Boeuf-Binninger, Regional
Dir.

Idaho Small Business Development
Center
305 E. Park St., Ste. 405
PO Box 1901
McCall, ID 83638
Phone: (208)634-2883
Larry Smith, Associate Business
Consultant

Idaho State University (Pocatello)
Small Business Development Center
1651 Alvin Ricken Dr.
Pocatello, ID 83201
Phone: (208)232-4921
Free: (800)232-4921
Fax: (208)233-0268
Paul Cox, Regional Dir.

North Idaho College
SBDC
525 W. Clearwater Loop
Post Falls, ID 83854
Phone: (208)769-3296
Fax: (208)769-3223
John Lynn, Regional Dir.

College of Southern Idaho
Small Business Development Center
315 Falls Ave.
PO Box 1238
Twin Falls, ID 83303
Phone: (208)733-9554
Fax: (208)733-9316
Cindy Bond, Regional Dir.

Illinois

Waubonsee Community College
(Aurora Campus)
Small Business Development Center
5 E. Galena Blvd.
Aurora, IL 60506-4178
Phone: (630)801-7900
Fax: (630)892-4668
Linda Garrison-Carlton, Dir.

Southern Illinois University at
Carbondale
Small Business Development Center
150 E. Pleasant Hill Rd.
Carbondale, IL 62901-4300
Phone: (618)536-2424
Fax: (618)453-5040
Dennis Cody, Dir.

John A. Logan College
Small Business Development Center
700 Logan College Rd.
Carterville, IL 62918-9802
Phone: (618)985-3741
Fax: (618)985-2248
Richard Fyke, Dir.

Kaskaskia College
Small Business Development Center
27210 College Rd.
Centralia, IL 62801-7878
Phone: (618)532-2049
Fax: (618)532-4983
Richard McCullum, Dir.

University of Illinois at Urbana-
Champaign
International Trade Center
Small Business Development Center
428 Commerce W.
1206 S. 6th St.
Champaign, IL 61820-6980
Phone: (217)244-1585
Fax: (217)333-7410
Tess Morrison, Dir.

Asian American Alliance
SBDC
222 W. Cermak, No. 302
Chicago, IL 60616
Phone: (312)326-2200
Fax: (312)326-0399
Emil Bernardo, Dir.

Back of the Yards Neighborhood
Council
Small Business Development Center
1751 W. 47th St.
Chicago, IL 60609-3889
Phone: (773)523-4419
Fax: (773)254-3525
Bill Przybylski, Dir.

Chicago Small Business
Development Center
DCCA / James R. Thompson Center
100 W. Randolph, Ste. 3-400
Chicago, IL 60601-3219
Phone: (312)814-6111
Fax: (312)814-5247
Carson A. Gallagher, Mgr.

Eighteenth Street Development Corp.
Small Business Development Center
1839 S. Carpenter
Chicago, IL 60608-3347
Phone: (312)733-2287

Fax: (312)733-8242
Maria Munoz, Dir.

Greater North Pulaski Development
Corp.
Small Business Development Center
4054 W. North Ave.
Chicago, IL 60639-5223
Phone: (773)384-2262
Fax: (773)384-3850
Kaushik Shah, Dir.

Industrial Council of Northwest
Chicago
Small Business Development Center
2023 W. Carroll
Chicago, IL 60612-1601
Phone: (312)421-3941
Fax: (312)421-1871
Melvin Eiland, Dir.

Latin American Chamber of
Commerce
Small Business Development Center
3512 W. Fullerton St.
Chicago, IL 60647-2655
Phone: (773)252-5211
Fax: (773)252-7065
Ed Diaz, Dir.

North Business and Industrial
Council (NORBIC)
SBDC
2500 W. Bradley Pl.
Chicago, IL 60618-4798
Phone: (773)588-5855
Fax: (773)588-0734
Tom Kamykowski, Dir.

Richard J. Daley College
Small Business Development Center
7500 S. Pulaski Rd., Bldg. 200
Chicago, IL 60652-1299
Phone: (773)838-0319
Fax: (773)838-0303
Jim Charney, Dir.

Women's Business Development
Center
Small Business Development Center
8 S. Michigan, Ste. 400
Chicago, IL 60603-3302
Phone: (312)853-3477
Fax: (312)853-0145
Joyce Wade, Dir.

McHenry County College
Small Business Development Center
8900 U.S. Hwy. 14

Crystal Lake, IL 60012-2761
Phone: (815)455-6098
Fax: (815)455-9319
Susan Whitfield, Dir.

Danville Area Community College
Small Business Development Center
28 W. North St.
Danville, IL 61832-5729
Phone: (217)442-7232
Fax: (217)442-6228
Ed Adrain, Dir.

Cooperative Extension Service
SBDC
Building 11, Ste. 1105
2525 E. Federal Dr.
Decatur, IL 62526-1573
Phone: (217)875-8284
Fax: (217)875-8288
Bill Wilkinson, Dir.

Sauk Valley Community College
Small Business Development Center
173 Illinois, Rte. 2
Dixon, IL 61021-9188
Phone: (815)288-5511
Fax: (815)288-5958
John Nelson, Dir.

Black Hawk College
Small Business Development Center
301 42nd Ave.
East Moline, IL 61244-4038
Phone: (309)755-2200
Fax: (309)755-9847
Donna Scalf, Dir.

East St. Louis Small Business
Development Center
Federal Building
650 Missouri Ave., Ste. G32
East St. Louis, IL 62201-2955
Phone: (618)482-3833
Fax: (618)482-3859
Robert Ahart, Dir.

Southern Illinois University at
Edwardsville
Small Business Development Center
Campus Box 1107
Edwardsville, IL 62026-0001
Phone: (618)692-2929
Fax: (618)692-2647
Alan Hauff, Dir.

Elgin Community College
Small Business Development Center
1700 Spartan Dr.

Elgin, IL 60123-7193
Phone: (847)888-7488
Fax: (847)931-3911
Craig Fowler, Dir.

Evanston Business and Technology
Center
Small Business Development Center
1840 Oak Ave.
Evanston, IL 60201-3670
Phone: (847)866-1817
Fax: (847)866-1808
Rick Holbrook, Dir.

College of DuPage
Small Business Development Center
425 22nd St.
Glen Ellyn, IL 60137-6599
Phone: (630)942-2771
Fax: (630)942-3789
David Gay, Dir.

Lewis and Clark Community College
SBDC
5800 Godfrey Rd.
Godfrey, IL 62035
Phone: (618)466-3411
Fax: (618)466-0810
Bob Duane, Dir.

College of Lake County
Small Business Development Center
19351 W. Washington St.
Grayslake, IL 60030-1198
Phone: (847)223-3633
Fax: (847)223-9371
Linda Jorn, Dir.

Southeastern Illinois College
Small Business Development Center
303 S. Commercial
Harrisburg, IL 62946-2125
Phone: (618)252-5001
Fax: (618)252-0210
Becky Williams, Dir.

Rend Lake College
Small Business Development Center
Rte. 1
Ina, IL 62846-9801
Phone: (618)437-5321
Fax: (618)437-5677
Lisa Payne, Dir.

Joliet Junior College
Small Business Development Center
Renaissance Center, Rm. 312
214 N. Ottawa St.
Joliet, IL 60431-4097
Phone: (815)727-6544

Fax: (815)722-1895
Denise Mikulski, Dir.

Kankakee Community College
Small Business Development Center
River Rd., Box 888
Kankakee, IL 60901-7878
Phone: (815)933-0376
Fax: (815)933-0217
Kelly Berry, Dir.

Western Illinois University
Small Business Development Center
214 Seal Hall
Macomb, IL 61455-1390
Phone: (309)298-2211
Fax: (309)298-2520
Dan Voorhis, Dir.

Maple City Business and Technology
Center
Small Business Development Center
620 S. Main St.
Monmouth, IL 61462-2688
Phone: (309)734-4664
Fax: (309)734-8579
Carol Cook, Dir.

Illinois Valley Community College
Small Business Development Center
815 N. Orlando Smith Ave., Bldg. 11
Oglesby, IL 61348-9692
Phone: (815)223-1740
Fax: (815)224-3033
Boyd Palmer, Dir.

Illinois Eastern Community College
Small Business Development Center
401 E. Main St.
Olney, IL 62450-2119
Phone: (618)395-3011
Fax: (618)395-1922
Debbie Chilson, Dir.

Moraine Valley Community College
Small Business Development Center
10900 S. 88th Ave.
Palos Hills, IL 60465-0937
Phone: (708)974-5468
Fax: (708)974-0078
Hilary Gereg, Dir.

Bradley University
Small Business Development Center
141 N. Jobst Hall, 1st Fl.
Peoria, IL 61625-0001
Phone: (309)677-2992
Fax: (309)677-3386
Roger Luman, Dir.

Illinois Central College
Procurement Technical Assistance
Center
Small Business Development Center
124 SW Adams St., Ste. 300
Peoria, IL 61602-1388
Phone: (309)676-7500
Fax: (309)676-7534
Susan Gorman, Dir.

John Wood Community College
Procurement Technical Assistance
Center
Small Business Development Center
301 Oak St.
Quincy, IL 62301-2500
Phone: (217)228-5511
Fax: (217)228-5501
Edward Van Leer, Dir.

Rock Valley College
Small Business Development Center
1220 Rock St.
Rockford, IL 61101-1437
Phone: (815)968-4087
Fax: (815)968-4157
Shirley DeBenedetto, Dir.

Department of Commerce &
Community Affairs
Illinois SBDC
620 East Adams St., Third Fl.
Springfield, IL 62701
Phone: (217)524-5856
Fax: (217)524-0171
Jeff Mitchell, State Dir.

Lincoln Land Community College
Small Business Development Center
100 N. 11th St.
Springfield, IL 62703-1002
Phone: (217)789-1017
Fax: (217)789-9838
Freida Schreck, Dir.

Shawnee Community College
Small Business Development Center
Shawnee College Rd.
Ullin, IL 62992
Phone: (618)634-9618
Fax: (618)634-2347
Donald Denny, Dir.

Governors State University
Small Business Development Center
College of Business, Rm. C-3370
University Park, IL 60466-0975
Phone: (708)534-4929

Fax: (708)534-1646
Christine Cochrane, Dir.

Indiana

Batesville Office of Economic
Development
SBDC
132 S. Main
Batesville, IN 47006
Phone: (812)933-6110

Bedford Chamber of Commerce
SBDC
1116 W. 16th St.
Bedford, IN 47421
Phone: (812)275-4493

Bloomfield Chamber of Commerce
SBDC
c/o Harrah Realty Co.
23 S. Washington St.
Bloomfield, IN 47424
Phone: (812)275-4493

Bloomington Area Regional Small
Business Development Center
216 Allen St.
Bloomington, IN 47403
Phone: (812)339-8937
Fax: (812)335-7352
David Miller, Dir.

Clay Count Chamber of Commerce
SBDC
12 N. Walnut St.
Brazil, IN 47834
Phone: (812)448-8457

Brookville Chamber of Commerce
SBDC
PO Box 211
Brookville, IN 47012
Phone: (317)647-3177

Clinton Chamber of Commerce
SBDC
292 N. 9th St.
Clinton, IN 47842
Phone: (812)832-3844

Columbia City Chamber of
Commerce
SBDC
112 N. Main St.
Columbia City, IN 46725
Phone: (219)248-8131

Columbus Regional Small Business
Development Center

4920 N. Warren Dr.
Columbus, IN 47203
Phone: (812)372-6480
Free: (800)282-7232
Fax: (812)372-0228
Jack Hess, Dir.

Connerville SBDC
504 Central
Connersville, IN 47331
Phone: (317)825-8328

Harrison County
Development Center
SBDC
405 N. Capitol, Ste. 308
Corydon, IN 47112
Phone: (812)738-8811

Montgomery County Chamber of
Commerce
SBDC
211 S. Washington St.
Crawfordsville, IN 47933
Phone: (317)654-5507

Decatur Chamber of Commerce
SBDC
125 E. Monroe St.
Decatur, IN 46733
Phone: (219)724-2604

City of Delphi Community
Development
SBDC
201 S. Union
Delphi, IN 46923
Phone: (317)564-6692

Southwestern Indiana Regional Small
Business Development Center
100 NW 2nd St., Ste. 200
Evansville, IN 47708
Phone: (812)425-7232
Fax: (812)421-5883
Kate Northrup, Dir.

Northeast Indiana Regional Small
Business Development Center
1830 Wayne Trace
Fort Wayne, IN 46803
Phone: (219)426-0040
Fax: (219)424-0024
E-mail: sbdc@mailfwi.com
Nick Adams, Dir.

Clinton County Chamber of
Commerce
SBDC
207 S. Main St.

Frankfort, IN 46041
Phone: (317)654-5507

Northlake Small Business
Development Center
487 Broadway, Ste. 201
Gary, IN 46402
Phone: (219)882-2000

Greencastle Partnership Center
SBDC
2 S. Jackson St.
Greencastle, IN 46135
Phone: (317)653-4517

Greensburg Area Chamber of
Commerce
SBDC
125 W. Main St.
Greensburg, IN 47240
Phone: (812)663-2832

Hammond Development Corp.
SBDC
649 Conkey St.
Hammond, IN 46324
Phone: (219)853-6399

Blackford County Economic
Development
SBDC
PO Box 43
Hartford, IN 47001-0043
Phone: (317)348-4944

Indiana SBDC Network
One North Capitol, Ste. 420
Indianapolis, IN 46204
Phone: (317)264-6871
Fax: (317)264-3102
E-mail: sthrash@in.net
Stephen Thrash, Exec. Dir.

Indianapolis Regional Small Business
Development Center
342 N. Senate Ave.
Indianapolis, IN 46204-1708
Phone: (317)261-3030
Fax: (317)261-3053
Glenn Dunlap, Dir.

Clark County Hoosier Falls
Private Industry Council Workforce
1613 E. 8th St.
Jeffersonville, IN 47130
Phone: (812)282-0456

Southern Indiana Regional Small
Business Development Center
1613 E. 8th St.

Jeffersonville, IN 47130
Phone: (812)288-6451
Fax: (812)284-8314
Patricia Stroud, Dir.

Kendallville Chamber of Commerce
SBDC
228 S. Main St.
Kendallville, IN 46755
Phone: (219)347-1554

Kokomo-Howard County Regional
Small Business Development Center
106 N. Washington
Kokomo, IN 46901
Phone: (317)454-7922
Fax: (317)452-4564
E-mail: sbdc5@holli.com
Kim Moyers, Dir.

LaPorte Small Business Development
Center
414 Lincolnway
La Porte, IN 46350
Phone: (219)326-7232

Greater Lafayette Regional Area
Small Business Development Center
122 N. 3rd
Lafayette, IN 47901
Phone: (765)742-2394
Fax: (765)742-6276
Susan Davis, Dir.

Union County Chamber of
Commerce
SBDC
102 N. Main St., No. 6
Liberty, IN 47353-1039
Phone: (317)458-5976

Linton/Stockton Chamber of
Commerce
SBDC
PO Box 208
Linton, IN 47441
Phone: (812)847-4846

Southeastern Indiana Regional Small
Business Development Center
975 Industrial Dr.
Madison, IN 47250
Phone: (812)265-3127
Fax: (812)265-5544
E-mail: seinsbdc@seidata.com
Rose Marie Roberts, Dir.

Crawford County
Private Industry Council Workforce
SBDC

Box 224 D, R.R. 1
Marengo, IN 47140
Phone: (812)365-2174

Greater Martinsville Chamber of
Commerce
SBDC
210 N. Marion St.
Martinsville, IN 46151
Phone: (317)342-8110

Lake County Public Library
Small Business Development Center
1919 W. 81st. Ave.
Merrillville, IN 46410-5382
Phone: (219)756-7232

First Citizens Bank
SBDC
515 N. Franklin Sq.
Michigan City, IN 46360
Phone: (219)874-9245

Mitchell Chamber of Commerce
SBDC
1st National Bank
Main Street
Mitchell, IN 47446
Phone: (812)849-4441

Mt. Vernon Chamber of Commerce
SBDC
405 E. 4th St.
Mt. Vernon, IN 47620
Phone: (812)838-3639

East Central Indiana Regional Small
Business Development Center
401 S. High St.
PO Box 842
Muncie, IN 47305
Phone: (765)284-8144
Fax: (765)751-9151
Barbara Armstrong, Dir.

Brown County Chamber of
Commerce
SBDC
PO Box 164
Nashville, IN 47448
Phone: (812)988-6647

Southern Indiana Small Business
Development Center
Private Industry Council Workforce
4100 Charleston Rd.
New Albany, IN 47150
Phone: (812)945-0266
Fax: (812)948-4664
Gretchen Mahaffey, Dir.

Henry County Economic
Development Corp.
SBDC
1325 Broad St., Ste. B
New Castle, IN 47362
Phone: (317)529-4635

Jennings County Chamber of
Commerce
SBDC
PO Box 340
North Vernon, IN 47265
Phone: (812)346-2339

Orange County
Private Industry Council Workforce
SBDC
326 B. N. Gospel
Paoli, IN 47454-1412
Phone: (812)723-4206

Northwest Indiana Regional Small
Business Development Center
Small Business Development Center
6100 Southport Rd.
Portage, IN 46368
Phone: (219)762-1696
Fax: (219)763-2653
Mark McLaughlin, Dir

Jay County Development Corp.
SBDC
121 W. Main St., Ste. A
Portland, IN 47371
Phone: (219)726-9311

Richmond-Wayne County Small
Business Development Center
33 S. 7th St.
Richmond, IN 47374
Phone: (765)962-2887
Fax: (765)966-0882
Cliff Fry, Dir.

Rochester and Lake Manitou
Chamber of Commerce
Fulton Economic Development
Center
SBDC
617 Main St.
Rochester, IN 46975
Phone: (219)223-6773

Rushville Chamber of Commerce
SBDC
PO Box 156
Rushville, IN 46173
Phone: (317)932-2222

St. Mary of the Woods College
SBDC
St. Mary-of-the-Woods, IN 47876
Phone: (812)535-5151

Washington County
Private Industry Council Workforce
SBDC
Hilltop Plaza
Salem, IN 47167
Phone: (812)883-2283

Scott County
Private Industry Council Workforce
SBDC
752 Lakeshore Dr.
Scottsburg, IN 47170
Phone: (812)752-3886

Seymour Chamber of Commerce
SBDC
PO Box 43
Seymour, IN 47274
Phone: (812)522-3681

Minority Business Development
Project Future
SBDC
401 Col
South Bend, IN 46634
Phone: (219)234-0051

South Bend Regional Small Business
Development Center
300 N. Michigan
South Bend, IN 46601
Phone: (219)282-4350
Fax: (219)236-1056
Jim Gregar, Dir.

Economic Development Office
SBDC
46 E. Market St.
Spencer, IN 47460
Phone: (812)829-3245

Sullivan Chamber of Commerce
SBDC
10 S. Crt. St.
Sullivan, IN 47882
Phone: (812)268-4836

Tell City Chamber of Commerce
SBDC
645 Main St.
Tell City, IN 47586
Phone: (812)547-2385
Fax: (812)547-8378

Terre Haute Area Small Business
Development Center
School of Business, Rm. 510
Terre Haute, IN 47809
Phone: (812)237-7676
Fax: (812)237-7675
William Minnis, Dir.

Tipton County Economic
Development Corp.
SBDC
136 E. Jefferson
Tipton, IN 46072
Phone: (317)675-7300

Porter County
SBDC
911 Wall St.
Valparaiso, IN 46383
Phone: (219)477-5256

Vevay/Switzerland Country
Foundation
SBDC
PO Box 193
Vevay, IN 47043
Phone: (812)427-2533

Vincennes University
SBDC
PO Box 887
Vincennes, IN 47591
Phone: (812)885-5749

Wabash Area Chamber of Commerce
Wabash Economic Development
Corp.
SBDC
67 S. Wabash
Wabash, IN 46992
Phone: (219)563-1168

Washington Daviess County
SBDC
1 Train Depot St.
Washington, IN 47501
Phone: (812)254-5262
Fax: (812)254-2550
Mark Brochin, Dir.

Purdue University
SBDC
Business & Industrial Development
Center
1220 Potter Dr.
West Lafayette, IN 47906
Phone: (317)494-5858

Randolph County Economic
Development Foundation

SBDC
111 S. Main St.
Winchester, IN 47394
Phone: (317)584-3266

Iowa

Iowa SBDC
137 Lynn Ave.
Ames, IA 50014
Phone: (515)292-6351
Free: (800)373-7232
Fax: (515)292-0020
Ronald Manning, State Dir.

Iowa State University
Small Business Development Center
ISU Branch Office
Bldg. 1, Ste. 615
2501 N. Loop Dr.
Ames, IA 50010-8283
Phone: (515)296-7828
Free: (800)373-7232
Fax: (515)296-6714
Steve Carter, Dir.

DMACC Small Business
Development Center
Circle West Incubator
PO Box 204
Audubon, IA 50025
Phone: (712)563-2623
Fax: (712)563-2301
Lori Harmening, Dir.

University of Northern Iowa
Small Business Development Center
8628 University Ave.
Cedar Falls, IA 50614-0032
Phone: (319)273-2696
Fax: (319)273-7730
Lyle Bowlin, Dir.

Iowa Western Community College
Small Business Development Center
2700 College Rd., Box 4C
Council Bluffs, IA 51502
Phone: (712)325-3260
Fax: (712)325-3408
Ronald Helms, Dir.

Southwestern Community College
Small Business Development Center
1501 W. Townline Rd.
Creston, IA 50801
Phone: (515)782-4161
Fax: (515)782-3312
Robin Beech Travis, Dir.

Eastern Iowa Small Business
Development Center
304 W. 2nd St.
Davenport, IA 52801
Phone: (319)322-4499
Fax: (319)322-8241
Jon Ryan, Dir.

Drake University
Small Business Development Center
2507 University Ave.
Des Moines, IA 50311-4505
Phone: (515)271-2655
Fax: (515)271-1899
Benjamin Swartz, Dir.

Northeast Iowa Small Business
Development Center
770 Town Clock Plz.
Dubuque, IA 52001
Phone: (319)588-3350
Fax: (319)557-1591
Charles Tonn, Dir.

Iowa Central Community College
SBDC
900 Central Ave., Ste. 4
Ft. Dodge, IA 50501
Phone: (515)576-5090
Fax: (515)576-0826
Todd Madson, Dir.

University of Iowa
Small Business Development Center
108 Papajohn Business
Administration Bldg., Ste. S-160
Iowa City, IA 52242-1000
Phone: (319)335-3742
Free: (800)253-7232
Fax: (319)353-2445
Paul Heath, Dir.

Kirkwood Community College
Small Business Development Center
2901 10th Ave.
Marion, IA 52302
Phone: (319)377-8256
Fax: (319)377-5667
Steve Sprague, Dir.

North Iowa Area Community College
Small Business Development Center
500 College Dr.
Mason City, IA 50401
Phone: (515)422-4342
Fax: (515)422-4129
Richard Petersen, Dir.

Indian Hills Community College
Small Business Development Center

525 Grandview Ave.
Ottumwa, IA 52501
Phone: (515)683-5127
Fax: (515)683-5263
Bryan Ziegler, Dir.

Western Iowa Tech Community
College
Small Business Development Center
4647 Stone Ave.
PO Box 5199
Sioux City, IA 51102-5199
Phone: (712)274-6418
Free: (800)352-4649
Fax: (712)274-6429
Dennis Bogenrief, Dir.

Iowa Lakes Community College
(Spencer)
Small Business Development Center
1900 N. Grand Ave., Ste. 8
Hwy. 71 N
Spencer, IA 51301
Phone: (712)262-4213
Fax: (712)262-4047
John Beneke, Dir.

Southeastern Community College
Small Business Development Center
Drawer F
West Burlington, IA 52655
Phone: (319)752-2731
Free: (800)828-7322
Fax: (319)752-3407
Deb Dalziel, Dir.

Kansas

Bendictine College
SBDC
1020 N. 2nd St.
Atchison, KS 66002
Phone: (913)367-5340
Fax: (913)367-6102
Don Laney, Dir.

Butler County Community College
Small Business Development Center
600 Walnut
Augusta, KS 67010
Phone: (316)775-1124
Fax: (316)775-1370
Dorinda Rolle, Dir.

Neosho County Community College
SBDC
1000 S. Allen
Chanute, KS 66720
Phone: (316)431-2820

Fax: (316)431-0082
Duane Clum, Dir.

Coffeyville Community College
SBDC
11th and Willow Sts.
Coffeyville, KS 67337-5064
Phone: (316)251-7700
Fax: (316)252-7098
Charles Shaver, Dir.

Colby Community College
Small Business Development Center
1255 S. Range
Colby, KS 67701
Phone: (913)462-3984
Fax: (913)462-8315
Robert Selby, Dir.

Cloud County Community College
SBDC
2221 Campus Dr.
PO Box 1002
Concordia, KS 66901
Phone: (913)243-1435
Fax: (913)243-1459
Tony Foster, Dir.

Dodge City Community College
Small Business Development Center
2501 N. 14th Ave.
Dodge City, KS 67801
Phone: (316)227-9247
Fax: (316)227-9200
Wayne E. Shiplet, Dir.

Emporia State University
Small Business Development Center
130 Cremer Hall
Emporia, KS 66801
Phone: (316)342-7162
Fax: (316)341-5418
Lisa Brumbaugh, Regional Dir.

Ft. Scott Community College
SBDC
2108 S. Horton
Ft. Scott, KS 66701
Phone: (316)223-2700
Fax: (316)223-6530
Steve Pammenter, Dir.

Garden City Community College
SBDC
801 Campus Dr.
Garden City, KS 67846
Phone: (316)276-9632
Fax: (316)276-9630
Bill Sander, Regional Dir.

Ft. Hays State University
Small Business Development Center
109 W. 10th St.
Hays, KS 67601
Phone: (785)628-6786
Fax: (785)628-0533
Clare Gustin, Regional Dir.

Hutchinson Community College
Small Business Development Center
815 N. Walnut, Ste. 225
Hutchinson, KS 67501
Phone: (316)665-4950
Free: (800)289-3501
Fax: (316)665-8354
Clark Jacobs, Dir.

Independence Community College
SBDC
Arco Bldg.
11th and Main St.
Independence, KS 67301
Phone: (316)332-1420
Fax: (316)331-5344
Preston Haddan, Dir.

Allen County Community College
SBDC
1801 N. Cottonwood
Iola, KS 66749
Phone: (316)365-5116
Fax: (316)365-3284
Susan Thompson, Dir.

University of Kansas
Small Business Development Center
734 Vermont St., Ste. 104
Lawrence, KS 66044
Phone: (785)843-8844
Fax: (785)865-8878
Randy Brady, Regional Dir.

Seward County Community College
Small Business Development Center
1801 N. Kansas
PO Box 1137
Liberal, KS 67901
Phone: (316)629-2650
Fax: (316)629-2689
Dale Reed, Dir.

Kansas State University (Manhattan)
Small Business Development Center
College of Business Administration
2323 Anderson Ave., Ste. 100
Manhattan, KS 66502-2947
Phone: (785)532-5529

Fax: (785)532-5827
Fred Rice, Regional Dir.

Ottawa University
SBDC
College Ave., Box 70
Ottawa, KS 66067
Phone: (913)242-5200
Fax: (913)242-7429
Lori Kravets, Dir.

Johnson County Community College
Small Business Development Center
CEC Bldg., Rm. 223
Overland Park, KS 66210-1299
Phone: (913)469-3878
Fax: (913)469-4415
Kathy Nadiman, Regional Dir.

Labette Community College
SBDC
200 S. 14th
Parsons, KS 67357
Phone: (316)421-6700
Fax: (316)421-0921
Mark Turnbull, Dir.

Pittsburg State University
Small Business Development Center
Shirk Hall
1501 S. Joplin
Pittsburg, KS 66762
Phone: (316)235-4920
Fax: (316)232-6440
Kathryn Richard

Pratt Community College
Small Business Development Center
Hwy. 61
Pratt, KS 67124
Phone: (316)672-5641
Fax: (316)672-5288
Pat Gordon, Dir.

Salina Area Chamber of Commerce
Small Business Development Center
PO Box 586
Salina, KS 67402
Phone: (785)827-9301
Fax: (785)827-9758
James Gaines, Regional Dir.

Kansas SBDC
214 SW 6th St., Ste. 205
Topeka, KS 66603-3261
Phone: (785)296-6514
Fax: (785)291-3261
E-mail: ksbdc@cjnetworks.com
Debbie Bishop, State Dir.

Washburn University of Topeka
SBDC
School of Business
101 Henderson Learning Center
Topeka, KS 66621
Phone: (785)231-1010
Fax: (785)231-1063
Don Kingman, Regional Dir.

Wichita State University
SBDC
1845 Fairmont
Wichita, KS 67260
Phone: (316)689-3193
Fax: (316)689-3647
Joann Ard, Regional Dir.

Kentucky

Morehead State University College of
Business
Boyd-Greenup County Chamber of
Commerce
SBDC
1401 Winchester Ave., Ste. 305
207 15th St.
Ashland, KY 41101
Phone: (606)329-8011
Fax: (606)324-4570
Kimberly A. Jenkins, Dir.

Western Kentucky University
Bowling Green Small Business
Development Center
2355 Nashville Rd.
Bowling Green, KY 42101
Phone: (502)745-1905
Fax: (502)745-1931
Richard S. Horn, Dir.

University of Kentucky
(Elizabethtown)
Small Business Development Center
133 W. Dixie Ave.
Elizabethtown, KY 42701
Phone: (502)765-6737
Fax: (502)769-5095
Lou Ann Allen, Dir.

Northern Kentucky University
SBDC
BEP Center 463
Highland Heights, KY 41099-0506
Phone: (606)572-6524
Fax: (606)572-6177
Sutton Landry, Dir.

Murray State University
(Hopkinsville)

Small Business Development Center
300 Hammond Dr.
Hopkinsville, KY 42240
Phone: (502)886-8666
Fax: (502)886-3211
Michael Cartner, Dir.

Small Business Development Center
Lexington Central Library, 4th Fl.
140 E. Main St.
Lexington, KY 40507-1376
Phone: (606)257-7666
Fax: (606)257-1751
Debbie McKnight, Dir.

University of Kentucky
Center for Entrepreneurship
Kentucky SBDC
225 Gatton Business and Economics
Bldg.
Lexington, KY 40506-0034
Phone: (606)257-7668
Fax: (606)323-1907
Janet S. Holloway, State Dir.

Bellarmine College
Small Business Development Center
School of Business
600 W. Main St., Ste. 219
Louisville, KY 40202
Phone: (502)574-4770
Fax: (502)574-4771
Thomas G. Daley, Dir.

University of Louisville
Center for Entrepreneurship and
Technology
Small Business Development Centers
Burhans Hall, Shelby Campus, Rm.
122
Louisville, KY 40292
Phone: (502)588-7854
Fax: (502)588-8573
Lou Dickie, Dir.

Southeast Community College
SBDC
1300 Chichester Ave.
Middlesboro, KY 40965-2265
Phone: (606)242-2145
Fax: (606)242-4514
Kathleen Moats, Dir.

Morehead State University
Small Business Development Center
309 Combs Bldg.
UPO 575
Morehead, KY 40351
Phone: (606)783-2895

Fax: (606)783-5020
Keith Moore, District Dir.

Murray State University
West Kentucky Small Business
Development Center
College of Business and Public
Affairs
PO Box 9
Murray, KY 42071
Phone: (502)762-2856
Fax: (502)762-3049
Rosemary Miller, Dir.

Murray State University
Owensboro Small Business
Development Center
3860 U.S. Hwy. 60 W
Owensboro, KY 42301
Phone: (502)926-8085
Fax: (502)684-0714
Mickey Johnson, District Dir.

Morehead State University
Pikeville Small Business
Development Center
3455 N. Mayo Trail, No. 4
110 Village St.
Pikeville, KY 41501
Phone: (606)432-5848
Fax: (606)432-8924
Michael Morley, Dir.

Eastern Kentucky University
South Central Small Business
Development Center
The Center for Rural Development,
Ste. 260
2292 S. Hwy. 27
Somerset, KY 42501
Phone: (606)677-6120
Fax: (606)677-6083
Kathleen Moats, Dir.

Louisiana

Alexandria SBDC
Hibernia National Bank Bldg., Ste.
510
934 3rd St.
Alexandria, LA 71301
Phone: (318)484-2123
Fax: (318)484-2126
Kathey Hunter, Consultant

Southern University
Capital Small Business Development
Center
1933 Wooddale Blvd., Ste. E

Baton Rouge, LA 70806
Phone: (504)922-0998
Fax: (504)922-0024
Gregory Spann, Dir.

Southeastern Louisiana University
Small Business Development Center
College of Business Administration
Box 522, SLU Sta.
Hammond, LA 70402
Phone: (504)549-3831
Fax: (504)549-2127
William Joubert, Dir.

University of Southwestern Louisiana
Acadiana Small Business
Development Center
College of Business Administration
Box 43732
Lafayette, LA 70504
Phone: (318)262-5344
Fax: (318)262-5296
Kim Spence, Dir.

McNeese State University
Small Business Development Center
College of Business Administration
Lake Charles, LA 70609
Phone: (318)475-5529
Fax: (318)475-5012
Paul Arnold, Dir.

Louisiana Electronic Assistance
Program
SBDC
NE Louisiana, College of Business
Administration
Monroe, LA 71209
Phone: (318)342-1215
Fax: (318)342-1209
Dr. Jerry Wall, Dir.

Northeast Louisiana University
SBDC
Louisiana SBDC
College of Business Administration,
Rm. 2-57
Monroe, LA 71209
Phone: (318)342-5506
Fax: (318)342-5510
Dr. John Baker, State Dir.

Northwestern State University
Small Business Development Center
College of Business Administration
Natchitoches, LA 71497
Phone: (318)357-5611
Fax: (318)357-6810
Mary Lynn Wilkerson, Dir.

Louisiana International Trade Center
SBDC
World Trade Center, Ste. 2926
2 Canal St.
New Orleans, LA 70130
Phone: (504)568-8222
Fax: (504)568-8228
Ruperto Chavarri, Dir.

Loyola University
Small Business Development Center
College of Business Administration
Box 134
New Orleans, LA 70118
Phone: (504)865-3474
Fax: (504)865-3496
Ronald Schroeder, Dir.

Southern University at New Orleans
Small Business Development Center
College of Business Administration
New Orleans, LA 70126
Phone: (504)286-5308
Fax: (504)286-5131
Jon Johnson, Dir.

University of New Orleans
Small Business Development Center
1600 Canal St., Ste. 620
New Orleans, LA 70112
Phone: (504)539-9292
Fax: (504)539-9205
Norma Grace, Dir.

Louisiana Tech University
Small Business Development Center
College of Business Administration
Box 10318, Tech Sta.
Ruston, LA 71272
Phone: (318)257-3537
Fax: (318)257-4253
Tracey Jeffers, Dir.

Louisiana State University at
Shreveport
Small Business Development Center
College of Business Administration
1 University Dr.
Shreveport, LA 71115
Phone: (318)797-5144
Fax: (318)797-5208
Peggy Cannon, Dir.

Nicholls State University
Small Business Development Center
College of Business Administration
PO Box 2015
Thibodaux, LA 70310

Phone: (504)448-4242
Fax: (504)448-4922
Weston Hull, Dir.

Maine

Androscoggin Valley Council of
Governments
Small Business Development Center
125 Manley Rd.
Auburn, ME 04210
Phone: (207)783-9186
Fax: (207)783-5211
Jane Mickeriz, Counselor

Coastal Enterprises Inc.
SBDC
Weston Bldg.
7 N. Chestnut St.
Augusta, ME 04330
Phone: (207)621-0245
Fax: (207)622-9739
Robert Chiozzi, Counselor

Eastern Maine Development Corp.
Small Business Development Center
1 Cumberland Pl., Ste. 300
PO Box 2579
Bangor, ME 04402-2579
Phone: (207)942-6389
Free: (800)339-6389
Fax: (207)942-3548
Ron Loyd, Dir.

Belfast Satellite
Waldo County Development Corp.
SBDC
67 Church St.
Belfast, ME 04915
Phone: (207)942-6389
Free: (800)339-6389
Fax: (207)942-3548

Brunswick Satellite
Midcoast Council for Business
Development
SBDC
8 Lincoln St.
Brunswick, ME 04011
Phone: (207)882-4340

Northern Maine Development
Commission
Small Business Development Center
2 S. Main St.
PO Box 779
Caribou, ME 04736
Phone: (207)498-8736
Free: (800)427-8736

Fax: (207)498-3108
Rodney Thompson, Dir.

East Millinocket Satellite
Katahdin Regional Development
Corp.
SBDC
58 Main St.
East Millinocket, ME 04430
Phone: (207)746-5338
Fax: (207)746-9535

East Wilton Satellite
Robinhood Plaza
Rte. 2 & 4
East Wilton, ME 04234
Phone: (207)783-9186
Fax: (207)783-9186

Fort Kent Satellite
SBDC
Aroostook County Registry of Deeds
Elm and Hall Sts.
Fort Kent, ME 04743
Phone: (207)498-8736
Free: (800)427-8736
Fax: (207)498-3108

Houlton Satellite
SBDC
Superior Court House
Court St.
Houlton, ME 04730
Phone: (207)498-8736
Free: (800)427-8736
Fax: (207)498-3108

Lewiston Satellite
Business Information Center (BIC)
SBDC
Bates Mill Complex
35 Canal St.
Lewiston, ME 04240
Phone: (207)783-9186
Fax: (207)783-5211

Machias Satellite
Sunrise County Economic Council
(Calais Area)
SBDC
63 Main St.
PO Box 679
Machias, ME 04654
Phone: (207)454-2430
Fax: (207)255-0983

University of Southern Maine
Maine SBDC
96 Falmouth St.
PO Box 9300

Portland, ME 04104-9300
Phone: (207)780-4420
Fax: (207)780-4810
E-mail: msbdc@portland.maine.edu
Charles Davis, Dir.

Rockland Satellite
SBDC
331 Main St.
Rockland, ME 04841
Phone: (207)882-4340
Fax: (207)882-4456

Rumford Satellite
River Valley Growth Council
Hotel Harris Bldg.
23 Hartford St.
Rumford, ME 04276
Phone: (207)783-9186
Fax: (207)783-5211

Biddeford Satellite
Biddeford-Saco Chamber of
Commerce and Industry
SBDC
110 Main St.
Saco, ME 04072
Phone: (207)282-1567
Fax: (207)282-3149

Southern Maine Regional Planning
Commission
Small Business Development Center
255 Main St.
PO Box Q
Sanford, ME 04073
Phone: (207)324-0316
Fax: (207)324-2958
Joseph Vitko, Dir.

Skowhegan Satellite
SBDC
Norridgewock Ave.
Skowhegan, ME 04976
Phone: (207)621-0245
Fax: (207)622-9739

South Paris Satellite
SBDC
166 Main St.
South Paris, ME 04281
Phone: (207)783-9186
Fax: (207)783-5211

Waterville Satellite
Thomas College
SBDC
Administrative Bldg. - Library
180 W. River Rd.

Waterville, ME 04901
Phone: (207)621-0245
Fax: (207)622-9739

Coastal Enterprises, Inc. (Wiscasset)
Small Business Development Center
Water St.
PO Box 268
Wiscasset, ME 04578
Phone: (207)882-4340
Fax: (207)882-4456
James Burbank, Dir.

York Satellite
York Chamber of Commerce
SBDC
449 Rte. 1
York, ME 03909
Phone: (207)363-4422
Fax: (207)324-2958

Maryland

Anne Arundel, Office of Economic
Development
SBDC
2666 Riva Rd., Ste. 200
Annapolis, MD 21401
Phone: (410)224-4205
Fax: (410)222-7415
Mike Fish, Consultant

Central Maryland
SBDC
1420 N. Charles St., Rm 142
Baltimore, MD 21201-5779
Phone: (410)837-4141
Fax: (410)837-4151
Barney Wilson, Executive Dir.

Hartford County Economic
Development Office
SBDC
220 S. Main St.
Bel Air, MD 21014
Phone: (410)893-3837
Fax: (410)879-8043
Maurice Brown, Consultant

Maryland Small Business
Development Center
7100 Baltimore Ave., Ste. 401
College Park, MD 20740
Phone: (301)403-8300
Fax: (301)403-8303
James N. Graham, State Dir.

University of Maryland
SBDC
College of Business and Management

College Park, MD 20742-1815
Phone: (301)405-2144
Fax: (301)314-9152

Howard County Economic
Development Office
SBDC
6751 Gateway Dr., Ste. 500
Columbia, MD 21044
Phone: (410)313-6552
Fax: (410)313-6556
Ellin Dize, Consultant

Western Maryland Small Business
Development Center
Western Region, Inc.
3 Commerce Dr.
Cumberland, MD 21502
Phone: (301)724-6716
Free: (800)457-7232
Fax: (301)777-7504
Sam LaManna, Exec. Dir.

Cecil County Chamber of Commerce
SBDC
135 E. Main St.
Elkton, MD 21921
Phone: (410)392-0597
Fax: (410)392-6225
Maurice Brown, Consultant

Frederick Community College
SBDC
7932 Opossumtown Pike
Frederick, MD 21702
Phone: (301)846-2683
Fax: (301)846-2689
Website: http://SBDC
Mary Ann Garst, Program Dir.

Arundel Center N.
SBDC
101 Crain Hwy., NW, Rm. 110B
Glen Burnie, MD 21061
Phone: (410)766-1910
Fax: (410)766-1911
Mike Fish, Consultant

Community College at Saint Mary's
County
SBDC
PO Box 98, Great Mills Rd.
Great Mills, MD 20634
Phone: (301)868-6679
Fax: (301)868-7392
James Shepherd

Hagerstown Junior College
SBDC
Technology Innovation Center

11404 Robinwood Dr.
Hagerstown, MD 21740
Phone: (301)797-0327
Fax: (301)777-7504
Tonya Fleming Brockett, Dir.

Landover SBDC
7950 New Hampshire Ave., 2nd Fl.
Langley Park, MD 20783
Phone: (301)445-7324
Fax: (301)883-6479
Avon Evans, Consultant

Charles County Community College
Southern Maryland SBDC
SBDC
Mitchell Rd.
PO Box 910
LaPlata, MD 20646-0910
Phone: (301)934-7580
Free: (800)762-7232
Fax: (301)934-7681
Betsy Cooksey, Exec. Dir.

Garrett Community College
SBDC
Mosser Rd.
McHenry, MD 21541
Phone: (301)387-6666
Fax: (301)387-3096
Sandy Major, Business Analyst

Salisbury State University
Eastern Shore Region Small Business
Development Center
Power Professional Bldg., Ste. 170
Salisbury, MD 21801
Phone: (410)546-4325
Free: (800)999-7232
Fax: (410)548-5389
Marty Green, Exec. Dir.

Baltimore County Chamber of
Commerce
SBDC
102 W. Pennsylvania Ave., Ste. 402
Towson, MD 21204
Phone: (410)832-5866
Fax: (410)821-9901
John Casper, Consultant

Prince George's County Minority
Business Opportunities Commission
Suburban Washington Region Small
Business Development Center
1400 McCormick Dr., Ste. 282
Upper Marlboro, MD 20774
Phone: (301)883-6491
Fax: (301)883-6479
Avon Evans, Acting Executive Dir.

Carrol County Economic
Development Office
SBDC
125 N. Court St., Rm. 101
Westminster, MD 21157
Phone: (410)857-8166
Fax: (410)848-0003
Michael Fish, Consultant

Eastern Region - Upper Shore SBDC
PO Box 8
Wye Mills, MD 21679
Phone: (410)822-5400
Free: (800)762SBDC
Fax: (410)827-5286
Patricia Ann Marie Schaller,
Consultant

Massachusetts

International Trade Center
University of Massachusetts Amherst
SBDC
205 School of Management
Amherst, MA 01003-4935
Phone: (413)545-6301
Fax: (413)545-1273

University of Massachusetts
Massachusetts SBDC
205 School of Management
Amherst, MA 01003-4935
Phone: (413)545-6301
Fax: (413)545-1273
John Ciccarelli, State Dir.

Massachusetts Export Center
World Trade Center, Ste. 315
Boston, MA 02210
Phone: (617)478-4133
Free: (800)478-4133
Fax: (617)478-4135
Paula Murphy, Dir.

Minority Business Assistance Center
SBDC
University of Massachusetts (Boston)
College of Management, 5th Fl.
Boston, MA 02125-3393
Phone: (617)287-7750
Fax: (617)287-7767
Hank Turner, Dir.

Boston College
Capital Formation Service
SBDC
Rahner House
96 College Rd.
Chestnut Hill, MA 02167

Phone: (617)552-4091
Fax: (617)552-2730
Don Reilley, Dir.

Metropolitan Boston Small Business
Development Center Regional Office
Rahner House
96 College Rd.
Chestnut Hill, MA 02167
Phone: (617)552-4091
Fax: (617)552-2730
Dr. Jack McKiernan, Regional Dir.

Southeastern Massachusetts Small
Business Development Center
Regional Office
200 Pocasset St.
PO Box 2785
Fall River, MA 02722
Phone: (508)673-9783
Fax: (508)674-1929
Clyde Mitchell, Regional Dir.

North Shore Massachusetts Small
Business Development Center
Regional Office
197 Essex St.
Salem, MA 01970
Phone: (508)741-6343
Fax: (508)741-6345
Frederick Young, Regional Dir.

Western Massachusetts Small
Business Development Center
Regional Office
101 State St., Ste. 424
Springfield, MA 01103
Phone: (413)737-6712
Fax: (413)737-2312
Dianne Fuller Doherty, Regional Dir.

Clark University
Central Massachusetts Small
Business Development Center
Regional
Office
Dana Commons
950 Main St.
Worcester, MA 01610
Phone: (508)793-7615
Fax: (508)793-8890
Laurence March, Regional Dir.

Michigan

Lenawee County Chamber of
Commerce
SBDC
202 N. Main St., Ste. A

Adrian, MI 49221-2713
Phone: (517)266-1488
Fax: (517)263-6065
Sally Pinchock, Dir.

Allegan County Economic Alliance
SBDC
Allegan Intermediate School Bldg.
2891 M-277
PO Box 277
Allegan, MI 49010-8042
Phone: (616)673-8442
Fax: (616)650-8042
Chuck Birr, Dir.

Ottawa County Economic
Development Office, Inc.
Small Business Development Center
6676 Lake Michigan Dr.
PO Box 539
Allendale, MI 49401-0539
Phone: (616)892-4120
Fax: (616)895-6670
Ken Rizzio, Dir.

Gratiot Area Chamber of Commerce
SBDC
110 W. Superior St.
PO Box 516
Alma, MI 48801-0516
Phone: (517)463-5525

Alpena Community College
SBDC
666 Johnson St.
Alpena, MI 49707
Phone: (517)356-9021
Fax: (517)354-7507
Carl Bourdelais, Dir.

MMTC SBDC
2901 Hubbard Rd.
PO Box 1485
Ann Arbor, MI 48106-1485
Phone: (313)769-4110
Fax: (313)769-4064
Bill Loomis, Dir.

Huron County Economic
Development Corp.
Small Business Development Center
Huron County Bldg., Rm. 303
250 E. Huron
Bad Axe, MI 48413
Phone: (517)269-6431
Fax: (517)269-7221
Carl Osentoski, Dir.

Battle Creek Area Chamber of
Commerce
SBDC
4 Riverwalk Centre
34 W. Jackson, Ste. A
Battle Creek, MI 49017
Phone: (616)962-4076
Fax: (616)962-4076
Kathy Perrett, Dir.

Bay Area Chamber of Commerce
SBDC
901 Saginaw
Bay City, MI 48708
Phone: (517)893-4567
Fax: (517)893-7016
Cheryl Hiner, Dir.

Lake Michigan College
Corporation and Community
Development Department
Small Business Development Center
2755 E. Napier
Benton Harbor, MI 49022-1899
Phone: (616)927-8179
Fax: (616)927-8103
Milton E. Richter, Dir.

Ferris State University
Small Business Development Center
330 Oak St.
West 115
Big Rapids, MI 49307
Phone: (616)592-3553
Fax: (616)592-3539
Lora Swenson, Dir.

Northern Lakes Economic Alliance
SBDC
1048 East Main St.
PO Box 8
Boyne City, MI 49712-0008
Phone: (616)582-6482
Fax: (616)582-3213
Thomas Johnson, Dir.

Livingston County Small Business
Development Center
131 S. Hyne
Brighton, MI 48116
Phone: (810)227-3556
Fax: (810)227-3080
Dennis Whitney, Dir.

Buchanan Chamber of Commerce
SBDC
119 Main St.
Buchanan, MI 49107
Phone: (616)695-3291

Fax: (616)695-4250
Marlene Gauer, Dir.

Tuscola County Economic
Development Corp.
Small Business Development Center
194 N. State St., Ste. 200
Caro, MI 48723
Phone: (517)673-2849
Fax: (517)673-2517
James McLoskey, Dir.

Branch County Economic Growth
Alliance
SBDC
20 Division St.
Coldwater, MI 49036
Phone: (517)278-4146
Fax: (517)278-8369
Joyce Elferdink, Dir.

University of Detroit-Mercy
Small Business Development Center
Commerce and Finance Bldg., Rm.
105
4001 W. McNichols
PO Box 19900
Detroit, MI 48219-0900
Phone: (313)993-1115
Fax: (313)993-1052
Ram Kesavan, Dir.

Wayne State University
Michigan SBDC
2727 Second Ave., Ste. 107
Detroit, MI 48201
Phone: (313)964-1798
Fax: (313)964-3648
E-mail:
stateoffice@misbdc.wayne.edu
Ronald R. Hall, State Dir.

First Step, Inc.
Small Business Development Center
2415 14th Ave., S.
Escanaba, MI 49829
Phone: (906)786-9234
Fax: (906)786-4442
David Gillis, Dir.

Community Capital Development
Corp.
SBDC
Walter Ruether Center
711 N. Saginaw, Ste. 123
Flint, MI 48503
Phone: (810)239-5847
Fax: (810)239-5575
Kim Yarber, Dir.

Center for Continuing Education-
Macomb Community College
SBDC
32101 Caroline
Fraser, MI 48026
Phone: (810)296-3516
Fax: (810)293-0427

North Central Michigan College
SBDC
800 Livingston Blvd.
Gaylord, MI 49735
Phone: (517)731-0071

Association of Commerce and
Industry
SBDC
1 S. Harbor Ave.
PO Box 509
Grand Haven, MI 49417
Phone: (616)846-3153
Fax: (616)842-0379
Karen K. Benson, Dir.

Grand Valley State University
SBDC
Seidman School of Business, Ste.
718S
301 W. Fulton St.
Grand Rapids, MI 49504
Phone: (616)771-6693
Fax: (616)458-3872
Carol R. Lopucki, Dir.

The Right Place Program
SBDC
820 Monroe NW, Ste. 350
Grand Rapids, MI 49503-1423
Phone: (616)771-0571
Fax: (616)458-3768
Raymond P. DeWinkle, Dir.

Oceana County Economic
Development Corp.
SBDC
100 State St.
PO Box 168
Hart, MI 49420-0168
Phone: (616)873-7141
Fax: (616)873-5914
Charles Persenaire, Dir.

Hastings Industrial Incubator
SBDC
1035 E. State St.
Hastings, MI 49058
Phone: (616)948-2305
Fax: (616)948-2947
Joe Rahn, Dir.

Greater Gratiot Development, Inc.
Small Business Center
136 S. Main
Ithaca, MI 48847
Phone: (517)875-2083
Fax: (517)875-2990
Don Schurr, Dir.

Jackson Business Development
Center
SBDC
414 N. Jackson St.
Jackson, MI 49201
Phone: (517)787-0442
Fax: (517)787-3960
Duane Miller, Dir.

Kalamazoo College
Small Business Development Center
Stryker Center for Management
Studies
1327 Academy St.
Kalamazoo, MI 49006-3200
Phone: (616)337-7350
Fax: (616)337-7415
Carl R. Shook, Dir.

Lansing Community College
Small Business Development Center
Continental Bldg.
333 N. Washington Sq.
PO Box 40010
Lansing, MI 48901-7210
Phone: (517)483-1921
Fax: (517)483-9803
Deleski Smith, Dir.

Lapeer Development Corp.
Small Business Development Center
449 McCormick Dr.
Lapeer, MI 48446
Phone: (810)667-0080
Fax: (810)667-3541
Patricia Crawford Lucas, Dir.

Midland Chamber of Commerce
SBDC
300 Rodd St.
Midland, MI 48640
Phone: (517)839-9901
Fax: (517)835-3701
Sam Boeke, Dir.

Genesis Center for Entrepreneurial
Development
SBDC
111 Conant Ave.
Monroe, MI 48161
Phone: (313)243-5947

Fax: (313)242-0009
Dani Topolski, Dir.

Macomb County Business Assistance
Network
Small Business Development Center
115 S. Groesbeck Hwy.
Mt. Clemens, MI 48043
Phone: (810)469-5118
Fax: (810)469-6787
Donald L. Morandi, Dir.

Central Michigan University
Small Business Development Center
256 Applied Business Studies
Complex
Mt. Pleasant, MI 48859
Phone: (517)774-3270
Fax: (517)774-7992
Charles Fitzpatrick, Dir.

Muskegon Economic Growth
Alliance
Small Business Development Center
230 Terrace Plz.
PO Box 1087
Muskegon, MI 49443-1087
Phone: (616)722-3751
Fax: (616)728-7251
Mert Johnson, Dir.

Harbor County Chamber of
Commerce
SBDC
3 W. Buffalo
New Buffalo, MI 49117
Phone: (616)469-5409
Fax: (616)469-2257

Greater Niles Economic Development
Fund
SBDC
1105 N. Front St.
Niles, MI 49120
Phone: (616)683-1833
Fax: (616)683-7515
Chris Brynes, Dir.

Huron Shores Campus
SBDC
5800 Skeel Ave.
Oscoda, MI 48750
Phone: (517)739-1445
Fax: (517)739-1161
Dave Wentworth, Dir.

St. Clair County Community College
Small Business Development Center
800 Military St., Ste. 320

Port Huron, MI 48060-5015
Phone: (810)982-9511
Fax: (810)982-9531
Todd Brian, Dir.

Kirtland Community College
SBDC
10775 N. St. Helen Rd.
Roscommon, MI 48653
Phone: (517)275-5121
Fax: (517)275-8745
John Loiacano, Dir.

Saginaw County Chamber of
Commerce
SBDC
901 S. Washington Ave.
Saginaw, MI 48601
Phone: (517)752-7161
Fax: (517)752-9055
James Bockelman, Dir.

Saginaw Future, Inc.
Small Business Development Center
301 E. Genesee, 3rd Fl.
Saginaw, MI 48607
Phone: (517)754-8222
Fax: (517)754-1715
Matthew Hufnagel, Dir.

Washtenaw Community College
SBDC
740 Woodland
Saline, MI 48176
Phone: (313)944-1016
Fax: (313)944-0165
Kathleen Woodard, Dir.

West Shore Community College
Small Business Development Center
Business and Industrial Development
Institute
3000 N. Stiles Rd.
PO Box 277
Scottville, MI 49454-0277
Phone: (616)845-6211
Fax: (616)845-0207
Mark Bergstrom, Dir.

South Haven Chamber of Commerce
SBDC
300 Broadway
South Haven, MI 49090
Phone: (616)637-5171
Fax: (616)639-1570
Larry King, Dir.

Downriver Small Business
Development Center

15100 Northline Rd.
Southgate, MI 48195
Phone: (313)281-0700
Fax: (313)281-3418
Paula Boase, Dir.

Arenac County Extension Service
SBDC
County Bldg.
PO Box 745
Standish, MI 48658
Phone: (517)846-4111

Sterling Heights Area Chamber of
Commerce
Small Business Development Center
12900 Hall Rd., Ste. 110
Sterling Heights, MI 48313
Phone: (810)731-5400
Fax: (810)731-3521
Lillian Adams-Yanssens, Dir.

Northwest Michigan Council of
Governments
Small Business Development Center
2200 Dendrinos Dr.
PO Box 506
Traverse City, MI 49685-0506
Phone: (616)929-5000
Fax: (616)929-5017
Richard J. Beldin, Dir.

Northwestern Michigan College
Small Business Development Center
Center for Business and Industry
1701 E. Front St.
Traverse City, MI 49686
Phone: (616)922-1717
Fax: (616)922-1722
Cheryl Troop, Dir.

Traverse Bay Economic Development
Corp.
Small Business Development Center
202 E. Grandview Pkwy.
PO Box 387
Traverse City, MI 49684
Phone: (616)946-1596
Fax: (616)946-2565
Charles Blankenship, Dir.

Traverse City Area Chamber of
Commerce
Small Business Development Center
202 E. Grandview Pkwy.
PO Box 387
Traverse City, MI 49684
Phone: (616)947-5075

Fax: (616)946-2565
Matthew Meadors, Dir.

Oakland Count Small Business
Development Center
SOC Bldg.
4555 Corporate Dr., Ste. 201
PO Box 7085
Troy, MI 48098
Phone: (810)641-0088
Fax: (810)267-3809
Daniel V. Belknap, Dir.

Saginaw Valley State University
Small Business Development Center
7400 Bay Rd.
University Center, MI 48710-0001
Phone: (517)791-7746
Fax: (517)249-1955
Christine Greve, Dir.

Macomb Community College
SBDC
14500 12 Mile Rd.
Warren, MI 48093
Phone: (810)445-7348
Fax: (810)445-7316
Geary Maiurini, Dir.

Warren - Centerline - Sterling
Heights Chamber of Commerce
Small Business Development Center
30500 Van Dyke, Ste. 118
Warren, MI 48093
Phone: (313)751-3939
Fax: (313)751-3995
Janet Masi, Dir.

Minnesota

Northwest Technical College
SBDC
905 Grant Ave., SE
Bemidji, MN 56601
Phone: (218)755-4286
Fax: (218)755-4289
Susan Kozojed, Dir.

Normandale Community College
(Bloomington)
Small Business Development Center
9700 France Ave. S
Bloomington, MN 55431
Phone: (612)832-6398
Fax: (612)832-6352
Scott Harding, Dir.

Central Lakes College
Small Business Development Center

501 W. College Dr.
Brainerd, MN 56401
Phone: (218)825-2028
Fax: (218)828-2053
Pamela Thomsen, Dir.

University of Minnesota at Duluth
Small Business Development Center
School of Business and Economics,
Rm. 150
10 University Dr.
Duluth, MN 55812-2496
Phone: (218)726-8758
Fax: (218)726-6338
Lee Jensen, Dir.

Itasca Development Corp.
Grand Rapids Small Business
Development Center
19 NE 3rd St.
Grand Rapids, MN 55744
Phone: (218)327-2241
Fax: (218)327-2242
Kirk Bustrom, Dir.

Hibbing Community College
Small Business Development Center
1515 E. 25th St.
Hibbing, MN 55746
Phone: (218)262-6703
Fax: (218)262-6717
Jim Antilla, Dir.

Rainy River Community College
Small Business Development Center
1501 Hwy. 71
International Falls, MN 56649
Phone: (218)285-2255
Fax: (218)285-2239
Tom West, Dir.

Region Nine Development
Commission
SBDC
410 Jackson St.
PO Box 3367
Mankato, MN 56002-3367
Phone: (507)389-8863
Fax: (507)387-7105
Jill Miller, Dir.

Southwest State University
Small Business Development Center
Science and Technical Resource
Center, Ste. 105
1501 State St.
Marshall, MN 56258
Phone: (507)537-7386

Fax: (507)387-7105
Jack Hawk, Dir.

Minnesota Project Innovation
Small Business Development Center
111 3rd Ave. S., Ste. 100
Minneapolis, MN 55401
Phone: (612)347-6751
Fax: (612)338-3483
Pat Dillon, Dir.

University of St. Thomas
SBDC
Mail Stop 25H 225
Ste. MPL 100
Minneapolis, MN 55403
Phone: (612)962-4500
Fax: (612)962-4810
Gregg Schneider, Dir.

Moorhead State University
Small Business Development Center
1104 7th Ave. S.
MSU Box 303
Moorhead, MN 56563
Phone: (218)236-2289
Fax: (218)236-2280
Len Sliwoski, Dir.

Owatonna Incubator, Inc.
SBDC
560 Dunnell Dr., Ste. 203
PO Box 505
Owatonna, MN 55060
Phone: (507)451-0517
Fax: (507)455-2788
Ken Henrickson, Dir.

Pine Technical College
Small Business Development Center
1100 4th St.
Pine City, MN 55063
Phone: (320)629-7340
Fax: (320)629-7603
John Sparling, Dir.

Hennepin Technical College
SBDC
1820 N. Xenium Ln.
Plymouth, MN 55441
Phone: (612)550-7218
Fax: (612)550-7272
Danelle Wolf, Dir.

Pottery Business and Tech. Center
Small Business Development Center
2000 Pottery Pl. Dr., Ste. 339
Red Wing, MN 55066
Phone: (612)388-4079

Fax: (612)385-2251
Marv Bollum, Dir.

Rochester Community and Tech.
College
Small Business Development Center
Riverland Hall
851 30th Ave. SE
Rochester, MN 55904
Phone: (507)285-7425
Fax: (507)285-7110
Michelle Pyfferoen, Dir.

Dakota County Technical College
Small Business Development Center
1300 E. 145th St.
Rosemount, MN 55068
Phone: (612)423-8262
Fax: (612)322-5156
Tom Trutna, Dir.

Southeast Minnesota Development
Corp.
SBDC
111 W. Jessie St.
PO Box 684
Rushford, MN 55971
Phone: (507)864-7557
Fax: (507)864-2091
Terry Erickson, Dir.

St. Cloud State University
Small Business Development Center
720 4th Ave. S.
St. Cloud, MN 56301-3761
Phone: (320)255-4842
Fax: (320)255-4957
Dawn Jensen-Ragnier, Dir.

Department of Trade and Economic
Development
Minnesota SBDC
500 Metro Sq.
121 7th Pl. E.
St. Paul, MN 55101-2146
Phone: (612)297-5770
Fax: (612)296-1290
Mary Kruger, State Dir.

Minnesota Technology, Inc.
Small Business Development Center
Olcott Plaza Bldg., Ste. 140
820 N. 9th St.
Virginia, MN 55792
Phone: (218)741-4241
Fax: (218)741-4249
John Freeland, Dir.

Wadena Chamber of Commerce
SBDC
222 2nd St., SE
Wadena, MN 56482
Phone: (218)631-1502
Fax: (218)631-2396
Paul Kinn, Dir.

Century College
SBDC
3300 Century Ave., N., Ste. 200-D
White Bear Lake, MN 55110-1894
Phone: (612)773-1794
Fax: (612)779-5802
Ernie Brodtmann, Dir.

Mississippi

Northeast Mississippi Community
College
SBDC
Holiday Hall, 2nd Fl.
Cunningham Blvd.
Booneville, MS 38829
Phone: (601)720-7448
Fax: (601)720-7464
Kenny Holt, Dir.

Delta State University
Small Business Development Center
PO Box 3235 DSU
Cleveland, MS 38733
Phone: (601)846-4236
Fax: (601)846-4235
David Holman, Dir.

East Central Community College
SBDC
Broad St.
PO Box 129
Decatur, MS 39327
Phone: (601)635-2111
Fax: (601)635-4031
Ronald Westbrook, Dir.

Jones County Junior College
SBDC
900 Court St.
Ellisville, MS 39437
Phone: (601)477-4165
Fax: (601)477-4166
Gary Suddith, Dir.

Mississippi Gulf Coast Community
College
SBDC
Jackson County Campus
PO Box 100
Gautier, MS 39553

Phone: (601)497-7723
Fax: (601)497-7788
Janice Mabry, Dir.

Mississippi Delta Community
College
Small Business Development Center
PO Box 5607
Greenville, MS 38704-5607
Phone: (601)378-8183
Fax: (601)378-5349
Chuck Herring, Dir.

Mississippi Contract Procurement
Center
SBDC
3015 12th St.
PO Box 610
Gulfport, MS 39502-0610
Phone: (601)864-2961
Fax: (601)864-2969
C. W. "Skip" Ryland, Exec. Dir.

Pearl River Community College
Small Business Development Center
5448 U.S. Hwy. 49 S.
Hattiesburg, MS 39401
Phone: (601)544-0030
Fax: (601)544-9149
Heidi McDuffie, Dir.

Mississippi Valley State University
Affiliate SBDC
PO Box 992
Itta Bena, MS 38941
Phone: (601)254-3601
Fax: (601)254-6704
Dr. Jim Breyley, Dir.

Jackson State University
Small Business Development Center
Jackson Enterprise Center, Ste. A-1
931 Hwy. 80 W
Box 43
Jackson, MS 39204
Phone: (601)968-2795
Fax: (601)968-2796
Henry Thomas, Dir.

University of Southern Mississippi
Small Business Development Center
136 Beach Park Pl.
Long Beach, MS 39560
Phone: (601)865-4578
Fax: (601)865-4581
Lucy Betcher, Dir.

Alcorn State University
SBDC
552 West St.

PO Box 90
Lorman, MS 39096-9402
Phone: (601)877-6684
Fax: (601)877-6256
Sharon Witty, Dir.

Meridian Community College
Small Business Development Center
910 Hwy. 19 N
Meridian, MS 39307
Phone: (601)482-7445
Fax: (601)482-5803
Mac Hodges, Dir.

Mississippi State University
Small Business Development Center
1 Research Bldg., Ste 201
PO Drawer 5288
Mississippi State, MS 39762
Phone: (601)325-8684
Fax: (601)325-4016
Sonny Fisher, Dir.

Copiah-Lincoln Community College
Small Business Development Center
11 County Line Circle
Natchez, MS 39120
Phone: (601)445-5254
Fax: (601)446-1221
Bob D. Russ, Dir.

Hinds Community College
Small Business Development Center/
International Trade Center
1500 Raymond Lake Rd., 2nd Fl.
Raymond, MS 39154
Phone: (601)857-3536
Fax: (601)857-3474
Marguerite Wall, Dir.

Holmes Community College
SBDC
412 W. Ridgeland Ave.
Ridgeland, MS 39157
Phone: (601)853-0827
Fax: (601)853-0844
John Deddens, Dir.

Northwest Mississippi Community
College
SBDC
DeSoto Ctr.
5197 W.E. Ross Pkwy.
Southaven, MS 38671
Phone: (601)280-7648
Fax: (601)280-7648
Jody Dunning, Dir.

Southwest Mississippi Community
College
SBDC
College Dr.
Summit, MS 39666
Phone: (601)276-3890
Fax: (601)276-3883
Kathryn Durham, Dir.

Itawamba Community College
Small Business Development Center
653 Eason Blvd.
Tupelo, MS 38801
Phone: (601)680-8515
Fax: (601)680-8547
Rex Hollingsworth, Dir.

University of Mississippi
Mississippi SBDC
N.C.P.A., Rm. 1082
University, MS 38677
Phone: (601)234-2120
Fax: (601)232-4220
Michael Vanderlip, Dir.

University of Mississippi
SBDC
Old Chemistry Bldg., Ste. 216
University, MS 38677
Phone: (601)232-5001
Fax: (601)232-5650
Walter D. Gurley, Jr.

Missouri

Camden County
SBDC Extension Center
113 Kansas
PO Box 1405
Camdenton, MO 65020
Phone: (573)882-0344
Fax: (573)884-4297
Jackie Rasmussen, B&I Spec.

Missouri PAC—Southeastern
Missouri State University
SBDC
222 N. Pacific
Cape Girardeau, MO 63701
Phone: (573)290-5965
Fax: (573)651-5005
George Williams, Dir.

Southeast Missouri State University
Small Business Development Center
University Plaza
MS 5925
Cape Girardeau, MO 63701
Phone: (573)290-5965

Fax: (573)651-5005
E-mail: sbdc-cg@ext.missouri.edu
Frank "Buz" Sutherland, Dir.

Chillicothe City Hall
SBDC
715 Washington St.
Chillicothe, MO 64601-2229
Phone: (660)646-6920
Fax: (660)646-6811
Nanette Anderjaska, Dir.

East Central Missouri - St. Louis
County
Extension Center
121 S. Meramac, Ste. 501
Clayton, MO 63105
Phone: (314)889-2911
Fax: (314)854-6147
Carole Leriche-Price, B&I Specialist

Boone County Extension Center
SBDC
1012 N. Hwy. UU
Columbia, MO 65203
Phone: (573)445-9792
Fax: (573)445-9807
Mr. Casey Venters, B&I Specialist

MO PAC-Central Region
University of Missouri-Columbia
SBDC
University Pl., Ste. 1800
1205 University Ave.
Columbia, MO 65211
Phone: (573)882-3597
Fax: (573)884-4297
E-mail: mopcol@ext.missouri.edu
Morris Hudson, Dir.

University of Missouri
Missouri SBDC System
1205 University Ave., Ste. 300
Columbia, MO 65211
Phone: (573)882-0344
Fax: (573)884-4297
E-mail: sbdc-mso@ext.missouri.edu
Max E. Summers, State Dir.

University of Missouri—Columbia
Small Business Development Center
University Pl., Ste. 1800
1205 University Ave.
Columbia, MO 65211
Phone: (573)882-7096
Fax: (573)882-6156
E-mail: sbdc-c@ext.missouri.edu
Frank Siebert, Dir.

Hannibal Satellite Center
Hannibal, MO 63401
Phone: (816)385-6550
Fax: (816)385-6568

Jefferson County
Extension Center
Courthouse, Annex 203
725 Maple St.
PO Box 497
Hillsboro, MO 63050
Phone: (573)789-5391
Fax: (573)789-5059

Cape Girardeau County
SBDC Extension Center
815 Hwy. 25S
PO Box 408
Jackson, MO 63755
Phone: (573)243-3581
Fax: (573)243-1606
Richard Sparks, B&I Specialist

Cole County Extension Center
SBDC
2436 Tanner Bridge Rd.
Jefferson City, MO 65101
Phone: (573)634-2824
Fax: (573)634-5463
Mr. Chris Bouchard, B&I Specialist

Missouri Southern State College
Small Business Development Center
Matthews Hall, Ste. 107
3950 Newman Rd.
Joplin, MO 64801-1595
Phone: (417)625-9313
Fax: (417)625-9782
E-mail: sbdc-j@ext.missouri.edu
Jim Krudwig, Dir.

Rockhurst College
Small Business Development Center
1100 Rockhurst Rd.
VanAckeren Hall, Rm. 205
Kansas City, MO 64110-2508
Phone: (816)501-4572
Fax: (816)501-4646
Rhonda Gerke, Dir.

Truman State University
Small Business Development Center
100 E. Norman
Kirksville, MO 63501-4419
Phone: (816)785-4307
Fax: (816)785-4357
E-mail: sbdc-k@ext.missouri.edu
Glen Giboney, Dir.

Thomas Hill Enterprise Center
SBDC
1409 N. Prospect Dr.
PO Box 246
Macon, MO 63552
Phone: (816)385-6550
Fax: (816)562-3071
Jane Vanderham, Dir.

Northwest Missouri State University
Small Business Development Center
423 N. Market St.
Maryville, MO 64468-1614
Phone: (660)562-1701
Fax: (660)582-3071
Brad Anderson, Dir.

Audrain County Extension Center
SBDC
Courthouse, 4th Fl.
101 Jefferson
Mexico, MO 65265
Phone: (573)581-3231
Fax: (573)581-2766
Virgil Woolridge, B&I Specialist

Randolph County
Extension Center
417 E. Urbandale
Moberly, MO 65270
Phone: (816)263-3534
Fax: (816)263-1874
Ray Marshall, B&I Specialist

Mineral Area College
SBDC
PO Box 1000
Park Hills, MO 63601-1000
Phone: (573)431-4593
Fax: (573)431-2144
E-mail: sbdc-fr@ext.missouri.edu
Eugene Cherry, Dir.

Telecommunications Community
Resource Center
Longhead Learning Center
Small Business Development Center
1121 Victory Ln.
3019 Fair St.
Poplar Bluff, MO 63901
Phone: (573)840-9450
Fax: (573)840-9456
Judy Moss, Dir.

Washington County SBDC
102 N. Missouri
Potosi, MO 63664
Phone: (573)438-2671

Fax: (573)438-2079
LaDonna McCuan, B&I Specialist

Center for Technology Transfer and
Economic Development
Nagogami Ter., Bldg. 1, Rm. 104
Rolla, MO 65401-0249
Phone: (573)341-4559
Fax: (573)346-2694
Fred Goss, Dir.

Phelps County
SBDC Extension Center
Courthouse
200 N. Main
PO Box 725
Rolla, MO 65401
Phone: (573)364-3147
Fax: (573)364-0436
Paul Cretin, B&I Specialist

University of Missouri at Rolla
SBDC
Nagogami Terrace, Bldg. 1, Rm. 104
Rolla, MO 65401-0249
Phone: (573)341-4559
Fax: (573)341-6495
E-mail: sbdc-rt@ext.missouri.edu
Fred Goss, Dir.

Missouri PAC - Eastern Region
SBDC
3830 Washington Ave.
St. Louis, MO 63108
Phone: (314)534-4413
Fax: (314)534-3237
E-mail: mopstl@ext.missouri.edu
Ken Konchel, Dir.

St. Louis County
Extension Center
207 Marillac, UMSL
8001 Natural Bridge Rd.
St. Louis, MO 63121
Phone: (314)553-5944
John Henschke, Specialist

St. Louis University
Small Business State University
SBDC
3750 Lindell Blvd.
St. Louis, MO 63108-3412
Phone: (314)977-7232
Fax: (314)977-7241
E-mail: sbdc-stl@ext.missouri.edu
Virginia Campbell, Dir.

St. Louis / St. Charles County
Economic Council

SBDC Extension Center
260 Brown Rd.
St. Peters, MO 63376
Phone: (314)970-3000
Fax: (314)274-3310
Tim Wathen, B&I Specialist

Pettis County
Extension Center
1012A Thompson Blvd.
Sedalia, MO 65301
Phone: (816)827-0591
Fax: (816)827-4888
Betty Lorton, B&I Specialist

Southwest Missouri State University
Center for Business Research
Small Business Development Center
901 S. National
Box 88
Springfield, MO 65804-0089
Phone: (417)836-5685
Fax: (417)836-7666
Jane Peterson, Dir.

Franklin County
SBDC Extension Center
414 E. Main
PO Box 71
Union, MO 63084
Phone: (573)583-5141
Fax: (573)583-5145
Rebecca How, B&I Specialist

Central Missouri State University
Center for Technology
Grinstead, No. 75
Warrensburg, MO 64093-5037
Phone: (816)543-4402
Fax: (816)747-1653
Cindy Tanck, Coordinator

Central Missouri State University
SBDC
Grinstead, No. 9
Warrensburg, MO 64093-5037
Phone: (816)543-4402
Fax: (816)543-8159
Wes Savage, Coordinator

Howell County
SBDC Extension Center
217 S. Aid Ave.
West Plains, MO 65775
Phone: (417)256-2391
Fax: (417)256-8569
Mick Gilliam, B&I Specialist

Montana

Montana Tradepost Authority
Small Business Development Center
2722 3rd Ave., Ste. W300
Billings, MT 59101
Phone: (406)256-6871
Fax: (406)256-6877
Tom McKerlick, Contact

Bozeman Small Business
Development Center
222 E. Main St., Ste. 102
Bozeman, MT 59715
Phone: (406)587-3113
Fax: (406)587-9565
Michele DuBose, Contact

Butte Small Business Development
Center
305 W. Mercury, Ste. 211
Butte, MT 59701
Phone: (406)782-7333
Fax: (406)782-9675
John Donovan, Contact

High Plains Development Authority
Great Falls SBDC
710 1st. Ave. N.
PO Box 2568
Great Falls, MT 59403
Phone: (406)454-1934
Fax: (406)454-2995
Suzie David

Havre Small Business Development
Center
PO Box 170
Havre, MT 59501
Phone: (406)265-9226
Fax: (406)265-5602
Randy Hanson, Contact

Montana Department of Commerce
Montana SBDC
1424 9th Ave.
PO Box 200505
Helena, MT 59620
Phone: (406)444-2463
Fax: (406)444-1872
Ralph Kloser, State Dir.

Kalispell Small Business
Development Center
PO Box 8300
Kalispell, MT 59901
Phone: (406)758-5412
Fax: (406)758-6582
Dan Manning, Contact

Missoula Small Business
Development Center
127 N. Higgins, 3rd Fl.
Missoula, MT 59802
Phone: (406)728-9234
Fax: (406)721-4584
Brett George, Contact

Sidney Small Business Development
Center
123 W. Main
Sidney, MT 59270
Phone: (406)482-5024
Fax: (406)482-5306
Dwayne Heintz, Contact

Nebraska

Chadron State College
SBDC
Administration Bldg.
1000 Main St.
Chadron, NE 69337
Phone: (308)432-6282
Fax: (308)432-6430
Cliff Hanson, Dir.

University of Nebraska at Kearney
SBDC
Welch Hall
19th St. and College Dr.
Kearney, NE 68849-3035
Phone: (308)865-8344
Fax: (308)865-8153
Susan Jensen, Dir.

University of Nebraska at Lincoln
SBDC
1135 M St., No. 200
11th and Cornhusker Hwy.
Lincoln, NE 68521
Phone: (402)472-3358
Fax: (402)472-3363
Cliff Mosteller, Dir.

Mid-Plains Community College
SBDC
416 N. Jeffers, Rm. 26
North Platte, NE 69101
Phone: (308)534-5115
Fax: (308)534-5117
Dean Kurth, Dir.

Nebraska Small Business
Development Center
Omaha Business and Technology
Center
2505 N. 24 St., Ste. 101
Omaha, NE 68110

Phone: (402)595-3511
Fax: (402)595-3524
Tom McCabe, Dir.

University of Nebraska at Omaha
Nebraska Business Development
Center
College of Business Administration,
Rm. 407
60th & Dodge Sts.
CBA Rm. 407
Omaha, NE 68182
Phone: (402)554-2521
Fax: (402)554-3747
Robert Bernier, State Dir.

University of Nebraska at Omaha
Peter Kiewit Conference Center
SBDC
1313 Farnam-on-the-Mall, Ste. 132
Omaha, NE 68182-0248
Phone: (402)595-2381
Fax: (402)595-2385
Nate Brei, Dir.

Peru State College
SBDC
T.J. Majors Hall, Rm. 248
Peru, NE 68421
Phone: (402)872-2274
Fax: (402)872-2422
Jerry Brazil, Dir.

Western Nebraska Community
College
SBDC
Nebraska Public Power Bldg., Rm.
408
1721 Broadway
Scottsbluff, NE 69361
Phone: (308)635-7513
Fax: (308)635-6596
Ingrid Battershell, Dir.

Wayne State College
SBDC
Gardner Hall
1111 Main St.
Wayne, NE 68787
Phone: (402)375-7575
Fax: (402)375-7574
Loren Kucera, Dir.

Nevada

Carson City Chamber of Commerce
Small Business Development Center
1900 S. Carson St., Ste. 100
Carson City, NV 89701

Phone: (702)882-1565
Fax: (702)882-4179
Larry Osborne, Dir.

Great Basin College
Small Business Development Center
1500 College Pkwy.
Elko, NV 89801
Phone: (702)753-2205
Fax: (702)753-2242
John Pryor, Dir.

Incline Village Chamber of
Commerce
SBDC
969 Tahoe Blvd.
Incline Village, NV 89451
Phone: (702)831-4440
Fax: (702)832-1605
Sheri Woods, Exec. Dir.

Las Vegas SBDC
SBDC
3720 Howard Hughes Pkwy., Ste.
130
Las Vegas, NV 89109
Phone: (702)734-7575
Fax: (702)734-7633
Robert Holland, Bus. Dev. Specialist

University of Nevada at Las Vegas
Small Business Development Center
4505 Maryland Pkwy.
Box 456011
Las Vegas, NV 89154-6011
Phone: (702)895-0852
Fax: (702)895-4095
Nancy Buist, Business Development
Specialist

North Las Vegas Small Business
Development Center
19 W. Brooks Ave., Ste. B
North Las Vegas, NV 89030
Phone: (702)399-6300
Fax: (702)895-4095
Janis Stevenson, Business
Development Specialist

University of Nevada at Reno
Small Business Development Center
College of Business Administration
Nazir Ansari Business Bldg., Rm.
411
Reno, NV 89557-0100
Phone: (702)784-1717
Fax: (702)784-4337
E-mail: nsbdc@scs.unr.edu
Sam Males, Dir.

Tri-County Development Authority
Small Business Development Center
50 W. 4th St.
PO Box 820
Winnemucca, NV 89446
Phone: (702)623-5777
Fax: (702)623-5999
Teri Williams, Dir.

New Hampshire

University of New Hampshire
Small Business Development Center
108 McConnell Hall
15 College Rd.
Durham, NH 03824-3593
Phone: (603)862-2200
Fax: (603)862-4876
Mary Collins, State Dir.

Keene State College
Small Business Development Center
Mail Stop 210
Keene, NH 03435-2101
Phone: (603)358-2602
Fax: (603)358-2612
Gary Cloutier, Regional Mgr.

Littleton Small Business
Development Center
120 Main St.
Littleton, NH 03561
Phone: (603)444-1053
Fax: (603)444-5463
Liz Ward, Regional Mgr.

Manchester Small Business
Development Center
1000 Elm St., 14th Fl.
Manchester, NH 03101
Phone: (603)624-2000
Fax: (603)634-2449
Bob Ebberson, Regional Mgr.

Office of Economic Initiatives
SBDC
1000 Elm St., 14th Fl.
Manchester, NH 03101
Phone: (603)634-2796
E-mail: ahj@hopper.unh.edu
Amy Jennings, Dir.

New Hampshire Small Business
Development Center
1 Indian Head Plz., Ste. 510
Nashua, NH 03060
Phone: (603)886-1233
Fax: (603)598-1164
Bob Wilburn, Regional Mgr.

Plymouth State College
Small Business Development Center
Outreach Center, MSC24A
Plymouth, NH 03264-1595
Phone: (603)535-2523
Fax: (603)535-2850
Janice Kitchen, Regional Mgr.

Small Business Development Center,
Rochester
18 S. Main St., Ste. 3A
Rochester, NH 03867
Phone: (603)330-1929
Fax: (603)330-1948

New Jersey

Greater Atlantic City Chamber of
Commerce
Small Business Development Center
1301 Atlantic Ave.
Atlantic City, NJ 08401
Phone: (609)345-5600
Fax: (609)345-1666
William R. McGinley, Dir.

Rutgers University At Camden
Small Business Development Center
227 Penn St., 3rd Fl., Rm. 334
Camden, NJ 08102
Phone: (609)757-6221
Fax: (609)225-6231
Patricia Peacock, Dir.

Brookdale Community College
Small Business Development Center
Newman Springs Rd.
Lincroft, NJ 07738
Phone: (732)842-1900
Fax: (732)842-0203
Larry Novick, Dir.

Rutgers University
New Jersey SBDC
Graduate School of Management
49 Bleeker St.
Newark, NJ 07102
Phone: (973)353-5950
Fax: (973)353-1110
Brenda B. Hopper, State Dir.

Bergen County Community College
SBDC
400 Paramus Rd., Rm. A333
Paramus, NJ 07652-1595
Phone: (201)447-7841
Fax: (201)447-7495
Melody Irvin, Dir.

Mercer County Community College
Small Business Development Center
West Windsor Campus
1200 Old Trenton Rd.
PO Box B
Trenton, NJ 08690
Phone: (609)586-4800
Fax: (609)890-6338
Herb Spiegel, Dir.

Kean College
Small Business Development Center
East Campus, Rm. 242
Union, NJ 07083
Phone: (908)527-2946
Fax: (908)527-2960
Mira Kostak, Dir.

Warren County Community College
Small Business Development Center
Skylands 475
Rte. 57 W.
Washington, NJ 07882-9605
Phone: (908)689-9620
Fax: (908)689-2247
James Smith, Dir.

New Mexico

New Mexico State University at
Alamogordo
Small Business Development Center
2230 Lawrence Blvd.
Alamogordo, NM 88310
Phone: (505)434-5272
Fax: (505)439-3643
Dwight Harp, Dir.

Albuquerque Technical-Vocational
Institute
Small Business Development Center
525 Buena Vista SE
Albuquerque, NM 87106
Phone: (505)224-4246
Fax: (505)224-4251
Ray Garcia, Dir.

South Valley SBDC
SBDC
70 4th St. SW, Ste. A
Albuquerque, NM 87102
Phone: (505)248-0132
Fax: (505)248-0127
Steven Becerra, Dir.

New Mexico State University at
Carlsbad
Small Business Development Center
301 S. Canal St.

PO Box 1090
Carlsbad, NM 88220
Phone: (505)887-6562
Fax: (505)885-0818
Larry Coalson, Dir.

Clovis Community College
Small Business Development Center
417 Schepps Blvd.
Clovis, NM 88101
Phone: (505)769-4136
Fax: (505)769-4190
Sandra Taylor-Smith

Northern New Mexico Community
College
Small Business Development Center
1002 N. Onate St.
Espanola, NM 87532
Phone: (505)747-2236
Fax: (505)757-2234
Ralph Prather, Dir.

San Juan College
Small Business Development Center
4601 College Blvd.
Farmington, NM 87402
Phone: (505)599-0528
Fax: (505)599-0385
Cal Tingey, Dir.

University of New Mexico at Gallup
Small Business Development Center
103 W. Hwy. 66
Gallup, NM 87305
Phone: (505)722-2220
Fax: (505)863-6006
Elsie Sanchez, Dir.

New Mexico State University at
Grants
Small Business Development Center
709 E. Roosevelt Ave.
Grants, NM 87020
Phone: (505)287-8221
Fax: (505)287-2125
Clemente Sanchez, Dir.

New Mexico Junior College
Small Business Development Center
5317 Lovington Hwy.
Hobbs, NM 88240
Phone: (505)392-5549
Fax: (505)392-2527
Don Leach, Dir.

Dona Ana Branch Community
College
Small Business Development Center

3400 S. Espina St.
Dept. 3DA, Box 30001
Las Cruces, NM 88003-0001
Phone: (505)527-7601
Fax: (505)527-7515
Terry Sullivan, Dir.

Luna Vocational-Technical Institute
Small Business Development Center
Camp Luna Site
Hot Springs Blvd.
PO Box 1510
Las Vegas, NM 87701
Phone: (505)454-2595
Fax: (505)454-2588
Don Bustos, Dir.

University of New Mexico at Los
Alamos
Small Business Development Center
901 18th St., No. 18
PO Box 715
Los Alamos, NM 87544
Phone: (505)662-0001
Fax: (505)662-0099
Jay Wechsler, Interim Dir.

University of New Mexico at
Valencia
Small Business Development Center
280 La Entrada
Los Lunas, NM 87031
Phone: (505)925-8980
Fax: (505)925-8987
David Ashley, Dir.

Eastern New Mexico University at
Roswell
Small Business Development Center
57 University Ave.
PO Box 6000
Roswell, NM 88201-6000
Phone: (505)624-7133
Fax: (505)624-7132
Eugene D. Simmons, Dir.

Santa Fe Community College
New Mexico SBDC
6401 Richards Ave.
Santa Fe, NM 87505
Phone: (505)438-1362
Free: (800)281-SBDC
Fax: (505)471-1469
Roy Miller, State Dir.

Western New Mexico University
Small Business Development Center
PO Box 2672
Silver City, NM 88062

Phone: (505)538-6320
Fax: (505)538-6341
Linda K. Jones, Dir.

Mesa Technical College
Small Business Development Center
911 S. 10th St.
Tucumcari, NM 88401
Phone: (505)461-4413
Fax: (505)461-1901
Carl Reiney, Dir.

New York

State University of New York at
Albany
Small Business Development Center
Draper Hall, Rm. 107
135 Western Ave.
Albany, NY 12222
Phone: (518)442-5577
Fax: (518)442-5582
Peter George, III

State University of New York (Suny)
New York SBDC
Suny Plaza, S-523
Albany, NY 12246
Phone: (518)443-5398
Free: (800)732-SBDC
Fax: (518)465-4992
E-mail: kingjl@cc.sunycentral.edu
James L. King, State Dir.

Binghamton University
Small Business Development Center
PO Box 6000
Binghamton, NY 13902-6000
Phone: (607)777-4024
Fax: (607)777-4029
E-mail: sbdcbu@spectra.net
Joanne Bauman, Dir.

State University of New York
Small Business Development Center
74 N. Main St.
Brockport, NY 14420
Phone: (716)637-6660
Fax: (716)637-2102
Wilfred Bordeau, Dir.

Bronx Community College
Small Business Development Center
McCracken Hall, Rm. 14
W. 181st St. & University Ave.
Bronx, NY 10453
Phone: (718)563-3570
Fax: (718)563-3572
Adi Israeli, Dir.

Bronx Outreach Center
Con Edison
SBDC
560 Cortlandt Ave.
Bronx, NY 10451
Phone: (718)563-9204
David Bradley

Downtown Brooklyn Outreach
Center
Kingsborough Community College
SBDC
395 Flatbush Ave., Extension Rm.
413
Brooklyn, NY 11201
Phone: (718)260-9783
Fax: (718)260-9797
Stuart Harker, Assoc. Dir.

Kingsborough Community College
Small Business Development Center
2001 Oriental Blvd., Bldg. T4, Rm.
4204
Manhattan Beach
Brooklyn, NY 11235
Phone: (718)368-4619
Fax: (718)368-4629
Edward O'Brien, Dir.

State University of New York at
Buffalo
Small Business Development Center
Bacon Hall 117
1300 Elmwood Ave.
Buffalo, NY 14222
Phone: (716)878-4030
Fax: (716)878-4067
Susan McCartney, Dir.

Canton Outreach Center (SUNY)
Jefferson Community College
SBDC
Canton, NY 13617
Phone: (315)386-7312
Fax: (315)386-7945

Cobleskill Outreach Center
SBDC
SUNY Cobleskill
Warner Hall, Rm. 218
Cobleskill, NY 12043
Phone: (518)234-5528
Fax: (518)234-5272
Peter Desmond, Business Advisor

Corning Community College
Small Business Development Center
24 Denison Pkwy. W
Corning, NY 14830

Phone: (607)962-9461
Free: (800)358-7171
Fax: (607)936-6642
Bonnie Gestwicki, Dir.

Mercy College/Westchester Outreach
Center
SBDC
555 Broadway
Dobbs Ferry, NY 10522-1189
Phone: (914)674-7485
Fax: (914)693-4996
Tom Milton, Coordinator

State University of New York at
Farmingdale
Small Business Development Center
Campus Commons Bldg.
2350 Route 110
Farmingdale, NY 11735
Phone: (516)420-2765
Fax: (516)293-5343
Joseph Schwartz, Dir.

Dutchess Outreach Center
SBDC
Fishkill Extension Center
2600 Rte. 9, Unit 90
Fishkill, NY 12524-2001
Phone: (914)897-2607
Fax: (914)897-4653

Suny Geneseo Outreach Center
SBDC
South Hall, No. 111
1 College Circle
Geneseo, NY 14454
Phone: (716)245-5429
Fax: (716)245-5430
Charles VanArsdale, Dir.

Geneva Outreach Center
SBDC
122 N. Genesee St.
Geneva, NY 14456
Phone: (315)781-1253
Sandy Bordeau, Administrative Dir.

Hempstead Outreach Center
SBDC
269 Fulton Ave.
Hempstead, NY 11550
Phone: (516)564-8672
Fax: (516)481-4938
Lloyd Clarke, Asst. Dir.

York College/City University of New
York
Small Business Development Center
Science Bldg., Rm. 107

94-50 159th St.
Jamaica, NY 11451
Phone: (718)262-2880
Fax: (718)262-2881
James A. Heyliger

Jamestown Community College
Small Business Development Center
525 Falconer St.
PO Box 20
Jamestown, NY 14702-0020
Phone: (716)665-5754
Free: (800)522-7232
Fax: (716)665-6733
Irene Dobies, Dir.

Kingston Small Business
Development Center
1 Development Ct.
Kingston, NY 12401
Phone: (914)339-0025
Fax: (914)339-1631
Patricia La Susa, Dir.

Baruch College
Mid-Town Outreach Center
SBDC
360 Park Ave. S., Rm. 1101
New York, NY 10010
Phone: (212)802-6620
Fax: (212)802-6613
Cheryl Fenton, Dir.

East Harlem Outreach Center
SBDC
145 E. 116th St., 3rd Fl.
New York, NY 10029
Phone: (212)346-1900
Fax: (212)534-4576
Anthony Sanchez, Coordinator

Harlem Outreach Center
SBDC
163 W. 125th St., Rm. 1307
New York, NY 10027
Phone: (212)346-1900
Fax: (212)534-4576
Anthony Sanchez, Coordinator

Mid-Town Outreach Ctr.
Baruch College
SBDC
360 Park Ave. S. Rm. 1101
New York, NY 10010
Phone: (212)802-6620
Fax: (212)802-6613
Barrie Phillip, Coordinator

Pace University
Small Business Development Center

1 Pace Plz., Rm. W483
New York, NY 10038
Phone: (212)346-1900
Fax: (212)346-1613
Ira Davidson, Dir.

Niagara Falls Satellite Office
SBDC/International Trade Center
Carborundum Center
345 3rd St.
Niagara Falls, NY 14303-1117
Phone: (716)285-4793
Fax: (716)285-4797

SUNY at Oswego
Operation Oswego County
SBDC
44 W. Bridge St.
Oswego, NY 13126
Phone: (315)343-1545
Fax: (315)343-1546

Clinton Community College
SBDC
Lake Shore Rd., Rte. 9 S.
136 Clinton Point Dr.
Plattsburgh, NY 12901
Phone: (518)562-4260
Fax: (518)563-9759
Merry Gwynn, Coordinator

Suffolk County Community College
Riverhead Outreach Center
SBDC
Orient Bldg., Rm. 132
Riverhead, NY 11901
Phone: (516)369-1409
Fax: (516)369-3255
Al Falkowski, Contact

SUNY at Brockport
SBDC
Sibley Bldg.
228 E. Main St.
Rochester, NY 14604
Phone: (716)232-7310
Fax: (716)637-2182

Niagara County Community College
at Sanborn
Small Business Development Center
3111 Saunders Settlement Rd.
Sanborn, NY 14132
Phone: (716)693-1910
Fax: (716)731-3595
Richard Gorko, Dir.

Long Island University at
Southhampton/Southampton
Outreach Center

SBDC
Abney Peak, Montauk Hwy.
Southampton, NY 11968
Phone: (516)287-0059
Fax: (516)287-8287
George Tulmany, Business Advisor

College of Staten Island
SBDC
Bldg. 1A, Rm. 111
2800 Victory Blvd.
Staten Island, NY 10314-9806
Phone: (718)982-2560
Fax: (718)982-2323
Dr. Martin Schwartz, Dir.

SUNY at Stony Brook
SBDC
Harriman Hall, Rm. 103
Stony Brook, NY 11794-3775
Phone: (516)632-9070
Fax: (516)632-7176
Judith McEvoy, Dir.

Rockland Community College
Small Business Development Center
145 College Rd.
Suffern, NY 10901-3620
Phone: (914)356-0370
Fax: (914)356-0381
Thomas J. Morley, Dir.

Onondaga Community College
Small Business Development Center
Excell Bldg., Rm. 108
4969 Onondaga Rd.
Syracuse, NY 13215-1944
Phone: (315)498-6070
Fax: (315)492-3704
Robert Varney, Dir.

Manufacturing Field Office
SBDC
Rensselaer Technology Park
385 Jordan Rd.
Troy, NY 12180-7602
Phone: (518)286-1014
Fax: (518)286-1006
Bill Brigham, Dir.

State University Institute of
Technology
Small Business Development Center
PO Box 3050
Utica, NY 13504-3050
Phone: (315)792-7546
Fax: (315)792-7554
David Mallen, Dir.

SUNY Institute of Technology at
Utica/Rome
SBDC
PO Box 3050
Utica, NY 13504-3050
Phone: (315)792-7546
Fax: (315)792-7554
David Mallen, Dir.

Jefferson Community College
Small Business Development Center
Coffeen St.
Watertown, NY 13601
Phone: (315)782-9262
Fax: (315)782-0901
John F. Tanner, Dir.

SBDC Outreach Small Business
Resource Center
222 Bloomingdale Rd., 3rd Fl.
White Plains, NY 10605-1500
Phone: (914)644-4116
Fax: (914)644-2184
Kathleen Cassels, Coordinator

North Carolina

Asheville SBTDC
Haywood St.
PO Box 2570
Asheville, NC 28805
Phone: (704)251-6025
Fax: (704)251-6025

Appalachian State University
Small Business and Technology
Development Center (Northwestern
Region)
Walker College of Business
2123 Raley Hall
Boone, NC 28608
Phone: (704)262-2492
Fax: (704)262-2027
Bill Parrish, Regional Dir.

University of North Carolina at
Chapel Hill
Central Carolina Regional Small
Business Development Center
608 Airport Rd., Ste. B
Chapel Hill, NC 27514
Phone: (919)962-0389
Fax: (919)962-3291
Dan Parks, Dir.

University of North Carolina at
Charlotte
Small Business and Technology
Development Center (Southern

Piedmont Region)
The Ben Craig Center
8701 Mallard Creek Rd.
Charlotte, NC 28262
Phone: (704)548-1090
Fax: (704)548-9050
George McAllister, Dir.

Western Carolina University
Small Business and Technology
Development Center (Western
Region)
Center for Improving Mountain
Living
Bird Bldg.
Cullowhee, NC 28723
Phone: (704)227-7494
Fax: (704)227-7422
Allan Steinburg, Dir.

Elizabeth City State University
Small Business and Technology
Development Center (Northeastern
Region)
1704 Weeksville Rd.
PO Box 874
Elizabeth City, NC 27909
Phone: (919)335-3247
Fax: (919)335-3648
Wauna Dooms, Dir.

Fayetteville State University
Cape Fear Small Business and
Technology Development Center
PO Box 1334
Fayetteville, NC 28302
Phone: (910)486-1727
Fax: (910)486-1949
Dr. Sid Gautam, Regional Dir.

North Carolina A&T State University
Northern Piedmont Small Business
and Technology Development
Center (Eastern Region)
C. H. Moore Agricultural Research
Center
1601 E. Market St.
PO Box D-22
Greensboro, NC 27411
Phone: (910)334-7005
Fax: (910)334-7073
Cynthia Clemons, Dir.

East Carolina University
Small Business and Technology
Development Center (Eastern
Region)
Willis Bldg.
300 East 1st St.

Greenville, NC 27858-4353
Phone: (919)328-6157
Fax: (919)328-6992
Walter Fitts, Dir.

Catawba Valley Region
SBTDC
514 Hwy. 321 NW, Ste. A
Hickory, NC 28601
Phone: (704)345-1110
Fax: (704)326-9117
Rand Riedrich, Dir.

Pembroke State University
Office of Economic Development and
SBTDC
SBDC
Pembroke, NC 28372
Phone: (910)521-6603
Fax: (910)521-6550

North Carolina SBTDC
SBDC
333 Fayette St. Mall, Ste. 1150
Raleigh, NC 27601
Phone: (919)715-7272
Fax: (919)715-7777
Scott R. Daugherty, Executive Dir.

North Carolina State University
Capital Region
SBTDC
MCI Small Business Resource Center
800 S. Salisbury St.
Raleigh, NC 27601
Phone: (919)715-0520
Fax: (919)715-0518
Mike Seibert, Dir.

North Carolina Wesleyan College
SBTDC
3400 N. Wesleyan Blvd.
Rocky Mount, NC 27804
Phone: (919)985-5130
Fax: (919)977-3701

University of North Carolina at
Wilmington
Small Business and Technology
Development Center (Southeast
Region)
601 S. College Rd.
Cameron Hall, Rm. 131
Wilmington, NC 28403
Phone: (910)395-3744
Fax: (910)350-3990
Mike Bradley, Dir.

University of North Carolina at
Wilmington
Southeastern Region
SBTDC
601 S. College Rd.
Wilmington, NC 28403
Phone: (910)395-3744
Fax: (910)350-3014
Dr. Warren Guiko, Acting Dir.

Winston-Salem State University
Northwestern Piedmont Region Small
Business and Technology
Center
PO Box 13025
Winston Salem, NC 27110
Phone: (910)750-2030
Fax: (910)750-2031
Bill Dowe, Dir.

North Dakota

Bismarck Regional Small Business
Development Center
700 E. Main Ave., 2nd Fl.
Bismarck, ND 58502
Phone: (701)328-5865
Fax: (701)250-4304
Jan M. Peterson, Regional Dir.

Devils Lake Outreach Center
SBDC
417 5th St.
Devils Lake, ND 58301
Free: (800)445-7232
Gordon Synder, Regional Dir.

Dickinson Regional Small Business
Development Center
Small Business Development Center
314 3rd Ave. W
Drawer L
Dickinson, ND 58602
Phone: (701)227-2096
Fax: (701)225-0049
Bryan Vendsel, Regional Dir.

Procurement Assistance Center
SBDC
PO Box 1309
Fargo, ND 58107-1309
Phone: (701)237-9678
Free: (800)698-5726
Fax: (701)237-9734
Eric Nelson

Tri-County Economic Development
Corp.
Fargo Regional Small Business
Development Center
657 2nd Ave. N, Rm. 279
PO Box 1309
Fargo, ND 58103
Phone: (701)237-0986
Fax: (701)237-9734
Jon Grinager, Regional Mgr.

Grafton Outreach Center
Red River Regional Planning Council
SBDC
PO Box 633
Grafton, ND 58237
Free: (800)445-7232
Gordon Snyder, Regional Dir.

Grand Forks Regional Small Business
Development Center
202 N. 3rd St., Ste. 200
The Hemmp Center
Grand Forks, ND 58203
Phone: (701)772-8502
Fax: (701)772-9238
Gordon Snyder, Regional Dir.

University of North Dakota
North Dakota SBDC
118 Gamble Hall
University Station, Box 7308
Grand Forks, ND 58202-7308
Phone: (701)777-3700
Fax: (701)777-3225
Walter "Wally" Kearns, State Dir.

Jamestown Outreach Center
North Dakota Small Business
Development Center
210 10th St. SE
PO Box 1530
Jamestown, ND 58402
Phone: (701)252-9243
Fax: (701)251-2488
Jon Grinager, Regional Dir.

Jamestown Outreach Ctr.
SBDC
210 10th St.
S.E.P.O Box 1530
Jamestown, ND 58402
Phone: (701)252-9243
Fax: (701)251-2488
Jon Grinager, Regional Dir.

Minot Regional Small Business
Development Center
SBDC

900 N. Broadway, Ste. 300
Minot, ND 58703
Phone: (701)852-8861
Fax: (701)858-3831
Brian Argabright, Regional Dir.

Williston Outreach Center
SBDC
PO Box 2047
Williston, ND 58801
Free: (800)445-7232
Bryan Vendsel, Regional Dir.

Ohio

Akron Regional Development Board
Small Business Development Center
1 Cascade Plz., 8th Fl.
Akron, OH 44308-1192
Phone: (330)379-3170
Fax: (330)379-3164
Charles Smith, Dir.

Women's Entrepreneurial Growth
Organization
Small Business Development Center
Buckingham Bldg., Rm. 55
PO Box 544
Akron, OH 44309
Phone: (330)972-5179
Fax: (330)972-5513
Dr. Penny Marquette, Exec. Dir.

Women's Network
SBDC
1540 West Market St., Ste. 100
Akron, OH 44313
Phone: (330)864-5636
Fax: (330)884-6526
Marlene Miller, Dir.

Enterprise Development Corp.
SBDC
900 E. State St.
Athens, OH 45701
Phone: (614)592-1188
Fax: (614)593-8283
Karen Patton, Dir.

Ohio University Innovation Center
Small Business Development Center
Enterprise & Technical Bldg., Rm.
155
20 East Circle Dr.
Athens, OH 45701
Phone: (614)593-1797
Fax: (614)593-1795
Debra McBride, Dir.

WSOS Community Action
Commission, Inc.
Wood County SBDC
121 E. Wooster St.
PO Box 539
Bowling Green, OH 43402
Phone: (419)352-3817
Fax: (419)353-3291
Pat Fligor, Dir.

Kent State University, Stark Campus
SBDC
6000 Frank Ave., NW
Canton, OH 44720
Phone: (330)499-9600
Fax: (330)494-6121
Annette Chunko, Contact

Women's Business Development
Center
SBDC
2400 Cleveland Ave., NW
Canton, OH 44709
Phone: (330)453-3867
Fax: (330)773-2992

Wright State University—Lake
Campus
Small Business Development Center
West Central Office
7600 State Rte. 703
Celina, OH 45882
Phone: (419)586-0355
Free: (800)237-1477
Fax: (419)586-0358
Tom Knapke, Dir.

Clermont County Chamber of
Commerce
Clermont County Area SBDC
4440 Glen Este-Withamsville Rd.
Cincinnati, OH 45245
Phone: (513)753-7141
Fax: (513)753-7146
Matt VanSant, Dir.

University of Cincinnati
SBDC
1111 Edison Ave.
Cincinnati, OH 45216-2265
Phone: (513)948-2051
Fax: (513)948-2109
Mark Sauter, Dir.

Greater Cleveland Growth
Association
Small Business Development Center
200 Tower City Center
50 Public Sq.

Cleveland, OH 44113-2291
Phone: (216)621-1294
Fax: (216)621-4617
JoAnn Uhlik, Dir.

Northern Ohio Manufacturing
SBDC
Prospect Park Bldg.
4600 Prospect Ave.
Cleveland, OH 44103-4314
Phone: (216)432-5300
Fax: (216)361-2900
Gretchen Faro, Dir.

Central Ohio Manufacturing
SBDC
1250 Arthur E. Adams Dr.
Columbus, OH 43221
Phone: (614)688-5136
Fax: (614)688-5001

Department of Development
Ohio SBDC
77 S. High St., 28th Fl.
Columbus, OH 43216-1001
Phone: (614)466-2711
Fax: (614)466-0829
Holly I. Schick, State Dir.

Greater Columbus Area Chamber of
Commerce
Central Ohio SBDC
37 N. High St.
Columbus, OH 43215-3065
Phone: (614)225-6910
Fax: (614)469-8250
Linda Steward, Dir.

Dayton Area Chamber of Commerce
Small Business Development Center
Chamber Plz.
5th & Main Sts.
Dayton, OH 45402-2400
Phone: (937)226-8239
Fax: (937)226-8254
Harry Bumgarner, Dir.

Wright State University/Dayton
SBDC
Center for Small Business Assistance
College of Business
Rike Hall, Rm. 120C
Dayton, OH 45435
Phone: (937)873-3503
Dr. Mike Body, Dir.

Northwest Private Industry Council
SBDC
197-2-B1 Park Island Ave.

Defiance, OH 43512
Phone: (419)784-6270
Fax: (419)782-6273
Don Wright, Dir.

Northwest Technical College
Small Business Development Center
1935 E. 2nd St., Ste. D
Defiance, OH 43512
Phone: (419)784-3777
Fax: (419)782-4649
Don Wright, Dir.

Terra Community College
Small Business Development Center
North Central Fremont Office
1220 Cedar St.
Fremont, OH 43420
Phone: (419)334-8400
Fax: (419)334-9414
Joe Wilson, Dir.

Enterprise Center
Small Business Development Center
129 E. Main St.
PO Box 756
Hillsboro, OH 45133
Phone: (937)393-9599
Fax: (937)393-8159
Bill Grunkemeyer, Interim Dir.

Ashtabula County Economic
Development Council, Inc.
Small Business Development Center
36 W. Walnut St.
Jefferson, OH 44047
Phone: (216)576-9134
Fax: (216)576-5003
Sarah Bogardus, Dir.

Kent State University Partnership
SBDC
College of Business Administration,
Rm. 300A
Summit and Terrace
Kent, OH 44242
Phone: (330)672-2772
Fax: (330)672-2448
Linda Yost, Dir.

EMTEC/Southern Area
Manufacturing
SBDC
3155 Research Park, Ste. 206
Kettering, OH 45420
Phone: (513)258-6180
Fax: (513)258-8189
Harry Bumgarner, Dir.

Lake County Economic Development
Center
SBDC
Lakeland Community College
7750 Clocktower Dr.
Kirtland, OH 44080
Phone: (216)951-1290
Fax: (216)951-7336
Cathy Haworth, Dir.

Lima Technical College
Small Business Development Center
West Central Office
545 W. Market St., Ste. 305
Lima, OH 45801-4717
Phone: (419)229-5320
Fax: (419)229-5424
Gerald J. Biedenharn, Dir.

Lorain County Chamber of
Commerce
SBDC
6100 S. Boadway
Lorain, OH 44053
Phone: (216)233-6500
Dennis Jones, Dir.

Mid-Ohio Small Business
Development Center
246 E. 4th St.
PO Box 1208
Mansfield, OH 44901
Phone: (419)521-2655
Free: (800)366-7232
Fax: (419)522-6811
Barbara Harmony, Dir.

Marietta College
SBDC
213 Fourth St., 2nd Fl.
Marietta, OH 45750
Phone: (614)376-4832
Fax: (614)376-4832
Emerson Shimp, Dir.

Marion Area Chamber of Commerce
SBDC
206 S. Prospect St.
Marion, OH 43302
Phone: (614)387-0188
Fax: (614)387-7722
Lynn Lovell, Dir.

Tuscarawas SBDC
300 University Dr., NE
Kent State University
300 University Dr., NE
New Philadelphia, OH 44663-9447
Phone: (330)339-3391

Fax: (330)339-2637
Tom Farbizo, Dir.

Miami University
Small Business Development Center
Department of Decision Sciences
336 Upham Hall
Oxford, OH 45056
Phone: (513)529-4841
Fax: (513)529-1469
Dr. Michael Broida, Dir.

Upper Valley Joint Vocational School
Small Business Development Center
8811 Career Dr.
N. Country Rd., 25A
Piqua, OH 45356
Phone: (937)778-8419
Free: (800)589-6963
Fax: (937)778-9237
Jon Heffner, Dir.

Ohio Valley Minority Business
Association
SBDC
1208 Waller St.
PO Box 847
Portsmouth, OH 45662
Phone: (614)353-8395
Fax: (614)353-3695
Clemmy Womack, Dir.

Department of Development
CIC of Belmont County
Small Business Development Center
100 E. Main St.
St. Clairsville, OH 43950
Phone: (614)695-9678
Fax: (614)695-1536
Mike Campbell, Dir.

Kent State University/Salem Campus
SBDC
2491 State Rte. 45 S.
Salem, OH 44460
Phone: (330)332-0361
Fax: (330)332-9256
Deanne Taylor, Dir.

Lawrence County Chamber of
Commerce
Small Business Development Center
U.S. Rte. 52 & Solida Rd.
PO Box 488
South Point, OH 45680
Phone: (740)894-3838
Fax: (740)894-3836
Lou-Ann Walden, Dir.

Springfield Small Business
Development Center
300 E. Auburn Ave.
Springfield, OH 45505
Phone: (937)322-7821
Fax: (937)322-7824
Ed Levanthal, Dir.

Greater Steubenville Chamber of
Commerce
Jefferson County Small Business
Development Center
630 Market St.
PO Box 278
Steubenville, OH 43952
Phone: (614)282-6226
Fax: (614)282-6285
Tim McFadden, Dir.

Toledo Small Business Development
Center
300 Madison Ave., Ste. 200
Toledo, OH 43604-1575
Phone: (419)243-8191
Fax: (419)241-8302
Wendy Gramza, Dir.

Youngstown/Warren SBDC
Region Chamber of Commerce
180 E. Market St., Ste. 225
Warren, OH 44482
Phone: (330)393-2565
Jim Rowlands, Mgr.

Youngstown State University
SBDC
241 Federal Plaza W.
Youngstown, OH 44503
Phone: (330)746-3350
Fax: (330)746-3324
Patricia Veisz, Mgr.

Zanesville Area Chamber of
Commerce
Mid-East Small Business
Development Center
217 N. 5th St.
Zanesville, OH 43701
Phone: (614)452-4868
Fax: (614)454-2963
Bonnie J. Winnett, Dir.

Oklahoma

East Central University
Small Business Development Center
1036 E. 10th St.
Ada, OK 74820
Phone: (405)436-3190

Fax: (405)436-3190
Frank Vater

Northwestern Oklahoma State
University
Small Business Development Center
709 Oklahoma Blvd.
Alva, OK 73717
Phone: (405)327-8608
Fax: (405)327-0560
Clance Doelling, Dir.

Southeastern Oklahoma State
University
Oklahoma SBDC
517 University
Station A, Box 2584
Durant, OK 74701
Phone: (405)924-0277
Free: (800)522-6154
Fax: (405)920-7471
Dr. Grady Pennington, State Dir.

Phillips University
Small Business Development Center
100 S. University Ave.
Enid, OK 73701
Phone: (405)242-7989
Fax: (405)237-1607
Bill Gregory, Coordinator

Langston University Center
Small Business Development Center
Minority Assistance Center
Hwy. 33 E.
Langston, OK 73050
Phone: (405)466-3256
Fax: (405)466-2909
Robert Allen, Dir.

Lawton Satellite
Small Business Development Center
American National Bank Bldg.
601 SW D Ave., Ste. 209
Lawton, OK 73501
Phone: (405)248-4946
Fax: (405)355-3560
Jim Elliot, Business Development
Specialists

Northeastern Oklahoma A&M
Miami Satellite
SBDC
Dyer Hall, Rm. 307
215 I St.
Miami, OK 74354
Phone: (918)540-0575
Fax: (918)540-0575
Hugh Simon, Business Development
Specialist

Rose State College
SBDC
Procurement Speciality Center
6420 Southeast 15th St.
Midwest City, OK 73110
Phone: (405)733-7348
Fax: (405)733-7495
Judy Robbins, Dir.

University of Central Oklahoma
Small Business Development Center
115 Park Ave.
Oklahoma City, OK 73102-9005
Phone: (405)232-1968
Fax: (405)232-1967
E-mail: sbdc@aix1.ucok.edu
Website: http://www.osbdc.org/
osbdc.htm
Susan Urbach

Carl Albert College
Small Business Development Center
1507 S. McKenna
Poteau, OK 74953
Phone: (918)647-4019
Fax: (918)647-1218
Dean Qualls, Dir.

Northeastern Oklahoma State
University
Small Business Development Center
Oklahoma Small Business
Development Center
Tahlequah, OK 74464
Phone: (918)458-0802
Fax: (918)458-2105
Danielle Coursey, Business
Development Specialist

Tulsa Satellite
Small Business Development Center
State Office Bldg.
616 S. Boston, Ste. 100
Tulsa, OK 74119
Phone: (918)583-2600
Fax: (918)599-6173
Jeff Horvath, Dir.

Southwestern Oklahoma State
University
Small Business Development Center
100 Campus Dr.
Weatherford, OK 73096
Phone: (405)774-1040
Fax: (405)774-7091
Chuck Felz, Dir.

Oregon

Linn-Benton Community College
Small Business Development Center
6500 SW Pacific Blvd.
Albany, OR 97321
Phone: (541)917-4923
Fax: (541)917-4445
Dennis Sargent, Dir.

Southern Oregon State College/
Ashland
Small Business Development Center
Regional Services Institute
Ashland, OR 97520
Phone: (541)482-5838
Fax: (541)482-1115
Liz Shelby, Dir.

Central Oregon Community College
Small Business Development Center
2600 NW College Way
Bend, OR 97701
Phone: (541)383-7290
Fax: (541)317-3445
Bob Newhart, Dir.

Southwestern Oregon Community
College
Small Business Development Center
2110 Newmark Ave.
Coos Bay, OR 97420
Phone: (541)888-7100
Fax: (541)888-7113
Jon Richards, Dir.

Columbia Gorge Community College
SBDC
400 E. Scenic Dr., Ste. 257
The Dalles, OR 97058
Phone: (541)298-3118
Fax: (541)298-3119
Mr. Bob Cole, Dir.

Lane Community College
Oregon SBDC
44 W. Broadway, Ste. 501
Eugene, OR 97401-3021
Phone: (541)726-2250
Fax: (541)345-6006
Dr. Edward Cutler, State Dir

Rogue Community College
Small Business Development Center
214 SW 4th St.
Grants Pass, OR 97526
Phone: (541)471-3515
Fax: (541)471-3589
Lee Merritt, Dir.

Mount Hood Community College
Small Business Development Center
323 NE Roberts St.
Gresham, OR 97030
Phone: (503)667-7658
Fax: (503)666-1140
Don King, Dir.

Oregon Institute of Technology
Small Business Development Center
3201 Campus Dr. S. 314
Klamath Falls, OR 97601
Phone: (541)885-1760
Fax: (541)885-1855
Jamie Albert, Dir.

Eastern Oregon State College
Small Business Development Center
Regional Services Institute
1410 L Ave.
La Grande, OR 97850
Phone: (541)962-3391
Free: (800)452-8639
Fax: (541)962-3668
John Prosnik, Dir.

Oregon Coast Community College
Small Business Development Center
4157 NW Hwy. 101, Ste. 123
PO Box 419
Lincoln City, OR 97367
Phone: (541)994-4166
Fax: (541)996-4958
Guy Faust, Contact

Southern Oregon State College/
Medford
Small Business Development Center
Regional Services Institute
332 W. 6th St.
Medford, OR 97501
Phone: (541)772-3478
Fax: (541)734-4813
Liz Shelby, Dir.

Clackamas Community College
Small Business Development Center
7616 SE Harmony Rd.
Milwaukie, OR 97222
Phone: (503)656-4447
Fax: (503)652-0389
Jan Stennick, Dir.

Treasure Valley Community College
Small Business Development Center
650 College Blvd.
Ontario, OR 97914
Phone: (541)889-6493

Business Plans Handbook, Volume 9

Fax: (541)881-2743
Kathy Simko, Dir.

Blue Mountain Community College
Small Business Development Center
37 SE Dorion
Pendleton, OR 97801
Phone: (541)276-6233
Fax: (541)276-6819
Gerald Wood, Dir.

Portland Community College
Small Business Development Center
2701 NW Vaughn St., No. 499
Portland, OR 97209
Phone: (503)978-5080
Fax: (503)228-6350
Robert Keyser, Dir.

Portland Community College
Small Business International Trade
Program
121 SW Salmon St., Ste. 210
Portland, OR 97204
Phone: (503)274-7482
Fax: (503)228-6350
Tom Niland, Dir.

Umpqua Community College
Small Business Development Center
744 SE Rose
Roseburg, OR 97470
Phone: (541)672-2535
Fax: (541)672-3679
Terry Swagerty, Dir.

Chemeketa Community College
Small Business Development Center
365 Ferry St. SE
Salem, OR 97301
Phone: (503)399-5088
Fax: (503)581-6017
Tom Nelson, Dir.

Clatsop Community College
Small Business Development Center
1761 N. Holladay
Seaside, OR 97138
Phone: (503)738-3347
Fax: (503)738-7843
Lori Martin, Dir.

Tillamook Bay Community College
Small Business Development Center
401 B Main St.
Tillamook, OR 97141
Phone: (503)842-2551
Fax: (503)842-2555
Kathy Wilkes, Dir.

Pennsylvania

Lehigh University
Small Business Development Center
Rauch Business Ctr., No. 37
621 Taylor St.
Bethlehem, PA 18015
Phone: (610)758-3980
Fax: (610)758-5205
Dr. Larry A. Strain, Dir.

Clarion University of Pennsylvania
Small Business Development Center
Dana Still Bldg., Rm. 102
Clarion, PA 16214
Phone: (814)226-2060
Fax: (814)226-2636
Dr. Woodrow Yeaney, Dir.

Bucks County SBDC Outreach
Center
2 E. Court St.
Doylestown, PA 18901
Phone: (215)230-7150
Bruce Love, Dir.

Gannon University
Small Business Development Center
120 W. 9th St.
Erie, PA 16501
Phone: (814)871-7714
Fax: (814)871-7383
Ernie Post, Dir.

Kutztown University
Small Business Development Center
2986 N. 2nd St.
Harrisburg, PA 17110
Phone: (717)720-4230
Fax: (717)720-4262
Katherine Wilson, Dir.

Indiana University of Pennsylvania
SBDC
208 Eberly College of Business
Indiana, PA 15705
Phone: (412)357-7915
Fax: (412)357-5985
Dr. Tony Palamone, Dir.

St. Vincent College
Small Business Development Center
Alfred Hall, 4th Fl.
300 Fraser Purchase Rd.
Latrobe, PA 15650
Phone: (412)537-4572
Fax: (412)537-0919
Jack Fabean, Dir.

Bucknell University
Small Business Development Center
126 Dana Engineering Bldg., 1st Fl.
Lewisburg, PA 17837
Phone: (717)524-1249
Fax: (717)524-1768
Charles Knisely, Dir.

St. Francis College
Small Business Development Center
Business Resource Center
Loretto, PA 15940
Phone: (814)472-3200
Fax: (814)472-3202
Edward Huttenhower, Dir.

LaSalle University
Small Business Development Center
1900 W. Olney Ave.
Box 365
Philadelphia, PA 19141
Phone: (215)951-1416
Fax: (215)951-1597
Andrew Lamas, Dir.

Temple University
Small Business Development Center
1510 Cecil B. Moore Ave.
Philadelphia, PA 19121
Phone: (215)204-7282
Fax: (215)204-4554
Geraldine Perkins, Dir.

University of Pennsylvania
Pennsylvania SBDC
The Wharton School
423 Vance Hall
3733 Spruce St.
Philadelphia, PA 19104-6374
Phone: (215)898-1219
Fax: (215)573-2135
E-mail:
ghiggins@sec1.wharton.upenn.edu
Gregory L. Higgins, Jr.

Duquesne University
Small Business Development Center
Rockwell Hall, Rm. 10, Concourse
600 Forbes Ave.
Pittsburgh, PA 15282
Phone: (412)396-6233
Fax: (412)396-5884
Dr. Mary T. McKinney, Dir.

University of Pittsburgh
Small Business Development Center
The Joseph M. Katz Graduate School
of Business
208 Bellefield Hall

315 S. Bellefield Ave.
Pittsburgh, PA 15213
Phone: (412)648-1544
Fax: (412)648-1636
Ann Dugan, Dir.

University of Scranton
Small Business Development Center
St. Thomas Hall, Rm. 588
Scranton, PA 18510
Phone: (717)941-7588
Fax: (717)941-4053
Elaine M. Tweedy, Dir.

West Chester University
SBDC
319 Anderson Hall
211 Carter Dr.
West Chester, PA 19383
Phone: (610)436-2162
Fax: (610)436-2577

Wilkes University
Small Business Development Center
Hollenback Hall
192 S. Franklin St.
Wilkes Barre, PA 18766-0001
Phone: (717)831-4340
Free: (800)572-4444
Fax: (717)824-2245
Jeffrey Alves, Dir.

Puerto Rico

Small Business Development Center
Edificio Union Plaza, Ste. 701
416 Ponce de Leon Ave.
Hato Rey, PR 00918
Phone: (787)763-6811
Fax: (787)763-4629
Carmen Marti, State Dir.

Rhode Island

Northern Rhode Island Chamber of
Commerce
SBDC
6 Blackstone Valley Pl., Ste. 105
Lincoln, RI 02865-1105
Phone: (401)334-1000
Fax: (401)334-1009
Shelia Hoogeboom, Program Mgr.

Newport County Chamber of
Commerce
E. Bay Small Business Development
Center
45 Valley Rd.
Middletown, RI 02842-6377

Phone: (401)849-6900
Fax: (401)841-0570
Samuel Carr, Program Mgr.

Fishing Community Program Office
SBDC
PO Box 178
Narragansett, RI 02882
Phone: (401)783-2466
Angela Caporelli, Program Mgr.

South County SBDC
QP/D Industrial Park
35 Belver Ave., Rm. 212
North Kingstown, RI 02852-7556
Phone: (401)294-1227
Fax: (401)294-6897
Elizabeth Kroll, Program Mgr.

Bryant College
Small Business Development Center
30 Exchange Terrace, 4th Fl.
Providence, RI 02903-1793
Phone: (401)831-1330
Fax: (401)274-5410
Ann Marie Marshall, Case Mgr.

Enterprise Community SBDC/BIC
550 Broad St.
Providence, RI 02907
Phone: (401)272-1083
Fax: (401)272-1186
Simon Goudiaby, Program Mgr.

Bell Atlantic Telecommunications
Center
1150 Douglas Pke.
Smithfield, RI 02917-1284
Phone: (401)232-0220
Fax: (401)232-0242
Kate Dolan, Managing Dir.

Bryant College
Export Assistance Center
SBDC
1150 Douglas Pike
Smithfield, RI 02917
Phone: (401)232-6407
Fax: (401)232-6416
Raymond Fogarty, Dir.

Bryant College
Rhode Island SBDC
1150 Douglas Pike
Smithfield, RI 02917-1284
Phone: (401)232-6111
Fax: (401)232-6933
Douglas H. Jobling, State Dir.

Entrepreneurship Training Program
Bryant College
SBDC
1150 Douglas Pike
Smithfield, RI 02917-1284
Phone: (401)232-6115
Fax: (401)232-6933
Sydney Okashige, Program Mgr.

Bristol County Chamber of
Commerce
SBDC
PO Box 250
Warren, RI 02885-0250
Phone: (401)245-0750
Fax: (401)245-0110
Samuel Carr, Program Mgr.

Central Rhode Island Chamber of
Commerce
SBDC
3288 Post Rd.
Warwick, RI 02886-7151
Phone: (401)732-1100
Fax: (401)732-1107
Mr. Elizabeth Kroll, Program Mgr.

South Carolina

University of South Carolina at Aiken
Aiken Small Business Development
Center
171 University Pkwy.
Box 9
Aiken, SC 29801
Phone: (803)641-3646
Fax: (803)641-3647
Jackie Moore, Area Mgr.

University of South Carolina at
Beaufort
Small Business Development Center
800 Carteret St.
Beaufort, SC 29902
Phone: (803)521-4143
Fax: (803)521-4142
Martin Goodman, Area Mgr.

Clemson University
Small Business Development Center
College of Business and Public
Affairs
425 Sirrine Hall
Box 341392
Clemson, SC 29634-1392
Phone: (803)656-3227
Fax: (803)656-4869
Becky Hobart, Regional Dir.

University of South Carolina
College of Business Administration
South Carolina SBDC
Hipp Bldg.
1710 College St.
Columbia, SC 29208
Phone: (803)777-4907
Fax: (803)777-4403
John Lenti, State Director

University of South Carolina
Small Business Development Center
College of Business Administration
Columbia, SC 29208
Phone: (803)777-5118
Fax: (803)777-4403
James Brazell, Dir.

Coastal Carolina College
Small Business Development Center
School of Business Administration
PO Box 261954
Conway, SC 29526-6054
Phone: (803)349-2170
Fax: (803)349-2455
Tim Lowery, Area Mgr.

Florence-Darlington Technical
College
Small Business Development Center
PO Box 100548
Florence, SC 29501-0548
Phone: (803)661-8256
Fax: (803)661-8041
David Raines, Area Mgr.

Greenville Manufacturing Field
Office
SBDC
53 E. Antrim Dr.
Greenville, SC 29607
Phone: (803)271-3005

University Center
Upstate Area Office Small Business
Development Center
216 S. Pleasantburg Dr., Rm. 140
Greenville, SC 29607
Phone: (864)250-8894
Fax: (864)250-8897

Upper Savannah Council of
Government
Small Business Development Center
Exchange Building
222 Phoenix St., Ste. 200
PO Box 1366
Greenwood, SC 29648
Phone: (803)941-8071

Fax: (803)941-8090
George Long, Area Mgr.

University of South Carolina at
Hilton Head
Small Business Development Center
1 College Center Dr.
10 Office Park Rd.
Hilton Head, SC 29928-7535
Phone: (803)785-3995
Fax: (803)785-3995
Pat Cameron, Consultant

Charleston SBDC
5900 Core Dr., Ste. 104
North Charleston, SC 29406
Phone: (803)740-6160
Fax: (803)740-1607
Merry Boone, Area Mgr.

South Carolina State College
Small Business Development Center
School of Business Administration
Algernon Belcher Hall
300 College Ave.
Campus Box 7176
Orangeburg, SC 29117
Phone: (803)536-8445
Fax: (803)536-8066
John Gadson, Regional Dir.

Winthrop University
Winthrop Regional Small Business
Development Center
College of Business Administration
118 Thurmond Bldg.
Rock Hill, SC 29733
Phone: (803)323-2283
Fax: (803)323-4281
Nate Barber, Regional Dir.

Spartanburg Chamber of Commerce
Small Business Development Center
105 Pine St.
PO Box 1636
Spartanburg, SC 29304
Phone: (803)594-5080
Fax: (803)594-5055
John Keagle, Area Mgr.

South Dakota

Aberdeen Small Business
Development Center (Northeast
Region)
620 15th Ave., SE
Aberdeen, SD 57401
Phone: (605)626-2565

Fax: (605)626-2667
Belinda Engelhart, Regional Dir.

Pierre Small Business Development
Center
105 S. Euclid, Ste. C
Pierre, SD 57501
Phone: (605)773-5941
Fax: (605)773-5942
Greg Sund, Dir.

Rapid City Small Business
Development Center (Western
Region)
444 N. Mount Rushmore Rd., Rm.
208
Rapid City, SD 57701
Phone: (605)394-5311
Fax: (605)394-6140
Carl Gustafson, Regional Dir.

Sioux Falls Region
SBDC
405 S. 3rd Ave., Ste. 101
Sioux Falls, SD 57104
Phone: (605)367-5757
Fax: (605)367-5755
Wade Bruin, Regional Dir.

University of South Dakota
South Dakota SBDC
School of Business
414 E. Clark
Vermillion, SD 57069
Phone: (605)677-5498
Fax: (605)677-5272
E-mail: sbdc@sundance.usd.edu
Robert E. Ashley. Jr.

Watertown Small Business
Development Center
124 1st. Ave., NW
PO Box 1207
Watertown, SD 57201
Phone: (605)886-7224
Fax: (605)882-5049
Belinda Engelhart, Regional Dir.

Tennessee

Chattanooga State Technical
Community College
SBDC
100 Cherokee Blvd., No. 202
Chattanooga, TN 37405-3878
Phone: (423)752-1774
Fax: (423)752-1925
Donna Marsh, Specialist

Southeast Tennessee Development
District
Small Business Development Center
25 Cherokee Blvd.
PO Box 4757
Chattanooga, TN 37405-0757
Phone: (423)266-5781
Fax: (423)267-7705
Sherri Bishop, Dir.

Austin Peay State University
Small Business Development Center
College of Business
Clarksville, TN 37044
Phone: (615)648-7764
Fax: (615)648-5985
John Volker, Dir.

Cleveland State Community College
Small Business Development Center
PO Box 3570
Cleveland, TN 37320-3570
Phone: (423)478-6247
Fax: (423)478-6251
Don Green, Dir.

Small Business Development Center
(Columbia)
Maury County Chamber of
Commerce Bldg.
106 W. 6th St.
PO Box 8069
Columbia, TN 38402-8069
Phone: (615)898-2745
Fax: (615)893-7089
Eugene Osekowsky, Small Business
Specialist

Tennessee Technological University
SBDC
College of Business Administration
PO Box 5023
Cookeville, TN 38505
Phone: (931)372-3648
Fax: (931)372-6249
Dorothy Vaden, Senior Small Bus.
Specialist

Dyersburg State Community College
Small Business Development Center
1510 Lake Rd.
Dyersburg, TN 38024-2450
Phone: (901)286-3201
Fax: (901)286-3271
Bob Wylie

Four Lakes Regional Industrial
Development Authority
SBDC

PO Box 63
Hartsville, TN 37074-0063
Phone: (615)374-9521
Fax: (615)374-4608
Dorothy Vaden, Senior Small Bus.
Specialist

Jackson State Community College
Small Business Development Center
McWherter Center, Rm. 213
2046 N. Parkway St.
Jackson, TN 38301-3797
Phone: (901)424-5389
Fax: (901)425-2641
David L. Brown

Lambuth University
SBDC
705 Lambuth Blvd.
Jackson, TN 38301
Phone: (901)425-3326
Fax: (901)425-3327
Phillip Ramsey, SB Specialist

East Tennessee State University
College of Business
SBDC
PO Box 70625
Johnson City, TN 37614-0625
Phone: (423)929-5630
Fax: (423)461-7080
Bob Justice, Dir.

Knoxville Area Chamber Partnership
International Trade Center
SBDC
Historic City Hall
601 W. Summit Hill Dr.
Knoxville, TN 37902-2011
Phone: (423)632-2990
Fax: (423)521-6367
Richard Vogler, IT Specialist

Pellissippi State Technical
Community College
Small Business Development Center
Historic City Hall
601 W. Summit Hill Dr.
Knoxville, TN 37902-2011
Phone: (423)632-2980
Fax: (423)971-4439
Teri Brahams, Consortium Dir.

University of Memphis
International Trade Center
SBDC
320 S. Dudley St.
Memphis, TN 38152-0001
Phone: (901)678-4174

Fax: (901)678-4072
Philip Johnson, Dir.

University of Memphis
Tennessee SBDC
320 S. Dudley St.
Building No. 1
Memphis, TN 38152
Phone: (901)678-2500
Fax: (901)678-4072
Dr. Kenneth J. Burns, State Dir.

Walters State Community College
Tennessee Small Business
Development Center
500 S. Davy Crockett Pkwy.
Morristown, TN 37813
Phone: (423)585-2675
Fax: (423)585-2679
Jack Tucker, Dir.

Middle Tennessee State University
Small Business Development Center
Chamber of Commerce Bldg.
501 Memorial Blvd.
PO Box 487
Murfreesboro, TN 37129-0001
Phone: (615)898-2745
Fax: (615)890-7600
Patrick Geho, Dir.

Tennessee State University
Small Business Development Center
College of Business
330 10th Ave. N.
Nashville, TN 37203-3401
Phone: (615)963-7179
Fax: (615)963-7160
Billy E. Lowe, Dir.

Texas

Abilene Christian University
Small Business Development Center
College of Business Administration
648 E. Hwy. 80
Abilene, TX 79601
Phone: (915)670-0300
Fax: (915)670-0311
Judy Wilhelm, Dir.

Sul Ross State University
Big Bend SBDC Satellite
PO Box C-47, Rm. 319
Alpine, TX 79832
Phone: (915)837-8694
Fax: (915)837-8104
Michael Levine, Dir.

Alvin Community College
Small Business Development Center
3110 Mustang Rd.
Alvin, TX 77511-4898
Phone: (713)388-4686
Fax: (713)388-4903
Gina Mattei, Dir.

West Texas A&M University
Small Business Development Center
T. Boone Pickens School of Business
1800 S. Washington, Ste. 209
Amarillo, TX 79102
Phone: (806)372-5151
Fax: (806)372-5261
Don Taylor, Dir.

Trinity Valley Community College
Small Business Development Center
500 S. Prairieville
Athens, TX 75751
Phone: (903)675-7403
Free: (800)335-7232
Fax: (903)675-5199
Judy Loden, Dir.

Lower Colorado River Authority
Small Business Development Center
3701 Lake Austin Blvd.
PO Box 220
Austin, TX 78703
Phone: (512)473-3510
Fax: (512)473-3285
Larry Lucero, Dir.

Lee College
Small Business Development Center
Rundell Hall
PO Box 818
Baytown, TX 77522-0818
Phone: (281)425-6309
Fax: (713)425-6309
Tommy Hathaway, Dir.

Lamar University
Small Business Development Center
855 Florida Ave.
Beaumont, TX 77705
Phone: (409)880-2367
Fax: (409)880-2201
Gene Arnold, Dir.

Bonham Satellite
Small Business Development Center
SBDC
Sam Rayburn Library, Bldg. 2
1201 E. 9th St.
Bonham, TX 75418
Phone: (903)583-7565

Fax: (903)583-6706
Darroll Martin, Coordinator

Blinn College
Small Business Development Center
902 College Ave.
Brenham, TX 77833
Phone: (409)830-4137
Fax: (409)830-4135
Phillis Nelson, Dir.

Brazos Valley Small Business
Development Center
Small Business Development Center
4001 E. 29th St., Ste. 175
PO Box 3695
Bryan, TX 77805-3695
Phone: (409)260-5222
Fax: (409)260-5229
Sam Harwell, Dir.

Greater Corpus Christi Business
Alliance
Small Business Development Center
1201 N. Shoreline
Corpus Christi, TX 78401
Phone: (512)881-1847
Fax: (512)882-4256
Rudy Ortiz, Dir.

Navarro Small Business Development
Center
120 N. 12th St.
Corsicana, TX 75110
Phone: (903)874-0658
Free: (800)320-7232
Fax: (903)874-4187
Leon Allard, Dir.

Dallas County Community College
North Texas SBDC
1402 Corinth St.
Dallas, TX 75215
Phone: 800-350-7232
Fax: (214)860-5813
Elizabeth (Liz) Klimback, Regional
Dir.

International Assistance Center
SBDC
2050 Stemmons Fwy.
PO Box 420451
Dallas, TX 75258
Phone: (214)747-1300
Free: (800)337-7232
Fax: (214)748-5774
Beth Huddleston, Dir.

Bill J. Priest Institute for Economic
Development
North Texas-Dallas Small Business
Development Center
1402 Corinth St.
Dallas, TX 75215
Phone: (214)860-5842
Free: (800)348-7232
Fax: (214)860-5881
Pamela Speraw, Dir.

Technology Assistance Center
SBDC
1402 Corinth St.
Dallas, TX 75215
Phone: 800-355-7232
Fax: (214)860-5881
Pamela Speraw, Dir.

Texas Center for Government
Contracting and Technology
Assistance
Small Business Development Center
1402 Corinth St.
Dallas, TX 75215
Phone: (214)860-5841
Fax: (214)860-5881
Gerald Chandler, Dir.

Grayson County College
Small Business Development Center
6101 Grayson Dr.
Denison, TX 75020
Phone: (903)463-8787
Free: (800)316-7232
Fax: (903)463-5437
Cynthia Flowers-Whitfield, Dir.

Denton Small Business Development
Center
PO Drawer P
Denton, TX 76201
Phone: (254)380-1849
Fax: (254)382-0040
Carolyn Birkhead, Coordinator

Best Southwest Small Business
Development Center
214 S. Main, Ste. 102A
Duncanville, TX 75116
Phone: (972)709-5878
Free: (800)317-7232
Fax: (972)709-6089
Neil Small, Dir.

University of Texas—Pan American
Small Business Development Center
1201 W. University Dr., Rm. BA-124

Center for Entrepreneurship &
Economic Development
Edinburg, TX 78539-2999
Phone: (956)316-2610
Fax: (956)316-2612
Juan Garcia, Dir.

El Paso Community College
Small Business Development Center
103 Montana Ave., Ste. 202
El Paso, TX 79902-3929
Phone: (915)831-4410
Fax: (915)831-4625
Roque R. Segura, Dir.

Small Business Development Center
for Enterprise Excellence
SBDC
7300 Jack Newell Blvd., S.
Fort Worth, TX 76118
Phone: (817)272-5930
Fax: (817)272-5932
Jo An Weddle, Dir.

Tarrant County Junior College
Small Business Development Center
Mary Owen Center, Rm. 163
1500 Houston St.
Ft. Worth, TX 76102
Phone: (817)871-2068
Fax: (817)871-0031
David Edmonds, Dir.

North Central Texas College
Small Business Development Center
1525 W. California
Gainesville, TX 76240
Phone: (254)668-4220
Free: (800)351-7232
Fax: (254)668-6049
Cathy Keeler, Dir.

Galveston College
Small Business Development Center
4015 Avenue Q
Galveston, TX 77550
Phone: (409)740-7380
Fax: (409)740-7381
Georgette Peterson, Dir.

Western Bank and Trust Satellite
SBDC
PO Box 461545
Garland, TX 75046
Phone: (214)860-5850
Fax: (214)860-5857
Al Salgado, Dir.

Grand Prairie Satellite
SBDC

Chamber of Commerce
900 Conover Dr.
Grand Prairie, TX 75053
Phone: (214)860-5850
Fax: (214)860-5857
Al Salgado, Dir.

Houston Community College System
Small Business Development Center
10450 Stancliff, Ste. 100
Houston, TX 77099
Phone: (281)933-7932
Fax: (281)568-3690
Joe Harper, Dir.

Houston International Trade Center
Small Business Development Center
1100 Louisiana, Ste. 500
Houston, TX 77002
Phone: (713)752-8404
Fax: (713)756-1500
Mr. Carlos Lopez, Dir.

North Harris Montgomery
Community College District
Small Business Development Center
250 N. Sam Houston Pkwy. E.
Houston, TX 77060
Phone: (281)260-3174
Fax: (713)591-3513
Kay Hamilton, Dir.

University of Houston
Southeastern Texas SBDC
1100 Louisiana, Ste. 500
Houston, TX 77002
Phone: (713)752-8444
Fax: (713)756-1500
J.E. "Ted" Cadou, Reg. Dir.

University of Houston
Texas Information Procurement
Service
Small Business Development Center
1100 Louisiana, Ste. 500
Houston, TX 77002
Phone: (713)752-8477
Fax: (713)756-1515
Jacqueline Taylor, Dir.

University of Houston
Texas Manufacturing Assistance
Center (Gulf Coast)
1100 Louisiana, Ste. 500
Houston, TX 77002
Phone: (713)752-8440
Fax: (713)756-1500
Roy Serpa, Regional Dir.

Sam Houston State University
Small Business Development Center
843 S. Sam Houston Ave.
PO Box 2058
Huntsville, TX 77341-3738
Phone: (409)294-3737
Fax: (409)294-3612
Bob Barragan, Dir.

Kingsville Chamber of Commerce
Small Business Development Center
635 E. King
Kingsville, TX 78363
Phone: (512)595-5088
Fax: (512)592-0866
Marco Garza, Dir.

Brazosport College
Small Business Development Center
500 College Dr.
Lake Jackson, TX 77566
Phone: (409)266-3380
Fax: (409)265-3482
Patricia Leyendecker, Dir.

Laredo Development Foundation
Small Business Development Center
Division of Business Administration
616 Leal St.
Laredo, TX 78041
Phone: (956)722-0563
Fax: (956)722-6247
Araceli Lozano, Acting Dir.

Kilgore College
SBDC
Triple Creek Shopping Plaza
110 Triple Creek Dr., Ste. 70
Longview, TX 75601
Phone: (903)757-5857
Free: (800)338-7232
Fax: (903)753-7920
Brad Bunt, Dir.

Texas Tech University
Northwestern Texas SBDC
Spectrum Plaza
2579 S. Loop 289, Ste. 114
Lubbock, TX 79423
Phone: (806)745-3973
Fax: (806)745-6207
E-mail: odbea@ttacs.ttu.edu
Craig Bean, Regional Dir.

Angelina Community College
Small Business Development Center
Hwy. 59 S.
PO Box 1768
Lufkin, TX 75902

Phone: (409)639-1887
Fax: (409)639-3863
Brian McClain, Dir.

Midlothian SBDC
330 N. 8th St., Ste. 203
Midlothian, TX 76065-0609
Phone: (214)775-4336
Fax: (214)775-4337

Northeast Texarkana
Small Business Development Center
PO Box 1307
Mt. Pleasant, TX 75455
Phone: (903)572-1911
Free: (800)357-7232
Fax: (903)572-0598
Bob Wall, Dir.

University of Texas—Permian Basin
Small Business Development Center
College of Management
4901 E. University Blvd.
Odessa, TX 79762
Phone: (915)552-2455
Fax: (915)552-2433
Arthur L. Connor, III

Paris Junior College
Small Business Development Center
2400 Clarksville St.
Paris, TX 75460
Phone: (903)784-1802
Fax: (903)784-1801
Pat Bell, Dir.

Courtyard Center for Professional and
Economic Development
Collin Small Business Development
Center
4800 Preston Park Blvd., Ste. A126
Box 15
Plano, TX 75093
Phone: (972)985-3770
Fax: (972)985-3775
Chris Jones, Dir.

Angelo State University
Small Business Development Center
2610 West Ave. N.
Campus Box 10910
San Angelo, TX 76909
Phone: (915)942-2098
Fax: (915)942-2096
Harlan Bruha, Dir.

University of Texas (Downtown San
Antonio)
South Texas Border SBDC
1222 N. Main, Ste. 450

San Antonio, TX 78212
Phone: (210)458-2450
Fax: (210)458-2464
E-mail: rmckinle@utsadt.utsa.edu
Robert McKinley, Regional Dir.

University of Texas at San Antonio
International Trade Center
SBDC
1222 N. Main, Ste. 450
San Antonio, TX 78212
Phone: (210)458-2470
Fax: (210)458-2464
Sara Jackson, Dir.

Houston Community College System
Small Business Development Center
13600 Murphy Rd.
Stafford, TX 77477
Phone: (713)499-4870
Fax: (713)499-8194
Ted Charlesworth, Acting Dir.

Tarleton State University
Small Business Development Center
College of Business Administration
Box T-0650
Stephenville, TX 76402
Phone: (817)968-9330
Fax: (817)968-9329
Jim Choate, Dir.

College of the Mainland
Small Business Development Center
1200 Amburn Rd.
Texas City, TX 77591
Phone: (409)938-1211
Free: (800)246-7232
Fax: (409)938-7578
Elizabeth Boudreau, Dir.

Tyler Junior College
Small Business Development Center
1530 South SW Loop 323, Ste. 100
Tyler, TX 75701
Phone: (903)510-2975
Fax: (903)510-2978
Frank Viso, Dir.

Middle Rio Grande Development
Council
Small Business Development Center
209 N. Getty St.
Uvalde, TX 78801
Phone: (830)278-2527
Fax: (830)278-2929
Sheri Rutledge, Dir.

University of Houston—Victoria
Small Business Development Center

700 Main Center, Ste. 102
Victoria, TX 77901
Phone: (512)575-8944
Fax: (512)575-8852
Carole Parks, Dir.

McLennan Community College
Small Business Development Center
401 Franklin
Waco, TX 76708
Phone: (254)714-0077
Free: (800)349-7232
Fax: (254)714-1668
Lu Billings, Dir.

LCRA Coastal Plains
SBDC
PO Box 148
Wharton, TX 77488
Phone: (409)532-1007
Fax: (409)532-0056
Lynn Polson, Dir.

Midwestern State University
Small Business Development Center
3410 Taft Blvd.
Wichita Falls, TX 76308
Phone: (817)397-4373
Fax: (817)397-4374
Tim Thomas, Dir.

Utah

Southern Utah University
Small Business Development Center
351 W. Center
Cedar City, UT 84720
Phone: (435)586-5400
Fax: (435)586-5493
Derek Snow, Dir.

Snow College
Small Business Development Center
345 West 100 North
Ephraim, UT 84627
Phone: (435)283-7472
Fax: (435)283-6913
Russell Johnson, Dir.

Utah State University
Small Business Development Center
East Campus Bldg., Rm. 124
Logan, UT 84322
Phone: (435)797-2277
Fax: (435)797-3317
Franklin C. Prante, Dir.

Weber State University
Small Business Development Center
School of Business and Economics

Ogden, UT 84408-3815
Phone: (435)626-6070
Fax: (435)626-7423
Bruce Davis, Dir.

Utah Valley State College
Utah Small Business Development
Center
800 West 200 South
Orem, UT 84058
Phone: (435)222-8230
Fax: (435)225-1229
Chuck Cozzens, Contact

South Eastern Utah AOG
Small Business Development Center
Price Center
PO Box 1106
Price, UT 84501
Phone: (435)637-5444
Fax: (435)637-7336
Dennis Rigby, Dir.

Utah State University Extension
Office
SBDC
987 E. Lagoon St.
Roosevelt, UT 84066
Phone: (435)722-2294
Fax: (435)789-3689
Mark Holmes, Dir.

Dixie College
Small Business Development Center
225 South 700 East
St. George, UT 84770-3876
Phone: (435)652-7751
Fax: (435)652-7870
Jill Ellis, Dir.

Salt Lake Community College
SBDC
1623 S. State St.
Salt Lake City, UT 84115
Phone: (801)957-3480
Fax: (801)957-3489
Mike Finnerty, State Dir.

Salt Lake Community College
Sandy SBDC
8811 South 700 East
Sandy, UT 84070
Phone: (435)255-5878
Fax: (435)255-6393
Barry Bartlett, Dir.

Vermont

Brattleboro Development Credit
Corp.
SBDC
72 Cotton Mill Hill
PO Box 1177
Brattleboro, VT 05301-1177
Phone: (802)257-7731
Fax: (802)258-3886
William McGrath, Executive V. P.

Greater Burlington Industrial Corp.
Northwestern Vermont Small
Business Development Center
PO Box 786
Burlington, VT 05402-0786
Phone: (802)658-9228
Fax: (802)860-1899
Thomas D. Schroeder, Specialist

Addison County Economic
Development Corp.
SBDC
RD4, Box 1309A
Middlebury, VT 05753
Phone: (802)388-7953
Fax: (802)388-8066
James Stewart, Exec. Dir.

Central Vermont Economic
Development Center
SBDC
PO Box 1439
Montpelier, VT 05601-1439
Phone: (802)223-4654
Fax: (802)223-4655
Donald Rowan, Exec. Dir.

Lamoille Economic Development
Corp.
SBDC
Sunset Dr.
PO Box 455
Morrisville, VT 05661-0455
Phone: (802)888-4542
Chris D'Elia, Executive Dir.

Bennington County Industrial Corp.
SBDC
PO Box 357
North Bennington, VT 05257-0357
Phone: (802)442-8975
Fax: (802)442-1101
Chris Hunsinger, Executive Dir.

Lake Champlain Islands Chamber of
Commerce
SBDC

PO Box 213
North Hero, VT 05474-0213
Phone: (802)372-5683
Fax: (802)372-6104
Barbara Mooney, Exec. Dir.

Vermont Technical College
Small Business Development Center
PO Box 422
Randolph Center, VT 05060-0422
Phone: (802)728-9101
Free: (800)464-7232
Fax: (802)728-3026
Donald L. Kelpinski, State Dir.

Rutland Economic Development
Corp.
Southwestern Vermont Small
Business Development Center
256 N. Main St.
Rutland, VT 05701-0039
Phone: (802)773-9147
Fax: (802)773-2772
Wendy Wilton, Regional Dir.

Franklin County Industrial
Development Corp.
SBDC
PO Box 1099
St. Albans, VT 05478-1099
Phone: (802)524-2194
Fax: (802)527-5258
Timothy J. Soule, Executive Dir.

Northeastern Vermont Small
Business Development Center
44 Main St.
PO Box 630
St. Johnsbury, VT 05819-0630
Phone: (802)748-1014
Fax: (802)748-1223
Charles E. E. Carter, Exec. Dir.

Springfield Development Corp.
Southeastern Vermont Small
Business Development Center
PO Box 58
Springfield, VT 05156-0058
Phone: (802)885-2071
Fax: (802)885-3027
Steve Casabona, Specialist

Green Mountain Economic
Development Corporation
SBDC
PO Box 246
White River Jct., VT 05001-0246
Phone: (802)295-3710
Fax: (802)295-3779

Lenae Quillen-Blume, SBDC
Specialist

Virgin Islands

University of the Virgin Islands
(Charlotte Amalie)
Small Business Development Center
8000 Nisky Center, Ste. 202
Charlotte Amalie, VI 00802-5804
Phone: (809)776-3206
Fax: (809)775-3756
Ian Hodge, Assoc. State Dir.

University of the Virgin Islands
Small Business Development Center
Sunshine Mall
No.1 Estate Cane, Ste. 104
Frederiksted, VI 00840
Phone: (809)692-5270
Fax: (809)692-5629
Chester Williams, State Dir.

Virginia

Virginia Highlands SBDC
Rte. 382
PO Box 828
Abingdon, VA 24212
Phone: (540)676-5615
Fax: (540)628-7576
Jim Tilley, Dir.

Arlington Small Business
Development Center
George Mason University, Arlington
Campus
4001 N. Fairfax Dr., Ste. 450
Arlington, VA 22203-1640
Phone: (703)993-8129
Fax: (703)430-7293
Paul Hall, Dir.

Virginia Eastern Shore Corp.
SBDC
36076 Lankford Hwy.
PO Box 395
Belle Haven, VA 23306
Phone: (757)442-7179
Fax: (757)442-7181

Mount Empire Community College
Southwest Small Business
Development Center
Drawer 700, Rte. 23, S.
Big Stone Gap, VA 24219
Phone: (540)523-6529
Fax: (540)523-2400
Tim Blankenbecler, Dir.

Central Virginia Small Business
Development Center
918 Emmet St., N., Ste. 200
Charlottesville, VA 22903-4878
Phone: (804)295-8198
Fax: (804)295-7066
Robert A. Hamilton, Jr.

Hampton Roads Chamber of
Commerce
SBDC
400 Volvo Pkwy.
PO Box 1776
Chesapeake, VA 23320
Phone: (757)664-2590
Fax: (757)548-1835
William J. Holoran, Jr.

George Mason University
Northern Virginia Small Business
Development Center
4031 University Dr., Ste. 200
Fairfax, VA 22030
Phone: (703)277-7700
Fax: (703)993-2126
Michael Kehoe, Exec. Dir.

Longwood College (Farmville)
Small Business Development Center
515 Main St.
Farmville, VA 23909
Phone: (804)395-2086
Fax: (804)395-2359
Gerald L. Hughes, Jr.

Rappahannock Region Small
Business Development Center
1301 College Ave.
Seacobeck Hall, Rm. 102
Fredericksburg, VA 22401
Phone: (540)654-1060
Fax: (540)654-1070
Jeffrey R. Sneddon, Exec. Dir.

Hampton Roads Inc.
Small Business Development Center
525 Butler Farm Rd., Ste. 102
Hampton, VA 23666
Phone: (757)825-2957
Fax: (757)825-2960
James Carroll, Dir.

James Madison University
Small Business Development Center
College of Business
Zane Showker Hall, Rm. 527
PO Box MSC 0206
Harrisonburg, VA 22807
Phone: (540)568-3227

Fax: (540)568-3106
Karen Wigginton, Dir.

Lynchburg Regional Small Business
Development Center
147 Mill Ridge Rd.
Lynchburg, VA 24502-4341
Phone: (804)582-6170
Free: (800)876-7232
Fax: (804)582-6106
Barry Lyons, Dir.

Flory Small Business Development
Center
10311 Sudley Manor Dr.
Manassas, VA 20109-2962
Phone: (703)335-2500
Linda Decker, Dir.

SBDC Satellite Office of Longwood
PO Box 709
115 Broad St.
Martinsville, VA 24114
Phone: (540)632-4462
Fax: (540)632-5059
Ken Copeland, Dir

Lord Fairfax Community College
SBDC
173 Skirmisher Ln.
PO Box 47
Middletown, VA 22645
Phone: (540)869-6649
Fax: (540)868-7002
Robert Crosen, Dir.

Small Business Development Center
of Hampton Roads, Inc. (Norfolk)
420 Bank St.
PO Box 327
Norfolk, VA 23501
Phone: (757)664-2528
Fax: (757)622-5563
Warren Snyder, Dir.

New River Valley
SBDC
600-H Norwood St.
PO Box 3726
Radford, VA 24141
Phone: (540)831-6056
Fax: (540)831-6057
David Shanks, Dir.

Southwest Virginia Community
College
Southwest Small Business
Development Center
PO Box SVCC, Rte. 19
Richlands, VA 24641

Phone: (540)964-7345
Fax: (540)964-5788
Jim Boyd, Dir.

Department of Business Assistance
Virginia SBDC
707 E. Main St., Ste. 300
Richmond, VA 23219
Phone: (804)371-8253
Fax: (804)225-3384
Bob Wilburn, State Dir.

Greater Richmond Small Business
Development Center
1 N. 5th St., Ste. 510
Richmond, VA 23219
Phone: (804)648-7838
Free: (800)646-SBDC
Fax: (804)648-7849
Charlie Meacham, Dir.

Regional Chamber Small Business
Development Center
Western Virginia SBDC Consortium
212 S. Jefferson St.
Roanoke, VA 24011
Phone: (540)983-0717
Fax: (540)983-0723
Ian Webb, Dir.

South Boston Satellite Office of
Longwood
Small Business Development Center
515 Broad St.
PO Box 1116
South Boston, VA 24592
Phone: (804)575-0044
Fax: (804)572-1762
Vincent Decker, Dir.

Loudoun County Small Business
Development Center
Satellite Office of Northern Virginia
207 E. Holly Ave., Ste. 214
Sterling, VA 20164
Phone: (703)430-7222
Fax: (703)430-7258
Ted London, Dir.

Warsaw Small Business Development
Center
Satellite Office of Rappahannock
5559 W. Richmond Rd.
PO Box 490
Warsaw, VA 22572
Phone: (804)333-0286
Free: (800)524-8915
Fax: (804)333-0187
John Clickener, Dir.

Wytheville Community College
Wytheville Small Business
Development Center
1000 E. Main St.
Wytheville, VA 24382
Phone: (540)223-4798
Free: (800)468-1195
Fax: (540)223-4716
Rob Edwards, Dir.

Washington

Bellevue Small Business
Development Center
Bellevue Community College
3000 Landerholm Circle SE
Bellevue, WA 98007-6484
Phone: (425)643-2888
Fax: (425)649-3113
Bill Huenefeld, Business Dev.
Specialist

Western Washington University
Small Business Development Center
College of Business and Economics
308 Parks Hall
Bellingham, WA 98225-9073
Phone: (360)650-4831
Fax: (360)650-4844
Tom Dorr, Business Dev. Specialist

Centralia Community College
Small Business Development Center
600 W. Locust St.
Centralia, WA 98531
Phone: (360)736-9391
Fax: (360)730-7504
Joanne Baria, Business Dev.
Specialist

Columbia Basin College—TRIDEC
Small Business Development Center
901 N. Colorado
Kennewick, WA 99336
Phone: (509)735-6222
Fax: (509)735-6609
Blake Escudier, Business Dev.
Specialist

Edmonds Community College
Small Business Development Center
20000 68th Ave. W.
Lynnwood, WA 98036
Phone: (425)640-1435
Fax: (425)640-1532
Jack Wicks, Business Dev. Specialist

Big Bend Community College
Small Business Development Center

7662 Chanute St.
Moses Lake, WA 98837-3299
Phone: (509)762-6306
Fax: (509)762-6329
Ed Baroch, Business Dev. Specialist

Skagit Valley College
Small Business Development Center
2405 College Way
Mount Vernon, WA 98273
Phone: (360)428-1282
Fax: (360)336-6116
Peter Stroosma, Business Dev.
Specialist

Wenatchee Valley College
SBDC
PO Box 741
Okanogan, WA 98840
Phone: (509)826-5107
Fax: (509)826-1812
John Rayburn, Business Dev.
Specialist

South Puget Sound Community
College
Small Business Development Center
721 Columbia St. SW
Olympia, WA 98501
Phone: (360)753-5616
Fax: (360)586-5493
Douglas Hammel, Business Dev.
Specialist

Washington State University
(Pullman)
Small Business Development Center
501 Johnson Tower
PO Box 644851
Pullman, WA 99164-4727
Phone: (509)335-1576
Fax: (509)335-0949
Carol Riesenberg, State Dir.

International Trade Institute
North Seattle Community College
Small Business Development Center
2001 6th Ave., Ste. 650
Seattle, WA 98121
Phone: (206)553-0052
Fax: (206)553-7253
Ann Tamura, IT Specialist

South Seattle Community College
Duwamish Industrial Education
Center
Small Business Development Center
6770 E. Marginal Way S
Seattle, WA 98108-3405

Phone: (206)768-6855
Fax: (206)764-5838
Henry Burton, Business Dev.
Specialist

Washington Small Business
Development Center (Seattle)
180 Nickerson, Ste. 207
Seattle, WA 98109
Phone: (206)464-5450
Fax: (206)464-6357
Warner Wong, Business Dev.
Specialist

Washington State University
(Spokane)
Small Business Development Center
665 North Riverpoint Blvd.
Spokane, WA 99202
Phone: (509)358-7894
Fax: (509)358-7896
Richard Thorpe, Business Dev.
Specialist

Washington Small Business
Development Center (Tacoma)
950 Pacific Ave., Ste. 300
PO Box 1933
Tacoma, WA 98401-1933
Phone: (253)272-7232
Fax: (253)597-7305
Neil Delisanti, Business Dev.
Specialist

Columbia River Economic
Development Council
Small Business Development Center
217 SE 136th Ave., Ste. 105
Vancouver, WA 98660
Phone: (360)260-6372
Fax: (360)260-6369
Janet Harte, Business Dev. Specialist

Port of Walla Walla SBDC
500 Tausick Way
Rte. 4, Box 174
Walla Walla, WA 99362
Phone: (509)527-4681
Fax: (509)525-3101
Rich Monacelli, Business Dev.
Specialist

Quest Small Business Development
Center
37 S. Wenatchee Ave., Ste. C
Industrial Bldg. 2, Ste. D.
Wenatchee, WA 98801-2443
Phone: (509)662-8016

Fax: (509)663-0455
Rich Reim, Business Dev. Specialist

Yakima Valley College
Small Business Development Center
PO Box 1647
Yakima, WA 98907
Phone: (509)454-3608
Fax: (509)454-4155
Audrey Rice, Business Dev.
Specialist

West Virginia

College of West Virginia
SBDC
PO Box AG
Beckley, WV 25802
Phone: (304)252-7885
Fax: (304)252-9584
Tom Hardiman, Program Mgr.

West Virginia Department Office
West Virginia SBDC
950 Kanawha Blvd. E., Ste. 200
Charleston, WV 25301
Phone: (304)558-2960
Free: (888)WVA-SBDC
Fax: (304)348-0127
Dr. Hazel Kroesser-Palmer, State-Dir.

Fairmont State College (Elkins
Satellite)
SBDC
10 Eleventh St., Ste. 1
Elkins, WV 26241
Phone: (304)637-7205
Fax: (304)637-4902
James Martin, Business Analyst

Fairmont State College
Small Business Development Center
1000 Technology Dr., Ste. 1120
Fairmont, WV 26554
Phone: (304)367-2712
Fax: (304)367-2717
Jack Kirby, Program Mgr.

Marshall University
Small Business Development Center
1050 4th Ave.
Huntington, WV 25755-2126
Phone: (304)696-6246
Fax: (304)696-6277
Edna McClain, Program Mgr.

West Virginia Institute of Technology
Small Business Development Center
Engineering Bldg., Rm. 102

Montgomery, WV 25136
Phone: (304)442-5501
Fax: (304)442-3307
James Epling, Program Mgr.

West Virginia University
Fairmont State College Satellite
Small Business Development Center
PO Box 6025
Morgantown, WV 26506-6025
Phone: (304)293-5839
Fax: (304)293-7061
Sharon Stratton, Business Analyst

West Virginia University
(Parkersburg)
Small Business Development Center
Rte. 5, Box 167-A
Parkersburg, WV 26101
Phone: (304)424-8277
Fax: (304)424-8315
Greg Hill, Program Mgr.

Shepherd College
Small Business Development Center
120 N. Princess St.
Shepherdstown, WV 25443
Phone: (304)876-5261
Fax: (304)876-5467
Fred Baer, Program Mgr.

West Virginia Northern Community
College
Small Business Development Center
1701 Market St.
College Sq.
Wheeling, WV 26003
Phone: (304)233-5900
Fax: (304)232-0965
Ron Trevellini, Program Mgr.

Wisconsin

University of Wisconsin—Eau Claire
Small Business Development Center
Schneider Hall, Rm. 113
PO Box 4004
Eau Claire, WI 54702-4004
Phone: (715)836-5811
Fax: (715)836-5263
Fred Waedt, Dir.

University of Wisconsin—Green Bay
Small Business Development Center
Wood Hall, Rm. 480
2420 Nicolet Dr.
Green Bay, WI 54311
Phone: (920)465-2089

Fax: (920)465-2552
Jan Thornton, Dir.

University of Wisconsin—Parkside
Small Business Development Center
Tallent Hall, Rm. 284
900 Wood Rd.
Kenosha, WI 53141-2000
Phone: (414)595-2189
Fax: (414)595-2471
Patricia Deutsch, Dir.

University of Wisconsin—La Crosse
Small Business Development Center
North Hall, Rm. 120
1701 Farwell St.
La Crosse, WI 54601
Phone: (608)785-8782
Fax: (608)785-6919
Jan Gallagher, Dir.

University of Wisconsin
Wisconsin SBDC
432 N. Lake St., Rm. 423
Madison, WI 53706
Phone: (608)263-7794
Fax: (608)263-7830
Erica McIntire, State Dir.

University of Wisconsin—Madison
Small Business Development Center
975 University Ave., Rm. 3260
Grainger Hall
Madison, WI 53706
Phone: (608)263-2221
Fax: (608)263-0818
Neil Lerner, Dir.

University of Wisconsin—Milwaukee
Small Business Development Center
161 W. Wisconsin Ave., Ste. 600
Milwaukee, WI 53203
Phone: (414)227-3240
Fax: (414)227-3142
Sara Thompson, Dir.

University of Wisconsin—Oshkosh
Small Business Development Center
800 Algoma Blvd.
Oshkosh, WI 54901
Phone: (920)424-1453
Fax: (920)424-7413
John Mozingo, Dir.

University of Wisconsin—Stevens
Point
Small Business Development Center
Old Main Bldg., Rm. 103
Stevens Point, WI 54481

Phone: (715)346-3838
Fax: (715)346-4045
Vicki Lobermeier, Acting Dir.

University of Wisconsin—Superior
Small Business Development Center
1800 Grand Ave.
Superior, WI 54880-2898
Phone: (715)394-8352
Fax: (715)394-8592
Laura Urban, Dir.

University of Wisconsin at
Whitewater
Wisconsin Innovation Service Center
SBDC
416 McCutchen Hall
Whitewater, WI 53190
Phone: (414)472-1365
Fax: (414)472-1600
E-mail:
malewicd@uwwvax.uww.edu
Debra Malewicki, Dir.

Wyoming

Casper Small Business Development
Center
Region III
111 W. 2nd St., Ste. 502
Casper, WY 82601
Phone: (307)234-6683
Free: (800)348-5207
Fax: (307)577-7014
Leonard Holler, Dir.

Cheyenne SBDC
Region IV
1400 E. College Dr.
Cheyenne, WY 82007-3298
Phone: (307)632-6141
Free: (800)348-5208
Fax: (307)632-6061
Arlene Soto, Regional Dir.

Northwest Community College
Small Business Development Center
Region II
146 South Bent St.
John Dewitt Student Center
Powell, WY 82435
Phone: (307)754-2139
Free: (800)348-5203
Fax: (307)754-0368
Dwane Heintz, Dir.

Rock Springs Small Business
Development Center
Region I

PO Box 1168
Rock Springs, WY 82902
Phone: (307)352-6894
Free: (800)348-5205
Fax: (307)352-6876

SERVICE CORPS OF RETIRED EXECUTIVES (SCORE) OFFICES

This section contains a listing of all SCORE offices organized alphabetically by state/U.S. territory name, then by city, then by agency name.

Alabama

SCORE Office (Northeast Alabama)
1330 Quintard Ave.
Anniston, AL 36202
Phone: (256)237-3536

SCORE Office (North Alabama)
901 South 15th St, Rm. 201
Birmingham, AL 35294-2060
Phone: (205)934-6868
Fax: (205)934-0538

SCORE Office (Baldwin County)
29750 Larry Dee Cawyer Dr.
Daphne, AL 36526
Phone: (334)928-5838

SCORE Office (Shoals)
Florence, AL 35630
Phone: (256)760-9067

SCORE Office (Mobile)
600 S Court St.
Mobile, AL 36104
Phone: (334)240-6868
Fax: (334)240-6869

SCORE Office (Alabama Capitol
City)
600 S. Court St.
Montgomery, AL 36104
Phone: (334)240-6868
Fax: (334)240-6869

SCORE Office (East Alabama)
601 Ave. A
Opelika, AL 36801
Phone: (334)745-4861
E-mail: score636@hotmail.com
Website: http://www.angelfire.com/
sc/score636/

SCORE Office (Tuscaloosa)
2200 University Blvd.
Tuscaloosa, AL 35402
Phone: (205)758-7588

Alaska

SCORE Office (Anchorage)
222 W. 8th Ave.
Anchorage, AK 99513-7559
Phone: (907)271-4022
Fax: (907)271-4545

Arizona

SCORE Office (Lake Havasu)
10 S. Acoma Blvd.
Lake Havasu City, AZ 86403
Phone: (520)453-5951
E-mail: SCORE@ctaz.com
Website: http://
www.scorearizona.org/lake_havasu/

SCORE Office (East Valley)
Federal Bldg., Rm. 104
26 N. MacDonald St.
Mesa, AZ 85201
Phone: (602)379-3100
Fax: (602)379-3143
E-mail: 402@aol.com
Website: http://
www.scorearizona.org/mesa/

SCORE Office (Phoenix)
2828 N. Central Ave., Ste. 800
Central & One Thomas
Phoenix, AZ 85004
Phone: (602)640-2329
Fax: (602)640-2360
E-mail: e-mail@SCORE-phoenix.org
Website: http://www.score-phoenix.org/

SCORE Office (Prescott Arizona)
1228 Willow Creek Rd., Ste. 2
Prescott, AZ 86301
Phone: (520)778-7438
Fax: (520)778-0812
E-mail: score@northlink.com
Website: http://
www.scorearizona.org/prescott/

SCORE Office (Tucson)
110 E. Pennington St.
Tucson, AZ 85702
Phone: (520)670-5008
Fax: (520)670-5011
E-mail: score@azstarnet.com

Website: http://
www.scorearizona.org/tucson/

SCORE Office (Yuma)
281 W. 24th St., Ste. 116
Yuma, AZ 85364
Phone: (520)314-0480
E-mail: score@C2i2.com
Website: http://
www.scorearizona.org/yuma

Arkansas

SCORE Office (South Central)
201 N. Jackson Ave.
El Dorado, AR 71730-5803
Phone: (870)863-6113
Fax: (870)863-6115

SCORE Office (Ozark)
Fayetteville, AR 72701
Phone: (501)442-7619

SCORE Office (Northwest Arkansas)
Glenn Haven Dr., No. 4
Ft. Smith, AR 72901
Phone: (501)783-3556

SCORE Office (Garland County)
Grand & Ouachita
PO Box 6012
Hot Springs Village, AR 71902
Phone: (501)321-1700

SCORE Office (Little Rock)
2120 Riverfront Dr., Rm. 100
Little Rock, AR 72202-1747
Phone: (501)324-5893
Fax: (501)324-5199

SCORE Office (Southeast Arkansas)
121 W. 6th
Pine Bluff, AR 71601
Phone: (870)535-7189
Fax: (870)535-1643

California

SCORE Office (Golden Empire)
1706 Chester Ave., No. 200
Bakersfield, CA 93301
Phone: (805)322-5881
Fax: (805)322-5663

SCORE Office (Greater Chico Area)
1324 Mangrove St., Ste. 114
Chico, CA 95926
Phone: (916)342-8932
Fax: (916)342-8932

SCORE Office (Concord)
2151-A Salvio St., Ste. B
Concord, CA 94520
Phone: (510)685-1181
Fax: (510)685-5623

SCORE Office (Covina)
935 W. Badillo St.
Covina, CA 91723
Phone: (818)967-4191
Fax: (818)966-9660

SCORE Office (Rancho Cucamonga)
8280 Utica, Ste. 160
Cucamonga, CA 91730
Phone: (909)987-1012
Fax: (909)987-5917

SCORE Office (Culver City)
PO Box 707
Culver City, CA 90232-0707
Phone: (310)287-3850
Fax: (310)287-1350

SCORE Office (Danville)
380 Diablo Rd., Ste. 103
Danville, CA 94526
Phone: (510)837-4400

SCORE Office (Downey)
11131 Brookshire Ave.
Downey, CA 90241
Phone: (310)923-2191
Fax: (310)864-0461

SCORE Office (El Cajon)
109 Rea Ave.
El Cajon, CA 92020
Phone: (619)444-1327
Fax: (619)440-6164

SCORE Office (El Centro)
1100 Main St.
El Centro, CA 92243
Phone: (619)352-3681
Fax: (619)352-3246

SCORE Office (Escondido)
720 N. Broadway
Escondido, CA 92025
Phone: (619)745-2125
Fax: (619)745-1183

SCORE Office (Fairfield)
1111 Webster St.
Fairfield, CA 94533
Phone: (707)425-4625
Fax: (707)425-0826

SCORE Office (Fontana)
17009 Valley Blvd., Ste. B

Fontana, CA 92335
Phone: (909)822-4433
Fax: (909)822-6238

SCORE Office (Foster City)
1125 E. Hillsdale Blvd.
Foster City, CA 94404
Phone: (415)573-7600
Fax: (415)573-5201

SCORE Office (Fremont)
2201 Walnut Ave., Ste. 110
Fremont, CA 94538
Phone: (510)795-2244
Fax: (510)795-2240

SCORE Office (Central California)
2719 N. Air Fresno Dr., Ste. 200
Fresno, CA 93727-1547
Phone: (559)487-5605
Fax: (559)487-5636

SCORE Office (Gardena)
1204 W. Gardena Blvd.
Gardena, CA 90247
Phone: (310)532-9905
Fax: (310)515-4893

SCORE Office (Lompoc)
330 N. Brand Blvd., Ste. 190
Glendale, CA 91203-2304
Phone: (818)552-3206
Fax: (818)552-3323

SCORE Office (Los Angeles)
330 N. Brand Blvd., Ste. 190
Glendale, CA 91203-2304
Phone: (818)552-3206
Fax: (818)552-3323

SCORE Office (Glendora)
131 E. Foothill Blvd.
Glendora, CA 91740
Phone: (818)963-4128
Fax: (818)914-4822

SCORE Office (Grover Beach)
177 S. 8th St.
Grover Beach, CA 93433
Phone: (805)489-9091
Fax: (805)489-9091

SCORE Office (Hawthorne)
12477 Hawthorne Blvd.
Hawthorne, CA 90250
Phone: (310)676-1163
Fax: (310)676-7661

SCORE Office (Hayward)
22300 Foothill Blvd., Ste. 303

Hayward, CA 94541
Phone: (510)537-2424

SCORE Office (Hemet)
1700 E. Florida Ave.
Hemet, CA 92544-4679
Phone: (909)652-4390
Fax: (909)929-8543

SCORE Office (Hesperia)
16367 Main St.
PO Box 403656
Hesperia, CA 92340
Phone: (619)244-2135

SCORE Office (Holloster)
321 San Felipe Rd., No. 11
Hollister, CA 95023

SCORE Office (Hollywood)
7018 Hollywood Blvd.
Hollywood, CA 90028
Phone: (213)469-8311
Fax: (213)469-2805

SCORE Office (Indio)
82503 Hwy. 111
PO Drawer TTT
Indio, CA 92202
Phone: (619)347-0676

SCORE Office (Inglewood)
330 Queen St.
Inglewood, CA 90301
Phone: (818)552-3206

SCORE Office (La Puente)
218 N. Grendanda St. D.
La Puente, CA 91744
Phone: (818)330-3216
Fax: (818)330-9524

SCORE Office (La Verne)
2078 Bonita Ave.
La Verne, CA 91750
Phone: (909)593-5265
Fax: (714)929-8475

SCORE Office (Lake Elsinore)
132 W. Graham Ave.
Lake Elsinore, CA 92530
Phone: (909)674-2577

SCORE Office (Lakeport)
PO Box 295
Lakeport, CA 95453
Phone: (707)263-5092

SCORE Office (Lakewood)
5445 E. Del Amo Blvd., Ste. 2

Lakewood, CA 90714
Phone: (213)920-7737

SCORE Office (Long Beach)
1 World Trade Center
Long Beach, CA 90831

SCORE Office (Los Alamitos)
901 W. Civic Center Dr., Ste. 160
Los Alamitos, CA 90720

SCORE Office (Los Altos)
321 University Ave.
Los Altos, CA 94022
Phone: (415)948-1455

SCORE Office (Manhattan Beach)
PO Box 3007
Manhattan Beach, CA 90266
Phone: (310)545-5313
Fax: (310)545-7203

SCORE Office (Merced)
1632 N. St.
Merced, CA 95340
Phone: (209)725-3800
Fax: (209)383-4959

SCORE Office (Milpitas)
75 S. Milpitas Blvd., Ste. 205
Milpitas, CA 95035
Phone: (408)262-2613
Fax: (408)262-2823

SCORE Office (Yosemite)
1012 11th St., Ste. 300
Modesto, CA 95354
Phone: (209)521-9333

SCORE Office (Montclair)
5220 Benito Ave.
Montclair, CA 91763

SCORE Office (Monterey Bay)
380 Alvarado St.
PO Box 1770
Monterey, CA 93940-1770
Phone: (408)649-1770

SCORE Office (Moreno Valley)
25480 Alessandro
Moreno Valley, CA 92553

SCORE Office (Morgan Hill)
25 W. 1st St.
PO Box 786
Morgan Hill, CA 95038
Phone: (408)779-9444
Fax: (408)778-1786

SCORE Office (Morro Bay)
880 Main St.

Morro Bay, CA 93442
Phone: (805)772-4467

SCORE Office (Mountain View)
580 Castro St.
Mountain View, CA 94041
Phone: (415)968-8378
Fax: (415)968-5668

SCORE Office (Napa)
1556 1st St.
Napa, CA 94559
Phone: (707)226-7455
Fax: (707)226-1171

SCORE Office (North Hollywood)
5019 Lankershim Blvd.
North Hollywood, CA 91601
Phone: (818)552-3206

SCORE Office (Northridge)
8801 Reseda Blvd.
Northridge, CA 91324
Phone: (818)349-5676

SCORE Office (Novato)
807 De Long Ave.
Novato, CA 94945
Phone: (415)897-1164
Fax: (415)898-9097

SCORE Office (East Bay)
519 17th St.
Oakland, CA 94612
Phone: (510)273-6611
Fax: (510)273-6015
E-mail: webmaster@eastbayscore.org
Website: http://www.eastbayscore.org

SCORE Office (Oceanside)
928 N. Coast Hwy.
Oceanside, CA 92054
Phone: (619)722-1534

SCORE Office (Ontario)
121 West B. St.
Ontario, CA 91762
Fax: (714)984-6439

SCORE Office (Oxnard)
PO Box 867
Oxnard, CA 93032
Phone: (805)385-8860
Fax: (805)487-1763

SCORE Office (Pacifica)
450 Dundee Way, Ste. 2
Pacifica, CA 94044
Phone: (415)355-4122

SCORE Office (Palm Desert)
72990 Hwy. 111
Palm Desert, CA 92260
Phone: (619)346-6111
Fax: (619)346-3463

SCORE Office (Palm Springs)
650 E. Tahquitz Canyon Way Ste. D
Palm Springs, CA 92262-6706
Phone: (760)320-6682
Fax: (760)323-9426

SCORE Office (Lakeside)
2150 Low Tree
Palmdale, CA 93551
Phone: (805)948-4518
Fax: (805)949-1212

SCORE Office (Palo Alto)
325 Forest Ave.
Palo Alto, CA 94301
Phone: (415)324-3121
Fax: (415)324-1215

SCORE Office (Pasadena)
117 E. Colorado Blvd., Ste. 100
Pasadena, CA 91105
Phone: (818)795-3355
Fax: (818)795-5663

SCORE Office (Paso Robles)
1225 Park St.
Paso Robles, CA 93446-2234
Phone: (805)238-0506
Fax: (805)238-0527

SCORE Office (Petaluma)
799 Baywood Dr., Ste. 3
Petaluma, CA 94954
Phone: (707)762-2785
Fax: (707)762-4721

SCORE Office (Pico Rivera)
9122 E. Washington Blvd.
Pico Rivera, CA 90660

SCORE Office (Pittsburg)
2700 E. Leland Rd.
Pittsburg, CA 94565
Phone: (510)439-2181
Fax: (510)427-1599

SCORE Office (Pleasanton)
777 Peters Ave.
Pleasanton, CA 94566
Phone: (510)846-9697

SCORE Office (Monterey Park)
485 N. Garey
Pomona, CA 91769

SCORE Office (Pomona)
485 N. Garey Ave.
Pomona, CA 91766
Phone: (909)622-1256

SCORE Office (Antelope Valley)
4511 West Ave. M-4
Quartz Hill, CA 93536
Phone: (805)272-0087
E-mail: avscore@ptw.com
Website: http://www.score.av.org/

SCORE Office (Shasta)
737 Auditorium Dr.
Redding, CA 96099
Phone: (916)225-2770

SCORE Office (Redwood City)
1675 Broadway
Redwood City, CA 94063
Phone: (415)364-1722
Fax: (415)364-1729

SCORE Office (Richmond)
3925 MacDonald Ave.
Richmond, CA 94805

SCORE Office (Ridgecrest)
PO Box 771
Ridgecrest, CA 93555
Phone: (619)375-8331
Fax: (619)375-0365

SCORE Office (Riverside)
3685 Main St., Ste. 350
Riverside, CA 92501
Phone: (909)683-7100

SCORE Office (Sacramento)
9845 Horn Rd., 260-B
Sacramento, CA 95827
Phone: (916)361-2322
Fax: (916)361-2164
E-mail: sacchapter@directcon.net

SCORE Office (Salinas)
PO Box 1170
Salinas, CA 93902
Phone: (408)424-7611
Fax: (408)424-8639

SCORE Office (Inland Empire)
777 E. Rialto Ave.
Purchasing
San Bernardino, CA 92415-0760
Phone: (909)386-8278

SCORE Office (San Carlos)
San Carlos Chamber of Commerce
PO Box 1086
San Carlos, CA 94070

Phone: (415)593-1068
Fax: (415)593-9108

SCORE Office (Encinitas)
550 W. C St., Ste. 550
San Diego, CA 92101-3540
Phone: (619)557-7272
Fax: (619)557-5894

SCORE Office (San Diego)
550 West C. St., Ste. 550
San Diego, CA 92101-3540
Phone: (619)557-7272
Fax: (619)557-5894
Website: http://www.score-
sandiego.org

SCORE Office (Menlo Park)
1100 Merrill St.
San Francisco, CA 94105
Phone: (415)325-2818
Fax: (415)325-0920

SCORE Office (San Francisco)
455 Market St., 6th Fl.
San Francisco, CA 94105
Phone: (415)744-6827
Fax: (415)744-6750
E-mail: sfscore@sfscore.
Website: http://www.sfscore.com

SCORE Office (San Gabriel)
401 W. Las Tunas Dr.
San Gabriel, CA 91776
Phone: (818)576-2525
Fax: (818)289-2901

SCORE Office (San Jose)
Deanza College
208 S. 1st. St., Ste. 137
San Jose, CA 95113
Phone: (408)288-8479
Fax: (408)535-5541

SCORE Office (Santa Clara County)
280 S. 1st St., Rm. 137
San Jose, CA 95113
Phone: (408)288-8479
Fax: (408)535-5541
E-mail: svscore@Prodigy.net
Website: http://www.svscore.org

SCORE Office (San Luis Obispo)
3566 S. Hiquera, No. 104
San Luis Obispo, CA 93401
Phone: (805)547-0779

SCORE Office (San Mateo)
1021 S. El Camino, 2nd Fl.
San Mateo, CA 94402
Phone: (415)341-5679

SCORE Office (San Pedro)
390 W. 7th St.
San Pedro, CA 90731
Phone: (310)832-7272

SCORE Office (Orange County)
200 W. Santa Anna Blvd., Ste. 700
Santa Ana, CA 92701
Phone: (714)550-7369
Fax: (714)550-0191
Website: http://www.score114.org

SCORE Office (Santa Barbara)
3227 State St.
Santa Barbara, CA 93130
Phone: (805)563-0084

SCORE Office (Central Coast)
509 W. Morrison Ave.
Santa Maria, CA 93454
Phone: (805)347-7755

SCORE Office (Santa Maria)
614 S. Broadway
Santa Maria, CA 93454-5111
Phone: (805)925-2403
Fax: (805)928-7559

SCORE Office (Santa Monica)
501 Colorado, Ste. 150
Santa Monica, CA 90401
Phone: (310)393-9825
Fax: (310)394-1868

SCORE Office (Santa Rosa)
777 Sonoma Ave., Rm. 115E
Santa Rosa, CA 95404
Phone: (707)571-8342
Fax: (707)541-0331
Website: http://www.pressdemo.com/
community/score/score.html

SCORE Office (Scotts Valley)
4 Camp Evers Ln.
Scotts Valley, CA 95066
Phone: (408)438-1010
Fax: (408)438-6544

SCORE Office (Simi Valley)
40 W. Cochran St., Ste. 100
Simi Valley, CA 93065
Phone: (805)526-3900
Fax: (805)526-6234

SCORE Office (Sonoma)
453 1st St. E
Sonoma, CA 95476
Phone: (707)996-1033

SCORE Office (Los Banos)
222 S. Shepard St.

Sonora, CA 95370
Phone: (209)532-4212

SCORE Office (Tuolumne County)
39 North Washington St.
Sonora, CA 95370
Phone: (209)588-0128
E-mail: score@mlode.com

SCORE Office (South San Francisco)
445 Market St., Ste. 6th Fl.
South San Francisco, CA 94105
Phone: (415)744-6827
Fax: (415)744-6812

SCORE Office (Stockton)
401 N. San Joaquin St., Rm. 215
Stockton, CA 95202
Phone: (209)946-6293

SCORE Office (Taft)
314 4th St.
Taft, CA 93268
Phone: (805)765-2165
Fax: (805)765-6639

SCORE Office (Conejo Valley)
625 W. Hillcrest Dr.
Thousand Oaks, CA 91360
Phone: (805)499-1993
Fax: (805)498-7264

SCORE Office (Torrance)
3400 Torrance Blvd., Ste. 100
Torrance, CA 90503
Phone: (310)540-5858
Fax: (310)540-7662

SCORE Office (Truckee)
PO Box 2757
Truckee, CA 96160
Phone: (916)587-2757
Fax: (916)587-2439

SCORE Office (Visalia)
113 S. M St,
Tulare, CA 93274
Phone: (209)627-0766
Fax: (209)627-8149

SCORE Office (Upland)
433 N. 2nd Ave.
Upland, CA 91786
Phone: (909)931-4108

SCORE Office (Vallejo)
2 Florida St.
Vallejo, CA 94590
Phone: (707)644-5551
Fax: (707)644-5590

SCORE Office (Van Nuys)
14540 Victory Blvd.
Van Nuys, CA 91411
Phone: (818)989-0300
Fax: (818)989-3836

SCORE Office (Ventura)
5700 Ralston St., Ste. 310
Ventura, CA 93001
Phone: (805)658-2688
Fax: (805)658-2252
E-mail: scoreven@jps.net
Website: http://www.jps.net/scoreven

SCORE Office (Vista)
201 E. Washington St.
Vista, CA 92084
Phone: (619)726-1122
Fax: (619)226-8654

SCORE Office (Watsonville)
PO Box 1748
Watsonville, CA 95077
Phone: (408)724-3849
Fax: (408)728-5300

SCORE Office (West Covina)
811 S. Sunset Ave.
West Covina, CA 91790
Phone: (818)338-8496
Fax: (818)960-0511

SCORE Office (Westlake)
30893 Thousand Oaks Blvd.
Westlake Village, CA 91362
Phone: (805)496-5630
Fax: (818)991-1754

Colorado

SCORE Office (Colorado Springs)
2 N. Cascade Ave., Ste. 110
Colorado Springs, CO 80903
Phone: (719)636-3074
Website: http://www.cscc.org/
score02/index.html

SCORE Office (Denver)
US Custom's House, 4th Fl.
721 19th St.
Denver, CO 80201-0660
Phone: (303)844-3985
Fax: (303)844-6490
E-mail: score62@csn.net
Website: http://www.sni.net/score62

SCORE Office (Tri-River)
1102 Grand Ave.
Glenwood Springs, CO 81601
Phone: (970)945-6589

SCORE Office (Grand Junction)
2591 B & 3/4 Rd.
Grand Junction, CO 81503
Phone: (970)243-5242

SCORE Office (Gunnison)
608 N. 11th
Gunnison, CO 81230
Phone: (303)641-4422

SCORE Office (Montrose)
1214 Peppertree Dr.
Montrose, CO 81401
Phone: (970)249-6080

SCORE Office (Pagosa Springs)
PO Box 4381
Pagosa Springs, CO 81157
Phone: (970)731-4890

SCORE Office (Rifle)
0854 W. Battlement Pky., Apt. C106
Parachute, CO 81635
Phone: (970)285-9390

SCORE Office (Pueblo)
302 N. Santa Fe
Pueblo, CO 81003
Phone: (719)542-1704
Fax: (719)542-1624
E-mail: mackey@iex.net
Website: http://www.pueblo.org/score

SCORE Office (Ridgway)
143 Poplar Pl.
Ridgway, CO 81432

SCORE Office (Silverton)
PO Box 480
Silverton, CO 81433
Phone: (303)387-5430

SCORE Office (Minturn)
PO Box 2066
Vail, CO 81658
Phone: (970)476-1224

Connecticut

SCORE Office (Greater Bridgeport)
230 Park Ave.
Bridgeport, CT 06601-0999
Phone: (203)576-4369
Fax: (203)576-4388

SCORE Office (Bristol)
10 Main St. 1st. Fl.
Bristol, CT 06010
Phone: (203)584-4718
Fax: (203)584-4722

SCORE Office (Greater Danbury)
246 Federal Rd., Unit LL2, Ste. 7
Brookfield, CT 06804
Phone: (203)775-1151

SCORE Office (Eastern Connecticut)
Administration Bldg., Rm. 313
PO 625
61 Main St. (Chapter 579)
Groton, CT 06475
Phone: (203)388-9508

SCORE Office (Greater Hartford
County)
330 Main St.
Hartford, CT 06106
Phone: (860)548-1749
Fax: (860)240-4659
Website: http://www.score56.org

SCORE Office (Manchester)
20 Hartford Rd.
Manchester, CT 06040
Phone: (203)646-2223
Fax: (203)646-5871

SCORE Office (New Britain)
185 Main St., Ste. 431
New Britain, CT 06051
Phone: (203)827-4492
Fax: (203)827-4480

SCORE Office (New Haven)
25 Science Pk., Bldg. 25, Rm. 366
New Haven, CT 06511
Phone: (203)865-7645

SCORE Office (Fairfield County)
24 Beldon Ave., 5th Fl.
Norwalk, CT 06850
Phone: (203)847-7348
Fax: (203)849-9308

SCORE Office (Old Saybrook)
146 Main St.
Old Saybrook, CT 06475
Phone: (860)388-9508

SCORE Office (Simsbury)
Box 244
Simsbury, CT 06070
Phone: (203)651-7307
Fax: (203)651-1933

SCORE Office (Torrington)
23 North Rd.
Torrington, CT 06791
Phone: (203)482-6586

Delaware

SCORE Office (Dover)
Treadway Towers
PO Box 576
Dover, DE 19903
Phone: (302)678-0892
Fax: (302)678-0189

SCORE Office (Lewes)
PO Box 1
Lewes, DE 19958
Phone: (302)645-8073
Fax: (302)645-8412

SCORE Office (Milford)
204 NE Front St.
Milford, DE 19963
Phone: (302)422-3301

SCORE Office (Wilmington)
824 Market St., Ste. 610
Wilmington, DE 19801
Phone: (302)573-6652
Fax: (302)573-6092
Website: http://
www.scoredelaware.com

District of Columbia

SCORE Office (George Mason
University)
409 3rd St. SW, 4th Fl.
Washington, DC 20024
Free: (800)634-0245

SCORE Office (Washington DC)
1110 Vermont Ave. NW, 9th Fl.
Washington, DC 20043
Phone: (202)606-4000
Fax: (202)606-4225
E-mail: dcscore@hotmail.com
Website: http://www.scoredc.org/

Florida

SCORE Office (Desota County
Chamber of Commerce)
16 South Velucia Ave.
Arcadia, FL 34266
Phone: (941)494-4033

SCORE Office (Suncoast/Pinellas)
Airport Business Ctr.
4707 - 140th Ave. N, No. 311
Clearwater, FL 33755
Phone: (813)532-6800
Fax: (813)532-6800

SCORE Office (DeLand)
336 N. Woodland Blvd.
DeLand, FL 32720
Phone: (904)734-4331
Fax: (904)734-4333

SCORE Office (South Palm Beach)
1050 S. Federal Hwy., Ste. 132
Delray Beach, FL 33483
Phone: (561)278-7752
Fax: (561)278-0288

SCORE Office (Ft. Lauderdale)
Federal Bldg., Ste. 123
299 E. Broward Blvd.
Ft. Lauderdale, FL 33301
Phone: (954)356-7263
Fax: (954)356-7145

SCORE Office (Southwest Florida)
The Renaissance
8695 College Pky., Ste. 345 & 346
Ft. Myers, FL 33919
Phone: (941)489-2935
Fax: (941)489-1170

SCORE Office (Treasure Coast)
Professional Center, Ste. 2
3220 S. US, No. 1
Ft. Pierce, FL 34982
Phone: (561)489-0548

SCORE Office (Gainesville)
101 SE 2nd Pl., Ste. 104
Gainesville, FL 32601
Phone: (904)375-8278

SCORE Office (Hialeah Dade
Chamber)
59 W. 5th St.
Hialeah, FL 33010
Phone: (305)887-1515
Fax: (305)887-2453

SCORE Office (Daytona Beach)
921 Nova Rd., Ste. A
Holly Hills, FL 32117
Phone: (904)255-6889
Fax: (904)255-0229
E-mail: score87@dbeach.com

SCORE Office (South Broward)
3475 Sheridian St., Ste. 203
Hollywood, FL 33021
Phone: (305)966-8415

SCORE Office (Citrus County)
5 Poplar Ct.
Homosassa, FL 34446
Phone: (352)382-1037

SCORE Office (Jacksonville)
7825 Baymeadows Way, Ste. 100-B
Jacksonville, FL 32256
Phone: (904)443-1911
Fax: (904)443-1980
E-mail: scorejax@juno.com
Website: http://www.scorejax.org/

SCORE Office (Jacksonville
Satellite)
3 Independent Dr.
Jacksonville, FL 32256
Phone: (904)366-6600
Fax: (904)632-0617

SCORE Office (Central Florida)
5410 S. Florida Ave., No. 3
Lakeland, FL 33801
Phone: (941)687-5783
Fax: (941)687-6225

SCORE Office (Lakeland)
100 Lake Morton Dr.
Lakeland, FL 33801
Phone: (941)686-2168

SCORE Office (St. Petersburg)
800 W. Bay Dr., Ste. 505
Largo, FL 33712
Phone: (813)585-4571

SCORE Office (Leesburg)
9501 US Hwy. 441
Leesburg, FL 34788-8751
Phone: (352)365-3556
Fax: (352)365-3501

SCORE Office (Cocoa)
1600 Farno Rd., Unit 205
Melbourne, FL 32935
Phone: (407)254-2288

SCORE Office (Melbourne)
Melbourne Professional Complex
1600 Sarno, Ste. 205
Melbourne, FL 32935
Phone: (407)254-2288
Fax: (407)245-2288

SCORE Office (Merritt Island)
1600 Sarno Rd., Ste. 205
Melbourne, FL 32935
Phone: (407)254-2288
Fax: (407)254-2288

SCORE Office (Space Coast)
Melbourn Professional Complex
1600 Sarno, Ste. 205
Melbourne, FL 32935
Phone: (407)254-2288
Fax: (407)254-2288

SCORE Office (Dade)
49 NW 5th St.
Miami, FL 33128
Phone: (305)371-6889
Fax: (305)374-1882
E-mail: score@netrox.net
Website: http://www.netrox.net/
~score/

SCORE Office (Naples of Collier)
International College
2654 Tamiami Trl. E
Naples, FL 34112
Phone: (941)417-1280
Fax: (941)417-1281
E-mail: score@naples.net
Website: http://www.naples.net/clubs/
score/index.htm

SCORE Office (Pasco County)
6014 US Hwy. 19, Ste. 302
New Port Richey, FL 34652
Phone: (813)842-4638

SCORE Office (Southeast Volusia)
115 Canal St.
New Smyrna Beach, FL 32168
Phone: (904)428-2449
Fax: (904)423-3512

SCORE Office (Ocala)
110 E. Silver Springs Blvd.
Ocala, FL 34470
Phone: (352)629-5959

Clay County SCORE Office
Clay County Chamber of Commerce
1734 Kingsdey Ave.
PO Box 1441
Orange Park, FL 32073
Phone: (904)264-2651
Fax: (904)269-0363

SCORE Office (Orlando)
80 N. Hughey Ave.
Rm. 445 Federal Bldg.
Orlando, FL 32801
Phone: (407)648-6476
Fax: (407)648-6425

SCORE Office (Emerald Coast)
19 W. Garden St., No. 325
Pensacola, FL 32501
Phone: (904)444-2060
Fax: (904)444-2070

SCORE Office (Charlotte County)
201 W. Marion Ave., Ste. 211
Punta Gorda, FL 33950
Phone: (941)575-1818

E-mail: score@gls3c.com
Website: http://www.charlotte-
florida.com/business/scorepg01.htm

SCORE Office (St. Augustine)
1 Riberia St.
St. Augustine, FL 32084
Phone: (904)829-5681
Fax: (904)829-6477

SCORE Office (Bradenton)
2801 Fruitville, Ste. 280
Sarasota, FL 34237
Phone: (813)955-1029

SCORE Office (Manasota)
2801 Fruitville Rd., Ste. 280
Sarasota, FL 34237
Phone: (941)955-1029
Fax: (941)955-5581
E-mail: score116@gte.net
Website: http://www.score-
suncoast.org/

SCORE Office (Tallahassee)
200 W. Park Ave.
Tallahassee, FL 32302
Phone: (850)487-2665

SCORE Office (Hillsborough)
4732 Dale Mabry Hwy. N, Ste. 400
Tampa, FL 33614-6509
Phone: (813)870-0125

SCORE Office (Lake Sumter)
122 E. Main St.
Tavares, FL 32778-3810
Phone: (352)365-3556

SCORE Office (Titusville)
2000 S. Washington Ave.
Titusville, FL 32780
Phone: (407)267-3036
Fax: (407)264-0127

SCORE Office (Venice)
257 N. Tamiami Trl.
Venice, FL 34285
Phone: (941)488-2236
Fax: (941)484-5903

SCORE Office (Palm Beach)
500 Australian Ave. S, Ste. 100
West Palm Beach, FL 33401
Phone: (561)833-1672
Fax: (561)833-1712

SCORE Office (Wildwood)
103 N. Webster St.
Wildwood, FL 34785

Georgia

SCORE Office (Atlanta)
Harris Tower, Suite 1900
233 Peachtree Rd., NE
Atlanta, GA 30309
Phone: (404)347-2442
Fax: (404)347-1227

SCORE Office (Augusta)
3126 Oxford Rd.
Augusta, GA 30909
Phone: (706)869-9100

SCORE Office (Columbus)
School Bldg.
PO Box 40
Columbus, GA 31901
Phone: (706)327-3654

SCORE Office (Dalton-Whitfield)
305 S. Thorton Ave.
Dalton, GA 30720
Phone: (706)279-3383

SCORE Office (Gainesville)
PO Box 374
Gainesville, GA 30503
Phone: (770)532-6206
Fax: (770)535-8419

SCORE Office (Macon)
711 Grand Bldg.
Macon, GA 31201
Phone: (912)751-6160

SCORE Office (Brunswick)
4 Glen Ave.
St. Simons Island, GA 31520
Phone: (912)265-0620
Fax: (912)265-0629

SCORE Office (Savannah)
111 E. Liberty St., Ste. 103
Savannah, GA 31401
Phone: (912)652-4335
Fax: (912)652-4184
E-mail: info@scoresav.org
Website: http://
www.coastalempire.com/score/
index.htm

Guam

SCORE Office (Guam)
Pacific News Bldg., Rm. 103
238 Archbishop Flores St.
Agana, GU 96910-5100
Phone: (671)472-7308

Hawaii

SCORE Office (Hawaii, Inc.)
1111 Bishop St., Ste. 204
PO Box 50207
Honolulu, HI 96813
Phone: (808)522-8132
Fax: (808)522-8135
E-mail: hnlscore@juno.com

SCORE Office (Kahului)
250 Alamaha, Unit N16A
Kahului, HI 96732
Phone: (808)871-7711

SCORE Office (Maui, Inc.)
590 E. Lipoa Pkwy., Ste. 227
Kihei, HI 96753
Phone: (808)875-2380

Idaho

SCORE Office (Treasure Valley)
1020 Main St., No. 290
Boise, ID 83702
Phone: (208)334-1696
Fax: (208)334-9353

SCORE Office (Eastern Idaho)
2300 N. Yellowstone, Ste. 119
Idaho Falls, ID 83401
Phone: (208)523-1022
Fax: (208)528-7127

Illinois

SCORE Office (Fox Valley)
40 W. Downer Pl.
PO Box 277
Aurora, IL 60506
Phone: (630)897-9214
Fax: (630)897-7002

SCORE Office (Greater Belvidere)
419 S. State St.
Belvidere, IL 61008
Phone: (815)544-4357
Fax: (815)547-7654

SCORE Office (Bensenville)
1050 Busse Hwy. Suite 100
Bensenville, IL 60106
Phone: (708)350-2944
Fax: (708)350-2979

SCORE Office (Central Illinois)
402 N. Hershey Rd.
Bloomington, IL 61704
Phone: (309)644-0549
Fax: (309)663-8270

E-mail: webmaster@central-illinois-score.org
Website: http://www.central-illinois-score.org/

SCORE Office (Southern Illinois)
150 E. Pleasant Hill Rd.
Box 1
Carbondale, IL 62901
Phone: (618)453-6654
Fax: (618)453-5040

SCORE Office (Chicago)
Northwest Atrium Ctr.
500 W. Madison St., No. 1250
Chicago, IL 60661
Phone: (312)353-7724
Fax: (312)886-5688
Website: http://www.mcs.net/~bic/

SCORE Office (Chicago—Oliver
Harvey College)
Pullman Bldg.
1000 E. 11th St., 7th Fl.
Chicago, IL 60628
Fax: (312)468-8086

SCORE Office (Danville)
28 W. N. Street
Danville, IL 61832
Phone: (217)442-7232
Fax: (217)442-6228

SCORE Office (Decatur)
Milliken University
1184 W. Main St.
Decatur, IL 62522
Phone: (217)424-6297
Fax: (217)424-3993
E-mail: charding@mail.millikin.edu
Website: http://www.millikin.edu/
academics/Tabor/score.html

SCORE Office (Downers Grove)
925 Curtis
Downers Grove, IL 60515
Phone: (708)968-4050
Fax: (708)968-8368

SCORE Office (Elgin)
24 E. Chicago, 3rd Fl.
PO Box 648
Elgin, IL 60120
Phone: (847)741-5660
Fax: (847)741-5677

SCORE Office (Freeport Area)
26 S. Galena Ave.
Freeport, IL 61032

Phone: (815)233-1350
Fax: (815)235-4038

SCORE Office (Galesburg)
292 E. Simmons St.
PO Box 749
Galesburg, IL 61401
Phone: (309)343-1194
Fax: (309)343-1195

SCORE Office (Glen Ellyn)
500 Pennsylvania
Glen Ellyn, IL 60137
Phone: (708)469-0907
Fax: (708)469-0426

SCORE Office (Greater Alton)
Alden Hall
5800 Godfrey Rd.
Godfrey, IL 62035-2466
Phone: (618)467-2280
Fax: (618)466-8289
Website: http://www.altonweb.com/
score/

SCORE Office (Grayslake)
19351 W. Washington St.
Grayslake, IL 60030
Phone: (708)223-3633
Fax: (708)223-9371

SCORE Office (Harrisburg)
303 S. Commercial
Harrisburg, IL 62946-1528
Phone: (618)252-8528
Fax: (618)252-0210

SCORE Office (Joliet)
100 N. Chicago
Joliet, IL 60432
Phone: (815)727-5371
Fax: (815)727-5374

SCORE Office (Kankakee)
101 S. Schuyler Ave.
Kankakee, IL 60901
Phone: (815)933-0376
Fax: (815)933-0380

SCORE Office (Macomb)
216 Seal Hall, Rm. 214
Macomb, IL 61455
Phone: (309)298-1128
Fax: (309)298-2520

SCORE Office (Matteson)
210 Lincoln Mall
Matteson, IL 60443
Phone: (708)709-3750
Fax: (708)503-9322

SCORE Office (Mattoon)
1701 Wabash Ave.
Mattoon, IL 61938
Phone: (217)235-5661
Fax: (217)234-6544

SCORE Office (Quad Cities)
622 19th St.
Moline, IL 61265
Phone: (309)797-0082
Fax: (309)757-5435
E-mail: score@qconline.com
Website: http://www.qconline.com/
business/score/

SCORE Office (Naperville)
131 W. Jefferson Ave.
Naperville, IL 60540
Phone: (708)355-4141
Fax: (708)355-8355

SCORE Office (Northbrook)
2002 Walters Ave.
Northbrook, IL 60062
Phone: (847)498-5555
Fax: (847)498-5510

SCORE Office (Palos Hills)
10900 S. 88th Ave.
Palos Hills, IL 60465
Phone: (847)974-5468
Fax: (847)974-0078

SCORE Office (Peoria)
124 SW Adams, Ste. 300
Peoria, IL 61602
Phone: (309)676-0755
Fax: (309)676-7534

SCORE Office (Prospect Heights)
1375 Wolf Rd.
Prospect Heights, IL 60070
Phone: (847)537-8660
Fax: (847)537-7138

SCORE Office (Quincy Tri-State)
300 Civic Center Plz., Ste. 245
Quincy, IL 62301
Phone: (217)222-8093
Fax: (217)222-3033

SCORE Office (River Grove)
2000 5th Ave.
River Grove, IL 60171
Phone: (708)456-0300
Fax: (708)583-3121

SCORE Office (Northern Illinois)
515 N. Court St.
Rockford, IL 61103

Phone: (815)962-0122
Fax: (815)962-0122

SCORE Office (St. Charles)
103 N. 1st Ave.
St. Charles, IL 60174-1982
Phone: (847)584-8384
Fax: (847)584-6065

SCORE Office (Springfield)
511 W. Capitol Ave., Ste. 302
Springfield, IL 62704
Phone: (217)492-4416
Fax: (217)492-4867

SCORE Office (Sycamore)
112 Somunak St.
Sycamore, IL 60178
Phone: (815)895-3456
Fax: (815)895-0125

SCORE Office (University)
Hwy. 50 & Stuenkel Rd. Ste. C3305
University Park, IL 60466
Phone: (708)534-5000
Fax: (708)534-8457

Indiana

SCORE Office (Anderson)
205 W. 11th St.
Anderson, IN 46015
Phone: (317)642-0264

SCORE Office (Bloomington)
Star Center
216 W. Allen
Bloomington, IN 47403
Phone: (812)335-7334
E-mail: wtfische@indiana.edu
Website: http://
www.brainfreezemedia.com/
score527/

SCORE Office (South East Indiana)
500 Franklin St.
Box 29
Columbus, IN 47201
Phone: (812)379-4457

SCORE Office (Corydon)
310 N. Elm St.
Corydon, IN 47112
Phone: (812)738-2137
Fax: (812)738-6438

SCORE Office (Crown Point)
Old Courthouse Sq. Ste. 206
PO Box 43
Crown Point, IN 46307
Phone: (219)663-1800

SCORE Office (Elkhart)
418 S. Main St.
Elkhart, IN 46515
Phone: (219)293-1531
Fax: (219)294-1859

SCORE Office (Evansville)
1100 W. Lloyd Expy., Ste. 105
Evansville, IN 47708
Phone: (812)426-6144

SCORE Office (Fort Wayne)
1300 S. Harrison St.
Ft. Wayne, IN 46802
Phone: (219)422-2601
Fax: (219)422-2601

SCORE Office (Gary)
973 W. 6th Ave., Rm. 326
Gary, IN 46402
Phone: (219)882-3918

SCORE Office (Hammond)
7034 Indianapolis Blvd.
Hammond, IN 46324
Phone: (219)931-1000
Fax: (219)845-9548

SCORE Office (Indianapolis)
429 N. Pennsylvania St., Ste. 100
Indianapolis, IN 46204-1873
Phone: (317)226-7264
Fax: (317)226-7259
E-mail: inscore@indy.net
Website: http://www.score-
indianapolis.org/

SCORE Office (Jasper)
PO Box 307
Jasper, IN 47547-0307
Phone: (812)482-6866

SCORE Office (Kokomo/Howard
Counties)
106 N. Washington St.
Kokomo, IN 46901
Phone: (765)457-5301
Fax: (765)452-4564

SCORE Office (Logansport)
300 E. Broadway, Ste. 103
Logansport, IN 46947
Phone: (219)753-6388

SCORE Office (Madison)
301 E. Main St.
Madison, IN 47250
Phone: (812)265-3135
Fax: (812)265-2923

SCORE Office (Marengo)
Rt. 1 Box 224D
Marengo, IN 47140
Fax: (812)365-2793

SCORE Office (Marion/Grant
Counties)
215 S. Adams
Marion, IN 46952
Phone: (765)664-5107

SCORE Office (Merrillville)
255 W. 80th Pl.
Merrillville, IN 46410
Phone: (219)769-8180
Fax: (219)736-6223

SCORE Office (Michigan City)
200 E. Michigan Blvd.
Michigan City, IN 46360
Phone: (219)874-6221
Fax: (219)873-1204

SCORE Office (South Central
Indiana)
4100 Charleston Rd.
New Albany, IN 47150-9538
Phone: (812)945-0066

SCORE Office (Rensselaer)
104 W. Washington
Rensselaer, IN 47978

SCORE Office (Salem)
210 N. Main St.
Salem, IN 47167
Phone: (812)883-4303
Fax: (812)883-1467

SCORE Office (South Bend)
300 N. Michigan St.
South Bend, IN 46601
Phone: (219)282-4350
E-mail: chair@southbend-score.org
Website: http://www.southbend-
score.org/

SCORE Office (Valparaiso)
150 Lincolnway
Valparaiso, IN 46383
Phone: (219)462-1105
Fax: (219)469-5710

SCORE Office (Vincennes)
27 N. 3rd
PO Box 553
Vincennes, IN 47591
Phone: (812)882-6440
Fax: (812)882-6441

SCORE Office (Wabash)
PO Box 371
Wabash, IN 46992
Phone: (219)563-1168
Fax: (219)563-6920

Iowa

SCORE Office (Burlington)
Federal Bldg.
300 N. Main St.
Burlington, IA 52601
Phone: (319)752-2967

SCORE Office (Cedar Rapids)
Lattner Bldg., Ste. 200
215-4th Avenue, SE, No. 200
Cedar Rapids, IA 52401-1806
Phone: (319)362-6405
Fax: (319)362-7861

SCORE Office (Illowa)
333 4th Ave. S
Clinton, IA 52732
Phone: (319)242-5702

SCORE Office (Council Bluffs)
7 N. 6th St.
Council Bluffs, IA 51502
Phone: (712)325-1000

SCORE Office (Northeast Iowa)
3404 285th St.
Cresco, IA 52136
Phone: (319)547-3377

SCORE Office (Des Moines)
Federal Bldg., Rm. 749
210 Walnut St.
Des Moines, IA 50309-2186
Phone: (515)284-4760

SCORE Office (Ft. Dodge)
Federal Bldg., Rm. 436
205 S. 8th St.
Ft. Dodge, IA 50501
Phone: (515)955-2622

SCORE Office (Independence)
110 1st. St. East
Independence, IA 50644
Phone: (319)334-7178
Fax: (319)334-7179

SCORE Office (Iowa City)
210 Federal Bldg.
PO Box 1853
Iowa City, IA 52240-1853
Phone: (319)338-1662

SCORE Office (Keokuk)
401 Main St.
Pierce Bldg., No. 1
Keokuk, IA 52632
Phone: (319)524-5055

SCORE Office (Central Iowa)
Fisher Community College
709 S. Center
Marshalltown, IA 50158
Phone: (515)753-6645

SCORE Office (River City)
15 West State St.
Mason City, IA 50401
Phone: (515)423-5724

SCORE Office (South Central)
SBDC, Indian Hills Community
College
525 Grandview Ave.
Ottumwa, IA 52501
Phone: (515)683-5127
Fax: (515)683-5263

SCORE Office (Dubuque)
10250 Sundown Rd.
Peosta, IA 52068
Phone: (319)556-5110

SCORE Office (Southwest Iowa)
614 W. Sheridan
Shenandoah, IA 51601
Phone: (712)246-3260

SCORE Office (Sioux City)
Federal Bldg.
320 6th St.
Sioux City, IA 51101
Phone: (712)277-2324
Fax: (712)277-2325

SCORE Office (Iowa Lakes)
122 W. 5th St.
Spencer, IA 51301
Phone: (712)262-3059

SCORE Office (Vista)
119 W. 6th St.
Storm Lake, IA 50588
Phone: (712)732-3780

SCORE Office (Waterloo)
215 E. 4th
Waterloo, IA 50703
Phone: (319)233-8431

Kansas

SCORE Office (Southwest Kansas)
501 W. Spruce

Dodge City, KS 67801
Phone: (316)227-3119

SCORE Office (Emporia)
811 Homewood
Emporia, KS 66801
Phone: (316)342-1600

SCORE Office (Golden Belt)
1307 Williams
Great Bend, KS 67530
Phone: (316)792-2401

SCORE Office (Hays)
PO Box 400
Hays, KS 67601
Phone: (913)625-6595

SCORE Office (Hutchinson)
1 E. 9th St.
Hutchinson, KS 67501
Phone: (316)665-8468
Fax: (316)665-7619

SCORE Office (Southeast Kansas)
404 Westminster Pl.
PO Box 886
Independence, KS 67301
Phone: (316)331-4741

SCORE Office (McPherson)
306 N. Main
PO Box 616
McPherson, KS 67460
Phone: (316)241-3303

SCORE Office (Salina)
120 Ash St.
Salina, KS 67401
Phone: (785)243-4290
Fax: (785)243-1833

SCORE Office (Topeka)
1700 College
Topeka, KS 66621
Phone: (785)231-1010

SCORE Office (Wichita)
100 E. English, Ste. 510
Wichita, KS 67202
Phone: (316)269-6273
Fax: (316)269-6499

SCORE Office (Ark Valley)
205 E. 9th St.
Winfield, KS 67156
Phone: (316)221-1617

Kentucky

SCORE Office (Ashland)
PO Box 830
Ashland, KY 41105
Phone: (606)329-8011
Fax: (606)325-4607

SCORE Office (Bowling Green)
812 State St.
PO Box 51
Bowling Green, KY 42101
Phone: (502)781-3200
Fax: (502)843-0458

SCORE Office (Tri-Lakes)
508 Barbee Way
Danville, KY 40422-1548
Phone: (606)231-9902

SCORE Office (Glasgow)
301 W. Main St.
Glasgow, KY 42141
Phone: (502)651-3161
Fax: (502)651-3122

SCORE Office (Hazard)
B & I Technical Center
100 Airport Gardens Rd.
Hazard, KY 41701
Phone: (606)439-5856
Fax: (606)439-1808

SCORE Office (Lexington)
410 W. Vine St., Ste. 290, Civic C
Lexington, KY 40507
Phone: (606)231-9902
Fax: (606)253-3190
E-mail:
scorelex@uky.campus.mci.net

SCORE Office (Louisville)
188 Federal Office Bldg.
600 Dr. Martin L. King Jr. Pl.
Louisville, KY 40202
Phone: (502)582-5976

SCORE Office (Madisonville)
257 N. Main
Madisonville, KY 42431
Phone: (502)825-1399
Fax: (502)825-1396

SCORE Office (Paducah)
Federal Office Bldg.
501 Broadway, Rm. B-36
Paducah, KY 42001
Phone: (502)442-5685

Louisiana

SCORE Office (Central Louisiana)
802 3rd St.
Alexandria, LA 71309
Phone: (318)442-6671

SCORE Office (Baton Rouge)
564 Laurel St.
PO Box 3217
Baton Rouge, LA 70801
Phone: (504)381-7130
Fax: (504)336-4306

SCORE Office (North Shore)
2 W. Thomas
Hammond, LA 70401
Phone: (504)345-4457
Fax: (504)345-4749

SCORE Office (Lafayette)
804 St. Mary Blvd.
Lafayette, LA 70505-1307
Phone: (318)233-2705
Fax: (318)234-8671
E-mail: score302@aol.com

SCORE Office (Lake Charles)
120 W. Pujo St.
Lake Charles, LA 70601
Phone: (318)433-3632

SCORE Office (New Orleans)
365 Canal St., Ste. 3100
New Orleans, LA 70130
Phone: (504)589-2356
Fax: (504)589-2339

SCORE Office (Shreveport)
400 Edwards St.
Shreveport, LA 71101
Phone: (318)677-2536
Fax: (318)677-2541

Maine

SCORE Office (Augusta)
40 Western Ave.
Augusta, ME 04330
Phone: (207)622-8509

SCORE Office (Bangor)
Peabody Hall, Rm. 229
One College Cir.
Bangor, ME 04401
Phone: (207)941-9707

SCORE Office (Central & Northern
Arroostock)
111 High St.
Caribou, ME 04736

Phone: (207)492-8010
Fax: (207)492-8010

SCORE Office (Penquis)
South St.
Dover Foxcroft, ME 04426
Phone: (207)564-7021

SCORE Office (Maine Coastal)
Mill Mall
Box 1105
Ellsworth, ME 04605-1105
Phone: (207)667-5800
E-mail: score@arcadia.net

SCORE Office (Lewiston-Auburn)
BIC of Maine-Bates Mill Complex
35 Canal St.
Lewiston, ME 04240-7764
Phone: (207)782-3708
Fax: (207)783-7745

SCORE Office (Portland)
66 Pearl St., Rm. 210
Portland, ME 04101
Phone: (207)772-1147
Fax: (207)772-5581
E-mail: Score53@score.maine.org
Website: http://www.score.maine.org/
chapter53/

SCORE Office (Western Mountains)
255 River St.
PO Box 252
Rumford, ME 04257-0252
Phone: (207)369-9976

SCORE Office (Oxford Hills)
166 Main St.
South Paris, ME 04281
Phone: (207)743-0499

Maryland

SCORE Office (Southern Maryland)
2525 Riva Rd., Ste. 110
Annapolis, MD 21401
Phone: (410)266-9553
Fax: (410)573-0981
E-mail: score390@aol.com
Website: http://members.aol.com/
score390/index.htm

SCORE Office (Baltimore)
The City Crescent Bldg., 6th Fl.
10 S. Howard St.
Baltimore, MD 21201
Phone: (410)962-2233
Fax: (410)962-1805

SCORE Office (Bel Air)
108 S. Bond St.
Bel Air, MD 21014
Phone: (410)838-2020
Fax: (410)893-4715

SCORE Office (Bethesda)
7910 Woodmont Ave., Ste. 1204
Bethesda, MD 20814
Phone: (301)652-4900
Fax: (301)657-1973

SCORE Office (Bowie)
6670 Race Track Rd.
Bowie, MD 20715
Phone: (301)262-0920
Fax: (301)262-0921

SCORE Office (Dorchester County)
203 Sunburst Hwy.
Cambridge, MD 21613
Phone: (410)228-3575

SCORE Office (Upper Shore)
210 Marlboro Ave.
Easton, MD 21601
Phone: (410)822-4606
Fax: (410)822-7922

SCORE Office (Frederick County)
43A S. Market St.
Frederick, MD 21701
Phone: (301)662-8723
Fax: (301)846-4427

SCORE Office (Gaithersburg)
9 Park Ave.
Gaithersburg, MD 20877
Phone: (301)840-1400
Fax: (301)963-3918

SCORE Office (Glen Burnie)
103 Crain Hwy. SE
Glen Burnie, MD 21061
Phone: (410)766-8282
Fax: (410)766-9722

SCORE Office (Hagerstown)
111 W. Washington St.
Hagerstown, MD 21740
Phone: (301)739-2015
Fax: (301)739-1278

SCORE Office (Laurel)
7901 Sandy Spring Rd. Ste. 501
Laurel, MD 20707
Phone: (301)725-4000
Fax: (301)725-0776

SCORE Office (Salisbury)
300 E. Main St.

Salisbury, MD 21801
Phone: (410)749-0185
Fax: (410)860-9925

Massachusetts

SCORE Office (NE Massachusetts)
100 Cummings Ctr., Ste. 101 K
Beverly, MA 01923
Phone: (978)922-9441
Website: http://www1.shore.net/
~score/

SCORE Office (Boston)
10 Causeway St., Rm. 265
Boston, MA 02222-1093
Phone: (617)565-5591
Fax: (617)565-5598
E-mail: boston-score-
20@worldnet.att.net
Website: http://www.scoreboston.org/

SCORE Office (Bristol/Plymouth
County)
53 N. 6th St., Federal Bldg.
Bristol, MA 02740
Phone: (508)994-5093

SCORE Office (SE Massachusetts)
60 School St.
Brockton, MA 02401
Phone: (508)587-2673
Fax: (508)587-1340
Website: http://
www.metrosouthchamber.com/
score.html

SCORE Office (North Adams)
820 N. State Rd.
Cheshire, MA 01225
Phone: (413)743-5100

SCORE Office (Clinton Satellite)
1 Green St.
Clinton, MA 01510
Fax: (508)368-7689

SCORE Office (Greenfield)
PO Box 898
Greenfield, MA 01302
Phone: (413)773-5463
Fax: (413)773-7008

SCORE Office (Haverhill)
87 Winter St.
Haverhill, MA 01830
Phone: (508)373-5663
Fax: (508)373-8060

SCORE Office (Hudson Satellite)
PO Box 578
Hudson, MA 01749
Phone: (508)568-0360
Fax: (508)568-0360

SCORE Office (Cape Cod)
Independence Pk., Ste. 5B
270 Communications Way
Hyannis, MA 02601
Phone: (508)775-4884
Fax: (508)790-2540

SCORE Office (Lawrence)
264 Essex St.
Lawrence, MA 01840
Phone: (508)686-0900
Fax: (508)794-9953

SCORE Office (Leominster Satellite)
110 Erdman Way
Leominster, MA 01453
Phone: (508)840-4300
Fax: (508)840-4896

SCORE Office (Bristol/Plymouth
Counties)
53 N. 6th St., Federal Bldg.
New Bedford, MA 02740
Phone: (508)994-5093

SCORE Office (Newburyport)
29 State St.
Newburyport, MA 01950
Phone: (617)462-6680

SCORE Office (Pittsfield)
66 West St.
Pittsfield, MA 01201
Phone: (413)499-2485

SCORE Office (Haverhill-Salem)
32 Derby Sq.
Salem, MA 01970
Phone: (508)745-0330
Fax: (508)745-3855

SCORE Office (Springfield)
1350 Main St.
Federal Bldg.
Springfield, MA 01103
Phone: (413)785-0314

SCORE Office (Carver)
12 Taunton Green, Ste. 201
Taunton, MA 02780
Phone: (508)824-4068
Fax: (508)824-4069

SCORE Office (Worcester)
33 Waldo St.

Worcester, MA 01608
Phone: (508)753-2929
Fax: (508)754-8560

Michigan

SCORE Office (Allegan)
PO Box 338
Allegan, MI 49010
Phone: (616)673-2479

SCORE Office (Ann Arbor)
425 S. Main St., Ste. 103
Ann Arbor, MI 48104
Phone: (313)665-4433

SCORE Office (Battle Creek)
34 W. Jackson Ste. 4A
Battle Creek, MI 49017-3505
Phone: (616)962-4076
Fax: (616)962-6309

SCORE Office (Cadillac)
222 Lake St.
Cadillac, MI 49601
Phone: (616)775-9776
Fax: (616)768-4255

SCORE Office (Detroit)
477 Michigan Ave., Rm. 515
Detroit, MI 48226
Phone: (313)226-7947
Fax: (313)226-3448

SCORE Office (Flint)
708 Root Rd., Rm. 308
Flint, MI 48503
Phone: (810)233-6846

SCORE Office (Grand Rapids)
111 Pearl St. NW
Grand Rapids, MI 49503-2831
Phone: (616)771-0305
Fax: (616)771-0328
E-mail: scoreone@iserv.net
Website: http://www.iserv.net/
~scoreone/

SCORE Office (Holland)
480 State St.
Holland, MI 49423
Phone: (616)396-9472

SCORE Office (Jackson)
209 East Washington
PO Box 80
Jackson, MI 49204
Phone: (517)782-8221
Fax: (517)782-0061

SCORE Office (Kalamazoo)
345 W. Michigan Ave.
Kalamazoo, MI 49007
Phone: (616)381-5382
Fax: (616)384-0096
E-mail: score@nucleus.net

SCORE Office (Lansing)
117 E. Allegan
PO Box 14030
Lansing, MI 48901
Phone: (517)487-6340
Fax: (517)484-6910

SCORE Office (Livonia)
15401 Farmington Rd.
Livonia, MI 48154
Phone: (313)427-2122
Fax: (313)427-6055

SCORE Office (Madison Heights)
26345 John R
Madison Heights, MI 48071
Phone: (810)542-5010
Fax: (810)542-6821

SCORE Office (Monroe)
111 E. 1st
Monroe, MI 48161
Phone: (313)242-3366
Fax: (313)242-7253

SCORE Office (Mt. Clemens)
58 S/B Gratiot
Mt. Clemens, MI 48043
Phone: (810)463-1528
Fax: (810)463-6541

SCORE Office (Muskegon)
PO Box 1087
230 Terrace Plz.
Muskegon, MI 49443
Phone: (616)722-3751
Fax: (616)728-7251

SCORE Office (Petoskey)
401 E. Mitchell St.
Petoskey, MI 49770
Phone: (616)347-4150

SCORE Office (Pontiac)
Executive Office Bldg.
1200 N. Telegraph Rd.
Pontiac, MI 48341
Phone: (810)975-9555

SCORE Office (Pontiac)
PO Box 430025
Pontiac, MI 48343
Phone: (810)335-9600

SCORE Office (Port Huron)
920 Pinegrove Ave.
Port Huron, MI 48060
Phone: (810)985-7101

SCORE Office (Rochester)
71 Walnut Ste. 110
Rochester, MI 48307
Phone: (810)651-6700
Fax: (810)651-5270

SCORE Office (Saginaw)
901 S. Washington Ave.
Saginaw, MI 48601
Phone: (517)752-7161
Fax: (517)752-9055

SCORE Office (Upper Peninsula)
2581 I-75 Business Spur
Sault Ste. Marie, MI 49783
Phone: (906)632-3301

SCORE Office (Southfield)
21000 W. 10 Mile Rd.
Southfield, MI 48075
Phone: (810)204-3050
Fax: (810)204-3099

SCORE Office (Traverse City)
202 E. Grandview Pkwy.
PO Box 387
Traverse City, MI 49685
Phone: (616)947-5075
Fax: (616)946-2565

SCORE Office (Warren)
30500 Van Dyke, Ste. 118
Warren, MI 48093
Phone: (810)751-3939

Minnesota

SCORE Office (Aitkin)
Aitkin, MN 56431
Phone: (218)741-3906

SCORE Office (Albert Lea)
202 N. Broadway Ave.
Albert Lea, MN 56007
Phone: (507)373-7487

SCORE Office (Austin)
PO Box 864
Austin, MN 55912
Phone: (507)437-4561
Fax: (507)437-4869

SCORE Office (South Metro)
Ames Business Ctr.
2500 W. County Rd., No. 42
Burnsville, MN 55337

Phone: (612)898-5645
Fax: (612)435-6972
E-mail: southmetro@scoreminn.org
Website: http://www.scoreminn.org/
southmetro/

SCORE Office (Duluth)
1717 Minnesota Ave.
Duluth, MN 55802
Phone: (218)727-8286
Fax: (218)727-3113
E-mail: duluth@scoreminn.org
Website: http://www.scoreminn.org

SCORE Office (Fairmont)
PO Box 826
Fairmont, MN 56031
Phone: (507)235-5547
Fax: (507)235-8411

SCORE Office (Southwest
Minnesota)
112 Riverfront St.
Box 999
Mankato, MN 56001
Phone: (507)345-4519
Fax: (507)345-4451
Website: http://www.scoreminn.org/

SCORE Office (Minneapolis)
North Plaza Bldg., Ste. 51
5217 Wayzata Blvd.
Minneapolis, MN 55416
Phone: (612)591-0539
Fax: (612)544-0436
Website: http://www.scoreminn.org/

SCORE Office (Owatonna)
PO Box 331
Owatonna, MN 55060
Phone: (507)451-7970
Fax: (507)451-7972

SCORE Office (Red Wing)
2000 W. Main St., Ste. 324
Red Wing, MN 55066
Phone: (612)388-4079

SCORE Office (Southeastern
Minnesota)
220 S. Broadway, Ste. 100
Rochester, MN 55901
Phone: (507)288-1122
Fax: (507)282-8960
Website: http://www.scoreminn.org/

SCORE Office (Brainerd)
St. Cloud, MN 56301

SCORE Office (Central Area)
1527 Northway Dr.
St. Cloud, MN 56301
Phone: (320)240-1332
Fax: (320)255-9050
Website: http://www.scoreminn.org/

SCORE Office (St. Paul)
350 St. Peter St., No. 295
Lowry Professional Bldg.
St. Paul, MN 55102
Phone: (651)223-5010
Fax: (651)223-5048
Website: http://www.scoreminn.org/

SCORE Office (Winona)
Box 870
Winona, MN 55987
Phone: (507)452-2272
Fax: (507)454-8814

SCORE Office (Worthington)
1121 3rd Ave.
Worthington, MN 56187
Phone: (507)372-2919
Fax: (507)372-2827

Mississippi

SCORE Office (Delta)
915 Washington Ave.
PO Box 933
Greenville, MS 38701
Phone: (601)378-3141

SCORE Office (Gulf Coast)
1 Government Plaza
2909 13th St., Ste. 203
Gulfport, MS 39501
Phone: (228)863-0054

SCORE Office (Jackson)
1st Jackson Center, Ste. 400
101 W. Capitol St.
Jackson, MS 39201
Phone: (601)965-5533

SCORE Office (Meridian)
5220 16th Ave.
Meridian, MS 39305
Phone: (601)482-4412

Missouri

SCORE Office (Lake of the Ozark)
University Extension
113 Kansas St.
PO Box 1405
Camdenton, MO 65020
Phone: (573)346-2644

Fax: (573)346-2694
E-mail: score@cdoc.net
Website: http://sites.cdoc.net/score/

Chamber of Commerce (Cape
Girardeau)
PO Box 98
Cape Girardeau, MO 63702-0098
Phone: (314)335-3312

SCORE Office (Mid-Missouri)
1705 Halstead Ct.
Columbia, MO 65203
Phone: (573)874-1132

SCORE Office (Ozark-Gateway)
1486 Glassy Rd.
Cuba, MO 65453-1640
Phone: (573)885-4954

SCORE Office (Kansas City)
323 W. 8th St., Ste. 104
Kansas City, MO 64105
Phone: (816)374-6675
Fax: (816)374-6692
E-mail: SCOREBIC@AOL.COM
Website: http://www.crn.org/score/

SCORE Office (Sedalia)
Lucas Place
323 W. 8th St., Ste.104
Kansas City, MO 64105
Phone: (816)374-6675

SCORE Office (Tri-Lakes)
PO Box 1148
Kimberling, MO 65686
Phone: (417)739-3041

SCORE Office (Tri-Lakes)
HCRI Box 85
Lampe, MO 65681
Phone: (417)858-6798

SCORE Office (Mexico)
111 N. Washington St.
Mexico, MO 65265
Phone: (314)581-2765

SCORE Office (Southeast Missouri)
Rte. 1, Box 280
Neelyville, MO 63954
Phone: (573)989-3577

SCORE Office (Poplar Bluff Area)
806 Emma St.
Poplar Bluff, MO 63901
Phone: (573)686-8892

SCORE Office (St. Joseph)
3003 Frederick Ave.

St. Joseph, MO 64506
Phone: (816)232-4461

SCORE Office (St. Louis)
815 Olive St., Rm. 242
St. Louis, MO 63101-1569
Phone: (314)539-6970
Fax: (314)539-3785
E-mail: info@stlscore.org
Website: http://www.stlscore.org/

SCORE Office (Lewis & Clark)
425 Spencer Rd.
St. Peters, MO 63376
Phone: (314)928-2900
Fax: (314)928-2900
E-mail: score01@mail.win.org

SCORE Office (Springfield)
620 S. Glenstone, Ste. 110
Springfield, MO 65802-3200
Phone: (417)864-7670
Fax: (417)864-4108

SCORE Office (Southeast Kansas)
1206 W. First St.
Webb City, MO 64870
Phone: (417)673-3984

Montana

SCORE Office (Billings)
815 S. 27th St.
Billings, MT 59101
Phone: (406)245-4111

SCORE Office (Bozeman)
1205 E. Main St.
Bozeman, MT 59715
Phone: (406)586-5421

SCORE Office (Butte)
1000 George St.
Butte, MT 59701
Phone: (406)723-3177

SCORE Office (Great Falls)
710 First Ave. N
Great Falls, MT 59401
Phone: (406)761-4434
E-mail: scoregtf@in.tch.com

SCORE Office (Havre, Montana)
518 First St.
Havre, MT 59501
Phone: (406)265-4383

SCORE Office (Helena)
Federal Bldg.
301 S. Park

Helena, MT 59626-0054
Phone: (406)441-1081

SCORE Office (Kalispell)
2 Main St.
Kalispell, MT 59901
Phone: (406)756-5271
Fax: (406)752-6665

SCORE Office (Missoula)
723 Ronan
Missoula, MT 59806
Phone: (406)327-8806
E-mail: score@safeshop.com
Website: http://missoula.bigsky.net/
score/

Nebraska

SCORE Office (Columbus)
Columbus, NE 68601
Phone: (402)564-2769

SCORE Office (Fremont)
92 W. 5th St.
Fremont, NE 68025
Phone: (402)721-2641

SCORE Office (Hastings)
Hastings, NE 68901
Phone: (402)463-3447

SCORE Office (Lincoln)
8800 O St.
Lincoln, NE 68520
Phone: (402)437-2409

SCORE Office (Panhandle)
150549 CR 30
Minatare, NE 69356
Phone: (308)632-2133
Website: http://www.tandt.com/
SCORE

SCORE Office (Norfolk)
3209 S. 48th Ave.
Norfolk, NE 68106
Phone: (402)564-2769

SCORE Office (North Platte)
3301 W. 2nd St.
North Platte, NE 69101
Phone: (308)532-4466

SCORE Office (Omaha)
11145 Mill Valley Rd.
Omaha, NE 68154
Phone: (402)221-3606
Fax: (402)221-3680
E-mail: infoctr@ne.uswest.net
Website: http://www.tandt.com/score/

Nevada

SCORE Office (Incline Village)
969 Tahoe Blvd.
Incline Village, NV 89451
Phone: (702)831-7327
Fax: (702)832-1605

SCORE Office (Carson City)
301 E. Stewart
PO Box 7527
Las Vegas, NV 89125
Phone: (702)388-6104

SCORE Office (Las Vegas)
300 Las Vegas Blvd. S, Ste. 1100
Las Vegas, NV 89101
Phone: (702)388-6104

SCORE Office (Northern Nevada)
SBDC, College of Business
Administration
Univ. of Nevada
Reno, NV 89557-0100
Phone: (702)784-4436
Fax: (702)784-4337

New Hampshire

SCORE Office (North Country)
PO Box 34
Berlin, NH 03570
Phone: (603)752-1090

SCORE Office (Concord)
143 N. Main St., Rm. 202A
PO Box 1258
Concord, NH 03301
Phone: (603)225-1400
Fax: (603)225-1409

SCORE Office (Dover)
299 Central Ave.
Dover, NH 03820
Phone: (603)742-2218
Fax: (603)749-6317

SCORE Office (Monadnock)
34 Mechanic St.
Keene, NH 03431-3421
Phone: (603)352-0320

SCORE Office (Lakes Region)
67 Water St., Ste. 105
Laconia, NH 03246
Phone: (603)524-9168

SCORE Office (Upper Valley)
Citizens Bank Bldg., Rm. 310
20 W. Park St.
Lebanon, NH 03766

Phone: (603)448-3491
Fax: (603)448-1908
E-mail: billt@valley.net
Website: http://www.valley.net/
~score/

SCORE Office (Merrimack Valley)
275 Chestnut St., Rm. 618
Manchester, NH 03103
Phone: (603)666-7561
Fax: (603)666-7925

SCORE Office (Mt. Washington
Valley)
PO Box 1066
North Conway, NH 03818
Phone: (603)383-0800

SCORE Office (Seacoast)
195 Commerce Way, Unit-A
Portsmouth, NH 03801-3251
Phone: (603)433-0575

New Jersey

SCORE Office (Somerset)
Paritan Valley Community College,
Rte. 28
Branchburg, NJ 08807
Phone: (908)218-8874
E-mail: nj-score@grizbiz.com.
Website: http://www.nj-score.org/

SCORE Office (Chester)
5 Old Mill Rd.
Chester, NJ 07930
Phone: (908)879-7080

SCORE Office (Greater Princeton)
4 A George Washington Dr.
Cranbury, NJ 08512
Phone: (609)520-1776

SCORE Office (Freehold)
36 W. Main St.
Freehold, NJ 07728
Phone: (908)462-3030
Fax: (908)462-2123

SCORE Office (North West)
Picantinny Innovation Ctr.
3159 Schrader Rd.
Hamburg, NJ 07419
Phone: (973)209-8525
Fax: (973)209-7252
E-mail: nj-score@grizbiz.com
Website: http://www.nj-score.org/

SCORE Office (Monmouth)
765 Newman Springs Rd.

Lincroft, NJ 07738
Phone: (908)224-2573
E-mail: nj-score@grizbiz.com
Website: http://www.nj-score.org/

SCORE Office (Manalapan)
125 Symmes Dr.
Manalapan, NJ 07726
Phone: (908)431-7220

SCORE Office (Jersey City)
2 Gateway Ctr., 4th Fl.
Newark, NJ 07102
Phone: (973)645-3982
Fax: (973)645-2375

SCORE Office (Newark)
2 Gateway Center, 15th Fl.
Newark, NJ 07102-5553
Phone: (973)645-3982
Fax: (973)645-2375
E-mail: nj-score@grizbiz.com
Website: http://www.nj-score.org

SCORE Office (Bergen County)
327 E. Ridgewood Ave.
Paramus, NJ 07652
Phone: (201)599-6090
E-mail: nj-score@grizbiz.com
Website: http://www.nj-score.org/

SCORE Office (Pennsauken)
4900 Rte. 70
Pennsauken, NJ 08109
Phone: (609)486-3421

SCORE Office (Southern New
Jersey)
4900 Rte. 70
Pennsauken, NJ 08109
Phone: (609)486-3421
E-mail: nj-score@grizbiz.com
Website: http://www.nj-score.org/

SCORE Office (Greater Princeton)
216 Rockingham Row
Princeton Forrestal Village
Princeton, NJ 08540
Phone: (609)520-1776
Fax: (609)520-9107
E-mail: nj-score@grizbiz.com
Website: http://www.nj-score.org/

SCORE Office (Shrewsbury)
Hwy. 35
Shrewsbury, NJ 07702
Phone: (908)842-5995
Fax: (908)219-6140

SCORE Office (Ocean County)
33 Washington St.
Toms River, NJ 08754
Phone: (732)505-6033
E-mail: nj-score@grizbiz.com
Website: http://www.nj-score.org/

SCORE Office (Wall)
2700 Allaire Rd.
Wall, NJ 07719
Phone: (908)449-8877

SCORE Office (Wayne)
2055 Hamburg Tpke.
Wayne, NJ 07470
Phone: (201)831-7788
Fax: (201)831-9112

New Mexico

SCORE Office (Albuquerque)
525 Buena Vista, SE
Albuquerque, NM 87106
Phone: (505)272-7999
Fax: (505)272-7963

SCORE Office (Las Cruces)
Loretto Towne Center
505 S. Main St., Ste. 125
Las Cruces, NM 88001
Phone: (505)523-5627
Fax: (505)524-2101
E-mail: score.397@zianet.com

SCORE Office (Roswell)
Federal Bldg., Rm. 237
Roswell, NM 88201
Phone: (505)625-2112
Fax: (505)623-2545

SCORE Office (Santa Fe)
Montoya Federal Bldg.
120 Federal Place, Rm. 307
Santa Fe, NM 87501
Phone: (505)988-6302
Fax: (505)988-6300

New York

SCORE Office (Northeast)
1 Computer Dr. S
Albany, NY 12205
Phone: (518)446-1118
Fax: (518)446-1228

SCORE Office (Auburn)
30 South St.
PO Box 675
Auburn, NY 13021
Phone: (315)252-7291

SCORE Office (South Tier
Binghamton)
Metro Center, 2nd Fl.
49 Court St.
PO Box 995
Binghamton, NY 13902
Phone: (607)772-8860

SCORE Office (Queens County City)
12055 Queens Blvd., Rm. 333
Borough Hall, NY 11424
Phone: (718)263-8961

SCORE Office (Buffalo)
Federal Bldg., Rm. 1311
111 W. Huron St.
Buffalo, NY 14202
Phone: (716)551-4301
Website: http://www2.pcom.net/
score/buf45.html

SCORE Office (Canandaigua)
Chamber of Commerce Bldg.
113 S. Main St.
Canandaigua, NY 14424
Phone: (716)394-4400
Fax: (716)394-4546

SCORE Office (Chemung)
333 E. Water St., 4th Fl.
Elmira, NY 14901
Phone: (607)734-3358

SCORE Office (Geneva)
Chamber of Commerce Bldg.
PO Box 587
Geneva, NY 14456
Phone: (315)789-1776
Fax: (315)789-3993

SCORE Office (Glens Falls)
84 Broad St.
Glens Falls, NY 12801
Phone: (518)798-8463
Fax: (518)745-1433

SCORE Office (Orange County)
40 Matthews St.
Goshen, NY 10924
Phone: (914)294-8080
Fax: (914)294-6121

SCORE Office (Huntington Area)
151 W. Carver St.
Huntington, NY 11743
Phone: (516)423-6100

SCORE Office (Tompkins County)
904 E. Shore Dr.
Ithaca, NY 14850
Phone: (607)273-7080

SCORE Office (Long Island City)
120-55 Queens Blvd.
Jamaica, NY 11424
Phone: (718)263-8961
Fax: (718)263-9032

SCORE Office (Chatauqua)
101 W. 5th St.
Jamestown, NY 14701
Phone: (716)484-1103

SCORE Office (Westchester)
2 Caradon Ln.
Katonah, NY 10536
Phone: (914)948-3907
Fax: (914)948-4645
E-mail: score@w-w-w.com
Website: http://w-w-w.com/score/

SCORE Office (Queens County)
Queens Borough Hall
120-55 Queens Blvd. Rm. 333
Kew Gardens, NY 11424
Phone: (718)263-8961
Fax: (718)263-9032

SCORE Office (Brookhaven)
3233 Rte. 112
Medford, NY 11763
Phone: (516)451-6563
Fax: (516)451-6925

SCORE Office (Melville)
35 Pinelawn Rd., Rm. 207-W
Melville, NY 11747
Phone: (516)454-0771

SCORE Office (Nassau County)
400 County Seat Dr., No. 140
Mineola, NY 11501
Phone: (516)571-3303
E-mail: Counse1998@aol.com
Website: http://members.aol.com/
Counse1998/Default.htm

SCORE Office (Mt. Vernon)
4 N. 7th Ave.
Mt. Vernon, NY 10550
Phone: (914)667-7500

SCORE Office (New York)
26 Federal Plz., Rm. 3100
New York, NY 10278
Phone: (212)264-4507
Fax: (212)264-4963
E-mail: score1000@erols.com
Website: http://users.erols.com/score-
nyc/

SCORE Office (Newburgh)
47 Grand St.

Newburgh, NY 12550
Phone: (914)562-5100

SCORE Office (Owego)
188 Front St.
Owego, NY 13827
Phone: (607)687-2020

SCORE Office (Peekskill)
1 S. Division St.
Peekskill, NY 10566
Phone: (914)737-3600
Fax: (914)737-0541

SCORE Office (Penn Yan)
2375 Rte. 14A
Penn Yan, NY 14527
Phone: (315)536-3111

SCORE Office (Dutchess)
110 Main St.
Poughkeepsie, NY 12601
Phone: (914)454-1700

SCORE Office (Rochester)
601 Keating Federal Bldg., Rm. 410
100 State St.
Rochester, NY 14614
Phone: (716)263-6473
Fax: (716)263-3146
Website: http://www.ggw.org/score/

SCORE Office (Saranac Lake)
30 Main St.
Saranac Lake, NY 12983
Phone: (315)448-0415

SCORE Office (Suffolk)
286 Main St.
Setauket, NY 11733
Phone: (516)751-3886

SCORE Office (Staten Island)
130 Bay St.
Staten Island, NY 10301
Phone: (718)727-1221

SCORE Office (Ulster)
Clinton Bldg., Rm. 107
Stone Ridge, NY 12484
Phone: (914)687-5035
Fax: (914)687-5015
Website: http://www.scoreulster.org/

SCORE Office (Syracuse)
401 S. Salina, 5th Fl.
Syracuse, NY 13202
Phone: (315)471-9393

SCORE Office (Utica)
SUNY Institute of Technology, Rte 12

Utica, NY 13504-3050
Phone: (315)792-7553

SCORE Office (Watertown)
518 Davidson St.
Watertown, NY 13601
Phone: (315)788-1200
Fax: (315)788-8251

North Carolina

SCORE Office (Asheboro)
317 E. Dixie Dr.
Asheboro, NC 27203
Free: (336)626-2626
Fax: (336)626-7077

SCORE Office (Asheville)
Federal Bldg., Rm. 259
151 Patton
Asheville, NC 28801-5770
Phone: (828)271-4786
Fax: (828)271-4009

SCORE Office (Chapel Hill)
104 S. Estes Dr.
PO Box 2897
Chapel Hill, NC 27514
Phone: (919)967-7075

SCORE Office (Coastal Plains)
PO Box 2897
Chapel Hill, NC 27515
Phone: (919)967-7075
Fax: (919)968-6874

SCORE Office (Charlotte)
200 N. College St., Ste. A-2015
Charlotte, NC 28202
Phone: (704)344-6576
Fax: (704)344-6769
E-mail:
CharlotteSCORE47@AOL.com
Website: http://www.charweb.org/
business/score/

SCORE Office (Durham)
411 W. Chapel Hill St.
Durham, NC 27707
Phone: (919)541-2171

SCORE Office (Gastonia)
PO Box 2168
Gastonia, NC 28053
Phone: (704)864-2621
Fax: (704)854-8723

SCORE Office (Greensboro)
400 W. Market St., Ste. 103
Greensboro, NC 27401-2241
Phone: (910)333-5399

SCORE Office (Henderson)
PO Box 917
Henderson, NC 27536
Phone: (919)492-2061
Fax: (919)430-0460

SCORE Office (Hendersonville)
Federal Bldg., Rm. 108
W. 4th Ave. & Church St.
Hendersonville, NC 28792
Phone: (828)693-8702
E-mail: score@circle.net
Website: http://www.wncguide.com/
score/Welcome.html

SCORE Office (Unifour)
PO Box 1828
Hickory, NC 28603
Phone: (704)328-6111

SCORE Office (High Point)
1101 N. Main St.
High Point, NC 27262
Phone: (336)882-8625
Fax: (336)889-9499

SCORE Office (Outer Banks)
Collington Rd. and Mustain
Kill Devil Hills, NC 27948
Phone: (252)441-8144

SCORE Office (Down East)
312 S. Front St., Ste. 6
New Bern, NC 28560
Phone: (252)633-6688
Fax: (252)633-9608

SCORE Office (Kinston)
PO Box 95
New Bern, NC 28561
Phone: (919)633-6688

SCORE Office (Raleigh)
Century Post Office Bldg., Ste. 306
300 Federal St. Mall
Raleigh, NC 27601
Phone: (919)856-4739
E-mail: jendres@ibm.net
Website: http://www.intrex.net/
score96/score96.htm

SCORE Office (Sanford)
1801 Nash St.
Sanford, NC 27330
Phone: (919)774-6442
Fax: (919)776-8739

SCORE Office (Sandhills Area)
1480 Hwy. 15-501
PO Box 458

Southern Pines, NC 28387
Phone: (910)692-3926

SCORE Office (Wilmington)
Corps of Engineers Bldg.
96 Darlington Ave., Ste. 207
Wilmington, NC 28403
Phone: (910)815-4576
Fax: (910)815-4658

North Dakota

SCORE Office (Bismarck-Mandan)
700 E. Main Ave., 2nd Fl.
PO Box 5509
Bismarck, ND 58506-5509
Phone: (701)250-4303

SCORE Office (Fargo)
657 2nd Ave., Rm. 225
Fargo, ND 58108-3083
Phone: (701)239-5677

SCORE Office (Upper Red River)
4275 Technology Dr., Rm. 156
Grand Forks, ND 58202-8372
Phone: (701)777-3051

SCORE Office (Minot)
100 1st St. SW
Minot, ND 58701-3846
Phone: (701)852-6883
Fax: (701)852-6905

Ohio

SCORE Office (Akron)
1 Cascade Plz., 7th Fl.
Akron, OH 44308
Phone: (330)379-3163
Fax: (330)379-3164

SCORE Office (Ashland)
Gill Center
47 W. Main St.
Ashland, OH 44805
Phone: (419)281-4584

SCORE Office (Canton)
116 Cleveland Ave. NW, Ste. 601
Canton, OH 44702-1720
Phone: (330)453-6047

SCORE Office (Chillicothe)
165 S. Paint St.
Chillicothe, OH 45601
Phone: (614)772-4530

SCORE Office (Cincinnati)
Ameritrust Bldg., Rm. 850

525 Vine St.
Cincinnati, OH 45202
Phone: (513)684-2812
Fax: (513)684-3251
Website: http://
www.score.chapter34.org/

SCORE Office (Cleveland)
Eaton Center, Ste. 620
1100 Superior Ave.
Cleveland, OH 44114-2507
Phone: (216)522-4194
Fax: (216)522-4844

SCORE Office (Columbus)
2 Nationwide Plz., Ste. 1400
Columbus, OH 43215-2542
Phone: (614)469-2357
Fax: (614)469-2391
E-mail: info@scorecolumbus.org
Website: http://
www.scorecolumbus.org/

SCORE Office (Dayton)
Dayton Federal Bldg., Rm. 505
200 W. Second St.
Dayton, OH 45402-1430
Phone: (513)225-2887
Fax: (513)225-7667

SCORE Office (Defiance)
615 W. 3rd St.
PO Box 130
Defiance, OH 43512
Phone: (419)782-7946

SCORE Office (Findlay)
123 E. Main Cross St.
PO Box 923
Findlay, OH 45840
Phone: (419)422-3314

SCORE Office (Lima)
147 N. Main St.
Lima, OH 45801
Phone: (419)222-6045
Fax: (419)229-0266

SCORE Office (Mansfield)
55 N. Mulberry St.
Mansfield, OH 44902
Phone: (419)522-3211

SCORE Office (Marietta)
Thomas Hall
Marietta, OH 45750
Phone: (614)373-0268

SCORE Office (Medina)
County Administrative Bldg.

144 N. Broadway
Medina, OH 44256
Phone: (216)764-8650

SCORE Office (Licking County)
50 W. Locust St.
Newark, OH 43055
Phone: (614)345-7458

SCORE Office (Salem)
2491 State Rte. 45 S
Salem, OH 44460
Phone: (216)332-0361

SCORE Office (Tiffin)
62 S. Washington St.
Tiffin, OH 44883
Phone: (419)447-4141
Fax: (419)447-5141

SCORE Office (Toledo)
608 Madison Ave, Ste. 910
Toledo, OH 43624
Phone: (419)259-7598
Fax: (419)259-6460

SCORE Office (Heart of Ohio)
377 W. Liberty St.
Wooster, OH 44691
Phone: (330)262-5735
Fax: (330)262-5745

SCORE Office (Youngstown)
306 Williamson Hall
Youngstown, OH 44555
Phone: (330)746-2687

Oklahoma

SCORE Office (Anadarko)
PO Box 366
Anadarko, OK 73005
Phone: (405)247-6651

SCORE Office (Ardmore)
410 W. Main
Ardmore, OK 73401
Phone: (580)226-2620

SCORE Office (Northeast Oklahoma)
210 S. Main
Grove, OK 74344
Phone: (918)787-2796
Fax: (918)787-2796
E-mail: Score595@greencis.net

SCORE Office (Lawton)
4500 W. Lee Blvd., Bldg. 100, Ste.
107
Lawton, OK 73505

Phone: (580)353-8727
Fax: (580)250-5677

SCORE Office (Oklahoma City)
210 Park Ave., No. 1300
Oklahoma City, OK 73102
Phone: (405)231-5163
Fax: (405)231-4876
E-mail: score212@usa.net

SCORE Office (Stillwater)
439 S. Main
Stillwater, OK 74074
Phone: (405)372-5573
Fax: (405)372-4316

SCORE Office (Tulsa)
616 S. Boston, Ste. 406
Tulsa, OK 74119
Phone: (918)581-7462
Fax: (918)581-6908
Website: http://www.ionet.net/
~tulscore/

Oregon

SCORE Office (Bend)
63085 N. Hwy. 97
Bend, OR 97701
Phone: (541)923-2849
Fax: (541)330-6900

SCORE Office (Willamette)
1401 Willamette St.
PO Box 1107
Eugene, OR 97401-4003
Phone: (541)465-6600
Fax: (541)484-4942

SCORE Office (Florence)
3149 Oak St.
Florence, OR 97439
Phone: (503)997-8444
Fax: (503)997-8448

SCORE Office (Southern Oregon)
33 N. Central Ave., Ste. 216
Medford, OR 97501
Phone: (541)776-4220
E-mail: pgr134f@prodigy.com

SCORE Office (Portland)
1515 SW 5th Ave., Ste. 1050
Portland, OR 97201
Phone: (503)326-3441
Fax: (503)326-2808
E-mail: gr134@prodigy.com

SCORE Office (Salem)
416 State St. (corner of Liberty)

Salem, OR 97301
Phone: (503)370-2896

Pennsylvania

SCORE Office (Altoona-Blair)
1212 12th Ave.
Altoona, PA 16601-3493
Phone: (814)943-8151

SCORE Office (Lehigh Valley)
Rauch Bldg. 37
Lehigh University
621 Taylor St.
Bethlehem, PA 18015
Phone: (610)758-4496
Fax: (610)758-5205

SCORE Office (Butler County)
100 N. Main St.
PO Box 1082
Butler, PA 16003
Phone: (412)283-2222
Fax: (412)283-0224

SCORE Office (Harrisburg)
4211 Trindle Rd.
Camp Hill, PA 17011
Phone: (717)761-4304
Fax: (717)761-4315

SCORE Office (Cumberland Valley)
75 S. 2nd St.
Chambersburg, PA 17201
Phone: (717)264-2935

SCORE Office (Monroe County-
Stroudsburg)
556 Main St.
East Stroudsburg, PA 18301
Phone: (717)421-4433

SCORE Office (Erie)
120 W. 9th St.
Erie, PA 16501
Phone: (814)871-5650
Fax: (814)871-7530

SCORE Office (Bucks County)
409 Hood Blvd.
Fairless Hills, PA 19030
Phone: (215)943-8850
Fax: (215)943-7404

SCORE Office (Hanover)
146 Broadway
Hanover, PA 17331
Phone: (717)637-6130
Fax: (717)637-9127

SCORE Office (Harrisburg)
100 Chestnut, Ste. 309
Harrisburg, PA 17101
Phone: (717)782-3874

SCORE Office (East Montgomery
County)
Baederwood Shopping Center
1653 The Fairways, Ste. 204
Jenkintown, PA 19046
Phone: (215)885-3027

SCORE Office (Kittanning)
2 Butler Rd.
Kittanning, PA 16201
Phone: (412)543-1305
Fax: (412)543-6206

SCORE Office (Lancaster)
118 W. Chestnut St.
Lancaster, PA 17603
Phone: (717)397-3092

SCORE Office (Westmoreland
County)
300 Fraser Purchase Rd.
Latrobe, PA 15650-2690
Phone: (412)539-7505
Fax: (412)539-1850

SCORE Office (Lebanon)
252 N. 8th St.
PO Box 899
Lebanon, PA 17042-0899
Phone: (717)273-3727
Fax: (717)273-7940

SCORE Office (Lewistown)
3 W. Monument Sq., Ste. 204
Lewistown, PA 17044
Phone: (717)248-6713
Fax: (717)248-6714

SCORE Office (Delaware County)
602 E. Baltimore Pike
Media, PA 19063
Phone: (610)565-3677
Fax: (610)565-1606

SCORE Office (Milton Area)
112 S. Front St.
Milton, PA 17847
Phone: (717)742-7341
Fax: (717)792-2008

SCORE Office (Mon-Valley)
435 Donner Ave.
Monessen, PA 15062
Phone: (412)684-4277
Fax: (412)684-7688

SCORE Office (Monroeville)
William Penn Plaza
2790 Mosside Blvd., Ste. 295
Monroeville, PA 15146
Phone: (412)856-0622
Fax: (412)856-1030

SCORE Office (Airport Area)
986 Brodhead Rd.
Moon Township, PA 15108-2398
Phone: (412)264-6270
Fax: (412)264-1575

SCORE Office (Northeast)
8601 E. Roosevelt Blvd.
Philadelphia, PA 19152
Phone: (215)332-3400
Fax: (215)332-6050

SCORE Office (Philadelphia)
1315 Walnut St., Ste. 500
Philadelphia, PA 19107
Phone: (215)790-5050
Fax: (215)790-5057
E-mail: score46@bellatlantic.net
Website: http://www.pgweb.net/
score46/

SCORE Office (Pittsburgh)
1000 Liberty Ave., Rm. 1122
Pittsburgh, PA 15222
Phone: (412)395-6560
Fax: (412)395-6562

SCORE Office (Tri-County)
801 N. Charlotte St.
Pottstown, PA 19464
Phone: (610)327-2673

SCORE Office (Reading)
601 Penn St.
Reading, PA 19601
Phone: (610)376-3497

SCORE Office (Scranton)
Oppenheim Bldg.
116 N. Washington Ave., Ste. 650
Scranton, PA 18503
Phone: (717)347-4611
Fax: (717)347-4611

SCORE Office (Central
Pennsylvania)
200 Innovation Blvd., Ste. 242-B
State College, PA 16803
Phone: (814)234-9415
Fax: (814)238-9686
Website: http://countrystore.org/
business/score.htm

SCORE Office (Monroe-
Stroudsburg)
556 Main St.
Stroudsburg, PA 18360
Phone: (717)421-4433

SCORE Office (Uniontown)
Federal Bldg.
Pittsburg St.
PO Box 2065 DTS
Uniontown, PA 15401
Phone: (412)437-4222
E-mail: uniontownscore@lcsys.net

SCORE Office (Warren County)
315 2nd Ave.
Warren, PA 16365
Phone: (814)723-9017

SCORE Office (Waynesboro)
323 E. Main St.
Waynesboro, PA 17268
Phone: (717)762-7123
Fax: (717)962-7124

SCORE Office (Chester County)
Government Service Center, Ste. 281
601 Westtown Rd.
West Chester, PA 19382-4538
Phone: (610)344-6910
Fax: (610)344-6919
E-mail: score@locke.ccil.org

SCORE Office (Wilkes-Barre)
7 N. Wilkes-Barre Blvd.
Wilkes Barre, PA 18702-5241
Phone: (717)826-6502
Fax: (717)826-6287

SCORE Office (North Central
Pennsylvania)
240 W. 3rd St., Rm. 227
PO Box 725
Williamsport, PA 17703
Phone: (717)322-3720
Fax: (717)322-1607
E-mail: score234@mail.csrlink.net
Website: http://www.lycoming.org/
score/

SCORE Office (York)
Cyber Center
2101 Pennsylvania Ave.
York, PA 17404
Phone: (717)845-8830
Fax: (717)854-9333

Puerto Rico

SCORE Office (Puerto Rico & Virgin
Islands)
PO Box 12383-96
San Juan, PR 00914-0383
Phone: (787)726-8040
Fax: (787)726-8135

Rhode Island

SCORE Office (Barrington)
281 County Rd.
Barrington, RI 02806
Phone: (401)247-1920
Fax: (401)247-3763

SCORE Office (Woonsocket)
640 Washington Hwy.
Lincoln, RI 02865
Phone: (401)334-1000
Fax: (401)334-1009

SCORE Office (Wickford)
8045 Post Rd.
North Kingstown, RI 02852
Phone: (401)295-5566
Fax: (401)295-8987

SCORE Office (J.G.E. Knight)
380 Westminster St.
Providence, RI 02903
Phone: (401)528-4571
Fax: (401)528-4539
E-mail: feedback@ch13.score.org.
Website: http://chapters.score.org/
ch13

SCORE Office (Warwick)
3288 Post Rd.
Warwick, RI 02886
Phone: (401)732-1100
Fax: (401)732-1101

SCORE Office (Westerly)
74 Post Rd.
Westerly, RI 02891
Phone: (401)596-7761
Free: (800)732-7636
Fax: (401)596-2190

South Carolina

SCORE Office (Aiken)
PO Box 892
Aiken, SC 29802
Phone: (803)641-1111
Free: (800)542-4536
Fax: (803)641-4174

SCORE Office (Anderson)
Anderson Mall
3130 N. Main St.
Anderson, SC 29621
Phone: (864)224-0453

SCORE Office (Coastal)
284 King St.
Charleston, SC 29401
Phone: (803)727-4778
Fax: (803)853-2529

SCORE Office (Midlands)
Strom Thurmond Bldg., Rm. 358
1835 Assembly St., Rm 358
Columbia, SC 29201
Phone: (803)765-5131
Fax: (803)765-5962
Website: http://
www.scoremidlands.org/

SCORE Office (Piedmont)
Federal Bldg., Rm. B-02
300 E. Washington St.
Greenville, SC 29601
Phone: (864)271-3638

SCORE Office (Greenwood)
PO Drawer 1467
Greenwood, SC 29648
Phone: (864)223-8357

SCORE Office (Hilton Head Island)
52 Savannah Trail
Hilton Head, SC 29926
Phone: (803)785-7107
Fax: (803)785-7110

SCORE Office (Grand Strand)
937 Broadway
Myrtle Beach, SC 29577
Phone: (803)918-1079
Fax: (803)918-1083
E-mail: score381@aol.com

SCORE Office (Spartanburg)
PO Box 1636
Spartanburg, SC 29304
Phone: (864)594-5000
Fax: (864)594-5055

South Dakota

SCORE Office (West River)
Rushmore Plz. Civic Ctr.
444 Mount Rushmore Rd., No. 209
Rapid City, SD 57701
Phone: (605)394-5311
E-mail: score@gwtc.net

SCORE Office (Sioux Falls)
First Financial Center
110 S. Phillips Ave., Ste. 200
Sioux Falls, SD 57104-6727
Phone: (605)330-4231
Fax: (605)330-4231

Tennessee

SCORE Office (Chattanooga)
Federal Bldg., Rm. 26
900 Georgia Ave.
Chattanooga, TN 37402
Phone: (423)752-5190
Fax: (423)752-5335

SCORE Office (Cleveland)
PO Box 2275
Cleveland, TN 37320
Phone: (423)472-6587
Fax: (423)472-2019

SCORE Office (Upper Cumberland Center)
1225 S. Willow Ave.
Cookeville, TN 38501
Phone: (615)432-4111
Fax: (615)432-6010

SCORE Office (Unicoi County)
PO Box 713
Erwin, TN 37650
Phone: (423)743-3000
Fax: (423)743-0942

SCORE Office (Greeneville)
115 Academy St.
Greeneville, TN 37743
Phone: (423)638-4111
Fax: (423)638-5345

SCORE Office (Jackson)
194 Auditorium St.
Jackson, TN 38301
Phone: (901)423-2200

SCORE Office (Northeast Tennessee)
1st Tennessee Bank Bldg.
2710 S. Roan St., Ste. 584
Johnson City, TN 37601
Phone: (423)929-7686
Fax: (423)461-8052

SCORE Office (Kingsport)
151 E. Main St.
Kingsport, TN 37662
Phone: (423)392-8805

SCORE Office (Greater Knoxville)
Farragot Bldg., Ste. 224

530 S. Gay St.
Knoxville, TN 37902
Phone: (423)545-4203
E-mail: scoreknox@ntown.com
Website: http://www.scoreknox.org/

SCORE Office (Maryville)
201 S. Washington St.
Maryville, TN 37804-5728
Phone: (423)983-2241
Free: (800)525-6834
Fax: (423)984-1386

SCORE Office (Memphis)
Federal Bldg., Ste. 390
167 N. Main St.
Memphis, TN 38103
Phone: (901)544-3588

SCORE Office (Nashville)
50 Vantage Way, Ste. 201
Nashville, TN 37228-1500
Phone: (615)736-7621

Texas

SCORE Office (Abilene)
2106 Federal Post Office and Court Bldg.
Abilene, TX 79601
Phone: (915)677-1857

SCORE Office (Austin)
2501 S. Congress
Austin, TX 78701
Phone: (512)442-7235
Fax: (512)442-7528

SCORE Office (Golden Triangle)
450 Boyd St.
Beaumont, TX 77704
Phone: (409)838-6581
Fax: (409)833-6718

SCORE Office (Brownsville)
3505 Boca Chica Blvd., Ste. 305
Brownsville, TX 78521
Phone: (210)541-4508

SCORE Office (Brazos Valley)
3000 Briarcrest, Ste. 302
Bryan, TX 77802
Phone: (409)776-8876
E-mail:
102633.2612@compuserve.com

SCORE Office (Cleburne)
Watergarden Pl., 9th Fl., Ste. 400
Cleburne, TX 76031
Phone: (817)871-6002

SCORE Office (Corpus Christi)
651 Upper North Broadway, Ste. 654
Corpus Christi, TX 78477
Phone: (512)888-4322
Fax: (512)888-3418

SCORE Office (Dallas)
6260 E. Mockingbird
Dallas, TX 75214-2619
Phone: (214)828-2471
Fax: (214)821-8033

SCORE Office (El Paso)
10 Civic Center Plaza
El Paso, TX 79901
Phone: (915)534-0541
Fax: (915)534-0513

SCORE Office (Bedford)
100 E. 15th St., Ste. 400
Ft. Worth, TX 76102
Phone: (817)871-6002

SCORE Office (Ft. Worth)
100 E. 15th St., No. 24
Ft. Worth, TX 76102
Phone: (817)871-6002
Fax: (817)871-6031
E-mail: fwbac@onramp.net

SCORE Office (Garland)
2734 W. Kingsley Rd.
Garland, TX 75041
Phone: (214)271-9224

SCORE Office (Granbury Chamber
of Commerce)
416 S. Morgan
Granbury, TX 76048
Phone: (817)573-1622
Fax: (817)573-0805

SCORE Office (Lower Rio Grande
Valley)
222 E. Van Buren, Ste. 500
Harlingen, TX 78550
Phone: (956)427-8533
Fax: (956)427-8537

SCORE Office (Houston)
9301 Southwest Fwy., Ste. 550
Houston, TX 77074
Phone: (713)773-6565
Fax: (713)773-6550

SCORE Office (Irving)
3333 N. MacArthur Blvd., Ste. 100
Irving, TX 75062
Phone: (214)252-8484
Fax: (214)252-6710

SCORE Office (Lubbock)
1205 Texas Ave., Rm. 411D
Lubbock, TX 79401
Phone: (806)472-7462
Fax: (806)472-7487

SCORE Office (Midland)
Post Office Annex
200 E. Wall St., Rm. P121
Midland, TX 79701
Phone: (915)687-2649

SCORE Office (Orange)
1012 Green Ave.
Orange, TX 77630-5620
Phone: (409)883-3536
Free: (800)528-4906
Fax: (409)886-3247

SCORE Office (Plano)
1200 E. 15th St.
PO Drawer 940287
Plano, TX 75094-0287
Phone: (214)424-7547
Fax: (214)422-5182

SCORE Office (Port Arthur)
4749 Twin City Hwy., Ste. 300
Port Arthur, TX 77642
Phone: (409)963-1107
Fax: (409)963-3322

SCORE Office (Richardson)
411 Belle Grove
Richardson, TX 75080
Phone: (214)234-4141
Free: (800)777-8001
Fax: (214)680-9103

SCORE Office (San Antonio)
Federal Bldg., Rm. A527
727 E. Durango
San Antonio, TX 78206
Phone: (210)472-5931
Fax: (210)472-5935

SCORE Office (Texarkana State
College)
819 State Line Ave.
Texarkana, TX 75501
Phone: (903)792-7191
Fax: (903)793-4304

SCORE Office (East Texas)
RTDC
1530 SSW Loop 323, Ste. 100
Tyler, TX 75701
Phone: (903)510-2975
Fax: (903)510-2978

SCORE Office (Waco)
401 Franklin Ave.
Waco, TX 76701
Phone: (817)754-8898
Fax: (817)756-0776
Website: http://www.brc-waco.com/

SCORE Office (Wichita Falls)
Hamilton Bldg.
900 8th St.
Wichita Falls, TX 76307
Phone: (940)723-2741
Fax: (940)723-8773

Utah

SCORE Office (Northern Utah)
160 N. Main
Logan, UT 84321
Phone: (435)752-2161

SCORE Office (Ogden)
1701 E. Windsor Dr.
Ogden, UT 84604
Phone: (801)226-0881
E-mail: score158@netscape.net

SCORE Office (Central Utah)
1071 E. Windsor Dr.
Provo, UT 84604
Phone: (801)226-0881

SCORE Office (Southern Utah)
225 South 700 East
St. George, UT 84770
Phone: (801)652-7741

SCORE Office (Salt Lake)
169 E. 100 S.
Salt Lake City, UT 84111
Phone: (801)364-1331
Fax: (801)364-1310

Vermont

SCORE Office (Champlain Valley)
Winston Prouty Federal Bldg.
11 Lincoln St., Rm. 106
Essex Junction, VT 05452
Phone: (802)951-6762

SCORE Office (Montpelier)
87 State St., Rm. 205
PO Box 605
Montpelier, VT 05601
Phone: (802)828-4422
Fax: (802)828-4485

SCORE Office (Marble Valley)
256 N. Main St.
Rutland, VT 05701-2413
Phone: (802)773-9147

SCORE Office (Northeast Kingdom)
20 Main St.
PO Box 904
St. Johnsbury, VT 05819
Phone: (802)748-5101

Virgin Islands

SCORE Office (St. Croix)
United Plaza Shopping Center
PO Box 4010, Christiansted
St. Croix, VI 00822
Phone: (809)778-5380

SCORE Office (St. Thomas-St. John)
Federal Bldg., Rm. 21
Veterans Dr.
St. Thomas, VI 00801
Phone: (809)774-8530

Virginia

SCORE Office (Arlington)
2009 N. 14th St., Ste. 111
Arlington, VA 22201
Phone: (703)525-2400

SCORE Office (Blacksburg)
141 Jackson St.
Blacksburg, VA 24060
Phone: (540)552-4061

SCORE Office (Bristol)
20 Volunteer Pkwy.
Bristol, VA 24203
Phone: (540)989-4850

SCORE Office (Central Virginia)
1001 E. Market St., Ste. 101
Charlottesville, VA 22902
Phone: (804)295-6712
Fax: (804)295-7066

SCORE Office (Alleghany Satellite)
241 W. Main St.
Covington, VA 24426
Phone: (540)962-2178
Fax: (540)962-2179

SCORE Office (Central Fairfax)
3975 University Dr., Ste. 350
Fairfax, VA 22030
Phone: (703)591-2450

SCORE Office (Falls Church)
PO Box 491

Falls Church, VA 22040
Phone: (703)532-1050
Fax: (703)237-7904

SCORE Office (Glenns)
Glenns Campus
Box 287
Glenns, VA 23149
Phone: (804)693-9650

SCORE Office (Peninsula)
6 Manhattan Sq.
PO Box 7269
Hampton, VA 23666
Phone: (757)766-2000
Fax: (757)865-0339
E-mail: score100@seva.net

SCORE Office (Tri-Cities)
108 N. Main St.
Hopewell, VA 23860
Phone: (804)458-5536

SCORE Office (Lynchburg)
Federal Bldg.
1100 Main St.
Lynchburg, VA 24504-1714
Phone: (804)846-3235

SCORE Office (Greater Prince
William)
8963 Center St
Manassas, VA 20110
Phone: (703)368-4813
Fax: (703)368-4733

SCORE Office (Martinsvile)
115 Broad St.
Martinsville, VA 24112-0709
Phone: (540)632-6401
Fax: (540)632-5059

SCORE Office (Hampton Roads)
Federal Bldg., Rm. 737
200 Grandby St.
Norfolk, VA 23510
Phone: (757)441-3733
Fax: (757)441-3733
E-mail: scorehr60@juno.com

SCORE Office (Norfolk)
Federal Bldg., Rm. 737
200 Granby St.
Norfolk, VA 23510
Phone: (757)441-3733
Fax: (757)441-3733

SCORE Office (Virginia Beach)
Chamber of Commerce
200 Grandby St., Rm 737

Norfolk, VA 23510
Phone: (804)441-3733

SCORE Office (Radford)
1126 Norwood St.
Radford, VA 24141
Phone: (540)639-2202

SCORE Office (Richmond)
Federal Bldg.
400 N. 8th St., Ste. 1150
PO Box 10126
Richmond, VA 23240-0126
Phone: (804)771-2400
Fax: (804)771-8018
E-mail: scorechapter12@yahoo.com
Website: http://www.cvco.org/score/

SCORE Office (Roanoke)
Federal Bldg., Rm. 716
250 Franklin Rd.
Roanoke, VA 24011
Phone: (540)857-2834
Fax: (540)857-2043
E-mail: scorerva@juno.com
Website: http://hometown.aol.com/
scorerv/Index.html

SCORE Office (Fairfax)
8391 Old Courthouse Rd., Ste. 300
Vienna, VA 22182
Phone: (703)749-0400

SCORE Office (Greater Vienna)
513 Maple Ave. West
Vienna, VA 22180
Phone: (703)281-1333
Fax: (703)242-1482

SCORE Office (Shenandoah Valley)
301 W. Main St.
Waynesboro, VA 22980
Phone: (540)949-8203
Fax: (540)949-7740
E-mail: score427@intelos.net

SCORE Office (Williamsburg)
201 Penniman Rd.
Williamsburg, VA 23185
Phone: (757)229-6511
E-mail: wacc@williamsburgcc.com

SCORE Office (Northern Virginia)
1360 S. Pleasant Valley Rd.
Winchester, VA 22601
Phone: (540)662-4118

Washington

SCORE Office (Gray's Harbor)
506 Duffy St.

Aberdeen, WA 98520
Phone: (360)532-1924
Fax: (360)533-7945

SCORE Office (Bellingham)
101 E. Holly St.
Bellingham, WA 98225
Phone: (360)676-3307

SCORE Office (Everett)
2702 Hoyt Ave.
Everett, WA 98201-3556
Phone: (206)259-8000

SCORE Office (Gig Harbor)
3125 Judson St.
Gig Harbor, WA 98335
Phone: (206)851-6865

SCORE Office (Kennewick)
PO Box 6986
Kennewick, WA 99336
Phone: (509)736-0510

SCORE Office (Puyallup)
322 2nd St. SW
PO Box 1298
Puyallup, WA 98371
Phone: (206)845-6755
Fax: (206)848-6164

SCORE Office (Seattle)
1200 6th Ave., Ste. 1700
Seattle, WA 98101
Phone: (206)553-7320
Fax: (206)553-7044
E-mail: score55@aol.com
Website: http://www.scn.org/civic/
score-online/index55.html

SCORE Office (Spokane)
801 W. Riverside Ave., No. 240
Spokane, WA 99201
Phone: (509)353-2820
Fax: (509)353-2600
E-mail: score@dmi.net
Website: http://www.dmi.net/score/

SCORE Office (Clover Park)
PO Box 1933
Tacoma, WA 98401-1933
Phone: (206)627-2175

SCORE Office (Tacoma)
1101 Pacific Ave.
Tacoma, WA 98402
Phone: (253)274-1288
Fax: (253)274-1289

SCORE Office (Fort Vancouver)
1701 Broadway, S-1

Vancouver, WA 98663
Phone: (360)699-1079

SCORE Office (Walla Walla)
500 Tausick Way
Walla Walla, WA 99362
Phone: (509)527-4681

SCORE Office (Mid-Columbia)
1113 S. 14th Ave.
Yakima, WA 98907
Phone: (509)574-4944
Fax: (509)574-2943
Website: http://www.ellensburg.com/
~score/

West Virginia

SCORE Office (Charleston)
1116 Smith St.
Charleston, WV 25301
Phone: (304)347-5463
E-mail: score256@juno.com

SCORE Office (Virginia Street)
1116 Smith St., Ste. 302
Charleston, WV 25301
Phone: (304)347-5463

SCORE Office (Marion County)
PO Box 208
Fairmont, WV 26555-0208
Phone: (304)363-0486

SCORE Office (Upper Monongahela
Valley)
1000 Technology Dr., Ste. 1111
Fairmont, WV 26555
Phone: (304)363-0486
E-mail: score537@hotmail.com

SCORE Office (Huntington)
1101 6th Ave., Ste. 220
Huntington, WV 25701-2309
Phone: (304)523-4092

SCORE Office (Wheeling)
1310 Market St.
Wheeling, WV 26003
Phone: (304)233-2575
Fax: (304)233-1320

Wisconsin

SCORE Office (Fox Cities)
227 S. Walnut St.
Appleton, WI 54913
Phone: (920)734-7101
Fax: (920)734-7161

SCORE Office (Beloit)
136 W. Grand Ave., Ste. 100
PO Box 717
Beloit, WI 53511
Phone: (608)365-8835
Fax: (608)365-9170

SCORE Office (Eau Claire)
Federal Bldg., Rm. B11
510 S. Barstow St.
Eau Claire, WI 54701
Phone: (715)834-1573
E-mail: score@ecol.net
Website: http://www.ecol.net/~score/

SCORE Office (Fond du Lac)
207 N. Main St.
Fond du Lac, WI 54935
Phone: (414)921-9500
Fax: (414)921-9559

SCORE Office (Green Bay)
835 Potts Ave.
Green Bay, WI 54304
Phone: (414)496-8930
Fax: (414)496-6009

SCORE Office (Janesville)
20 S. Main St., Ste. 11
PO Box 8008
Janesville, WI 53547
Phone: (608)757-3160
Fax: (608)757-3170

SCORE Office (La Crosse)
712 Main St.
La Crosse, WI 54602-0219
Phone: (608)784-4880

SCORE Office (Madison)
505 S. Rosa Rd.
Madison, WI 53719
Phone: (608)441-2820

SCORE Office (Manitowoc)
1515 Memorial Dr.
PO Box 903
Manitowoc, WI 54221-0903
Phone: (414)684-5575
Fax: (414)684-1915

SCORE Office (Milwaukee)
310 W. Wisconsin Ave., Ste. 425
Milwaukee, WI 53203
Phone: (414)297-3942
Fax: (414)297-1377

SCORE Office (Central Wisconsin)
1224 Lindbergh Ave.
Stevens Point, WI 54481
Phone: (715)344-7729

SCORE Office (Superior)
Superior Business Center Inc.
1423 N. 8th St.
Superior, WI 54880
Phone: (715)394-7388
Fax: (715)393-7414

SCORE Office (Waukesha)
223 Wisconsin Ave.
Waukesha, WI 53186-4926
Phone: (414)542-4249

SCORE Office (Wausau)
300 3rd St., Ste. 200
Wausau, WI 54402-6190
Phone: (715)845-6231

SCORE Office (Wisconsin Rapids)
2240 Kingston Rd.
Wisconsin Rapids, WI 54494
Phone: (715)423-1830

Wyoming

SCORE Office (Casper)
Federal Bldg., No. 2215
100 East B St.
Casper, WY 82602
Phone: (307)261-6529
Fax: (307)261-6530

VENTURE CAPITAL & FINANCING COMPANIES

This section contains a listing of financing and loan companies in the United States and Canada. These listings are arranged alphabetically by country, state or province, then by city, then by organization name.

CANADA

Alberta

Launchworks Inc.
1902J 11th St., S.E.
Calgary, AB, Canada T2G 3G2
Phone: (403)269-1119
Fax: (403)269-1141
Website: http://
www.launchworks.com
Investment Types: Start-up. Industry
Preferences: Diversified. Geographic
Preferences: Canada.

Native Venture Capital Company,
Inc.
21 Artist View Point, Box 7
Site 25, RR 12
Calgary, AB, Canada T3E 6W3
Phone: (903)208-5380
Milt Pahl, President
Investment Types: Seed, start-up, first
stage, second stage, and leveraged
buyout. Industry Preferences:
Diversified. Geographic Preferences:
Western Canada.

Miralta Capital Inc.
4445 Calgary Trail South
888 Terrace Plaza Alberta
Edmonton, AB, Canada T6H 5R7
Phone: (780)438-3535
Fax: (780)438-3129
Michael Welsh
Preferred Investment Size:
$1,000,000 minimum. Investment
Types: First and second stage, and
leveraged buyout. Industry
Preferences: Diversified
communications, computer related,
electronics, consumer products,
industrial products and equipment.
Geographic Preferences: Canada.

Vencap Equities Alberta Ltd.
10180-101st St., Ste. 1980
Edmonton, AB, Canada T5J 3S4
Phone: (403)420-1171
Fax: (403)429-2541
Preferred Investment Size:
$1,000,000 minimum. Investment
Types: Start-up, first and second
stage, control-block purchases,
leveraged buyout, and mezzanine.
Industry Preferences: Diversified.
Geographic Preferences:
Northwest, Rocky Mountain region,
and Western Canada.

British Columbia

Discovery Capital
5th Fl., 1199 West Hastings
Vancouver, BC, Canada V6E 3T5
Phone: (604)683-3000
Fax: (604)662-3457
E-mail: info@discoverycapital.com
Website: http://
www.discoverycapital.com
Investment Types: Early stage and
start-up. Industry Preferences:

Internet related. Geographic
Preferences: Canada.

Greenstone Venture Partners
1177 West Hastings St.
Ste. 400
Vancouver, BC, Canada V6E 2K3
Phone: (604)717-1977
Fax: (604)717-1976
Website: http://
www.greenstonevc.com
Investment Types: Diversified.
Industry Preferences: Diversified.
Geographic Preferences: Canada.

Growthworks Capital
2600-1055 West Georgia St.
Box 11170 Royal Centre
Vancouver, BC, Canada V6E 3R5
Phone: (604)895-7259
Fax: (604)669-7605
Website: http://www.wofund.com
Mike Philips
Preferred Investment Size: $330,000
to $3,300,000. Investment Types:
Seed, start-up, first and second stage,
balanced, joint ventures, mezzanine,
private placement, research and
development, and management
buyout. Industry Preferences:
Diversified. Geographic Preferences:
British Columbia, Canada.

MDS Discovery Venture
Management, Inc.
555 W. Eighth Ave., Ste. 305
Vancouver, BC, Canada V5Z 1C6
Phone: (604)872-8464
Fax: (604)872-2977
E-mail: info@mds-ventures.com
David Scott, President
Investment Types: Seed, research and
development, start-up, first and
second stages. Industry Preferences:
Biotechnology and communications.
Geographic Preferences: Western
Canada and Northwestern U.S.

Ventures West Management Inc.
1285 W. Pender St., Ste. 280
Vancouver, BC, Canada V6E 4B1
Phone: (604)688-9495
Fax: (604)687-2145
Website: http://
www.ventureswest.com
Investment Types: Seed, research and
development, start-up, first and

second stages. Industry Preferences: Diversified technology. Geographic Preferences: Northeast and Western U.S., Canada.

Nova Scotia

ACF Equity Atlantic Inc.
Purdy's Wharf Tower II
Ste. 2106
Halifax, NS, Canada B3J 3R7
Phone: (902)421-1965
Fax: (902)421-1808
David Wilson
Investment Types: Seed, start-up, first and second stage, balanced, mezzanine, and leveraged buyout. Industry Preferences: Diversified. Geographic Preferences: Canada.

Montgomerie, Huck & Co.
146 Bluenose Dr.
PO Box 538
Lunenburg, NS, Canada B0J 2C0
Phone: (902)634-7125
Fax: (902)634-7130
Christopher Huck
Preferred Investment Size: $300,000 to $500,000. Investment Types: First and second stage, leveraged buyout, mezzanine, and special situation. Industry Preferences: Diversified communications, computer related, and industrial machinery. Geographic Preferences: Canada.

Ontario

IPS Industrial Promotion Services Ltd.
60 Columbia Way, Ste. 720
Markham, ON, Canada L3R 0C9
Phone: (905)475-9400
Fax: (905)475-5003
Azim Lalani
Preferred Investment Size: $500,000 minimum. Investment Types: Control-block purchases, leveraged buyout, second stage, and special situation. Industry Preferences: Diversified. Geographic Preferences: U.S. and Canada.

Betwin Investments Inc.
Box 23110
Sault Ste. Marie, ON, Canada P6A 6W6
Phone: (705)253-0744

Fax: (705)253-0744
D.B. Stinson
Preferred Investment Size: $500,000 to $1,000,000. Investment Types: Second stage. Industry Preferences: Diversified. Geographic Preferences: U.S. and Canada.

Bailey & Company, Inc.
594 Spadina Ave.
Toronto, ON, Canada M5S 2H4
Phone: (416)921-6930
Fax: (416)925-4670
Preferred Investment Size: $500,000 to $1,000,000. Investment Types: Research and development, first stage, and special situations. Industry Preferences: Diversified technology. Geographic Preferences: No preference.

BCE Capital
200 Bay St.
South Tower, Ste. 3120
Toronto, ON, Canada M5J 2J2
Phone: (416)815-0078
Fax: (416)941-1073
Website: http://www.bcecapital.com
Preferred Investment Size: $350,000 to $2,000,000. Investment Types: Seed, start-up, early stage, expansion, and research and development. Industry Preferences: Communications, Internet related, electronics, and computer software and services. Geographic Preferences: Ontario and Western Canada.

Castlehill Ventures
55 University Ave., Ste. 500
Toronto, ON, Canada M5J 2H7
Phone: (416)862-8574
Fax: (416)862-8875
Investment Types: Start-up. Industry Preferences: Telecommunications and computer related. Geographic Preferences: Ontario, Canada.

CCFL Mezzanine Partners of Canada
70 University Ave.
Ste. 1450
Toronto, ON, Canada M5J 2M4
Phone: (416)977-1450
Fax: (416)977-6764
E-mail: info@ccfl.com
Website: http://www.ccfl.com
Paul Benson

Preferred Investment Size: $10,000,000. Investment Types: Generalist PE. Industry Preferences: Diversified. Geographic Preferences: U.S. and Canada.

Celtic House International
100 Simcoe St., Ste. 100
Toronto, ON, Canada M5H 3G2
Phone: (416)542-2436
Fax: (416)542-2435
Website: http://www.celtic-house.com
Investment Types: Early stage. Industry Preferences: Computer software and services, electronics, Internet related, communications, and computer hardware. Geographic Preferences: U.S. and Canada.

Clairvest Group Inc.
22 St. Clair Ave. East
Ste. 1700
Toronto, ON, Canada M4T 2S3
Phone: (416)925-9270
Fax: (416)925-5753
Jeff Parr
Preferred Investment Size: $5,000,000 minimum. Investment Types: Balanced, control-block purchases, later stage, leveraged buyout, and special situation. Industry Preferences: Diversified. Geographic Preferences: U.S. and Canada.

Crosbie & Co., Inc.
One First Canadian Place
9th Fl.
PO Box 116
Toronto, ON, Canada M5X 1A4
Phone: (416)362-7726
Fax: (416)362-3447
E-mail: info@crosbieco.com
Website: http://www.crosbieco.com
Investment Types: Acquisition, distressed debt, expansion, generalist PE, later stage, leveraged and management buyouts, mezzanine, private placement, recaps, special situations, and turnarounds. Industry Preferences: Diversified. Geographic Preferences: Ontario, Canada.

Drug Royalty Corp.
Eight King St. East
Ste. 202
Toronto, ON, Canada M5C 1B5
Phone: (416)863-1865

Fax: (416)863-5161
Harry K. Loveys
Preferred Investment Size:
$4,000,000 to $5,000,000. Investment
Types: Research and development
and special situation. Industry
Preferences: Biotechnology and
medical/health related. Geographic
Preferences: No preference.

Grieve, Horner, Brown & Asculai
8 King St. E, Ste. 1704
Toronto, ON, Canada M5C 1B5
Phone: (416)362-7668
Fax: (416)362-7660
Preferred Investment Size: $300,000
to $500,000. Investment Types:
Start-up, first and second stages.
Industry Preferences: Diversified.
Geographic Preferences: Entire U.S.
and Canada.

Jefferson Partners
77 King St. West
Ste. 4010
PO Box 136
Toronto, ON, Canada M5K 1H1
Phone: (416)367-1533
Fax: (416)367-5827
Website: http://www.jefferson.com
Preferred Investment Size:
$3,000,000 to $10,000,000.
Investment Types: Seed and
expansion. Industry Preferences:
Communications and media,
software, and Internet related.
Geographic Preferences: Northeastern
U.S. and Canada.

J.L. Albright Venture Partners
Canada Trust Tower, 161 Bay St.
Ste. 4440
PO Box 215
Toronto, ON, Canada M5J 2S1
Phone: (416)367-2440
Fax: (416)367-4604
Website: http://www.jlaventures.com
Jon Prosser
Investment Types: First and second
stage. Industry Preferences: Internet
related, communications, and
computer related. Geographic
Preferences: Canada.

McLean Watson Capital Inc.
One First Canadian Place
Ste. 1410
PO Box 129

Toronto, ON, Canada M5X 1A4
Phone: (416)363-2000
Fax: (416)363-2010
Website: http://
www.mcleanwatson.com
Matt H. Lawton
Investment Types: First and second
stage. Industry Preferences:
Diversified communications,
computer related, laser related, and
fiber optics. Geographic Preferences:
U.S. and Canada.

Middlefield Capital Fund
One First Canadian Place
85th Fl.
PO Box 192
Toronto, ON, Canada M5X 1A6
Phone: (416)362-0714
Fax: (416)362-7925
Website: http://www.middlefield.com
David Roode
Preferred Investment Size:
$3,000,000 minimum. Investment
Types: Second stage, control-block
purchases, industry rollups, leveraged
buyout, and mezzanine. Industry
Preferences: Diversified. Geographic
Preferences: U.S. and Canada.

Mosaic Venture Partners
24 Duncan St.
Ste. 300
Toronto, ON, Canada M5V 3M6
Phone: (416)597-8889
Fax: (416)597-2345
Investment Types: Early stage.
Industry Preferences: Internet related.
Geographic Preferences: U.S. and
Canada.

Onex Corp.
161 Bay St.
PO Box 700
Toronto, ON, Canada M5J 2S1
Phone: (416)362-7711
Fax: (416)362-5765
Anthony Munk
Preferred Investment Size:
$10,000,000 minimum. Investment
Types: Control-block purchases,
leveraged buyout, and special
situations. Industry Preferences:
Diversified. Geographic Preferences:
U.S. and Canada.

Penfund Partners Inc.
145 King St. West

Ste. 1920
Toronto, ON, Canada M5H 1J8
Phone: (416)865-0300
Fax: (416)364-6912
Website: http://www.penfund.com
David Collins
Preferred Investment Size: $667,000
to $4,670,000. Investment Types:
Generalist PE, leveraged and
management buyouts, and mezzanine.
Industry Preferences: Diversified.
Geographic Preferences: Canada.

Primaxis Technology Ventures Inc.
1 Richmond St. West, 8th Fl.
Toronto, ON, Canada M5H 3W4
Phone: (416)313-5210
Fax: (416)313-5218
Website: http://www.primaxis.com
Investment Types: Seed and early
stage. Industry Preferences:
Telecommunications, electronics, and
manufacturing. Geographic
Preferences: Canada.

Priveq Capital Funds
240 Duncan Mill Rd., Ste. 602
Toronto, ON, Canada M3B 3P1
Phone: (416)447-3330
Fax: (416)447-3331
E-mail: priveq@sympatico.ca
Preferred Investment Size:
$1,000,000 minimum. Investment
Types: Industry rollups, leveraged
buyout, mezzanine, recaps, second
stage, and special situation. Industry
Preferences: Diversified. Geographic
Preferences: Mid Atlantic, Midwest,
Northeast, Northwest, and
Southeastern U.S., and Canada.

Roynat Ventures
40 King St. West, 26th Fl.
Toronto, ON, Canada M5H 1H1
Phone: (416)933-2667
Fax: (416)933-2783
Website: http://
www.roynatcapital.com
Bob Roy
Investment Types: Early stage and
expansion. Industry Preferences:
Diversified. Geographic Preferences:
Canada.

Tera Capital Corp.
366 Adelaide St. East, Ste. 337
Toronto, ON, Canada M5A 3X9
Phone: (416)368-1024

Fax: (416)368-1427
Investment Types: Balanced. Industry Preferences: Computer related and biotechnology. Geographic Preferences: U.S. and Canada.

Working Ventures Canadian Fund Inc.
250 Bloor St. East, Ste. 1600
Toronto, ON, Canada M4W 1E6
Phone: (416)934-7718
Fax: (416)929-0901
Website: http://
www.workingventures.ca
Preferred Investment Size: $334,000 minimum. Investment Types: No preference. Industry Preferences: Diversified. Geographic Preferences: Ontario and Western Canada.

Quebec

Altamira Capital Corp.
202 University
Niveau de Maisoneuve, Bur. 201
Montreal, QC, Canada H3A 2A5
Phone: (514)499-1656
Fax: (514)499-9570
Preferred Investment Size: $1,000,000 minimum. Investment Types: First stage. Industry Preferences: Diversified. Geographic Preferences: No preference.

Federal Business Development Bank
Venture Capital Division
Five Place Ville Marie, Ste. 600
Montreal, QC, Canada H3B 5E7
Phone: (514)283-1896
Fax: (514)283-5455
Preferred Investment Size: $1,000,000. Investment Types: Seed, start-up, first and second stage, mezzanine, research and development, and leveraged buyout. Industry Preferences: Biotechnology; Internet related; computer software, hardware, and services. Geographic Preferences: Canada.

Hydro-Quebec Capitech Inc.
75 Boul, Rene Levesque Quest
Montreal, QC, Canada H2Z 1A4
Phone: (514)289-4783
Fax: (514)289-5420
Website: http://www.hqcapitech.com
Investment Types: Seed, start-up, early, first and second stage,

balanced, expansion, and mezzanine. Industry Preferences: Diversified. Geographic Preferences: U.S. and Canada.

Investissement Desjardins
2 complexe Desjardins
C.P. 760
Montreal, QC, Canada H5B 1B8
Phone: (514)281-7131
Fax: (514)281-7808
Website: http://www.desjardins.com/id
Preferred Investment Size: $5,000,000 minimum. Investment Types: Start-up, first and second stage, control-block purchases, mezzanine, and leveraged buyout. Industry Preferences: Diversified. Geographic Preferences: Quebec, Canada.

Marleau Lemire Inc.
One Place Ville-Marie, Ste. 3601
Montreal, QC, Canada H3B 3P2
Phone: (514)877-3800
Fax: (514)875-6415
Jean Francois Perrault
Preferred Investment Size: $3,000,000 minimum. Investment Types: Second stage, mezzanine, leveraged buyout, and special situation. Industry Preferences: Diversified. Geographic Preferences: Canada.

Speirs Consultants Inc.
365 Stanstead
Montreal, QC, Canada H3R 1X5
Phone: (514)342-3858
Fax: (514)342-1977
Derek Speirs
Preferred Investment Size: $1,000,000 minimum. Investment Types: Start-up, first and second stage, control-block purchases, industry rollups, leveraged buyout, mezzanine, research and development, and special situation. Industry Preferences: Diversified. Geographic Preferences: Canada.

Tecnocap Inc.
4028 Marlowe
Montreal, QC, Canada H4A 3M2
Phone: (514)483-6009
Fax: (514)483-6045
Website: http://www.technocap.com

Preferred Investment Size: $1,000,000 minimum. Investment Types: Early stage and expansion. Industry Preferences: Diversified. Geographic Preferences: Northeast and Southwest U.S., and Central Canada.

Telsoft Ventures
1000, Rue de la Gauchetiere
Quest, 25eme Etage
Montreal, QC, Canada H3B 4W5
Phone: (514)397-8450
Fax: (514)397-8451
Investment Types: First and second stage, and mezzanine. Industry Preferences: Computer related. Geographic Preferences: West Coast, and Western Canada.

Saskatchewan

Saskatchewan Government Growth Fund
1801 Hamilton St., Ste. 1210
Canada Trust Tower
Regina, SK, Canada S4P 4B4
Phone: (306)787-2994
Fax: (306)787-2086
Rob M. Duguid, Vice President, Investing
Investment Types: Start-up, first stage, second stage, and mezzanine. Industry Preferences: Diversified. Geographic Preferences: Western Canada.

UNITED STATES

Alabama

FHL Capital Corp.
600 20th Street North
Suite 350
Birmingham, AL 35203
Phone: (205)328-3098
Fax: (205)323-0001
Kevin Keck, Vice President
Preferred Investment Size: Between $500,000 and $1,000,000. Investment Types: Mezzanine, leveraged buyout, and special situations. Geographic Preferences: Southeast.

Harbert Management Corp.
One Riverchase Pkwy. South
Birmingham, AL 35244

Phone: (205)987-5500
Fax: (205)987-5707
Website: http://www.harbert.net
Charles Miller, Vice President
Preferred Investment Size:
$5,000,000 to $25,000,000.
Investment Types: Leveraged buyout,
special situations and industry roll
ups. Industry Preferences: Oil and gas
not considered. Geographic
Preferences: Entire U.S.

Jefferson Capital Fund
PO Box 13129
Birmingham, AL 35213
Phone: (205)324-7709
Preferred Investment Size: From
$1,000,000. Investment Types:
Leveraged buyout, special situations
and control block purchases. Industry
Preferences: Telephone
communications; consumer leisure
and recreational products; consumer
and industrial, medical and catalog
specialty distribution; industrial
products and equipment; medical/
health related; publishing and
education related. Geographic
Preferences: Northeast, Southeast,
and Middle Atlantic.

Private Capital Corp.
100 Brookwood Pl., 4th Fl.
Birmingham, AL 35209
Phone: (205)879-2722
Fax: (205)879-5121
William Acker, Vice President
Preferred Investment Size:
$1,000,000 to $5,000,000. Investment
Types: Start-up, first stage, second
stage, mezzanine, leveraged buyout,
and special situations. Industry
Preferences: Communications;
computer related; industrial, and
medical product distribution;
electronic components and
instrumentation; energy/natural
resources; medical/health related;
education; and finance and insurance.
Geographic Preferences: Southeast.

21st Century Health Ventures
One Health South Pkwy.
Birmingham, AL 35243
Phone: (256)268-6250
Fax: (256)970-8928
W. Barry McRae

Preferred Investment Size:
$5,000,000. Investment Types: First
stage, second stage, and leveraged
buyout. Industry Preferences:
Medical/Health related. Geographic
Preferences: Entire U.S.

FJC Growth Capital Corp.
200 W. Side Sq., Ste. 340
Huntsville, AL 35801
Phone: (256)922-2918
Fax: (256)922-2909
William B. Noojin, President
Preferred Investment Size: $300,000
and $500,000. Investment Types:
Mezzanine and second stage. Industry
Preferences: Communications,
electronics, hotels, and resort.
Geographic Preferences: Southeast.

Hickory Venture Capital Corp.
301 Washington St. NW
Suite 301
Huntsville, AL 35801
Phone: (256)539-1931
Fax: (256)539-5130
E-mail: hvcc@hvcc.com
Website: http://www.hvcc.com
J. Thomas Noojin, President
Preferred Investment Size:
$1,000,000 - $7,000,000. Investment
Types: First stage, late stage, and
leverage buyout. Industry
Preferences: Communications,
computer and Internet-related,
energy, consumer, and biotechnology.
Geographic Preferences: Southeast,
Midwest, and Texas.

Southeastern Technology Fund
7910 South Memorial Pkwy., Ste. F
Huntsville, AL 35802
Phone: (256)883-8711
Fax: (256)883-8558
Preferred Investment Size: $500,000
to $5,000,000. Investment Types:
Early, first and second stage, and
expansion. Industry Preferences:
Internet related, computer related, and
communications. Geographic
Preferences: Southeast.

Cordova Ventures
4121 Carmichael Rd., Ste. 301
Montgomery, AL 36106
Phone: (334)271-6011
Fax: (334)260-0120
Website: http://
www.cordovaventures.com

Teo F. Dagi
Investment Types: Start-up, early,
second and late stage, and expansion.
Industry Preferences: Diversified.
Geographic Preferences: Southeast.

Small Business Clinic of Alabama/
AG Bartholomew & Associates
PO Box 231074
Montgomery, AL 36123-1074
Phone: (334)284-3640
Preferred Investment Size: From
$2,000,000. Investment Types: Start-
up, first stage, second stage,
leveraged buyout, and special
situations. Industry Preferences:
Communications, computer related,
consumer, distribution, industrial
products and equipment, medical/
health related, education, finance
and insurance, real estate, specialty
consulting, and transportation.
Geographic Preferences: Southeast.

Arizona

Miller Capital Corp.
4909 E. McDowell Rd.
Phoenix, AZ 85008
Phone: (602)225-0504
Fax: (602)225-9024
Website: http://
www.themillergroup.com
Rudy R. Miller, Chairman and
President
Preferred Investment Size:
$1,000,000 to $20,000,000.
Investment Types: First stage, second
stage, and recapitalizations. Industry
Preferences: Communications,
computer-related, electronics,
financial and business services, and
consumer-related. Geographic
Preferences: Entire U.S.

The Columbine Venture Funds
9449 North 90th St., Ste. 200
Scottsdale, AZ 85258
Phone: (602)661-9222
Fax: (602)661-6262
Preferred Investment Size: $300,000 -
$800,000. Investment Types: Seed,
research and development, start-up,
and first stage. Industry Preferences:
Diversified technology. Geographic
Preferences: Southwest, Rocky
Mountains, and West Coast.

Koch Ventures
17767 N. Perimeter Dr., Ste. 101
Scottsdale, AZ 85255
Phone: (480)419-3600
Fax: (480)419-3606
Website: http://
www.kochventures.com
Preferred Investment Size:
$2,000,000 to $10,000,000.
Investment Types: Early stage and
expansion. Industry Preferences:
Electronics, Internet and computer
related, and communications.
Geographic Preferences: U.S.

McKee & Co.
7702 E. Doubletree Ranch Rd.
Suite 230
Scottsdale, AZ 85258
Phone: (480)368-0333
Fax: (480)607-7446
Mark Jazwin, Corporate Finance
Preferred Investment Size: From
$1,000,000. Investment Types:
Second stage, mezzanine, and
leveraged buyout. Industry
Preferences: Communications,
computer related, consumer,
distribution, electronic
components and instrumentation,
energy/natural resources, biosensors,
industrial products and equipment,
medical and health related, finance,
and transportation. Geographic
Preferences: Entire U.S.

Merita Capital Ltd.
7350 E. Stetson Dr., Ste. 108-A
Scottsdale, AZ 85251
Phone: (480)947-8700
Fax: (480)947-8766
Investment Types: First and second
stage, mezzanine, and special
situation. Industry Preferences:
Diversified. Geographic Preferences:
Western U.S.

Valley Ventures/Arizona Growth
Partners L.P.
6720 N. Scottsdale Rd., Ste. 208
Scottsdale, AZ 85253
Phone: (480)661-6600
Fax: (480)661-6262
Investment Types: Second stage,
mezzanine, and leveraged buyout.
Industry Preferences: Diversified.
Geographic Preferences: Southwest
and Rocky Mountains.

Estreetcapital.com
660 South Mill Ave., Ste. 315
Tempe, AZ 85281
Phone: (480)968-8400
Fax: (480)968-8480
Website: http://
www.estreetcapital.com
Industry Preferences: Internet related.
Geographic Preferences: Entire U.S.

Coronado Venture Fund
PO Box 65420
Tucson, AZ 85728-5420
Phone: (520)577-3764
Fax: (520)299-8491
Preferred Investment Size: $100,000
$500,000. Investment Types: Seed,
start-up, first and second stage.
Industry Preferences:
Communications, computer related,
electronic components and
instrumentation, genetic engineering,
industrial products and equipment,
medical and health related, retail, and
robotics. Geographic Preferences: No
preference.

Arkansas

Arkansas Capital Corp.
225 South Pulaski St.
Little Rock, AR 72201
Phone: (501)374-9247
Fax: (501)374-9425
Website: http://www.arcapital.com
Private firm investing own capital.
Interested in financing expansion.

California

Sundance Venture Partners, L.P.
100 Clocktower Place, Ste. 130
Carmel, CA 93923
Phone: (831)625-6500
Fax: (831)625-6590
Preferred Investment Size: $800,000
minimum. Investment Types: First
and second stage, mezzanine,
leveraged buyout, and special
situations. Industry Preferences: No
preference. Geographic Preferences:
Southwest and West Coast.

Westar Capital (Costa Mesa)
949 South Coast Dr., Ste. 650
Costa Mesa, CA 92626
Phone: (714)481-5160
Fax: (714)481-5166

E-mail: mailbox@westarcapital.com
Website: http://
www.westarcapital.com
Alan Sellers, General Partner
Preferred Investment Size:
$5,000,000 to $10,000,000.
Investment Types: Leveraged
buyouts, special situations, control
block purchases, and industry
roll ups. Industry Preferences:
Diversified. Geographic Preferences:
Northwest, Southwest, Rocky
Mountains, and West Coast.

Alpine Technology Ventures
20300 Stevens Creek Boulevard, Ste.
495
Cupertino, CA 95014
Phone: (408)725-1810
Fax: (408)725-1207
Website: http://
www.alpineventures.com
Investment Types: Seed, start-up,
research and development, first and
second stage. Industry Preferences:
Internet-related, communications,
computer-related, distribution,
electronic components and
instrumentation, industrial products
and equipment.

Bay Partners
10600 N. De Anza Blvd.
Cupertino, CA 95014-2031
Phone: (408)725-2444
Fax: (408)446-4502
Website: http://www.baypartners.com
Bob Williams, General Partner
Preferred Investment Size:
$5,000,000 to $15,000,000.
Investment Types: Seed and start-up.
Industry Preferences: Internet,
communications, and computer
related. Geographic Preferences:
National.

Novus Ventures
20111 Stevens Creek Blvd., Ste. 130
Cupertino, CA 95014
Phone: (408)252-3900
Fax: (408)252-1713
Website: http://
www.novusventures.com
Dan Tompkins, Managing General
Partner
Preferred Investment Size: $500,000
to $1 Million. Investment Types:
Start-up, first and early stage,

expansion, and buyouts. Industry Preferences: Information technology. Geographic Preferences: Western U.S.

Triune Capital
19925 Stevens Creek Blvd., Ste. 200
Cupertino, CA 95014
Phone: (310)284-6800
Fax: (310)284-3290
Preferred Investment Size: $1,000,000 minimum. Investment Types: First, second, and late stage; mezzanine; control block; and special situations. Industry Preferences: Diversified technology. Geographic Preferences: West Coast.

Acorn Ventures
268 Bush St., Ste. 2829
Daly City, CA 94014
Phone: (650)994-7801
Fax: (650)994-3305
Website: http:// www.acornventures.com
Preferred Investment Size: $250,000 minimum. Investment Types: Seed, first and second stage, and leveraged buyout. Industry Preferences: Diversified. Geographic Preferences: No preference.

Digital Media Campus
2221 Park Place
El Segundo, CA 90245
Phone: (310)426-8000
Fax: (310)426-8010
E-mail: info@thecampus.com
Website: http:// www.digitalmediacampus.com
Investment Types: Seed and early stage. Industry Preferences: Entertainment and leisure, sports, and media. Geographic Preferences: U.S.

BankAmerica Ventures / BA Venture Partners
950 Tower Ln., Ste. 700
Foster City, CA 94404
Phone: (650)378-6000
Fax: (650)378-6040
Website: http:// www.baventurepartners.com
George Rossman
Preferred Investment Size: $1,000,000 to $12,000,000. Investment Types: Start-up, first and second stage. Industry Preferences:

Computer and Internet related, communications, medical product distribution, electronic components and instrumentation, genetic engineering, and medical/health related. Geographic Preferences: National.

Starting Point Partners
666 Portofino Lane
Foster City, CA 94404
Phone: (650)722-1035
Website: http:// www.startingpointpartners.com
Preferred Investment Size: $100,000 to $1,000,000. Investment Types: Early stage. Industry Preferences: Diversified. Geographic Preferences: U.S.

Opportunity Capital Partners
2201 Walnut Ave., Ste. 210
Fremont, CA 94538
Phone: (510)795-7000
Fax: (510)494-5439
Website: http://www.ocpcapital.com
Peter Thompson, Managing Partner
Preferred Investment Size: $100,000 to $1,500,000. Investment Types: Second stage, late stage, mezzanine, leveraged buyout, and industry roll ups. Industry Preferences: Internet related, consumer related, communications, computer, and medical/health related. Geographic Preferences: Entire U.S.

Imperial Ventures Inc.
9920 S. La Cienega Boulevar, 14th Fl.
Inglewood, CA 90301
Phone: (310)417-5409
Fax: (310)338-6115
Preferred Investment Size: $500,000 to $2,000,000. Investment Types: Second stage and leveraged buyout. Industry Preferences: Diversified. Geographic Preferences: No preference.

Ventana Global (Irvine)
18881 Von Karman Ave., Ste. 1150
Irvine, CA 92612
Phone: (949)476-2204
Fax: (949)752-0223
Website: http:// www.ventanaglobal.com
Scott A. Burri, Managing Director

Preferred Investment Size: $1,000,000 minimum. Investment Types: First and second stage, seed, special situation, and mezzanine. Industry Preferences: Diversified technology. Geographic Preferences: Southwest.

Integrated Consortium Inc.
50 Ridgecrest Rd.
Kentfield, CA 94904
Phone: (415)925-0386
Fax: (415)461-2726
Preferred Investment Size: $1,000,000. Investment Types: First and second stage, control-block purchases, industry rollups, leveraged buyouts, and mezzanine. Industry Preferences: Entertainment and leisure, retail, computer stores, franchises, food/beverage, consumer products and services. Geographic Preferences: West Coast.

Enterprise Partners
979 Ivanhoe Ave., Ste. 550
La Jolla, CA 92037
Phone: (858)454-8833
Fax: (858)454-2489
Website: http://www.epvc.com
Preferred Investment Size: $1,000,000 to $20,000,000. Investment Types: Early stage. Industry Preferences: Diversified. Geographic Preferences: Entire U.S.

Domain Associates
28202 Cabot Rd., Ste. 200
Laguna Niguel, CA 92677
Phone: (949)347-2446
Fax: (949)347-9720
Website: http://www.domainvc.com
Preferred Investment Size: $1,000,000 to $20,000,000. Investment Types: Seed, first stage and second stage, expansion, private placement, research and development, and balanced. Industry Preferences: Electronics, computer, biotechnology, and medical/health related. Geographic Preferences: Entire U.S.

Cascade Communications Ventures
60 E. Sir Francis Drake Blvd., Ste. 300
Larkspur, CA 94939
Phone: (415)925-6500
Fax: (415)925-6501

Dennis Brush
Preferred Investment Size:
$1,000,000 to $5,000,000. Investment
Types: Leveraged buyout and special
situations. Industry Preferences:
Communications and franchises.
Geographic Preferences: Entire U.S
and Canada.

Allegis Capital
One First St., Ste. Two
Los Altos, CA 94022
Phone: (650)917-5900
Fax: (650)917-5901
Website: http://
www.allegiscapital.com
Robert R. Ackerman, Jr.
Investment Types: Seed and early
stage. Industry Preferences:
Diversified.
Geographic Preferences: West Coast
and District of Columbia.

Aspen Ventures
1000 Fremont Ave., Ste. 200
Los Altos, CA 94024
Phone: (650)917-5670
Fax: (650)917-5677
Website: http://
www.aspenventures.com
Alexander Cilento, Partner
Preferred Investment Size: $500,000
to $3,500,000. Investment Policies:
Equity. Investment Types: Seed, and
early stage. Industry Preferences:
Communications, computer related,
medical/health, biotechnology, and
electronics. Geographic Preferences:
West Coast.

AVI Capital L.P.
1 First St., Ste. 2
Los Altos, CA 94022
Phone: (650)949-9862
Fax: (650)949-8510
Website: http://www.avicapital.com
Brian J. Grossi, General Partner
Preferred Investment Size:
$1,000,000 to $2 million. Investment
Policies: Equity Only. Investment
Types: Seed, start-up, first and second
stage, and special situations. Industry
Preferences: Computer hardware,
software, and services; Internet
related; communications; electronics;
energy; and medical/health.
Geographic Preferences: West Coast.

Bastion Capital Corp.
1999 Avenue of the Stars, Ste. 2960
Los Angeles, CA 90067
Phone: (310)788-5700
Fax: (310)277-7582
E-mail: ga@bastioncapital.com
Website: http://
www.bastioncapital.com
James Villanueva, Vice President
Preferred Investment Size:
$10,000,000 minimum. Investment
Types: Leveraged buyout, special
situations and control block
purchases. Industry Preferences:
Diversified. Geographic Preferences:
Entire U.S. and Canada.

Davis Group
PO Box 69953
Los Angeles, CA 90069-0953
Phone: (310)659-6327
Fax: (310)659-6337
Roger W. Davis, Chairman
Preferred Investment Size: $100,000
minimum. Investment Types: Early
stages, leveraged buyouts, and special
situations. Industry Preferences:
Diversified. Geographic Preferences:
International.

Developers Equity Corp.
1880 Century Park East, Ste. 211
Los Angeles, CA 90067
Phone: (213)277-0300
Investment Types: Seed, start-up, and
leverage buyout. Industry
Preferences: Industrial products and
machinery, transportation, and real
estate.

Far East Capital Corp.
350 S. Grand Ave., Ste. 4100
Los Angeles, CA 90071
Phone: (213)687-1361
Fax: (213)617-7939
E-mail:
free@fareastnationalbank.com
Preferred Investment Size: $100,000
to $300,000. Investment Types: First
stage, second stage, mezzanine, and
special situations. Industry
Preferences: Communications,
computer and Internet related,
electronic components and
instrumentation, genetic engineering,
medical/health related. Geographic
Preferences: West Coast.

Kline Hawkes & Co.
11726 San Vicente Blvd., Ste. 300
Los Angeles, CA 90049
Phone: (310)442-4700
Fax: (310)442-4707
Website: http://
www.klinehawkes.com
Robert M. Freiland, Partner
Preferred Investment Size:
$4,000,000 to $10,000,000.
Investment Types: Second and later
stage, private placement, and
expansion. Industry Preferences:
Diversified technology. Geographic
Preferences: West Coast.

Lawrence Financial Group
701 Teakwood
PO Box 491773
Los Angeles, CA 90049
Phone: (310)471-4060
Fax: (310)472-3155
Larry Hurwitz
Preferred Investment Size: $500,000
to $1,000,000. Investment Types:
Second stage. Industry Preferences:
Diversified. Geographic Preferences:
West Coast.

Riordan Lewis & Haden
300 S. Grand Ave., 29th Fl.
Los Angeles, CA 90071
Phone: (213)229-8500
Fax: (213)229-8597
Jonathan Leach
Preferred Investment Size:
$2,000,000 minimum. Investment
Types: First and second stage, start-
up, leveraged buyouts, and special
situations. Industry Preferences:
Diversified. Geographic Preferences:
West Coast.

Union Venture Corp.
445 S. Figueroa St., 9th Fl.
Los Angeles, CA 90071
Phone: (213)236-4092
Fax: (213)236-6329
Preferred Investment Size: $300,000
to $500,000. Investment Types:
Second stage, mezzanine, leveraged
buyout, and special situations.
Industry Preferences:
Communications, computer related.
Geographic Preferences: National.

Wedbush Capital Partners
1000 Wilshire Blvd.

Los Angeles, CA 90017
Phone: (213)688-4545
Fax: (213)688-6642
Website: http://www.wedbush.com
Preferred Investment Size: $500,000 minimum. Investment Types: Second stage, mezzanine, and leveraged buyouts. Industry Preferences: Diversified computer technology, consumer related, distribution, and healthcare. Geographic Preferences: West Coast.

Advent International Corp.
2180 Sand Hill Rd., Ste. 420
Menlo Park, CA 94025
Phone: (650)233-7500
Fax: (650)233-7515
Website: http://
www.adventinternational.com
Preferred Investment Size:
$1,000,000 minimum. Investment Types: Start-up, first and second stage, mezzanine, leveraged buyout, special
situations, recaps, and acquisitions. Industry Preferences: Diversified. Geographic Preferences: Entire U.S. and Canada.

Altos Ventures
2882 Sand Hill Rd., Ste. 100
Menlo Park, CA 94025
Phone: (650)234-9771
Fax: (650)233-9821
Website: http://www.altosvc.com
Investment Types: Start-up, seed, first and second stage. Industry Preferences: Internet and computer related, consumer related, medical/ health. Geographic Preferences: West Coast.

Applied Technology
1010 El Camino Real, Ste. 300
Menlo Park, CA 94025
Phone: (415)326-8622
Fax: (415)326-8163
Ellie McCormack, Partner
Investment Types: Seed, start-up, first and second stage, research and development. Industry Preferences: Diversified. Geographic Preferences: Entire U.S.

APV Technology Partners
535 Middlefield, Ste. 150
Menlo Park, CA 94025

Phone: (650)327-7871
Fax: (650)327-7631
Website: http://www.apvtp.com
Preferred Investment Size:
$2,000,000 to $10,000,000.
Investment Types: Early stage.
Industry Preferences: Diversified.
Geographic Preferences: Entire U.S.

August Capital Management
2480 Sand Hill Rd., Ste. 101
Menlo Park, CA 94025
Phone: (650)234-9900
Fax: (650)234-9910
Website: http://www.augustcap.com
Andrew S. Rappaport, General Partner
Preferred Investment Size:
$1,000,000 to $5,000,000. Investment Types: Start-up, first stage and special situations. Industry Preferences: Communications, computer related, distribution, and electronic components and instrumentation. Geographic Preferences: Northwest, Southwest, Rocky Mountains and West Coast.

Baccharis Capital Inc.
2420 Sand Hill Rd., Ste. 100
Menlo Park, CA 94025
Phone: (650)324-6844
Fax: (650)854-3025
Michelle von Roedelbronn
Preferred Investment Size:
$1,000,000 minimum. Investment Types: Start-up, first stage and second stage, mezzanine and special situations. Industry Preferences: Diversified. Geographic Preferences: West Coast.

Benchmark Capital
2480 Sand Hill Rd., Ste. 200
Menlo Park, CA 94025
Phone: (650)854-8180
Fax: (650)854-8183
E-mail: info@benchmark.com
Website: http://www.benchmark.com
Investment Types: Seed, research and development, start-up, first and second stage, and special situations. Industry Preferences: Communications, computer related, and electronic components and instrumentation. Geographic Preferences: Southwest and West Coast.

Bessemer Venture Partners (Menlo Park)
535 Middlefield Rd., Ste. 245
Menlo Park, CA 94025
Phone: (650)853-7000
Fax: (650)853-7001
Website: http://www.bvp.com
Investment Types: Seed, research and development, start-up, first stages, leveraged buyout, special situations, and expansion. Industry Preferences: Communications, computer related, consumer products, distribution, and electronics. Geographic Preferences: Entire U.S.

The Cambria Group
1600 El Camino Real Rd., Ste. 155
Menlo Park, CA 94025
Phone: (650)329-8600
Fax: (650)329-8601
Website: http://
www.cambriagroup.com
Paul L. Davies, III, Managing Principal
Preferred Investment Size:
$3,000,000. Investment Types: Second stage, mezzanine, leveraged buyout, special situations, and control block purchases. Industry Preferences: Diversified. Geographic Preferences: Entire U.S.

Canaan Partners
2884 Sand Hill Rd., Ste. 115
Menlo Park, CA 94025
Phone: (650)854-8092
Fax: (650)854-8127
Website: http://www.canaan.com
Preferred Investment Size: $5,00,000 to $20,000,000. Investment Types: First and second stage, and expansion. Industry Preferences: Diversified.
Geographic Preferences: Entire U.S.

Capstone Ventures
3000 Sand Hill Rd., Bldg. One, Ste. 290
Menlo Park, CA 94025
Phone: (650)854-2523
Fax: (650)854-9010
Website: http://www.capstonevc.com
Eugene J. Fischer
Preferred Investment Size: $500,000 to $3,000,000. Investment Types: First and second stage, early, and expansion. Industry Preferences:

Diversified high technology.
Geographic Preferences: Diversified.

Comdisco Venture Group (Silicon
Valley)
3000 Sand Hill Rd., Bldg. 1, Ste. 155
Menlo Park, CA 94025
Phone: (650)854-9484
Fax: (650)854-4026
Preferred Investment Size: $300,000
to $20,000,000. Investment Types:
Seed, start-up, first and second stage.
Industry Preferences: Diversified.
Geographic Preferences: No
preference.

Commtech International
535 Middlefield Rd., Ste. 200
Menlo Park, CA 94025
Phone: (650)328-0190
Fax: (650)328-6442
Preferred Investment Size: $300,000
to $500,000. Investment Types: Seed
and start-up. Industry Preferences:
Diversified. Geographic Preferences:
West Coast.

Compass Technology Partners
1550 El Camino Real, Ste. 275
Menlo Park, CA 94025-4111
Phone: (650)322-7595
Fax: (650)322-0588
Website: http://
www.compasstechpartners.com
Leon Dulberger, General Partner
Investment Types: Mezzanine,
leveraged buyout, and special
situations. Industry Preferences:
Diversified high technology.
Geographic Preferences: National.

Convergence Partners
3000 Sand Hill Rd., Ste. 235
Menlo Park, CA 94025
Phone: (650)854-3010
Fax: (650)854-3015
Website: http://
www.convergencepartners.com
Preferred Investment Size:
$2,000,000 to $10,000,000.
Investment Types: Seed, start-up,
research and development, early and
late stage, and mezzanine. Industry
Preferences: Communications,
computer related, electronic
components and instrumentation, and
interactive media. Geographic
Preferences: West Coast.

The Dakota Group
PO Box 1025
Menlo Park, CA 94025
Phone: (650)853-0600
Fax: (650)851-4899
E-mail: info@dakota.com
Stephen A. Meyer, General Partner
Preferred Investment Size: $300,000
to $500,000. Investment Types: Early
and later stages, and special
situations. Industry Preferences:
Diversified computer and
communications technology,
education, and publishing.
Geographic Preferences: National.

Delphi Ventures
3000 Sand Hill Rd.
Bldg. One, Ste. 135
Menlo Park, CA 94025
Phone: (650)854-9650
Fax: (650)854-2961
Website: http://
www.delphiventures.com
Preferred Investment Size: $500,000
minimum. Investment Types: Seed,
start-up, first and second stage.
Industry Preferences: Medical/health
related, Internet related,
biotechnology, computer software
and services. Geographic Preferences:
Entire U.S.

El Dorado Ventures
2884 Sand Hill Rd., Ste. 121
Menlo Park, CA 94025
Phone: (650)854-1200
Fax: (650)854-1202
Website: http://
www.eldoradoventures.com
Preferred Investment Size: $500,000
to $5,000,000. Investment Types:
Seed, start-up, first and second stage.
Industry Preferences:
Communications, computer and
Internet related, electronics, and
industrial products and equipment.
Geographic Preferences: West Coast.

Glynn Ventures
3000 Sand Hill Rd., Bldg. 4, Ste. 235
Menlo Park, CA 94025
Phone: (650)854-2215
John W. Glynn, Jr., General Partner
Preferred Investment Size: $300,000
to $500,000. Investment Types:
Start-up, first and second stage,
leveraged buyout, and mezzanine.

Industry Preferences: Diversified
computer and communications
technology, and medical/health.
Geographic Preferences: East and
West Coast.

Indosuez Ventures
2180 Sand Hill Rd., Ste. 450
Menlo Park, CA 94025
Phone: (650)854-0587
Fax: (650)323-5561
Website: http://
www.indosuezventures.com
Preferred Investment Size: $250,000
to $1,500,000. Investment Types:
Start-up, first and second stage, and
mezzanine. Industry Preferences:
Diversified. Geographic Preferences:
West Coast.

Institutional Venture Partners
3000 Sand Hill Rd., Bldg. 2, Ste. 290
Menlo Park, CA 94025
Phone: (650)854-0132
Fax: (650)854-5762
Website: http://www.ivp.com
Preferred Investment Size: $500,000
minimum. Investment Types: Seed,
start-up, first and second stage, and
special situations. Industry
Preferences: Diversified. Geographic
Preferences: International.

Interwest Partners (Menlo Park)
3000 Sand Hill Rd., Bldg. 3, Ste. 255
Menlo Park, CA 94025-7112
Phone: (650)854-8585
Fax: (650)854-4706
Website: http://www.interwest.com
Preferred Investment Size:
$2,000,000 to $25,000,000.
Investment Types: Seed, research and
development, start-up, first and
second stage, expansion, and special
situations. Industry Preferences:
Diversified. Geographic Preferences:
Entire U.S.

Kleiner Perkins Caufield & Byers
(Menlo Park)
2750 Sand Hill Rd.
Menlo Park, CA 94025
Phone: (650)233-2750
Fax: (650)233-0300
Website: http://www.kpcb.com
Preferred Investment Size: $500,000.
Investment Types: Seed, start-up,

first and second stage. Industry Preferences: Diversified. Geographic Preferences: West Coast.

Magic Venture Capital LLC
1010 El Camino Real, Ste. 300
Menlo Park, CA 94025
Phone: (650)325-4149
Patrick Lynn
Preferred Investment Size: $100,000 to $1,000,000. Investment Types: Seed, start-up, first stage. Industry Preferences: Medical/health related. Geographic Preferences: West Coast.

Matrix Partners
2500 Sand Hill Rd., Ste. 113
Menlo Park, CA 94025
Phone: (650)854-3131
Fax: (650)854-3296
Website: http://
www.matrixpartners.com
Andrew W. Verlahen, General Partner
Preferred Investment Size: $500,000 to $1,000,000. Investment Types: Start-up, early, first and second stage, and leveraged buyout. Industry Preferences: Communications, computer related, medical/health, and electronic components and instrumentation. Geographic Preferences: Entire U.S.

Mayfield Fund
2800 Sand Hill Rd.
Menlo Park, CA 94025
Phone: (650)854-5560
Fax: (650)854-5712
Website: http://www.mayfield.com
Preferred Investment Size: $250,000 minimum. Investment Types: Seed, start-up, first and second stage, and recapitalization. Industry Preferences: Diversified. Geographic Preferences: Northwest, Rocky Mountains, and West Coast.

McCown De Leeuw and Co. (Menlo Park)
3000 Sand Hill Rd., Bldg. 3, Ste. 290
Menlo Park, CA 94025-7111
Phone: (650)854-6000
Fax: (650)854-0853
Website: http://
www.mdcpartners.com
Christopher Crosby, Principal

Preferred Investment Size: $40,000,000 minimum. Investment Types: Leveraged buyout and special situations. Industry Preferences: Diversified. Geographic Preferences: Entire U.S.

Menlo Ventures
3000 Sand Hill Rd., Bldg. 4, Ste. 100
Menlo Park, CA 94025
Phone: (650)854-8540
Fax: (650)854-7059
Website: http://
www.menloventures.com
H. DuBose Montgomery, General Partner and Managing Director
Venture capital supplier. Provides start-up and expansion financing to companies with experienced management teams, distinctive product lines, and large growing markets. Primary interest is in technology-oriented, Internet, and computer related companies. Investments range from $5,000,000 to $30 million; also provides capital for research and development.

Merrill Pickard Anderson & Eyre
2480 Sand Hill Rd., Ste. 200
Menlo Park, CA 94025
Phone: (650)854-8600
Fax: (650)854-0345
Preferred Investment Size: $1,000,000 maximum. Investment Types: Seed, start-up, first and second stage. Industry Preferences: Diversified technology. Geographic Preferences: No preference.

New Enterprise Associates (Menlo Park)
2490 Sand Hill Rd.
Menlo Park, CA 94025
Phone: (650)854-9499
Fax: (650)854-9397
Website: http://www.nea.com
Ronald H. Kase, General Partner
Preferred Investment Size: $100,000 minimum. Investment Types: Seed, early, start-up, first and second stage, and mezzanine. Industry Preferences: Diversified technology. Geographic Preferences: No preference.

Onset Ventures
2400 Sand Hill Rd., Ste. 150
Menlo Park, CA 94025

Phone: (650)529-0700
Fax: (650)529-0777
Website: http://www.onset.com
Preferred Investment Size: $100,000 minimum. Investment Types: Early stage. Industry Preferences: communications, computer related, medical and health related. Geographic Preferences: West Coast.

Paragon Venture Partners
3000 Sand Hill Rd., Bldg. 1, Ste. 275
Menlo Park, CA 94025
Phone: (650)854-8000
Fax: (650)854-7260
Preferred Investment Size: $500,000 to $1,500,000. Investment Types: Start-up, seed, first and second stage, special situation. Industry Preferences: Diversified. Geographic Preferences: No preference.

Pathfinder Venture Capital Funds (Menlo Park)
3000 Sand Hill Rd., Bldg. 3, Ste. 255
Menlo Park, CA 94025
Phone: (650)854-0650
Fax: (650)854-4706
Jack K. Ahrens, II, Investment Officer
Preferred Investment Size: $200,000 minimum. Investment Types: Seed, start-up, first and second stage, mezzanine, leveraged buyout, and special situations. Industry Preferences: Diversified technology. Geographic Preferences: Entire U.S. and Canada.

Rocket Ventures
3000 Sandhill Rd., Bldg. 1, Ste. 170
Menlo Park, CA 94025
Phone: (650)561-9100
Fax: (650)561-9183
Website: http://
www.rocketventures.com
Preferred Investment Size: $100,000 to $5,000,000. Investment Types: Seed, start-up, and early stage. Industry Preferences: Communications, software, and Internet related. Geographic Preferences: West Coast.

Sequoia Capital
3000 Sand Hill Rd., Bldg. 4, Ste. 280
Menlo Park, CA 94025
Phone: (650)854-3927

Fax: (650)854-2977
E-mail: sequoia@sequioacap.com
Website: http://www.sequoiacap.com
Investment Types: Early, seed, start-up, first and second stage. Industry Preferences: Diversified technology. Geographic Preferences: Western U.S. and international.

Sierra Ventures
3000 Sand Hill Rd., Bldg. 4, Ste. 210
Menlo Park, CA 94025
Phone: (650)854-1000
Fax: (650)854-5593
Website: http://
www.sierraventures.com
Preferred Investment Size: $100,000 minimum. Investment Types: Seed, start-up, first and second stage, recapitalization, and leveraged buyout. Industry Preferences: Diversified. Geographic Preferences: No preference.

Sigma Partners
2884 Sand Hill Rd., Ste. 121
Menlo Park, CA 94025-7022
Phone: (650)853-1700
Fax: (650)853-1717
E-mail: info@sigmapartners.com
Website: http://
www.sigmapartners.com
Lawrence G. Finch, Partner
Investment Types: Seed, start-up, first and second stage, special situation, recap, and control block purchases. Industry Preferences: Diversified technology. Geographic Preferences: U.S.

Sprout Group (Menlo Park)
3000 Sand Hill Rd.
Bldg. 3, Ste. 170
Menlo Park, CA 94025
Phone: (650)234-2700
Fax: (650)234-2779
Website: http://
www.sproutgroup.com
Investment Types: Seed, start-up, first and second stage, mezzanine, leveraged buyout, and special situations. Industry Preferences: Diversified technology. Geographic Preferences: U.S. and foreign countries.

TA Associates (Menlo Park)
70 Willow Rd., Ste. 100

Menlo Park, CA 94025
Phone: (650)328-1210
Fax: (650)326-4933
Website: http://www.ta.com
Michael C. Child, Managing Director
Preferred Investment Size:
$20,000,000 to $60,000,000.
Investment Types: Control-block purchases, leveraged buyout, and special situations. Industry Preferences: Diversified. Geographic Preferences: No preference.

Thompson Clive & Partners Ltd.
3000 Sand Hill Rd., Bldg. 1, Ste. 185
Menlo Park, CA 94025-7102
Phone: (650)854-0314
Fax: (650)854-0670
E-mail: mail@tcvc.com
Website: http://www.tcvc.com
Greg Ennis, Principal
Preferred Investment Size: $500,000 to $1,000,000. Investment Types: Early stage, management buyouts, and special situations. Industry Preferences: Diversified computer and communications technology, electronic instrumentation, genetic engineering, and medical/health. Geographic Preferences: Entire U.S. and International.

Trinity Ventures Ltd.
3000 Sand Hill Rd., Bldg. 1, Ste. 240
Menlo Park, CA 94025
Phone: (650)854-9500
Fax: (650)854-9501
Website: http://
www.trinityventures.com
Lawrence K. Orr, General Partner
Preferred Investment Size:
$5,000,000 to $20,000,000.
Investment Types: Early stage.
Industry Preferences:
Communications, computer and Internet related, consumer products and services, and electronics. Geographic Preferences: Mid-Atlantic and Western U.S.

U.S. Venture Partners
2180 Sand Hill Rd., Ste. 300
Menlo Park, CA 94025
Phone: (650)854-9080
Fax: (650)854-3018
Website: http://www.usvp.com
William K. Bowes, Jr., Founding Partner

Preferred Investment Size: $500,000 minimum. Investment Types: Seed, start-up, first and second stage, and late stage. Industry Preferences: Communications, computer related, consumer products and services, distribution, electronics, and medical/health related. Geographic Preferences: Northwest and West Coast.

USVP-Schlein Marketing Fund
2180 Sand Hill Rd., Ste. 300
Menlo Park, CA 94025
Phone: (415)854-9080
Fax: (415)854-3018
Website: http://www.usvp.com
Venture capital fund. Prefers specialty retailing/consumer products companies.

Venrock Associates
2494 Sand Hill Rd., Ste. 200
Menlo Park, CA 94025
Phone: (650)561-9580
Fax: (650)561-9180
Website: http://www.venrock.com
Ted H. McCourtney, Managing General Partner
Preferred Investment Size: $500,000 minimum. Investment Types: Seed, research and development, start-up, first and second stage. Industry Preferences: Diversified. Geographic Preferences: No preference.

Brad Peery Capital Inc.
145 Chapel Pkwy.
Mill Valley, CA 94941
Phone: (415)389-0625
Fax: (415)389-1336
Brad Peery, Chairman
Preferred Investment Size: $100,000 to $300,000. Investment Types: Second stage financing. Industry Preferences: Communications and media. Geographic Preferences: Entire U.S.

Dot Edu Ventures
650 Castro St., Ste. 270
Mountain View, CA 94041
Phone: (650)575-5638
Fax: (650)325-5247
Website: http://
www.doteduventures.com
Investment Types: Early stage and seed. Industry Preferences: Internet

related. Geographic Preferences:
Entire U.S.

Forrest, Binkley & Brown
840 Newport Ctr. Dr., Ste. 480
Newport Beach, CA 92660
Phone: (949)729-3222
Fax: (949)729-3226
Website: http://www.fbbvc.com
Jeff Brown, Partner
Investment Policies: $1,000,000 to
$10,000,000. Investment Types: First
stage, second stage, expansion, and
balanced. Industry Preferences:
Communications, computer and
Internet related, consumer, electronic
components and instrumentation,
genetic engineering, industrial
products and equipment, and medical/
health related. Geographic
Preferences: National.

Marwit Capital LLC
180 Newport Center Dr., Ste. 200
Newport Beach, CA 92660
Phone: (949)640-6234
Fax: (949)720-8077
Website: http://www.marwit.com
Thomas W. Windsor, Vice President
Preferred Investment Size: $250,000
minimum. Investment Types:
Acquisition, control-block, leveraged
buyout, and mezzanine. Industry
Preferences: Software, transportation,
distribution, and manufacturing.
Geographic Preferences: Entire U.S.

Kaiser Permanente/National Venture
Development
1800 Harrison St., 22nd Fl.
Oakland, CA 94612
Phone: (510)267-4010
Fax: (510)267-4036
Website: http://www.kpventures.com
Preferred Investment Size: $500,000
to $2,000,000. Investment Types:
Balanced, first and second stage,
expansion, joint ventures, and private
placement. Industry Preferences:
Diversified. Geographic Preferences:
Entire U.S. and Canada.

Nu Capital Access Group, Ltd.
7677 Oakport St., Ste. 105
Oakland, CA 94621
Phone: (510)635-7345
Fax: (510)635-7068

Preferred Investment Size: $500,000
to $1,000,000. Investment Types:
First and second stages, leveraged
buyouts, industry rollups, and special
situations. Industry Preferences:
Diversified consumer products and
services, food and industrial product
distribution. Geographic Preferences:
Western U.S.

Inman and Bowman
4 Orinda Way, Bldg. D, Ste. 150
Orinda, CA 94563
Phone: (510)253-1611
Fax: (510)253-9037
Preferred Investment Size:
$1,000,000 minimum. Investment
Types: Start-up, first and second
stage, leveraged buyout, and special
situations. Industry Preferences:
Diversified technology. Geographic
Preferences: West Coast.

Accel Partners (San Francisco)
428 University Ave.
Palo Alto, CA 94301
Phone: (650)614-4800
Fax: (650)614-4880
Website: http://www.accel.com
Preferred Investment Size:
$1,000,000 minimum. Investment
Types: Seed, start-up, and early stage.
Industry Preferences:
Communications, computer related,
medical/health, biotechnology, and
electronic components and
instrumentation. Geographic
Preferences: No preference.

Accenture Technology Ventures
1661 Page Mill Rd.
Palo Alto, CA 94304
Phone: (650)213-2500
Fax: (650)213-2222
Website: http://
www.accenturetechventures.com
Investment Types: Start-up, early and
later stage, balanced, expansion, and
mezzanine. Industry Preferences:
Internet and computer related, and
communications. Geographic
Preferences: Entire U.S.

Advanced Technology Ventures
485 Ramona St., Ste. 200
Palo Alto, CA 94301
Phone: (650)321-8601
Fax: (650)321-0934

Website: http://www.atvcapital.com
Steven Baloff, General Partner
Investment Types: Start-up, first
stage, second stage, and balanced.
Industry Preferences: Diversified.
Geographic Preferences: National.

Anila Fund
400 Channing Ave.
Palo Alto, CA 94301
Phone: (650)833-5790
Fax: (650)833-0590
Website: http://www.anila.com
Investment Types: Early stage.
Industry Preferences:
Telecommunications and Internet
related. Geographic Preferences:
Entire U.S.

Asset Management Company Venture
Capital
2275 E. Bayshore, Ste. 150
Palo Alto, CA 94303
Phone: (650)494-7400
Fax: (650)856-1826
E-mail: postmaster@assetman.com
Website: http://www.assetman.com
Preferred Investment Size: $750,000
minimum. Investment Types: Seed,
start-up, and first stage. Industry
Preferences: Diversified technology.
Geographic Preferences: Northeast,
West Coast.

BancBoston Capital / BancBoston
Ventures
435 Tasso St., Ste. 250
Palo Alto, CA 94305
Phone: (650)470-4100
Fax: (650)853-1425
Website: http://
www.bancbostoncapital.com
Preferred Investment Size:
$1,000,000 to $10,000,000.
Investment Types: Seed, early stage,
acquisition, expansion, later stage,
management buyouts, and
recapitalizations. Industry
Preferences: Diversified. Geographic
Preferences: Entire U.S. and Eastern
Canada.

Charter Ventures
525 University Ave., Ste. 1400
Palo Alto, CA 94301
Phone: (650)325-6953
Fax: (650)325-4762

Website: http://
www.charterventures.com
Investment Types: Seed, start-up, first
and second stage, mezzanine,
leveraged buyout, and special
situations. Industry Preferences:
Diversified. Geographic Preferences:
No preference.

Communications Ventures
505 Hamilton Avenue, Ste. 305
Palo Alto, CA 94301
Phone: (650)325-9600
Fax: (650)325-9608
Website: http://www.comven.com
Clifford Higgerson, General Partner
Preferred Investment Size: $500,000
to $25,000,000. Investment Types:
Seed, start-up, early, first, and second
stage. Industry Preferences:
Communications, Internet related,
electronics, and computer related.
Geographic Preferences: No
preference.

HMS Group
2468 Embarcadero Way
Palo Alto, CA 94303-3313
Phone: (650)856-9862
Fax: (650)856-9864
Industry Preferences:
Communications, computer related,
electronics, and industrial products.
Geographic Preferences: No
preference.

New Vista Capital
540 Cowper St., Ste. 200
Palo Alto, CA 94301
Phone: (650)329-9333
Fax: (650)328-9434
E-mail: fgreene@nvcap.com
Website: http://www.nvcap.com
Frank Greene
Investment Types: Seed, start-up, first
stage, second stage. Industry
Preferences: Communications,
computer related, electronics, and
consumer related. Geographic
Preferences: Western U.S., Rocky
Mountains.

Norwest Equity Partners (Palo Alto)
245 Lytton Ave., Ste. 250
Palo Alto, CA 94301-1426
Phone: (650)321-8000
Fax: (650)321-8010
Website: http://www.norwestvp.com

Charles B. Lennin, Partner
Preferred Investment Size:
$1,000,000 to $25,000,000.
Investment Types: Seed, early and
later stage, and expansion. Industry
Preferences: Diversified. Geographic
Preferences: No preference.

Oak Investment Partners
525 University Ave., Ste. 1300
Palo Alto, CA 94301
Phone: (650)614-3700
Fax: (650)328-6345
Website: http://www.oakinv.com
Preferred Investment Size: $250,000
to $5,000,000. Investment Types:
Seed, start-up, first stage, leveraged
buyout, open market, control-block
purchases, and special situations.
Industry Preferences:
Communications, computer related,
consumer restaurants and retailing,
electronics, genetic engineering, and
medical/health related. Geographic
Preferences: No preference.

Patricof & Co. Ventures, Inc. (Palo
Alto)
2100 Geng Rd., Ste. 150
Palo Alto, CA 94303
Phone: (650)494-9944
Fax: (650)494-6751
Website: http://www.patricof.com
Preferred Investment Size:
$5,000,000 minimum. Investment
Types: Seed, start-up, first and second
stage, mezzanine, and leveraged
buyout. Industry Preferences:
Diversified. Geographic Preferences:
No preference.

RWI Group
835 Page Mill Rd.
Palo Alto, CA 94304
Phone: (650)251-1800
Fax: (650)213-8660
Website: http://www.rwigroup.com
Preferred Investment Size: $500,000
to $4,000,000. Investment Types:
Seed, start-up, first and second stage.
Industry Preferences: Diversified.
Geographic Preferences: West Coast.

Summit Partners (Palo Alto)
499 Hamilton Ave., Ste. 200
Palo Alto, CA 94301
Phone: (650)321-1166
Fax: (650)321-1188

Website: http://
www.summitpartners.com
Christopher W. Sheeline
Preferred Investment Size:
$1,500,000 minimum. Investment
Types: First and second stage,
mezzanine, leveraged buyout, special
situations, and control block
purchases. Industry Preferences:
Diversified. Geographic
Preferences: Entire U.S. and Canada.

Sutter Hill Ventures
755 Page Mill Rd., Ste. A-200
Palo Alto, CA 94304
Phone: (650)493-5600
Fax: (650)858-1854
E-mail: shv@shv.com
Preferred Investment Size: $100,000
minimum. Investment Types: Seed,
start-up, first and second stage.
Industry Preferences: Diversified.
Geographic Preferences: Entire U.S.

Vanguard Venture Partners
525 University Ave., Ste. 600
Palo Alto, CA 94301
Phone: (650)321-2900
Fax: (650)321-2902
Website: http://
www.vanguardventures.com
Donald F. Wood, Partner
Preferred Investment Size: $500,000
to $1,000,000. Investment Types:
Early stages. Industry Preferences:
Diversified computer and
communications technology, genetic
engineering, and electronics.
Geographic Preferences: National.

Venture Growth Associates
2479 East Bayshore St., Ste. 710
Palo Alto, CA 94303
Phone: (650)855-9100
Fax: (650)855-9104
James R. Berdell, Managing Partner
Preferred Investment Size:
$1,000,000 to $5,000,000. Investment
Types: First and second stage,
leveraged buyout, and mezzanine.
Industry Preferences: Diversified
technology, finance and consumer
related. Geographic Preferences:
West Coast.

Worldview Technology Partners
435 Tasso St., Ste. 120
Palo Alto, CA 94301

Phone: (650)322-3800
Fax: (650)322-3880
Website: http://www.worldview.com
Mike Orsak, General Partner
Investment Types: Seed, research and development, start-up, first stage, second stage, mezzanine. Industry Preferences: Diversified technology. Geographic Preferences: National.

Jafco America Ventures, Inc.
505 Hamilton Ste. 310
Palto Alto, CA 94301
Phone: (650)463-8800
Fax: (650)463-8801
Website: http://www.jafco.com
Andrew P. Goldfarb, Senior Managing Director
Preferred Investment Size: $500,000 minimum. Investment Types: First and second stage and mezzanine. Industry Preferences: Diversified technology. Geographic Preferences: No preference.

Draper, Fisher, Jurvetson / Draper Associates
400 Seaport Ct., Ste.250
Redwood City, CA 94063
Phone: (415)599-9000
Fax: (415)599-9726
Website: http://www.dfj.com
J.B. Fox
Preferred Investment Size: $1,000,000 to $5,000,000. Investment Types: Seed, start-up, and first stage. Industry Preferences: Communications, computer and Internet related, electronic components and instrumentation. Geographic Preferences: No preference.

Gabriel Venture Partners
350 Marine Pkwy., Ste. 200
Redwood Shores, CA 94065
Phone: (650)551-5000
Fax: (650)551-5001
Website: http://www.gabrielvp.com
Preferred Investment Size: $500,000 to $7,000,000. Investment Types: Seed, early and first stage. Industry Preferences: Internet and computer related, communications, and electronics. Geographic Preferences: West Coast and Mid Atlantic.

Hallador Venture Partners, L.L.C.
740 University Ave., Ste. 110
Sacramento, CA 95825-6710
Phone: (916)920-0191
Fax: (916)920-5188
E-mail: chris@hallador.com
Chris L. Branscum, Managing Director
Preferred Investment Size: $500,000 to $1,000,000. Investment Types: Early and later stages, and research and development. Industry Preferences: Diversified computer and communications technology, and electronic semiconductors. Geographic Preferences: Western U.S.

Emerald Venture Group
12396 World Trade Dr., Ste. 116
San Diego, CA 92128
Phone: (858)451-1001
Fax: (858)451-1003
Website: http://www.emeraldventure.com
Cherie Simoni
Preferred Investment Size: $100,000 to $50,000,000. Investment Types: Start-up, seed, first and second stage, leveraged buyout, mezzanine, and research and development. Industry Preferences: Diversified. Geographic Preferences: No preference.

Forward Ventures
9255 Towne Centre Dr.
San Diego, CA 92121
Phone: (858)677-6077
Fax: (858)452-8799
E-mail: info@forwardventure.com
Website: http://www.forwardventure.com
Standish M. Fleming, Partner
Preferred Investment Size: $500,000 to $10,000,000. Investment Types: Seed, research and development, start-up, first and second stage, mezzanine, and private placement. Industry Preferences: Biotechnology, and medical/health related. Geographic Preferences: Entire U.S.

Idanta Partners Ltd.
4660 La Jolla Village Dr., Ste. 850
San Diego, CA 92122
Phone: (619)452-9690
Fax: (619)452-2013
Website: http://www.idanta.com

Preferred Investment Size: $500,000 minimum. Investment Types: Seed, start-up, first and second stage. Industry Preferences: Diversified. Geographic Preferences: Entire U.S.

Kingsbury Associates
3655 Nobel Dr., Ste. 490
San Diego, CA 92122
Phone: (858)677-0600
Fax: (858)677-0800
Preferred Investment Size: $500,000 to $1,000,000. Investment Types: Start-up, first and second stage. Industry Preferences: Medical/health, biotechnology, computer and Internet related. Geographic Preferences: West Coast.

Kyocera International Inc.
Corporate Development
8611 Balboa Ave.
San Diego, CA 92123
Phone: (858)576-2600
Fax: (858)492-1456
Preferred Investment Size: $300,000 to $500,000. Investment Types: Second stage. Industry Preferences: Diversified. Geographic Preferences: Northeast, Northwest, West Coast.

Sorrento Associates, Inc.
4370 LaJolla Village Dr., Ste. 1040
San Diego, CA 92122
Phone: (619)452-3100
Fax: (619)452-7607
Website: http://www.sorrentoventures.com
Vincent J. Burgess, Vice President
Preferred Investment Size: $500,000 TO $7,000,000. Investment Policies: Equity only. Investment Types: Start-up, first and second stage, leveraged buyout, special situations, and control block purchases. Industry Preferences: Medicine, health, communications, electronics, special retail. Geographic Preferences: West Coast.

Western States Investment Group
9191 Towne Ctr. Dr., Ste. 310
San Diego, CA 92122
Phone: (619)678-0800
Fax: (619)678-0900
Investment Types: Seed, research and development, start-up, first stage,

leveraged buyout. Industry
Preferences: Computer related,
consumer, electronic components and
instrumentation, medical/health
related. Geographic Preferences:
Western U.S.

Aberdare Ventures
One Embarcadero Center, Ste. 4000
San Francisco, CA 94111
Phone: (415)392-7442
Fax: (415)392-4264
Website: http://www.aberdare.com
Preferred Investment Size: $500,000
to $7,000,000. Investment Types:
Start-up, first and second stage.
Industry Preferences: Diversified.
Geographic Preferences: Entire U.S.

Acacia Venture Partners
101 California St., Ste. 3160
San Francisco, CA 94111
Phone: (415)433-4200
Fax: (415)433-4250
Website: http://www.acaciavp.com
Brian Roberts, Senior Associate
Preferred Investment Size:
$2,000,000 to $10,000,000.
Investment Types:
Seed, start-up, first and second stage,
mezzanine and leveraged buyout.
Industry Preferences: Computer, and
medical/health related. Geographic
Preferences: Entire U.S.

Access Venture Partners
319 Laidley St.
San Francisco, CA 94131
Phone: (415)586-0132
Fax: (415)392-6310
Website: http://
www.accessventurepartners.com
Robert W. Rees, II, Managing
Director
Preferred Investment Size: $250,000
to $5 million. Investment Types:
Seed, start-up, and first stage.
Industry Preferences: Internet related,
biotechnology, communications, and
computer software and services.
Geographic Preferences: Southwest
and Rocky Mountain region.

Alta Partners
One Embarcadero Center, Ste. 4050
San Francisco, CA 94111
Phone: (415)362-4022
Fax: (415)362-6178

E-mail: alta@altapartners.com
Website: http://www.altapartners.com
Jean Deleage, Partner
Preferred Investment Size:
$1,000,000 to $10,000,000.
Investment Types: Seed, start-up, first
and second stage, and mezzanine.
Industry Preferences:
Communications, computer related,
distribution, electronic components
and instrumentation, genetic
engineering, industrial products and
equipment, medical/health related.
Real estate, oil and natural gas
exploration, and environmental not
considered. Geographic Preferences:
West Coast.

Bangert Dawes Reade Davis & Thom
220 Montgomery St., Ste. 424
San Francisco, CA 94104
Phone: (415)954-9900
Fax: (415)954-9901
E-mail: bdrdt@pacbell.net
Lambert Thom, Vice President
Preferred Investment Size: $500,000
to $5,000,000. Investment Types:
Second stage, mezzanine, leveraged
buyout and special situations.
Industry Preferences: Diversified.
Geographic Preferences: No
preference.

Berkeley International Capital Corp.
650 California St., Ste. 2800
San Francisco, CA 94108-2609
Phone: (415)249-0450
Fax: (415)392-3929
Website: http://www.berkeleyvc.com
Arthur I. Trueger, Chairman
Preferred Investment Size:
$3,000,000 to $15,000,000.
Investment Types: Second stage,
mezzanine, leveraged buyout and
special situations. Industry
Preferences: Communications,
computer related, distribution,
electronic components and
instrumentation, industrial products
and equipment, and medical/health
related. Geographic Preferences:
Entire U.S.

Blueprint Ventures LLC
456 Montgomery St., 22nd Fl.
San Francisco, CA 94104
Phone: (415)901-4000
Fax: (415)901-4035

Website: http://
www.blueprintventures.com
Preferred Investment Size:
$3,000,000 to $10,000,000.
Investment Types: Early stage.
Industry Preferences:
Communications and Internet related.
Geographic Preferences: Entire U.S.

Blumberg Capital Ventures
580 Howard St., Ste. 401
San Francisco, CA 94105
Phone: (415)905-5007
Fax: (415)357-5027
Website: http://www.blumberg-
capital.com
Mark Pretorius, Principal
Preferred Investment Size: $500,000
to $5,000,000. Investment Types:
Seed, start-up, first and early stage,
and expansion. Industry Preferences:
Diversified. Geographic Preferences:
Entire U.S.

Burr, Egan, Deleage, and Co. (San
Francisco)
1 Embarcadero Center, Ste. 4050
San Francisco, CA 94111
Phone: (415)362-4022
Fax: (415)362-6178
Private venture capital supplier.
Invests start-up, expansion, and
acquisitions capital nationwide.
Principal concerns are strength of the
management team; large, rapidly
expanding markets; and unique
products for services. Past
investments have been made in the
fields of biotechnology and
pharmaceuticals, cable TV,
chemicals/plastics, communications,
software, computer systems and
peripherals, distributorships, radio
common carriers, electronics and
electrical components, environmental
control, health services, medical
devices and instrumentation, and
radio and cellular
telecommunications. Primarily
interested in medical, electronics, and
media industries.

Burrill & Company
120 Montgomery St., Ste. 1370
San Francisco, CA 94104
Phone: (415)743-3160
Fax: (415)743-3161

Website: http://
www.burrillandco.com
David Collier, Managing Director
Preferred Investment Size: $500,000
to $5,000,000. Investment Types:
Start-up, first and second stage, and
mezzanine. Industry Preferences:
Diversified. Geographic Preferences:
No preference.

CMEA Ventures
235 Montgomery St., Ste. 920
San Francisco, CA 94401
Phone: (415)352-1520
Fax: (415)352-1524
Website: http://
www.cmeaventures.com
Thomas R. Baruch, General Partner
Preferred Investment Size: $100,000
to $1,000,000. Investment Types:
Seed, start-up, first and second stage.
Industry Preferences: Diversified high
technology. Geographic Preferences:
No preference.

Crocker Capital
1 Post St., Ste. 2500
San Francisco, CA 94101
Phone: (415)956-5250
Fax: (415)959-5710
Investment Types: Second stage,
leveraged buyout, and start-up.
Industry Preferences:
Communications, medical/health
related, consumer, retail, food/
beverage, education, industrial
materials, and manufacturing.
Geographic Preferences: West Coast.

Dominion Ventures, Inc.
44 Montgomery St., Ste. 4200
San Francisco, CA 94104
Phone: (415)362-4890
Fax: (415)394-9245
Preferred Investment Size:
$1,000,000 to $10,000,000.
Investment Types: First and second
stage, and mezzanine. Industry
Preferences: Diversified. Geographic
Preferences: No preference.

Dorset Capital
Pier 1, Bay 2
San Francisco, CA 94111
Phone: (415)398-7101
Fax: (415)398-7141
Website: http://
www.dorsetcapital.com

Preferred Investment Size:
$1,000,000 to $10,000,000.
Investment Types: Second and later
stage, expansion, generalist PE,
leveraged and management
buyouts. Industry Preferences:
Consumer retail, food and beverage,
and business services. Geographic
Preferences: Entire U.S.

Gatx Capital
Four Embarcadero Center, Ste. 2200
San Francisco, CA 94904
Phone: (415)955-3200
Fax: (415)955-3449
Preferred Investment Size: $500,000
to $5,000,000. Investment Types:
Early and later stages, and leveraged
buyouts. Industry Preferences:
Diversified technologies, forestry,
and agriculture. Geographic
Preferences:
National and Canada.

IMinds
135 Main St., Ste. 1350
San Francisco, CA 94105
Phone: (415)547-0000
Fax: (415)227-0300
Website: http://www.iminds.com
Preferred Investment Size: $500,000
to $2,000,000. Investment Types:
Seed, start-up, and early stage.
Industry Preferences: Internet and
computer related. Geographic
Preferences: West Coast.

LF International Inc.
360 Post St., Ste. 705
San Francisco, CA 94108
Phone: (415)399-0110
Fax: (415)399-9222
Website: http://www.lfvc.com
Preferred Investment Size: $500,000
to $1,000,000. Investment Types:
Control-block purchases, first and
second stage, expansion, industry
rollups, management buyouts, and
special situations. Industry
Preferences: Consumer related, retail.
Geographic Preferences: Entire U.S.

Newbury Ventures
535 Pacific Ave., 2nd Fl.
San Francisco, CA 94133
Phone: (415)296-7408
Fax: (415)296-7416

Website: http://
www.newburyven.com
Preferred Investment Size: $500,000
to $1,000,000. Investment Types:
Early and later stages, and leveraged
buyout. Industry Preferences:
Diversified high technology.
Geographic Preferences: Eastern and
Western U.S. and Canada.

Quest Ventures (San Francisco)
333 Bush St., Ste. 1750
San Francisco, CA 94104
Phone: (415)782-1414
Fax: (415)782-1415
E-mail: ruby@crownadvisors.com
Lucien Ruby, General Partner
Preferred Investment Size: $100,000
maximum. Investment Types: Seed
and special situations. Industry
Preferences: Diversified. Geographic
Preferences: No preference.

Robertson-Stephens Co.
555 California St., Ste. 2600
San Francisco, CA 94104
Phone: (415)781-9700
Fax: (415)781-2556
Website: http://
www.omegaadventures.com
Private venture capital firm.
Considers investments in any
attractive merging-growth area,
including product and service
companies. Key preferences include
health care, communications and
technology, biotechnology, software,
and information services. Maximum
investment is $5 million.

Rosewood Capital, L.P.
One Maritime Plaza, Ste. 1330
San Francisco, CA 94111-3503
Phone: (415)362-5526
Fax: (415)362-1192
Website: http://
www.rosewoodvc.com
Kevin Reilly, Vice President
Preferred Investment Size:
$1,000,000 to $3,000,000. Investment
Policies: Equity. Investment Types:
Later stages, leveraged buyout, and
special situations. Industry
Preferences: Consumer and Internet
related. Geographic Preferences:
National.

Ticonderoga Capital Inc.
555 California St., No. 4950
San Francisco, CA 94104
Phone: (415)296-7900
Fax: (415)296-8956
Graham K Crooke, Partner
Preferred Investment Size:
$5,000,000 maximum. Investment
Types: Second stage, mezzanine,
leveraged buyout, and consolidation
strategies. Industry Preferences:
Diversified. Geographic Preferences:
Entire U.S. and Canada.

21st Century Internet Venture
Partners
Two South Park
2nd Floor
San Francisco, CA 94107
Phone: (415)512-1221
Fax: (415)512-2650
Website: http://www.21vc.com
Shawn Myers
Preferred Investment Size:
$5,000,000 maximum. Investment
Types: Seed, research and
development, start-up, first and
second stage, mezzanine, leveraged
buyout, and special situations.
Industry Preferences: Diversified.
Geographic Preferences: Entire U.S.
and Canada.

VK Ventures
600 California St., Ste.1700
San Francisco, CA 94111
Phone: (415)391-5600
Fax: (415)397-2744
David D. Horwich, Senior Vice
President
Preferred Investment Size: $100,000
to $250,000. Investment Types:
Second stage, mezzanine, and
leveraged buyout. Industry
Preferences: Diversified. Geographic
Preferences: West Coast.

Walden Group of Venture Capital
Funds
750 Battery St., Seventh Floor
San Francisco, CA 94111
Phone: (415)391-7225
Fax: (415)391-7262
Arthur Berliner
Preferred Investment Size:
$1,000,000 to $7,000,000. Investment
Types Seed, start-up, first and second
stage. Industry Preferences:

Diversified technology. Geographic
Preferences: Entire U.S.

Acer Technology Ventures
2641 Orchard Pkwy.
San Jose, CA 95134
Phone: (408)433-4945
Fax: (408)433-5230
James C. Lu, Managing Director
Preferred Investment Size: $500,000
to $5,000,000. Investment Types:
Seed, start-up, first and second stage.
Industry Preferences: Diversified.
Geographic Preferences: Entire U.S.
and Canada.

Authosis
226 Airport Pkwy., Ste. 405
San Jose, CA 95110
Phone: (650)814-3603
Website: http://www.authosis.com
Investment Types: Seed, first and
second stage. Industry Preferences:
Computer software. Geographic
Preferences: Entire U.S.

Western Technology Investment
2010 N. First St., Ste. 310
San Jose, CA 95131
Phone: (408)436-8577
Fax: (408)436-8625
E-mail: mktg@westerntech.com
Investment Types: Seed, research and
development, start-up, first stage,
second stage, mezzanine, leveraged
buyout, and special situations.
Industry Preferences: Diversified.
Geographic Preferences: National.

Drysdale Enterprises
177 Bovet Rd., Ste. 600
San Mateo, CA 94402
Phone: (650)341-6336
Fax: (650)341-1329
E-mail: drysdale@aol.com
George M. Drysdale, President
Preferred Investment Size: $500,000
to $5,000,000. Investment Types:
First and second stage, mezzanine,
leveraged buyout, and special
situations. Industry Preferences:
Diversified. Geographic Preferences:
West Coast.

Greylock
2929 Campus Dr., Ste. 400
San Mateo, CA 94401
Phone: (650)493-5525
Fax: (650)493-5575

Website: http://www.greylock.com
Preferred Investment Size: $250,000
minimum. Investment Types: Seed,
start-up, early and first stage, and
expansion. Industry Preferences:
Diversified. Geographic Preferences:
Entire U.S.

Technology Funding
2000 Alameda de las Pulgas, Ste. 250
San Mateo, CA 94403
Phone: (415)345-2200
Fax: (415)345-1797
Peter F. Bernardoni, Partner
Small business investment
corporation. Provides primarily late
first-stage, early second-stage, and
mezzanine equity financing. Also
offers secured debt with equity
participation to venture capital backed
companies. Investments range from
$250,000 to $500,000.

2M Invest Inc.
1875 S. Grant St.
Suite 750
San Mateo, CA 94402
Phone: (650)655-3765
Fax: (650)372-9107
E-mail: 2minfo@2minvest.com
Website: http://www.2minvest.com
Preferred Investment Size: $500,000
to $5 million. Investment Types:
Start-up. Industry Preferences:
Communications, computer related,
electronic components and
instrumentation. Non-information
technology companies not
considered. Geographic Preferences:
West Coast.

Phoenix Growth Capital Corp.
2401 Kerner Blvd.
San Rafael, CA 94901
Phone: (415)485-4569
Fax: (415)485-4663
E-mail: nnelson@phxa.com
Preferred Investment Size: $250,000
to $1,000,000. Investment Types:
First and second stage, and
mezzanine. Industry Preferences:
Communications, computer related,
consumer retailing, distribution,
electronics, genetic engineering,
medical/health related, education,
publishing, and transportation.
Geographic Preferences: Entire U.S.

NextGen Partners LLC
1705 East Valley Rd.
Santa Barbara, CA 93108
Phone: (805)969-8540
Fax: (805)969-8542
Website: http://
www.nextgenpartners.com
Preferred Investment Size: $100,000
to $3,000,000. Investment Types:
Seed, start-up, first and second stage,
expansion, and research and
development. Industry Preferences:
Diversified. Geographic Preferences:
Entire U.S. and Canada.

Denali Venture Capital
1925 Woodland Ave.
Santa Clara, CA 95050
Phone: (408)690-4838
Fax: (408)247-6979
E-mail:
wael@denaliventurecapital.com
Website: http://
www.denaliventurecapital.com
Preferred Investment Size: $100,000
to $5,000,000. Investment Types:
Early stage. Industry Preferences:
Medical/health related. Geographic
Preferences: West Coast.

Dotcom Ventures LP
3945 Freedom Circle, Ste. 740
Santa Clara, CA 95045
Phone: (408)919-9855
Fax: (408)919-9857
Website: http://
www.dotcomventuresatl.com
Investment Types: Early, first stage,
and seed. Industry Preferences:
Telecommunications and Internet
related. Geographic Preferences:
Entire U.S.

Silicon Valley Bank
3003 Tasman
Santa Clara, CA 95054
Phone: (408)654-7400
Fax: (408)727-8728
Investment Types: Start-up, first
stage, second stage, mezzanine.
Industry
Preferences: Diversified. Geographic
Preferences: National.

Al Shugart International
920 41st Ave.
Santa Cruz, CA 95062
Phone: (831)479-7852

Fax: (831)479-7852
Website: http://www.alshugart.com
Investment Types: Seed, start-up, and
early stage. Industry Preferences:
Diversified. Geographic Preferences:
U.S.

Leonard Mautner Associates
1434 Sixth St.
Santa Monica, CA 90401
Phone: (213)393-9788
Fax: (310)459-9918
Leonard Mautner
Preferred Investment Size: $100,000
to $300,000. Investment Types: Seed,
start-up, first stage, and special
situation. Industry Preferences:
Diversified. Geographic Preferences:
West Coast.

Palomar Ventures
100 Wilshire Blvd., Ste. 450
Santa Monica, CA 90401
Phone: (310)260-6050
Fax: (310)656-4150
Website: http://
www.palomarventures.com
Preferred Investment Size: $250,000
to $15,000,000. Investment Types:
Seed, start-up, first and early stage,
and expansion. Industry Preferences:
Communications, Internet related,
computer software and services.
Geographic Preferences: West Coast
and Southwest.

Medicus Venture Partners
12930 Saratoga Ave., Ste. D8
Saratoga, CA 95070
Phone: (408)447-8600
Fax: (408)447-8599
Website: http://www.medicusvc.com
Fred Dotzler, General Partner
Preferred Investment Size: $100,000
to $5,000,000. Investment Types:
Early stages. Industry Preferences:
Genetic engineering and healthcare
industry. Geographic Preferences:
Western U.S.

Redleaf Venture Management
14395 Saratoga Ave., Ste. 130
Saratoga, CA 95070
Phone: (408)868-0800
Fax: (408)868-0810
E-mail: nancy@redleaf.com
Website: http://www.redleaf.com
Robert von Goeben, Director

Preferred Investment Size:
$1,000,000 to $4,000,000. Investment
Policies: Equity. Investment Types:
Early and late stage. Industry
Preferences: Internet business related.
Geographic Preferences: Northwest
and Silicon Valley.

Artemis Ventures
207 Second St., Ste. E
3rd Fl.
Sausalito, CA 94965
Phone: (415)289-2500
Fax: (415)289-1789
Website: http://
www.artemisventures.com
Investment Types: Seed, first and
second stage. Industry Preferences:
Internet and computer related,
electronics, and various products.
Geographic Preferences: Northern
U.S. and West Coast.

Deucalion Venture Partners
19501 Brooklime
Sonoma, CA 95476
Phone: (707)938-4974
Fax: (707)938-8921
Preferred Investment Size: $500,000
minimum. Investment Types: Seed,
start-up, first and second stage.
Industry Preferences: Computer
software, biotechnology, education,
energy conservation, industrial
machinery, transportation, financial
services, and publishing. Geographic
Preferences: West Coast.

Windward Ventures
PO Box 7688
Thousand Oaks, CA 91359-7688
Phone: (805)497-3332
Fax: (805)497-9331
Investment Types: Seed, start-up, first
stage, second stage. Industry
Preferences: Communications,
computer related, electronic
components and instrumentation,
genetic engineering, industrial
products and equipment, medical and
health related. Geographic
Preferences: West Coast.

National Investment Management,
Inc.
2601 Airport Dr., Ste.210
Torrance, CA 90505
Phone: (310)784-7600

Fax: (310)784-7605
E-mail: robins621@aol.com
Preferred Investment Size:
$1,000,000 to $5,000,000. Investment
Types: Leveraged buyout. Industry
Preferences: Consumer products and
retailing, distribution, industrial
products and equipment, medical/
health related, and publishing. Real
estate deals not considered.
Geographic Preferences: Entire U.S.

Southern California Ventures
406 Amapola Ave. Ste. 125
Torrance, CA 90501
Phone: (310)787-4381
Fax: (310)787-4382
Preferred Investment Size: $300,000
to $1,000,000. Investment Types:
Seed, start-up, and first stage.
Industry Preferences:
Communications, and medical/health
related. Geographic Preferences:
West Coast.

Sandton Financial Group
21550 Oxnard St., Ste. 300
Woodland Hills, CA 91367
Phone: (818)702-9283
Preferred Investment Size: $100,000
to $250,000. Investment Types: Early
and later stages, and special
situations. Industry Preferences: No
preference. Geographic Preferences:
National and Canada.

Woodside Fund
850 Woodside Dr.
Woodside, CA 94062
Phone: (650)368-5545
Fax: (650)368-2416
Website: http://
www.woodsidefund.com
Matthew Bolton, Analyst
Investment Types: Seed, start-up, first
stage, second stage, and special
situations. Industry Preferences:
Diversified technology. Geographic
Preferences: Western U.S.

Colorado

Colorado Venture Management
Ste. 300
Boulder, CO 80301
Phone: (303)440-4055
Fax: (303)440-4636

Preferred Investment Size: $250,000
to $1,000,000. Investment Types:
Seed, start-up, early, and first and
second stage. Industry Preferences:
Diversified. Geographic Preferences:
Midwest and Rocky Mountain region.

Dean & Associates
4362 Apple Way
Boulder, CO 80301
Fax: (303)473-9900
Investment Types: First stage, second
stage, and mezzanine. Industry
Preferences: Internet related.
Geographic Preferences: Western
U.S.

Roser Ventures LLC
1105 Spruce St.
Boulder, CO 80302
Phone: (303)443-6436
Fax: (303)443-1885
Website: http://
www.roserventures.com
Steven T. Joanis, Associate
Investment Types: Start-up, first
stage, second stage, and special
situations.
Industry Preferences:
Communications, computer related,
distribution, electronic components
and instrumentation, energy/natural
resources, industrial products and
equipment, medical and health
related. Geographic Preferences:
National.

Sequel Venture Partners
4430 Arapahoe Ave., Ste. 220
Boulder, CO 80303
Phone: (303)546-0400
Fax: (303)546-9728
E-mail: tom@sequelvc.com
Website: http://www.sequelvc.com
Kinney Johnson, Partner
Preferred Investment Size: $100,000
to $5,000,000. Investment Types:
Seed, start-up, and early stage.
Industry Preferences: Diversified
technology. Geographic Preferences:
Rocky Mountains.

New Venture Resources
445C E. Cheyenne Mtn. Blvd.
Colorado Springs, CO 80906-4570
Phone: (719)598-9272
Fax: (719)598-9272

Jeffrey M. Cooper, Managing
Director
Preferred Investment Size: $100,000
to $250,000. Investment Types: Seed
and start-up. Industry Preferences:
Diversified technology. Geographic
Preferences: Southwest, Rocky
Mountains.

The Centennial Funds
1428 15th St.
Denver, CO 80202-1318
Phone: (303)405-7500
Fax: (303)405-7575
Website: http://www.centennial.com
Preferred Investment Size: $250,000
to $5,000,000. Investment Types:
Seed, start-up, first and second stage,
and national consolidations. Industry
Preferences: Diversified. Geographic
Preferences: No preference.

Rocky Mountain Capital Partners
1125 17th St., Ste. 2260
Denver, CO 80202
Phone: (303)291-5200
Fax: (303)291-5327
Investment Types: Mezzanine and
leveraged buyout. Industry
Preferences: Diversified.
Communications, computer related,
consumer, distribution, electronic
components and instrumentation, and
industrial products and equipment.
Geographic Preferences: Western
U.S.

Sandlot Capital LLC
600 South Cherry St., Ste. 525
Denver, CO 80246
Phone: (303)893-3400
Fax: (303)893-3403
Website: http://
www.sandlotcapital.com
Preferred Investment Size: $250,000
to $20,000,000. Investment Types:
Seed, start-up, early and first stage,
and special situation. Industry
Preferences: Diversified. Geographic
Preferences: U.S.

Wolf Ventures
50 South Steele St., Ste. 777
Denver, CO 80209
Phone: (303)321-4800
Fax: (303)321-4848
E-mail:
businessplan@wolfventures.com

Website: http://
www.wolfventures.com
David O. Wolf
Preferred Investment Size: $500,000
to $3,000,000. Investment Types:
First stage, second stage, and special
situations. Industry Preferences:
Diversified. Geographic Preferences:
Rocky Mountains.

The Columbine Venture Funds
5460 S. Quebec St., Ste. 270
Englewood, CO 80111
Phone: (303)694-3222
Fax: (303)694-9007
Preferred Investment Size: $100,000
to $250,000. Investment Types: Seed,
research and development, start-up,
and first stage. Industry Preferences:
Diversified technology. Geographic
Preferences: Southwest, Rocky
Mountains, and West Coast.

Investment Securities of Colorado,
Inc.
4605 Denice Dr.
Englewood, CO 80111
Phone: (303)796-9192
Preferred Investment Size: $100,000
to $300,000. Investment Types: Seed
and start-up. Industry Preferences:
Electronic components, industrial
controls and sensors, healthcare
industry. Geographic Preferences:
Rocky Mountain area.

Kinship Partners
6300 S. Syracuse Way, Ste. 484
Englewood, CO 80111
Phone: (303)694-0268
Fax: (303)694-1707
E-mail: block@vailsys.com
Preferred Investment Size: $250,000
to $1,000,000. Investment Types:
Seed, start-up, and early stage.
Industry Preferences: Diversified
computer and communication
technology, specialty retailing,
genetic engineering, and
healthcare. Geographic Preferences:
Within two hours of office.

Boranco Management, L.L.C.
1528 Hillside Dr.
Fort Collins, CO 80524-1969
Phone: (970)221-2297
Fax: (970)221-4787

Preferred Investment Size: $100,000.
Investment Types: Early and late
stage. Industry Preferences:
Agricultural and animal
biotechnology. Geographic
Preferences: Within two hours of
office.

Aweida Ventures
890 West Cherry St., Ste. 220
Louisville, CO 80027
Phone: (303)664-9520
Fax: (303)664-9530
Website: http://www.aweida.com
Investment Types: Seed and first and
second stage. Industry Preferences:
Software, Internet related, and
medical/health related. Geographic
Preferences: West Coast.

Access Venture Partners
8787 Turnpike Dr., Ste. 260
Westminster, CO 80030
Phone: (303)426-8899
Fax: (303)426-8828
E-mail: robert.rees@juno.com
Robert W. Rees, Managing Director
Investment Types: Seed, start-up, first
stage, and special situations.
Industry Preferences: Diversified.
Geographic Preferences: Western and
Midwestern U.S.

Connecticut

Medmax Ventures LP
1 Northwestern Dr., Ste. 203
Bloomfield, CT 06002
Phone: (860)286-2960
Fax: (860)286-9960
Noam Karstaedt
Preferred Investment Size: $500,000
minimum. Investment Types: Seed,
start-up, first and second stage, and
research and development. Industry
Preferences: Biotechnology and
medical/health related. Geographic
Preferences: Northeast.

James B. Kobak & Co.
Four Mansfield Place
Darien, CT 06820
Phone: (203)656-3471
Fax: (203)655-2905
Preferred Investment Size: $100,000
maximum. Investment Types: First
stage. Industry Preferences:
Publishing. Geographic Preferences:
National.

Orien Ventures
1 Post Rd.
Fairfield, CT 06430
Phone: (203)259-9933
Fax: (203)259-5288
Anthony Miadich, Managing General
Partner
Preferred Investment Size: $500,000
minimum. Investment Types: Start-
up, seed, early and first stage.
Industry Preferences: Diversified
technology. Geographic Preferences:
No preference.

ABP Acquisition Corporation
115 Maple Ave.
Greenwich, CT 06830
Phone: (203)625-8287
Fax: (203)447-6187
Preferred Investment Size:
$10,000,000 to $30,000,000.
Investment Types: Leveraged buyout
and acquisition. Industry Preferences:
Diversified. Geographic Preferences:
Mid Atlantic, Northeast, Ontario, and
Quebec.

Catterton Partners
9 Greenwich Office Park
Greenwich, CT 06830
Phone: (203)629-4901
Fax: (203)629-4903
Website: http://www.cpequity.com
Andrew C. Taub
Preferred Investment Size:
$5,000,000 minimum. Investment
Types: First stage, second stage,
leveraged buyout, and special
situations. Industry Preferences:
Consumer products and services,
Internet related, biotechnology.
Geographic Preferences: U.S. and
Canada.

Consumer Venture Partners
3 Pickwick Plz.
Greenwich, CT 06830
Phone: (203)629-8800
Fax: (203)629-2019
E-mail: lcummin@consumer-
venture.com
Linda Cummin, Business Manager
Preferred Investment Size:
$10,000,000 minimum. Investment
Types: Start-up, first and second
stage, and leveraged buyout. Industry

Preferences: Internet related, consumer related. Geographic Preferences: Entire U.S.

Insurance Venture Partners
31 Brookside Dr., Ste. 211
Greenwich, CT 06830
Phone: (203)861-0030
Fax: (203)861-2745
Preferred Investment Size: $500,000 to $50,000,000. Investment Types: First and second stage, and leveraged buyouts. Industry Preferences: Insurance. Geographic Preferences: U.S.

The NTC Group
Three Pickwick Plaza
Ste. 200
Greenwich, CT 06830
Phone: (203)862-2800
Fax: (203)622-6538
Preferred Investment Size: $1,000,000 minimum. Investment Types: Seed, first stage, control-block purchases, and leveraged buyout. Industry Preferences: Electronic components, factory automation, and machinery. Geographic Preferences: Entire U.S.

Regulus International Capital Co., Inc.
140 Greenwich Ave.
Greenwich, CT 06830
Phone: (203)625-9700
Fax: (203)625-9706
E-mail: lee@chaossystems.com
Preferred Investment Size: $100,000 minimum. Investment Types: Start-up, seed, research and development. Industry Preferences: Computer software, industrial materials and machinery, and publishing. Geographic Preferences: National.

Axiom Venture Partners
City Place II
185 Asylum St., 17th Fl.
Hartford, CT 06103
Phone: (860)548-7799
Fax: (860)548-7797
Website: http://
www.axiomventures.com
Preferred Investment Size: $2,000,000 to $5,000,000. Investment Types: Seed, early and later stages, and expansion. Industry Preferences:

Communications, computer and Internet related, distribution, genetic engineering, medical/health related. Geographic Preferences: National.

Conning Capital Partners
City Place II
185 Asylum St.
Hartford, CT 06103-4105
Phone: (860)520-1289
Fax: (860)520-1299
E-mail: pe@conning.com
Website: http://www.conning.com
John B. Clinton, Executive Vice President
Preferred Investment Size: $5,000,000 to $35,000,000. Investment Types: Second and late stage, and expansion. Industry Preferences: Computer related, consumer related, and medical/health related. Geographic Preferences: National.

First New England Capital L.P.
100 Pearl St.
Hartford, CT 06103
Phone: (860)293-3333
Fax: (860)293-3338
E-mail: info@firstnewenglandcapital.com
Website: http://
www.firstnewenglandcapital.com
Preferred Investment Size: $100,000 to $1,000,000. Investment Types: Mezzanine, expansion, and management buyouts. Industry Preferences: Communications, computer related, electronics, consumer related, and medical/health related. Geographic Preferences: Northeastern U.S.

Northeast Ventures
One State St., Ste. 1720
Hartford, CT 06103
Phone: (860)547-1414
Fax: (860)246-8755
Preferred Investment Size: $1,000,000 minimum. Investment Types: Secondary. Industry Preferences: Diversified. Geographic Preferences: National.

Windward Holdings
38 Sylvan Rd.
Madison, CT 06443
Phone: (203)245-6870

Fax: (203)245-6865
Preferred Investment Size: $300,000 minimum. Investment Types: Leveraged buyouts, mezzanine, recaps, and special situations. Industry Preferences: Electronics, food/beverage, and industrial products. Geographic Preferences: Northeastern U.S.

Advanced Materials Partners, Inc.
45 Pine St.
PO Box 1022
New Canaan, CT 06840
Phone: (203)966-6415
Fax: (203)966-8448
E-mail: wkb@amplink.com
Preferred Investment Size: $500,000 to $25,000,000. Investment Types: Seed, start-up, early and late stage, leveraged buyout, research and development, and special situations. Industry Preferences: Diversified. Geographic Preferences: National and Canada.

RFE Investment Partners
36 Grove St.
New Canaan, CT 06840
Phone: (203)966-2800
Fax: (203)966-3109
Website: http://www.rfeip.com
James A. Parsons, General Partner
Preferred Investment Size: $15,000,000 minimum. Investment Policies: Prefer equity investments. Investment Types: Later stage, industry rollups, leveraged buyout, mezzanine, and special situations. Industry Preferences: Diversified. Geographic Preferences: Entire U.S.

Connecticut Innovations, Inc.
999 West St.
Rocky Hill, CT 06067
Phone: (860)563-5851
Fax: (860)563-4877
E-mail: pamela.hartley@ctinnovations.com
Website: http://
www.ctinnovations.com
Preferred Investment Size: $50,000 minimum to $1,000,000. Investment Types: Start-up, first and second stage, joint ventures, and mezzanine. Industry Preferences: Diversified technology. Geographic Preferences: Northeast.

Canaan Partners
105 Rowayton Ave.
Rowayton, CT 06853
Phone: (203)855-0400
Fax: (203)854-9117
Website: http://www.canaan.com
Preferred Investment Size:
$5,000,000 to $20,000,000.
Investment Types: Early, first, and
second stage; and expansion. Industry
Preferences: Diversified. Geographic
Preferences: National.

Landmark Partners, Inc.
10 Mill Pond Ln.
Simsbury, CT 06070
Phone: (860)651-9760
Fax: (860)651-8890
Website: http://
www.landmarkpartners.com
James P. McConnell, Partner
Preferred Investment Size: $500,000
to $5,000,000. Investment Types:
Seed, start-up, first and second stage,
and special situations. Industry
Preferences: Diversified technology.
Geographic Preferences: U.S. and
Canada.

Sweeney & Company
PO Box 567
Southport, CT 06490
Phone: (203)255-0220
Fax: (203)255-0220
E-mail: sweeney@connix.com
Preferred Investment Size:
$1,000,000 minimum. Investment
Types: Seed, research and
development, start-up, first stage,
second stage, mezzanine,
leveraged buyout, and special
situations. Industry Preferences:
Diversified. Geographic Preferences:
Northeast U.S. and Eastern Canada.

Baxter Associates, Inc.
PO Box 1333
Stamford, CT 06904
Phone: (203)323-3143
Fax: (203)348-0622
Preferred Investment Size:
$2,000,000 minimum. Investment
Types: Seed, start-up, first stage,
research and development, leveraged
buyout, and special situations.
Industry Preferences: Diversified.
Geographic Preferences: National.

Beacon Partners Inc.
6 Landmark Sq., 4th Fl.
Stamford, CT 06901-2792
Phone: (203)359-5776
Fax: (203)359-5876
Preferred Investment Size: $300,000
to $1,000,000. Investment Types:
First stage, second stage, mezzanine,
and leveraged buyout. Industry
Preferences: Diversified. Geographic
Preferences: Northeast.

Collinson, Howe, and Lennox, LLC
1055 Washington Blvd., 5th Fl.
Stamford, CT 06901
Phone: (203)324-7700
Fax: (203)324-3636
E-mail: info@chlmedical.com
Website: http://www.chlmedical.com
Investment Types: Seed, research and
development, start-up, and first
stage. Industry Preferences: Medical/
health related, biotechnology, and
Internet related. Geographic
Preferences: National.

Prime Capital Management Co.
550 West Ave.
Stamford, CT 06902
Phone: (203)964-0642
Fax: (203)964-0862
Preferred Investment Size: $300,000
to $800,000. Investment Types: First
and second stage, and recaps.
Industry Preferences: Diversified.
Geographic
Preferences: Northeast.

Saugatuck Capital Co.
1 Canterbury Green
Stamford, CT 06901
Phone: (203)348-6669
Fax: (203)324-6995
Website: http://
www.saugatuckcapital.com
Preferred Investment Size:
$25,000,000 maximum. Investment
Types: Leveraged buyout,
acquisition, control-block purchases,
expansion, later stage, and recaps.
Industry Preferences: Diversified.
Geographic
Preferences: Entire U.S.

Soundview Financial Group Inc.
22 Gatehouse Rd.
Stamford, CT 06902
Phone: (203)462-7200

Fax: (203)462-7350
Website: http://www.sndv.com
Brian Bristol, Managing Director
Preferred Investment Size: $100,000
to $500,000. Investment Types:
Second stage and mezzanine. Industry
Preferences: Diversified information
technology. Geographic Preferences:
United States and Canada.

TSG Ventures, L.L.C.
177 Broad St., 12th Fl.
Stamford, CT 06901
Phone: (203)406-1500
Fax: (203)406-1590
Darryl Thompson
Preferred Investment Size:
$30,000,000 minimum. Investment
Types: Second stage and leveraged
buyout. Industry Preferences:
Diversified. Geographic Preferences:
Entire U.S. and Canada.

Whitney & Company
177 Broad St.
Stamford, CT 06901
Phone: (203)973-1400
Fax: (203)973-1422
Website: http://www.jhwhitney.com
Preferred Investment Size:
$1,000,000. Investment Types:
Leveraged buyout and expansion.
Industry Preferences: Diversified
technology. Geographic Preferences:
No preference.

Cullinane & Donnelly Venture
Partners L.P.
970 Farmington Ave.
West Hartford, CT 06107
Phone: (860)521-7811
Fax: (860)521-7911
Preferred Investment Size: $300,000
to $1,000,000. Investment Types:
Seed, first and second stage, and
recaps. Industry Preferences:
Diversified. Geographic Preferences:
Northeast.

The Crestview Investment and
Financial Group
431 Post Rd. E, Ste. 1
Westport, CT 06880-4403
Phone: (203)222-0333
Fax: (203)222-0000
Norman Marland, Pres.
Preferred Investment Size: $500,000
to $3,000,000. Investment Types:

Seed, research and development, first stage, second stage, and mezzanine. Industry Preferences: Diversified. Geographic Preferences: U.S. and Canada.

Marketcorp Venture Associates, L.P. (MCV)
274 Riverside Ave.
Westport, CT 06880
Phone: (203)222-3030
Fax: (203)222-3033
E. Bulkeley Griswold, General Partner
Preferred Investment Size: $500,000 to $1,000,000. Investment Types: First and second stage, mezzanine, and leveraged buyout. Industry Preferences: Consumer products and services, and computer services. Geographic Preferences: Entire U.S.

Oak Investment Partners (Westport)
1 Gorham Island
Westport, CT 06880
Phone: (203)226-8346
Fax: (203)227-0372
Website: http://www.oakinv.com
Preferred Investment Size: $250,000 to $5,000,000. Investment Types: Start-up; early, first, second, and late stage; leveraged buyout; open market; control-block purchases; open market; and special situations. Industry Preferences: Diversified technology. Geographic Preferences: National.

Oxford Bioscience Partners
315 Post Rd. W
Westport, CT 06880-5200
Phone: (203)341-3300
Fax: (203)341-3309
Website: http://www.oxbio.com
William Greenman
Preferred Investment Size: $500,000 to $5,000,000. Investment Types: Early and first stage, and research and development. Industry Preferences: Genetic engineering and medical/ health related, computer related. Geographic Preferences: Entire U.S. and Canada.

Prince Ventures (Westport)
25 Ford Rd.
Westport, CT 06880
Phone: (203)227-8332

Fax: (203)226-5302
Preferred Investment Size: $500,000 to $1,000,000. Investment Types: Seed, start-up, first and second stage, and leveraged buyout. Industry Preferences: Genetic engineering and medical/health related, computer software and services, industrial, and communications. Geographic Preferences: No preference.

LTI Venture Leasing Corp.
221 Danbury Rd.
Wilton, CT 06897
Phone: (203)563-1100
Fax: (203)563-1111
Website: http://www.ltileasing.com
Richard Livingston, Vice President
Preferred Investment Size: $500,000 to $2,000,000. Investment Types: Early, first, second, and late stage; mezzanine; and special situation. Industry Preferences: Communications, computer related, consumer, electronic components and instrumentation, industrial products and equipment, medical and health related. Geographic Preferences: National.

Delaware

Blue Rock Capital
5803 Kennett Pike, Ste. A
Wilmington, DE 19807
Phone: (302)426-0981
Fax: (302)426-0982
Website: http://www.bluerockcapital.com
Preferred Investment Size: $250,000 to $3,000,000. Investment Types: Seed, start-up, and first stage. Industry Preferences: Communication, Internet related, computer, semiconductors, and consumer related. Geographic Preferences: Northeast, Middle Atlantic.

District of Columbia

Allied Capital Corp.
1919 Pennsylvania Ave. NW
Washington, DC 20006-3434
Phone: (202)331-2444
Fax: (202)659-2053
Website: http://www.alliedcapital.com

Tricia Daniels, Sales & Marketing
Preferred Investment Size: $5,000,000 to $40,000,000. Investment Types: Mezzanine, leveraged buyout, acquisition, management buyouts, and recapitalization. Industry Preferences: Diversified. Geographic Preferences: No preference.

Atlantic Coastal Ventures, L.P.
3101 South St. NW
Washington, DC 20007
Phone: (202)293-1166
Fax: (202)293-1181
Website: http://www.atlanticcv.com
Preferred Investment Size: $300,000 minimum. Investment Types: Leveraged buyout, mezzanine, and special situations. Industry Preferences: Communication and computer related, and electronics. Geographic Preferences: East Coast.

Columbia Capital Group, Inc.
1660 L St. NW, Ste. 308
Washington, DC 20036
Phone: (202)775-8815
Fax: (202)223-0544
Erica Batie, Director of Investments
Preferred Investment Size: $100,000 to $250,000. Investment Types: First and second stage, and mezzanine. Industry Preferences: Communication and computer related, electronics, and biotechnology. Geographic Preferences: Mid Atlantic.

Core Capital Partners
901 15th St., NW
9th Fl.
Washington, DC 20005
Phone: (202)589-0090
Fax: (202)589-0091
Website: http://www.core-capital.com
Preferred Investment Size: $1,000,000 to $10,000,000. Investment Types: Start-up, first and second stage, expansion, and later stage. Industry Preferences: Diversified. Geographic Preferences: Mid Atlantic, Northeast, and Southeast.

Next Point Partners
701 Pennsylvania Ave. NW, Ste. 900
Washington, DC 20004
Phone: (202)661-8703

Fax: (202)434-7400
E-mail: mf@nextpoint.vc
Website: http://www.nextpointvc.com
Michael Faber, Managing General
Partner
Investment Types: First and second
stage. Industry Preferences:
Communications, computer related,
and electronic components.
Geographic Preferences: National.

Telecommunications Development
Fund
2020 K. St. NW
Ste. 375
Washington, DC 20006
Phone: (202)293-8840
Fax: (202)293-8850
Website: http://www.tdfund.com
Preferred Investment Size: $375,000
to $1,000,000. Investment Types:
Seed, early stage, and expansion.
Industry Preferences: Internet related,
computer hardware/software and
services, and communications.
Geographic Preferences: Entire U.S.

Wachtel & Co., Inc.
1101 4th St. NW
Washington, DC 20005-5680
Phone: (202)898-1144
Preferred Investment Size: $100,000
to $300,000. Investment Types:
Start-up, first and second stage, and
recaps. Industry Preferences:
Diversified. Geographic Preferences:
East Coast.

Winslow Partners LLC
1300 Connecticut Ave. NW
Washington, DC 20036-1703
Phone: (202)530-5000
Fax: (202)530-5010
E-mail:
winslow@winslowpartners.com
Robert Chartener, Partner
Investment Types: Later stage,
acquisition, control-block purchases,
expansion, management and leverage
buyouts. Industry Preferences:
Diversified. Geographic Preferences:
Entire U.S.

Women's Growth Capital Fund
1054 31st St., NW
Ste. 110
Washington, DC 20007
Phone: (202)342-1431

Fax: (202)341-1203
Website: http://www.wgcf.com
Preferred Investment Size: $500,000
to $2,000,000. Investment Types:
First, second, and later stage. Industry
Preferences: Internet related,
communications, and computer
software and services. Geographic
Preferences: Entire U.S.

Florida

Sigma Capital Corp.
22668 Caravelle Circle
Boca Raton, FL 33433
Phone: (561)368-9783
Preferred Investment Size: $100,000
to $300,000. Investment Types:
Second stage. Industry Preferences:
Diversified communication and
computer, consumer products and
services, distribution, electronics,
genetic engineering, finance, and real
estate. Geographic Preferences:
Southeast.

North American Business
Development Co., L.L.C.
111 East Las Olas Blvd.
Ft. Lauderdale, FL 33301
Phone: (305)463-0681
Fax: (305)527-0904
Website: http://
www.northamericanfund.com
Robert Underwood
PIS $10,000,000 minimum.
Investment Types: Leveraged buyout,
special situations, control block
purchases, industry roll ups, and
small business with growth potential.
Industry Preferences: No preference.
Geographic Preferences: Southeast
and Midwest.

Chartwell Capital Management Co.
Inc.
1 Independent Dr., Ste. 3120
Jacksonville, FL 32202
Phone: (904)355-3519
Fax: (904)353-5833
E-mail: info@chartwellcap.com
Anthony Marinatos
Preferred Investment Size:
$5,000,000 minimum. Investment
Types: First stage, second stage and
leveraged buyout. Industry
Preferences: Diversified. Geographic

Preferences: Northwest and
Southeast.

CEO Advisors
1061 Maitland Center Commons
Ste. 209
Maitland, FL 32751
Phone: (407)660-9327
Fax: (407)660-2109
Preferred Investment Size: $300,000
to $500,000. Investment Types: Seed
start-up, first stage, and research and
development. Industry Preferences:
Diversified. Geographic Preferences:
Southeast.

Henry & Co.
8201 Peters Rd., Ste. 1000
Plantation, FL 33324
Phone: (954)797-7400
June Knaudt
Preferred Investment Size: $500,000
to $1,000,000. Investment Types:
First and second stage. Industry
Preferences: Healthcare industry.
Geographic Preferences: West Coast.

Avery Business Development
Services
2506 St. Michel Ct.
Ponte Vedra, FL 32082
Phone: (904)285-6033
Preferred Investment Size:
$2,000,000. Investment Types: Seed,
research and development, start-up,
first stage, leveraged buyout, and
special situations. Industry
Preferences: Diversified. Geographic
Preferences: National.

New South Ventures
5053 Ocean Blvd.
Sarasota, FL 34242
Phone: (941)358-6000
Fax: (941)358-6078
Website: http://
www.newsouthventures.com
Preferred Investment Size: $300,000
to $3,000,000. Investment Types:
Seed and early stage. Industry
Preferences: Diversified. Geographic
Preferences: Southeast.

Venture Capital Management Corp.
PO Box 2626
Satellite Beach, FL 32937
Phone: (407)777-1969
Preferred Investment Size: $100,000
to $300,000. Investment Types: First

and second stage, and leveraged buyout. Industry Preferences: Diversified. Geographic Preferences: National.

Florida Capital Venture Ltd.
325 Florida Bank Plaza
100 W. Kennedy Blvd.
Tampa, FL 33602
Phone: (813)229-2294
Fax: (813)229-2028
Warren Miller
Preferred Investment Size: $500,000 minimum. Investment Types: Start-up,
first and second stage, leveraged buyout, and special situations. Industry Preferences: Diversified. Geographic Preferences: Southeast.

Quantum Capital Partners
339 South Plant Ave.
Tampa, FL 33606
Phone: (813)250-1999
Fax: (813)250-1998
Website: http://www.quantumcapitalpartners.com
Preferred Investment Size: $1,000,000 to $5,000,000. Investment Types: Expansion, later stage, and mezzanine. Industry Preferences: Diversified technology, medical/health, consumer, retail, financial and business services, and manufacturing. Geographic Preferences: Florida.

South Atlantic Venture Fund
614 W. Bay St.
Tampa, FL 33606-2704
Phone: (813)253-2500
Fax: (813)253-2360
E-mail: venture@southatlantic.com
Website: http://www.southatlantic.com
Donald W. Burton, Chairman and Managing Director
Preferred Investment Size: $1,500,000 minimum. Investment Types: First and second stage, special situations, expansion and control block purchases. Industry Preferences: Diversified. Geographic Preferences: Southeast, Middle Atlantic, and Texas.

LM Capital Corp.
120 S. Olive, Ste. 400
West Palm Beach, FL 33401

Phone: (561)833-9700
Fax: (561)655-6587
Website: http://www.lmcapitalsecurities.com
Preferred Investment Size: $5,000,000 minimum. Investment Types: Leveraged buyout. Industry Preferences: Diversified. Geographic Preferences: No preference.

Georgia

Venture First Associates
4811 Thornwood Dr.
Acworth, GA 30102
Phone: (770)928-3733
Fax: (770)928-6455
J. Douglas Mullins
Preferred Investment Size: $500,000 to $5,000,000. Investment Types: Seed, start-up, first and second stage. Industry Preferences: Diversified technology and electronics. Geographic Preferences: Southeast.

Alliance Technology Ventures
8995 Westside Pkwy., Ste. 200
Alpharetta, GA 30004
Phone: (678)336-2000
Fax: (678)336-2001
E-mail: info@atv.com
Website: http://www.atv.com
Preferred Investment Size: $250,000 to $1,000,000. Investment Types: Seed, start-up, first and second stage. Industry Preferences: Diversified technology. Geographic Preferences: Southeast.

Cordova Ventures
2500 North Winds Pkwy., Ste. 475
Alpharetta, GA 30004
Phone: (678)942-0300
Fax: (678)942-0301
Website: http://www.cordovaventures.com
Teo F. Dagi
Preferred Investment Size: $250,000 to $4,000,000. Investment Policies: Equity and/or debt. Investment Types: Early and late stage, start-up expansion, and balanced. Industry Preferences: Diversified. Geographic Preferences: Southeast.

Advanced Technology Development Fund
1000 Abernathy, Ste. 1420

Atlanta, GA 30328-5614
Phone: (404)668-2333
Fax: (404)668-2333
Preferred Investment Size: $500,000 to $1,500,000. Investment Types: Seed, start-up, first and second stage, and leveraged buyout. Industry Preferences: Diversified. Geographic Preferences: No preference.

CGW Southeast Partners
12 Piedmont Center, Ste. 210
Atlanta, GA 30305
Phone: (404)816-3255
Fax: (404)816-3258
Website: http://www.cgwlp.com
Garrison M. Kitchen, Managing Partner
Preferred Investment Size: $25,000,000 to $200,000,000. Investment Types: Management buyout. Industry Preferences: Diversified. Geographic Preferences: Entire U.S.

Cyberstarts
1900 Emery St., NW
3rd Fl.
Atlanta, GA 30318
Phone: (404)267-5000
Fax: (404)267-5200
Website: http://www.cyberstarts.com
Investment Types: Seed and start-up. Industry Preferences: Internet and financial services. Geographic Preferences: Entire U.S.

EGL Holdings, Inc.
10 Piedmont Center, Ste. 412
Atlanta, GA 30305
Phone: (404)949-8300
Fax: (404)949-8311
Salvatore A. Massaro, Partner
Preferred Investment Size: $1,000,000 minimum. Investment Types: Mezzanine, leveraged buyout, industry roll ups, recapitalization, and second stage. Industry Preferences: Diversified. Geographic Preferences: Southeast and East Coast, Midwest.

Equity South
1790 The Lenox Bldg.
3399 Peachtree Rd. NE
Atlanta, GA 30326
Phone: (404)237-6222
Fax: (404)261-1578

Douglas L. Diamond, Managing Director
Preferred Investment Size: $2,000,000 to $3,000,000. Investment Types: Mezzanine, leveraged buyout, recapitalization, and control block purchases. Industry Preferences: Diversified. Geographic Preferences: Northeast, Southeast, and Southwest.

Five Paces
3400 Peachtree Rd., Ste. 200
Atlanta, GA 30326
Phone: (404)439-8300
Fax: (404)439-8301
Website: http://www.fivepaces.com
Investment Types: Balanced. Industry Preferences: Diversified. Geographic Preferences: Entire U.S.

Frontline Capital, Inc.
3475 Lenox Rd., Ste. 400
Atlanta, GA 30326
Phone: (404)240-7280
Fax: (404)240-7281
Preferred Investment Size: $1,000,000 minimum. Investment Types: First stage. Industry Preferences: Diversified communication and computer technology, consumer products and services, distribution, electronics, business and financial services, and publishing. Geographic Preferences: Southeast.

Fuqua Ventures LLC
1201 W. Peachtree St. NW, Ste. 5000
Atlanta, GA 30309
Phone: (404)815-4500
Fax: (404)815-4528
Website: http://www.fuquaventures.com
Investment Types: Early stage. Industry Preferences: Internet related, biotechnology, communications, and computer software and services. Geographic Preferences: Entire U.S.

Noro-Moseley Partners
4200 Northside Pkwy., Bldg. 9
Atlanta, GA 30327
Phone: (404)233-1966
Fax: (404)239-9280
Website: http://www.noro-moseley.com
Preferred Investment Size: $1,000,000 to $5,000,000. Investment

Types: Start-up, first and second stage, mezzanine, leveraged buyout, special situations, and control block purchases. Industry Preferences: Diversified. Geographic Preferences: Southeast.

Renaissance Capital Corp.
34 Peachtree St. NW, Ste. 2230
Atlanta, GA 30303
Phone: (404)658-9061
Fax: (404)658-9064
Larry Edler
Preferred Investment Size: $300,000 minimum. Investment Types: Second stage, mezzanine, and leveraged buyout. Industry Preferences: Diversified. Geographic Preferences: Southeast.

River Capital, Inc.
Two Midtown Plaza
1360 Peachtree St. NE, Ste. 1430
Atlanta, GA 30309
Phone: (404)873-2166
Fax: (404)873-2158
Jerry D. Wethington
Preferred Investment Size: $3,000,000 minimum. Investment Types: Mezzanine, recapitalization, and leveraged buyout. Industry Preferences: Diversified. Geographic Preferences: Southeast, Southwest, Midwest, and Middle Atlantic.

State Street Bank & Trust Co.
3414 Peachtree Rd. NE, Ste. 1010
Atlanta, GA 30326
Phone: (404)364-9500
Fax: (404)261-4469
Preferred Investment Size: $10,000,000 minimum. Investment Types: Leveraged buyout and special situations. Industry Preferences: Diversified technology. Geographic Preferences: National.

UPS Strategic Enterprise Fund
55 Glenlake Pkwy. NE
Atlanta, GA 30328
Phone: (404)828-8814
Fax: (404)828-8088
E-mail: jcacyce@ups.com
Website: http://www.ups.com/sef/sef_home
Preferred Investment Size: $1,000,000. Investment Types: Early

and late stage. Industry Preferences: Diversified communication and computer technology. Geographic Preferences: United States and Canada.

Wachovia
191 Peachtree St. NE, 26th Fl.
Atlanta, GA 30303
Phone: (404)332-1000
Fax: (404)332-1392
Website: http://www.wachovia.com/wca
Preferred Investment Size: $5,000,000 to $15,000,000. Investment Types: Expansion, later stage, management buyouts, mezzanine, private placement, and recaps. Industry Preferences: Diversified. Geographic Preferences: Southeast.

Brainworks Ventures
4243 Dunwoody Club Dr.
Chamblee, GA 30341
Phone: (770)239-7447
Investment Types: Balanced and early and later stage. Industry Preferences: Telecommunications and computers. Geographic Preferences: Southeast.

First Growth Capital Inc.
Best Western Plaza, Ste. 105
PO Box 815
Forsyth, GA 31029
Phone: (912)781-7131
Fax: (912)781-0066
Preferred Investment Size: $100,000 to $300,000. Investment Types: Second stage and special situation. Industry Preferences: Diversified. Geographic Preferences: No preference.

Financial Capital Resources, Inc.
21 Eastbrook Bend, Ste. 116
Peachtree City, GA 30269
Phone: (404)487-6650
Preferred Investment Size: $5,000,000 minimum. Investment Types: Leveraged buyout. Industry Preferences: Machinery. Geographic Preferences: National.

Hawaii

HMS Hawaii Management Partners
Davies Pacific Center

841 Bishop St., Ste. 860
Honolulu, HI 96813
Phone: (808)545-3755
Fax: (808)531-2611
Preferred Investment Size: $500,000
to $1,500,000. Investment Types:
Seed, start-up, first stage, and
leveraged buyout. Industry
Preferences: Internet related,
communications, and consumer
related. Geographic Preferences:
Entire U.S.

Idaho

Sun Valley Ventures
160 Second St.
Ketchum, ID 83340
Phone: (208)726-5005
Fax: (208)726-5094
Preferred Investment Size:
$5,000,000. Investment Types:
Second stage, leveraged buyout,
control-block purchases, and special
situations. Industry Preferences:
Diversified. Geographic Preferences:
Entire U.S. and Canada.

Illinois

Open Prairie Ventures
115 N. Neil St., Ste. 209
Champaign, IL 61820
Phone: (217)351-7000
Fax: (217)351-7051
E-mail: inquire@openprairie.com
Website: http://www.openprairie.com
Dennis D. Spice, Managing Member
Preferred Investment Size: $250,000
to $2,500,000. Investment Types:
Early stage. Industry Preferences:
Diversified communication and
computer technology, electronics, and
genetic engineering. Geographic
Preferences: Midwest.

ABN AMRO Private Equity
208 S. La Salle St., 10th Fl.
Chicago, IL 60604
Phone: (312)855-7079
Fax: (312)553-6648
Website: http://www.abnequity.com
David Bogetz, Managing Director
Preferred Investment Size:
$10,000,000 maximum. Investment
Types: Early stage and expansion.
Industry Preferences: Diversified.

Geographic Preferences: Entire U.S.
and Canada.

Alpha Capital Partners, Ltd.
122 S. Michigan Ave., Ste. 1700
Chicago, IL 60603
Phone: (312)322-9800
Fax: (312)322-9808
E-mail: acp@alphacapital.com
William J. Oberholtzer, Vice
President
Preferred Investment Size:
$2,000,000 minimum. Investment
Types: First and second stage,
leveraged buyout, and special
situations. Industry Preferences:
Diversified. Geographic Preferences:
Midwest.

Ameritech Development Corp.
30 S. Wacker Dr., 37th Fl.
Chicago, IL 60606
Phone: (312)750-5083
Fax: (312)609-0244
Craig Lee, Director
Preferred Investment Size:
$5,000,000 minimum. Investment
Types: Start-up, first and second
stage. Industry Preferences:
Communications, computer related,
and electronics. Geographic
Preferences: Entire U.S.

Apex Investment Partners
225 W. Washington, Ste. 1450
Chicago, IL 60606
Phone: (312)857-2800
Fax: (312)857-1800
E-mail: apex@apexvc.com
Website: http://www.apexvc.com
Preferred Investment Size: $500,000
to $15,000,000. Investment Types:
Early stage. Industry Preferences:
Diversified communication and
computer technology, consumer
products and services, industrial/
energy, and electronics. Geographic
Preferences: Entire U.S.

Arch Venture Partners
8725 W. Higgins Rd., Ste. 290
Chicago, IL 60631
Phone: (773)380-6600
Fax: (773)380-6606
Website: http://www.archventure.com
Steven Lazarus, Managing Director
Preferred Investment Size: $100,000
to $1,000,000. Investment Types:

Seed, start-up, early stage. Industry
Preferences: Diversified
communication and computer
technology, electronics, and genetic
engineering. Geographic Preferences:
National.

The Bank Funds
208 South LaSalle St., Ste. 1680
Chicago, IL 60604
Phone: (312)855-6020
Fax: (312)855-8910
Investment Types: Control-block
purchases, later stage, leveraged
buyout, second stage, and special
situation. Industry Preferences:
Diversified. Geographic Preferences:
No preference.

Batterson Venture Partners
303 W. Madison St., Ste. 1110
Chicago, IL 60606-3309
Phone: (312)269-0300
Fax: (312)269-0021
Website: http://www.battersonvp.com
Preferred Investment Size: $500,000
to $3,000,000. Investment Types:
Seed, start-up, first and second stage.
Industry Preferences: Diversified.
Geographic Preferences: Entire U.S.

William Blair Capital Partners, L.L.C.
222 W. Adams St., Ste. 1300
Chicago, IL 60606
Phone: (312)364-8250
Fax: (312)236-1042
E-mail: privateequity@wmblair.com
Website: http://www.wmblair.com
Maureen Naddy, Office Manager
Preferred Investment Size:
$5,000,000 minimum. Investment
Types: First and early stage,
acquisition and leveraged buyout.
Industry Preferences:
Communications, computer related,
consumer, electronics, energy/natural
resources, genetic engineering, and
medical/health related. Geographic
Preferences: Mid Atlantic, Midwest,
and Northeast.

Bluestar Ventures
208 South LaSalle St., Ste. 1020
Chicago, IL 60604
Phone: (312)384-5000
Fax: (312)384-5005
Website: http://
www.bluestarventures.com

Preferred Investment Size: $1,000,000 to $3,000,000. Investment Types: Early, first, and second stage. Industry Preferences: Diversified. Geographic Preferences: Midwest.

The Capital Strategy Management Co.
233 S. Wacker Dr.
Box 06334
Chicago, IL 60606
Phone: (312)444-1170
Eric Von Bauer
Preferred Investment Size: $200,000 to $50,000,000. Investment Types: Various types. Industry Preferences: Diversified communication and computer technology, medical/health, industrial/energy, consumer products and services, distribution, electronics, and utilities. Geographic Preferences: Midwest, Northwest, Southeast, Mid Atlantic.

DN Partners
77 West Wacker Dr., Ste. 4550
Chicago, IL 60601
Phone: (312)332-7960
Fax: (312)332-7979
Investment Types: Leveraged buyout. Industry Preferences: Communications, computer related, electronics, medical/health, consumer related, industrial products, transportation, financial services, publishing, and agriculture related. Geographic Preferences: U.S.

Dresner Capital Inc.
29 South LaSalle St., Ste. 310
Chicago, IL 60603
Phone: (312)726-3600
Fax: (312)726-7448
John Riddle
Preferred Investment Size: $500,000 to $1,000,000. Investment Types: Leveraged buyout, mezzanine, and second stage. Industry Preferences: Diversified. Geographic Preferences: No preference.

Eblast Ventures LLC
11 South LaSalle St., 5th Fl.
Chicago, IL 60603
Phone: (312)372-2600
Fax: (312)372-5621
Website: http://
www.eblastventures.com

Preferred Investment Size: $100,000 to $500,000. Investment Types: Early,
seed, start-up, and turnaround. Industry Preferences: Diversified. Geographic Preferences: Midwest.

Essex Woodlands Health Ventures, L.P.
190 S. LaSalle St., Ste. 2800
Chicago, IL 60603
Phone: (312)444-6040
Fax: (312)444-6034
Website: http://
www.essexwoodlands.com
Marc S. Sandroff, General Partner
Preferred Investment Size: $1,000,000 to $12,000,000. Investment Types: Start-up, early and second stage, private placement, and mezzanine. Industry Preferences: Healthcare, biotechnology, Internet related. Geographic Preferences: No preference.

First Analysis Venture Capital
233 S. Wacker Dr., Ste. 9500
Chicago, IL 60606
Phone: (312)258-1400
Fax: (312)258-0334
Website: http://
www.firstanalysis.com
Bret Maxwell, CEO
Preferred Investment Size: $3,000,000 to $15,000,000. Investment Types: Early and later stage, and expansion. Industry Preferences: Diversified. Geographic Preferences: No preference.

Frontenac Co.
135 S. LaSalle St., Ste.3800
Chicago, IL 60603
Phone: (312)368-0044
Fax: (312)368-9520
Website: http://www.frontenac.com
Preferred Investment Size: $500,000 minimum. Investment Types: Start-up, first and second stage, leveraged buyout, special situation, and industry roll ups. Industry Preferences: Diversified. Geographic Preferences: Entire U.S.

GTCR Golder Rauner, LLC
6100 Sears Tower
Chicago, IL 60606
Phone: (312)382-2200

Fax: (312)382-2201
Website: http://www.gtcr.com
Bruce V. Rauner
Preferred Investment Size: $10,000,000 minimum. Investment Types: Leveraged buyout, acquisition, expansion, management buyouts, and recapitalization. Industry Preferences: Diversified. Geographic Preferences: No preference.

High Street Capital LLC
311 South Wacker Dr., Ste. 4550
Chicago, IL 60606
Phone: (312)697-4990
Fax: (312)697-4994
Website: http://www.highstr.com
Preferred Investment Size: $2,000,000 to $10,000,000. Investment Types: Acquisition, control-block purchases, expansion, generalist PE, leveraged and management buyouts, recaps, and special situations. Industry Preferences: Diversified. Geographic Preferences: Entire U.S.

IEG Venture Management, Inc.
70 West Madison
Chicago, IL 60602
Phone: (312)644-0890
Fax: (312)454-0369
Website: http://www.iegventure.com
Preferred Investment Size: $100,000 to $500,000. Investment Types: Seed, start-up, first and second stage. Industry Preferences: Diversified. Geographic Preferences: Midwest.

JK&B Capital
180 North Stetson, Ste. 4500
Chicago, IL 60601
Phone: (312)946-1200
Fax: (312)946-1103
E-mail: gspencer@jkbcapital.com
Website: http://www.jkbcapital.com
Preferred Investment Size: $5,000,000 to $20,000,000. Investment Types: Early and late stage, and expansion. Industry Preferences: Diversified. Geographic Preferences: National.

Kettle Partners L.P.
350 W. Hubbard, Ste. 350
Chicago, IL 60610
Phone: (312)329-9300

Fax: (312)527-4519
Website: http://www.kettlevc.com
Preferred Investment Size:
$1,000,000 to $5,000,000. Investment
Types: Early, first and second stage,
seed, and start-up. Industry
Preferences: Internet related,
communications, computer related.
Geographic Preferences: Entire U.S.

Lake Shore Capital Partners
20 N. Wacker Dr., Ste. 2807
Chicago, IL 60606
Phone: (312)803-3536
Fax: (312)803-3534
Preferred Investment Size:
$1,000,000 to $10,000,000.
Investment Types: First and second
stage, mezzanine, and leveraged
buyout. Industry Preferences:
Diversified. Geographic Preferences:
National.

LaSalle Capital Group Inc.
70 W. Madison St., Ste. 5710
Chicago, IL 60602
Phone: (312)236-7041
Fax: (312)236-0720
Anthony Pesavento
Preferred Investment Size:
$1,000,000 minimum. Investment
Types: Leveraged buyout and special
situation. Industry Preferences:
Entertainment and leisure, consumer
products, industrial products, and
machinery. Geographic Preferences:
No preference.

Linc Capital, Inc.
303 E. Wacker Pkwy., Ste. 1000
Chicago, IL 60601
Phone: (312)946-2670
Fax: (312)938-4290
E-mail: bdemars@linccap.com
Martin E. Zimmerman, Chairman
Preferred Investment Size: $500,000
to $2,000,000. Investment Types:
Seed, start-up, early and late stage,
mezzanine, research and
development, and special situations.
Industry Preferences: Diversified
communication and computer
technology, electronics, and medical/
health related. Geographic
Preferences: National.

Madison Dearborn Partners, Inc.
3 First National Plz., Ste. 3800

Chicago, IL 60602
Phone: (312)895-1000
Fax: (312)895-1001
E-mail: invest@mdcp.com
Website: http://www.mdcp.com
Preferred Investment Size:
$20,000,000 to $400,000,000.
Investment Types: Start-up, early
stage, leveraged buyout, special
situations, and expansion. Industry
Preferences: Diversified. Geographic
Preferences: Entire U.S. and Canada.

Mesirow Private Equity Investments
Inc.
350 N. Clark St.
Chicago, IL 60610
Phone: (312)595-6950
Fax: (312)595-6211
Website: http://
www.meisrowfinancial.com
Preferred Investment Size:
$4,000,000 to $10,000,000.
Investment Types: Second stage,
mezzanine, and leveraged buyout.
Industry Preferences: Diversified.
Geographic Preferences: Entire U.S.

Mosaix Ventures LLC
1822 North Mohawk
Chicago, IL 60614
Phone: (312)274-0988
Fax: (312)274-0989
Website: http://
www.mosaixventures.com
Preferred Investment Size: $500,000
to $3,000,000. Investment Types:
Early and later stage, and expansion.
Industry Preferences: Medical/health
related. Geographic Preferences: U.S.

Nesbitt Burns
111 West Monroe St.
Chicago, IL 60603
Phone: (312)416-3855
Fax: (312)765-8000
Website: http://www.harrisbank.com
I. David Burn
Investment Types: Control-block
purchases, leveraged buyout, and
special situation. Industry
Preferences: Diversified. Geographic
Preferences: U.S. and Canada.

Polestar Capital, Inc.
180 N. Michigan Ave., Ste. 1905
Chicago, IL 60601
Phone: (312)984-9090

Fax: (312)984-9877
E-mail: wl@polestarvc.com
Website: http://www.polestarvc.com
Preferred Investment Size: $250,000
to $1,000,000. Investment Policies:
Primarily equity. Investment Types:
Start-up, first and second stage.
Industry Preferences:
communications, computer related.
Geographic Preferences: Entire U.S.

Prince Ventures (Chicago)
10 S. Wacker Dr., Ste. 2575
Chicago, IL 60606-7407
Phone: (312)454-1408
Fax: (312)454-9125
Preferred Investment Size: $500,000
to $1,000,000. Investment Types:
Seed, start-up, first and second stage,
leveraged buyout. Industry
Preferences: Genetic engineering and
medical/health related. Geographic
Preferences: No preference.

Prism Capital
444 N. Michigan Ave.
Chicago, IL 60611
Phone: (312)464-7900
Fax: (312)464-7915
Website: http://www.prismfund.com
Investment Types: First and second
stage, mezzanine, leveraged buyout,
and special situations. Industry
Preferences: Diversified technology.
Geographic Preferences: National.

Third Coast Capital
900 N. Franklin St., Ste. 700
Chicago, IL 60610
Phone: (312)337-3303
Fax: (312)337-2567
E-mail: manic@earthlink.com
Website: http://
www.thirdcoastcapital.com
Preferred Investment Size:
$2,000,000 to $5,000,000. Industry
Preferences: Telecommunications and
fiber optics. Geographic Preferences:
National.

Thoma Cressey Equity Partners
4460 Sears Tower, 92nd Fl.
233 S. Wacker Dr.
Chicago, IL 60606
Phone: (312)777-4444
Fax: (312)777-4445
Website: http://
www.thomacressey.com

Investment Types: Early and later stage, leveraged buyouts, and recapitalization. Industry Preferences: Diversified. Geographic Preferences: U.S. and Canada.

Tribune Ventures
435 N. Michigan Ave., Ste. 600
Chicago, IL 60611
Phone: (312)527-8797
Fax: (312)222-5993
Website: http://
www.tribuneventures.com
Frances McCaughan
Preferred Investment Size:
$1,000,000 to $10,000,000.
Investment Types: Early stage, expansion, first and second stage, seed, and start-up. Industry Preferences: Diversified. Geographic Preferences: Entire U.S.

Wind Point Partners (Chicago)
676 N. Michigan Ave., Ste. 330
Chicago, IL 60611
Phone: (312)649-4000
Website: http://www.wppartners.com
Preferred Investment Size:
$10,000,000 to $60,000,000.
Investment Types: Later stage, leveraged buyout, acquisition, expansion, and recapitalization. Industry Preferences: Diversified. Geographic Preferences: Midwest.

Marquette Venture Partners
520 Lake Cook Rd., Ste. 450
Deerfield, IL 60015
Phone: (847)940-1700
Fax: (847)940-1724
Website: http://
www.marquetteventures.com
Preferred Investment Size:
$1,000,000 to $5,000,000. Investment Types: Start-up, first and second stage. Industry Preferences: Diversified.
Geographic Preferences: Mid Atlantic, Midwest, Rocky Mountain, and West Coast.

Duchossois Investments Limited, LLC
845 Larch Ave.
Elmhurst, IL 60126
Phone: (630)530-6105
Fax: (630)993-8644
Website: http://www.duchtec.com

Preferred Investment Size: $500,000 to $5,000,000. Investment Types: Early, first and second stage. Industry Preferences: Diversified. Communications and computer related. Geographic Preferences: National.

Evanston Business Investment Corp.
1840 Oak Ave.
Evanston, IL 60201
Phone: (847)866-1840
Fax: (847)866-1808
E-mail: t-parkinson@nwu.com
Website: http://www.ebic.com
Preferred Investment Size: $250,000 to $500,000. Investment Types: Early stages. Industry Preferences: Diversified communication and computer technology, consumer products and services, medical/health, electronics, and publishing. Geographic Preferences: Chicago metropolitan area.

Inroads Capital Partners L.P.
1603 Orrington Ave., Ste. 2050
Evanston, IL 60201-3841
Phone: (847)864-2000
Fax: (847)864-9692
Preferred Investment Size:
$1,000,000 to $5,000,000. Investment Types: Expansion and later stage. Industry Preferences: Diversified. Geographic Preferences: Entire U.S.

The Cerulean Fund/WGC Enterprises
1701 E. Lake Ave., Ste. 170
Glenview, IL 60025
Phone: (847)657-8002
Fax: (847)657-8168
Walter G. Cornett, III, Managing Director
Preferred Investment Size:
$5,000,000 minimum. Investment Types: Seed, start-up, leveraged buyout, special situations, control block purchases, and research and development. Industry Preferences: Diversified. Geographic Preferences: Midwest.

Ventana Financial Resources, Inc.
249 Market Sq.
Lake Forest, IL 60045
Phone: (847)234-3434
Preferred Investment Size:
$5,000,000 minimum. Investment

Types: Seed, start-up, first and second stage, research and development, leveraged buyout, and mezzanine. Industry Preferences: Diversified. Geographic Preferences: Midwest, Southeast, and Southwest.

Beecken, Petty & Co.
901 Warrenville Rd., Ste. 205
Lisle, IL 60532
Phone: (630)435-0300
Fax: (630)435-0370
E-mail: hep@bpcompany.com
Website: http://www.bpcompany.com
Preferred Investment Size:
$2,000,000 to $12,000,000.
Investment Types: Early, first, second, and late stage; expansion; management buyouts; private placement; recapitalization. Industry Preferences: Communications, computer related, genetic engineering, medical and health related. Geographic Preferences: National.

Allstate Private Equity
3075 Sanders Rd., Ste. G5D
Northbrook, IL 60062-7127
Phone: (847)402-8247
Fax: (847)402-0880
Preferred Investment Size:
$5,000,000 minimum. Investment Types: Start-up, first and second stage, mezzanine, leveraged buyout, and special situations. Industry Preferences: Diversified. Geographic Preferences: Entire U.S.

KB Partners
1101 Skokie Blvd., Ste. 260
Northbrook, IL 60062-2856
Phone: (847)714-0444
Fax: (847)714-0445
E-mail: keith@kbpartners.com
Website: http://www.kbpartners.com
Keith Bank, Managing Partner
Preferred Investment Size:
$1,000,000 to $5,000,000. Investment Types: Seed, start-up, and early, first and second stage. Industry Preferences: Diversified. Geographic Preferences: National.

Transcap Associates Inc.
900 Skokie Blvd., Ste. 210
Northbrook, IL 60062
Phone: (847)753-9600

Fax: (847)753-9090
Ira J. Ederson
Preferred Investment Size: $500,000
to $5,000,000. Investment Types:
Mezzanine, second stage, and special
situation. Industry Preferences:
Diversified. Geographic Preferences:
Entire U.S.

Graystone Venture Partners, L.L.C. /
Portage Venture Partners
One Northfield Plaza, Ste. 530
Northfield, IL 60093
Phone: (847)446-9460
Fax: (847)446-9470
Website: http://
www.portageventures.com
Mathew B. McCall, Vice President
Preferred Investment Size: $250,000
to $3,000,000. Investment Types:
Early stage. Industry Preferences:
Diversified communication and
computer technology, consumer
products and services, genetic
engineering, and medical/health.
Geographic Preferences: National.

Motorola Inc.
1303 E. Algonquin Rd.
Schaumburg, IL 60196-1065
Phone: (847)576-4929
Fax: (847)538-2250
Website: http://www.mot.com/mne
James Burke, New Business
Development Manager
Investment Types: Start-up, first and
second stage. Industry Preferences:
Diversified technology. Geographic
Preferences: National.

Indiana

Irwin Ventures LLC
500 Washington St.
Columbus, IN 47202
Phone: (812)373-1434
Fax: (812)376-1709
Website: http://
www.irwinventures.com
Preferred Investment Size: $750,000
to $1,250,000. Investment Types:
Early and first stage. Industry
Preferences: Internet related and
financial services. Geographic
Preferences: Northeast and
Northwest.

Cambridge Venture Partners
4181 East 96th St., Ste. 200
Indianapolis, IN 46240
Phone: (317)814-6192
Fax: (317)944-9815
Jean Wojtowicz, President
Preferred Investment Size: $100,000
maximum. Investment Types: Second
stage, mezzanine, and leveraged
buyout. Industry Preferences: No
preference. Geographic Preferences:
Midwest, within 200 miles of office.

CID Equity Partners
One American Square, Ste. 2850
Box 82074
Indianapolis, IN 46282
Phone: (317)269-2350
Fax: (317)269-2355
Website: http://www.cidequity.com
Chris Gough, Associate
Preferred Investment Size:
$1,000,000 minimum. Investment
Types: Start-up, early and first stage,
industry rollups, leveraged buyout,
and special situations. Industry
Preferences: Diversified. Geographic
Preferences: Midwest and Rocky
Mountain region.

Gazelle Techventures
6325 Digital Way, Ste. 460
Indianapolis, IN 46278
Phone: (317)275-6800
Fax: (317)275-1101
Website: http://www.gazellevc.com
Preferred Investment Size:
$2,000,000 maximum. Investment
Types: Early and later stage. Industry
Preferences: Diversified. Geographic
Preferences: Indiana.

Monument Advisors Inc.
Bank One Center/Circle
111 Monument Circle, Ste. 600
Indianapolis, IN 46204-5172
Phone: (317)656-5065
Fax: (317)656-5060
Website: http://
www.monumentadv.com
Preferred Investment Size: $500,000
to $7,000,000. Investment Types:
Balanced, leveraged buyout,
management buyouts, and mezzanine.
Industry Preferences: Business
services, distribution, and
manufacturing. Geographic
Preferences: Midwest and Southeast.

MWV Capital Partners
201 N. Illinois St., Ste. 300
Indianapolis, IN 46204
Phone: (317)237-2323
Fax: (317)237-2325
Website: http://www.mwvcapital.com
Garth Dickey, Managing Director
Preferred Investment Size:
$1,000,000 to $5,000,000. Investment
Types: Balanced, second and later
stage. Industry Preferences:
Diversified. Geographic Preferences:
Midwest.

First Source Capital Corp.
100 North Michigan St.
PO Box 1602
South Bend, IN 46601
Phone: (219)235-2180
Fax: (219)235-2227
Eugene L. Cavanaugh, Vice President
Preferred Investment Size: $300,000
to $500,000. Investment Types:
Second stage, mezzanine, leveraged
buyout, and special situations.
Industry Preferences: Diversified.
Geographic Preferences: Midwest.

Iowa

Allsop Venture Partners
118 Third Ave. SE, Ste. 837
Cedar Rapids, IA 52401
Phone: (319)368-6675
Fax: (319)363-9515
Preferred Investment Size: $500,000
minimum. Investment Types: First
stage, industry rollups, leveraged
buyout, mezzanine, second stage, and
special situation. Industry
preferences: Diversified. Geographic
Preferences: Entire U.S.

InvestAmerica Investment Advisors,
Inc.
101 2nd St. SE, Ste. 800
Cedar Rapids, IA 52401
Phone: (319)363-8249
Fax: (319)363-9683
Kevin F. Mullane, Vice President
Preferred Investment Size: $500,000
to $1,000,000. Investment Types:
First and second stage, leveraged
buyout, and special situations.
Industry Preferences: Diversified.
Geographic Preferences: Entire U.S.

Pappajohn Capital Resources
2116 Financial Center
Des Moines, IA 50309
Phone: (515)244-5746
Fax: (515)244-2346
Website: http://www.pappajohn.com
Joe Dunham, President
Preferred Investment Size: $500,000
to $1,000,000. Investment Policies:
Equity. Investment Types: Seed, start-
up, first and second stage, leveraged
buyout, and special situations.
Industry Preferences: Diversified
communication and computer
technology, electronics, genetic
engineering, and healthcare.
Geographic Preferences: National.

Berthel Fisher & Company Planning
Inc.
701 Tama St.
PO Box 609
Marion, IA 52302
Phone: (319)497-5700
Fax: (319)497-4244
Investment Types: Later stage.
Industry Preferences: Diversified.
Geographic Preferences: Midwest.

Kansas

Enterprise Merchant Bank
7400 West 110th St., Ste. 560
Overland Park, KS 66210
Phone: (913)327-8500
Fax: (913)327-8505
Preferred Investment Size:
$1,000,000 minimum. Investment
Types: Second stage, leveraged
buyout, mezzanine, and special
situations. Geographic Preferences:
Midwest.

Kansas Venture Capital, Inc.
(Overland Park)
6700 Antioch Plz., Ste. 460
Overland Park, KS 66204
Phone: (913)262-7117
Fax: (913)262-3509
E-mail: jdalton@kvci.com
John S. Dalton, President
Preferred Investment Size:
$1,000,000 minimum. Investment
Types: First and second stage,
mezzanine, and leveraged buyout.
Industry Preferences: Diversified.
Geographic Preferences: Midwest.

Child Health Investment Corp.
6803 W. 64th St., Ste. 208
Shawnee Mission, KS 66202
Phone: (913)262-1436
Fax: (913)262-1575
Website: http://www.chca.com
Investment Types: Balanced, early
stage, first stage, seed, and start-up.
Industry Preferences: Diversified.
Geographic Preferences: Entire U.S.

Kansas Technology Enterprise Corp.
214 SW 6th, 1st Fl.
Topeka, KS 66603-3719
Phone: (785)296-5272
Fax: (785)296-1160
E-mail: ktec@ktec.com
Website: http://www.ktec.com
Preferred Investment Size: $300,000.
Investment Types: Seed, start-up,
research and development. Industry
Preferences: Diversified
communication and computer
technology, electronics, genetic
engineering, and healthcare.
Geographic Preferences: Within two
hours of office.

Kentucky

Kentucky Highlands Investment
Corp.
362 Old Whitley Rd.
London, KY 40741
Phone: (606)864-5175
Fax: (606)864-5194
Website: http://www.khic.org
Investment Types: Second stage,
special situation, and start-up.
Industry Preferences: Manufacturing.
Geographic Preferences: Kentucky.

Chrysalis Ventures, L.L.C.
1850 National City Tower
Louisville, KY 40202
Phone: (502)583-7644
Fax: (502)583-7648
E-mail:
bobsany@chrysalisventures.com
Website: http://
www.chrysalisventures.com
Preferred Investment Size:
$3,000,000 to $5,000,000. Investment
Types: Start-up, first and second
stage. Industry Preferences:
Diversified communication and
computer technology. Geographic
Preferences: Southeast and Midwest.

Humana Venture Capital
500 West Main St.
Louisville, KY 40202
Phone: (502)580-3922
Fax: (502)580-2051
E-mail: gemont@humana.com
George Emont, Director
Preferred Investment Size:
$10,000,000 minimum. Investment
Types: Seed, start-up, first and second
stage, leveraged buyout, mezzanine,
and research and development.
Industry Preferences: Medical/health
related, Internet and computer related,
and biotechnology. Geographic
Preferences: National.

Summit Capital Group, Inc.
6510 Glenridge Park Pl., Ste. 8
Louisville, KY 40222
Phone: (502)332-2700
Preferred Investment Size:
$10,000,000 to $40,000,000.
Investment Types: Control-block
purchases, expansion, leveraged and
management buyouts. Industry
Preferences: Diversified. Geographic
Preferences: Southeast and
Southwest.

Louisiana

Bank One Equity Investors, Inc.
451 Florida St.
Baton Rouge, LA 70801
Phone: (504)332-4421
Fax: (504)332-7377
Michael P. Kriby
Preferred Investment Size:
$8,000,000 minimum. Investment
Types: First and second stage,
mezzanine, leveraged buyout, and
special situations. Industry
Preferences: Diversified. Geographic
Preferences: Southeast and
Southwest.

Advantage Capital Partners
LLE Tower
909 Poydras St., Ste. 2230
New Orleans, LA 70112
Phone: (504)522-4850
Fax: (504)522-4950
Website: http://
www.advantagecap.com
Steven T. Stull, President
Preferred Investment Size:
$1,000,000 to $10,000,000.

Investment Types: Seed, start-up, early and second stage, and mezzanine. Industry Preferences: Diversified. Geographic Preferences: North and Southeast, and Midwest.

Maine

CEI Ventures / Coastal Ventures LP
2 Portland Fish Pier, Ste. 201
Portland, ME 04101
Phone: (207)772-5356
Fax: (207)772-5503
Website: http://www.ceiventures.com
Investment Types: No preference.
Industry Preferences: Diversified.
Geographic Preferences: Entire U.S.

Commwealth Bioventures, Inc.
4 Milk St.
Portland, ME 04101
Phone: (207)780-0904
Fax: (207)780-0913
E-mail: cbi4milk@aol.com
Investment Types: Seed. Industry Preferences: Biotechnology based start-ups. Geographic Preferences: No preference.

Maryland

Annapolis Ventures LLC
151 West St., Ste. 302
Annapolis, MD 21401
Phone: (443)482-9555
Fax: (443)482-9565
Website: http://
www.annapolisventures.com
Preferred Investment Size:
$2,000,000 to $5,000,000. Investment Types: Later stage. Industry Preferences: Diversified. Geographic Preferences: Midwest, Northeast, and Southeast.

Delmag Ventures
220 Wardour Dr.
Annapolis, MD 21401
Phone: (410)267-8196
Fax: (410)267-8017
Website: http://
www.delmagventures.com
Preferred Investment Size: $250,000 to $1,000,000. Investment Types: Early stage and seed. Industry Preferences: Diversified. Geographic Preferences: Mid Atlantic.

Abell Venture Fund
111 S. Calvert St., Ste. 2300
Baltimore, MD 21202
Phone: (410)547-1300
Fax: (410)539-6579
Website: http://www.abell.org
Investment Types: Early stage, expansion, first and second stage, and private placement. Industry preferences: Internet related, electronics, communications, and medical/health related. Geographic Preferences: Maryland.

ABS Ventures (Baltimore)
1 South St., Ste. 2150
Baltimore, MD 21202
Phone: (410)895-3895
Fax: (410)895-3899
Website: http://www.absventures.com
Preferred Investment Size: $500,000 maximum. Investment Types: Start-up, first and second stage, and mezzanine. Industry Preferences: Communications, computer related, genetic engineering, and medical/health related. Geographic Preferences: Entire U.S.

Anthem Capital, L.P.
16 S. Calvert St., Ste. 800
Baltimore, MD 21202-1305
Phone: (410)625-1510
Fax: (410)625-1735
Website: http://
www.anthemcapital.com
Preferred Investment Size: $500,000 to $1,000,000. Investment Types: Early and later stage, mezzanine, and special situations. Industry Preferences: Diversified. Geographic Preferences: Middle Atlantic.

Catalyst Ventures
1119 St. Paul St.
Baltimore, MD 21202
Phone: (410)244-0123
Fax: (410)752-7721
Preferred Investment Size: $500,000 maximum. Investment Policies: Equity. Investment Types: Research and development, and early stage. Industry Preferences: Data communications, biotechnology, and medical related. Geographic Preferences: Middle Atlantic.

Maryland Venture Capital Trust
217 E. Redwood St., Ste. 2200

Baltimore, MD 21202
Phone: (410)767-6361
Fax: (410)333-6931
E-mail:
rblank@mdbusiness.state.md.us
Preferred Investment Size:
$1,000,000 to $5,000,000. Investment Types: Seed, start-up, first and second stage. Industry Preferences: Diversified. Geographic Preferences: Maryland.

New Enterprise Associates
(Baltimore)
1119 St. Paul St.
Baltimore, MD 21202
Phone: (410)244-0115
Fax: (410)752-7721
Website: http://www.nea.com
Frank A. Bonsal, Jr., Founding Partner
Preferred Investment Size: $100,000 minimum. Investment Types: Seed, start-up, first and second stage, and mezzanine. Industry Preferences: Diversified. Geographic Preferences: Entire U.S.

T. Rowe Price Threshold Partnerships
100 E. Pratt St., 8th Fl.
Baltimore, MD 21202
Phone: (410)345-2000
Fax: (410)345-2800
Terral Jordan
Preferred Investment Size:
$3,000,000 to $5,000,000. Investment Types: Mezzanine and special situations. Industry Preferences: Diversified. Geographic Preferences: Entire U.S.

Spring Capital Partners
16 W. Madison St.
Baltimore, MD 21201
Phone: (410)685-8000
Fax: (410)727-1436
E-mail: mailbox@springcap.com
Robert M. Stewart
Preferred Investment Size:
$2,000,000 minimum. Investment Types: Second stage, acquisition, industry rollups, mezzanine, and leveraged buyout. Industry Preferences: Diversified. Geographic Preferences: Mid-Atlantic.

Arete Corporation
3 Bethesda Metro Ctr., Ste. 770
Bethesda, MD 20814

Phone: (301)657-6268
Fax: (301)657-6254
Website: http://www.arete-
microgen.com
Jill Wilmoth
Investment Types: Seed, start-up, first
stage, and research and development.
Industry Preferences: Alternative
energy. Geographic Preferences:
Entire U.S. and Canada.

Embryon Capital
7903 Sleaford Place
Bethesda, MD 20814
Phone: (301)656-6837
Fax: (301)656-8056
Preferred Investment Size: $300,000
to $1,000,000. Investment Types:
Diversified. Industry Preferences:
Diversified. Geographic Preferences:
Entire U.S.

Potomac Ventures
7920 Norfolk Ave., Ste. 1100
Bethesda, MD 20814
Phone: (301)215-9240
Website: http://
www.potomacventures.com
Preferred Investment Size: $400,000
to $1,000,000. Investment Types:
Early stage. Industry Preferences:
Internet related. Geographic
Preferences: Mid Atlantic.

Toucan Capital Corp.
3 Bethesda Metro Center, Ste. 700
Bethesda, MD 20814
Phone: (301)961-1970
Fax: (301)961-1969
Website: http://
www.toucancapital.com
Preferred Investment Size:
$1,000,000 to $1,000,000. Investment
Types: Early stage, seed, and start-up.
Industry Preferences: Diversified.
Geographic Preferences: Entire U.S.

Kinetic Ventures LLC
2 Wisconsin Cir., Ste. 620
Chevy Chase, MD 20815
Phone: (301)652-8066
Fax: (301)652-8310
Website: http://
www.kineticventures.com
Investment Types: Start-up, first
stage, second stage, and leveraged
buyout. Industry Preferences:
Diversified technology. Geographic
Preferences: National.

Boulder Ventures Ltd.
4750 Owings Mills Blvd.
Owings Mills, MD 21117
Phone: (410)998-3114
Fax: (410)356-5492
Website: http://
www.boulderventures.com
Preferred Investment Size:
$2,000,000 to $5,000,000. Investment
Types: Early stage, expansion, first
stage, and start-up. Industry
Preferences: Diversified. Geographic
Preferences: Entire U.S.

Grotech Capital Group
9690 Deereco Rd., Ste. 800
Timonium, MD 21093
Phone: (410)560-2000
Fax: (410)560-1910
Website: http://www.grotech.com
Frank A. Adams, President and CEO
Preferred Investment Size:
$1,000,000 to $5,000,000. Investment
Types: First and second stage, start-
up, mezzanine, leveraged buyouts,
and special situations. Industry
Preferences: Diversified. Geographic
Preferences: Southeast and Middle
Atlantic.

Massachusetts

Adams, Harkness & Hill, Inc.
60 State St.
Boston, MA 02109
Phone: (617)371-3900
Tim McMahan, Managing Director
Preferred Investment Size:
$1,000,000 minimum. Investment
Types: Second stage, balanced,
mezzanine, and special situation.
Industry Preferences: Computer,
consumer, electronics, business
services, industrial products and
equipment, and medical. Geographic
Preferences: Northeast.

Advent International
75 State St., 29th Fl.
Boston, MA 02109
Phone: (617)951-9400
Fax: (617)951-0566
Website: http://
www.adventinternational.com
Will Schmidt, Managing Director
Preferred Investment Size:
$1,000,000 minimum. Investment
Types: Seed, first and second stage,

mezzanine, leveraged buyout, special
situations, research and development,
and acquisitions. Industry
Preferences: Diversified. Geographic
Preferences: Entire U.S. and Canada.

American Research and Development
30 Federal St.
Boston, MA 02110-2508
Phone: (617)423-7500
Fax: (617)423-9655
Maureen A. White, Administrative
Manager
Preferred Investment Size: $100,000
minimum. Investment Types: Seed,
start-up, first and second stage.
industry Preferences: Diversified
technology. Geographic Preferences:
Northeast.

Ascent Venture Partners
255 State St., 5th Fl.
Boston, MA 02109
Phone: (617)270-9400
Fax: (617)270-9401
E-mail: info@ascentvp.com
Website: http://www.ascentvp.com
Leigh E. Michl, Managing Director
Investment Types: First stage and
acquisition. Industry Preferences:
Diversified. Geographic Preferences:
Northeast.

Atlas Venture
222 Berkeley St.
Boston, MA 02116
Phone: (617)488-2200
Fax: (617)859-9292
Website: http://
www.atlasventure.com
Preferred Investment Size: $500,000
to $20,000,000. Investment Types:
Seed, start-up, research and
development, first and second stage,
mezzanine, and balanced. Industry
Preferences: Communications,
computer, genetic engineering,
electronics, medical and health
related. Geographic Preferences:
Entire U.S. and Canada.

Axxon Capital
28 State St., 37th Fl.
Boston, MA 02109
Phone: (617)722-0980
Fax: (617)557-6014
Website: http://
www.axxoncapital.com

Preferred Investment Size: $300,000 to $2,500,000. Investment Types: Balanced. Industry Preferences: Communications and media. Geographic Preferences: Northeast.

BancBoston Capital/BancBoston Ventures
175 Federal St., 10th Fl.
Boston, MA 02110
Phone: (617)434-2509
Fax: (617)434-6175
Website: http://
www.bancbostoncapital.com
Frederick M. Fritz, President
Preferred Investment Size:
$1,000,000 to $100,000,000.
Investment Types: Seed, early stage, acquisition, recaps, later stage, management buyouts, expansion, and mezzanine. Industry Preferences: Diversified. Geographic Preferences: Entire U.S. and Eastern Canada.

Boston Capital Ventures
Old City Hall
45 School St.
Boston, MA 02108
Phone: (617)227-6550
Fax: (617)227-3847
E-mail: info@bcv.com
Website: http://www.bcv.com
Alexander Wilmerding
Preferred Investment Size: $250,000 to $8,000,000. Investment Types: Start-up, first and second stage, recaps, and leveraged buyouts. Industry Preferences: Diversified. Geographic Preferences: Entire U.S.

Boston Financial & Equity Corp.
20 Overland St.
PO Box 15071
Boston, MA 02215
Phone: (617)267-2900
Fax: (617)437-7601
E-mail: debbie@bfec.com
Deborah J. Monosson, Senior Vice President
Preferred Investment Size: $500,000 to $1,000,000. Investment Types: Seed, start-up, first and second stage, leveraged buyout, mezzanine, and research and development. Industry Preferences: Diversified. Geographic Preferences: National.

Boston Millennia Partners
30 Rowes Wharf

Boston, MA 02110
Phone: (617)428-5150
Fax: (617)428-5160
Website: http://
www.millenniapartners.com
Dana Callow, Managing General Partner
Preferred Investment Size:
$5,000,000 to $25,000,000.
Investment Policies: Equity.
Investment Types: First and second stage, start-up, leveraged buyout, and mezzanine. Industry Preferences: Communication, computer related, consumer services, electronics, genetic engineering, medical, and education. Geographic Preferences: National.

Bristol Investment Trust
842A Beacon St.
Boston, MA 02215-3199
Phone: (617)566-5212
Fax: (617)267-0932
E-mail: bernardberkman@prodigy.net
Preferred Investment Size: $100,000 minimum. Investment Policies: Equity. Investment Types: First and second stage, and mezzanine. Industry Preferences: Restaurants, retailing, consumer distribution, medical/health, and real estate. Geographic Preferences: Northeast.

Brook Venture Management LLC
50 Federal St., 5th Fl.
Boston, MA 02110
Phone: (617)451-8989
Fax: (617)451-2369
Website: http://
www.brookventure.com
Preferred Investment Size: $500,000 to $2,500,000. Investment Types: Early and first stage. Industry Preferences: Diversified. Geographic Preferences: Northeast.

Burr, Egan, Deleage, and Co. (Boston)
200 Clarendon St., Ste. 3800
Boston, MA 02116
Phone: (617)262-7770
Fax: (617)262-9779
Preferred Investment Size: $2,000,000. Investment Types: No preference. Industry Preferences: Communications, computer, and

medical/health related. Geographic Preferences: Entire U.S.

Cambridge/Samsung Partners
One Exeter Plaza
Ninth Fl.
Boston, MA 02116
Phone: (617)262-4440
Fax: (617)262-5562
Aashish Kalra, Associate
Preferred Investment Size: $100,000 minimum. Investment Policies: Equity. Investment Types: Early stage. Industry Preferences: Diversified. Geographic Preferences: National.

Chestnut Street Partners, Inc.
75 State St., Ste. 2500
Boston, MA 02109
Phone: (617)345-7220
Fax: (617)345-7201
E-mail: chestnut@chestnutp.com
Drew Zalkind, Senior Vice President
Preferred Investment Size: $100,000 to $1,000,000. Investment Types: Seed, research and development, start-up, and first stage. Industry Preferences: Diversified. Geographic Preferences: No preference.

Claflin Capital Management, Inc.
10 Liberty Sq., Ste. 300
Boston, MA 02109
Phone: (617)426-6505
Fax: (617)482-0016
Website: http://
www.claflincapital.com
William Wilcoxson, General Partner
Preferred Investment Size: $100,000 minimum. Investment Types: Seed, start-up, and first stage. Industry Preferences: Diversified. Geographic Preferences: Northeast.

Copley Venture Partners
99 Summer St., Ste. 1720
Boston, MA 02110
Phone: (617)737-1253
Fax: (617)439-0699
Preferred Investment Size:
$1,000,000 minimum. Investment Types: First and second stage, and start-up. Industry Preferences: Diversified. Geographic Preferences: No preference.

Corning Capital / Corning Technology Ventures

121 High Street, Ste. 400
Boston, MA 02110
Phone: (617)338-2656
Fax: (617)261-3864
Website: http://
www.corningventures.com
Preferred Investment Size: $100,000
to $500,000. Investment Policies:
Equity. Investment Types: Early
stage. Industry Preferences:
Diversified technology. Geographic
Preferences: Northeast.

Downer & Co.
211 Congress St.
Boston, MA 02110
Phone: (617)482-6200
Fax: (617)482-6201
E-mail: cdowner@downer.com
Website: http://www.downer.com
Charles W. Downer
Preferred Investment Size: $300,000
to $500,000. Investment Types: Start-
up, first and second stage, and
mezzanine. Industry Preferences:
Diversified. Geographic Preferences:
Northeastern U.S. and Canada.

Fidelity Ventures
82 Devonshire St.
Boston, MA 02109
Phone: (617)563-6370
Fax: (617)476-9023
Website: http://
www.fidelityventures.com
Neal Yanofsky, Vice President
Preferred Investment Size:
$1,000,000 to $10,000,000.
Investment Types: Start-up, first and
second stage, leveraged buyout, and
special situations. Industry
Preferences: Diversified. Geographic
Preferences: Northeast.

Greylock Management Corp.
(Boston)
1 Federal St.
Boston, MA 02110-2065
Phone: (617)423-5525
Fax: (617)482-0059
Chris Surowiec
Preferred Investment Size: $250,000
minimum. Investment Types: Seed,
start-up, first and early stage, and
expansion. Industry Preferences:
Diversified. Geographic Preferences:
No preference.

Gryphon Ventures
222 Berkeley St., Ste.1600
Boston, MA 02116
Phone: (617)267-9191
Fax: (617)267-4293
E-mail: all@gryphoninc.com
Andrew J. Atkinson, Vice President
Preferred Investment Size:
$1,000,000 minimum. Investment
Types: Start-up, first stage, second
stage. Industry Preferences: Energy/
natural resources, genetic
engineering, and industrial products
and equipment. Geographic
Preferences: National.

Halpern, Denny & Co.
500 Boylston St.
Boston, MA 02116
Phone: (617)536-6602
Fax: (617)536-8535
David P. Malm, Partner
Preferred Investment Size:
$5,000,000 to $40,000,000.
Investment Types: First stage, second
stage, control-black purchases, and
leveraged buyouts. Industry
Preferences: Consumer related,
Internet and computer related,
communications, industrial/energy,
and medical/health. Geographic
Preferences: National.

Harbourvest Partners, LLC
1 Financial Center, 44th Fl.
Boston, MA 02111
Phone: (617)348-3707
Fax: (617)350-0305
Website: http://www.hvpllc.com
Kevin Delbridge, Managing Partner
Preferred Investment Size:
$5,000,000 minimum. Investment
Types: All types. Industry
Preferences: Diversified. Geographic
Preferences: No preference.

Highland Capital Partners
2 International Pl.
Boston, MA 02110
Phone: (617)981-1500
Fax: (617)531-1550
E-mail: info@hcp.com
Website: http://www.hcp.com
Keith Benjamin, General Partner
Preferred Investment Size: $500,000
to $5,000,000. Investment Types:
Seed, start-up, and early, first and
second stage. Industry Preferences:

Communications, computer and
Internet related, genetic engineering,
and medical/health related.
Geographic Preferences: Entire U.S.
and Canada.

Lee Munder Venture Partners
John Hancock Tower T-53
200 Clarendon St.
Boston, MA 02103
Phone: (617)380-5600
Fax: (617)380-5601
Website: http://www.leemunder.com
Investment Types: Early, first,
second, and later stage; expansion;
mezzanine; seed; start-up; and special
situation. Industry Preferences:
Diversified. Geographic Preferences:
East Coast, Mid Atlantic, Northeast,
and Southeast.

M/C Venture Partners
75 State St., Ste. 2500
Boston, MA 02109
Phone: (617)345-7200
Fax: (617)345-7201
Website: http://
www.mcventurepartners.com
Matthew J. Rubins
Preferred Investment Size:
$5,000,000 to $20,000,000.
Investment Types: Early stage.
Industry Preferences:
communications, computer software
and services, Internet related.
Geographic Preferences: Entire U.S.
and Canada.

Massachusetts Capital Resources Co.
420 Boylston St.
Boston, MA 02116
Phone: (617)536-3900
Fax: (617)536-7930
William J. Torpey, Jr., President
Preferred Investment Size: $500,000
to $1,000,000. Investment Policies:
Equity. Investment Types: Second
stage, leveraged buyout, and
mezzanine. Industry Preferences: No
preference. Geographic Preferences:
Northeast.

Massachusetts Technology
Development Corp. (MTDC)
148 State St.
Boston, MA 02109
Phone: (617)723-4920
Fax: (617)723-5983

E-mail: jhodgman@mtdc.com
Website: http://www.mtdc.com
John F. Hodgman, President
Preferred Investment Size: $200,000
to $1,000,000. Investment Types:
Early, seed, and start-up. Industry
Preferences: Diversified. Geographic
Preferences: Massachusetts.

New England Partners
One Boston Place, Ste. 2100
Boston, MA 02108
Phone: (617)624-8400
Fax: (617)624-8999
Website: http://www.nepartners.com
Christopher P. Young
Preferred Investment Size:
$1,000,000 to $5,000,000. Investment
Types: Balanced, early, and first and
second stage. Industry Preferences:
Diversified. Geographic Preferences:
Entire U.S.

North Hill Ventures
Ten Post Office Square
11th Fl.
Boston, MA 02109
Phone: (617)788-2112
Fax: (617)788-2152
Website: http://
www.northhillventures.com
Preferred Investment Size:
$1,500,000 to $7,000,000. Investment
Types: Balanced, expansion, and later
and second stage. Industry
Preferences: Communications,
computer software, Internet related,
consumer and retail related, business
services, and financial services.
Geographic Preferences: Entire U.S.

OneLiberty Ventures
150 Cambridge Park Dr.
Boston, MA 02140
Phone: (617)492-7280
Fax: (617)492-7290
Website: http://www.oneliberty.com
Stephen J. McCullen, General Partner
Preferred Investment Size:
$1,000,000 to $8,000,000. Investment
Policies: Equity. Investment Types:
Early and late stage. Industry
Preferences: Diversified technology.
Geographic Preferences: Northeast.

Schroder Ventures
Life Sciences
60 State St., Ste. 3650

Boston, MA 02109
Phone: (617)367-8100
Fax: (617)367-1590
Website: http://
www.shroderventures.com
Preferred Investment Size: $250,000
minimum. Investment Types:
Balanced, first stage, leveraged
buyout, mezzanine, second stage,
special situation, and start-up.
Industry Preferences: Diversified.
Geographic Preferences: Entire U.S.
and Canada.

Shawmut Capital Partners
75 Federal St., 18th Fl.
Boston, MA 02110
Phone: (617)368-4900
Fax: (617)368-4910
Website: http://
www.shawmutcapital.com
Daniel Doyle, Managing Director
Preferred Investment Size:
$5,000,000 minimum. Investment
Types: Start-up, first stage, second
stage, mezzanine, leveraged buyout,
and special situations. Industry
Preferences: Financial services and
applications. Geographic Preferences:
Entire U.S. and Canada.

Solstice Capital LLC
15 Broad St., 3rd Fl.
Boston, MA 02109
Phone: (617)523-7733
Fax: (617)523-5827
E-mail: solticecapital@solcap.com
Henry Newman, Partner
Preferred Investment Size: $250,000
to $1,000,000. Investment Types:
Early and seed. Industry Preferences:
Diversified. Geographic Preferences:
Northeast, Rocky Mountain,
Southwest, West Coast.

Spectrum Equity Investors
One International Pl., 29th Fl.
Boston, MA 02110
Phone: (617)464-4600
Fax: (617)464-4601
Website: http://
www.spectrumequity.com
William Collatos, Managing General
Partner
Preferred Investment Size:
$5,000,000 minimum. Investment
Types: Balanced. Industry
Preferences: Communications and

computer related. Geographic
Preferences: U.S. and Canada.

Spray Venture Partners
One Walnut St.
Boston, MA 02108
Phone: (617)305-4140
Fax: (617)305-4144
Website: http://
www.sprayventure.com
Preferred Investment Size: $50,000 to
$4,000,000. Investment Policies:
Equity. Investment Types: Seed, start-
up, first and second stage, and
research and development. Industry
Preferences: Medical and health
related, and genetic engineering.
Geographic Preferences: National.

The Still River Fund
100 Federal St., 29th Fl.
Boston, MA 02110
Phone: (617)348-2327
Fax: (617)348-2371
Website: http://
www.stillriverfund.com
Preferred Investment Size: $300,000
to $4,000,000. Investment Types:
Early stage, expansion, first and
second stage, seed, and start-up.
Industry Preferences: Diversified.
Geographic Preferences: Entire U.S.

Summit Partners
600 Atlantic Ave., Ste. 2800
Boston, MA 02210-2227
Phone: (617)824-1000
Fax: (617)824-1159
Website: http://
www.summitpartners.com
Christopher W. Sheeline
Preferred Investment Size:
$1,500,000 minimum. Investment
Types: First and second stage,
mezzanine, leveraged buyout, special
situations, and control block
purchases. Industry Preferences:
Diversified. Geographic Preferences:
Entire U.S. and Canada.

TA Associates, Inc. (Boston)
High Street Tower
125 High St., Ste. 2500
Boston, MA 02110
Phone: (617)574-6700
Fax: (617)574-6728
Website: http://www.ta.com
Brian Conway, Managing Director

Preferred Investment Size: $60,000,000 maximum. Investment Types: Leveraged buyout, special situations, control block purchases. Industry Preferences: Diversified. Geographic Preferences: No preference.

TVM Techno Venture Management
101 Arch St., Ste. 1950
Boston, MA 02110
Phone: (617)345-9320
Fax: (617)345-9377
E-mail: info@tvmvc.com
Website: http://www.tvmvc.com
Helmut Schuehsler, Partner
Investment Types: Seed, start-up, first and early stage. Industry Preferences: Diversified. Geographic Preferences: Entire U.S.

UNC Ventures
64 Burough St.
Boston, MA 02130-4017
Phone: (617)482-7070
Fax: (617)522-2176
Preferred Investment Size: $500,000 to $1,000,000. Investment Types: Leveraged buyout, mezzanine, and second stage. Industry Preferences: Radio and television broadcasting, environmental related, and financial services. Geographic Preferences: Entire U.S.

Venture Investment Management Company (VIMAC)
177 Milk St.
Boston, MA 02190-3410
Phone: (617)292-3300
Fax: (617)292-7979
E-mail: bzeisig@vimac.com
Website: http://www.vimac.com
Preferred Investment Size: $1,000,000 to $7,000,000. Investment Types: Seed, start-up, first and second stage. Industry Preferences: Diversified technology. Geographic Preferences: Northeast U.S. and Eastern Canada.

MDT Advisers, Inc.
125 Cambridge Park Dr.
Cambridge, MA 02140-2314
Phone: (617)234-2200
Fax: (617)234-2210
Website: http://www.mdtai.com
Michael E.A. O'Malley

Preferred Investment Size: $500,000 to $5,000,000. Investment Types: Early stage and expansion. Industry Preferences: Diversified. Geographic Preferences: Northeast.

TTC Ventures
One Main St., 6th Fl.
Cambridge, MA 02142
Phone: (617)528-3137
Fax: (617)577-1715
E-mail: info@ttcventures.com
Investment Types: Seed, start-up, first stage, second stage, and mezzanine. Industry Preferences: Computer related. Geographic Preferences: National.

Zero Stage Capital Co. Inc.
101 Main St., 17th Fl.
Cambridge, MA 02142
Phone: (617)876-5355
Fax: (617)876-1248
Website: http://www.zerostage.com
Paul Kelley, President
Preferred Investment Size: $10,000 to $15,000,000. Investment Types: Early and later stage. Industry Preferences: Diversified technology. Geographic Preferences: Entire U.S.

Atlantic Capital
164 Cushing Hwy.
Cohasset, MA 02025
Phone: (617)383-9449
Fax: (617)383-6040
E-mail: info@atlanticcap.com
Website: http://www.atlanticcap.com
Preferred Investment Size: $300,000 to $500,000. Investment Types: Start-up and first stage. Industry Preferences: Diversified. Geographic Preferences: National.

Seacoast Capital Partners
55 Ferncroft Rd.
Danvers, MA 01923
Phone: (978)750-1300
Fax: (978)750-1301
E-mail: gdeli@seacoastcapital.com
Website: http://www.seacoastcapital.com
Gregory A. Hulecki
Preferred Investment Size: $3,000,000 minimum. Investment Policies: Loans and equity investments. Investment Types: Second stage, industry rollups,

leveraged buyout, mezzanine, and special situations. Industry Preferences: Diversified. Geographic Preferences: National.

Sage Management Group
44 South Street
PO Box 2026
East Dennis, MA 02641
Phone: (508)385-7172
Fax: (508)385-7272
E-mail: sagemgt@capecod.net
Charles Bauer
Preferred Investment Size: $500,000 to $1,000,000. Investment Policies: Equity. Investment Types: First and second stage, leveraged buyout, mezzanine, and special situations. Industry Preferences: Diversified technology. Geographic Preferences: National.

Applied Technology
1 Cranberry Hill
Lexington, MA 02421-7397
Phone: (617)862-8622
Fax: (617)862-8367
Ellie McCormack, Analyst
Preferred Investment Size: $100,000 to $2,000,000. Investment Types: Seed, start-up, first and second stage, leveraged buyout, and research and development. Industry Preferences: Diversified. Geographic Preferences: Entire U.S.

Royalty Capital Management
5 Downing Rd.
Lexington, MA 02421-6918
Phone: (781)861-8490
Preferred Investment Size: $100,000 to $300,000. Investment Types: Start-up, first stage, second stage, leveraged buyout, and special situations. Industry Preferences: Diversified. Geographic Preferences: Northeast.

Argo Global Capital
210 Broadway, Ste. 101
Lynnfield, MA 01940
Phone: (781)592-5250
Fax: (781)592-5230
Website: http://www.gsmcapital.com
Investment Types: Balanced and expansion. Industry Preferences: Communications, computer, and

Internet related. Geographic
Preferences: No preference.

Industry Ventures
6 Bayne Lane
Newburyport, MA 01950
Phone: (978)499-7606
Fax: (978)499-0686
Website: http://
www.industryventures.com
Preferred Investment Size: $250,000
to $2,000,000. Investment Types:
Early, first, and second stage; seed,
start-up. Industry Preferences:
Wireless communications, computer
software, Internet related, retail, and
media. Geographic Preferences: Mid
Atlantic, Northeast, West Coast.

Softbank Capital Partners
10 Langley Rd., Ste. 202
Newton Center, MA 02459
Phone: (617)928-9300
Fax: (617)928-9305
E-mail: clax@bvc.com
Gary Rieschel
Investment Types: Seed, start-up, first
stage, second stage, mezzanine,
leveraged buyout, and special
situations. Industry Preferences:
Communications and Internet.
Geographic Preferences: Entire U.S.
and Canada.

Advanced Technology Ventures
(Boston)
281 Winter St., Ste. 350
Waltham, MA 02451
Phone: (781)290-0707
Fax: (781)684-0045
E-mail: info@atvcapital.com
Website: http://www.atvcapital.com
Preferred Investment Size:
$15,000,000 to $35,000,000.
Investment Types: Start-up, first
stage, second stage, and balanced.
Industry Preferences: Diversified.
Geographic Preferences: No
preference.

Castile Ventures
890 Winter St., Ste. 140
Waltham, MA 02451
Phone: (781)890-0060
Fax: (781)890-0065
Website: http://
www.castileventures.com

Preferred Investment Size: $100,000
to $15,000,000. Investment Types:
Early, first, and second stage; seed;
and start-up. Industry Preferences:
Communications and media, and
Internet related. Geographic
Preferences: Mid Atlantic, Northeast,
and Southeast.

Charles River Ventures
1000 Winter St., Ste. 3300
Waltham, MA 02451
Phone: (781)487-7060
Fax: (781)487-7065
Website: http://www.crv.com
Richard M. Burnes, Jr., General
Partner
Preferred Investment Size:
$1,000,000 to $20,000,000.
Investment Types: Seed, start-up, first
and second stage. Industry
Preferences: Diversified. Geographic
Preferences: No preference.

Comdisco Venture Group (Waltham)
Totton Pond Office Center
400-1 Totten Pond Rd.
Waltham, MA 02451
Phone: (617)672-0250
Fax: (617)398-8099
Preferred Investment Size: $300,000
to $20,000,000. Investment Types:
Seed, start-up, first and second stage.
Industry Preferences: Diversified.
Geographic Preferences: National.

Marconi Ventures
890 Winter St., Ste. 310
Waltham, MA 02451
Phone: (781)839-7177
Fax: (781)522-7477
Website: http://www.marconi.com
Preferred Investment Size:
$1,000,000 to $10,000,000.
Investment Types: Balanced; first,
second, and later stage; and start-up.
Industry Preferences: Diversified.
Geographic Preferences: U.S. and
Canada.

Matrix Partners
Bay Colony Corporate Center
1000 Winter St., Ste.4500
Waltham, MA 02451
Phone: (781)890-2244
Fax: (781)890-2288
Website: http://
www.matrixpartners.com

Andrew Marcuvitz, General Partner
Preferred Investment Size: $500,000
to $1,000,000. Investment Types:
Start-up, first and second stage, and
leveraged buyout. Industry
Preferences: Diversified. Geographic
Preferences: Entire U.S.

North Bridge Venture Partners
950 Winter St. Ste. 4600
Waltham, MA 02451
Phone: (781)290-0004
Fax: (781)290-0999
E-mail: eta@nbvp.com
Preferred Investment Size:
$2,000,000 to $3,000,000. Investment
Types: Seed, research and
development, start-up, first and
second stage. Industry Preferences:
Communications, computer related,
medical/health, and electronics.
Geographic Preferences: Entire U.S.
and Canada.

Polaris Venture Partners
Bay Colony Corporate Ctr.
1000 Winter St., Ste. 3500
Waltham, MA 02451
Phone: (781)290-0770
Fax: (781)290-0880
E-mail:
partners@polarisventures.com
Website: http://
www.polarisventures.com
Michael Hirschland
Preferred Investment Size: $250,000
to $15,000,000. Investment Types:
Seed, start-up, first and second stages.
Industry Preferences: Information
technology, medical and health
related. Geographic Preferences:
National.

Seaflower Ventures
Bay Colony Corporate Ctr.
1000 Winter St. Ste. 1000
Waltham, MA 02451
Phone: (781)466-9552
Fax: (781)466-9553
E-mail: moot@seaflower.com
Website: http://www.seaflower.com
Alexander Moot, Partner
Investment Types: Seed, research and
development, start-up, first and
second stage, recaps, and strategic
alliances. Industry Preferences:

Diversified technology. Geographic Preferences: Eastern U.S. and Midwest.

Ampersand Ventures
55 William St., Ste. 240
Wellesley, MA 02481
Phone: (617)239-0700
Fax: (617)239-0824
E-mail: info@ampersandventures.com
Website: http://www.ampersandventures.com
Paul C. Zigman, Partner
Preferred Investment Size: $5,000,000 to $15,000,000. Investment Types: All types. Industry Preferences: Diversified. Geographic Preferences: No preference.

Battery Ventures (Boston)
20 William St., Ste. 200
Wellesley, MA 02481
Phone: (781)577-1000
Fax: (781)577-1001
Website: http://www.battery.com
David A. Hartwig
Preferred Investment Size: $3,000,000 to $35,000,000. Investment Types: Seed, start-up, first and second stage, mezzanine, and leveraged buyout. Industry Preferences: Communications, computer, computer and communications distribution. Geographic Preferences: No preference.

Commonwealth Capital Ventures, L.P.
20 William St., Ste.225
Wellesley, MA 02481
Phone: (781)237-7373
Fax: (781)235-8627
Website: http://www.ccvlp.com
Preferred Investment Size: $500,000 to $5,000,000. Investment Policies: Equity. Investment Types: Seed, start-up, first stage, leveraged buyout, mezzanine, and special situation. Industry Preferences: Diversified communication and computer technology, consumer products and services, retailing, distribution, electronics, medical and health related. Geographic Preferences: Northeast.

Fowler, Anthony & Company
20 Walnut St.
Wellesley, MA 02481
Phone: (781)237-4201
Fax: (781)237-7718
Preferred Investment Size: $4,000,000 to $5,000,000. Investment Types: All types. Industry Preferences: Diversified. Geographic Preferences: Entire U.S. and Canada.

Gemini Investors
20 William St.
Wellesley, MA 02481
Phone: (781)237-7001
Fax: (781)237-7233
C. Redington Barrett, III, Managing Director
Investment Types: Second stage, mezzanine, leveraged buyout, and special situations. Industry Preferences: Diversified. Geographic Preferences: National.

Grove Street Advisors Inc.
20 William St., Ste. 230
Wellesley, MA 02481
Phone: (781)263-6100
Fax: (781)263-6101
Website: http://www.grovestreetadvisors.com
Preferred Investment Size: $1,000,000 to $7,500,000. Investment Types: First stage, mezzanine, second stage, special situation, and start-up. Industry Preferences: Diversified. Geographic Preferences: U.S.

Mees Pierson Investeringsmaat B.V.
20 William St., Ste. 210
Wellesley, MA 02482
Phone: (781)239-7600
Fax: (781)239-0377
Dennis P. Cameron
Investment Types: First and second stage, and start-up. Industry Preferences: Diversified technology. Geographic Preferences: Entire U.S. and Canada.

Norwest Equity Partners
40 William St., Ste. 305
Wellesley, MA 02481-3902
Phone: (781)237-5870
Fax: (781)237-6270
Website: http://www.norwestvp.com
Charles B. Lennin

Preferred Investment Size: $1,000,000 to $25,000,000. Investment Types: Seed, early and later stage, and expansion. Industry Preferences: Diversified. Geographic Preferences: National.

Bessemer Venture Partners (Wellesley Hills)
83 Walnut St.
Wellesley Hills, MA 02481
Phone: (781)237-6050
Fax: (781)235-7576
E-mail: travis@bvpny.com
Website: http://www.bvp.com
Preferred Investment Size: $100,000 to $15,000,000. Investment Types: Seed, start-up, early stage, first and second stage, and expansion. Industry Preferences: Communications, computer related, consumer products, distribution, and electronics. Geographic Preferences: National.

Venture Capital Fund of New England
20 Walnut St., Ste. 120
Wellesley Hills, MA 02481-2175
Phone: (781)239-8262
Fax: (781)239-8263
E-mail: kjdvcfne3@aol.com
Kevin J. Dougherty, General Partner
Preferred Investment Size: $750,000 to $3,000,000. Investment Types: Start-up, first and second stage. Industry Preferences: Diversified. Geographic Preferences: Northeast.

Prism Venture Partners
100 Lowder Brook Dr., Ste. 2500
Westwood, MA 02090
Phone: (781)302-4000
Fax: (781)302-4040
E-mail: dwbaum@prismventure.com
Preferred Investment Size: $2,000,000 to $10,000,000. Investment Types: Start-up, first stage, second stage, and mezzanine. Industry Preferences: Communications, computer and Internet related, electronic components and instrumentation, medical and health. Geographic Preferences: U.S. and Canada.

Palmer Partners LP
200 Unicorn Park Dr.
Woburn, MA 01801

Phone: (781)933-5445
Fax: (781)933-0698
John Shane
Preferred Investment Size: $250,000 to $1,000,000. Investment Types: Start-up, first and second stage, and special situations. Industry Preferences: Communications, computer, energy/natural resources, industrial, education, finance, and publishing. Geographic Preferences: Northeast, Southeast, Southwest, Midwest, and Middle Atlantic; Central and Eastern Canada.

Michigan

Arbor Partners, L.L.C.
130 South First St.
Ann Arbor, MI 48104
Phone: (734)668-9000
Fax: (734)669-4195
Website: http://www.arborpartners.com
Preferred Investment Size: $250,000 minimum. Investment Policies: Equity. Investment Types: Early and expansion. Industry Preferences: Diversified technology. Geographic Preferences: Midwest.

EDF Ventures
425 N. Main St.
Ann Arbor, MI 48104
Phone: (734)663-3213
Fax: (734)663-7358
E-mail: edf@edfvc.com
Website: http://www.edfvc.com
Mary Campbell, Partner
Preferred Investment Size: $500,000 to $10,000,000. Investment Types: Seed, start-up, first stage, second stage, expansion, and research and development. Industry Preferences: Diversified technology. Geographic Preferences: Midwest.

White Pines Management, L.L.C.
2401 Plymouth Rd., Ste. B
Ann Arbor, MI 48105
Phone: (734)747-9401
Fax: (734)747-9704
E-mail: ibund@whitepines.com
Website: http://www.whitepines.com
Preferred Investment Size: $1,000,000 to $4,000,000. Investment Types: Second stage, mezzanine, leveraged buyout, and special

situations. Industry Preferences: Diversified. Geographic Preferences: Southeast and Midwest.

Wellmax, Inc.
3541 Bendway Blvd., Ste. 100
Bloomfield Hills, MI 48301
Phone: (248)646-3554
Fax: (248)646-6220
Preferred Investment Size: $100,000 to $1,000,000. Investment Policies: Equity. Investment Types: Start-up, early and late stage, leveraged buyout, and special situations. Industry Preferences: Diversified. Geographic Preferences: Midwest, Southeast.

Venture Funding, Ltd.
Fisher Bldg.
3011 West Grand Blvd., Ste. 321
Detroit, MI 48202
Phone: (313)871-3606
Fax: (313)873-4935
Monis Schuster, Vice President
Preferred Investment Size: $1,000,000 minimum. Investment Policies: Equity. Investment Types: Start-up, seed, leveraged buyout, research and development, and special situations. Industry Preferences: Diversified. Geographic Preferences: National.

Investcare Partners L.P. / GMA Capital LLC
32330 W. Twelve Mile Rd.
Farmington Hills, MI 48334
Phone: (248)489-9000
Fax: (248)489-8819
E-mail: gma@gmacapital.com
Website: http://www.gmacapital.com
Malcolm Moss, Managing Director
Investment Types: Second stage and leveraged buyout. Industry Preferences: Medical and health related. Geographic Preferences: National.

Liberty Bidco Investment Corp.
30833 Northwestern Highway, Ste. 211
Farmington Hills, MI 48334
Phone: (248)626-6070
Fax: (248)626-6072
James Zabriskie, Vice President
Preferred Investment Size: $500,000 minimum. Investment Types: Second

stage, leveraged buyout, mezzanine, and special situations. Industry Preferences: Diversified. Geographic Preferences: Midwestern U.S. and Ontario, Canada.

Seaflower Ventures
5170 Nicholson Rd.
PO Box 474
Fowlerville, MI 48836
Phone: (517)223-3335
Fax: (517)223-3337
E-mail: gibbons@seaflower.com
Website: http://www.seaflower.com
M. Christine Gibbons, Partner
Investment Types: Seed, research and development, start-up, recaps, strategic alliances, first and second stage. Industry Preferences: Genetic engineering, industrial products and equipment, medical and health related. Geographic Preferences: Midwest, Northeast, and Mid Atlantic.

Ralph Wilson Equity Fund LLC
15400 E. Jefferson Ave.
Gross Pointe Park, MI 48230
Phone: (313)821-9122
Fax: (313)821-9101
Website: http://www.RalphWilsonEquityFund.com
J. Skip Simms, President
Preferred Investment Size: $200,000 to $1,000,000. Investment Types: Balanced, early stage, expansion, and first and second stage. Industry Preferences: Diversified. Geographic Preferences: Entire U.S.

Minnesota

Development Corp. of Austin
1900 Eighth Ave., NW
Austin, MN 55912
Phone: (507)433-0346
Fax: (507)433-0361
E-mail: dca@smig.net
Website: http://www.spamtownusa.com
Preferred Investment Size: $100,000. Investment Types: Start-up, seed, and first stage. Industry Preferences: Diversified. Geographic Preferences: No preference.

Northeast Ventures Corp.
802 Alworth Bldg.

Duluth, MN 55802
Phone: (218)722-9915
Fax: (218)722-9871
Greg Sandbulte, President
Preferred Investment Size: $100,000
to $500,000. Investment Policies:
Equity. Investment Types: Start-up,
early and late stage, mezzanine,
leveraged buyout, and research and
development. Industry Preferences:
No preference. Geographic
Preferences: Midwest.

Medical Innovation Partners, Inc.
6450 City West Pkwy.
Eden Prairie, MN 55344-3245
Phone: (612)828-9616
Fax: (612)828-9596
Mark B. Knudson, Ph.D., Managing
Partner
Preferred Investment Size: $100,000
to $5,000,000. Investment Types:
Seed, start-up, and first stage.
Industry Preferences: Medical
technology and healthcare, and
communications. Geographic
Preferences: Northwest and Midwest.

St. Paul Venture Capital, Inc.
10400 Vicking Dr., Ste. 550
Eden Prairie, MN 55344
Phone: (612)995-7474
Fax: (612)995-7475
Website: http://www.stpaulvc.com
Preferred Investment Size: $500,000
minimum. Investment Types: Early
stage. Industry Preferences:
Diversified. Geographic Preferences:
California, Massachusetts, and
Minnesota.

Cherry Tree Investments, Inc.
7601 France Ave. S, Ste. 150
Edina, MN 55435
Phone: (612)893-9012
Fax: (612)893-9036
Website: http://www.cherrytree.com
Sandy Trump
Preferred Investment Size: $100,000
minimum. Investment Types:
Balanced and early second stage.
Industry Preferences: Diversified.
Geographic Preferences: Midwest.

Shared Ventures, Inc.
6550 York Ave. S
Edina, MN 55435
Phone: (612)925-3411

Howard Weiner
Preferred Investment Size: $100,000
to $300,000. Investment Types: First
and second stage, start-up, leveraged
buyout, control-block purchases, and
special situations. Industry
Preferences: Consumer, electronics,
distribution, energy/natural resources,
industrial products and equipment,
medical and health related.
Geographic Preferences: Midwest.

Sherpa Partners LLC
5050 Lincoln Dr., Ste. 490
Edina, MN 55436
Phone: (952)942-1070
Fax: (952)942-1071
Website: http://
www.sherpapartners.com
Preferred Investment Size: $250,000
to $5,000,000. Investment Types:
Early stage. Industry Preferences:
Telecommunications, computer
software, and Internet related.
Geographic Preferences: Midwest.

Affinity Capital Management
901 Marquette Ave., Ste. 1810
Minneapolis, MN 55402
Phone: (612)252-9900
Fax: (612)252-9911
Website: http://
www.affinitycapital.com
Edson W. Spencer
Preferred Investment Size: $250,000
to $1,100,000. Investment Types:
Seed, start-up, first and second stage.
Industry Preferences: Medical/Health
related, Internet and computer related.
Geographic Preferences: Midwest.

Artesian Capital
1700 Foshay Tower
821 Marquette Ave.
Minneapolis, MN 55402
Phone: (612)334-5600
Fax: (612)334-5601
E-mail: artesian@artesian.com
Frank B. Bennett, President
Preferred Investment Size: $300,000
to $500,000. Investment Types: Seed,
research and development, leveraged
buyout, and start-up. Industry
Preferences: Diversified. Geographic
Preferences: Midwest.

Coral Ventures
60 S. 6th St., Ste. 3510

Minneapolis, MN 55402
Phone: (612)335-8666
Fax: (612)335-8668
Website: http://
www.coralventures.com
Preferred Investment Size:
$1,000,000 to $11,000,000.
Investment Types: Seed, start-up, first
and second stage. Industry
Preferences: Diversified technology.
Geographic Preferences: No
preference.

Crescendo Venture Management,
L.L.C.
800 LaSalle Ave., Ste. 2250
Minneapolis, MN 55402
Phone: (612)607-2800
Fax: (612)607-2801
Website: http://
www.crescendoventures.com
Jeffrey R. Tollefson, Partner
Preferred Investment Size:
$1,000,000 to $5,000,000. Investment
Types: Start-up, seed, early and late
stage. Industry Preferences:
Diversified information technology.
Geographic Preferences: U.S. and
Canada.

Gideon Hixon Venture
1900 Foshay Tower
821 Marquette Ave.
Minneapolis, MN 55402
Phone: (612)904-2314
Fax: (612)204-0913
E-mail:
bkwhitney@gideonhixon.com
Preferred Investment Size: $300,000
to $500,000. Investment Policies:
Equity. Investment Types: Start-up,
seed, early and late stage. Industry
Preferences: Diversified
communication and computer
technology, medical/health, and
electronics. Geographic Preferences:
West Coast.

Norwest Equity Partners
3600 IDS Center
80 S. 8th St.
Minneapolis, MN 55402
Phone: (612)215-1600
Fax: (612)215-1601
Website: http://www.norwestvp.com
Charles B. Lennin, Partner
Preferred Investment Size:
$1,000,000 to $25,000,000.

Investment Policies: Equity.
Investment Types: Seed, expansion,
early and later stage. Industry
Preferences: Diversified. Geographic
Preferences: National.

Oak Investment Partners
(Minneapolis)
4550 Norwest Center
90 S. 7th St.
Minneapolis, MN 55402
Phone: (612)339-9322
Fax: (612)337-8017
Website: http://www.oakinv.com
Preferred Investment Size: $250,000
to $5,000,000. Investment Types:
Start-up, first stage, second and late
stage, leveraged buyout, control-
block purchases, open market, and
special situations. Industry
Preferences: Diversified. Geographic
Preferences: Entire U.S.

Pathfinder Venture Capital Funds
(Minneapolis)
7300 Metro Blvd., Ste. 585
Minneapolis, MN 55439
Phone: (612)835-1121
Fax: (612)835-8389
E-mail: jahrens620@aol.com
Jack K. Ahrens, II, Investment
Officer
Preferred Investment Size:
$2,000,000 minimum. Investment
Types: Seed, start-up, first and second
stage, mezzanine, leveraged buyouts,
and special situations. Industry
Preferences: Diversified. Geographic
Preferences: Entire U.S. and Canada.

U.S. Bancorp Piper Jaffray Ventures,
Inc.
800 Nicollet Mall, Ste. 800
Minneapolis, MN 55402
Phone: (612)303-5686
Fax: (612)303-1350
Website: http://
www.paperjaffreyventures.com
Preferred Investment Size: $250,000
minimum. Investment Types: Early
and late stage, and mezzanine.
Industry Preferences: Diversified.
Geographic Preferences: Entire U.S.

The Food Fund, Ltd. Partnership
5720 Smatana Dr., Ste. 300
Minnetonka, MN 55343
Phone: (612)939-3950

Fax: (612)939-8106
John Trucano, Managing General
Partner
Preferred Investment Size: $800,000
minimum. Investment Types: Start-
up, first and second stage, leveraged
buyout, and special situations.
Industry Preferences: Consumer
related, industrial and energy, and
electronics. Geographic Preferences:
Entire U.S.

Mayo Medical Ventures
200 First St. SW
Rochester, MN 55905
Phone: (507)266-4586
Fax: (507)284-5410
Website: http://www.mayo.edu
Preferred Investment Size:
$1,000,000 minimum. Investment
Types: Early stage. Industry
Preferences: Diversified. Geographic
Preferences: Entire U.S.

Missouri

Bankers Capital Corp.
3100 Gillham Rd.
Kansas City, MO 64109
Phone: (816)531-1600
Fax: (816)531-1334
Lee Glasnapp, Vice President
Preferred Investment Size: $100,000
minimum. Investment Types:
Leveraged buyout. Industry
Preferences: Consumer product and
electronics distribution, and industrial
equipment and machinery.
Geographic Preferences: Midwest.

Capital for Business, Inc. (Kansas
City)
1000 Walnut St., 18th Fl.
Kansas City, MO 64106
Phone: (816)234-2357
Fax: (816)234-2952
Website: http://
www.capitalforbusiness.com
Hollis A. Huels
Preferred Investment Size: $500,000
to $5,000,000. Investment Types:
Expansion, leveraged and
management buyouts, and later stage.
Industry Preferences: Diversified.
Geographic Preferences: Midwest.

De Vries & Co. Inc.
800 West 47th St.

Kansas City, MO 64112
Phone: (816)756-0055
Fax: (816)756-0061
Preferred Investment Size: $500,000
minimum. Investment Types:
Acquisition, expansion, later stage,
leveraged and management buyout,
mezzanine, private placement, recaps,
and second stage. Industry
Preferences: Diversified. Geographic
Preferences: No preference.

InvestAmerica Venture Group Inc.
(Kansas City)
Commerce Tower
911 Main St., Ste. 2424
Kansas City, MO 64105
Phone: (816)842-0114
Fax: (816)471-7339
Kevin F. Mullane, Vice President
Preferred Investment Size: $500,000
to $1,000,000. Investment Types:
First and second stage, leveraged
buyout, and special situations.
Industry Preferences: Diversified.
Geographic Preferences: Entire U.S.

Kansas City Equity Partners
233 W. 47th St.
Kansas City, MO 64112
Phone: (816)960-1771
Fax: (816)960-1777
Website: http://www.kcep.com
Preferred Investment Size:
$2,000,000 to $8,000,000. Investment
Types: Start-up, early stage,
expansion, and joint ventures.
Industry Preferences: Diversified.
Geographic Preferences: Midwest.

Bome Investors, Inc.
8000 Maryland Ave., Ste. 1190
St. Louis, MO 63105
Phone: (314)721-5707
Fax: (314)721-5135
Website: http://
www.gatewayventures.com
Gregory R. Johnson
Preferred Investment Size: $500,000
to $1,000,000. Investment Types:
Start-up, early and late stage. Industry
Preferences: Diversified. Geographic
Preferences: Midwest.

Capital for Business, Inc. (St. Louis)
11 S. Meramac St., Ste. 1430
St. Louis, MO 63105
Phone: (314)746-7427

Fax: (314)746-8739
Website: http://
www.capitalforbusiness.com
Hollis A. Huels
Preferred Investment Size: $500,000
to $5,000,000. Investment Types:
Expansion, leveraged and
management buyouts, and later stage.
Industry Preferences: Diversified.
Geographic Preferences: Midwest.

Crown Capital Corp.
540 Maryville Centre Dr., Ste. 120
Saint Louis, MO 63141
Phone: (314)576-1201
Fax: (314)576-1525
Website: http://www.crown-cap.com
Investment Types: Control-block
purchases, first stage, leveraged
buyout, mezzanine, second stage, and
special situation. Industry
Preferences: Diversified. Geographic
Preferences: Entire U.S. and Canada.

Gateway Associates L.P.
8000 Maryland Ave., Ste. 1190
St. Louis, MO 63105
Phone: (314)721-5707
Fax: (314)721-5135
John S. McCarthy, Managing General
Partner
Preferred Investment Size:
$1,000,000 minimum. Investment
Types: Start-up, second stage,
mezzanine, leveraged buyout, special
situations, control block purchases.
Industry Preferences:
Communications, computer related,
electronics, and hospital and other
institutional management. Geographic
Preferences: Entire U.S.

Harbison Corp.
8112 Maryland Ave., Ste. 250
Saint Louis, MO 63105
Phone: (314)727-8200
Fax: (314)727-0249
Keith Harbison
Preferred Investment Size: $500,000
minimum. Investment Types:
Control-block purchases, leveraged
buyout, and special situation. Industry
Preferences: Diversified. Geographic
Preferences: Mid Atlantic and
Southeast; Ontario and Quebec,
Canada.

Nebraska

Heartland Capital Fund, Ltd.
PO Box 642117
Omaha, NE 68154
Phone: (402)778-5124
Fax: (402)445-2370
Website: http://
www.heartlandcapitalfund.com
John G. Gustafson, Vice President
Preferred Investment Size: $500,000
to $3,000,000. Investment Policies:
Equity. Investment Types: First and
second stage, and expansion. Industry
Preferences: Diversified technology.
Geographic Preferences: Southwest
and Midwest.

Odin Capital Group
1625 Farnam St., Ste. 700
Omaha, NE 68102
Phone: (402)346-6200
Fax: (402)342-9311
Website: http://www.odincapital.com
Preferred Investment Size:
$1,000,000 to $5,000,000. Investment
Types: Early, first, and second stage,
and expansion. Industry Preferences:
Internet related and financial services.
Geographic Preferences: U.S.

Nevada

Edge Capital Investment Co. LLC
1350 E. Flamingo Rd., Ste. 3000
Las Vegas, NV 89119
Phone: (702)438-3343
E-mail: info@edgecapital.net
Website: http://www.edgecapital.net
Preferred Investment Size: $500,000
to $15,000,000. Investment Types:
Seed, start-up, first stage, second
stage, mezzanine, leveraged buyout,
and special situations. Industry
Preferences: Diversified technology.
Geographic Preferences: U.S. and
Canada.

The Benefit Capital Companies Inc.
PO Box 542
Logandale, NV 89021
Phone: (702)398-3222
Fax: (702)398-3700
Robert Smiley
Preferred Investment Size:
$2,500,000 minimum. Investment
Types: Leveraged buyout and
mezzanine. Industry Preferences:

Diversified. Geographic Preferences:
Entire U.S.

Millennium Three Venture Group
LLC
6880 South McCarran Blvd., Ste. A-
11
Reno, NV 89509
Phone: (775)954-2020
Fax: (775)954-2023
Website: http://www.m3vg.com
Preferred Investment Size: $500,000
to $2,000,000. Investment Types:
Early stage, expansion, first stage,
mezzanine, second stage, and seed.
Industry Preferences: Diversified.
Geographic Preferences: West Coast.

New Jersey

Alan I. Goldman & Associates
497 Ridgewood Ave.
Glen Ridge, NJ 07028
Phone: (973)857-5680
Fax: (973)509-8856
Alan Goldman
Preferred Investment Size: $500,000
minimum. Investment Types:
Control-block purchases, leveraged
buyout, mezzanine, second stage, and
special situation. Industry
Preferences: Diversified. Geographic
Preferences: Entire U.S. and Canada.

CS Capital Partners LLC
328 Second St., Ste. 200
Lakewood, NJ 08701
Phone: (732)901-1111
Fax: (212)202-5071
Website: http://www.cs-capital.com
Preferred Investment Size: $500,000
to $3,000,000. Investment Types:
Distressed debt, early stage,
expansion, first and second stage, and
turnaround. Industry Preferences:
Internet and computer related,
communications, and medical/health
related. Geographic Preferences:
Entire U.S. and Ontario and Quebec,
Canada.

Edison Venture Fund
1009 Lenox Dr., Ste. 4
Lawrenceville, NJ 08648
Phone: (609)896-1900
Fax: (609)896-0066
E-mail: info@edisonventure.com

Website: http://
www.edisonventure.com
John H. Martinson, Managing Partner
Preferred Investment Size:
$1,000,000 to $6,000,000. Investment
Types: Early and later stage,
expansion, and management buyouts.
Industry Preferences: Diversified.
Geographic Preferences: Northeast
and Middle Atlantic.

Tappan Zee Capital Corp. (New
Jersey)
201 Lower Notch Rd.
PO Box 416
Little Falls, NJ 07424
Phone: (973)256-8280
Fax: (973)256-2841
Jeffrey Birnberg, President
Preferred Investment Size: $100,000
to $250,000. Investment Types:
Leveraged buyout. Industry
Preferences: Diversified. Geographic
Preferences: No preference.

The CIT Group/Venture Capital, Inc.
650 CIT Dr.
Livingston, NJ 07039
Phone: (973)740-5429
Fax: (973)740-5555
Website: http://www.cit.com
Preferred Investment Size:
$3,000,000 minimum. Investment
Types: First and second stage,
mezzanine, and leveraged buyout.
Industry Preferences: Diversified.
Geographic Preferences: Entire U.S.

Capital Express, L.L.C.
1100 Valleybrook Ave.
Lyndhurst, NJ 07071
Phone: (201)438-8228
Fax: (201)438-5131
E-mail: niles@capitalexpress.com
Website: http://
www.capitalexpress.com
Niles Cohen
Preferred Investment Size: $300,000
to $500,000. Investment Policies:
Equity. Investment Types: Start-up,
first and second stage, and recaps.
Industry Preferences: Internet and
consumer related, and publishing.
Geographic Preferences: East Coast.

Westford Technology Ventures, L.P.
17 Academy St.
Newark, NJ 07102

Phone: (973)624-2131
Fax: (973)624-2008
Preferred Investment Size: $300,000
to $500,000. Investment Types: Start-
up, first and second stage. Industry
Preferences: Diversified
communication and computer
technology, electronics, industrial
products and equipment. Geographic
Preferences: No preference.

Accel Partners
1 Palmer Sq.
Princeton, NJ 08542
Phone: (609)683-4500
Fax: (609)683-4880
Website: http://www.accel.com
Preferred Investment Size:
$1,000,000 minimum. Investment
Types: Seed, start-up and early stage.
Industry Preferences: Diversified.
Geographic Preferences: National.

Cardinal Partners
221 Nassau St.
Princeton, NJ 08542
Phone: (609)924-6452
Fax: (609)683-0174
Website: http://
www.cardinalhealthpartners.com
Lisa Skeete Tatum, Associate
Preferred Investment Size:
$1,000,000 to $8,000,000. Investment
Types: Seed, start-up, first and second
stage. Industry Preferences:
Diversified. Geographic Preferences:
U.S. and Canada.

Domain Associates L.L.C.
One Palmer Sq., Ste. 515
Princeton, NJ 08542
Phone: (609)683-5656
Fax: (609)683-9789
Website: http://www.domainvc.com
Preferred Investment Size:
$1,000,000 to $20,000,000.
Investment Types: Seed, start-up, first
and second stage, balanced,
expansion, mezzanine, private
placement, research and development,
and late stage. Industry Preferences:
Electronic components and
instrumentation, genetic engineering,
industrial products and equipment,
medical and health related.
Geographic Preferences: National.

Johnston Associates, Inc.
181 Cherry Valley Rd.
Princeton, NJ 08540
Phone: (609)924-3131
Fax: (609)683-7524
E-mail: jaincorp@aol.com
Preferred Investment Size: $500,000
to $5,000,000. Investment Types:
Start-up and early stage. Industry
Preferences: Science and healthcare
industry. Geographic Preferences:
Northeast.

Kemper Ventures
Princeton Forrestal Village
155 Village Blvd.
Princeton, NJ 08540
Phone: (609)936-3035
Fax: (609)936-3051
Richard Secchia, Partner
Investment Types: Seed, research and
development, start-up, first and
second stage. Industry Preferences:
Computer related, medical and health
related, financial services.
Geographic Preferences: National.

Penny Lane Parnters
One Palmer Sq., Ste. 309
Princeton, NJ 08542
Phone: (609)497-4646
Fax: (609)497-0611
Preferred Investment Size:
$1,000,000. Investment Types:
Recaps, second stage, and leveraged
buyouts. Industry Preferences:
Computer related, genetic
engineering, medical/health related,
and electronics. Geographic
Preferences: Eastern U.S.

Early Stage Enterprises L.P.
995 Route 518
Skillman, NJ 08558
Phone: (609)921-8896
Fax: (609)921-8703
Website: http://www.esevc.com
Ronald R. Hahn, Managing Director
Preferred Investment Size: $250,000
to $1,000,000. Investment Types:
Seed, start-up, and early stage.
Industry Preferences: Diversified.
Geographic Preferences: Mid
Atlantic.

MBW Management Inc.
1 Springfield Ave.
Summit, NJ 07901

Phone: (908)273-4060
Fax: (908)273-4430
Preferred Investment Size:
$1,000,000 minimum. Investment
Types: First stage, leveraged buyout,
second stage, special situation, and
start-up. Industry Preferences:
Diversified. Geographic Preferences:
No preference.

BCI Advisors, Inc.
Glenpointe Center W.
Teaneck, NJ 07666
Phone: (201)836-3900
Fax: (201)836-6368
E-mail: info@bciadvisors.com
Website: http://www.bcipartners.com
Thomas J. Cusick, General Partner
Preferred Investment Size:
$5,000,000 to $25,000,000.
Investment Types: Expansion.
Industry Preferences: Diversified.
Geographic Preferences: Entire U.S.

Demuth, Folger & Wetherill / DFW
Capital Partners
Glenpointe Center E., 5th Fl.
300 Frank W. Burr Blvd.
Teaneck, NJ 07666
Phone: (201)836-2233
Fax: (201)836-5666
Website: http://www.dfwcapital.com
Donald F. DeMuth, General Partner
Preferred Investment Size: $500,000
minimum. Investment Policies:
Equity. Investment Types:
Acquisition, control-block purchases,
later stage, leveraged buyout,
management buyout, recaps, and
special situations. Industry
Preferences: Healthcare, computer,
communication, diversified.
Geographic Preferences: National.

First Princeton Capital Corp.
189 Berdan Ave., No. 131
Wayne, NJ 07470-3233
Phone: (973)278-3233
Fax: (973)278-4290
Website: http://www.lytellcatt.net
Michael Lytell
Preferred Investment Size: $200,000
minimum. Investment Types: First
and second stage, mezzanine, recaps,
control-block purchases, and
leveraged buyout. Industry
Preferences: Diversified. Geographic

Preferences: Northeast and East
Coast.

Edelson Technology Partners
300 Tice Blvd.
Woodcliff Lake, NJ 07675
Phone: (201)930-9898
Fax: (201)930-8899
Website: http://www.edelsontech.com
Harry Edelson, Managing Partner
Preferred Investment Size: $500,000
to $1,000,000. Investment Types:
Seed, start-up, first and second stage,
leveraged buyout, and mezzanine.
Industry Preferences: Diversified.
Geographic Preferences: No
preference.

New Mexico

Bruce F. Glaspell & Associates
10400 Academy Rd. NE, Ste. 313
Albuquerque, NM 87111
Phone: (505)292-4505
Fax: (505)292-4258
Bruce Glaspell
Preferred Investment Size: $100,000
to $5,000,000. Investment Types:
Seed, start-up, first stage, second
stage, late stage, private placement,
and expansion. Industry Preferences:
Diversified. Geographic Preferences:
Entire U.S. and Canada.

High Desert Ventures, Inc.
6101 Imparata St. NE, Ste. 1721
Albuquerque, NM 87111
Phone: (505)797-3330
Fax: (505)338-5147
E-mail: zilenziger@aol.com
Preferred Investment Size: $500,000
to $2,500,000. Investment Types:
Start-up and early stage. Industry
Preferences: Diversified. Geographic
Preferences: Northeast and
Southwest.

New Business Capital Fund, Ltd.
5805 Torreon NE
Albuquerque, NM 87109
Phone: (505)822-8445
Preferred Investment Size: $100,000.
Investment Policies: Equity.
Investment Types: Seed, start-up, and
first stage. Industry Preferences:
Diversified. Geographic Preferences:
No preference.

SBC Ventures
10400 Academy Rd. NE, Ste. 313
Albuquerque, NM 87111
Phone: (505)292-4505
Fax: (505)292-4528
Viviana Cloninger, General Partner
Preferred Investment Size: $300,000
to $3,000,000. Investment Types:
Seed, research and development,
start-up, and first stage. Industry
Preferences: Diversified. Geographic
Preferences: Entire U.S. and Canada.

Technology Ventures Corp.
1155 University Blvd. SE
Albuquerque, NM 87106
Phone: (505)246-2882
Fax: (505)246-2891
Beverly Bendicksen
Investment Types: Seed, start-up, first
and second stage. Industry
Preferences: Diversified. Geographic
Preferences: Southwest.

New York

New York State Science &
Technology Foundation
Small Business Technology
Investment Fund
99 Washington Ave., Ste. 1731
Albany, NY 12210
Phone: (518)473-9741
Fax: (518)473-6876
E-mail: jvanwie@empire.state.ny.us
Preferred Investment Size: $100,000
to $300,000. Investment Types: Seed,
start-up, first and second stage.
Industry Preferences: Diversified
technology. Geographic Preferences:
Northeast.

Rand Capital Corp.
2200 Rand Bldg.
Buffalo, NY 14203
Phone: (716)853-0802
Fax: (716)854-8480
Website: http://www.randcapital.com
Allen F. Grum, President and CEO
Preferred Investment Size: $25,000 to
$500,000. Investment Types: Second
stage. Industry Preferences:
Diversified. Geographic Preferences:
Northeast and Ontario, Canada.

Seed Capital Partners
620 Main St.
Buffalo, NY 14202

Phone: (716)845-7520
Fax: (716)845-7539
Website: http://www.seedcp.com
Investment Types: Early stage.
Industry Preferences: Diversified
technology, communications, and
other products. Geographic
Preferences: Northeast.

Coleman Venture Group
5909 Northern Blvd.
PO Box 224
East Norwich, NY 11732
Phone: (516)626-3642
Fax: (516)626-9722
Preferred Investment Size: $100,000
to $1,000,000. Investment Types:
First stage, recaps, seed, start-up, and
special situation. Industry
Preferences: Electronics and
consumer products. Geographic
Preferences: Northeast and West
Coast, and Canada.

Vega Capital Corp.
45 Knollwood Rd.
Elmsford, NY 10523
Phone: (914)345-9500
Fax: (914)345-9505
Ronald Linden
Preferred Investment Size: $300,000
minimum. Investment Types: Second
stage, mezzanine, leveraged buyout,
and special situations. Industry
Preferences: Diversified. Geographic
Preferences: Northeast, Southeast,
and Middle Atlantic.

Herbert Young Securities, Inc.
98 Cuttermill Rd.
Great Neck, NY 11021
Phone: (516)487-8300
Fax: (516)487-8319
Herbert D. Levine, President
Preferred Investment Size:
$1,000,000 minimum. Investment
Types: First and second stage,
leveraged buyout, mezzanine, and
special situation. Industry
Preferences: Diversified
communications and computer
technology, consumer products and
services, electronics, genetic
engineering, healthcare, and real
estate. Geographic Preferences:
National.

Sterling/Carl Marks Capital, Inc.
175 Great Neck Rd., Ste. 408
Great Neck, NY 11021
Phone: (516)482-7374
Fax: (516)487-0781
E-mail: stercrlmar@aol.com
Website: http://
www.serlingcarlmarks.com
Preferred Investment Size:
$1,000,000 to $2,000,000. Investment
Types: Second stage, expansion,
management buyouts, and mezzanine.
Industry Preferences: Consumer
related; distribution of electronics
equipment, food and industrial
products; and industrial equipment
and machinery. Geographic
Preferences: Northeast.

Impex Venture Management Co.
PO Box 1570
Green Island, NY 12183
Phone: (518)271-8008
Fax: (518)271-9101
Jay Banker
Preferred Investment Size:
$1,000,000 minimum. Investment
Types: First stage, leveraged buyout,
second stage, special situation, and
start-up. Industry Preferences:
Diversified. Geographic Preferences:
Mid Atlantic and Northeast, and
Quebec, Canada.

Corporate Venture Partners L.P.
200 Sunset Park
Ithaca, NY 14850
Phone: (607)257-6323
Fax: (607)257-6128
Preferred Investment Size: $500,000
to $1,000,000. Investment Types:
First stage. Industry Preferences:
Diversified. Geographic Preferences:
Northeast.

Arthur P. Gould & Co.
One Wilshire Dr.
Lake Success, NY 11020
Phone: (516)773-3000
Fax: (516)773-3289
Andrew Gould, Vice President
Preferred Investment Size:
$5,000,000 minimum. Investment
Types: Seed, research and
development, start-up, first stage,
second stage, mezzanine, and
leveraged buyout. Industry

Preferences: Diversified. Geographic
Preferences: National.

Dauphin Capital Partners
108 Forest Ave.
Locust Valley, NY 11560
Phone: (516)759-3339
Fax: (516)759-3322
Website: http://
www.dauphincapital.com
Preferred Investment Size:
$1,000,000 to $3,000,000. Investment
Types: Balanced; and early, first,
second, and later stage. Industry
Preferences: Diversified technology,
education, and business services.
Geographic Preferences: Entire U.S.

550 Digital Media Ventures
555 Madison Ave., 10th Fl.
New York, NY 10022
Website: http://www.550dmv.com
Investment Types: Early stage.
Industry Preferences: Entertainment
and leisure, and media. Geographic
Preferences: Entire U.S.

Aberlyn Capital Management Co.,
Inc.
500 Fifth Ave.
New York, NY 10110
Phone: (212)391-7750
Fax: (212)391-7762
Lawrence Hoffman, Chairman and
CEO
Preferred Investment Size:
$25,000,000 minimum. Investment
Types: Start-up, first and second
stage, leveraged buyout, and special
situation. Industry Preferences:
Diversified computer technology,
food and beverage products, genetic
engineering, and healthcare.
Geographic Preferences: National.

Adler & Company
342 Madison Ave., Ste. 807
New York, NY 10173
Phone: (212)599-2535
Fax: (212)599-2526
Jay Nickse, Treasurer & Chief
Financial Officer
Investment Types: Start-up, first and
second stage, leveraged buyout, and
control-block purchases. Industry
Preferences: Diversified. Geographic
Preferences: National.

Alimansky Capital Group, Inc.
605 Madison Ave., Ste. 300
New York, NY 10022-1901
Phone: (212)832-7300
Fax: (212)832-7338
Howard Duby, Managing Director
Preferred Investment Size:
$2,000,000. Investment Types: First
stage, second stage, mezzanine,
leveraged buyout, and special
situations. Industry Preferences:
Diversified. Geographic Preferences:
Entire U.S. and Canada.

Allegra Partners
515 Madison Ave., 29th Fl.
New York, NY 10022
Phone: (212)826-9080
Fax: (212)759-2561
Preferred Investment Size:
$1,000,000 minimum. Investment
Types: First stage, leveraged buyout,
recaps, second stage, and special
situation. Industry Preferences:
Communications, computer related,
and consumer related. Geographic
Preferences: Mid Atlantic, and
Eastern and Western U.S.

The Argentum Group
The Chyrsler Bldg.
405 Lexington Ave.
New York, NY 10174
Phone: (212)949-6262
Fax: (212)949-8294
Website: http://
www.argentumgroup.com
Walter H. Barandiaran, Managing
Dir.
Preferred Investment Size:
$10,000,000 minimum. Investment
Types: Second stage, mezzanine,
leveraged buyout, and special
situations. Industry Preferences:
Diversified. Geographic Preferences:
Entire U.S.

Axavision Inc.
14 Wall St., 26th Fl.
New York, NY 10005
Phone: (212)619-4000
Fax: (212)619-7202
Preferred Investment Size: $100,000
to $300,000. Investment Types: Seed
and start-up. Industry Preferences:
Computer services and software,
Internet related, and financial

services. Geographic Preferences: No
preference.

Bedford Capital Corp.
18 East 48th St., Ste. 1800
New York, NY 10017
Phone: (212)688-5700
Fax: (212)754-4699
E-mail: info@bedfordnyc.com
Website: http://www.bedfordnyc.com
Nathan Bernstein
Preferred Investment Size: $100,000
to $300,000. Investment Types: First
and second stage, industry rollups,
recaps, and leveraged buyout.
Industry Preferences: Diversified.
Geographic Preferences: Midwest.

Bloom & Co.
950 Third Ave.
New York, NY 10022
Phone: (212)838-1858
Fax: (212)838-1843
Jack S. Bloom, President
Preferred Investment Size:
$3,000,000 minimum. Investment
Types: Start-up, first and second
stage, control-block purchases,
leveraged buyout, mezzanine, and
special situation. Industry
Preferences: No preference.
Geographic Preferences: No
preference.

Bristol Capital Management
300 Park Ave., 17th Fl.
New York, NY 10022
Phone: (212)572-6306
Fax: (212)705-4292
Investment Types: Leveraged buyout,
mezzanine, second stage, and special
situation. Industry Preferences:
Communications, computer related,
electronics, medical/health related,
entertainment and leisure, retail, food/
beverage, consumer services,
machinery, and publishing.
Geographic Preferences: Entire U.S.

Citicorp Venture Capital Ltd. (New
York City)
399 Park Ave., 14th Fl.
Zone 4
New York, NY 10043
Phone: (212)559-1127
Fax: (212)888-2940
Preferred Investment Size:
$5,000,000. Investment Types:

Leveraged buyout, second stage, and
special situations. Industry
Preferences: Diversified. Geographic
Preferences: No preference.

CM Equity Partners
135 E. 57th St.
New York, NY 10022
Phone: (212)909-8428
Fax: (212)980-2630
Preferred Investment Size:
$2,000,000 minimum. Investment
Types: First and second stage, start-
up, mezzanine, leveraged buyout,
special situations, and industry
rollups. Industry Preferences:
Diversified. Geographic Preferences:
No preference.

Cohen & Co., L.L.C.
800 Third Ave.
New York, NY 10022
Phone: (212)317-2250
Fax: (212)317-2255
E-mail: nlcohen@aol.com
Neil L. Cohen, President
Preferred Investment Size:
$10,000,000 minimum. Investment
Types: Start-up, seed, early and late
stage, mezzanine, leveraged buyout,
control-block purchases, and special
situations. Industry Preferences:
Communications, consumer,
distribution, electronics, energy, and
healthcare. Geographic Preferences:
National.

Cornerstone Equity Investors, L.L.C.
717 5th Ave., Ste. 1100
New York, NY 10022
Phone: (212)753-0901
Fax: (212)826-6798
Website: http://www.cornerstone-
equity.com
Mark Rossi, Senior Managing
Director
Preferred Investment Size:
$50,000,000 maximum. Investment
Types: Leveraged buyout, and special
situations. Industry Preferences:
Diversified. Geographic Preferences:
No preference.

CW Group, Inc.
1041 3rd Ave., 2nd fl.
New York, NY 10021
Phone: (212)308-5266
Fax: (212)644-0354

Website: http://www.cwventures.com
Christopher Fenimore
Preferred Investment Size: $100,000
to $5,000,000. Investment Types:
Seed, research and development,
start-up, first and second stage,
leveraged buyout, special situations,
and control block purchases. Industry
Preferences: Specialize in the
medical/health business and
biotechnology. Geographic
Preferences: Entire U.S.

DH Blair Investment Banking Corp.
44 Wall St., 2nd Fl.
New York, NY 10005
Phone: (212)495-5000
Fax: (212)269-1438
J. Morton Davis, Chairman
Preferred Investment Size: $100,000.
Investment Types: Research and
development, start-up, first stage, and
leveraged buyout. Industry
Preferences: Diversified. Geographic
Preferences: No preference.

Dresdner Kleinwort Capital
75 Wall St.
New York, NY 10005
Phone: (212)429-3131
Fax: (212)429-3139
Website: http://www.dresdnerkb.com
Richard Wolf, Partner
Preferred Investment Size:
$5,000,000 minimum. Investment
Types: Early and second stage,
expansion, mezzanine, and leveraged
buyout. Industry Preferences:
Diversified. Geographic Preferences:
National.

East River Ventures, L.P.
645 Madison Ave., 22nd Fl.
New York, NY 10022
Phone: (212)644-2322
Fax: (212)644-5498
Montague H. Hackett
Preferred Investment Size: $500,000
to $5,000,000. Investment Types:
Early and late stage, and mezzanine.
Industry Preferences: Diversified
communication and computer
technology, consumer services, and
medical. Geographic Preferences:
National.

Easton Hunt Capital Partners
641 Lexington Ave., 21st Fl.

New York, NY 10017
Phone: (212)702-0950
Fax: (212)702-0952
Website: http://
www.eastoncapital.com
Investment Types: First stage,
mezzanine, and special situations.
Industry Preferences: Diversified.
Geographic Preferences: Entire U.S.

Elk Associates Funding Corp.
747 3rd Ave., Ste. 4C
New York, NY 10017
Phone: (212)355-2449
Fax: (212)759-3338
Gary C. Granoff, Pres.
Preferred Investment Size: $100,000
to $300,000. Investment Types:
Second stage and leveraged buyout.
Industry Preferences: Radio and TV,
consumer franchise businesses, hotel
and resort areas, and transportation.
Geographic Preferences: Southeast
and Midwest.

EOS Partners, L.P.
320 Park Ave., 22nd Fl.
New York, NY 10022
Phone: (212)832-5800
Fax: (212)832-5815
E-mail: mfirst@eospartners.com
Website: http://www.eospartners.com
Mark L. First, Managing Director
Preferred Investment Size:
$3,000,000. Investment Policies:
Equity and equity-oriented debt.
Investment Types: Industry rollups,
leveraged buyout, mezzanine, second
stage, and special situation. Industry
Preferences: Diversified. Geographic
Preferences: Entire United States and
Canada.

Euclid Partners
45 Rockefeller Plaza, Ste. 3240
New York, NY 10111
Phone: (212)218-6880
Fax: (212)218-6877
E-mail: graham@euclidpartners.com
Website: http://
www.euclidpartners.com
Preferred Investment Size: $500,000
to $5,000,000. Investment Types:
Start-up, first and second stage.
Industry Preferences: Internet related,
computer software and services,
genetic engineering, and medical/

health related. Geographic
Preferences: No preference.

Evergreen Capital Partners, Inc.
150 East 58th St.
New York, NY 10155
Phone: (212)813-0758
Fax: (212)813-0754
E-mail:
rysmith@evergreencapital.com
Preferred Investment Size:
$1,000,000 to $300,000,000.
Investment Types: No preference.
Industry Preferences: Diversified.
Geographic Preferences: National.

Exeter Capital L.P.
10 E. 53rd St.
New York, NY 10022
Phone: (212)872-1172
Fax: (212)872-1198
E-mail: exeter@usa.net
Karen J. Watai, Partner
Preferred Investment Size:
$1,000,000 minimum. Investment
Policies: Loans and equity
investments. Investment Types:
Leveraged buyout, mezzanine, second
stage, and special situation. Industry
Preferences: Diversified. Geographic
Preferences: National.

Financial Technology Research Corp.
518 Broadway
Penthouse
New York, NY 10012
Phone: (212)625-9100
Fax: (212)431-0300
E-mail: fintek@financier.com
Neal Bruckman, President
Preferred Investment Size: $300,000
to $500,000. Investment Types: Seed,
research and development, start-up,
first stage, second stage, and special
situations. Industry Preferences:
Diversified. Geographic Preferences:
Entire U.S. and Canada.

4C Ventures
237 Park Ave., Ste. 801
New York, NY 10017
Phone: (212)692-3680
Fax: (212)692-3685
Website: http://www.4cventures.com
Ted Hobart, Partner
Preferred Investment Size: $500,000
to $1,000,000. Investment Types:

Seed, research and development,
start-up, first and second stage.
Industry Preferences:
Communications, computer related,
and consumer. Geographic
Preferences: Entire U.S. and Canada.

Fusient Ventures
99 Park Ave., 20th Fl.
New York, NY 10016
Phone: (212)972-8999
Fax: (212)972-9876
E-mail: info@fusient.com
Website: http://www.fusient.com
Preferred Investment Size: $500,000
to $3,000,000. Investment Types:
Early and first stage, and seed.
Industry Preferences: Internet,
entertainment and leisure, and media.
Geographic Preferences: U.S.

Generation Capital Partners
551 Fifth Ave., Ste. 3100
New York, NY 10176
Phone: (212)450-8507
Fax: (212)450-8550
Website: http://www.genpartners.com
Preferred Investment Size:
$5,000,000. Investment Types: Start-
up, early and late stage, and leveraged
buyout. Industry Preferences:
Diversified communications and
computer technology, consumer
products and services, and industrial
products and equipment. Geographic
Preferences: United States and
Canada.

Golub Associates, Inc.
555 Madison Ave.
New York, NY 10022
Phone: (212)750-6060
Fax: (212)750-5505
Evelyn Mordechai, Vice President
Preferred Investment Size:
$1,000,000 to $10,000,000.
Investment Types: Second stage,
mezzanine, leveraged buyout, recaps,
and special situations. Industry
Preferences: Diversified. Geographic
Preferences: Eastern U.S.

Hambro America Biosciences Inc.
650 Madison Ave., 21st Floor
New York, NY 10022
Phone: (212)223-7400
Fax: (212)223-0305

Preferred Investment Size:
$2,500,000 to $5,000,000. Investment
Types: First and second stage, and
special situations. Industry
Preferences: Genetic engineering,
chemicals and materials, and medical/
health related. Geographic
Preferences: Entire U.S.

Hanover Capital Corp.
505 Park Ave., 15th Fl.
New York, NY 10022
Phone: (212)755-1222
Fax: (212)935-1787
Michael Wainstein
Preferred Investment Size: $300,000
minimum. Investment Types:
Leveraged buyout, mezzanine, and
second stage. Industry Preferences:
Diversified. Geographic Preferences:
Entire U.S.

Harvest Partners, Inc.
280 Park Ave, 33rd Fl.
New York, NY 10017
Phone: (212)559-6300
Fax: (212)812-0100
Website: http://www.harvpart.com
Harvey Mallement
Preferred Investment Size:
$15,000,000 to $100,000,000.
Investment Types: Acquisition,
leveraged buyout, management
buyouts, private placements, special
situations, and turnaround. Industry
Preferences: Consumer products and
services, communications,
distribution, fiberoptics, and medical/
health related. Geographic
Preferences: No preference.

Holding Capital Group, Inc.
10 E. 53rd St., 30th Fl.
New York, NY 10022
Phone: (212)486-6670
Fax: (212)486-0843
James W. Donaghy, President
Preferred Investment Size:
$5,000,000. Investment Types:
Leveraged buyout. Industry
Preferences: No preference.
Geographic Preferences: Entire U.S.

Hudson Venture Partners
660 Madison Ave., 14th Fl.
New York, NY 10021-8405
Phone: (212)644-9797
Fax: (212)644-7430

Website: http://www.hudsonptr.com
Marilyn Adler
Preferred Investment Size: $500,000
to $2,800,000. Investment Types:
Seed, start-up, first and early stages,
and expansion. Industry Preferences:
Diversified. Geographic Preferences:
Entire U.S.

IBJS Capital Corp.
1 State St., 9th Fl.
New York, NY 10004
Phone: (212)858-2018
Fax: (212)858-2768
George Zombeck, Chief Operating
Officer
Preferred Investment Size:
$2,000,000. Investment Types:
Mezzanine, leveraged buyout, and
special situations. Industry
Preferences: Consumer products and
services, and chemicals and materials.
Geographic Preferences: Entire U.S.

InterEquity Capital Partners, L.P.
220 5th Ave.
New York, NY 10001
Phone: (212)779-2022
Fax: (212)779-2103
Website: http://www.interequity-
capital.com
Preferred Investment Size:
$1,000,000 to $3,000,000. Investment
Types: First and second stage,
mezzanine, leveraged buyout, and
special situations. Industry
Preferences: Diversified. Geographic
Preferences: Entire U.S.

The Jordan Edmiston Group Inc.
150 East 52nd St., 18th Fl.
New York, NY 10022
Phone: (212)754-0710
Fax: (212)754-0337
Scott Peters
Preferred Investment Size:
$1,000,000. Investment Types:
Leveraged buyout, mezzanine, second
stage, and special situation. Industry
Preferences: Publishing. Geographic
Preferences: No preference.

Josephberg, Grosz and Co., Inc.
633 3rd Ave., 13th Fl.
New York, NY 10017
Phone: (212)974-9926
Fax: (212)397-5832
Richard Josephberg

Preferred Investment Size: $1,000,000 to $30,000,000. Investment Types: Many types including seed, research and development, start-up, first and second stage, mezzanine, and leveraged buyout. Industry Preferences: Diversified. Geographic Preferences: Entire U.S.

J.P. Morgan Capital Corp.
60 Wall St.
New York, NY 10260-0060
Phone: (212)648-9000
Fax: (212)648-5002
Website: http://www.jpmorgan.com
Lincoln E. Frank, Chief Operating Officer
Preferred Investment Size: $10,000,000 to $20,000,000. Investment Types: Second stage and special situations. Industry Preferences: Diversified. Geographic Preferences: Entire U.S. and Canada.

The Lambda Funds
380 Lexington Ave., 54th Fl.
New York, NY 10168
Phone: (212)682-3454
Fax: (212)682-9231
Preferred Investment Size: $200,000 to $500,000. Investment Types: Early stage, expansion, first and second stage, and management buyout. Industry Preferences: Diversified. Geographic Preferences: Mid Atlantic, Northeast, and West Coast.

Lepercq Capital Management Inc.
1675 Broadway
New York, NY 10019
Phone: (212)698-0795
Fax: (212)262-0155
Michael J. Connelly
Preferred Investment Size: $1,000,000 to $10,000,000. Investment Types: Control-block purchases, leveraged buyout, and second stage. Industry Preferences: Diversified. Geographic Preferences: No preference.

Loeb Partners Corp.
61 Broadway, Ste. 2400
New York, NY 10006
Phone: (212)483-7000
Fax: (212)574-2001

Preferred Investment Size: $100,000. Investment Types: Early stage, acquisition, expansion, leveraged and management buyout. Industry Preferences: Diversified. Geographic Preferences: National.

Madison Investment Partners
660 Madison Ave.
New York, NY 10021
Phone: (212)223-2600
Fax: (212)223-8208
Preferred Investment Size: $5,000,000. Investment Types: Second stage, leveraged buyout, and industry roll ups. Industry Preferences: Diversified. Geographic Preferences: National.

MC Capital Inc.
520 Madison Ave., 16th Fl.
New York, NY 10022
Phone: (212)644-0841
Fax: (212)644-2926
Shunichi Maeda
Preferred Investment Size: $1,000,000 to $30,000,000. Investment Types: Acquisition, expansion, first stage, fund of funds, generalist PE, joint ventures, later stage, leveraged buyout, private placement, second stage, special situation, and turnaround. Industry Preferences: Communications, computers, electronics, biotechnology, and medical/health related. Geographic Preferences: Entire U.S. and Canada.

McCown, De Leeuw and Co. (New York)
65 E. 55th St., 36th Fl.
New York, NY 10022
Phone: (212)355-5500
Fax: (212)355-6283
Website: http://www.mdcpartners.com
Christopher Crosby, Principal
Preferred Investment Size: $40,000,000 minimum. Investment Types: Leveraged buyout and special situations. Industry Preferences: Diversified. Geographic Preferences: Entire U.S.

Morgan Stanley Venture Partners
1221 Avenue of the Americas, 33rd Fl.

New York, NY 10020
Phone: (212)762-7900
Fax: (212)762-8424
E-mail: msventures@ms.com
Website: http://www.msvp.com
Preferred Investment Size: $2,000,000. Investment Types: Second stage, mezzanine, leveraged buyout, and industry roll ups. Industry Preferences: Diversified technology. Geographic Preferences: Entire U.S. and Canada.

Nazem and Co.
645 Madison Ave., 12th Fl.
New York, NY 10022
Phone: (212)371-7900
Fax: (212)371-2150
E-mail: nazem@msn.com
Fred F. Nazem, Managing General Partner
Preferred Investment Size: $1,000,000 minimum. Investment Types: Seed, start-up, first and second stage, mezzanine, leveraged buyout, and special situations. Industry Preferences: Diversified. Geographic Preferences: No preference.

Needham Capital Management, L.L.C.
445 Park Ave.
New York, NY 10022
Phone: (212)371-8300
Fax: (212)705-0299
Website: http://www.needhamco.com
Joseph Abramoff
Preferred Investment Size: $1,000,000 to $10,000,000. Investment Policies: Equity. Investment Types: Expansion, later stage, leveraged buyout, management buyout, and mezzanine. Industry Preferences: Diversified technology. Geographic Preferences: National.

Norwood Venture Corp.
1430 Broadway, Ste. 1607
New York, NY 10018
Phone: (212)869-5075
Fax: (212)869-5331
E-mail: nvc@mail.idt.net
Website: http://www.norven.com
Mark Littell
Preferred Investment Size: $500,000 to $1,000,000. Investment Types: Mezzanine, leveraged buyout, and special situations. Industry

Preferences: Diversified. Geographic Preferences: National.

Noveltek Venture Corp.
521 Fifth Ave., Ste. 1700
New York, NY 10175
Phone: (212)286-1963
Preferred Investment Size: $1,000,000 minimum. Investment Types: Control-block purchases, first stage, mezzanine, second stage, special situation, and start-up. Industry Preferences: Diversified. Geographic Preferences: Entire U.S. and Canada.

Paribas Principal, Inc.
787 7th Ave.
New York, NY 10019
Phone: (212)841-2005
Fax: (212)841-3558
Gary Binning
Preferred Investment Size: $50,000,000. Investment Types: Leveraged buyout, special situations, and control block purchases. Industry Preferences: Diversified. Geographic Preferences: Entire U.S.

Patricof & Co. Ventures, Inc. (New York)
445 Park Ave.
New York, NY 10022
Phone: (212)753-6300
Fax: (212)319-6155
Website: http://www.patricof.com
Preferred Investment Size: $500,000 minimum. Investment Types: Seed, start-up, first and second stage, mezzanine, and leveraged buyout. Industry Preferences: Diversified. Geographic Preferences: No preference.

The Platinum Group, Inc.
350 Fifth Ave, Ste. 7113
New York, NY 10118
Phone: (212)736-4300
Fax: (212)736-6086
Website: http://www.platinumgroup.com
Michael Grant, Analyst
Investment Types: Start-up, first stage, second stage, and leveraged buyout. Industry Preferences: Diversified. Geographic Preferences: National.

Pomona Capital
780 Third Ave., 28th Fl.
New York, NY 10017
Phone: (212)593-3639
Fax: (212)593-3987
Website: http://www.pomonacapital.com
Karen Macleod
Preferred Investment Size: $1,000,000 minimum. Investment Types: Various investment types. Industry Preferences: Diversified. Geographic Preferences: Entire U.S.

Prospect Street Ventures
10 East 40th St., 44th Fl.
New York, NY 10016
Phone: (212)448-0702
Fax: (212)448-9652
E-mail: wkohler@prospectstreet.com
Website: http://www.prospectstreet.com
Edward Ryeom, Vice President
Preferred Investment Size: $1,000,000 minimum. Investment Types: First and second stage, start-up, control-block purchases, recaps, and special situations. Industry Preferences: Internet related, computer software and services, computer hardware, and communications. Geographic Preferences: East and West Coast, and Eastern Canada.

Regent Capital Management
505 Park Ave., Ste. 1700
New York, NY 10022
Phone: (212)735-9900
Fax: (212)735-9908
E-mail: ninamcle@aol.com
Richard Hochman, Managing Director
Preferred Investment Size: $3,500,000 minimum. Investment Types: Second stage, mezzanine, and leveraged buyout. Industry Preferences: Communications, consumer products and services. Geographic Preferences: National.

Rothschild Ventures, Inc.
1251 Avenue of the Americas, 51st Fl.
New York, NY 10020
Phone: (212)403-3500
Fax: (212)403-3652

Website: http://www.nmrothschild.com
Preferred Investment Size: $500,000 to $5,000,000. Investment Types: Seed, research and development, start-up, first and second stage, mezzanine, and leveraged buyout. Industry Preferences: Diversified. Geographic Preferences: Entire U.S. and Canada.

Sandler Capital Management
767 Fifth Ave., 45th Fl.
New York, NY 10153
Phone: (212)754-8100
Fax: (212)826-0280
Preferred Investment Size: $20,000,000 minimum. Investment Policies: Equity. Investment Types: Seed, start-up, first and second stage, control-block purchases, leveraged buyout, mezzanine, research and development, and special situation. Industry Preferences: Diversified communication and computer technology, consumer products and services, education, and publishing. Geographic Preferences: United States and Canada.

Siguler Guff & Company
630 Fifth Ave., 16th Fl.
New York, NY 10111
Phone: (212)332-5100
Fax: (212)332-5120
Maria Boyazny, Associate
Investment Types: Start-up, first stage, second stage, control-block purchases, mezzanine, leveraged buyout, and special situations. Industry Preferences: Diversified. Geographic Preferences: National.

Spencer Trask Ventures Inc.
535 Madison Ave.
New York, NY 10022
Phone: (212)355-5565
Fax: (212)751-3362
Website: http://www.spencertrask.com
A. Emerson Martin, II, Senior Managing Director
Preferred Investment Size: $3,000,000 minimum. Investment Types: Start-up, first stage, second stage, and special situations. Industry Preferences: Diversified. Geographic Preferences: National.

Sprout Group (New York City)
277 Park Ave.
New York, NY 10172
Phone: (212)892-3600
Fax: (212)892-3444
E-mail: info@sproutgroup.com
Website: http://
www.sproutgroup.com
Patrick J. Boroian, General Partner
Preferred Investment Size:
$5,000,000 to $50,000,000.
Investment Types: Seed, start-up, first
and second stage, mezzanine,
leveraged buyout, and special
situations. Industry Preferences:
Diversified technology. Geographic
Preferences: Entire U.S.

US Trust Private Equity
114 W.47th St.
New York, NY 10036
Phone: (212)852-3949
Fax: (212)852-3759
Website: http://www.ustrust.com/
privateequity
Jim Ruler
Preferred Investment Size:
$5,000,000 minimum. Investment
Types: Early, first stage, and second
stage. Industry Preferences:
Diversified. Geographic Preferences:
National.

Vencon Management Inc.
301 West 53rd St., Ste. 10F
New York, NY 10019
Phone: (212)581-8787
Fax: (212)397-4126
Website: http://www.venconinc.com
Ingrid Yang
Preferred Investment Size: $500,000
to $10,000,000. Investment Types:
First and second stage, leveraged
buyout, seed, special situation, and
start-up. Industry Preferences:
Diversified. Geographic Preferences:
Entire U.S. and Canada.

Venrock Associates
30 Rockefeller Plaza, Ste. 5508
New York, NY 10112
Phone: (212)649-5600
Fax: (212)649-5788
Website: http://www.venrock.com
Preferred Investment Size: $500,000
minimum. Investment Types: Seed,
research and development, start-up,
first and second stages. Industry

Preferences: Diversified. Geographic
Preferences: National.

Venture Capital Fund of America,
Inc.
509 Madison Ave., Ste. 812
New York, NY 10022
Phone: (212)838-5577
Fax: (212)838-7614
E-mail: mail@vcfa.com
Website: http://www.vcfa.com
Dayton T. Carr, General Partner
Preferred Investment Size: $500,000
to $100,000,000. Investment Types:
Secondary partnership interests.
Industry Preferences: Does not
consider tax shelters, real estate, or
direct investments in companies.
Geographic Preferences: Entire U.S.

Venture Opportunities Corp.
150 E. 58th St.
New York, NY 10155
Phone: (212)832-3737
Fax: (212)980-6603
E-mail: jerryvoc@aol.com
Jerry March
Preferred Investment Size:
$2,000,000 minimum. Investment
Types: Start-up, first and second
stage, mezzanine, leveraged buyout,
and special situations. Industry
Preferences: Diversified. Geographic
Preferences: Entire U.S.

Warburg Pincus Ventures, Inc.
466 Lexington Ave., 11th Fl.
New York, NY 10017
Phone: (212)878-9309
Fax: (212)878-9200
Website: http://
www.warburgpincus.com
Preferred Investment Size:
$1,000,000 to $500,000,000.
Investment Types: Many types
including seed, start-up, first and
second stage, mezzanine, leveraged
buyouts, private placements, recaps,
and special situations. Industry
Preferences: Diversified. Geographic
Preferences: U.S. and Canada.

Wasserstein, Perella & Co. Inc.
31 W. 52nd St., 27th Fl.
New York, NY 10019
Phone: (212)702-5691
Fax: (212)969-7879
Perry W. Steiner

Investment Types: Leveraged buyout.
Industry Preferences: Diversified.
Geographic Preferences: National.

Welsh, Carson, Anderson, & Stowe
320 Park Ave., Ste. 2500
New York, NY 10022-6815
Phone: (212)893-9500
Fax: (212)893-9575
Patrick J. Welsh, General Partner
Preferred Investment Size:
$25,000,000 minimum. Investment
Types: Leveraged buyout and special
situations. Industry Preferences:
Computer related and medical/health
related. Geographic Preferences:
Entire U.S.

Whitney and Co. (New York)
630 Fifth Ave. Ste. 3225
New York, NY 10111
Phone: (212)332-2400
Fax: (212)332-2422
Website: http://www.jhwitney.com
Preferred Investment Size:
$1,000,000. Investment Types:
Leveraged buyout and expansion.
Industry Preferences: Diversified
technology. Geographic Preferences:
No preference.

Winthrop Ventures
74 Trinity Place, Ste. 600
New York, NY 10006
Phone: (212)422-0100
Cyrus Brown
Preferred Investment Size:
$1,000,000 minimum. Investment
Types: Start-up, early and late stage,
and leveraged buyout. Industry
Preferences: Diversified. Geographic
Preferences: National.

The Pittsford Group
8 Lodge Pole Rd.
Pittsford, NY 14534
Phone: (716)223-3523
Preferred Investment Size: $100,000
to $300,000. Investment Types: Start-
up, first and second stage, and
control-block purchases. Industry
Preferences: Diversified technology.
Geographic Preferences: Eastern U.S.
and Canada.

Genesee Funding
70 Linden Oaks, 3rd Fl.
Rochester, NY 14625
Phone: (716)383-5550

Fax: (716)383-5305
Preferred Investment Size: $200,000.
Investment Types: Second stage,
mezzanine, and leveraged buyout.
Industry Preferences: Diversified.
Geographic Preferences: Northeast.

Gabelli Multimedia Partners
One Corporate Center
Rye, NY 10580
Phone: (914)921-5395
Fax: (914)921-5031
E-mail: fsommer@gabelli.com
Preferred Investment Size: $250,000
to $500,000. Investment Policies:
Equity. Investment Types: Seed, start-
up, first and second stage. Industry
Preferences: Diversified
communications. Geographic
Preferences: Northeast.

Stamford Financial
108 Main St.
Stamford, NY 12167
Phone: (607)652-3311
Fax: (607)652-6301
Website: http://
www.stamfordfinancial.com
Alexander C. Brosda
Preferred Investment Size:
$1,000,000 to $2,500,000. Investment
Types: Expansion and mezzanine.
Industry Preferences: Diversified.
Geographic Preferences: Entire U.S.

Northwood Ventures LLC
485 Underhill Blvd., Ste. 205
Syosset, NY 11791
Phone: (516)364-5544
Fax: (516)364-0879
E-mail: northwood@northwood.com
Website: http://
www.northwoodventures.com
Paul Homer, Associate
Preferred Investment Size:
$1,000,000 to $10,000,000.
Investment Types: First and second
stage, acquisition, expansion,
leveraged buyout, private placement,
special situations, and industry roll
ups. Industry Preferences:
Diversified. Geographic Preferences:
Entire U.S. and Canada.

Exponential Business Development
Co.
216 Walton St.
Syracuse, NY 13202-1227

Phone: (315)474-4500
Fax: (315)474-4682
E-mail: dirksonn@aol.com
Website: http://www.exponential-
ny.com
Dirk E. Sonneborn, Partner
Preferred Investment Size: $100,000
to $600,000. Investment Types: Early
and first stage. Industry Preferences:
No preference. Geographic
Preferences: New York.

Onondaga Venture Capital Fund Inc.
714 State Tower Bldg.
Syracuse, NY 13202
Phone: (315)478-0157
Fax: (315)478-0158
Irving Schwartz
Preferred Investment Size: $100,000
to $250,000. Investment Types:
Expansion, later stage, and
mezzanine. Industry Preferences:
Diversified. Geographic Preferences:
Mid Atlantic and Northeast.

Bessemer Venture Partners
(Westbury)
1400 Old Country Rd., Ste. 109
Westbury, NY 11590
Phone: (516)997-2300
Fax: (516)997-2371
E-mail: bob@bvpny.com
Website: http://www.bvp.com
Investment Types: Seed, research and
development, start-up, first stages,
leveraged buyout, special situations,
and expansion. Industry Preferences:
Communications, computer related,
consumer products, distribution, and
electronics. Geographic Preferences:
Entire U.S.

Ovation Capital Partners
120 Bloomingdale Rd., 4th Fl.
White Plains, NY 10605
Phone: (914)258-0011
Fax: (914)684-0848
Website: http://
www.ovationcapital.com
Preferred Investment Size: $500,000
to $4,000,000. Investment Types:
Early stage. Industry Preferences:
Internet related. Geographic
Preferences: Northeast.

North Carolina

Carolinas Capital Investment Corp.
1408 Biltmore Dr.

Charlotte, NC 28207
Phone: (704)375-3888
Fax: (704)375-6226
E-mail: ed@carolinacapital.com
Edward Goode
Preferred Investment Size: $200,000
to $1,000,000. Investment Types:
Seed, research and development,
leveraged buyout, start-up, first and
second stages. Industry Preferences:
Communications, electronic
components and instrumentation.
Geographic Preferences: No
preference.

First Union Capital Partners
1st Union Center, 12th Fl.
301 S. College St.
Charlotte, NC 28288-0732
Phone: (704)383-0000
Fax: (704)374-6711
Website: http://www.fucp.com
L. Watts Hamrick, III, Partner
Preferred Investment Size:
$5,000,000 minimum. Investment
Types: Seed, start-up, first and second
stage, mezzanine, expansion,
leveraged buyout, special situations,
and control block purchases. Industry
Preferences: Diversified. Geographic
Preferences: No preference.

Frontier Capital LLC
525 North Tryon St., Ste. 1700
Charlotte, NC 28202
Phone: (704)414-2880
Fax: (704)414-2881
Website: http://
www.frontierfunds.com
Preferred Investment Size: $500,000
to $3,000,000. Investment Types:
Early stage and expansion. Industry
Preferences: Telecommunications,
computer related, electronics, and
energy. Geographic Preferences: Mid
Atlantic and Southeast.

Kitty Hawk Capital
2700 Coltsgate Rd., Ste. 202
Charlotte, NC 28211
Phone: (704)362-3909
Fax: (704)362-2774
Website: http://
www.kittyhawkcapital.com
Stephen W. Buchanan, General
Partner
Preferred Investment Size:
$1,000,000 to $7,000,000. Investment

Types: Expansion, first and early stage. Industry Preferences: Diversified. Geographic Preferences: Southeast.

Piedmont Venture Partners
One Morrocroft Centre
6805 Morisson Blvd., Ste. 380
Charlotte, NC 28211
Phone: (704)731-5200
Fax: (704)365-9733
Website: http://
www.piedmontvp.com
Preferred Investment Size: $250,000
to $5,000,000. Investment Types:
Early stage. Industry Preferences:
Diversified. Geographic Preferences:
Southeast.

Ruddick Investment Co.
1800 Two First Union Center
Charlotte, NC 28282
Phone: (704)372-5404
Fax: (704)372-6409
Richard N. Brigden, Vice President
Preferred Investment Size: $500,000
to $1,000,000. Investment Types:
First and second stage, and
mezzanine. Industry Preferences:
Diversified. Geographic Preferences:
Southeast.

The Shelton Companies Inc.
3600 One First Union Center
301 S. College St.
Charlotte, NC 28202
Phone: (704)348-2200
Fax: (704)348-2260
Preferred Investment Size:
$1,000,000 to $10,000,000.
Investment Types: Control-block
purchases, leveraged buyouts, recaps,
and second stage. Industry
Preferences: Diversified. Geographic
Preferences: Mid Atlantic, Midwest,
Southeast, and Southwest.

Wakefield Group
1110 E. Morehead St.
PO Box 36329
Charlotte, NC 28236
Phone: (704)372-0355
Fax: (704)372-8216
Website: http://
www.wakefieldgroup.com
Anna Nelson, Partner
Preferred Investment Size:
$1,000,000 to $5,000,000. Investment

Types: Early stage. Industry
Preferences: Diversified. Geographic
Preferences: Southeast.

Aurora Funds, Inc.
2525 Meridian Pkwy., Ste. 220
Durham, NC 27713
Phone: (919)484-0400
Fax: (919)484-0444
Website: http://
www.aurorafunds.com
Preferred Investment Size: $250,000
to $1,500,000. Investment Types:
Start-up, seed, early and first stage.
Industry Preferences: Diversified.
Geographic Preferences: Eastern
United States.

Intersouth Partners
3211 Shannon Rd., Ste. 610
Durham, NC 27707
Phone: (919)493-6640
Fax: (919)493-6649
E-mail: info@intersouth.com
Website: http://www.intersouth.com
Jonathan Perl
Preferred Investment Size:
$2,000,000 to $10,000,000.
Investment Types: Seed, start-up, first
and early stages. Industry
Preferences: Diversified. Geographic
Preferences: Southeast and
Southwest.

Geneva Merchant Banking Partners
PO Box 21962
Greensboro, NC 27420
Phone: (336)275-7002
Fax: (336)275-9155
Website: http://
www.genevamerchantbank.com
Preferred Investment Size:
$1,000,000 to $7,000,000. Investment
Types: Balanced, distressed debt,
expansion, leveraged and
management buyout, mezzanine,
second stage, and special situation.
Industry Preferences: Diversified.
Geographic Preferences: Mid
Atlantic, Midwest, and Southeast.

The North Carolina Enterprise Fund,
L.P.
3600 Glenwood Ave., Ste. 107
Raleigh, NC 27612
Phone: (919)781-2691
Fax: (919)783-9195
Website: http://www.ncef.com

Charles T. Closson, President and
CEO
Preferred Investment Size:
$2,000,000 minimum. Investment
Policies: Equity. Investment Types:
Start-up, first stage, and mezzanine.
Industry Preferences: Diversified.
Geographic Preferences: North
Carolina and Southeast.

Ohio

Senmend Medical Ventures
4445 Lake Forest Dr., Ste. 600
Cincinnati, OH 45242
Phone: (513)563-3264
Fax: (513)563-3261
Preferred Investment Size: $500,000
to $1,000,000. Investment Types:
Second stage and mezzanine. Industry
Preferences: Genetic engineering,
medical and health related.
Geographic Preferences: National.

The Walnut Group
312 Walnut St., Ste. 1151
Cincinnati, OH 45202
Phone: (513)651-3300
Fax: (513)929-4441
Website: http://
www.thewalnutgroup.com
Preferred Investment Size: $500,000
to $5,000,000. Investment Types:
Balanced. Geographic Preferences:
Northeast.

Brantley Venture Partners
20600 Chagrin Blvd., Ste. 1150
Cleveland, OH 44122
Phone: (216)283-4800
Fax: (216)283-5324
Kevin J. Cook, Associate
Preferred Investment Size:
$1,000,000 to $5,000,000. Investment
Types: Industry rollups, seed, start-
up, and first stage. Industry
Preferences: Diversified. Geographic
Preferences: Entire U.S.

Clarion Capital Corp.
1801 E. 9th St., Ste. 1120
Cleveland, OH 44114
Phone: (216)687-1096
Fax: (216)694-3545
Preferred Investment Size: $250,000
to $500,000. Investment Types:
Early, first and second stage. Industry
Preferences: Diversified. Geographic

Preferences: East Coast, Midwest, and West Coast.

Crystal Internet Venture Fund, L.P.
1120 Chester Ave., Ste. 418
Cleveland, OH 44114
Phone: (216)263-5515
Fax: (216)263-5518
E-mail: jf@crystalventure.com
Website: http://www.crystalventure.com
Daniel Kellog, Partner
Preferred Investment Size: $1,000,000 to $6,000,000. Investment Policies: Equity. Investment Types: Balanced and early stage. Industry Preferences: Diversified communications and computer technology. Geographic Preferences: National.

Key Equity Capital Corp.
127 Public Sq., 28th Fl.
Cleveland, OH 44114
Phone: (216)689-3000
Fax: (216)689-3204
Website: http://www.keybank.com
Cindy J. Babitt
Preferred Investment Size: $1,000,000 minimum. Investment Policies: Willing to make equity investments. Investment Types: Expansion, industry rollups, leveraged buyout, second stage, and special situation. Industry Preferences: Diversified. Geographic Preferences: National.

Morgenthaler Ventures
Terminal Tower
50 Public Square, Ste. 2700
Cleveland, OH 44113
Phone: (216)416-7500
Fax: (216)416-7501
Website: http://www.morgenthaler.com
Robert C. Belles, Jr., General Partner
Preferred Investment Size: $500,000 minimum. Investment Types: Start-up, first and second stage, acquisition, leveraged and management buyout, special situations, and expansion. Industry Preferences: Diversified. Geographic Preferences: Entire U.S. and Ontario, Canada.

National City Equity Partners Inc.
1965 E. 6th St.

Cleveland, OH 44114
Phone: (216)575-2491
Fax: (216)575-9965
E-mail: nccap@aol.com
Website: http://www.nccapital.com
Carl E. Baldassarre, Managing Director
Preferred Investment Size: $1,000,000 to $20,000,000. Investment Types: Second stage, mezzanine, leveraged buyout, special situations, recaps, management buyouts, and expansion. Industry Preferences: Diversified. Geographic Preferences: Entire U.S.

Primus Venture Partners, Inc.
5900 LanderBrook Dr., Ste. 2000
Cleveland, OH 44124-4020
Phone: (440)684-7300
Fax: (440)684-7342
E-mail: info@primusventure.com
Website: http://www.primusventure.com
Jeffrey J. Milius, Investment Manager
Preferred Investment Size: $5,000,000 minimum. Investment Types: Early stage, start-up, expansion and balanced. Industry Preferences: Diversified. Geographic Preferences: Entire U.S.

Banc One Capital Partners (Columbus)
150 East Gay St., 24th Fl.
Columbus, OH 43215
Phone: (614)217-1100
Fax: (614)217-1217
Suzanne B. Kriscunas, Managing Director
Preferred Investment Size: $1,000,000 minimum. Investment Types: Later stage, leveraged buyout, mezzanine, industry rollups, and special situations. Industry Preferences: Diversified. Geographic Preferences: Entire U.S.

Battelle Venture Partners
505 King Ave.
Columbus, OH 43201
Phone: (614)424-7005
Fax: (614)424-4874
Preferred Investment Size: $500,000 to $1,000,000. Investment Types: Start-up, first and second stage. Industry Preferences: Energy/natural resources, industrial products and

equipment. Geographic Preferences: National.

Ohio Partners
62 E. Board St., 3rd Fl.
Columbus, OH 43215
Phone: (614)621-1210
Fax: (614)621-1240
E-mail: mcox@ohiopartners.com
Investment Types: Start-up, first and second stage. Industry Preferences: Computer related. Geographic Preferences: Western U.S. and Midwest.

Capital Technology Group, L.L.C.
400 Metro Place North, Ste. 300
Dublin, OH 43017
Phone: (614)792-6066
Fax: (614)792-6036
E-mail: info@capitaltech.com
Website: http://www.capitaltech.com
Preferred Investment Size: $250,000 to $1,000,000. Investment Types: Seed, early and start-up. Industry Preferences: Diversified electronics, alternative energy, and Internet related. Geographic Preferences: National.

Northwest Ohio Venture Fund
4159 Holland-Sylvania R., Ste. 202
Toledo, OH 43623
Phone: (419)824-8144
Fax: (419)882-2035
E-mail: bwalsh@novf.com
Barry P. Walsh, Managing Partner
Preferred Investment Size: $250,000 minimum. Investment Types: Seed, early and late stage, leveraged buyout, mezzanine, research and development. Industry Preferences: Diversified. Geographic Preferences: Midwest.

Oklahoma

Moore & Associates
1000 W. Wilshire Blvd., Ste. 370
Oklahoma City, OK 73116
Phone: (405)842-3660
Fax: (405)842-3763
Preferred Investment Size: $500,000 minimum. Investment Types: Start-up, first and second stage, mezzanine, and leveraged buyout. Industry Preferences: Diversified technology. Geographic Preferences: National.

Chisholm Private Capital Partners
100 West 5th St., Ste. 805
Tulsa, OK 74103
Phone: (918)584-0440
Fax: (918)584-0441
Website: http://www.chisholmvc.com
James Bode, General Partner
Preferred Investment Size:
$1,000,000 to $4,000,000. Investment
Types: Start-up, early and late stage.
Industry Preferences: Diversified
communications and computer,
consumer products and retailing,
electronics, alternative energy, and
medical. Geographic Preferences:
Entire U.S.

Davis, Tuttle Venture Partners
(Tulsa)
320 S. Boston, Ste. 1000
Tulsa, OK 74103-3703
Phone: (918)584-7272
Fax: (918)582-3404
Website: http://www.davistuttle.com
Preferred Investment Size:
$5,000,000 minimum. Investment
Types: First and second stage,
mezzanine, and leveraged buyout.
Industry Preferences: Diversified.
Geographic Preferences: Southwest.

RBC Ventures
2627 E. 21st St.
Tulsa, OK 74114
Phone: (918)744-5607
Fax: (918)743-8630
K.Y. Vargas, Vice President
Preferred Investment Size:
$2,000,000 minimum. Investment
Policies: Equity. Investment Types:
Control-block purchases, leveraged
buyout, mezzanine, second stage, and
special situations. Industry
Preferences: Diversified
transportation. Geographic
Preferences: Southwest.

Oregon

Utah Ventures II LP
10700 SW Beaverton-Hillsdale Hwy.,
Ste. 548
Beaverton, OR 97005
Phone: (503)574-4125
E-mail: adishlip@uven.com
Website: http://www.uven.com
Preferred Investment Size:
$1,000,000 to $7,000,000. Investment

Types: Early stages. Industry
Preferences: Diversified technology.
Geographic Preferences: Northwest
and Rocky Mountains.

Orien Ventures
14523 SW Westlake Dr.
Lake Oswego, OR 97035
Phone: (503)699-1680
Fax: (503)699-1681
Anthony Miadich, Managing General
Partner
Preferred Investment Size: $500,000
minimum. Investment Types: Start-
up, seed, early and first stage.
Industry Preferences: Diversified
technology. Geographic Preferences:
No preference.

OVP Venture Partners (Lake
Oswego)
340 Oswego Pointe Dr., Ste. 200
Lake Oswego, OR 97034
Phone: (503)697-8766
Fax: (503)697-8863
E-mail: info@ovp.com
Website: http://www.ovp.com
Preferred Investment Size:
$1,000,000 to $10,000,000.
Investment Types: Seed, start-up, and
early stage. Industry Preferences:
Communications, computer and
Internet related, electronics, genetic
engineering, and medical health
related. Geographic Preferences:
Western U.S. and Western Canada.

Oregon Resource and Technology
Development Fund
4370 NE Halsey St., Ste. 233
Portland, OR 97213-1566
Phone: (503)282-4462
Fax: (503)282-2976
Preferred Investment Size: $100,000
to $300,000. Investment Types: Seed,
start-up, research and development.
Industry Preferences: Biotechnology,
electronics, computer software and
services, and medical/health related.
Geographic Preferences: West Coast.

Shaw Venture Partners
400 SW 6th Ave., Ste. 1100
Portland, OR 97204-1636
Phone: (503)228-4884
Fax: (503)227-2471
Website: http://
www.shawventures.com

Preferred Investment Size: $250,000
to $3,000,000. Investment Types:
Seed, start-up, first and second stage,
leveraged buyout, and special
situations. Industry Preferences:
Diversified. Geographic Preferences:
Northwest.

Pennsylvania

Mid-Atlantic Venture Funds
125 Goodman Dr.
Bethlehem, PA 18015
Phone: (610)865-6550
Fax: (610)865-6427
Website: http://www.mavf.com
Thomas A. Smith
Preferred Investment Size: $500,000
to $8,000,000. Investment Types:
Seed, research and development, first
and second stage, leveraged buyout.
Industry Preferences: Diversified.
Geographic Preferences: Middle
Atlantic and Northeast.

Newspring Ventures
100 W. Elm St., Ste. 101
Conshohocken, PA 19428
Phone: (610)567-2380
Fax: (610)567-2388
Website: http://
www.newsprintventures.com
Preferred Investment Size:
$1,000,000 minimum. Investment
Types: Early stage and expansion.
Industry Preferences:
Communications, computer related,
medical products, industrial products,
and business services. Geographic
Preferences: Mid Atlantic.

Patricof & Co. Ventures, Inc.
455 S. Gulph Rd., Ste. 410
King of Prussia, PA 19406
Phone: (610)265-0286
Fax: (610)265-4959
Website: http://www.patricof.com
Preferred Investment Size: $500,000
minimum. Investment Types: Seed,
start-up, first and second stage,
mezzanine, and leveraged buyout.
Industry Preferences: Diversified.
Geographic Preferences: No
preference.

Loyalhanna Venture Fund
527 Cedar Way, Ste. 104
Oakmont, PA 15139

Phone: (412)820-7035
Fax: (412)820-7036
James H. Knowles, Jr.
Preferred Investment Size: $300,000
to $1,000,000. Investment Types:
First and second stage, and leveraged
buyout. Industry Preferences: No
preference. Geographic Preferences:
Entire U.S.

Innovest Group Inc.
2000 Market St., Ste. 1400
Philadelphia, PA 19103
Phone: (215)564-3960
Fax: (215)569-3272
Richard Woosnam
Preferred Investment Size: $500,000
to $1,000,000. Investment Types:
First stage, leveraged buyout, recaps,
second stage, special situation, and
start-up. Industry Preferences:
Diversified. Geographic Preferences:
Mid Atlantic, Midwest, Northeast,
and Southeast.

Keystone Venture Capital
Management Co.
1601 Market St., Ste. 2500
Philadelphia, PA 19103
Phone: (215)241-1200
Fax: (215)241-1211
Website: http://www.keystonevc.com
Peter Ligeti
Preferred Investment Size:
$2,000,000 to $5,000,000. Investment
Types: First and second stage,
balanced, and expansion. Industry
Preferences: Diversified. Geographic
Preferences: Middle Atlantic.

Liberty Venture Partners
2005 Market St., Ste. 200
Philadelphia, PA 19103
Phone: (215)282-4484
Fax: (215)282-4485
E-mail: info@libertyvp.com
Website: http://www.libertyvp.com
Thomas Morse
Preferred Investment Size:
$3,000,000 to $7,000,000. Investment
Types: Early stage and expansion.
Industry Preferences: Diversified
technology. Geographic Preferences:
National.

Penn Janney Fund, Inc.
1801 Market St., 11th Fl.
Philadelphia, PA 19103

Phone: (215)665-4447
Fax: (215)557-0820
William Rulon-Miller
Preferred Investment Size:
$1,000,000 minimum. Investment
Types: Second stage, mezzanine,
leveraged buyout, and special
situations. Industry Preferences:
Diversified. Geographic Preferences:
Northeast, West Coast, and Middle
Atlantic.

Philadelphia Ventures, Inc.
The Bellevue
200 S. Broad St.
Philadelphia, PA 19102
Phone: (215)732-4445
Fax: (215)732-4644
Walter M. Aikman, Managing
Director
Preferred Investment Size: $500,000
maximum. Investment Types: Start-
up, first and second stage, mezzanine,
and leveraged buyout. Industry
Preferences: Diversified technology.
Geographic Preferences: Entire U.S.

Birchmere Ventures Inc.
2000 Technology Dr.
Pittsburgh, PA 15219-3109
Phone: (412)803-8000
Fax: (412)687-8139
Website: http://
www.birchmerevc.com
Investment Types: Early stage,
expansion, first and later stage, and
start-up. Industry Preferences:
Diversified. Geographic Preferences:
Mid Atlantic.

CEO Venture Fund
2000 Technology Dr., Ste. 160
Pittsburgh, PA 15219-3109
Phone: (412)687-3451
Fax: (412)687-8139
E-mail: ceofund@aol.com
Website: http://
www.ceoventurefund.com
Ned Renzi, General Partner
Preferred Investment Size:
$1,000,000 to $2,000,000. Investment
Types: Start-up, first stage, second
stage, leveraged buyout, and special
situations. Industry Preferences:
Diversified technology. Geographic
Preferences: Middle Atlantic states.

Innovation Works Inc.
2000 Technology Dr., Ste. 250
Pittsburgh, PA 15219
Phone: (412)681-1520
Fax: (412)681-2625
Website: http://
www.innovationworks.org
Preferred Investment Size: $100,000
to $500,000. Investment Types: Early
and first stage, seed, and start-up.
Industry Preferences: Diversified
technology. Geographic Preferences:
Pennsylvania.

Keystone Minority Capital Fund L.P.
1801 Centre Ave., Ste. 201
Williams Sq.
Pittsburgh, PA 15219
Phone: (412)338-2230
Fax: (412)338-2224
Earl Hord, General Partner
Preferred Investment Size: $500,000
minimum. Investment Types: Start-
up, first stage, second stage,
mezzanine, and leveraged buyout.
Industry Preferences: Diversified.
Geographic Preferences: Middle
Atlantic states.

Mellon Ventures, Inc.
One Mellon Bank Ctr., Rm. 3500
Pittsburgh, PA 15258
Phone: (412)236-3594
Fax: (412)236-3593
Website: http://
www.mellonventures.com
Preferred Investment Size:
$2,000,000 to $25,000,000.
Investment Types: Mezzanine,
leveraged buyout, and special
situations. Industry Preferences:
Diversified. Geographic Preferences:
National.

Pennsylvania Growth Fund
5850 Ellsworth Ave., Ste. 303
Pittsburgh, PA 15232
Phone: (412)661-1000
Fax: (412)361-0676
Barry Lhormer, Partner
Preferred Investment Size: $500,000
minimum. Investment Types:
Leveraged buyout, mezzanine, second
stage, and special situation. Industry
Preferences: Diversified. Geographic
Preferences: Middle Atlantic,
Midwest, Northeast, and Southeast.

Point Venture Partners
The Century Bldg.
130 Seventh St., 7th Fl.
Pittsburgh, PA 15222
Phone: (412)261-1966
Fax: (412)261-1718
Kent Engelmeier, General Partner
Preferred Investment Size:
$2,000,000. Investment Types: Start-up, first stage, second stage, mezzanine, recaps, and leveraged buyout. Industry Preferences: Diversified. Geographic Preferences: Eastern and Midwestern U.S.

Cross Atlantic Capital Partners
5 Radnor Corporate Center, Ste. 555
Radnor, PA 19087
Phone: (610)995-2650
Fax: (610)971-2062
Website: http://www.xacp.com
Preferred Investment Size:
$1,000,000 to $10,000,000.
Investment Types: Balanced, early stage, expansion, seed, and start-up. Industry Preferences: Diversified. Geographic Preferences: Entire U.S.

Meridian Venture Partners (Radnor)
The Radnor Court Bldg., Ste. 140
259 Radnor-Chester Rd.
Radnor, PA 19087
Phone: (610)254-2999
Fax: (610)254-2996
E-mail: mvpart@ix.netcom.com
Kenneth E. Jones
Preferred Investment Size:
$1,000,000 to $2,000,000. Investment Types: Second stage, leveraged buyout, and special situations. Industry Preferences: Diversified. Geographic Preferences: Entire U.S.

TDH
919 Conestoga Rd., Bldg. 1, Ste. 301
Rosemont, PA 19010
Phone: (610)526-9970
Fax: (610)526-9971
J.B. Doherty, Managing General Partner
Preferred Investment Size:
$1,500,000 minimum. Investment Types: Start-up, first and second stage, mezzanine, recaps, and leveraged buyout. Industry Preferences: Diversified. Geographic Preferences: Eastern U.S. and Midwest.

Adams Capital Management
500 Blackburn Ave.
Sewickley, PA 15143
Phone: (412)749-9454
Fax: (412)749-9459
Website: http://www.acm.com
Joel Adams, General Partner
Investment Types: Early and first stages. Industry Preferences: Diversified technology. Geographic Preferences: National.

S.R. One, Ltd.
Four Tower Bridge
200 Barr Harbor Dr., Ste. 250
W. Conshohocken, PA 19428
Phone: (610)567-1000
Fax: (610)567-1039
Barbara Dalton, Vice President
Preferred Investment Size: $500,000 to $5,000,000. Investment Types: Start-up, first and second stage, and late stage. Industry Preferences: Healthcare and genetic engineering, and computer software and services. Geographic Preferences: No preference.

Greater Philadelphia Venture Capital Corp.
351 East Conestoga Rd.
Wayne, PA 19087
Phone: (610)688-6829
Fax: (610)254-8958
Fred Choate, Manager
Preferred Investment Size: $100,000 to $300,000. Investment Types: First and second stage, leveraged buyout, mezzanine, and special situations. Industry Preferences: Diversified. Geographic Preferences: Middle Atlantic.

PA Early Stage
435 Devon Park Dr., Bldg. 500, Ste. 510
Wayne, PA 19087
Phone: (610)293-4075
Fax: (610)254-4240
Website: http://www.paearlystage.com
Preferred Investment Size: $100,000 to $10,000,000. Investment Types: Early, first, and second stage; seed; and start-up. Industry Preferences: Diversified. Geographic Preferences: Mid Atlantic.

The Sandhurst Venture Fund, L.P.
351 E. Constoga Rd.
Wayne, PA 19087
Phone: (610)254-8900
Fax: (610)254-8958
Preferred Investment Size: $500,000 to $1,000,000. Investment Types: Second stage, recaps, and leveraged buyout. Industry Preferences: Computer stores, disposable medical/ health related, and industrial products. Geographic Preferences: East Coast and Middle Atlantic.

TL Ventures
700 Bldg.
435 Devon Park Dr.
Wayne, PA 19087-1990
Phone: (610)975-3765
Fax: (610)254-4210
Website: http://www.tlventures.com
Pam Strisofsky,
pstrisofsky@tlventures.com
Preferred Investment Size:
$2,000,000 minimum. Investment Types: Seed and early stage. Industry Preferences: Diversified technology. Geographic Preferences: National.

Rockhill Ventures, Inc.
100 Front St., Ste. 1350
West Conshohocken, PA 19428
Phone: (610)940-0300
Fax: (610)940-0301
E-mail: chuck@rockhillventures.com
Preferred Investment Size:
$1,000,000 to $2,000,000. Investment Types: Seed, research and development, start-up, first and second stage, leveraged buyout, and recaps. Industry Preferences: Genetic engineering and medical/health related. Geographic Preferences: Eastern U.S.

Puerto Rico

Advent-Morro Equity Partners
Banco Popular Bldg.
206 Tetuan St., Ste. 903
San Juan, PR 00902
Phone: (787)725-5285
Fax: (787)721-1735
Cyril L. Meduna, General Partner
Preferred Investment Size: $500,000 to $3,000,000. Investment Types: No preference. Industry Preferences:

Diversified. Geographic Preferences: Puerto Rico.

North America Investment Corp.
Mercantil Plaza, Ste. 813
PO Box 191831
San Juan, PR 00919
Phone: (787)754-6178
Fax: (787)754-6181
Marcelino D. Pastrana-Torres, President
Preferred Investment Size: $25,000 to $250,000. Investment Types: Early stage and expansion. Industry Preferences: Consumer products and retailing, consumer distribution, industrial equipment, therapeutic equipment, real estate, and business services. Geographic Preferences: Puerto Rico.

Rhode Island

Manchester Humphreys, Inc.
40 Westminster St., Ste. 900
Providence, RI 02903
Phone: (401)454-0400
Fax: (401)454-0403
Preferred Investment Size: $500,000 minimum. Investment Types: Leveraged and management buyouts. Industry Preferences: Diversified. Geographic Preferences: National.

Navis Partners
50 Kennedy Plaza, 12th Fl.
Providence, RI 02903
Phone: (401)278-6770
Fax: (401)278-6387
Website: http://
www.navispartners.com
Rory B. Smith, General Partner
Preferred Investment Size:
$20,000,000 to $75,000,000.
Investment Policies: Equity.
Investment Types: Acquisition, early and later stage, leveraged and management buyouts, recaps, and expansion. Industry Preferences: Diversified. Geographic Preferences: U.S. and Canada.

South Carolina

Capital Insights, L.L.C.
PO Box 27162
Greenville, SC 29616-2162
Phone: (864)242-6832

Fax: (864)242-6755
E-mail: jwarner@capitalinsights.com
Website: http://
www.capitalinsights.com
Preferred Investment Size: $500,000 to $5,000,000. Investment Policies: Equity. Investment Types: Early and late stage. Industry Preferences: Communications and consumer-related services. Geographic Preferences: Southeast.

Transamerica Mezzanine Financing
7 N. Laurens St., Ste. 603
Greenville, SC 29601
Phone: (864)232-6198
Fax: (864)241-4444
J. Phillip Falls, Investment Officer
Investment Types: Seed, start-up, first stage, second stage, and mezzanine. Industry Preferences: Diversified technology. Geographic Preferences: Southeast.

Tennessee

Valley Capital Corp.
Krystal Bldg.
100 W. Martin Luther King Blvd., Ste. 212
Chattanooga, TN 37402
Phone: (423)265-1557
Fax: (423)265-1588
Faye Robinson
Preferred Investment Size: $200,000 minimum. Investment Types: Second stage, mezzanine, and leveraged buyout. Industry Preferences: Diversified. Geographic Preferences: Southeast.

Coleman Swenson Booth Inc.
237 2nd Ave. S
Franklin, TN 37064-2649
Phone: (615)791-9462
Fax: (615)791-9636
Website: http://
www.colemanswenson.com
Larry H. Coleman, Ph.D., Managing Partner
Preferred Investment Size:
$1,000,000 to $7,000,000. Investment Types: Seed, start-up, first and second stage, and mezzanine. Industry Preferences: Diversified. Geographic Preferences: No preference.

Capital Services & Resources, Inc.
5159 Wheelis Dr., Ste. 106
Memphis, TN 38117
Phone: (901)761-2156
Fax: (907)767-0060
Charles Y. Bancroft, Treasurer
Preferred Investment Size: $300,000 minimum. Investment Policies: Equity. Investment Types: Second stage, leveraged buyout, and special situations. Industry Preferences: Diversified. Geographic Preferences: United States and Canada.

Paradigm Capital Partners LLC
6410 Poplar Ave., Ste. 395
Memphis, TN 38119
Phone: (901)682-6060
Fax: (901)328-3061
Preferred Investment Size: $500,000 to $6,000,000. Investment Types: First and second stage, and seed. Industry Preferences: Diversified. Geographic Preferences: Southeast.

SSM Ventures
845 Crossover Ln., Ste. 140
Memphis, TN 38117
Phone: (901)767-1131
Fax: (901)767-1135
Website: http://
www.ssmventures.com
R. Wilson Orr, III
Preferred Investment Size:
$2,000,000 to $10,000,000.
Investment Types: Start-up, leveraged buyout, and expansion. Industry Preferences: Diversified. Geographic Preferences: Southeast and Southwest U.S.

Capital Across America L.P.
501 Union St., Ste. 201
Nashville, TN 37219
Phone: (615)254-1414
Fax: (615)254-1856
Website: http://
www.capitalacrossamerica.com
Investment Types: Balanced. Industry Preferences: Diversified; women/minority-owned businesses.
Geographic Preferences: Entire U.S.

Equitas L.P.
2000 Glen Echo Rd., Ste. 101
PO Box 158838
Nashville, TN 37215-8838
Phone: (615)383-8673

Fax: (615)383-8693
Preferred Investment Size: $500.000.
Investment Types: Second stage,
leveraged buyout, mezzanine, recaps,
and special situation. Industry
Preferences: Diversified. Geographic
Preferences: Southeast and Midwest.

Massey Burch Capital Corp.
One Burton Hills Blvd., Ste. 350
Nashville, TN 37215
Phone: (615)665-3221
Fax: (615)665-3240
E-mail: tcalton@masseyburch.com
Website: http://
www.masseyburch.com
Lucious E. Burch, IV, Partner
Preferred Investment Size:
$1,000,000 to $5,000,000. Investment
Types: Seed, start-up, early and first
stage. Industry Preferences:
Communication and computer
related. Geographic Preferences:
Southeast.

Nelson Capital Corp.
3401 West End Ave., Ste. 300
Nashville, TN 37203
Phone: (615)292-8787
Fax: (615)385-3150
Preferred Investment Size: $500,000
minimum. Investment Types: First
and second stage, leveraged buyout,
and mezzanine. Industry Preferences:
Diversified. Geographic Preferences:
Southeast.

Texas

Phillips-Smith Specialty Retail Group
5080 Spectrum Dr., Ste. 805 W
Addison, TX 75001
Phone: (972)387-0725
Fax: (972)458-2560
E-mail: pssrg@aol.com
Website: http://www.phillips-
smith.com
G. Michael Machens, General Partner
Preferred Investment Size:
$1,000,000 minimum. Investment
Types: Seed, start-up, first and second
stage, mezzanine, and leveraged
buyout. Industry Preferences: Retail
and Internet related. Geographic
Preferences: Entire U.S.

Austin Ventures, L.P.
701 Brazos St., Ste. 1400

Austin, TX 78701
Phone: (512)485-1900
Fax: (512)476-3952
E-mail: info@ausven.com
Website: http://
www.austinventures.com
Joseph C. Aragona, General Partner
Preferred Investment Size:
$1,000,000 to $15,000,000.
Investment Types: Seed, start-up, first
and second stage, leveraged buyout,
and special situations. Industry
Preferences: Diversified. Geographic
Preferences: Southwest and Texas.

The Capital Network
3925 West Braker Lane, Ste. 406
Austin, TX 78759-5321
Phone: (512)305-0826
Fax: (512)305-0836
Preferred Investment Size: $100,000
to $500,000. Investment Types: Seed,
early and late stage, leveraged
buyout, mezzanine, research and
development, and special situations.
Industry Preferences: Diversified.
Geographic Preferences: United
States and Canada.

Techxas Ventures LLC
5000 Plaza on the Lake
Austin, TX 78746
Phone: (512)343-0118
Fax: (512)343-1879
E-mail: bruce@techxas.com
Website: http://www.techxas.com
Bruce Ezell, General Partner
Preferred Investment Size: $500,000
to $5,000,000. Investment Types:
Seed, start-up, first stage, second
stage, balanced, joint ventures, and
special situations. Industry
Preferences: Diversified technology.
Geographic Preferences: Texas.

Alliance Financial of Houston
218 Heather Ln.
Conroe, TX 77385-9013
Phone: (936)447-3300
Fax: (936)447-4222
Preferred Investment Size: $300,000
to $500,000. Investment Types:
Second stage, mezzanine, leveraged
buyout, and special situations.
Industry Preferences: Sales,
distribution, and manufacturing.
Geographic Preferences: Gulf states.

Amerimark Capital Corp.
1111 W. Mockingbird, Ste. 1111
Dallas, TX 75247
Phone: (214)638-7878
Fax: (214)638-7612
E-mail: amerimark@amcapital.com
Website: http://www.amcapital.com
Preferred Investment Size: $500,000
minimum. Investment Types: Second
stage, mezzanine, and leveraged
buyout. Industry Preferences:
Diversified. Geographic Preferences:
National.

AMT Venture Partners / AMT
Capital Ltd.
5220 Spring Valley Rd., Ste. 600
Dallas, TX 75240
Phone: (214)905-9757
Fax: (214)905-9761
Website: http://www.amtcapital.com
Preferred Investment Size: $100,000
to $500,000. Investment Types: First
and second stages, and expanion.
Industry Preferences: Industrial
products and equipment, electronic
components and instruments.
Geographic Preferences: National.

Arkoma Venture Partners
5950 Berkshire Lane, Ste. 1400
Dallas, TX 75225
Phone: (214)739-3515
Fax: (214)739-3572
E-mail: joelf@arkomavp.com
Joel Fontenot, Executive Vice
President
Preferred Investment Size: $250,000
to $2,500,000. Investment Policies:
Equity. Investment Types: Seed, start-
up, early and second stage, and
expansion. Industry Preferences:
Communications, computer, and
electronics. Geographic Preferences:
Southwest.

Capital Southwest Corp.
12900 Preston Rd., Ste. 700
Dallas, TX 75230
Phone: (972)233-8242
Fax: (972)233-7362
Website: http://
www.capitalsouthwest.com
Howard Thomas, Investment
Associate
Preferred Investment Size:
$1,000,000 to $6,000,000. Investment
Types: First and second stage,

leveraged buyout, acquisition, expansion, management buyout, and late stage. Industry Preferences: Diversified. Geographic Preferences: Entire U.S.

Dali, Hook Partners
One Lincoln Center, Ste. 1550
5400 LBJ Freeway
Dallas, TX 75240
Phone: (972)991-5457
Fax: (972)991-5458
E-mail: dhook@hookpartners.com
Website: http://
www.hookpartners.com
David J. Hook
Preferred Investment Size: $100,000 to $5,000,000. Investment Types: Balanced, first, and second stage. Industry Preferences: Diversified. Geographic Preferences: Southwest and West Coast.

HO2 Partners
Two Galleria Tower
13455 Noel Rd., Ste. 1670
Dallas, TX 75240
Phone: (972)702-1144
Fax: (972)702-8234
Website: http://www.ho2.com
Preferred Investment Size: $750,000 to $3,000,000. Investment Types: First and second stage, and seed. Industry Preferences: Diversified technology. Geographic Preferences: Texas.

Interwest Partners (Dallas)
2 Galleria Tower
13455 Noel Rd., Ste. 1670
Dallas, TX 75240
Phone: (972)392-7279
Fax: (972)490-6348
Website: http://www.interwest.com
Preferred Investment Size: $2,000,000 to $25,000,000. Investment Types: Seed, research and development, start-up, first and second stage, expansion, and special situations. Industry Preferences: Diversified. Geographic Preferences: Entire U.S.

Kahala Investments, Inc.
8214 Westchester Dr., Ste. 715
Dallas, TX 75225
Phone: (214)987-0077
Fax: (214)987-2332

Lee R. Slaughter, Jr., President
Preferred Investment Size: $10,000,000 minimum. Investment Types: Mezzanine, leveraged buyout, special situations, control block purchases, and industry roll ups. Industry Preferences: Diversified. Geographic Preferences: Southeast and Southwest.

MESBIC Ventures Holding Co.
2435 North Central Expressway, Ste. 200
Dallas, TX 75080
Phone: (972)991-1597
Fax: (972)991-4770
Website: http://www.mvhc.com
Jeff Schaefer
Preferred Investment Size: $1,000,000 minimum. Investment Policies: Loans and/or equity. Investment Types: Leveraged buyout, mezzanine, and second stage. Industry Preferences: Diversified. Geographic Preferences: Southeast and Southwest.

North Texas MESBIC, Inc.
9500 Forest Lane, Ste. 430
Dallas, TX 75243
Phone: (214)221-3565
Fax: (214)221-3566
Preferred Investment Size: $300,000 minimum. Investment Types: Second stage, mezzanine, and leveraged buyout. Industry Preferences: Consumer food and beverage products, restaurants, retailing, consumer and food distribution. Geographic Preferences: Southwest.

Richard Jaffe & Company, Inc,
7318 Royal Cir.
Dallas, TX 75230
Phone: (214)265-9397
Fax: (214)739-1845
E-mail: rjaffe@pssi.net
Richard R. Jaffe, President
Preferred Investment Size: $100,000 to $300,000. Investment Types: Start-up, first stage, leveraged buyouts, and special situations. Industry Preferences: Diversified. Geographic Preferences: Southwest.

Sevin Rosen Management Co.
13455 Noel Rd., Ste. 1670
Dallas, TX 75240

Phone: (972)702-1100
Fax: (972)702-1103
E-mail: info@srfunds.com
Website: http://www.srfunds.com
John V. Jaggers, Partner
Preferred Investment Size: $500,000 minimum. Investment Types: Start-up, early and first stage. Industry Preferences: Diversified technology. Geographic Preferences: Entire U.S.

Stratford Capital Partners, L.P.
300 Crescent Ct., Ste. 500
Dallas, TX 75201
Phone: (214)740-7377
Fax: (214)720-7393
E-mail: stratcap@hmtf.com
Michael D. Brown, Managing Partner
Preferred Investment Size: $1,000,000 minimum. Investment Policies: Equity, sub debt with equity. Investment Types: Expansion, later stage, acquisition, leveraged and management buyout, mezzanine, and recaps. Industry Preferences: Diversified. Geographic Preferences: National.

Sunwestern Investment Group
12221 Merit Dr., Ste. 935
Dallas, TX 75251
Phone: (972)239-5650
Fax: (972)701-0024
Preferred Investment Size: $500,000 to $1,000,000. Investment Types: Second stage, leveraged buyout, and special situations. Industry Preferences: Diversified. Geographic Preferences: Southwest and West Coast.

Wingate Partners
750 N. St. Paul St., Ste. 1200
Dallas, TX 75201
Phone: (214)720-1313
Fax: (214)871-8799
Preferred Investment Size: $20,000,000 minimum. Investment Types: Leveraged buyout and control block purchases. Industry Preferences: Diversified. Geographic Preferences: Entire U.S. and Canada.

Buena Venture Associates
201 Main St., 32nd Fl.
Fort Worth, TX 76102
Phone: (817)339-7400
Fax: (817)390-8408

Website: http://
www.buenaventure.com
Preferred Investment Size:
$1,000,000 to $50,000,000.
Investment Types: Early, first and
second stage; seed; and start-up.
Industry Preferences: Diversified
technology, and health services.
Geographic Preferences: Entire U.S.

The Catalyst Group
3 Riverway, Ste. 770
Houston, TX 77056
Phone: (713)623-8133
Fax: (713)623-0473
E-mail: herman@thecatalystgroup.net
Website: http://
www.thecatalystgroup.net
Rick Herman, Partner
Preferred Investment Size:
$1,000,000 minimum. Investment
Types: Second stage, mezzanine,
leveraged buyout, and control block
purchases. Industry Preferences:
Diversified. Geographic Preferences:
No preference.

Cureton & Co., Inc.
1100 Louisiana, Ste. 3250
Houston, TX 77002
Phone: (713)658-9806
Fax: (713)658-0476
Stewart Cureton, Jr., President
Preferred Investment Size:
$10,000,000 minimum. Investment
Types: First and second stage,
leveraged buyout, and special
situations. Industry Preferences:
Diversified. Geographic Preferences:
Southwest.

Davis, Tuttle Venture Partners
(Dallas)
8 Greenway Plaza, Ste. 1020
Houston, TX 77046
Phone: (713)993-0440
Fax: (713)621-2297
Website: http://www.davistuttle.com
Phillip Tuttle, Partner
Preferred Investment Size:
$5,000,000 minimum. Investment
Types: First and second stage,
mezzanine, and leveraged buyout.
Industry Preferences: Diversified.
Geographic Preferences: Southwest.

Houston Partners
401 Louisiana, 8th Fl.

Houston, TX 77002
Phone: (713)222-8600
Fax: (713)222-8932
Preferred Investment Size: $500,000
to $1,000,000. Investment Types:
Start-up, first and second stage, and
expansion. Industry Preferences:
Diversified industry preference.
Geographic Preferences: Entire U.S.

Southwest Venture Group
10878 Westheimer, Ste. 178
Houston, TX 77042
Phone: (713)827-8947
Free: (713)461-1470
David M. Klausmeyer, Partner
Preferred Investment Size:
$50,000,000 minimum. Investment
Types: Diversified. Industry
Preferences: Diversified. Geographic
Preferences: U.S. and Canada.

Triad Ventures
AM Fund
4600 Post Oak Place, Ste. 100
Houston, TX 77027
Phone: (713)627-9111
Fax: (713)627-9119
David Mueller
Preferred Investment Size: $800,000
maximum. Investment Types: First
and second stage, and mezzanine.
Industry Preferences: Medical,
consumer, computer-related.
Geographic Preferences: Southwest
and Texas.

Ventex Management, Inc.
3417 Milam St.
Houston, TX 77002-9531
Phone: (713)659-7870
Fax: (713)659-7855
Preferred Investment Size:
$1,000,000 to $5,000,000. Investment
Types: Second stage, mezzanine,
leveraged buyout, and special
situations. Industry Preferences:
Diversified. Geographic Preferences:
Southwest.

MBA Venture Group
1004 Olde Town Rd., Ste. 102
Irving, TX 75061
Phone: (972)986-6703
John Mason
Preferred Investment Size:
$1,000,000 minimum. Investment
Types: First stage, leveraged buyout,

mezzanine, research and
development, second stage, seed,
start-up. Industry Preferences:
Diversified. Geographic Preferences:
Entire U.S.

First Capital Group Management Co.
750 East Mulberry St., Ste. 305
PO Box 15616
San Antonio, TX 78212
Phone: (210)736-4233
Fax: (210)736-5449
Jeffrey P. Blanchard, Managing
Partner
Preferred Investment Size:
$1,000,000 minimum. Investment
Types: First and second stage,
mezzanine, leveraged buyout, and
special situations. Industry
Preferences: Diversified. Geographic
Preferences: Southwest.

The Southwest Venture Partnerships
16414 San Pedro, Ste. 345
San Antonio, TX 78232
Phone: (210)402-1200
Fax: (210)402-1221
E-mail: swvp@aol.com
Preferred Investment Size: $500,000
to $5,000,000. Investment Types:
Start-up, first and second stage, and
leveraged buyout. Industry
Preferences: Diversified. Geographic
Preferences: Southwest.

Medtech International Inc.
1742 Carriageway
Sugarland, TX 77478
Phone: (713)980-8474
Fax: (713)980-6343
Dave Banker
Preferred Investment Size: $100,000
to $500,000. Investment Types: First
stage, leveraged buyout, mezzanine,
research and development, second
stage, seed, special situation, and
start-up. Industry Preferences:
Diversified. Geographic Preferences:
No preference.

Utah

First Security Business Investment
Corp.
15 East 100 South, Ste. 100
Salt Lake City, UT 84111
Phone: (801)246-5737
Fax: (801)246-5740

Preferred Investment Size: $300,000 to $800,000. Investment Policies: Loans and/or equity. Investment Types: Leveraged buyout, mezzanine, and second stage. Industry Preferences: Diversified. Geographic Preferences: West Coast, Rocky Mountains.

Utah Ventures II, L.P.
423 Wakara Way, Ste. 206
Salt Lake City, UT 84108
Phone: (801)583-5922
Fax: (801)583-4105
Website: http://www.uven.com
James C. Dreyfous, Managing General Partner
Preferred Investment Size: $1,000,000 to $7,000,000. Investment Types: Early stage. Industry Preferences: Diversified technology. Geographic Preferences: Northwest and Rocky Mountain region.

Wasatch Venture Corp.
1 S. Main St., Ste. 1400
Salt Lake City, UT 84133
Phone: (801)524-8939
Fax: (801)524-8941
E-mail: mail@wasatchvc.com
Todd Stevens, Manager
Preferred Investment Size: $500,000 to $2,000,000. Investment Policies: Equity and debt. Investment Types: Early stage. Industry Preferences: High technology. Geographic Preferences: Western U.S.

Vermont

North Atlantic Capital Corp.
76 Saint Paul St., Ste. 600
Burlington, VT 05401
Phone: (802)658-7820
Fax: (802)658-5757
Website: http://
www.northatlanticcapital.com
Preferred Investment Size: $1,500,000 minimum. Investment Types: First and second stage, mezzanine, and leveraged buyout. Industry Preferences: Diversified technology. Geographic Preferences: Northeast.

Green Mountain Advisors Inc.
PO Box 1230
Quechee, VT 05059

Phone: (802)296-7800
Fax: (802)296-6012
Website: http://www.gmtcap.com
Michael Sweatman, President
Preferred Investment Size: $100,000 to $500,000. Investment Types: Second stage, expansion, and mezzanine. Industry Preferences: Technology, communications. Geographic Preferences: Entire U.S.

Virginia

Oxford Financial Services Corp.
Alexandria, VA 22314
Phone: (703)519-4900
Fax: (703)519-4910
E-mail: oxford133@aol.com
J. Alden Philbrick
Preferred Investment Size: $1,000,000. Investment Types: Seed, research and development, start-up, first stage, second stage, and mezzanine. Industry Preferences: Diversified technology. Geographic Preferences: National.

Continental SBIC
4141 N. Henderson Rd.
Arlington, VA 22203
Phone: (703)527-5200
Fax: (703)527-3700
Michael W. Jones, Senior Vice President
Preferred Investment Size: $300,000 to $5,000,000. Investment Types: No preference. Industry Preferences: Diversified. Geographic Preferences: Northeast, Southeast, Middle Atlantic, and Central Canada.

Novak Biddle Venture Partners
1750 Tysons Blvd., Ste. 1190
McLean, VA 22102
Phone: (703)847-3770
Fax: (703)847-3771
E-mail: roger@novakbiddle.com
Website: http://
www.novakbiddle.com
Roger Novak, General Partner
Preferred Investment Size: $1,000,000 to $5,000,000. Investment Types: Seed and early stage. Industry Preferences: Communications and computer related. Geographic Preferences: Eastern U.S.

Spacevest
11911 Freedom Dr., Ste. 500
Reston, VA 20190
Phone: (703)904-9800
Fax: (703)904-0571
E-mail: spacevest@spacevest.com
Website: http://www.spacevest.com
Roger P. Widing, Managing Director
Preferred Investment Size: $250,000 to $10,000,000. Investment Policies: Equity. Investment Types: Early and late stage, expansion, and mezzanine. Industry Preferences: Diversified. Geographic Preferences: U.S. and Canada.

Virginia Capital
1801 Libbie Ave., Ste. 201
Richmond, VA 23226
Phone: (804)648-4802
Fax: (804)648-4809
E-mail: webmaster@vacapital.com
Website: http://www.vacapital.com
Thomas E. Deardorff, Vice President
Investment Types: Acquisition, balanced, expansion, and leveraged and management buyouts. Industry Preferences: Communications; consumer, medical and health related. Geographic Preferences: Mid Atlantic.

Calvert Social Venture Partners
402 Maple Ave. W
Vienna, VA 22180
Phone: (703)255-4930
Fax: (703)255-4931
E-mail: calven2000@aol.com
John May, Managing General Partner
Preferred Investment Size: $100,000 to $700,000. Investment Types: First stages. Industry Preferences: Diversified. Geographic Preferences: Middle Atlantic states.

Fairfax Partners
8000 Towers Crescent Dr., Ste. 940
Vienna, VA 22182
Phone: (703)847-9486
Fax: (703)847-0911
E-mail: bgouldey@fairfaxpartners.com
Bruce K. Gouldey, Managing Director
Investment Types: Start-up, first stage, second stage, and leveraged buyout. Industry Preferences: Computer related, Medical and health

related. Geographic Preferences: Middle Atlantic States.

Global Internet Ventures
8150 Leesburg Pike, Ste. 1210
Vienna, VA 22182
Phone: (703)442-3300
Fax: (703)442-3388
Website: http://www.givinc.com
Preferred Investment Size: $500,000 to $3,000,000. Investment Types: Early stage. Industry Preferences: Communications, computer, and Internet related. Geographic Preferences: Entire U.S.

Walnut Capital Corp. (Vienna)
8000 Towers Crescent Dr., Ste. 1070
Vienna, VA 22182
Phone: (703)448-3771
Fax: (703)448-7751
Preferred Investment Size: $300,000 to $500,000. Investment Types: Start-up, first and second stage, mezzanine, and leveraged buyout. Industry Preferences: Diversified. Geographic Preferences: No preference.

Washington

Encompass Ventures
777 108th Ave. NE, Ste. 2300
Bellevue, WA 98004
Phone: (425)486-3900
Fax: (425)486-3901
E-mail: info@evpartners.com
Website: http://www.encompassventures.com
Preferred Investment Size: $300,000 to $3,000,000. Investment Types: Research and development, start-up, first and second stages. Industry Preferences: Computer related, medical and health related. Geographic Preferences: Western U.S. and Canada.

Fluke Venture Partners
11400 SE Sixth St., Ste. 230
Bellevue, WA 98004
Phone: (425)453-4590
Fax: (425)453-4675
E-mail: gabelein@flukeventures.com
Website: http://www.flukeventures.com
Dennis Weston, Managing Director
Preferred Investment Size: $250,000 to $2,500,000. Investment Types:

Start-up, seed, first stage, second stage, expansion, and mezzanine. Industry Preferences: Diversified. Geographic Preferences: Northwest.

Pacific Northwest Partners SBIC, L.P.
15352 SE 53rd St.
Bellevue, WA 98006
Phone: (425)455-9967
Fax: (425)455-9404
Preferred Investment Size: $500,000 minimum. Investment Policies: Private equity investments. Investment Types: Seed, start-up, and early and first stage. Industry Preferences: Diversified. Geographic Preferences: Entire U.S.

Materia Venture Associates, L.P.
3435 Carillon Pointe
Kirkland, WA 98033-7354
Phone: (425)822-4100
Fax: (425)827-4086
Preferred Investment Size: $500,000 to $1,000,000. Investment Types: Start-up, first and second stage, and mezzanine. Industry Preferences: Advanced industrial products and equipment. Geographic Preferences: Entire U.S.

OVP Venture Partners (Kirkland)
2420 Carillon Pt.
Kirkland, WA 98033
Phone: (425)889-9192
Fax: (425)889-0152
E-mail: info@ovp.com
Website: http://www.ovp.com
Preferred Investment Size: $1,000,000 to $10,000,000. Investment Types: Seed, start-up, early stage. Industry Preferences: Diversified technology. Geographic Preferences: Western U.S. and Canada.

Digital Partners
999 3rd Ave., Ste. 1610
Seattle, WA 98104
Phone: (206)405-3607
Fax: (206)405-3617
Website: http://www.digitalpartners.com
Preferred Investment Size: $250,000 to $3,000,000. Investment Types: Early, first and second stage, and seed. Industry Preferences:

Diversified technology. Geographic Preferences: Northwest and Western Canada.

Frazier & Company
601 Union St., Ste. 3300
Seattle, WA 98101
Phone: (206)621-7200
Fax: (206)621-1848
E-mail: jon@frazierco.com
Jon Gilbert, General Partner
Preferred Investment Size: $2,000,000 to $3,000,000. Investment Types: No preference. Industry Preferences: Diversified. Geographic Preferences: National.

Kirlan Venture Capital, Inc.
221 First Ave. W, Ste. 108
Seattle, WA 98119-4223
Phone: (206)281-8610
Fax: (206)285-3451
E-mail: bill@kirlanventure.com
Website: http://www.kirlanventure.com
Preferred Investment Size: $300,000 to $500,000. Investment Types: First stage, second stage, and mezzanine. Industry Preferences: Diversified technology. Geographic Preferences: Western U.S. and Canada.

Phoenix Partners
1000 2nd Ave., Ste. 3600
Seattle, WA 98104
Phone: (206)624-8968
Fax: (206)624-1907
E-mail: djohnsto@interserv.com
William B. Horne, Chief Financial Officer
Preferred Investment Size: $2,000,000 to $3,000,000. Investment Types: Seed, research and development, start-up, first and second stage, and mezzanine. Industry Preferences: Diversified. Geographic Preferences: No preference.

Voyager Capital
800 5th St., Ste. 4100
Seattle, WA 98103
Phone: (206)470-1180
Fax: (206)470-1185
E-mail: info@voyagercap.com
Website: http://www.voyagercap.com
Erik Benson, Senior Associate

Preferred Investment Size: $5,000,000 to $10,000,000. Investment Policies: Equity. Investment Types: Start-up, early and late stage. Industry Preferences: Diversified communications and computer related. Geographic Preferences: West Coast and Western Canada.

Northwest Venture Associates
221 N. Wall St., Ste. 628
Spokane, WA 99201
Phone: (509)747-0728
Fax: (509)747-0758
Website: http://www.nwva.com
Christopher Brookfield
Preferred Investment Size: $1,000,000 to $2,000,000. Investment Types: Seed, research and development, start-up, first stage, second stage, and mezzanine. Industry Preferences: Diversified. Geographic Preferences: Northwest and Rocky Mountains.

Wisconsin

Venture Investors Management, L.L.C.
University Research Park
505 S. Rosa Rd.
Madison, WI 53719
Phone: (608)441-2700
Fax: (608)441-2727
E-mail: roger@ventureinvestors.com
Website: http://
www.ventureinvesters.com
Scott Button, Partner
Preferred Investment Size: $250,000 to $1,000,000. Investment Types: Seed, start-up, first and second stage, mezzanine, and special situations. Industry Preferences: Diversified. Geographic Preferences: Southeast and Midwest.

Capital Investments, Inc.
1009 West Glen Oaks Lane, Ste. 103
Mequon, WI 53092
Phone: (414)241-0303
Fax: (414)241-8451
E-mail:
dmayer@capitalinvestmentsinc.com
Website: http://
www.capitalinvestmentsinc.com
Preferred Investment Size: $500,000 to $1,000,000. Investment Types:

Second stage, mezzanine, and leveraged buyout. Industry Preferences: Diversified. Geographic Preferences: Southwest and Midwest.

Future Value Venture, Inc.
2745 N. Martin Luther King Dr., Ste. 204
Milwaukee, WI 53212-2300
Phone: (414)264-2252
Fax: (414)264-2253
E-mail: fvvventures@aol.com
William Beckett, President
Preferred Investment Size: $100,000 to $300,000. Investment Types: First and second stage, start-up, and mezzanine. Industry Preferences: No preference. Geographic Preferences: Entire U.S.

Lubar and Co., Inc.
700 N. Water St., Ste. 1200
Milwaukee, WI 53202
Phone: (414)291-9000
Fax: (414)291-9061
David J. Lubar, Partner
Preferred Investment Size: $10,000,000 minimum. Investment Types: Second stage, leveraged buyout, special situations, and control block purchases. Industry Preferences: Diversified. Geographic Preferences: Midwest.

GCI
20875 Crossroads Cir., Ste. 100
Waukesha, WI 53186
Phone: (262)798-5080
Fax: (262)798-5087
Preferred Investment Size: $2,000,000 minimum. Investment Types: First stage, second stage, and leveraged buyout. Industry Preferences: Diversified technology. Geographic Preferences: National.

Appendix C - Glossary of Small Business Terms

Glossary of Small Business Terms

Absolute liability
Liability that is incurred due to product defects or negligent actions. Manufacturers or retail establishments are held responsible, even though the defect or action may not have been intentional or negligent.

ACE
See Active Corps of Executives

Accident and health benefits
Benefits offered to employees and their families in order to offset the costs associated with accidental death, accidental injury, or sickness.

Account statement
A record of transactions, including payments, new debt, and deposits, incurred during a defined period of time.

Accounting system
System capturing the costs of all employees and/or machinery included in business expenses.

Accounts payable
See Trade credit

Accounts receivable
Unpaid accounts which arise from unsettled claims and transactions from the sale of a company's products or services to its customers.

Active Corps of Executives (ACE)
(See also Service Corps of Retired Executives)
A group of volunteers for a management assistance program of the U.S. Small Business Administration; volunteers provide one-on-one counseling and teach workshops and seminars for small firms.

ADA
See Americans with Disabilities Act

Adaptation
The process whereby an invention is modified to meet the needs of users.

Adaptive engineering
The process whereby an invention is modified to meet the manufacturing and commercial requirements of a targeted market.

Adverse selection
The tendency for higher-risk individuals to purchase health care and more comprehensive plans, resulting in increased costs.

Advertising
A marketing tool used to capture public attention and influence purchasing decisions for a product or service. Utilizes various forms of media to generate consumer response, such as flyers, magazines, newspapers, radio, and television.

Age discrimination
The denial of the rights and privileges of employment based solely on the age of an individual.

Agency costs
Costs incurred to insure that the lender or investor maintains control over assets while allowing the borrower or entrepreneur to use them. Monitoring and information costs are the two major types of agency costs.

Agribusiness
The production and sale of commodities and products from the commercial farming industry.

Americans with Disabilities Act (ADA)
Law designed to ensure equal access and opportunity to handicapped persons.

Annual report
(See also Securities and Exchange Commission)
Yearly financial report prepared by a business that adheres to the requirements set forth by the Securities and Exchange Commission (SEC).

Antitrust immunity

(See also Collective ratemaking)

Exemption from prosecution under antitrust laws. In the transportation industry, firms with antitrust immunity are permitted—under certain conditions—to set schedules and sometimes prices for the public benefit.

Applied research

Scientific study targeted for use in a product or process.

Assets

Anything of value owned by a company.

Audit

The verification of accounting records and business procedures conducted by an outside accounting service.

Average cost

Total production costs divided by the quantity produced.

Balance Sheet

A financial statement listing the total assets and liabilities of a company at a given time.

Bankruptcy

(See also Chapter 7 of the 1978 Bankruptcy Act; Chapter 11 of the 1978 Bankruptcy Act)

The condition in which a business cannot meet its debt obligations and petitions a federal district court either for reorganization of its debts (Chapter 11) or for liquidation of its assets (Chapter 7).

Basic research

Theoretical scientific exploration not targeted to application.

Basket clause

A provision specifying the amount of public pension funds that may be placed in investments not included on a state's legal list (see separate citation).

BBS

See Bulletin Board Service

BDC

See Business development corporation

Benefit

Various services, such as health care, flextime, day care, insurance, and vacation, offered to employees as part of a hiring package. Typically subsidized in whole or in part by the business.

BIDCO

See Business and industrial development company

Billing cycle

A system designed to evenly distribute customer billing throughout the month, preventing clerical backlogs.

Birth

See Business birth

Blue chip security

A low-risk, low-yield security representing an interest in a very stable company.

Blue sky laws

A general term that denotes various states' laws regulating securities.

Bond

(See also General obligation bond; Taxable bonds; Treasury bonds)

A written instrument executed by a bidder or contractor (the principal) and a second party (the surety or sureties) to assure fulfillment of the principal's obligations to a third party (the obligee or government) identified in the bond. If the principal's obligations are not met, the bond assures payment to the extent stipulated of any loss sustained by the obligee.

Bonding requirements

Terms contained in a bond (see separate citation).

Bonus

An amount of money paid to an employee as a reward for achieving certain business goals or objectives.

Brainstorming

A group session where employees contribute their ideas for solving a problem or meeting a company objective without fear of retribution or ridicule.

Brand name

The part of a brand, trademark, or service mark that can be spoken. It can be a word, letter, or group of words or letters.

Bridge financing

A short-term loan made in expectation of intermediate-term or long-term financing. Can be used when a company plans to go public in the near future.

Broker
One who matches resources available for innovation with those who need them.

Budget
An estimate of the spending necessary to complete a project or offer a service in comparison to cash-on-hand and expected earnings for the coming year, with an emphasis on cost control.

Bulletin Board Service (BBS)
An online service enabling users to communicate with each other about specific topics.

Business and industrial development company (BIDCO)
A private, for-profit financing corporation chartered by the state to provide both equity and long-term debt capital to small business owners (see separate citations for equity and debt capital).

Business birth
The formation of a new establishment or enterprise. The appearance of a new establishment or enterprise in the Small Business Data Base (see separate citation).

Business conditions
Outside factors that can affect the financial performance of a business.

Business contractions
The number of establishments that have decreased in employment during a specified time.

Business cycle
A period of economic recession and recovery. These cycles vary in duration.

Business death
The voluntary or involuntary closure of a firm or establishment. The disappearance of an establishment or enterprise from the Small Business Data Base (see separate citation).

Business development corporation (BDC)
A business financing agency, usually composed of the financial institutions in an area or state, organized to assist in financing businesses unable to obtain assistance through normal channels; the risk is spread among various members of the business development corporation, and interest rates may vary somewhat from those charged by member institutions. A venture capital firm in which

shares of ownership are publicly held and to which the Investment Act of 1940 applies.

Business dissolution
For enumeration purposes, the absence of a business that was present in the prior time period from any current record.

Business entry
See Business birth

Business ethics
Moral values and principles espoused by members of the business community as a guide to fair and honest business practices.

Business exit
See Business death

Business expansions
The number of establishments that added employees during a specified time.

Business failure
Closure of a business causing a loss to at least one creditor.

Business format franchising
(See also Franchising)
The purchase of the name, trademark, and an ongoing business plan of the parent corporation or franchisor by the franchisee.

Business license
A legal authorization issued by municipal and state governments and required for business operations.

Business name
(See also Business license; Trademark)
Enterprises must register their business names with local governments usually on a "doing business as" (DBA) form. (This name is sometimes referred to as a "fictional name.") The procedure is part of the business licensing process and prevents any other business from using that same name for a similar business in the same locality.

Business norms
See Financial ratios

Business permit
See Business license

Business plan
A document that spells out a company's expected course of action for a specified period, usually including a detailed listing and analysis of risks and uncertainties. For the small business, it should examine the proposed products, the market, the industry, the management policies, the marketing policies, production needs, and financial needs. Frequently, it is used as a prospectus for potential investors and lenders.

Business proposal
See Business plan

Business service firm
An establishment primarily engaged in rendering services to other business organizations on a fee or contract basis.

Business start
For enumeration purposes, a business with a name or similar designation that did not exist in a prior time period.

Cafeteria plan
See Flexible benefit plan

Capacity
Level of a firm's, industry's, or nation's output corresponding to full practical utilization of available resources.

Capital
Assets less liabilities, representing the ownership interest in a business. A stock of accumulated goods, especially at a specified time and in contrast to income received during a specified time period. Accumulated goods devoted to production. Accumulated possessions calculated to bring income.

Capital expenditure
Expenses incurred by a business for improvements that will depreciate over time.

Capital gain
The monetary difference between the purchase price and the selling price of capital. Capital gains are taxed at a rate of 28% by the federal government.

Capital intensity
(See also Debt capital; Equity midrisk venture capital; Informal capital; Internal capital; Owner's capital; Secondhand capital; Seed capital; Venture capital)
The relative importance of capital in the production process, usually expressed as the ratio of capital to labor but also sometimes as the ratio of capital to output.

Capital resource
The equipment, facilities and labor used to create products and services.

Caribbean Basin Initiative
An interdisciplinary program to support commerce among the businesses in the nations of the Caribbean Basin and the United States. Agencies involved include: the Agency for International Development, the U.S. Small Business Administration, the International Trade Administration of the U.S. Department of Commerce, and various private sector groups.

Catastrophic care
Medical and other services for acute and long-term illnesses that cost more than insurance coverage limits or that cost the amount most families may be expected to pay with their own resources.

CDC
See Certified development corporation

CD-ROM
Compact disc with read-only memory used to store large amounts of digitized data.

Certified development corporation (CDC)
A local area or statewide corporation or authority (for profit or nonprofit) that packages U.S. Small Business Administration (SBA), bank, state, and/or private money into financial assistance for existing business capital improvements. The SBA holds the second lien on its maximum share of 40 percent involvement. Each state has at least one certified development corporation. This program is called the SBA 504 Program.

Certified lenders
Banks that participate in the SBA guaranteed loan program (see separate citation). Such banks must have a good track record with the U.S. Small Business Administration (SBA) and must agree to certain conditions set forth by the agency. In return, the SBA agrees to process any guaranteed loan application within three business days.

Champion
An advocate for the development of an innovation.

Channel of distribution
The means used to transport merchandise from the manufacturer to the consumer.

Chapter 7 of the 1978 Bankruptcy Act

Provides for a court-appointed trustee who is responsible for liquidating a company's assets in order to settle outstanding debts.

Chapter 11 of the 1978 Bankruptcy Act

Allows the business owners to retain control of the company while working with their creditors to reorganize their finances and establish better business practices to prevent liquidation of assets.

Closely held corporation

A corporation in which the shares are held by a few persons, usually officers, employees, or others close to the management; these shares are rarely offered to the public.

Code of Federal Regulations

Codification of general and permanent rules of the federal government published in the Federal Register.

Code sharing

See Computer code sharing

Coinsurance

(See also Cost sharing)

Upon meeting the deductible payment, health insurance participants may be required to make additional health care cost-sharing payments. Coinsurance is a payment of a fixed percentage of the cost of each service; copayment is usually a fixed amount to be paid with each service.

Collateral

Securities, evidence of deposit, or other property pledged by a borrower to secure repayment of a loan.

Collective ratemaking

(See also Antitrust immunity)

The establishment of uniform charges for services by a group of businesses in the same industry.

Commercial insurance plan

See Underwriting

Commercial loans

Short-term renewable loans used to finance specific capital needs of a business.

Commercialization

The final stage of the innovation process, including production and distribution.

Common stock

The most frequently used instrument for purchasing ownership in private or public companies. Common stock generally carries the right to vote on certain corporate actions and may pay dividends, although it rarely does in venture investments. In liquidation, common stockholders are the last to share in the proceeds from the sale of a corporation's assets; bondholders and preferred shareholders have priority. Common stock is often used in first-round start-up financing.

Community development corporation

A corporation established to develop economic programs for a community and, in most cases, to provide financial support for such development.

Competitor

A business whose product or service is marketed for the same purpose/use and to the same consumer group as the product or service of another.

Computer code sharing

An arrangement whereby flights of a regional airline are identified by the two-letter code of a major carrier in the computer reservation system to help direct passengers to new regional carriers.

Consignment

A merchandising agreement, usually referring to second-hand shops, where the dealer pays the owner of an item a percentage of the profit when the item is sold.

Consortium

A coalition of organizations such as banks and corporations for ventures requiring large capital resources.

Consultant

An individual that is paid by a business to provide advice and expertise in a particular area.

Consumer price index

A measure of the fluctuation in prices between two points in time.

Consumer research

Research conducted by a business to obtain information about existing or potential consumer markets.

Continuation coverage

Health coverage offered for a specified period of time to employees who leave their jobs and to their widows, divorced spouses, or dependents.

Contractions
See Business contractions

Convertible preferred stock
A class of stock that pays a reasonable dividend and is convertible into common stock (see separate citation). Generally the convertible feature may only be exercised after being held for a stated period of time. This arrangement is usually considered second-round financing when a company needs equity to maintain its cash flow.

Convertible securities
A feature of certain bonds, debentures, or preferred stocks that allows them to be exchanged by the owner for another class of securities at a future date and in accordance with any other terms of the issue.

Copayment
See Coinsurance

Copyright
A legal form of protection available to creators and authors to safeguard their works from unlawful use or claim of ownership by others. Copyrights may be acquired for works of art, sculpture, music, and published or unpublished manuscripts. All copyrights should be registered at the Copyright Office of the Library of Congress.

Corporate financial ratios
(See also Industry financial ratios)
The relationship between key figures found in a company's financial statement expressed as a numeric value. Used to evaluate risk and company performance. Also known as Financial averages, Operating ratios, and Business ratios.

Corporation
A legal entity, chartered by a state or the federal government, recognized as a separate entity having its own rights, privileges, and liabilities distinct from those of its members.

Cost containment
Actions taken by employers and insurers to curtail rising health care costs; for example, increasing employee cost sharing (see separate citation), requiring second opinions, or preadmission screening.

Cost sharing
The requirement that health care consumers contribute to their own medical care costs through deductibles and coinsurance (see separate citations). Cost sharing does not include the amounts paid in premiums. It is used to control utilization of services; for example, requiring a fixed amount to be paid with each health care service.

Cottage industry
(See also Home-based business)
Businesses based in the home in which the family members are the labor force and family-owned equipment is used to process the goods.

Credit Rating
A letter or number calculated by an organization (such as Dun & Bradstreet) to represent the ability and disposition of a business to meet its financial obligations.

Customer service
Various techniques used to ensure the satisfaction of a customer.

Cyclical peak
The upper turning point in a business cycle.

Cyclical trough
The lower turning point in a business cycle.

DBA
See Business name

Death
See Business death

Debenture
A certificate given as acknowledgment of a debt (see separate citation) secured by the general credit of the issuing corporation. A bond, usually without security, issued by a corporation and sometimes convertible to common stock.

Debt
(See also Long-term debt; Mid-term debt; Securitized debt; Short-term debt)
Something owed by one person to another. Financing in which a company receives capital that must be repaid; no ownership is transferred.

Debt capital
Business financing that normally requires periodic interest payments and repayment of the principal within a specified time.

Debt financing
See Debt capital

Debt securities
Loans such as bonds and notes that provide a specified rate of return for a specified period of time.

Deductible
A set amount that an individual must pay before any benefits are received.

Demand shock absorbers
A term used to describe the role that some small firms play by expanding their output levels to accommodate a transient surge in demand.

Demographics
Statistics on various markets, including age, income, and education, used to target specific products or services to appropriate consumer groups.

Demonstration
Showing that a product or process has been modified sufficiently to meet the needs of users.

Deregulation
The lifting of government restrictions; for example, the lifting of government restrictions on the entry of new businesses, the expansion of services, and the setting of prices in particular industries.

Desktop Publishing
Using personal computers and specialized software to produce copy for publications.

Disaster loans
Various types of physical and economic assistance available to individuals and businesses through the U.S. Small Business Administration (SBA). This is the only SBA loan program available for residential purposes.

Discrimination
The denial of the rights and privileges of employment based on factors such as age, race, religion, or gender.

Diseconomies of scale
The condition in which the costs of production increase faster than the volume of production.

Dissolution
See Business dissolution

Distribution
Delivering a product or process to the user.

Distributor
One who delivers merchandise to the user.

Diversified company
A company whose products and services are used by several different markets.

Doing business as (DBA)
See Business name

Dow Jones
An information services company that publishes the Wall Street Journal and other sources of financial information.

Dow Jones Industrial Average
An indicator of stock market performance.

Earned income
A tax term that refers to wages and salaries earned by the recipient, as opposed to monies earned through interest and dividends.

Economic efficiency
The use of productive resources to the fullest practical extent in the provision of the set of goods and services that is most preferred by purchasers in the economy.

Economic indicators
Statistics used to express the state of the economy. These include the length of the average work week, the rate of unemployment, and stock prices.

Economically disadvantaged
See Socially and economically disadvantaged

Economies of scale
See Scale economies

EEOC
See Equal Employment Opportunity Commission

8(a) Program
A program authorized by the Small Business Act that directs federal contracts to small businesses owned and operated by socially and economically disadvantaged individuals.

Electronic mail (e-mail)
The electronic transmission of mail via phone lines.

E-mail
See Electronic mail

Employee leasing
A contract by which employers arrange to have their workers hired by a leasing company and then leased back to them for a management fee. The leasing company typically assumes the administrative burden of payroll and provides a benefit package to the workers.

Employee tenure
The length of time an employee works for a particular employer.

Employer identification number
The business equivalent of a social security number. Assigned by the U.S. Internal Revenue Service.

Enterprise
An aggregation of all establishments owned by a parent company. An enterprise may consist of a single, independent establishment or include subsidiaries and other branches under the same ownership and control.

Enterprise zone
A designated area, usually found in inner cities and other areas with significant unemployment, where businesses receive tax credits and other incentives to entice them to establish operations there.

Entrepreneur
A person who takes the risk of organizing and operating a new business venture.

Entry
See Business entry

Equal Employment Opportunity Commission (EEOC)
A federal agency that ensures nondiscrimination in the hiring and firing practices of a business.

Equal opportunity employer
An employer who adheres to the standards set by the Equal Employment Opportunity Commission (see separate citation).

Equity
(See also Common Stock; Equity midrisk venture capital)

The ownership interest. Financing in which partial or total ownership of a company is surrendered in exchange for capital. An investor's financial return comes from dividend payments and from growth in the net worth of the business.

Equity capital
See Equity; Equity midrisk venture capital

Equity financing
See Equity; Equity midrisk venture capital

Equity midrisk venture capital
An unsecured investment in a company. Usually a purchase of ownership interest in a company that occurs in the later stages of a company's development.

Equity partnership
A limited partnership arrangement for providing start-up and seed capital to businesses.

Equity securities
See Equity

Equity-type
Debt financing subordinated to conventional debt.

Establishment
A single-location business unit that may be independent (a single-establishment enterprise) or owned by a parent enterprise.

Establishment and Enterprise Microdata File
See U.S. Establishment and Enterprise Microdata File

Establishment birth
See Business birth

Establishment Longitudinal Microdata File
See U.S. Establishment Longitudinal Microdata File

Ethics
See Business ethics

Evaluation
Determining the potential success of translating an invention into a product or process.

Exit
See Business exit

Experience rating
See Underwriting

Export

A product sold outside of the country.

Export license

A general or specific license granted by the U.S. Department of Commerce required of anyone wishing to export goods. Some restricted articles need approval from the U.S. Departments of State, Defense, or Energy.

Failure

See Business failure

Fair share agreement

(See also Franchising)

An agreement reached between a franchisor and a minority business organization to extend business ownership to minorities by either reducing the amount of capital required or by setting aside certain marketing areas for minority business owners.

Feasibility study

A study to determine the likelihood that a proposed product or development will fulfill the objectives of a particular investor.

Federal Trade Commission (FTC)

Federal agency that promotes free enterprise and competition within the U.S.

Federal Trade Mark Act of 1946

See Lanham Act

Fictional name

See Business name

Fiduciary

An individual or group that hold assets in trust for a beneficiary.

Financial analysis

The techniques used to determine money needs in a business. Techniques include ratio analysis, calculation of return on investment, guides for measuring profitability, and break-even analysis to determine ultimate success.

Financial intermediary

A financial institution that acts as the intermediary between borrowers and lenders. Banks, savings and loan associations, finance companies, and venture capital companies are major financial intermediaries in the United States.

Financial ratios

See Corporate financial ratios; Industry financial ratios

Financial statement

A written record of business finances, including balance sheets and profit and loss statements.

Financing

See First-stage financing; Second-stage financing; Third-stage financing

First-stage financing

(See also Second-stage financing; Third-stage financing)

Financing provided to companies that have expended their initial capital, and require funds to start full-scale manufacturing and sales. Also known as First-round financing.

Fiscal year

Any twelve-month period used by businesses for accounting purposes.

504 Program

See Certified development corporation

Flexible benefit plan

A plan that offers a choice among cash and/or qualified benefits such as group term life insurance, accident and health insurance, group legal services, dependent care assistance, and vacations.

FOB

See Free on board

Format franchising

See Business format franchising; Franchising

401(k) plan

A financial plan where employees contribute a percentage of their earnings to a fund that is invested in stocks, bonds, or money markets for the purpose of saving money for retirement.

Four Ps

Marketing terms referring to Product, Price, Place, and Promotion.

Franchising

A form of licensing by which the owner—the franchisor—distributes or markets a product, method, or service through affiliated dealers called franchisees. The product, method, or service being marketed is identified by a brand name, and the franchisor maintains control over the marketing methods employed. The franchisee is often given exclusive access to a defined geographic area.

Free on board (FOB)
A pricing term indicating that the quoted price includes the cost of loading goods into transport vessels at a specified place.

Frictional unemployment
See Unemployment

FTC
See Federal Trade Commission

Fulfillment
The systems necessary for accurate delivery of an ordered item, including subscriptions and direct marketing.

Full-time workers
Generally, those who work a regular schedule of more than 35 hours per week.

Garment registration number
A number that must appear on every garment sold in the U.S. to indicate the manufacturer of the garment, which may or may not be the same as the label under which the garment is sold. The U.S. Federal Trade Commission assigns and regulates garment registration numbers.

Gatekeeper
A key contact point for entry into a network.

GDP
See Gross domestic product

General obligation bond
A municipal bond secured by the taxing power of the municipality. The Tax Reform Act of 1986 limits the purposes for which such bonds may be issued and establishes volume limits on the extent of their issuance.

GNP
See Gross national product

Good Housekeeping Seal
Seal appearing on products that signifies the fulfillment of the standards set by the Good Housekeeping Institute to protect consumer interests.

Goods sector
All businesses producing tangible goods, including agriculture, mining, construction, and manufacturing businesses.

GPO
See Gross product originating

Gross domestic product (GDP)
The part of the nation's gross national product (see separate citation) generated by private business using resources from within the country.

Gross national product (GNP)
The most comprehensive single measure of aggregate economic output. Represents the market value of the total output of goods and services produced by a nation's economy.

Gross product originating (GPO)
A measure of business output estimated from the income or production side using employee compensation, profit income, net interest, capital consumption, and indirect business taxes.

HAL
See Handicapped assistance loan program

Handicapped assistance loan program (HAL)
Low-interest direct loan program through the U.S. Small Business Administration (SBA) for handicapped persons. The SBA requires that these persons demonstrate that their disability is such that it is impossible for them to secure employment, thus making it necessary to go into their own business to make a living.

Health maintenance organization (HMO)
Organization of physicians and other health care professionals that provides health services to subscribers and their dependents on a prepaid basis.

Health provider
An individual or institution that gives medical care. Under Medicare, an institutional provider is a hospital, skilled nursing facility, home health agency, or provider of certain physical therapy services.

HMO
See Health maintenance organization

Home-based business
(See also Cottage industry)
A business with an operating address that is also a residential address (usually the residential address of the proprietor).

Hub-and-spoke system

A system in which flights of an airline from many different cities (the spokes) converge at a single airport (the hub). After allowing passengers sufficient time to make connections, planes then depart for different cities.

Human Resources Management

A business program designed to oversee recruiting, pay, benefits, and other issues related to the company's work force, including planning to determine the optimal use of labor to increase production, thereby increasing profit.

Idea

An original concept for a new product or process.

Import

Products produced outside the country in which they are consumed.

Income

Money or its equivalent, earned or accrued, resulting from the sale of goods and services.

Income statement

A financial statement that lists the profits and losses of a company at a given time.

Incorporation

The filing of a certificate of incorporation with a state's secretary of state, thereby limiting the business owner's liability.

Incubator

A facility designed to encourage entrepreneurship and minimize obstacles to new business formation and growth, particularly for high-technology firms, by housing a number of fledgling enterprises that share an array of services, such as meeting areas, secretarial services, accounting, research library, on-site financial and management counseling, and word processing facilities.

Independent contractor

An individual considered self-employed (see separate citation) and responsible for paying Social Security taxes and income taxes on earnings.

Indirect health coverage

Health insurance obtained through another individual's health care plan; for example, a spouse's employer-sponsored plan.

Industrial development authority

The financial arm of a state or other political subdivision established for the purpose of financing economic development in an area, usually through loans to nonprofit organizations, which in turn provide facilities for manufacturing and other industrial operations.

Industry financial ratios

(See also Corporate financial ratios)
Corporate financial ratios averaged for a specified industry. These are used for comparison purposes and reveal industry trends and identify differences between the performance of a specific company and the performance of its industry. Also known as Industrial averages, Industry ratios, Financial averages, and Business or Industrial norms.

Inflation

Increases in volume of currency and credit, generally resulting in a sharp and continuing rise in price levels.

Informal capital

Financing from informal, unorganized sources; includes informal debt capital such as trade credit or loans from friends and relatives and equity capital from informal investors.

Initial public offering (IPO)

A corporation's first offering of stock to the public.

Innovation

The introduction of a new idea into the marketplace in the form of a new product or service or an improvement in organization or process.

Intellectual property

Any idea or work that can be considered proprietary in nature and is thus protected from infringement by others.

Internal capital

Debt or equity financing obtained from the owner or through retained business earnings.

Internet

A government-designed computer network that contains large amounts of information and is accessible through various vendors for a fee.

Intrapreneurship

The state of employing entrepreneurial principles to nonentrepreneurial situations.

Invention

The tangible form of a technological idea, which could include a laboratory prototype, drawings, formulas, etc.

IPO

See Initial public offering

Job description

The duties and responsibilities required in a particular position.

Job tenure

A period of time during which an individual is continuously employed in the same job.

Joint marketing agreements

Agreements between regional and major airlines, often involving the coordination of flight schedules, fares, and baggage transfer. These agreements help regional carriers operate at lower cost.

Joint venture

Venture in which two or more people combine efforts in a particular business enterprise, usually a single transaction or a limited activity, and agree to share the profits and losses jointly or in proportion to their contributions.

Keogh plan

Designed for self-employed persons and unincorporated businesses as a tax-deferred pension account.

Labor force

Civilians considered eligible for employment who are also willing and able to work.

Labor force participation rate

The civilian labor force as a percentage of the civilian population.

Labor intensity

(See also Capital intensity)

The relative importance of labor in the production process, usually measured as the capital-labor ratio; i.e., the ratio of units of capital (typically, dollars of tangible assets) to the number of employees. The higher the capital-labor ratio exhibited by a firm or industry, the lower the capital intensity of that firm or industry is said to be.

Labor surplus area

An area in which there exists a high unemployment rate. In procurement (see separate citation), extra points are given to firms in counties that are designated a labor surplus area; this information is requested on procurement bid sheets.

Labor union

An organization of similarly-skilled workers who collectively bargain with management over the conditions of employment.

Laboratory prototype

See Prototype

LAN

See Local Area Network

Lanham Act

Refers to the Federal Trade Mark Act of 1946. Protects registered trademarks, trade names, and other service marks used in commerce.

Large business-dominated industry

Industry in which a minimum of 60 percent of employment or sales is in firms with more than 500 workers.

LBO

See Leveraged buy-out

Leader pricing

A reduction in the price of a good or service in order to generate more sales of that good or service.

Legal list

A list of securities selected by a state in which certain institutions and fiduciaries (such as pension funds, insurance companies, and banks) may invest. Securities not on the list are not eligible for investment. Legal lists typically restrict investments to high quality securities meeting certain specifications. Generally, investment is limited to U.S. securities and investment-grade blue chip securities (see separate citation).

Leveraged buy-out (LBO)

The purchase of a business or a division of a corporation through a highly leveraged financing package.

Liability

An obligation or duty to perform a service or an act. Also defined as money owed.

License

(See also Business license)

A legal agreement granting to another the right to use a technological innovation.

Limited partnerships
See Venture capital limited partnerships

Liquidity
The ability to convert a security into cash promptly.

Loans
See Commercial loans; Disaster loans; SBA direct loans; SBA guaranteed loans; SBA special lending institution categories

Local Area Network (LAN)
Computer networks contained within a single building or small area; used to facilitate the sharing of information.

Local development corporation
An organization, usually made up of local citizens of a community, designed to improve the economy of the area by inducing business and industry to locate and expand there. A local development corporation establishes a capability to finance local growth.

Long-haul rates
Rates charged by a transporter in which the distance traveled is more than 800 miles.

Long-term debt
An obligation that matures in a period that exceeds five years.

Low-grade bond
A corporate bond that is rated below investment grade by the major rating agencies (Standard and Poor's, Moody's).

Macro-efficiency
(See also Economic efficiency)
Efficiency as it pertains to the operation of markets and market systems.

Managed care
A cost-effective health care program initiated by employers whereby low-cost health care is made available to the employees in return for exclusive patronage to program doctors.

Management Assistance Programs
See SBA Management Assistance Programs

Management and technical assistance
A term used by many programs to mean business (as opposed to technological) assistance.

Mandated benefits
Specific treatments, providers, or individuals required by law to be included in commercial health plans.

Market evaluation
The use of market information to determine the sales potential of a specific product or process.

Market failure
The situation in which the workings of a competitive market do not produce the best results from the point of view of the entire society.

Market information
Data of any type that can be used for market evaluation, which could include demographic data, technology forecasting, regulatory changes, etc.

Market research
A systematic collection, analysis, and reporting of data about the market and its preferences, opinions, trends, and plans; used for corporate decision-making.

Market share
In a particular market, the percentage of sales of a specific product.

Marketing
Promotion of goods or services through various media.

Master Establishment List (MEL)
A list of firms in the United States developed by the U.S. Small Business Administration; firms can be selected by industry, region, state, standard metropolitan statistical area (see separate citation), county, and zip code.

Maturity
(See also Term)
The date upon which the principal or stated value of a bond or other indebtedness becomes due and payable.

Medicaid (Title XIX)
A federally aided, state-operated and administered program that provides medical benefits for certain low-income persons in need of health and medical care who are eligible for one of the government's welfare cash payment programs, including the aged, the blind, the disabled, and members of families with dependent children where one parent is absent, incapacitated, or unemployed.

Medicare (Title XVIII)

A nationwide health insurance program for disabled and aged persons. Health insurance is available to insured persons without regard to income. Monies from payroll taxes cover hospital insurance and monies from general revenues and beneficiary premiums pay for supplementary medical insurance.

MEL

See Master Establishment List

MESBIC

See Minority enterprise small business investment corporation

MET

See Multiple employer trust

Metropolitan statistical area (MSA)

A means used by the government to define large population centers that may transverse different governmental jurisdictions. For example, the Washington, D.C. MSA includes the District of Columbia and contiguous parts of Maryland and Virginia because all of these geopolitical areas comprise one population and economic operating unit.

Mezzanine financing

See Third-stage financing

Micro-efficiency

(See also Economic efficiency)

Efficiency as it pertains to the operation of individual firms.

Microdata

Information on the characteristics of an individual business firm.

Mid-term debt

An obligation that matures within one to five years.

Midrisk venture capital

See Equity midrisk venture capital

Minimum premium plan

A combination approach to funding an insurance plan aimed primarily at premium tax savings. The employer self-funds a fixed percentage of estimated monthly claims and the insurance company insures the excess.

Minimum wage

The lowest hourly wage allowed by the federal government.

Minority Business Development Agency

Contracts with private firms throughout the nation to sponsor Minority Business Development Centers which provide minority firms with advice and technical assistance on a fee basis.

Minority Enterprise Small Business Investment Corporation (MESBIC)

A federally funded private venture capital firm licensed by the U.S. Small Business Administration to provide capital to minority-owned businesses (see separate citation).

Minority-owned business

Businesses owned by those who are socially or economically disadvantaged (see separate citation).

Mom and Pop business

A small store or enterprise having limited capital, principally employing family members.

Moonlighter

A wage-and-salary worker with a side business.

MSA

See Metropolitan statistical area

Multi-employer plan

A health plan to which more than one employer is required to contribute and that may be maintained through a collective bargaining agreement and required to meet standards prescribed by the U.S. Department of Labor.

Multi-level marketing

A system of selling in which you sign up other people to assist you and they, in turn, recruit others to help them. Some entrepreneurs have built successful companies on this concept because the main focus of their activities is their product and product sales.

Multimedia

The use of several types of media to promote a product or service. Also, refers to the use of several different types of media (sight, sound, pictures, text) in a CD-ROM (see separate citation) product.

Multiple employer trust (MET)

A self-funded benefit plan generally geared toward small employers sharing a common interest.

NAFTA
See North American Free Trade Agreement

NASDAQ
See National Association of Securities Dealers Automated Quotations

National Association of Securities Dealers Automated Quotations
Provides price quotes on over-the-counter securities as well as securities listed on the New York Stock Exchange.

National income
Aggregate earnings of labor and property arising from the production of goods and services in a nation's economy.

Net assets
See Net worth

Net income
The amount remaining from earnings and profits after all expenses and costs have been met or deducted. Also known as Net earnings.

Net profit
Money earned after production and overhead expenses (see separate citations) have been deducted.

Net worth
(See also Capital)
The difference between a company's total assets and its total liabilities.

Network
A chain of interconnected individuals or organizations sharing information and/or services.

New York Stock Exchange (NYSE)
The oldest stock exchange in the U.S. Allows for trading in stocks, bonds, warrants, options, and rights that meet listing requirements.

Niche
A career or business for which a person is well-suited. Also, a product which fulfills one need of a particular market segment, often with little or no competition.

Nodes
One workstation in a network, either local area or wide area (see separate citations).

Nonbank bank
A bank that either accepts deposits or makes loans, but not both. Used to create many new branch banks.

Noncompetitive awards
A method of contracting whereby the federal government negotiates with only one contractor to supply a product or service.

Nonmember bank
A state-regulated bank that does not belong to the federal bank system.

Nonprofit
An organization that has no shareholders, does not distribute profits, and is without federal and state tax liabilities.

Norms
See Financial ratios

North American Free Trade Agreement (NAFTA)
Passed in 1993, NAFTA eliminates trade barriers among businesses in the U.S., Canada, and Mexico.

NYSE
See New York Stock Exchange

Occupational Safety & Health Administration (OSHA)
Federal agency that regulates health and safety standards within the workplace.

Optimal firm size
The business size at which the production cost per unit of output (average cost) is, in the long run, at its minimum.

Organizational chart
A hierarchical chart tracking the chain of command within an organization.

OSHA
See Occupational Safety & Health Administration

Overhead
Expenses, such as employee benefits and building utilities, incurred by a business that are unrelated to the actual product or service sold.

Owner's capital
Debt or equity funds provided by the owner(s) of a business; sources of owner's capital are personal savings, sales of assets, or loans from financial institutions.

P & L
See Profit and loss statement

Part-time workers
Normally, those who work less than 35 hours per week. The Tax Reform Act indicated that part-time workers who work less than 17.5 hours per week may be excluded from health plans for purposes of complying with federal nondiscrimination rules.

Part-year workers
Those who work less than 50 weeks per year.

Partnership
Two or more parties who enter into a legal relationship to conduct business for profit. Defined by the U.S. Internal Revenue Code as joint ventures, syndicates, groups, pools, and other associations of two or more persons organized for profit that are not specifically classified in the IRS code as corporations or proprietorships.

Patent
A grant made by the government assuring an inventor the sole right to make, use, and sell an invention for a period of 17 years.

PC
See Professional corporation

Peak
See Cyclical peak

Pension
A series of payments made monthly, semiannually, annually, or at other specified intervals during the lifetime of the pensioner for distribution upon retirement. The term is sometimes used to denote the portion of the retirement allowance financed by the employer's contributions.

Pension fund
A fund established to provide for the payment of pension benefits; the collective contributions made by all of the parties to the pension plan.

Performance appraisal
An established set of objective criteria, based on job description and requirements, that is used to evaluate the performance of an employee in a specific job.

Permit
See Business license

Plan
See Business plan

Pooling
An arrangement for employers to achieve efficiencies and lower health costs by joining together to purchase group health insurance or self-insurance.

PPO
See Preferred provider organization

Preferred lenders program
See SBA special lending institution categories

Preferred provider organization (PPO)
A contractual arrangement with a health care services organization that agrees to discount its health care rates in return for faster payment and/or a patient base.

Premiums
The amount of money paid to an insurer for health insurance under a policy. The premium is generally paid periodically (e.g., monthly), and often is split between the employer and the employee. Unlike deductibles and coinsurance or copayments, premiums are paid for coverage whether or not benefits are actually used.

Prime-age workers
Employees 25 to 54 years of age.

Prime contract
A contract awarded directly by the U.S. Federal Government.

Private company
See Closely held corporation

Private placement
A method of raising capital by offering for sale an investment or business to a small group of investors (generally avoiding registration with the Securities and Exchange Commission or state securities registration agencies). Also known as Private financing or Private offering.

Pro forma
The use of hypothetical figures in financial statements to represent future expenditures, debts, and other potential financial expenses.

Proactive

Taking the initiative to solve problems and anticipate future events before they happen, instead of reacting to an already existing problem or waiting for a difficult situation to occur.

Procurement

(See also 8(a) Program; Small business set asides)
A contract from an agency of the federal government for goods or services from a small business.

Product development

The stage of the innovation process where research is translated into a product or process through evaluation, adaptation, and demonstration.

Product franchising

An arrangement for a franchisee to use the name and to produce the product line of the franchisor or parent corporation.

Production

The manufacture of a product.

Production prototype

See Prototype

Productivity

A measurement of the number of goods produced during a specific amount of time.

Professional corporation (PC)

Organized by members of a profession such as medicine, dentistry, or law for the purpose of conducting their professional activities as a corporation. Liability of a member or shareholder is limited in the same manner as in a business corporation.

Profit and loss statement (P & L)

The summary of the incomes (total revenues) and costs of a company's operation during a specific period of time. Also known as Income and expense statement.

Proposal

See Business plan

Proprietorship

The most common legal form of business ownership; about 85 percent of all small businesses are proprietorships. The liability of the owner is unlimited in this form of ownership.

Prospective payment system

A cost-containment measure included in the Social Security Amendments of 1983 whereby Medicare payments to hospitals are based on established prices, rather than on cost reimbursement.

Prototype

A model that demonstrates the validity of the concept of an invention (laboratory prototype); a model that meets the needs of the manufacturing process and the user (production prototype).

Prudent investor rule or standard

A legal doctrine that requires fiduciaries to make investments using the prudence, diligence, and intelligence that would be used by a prudent person in making similar investments. Because fiduciaries make investments on behalf of third-party beneficiaries, the standard results in very conservative investments. Until recently, most state regulations required the fiduciary to apply this standard to each investment. Newer, more progressive regulations permit fiduciaries to apply this standard to the portfolio taken as a whole, thereby allowing a fiduciary to balance a portfolio with higher-yield, higher-risk investments. In states with more progressive regulations, practically every type of security is eligible for inclusion in the portfolio of investments made by a fiduciary, provided that the portfolio investments, in their totality, are those of a prudent person.

Public equity markets

Organized markets for trading in equity shares such as common stocks, preferred stocks, and warrants. Includes markets for both regularly traded and nonregularly traded securities.

Public offering

General solicitation for participation in an investment opportunity. Interstate public offerings are supervised by the U.S. Securities and Exchange Commission (see separate citation).

Quality control

The process by which a product is checked and tested to ensure consistent standards of high quality.

Rate of return

(See also Yield)
The yield obtained on a security or other investment based on its purchase price or its current market price. The total

rate of return is current income plus or minus capital appreciation or depreciation.

Real property
Includes the land and all that is contained on it.

Realignment
See Resource realignment

Recession
Contraction of economic activity occurring between the peak and trough (see separate citations) of a business cycle.

Regulated market
A market in which the government controls the forces of supply and demand, such as who may enter and what price may be charged.

Regulation D
A vehicle by which small businesses make small offerings and private placements of securities with limited disclosure requirements. It was designed to ease the burdens imposed on small businesses utilizing this method of capital formation.

Regulatory Flexibility Act
An act requiring federal agencies to evaluate the impact of their regulations on small businesses before the regulations are issued and to consider less burdensome alternatives.

Research
The initial stage of the innovation process, which includes idea generation and invention.

Research and development financing
A tax-advantaged partnership set up to finance product development for start-ups as well as more mature companies.

Resource mobility
The ease with which labor and capital move from firm to firm or from industry to industry.

Resource realignment
The adjustment of productive resources to interindustry changes in demand.

Resources
The sources of support or help in the innovation process, including sources of financing, technical evaluation, market evaluation, management and business assistance, etc.

Retained business earnings
Business profits that are retained by the business rather than being distributed to the shareholders as dividends.

Revolving credit
An agreement with a lending institution for an amount of money, which cannot exceed a set maximum, over a specified period of time. Each time the borrower repays a portion of the loan, the amount of the repayment may be borrowed yet again.

Risk capital
See Venture capital

Risk management
The act of identifying potential sources of financial loss and taking action to minimize their negative impact.

Routing
The sequence of steps necessary to complete a product during production.

S corporations
See Sub chapter S corporations

SBA
See Small Business Administration

SBA direct loans
Loans made directly by the U.S. Small Business Administration (SBA); monies come from funds appropriated specifically for this purpose. In general, SBA direct loans carry interest rates slightly lower than those in the private financial markets and are available only to applicants unable to secure private financing or an SBA guaranteed loan.

SBA 504 Program
See Certified development corporation

SBA guaranteed loans
Loans made by lending institutions in which the U.S. Small Business Administration (SBA) will pay a prior agreed-upon percentage of the outstanding principal in the event the borrower of the loan defaults. The terms of the

loan and the interest rate are negotiated between the borrower and the lending institution, within set parameters.

SBA loans
See Disaster loans; SBA direct loans; SBA guaranteed loans; SBA special lending institution categories

SBA Management Assistance Programs
(See also Active Corps of Executives; Service Corps of Retired Executives; Small business institutes program)
Classes, workshops, counseling, and publications offered by the U.S. Small Business Administration.

SBA special lending institution categories.
U.S. Small Business Administration (SBA) loan program in which the SBA promises certified banks a 72-hour turnaround period in giving its approval for a loan, and in which preferred lenders in a pilot program are allowed to write SBA loans without seeking prior SBA approval.

SBDB
See Small Business Data Base

SBDC
See Small business development centers

SBI
See Small business institutes program

SBIC
See Small business investment corporation

SBIR Program
See Small Business Innovation Development Act of 1982

Scale economies
The decline of the production cost per unit of output (average cost) as the volume of output increases.

Scale efficiency
The reduction in unit cost available to a firm when producing at a higher output volume.

SCORE
See Service Corps of Retired Executives

SEC
See Securities and Exchange Commission

SECA
See Self-Employment Contributions Act

Second-stage financing
(See also First-stage financing; Third-stage financing)
Working capital for the initial expansion of a company that is producing, shipping, and has growing accounts receivable and inventories. Also known as Second-round financing.

Secondary market
A market established for the purchase and sale of outstanding securities following their initial distribution.

Secondary worker
Any worker in a family other than the person who is the primary source of income for the family.

Secondhand capital
Previously used and subsequently resold capital equipment (e.g., buildings and machinery).

Securities and Exchange Commission (SEC)
Federal agency charged with regulating the trade of securities to prevent unethical practices in the investor market.

Securitized debt
A marketing technique that converts long-term loans to marketable securities.

Seed capital
Venture financing provided in the early stages of the innovation process, usually during product development.

Self-employed person
One who works for a profit or fees in his or her own business, profession, or trade, or who operates a farm.

Self-Employment Contributions Act (SECA)
Federal law that governs the self-employment tax (see separate citation).

Self-employment income
Income covered by Social Security if a business earns a net income of at least $400.00 during the year. Taxes are paid on earnings that exceed $400.00.

Self-employment retirement plan
See Keogh plan

Self-employment tax
Required tax imposed on self-employed individuals for the provision of Social Security and Medicare. The tax must be paid quarterly with estimated income tax statements.

Self-funding

A health benefit plan in which a firm uses its own funds to pay claims, rather than transferring the financial risks of paying claims to an outside insurer in exchange for premium payments.

Service Corps of Retired Executives (SCORE)

(See also Active Corps of Executives)

Volunteers for the SBA Management Assistance Program who provide one-on-one counseling and teach workshops and seminars for small firms.

Service firm

See Business service firm

Service sector

Broadly defined, all U.S. industries that produce intangibles, including the five major industry divisions of transportation, communications, and utilities; wholesale trade; retail trade; finance, insurance, and real estate; and services.

Set asides

See Small business set asides

Short-haul service

A type of transportation service in which the transporter supplies service between cities where the maximum distance is no more than 200 miles.

Short-term debt

An obligation that matures in one year.

SIC codes

See Standard Industrial Classification codes

Single-establishment enterprise

See Establishment

Small business

An enterprise that is independently owned and operated, is not dominant in its field, and employs fewer than 500 people. For SBA purposes, the U.S. Small Business Administration (SBA) considers various other factors (such as gross annual sales) in determining size of a business.

Small Business Administration (SBA)

An independent federal agency that provides assistance with loans, management, and advocating interests before other federal agencies.

Small Business Data Base

(See also U.S. Establishment and Enterprise Microdata File; U.S. Establishment Longitudinal Microdata File)

A collection of microdata (see separate citation) files on individual firms developed and maintained by the U.S. Small Business Administration.

Small business development centers (SBDC)

Centers that provide support services to small businesses, such as individual counseling, SBA advice, seminars and conferences, and other learning center activities. Most services are free of charge, or available at minimal cost.

Small business development corporation

See Certified development corporation

Small business-dominated industry

Industry in which a minimum of 60 percent of employment or sales is in firms with fewer than 500 employees.

Small Business Innovation Development Act of 1982

Federal statute requiring federal agencies with large extramural research and development budgets to allocate a certain percentage of these funds to small research and development firms. The program, called the Small Business Innovation Research (SBIR) Program, is designed to stimulate technological innovation and make greater use of small businesses in meeting national innovation needs.

Small business institutes (SBI) program

Cooperative arrangements made by U.S. Small Business Administration district offices and local colleges and universities to provide small business firms with graduate students to counsel them without charge.

Small business investment corporation (SBIC)

A privately owned company licensed and funded through the U.S. Small Business Administration and private sector sources to provide equity or debt capital to small businesses.

Small business set asides

Procurement (see separate citation) opportunities required by law to be on all contracts under $10,000 or a certain percentage of an agency's total procurement expenditure.

Smaller firms

For U.S. Department of Commerce purposes, those firms not included in the Fortune 1000.

SMSA
See Metropolitan statistical area

Socially and economically disadvantaged
Individuals who have been subjected to racial or ethnic prejudice or cultural bias without regard to their qualities as individuals, and whose abilities to compete are impaired because of diminished opportunities to obtain capital and credit.

Sole proprietorship
An unincorporated, one-owner business, farm, or professional practice.

Special lending institution categories
See SBA special lending institution categories

Standard Industrial Classification (SIC) codes
Four-digit codes established by the U.S. Federal Government to categorize businesses by type of economic activity; the first two digits correspond to major groups such as construction and manufacturing, while the last two digits correspond to subgroups such as home construction or highway construction.

Standard metropolitan statistical area (SMSA)
See Metropolitan statistical area

Start-up
A new business, at the earliest stages of development and financing.

Start-up costs
Costs incurred before a business can commence operations.

Start-up financing
Financing provided to companies that have either completed product development and initial marketing or have been in business for less than one year but have not yet sold their product commercially.

Stock
(See also Common stock; Convertible preferred stock)
A certificate of equity ownership in a business.

Stop-loss coverage
Insurance for a self-insured plan that reimburses the company for any losses it might incur in its health claims beyond a specified amount.

Strategic planning
Projected growth and development of a business to establish a guiding direction for the future. Also used to determine which market segments to explore for optimal sales of products or services.

Structural unemployment
See Unemployment

Sub chapter S corporations
Corporations that are considered noncorporate for tax purposes but legally remain corporations.

Subcontract
A contract between a prime contractor and a subcontractor, or between subcontractors, to furnish supplies or services for performance of a prime contract (see separate citation) or a subcontract.

Surety bonds
Bonds providing reimbursement to an individual, company, or the government if a firm fails to complete a contract. The U.S. Small Business Administration guarantees surety bonds in a program much like the SBA guaranteed loan program (see separate citation).

Swing loan
See Bridge financing

Target market
The clients or customers sought for a business' product or service.

Targeted Jobs Tax Credit
Federal legislation enacted in 1978 that provides a tax credit to an employer who hires structurally unemployed individuals.

Tax number
(See also Employer identification number)
A number assigned to a business by a state revenue department that enables the business to buy goods without paying sales tax.

Taxable bonds
An interest-bearing certificate of public or private indebtedness. Bonds are issued by public agencies to finance economic development.

Technical assistance
See Management and technical assistance

Technical evaluation
Assessment of technological feasibility.

Technology

The method in which a firm combines and utilizes labor and capital resources to produce goods or services; the application of science for commercial or industrial purposes.

Technology transfer

The movement of information about a technology or intellectual property from one party to another for use.

Tenure

See Employee tenure

Term

(See also Maturity)
The length of time for which a loan is made.

Terms of a note

The conditions or limits of a note; includes the interest rate per annum, the due date, and transferability and convertibility features, if any.

Third-party administrator

An outside company responsible for handling claims and performing administrative tasks associated with health insurance plan maintenance.

Third-stage financing

(See also First-stage financing; Second-stage financing)
Financing provided for the major expansion of a company whose sales volume is increasing and that is breaking even or profitable. These funds are used for further plant expansion, marketing, working capital, or development of an improved product. Also known as Third-round or Mezzanine financing.

Time deposit

A bank deposit that cannot be withdrawn before a specified future time.

Time management

Skills and scheduling techniques used to maximize productivity.

Trade credit

Credit extended by suppliers of raw materials or finished products. In an accounting statement, trade credit is referred to as "accounts payable."

Trade name

The name under which a company conducts business, or by which its business, goods, or services are identified. It may or may not be registered as a trademark.

Trade periodical

A publication with a specific focus on one or more aspects of business and industry.

Trade secret

Competitive advantage gained by a business through the use of a unique manufacturing process or formula.

Trade show

An exhibition of goods or services used in a particular industry. Typically held in exhibition centers where exhibitors rent space to display their merchandise.

Trademark

A graphic symbol, device, or slogan that identifies a business. A business has property rights to its trademark from the inception of its use, but it is still prudent to register all trademarks with the Trademark Office of the U.S. Department of Commerce.

Translation

See Product development

Treasury bills

Investment tender issued by the Federal Reserve Bank in amounts of $10,000 that mature in 91 to 182 days.

Treasury bonds

Long-term notes with maturity dates of not less than seven and not more than twenty-five years.

Treasury notes

Short-term notes maturing in less than seven years.

Trend

A statistical measurement used to track changes that occur over time.

Trough

See Cyclical trough

UCC

See Uniform Commercial Code

UL

See Underwriters Laboratories

Underwriters Laboratories (UL)

One of several private firms that tests products and processes to determine their safety. Although various firms can provide this kind of testing service, many local and insurance codes specify UL certification.

Underwriting

A process by which an insurer determines whether or not and on what basis it will accept an application for insurance. In an experience-rated plan, premiums are based on a firm's or group's past claims; factors other than prior claims are used for community-rated or manually rated plans.

Unfair competition

Refers to business practices, usually unethical, such as using unlicensed products, pirating merchandise, or misleading the public through false advertising, which give the offending business an unequitable advantage over others.

Unfunded accrued liability

The excess of total liabilities, both present and prospective, over present and prospective assets.

Unemployment

The joblessness of individuals who are willing to work, who are legally and physically able to work, and who are seeking work. Unemployment may represent the temporary joblessness of a worker between jobs (frictional unemployment) or the joblessness of a worker whose skills are not suitable for jobs available in the labor market (structural unemployment).

Uniform Commercial Code (UCC)

A code of laws governing commercial transactions across the U.S., except Louisiana. Their purpose is to bring uniformity to financial transactions.

Uniform product code (UPC symbol)

A computer-readable label comprised of ten digits and stripes that encodes what a product is and how much it costs. The first five digits are assigned by the Uniform Product Code Council, and the last five digits by the individual manufacturer.

Unit cost

See Average cost

UPC symbol

See Uniform product code

U.S. Establishment and Enterprise Microdata (USEEM) File

A cross-sectional database containing information on employment, sales, and location for individual enterprises and establishments with employees that have a Dun & Bradstreet credit rating.

U.S. Establishment Longitudinal Microdata (USELM) File

A database containing longitudinally linked sample microdata on establishments drawn from the U.S. Establishment and Enterprise Microdata file (see separate citation).

U.S. Small Business Administration 504 Program

See Certified development corporation

USEEM

See U.S. Establishment and Enterprise Microdata File

USELM

See U.S. Establishment Longitudinal Microdata File

VCN

See Venture capital network

Venture capital

(See also Equity; Equity midrisk venture capital)
Money used to support new or unusual business ventures that exhibit above-average growth rates, significant potential for market expansion, and are in need of additional financing to sustain growth or further research and development; equity or equity-type financing traditionally provided at the commercialization stage, increasingly available prior to commercialization.

Venture capital company

A company organized to provide seed capital to a business in its formation stage, or in its first or second stage of expansion. Funding is obtained through public or private pension funds, commercial banks and bank holding companies, small business investment corporations licensed by the U.S. Small Business Administration, private venture capital firms, insurance companies, investment management companies, bank trust departments, industrial companies seeking to diversify their investment, and investment bankers acting as intermediaries for other investors or directly investing on their own behalf.

Venture capital limited partnerships
Designed for business development, these partnerships are an institutional mechanism for providing capital for young, technology-oriented businesses. The investors' money is pooled and invested in money market assets until venture investments have been selected. The general partners are experienced investment managers who select and invest the equity and debt securities of firms with high growth potential and the ability to go public in the near future.

Venture capital network (VCN)
A computer database that matches investors with entrepreneurs.

WAN
See Wide Area Network

Wide Area Network (WAN)
Computer networks linking systems throughout a state or around the world in order to facilitate the sharing of information.

Withholding
Federal, state, social security, and unemployment taxes withheld by the employer from employees' wages; employers are liable for these taxes and the corporate umbrella and bankruptcy will not exonerate an employer from paying back payroll withholding. Employers should escrow these funds in a separate account and disperse them quarterly to withholding authorities.

Workers' compensation
A state-mandated form of insurance covering workers injured in job-related accidents. In some states, the state is the insurer; in other states, insurance must be acquired from commercial insurance firms. Insurance rates are based on a number of factors, including salaries, firm history, and risk of occupation.

Working capital
Refers to a firm's short-term investment of current assets, including cash, short-term securities, accounts receivable, and inventories.

Yield
(See also Rate of return)
The rate of income returned on an investment, expressed as a percentage. Income yield is obtained by dividing the current dollar income by the current market price of the security. Net yield or yield to maturity is the current income yield minus any premium above par or plus any discount from par in purchase price, with the adjustment spread over the period from the date of purchase to the date of maturity.

Appendix D - Cumulative Index

Cumulative Index

Listings in this index are arranged alphabetically by business plan type (in bold), then alphabetically by business plan name. Users are provided with the volume number in which the plan appears.

CUMULATIVE INDEX